The CD files for this title can be found on the website booksupport.wiley.com by entering the ISBN

9780471786320

# Derivatives

*Markets, Valuation, and Risk Management*

Founded in 1807, John Wiley & Sons is the oldest independent publishing company in the United States. With offices in North America, Europe, Australia, and Asia, Wiley is globally committed to developing and marketing print and electronic products and services for our customers' professional and personal knowledge and understanding.

The Wiley Finance series contains books written specifically for finance and investment professionals as well as sophisticated individual investors and their financial advisors. Book topics range from portfolio management to e-commerce, risk management, financial engineering, valuation and financial instrument analysis, as well as much more.

For a list of available titles, please visit our Web site at www.WileyFinance.com.

# Derivatives

*Markets, Valuation, and Risk Management*

ROBERT E. WHALEY

John Wiley & Sons, Inc.

Published by John Wiley & Sons, Inc., Hoboken, New Jersey.
Published simultaneously in Canada.



For general information on our other products and services or for technical support, please contact our Customer Care Department within the United States at (800) 762-2974, outside the United States at (317) 572-3993 or fax (317) 572-4002.

Wiley publishes in a variety of print and electronic formats and by print-on-demand. Some material included with standard print versions of this book may not be included in e-books or in print-on-demand. If this book refers to media such as a CD or DVD that is not included in the version you purchased, you may download this material at http://booksupport.wiley.com. For more information about Wiley products, visit www.wiley.com.

*Library of Congress Cataloging-in-Publication Data:*

Whaley, Robert E.
Derivatives : markets, valuation, and risk management / Robert E. Whaley.
p. cm. — (Wiley finance series)
Includes index.
ISBN-13: 978-0-471-78632-0 (cloth/cd-rom)
ISBN-10: 0-471-78632-2 (cloth/cd-rom)
1. Derivative securities—Marketing. 2. Derivative securities—Valuation. 3. Financial risk managment. I. Titile. II. Series.
HG6024.A3W475 2006
332.64'57—dc22

2006016190

# Contents

*Publisher's note:* Wiley publishes in a variety of print and electronic formats and by print-on-demand. If this book refers to media such as a CD or DVD that is not included in the version you purchased, you may download this material at http://booksupport.wiley.com. For more information about Wiley products, visit www.wiley.com.

# Preface

The book's title is *Derivatives: Markets, Valuation, and Risk Management.* In a nutshell, that is what it intends to provide—an understanding of derivatives markets, derivatives valuation, and risk management using derivative contracts. The first part of the book—*Markets*—sketches the landscape. What are derivative contracts? Where do they trade? Why do they exist? While a seemingly endless number of derivative contract structures will appear as we proceed through the chapters of the book, do not be misled. Only two basic contract structures exist—a forward and an option. All other product structures are nothing more than portfolios of forwards and options. Similarly, derivative products are offered by an almost endless number of firms and institutions in the marketplace—brokerages houses, banks, investment houses, commodity producers, importers, exporters, and so on. Again, do not be misled. Fundamentally there are only two types of derivatives markets—exchange-traded markets and over-the-counter (OTC) markets. Exchanges facilitate trading in standardized contracts. They offer deep and liquid markets, and the financial integrity of trades is guaranteed by the exchange's clearinghouse. OTC markets, on the other hand, can tailor contracts to meet customer needs, however, counterparties are left to their own devices to arrange protection from counterparty default. Finally, why do derivatives markets flourish, considering that they are *redundant securities*, that is, they derive their value from the price of the underlying security? The answer is plain and simple. They are generally less expensive to trade, or, in many instances, circumvent trading restrictions that impede trading in the underlying security market. Because derivative contracts are redundant means that they are effective risk management tools. Because they are cheaper to trade and may circumvent trading restrictions means that they are cost-effective.

The last two terms in the title—*Valuation* and *Risk Management*—are the other main focuses of the book. As we amply demonstrate throughout the book, derivative contracts are incredibly powerful tools for managing expected return and risk. In order to take full advantage of the opportunities they afford, we need to have a thorough understanding of how derivative contracts are valued. Without an understanding the economic factors that drive valuation, we cannot measure risk accurately, and, if we cannot measure risk accurately, we certainly cannot manage it effectively.

With this background in mind, we now outline the contents of the book. The sections of the book, and the chapters that comprise each section, are listed in Table 1. Here we provide a brief description of the each section's contents. As noted earlier, Part One sketches the derivatives landscape. Part Two, together

**TABLE 1** Section outline for *Derivatives: Markets, Valuation, Risk Management*

I. DERIVATIVE MARKETS
- 1. Derivative contracts and markets

II. FUNDAMENTALS OF VALUATION
- 2. Assumptions and interest rate mechanics
- 3. Relation between expected return and risk

III. FORWARD/FUTURES/SWAP VALUATION
- 4. No-arbitrage price relations: Forwards, futures, swaps
- 5. Risk management strategies: Futures

IV. OPTION VALUATION
- 6. No-arbitrage price relations: Options
- 7. Valuing standard option analytically
- 8. Valuing nonstandard option analytically
- 9. Valuing options numerically
- 10. Risk management strategies: Options

V. STOCK DERIVATIVES
- 11. Stock products
- 12. Corporate securities
- 13. Compensation agreements

VI. STOCK INDEX DERIVATIVES
- 14. Stock index products: Futures and options
- 15. Stock index products: Strategy based

VII. CURRENCY DERIVATIVES
- 16. Currency products

VIII. INTEREST RATE DERIVATIVES
- 17. Interest rate products: Futures and options
- 18. Interest rate products: Swaps
- 19. Credit products
- 20. Valuing interest rate products numerically

IX. COMMODITY DERIVATIVES
- 21. Commodity products

X. LESSONS LEARNED
- 22. Lessons and guidelines

APPENDICES
- A. Elementary statistics
- B. Regression analysis
- C. Statistical tables
- D. Glossary

with Appendixes A and B, review the basic principles of security valuation. The purpose of this section is to ensure that everyone is on the same page as we enter the discussions of derivative contract valuation and risk measurement. Parts Three and Four focus exclusively on derivatives valuation and risk measurement. These principles are developed in an environment in which the underlying asset is generic. We do this to emphasize the fact that the valuation and risk measurement principles are generally not asset-specific—the valuation equations/methods and risk management strategies for foreign currency derivatives are no different than those used for stock derivatives, stock index derivatives, interest rate derivatives, and commodity derivatives. With the general valuation/risk measurement framework in hand, we then focus in Parts Five through Nine on derivative contracts in specific asset categories. Aside from pointing out any asset market idiosyncrasies that may affect valuation, specific risk management strategies/practices, as they apply to the particular asset market, are discussed. Part Ten summarizes the key lessons contained in the chapters of the book and offers some general guidelines on derivatives use.

## DERIVATIVE MARKETS

The first section of the book is devoted to providing a broad overview of derivative contracts and the markets within which they trade. We start by describing and illustrating the basic types of derivative contracts—a forward and an option. With these generic contract designs in mind, we then discuss the fundamental issues regarding derivatives markets—why they exist, how they originated, how they work, and how they are regulated.

## FUNDAMENTALS OF VALUATION

The second section of the book together with the two supporting end-of-book appendices—Appendix A: Elementary Statistics, and Appendix B: Regression Analysis—are not specific to derivative contract valuation. They focus on security valuation in general. The reason is simple. The problem is risk management. What risks? You name it. Corporations, institutions, governments, and governmental agencies incur all sorts of risks in their day-to-day operations. For corporate producers such as oil refiners, managing price risk of input costs (i.e., crude oil) as well as output prices (i.e., heating oil and unleaded gasoline) are relevant. For end-users such as airlines, managing its exposure to jet fuel prices is important. Depending upon user, some risks may be acceptable, while others may not. A gold company, for example, may have a thorough understanding of the world's supply and demand for gold production and, consequently, may be better able to predict gold price movements in the short- and long-run. On the other hand, it may have little or no awareness of probable movements in exchange rates. For this company to accept the gold price risk exposure and, at the same time, to hedge foreign currency risk exposure of sales commitments in a different currency is perfectly sensible.

All of this is to say, we must begin at a more basic level. The key elements in financial decision making are the risk, return, and timing of cash flows. A security's value is driven by all three factors. A fundamental assumption that we will maintain throughout the book is the *absence of costless arbitrage opportunities*. If we identify two investments whose risk, return, and timing of cash flow properties are exactly the same, they must have the same price in the marketplace. Otherwise, market participants can make free money by simultaneously selling the more expensive one and buying the cheaper one. This economic premise was introduced nearly fifty years ago in the Nobel Prize-winning work of Modigliani and Miller (1958, 1961). We apply this premise again and again throughout the book in a context called *valuation-by-replication*. Suppose we are faced with the problem of valuing and measuring the risk of a seemingly complex security or derivative contract. If we can identify a set of securities/derivatives whose cash flow stream maps identically to the cash flow stream of the complex security, that security's value must be equal to the sum of the values of the constituent securities/derivatives. Then, since we know how to value the instrument, we can measure its risk.

After reviewing the no-arbitrage principles, we turn to reviewing the use of interest rate mechanics in moving expected future cash flows through time. To reenforce the relation between valuation and risk measurement, we examine simple security valuation problems such as bond valuation. After deriving the bond valuation formula, we show how to measure its risk. A bond's interest-rate price risk is called duration. We show how to measure it, and, then, how to hedge it.

Where Chapter 2 deals with projection of expected future cash flows and moving them back to the present at a specified rate of interest, Chapter 3 deals with the motivation for and the measurement of risk-adjusted rates of interest. In financial economics, the capital asset pricing model (CAPM) provides the structural relation between expected return and risk. Like the work of Modigliani and Miller, the precepts are not new. They begin with the work of Markowitz (1952, 1959) who demonstrates how risk-averse individuals should go about allocating their wealth among risky securities on a single-period model. Tobin (1958) extends the model to include risk-free borrowing and lending extends an individual's set of return/risk opportunities. Finally, Sharpe (1964) and Lintner (1965) show how individuals' security demands can be aggregated and identify the equilibrium expected return/risk relation for the marketplace. The continuous-time version of the CAPM, which we use repeatedly throughout the book, was derived by Merton (1973a). The central role that the CAPM plays in financial economics in general is attested to by the fact that five of the key players in its development—Harry Markowitz, James Tobin, William Sharpe, John Lintner, and Robert C. Merton—have received Nobel Prizes in Economics.

The expected return/risk relation is central to the understanding risk management using derivative contracts. Consider Figure 1. The vertical axis is expected return and the horizontal axis is risk. What derivatives risk management deals with is moving along the line by entering particular derivative contract positions. Point C on the figure might represent, for example, a farmer's current unhedged, expected return/risk profile. The coordinates of point C are determined by his assessment of the mean and the variance of the wheat price distribution. His decision about what to do depends on his risk preferences. He can engage in a risk-reducing strategy by committing to deliver part of his anticipated harvest of wheat

**FIGURE 1** Expected return/risk tradeoff.

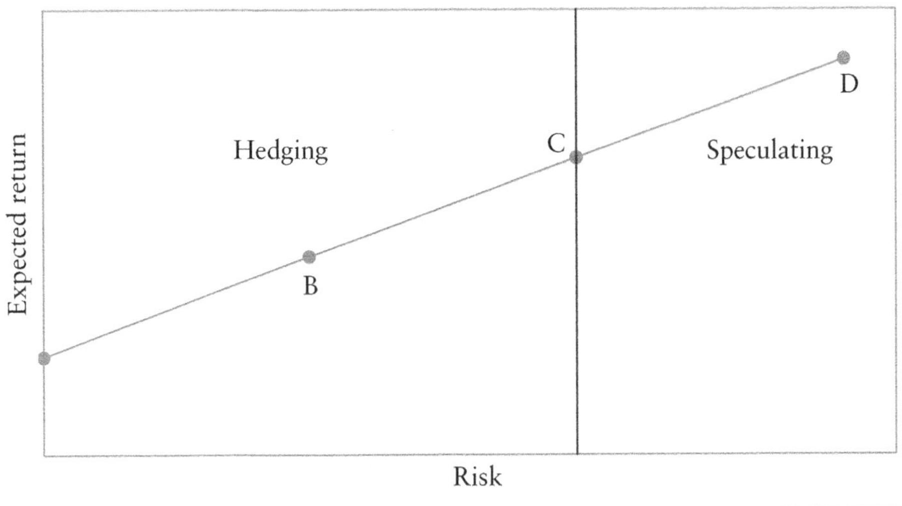


at a price that is fixed today. This short forward commitment would bring his return/risk profile toward the risk-free rate of return, say to point B, and would be referred to as *hedging*. On the other hand, if he is confident that wheat prices are going to be high as a result of poor weather during the summer and low yield in the fall, he may not hedge, keeping his risk profile at C, or he may attempt to profit from his directional view regarding wheat price movements and buy forward to increase his risk profile from C to, say, point D. All of this is to say that this book deals with moving along this line. There will be different types of risk to be managed, and we will handle each of them in turn. We should be clear, however, that risk management is synonymous with expected return/risk management. In equilibrium, we cannot move one without moving the other.

Appendices A and B to the book are intended to review the basic principles of elementary statistics and ordinary least squares regression. These are provided so as "... to leave no stone unturned." Having a basic understanding of statistics and regression analysis is a prerequisite for financial management. The implementation of the capital asset pricing model, for example, requires estimates of expected return, standard deviation of return, and covariance of returns of pairs of risky assets.

## FORWARD/FUTURES/SWAP VALUATION

The third section of the book focuses on the valuation of forward contracts, and the fourth section focuses on the valuation of option contracts. In both cases, the underlying asset is generic and is characterized only by its net cost of carry rate. Section three has two parts. Chapter 4 focuses on the valuation of forward contracts. Futures and swaps are also mentioned in the section heading because they are simply different types of forward commitments. In Chapter 4, we demonstrate that the price of a futures contract is identical to the price of a forward contract in an environment in which short-term interest rates are known. In addition, we demonstrate that a swap contract is nothing more than a portfolio of forward contracts. Hence, if we can value a forward, we can value a swap. We show that the forward price and the underlying spot price are inextricably linked by the *net cost of carry relation*. The intuition underlying this relation is straightforward. Suppose we need 5,000 bushels of wheat on hand in three months. To lock in the purchase price of the wheat today, we can buy it in the marketplace, store it, and then use it in three months. Under this action, we forego the opportunity cost of the funds that we used to buy the wheat and pay storage costs such as warehouse rent and insurance. Collectively, these items are called *carry costs*. A second strategy is to buy wheat forward at the price agreed upon today. Since both alternatives provide wheat in three months at a price known today, the costs of the two strategies must be the same. Otherwise, someone can earn a *costless* arbitrage profit.

Assuming individuals are constantly monitoring the marketplace for free money opportunities, we can depend on the net cost of carry relation between a forward contract and the spot price to hold at any point in time, which implies that the price movements of the forward and the underlying asset are perfectly positively correlated. The correlation between forward and spot price movements is at the heart of the risk management strategies discussed in Chapter 5. We simply rework the mechanics of the CAPM to handle the problem. We show that we can alter the expected return/risk attributes of any commodity or financial asset position by entering forward positions. It is only a matter of deciding what exposures to hedge and what exposures to retain. If we have the ability to pick underpriced stocks but have no ability to pick the direction of the market, for example, an appropriate risk management strategy is to buy the underpriced stocks and sell stock index futures. In this way, we accept the stock's idiosyncratic risk about which we are expert and lay off the market risk about which we have little knowledge.

## OPTION VALUATION

Section four is the longest of the book's ten sections.[1] But, it is arguably the most interesting and important. The ideas in this section have spawned an entire industry, which, as of December 2003, had more than USD 230 trillion in notional amount of contracts outstanding. Chapter 6 is the options counterpart to the no-arbitrage price relations for forward contracts provided in Chapter 4. The no-arbitrage price relations for options fall into one of three categories. First, because options are contingent claims (i.e., we have the right but not the obligation to engage in a future transaction), we can only develop lower bounds on call and put prices. Second, if we consider the call and put prices simultaneously, we can create a forward contract and, therefore, develop a net cost of carry relation for options. Called *put-call parity*, this relation resurfaces on many occasions throughout the chapters of the book. Finally, in countries such

[1] Much of the material for these chapters is drawn from Whaley (2003).

as the United States, options on assets as well as options on the futures written on those same assets are sometimes traded. When this happens, certain no-arbitrage price relations will govern prices in the adjacent markets.

Chapter 7 contains the development of the Black-Scholes (1973)/Merton (1973b) (hereafter, BSM) model. From the valuation of employee stock options to the dynamic risk management of securities/derivatives portfolios, this model plays a critical role in the valuation and risk management of hundreds of billions of dollars of derivatives transactions each day. A standard option contract, like any security, can be valued as the present value of its expected cash flows. For a European-style call option, the expected cash flow is at the option's expiration and equals the expected difference between the underlying asset price and the exercise price conditional upon the asset price being greater than the exercise price. Thus, the call's expected cash flow depends on, among other things, the expected risk-adjusted rate of price appreciation on the underlying asset between now and expiration. Once the call's expected terminal value is established, it must be discounted to the present. The discount rate applied to the expected terminal option value is the expected risk-adjusted rate of return for the option. The problem with this traditional approach to option valuation, provided by Samuelson (1965) eight years before BSM,[2] is that it is difficult, if not impossible, to estimate reliably the expected risk-adjusted return parameters.

A major theoretical breakthrough occurred in 1973 with the publication of research papers by Black and Scholes (1973) and Merton (1973b). They showed that, if a risk-free hedge between an option and its underlying asset can be formed, option valuation does not depend on individual risk preferences and therefore need not depend on estimating expected risk-adjusted returns.[3] Indeed, if option valuation does not depend on risk preferences, we are free to choose any type of individual risk behavior in valuing an option. An obvious choice is to assume individuals are risk-neutral. In a risk-neutral world, all assets are expected to have a rate of return equal to their risk-free rate of interest. Consequently, the need to estimate risk-adjusted rates of return is eliminated.

Chapter 7 begins by building the intuition underlying risk-neutral valuation using a simple, one-period binomial model. We show that BSM option values are the same as those obtained using risk-neutral individuals and risk-averse individuals. With the irrelevance of risk preferences established, we then turn to risk-neutral option valuation. The BSM model assumes that the price of the asset underlying the option is log-normally distributed. We develop the expressions for the expected value of the asset price given estimates of the mean and the variance of the normally distributed return distribution. With the expected terminal price of the option in hand, we present the valuation formulas for European-style call and put options. We then use the formulas to derive expressions to assess the option's risk characteristics.

Chapter 8 uses the BSM option valuation framework to value unusual or nonstandard types of option contracts. Many of these contracts emerged in the late 1980s and 1990s when the OTC markets were focused on designing new

[2] Interestingly enough, Paul Samuelson was also awarded the Nobel Prize in economics.

[3] If a risk-free hedge can be formed between two risky securities, the securities are *redundant*, and each can be priced in relation to the other as investors are risk neutral.

and ever more elaborate option contracts with wide-ranging payoff contingencies. For some contracts, the potential hedging properties are immediately obvious. For others, the contracts seem cleverly designed forms of speculation. Regardless of the purpose, all of the contracts discussed in this chapter have analytical valuation equations, that is, all of them are formulaic (rather than numerical) solutions to option valuation problems.

Where Chapter 7 and 8 focus on valuing options analytically, Chapter 9 focuses on numerical techniques that can be used to approximate the values of options with no analytical valuation equation. Here, the early contributors were Cox, Ross, and Rubinstein (1979) and Rendleman and Bartter (1979). What made the option valuation problem in Chapter 7 tractable is that we assumed the options were European style with only one exercise opportunity. For other types of options, the valuation problem is not so simple. With American-style options, for example, there are an infinite number of early exercise opportunities between now and the expiration date, and the decision to exercise early depends on a number of factors including all subsequent exercise opportunities. An analytical solution for the American-style option valuation problem (i.e., a valuation formula) has not been found. The same is true for many Asian-style options (e.g., options written on an arithmetic average) and many European-style options with multiple sources of underlying price risk (e.g., spread options). In such cases, options must be valued numerically. Moreover, even in instances where analytical solutions to option contract values are possible (e.g., accrual options), numerical methods are often easier to apply.

The numerical methods for valuing options described in Chapter 9 employ the BSM valuation assumptions. The underlying asset's price is assumed to follow a geometric Brownian motion (i.e., to be log-normally distributed at any future instant in time), and a risk-free hedge between the option and its underlying asset(s) is possible. Three of the methods involve replacing the continuous Brownian diffusion with a process that involves discrete jumps. The *binomial method,* for example, assumes that the asset price moves to one of two levels over the next increment in time. The size of the move and its likelihood are chosen in a manner so as to be consistent with the log-normal asset price distribution. In a similar fashion, the *trinomial method* allows the asset price to move to one of three levels over the next increment in time. The *Monte Carlo simulation* technique uses a discretized version of geometric Brownian motion to enumerate every possible path that the asset's price may take over the life of the option. A fourth method, called the *quadratic approximation method*, addresses the value of early exercise by modifying the BSM partial differential equation. As important as valuation, however, is risk measurement. The chapter concludes with a description of how the risk characteristics of options can be computed numerically.

Chapters 7 through 9 deal with option valuation. Knowing how to value options, in turn, provides a means for measuring risk. Chapter 10 focuses on option risk management strategies. Two major categories exist—dynamic strategies and passive strategies. Dynamic expected return/risk management, for example, attempts to manage changes in portfolio value caused by unexpected changes in the asset price, volatility, and interest rates, as well as the natural erosion of option's time value as it approaches expiration. These strategies are of particular importance to exchange-traded option market makers or OTC option dealers who, in the normal course of business, acquire option positions whose risks need to be managed on a day-to-day (minute-to-minute) basis.

Passive strategies, on the other hand, are those that involve holding an option over some discrete interval of time such as a week, a month, or even held to expiration. In this instance, the rates of return of the option and the asset are not perfectly correlated and the mechanics for analyzing the position are somewhat different. Specifically, we assess the expected return/risk characteristics of portfolios that are entered into and held to expiration. We discuss how to compute expected profits, expected returns, and risks under the assumption that the underlying asset price is log-normally distributed at the options' expiration. Finally, we show how to simulate the performance of option trading strategies using Monte Carlo simulation.

## STOCK DERIVATIVES

The remaining sections of the book are arranged by the nature of the asset underlying the derivatives contract—stocks first, then stock indexes, currencies, interest rates or bonds, and, finally, commodities. In each section, we provide a flavor for the history of each derivatives market as well as any market idiosyncrasies that may affect the valuation principles developed in earlier chapters.

We begin with stock derivatives. Three chapters are warranted. Chapter 11 is focused on stock products. Options on common stocks have been traded in the United States since the 1790s. Originally, trading took place in the over-the-counter market. Put/call dealers would advertise their prices in the financial press, and interested buyers would call a dealer. These contracts were not standardized with respect to exercise prices or expiration dates. Without standardization, option positions were often difficult to unwind prior to expiration. An investor wanting to reverse his option position was forced to negotiate with the dealer with whom the original trade was made.

On April 26, 1973, the Chicago Board Options Exchange (CBOE) became the world's first organized secondary market for standardized stock options. The beginnings were modest. The "exchange" was in a small smokers' lounge off the main floor of the Chicago Board of Trade. The only options traded were calls, and calls were available only on 16 New York Stock Exchange stocks. Today, the CBOE, together with the American Stock Exchange, the Philadelphia Stock Exchange, the Pacific Coast Exchange, and the International Securities Exchange, list call and put options on over 2,200 hundred different stocks in the United States alone. Worldwide, stock options trade on over 50 exchanges in 38 different countries. Futures contracts on individual stocks also trade on a handful of exchanges worldwide, but their popularity pales by comparison.

Chapter 12 deals with the valuation of corporate securities, which can also be viewed as stock derivatives. Firms issue different types of securities to finance the assets of the firm—common stock preferred stock, discount bonds, coupon bonds, convertible bonds, warrants, convertible bonds, and so on. Some are issued to the public and are actively traded in the secondary markets. Others are placed publicly, but trade infrequently. Yet others are privately placed, and trade seldom if at all. The purpose of this chapter is to show how all of the firm's securities outstanding can be valued using only information regarding the firm's common stock price and volatility rate. This is possible because all of the firm's securities have the same source of uncertainty—the overall market value of the firm's assets. To develop the corporate security valuation framework, we rely of the BSM option valuation results from Chapter 7. The underlying source of uncertainty is the firm's overall market value, which we assume is log-normally distributed in the future. We also assume that a risk-free hedge may be formed between each of the firm's securities and the firm's overall value. As a practical matter, the firm's overall value (i.e., the sum of the market values of all of the firm's constituent securities) does not trade as a single asset, however, small changes in the value of the firm are perfectly correlated with the changes in the value of its stock. This means that, as long as the firm's common stock is actively traded, we can apply the risk-neutral valuation principles with no loss in generality. We value bonds with varying degrees of seniority, rights and warrants, and convertible bonds.

Chapter 13 deals with the valuation of options awarded by the firm to its employees. By providing employees with the shares of the firm, or claims on the shares of the firm, management aligns the interests of employees with those of owners (i.e., the shareholders). Two common contracts are an *employee stock option* (ESO) and an *employee stock purchase plan* (ESPP). Like a warrant, an ESO is a call option contract issued by the firm. Typically, ESOs are at-the-money at the time of issuance (i.e., the exercise price is set equal to the stock price) and have terms to expiration of ten years. Over the first few (usually three) years, the options cannot be exercised. This is called the *vesting period*. If the employee leaves the firm during the vesting period, the options are forfeit. After the vesting date, the options can be exercised at any time but are *nontransferable*. Because they are nontransferable, the only way for the employee to capitalize on its value is to exercise the option. An ESPP allows the employee to buy the company's stock at a discount, usually 15%, within a certain period of time, typically six months. Some the ESPP includes a lookback provision that allows its holder to apply the discount to either the end-of-period or the beginning-of-period stock price, whichever is less. Our standard approach to stock option valuation is modified to handle all of these special considerations.

## STOCK INDEX DERIVATIVES

Arguably the most exciting financial innovation of the 1980s was the development of stock index derivative contracts. Although derivatives on the Dow were contemplated by the Chicago Board of Trade as early as the late 1960s, it was not until April 1982 that the Chicago Mercantile Exchange (CME) launched trading of the S&P 500 index futures contract. Options followed about a year later. Within a few years, stock index products appeared in most major financial centers worldwide. Included, for example, were contracts on the All Ordinaries index in Sydney, the FT-SE 100 index in London, and the Hang Seng index in Hong Kong. In spite of their relatively short history, billions of dollars in equities change hands every day through index derivatives trading in nearly 30 different countries.

Chapter 14 contains discussions of index derivatives markets and valuation. The primary focus is futures and option contracts. A return/risk management strategy discussed in detail in this chapter is the use of stock index futures to tailor the expected return-risk characteristics of a stock portfolio. This strategy is frequently in practice for purposes of market timing and asset allocation. Exchange-traded contracts are also used for structuring new and different products. Protected equity notes are one example. These notes allow individuals to protect the principal value of their investment, while, at the same time, share in the upside of a market index. We value protected equity notes using the valuation-by-replication principle and show that they are nothing more than a combination of risk-free bonds and a stock index call options.

A number of stock index products are based on trading strategies. These are the focus of Chapter 15. One such product is portfolio insurance. We examine several competing methods by which the value of stock portfolios may be insured against decline. These include passive insurance provided by index puts as well as dynamic insurance possible through continuous rebalancing of stocks and risk-free bonds, stocks and index futures, and index futures and risk-free bonds. Another product is funds based on particular option trading strategies. With options included in the mix, the properties of the return distribution can be dramatically altered, undermining conventional methods of portfolio performance. We examine this problem using the realized return/risk attributes of the BXM index—an index created from buying the S&P 500 index portfolio and selling one-month, at-the-money call options. The third set of products focus on stock market volatility. Two types exist—contracts on realized volatility and contracts on volatility implied by index option prices. We describe volatility contract specifications, valuation, and selected risk management strategies.

## CURRENCY DERIVATIVES

Chapter 16 deals with currency products. Futures on foreign exchange (FX) rates were the first financial futures contract introduced by an exchange. On May 16, 1972, the Chicago Mercantile Exchange launched trading futures on three currencies—the British pound, the Deutschemark, and the Japanese yen. Before that time there was little need for derivatives markets on currencies. Exchange rates were essentially fixed as a result of the Bretton Woods Agreement, which required each country to fix the price of its currency in relation to gold. With the failure of the Bretton Woods Agreement and the removal of the gold standard in 1971, exchange rates began to fluctuate more freely, motivating a need for exchange rate risk management tools. Chapter 16 illustrates a number important currency risk management strategies. We show, for example, how to redenominate fixed-rate debt in one currency into another using a currency swap or a strip of currency forwards. We also show how forward/option contracts can be used to manage the price risks of single and multiple transactions and balance sheet risk.

## INTEREST RATE DERIVATIVES

Where equity derivative products have the largest presence in exchange-traded markets, interest rate derivative products have the largest presence in the OTC market. Indeed, interest rate derivatives account for 72% of the USD 197.2 trillion in notional amount of OTC derivatives outstanding at the end of 2003. The popularity of these contracts is easy to imagine. Interest rate risk management is an important concern for most participants in the marketplace—corporations, agencies, municipalities, governments, and even individuals.

The interest rate derivatives section is divided into four chapters. Chapter 17 focuses on the interest rate derivative contracts traded on exchanges. For the most part, the principles and valuation methods of Chapters 4 through 10 can be applied directly to interest rate futures and options, with two notable exceptions. First, certain of the interest rate futures contracts have embedded delivery options that allow the short futures to deliver any one of a number of eligible bond issues. This "cheapest-to-deliver" option has value and affects the net cost of carry relation. Second, for options on short-term debt instruments, the log-normal price distribution assumption is inappropriate since the debt instrument cannot have a price that exceeds its par value. Consequently, we are required to develop a new methodology for valuing interest rate options. To do so, we invoke the assumption that the short-term interest rate is log-normally distributed, and then modify the valuation methods of Chapters 7 through 9. We then focus on some important interest rate risk management problems.

Chapter 18 focuses on interest rate swaps. The first interest rate swaps were consummated in the early 1980s. An early example occurred in 1982 when Sallie Mae swapped the interest payments on intermediate-term fixed rate debt for floating-rate payments indexed to the three-month T-bill yield. In the same year, a USD 300 million seven-year Deutsche Bank bond issue was swapped into USD LIBOR. While we discussed swaps on other types of assets in earlier chapters, interest rate swaps are far and away the largest asset category. As of year-end 2003, interest rate derivatives accounted for 72% of the notional amount of all OTC derivatives outstanding. Of this amount, more than 78% of interest rate derivatives were swaps. While plain vanilla swaps is certainly the largest category within this group, there are also a variety of other multiple-cash flow instruments including caps, collars, floors, and swaptions. We will address each in turn. A critical ingredient in the valuation of each of these contracts is the zero-coupon yield curve. The chapter, therefore, begins with a lengthy discussion of the zero-coupon yield curve and how it is estimated.

The first two interest rate derivatives chapters focus almost exclusively on interest-rate risk. Chapter 19 introduces a second source of risk often present in interest rate instruments—credit risk. For corporate bonds, credit risk is sometimes called default risk; for foreign bonds, it is called sovereign risk. Under either label, it refers to the fact that receiving the bond's promised interest payments and repayment of principal is uncertain. Credit derivatives come in a variety forms. We discuss three—credit default swaps, total return swaps, and credit-linked notes. In a credit default swap, the protection seller agrees, for an upfront fee or a continuing premium, to compensate the protection buyer upon a defined credit event. Since the buyer retains ownership of the underlying asset, a credit default swap isolates the credit risk inherent in the asset (e.g., the default risk of a corporate bond) from market risk (e.g., the interest rate risk of a corporate bond). With total return swaps, however, the buyer transfers all of the risks of the asset (e.g., the market risk and default risk of a corporate bond) to the seller in return for a risk-free interest payment. A credit-linked note is a corporate bond-like security structured by a bank to behave like a particular corporate or sovereign bond. This is done by buying risk-free bonds and selling credit default options. The success of this market is driven by the fact that the corporate bond is illiquid, at least relative to the stock market, and that many firms and institutions do not have authorization to trade derivative contracts or to engage in off-balance sheet transactions.

Chapter 20 focuses on the no-arbitrage valuation of interest rate options. The modeling is more intricate than it is the case for other asset categories for two reasons. The first is, as noted earlier, while an asset such as a stock price, an exchange rate or a commodity price can roam freely through time without constraint, fixed income security prices must converge to their par values as the security approaches its maturity. Second, in the fixed income markets, there is often a wide range of securities available on the *same* underlying source of uncertainty. The U.S. Treasury, for example, has T-bills, T-notes and T-bonds with a wide range of maturities. In modeling interest rate dynamics, care must be taken to ensure that all of these securities are simultaneously valued at levels consistent with observed market prices. Chapter 20 develops a binomial procedure for valuing interest rate derivative contracts where the short-term interest rate ("short rate") is the single underlying source of interest rate uncertainty and zero-coupon bond values are consistent with observed market prices. With the mechanics of no-arbitrage pricing in hand, we then turn to valuing coupon-bearing bonds, callable bonds, putable bonds, and bond options. Be forewarned, however. While the valuation framework provided in this chapter is intuitive and commonly applied in practice, it only begins to scratch the surface of the literature focused on no-arbitrage interest rate models. This literature is deep in multifactor theoretical models of interest rate movements and sophisticated numerical procedures for calibrating the models to observed market prices. Such technical discussions, however, are beyond the scope of this book.

## COMMODITY DERIVATIVES

Commodities are physical assets. Examples include precious metals, base metals, energy stores (e.g., crude oil and natural gas), refined products (e.g., heating oil and gasoline), and food (e.g., wheat, and livestock). Commodity derivatives have been traded in over-the-counter markets for centuries. The first modern-day commodity futures exchange began operation in 1865, when the Chicago Board of Trade launched trading of standardized futures contracts calling for the delivery of grain. With the passage of time, nonagricultural commodities were introduced—precious metal (silver) futures in 1933, livestock in 1961, petroleum and petroleum products in the late 1970s and early 1980s, liquefied propane in 1987, natural gas in 1990, and electricity in 1996. Chapter 21 focuses on derivatives contracts written on commodities. This chapter is organized by underlying commodity. The reason is that the price relations of commodity derivatives are influenced by idiosyncrasies in the underlying commodity market. Understanding commodity derivatives price behavior, therefore, involves understanding the factors that influence commodity price behavior. We discuss the fundamental differences between pricing commodity derivatives and pricing financial derivatives. Commodity derivatives require that we consider the storage costs such as warehouse rent and insurance as well as the convenience of having an inventory of the commodity on hand. Neither of these factors played an important role in the pricing of stock, stock index, currency, and interest rate derivatives products. We focus on the three major commodity categories—energy, agricultural, and metals—and on common types of commodity price risk management problems.

## LESSONS LEARNED

Chapter 22 summarizes the key lessons contained in the book. In spite of the book's length, the lessons are few.

1. Derivatives markets exist because of high trading costs and/or trading restrictions/regulations in the underlying asset market.
2. The expected return/risk relation for derivative contracts, like risky assets, is governed by the capital asset pricing model.
3. The absence of costless arbitrage opportunities (i.e., the law of one price) ensures that derivative contract price is inextricably linked to the prices of the underlying asset and risk-free bonds.
4. The no-arbitrage price relation between a derivative contract and its underlying asset ensures that derivative contracts are effective risk management tools.
5. The key insight into derivative contract valuation is that a risk-free hedge can be formed between a derivatives contract and its underlying asset.
6. Only two basic types of derivatives exist—a forward and an option.
7. Valuing and measuring the risk of complex derivatives is made possible by valuation by replication.
8. Derivatives valuation and risk measurement principles are not asset-specific.
9. Accurate parameter estimation is critical in applying derivative contract valuation models.
10. So-called "derivative disasters" reported in the financial press did not arise from a failing in the performance of a derivative contract or the market in which it traded.

## OPTVAL™

The book makes extensive use of OPTVAL™, a library of Microsoft Excel Visual Basic Add-Ins design to perform a wide range of valuation, risk measurement, and statistical computations. The logic in doing so is simple. By facilitating the computation of value/risk, the OPTVAL functions allow the reader to focus on the economic understanding of solving the valuation and risk management problems rather than the computational mechanics of valuation and risk measurement.

More specifically, accurate and reliable valuation/risk measurement has two important computational steps. The first is performing all of the computations that go into generating a model value conditional on knowing the values of the model's parameters. In some instances such as valuing a simple forward or futures contract, the numbers of intermediate computations are hundreds, perhaps, thousands. In other instances such as valuing an option on a dividend-paying stock, they are many. The second is estimating model parameters. All valuation models are function analytical or numerical functions of a set of parameters. Reliably estimating many of these parameters such as expected future return volatility involves collecting histories of price data and then applying statistical techniques. OPTVAL also contains a host of statistical functions to supplement what is already available in Microsoft Excel.

The add-in functions contained in OPTVAL are introduced and applied in each chapter's illustrations. In the early chapters of the book, the illustrations show all of the intermediate computations involved in addressing the valuation/risk measurement problem at hand as well as the OPTVAL function that allows the reader to find the solution without seeing the intermediate computations. This two-step procedure is designed to allow the reader to develop confidence that OPTVAL functions are not merely a "black box" but rather a set of computational routines that the reader can verify, if he or she chooses to do so. As the chapters progress, less emphasis is placed on showing intermediate steps and more emphasis is placed on addressing important, everyday valuation/risk management problems.

## REFERENCES

Black, Fischer, and Myron Scholes. 1973. The pricing of options and corporate liabilities. *Journal of Political Economy* 81: 637–659.

Cox, John C., Stephen A. Ross, and Mark Rubinstein. 1979. Option pricing: A simplified approach. *Journal of Financial Economics* 7 (September): 229–264.

Lintner, John. 1965. The valuation of risk assets and the selection of risky investments in stock portfolios and capital budgets. *Review of Economics and Statistics* 47: 13–37.

Markowitz, Harry. 1952. Portfolio selection. *Journal of Finance* 12 (March): 77–91.

Markowitz, Harry. 1959. *Portfolio Selection*. New York: John Wiley & Sons.

Merton, Robert C. 1973a. An intertemporal capital asset pricing model. *Econometrica* 41: 867–888.

Merton, Robert C. 1973b. Theory of rational option pricing. *Bell Journal of Economics and Management Science* 4: 141–183.

Miller, Merton H., and Franco Modigliani. 1961. Dividend policy, growth and the valuation of shares. *Journal of Business* 34 (October): 411–433.

Modigliani, Franco, and Merton H. Miller. 1958. The cost of capital, corporation finance and the theory of investment. *American Economic Review* 48 (June): 261–297.

Rendleman Jr., Richard J., and Brit J. Bartter. 1979. Two-state option pricing. *Journal of Finance* 34 (December): 1093–1110.

Samuelson, Paul A. 1965. Rational theory of warrant pricing. *Industrial Management Review* 10 (Winter): 13–31.

Sharpe, William F. 1964. Capital asset prices: A theory of market equilibrium under conditions of risk. *Journal of Finance* 19: 425–442.

Tobin, James. 1958. Liquidity preference as behavior towards risk. *Review of Economic Studies* 25 (February): 65–86.

Whaley, Robert E. 2003. Derivatives. In *Handbook of the Economics of Finance*, edited by George Constantinides, Milton Harris, and Rene Stulz. Elsevier North-Holland.

# Acknowledgments

Writing a comprehensive book on derivatives is an impossible task. Derivatives markets continue to grow at rapid rate, with thousands of new products or product variations being introduced every year. At best, all a derivatives book can hope to provide is a framework for understanding derivatives contract valuation and risk management as well as the structure of the markets within which they trade. My thinking about these issues has been influenced in many important ways by coauthors, professional colleagues, teachers, and students. Among those who deserve special recognition and gratitude are David Alexander, Fred Arditti, Lynn Bai, Giovanni Barone-Adesi, Messod D. Beneish, Fischer Black, Nicolas P. B. Bollen, Michael Bradley, Michael W. Brandt, Alon Brav, Alan Brudner, Pat Catania, Alger "Duke" Chapman, Joseph K. Cheung, Jeff Fleming, Theodore E. Day, Paul Dengel, Bernard Dumas, Frank J. Fabozzi, Myron J. Gordon, John Graham, Dwight Grant, Stephen Gray, Campbell R. Harvey, Edward Joyce, Runeet Kishore, T.E. "Rick" Kilcollin, Chris Kirby, Alan W. Kleidon, Albert "Pete" Kyle, Joseph Levin, Craig Lewis, Ravi Mattu, Robert C. Merton, Merton H. Miller, Matt Moran, Jay Muthuswamy, Barbara Ostdiek, Todd Petzel, Emma Rasiel, Ray Rezner, David T. Robinson, Mark Rubinstein, Eileen Smith, Bill Speth, Hans R. Stoll, René M. Stulz, Joseph R. Sweeney, and Guofu Zhou. I am especially indebted to Tom Smith of Australian National University in Canberra who carefully read and commented on all of the chapters of the book in preparation for final submission. Megan Orem provided professional and accurate typesetting. Finally, I would like to dedicate this book to my family, who have supported me during this long writing process—my wife, Sondra, and my children, Ryan, Justin, and Heather. Without their support and encouragement, this project would never have been completed.

# About the Author

Robert E. Whaley is the Valere Blair Potter Professor of Management at the Owen Graduate School of Management, Vanderbilt University. He received his bachelors of commerce degree from the University of Alberta, and his masters of business administration and doctorate degrees from the University of Toronto. His past academic appointments include Duke University, the University of Chicago, and the University of Alberta.

Professor Whaley's current research interests are in the areas of market microstructure, market volatility, hedge fund performance, index construction, and employee compensation. Much of his past work focused on investigations of the effects of program trading on stock prices, the expiration day effects of index futures and options, and the valuation of option and futures option contracts and the efficiency of the markets in which they trade. His research has been published in the top academic and practitioner journals, and he is a frequent presenter at major conferences and seminars. He has also published six books, including a textbook on the theory and applications of futures and option contracts.

Professor Whaley holds a number of editorial positions including Associate Editor of *Journal of Futures Markets*, *Journal of Derivatives*, *Journal of Risk*, *Pacific-Basin Finance Journal* and *Advances in Futures and Options Research*. His past editorial positions included *Review of Futures Markets*, *Journal of Finance*, *Journal of Financial Economics*, *Management Science*, *China Accounting and Finance Review*, and *Canadian Journal of Administrative Science*. He also has served as a referee for more than fifty journals and granting agencies and is a former member of the Board of Directors of the Western Finance Association and the American Finance Association. He is currently a member of the International Advisory Board of the University Centre for Financial Engineering at the National University of Singapore.

Professor Whaley is an established expert in derivative contract valuation and risk management, and market operation. He has been a consultant for many major investment houses, security (futures, option and stock) exchanges, governmental agencies, and accounting and law firms. Whaley work with the Chicago Board Options Exchange in the development of the Market Volatility Index (i.e., the "VIX") in 1993, the NASDAQ Market Volatility Index (i.e., the "VXN") in 2000, and the BuyWrite Monthly Index (the "BXM") in 2001.

During his career, Professor Whaley received a number of grants and awards including the 1989 Richard and Hinda Rosenthal Foundation Award for innovation in finance research, the 1991 NCNB Faculty Award for contributions in research, teaching and service at the Fuqua School of Business, and the 1993 Earl M. Combs, Jr. Award for contributions to the futures industry. Many of his research papers have received awards, including Graham and Dodd Scrolls for Excellence in Financial Writing from the *Financial Analysts Journal* in 1986 and 1987, the Bernstein Fabozzi/Jacobs Levy Award for Outstanding Article published in *Journal of Portfolio Management* during the volume year 1999–2000, the E. Yetton Award for Best Paper in *Australian Journal of Management*, 1997 for his work on program trading and futures option valuation, the CBOT Award for Best Paper on Futures at the Western Finance Association meetings in 1993 for his work on dual trading, the Canadian Securities Institute Award for Best Paper in Investments at the Northern Finance Association meetings in 1989 for his work on market volatility prediction, and an EOE Prize from the Institute for Quantitative Investment Research—Europe in 1995 for his work on deterministic volatility functions.

# PART One

# Derivative Markets

# 1

# Derivative Contracts and Markets

A *derivative contract* is a contractual agreement to execute an exchange at some future date. The term "derivative" arises from the fact that the agreement "derives" its value from the price of an underlying asset such as a stock, bond, currency, or commodity. A stock index futures derives its value from an underlying stock index, a foreign currency option derives its value from an underlying exchange rate, and so on. The key feature of the transaction specified in a derivative contract is that it will be executed in the future rather than today.

One can easily become overwhelmed by the apparently countless types of derivative contracts traded in the marketplace. The pages of the *Wall Street Journal* (*WSJ*) list the prices of tens of thousands of standardized, exchange-traded futures, options, and futures option contracts on hundreds of different underlying assets. And this only begins to scratch the surface. The *WSJ* reports only trading summaries for U.S. derivatives exchanges. Other exchanges worldwide have derivatives trading volume roughly equal to that in the United States. Moreover, the notional amount of exchange-traded derivatives worldwide represents only about 16% of all derivatives outstanding (i.e., USD 233.9 trillion as of December 2003). About 84% of derivatives are private contracts arranged with banks and various other financial houses. Many of these contracts are plain-vanilla forwards, swaps, caps, collars, or floors, but you will also hear of inverse floaters, protected equity notes, ratio swaps, time swaps, knockout options, spread locks, wedding-band swaps, and the like.

Do not be misled, however. Derivatives are not nearly as mystifying as they may seem. Fundamentally, there are only two different types of contracts—a forward and an option. A *forward* is a contract to buy or sell an underlying asset at some prespecified future date at a price agreed upon today. No money changes hands until the expiration date, at which time the buyer pays the amount of cash specified in the contract and the seller delivers the underlying asset. An *option* is also a contract to buy or sell an underlying asset at some prespecified future date at a price agreed upon today. Unlike a forward, however, the buyer of the option has the right but not the obligation to buy or sell the underlying asset at the option's expiration. The seller's obligation depends on whether or not the buyer chooses to exercise the option.

The purpose of this chapter is to provide a general understanding of derivative contracts and derivative-contract market operation. We begin by describing and illustrating the nature of forward and option contracts. With these generic contract designs in mind, we then discuss fundamental issues such as why derivative contracts exist, how they originated, and where and how they trade.

## FORWARDS

A *cash* (or *spot*) *transaction* refers to an exchange of an asset that takes place *today*. The buyer pays the seller an agreed-upon price in cash and the seller delivers the asset. A *forward transaction*, on the other hand, is an agreement to an exchange that will take place in the future (i.e., at some time "forward"). No money changes hands today. The buyer and seller simply agree upon the terms of the exchange. The terms are formalized in a contract called a *forward*. The terms include (a) the price per unit of the asset that the buyer will pay the seller of the asset; (b) the number of units of the asset that will be delivered; and (c) the date on which the delivery will take place.[1] On the delivery date, the seller is contractually obliged to deliver the underlying asset to the buyer, and the buyer is obliged to pay the seller the prespecified price in cash.

To illustrate the mechanics of a forward transaction, suppose it is March and the price of a 180-day forward contract on 5,000 bushels of wheat is $3.00 a bushel.[2] If you buy this contract, you are agreeing to take delivery of 5,000 bushels of wheat in 180 days at a cost of $3.00 a bushel. You pay nothing today. You pay $15,000 in 180 days.

What motivates such a transaction? One possibility is *speculation*. Suppose that a meteorologist has, through his study of weather patterns over the past few months, become convinced that the summer will be very dry, and the Midwest will experience drought conditions. Under such conditions, he speculates that the size of the wheat harvest in the fall will be abnormally low and the price of wheat high. Indeed, he predicts that the price will be $5.00 a bushel in September. If, when September arrives, the price of wheat is $5.00 a bushel, he posts a *speculative gain*. While he pays $3.00 a bushel, or $15,000 in total, to take delivery of the wheat, he can turn around and sell it for $5.00 a bushel, thereby posting a $10,000 profit. But, if he makes $10,000, who loses? The answer is the person who sold him the forward contract (i.e., his *counterparty*). His counterparty gets paid $3.00 a bushel for delivering wheat now worth $5.00 a bushel in the spot market and thereby loses $10,000. Derivative contracts are a *zero-sum* game. What the buyer gains, the seller loses, and vice versa.

---

[1] Forward contracts also contain other terms such as the location of delivery or the method of settlement. These are not germane to the illustration at hand, however, and are therefore omitted.

[2] The fact that the intermediate gains (losses) of the futures position can (must) be invested (financed) leads to a small difference in the terminal values of a forward and a futures position. We discuss this matter in greater detail in Chapter 3.

Speculation is not the only motive for buying the wheat forward contract, however. The other motive is *hedging*. Often manufacturers commit to forward transactions with customers. Suppose a breakfast cereal producer commits to deliver 1,000 cases of a particular product at $25 a case to a grocery chain customer in September. Processing the wheat into cereal takes one day. To lock in the cost of the wheat for September production, the cereal producer can buy a forward contract expiring in September. Is he speculating? No, just the opposite. It is because the price of wheat in six months is uncertain that he buys the forward. Indeed, if he does not buy the forward, he is speculating that the price of wheat will fall. Buying a forward contract to lock in the price at which the asset will be acquired is known as an *anticipatory hedge*. The breakfast cereal producer is said to be a long hedger because he is buying (i.e., *going long*) the forward to hedge the price risk.

Someone's motive in buying the forward contract on wheat may be to speculate or to hedge, but what about the motive of his counterparty's motive? Is she speculating or hedging? The answer is one or the other. Suppose she is a farmer in the Midwest and has just seeded her land with wheat for September harvest. Standing in March, she faces two types of risk. She knows neither how plentiful her harvest will be nor the price per bushel at which she will be able to sell her crop. To hedge her price risk, she may want to sell a September wheat forward contract. If she does, she is said to be a *short hedger*, that is, she is selling (i.e., *going short*) the forward to lock in the price at which she can sell her crop. Is she speculating? No, again, just the opposite. She does not want to bet on the price at which she can sell her crop in September, so she sells the wheat forward. On the other hand, suppose your counterparty is involved in international grain trade and understands that there has been a significant increase in wheat production in virtually every grain-producing nation. Based on her knowledge about world oversupply, she predicts that the market price of wheat will be $2.00 a bushel in September. To act on her prediction, she may sell a forward contract on wheat for September delivery. If she does so, she is speculating. In September, she must buy 5,000 bushels of wheat in the cash market and then will deliver it to fulfill her obligation on the forward. If she is correct in her prediction, she will buy the wheat at $2.00 a bushel and then sell it at $3.00, thereby posting a $5,000 speculative gain.

The wheat forward contract described above has *delivery settlement*, that is, when the forward contract expires, the seller must deliver and the buyer must take delivery of the underlying asset. The forward contract will specify the location of delivery. For physical commodities such as wheat, the delivery process can be cumbersome and costly. The woman in the last example was speculating that the price of wheat would fall, and, when it fell as she predicted, she posted a *gross* speculative gain of $5,000. But, to realize her gain, she has to buy the wheat in the spot market for $2.00 a bushel and then transport it to the location specified in her forward contract. If such freight costs amount to, say, $1,000, her net gain from speculation is only $4,000.

To circumvent such costs, some derivative contracts specify *cash settlement* rather than delivery settlement. When the forward contract expires, the difference between the spot price and the forward price is paid in cash. If the spot price at the time of expiration exceeds the forward price, the short pays the difference in cash to the long. If the long is hedging and requires the delivery of the wheat, he will take his original commitment price (i.e., the forward price at inception) plus the profit on the forward trade to buy the commodity in the local spot market (thereby avoiding the transportation costs that may be associated with taking delivery at a different geographical location). Conversely, if the spot price at expiration is less than the forward price, the long pays the difference to the short. With cash settlement, the woman in the above illustration receives $5,000 in cash, thereby circumventing the cost (and the annoyance) of dealing with the delivery process. All derivative contracts including forwards specify whether settlement is *through delivery* or *in cash*. Absent significant delivery costs, the method of settlement is moot.

### Futures

A *futures contract* is virtually identical to a forward contract. The only difference is that the gains and/or losses on a futures position are posted each day. Suppose that you see that the price of a wheat futures contract with two days to expiration and a denomination of 5,000 bushels is $3.00 a bushel. If you buy this contract, you are in effect agreeing to buy 5,000 bushels of wheat in two days at $3.00 a bushel. The payment is made in stages, however. Suppose that after one day the price of the futures (now with one day remaining to expiration) has risen to $3.50 a bushel. With a futures contract, you are immediately entitled to the $.50 per bushel gain and will receive a deposit of $2,500 in your trading account. This process is known as *marking-to-market* and occurs at the end of each trading day. Who pays? The answer is the person on the other side of your trade. He is marked-to-market with a $.50 a bushel loss.

Suppose that at the end of the second day the price of wheat is $4.50 a bushel. The marking-to-market process provides you a gain of $1.00 a bushel or $5,000. Since your futures contract has expired, you are required to buy 5,000 bushels of wheat at the market price of $4.50 a bushel, for a total cost of $22,500. But, you have already pocketed $7,500 in cash, so your net outlay is $15,000, or $3.00 a bushel. At the end of the second day, you are in the same position had you been if you had purchased a two-day forward contract at $3.00 a bushel. In most risk management applications, forwards and futures contracts can be used interchangeably.

### Open Interest

Figure 1.1 illustrates a concept called *open interest*. Suppose you consider all of the open positions in a given futures contract (e.g., the September wheat futures contract traded on the Chicago Board of Trade) on a given day. At any given time, by virtue of the fact that derivatives markets are a zero-sum game, the total number of contracts outstanding as long positions *must equal* the total number of contracts outstanding as short positions, as illustrated in Figure 1.1. The total number of contracts outstanding (long or short) is called *open interest*. The total number of long contracts can be broken down into two groups—hedgers who trade to lock in the price at which the asset can be purchased (i.e, long

**FIGURE 1.1** Breakdown of open interest between hedgers and speculators.

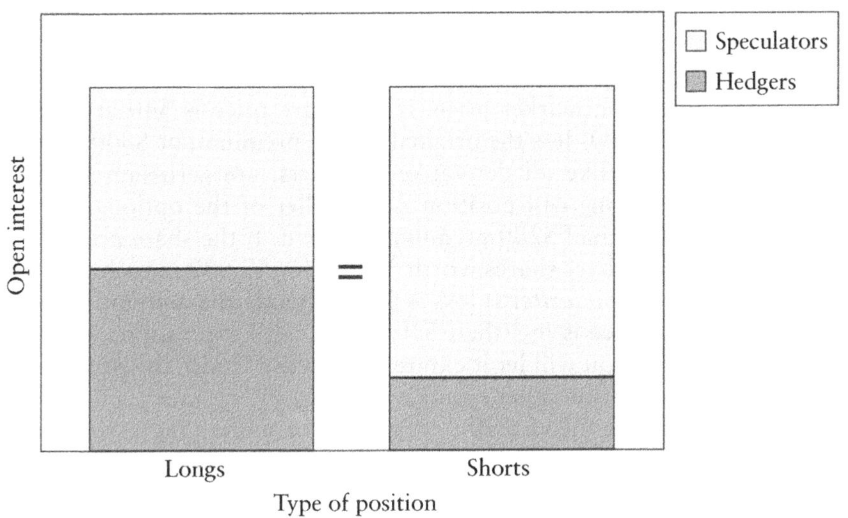


hedgers) and speculators who trade to benefit from an anticipated price increase. The total number of short contracts can also be broken down into two groups—hedgers who trade to lock in the price at which the asset can be sold (i.e., short hedgers) and speculators who trade to benefit from an anticipated price drop. The breakdown of the long and short positions in outstanding contracts between hedgers and speculators varies by underlying commodity and through time.

## OPTIONS

An option contract is the other fundamental type of derivative. Like a forward, an option is an agreement to exchange an underlying asset at a fixed price (called the option's *exercise price* or *striking price*) on some future date. Unlike a forward, however, an option provides the *right*, but not the *obligation*, to buy or sell the underlying asset.[3] The right to buy the underlying asset at a specified price on or before some specified future date is called a *call option*; the right to sell the underlying asset is called a *put option*. The amount that the option buyer pays the seller for the right is called the *option premium*.

To illustrate the mechanics of an option, suppose it is July and you predict that back-to-school software sales will drive Microsoft's share price from its current level of $25 a share to over $30 a share within three months. One way to act on your prediction is to buy a call option on the shares of Microsoft. You peruse the *Wall Street Journal* and find a Microsoft call that expires in October, has an exercise price of $30, has a contract denomination of 100 shares, and has a pre-

[3] Since an option is a right rather than an obligation, it is often referred to as a *contingent claim*.

mium of $2 a share. If you buy this call at $2.00 per share (i.e., a total option premium of $200), you have the right to buy 100 shares of Microsoft at $30 a share between now and October. If Microsoft's share price is above $30 when the contract expires, you will exercise your call by paying the option seller $3,000. The option seller, in turn, will deliver to you 100 shares of Microsoft, which you can sell at the prevailing market price. If the share price is $40 at expiration, your profit will be $1,000[4] less the original option premium, or $800.

Microsoft options, like all derivative contracts, are zero-sum games. The counterparty to your long call position is the seller of the option. The option seller received your original $200 premium payment. If the share price is $40 at expiration, he has to deliver shares worth $4,000 for $3,000 in cash. The option seller's (also called *option writer's*) loss is $800, exactly the amount you earned. If Microsoft's share price is less than $30 at the call's expiration, you will not exercise the call[5] (i.e., you will let it expire worthless). Under this scenario, your loss is $200, and the option seller's gain is $200.

Options are written on virtually every type of underlying asset, including stocks, bonds, currencies, and commodities. The nature of the underlying asset is usually used as a descriptor on the word "option." Options on stocks are called *stock options*, options on bonds *bond options*, options on currencies *currency options*, and so on. Options are also written on forward and futures contracts. The forward and futures contracts, in turn, are written on specific types of underlying assets. An option written on a stock index futures is called a *stock index futures option*, and an option written on a foreign currency forward contract is called a *currency forward option*.

## WHY DO DERIVATIVES MARKETS EXIST?

With a basic understanding of forward and option contracts in hand, we now turn to a critically important question—why do derivative contract markets exist? The answer is surprisingly simple. Derivative contracts exist because of trading costs or trading restrictions/regulations in the underlying asset market.

### Trading Costs

Trading costs are just that—costs incurred in a trade. Depending upon the type of market and the nature of the asset or derivative contract, trading costs vary. In general, however, the trading costs for derivative contracts are less than the trading costs for the underlying asset, holding the dollar value of the transaction constant. Consequently, cost-conscious risk managers prefer to trade derivatives rather than the underlying asset.

[4] Like forwards, options can be settled by delivery or in cash. In general, stock options traded on exchanges are delivery contracts. Stock index options, on the other hand, are generally cash settled.

[5] If you exercised the call, you would pay more than the current market price for the shares of Microsoft.

In securities markets, trading costs are incurred on transactions executed in both the primary and secondary markets. The *primary market* refers to the market in which securities are traded for the first time. These include *brand new issues* such as *initial public offerings* (or IPOs) of stocks, in which privately owned companies sell shares to the public for the first time or new bond offerings in which the firm floats new issue of debt, and *seasoned new issues* in which more units of an existing publicly traded security are issued. In either case, the firm enlists the help of an investment banker who *underwrites* the issue. For this service, he charges an underwriting fee. In most cases, this underwriting fee is a fairly significant proportion of the issue proceeds.

To illustrate the trading cost savings afforded by derivatives markets, consider a firm that has a significant amount of floating rate debt in its capital structure. The firm's chief financial officer fears that interest rates are about to rise and that the firm's earnings after interest will fall. Consequently, he decides to explore different hedging alternatives. One alternative is, of course, to retire the floating rate debt with a fixed rate bond issue. Issuing bonds, however, is expensive. The commission paid to the investment banker, together with the legal, auditing and printing costs associated with putting together a prospectus, average about 2.2% of issue proceeds.[6] Such costs can be avoided almost entirely by entering a *plain-vanilla interest rate swap* in which the firm agrees to receive a periodic floating rate and pay a periodic fixed rate. The market for interest rate swaps is very liquid, and trading costs can be as little as 4 basis points (0.04%).[7] From the firm's perspective, the risk management properties of the two strategies are virtually perfect substitutes. The costs of the two alternatives, however, differ by a factor of 55.

The *secondary market* refers to the market in which existing securities are traded. Securities exchanges, for example, are secondary markets. If you decide to buy or sell a security, you will incur at least two forms of trading costs: (a) a commission paid to the broker for executing the trade; and (b) the bid/ask spread charged by the market maker for providing immediacy of exchange. To execute a trade, you call your broker or sign in to your online brokerage service and place an order. The broker then turns around and communicates your order to the appropriate market maker. The market maker stands ready to buy at his quoted bid price and sell at his quoted ask price. The difference between the two prices is called the *quoted bid/ask spread* and represents the revenue the market maker earns for providing immediate exchange.[8] Once the order is consummated, the broker is informed, and he, in turn, informs you.

To illustrate the potential savings of the derivatives market in this case, suppose that you manage a portfolio of U.S. stocks and that you believe that the stock market will fall over the next month. After careful consideration, you decide that you want to eliminate entirely your stock market price risk exposure. One way to hedge the stock market risk is to sell all of your stocks and buy short-term money market instruments. Then, after you are convinced that the worst is over, you can liquidate your money market holdings and buy back your

[6] See Lee, Lochhead, Ritter, and Zhao (1996, p. 62, table 1).

[7] A basis point is 1/100 of 1%. Sample interest rate swap rates are reported in Table 1.8.

[8] In many electronic markets, buy and sell orders are matched automatically in the computer system of the exchange without the intermediation of market makers.

stocks. Another way to hedge this market risk exposure is to sell stock index futures contracts. This action, too, negates your market risk. When the worst is over, you unwind the hedge by buying an equivalent number of index futures. While these two strategies are equivalent in terms of their ability to hedge market risk, the second hedging strategy is much cheaper. In U.S. markets, the trading costs associated with the futures hedge are less than 1/20th of those incurred in liquidating and then buying back shares of stock.

### Trading Restrictions

Trading restrictions come in a variety of forms. Some arise because it is infeasible to trade the underlying asset. A farmer seeding his land in the spring for harvest in the fall, for example, has no means of selling his crop until it is harvested. Others arise from regulation. In Australia and Hong Kong, short-selling is permitted for only designated securities. In situations such as these, derivative contracts have been introduced to circumvent trading restrictions.

**Hedging by Selling an Unharvested Crop** Suppose that you are a farmer in the Midwest and have just seeded your land with wheat for a September harvest. Standing in March, you face *yield risk* (i.e., the number of bushels per acre your land will produce) and *price risk* (i.e., the price per bushel at which you will be able to sell your crop). Without derivative contracts, you have no means of offsetting either risk. With actively traded futures contracts traded on wheat, you can sell wheat futures and reduce the uncertainty of the revenue that you will earn at the time of harvest.

**Speculating by Circumventing Trading Restriction/Regulation** Suppose that you live in Australia and have noticed a frightening decline in beer consumption. Figuring that this decline will soon have an adverse effect on the earnings of Foster Brewing, you begin considering alternatives ways to profit from your belief. If you cannot short sell the shares of Foster Brewing on the Australian Stock Exchange, you cannot profit by trading in the stock market directly. It should not be surprising, therefore, to learn that the Sydney Futures Exchange was one of the first futures exchanges worldwide to launch trading in stock futures contracts. Selling stock futures enables individual investors to effectively short-sell stocks.

**Summary** Derivative contracts exist and, indeed, flourish because of trading costs and trading restrictions in the underlying asset market. Trading takes place for only two reasons—hedging or speculating. Hedging reduces risk and hence reduces expected return; speculation increases risk and hence increases expected return. Managing risk and return can be accomplished in only two ways—by changing the amount of the asset being held or by taking a position in derivative contracts written on the underlying asset. When both strategies are feasible, trading activity will tend to be concentrated in the lowest cost market, and the lowest cost market is usually the derivatives market. Sometimes, however, both strategies are not feasible. If an asset cannot be traded or if regulation limits the types of trades that can be placed, derivative contracts can serve as an effective substitute.

## EVOLUTION OF DERIVATIVES MARKETS

Derivatives, while seemingly new financial instruments, have actually been around for thousands of years. The earliest written example is contained in the Code of Hammurabi, a body of laws written by Hammurabi who reigned as king of Babylon from 1795 to 1750 BCE. Hammurabi's laws regulated all aspects of society. One law dealt with the relationship of farmers with their mortgage-holders, that is,

> 48. If any one owe a debt for a loan, and a storm prostrates the grain, or the harvest fail, or the grain does not grow for lack of water; in that year he need not give his creditor any grain, he washes his debt-tablet in water and pays no rent for the year.[9]

What this says, it seems, is that a typical farmer at the time carried a mortgage on his property and was required to make annual interest payments in the form of grain. In the event of crop failure, the farmer had the right to pay nothing and the mortgagor had no alternative but to forgive the interest. This decree by the king gave grain farmers an asset-or-nothing put option.[10] If the harvest was plentiful and the farmer had enough grain to pay his mortgage interest, the put option would expire worthless. If his harvest fell short, however, he would exercise his right to walk away from making the payment.

Another example of early derivatives use appears in Aristotle's *Politics* (350 BCE). Aristotle tells the story of Thales, a philosopher (and reasonably good meteorologist) who, based on studying the winter sky, predicted an unusually large olive harvest.[11] He was so confident of his prediction that he bought rights to rent all of the olive presses in the region for the following fall. The fall arrived, and the harvest was unusually plentiful. The demand and price for the use of olive presses soared.

These anecdotes serve to show that, while derivatives are sometimes thought of as being recent innovations, they have been used throughout recorded history. Hammurabi's put and Thales' call are examples of *over-the-counter* (OTC) derivatives. OTC derivatives are private contracts negotiated between parties. In the first example, the farmer bought, and the mortgagor sold, the asset-or-nothing put. The put premium was presumably embedded in the amount of the mortgage payment negotiated between the buyer and the seller. In the second example, Thales bought, and the olive press owners sold, call options. The prices of the options were negotiated, and Thales paid for them in the form of cash deposits. The chief advantage of OTC derivatives markets is the limitless flexibility in contract design. The underlying asset can be anything, the size of the contract can be any amount, and the delivery can be made at any time and in any location. All that an OTC contract requires is a willing buyer and a willing seller.

Among the disadvantages of OTC markets, however, is that willing buyers and sellers must spend time identifying each other. Thousands of years ago, before the

---

[9] The Avalon Project at the Yale Law School has made the Code of Hammurabi available on the website http://www.yale.edu/lawweb/avalon/hamcode.htm.

[10] All-or-nothing options are discussed in detail in Chapters 5 and 6.

[11] See *Politics* by Aristotle (1885, Book 1, Part XI).

advent of high-speed communication and computer technology, such searches were costly. Consequently, *centralized markets* evolved. The Romans organized commodity markets with specific locations and fixed times for trading. Medieval fairs in England and France during the 12th and 13th centuries served the same purpose. While centralized commodity markets were originally developed to facilitate immediate cash transactions, the practice of contracting for future delivery (i.e., forward transactions) was also introduced. So, while the contracts remained over-the-counter, there was at least some agreement about where the "counters" were.

Another disadvantage of OTC derivatives is *credit risk*, that is, the risk that a counterparty will renege on his contractual obligation. Perhaps the most colorful example of this type of risk involves forward and option contracts on tulip bulbs. In what can be characterized as a *speculative bubble*, rare and beautiful tulips became collectors' items for the upper class in Holland in the early 17th century. Prices soared to incredible levels.[12] Homes, jewels, livestock—nothing was too precious that it could not be sacrificed for the purchase of tulip bulbs. In an attempt to cash in on this craze, it was not uncommon for tulip bulb dealers to sell bulbs for future delivery. They did so based on call options provided by tulip bulb growers. In this way, if bulb prices rose significantly prior to delivery, the dealers would simply exercise their options and acquire the bulbs to be delivered on the forward commitments at a fixed (lower) price. The tulip bulb growers also engaged in risk management by buying put options from the dealers. In this way, if prices fell, the growers could exercise their puts and sell their bulbs at a price higher than that prevailing in the market. In retrospect, both the tulip bulb dealers and growers were managing the risk of their positions quite sensibly.

Everything could have worked out just fine, except that the bubble burst in the winter of 1637 when a gathering of bulb merchants could not get the usual inflated prices for their bulbs. Panic ensued. Prices sank to levels of 1/100th of what they had once been. This set off an unfortunate chain of events. Individuals who had agreed to buy bulbs from dealers did not do so. Consequently, dealers did not have the cash necessary to buy the bulbs when the growers attempted to exercise their puts. Some legal attempts were made to enforce the contracts, but the bottom line was that it was "as difficult to get blood out of a tulip bulb as out of a turnip."[13] These contract defaults left an indelible mark on OTC derivatives trading.

By the 1800s, the pendulum had swung from undisciplined derivatives trading in OTC markets toward more structured and secured trading on organized exchanges. The first derivatives exchange in the United States was the Chicago Board of Trade (CBT), as is noted in Table 1.1. While the CBT was originally formed in 1848 as a centralized marketplace for exchanging grain, forward contracts were also negotiated. The earliest recorded forward contract trade was made on March 13, 1851 and called for 3,000 bushels of corn to be delivered in June at a price of one cent per bushel below the March 13 spot price.[14] Forward contracts had their drawbacks, however. They were not standardized according to quality or delivery time. In addition, as in the case of the tulip bulb fiasco, merchants and traders often did not fulfill their forward commitments.

[12] Garber (2000) provides a detailed account of tulip bulb prices during this period.
[13] Gastineau (1988, ch. 3, p.14).
[14] See Chicago Board of Trade (1994, ch.1, p.14).

**TABLE 1.1** Milestones in the history of derivative contract markets (with emphasis on U.S. markets)

1750 BCE

- Options to default on interest payments are described in the Code of Hammurabi.

350 BCE

- Options to rent olive presses are described in Aristotle's Politics.

1600 CE

- Forward and option contracts on tulip bulbs flourish in Holland. Tulip bulb prices collapse in the winter of 1637, causing significant contract default.

1848 CE

- Chicago Board of Trade (CBT) is formed to provide a centralized marketplace for cash and forward transactions in grains.

1865 CE

- CBT revamps forward markets by introducing futures contracts on agricultural commodities. These new contracts were standardized contracts in terms of quality, quantity, and time and place of delivery, and involved the use of a clearinghouse and a system of margining.

1870 CE

- New York Cotton Exchange (NYCE) is formed to trade futures on cotton.

1874 CE

- Chicago Produce Exchange (CPE) is formed to trade futures on butter, eggs, poultry, and other perishable products.

1878 CE

- London Corn Trade Association introduces the first futures contract in the United Kingdom.

1882 CE

- Coffee Exchange (CE) is formed by a group of coffee merchants to trade futures on coffee.

1898 CE

- Butter and egg dealers withdraw from the CPE to form the Chicago Butter and Egg Board (CBEB).

1904 CE

- Winnipeg Commodity Exchange (WCE) introduces first commodity (oat) futures contracts in Canada.

1919 CE

- São Paulo Commodities Exchange (BMSP) introduces first commodity futures in Brazil.
- CBEB becomes the Chicago Mercantile Exchange (CME).

1933 CE

- Commodity Exchange (COMEX) is formed and introduces first futures contract on a non-agricultural commodity—silver.

1952 CE

- October: London Metal Exchange (LME) lists the first metal (lead) futures contract in the United Kingdom.

1960 CE

- Sydney Futures Exchange (SFE), originally called the Greasy Wool Futures Exchange, is formed to trade greasy wool futures.

**TABLE 1.1** (Continued)

1961 CE

- September: CME introduces first futures contract on livestock—frozen pork bellies.

1972 CE

- February: CME introduces first futures contract written on a financial instrument—foreign currencies.

1973 CE

- April: CBT organizes the Chicago Board Options Exchange (CBOE) for the purpose of trading call options on 16 New York Stock Exchange (NYSE) common stocks. Trading begins in a small smokers' lounge overlooking the futures exchange.

1975 CE

- CBT introduces first interest rate futures contracts—Government National Mortgage Association (GNMA) futures.
- Montreal Exchange (ME) launches stock options in Canada.
- January: American Stock Exchange (AMEX) launches call options on stocks.
- June: Philadelphia Stock Exchange (PHLX) launches call options on stocks.

1976 CE

- Pacific Stock Exchange (PSE) launches stock options.
- Australian Options Market (AOA) is formed in Australia to list stock options.
- January: CME launches T-bill futures contracts.
- March: Toronto Stock Exchange (TSE) lists stock options in Canada.

1977 CE

- June: Put options on common stocks are listed for the first time in the United States on the CBOE, AMEX, PHLX, and PSE.
- August: CBT launches T-bond futures contracts.

1978 CE

- London Traded Options Market (LTOM) is formed and launches stock options.
- European Options Exchange (EOE), formed in November 1977, launches stock options in The Netherlands.
- November: New York Mercantile Exchange (NYMEX) introduces first energy futures—heating oil.

1980 CE

- International Petroleum Exchange (IPE) is formed in the United Kingdom to list futures on petroleum and petroleum products.
- First over-the-counter (OTC) Treasury bond option takes place.
- September: Toronto Futures Exchange (TFE) is formed to list futures contracts on financial assets in Canada.

1981 CE

- First over-the-counter (OTC) interest rate swap transaction takes place.
- December: CME introduces the first cash settlement futures contract—the Eurodollar futures.

1982 CE

- London International Financial Futures Exchange (LIFFE) is formed in the United Kingdom to trade futures on financial instruments.
- February: Kansas City Board of Trade (KCBT) introduces first futures on a stock index (the Value Line stock index).
- April: CME launches S&P 500 index futures.
- October: First options listed on instruments other than common stocks.
- CBOE and AMEX launch options on Treasury bonds, notes, and bills.
- CBT launches options on T-bond futures.
- Coffee, Sugar, and Cocoa (CSCE) launches options on sugar futures.

**TABLE 1.1** (Continued)

1982 CE

- COMEX launches options on gold futures.
- December: PHLX launch options on currencies.

1983 CE

- January: CME and New York Futures Exchange (NYFE) launch options on stock index futures.
- February: SFE launches futures on the All Ordinaries Share Price Index in Australia.
- March: CBOE launches options on stock indexes, and NYMEX launches crude oil futures.

1984 CE

- Singapore International Monetary Exchange (SIMEX) is inaugurated as the first financial futures exchange in Asia.
- May: LIFFE launches futures on the FT-SE index in the United Kingdom.
- December: NYMEX launches futures on unleaded gasoline.

1986 CE

- May: Hong Kong Futures Exchange launches futures on the Hang Seng Index.
- September: SIMEX launches futures on the Nikkei 225 Stock Average.

1987 CE

- August: NYMEX launches futures on liquefied propane.

1991 CE

- Notional amount of OTC derivatives trading surpasses exchange-traded derivatives.

1992 CE

- Credit derivative contracts begin trading in OTC market.

1996 CE

- March: NYMEX launches futures on electricity.

2004 CE

- March: CBOE launches futures contract written on CBOE Market Volatility Index (VIX).
- May: CBOE launches futures contract written on three-month S&P 500 realized variance.

In 1865, the CBT made three important changes to the structure of its grain trading market. First, it introduced the use of standardized contracts called *futures contracts*. Unlike forward contracts in which the parties are free to choose the terms of the contract, the terms of futures contracts are set by the exchange and are standardized with respect to quality, quantity, and time and place of delivery for the underlying commodity. By concentrating hedging and speculative demands on fewer contracts, the depth and liquidity of the market are enhanced. This facilitates position unwinding. If a party to a trade wants to exit his position prior to the delivery date of the contract, he need only execute an opposite trade (i.e., *reverse* his trade) in the same contract. There is no need to seek out the counterparty of the original trade and attempt to negotiate the contract's termination.

The second and third changes were made in an effort to promote *market integrity*. The second was the introduction of a *clearinghouse* to stand between the buyer and the seller and guarantee the performance of each party. This crucial step eliminated the *counterparty risk* that had plagued OTC trading. In the event a buyer defaults, the clearinghouse "makes good" on the seller's position, and then holds the buyer's clearing firm liable for the consequences. The buyer's clearing firm, in turn, passes the liability onto the buyer's broker, and ultimately the buyer. Note that, at any point in time, the clearinghouse has no net position since there are as many long contracts outstanding as there are short. The third change was the introduction of a *margining system*. When the buyer and seller enter a futures position, they are both required to deposit good-faith collateral designed to show that they can fulfill the terms of the contract.

From the late 1800s through the early 1980s, the lion's share of derivatives trading took place on exchanges. Over most of this period, the dominant form of derivatives trading was with futures contracts, and the futures contracts were written primarily on agricultural commodities. The CBT began trading corn, oat, and wheat contracts in 1865. In 1870, the New York Cotton Exchange was formed by a group of cotton brokers and merchants to trade futures on cotton; in 1874, the Chicago Produce Exchange was formed by a group of agricultural dealers to trade futures on butter, eggs, and other perishable agricultural commodities; and, in 1882, the Coffee Exchange was formed by a group of coffee merchants who wished to avoid the risk of a cash market collapse by organizing a market for trading coffee futures. The first commodity futures contract in the United Kingdom was listed by the London Corn Trade Association in 1878, and the first contract in Canada was listed by the Winnipeg Commodity Exchange in 1904.

The move to nonagricultural commodities was slow. Indeed, more than 50 years elapsed before the Commodity Exchange (COMEX) in New York was formed in July 1933 to trade the first metals contract—silver futures. The London Metal Exchange (LME) launched lead futures in the United Kingdom in October 1952. The New York Mercantile Exchange (NYMEX) followed in the United States with platinum futures in December 1956 and palladium futures in January 1968. The introduction of futures on livestock occurred in the 1960s. The Chicago Mercantile Exchange (CME) launched pork belly futures in September 1961, live cattle futures in November 1964, and live hog futures in February 1966. Futures contracts on energy products did not emerge until November 1978, at which time the NYMEX introduced the heating oil futures contract. The International Petroleum Exchange (IPE) was formed in 1980 to make markets in futures on petroleum and petroleum products in the United Kingdom.

The pace of innovation in derivatives markets increased remarkably in the 1970s. Many of the important events occurring during this decade, as well as the next, are summarized in Table 1.1. The first major innovation occurred in February 1972, when the CME began trading futures on currencies in its International Monetary Market (IMM) division. This marked the first time a futures contract was written on anything other than a physical commodity. The second was in April 1973, when the CBT formed the Chicago Board Options Exchange (CBOE) to trade options on common stocks.[15] This marked the first time an option was traded on an exchange. The American Stock Exchange (AMEX) and

[15] Initially, only call options were listed in the United States. Put option trading were not listed until June 1977, and, even then, only on an experimental basis.

the Philadelphia Stock Exchange (PHLX) followed suit by listing options on U.S. stocks in 1975, and the Pacific Stock Exchange (PSE) in 1976. Other countries entered the picture around the same time. Options on the shares of Canadian stocks were listed by the Montreal Exchange in 1975 and the Toronto Stock Exchange in 1976. The Australian Options Market began listing stock options in 1976, and, in 1978, the London Traded Option Market (LTOM) was formed to list stock options in the United Kingdom. The third major innovation occurred in October 1975, when the CBT introduced the first futures contract on an interest rate instrument—Government National Mortgage Association futures. In January 1976, the CME launched Treasury bill futures, and, in August 1977, the CBT launched Treasury bond futures.

The 1980s brought yet another round of important innovations. The first was the use of cash settlement. In December 1981, the IMM launched the first cash settlement contracts, the 3-month Eurodollar futures. At expiration, the Eurodollar futures is settled in cash based on the interest rate prevailing for a 3-month Eurodollar time deposit.[16] Cash settlement made feasible the introduction of derivatives on stock index futures, the second major innovation of the 1980s. In February 1982, the Kansas City Board of Trade (KCBT) listed futures on the Value Line Composite stock index, and, in April 1982, the CME listed futures on the S&P 500. These contract introductions marked the first time that futures contracts were written on stock indexes. Other countries quickly followed suit. The Sydney Futures Exchange (SFE) listed futures on the All Ordinaries Share Price Index in February 1983, the London International Financial Futures and Options Exchange (LIFFE) listed futures on the FT-SE 100 in May 1984, the Hong Kong Futures Exchange (HKFE) listed futures on the Hang Seng Index in May 1986, and the Singapore International Monetary Exchange (SIMEX) listed futures on the Nikkei 225 Stock Average in September 1986. The third major innovation of the 1980s was the introduction of exchange-traded option contracts written on *underlyings*[17] other than individual common stocks.[18] The CBOE and AMEX listed interest rate options in October 1982 and the Philadelphia Stock Exchange (PHLX) listed currency options in December 1982. In the same year, options on futures appeared for the first time. In October 1982, the CBT began to list Treasury bond futures options, and the Coffee, Sugar, and Cocoa Exchange (CSCE) began to list options on sugar and gold futures. In January 1983, the CME and the New York Futures Exchange (NYFE) began to list options directly on stock index futures, and, in March 1983, the CBOE began to list options on stock indexes.

These two decades of innovation have had an enormous impact on the balance of derivatives trading activity on exchanges worldwide. While derivatives exchanges were originally developed to help market participants manage com-

[16] A Eurodollar time deposit is a U.S. dollar deposit in a London bank, and the interest rate quoted on such deposits is called the London Interbank Offer Rate (LIBOR). Since different banks may offer different rates on deposits of the same maturity, the settlement rate is based on an average of rates across banks.

[17] From this point forward, the term "underlying" refers to the asset or instrument that underlies the derivative contract.

[18] For a comprehensive review of these new option introductions and their economic purposes, see Stoll and Whaley (1985).

modity price risk, most of the trading activity today is concentrated in the risks of financial assets such as stocks, bonds, and currencies. Table 1.2 summarizes exchange-traded derivatives contract volume worldwide for the year 2003. Commodity futures accounted for about 17% of total futures volume worldwide, and commodity options accounted for less than 1%. At the same time, futures contracts on different interest rate instruments accounted for more than 55% of total futures volume and options on stocks/stock indexes accounted for more than 93% of total option volume. Thirty years ago, there were no exchange-traded derivatives on any financial asset at all.

The 1980s also saw the reemergence of OTC derivatives trading. With the derivatives on financial assets coming to the forefront, investment banks began to think of new ways to tailor contracts to meet customers' needs. Some ideas were standard forward and option contracts on financial instruments or indexes. In 1980, for example, the first OTC Treasury bond option was traded. Other contracts were seemingly new and different. Most fall under the generic heading, "swaps." A *swap contract* is a contract to exchange (or swap) a series of periodic future cash flows, where the terms of the contract are usually set such that the up-front payment is zero. The first *interest rate swap* was in 1981, when the Student Loan Marketing Association (Sallie Mae) swapped interest payments on intermediate-term, fixed rate debt for floating rate payments indexed to the three-month Treasury bill rate. The cash flows of the two legs of a swap can be linked to virtually any reference rate, asset price, or index level. A *basis rate swap*, for example, is an exchange of floating rate payments where the two floating rates are linked to, say, a three-month Treasury bill rate and a three-month Eurodollar time deposit rate, respectively. A *currency swap* is an exchange of interest payments (either fixed or floating) in one currency for payments (either fixed or floating) in another.[19] An *equity swap* involves the exchange of an inter-

**TABLE 1.2** Exchange-traded and over-the-counter derivatives activity during 2003.

| Underlying | Exchange-Traded Markets: Millions of Contracts Traded in 2003 | | | | OTC Markets: Notional Amount in Billions as of December 2003 | |
|---|---|---|---|---|---|---|
| | Futures | | Options | | | |
| Currencies | 59 | 2.06% | 14 | 0.28% | 24,484 | 12.42% |
| Interest rates | 1,577 | 55.37% | 302 | 5.80% | 141,991 | 72.01% |
| Equities | 726 | 25.48% | 4,843 | 92.94% | 3,787 | 1.92% |
| Commodities | 486 | 17.08% | 51 | 0.98% | 1,406 | 0.71% |
| Other | | | | | 25,510 | 12.94% |
| Total | 2,848 | 100% | 5,210 | 100% | 197,178 | 100% |

*Source:* This table was constructed from information provided in the Bank of International Settlements (www.bis.org), *BIS Quarterly Review*, June 2004.

[19] Currency swaps are unusual to the extent that the principal amounts are also usually exchanged at the beginning and the end of the swap. The principal amounts are typically chosen to be approximately equivalent at the prevailing spot rate when the contract is entered.

est rate payment and a payment based on the performance of a stock index, while an *equity basis swap* involves an exchange of payments on two different indexes. While swap agreements appear different from standard forward and option contracts, they are not new in the sense that each can be decomposed into a portfolio of forwards and options, as we discuss in great detail in subsequent chapters. What makes the swap attractive to the customer, however, is that one transaction can replace several.

Table 1.2 shows the notional amount of OTC derivatives outstanding at the end of 2003 by asset category. Clearly, the introduction of derivatives on financial assets has been crucial to the success of modern-day OTC derivatives markets. Interest rate derivatives accounted for about 72% of the USD 197.2 trillion of contracts outstanding at the end of 2003, and currency derivatives accounted for another 12.5%. In addition to using financial assets as the underlying, the "package" nature of swap agreements has met with widespread market approval. According to the Bank for International Settlements, the total notional amount of single-currency, interest rate derivatives outstanding worldwide as of December 2003 was USD 141.99 trillion with swaps being 78.32%, options 14.09%, and forwards 7.58%.

Another way to view the success of modern-day OTC derivatives markets is to compare the notional amount outstanding against exchange-traded derivatives.[20] At the beginning of 1980, virtually all derivatives traded were on exchanges. By 1991, the notional amount of derivatives traded in the OTC market was about equal to that of exchange-traded markets. According to the Bank for International Settlements, the total notional amount of derivatives outstanding worldwide as of December 2003 was USD 233.9 trillion, 15.7% being exchange-traded and 83.3% over-the-counter.

Does this enormous rate of growth in OTC markets imply the demise of exchange-traded derivative contract markets? Not necessarily. In many ways, the markets are complementary. In standing on the other side of customer transactions, investment banks wind up with large portfolios (i.e., "books") of OTC agreements. Some of the risks of the individual contracts in the dealer's book offset each other, however, at any point in time, the dealer's book is likely to have significant net exposures to equity, interest rate, currency, and/or commodity price risks. These exposures can be laid off conveniently and inexpensively using the standardized contracts that exchanges provide.

## ATTRIBUTES OF EXCHANGE-TRADED DERIVATIVE MARKETS

Exchange-traded derivatives arose in response to controversies such as the tulip bulb fiasco. The key ingredients to the success of exchange-traded derivative markets are: (1) standardized contracts, (2) a clearinghouse, (3) a system of margining, and (4) market transparency. After discussions of these attributes, we describe regulations governing exchanges in the United States and provide some examples of exchange-traded derivative contracts.

[20] The figures, compiled and reported by the Bank for International Settlements (BIS) may be somewhat misleading, as we discuss later in the chapter.

## Standardized Contracts

Exchange-traded contracts are standardized by underlying asset, time and location of delivery, method of settlement, and other factors. By concentrating trading activity in fewer types of contracts, the exchange promotes market depth and liquidity. Deep and liquid markets are desirable for two reasons. First, it permits secondary market trading "in size" with little impact on price. An OTC dealer with a large exposure to U.S. stock market risk, for example, can lay off that risk quickly and inexpensively using the CME's S&P 500 futures contracts. In addition, it permits easy *unwinding* of existing positions. If a farmer hedges his price risk by selling a September wheat futures contract on the CBT in the spring but later decides he wants to unwind his futures position before harvest, he can simply buy the same futures contract to offset (or reverse) his short position. In contrast, if the farmer sold a forward contract with the same terms in the OTC market, he would be faced with the prospect of calling the OTC derivatives dealer and negotiating his way out of the agreement. This places the farmer at a competitive disadvantage.[21]

The second reason that deep and liquid markets are important is that they limit the prospect of corners and short-squeezes. These are attempts to profit from futures trading by manipulating price. A *corner* refers to an individual or firm gaining control of the entire deliverable supply of the commodity underlying the futures. If this individual also simultaneously buys futures contracts, he may be attempting a *short-squeeze*. To understand how a short-squeeze works, recall that those who are short futures at the contract expiration must liquidate by either (a) delivering the underlying commodity or (b) buying an offsetting number of futures. In a short-squeeze, both actions are encumbered. The individual attempting the short-squeeze refuses to sell either the commodity or the futures. As the shorts[22] scramble to buy futures and cover their positions, the futures price rises. When the price rises high enough in the eyes of those squeezing the market, they sell their futures and realize their gains.

A telltale sign of an attempted short-squeeze is that the futures price in the delivery month rises relative to the prices of more distant contracts and to the underlying commodity price. Exchanges and the CFTC monitor futures markets for such signs in an attempt to guard against possible short-squeeze activity. If such activity is suspected, the person or firm undertaking the squeeze may be required to liquidate the long futures positions. The most recent example of a near short-squeeze was the attempt by an Italian grain-trading firm, Ferruzzi Finanziaria S.p.A., to corner the July 1989 soybean contract.[23] The July contract expired on July 19. At the beginning of July, Ferruzzi held more than half of the net long July futures positions, which was double the deliverable supply, and owned 85% of the

[21] OTC positions could also be offset by taking an opposite position with another OTC derivatives dealer. In this way, you can "shop around" to find the best terms. In contrast to exchange-traded derivatives where "two-sided" markets are quoted at all times, you will have to identify to the OTC dealer whether you plan to be a buyer or a seller before he quotes you the terms of the agreement.

[22] A "short" is someone who is currently short a futures or option contract. Conversely, a "long" is someone who is currently long.

[23] See Chicago Board of Trade (1990). Daily price and open interest data for the soybean futures contracts traded during the period are contained in the Excel file, **Soybean Data (Ferruzzi).xls**.

soybeans in deliverable position. The shorts would have had to move massive amounts of soybeans to the approved delivery points (in Chicago and Toledo) in order to make delivery of their futures contracts, an impossible task in the short time remaining to expiration. In reaction to the potential corner, the Chicago Board of Trade ordered those holding futures positions in excess of 3 million bushels to liquidate. This meant that Ferruzzi had to sell much of its long position to the shorts, thereby avoiding a short-squeeze. July soybean futures prices, which had risen in reaction to the developing short-squeeze, fell back to normal levels. A more detailed account of the events is included in Appendix 1 of this chapter.

### The Clearinghouse

A second attribute that distinguishes an exchange from a OTC market is the clearinghouse. The role of a *clearinghouse* is to stand between the buyer and the seller and guarantee the transaction of each party. Figure 1.2 illustrates the process. The buyer and the seller agree to the price of the contract. Historically, this agreement has taken place on a trading floor, however, with the advent of computers and high-speed communication, most exchanges are now moving toward electronic trading. Regardless of where the agreement takes place, the buyer's and the seller's brokers then report the trade to their respective clearing firms. Some brokers are clearing firms. Those that are not simply clear their trades through firms that are. The clearing firms then report the trade to the clearinghouse. By interposing itself between the buyer and the seller, the clearinghouse acts as a guarantor by, in effect, becoming the party to whom delivery is made and from whom delivery is taken. In the event the buyer defaults, the clearinghouse "makes good" on the seller's position, and then holds the buyer's clearing firm liable for the consequences.[24] The buyer's clearing firm, in turn, passes the

**FIGURE 1.2** Derivatives trading on exchanges.

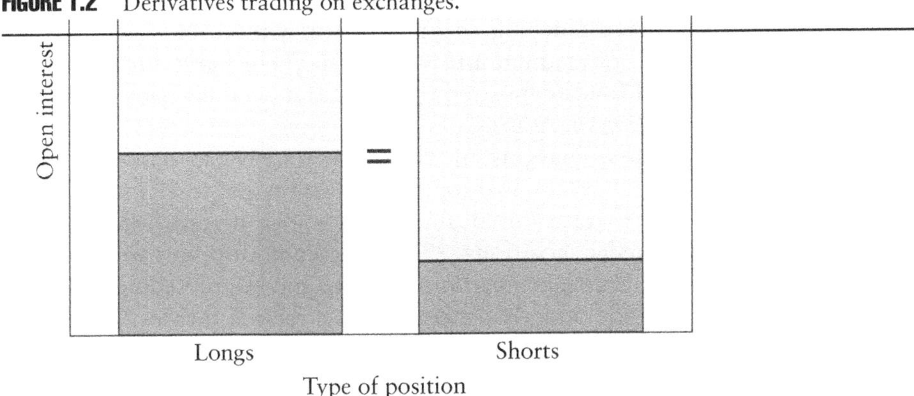


[24] The efficacy of clearinghouse operations depends critically on the solvency of the clearing members. To protect the integrity of operations, clearinghouses impose minimum capital requirements and position limits on clearing members, and exchanges set price limits on most contracts.

liability onto the buyer's broker, and ultimately the buyer. Note that the clearinghouse has no net position. At any point in time, there are as many long contracts outstanding as there are short. Note also that the exchange or clearinghouse's netting process is what allows customers to easily offset existing contract positions. If you buy (or sell) and then later sell (or buy) the same contract, your net position will be zero, and the position will disappear from your account statement. Any long option positions exercised during their life or at expiration will be randomly assigned to someone who has a short option position. Any deliveries made on open short futures positions during the delivery month will be either randomly assigned to open long positions or to the long position which has had the longest duration, depending on the contract. In the United States, all options exchanges use the same clearinghouse, that is, the Options Clearing Corporation (OCC). Historically, each U.S. futures exchange has had its own clearinghouse, although recently certain exchanges have agreed to a common clearing mechanism.[25]

### Margins

A third attribute that distinguishes an exchange from a OTC market is the imposition of margins. *Margin* is essentially a performance bond designed to show that you can fulfill your financial obligations resulting from your trade in the event that the market moves against you. Margins are of two types—*initial margin* and *maintenance margin*. The *initial margin* is the per contract amount deposited when you open a position. If the market moves against you on the opening day, your position is marked-to-market with a loss. The loss reduces the amount of your original deposit. If the balance in your account at the end of the day falls below a level called the *maintenance margin*, you will receive a *margin call* and will be required to bring the total amount of the margin back up to the initial margin level (as opposed to the maintenance margin level) by the opening of trading on the following morning. If you do not, your broker will reverse your position at the open of trading, and you will be held liable for the consequences. The incremental funds deposited to bring your account back to the initial level are called *variation margin*.

Initial and maintenance margins on the same underlying asset can vary depending on the nature of your position. With futures contract markets, for example, there may be separate initial and maintenance margin levels for (1) outright positions, (2) hedge positions, (3) intracommodity spreads, and (4) intercommodity spreads. *Outright positions* refer to buying or selling a futures with no other position in the underlying asset or in a related futures. In general, these margins are referred to as speculative margins and are the highest of the four positions listed. *Hedge positions* refer to selling (buying) the futures when you hold a long (short) position in the underlying asset. Since the riskiness of the individual legs of the hedge tend to offset each, hedge margins are lower

[25] In April 2003, for example, the CME signed an agreement with the CBT to provide clearing services for all CBT products. The clearing firm is now known as "The Clearing Corporation." In addition, The Clearing Corporation and the Options Clearing Corporation have a joint system for the clearing of stock futures.

than speculative margins. If a farmer can document the fact that he is in the business of growing wheat, his broker will likely require only hedge margin when the farmer sells wheat futures.[26] *Intracommodity* (or *calendar*) *spreads* refer to buying a futures and selling a futures on the same underlying asset but with different contract maturities. Since the trader is both long and short the same underlying, the risk of the position is negligible. Hence, the margin levels on intracommodity spreads are quite low. Finally, *intercommodity spreads* refer to buying a futures and selling a futures with the same maturity month but with a different (albeit related) asset. Buying a *crack spread*, for example, means buying a heating oil futures and selling a crude oil futures of the same maturity. The margin levels of such intercommodity spreads are generally lower than outright positions, but are considerably higher than intracommodity spreads.

It is important to recognize that cash balances held in your margin account should not be considered costly. Since you are allowed to post margin in the form of Treasury bills or, alternatively, since your broker may simply pay you a money market interest rate on your cash balance, your money is earning a fair rate of return.[27] Margin deposits are only costly when your broker does not allow Treasury bill deposits or is unwilling to pay a market interest rate on your cash deposit.

**ILLUSTRATION 1.1** Compute the margin balances in a futures account.

*Compute the margin account balances at the end of each day assuming that you sold outright 10 Canadian dollar futures on the CME at a price of USD 0.6760/CDN midday on June 1, 1999. The CME's contract denomination is CDN 100,000, and their initial and maintenance margin requirements on this contract are USD 675 and USD 500, respectively. Assume your broker pays 5% simple interest on your margin account balance. The subsequent prices of the futures over the next nine trading days are given in the table below.*

On June 1, 1999, you sold 10 contracts midday at a price of USD 0.6760/CDN. By the end of the day, the market has moved against your position and the settlement price is 0.6770. This means you will be marked-to-market with a USD 1,000 loss, that is, 0.001 per contract times 10 contracts times the CDN 100,000 contract denomination. This amount is netted from your initial margin deposit, leaving you with an ending balance on June 1 of USD 5,750.

On June 2, the futures price settles at 0.6787. Over the day, you earned USD 0.79 interest on your margin account balance, that is, USD 5,750 times 0.05 times 1/365. The futures price, again, moved adversely to your position, causing a mark-to-market loss of USD 1,700. Adding your previous end-of-day balance, your earned interest, and your mark-to-market adjustment, you have USD 4,050.79 in your margin account when the minimum required maintenance level is USD 5,000 (i.e., USD 500 per contract times 10 contracts). The exchange issues you a margin call, whereupon you must deposit enough extra funds (i.e., variation margin) to bring your account balance back up to the initial margin level. The variation margin payment is USD 2,699.21.

[26] A wheat farmer who buys wheat futures is said to be *Texas hedging*. In this case, the farmer would pay the speculative margin levels.

[27] In the third chapter, we review the mechanics of the capital asset pricing model (CAPM). The CAPM specifies the "fair" rate of return on an asset given its risk. The fair rate of return on a risk-free asset is the rate of return on a default-free security such as the Treasury bill rate.

On June 3, the futures settles at 0.6802. You have earned USD 0.92 interest and are marked-to-market with a USD 1,500 loss. Your account balance remains above USD 5,000 so no additional variation margin is necessary. You are not so lucky on June 4, when the futures settles at 0.6831. You earn USD 0.72 interest and are marked-to-market with a USD 2,900 loss. Your account balance, USD 4,398.36, is now below the maintenance margin level and you are required to bring the balance back up to the initial level of USD 6,750.

The remaining entries in the table are computed in a similar fashion. Larger amounts of interest are earned on June 7 and June 14 resulting from the 3 days of interest earned over the weekend.

**USD Margin Balances in Futures Account**

| End of Day | Settlement Price | Interest Earned | Mark-to-Market | Maintenance Check | Cash Deposit | Ending Balance |
|---|---|---|---|---|---|---|
| 6/1/1999 | 0.6770 | | −1,000.00 | | 6,750.00 | 5,750.00 |
| 6/2/1999 | 0.6787 | 0.79 | −1,700.00 | 4,050.79 | 2,699.21 | 6,750.00 |
| 6/3/1999 | 0.6802 | 0.92 | −1,500.00 | 5,250.92 | 0.00 | 5,250.92 |
| 6/4/1999 | 0.6831 | 0.72 | −2,900.00 | 2,351.64 | 4,398.36 | 6,750.00 |
| 6/7/1999 | 0.6837 | 2.77 | −600.00 | 6,152.77 | 0.00 | 6,152.77 |
| 6/8/1999 | 0.6827 | 0.84 | 1,000.00 | 7,153.62 | 0.00 | 7,153.62 |
| 6/9/1999 | 0.6818 | 0.98 | 900.00 | 8,054.60 | 0.00 | 8,054.60 |
| 6/10/1999 | 0.6867 | 1.10 | −4,900.00 | 3,155.70 | 3,594.30 | 6,750.00 |
| 6/11/1999 | 0.6873 | 0.92 | −600.00 | 6,150.92 | 0.00 | 6,150.92 |
| 6/14/1999 | 0.6879 | 2.53 | −600.00 | 5,553.45 | 0.00 | 5,553.45 |

The amounts of the initial and maintenance margin levels are set by the exchange and are different for different futures contracts.[28] Since the margin is designed only to protect the integrity of the market over a single day, the margin must be large enough to cover a reasonable range of price movements over a single day. Exchanges commonly set the initial margin to cover the mean absolute daily price change of the contract plus 3 standard deviations.[29] The mean absolute daily price change of the Canadian dollar futures contract during the month of June 1999 was 0.0019 and the standard deviation was 0.0017. This rule implies, therefore, that the initial speculative margin should be $(0.0019 + 3 \times 0.0017) \times$ 100,000 or \$700 per contract, which is very close to the actual level of \$675. Note how both price volatility *and* contract size figure into the computation of the initial margin. Note also that with a pronounced change in price volatility, an exchange may elect to change the contract's margin levels.

## Transparency

A fourth important attribute of exchange-traded derivatives markets is that they are *transparent*—you can see what goes on. During the trading day, the price

[28] The margin levels set by the exchanges apply to the deposits made by clearing firms with the clearinghouse. The margin levels charged by brokers (and/or the clearing firms) to customers often exceed the exchange-mandated levels.

[29] See Edwards and Ma (1992, p.39).

quotes and trade prices/volumes stream across the screens of various on line data services. Then, at the end of the day, many financial publications such as the *Wall Street Journal* summarize each derivatives exchange's trading activity. An important figure provided to the financial press by the exchange's clearinghouse is the open interest in each contract. *Open interest* is a figure that expresses the amount of delivery that would take place if the contract was liquidated immediately.[30] To understand its computation each day, consider Table 1.3, which takes you through a hypothetical sequence of trades over five days. During the first day, A buys 30 contracts—10 from B, 5 from C, and 15 from D. The total trading volume over the day is 30 contracts.[31] The open interest is also 30 contracts. The total number of contracts outstanding is 30, which can be obtained by summing across all the open long positions (i.e., the total demand for delivery) *or* by summing across all the open short positions (i.e., the total supply promised).

**TABLE 1.3** Illustration of the computation of trading volume and open interest.

| | | | | End of Days | |
|---|---|---|---|---|---|
| Day | Buyer | Seller | Number of Contracts | Contract Volume | Open Interest |
| 1 | A | B | 10 | | |
| | A | C | 5 | | |
| | A | D | 15 | | |
| | | | | 30 | 30 |
| 2 | A | E | 15 | | |
| | B | A | 10 | | |
| | B | D | 20 | | |
| | | | | 45 | 55 |
| 3 | D | F | 40 | | |
| | F | G | 30 | | |
| | F | A | 15 | | |
| | | | | 85 | 50 |
| 4 | A | G | 20 | | |
| | D | B | 30 | | |
| | E | C | 25 | | |
| | | | | 75 | 90 |
| 5 | C | A | 40 | | |
| | G | B | 15 | | |
| | C | D | 10 | | |
| | | | | 65 | 60 |

[30] That is not to say that delivery *will* be made immediately. Open interest merely reflects the aggregate hedging and speculative demand in a particular commodity contract.

[31] Occasionally you will see the total trading volume reported by an exchange on such a day as 60 contracts. The rationale for such computation is that 30 contracts were purchased and 30 contracts were sold. For our purposes, we ignore this practice.

On the second day, A buys 15 more contracts but sells 10. Thus, his open long positions have increased from 30 to 35 contracts. B, on the other hand, entered the day short 10 contracts. He then proceeded to close his short position by buying 10 contracts and by buying 20 more contracts to enter a long position. At the end of the day, A is long 35 contracts and B is long 20 contracts, so the total open interest at the end of the second day is 55 contracts. Note that we could also arrive at the same open interest figure by considering only open short positions. At the end of the first day, B is short 10 contracts, C is short 5, and D is short 15. During day 2, B closes his short position, C does nothing, D sells 20 more contracts bringing his total to 25, and E establishes a new short position of 15 contracts. Summing across all open short positions, you have open interest of 5 + 35 + 15 or 55 contracts.

It is important to recognize that there is no direct linkage between trading volume and open interest. While open interest cannot change without trading volume, trading volume may increase, decrease or have no effect on the level of open interest prior to expiration. As a practical matter, open interest in delivery contracts such as grain futures tends to disappear prior to the delivery month. This reflects contract buyers and sellers reversing and closing their positions to avoid the transportation costs associated with accepting or making delivery of the underlying commodity. Open interest in cash settlement contracts, on the other hand, tends to carried into the delivery month and may even be quite large on the day before expiration. On the expiration day, all open positions are settled in cash and the open interest disappears.

### Regulation

In the United States, two regulatory bodies oversee derivatives traded on exchanges. The Securities and Exchange Commission (SEC) governs the markets for options on securities and the Commodity Futures Trading Commission (CFTC) governs futures and futures options. Option exchanges list options on stocks, bonds, and currencies, hence fall under the regulatory jurisdiction of the SEC. Futures and futures options exchanges fall under the jurisdiction of the CFTC. These regulatory authorities are both a blessing and a curse. On one hand, having the operation of exchanges monitored by a federal agency further enhances market integrity. The CFTC, for example, establishes *position limits* on the maximum number of contracts that a single trader may have at any one time. This safeguards against illicit activities such as short squeezes. On the other hand, these regulatory authorities may slow the pace of financial innovation. Each time an exchange considers introducing a new type of derivative contract, it must apply to the appropriate regulatory authority, specifying all terms and conditions of the contract, as well as explaining how its presence in the marketplace will benefit society. Such contract applications may go through several rounds of revision and take months (and sometimes years) to get approved.

### Examples of Exchange-Traded Derivatives

All derivatives exchanges summarize the trading activity of *all* of the contracts they list on a daily basis, and most make the summaries available on their internet websites. To provide a flavor for this type of information, we discuss three examples—stock options, U.S. Treasury-bond futures, and corn futures options. Many other examples appear in later chapters.

**Stock Options** The first example is options listed on the shares of Dell. Viewed in whole, exchange-traded options written on the same underlying asset are called an *option class*. Table 1.4A reports the prices of Dell stock options as of 1:53 PM (CST) on Tuesday, January 6, 2004 on the Chicago Board Options Exchange's website, www.cboe.com. At the time, Dell's shares had a quoted bid/ask spread of 35.05/35.06. The expiration month and the exercise price are reported in the columns headed "Calls" and "Puts." The first row in the table is for the January 2004 call and put with an exercise price of 5, as indicated by the prefix "04 Jan 5.00." By convention, all stock options traded in the United States expire on the Saturday following the third Friday of the contract month. The first five characters of the term in parenthesis is the option series ticker symbol. The call's ticker symbol, for example, is "DLYAA." Note that each ticker symbol in the table is unique. This is its identifier for trading purposes. Each ticker represents an option series, where an *option series* is identified by a unique triplet of attributes: (1) call or put, (2) exercise price, and (3) expiration day.

The table shows that neither the call nor the put traded on January 6, at least as of the time the prices were downloaded (i.e., their volumes of trading are 0). Both options have traded at some time in the past, however, since the call has open interest of 580 and the put has open interest of 245. The call has a bid/ask price quote of 30.00/30.10. The last trade price, 28.60, lies outside the option's prevailing bid/ask quotes. This merely indicates that the market price of the option has moved since the time of the last trade. When the last trade occurred cannot be inferred from the information in the table. All that can be inferred is that the trade did not occur on January 6, 2004. By exchange convention, each option contract is written on 100 shares of stock, although the option premiums are reported on a per share basis. The January 2004 call with an exercise price of 5, for example, has a quoted ask price of $30.10. If you were to buy this option, you would pay $3,010 for the right to buy 100 shares of Dell at $5 a share. All stock options traded in the United States are *American-style*, meaning that the buyer can exercised at any time up to and including the expiration day.[32]

Table 1.4A reveals two interesting characteristics about stock option markets. First, at-the-money options tend to be the most active. The table shows that more than 99 percent of call option trading volume and 85 percent of put option trading volume on January 6, 2004 was in option series with exercise prices between 32.50 and 37.50 (i.e., at-the-money options). Second, the total

[32] Many other styles of options exist. A *European-style* option, perhaps the most common, can be exercised only on the expiration date. A *Bermuda-style* option can be exercised on prespecified dates during the option's life.

**TABLE 1.4A** Summary of price, volume, and open interest information for Dell stock options drawn from www.cboe.com at 1:53 PM on Tuesday, January 6, 2004. Underlying stock has contemporaneous bid (ask) price of 35.05 (35.06).

| Calls | Last Sale | Bid | Ask | Vol | Open Int | Puts | Last Sale | Bid | Ask | Vol | Open Int |
|---|---|---|---|---|---|---|---|---|---|---|---|
| 04 Jan 5.00 (DLY AA-E) | 28.60 | 30.00 | 30.10 | 0 | 580 | 04 Jan 5.00 (DLY MA-E) | 0.05 | 0.00 | 0.05 | 0 | 245 |
| 04 Jan 7.50 (DLY AU-E) | 27.40 | 27.50 | 27.60 | 0 | 935 | 04 Jan 7.50 (DLY MU-E) | 0.45 | 0.00 | 0.05 | 0 | 1,012 |
| 04 Jan 10.00 (DLY AB-E) | 25.60 | 25.00 | 25.10 | 0 | 2,554 | 04 Jan 10.00 (DLY MB-E) | 0.05 | 0.00 | 0.05 | 0 | 12,981 |
| 04 Jan 12.50 (DLY AV-E) | 22.30 | 22.50 | 22.60 | 0 | 1,872 | 04 Jan 12.50 (DLY MV-E) | 0.05 | 0.00 | 0.05 | 0 | 1,209 |
| 04 Jan 15.00 (DLY AC-E) | 19.90 | 20.00 | 20.10 | 0 | 2,886 | 04 Jan 15.00 (DLY MC-E) | 0.05 | 0.00 | 0.05 | 0 | 7,190 |
| 04 Jan 17.50 (DLY AW-E) | 17.30 | 17.50 | 17.60 | 0 | 2,554 | 04 Jan 17.50 (DLY MW-E) | 0.10 | 0.00 | 0.05 | 0 | 9,807 |
| 04 Jan 20.00 (DLY AD-E) | 14.50 | 15.00 | 15.10 | 0 | 10,362 | 04 Jan 20.00 (DLY MD-E) | 0.05 | 0.00 | 0.05 | 0 | 27,524 |
| 04 Jan 22.50 (DLQ AX-E) | 11.70 | 12.50 | 12.60 | 0 | 4,120 | 04 Jan 22.50 (DLQ MX-E) | 0.05 | 0.00 | 0.05 | 0 | 7,753 |
| 04 Jan 25.00 (DLQ AE-E) | 10.20 | 10.00 | 10.10 | 2 | 22,611 | 04 Jan 25.00 (DLQ ME-E) | 0.05 | 0.00 | 0.05 | 0 | 23,350 |
| 04 Jan 27.50 (DLQ AY-E) | 7.70 | 7.50 | 7.60 | 0 | 32,333 | 04 Jan 27.50 (DLQ MY-E) | 0.05 | 0.00 | 0.05 | 0 | 21,488 |
| 04 Jan 30.00 (DLQ AF-E) | 5.10 | 5.00 | 5.10 | 2 | 42,340 | 04 Jan 30.00 (DLQ MF-E) | 0.05 | 0.00 | 0.05 | 0 | 39,133 |
| 04 Jan 32.50 (DLQ AZ-E) | 2.65 | 2.55 | 2.65 | 140 | 47,599 | 04 Jan 32.50 (DLQ MZ-E) | 0.05 | 0.00 | 0.10 | 70 | 34,591 |
| 04 Jan 35.00 (DLQ AG-E) | 0.55 | 0.55 | 0.65 | 1,490 | 126,530 | 04 Jan 35.00 (DLQ MG-E) | 0.55 | 0.45 | 0.55 | 485 | 39,290 |
| 04 Jan 37.50 (DLQ AT-E) | 0.05 | 0.00 | 0.05 | 0 | 49,257 | 04 Jan 37.50 (DLQ MT-E) | 2.55 | 2.40 | 2.50 | 10 | 4,404 |
| 04 Jan 40.00 (DLQ AH-E) | 0.05 | 0.00 | 0.05 | 0 | 42,460 | 04 Jan 40.00 (DLQ MH-E) | 5.10 | 4.90 | 5.00 | 0 | 6,914 |
| 04 Jan 42.50 (DLQ AS-E) | 0.05 | 0.00 | 0.05 | 0 | 255 | 04 Jan 42.50 (DLQ MS-E) | 0.00 | 7.40 | 7.50 | 0 | 147 |
| 04 Jan 45.00 (DLQ AI-E) | 0.05 | 0.00 | 0.05 | 0 | 8,573 | 04 Jan 45.00 (DLQ MI-E) | 10.50 | 9.90 | 10.00 | 0 | 149 |
| 04 Jan 50.00 (DLQ AJ-E) | 0.10 | 0.00 | 0.05 | 0 | 9,076 | 04 Jan 50.00 (DLQ MJ-E) | 14.20 | 14.90 | 15.00 | 0 | 168 |
| 04 Feb 20.00 (DLY BD-E) | 14.90 | 15.00 | 15.20 | 0 | 1,313 | 04 Feb 20.00 (DLY ND-E) | 0.05 | 0.00 | 0.05 | 0 | 45 |
| 04 Feb 22.50 (DLQ BX-E) | 12.30 | 12.50 | 12.70 | 0 | 1,165 | 04 Feb 22.50 (DLQ NX-E) | 0.05 | 0.00 | 0.05 | 0 | 620 |
| 04 Feb 25.00 (DLQ BE-E) | 8.50 | 10.00 | 10.20 | 0 | 1,954 | 04 Feb 25.00 (DLQ NE-E) | 0.05 | 0.00 | 0.05 | 0 | 3,275 |
| 04 Feb 27.50 (DLQ BY-E) | 6.80 | 7.60 | 7.70 | 0 | 1,657 | 04 Feb 27.50 (DLQ NY-E) | 0.10 | 0.05 | 0.10 | 0 | 3,721 |
| 04 Feb 30.00 (DLQ BF-E) | 5.40 | 5.20 | 5.30 | 0 | 2,477 | 04 Feb 30.00 (DLQ NF-E) | 0.15 | 0.10 | 0.20 | 200 | 7,054 |
| 04 Feb 32.50 (DLQ BZ-E) | 3.20 | 3.00 | 3.10 | 438 | 15,854 | 04 Feb 32.50 (DLQ NZ-E) | 0.50 | 0.40 | 0.45 | 15 | 18,014 |
| 04 Feb 35.00 (DLQ BG-E) | 1.45 | 1.30 | 1.40 | 88 | 32,620 | 04 Feb 35.00 (DLQ NG-E) | 1.25 | 1.20 | 1.30 | 265 | 10,863 |
| 04 Feb 37.50 (DLQ BT-E) | 0.40 | 0.35 | 0.45 | 3,784 | 23,799 | 04 Feb 37.50 (DLQ NT-E) | 3.00 | 2.75 | 2.85 | 20 | 2,117 |

**TABLE 1.4A** (Continued)

| Calls | Last Sale | Bid | Ask | Vol | Open Int | Puts | Last Sale | Bid | Ask | Vol | Open Int |
|---|---|---|---|---|---|---|---|---|---|---|---|
| 04 Feb 40.00 (DLQ BH-E) | 0.10 | 0.05 | 0.10 | 0 | 8,146 | 04 Feb 40.00 (DLQ NH-E) | 5.80 | 4.90 | 5.10 | 0 | 1,051 |
| 04 Feb 42.50 (DLQ BS-E) | 0.05 | 0.00 | 0.05 | 0 | 1,285 | 04 Feb 42.50 (DLQ NS-E) | 7.90 | 7.40 | 7.50 | 0 | 32 |
| 04 Feb 45.00 (DLQ BI-E) | 0.05 | 0.00 | 0.05 | 0 | 1,318 | 04 Feb 45.00 (DLQ NI-E) | 10.50 | 9.90 | 10.00 | 0 | 97 |
| 04 May 20.00 (DLY ED-E) | 15.00 | 15.10 | 15.20 | 0 | 2,194 | 04 May 20.00 (DLY QD-E) | 0.00 | 0.00 | 0.05 | 0 | 0 |
| 04 May 22.50 (DLQ EX-E) | 12.40 | 12.60 | 12.80 | 0 | 1,066 | 04 May 22.50 (DLQ QX-E) | 0.15 | 0.05 | 0.10 | 0 | 670 |
| 04 May 25.00 (DLQ EE-E) | 9.50 | 10.20 | 10.40 | 0 | 862 | 04 May 25.00 (DLQ QE-E) | 0.20 | 0.10 | 0.15 | 0 | 1,252 |
| 04 May 27.50 (DLQ EY-E) | 7.40 | 7.90 | 8.00 | 0 | 695 | 04 May 27.50 (DLQ QY-E) | 0.35 | 0.25 | 0.30 | 0 | 1,959 |
| 04 May 30.00 (DLQ EF-E) | 5.30 | 5.70 | 5.80 | 0 | 1,981 | 04 May 30.00 (DLQ QF-E) | 0.55 | 0.50 | 0.60 | 0 | 11,585 |
| 04 May 32.50 (DLQ EZ-E) | 3.90 | 3.70 | 3.90 | 0 | 2,664 | 04 May 32.50 (DLQ QZ-E) | 1.10 | 1.05 | 1.15 | 50 | 7,858 |
| 04 May 35.00 (DLQ EG-E) | 2.25 | 2.20 | 2.30 | 84 | 16,581 | 04 May 35.00 (DLQ QG-E) | 2.10 | 2.00 | 2.05 | 0 | 6,313 |
| 04 May 37.50 (DLQ ET-E) | 1.15 | 1.15 | 1.20 | 54 | 11,003 | 04 May 37.50 (DLQ QT-E) | 3.20 | 3.40 | 3.50 | 40 | 893 |
| 04 May 40.00 (DLQ EH-E) | 0.55 | 0.50 | 0.60 | 8 | 11,819 | 04 May 40.00 (DLQ QH-E) | 5.70 | 5.30 | 5.40 | 0 | 910 |
| 04 May 42.50 (DLQ ES-E) | 0.15 | 0.20 | 0.25 | 0 | 3,187 | 04 May 42.50 (DLQ QS-E) | 0.00 | 7.50 | 7.60 | 0 | 1,155 |
| 04 May 45.00 (DLQ EI-E) | 0.10 | 0.05 | 0.10 | 0 | 183 | 04 May 45.00 (DLQ QI-E) | 0.00 | 9.90 | 10.00 | 0 | 380 |
| 04 Aug 20.00 (DLY HD-E) | 0.00 | 15.20 | 15.30 | 0 | 0 | 04 Aug 20.00 (DLY TD-E) | 0.00 | 0.05 | 0.10 | 0 | 0 |
| 04 Aug 22.50 (DLQ HX-E) | 0.00 | 12.80 | 12.90 | 0 | 10 | 04 Aug 22.50 (DLQ TX-E) | 0.00 | 0.10 | 0.20 | 0 | 0 |
| 04 Aug 25.00 (DLQ HE-E) | 10.10 | 10.40 | 10.60 | 0 | 18 | 04 Aug 25.00 (DLQ TE-E) | 0.00 | 0.25 | 0.35 | 0 | 29 |
| 04 Aug 27.50 (DLQ HY-E) | 7.60 | 8.20 | 8.30 | 0 | 110 | 04 Aug 27.50 (DLQ TY-E) | 0.65 | 0.50 | 0.60 | 0 | 55 |
| 04 Aug 30.00 (DLQ HF-E) | 6.30 | 6.20 | 6.30 | 0 | 71 | 04 Aug 30.00 (DLQ TF-E) | 1.00 | 0.90 | 1.05 | 0 | 339 |
| 04 Aug 32.50 (DLQ HZ-E) | 4.40 | 4.40 | 4.50 | 0 | 221 | 04 Aug 32.50 (DLQ TZ-E) | 1.60 | 1.60 | 1.70 | 100 | 611 |
| 04 Aug 35.00 (DLQ HG-E) | 2.95 | 2.90 | 3.00 | 8 | 823 | 04 Aug 35.00 (DLQ TG-E) | 2.70 | 2.60 | 2.70 | 0 | 1,153 |
| 04 Aug 37.50 (DLQ HT-E) | 1.70 | 1.75 | 1.85 | 104 | 365 | 04 Aug 37.50 (DLQ TT-E) | 4.20 | 4.00 | 4.10 | 110 | 141 |
| 04 Aug 40.00 (DLQ HH-E) | 1.00 | 1.00 | 1.05 | 38 | 213 | 04 Aug 40.00 (DLQ TH-E) | 0.00 | 5.70 | 5.80 | 0 | 121 |
| 04 Aug 42.50 (DLQ HS-E) | 0.00 | 0.50 | 0.60 | 0 | 207 | 04 Aug 42.50 (DLQ TS-E) | 0.00 | 7.70 | 7.90 | 0 | 1 |
| 04 Aug 45.00 (DLQ HI-E) | 0.00 | 0.25 | 0.30 | 0 | 6 | 04 Aug 45.00 (DLQ TI-E) | 0.00 | 10.00 | 10.10 | 0 | 0 |
| Total | | | | 6,240 | 552,764 | | | | | 1,365 | 319,669 |

**TABLE 1.4B** Summary of price, volume, and open interest information for Dell leaps drawn from www.cboe.com at 1:53 PM on Tuesday, January 6, 2004. Underlying stock has contemporaneous bid (ask) price of 35.05 (35.06).

| Calls | Last Sale | Bid | Ask | Vol | Open Int | Puts | Last Sale | Bid | Ask | Vol | Open Int |
|---|---|---|---|---|---|---|---|---|---|---|---|
| 05 Jan 5.00 (ZDE AA-E) | 29.30 | 30.00 | 30.20 | 0 | 237 | 05 Jan 5.00 (ZDE MA-E) | 0.00 | 0.00 | 0.15 | 0 | 0 |
| 05 Jan 10.00 (ZDE AB-E) | 25.30 | 25.10 | 25.30 | 0 | 1,000 | 05 Jan 10.00 (ZDE MB-E) | 0.05 | 0.00 | 0.15 | 0 | 1,316 |
| 05 Jan 15.00 (ZDE AC-E) | 17.90 | 20.20 | 20.40 | 0 | 1,464 | 05 Jan 15.00 (ZDE MC-E) | 0.10 | 0.00 | 0.15 | 0 | 4,597 |
| 05 Jan 17.50 (ZDE AW-E) | 18.70 | 17.80 | 18.00 | 0 | 570 | 05 Jan 17.50 (ZDE MW-E) | 0.20 | 0.05 | 0.15 | 0 | 1,044 |
| 05 Jan 20.00 (ZDE AD-E) | 13.70 | 15.40 | 15.60 | 0 | 5,759 | 05 Jan 20.00 (ZDE MD-E) | 0.25 | 0.15 | 0.25 | 0 | 4,618 |
| 05 Jan 22.50 (ZDE AX-E) | 11.90 | 13.10 | 13.30 | 0 | 3,021 | 05 Jan 22.50 (ZDE MX-E) | 0.60 | 0.30 | 0.40 | 0 | 6,358 |
| 05 Jan 25.00 (ZDE AE-E) | 11.00 | 10.90 | 11.10 | 0 | 6,291 | 05 Jan 25.00 (ZDE ME-E) | 0.65 | 0.60 | 0.70 | 50 | 7,969 |
| 05 Jan 27.50 (ZDE AY-E) | 8.20 | 8.90 | 9.00 | 0 | 11,869 | 05 Jan 27.50 (ZDE MY-E) | 1.00 | 1.00 | 1.10 | 0 | 4,784 |
| 05 Jan 30.00 (ZDE AF-E) | 6.40 | 7.00 | 7.20 | 0 | 18,903 | 05 Jan 30.00 (ZDE MF-E) | 1.75 | 1.60 | 1.70 | 0 | 7,978 |
| 05 Jan 32.50 (ZDE AZ-E) | 5.50 | 5.30 | 5.50 | 6 | 9,914 | 05 Jan 32.50 (ZDE MZ-E) | 2.65 | 2.35 | 2.50 | 0 | 6,032 |
| 05 Jan 35.00 (ZDE AG-E) | 4.00 | 3.90 | 4.10 | 13 | 47,104 | 05 Jan 35.00 (ZDE MG-E) | 3.60 | 3.40 | 3.60 | 0 | 16,575 |
| 05 Jan 37.50 (ZDE AT-E) | 2.90 | 2.80 | 2.90 | 76 | 8,299 | 05 Jan 37.50 (ZDE MT-E) | 5.10 | 4.80 | 5.00 | 0 | 1,605 |
| 05 Jan 40.00 (ZDE AH-E) | 1.90 | 1.90 | 2.00 | 72 | 19,980 | 05 Jan 40.00 (ZDE MH-E) | 6.50 | 6.40 | 6.60 | 0 | 3,127 |
| 05 Jan 42.50 (ZDE AS-E) | 1.35 | 1.25 | 1.35 | 50 | 2,990 | 05 Jan 42.50 (ZDE MS-E) | 8.90 | 8.20 | 8.40 | 0 | 1,418 |
| 05 Jan 45.00 (ZDE AI-E) | 0.75 | 0.80 | 0.90 | 0 | 7,157 | 05 Jan 45.00 (ZDE MI-E) | 12.30 | 10.30 | 10.50 | 0 | 1,132 |
| 05 Jan 50.00 (ZDE AJ-E) | 0.35 | 0.30 | 0.40 | 150 | 4,766 | 05 Jan 50.00 (ZDE MJ-E) | 15.60 | 14.90 | 15.00 | 0 | 2,833 |
| 06 Jan 20.00 (WDQ AD-E) | 16.40 | 16.20 | 16.40 | 0 | 1,078 | 06 Jan 20.00 (WDQ MD-E) | 0.55 | 0.55 | 0.65 | 0 | 426 |
| 06 Jan 22.50 (WDQ AX-E) | 0.00 | 14.10 | 14.40 | 0 | 220 | 06 Jan 22.50 (WDQ MX-E) | 0.95 | 0.90 | 1.00 | 0 | 391 |
| 06 Jan 25.00 (WDQ AE-E) | 12.30 | 12.20 | 12.40 | 10 | 543 | 06 Jan 25.00 (WDQ ME-E) | 1.50 | 1.35 | 1.45 | 0 | 311 |
| 06 Jan 27.50 (WDQ AY-E) | 10.80 | 10.40 | 10.60 | 0 | 642 | 06 Jan 27.50 (WDQ MY-E) | 2.40 | 1.95 | 2.05 | 0 | 476 |
| 06 Jan 30.00 (WDQ AF-E) | 8.50 | 8.70 | 9.00 | 0 | 1,310 | 06 Jan 30.00 (WDQ MF-E) | 2.80 | 2.70 | 2.80 | 20 | 1,249 |
| 06 Jan 32.50 (WDQ AZ-E) | 6.70 | 7.20 | 7.50 | 0 | 674 | 06 Jan 32.50 (WDQ MZ-E) | 3.80 | 3.60 | 3.80 | 0 | 5,498 |
| 06 Jan 35.00 (WDQ AG-E) | 5.50 | 5.90 | 6.10 | 0 | 7,414 | 06 Jan 35.00 (WDQ MG-E) | 5.40 | 4.80 | 4.90 | 0 | 8,683 |
| 06 Jan 37.50 (WDQ AT-E) | 4.40 | 4.80 | 5.00 | 0 | 369 | 06 Jan 37.50 (WDQ MT-E) | 7.10 | 6.10 | 6.20 | 0 | 4,621 |
| 06 Jan 40.00 (WDQ AH-E) | 3.40 | 3.80 | 4.00 | 0 | 3,826 | 06 Jan 40.00 (WDQ MH-E) | 9.40 | 7.50 | 7.80 | 0 | 834 |
| 06 Jan 42.50 (WDQ AS-E) | 2.55 | 2.95 | 3.10 | 0 | 801 | 06 Jan 42.50 (WDQ MS-E) | 0.00 | 9.20 | 9.50 | 0 | 695 |
| 06 Jan 45.00 (WDQ AI-E) | 2.10 | 2.30 | 2.45 | 0 | 1,642 | 06 Jan 45.00 (WDQ MI-E) | 11.10 | 11.10 | 11.30 | 0 | 1,911 |
| 06 Jan 50.00 (WDQ AJ-E) | 1.35 | 1.30 | 1.50 | 0 | 1,387 | 06 Jan 50.00 (WDQ MJ-E) | 15.10 | 15.20 | 15.40 | 0 | 1,188 |
| Total | | | | 377 | 169,230 | | | | | 70 | 97,669 |

open interest for calls, 552,764, exceeds that of puts, 319,669. In stock option markets, there seems to be greater interest in speculating that the stock price will rise rather than fall. Table 1.4B has the same columns as Table 1.4A. The only difference is that Table 1.4B contains "Leaps" written on Dell's stock. In the 1980s, the CBOE, in response to investor demand, began trading "Long-term Equity Anticipation Securities," or Leaps. Where stock options have times to expiration up to nine months, Leaps have times to expiration up to three years. As of January 6, 2004, Dell had leaps expiring in January 2005 and January 2006. When Dell's January 2004 stock options expire on January 17, 2004, leaps with a January 2007 expiration will be introduced. Note that there is significant open interest in long-term options. Apparently a large number of traders have long-term directional views on Dell's stock price.

**S&P 500 Futures** Table 1.5 reports a summary of the daily trading activity of the Chicago Mercantile Exchange's (CME's) S&P 500 futures contract on Friday, July 20, 2004. The data were downloaded from the CME's website, www.cme.com. The reporting conventions are different than those used for stock options. Futures exchanges provide daily summaries, showing the open, high, low and last trade prices as well as the settlement price of each futures/futures option contract. Some of the prices that appear have a suffix "B" or "A." Such prices are not trades but are quotes. If a bid price quote exceeds the highest trade price in a given day, it appears as the "high." Conversely, if the lowest ask price quote is beneath the lowest trade price as for the day, it appears as the low. The last trade and settlement prices may differ because of market movements between the time of the last trade and the market close. The settlement price is used for the marking-to-market of futures positions.

The leftmost column contains the contract month. The S&P 500 futures is on a quarterly contract expiration cycle and expire at the open on the third Friday of the contract month. Elsewhere on the exchange's website are the specifications of the contract. The S&P 500 futures has a multiplier of 250, which means that the September 2004 futures contract settled at a dollar value of $1,093.40 \times \$250 = \$273,425$ on July 20, 2004. With an estimated contract volume of 44,681, this means that approximately $12.2 billion of stocks traded hands through this contract on this day. Futures exchanges disseminate their daily summaries shortly after the market closes each day. At that time, precise figures on the trading volume and current open interest are not known. Consequently, the exchanges report an estimate volume as well as the actual volume and open interest for the previous day, as is shown in Table 1.5. The open interest (i.e., number of contracts outstanding) for the September 2004 futures is 579,019. Since each contract has a face value of $273,425, this means that the aggregate hedging and speculative demand for the S&P 500 index portfolio, as reflected by the September 2004 futures contract, exceeds $158 billion.

**Eurodollar Futures Options** Table 1.6 contains a market summary for the CME's Eurodollar futures option contracts traded on Friday, July 20, 2004. The table includes only activity for September 2004 call options and was downloaded from www.cme.com. Other call option contract expirations as well as put options are also available of the exchange's website. Options on futures are like

**TABLE 1.5** Summary of daily trading for S&P 500 futures contract drawn from www.cme.com for Friday, July 20, 2004.

| | | | | | | | | Prior Day | | |
|---|---|---|---|---|---|---|---|---|---|---|
| Month | Open | High | Low | Last | Settlement | Point Change | Estimated Volume | Settlement | Volume | Open Interest |
| Sep04 | 1090.20 | 1099.20 | 1083.10 | 1094.00 | 1093.70 | 310 | 44,681 | 1090.60 | 57,203 | 579,019 |
| Dec04 | 1089.50 | 1099.00B | 1085.00 | 1098.00A | 1094.00 | 300 | 225 | 1091.00 | 6,547 | 12,623 |
| Mar04 | 1085.00 | 1101.40B | 1085.00 | 1098.40A | 1095.40 | 300 | 68 | 1092.40 | | 465 |
| Jun04 | ---- | 1104.50B | 1089.50A | 1101.50A | 1098.50 | 300 | | 1095.50 | | 268 |
| Sep04 | ---- | 1108.50B | 1093.50A | 1105.50A | 1102.50 | 300 | | 1099.50 | | 16 |
| Dec04 | ---- | 1113.00B | 1098.00A | 1110.00A | 1107.00 | 300 | | 1104.00 | | 16 |
| Mar04 | ---- | 1118.50B | 1103.50A | 1115.50A | 1112.50 | 300 | | 1109.50 | | 6 |
| Jun04 | ---- | 1124.00B | 1109.00A | 1121.00A | 1118.00 | 300 | | 1115.00 | | 6 |
| Total | | | | | | | 44,974 | | 63,750 | 592,419 |

options on assets except that when a futures option is exercised, a futures position rather than an asset is delivered.[33] The options are American-style, and expire together with the underlying futures on the second London business day before the third Wednesday of the contract month. Exercising a Eurodollar option before expiration results in the delivery of the underlying futures, with each futures contract having a denomination of 1 million dollars.[34]

The leftmost column of Table 1.6 contains the option's exercise price. The first row shows a value of 9625. This means that the call provides its holder to buy the underlying futures contract at an index level of 96.25.[35] To identify the rate of interest on the underlying Eurodollar time deposit, the index level is subtracted from 100. Thus, buying the September 2004 futures call option with an exercise price of 9800, means acquiring the right to lend your money at 100.00 – 98.00 = 2.00 beginning in September 2004, where the amount of your deposit is 1 million dollars. The cost of acquiring this right (using the last trade price for illustrative purposes) is 0.09% of par or 0.0009 cents per dollar of deposit times the 1 million dollar contract denomination of $900.

## ATTRIBUTES OF OTC DERIVATIVE MARKETS

Early derivatives use was in the form of OTC contracts. Markets lacked depth and liquidity, which meant that early unwinding of a contract involved negotiating with your counterparty, frequently at unfavorable terms. In addition, contract defaults were commonplace, undermining the integrity of the market. Gradually, exchange-traded derivatives markets took over. Having a centralized market with standardized contracts and transparency provided needed depth and liquidity. Having a clearinghouse with a system of margining provided needed assurance that the terms of contracts would be honored. Exchange-traded markets continued to dominate, reaching market dominance in 1970s and 1980s—a period of major financial innovation. Exchanges introduced derivatives on financial assets such as stocks, stock indexes, bonds, and currencies. In addition, contract designs were streamlined with the use of cash settlement. The banking community was quick to realize that they, too, could design such structures for customers. Indeed, they could design any type of contract the customer wanted without the encumbrance of obtaining regulatory approval. We now turn to describing the key attributes of OTC derivative contract markets: contract flexibility and the regulatory environment within which OTC derivatives markets

[33] The Eurodollar futures contract has a denomination of USD 1,000,000 and is cash-settled to the interest rate on a USD 1,000,000 Eurodollar deposit with three months to maturity. Its price is quoted as an index level and is created by subtracting the Eurodollar rate from 100. A price of 94.50 therefore means that the contract buyer is willing to lend USD 1,000,000 at 5.50 percent for a three-month period beginning on the date the futures contract expires.

[34] As a rule of thumb, futures options will expire in the month before the underlying futures if the futures is settled by delivery. If the underlying futures is cash settled, the futures options and the futures will both be cash settled in the contract month.

[35] Available space in the financial is limited, so various abbreviations are used. One abbreviation is that decimal points are excluded from the strike price. Another is that only two places to the right of the decimal are reported. The strike price of 9787 is actually 97.875.

**TABLE 1.6** Summary of daily trading for September 2004 Eurodollar futures call options traded drawn from www.cme.com for Friday, July 20, 2004.

| | | | | | | | | Prior Day | | |
|---|---|---|---|---|---|---|---|---|---|---|
| Strike | Open | High | Low | Last | Settlement | Point Change | Estimated Volume | Settlement | Volume | Open Interest |
| 9625 | — | — | — | — | 1.8000 | 1.00 | | 1.79000 | | 1,050 |
| 9650 | — | — | — | — | 1.5500 | 1.00 | | 1.54000 | | 9,381 |
| 9675 | — | — | — | — | 1.3000 | 1.00 | | 1.29000 | | 612 |
| 9700 | — | — | — | — | 1.0500 | 1.00 | | 1.04000 | | 6,121 |
| 9725 | — | — | — | — | 0.8000 | 1.00 | | 0.79000 | | 3,434 |
| 9750 | — | — | — | — | 0.5500 | 0.75 | | 0.54250 | | 25,851 |
| 9775 | — | — | — | — | 0.3050 | 0.50 | | 0.30000 | | 56,199 |
| 9787 | 0.1850 | 0.1850 | 0.1850 | 0.1850 | 0.1875 | 0.50 | 900 | 0.18250 | 51 | 61,368 |
| 9800 | 0.0950 | 0.0950 | 0.0900 | 0.0900 | 0.0875 | UNCH | 5,455 | 0.08750 | 10,783 | 219,220 |
| 9812 | 0.0350 | 0.0400 | 0.0350 | 0.0350 | 0.0325 | –0.50 | 3,102 | 0.03750 | 17,890 | 226,158 |
| 9825 | 0.0150 | 0.0150 | 0.0150 | 0.0150 | 0.0125 | –0.25 | 3,050 | 0.01500 | 16,450 | 269,037 |
| 9837 | 0.0050 | 0.0050 | 0.0050 | 0.0050 | 0.0075 | UNCH | 1,400 | 0.00750 | 8,101 | 190,439 |
| 9850 | — | — | — | — | 0.0050 | UNCH | 3,450 | 0.00500 | 6,118 | 282,240 |
| 9862 | — | — | — | — | 0.0025 | UNCH | | 0.00250 | 1,000 | 227,693 |
| 9875 | — | — | — | — | CAB | UNCH | | CAB | | 271,862 |
| 9887 | — | — | — | — | CAB | UNCH | | CAB | | 215,882 |
| 9900 | — | — | — | — | CAB | UNCH | | CAB | | 135,934 |
| 9912 | — | — | — | — | CAB | UNCH | | CAB | | 9,610 |
| 9925 | — | — | — | — | CAB | UNCH | | CAB | | 59,567 |
| 9950 | — | — | — | — | CAB | UNCH | | CAB | | 6,756 |

operate. Discussions of the transparency and credit risk issues follow, along with descriptions to two actively traded OTC derivative contract designs.

### Contract Flexibility

The chief virtue of OTC markets is contract flexibility. A customer can virtually be assured that he can find someone who is willing to tailor a derivatives contract to meet his needs. You might go to your local wine merchant, for example, and negotiate a contract for the future delivery of Penfolds Bin 389 Cabernet Shiraz from South Australia though the grapes have not yet been harvested. As noted earlier in the chapter, however, the primary interest is not in commodities but rather in financial assets. As the OTC markets grew in the early 1980s, it quickly became apparent more structure was needed to help avoid the controversies of the past. A global trade association called the International Swaps and Derivatives Association (ISDA) was chartered in 1985,[36] and today ISDA has over 450 members (largely banks who make markets in OTC derivatives) in 37 countries on five continents. Its primary purpose is to encourage the prudent and efficient development of the privately negotiated derivatives business by, among other things, promoting practices conducive to the efficient conduct of the business, including the development and maintenance of derivatives documentation.

The ISDA derivatives documentation comes in two forms. Documents such as *2000 ISDA Definitions and Annex to the 2000 ISDA Definitions*[37] lay out the industry's "language" for communicating the terms of derivatives transactions. Other documents such as the *ISDA Master Agreement (Local Currency – Single Jurisdiction)* and the *ISDA Master Agreement (Multicurrency – Cross Border)* provide the text for actual contracts. If two parties are about to enter their first OTC derivative transaction with each other, they will first sign a general agreement called the *ISDA Master Agreement.* The purpose of this agreement is to specify the general (nontransaction specific) conditions under which all transactions between the two parties will be carried out. With the definitions and master agreement in hand, individual trades can be negotiated between parties and confirmed in writing within minutes. The faxed confirmation will contain references to the ISDA documents such as:

> The definitions and provisions contained in the 1991 ISDA Definitions (as published by the International Swaps and Derivatives Association, Inc.) are incorporated into this Confirmation.

and

> The Confirmation supplements, forms part of, and is subject to, the following ISDA Master Agreement:

[36] Originally the association was called the International Swap Dealers Association.

[37] See International Swap Dealers Association (2000a, 2000b). ISDA's website can be viewed at www.isda.org.

| | |
|---|---|
| Dated as of: | July 28, 2000 |
| Between: | Counterparty A |
| And: | Counterparty B |
| Master agreement number: | 12345 |

The rest of the confirmation will include the specific terms of the trade. Prior to reviewing the terms of specific types of OTC trades, however, it is worth discussing some other important attributes of the OTC market.

### Regulation

Aside from the self-imposed working standards of ISDA, OTC markets are unregulated. For OTC markets, the arguments regarding transparency are the opposite of what they were for exchanges. On one hand, trading participants in OTC derivatives markets do not have the extra layer of protection provided by a federal agency overseeing trading, making sure that everyone is operating according to the same set of rules and safeguarding against manipulative practices. On the other, OTC markets can introduce new types of derivative contracts at the drop of a hat—an important competitive advantage over exchanges that must seek governmental approval. All that an OTC transaction requires is a willing buyer and a willing seller.

### Transparency

*Market transparency* refers to the amount of information provided about the derivatives being traded. Exchange markets are transparent in the sense that information about trade prices, volumes, and open interest figures are publicly disseminated. OTC markets, on the other hand, are privately negotiated transactions. At any point in time, it is virtually impossible to predicted the amount of interest in a particular underlying commodity. Prior to the collapse of the tulip bulb derivatives trading in Holland, for example, no one could have gauged the full repercussions of the precipitous price decline. In an attempt to provide at least some transparency, both ISDA and the Bank for International Settlements (BIS) perform semiannual surveys of banks, asking that they itemize the notional amounts of outstanding derivatives positions by underlying asset and type of contract. Indeed, the OTC figures shown earlier in the chapter were drawn from the latest BIS survey. But surveys such as these are not comprehensive, take a long time to complete, and are reported with a considerable lag. In addition, notional amount is a misleading figure. The notional amount of an interest rate swap agreement, for example, is simply the principal amount upon which interest payments are computed. The market value of the agreement pales by comparison. Moreover, the aggregate notional amount (and even aggregate market value) are overstated since more than one bank may be reporting the same contract (i.e., the banks may be counterparties on the same trade). Nonetheless, looking at changes in notional amount through time, as well as the levels across asset categories, countries, and types of markets, is informative.

**FIGURE 1.3** OTC derivatives trading.

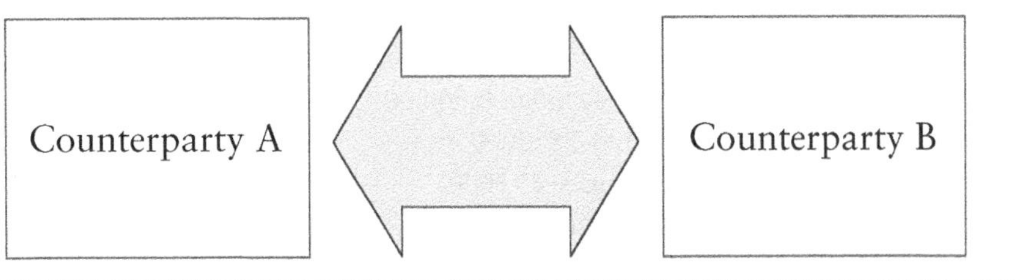


### Credit Risk

Unlike contracts in exchange markets, contracts in the OTC market have *credit risk*, that is, risk that your counterparty will default. We discussed some examples earlier in the chapter. The tulip bulb fiasco was caused by put option writers reneging on their obligation to buy bulbs from the growers. Similarly, futures markets evolved because traders and merchants sometimes did not fulfill promised deliveries on forward contracts. With OTC contracts, the parties are forced to deal with credit on their own. The counterparties to an OTC derivatives transaction (see Figure 1.3) are usually dealer versus user (i.e., a bank versus a firm) or dealer versus dealer (i.e., a bank versus a bank). Hence, the issue of creditworthiness is asymmetric. While large banks may be extremely creditworthy, some firms or smaller banks may not be.

One possible way to deal with credit risk is to trade only with creditworthy counterparties. A bank with such a credit risk policy may not be acting in the best interests of its shareholders, however, since there is probably a good deal of profitable trading that can be conducted with less creditworthy customers. Another way to handle credit risk is by asking the customer to provide a guarantor. Under such an arrangement, the firm will pay a premium (e.g., a fixed percentage of the notional amount) to a third party who acts as guarantor. Yet another way to handle the credit risk is to embed the expected cost of default by adjusting the terms of the contract.[38]

### Examples of OTC Derivative Contracts

Without standardized contracts and a central marketplace, finding information on OTC derivative contract specifications involves talking directly with OTC dealers. The terms of some generic types of instruments are well known. Below we describe two—plain-vanilla interest rates swaps and currency forward contracts.

**Plain-Vanilla Interest Rate Swap** The terms of a particular swap agreement are usually negotiated over the phone. Once an oral agreement is reached, the OTC derivatives dealer will fax a confirmation to the customer. Table 1.7 illustrates selected terms from the confirmation of a plain-vanilla, *fixed-for-floating* inter-

[38] Credit risk and credit risk derivatives are discussed in Chapter 19.

**TABLE 1.7** Selected terms from the confirmation of an OTC interest rate swap.

The terms of the particular swap transaction to which this confirmation relates are as follows:

| | |
|---|---|
| Calculation amount | USD 30,000,000.00 |
| Trade date | July 28, 2000 |
| Effective date | August 1, 2000 |
| Termination date | August 1, 2005 |

The fixed rate payer pays on each payment date an amount determined in accordance with the following:

| | |
|---|---|
| Fixed rate payer | BANK A |
| Payment dates | Commencing on February 1, 2001 and semiannually thereafter on the first calendar day of each calendar day of February and August up to and including the termination date. |
| Fixed rate | 7.036% |
| Fixed rate, day-count fraction | 30/360 |

The floating rate payer pays on each payment date an amount determined in accordance with the following:

| | |
|---|---|
| Floating rate payer | COMPANY B |
| Payment dates | Commencing on February 1, 2001 and semiannually thereafter on the first calendar day of each calendar day of February and August up to and including the termination date. |
| Floating rate option | USD-LIBOR-LIBO |
| Designated maturity | 6 months |
| Reset dates | The first day of the relevant calculation period |
| Rounding factor | One hundred-thousandth of one percent |
| Floating rate, day-count fraction | Actual/360 |

est rate swap. The sheet is divided into three panels of information. The first panel provides the calculation amount, trade date, and termination date. The *calculation amount* is the notional amount upon which interest payments are computed. The *trade date* is the day on which the parties enter into the agreement, the *effective date* is the first day of the term of the agreement, and the *termination date* is the last day of the agreement.

The second and third panels of information specify obligations of the fixed rate and floating rate payers, respectively. The fixed rate payer, in this case, is BANK A, which promises to make semiannual, fixed interest payments at a rate of 7.036 percent. The "30/360" fixed rate, day-count fraction implies that each month (year) is assumed to have 30 (360) days. Thus, BANK A is obliged to pay COMPANY B an amount equal to

$$\$30{,}000{,}000 \times 0.07036 \times \frac{180}{360} = \$1{,}055{,}400$$

every six months for five years, with the first payment commencing on February 1, 2001.

At the same time, the floating rate payer, COMPANY B, is obliged to make semiannual interest payments on the same dates. The *floating rate option* is specified to be "USD-LIBOR-LIBO" and the *designated maturity* is 6 months. The term, USD-LIBOR-LIBO, is defined in the *Annex to the 2000 ISDA Definitions*[39] and means the offered rate on U.S. dollar deposits for the period of the designated maturity as they appear on the Reuters Screen LIBO Page. Since the *reset date* is the first day of the calculation period, the first floating rate payment becomes known as of the effective date of the swap. If the rate is 6.8125 percent on August 1, 2000, the floating rate interest payment on February 1, 2001 will be computed as follows. First, you compute the actual number of days between August 1, 2000 and February 1, 2001. The actual number of days is 184. Next, we compute the semiannual interest rate by taking the annual interest rate, 6.8125 percent, and multiplying by the *floating rate, day-count fraction*,

$$\frac{184}{360}$$

to get percent, which gets rounded to 3.48194 percent by virtue of the stated *rounding factor*. The floating rate payment that COMPANY B is obliged to make on February 1, 2001 is $1,044,582. The fixed rate and floating rate payments are then *netted* so that only one party pays on a particular payment date. In our illustration, this means BANK A will pay COMPANY B $10,818 on February 1, 2001. Who pays and the amount of subsequent payments will depend on the level of the floating rates on the remaining reset dates.

We called the interest rate swap illustrated in Table 1.7 a *fixed-for-floating* swap. It also goes by other names including a *fixed-to-floating* swap, a *fixed-against-floating* swap, and a *coupon* swap. In order to distinguish the counterparties to a fixed-for-floating swap, one is termed the *payer* and the other, the *receiver*. The paying and receiving refer to the *fixed* interest payment. Thus, BANK A is the payer of the interest swap illustrated in Table 1.7, and COMPANY B is the receiver. Sometimes, the terms *buyer* and *seller* are used to describe swap counterparties. Since these terms are not intuitively obvious, their use in the swap market is discouraged. With fixed-for-floating swaps, however, the terms refer to the *obligation to pay fixed*. Thus, a swap *buyer pays fixed* and receives the floating interest stream. A swap *seller receives fixed* and pays floating. Thus, in our illustration, BANK A is the buyer of the interest rate swap and COMPANY B is the seller.

In general, terms of OTC derivative contracts are not available in financial publications such as the *Wall Street Journal*. Indeed, since OTC derivatives are privately negotiated and have wide-ranging terms, there are no means to systematically collect and report such information. One way to obtain indicative prices or rates of certain "generic" OTC derivatives deals is to subscribe to a service such as Bloomberg, Reuters, and Telerate that provides such quotes on a real-

[39] See International Swaps and Derivatives Association (2000b, p.41).

**TABLE 1.8** Fixed-for-floating interest rate swap quotes from Bloomberg at 3:50 PM (EST) on Monday, August 7, 2000.

| Term | Bid | Ask |
|---|---|---|
| 2 yr | 6.983 | 7.024 |
| 3 yr | 6.985 | 7.026 |
| 4 yr | 7.013 | 7.053 |
| 5 yr | 7.036 | 7.077 |
| 6 yr | 7.059 | 7.100 |
| 7 yr | 7.079 | 7.120 |
| 8 yr | 7.084 | 7.125 |
| 9 yr | 7.100 | 7.141 |
| 10 yr | 7.112 | 7.153 |
| 15 yr | 7.139 | 7.180 |
| 20 yr | 7.123 | 7.164 |
| 30 yr | 7.083 | 7.123 |

time basis. Essentially, what these services provide is access to a number of pages (computer screens), each page containing the current market quotes of generic types of trades. The rates shown in Table 1.8, for example, are fixed-for-floating swap rates provided on one of Bloomberg's screens at 3:50 PM (EST) on Monday, August 7, 2000. While interest rate swaps can have a wide variety of terms, the terms of these swaps are "standardized." The periodic payments of all these swaps are made semiannually, with the first payment occurring in 6 months. All of the rates are set in such a manner that the swaps have a zero upfront payment. The floating rate interest payment is indexed to the 6-month LIBOR rate with an "actual/360" day-count fraction convention, and the fixed rate interest payment is based on the quotes appearing in the table and is calculated using a "30/360" day-count fraction convention. So, given these standard practices, the terms of the entire swap are summarized by the term and by the fixed rate. Bid and ask rates appear in the table (on the Bloomberg screen). These represent the highest bid rate and the lowest ask rate of all OTC dealers supplying Bloomberg with intraday quotes. If you buy the swap, you will pay the ask rate and receive LIBOR. If you sell the swap, you will receive the bid rate and pay LIBOR. The difference between the bid and ask rates is the dealer's spread. As the table shows, spreads in the plain-vanilla interest rate market are incredibly small, averaging about 4 basis points.

### Currency Forwards

Currency forward prices are also reported on a real-time basis by a number of data vendors. The prices reported in Table 1.9, for example, were drawn from Bloomberg. The table contains U.S. dollar (USD) bid and ask price quotes of one Great Britain pound (GBP) in the spot and forward markets as of 2:25 PM (EST) on March 27, 2006. To buy one pound in the spot market costs USD 1.7478. To buy one pound in one week (i.e., a 1-week forward contract) costs USD 1.7479, and so on. Forward rates are quoted with terms to maturity as

**TABLE 1.9** USD/GBP spot and forward exchange rate quotes drawn from Bloomberg at 2:25 PM (EST), March 27, 2006.

| | | USD/GBP | |
|---|---|---|---|
| Term | Bid Rate | Ask Rate | Bid/Ask Spread |
| Spot | 1.7475 | 1.7478 | 0.0003 |
| 1 week | 1.7476 | 1.7479 | 0.0003 |
| 1 month | 1.7480 | 1.7483 | 0.0003 |
| 2 month | 1.7487 | 1.7490 | 0.0003 |
| 3 month | 1.7494 | 1.7497 | 0.0003 |
| 4 month | 1.7503 | 1.7506 | 0.0003 |
| 5 month | 1.7510 | 1.7514 | 0.0004 |
| 6 month | 1.7519 | 1.7522 | 0.0003 |
| 9 month | 1.7543 | 1.7547 | 0.0004 |
| 1 year | 1.7562 | 1.7567 | 0.0005 |
| 2 year | 1.7602 | 1.7615 | 0.0013 |
| 3 year | 1.7645 | 1.7688 | 0.0043 |
| 4 year | 1.7685 | 1.7763 | 0.0078 |
| 5 year | 1.7760 | 1.7853 | 0.0093 |

long as five years. Note that as the time to maturity increases, the spread between the bid and ask rates increases. This is a reflection of the fact that the markets for longer term forward contracts are less liquid.

## SUMMARY

This chapter provides a broad-ranging overview of derivative contract markets. The first lesson of the chapter is that there exist only *two* types of derivative contracts—a forward and an option. Buying a forward means that you are obliged to buy the asset specified in the contract at some future date at a price agreed upon today. Buying an option means that you have the right, but not the obligation, to buy (in the case of a call) or sell (in the case of a put) the underlying asset at some future date at a price agreed upon today. So, although current day markets appear to have different types of derivative contracts trading, do not be overwhelmed. Each and every one can be decomposed into a portfolio of forwards and options.

The second lesson is that derivatives markets exist because it is either expensive to trade the underlying asset, or trading in the underlying asset is restricted in some way. Derivative contract trading is merely an inexpensive and effective means of trading the underlying asset.

The third lesson involves developing an understanding of the evolution of derivatives markets. Derivative contracts have been around thousands of years. The first recorded use dates back to 18th century BCE in ancient Babylon. Early derivative contracts resulted from private (or "over-the-counter") negotiations, hence trading was relatively undisciplined, and contract defaults were not uncommon. By the mid-1860s, it became clear that centralized markets with standardized contracts and a clearinghouse would add structure to the market, improving market depth and liquidity, and would eliminate the undesirable consequences of contract default. Hence, the birth of the first futures exchange—the Chicago Board of Trade in 1985. From the late 1800s through the 1960s, futures contracts written on physical commodities were the dominant form of derivatives trading. While grains were the first to be introduced, physical commodities such as metals and livestock were added during this period. In addition, many more futures exchanges were introduced in the United States as well as other countries worldwide including Canada, Brazil, the United Kingdom, and Australia.

Beginning in the early 1970s, derivatives markets have gone through some dramatic changes. The 1970s saw the introduction of exchange-traded futures on financial assets such as currencies and interest rates as well as exchange-traded options on common stocks. The 1980s saw even more interesting and important innovations in exchange-traded derivatives market—cash settlement of derivative contracts, stock index futures, and options on underlyings including currencies, interest rates, and stock indexes. The 1980s also saw the rebirth of OTC derivatives markets. The newfound interest in derivatives on financial assets, together with the OTC markets' flexibility in contract design, spawned the development of contracts tailor-made to meet the risk management needs of customers. Where the notional amount of OTC contracts was negligible in the early 1980s, it matched exchange-traded derivatives by 1991 and is nearly seven times larger today.

## REFERENCES AND SUGGESTED READINGS


Aristotle, 1885. *Politics*. Translated by Benjamin Jowett. The Internet Classics Archive. <http://classics.mit.edu/Aristotle/politics.html>.

Bank for International Settlements. 2004. 74th Annual Report.

Chicago Board of Trade. 1994. *Commodities Trading Manual*. Chicago: Chicago Board of Trade.

Chicago Board of Trade. 1990. *Emergency Action*. Chicago: Chicago Board of Trade.

Edwards, Franklin R., and Cindy W. Ma. 1992. *Futures and Options*. New York: McGraw-Hill, Inc.

Garber, Peter M. 2000. *Famous First Bubbles: The Fundamentals of Early Manias*. Cambridge, Massachusetts: MIT Press.

Gastineau, Gary. 1988. *The Options Manual,* 3rd ed. New York: McGraw-Hill.

International Swaps and Derivatives Association, 2000a. *2000 ISDA Definitions*. New York, NY: International Swaps and Derivatives Association).

International Swaps and Derivatives Association. 2000b. *Annex to the 2000 ISDA Definitions*. June 2000 version. New York: International Swaps and Derivatives Association.

Lee, Inmoo, Scott Lochhead, Jay Ritter, and Quanshui Zhao. 1996. The costs of raising capital. *Journal of Financial Research* 19 (Spring): 59–74.

Stoll, Hans R. and Robert E. Whaley. 1985. The new options markets, in *Futures Markets: Their Economic Role,* edited by Anne Peck. Washington, D.C.: American Enterprise Institute.

## APPENDIX 1: SQUEEZING THE SOYBEAN MARKET[40]

In the spring of 1989, an Italian grain-trading firm by the name of Ferruzzi Finanziaria S.p.A. began acquiring soybean futures contracts. Simultaneously, the firm purchased a significant percentage of the cash-market soybeans available for delivery against these contracts. Whether the firm's intentions were to squeeze markets it is impossible to say. Regardless of the Ferruzzi's intentions, however, on July 12, 1989, the size of the firm's holdings compelled the Chicago Board of Traded (CBT) to order all market participants to liquidate soybean futures positions in excess of the speculative trading limit. Exchanges rarely actively interfere with markets and news of the CBT's directive made headlines worldwide. This appendix describes the events and the aftermath of the CBT's decision to take emergency action.

### Soybean Markets in the Spring of 1989

Soybean markets were in peril as early as 1988. The worst drought in nearly half a century was devastating farmers in the United States and rapidly shrinking soybean reserves. The U.S. Department of Agriculture forecast that by the end of August 1989 there would be only 125 million bushels of soybeans remaining in silos: a mere three-week supply! The scarcity of domestic reserves stood to significantly increase the probability that market participants with short positions in soybean futures markets would default. Market defaults are borne by clearinghouses and impede normal exchange activity. Consequently, the grim state of soybean markets had regulators on edge. It was apparent that soybean markets would only maintain their integrity "if all market participants conducted their business in an economic and responsible manner." Any deviation from this standard had the potential to instigate a disastrous string of events.

### A Crisis Develops

Hedgers holding long futures contracts unwind positions if and when an underlying commodity can be purchased cheaply enough on the cash market to cover costs of carry. Upon purchase of the underlying commodity, futures contracts become redundant. After all, there is no need to lock in the price of an asset already owned.

For this reason, given the current state of soybean markets, regulators grew anxious as an international grain-trading organization named Ferruzzi Finanziaria purchased soybean futures and soybean stocks simultaneously. If the company's intention was to hedge against increases in the price of soybeans (as company spokespeople claimed), this behavior was illogical. Indeed, at the same time Ferruzzi was aggressively buying soybean and soybean future contracts, the

[40] I am grateful for the help of Seth James Wechsler in preparing the first draft of this appendix. The dates and details of the emergency actions taken in response to the apparent squeeze in the soybean market were taken from Chicago Board of Trade (1990). The quotes appearing in this appendix were also taken from CBT (1990).

majority of firms hedging soybean prices were unwinding their long positions and acquiring soybeans on the cash market. If Ferruzzi continued to hold dominant positions in both the futures and cash market, regulators were concerned that prices might become artificially inflated.

### A Crisis Postponed

On May 16, with just three days remaining until the expiration date of the May futures contract, the Commodity and Futures Trading Commission delivered a written warning to Ferruzzi:

> We are further concerned by the large long position that you hold in the May future. We believe that because of your holding of about 16.2 million bushels relative to the amount of soybeans available for delivery, your further actions can have a substantial impact on whether or not the price of the May future becomes artificial relative to commercial values. You are prohibited by law from causing an artificial price. Price manipulation is a violation of .... the Commodity Exchange Act.[41]

and

> if prices of the May future have been, are now, or should become artificial during the liquidation due to your action or inaction, we will consider whether or not to pursue an investigation that could result in charges of price manipulation.[42]

As of May 18, however, Ferruzzi still had not liquidated its position. At this point, the CTFC took a more aggressive approach. Ferruzzi Finanziaria was contacted by phone and informed that its hedging exemptions were revoked.[43]

Ferruzzi responded by engaging in a number of spread transactions. More specifically, it sold its May futures contracts and bought July. Markets would maintain their integrity in May, but the stage was set for a fierce, potentially disruptive confrontation in July.

### A Tightening Fist—Ferruzzi Increases Size of its Holdings

By early June Ferruzzi had acquired a 32-million-bushel net long position in the July futures contract. This position was almost double the size of the long position the firm had been ordered to unwind only three weeks earlier! When asked to explain the size of its position, Ferruzzi claimed that its futures holdings were

[41] CBT (1990, p. 20).
[42] CBT (1990, p. 9).
[43] A hedging exemption permits a firm to hold contracts in excess of the speculative trading limit. In the case of soybeans, the speculative trading limit is 3 million bushels. Firms are granted hedging exemptions routinely, however exchanges can revoke these exemptions at any time should it be judged that the exemptions are being used for speculative purposes.

hedges against export sales and the anticipated crushing requirements of Central Soya, a major U.S. soybean processor and wholly owned subsidiary of Ferruzzi Finanziaria. Because the expiration date of Ferruzzi's contracts was two months away, regulators deemed immediate action to be unnecessary. Ferruzzi Finanziaria's holdings would be closely monitored and action would be taken (if necessary), as the firm's contracts reached maturity.

Would Ferruzzi actually purchase the soybean requirements it claimed to be hedging? If and when the soybeans were acquired, would Ferruzzi proceed with an orderly liquidation of its long futures positions? Only time would tell.

### Crisis and Confrontation

As July approached, Ferruzzi remained virtually the sole holder of soybean stocks in approved-for-delivery locations. Assuming Ferruzzi intended to refrain from price manipulation, this behavior was highly irregular. To appreciate this, one must examine the differences between futures prices expiring in July and in August. At the end of May, the July futures contract was priced 7 cents higher than the August contract. By June, this differential had climbed to 30 cents. As June drew to a close, the difference was 40 cents! Despite the enormous profits it could have reaped by selling its futures contracts, Ferruzzi chose to maintain its prodigious long position. Additionally, Ferruzzi failed to liquidate futures contracts at critical times when soybeans could have been purchased for lower net costs than those resulting from soybean delivery via the July futures. Taking into account expenses associated with load-out, weighing and grading, transportation, and allowance for grade difference, local soybean prices were substantially below the cost of acquiring soybeans via the futures-delivery mechanism.

The size of Ferruzzi's holdings measured on a per bushel basis decreased as the end of July approached, but Ferruzzi's holdings in terms of the percentage of the contract's open interest increased drastically. As of June, the firm owned 18% of the contract's open interest. By the second week in July, Ferruzzi owned 53% of the contract's open interest!

As July 19 drew near, regulators felt that Ferruzzi had disregarded normal hedging practices to such a large extent that interference in markets was once again necessary. If the CBT or the CFTC did not intervene, a price distortion, and the market failures that could accompany it, would be nearly unavoidable.

Both the CBT and the CFTC had been in almost daily contact with Ferruzzi since May:

> June 1: CFTC staff urges Ferruzzi to buy cash and liquidate July futures.
>
> June 5: CBT's Business Conduct Committee calls in all major market participants, long and short, and reminds them of their obligation to effect orderly liquidation of the next expiring contract.
>
> June 12: CFTC staff urges Ferruzzi to buy cash and liquidate futures.

> June 13 and June 14: CFTC staff again urges Ferruzzi to buy cash and liquidate futures.
>
> June 15: Senior staffs of CBT and CFTC meet in Chicago to discuss concerns about orderly liquidation of July futures.
>
> June 19 and 28: CFTC staff once more urges Ferruzzi to buy cash and sell futures.

By July it had become apparent that Ferrruzzi would not liquidate its contracts unless forced to do so. On July 5, the CBT's Business Conduct Committee summoned representatives of Ferruzzi Finanziaria. These representatives were informed that unless immediate steps were taken to liquidate July futures contracts the CBT's Board of Directors would be asked to consider emergency action. The CFTC relayed a similar message to Ferruzzi representatives on July 6. On July 7, the CBT's Business Conduct Committee delivered a final warning. Continued failure to comply by July 10, Ferruzzi was warned, would almost certainly result in emergency action by the exchange.

Despite these warnings, however, Ferruzzi representatives made it quite clear that the company had no intention of reducing its holdings.

## Emergency Action

Upon concluding that Ferruzzi had little intention of complying with federal and exchange regulations the CFTC's reaction was immediate. On July 11, Ferruzzi's hedging exemptions were revoked. The chairman of the CBT's Board of Directors was notified that emergency action in soybean markets might be necessary.

The Board of Directors met immediately following the close of trading on July 11. Information concerning Ferruzzi's holdings was presented to the committee and the consequences of emergency action were discussed. The board adopted the following Emergency Resolution by a vote of 16 to 1:

> RESOLVED, that the Board of Directors of the Board of Trade of the City of Chicago hereby determines that an emergency exists with regard to the July 1989 soybean futures contract traded on the exchange that requires immediate action and threatens or may threaten fair and orderly trading in, the liquidation of, and delivery pursuant to, the July 1989 soybean futures contract, and hereby adopts the following measure to deal with this emergency.
>
> Effective as of the opening of the market on July 12, 1989, any person or entity either alone or in conjunction with any other person or entity, who owns or controls a gross long or short position for any purpose whatsoever in excess of three million bushels in the July 1989 soybean futures contract traded on the Exchange must reduce said position and subsequent positions by at least 20% per trading day subject to the following absolute limits . . .

> [The limits precluded any person from owning or controlling a July 1989 soybean futures position of more than 3 million bushels on July 18 or more than 1 million bushels as of the expiration of trading on July 20][44]

### The Aftermath—Soybean Market Stability Ensured

Overall, financial institutions were supportive of the CBT's intervention in soybean markets. There were critiques of the action, however. Critics contended that Ferruzzi's liquidation triggered an artificially large decline in futures prices.

July futures prices did decline following the CBT's announcement that emergency action was to be taken. On the first day of Ferruzzi's mandated liquidation, futures prices closed 39.5 cents a bushel lower than at the opening bell. As Ferruzzi continued to carry out its liquidation, however, soybean prices actually rose. In fact, by the time Ferruzzi had completed unwinding its holdings, futures prices were actually 1.5 cents higher than they had been at the start of the liquidation. An appraisal of the effects of the emergency action conducted by an independent government agency later confirmed that the CBT's intervention had "no significant effect" on either farm or consumer soybean prices.

As for Ferruzzi Finanziaria, the firm underwent a major reorganization of its international trading operations. On September 15, 1989, Ferruzzi announced that its three principal grain and oilseed traders had resigned because of "differences over trading."

[44] CBT (1990, p. 20).

# PART Two

# Fundamentals of Valuation

# 2

# Assumptions and Interest Rate Mechanics

This book deals with risk management using derivatives. Effective risk management, however, requires accurate risk measurement, and accurate risk measurement requires a thorough understanding of valuation. The purpose of this chapter and the next is to review the fundamental principles of security valuation. This chapter focuses on the key assumptions that underlie security valuation models and reviews the use of interest rate mechanics in moving expected future cash flows through time. The next chapter focuses on estimating appropriate discount rates for securities given their risk characteristics.

The outline of this chapter is as follows. The first section presents the set of assumptions that underlie our valuation framework. The second section deals with the interest rate mechanics that allow us to move cash flows through time. The third and fourth sections then apply the assumptions and interest rate mechanics to value fixed income securities—discount bonds and coupon bonds. The fifth section focuses on the relation between interest rates and term to maturity as well as the meaning and computation of forward rates of interest. The sixth section describes common stock valuation. The chapter concludes with a summary.

## UNDERLYING ASSUMPTIONS

Building valuation models requires making assumptions. Two assumptions that lay the foundation for security valuation are the absence of costless arbitrage opportunities and frictionless markets. The first assumption is critical; the second is made largely for expositional convenience.

### Absence of Costless Arbitrage Opportunities

The absence of costless arbitrage opportunities is driven by a basic tenet of human behavior—individuals prefer more wealth to less, holding other factors constant. "Greed is good!"[1] If two perfect substitutes are traded in the marketplace and they do not have the same price, someone will immediately step in to earn a risk-free profit by simultaneously buying the cheaper asset and selling the more expensive one. Because the asset is both bought and sold simultaneously (albeit in different markets), there is no risk. This is the single key element of an *arbitrage* strategy.[2] Because this particular arbitrage involves no cash outlay, it is a *costless arbitrage*. The person enacting the strategy is called an *arbitrageur*. Because the prices of perfect substitutes must be the same in equilibrium, this principle is also known as the *law of one price*.

Arbitrageurs are at work in all markets where perfect substitutes are traded simultaneously. The shares of IBM, for example, trade on many exchanges in the U.S., not to mention other countries worldwide. Suppose that we see that IBM's stock has a bid price of $120.75 per share on the New York Stock Exchange (NYSE) and an ask price of $120.25 per share on the Pacific Coast Exchange (PCE). We can earn a costless arbitrage profit of $0.50 per share by simultaneously selling IBM on the NYSE and buying it on the PCE. Do not expect to find such opportunities, however. Market makers on the various exchanges continuously monitor markets for such anomalies, and act immediately upon finding any pricing distortion that exceeds trading costs.

### Frictionless Markets

Frictionless markets is an assumption made more for convenience than necessity. Invoking it permits sharper focus on the economics of the situation at hand, absent the effects of market idiosyncrasies. Once the economic intuition is developed, the effects of trading costs, taxes, divergent borrowing and lending rates, and the like can be added straightforwardly. For now, however, we wipe the slate clean.

The assumption of frictionless markets requires:

- No trading costs.
- No taxes.
- Unlimited borrowing and lending at the risk-free rate of interest.
- Freedom to sell (short) with full use of any proceeds.
- Can trade at any time.

**No Trading Costs** Trading costs are costs associated with executing a transaction. These include (1) commissions paid to brokers as well as (2) bid/ask spreads and (3) market impact costs paid to market makers. The effects of trading costs can modeled quite easily. Take, for example, the IBM arbitrage illustration provided earlier in the chapter. Recall that we implicitly incorporated the effect of the bid/

[1] This is from a speech by Gordon Gekko to Teldar Paper Shareholders in the 1987 movie, *Wall Street*, directed by Oliver Stone. See www.americanrhetoric.com/Movie Speeches/moviespeechwallstreet.html.

[2] The term, arbitrage, is frequently misapplied. *Risk arbitrage*, for example, refers to a trading strategy in which the shares of a firm rumored to be on the verge of being acquired are purchased and the shares of the acquiring firm are simultaneously purchased. Since the merger may or may not take place, this activity is *not* arbitrage.

ask spread by comparing the bid price (the price at which we can sell immediately) on the NYSE with the ask price (i.e., the price at which we can buy immediately) on the PCE. Suppose that, in addition to the market maker's spread, our broker charges a commission rate of $0.10 per share. We can still earn a costless arbitrage profit of $0.40. Beyond commissions and spreads, we may face market impact costs if you attempt to trade in large quantities. Since exchanges are obliged to have a minimum market depth at the prevailing market quotes, some amount of profitable arbitrage can be earned. Going beyond that posted levels of depth requires estimating the price elasticity of the stock. Thus, in general, we can account for the effects of trading costs in a logical and coherent fashion because they are known or can be estimated reasonably precisely.

**No Taxes** Taxes affects valuation in two ways: first, it reduces the amount of the gain (loss), and, second, it may affect the gain (loss) differentially depending upon whether it comes in the form of ordinary income or capital gain. In some models, the first consideration is unimportant. In the IBM arbitrage illustration, the after-trading cost gain was $0.40. Assuming the marginal tax rate is less than 100%, the arbitrage opportunity still exists. The second consideration can have more far reaching consequences, however. Consider two identical firms, one that pays a generous cash dividend each quarter (and raises capital for new investment by issuing new securities) and another that pays no dividends (and uses the cash for new investment). If our long-term capital gains tax rate is less than our ordinary income tax rate, we will prefer to hold the shares of the second firm, holding other factors constant. Taxes, per se, do not make the security valuation problem more complicated, just more tedious. Because the marginal tax rates on the different forms of income are known or can be estimated, incorporating them directly in the valuation problem is straightforward.

**Unlimited Borrowing and Lending at the Risk-Free Interest Rate** This assumption has two important facets. First, it says that the borrowing and lending rates are equal. Obviously, this is not the case. A bank has a margin between the rate it pays on demand deposits and the rate it charges on short-term loans. Second, it assumes that everyone is equally creditworthy. Borrowing and lending rates vary by customer, with the largest and most secure customers receiving the most favorable rates (i.e., the lowest margin). Because rates are known, accountingfor the effects of divergent borrowing and lending rates within the valuation framework, like trading costs and taxes, is manageable.

**Freedom to Sell (Short) with Full Use of Any Proceeds** For large institutions, short selling of securities with full use of proceeds is common. Suppose, for example, that we believe that the price of IBM will fall from, say, $120 to $100 over the next month. If we short sell IBM, we will see $120 in cash appear in our account and will have a liability of one share of IBM. Since we have access to the cash, we can invest it immediately and earn interest while our short sale position is in place. When (or if) the price drops to $100, as we predicted, we buy a share of IBM to cover our short position. Our net gain is $120 plus interest less $100. For retail customers, short sales are costly in the sense that the broker may not pay interest on the cash generated from the short sale. Also, for securities in short supply, short sales may not be possible. Under the frictionless market assumption, we have full use of proceeds.

**Can Trade at Any Time** In order to execute arbitrage, the markets for the perfect substitutes must be open at the same time. Suppose that in late morning London time we see that IBM's shares are quoted at \$121.00 (bid) and \$121.25 (ask) on the London Stock Exchange, while IBM's shares closed at \$120.75 (bid) and \$120.875 (ask) at the NYSE on the previous day. Does that mean a costless arbitrage opportunity is available? Obviously not! The NYSE is not open, so we cannot simultaneously sell in London and buy in New York. Under the frictionless markets assumption, the markets for all securities are open all of the time.

## INTEREST RATE MECHANICS

The next step in preparing to value securities is to review interest rate mechanics, that is, how to move expected cash flows through time. Throughout this book, we use *continuously compounded* interest rates. Continuous rates are realistic, convenient, and consistent with the practice of dynamic risk management. Other types of interest rates are mentioned periodically in the discussion, but only when it is necessary to unravel the mystery of the pricing conventions used in a particular market.

### Continuously Compounded Interest Rates

Interest rates follow a number of conventions. The first and, perhaps, simplest convention is that interest rates are quoted on an *annualized* basis. This is done to facilitate comparisons across different investment alternatives. If one investment promises a 40% return over five years and another promises a 23% return over three years, it is not immediately obvious which investment we prefer. On the other hand, if we are told that the first investment promises 6.96% annually and the second investment 7.14% annually, the choice is obvious. We are comparing apples with apples.

A second convention is that rates are usually quoted as *nominal rates*. If a bank advertises that it pays 6% *compounded* semiannually, they nominally pay 6% per year (recall the first convention). What they actually pay is, however, 3% each 6 months (i.e., the nominal interest rate divided by the number of compounding intervals in a year). Because interest on interest is earned in the second 6-month period, the effective annual interest rate is $(1 + 0.06/2)^2 = 6.09\%$. In general, given a nominal rate of interest $r$ and $m$ compounding intervals a year, the *effective* interest rate is determined by

$$\text{Effective rate} = (1 + r/m)^m - 1 \tag{2.1}$$

Holding the nominal interest rate constant, the effective interest rate rises with the number of compounding intervals. As $m$ approaches infinity, the effective interest rate becomes

$$\text{Effective rate} = e^r - 1 \tag{2.2}$$

In (2.2), $r$ is referred to as a *continuously compounded* nominal rate of interest.

On first appearance, continuous interest rates may seem unrealistic, but just the opposite is true. Suppose we are interested in modeling the growth of a tree. A tree does not grow by a discrete amount each few months throughout the year. It grows continuously. If the current height of the tree is 50 feet and it grows at a rate of 5% a year, the height of the tree in 6 months will be $50e^{0.05(0.5)} = 51.266$ feet.

The prices of financial instruments grow in exactly the same way. For risky securities such as stocks, prices evolve through time as new information arrives in the marketplace. Growth is continuous in the sense that the movement of the stock price is smooth through the day, however, the rate of movement changes. For risk-free securities, the rate of price movement is constant. Assuming a zero-coupon bond grows at a rate of $r$ percent annually, an investment of $B$ will have a value of $F$ at time $T$, where $F$ is given by the formula,

$$F = Be^{rT} \tag{2.3}$$

If the growth rate is 6% and the bond's price is \$100, its price will be $F = 100e^{0.06(3/12)} = 101.511$ in three months, $F = 100e^{0.06(6/12)} = 103.045$ in six months, and so on.

## DISCOUNT BONDS

With the continuously compounded interest rate mechanics in hand, we now turn to the valuation of bonds or so-called *fixed income securities*. Bonds are of two types—*zero-coupon* (or *discount bonds*) and *coupon-bearing bonds*. This section focuses on the discount bonds. Coupon-bearing bonds follow in the next. We begin by describing discount bond valuation, and then use the valuation formula as a means of measuring interest rate risk exposure. We follow with a description of the discount instruments issued by the U.S. Treasury.

### Valuation

A *discount bond* or *zero-coupon bond* is a debt security with a *single* future cash payment, $F$. $F$ is usually called the *par amount* or *face value* of the bond. If the discount bond has an annualized yield of $r$ percent and a time to maturity of $T$ years, it is

$$B = Fe^{-rT} \tag{2.4}$$

The term, $e^{-rT}$, is called a *discount factor*. It is the current price of \$1 received at time $T$. Figure 2.1 shows the discount factors as a function of yield to maturity. Note that the yield and the discount factor are inversely related. The higher the yield, the lower the discount factor. Note also that the function is convex. As yield increases, the bond's value decreases at a decreasing rate. Rearranging (2.4), we can compute the rate of return on a discount bond given its current price, par amount, and term to maturity, that is,

**FIGURE 2.1** Discount factor as a function of yield to maturity.

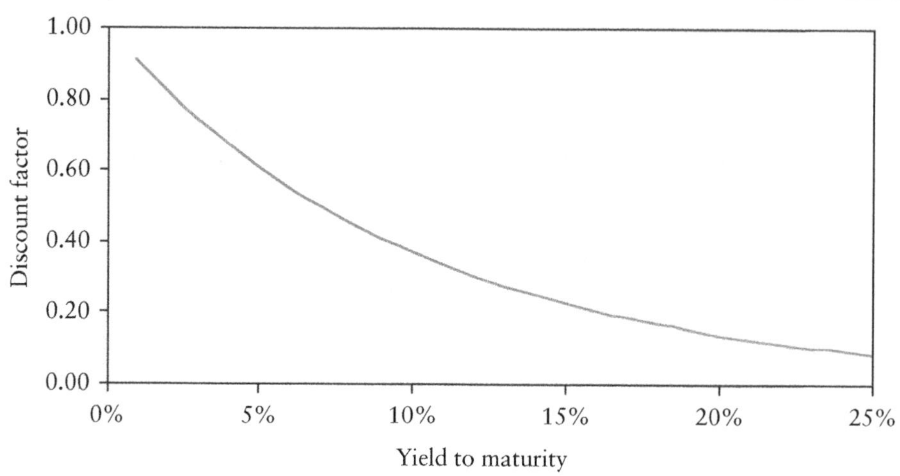


$$r = \frac{\ln(F/B)}{T} \tag{2.5}$$

**ILLUSTRATION 2.1** Compute implied yield of discount bond.

*In the early 1980s, a number of banks marketed discount bonds to retail customers as a long-term savings vehicle for future expenditures such as their children's college tuition. Interest rates were so high at the time that it was not uncommon to see advertisements saying that a four cent investment today will provide one dollar in 25 years. What is the implied annualized rate of return on this investment?*

The annualized rate of return or yield on this investment is

$$r = \frac{\ln(1/0.04)}{25} = 12.876\%$$

This value may be computed using the OPTVAL function,

OV_IR_DISCB_YIELD(*price*, *face*, *term*)

where *price* is the current price of the bond, *face* is its face value, and *term* is its term to maturity. Using the parameters of the problem,

B4 =OV_IR_DISCB_YIELD($B$1,$B$2,$B$3)

| | A | B | C | D | E |
|---|---|---|---|---|---|
| 1 | Present value | 0.040 | | | |
| 2 | Future value | 1.000 | | | |
| 3 | Years to maturity | 25 | | | |
| 4 | Implied interest rate | 12.876% | | | |
| 5 | | | | | |

### Risk Measurement

In holding a fixed income security such as a discount bond, we are often concerned with knowing what will happen to the value of our bond if interest rates change. Such risk measures are easy to develop once we know how to value the bond. One approach is to simply change the yield in the valuation formula (2.4) from its current level to see what happens to bond value. Indeed, this was the procedure used to generate Figure 2.1. Unfortunately, different bonds react to changes in interest rates in very different ways. To isolate the essential interest rate risk characteristics of a bond, we approximate the shape of the bond valuation function using a polynomial function. Specifically, we expand the bond valuation function (2.4) into a Taylor series about the current yield $r_0$,[3] that is,

$$dB = \frac{dB}{dr}(r - r_0) + \frac{1}{2}\frac{d^2B}{dr^2}(r - r_0)^2 + \frac{1}{6}\frac{d^3B}{dr^3}(r - r_0)^3 + \cdots \tag{2.6}$$

What (2.6) says is that the change in the bond valuation function (2.4) for a given change in yield equals a polynomial function with an infinite number of terms. As we proceed through the terms on the right-hand side of (2.6), however, they become progressively smaller in size. Interest rate risk management usually involves only the first or, perhaps, the first and the second terms of the series. Higher-order terms are usually ignored.

Let us begin with a first-order approximation. It goes by a variety of names including *DV01* and *duration*. Ignoring second- and higher-order terms on the right-hand side of (2.6), the approximate change in bond value for a given change in yield in given by

$$dB \approx \frac{dB}{dr}(r - r_0) \tag{2.7}$$

where the derivative *dB/dr* is determined from the valuation equation (2.4), that is,

$$\frac{dB}{dr} = -TFe^{-rT} \tag{2.8}$$

**DV01** The acronym, *DV01*, stands for the dollar value of one basis point (i.e., 0.01 of 1%). To create the appropriate formula for *DV01*, we substitute (2.8) into (2.7) and replace $r - r_0$ with 0.0001 and get

$$dB \approx -TFe^{-rT}(0.0001) \equiv DV01 \tag{2.9}$$

[3] A Taylor series expansion can be used to approximate any smooth nonlinear function such as the bond valuation equation. For more details regarding this application, see Appendix 2A.

**Duration** *Duration* is the percent change in bond value for a given change in yield,[4] and is also commonly used as a measure of interest rate risk exposure. To understand its origin, divide (2.7) by the current bond price, that is,

$$dB/B \approx \frac{dB/B}{dr}(r - r_0) \tag{2.10}$$

Since duration is defined as minus the percent change in bond price with respect to a change in yield,

$$\text{DUR} \equiv -\frac{dB/B}{dr}$$

we have

$$\text{DUR} \equiv -\frac{dB/B}{dr} = -\frac{dB/dr}{B} = -\frac{-TFe^{-rT}}{Fe^{-rT}} = T \tag{2.11}$$

The duration of a discount bond equals the negative of its years to maturity, and, given the value of duration, the percent change in a discount bond value for a given change in interest rates can be approximated using

$$dB/B \approx -T(r - r_0) \tag{2.12}$$

In other words, if a bond has $T$ years to maturity, a one basis point increase in the bond's yield will cause its value to fall approximately $0.01 \times T\%$. Note that the *DV01* measure (2.9) gives the same result after we divide through by the bond value.

**ILLUSTRATION 2.2** Use duration to approximate discount bond price change.

*Suppose that 25 years ago you bought \$4,000 worth of the discount bonds in Illustration 2.1. What would have happened to the value of the bonds if interest rates would have immediately jumped by 100 basis points? Compute the actual change in price using the bond formula (2.4), and then the approximate change using duration (2.10).*

At a yield of 12.876%, the value of your investment at inception was \$4,000. If the interest rate jumps to 13.876%, your investment value will fall to

$$B = 100{,}000e^{-0.13876(25)} = 3{,}115.20$$

This can be verified using the OPTVAL Library function

OV_IR_DISCB(*face, rate, term, vdc*)

[4] The concept of duration was first introduced in Macaulay (1938). Other treatments are provided in Reddington (1952) and Samuelson (1945).

where *face* is the face value of the discount bond, *rate* and *term* are its yield and term to maturity, respectively. The indicator variable *vdc* instructs the function to return the bond's value ("*v*" or "*V*"), duration ("*d*" or "*D*"), or convexity ("*c*" or "C"). The bond's value is illustrated below. With a 100 basis point increase in the interest rate, the bond value falls by $884.20.

B10 =OV_IR_DISCB($B$2,$B$9,$B$3,"V")

| | A | B | C |
|---|---|---|---|
| 1 | Original bond price | 4,000 | |
| 2 | Face amount | 100,000 | |
| 3 | Years to maturity | 25 | |
| 4 | Original interest rate | 12.876% | |
| 5 | Duration | 25 | |
| 6 | Convexity | 625 | |
| 7 | | | |
| 8 | Change in interest rate | 1.00% | |
| 9 | New interest rate | 13.876% | |
| 10 | New bond value | 3,115.20 | |
| 11 | Actual change in bond value | -884.80 | |

The duration-based approximation is given by (2.10). Multiplying (2.10) by the bond price provides an estimate of the change in bond value. Since the duration of your bond is 25, an increase of 100 basis points implies that the value of your bond will fall by approximately 25% or $1,000, that is,

$$dB \approx -B \times T \times (r - r_0) = -4{,}000 \times 25 \times 0.01 = -1{,}000$$

The price discrepancy arises from the fact that the bond valuation function is convex. (See Figure 2.1.) First-order approximations such as duration are accurate for only small changes in yield. As yield changes become large, the degree of error using the duration approximation becomes large.

**Convexity** DV01 and duration first-order approximations of the bond valuation function that are based on the slope of a straight line that is tangent to the bond valuation function at the current yield, $r_0$, as shown is Figure 2.2. For small changes in yield, a first-order approximation will be reasonably accurate, however, the approximation error grows large with the size of the yield change. To improve the degree of accuracy in the approximation, we can also incorporate the second-order term of the Taylor series expansion (2.6). Using percent changes, the approximation is now

$$dB/B \approx \left(\frac{dB/B}{dr}\right)(r - r_0) + \frac{1}{2}\left(\frac{d^2B/B}{dr^2}\right)(r - r_0)^2 \tag{2.13}$$

The second term in parentheses on the right-hand side of (2.13) is called *convexity.* Since the second derivative of the bond valuation function is

**FIGURE 2.2** Slope of bond valuation formula.

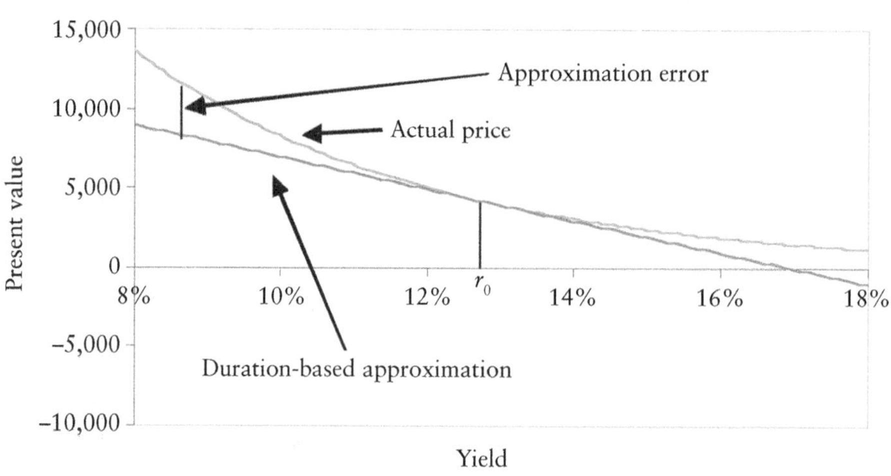


$$\frac{d^2B}{dr^2} = T^2Fe^{-rT} \tag{2.14}$$

the definition of convexity of a discount bond is

$$\text{CVX} = \frac{d^2B/B}{dr^2} = \frac{d^2B/dr^2}{B} = \frac{T^2Fe^{-rT}}{Fe^{-rT}} = T^2 \tag{2.15}$$

**ILLUSTRATION 2.3** Use duration and convexity to approximate discount bond price change.

*Reconsider Illustration 2.2 using duration and convexity to approximate the change in price of the discount bond.*

At a yield of 12.876%, the value of your investment at inception was \$4,000. If the interest rate immediately increases to 13.876%, your investment value would fall to \$3,115.20 or by \$884.80. The predicted value change using duration and convexity is

$$dB \approx B\left[-T(r-r_0)+\frac{1}{2}T^2(r-r_0)^2\right]$$

$$= 4{,}000\left[-25(0.01)+\frac{625}{2}(0.0001)\right] = -875.00$$

Note that the degree of approximation error has fallen from \$115.20 or 13.0% to –\$9.80 or –1.1%.

### Discount Bonds Traded in the Marketplace

The focus now turns to discount bonds traded in the marketplace. Since we need a proxy for the zero-coupon risk-free rate of interest in subsequent chapters, we focus here on only U.S. Treasury securities. For terms to maturity of one year or less, we use Treasury bills. For terms to maturity greater than one year, we use Treasury strip bonds.

**Treasury Bills** A number of different zero-coupon or discount bonds trade in the U.S. Perhaps the most commonly known are U.S. Treasury bills or, simply, T-bills. To finance the operations of the government, the U.S. Treasury auctions new 28-day, 91-day, and 182-day bills every Thursday. The prices of T-bills follow certain reporting conventions. It is important to understand these reporting conventions since the interest rate on T-bills is an excellent proxy for the risk-free rate of interest—a rate applied throughout the applications of this book. Table 2.1 contains a panel of T-bill price quotes obtained from *Bloomberg* on March 29, 2006. The first column contains the maturity date of each T-bill, and the second contains the number of days to maturity. The number of days to maturity equals the actual number of days from the close on March 29, 2006 to the maturity date less one business day since T-bills have one-business day delayed settlement. The columns headed "Bid" and "Ask" are *bank discounts* or simply *discounts*. They are *neither* prices *nor* interest rates. A bank discount is defined as

$$\text{Bank discount} = (360/n)(100 - \text{T-bill price}) \tag{2.16}$$

where $n$ is the number of days to maturity and 360 is the number of days in a "banker's year." To deduce the actual bid and ask prices for the T-bill, we must invert (2.16) and use

$$\text{T-bill price} = 100 - \text{Bank discount}(n/360) \tag{2.17}$$

If we again consider the T-bill with maturity date of 6/29/06, we see that the bid and ask discounts are 4.52 and 4.51, respectively. This means that if we bought this T-bill, you would pay

$$\text{T-bill price} = 100 - 4.51(91/360) = 98.6000\% \text{ of par}$$

If the T-bill has a par value of $1 million, you would pay $986,000.

At this juncture, it is important to digress and link the price to the continuously compounded rate of return on this T-bill. If you pay 98.83275% of par for the T-bill that matures in 69 days, the T-bill rate price promises to grow at an annualized rate of

$$r = \frac{\ln(100/98.6000)}{91/365} = 4.599\%$$

Note that 365 days rather than 360 days are used in the computation. This is because time should be measured in actual years rather than banker's years.

**TABLE 2.1** U.S. Treasury bill discounts drawn from Bloomberg on March 29, 2006.

| Maturity | Days to Maturity | Bid | Ask | Ask Yield |
|---|---|---|---|---|
| 4/6/06 | 7 | 4.46 | 4.45 | 4.52 |
| 4/13/06 | 14 | 4.60 | 4.56 | 4.63 |
| 4/20/06 | 21 | 4.59 | 4.55 | 4.63 |
| 4/27/06 | 28 | 4.61 | 4.60 | 4.68 |
| 5/4/06 | 35 | 4.54 | 4.51 | 4.59 |
| 5/11/06 | 42 | 4.52 | 4.51 | 4.60 |
| 5/18/06 | 49 | 4.54 | 4.53 | 4.62 |
| 5/25/06 | 56 | 4.50 | 4.49 | 4.58 |
| 6/1/06 | 63 | 4.55 | 4.53 | 4.63 |
| 6/8/06 | 70 | 4.53 | 4.52 | 4.62 |
| 6/16/06 | 78 | 4.53 | 4.52 | 4.63 |
| 6/22/06 | 84 | 4.53 | 4.52 | 4.63 |
| 6/29/06 | 91 | 4.52 | 4.51 | 4.63 |
| 7/6/06 | 98 | 4.55 | 4.53 | 4.65 |
| 7/13/06 | 105 | 4.56 | 4.53 | 4.65 |
| 7/20/06 | 112 | 4.54 | 4.53 | 4.66 |
| 7/27/06 | 119 | 4.60 | 4.58 | 4.71 |
| 8/3/06 | 126 | 4.57 | 4.56 | 4.70 |
| 8/10/06 | 133 | 4.60 | 4.59 | 4.73 |
| 8/17/06 | 140 | 4.60 | 4.59 | 4.74 |
| 8/24/06 | 147 | 4.62 | 4.61 | 4.76 |
| 8/31/06 | 154 | 4.63 | 4.62 | 4.78 |
| 9/7/06 | 161 | 4.64 | 4.63 | 4.79 |
| 9/14/06 | 168 | 4.65 | 4.64 | 4.81 |
| 9/21/06 | 175 | 4.65 | 4.64 | 4.81 |
| 9/28/06 | 182 | 4.65 | 4.64 | 4.82 |

The last column is the *bond equivalent yield* based on the ask price. It represents an attempt to make the yield on a T-bill comparable to the yield on other Treasury securities whose yields are based on a 365-day, as opposed to 360-day, calendar year. Note that the reported bond equivalent yield for the 6/29/06 T-bill is 4.63%. This rate is computed by solving

$$\text{T-bill price} \times \left[1 + \text{Bond equivalent yield}\left(\frac{n}{365}\right)\right] = 100 \tag{2.18}$$

Alternatively, the bond equivalent yield may be computed directly from the T-bill's discount:

$$\text{Bond equivalent yield} = \frac{365 \times \text{Bank discount}}{360 - \text{Bank discount} \times n} \tag{2.19}$$

Either way, the number is, at best, an *approximation* for the rate of return on the T-bill. The actual rate of return (growth) of the T-bill over its life is the continuously compounded interest rate, 4.599%.

**Stripped Treasury Bonds and Notes** U.S. Treasury *strips*[5] are also discount bonds. The U.S. Treasury does not issue these instruments directly. Instead, they issue only coupon-bearing bonds and notes with maturities as long as 30 years. What happens is that the original issue coupon bonds are "stripped," with each coupon as well as the principal amount sold as a separate unit. In the absence of costless arbitrage opportunities, the sum of the prices of the discount bonds stripped from the original coupon issue must be equal to the price of the coupon bond.

Table 2.2 contains the ask price quotes for STRIPS of different maturities. The price data were drawn from *Bloomberg* on March 29, 2006. The last col-

**TABLE 2.2** Selected U.S. Treasury STRIP prices drawn from Bloomberg on March 29, 2006.

| Maturity | Ask Price | Years to Maturity | Continuous Yield |
|---|---|---|---|
| 6/15/06 | 99.04 | 0.21 | 4.51% |
| 9/30/06 | 97.68 | 0.51 | 4.63% |
| 3/15/07 | 95.55 | 0.96 | 4.73% |
| 3/15/08 | 91.05 | 1.96 | 4.77% |
| 3/15/09 | 86.72 | 2.96 | 4.81% |
| 3/15/10 | 82.91 | 3.96 | 4.73% |
| 2/15/11 | 79.48 | 4.89 | 4.70% |
| 2/15/12 | 75.62 | 5.89 | 4.75% |
| 2/15/13 | 71.85 | 6.89 | 4.80% |
| 2/15/14 | 68.30 | 7.89 | 4.83% |
| 2/15/15 | 65.11 | 8.89 | 4.83% |
| 2/15/16 | 61.88 | 9.89 | 4.85% |
| 2/15/17 | 58.66 | 10.89 | 4.90% |
| 2/15/18 | 55.54 | 11.89 | 4.94% |
| 2/15/19 | 52.71 | 12.89 | 4.97% |
| 2/15/20 | 49.91 | 13.89 | 5.00% |
| 2/15/21 | 47.45 | 14.90 | 5.00% |
| 2/15/22 | 45.23 | 15.90 | 4.99% |
| 2/15/23 | 42.98 | 16.90 | 5.00% |
| 2/15/24 | 40.89 | 17.90 | 5.00% |
| 2/15/25 | 38.87 | 18.90 | 5.00% |
| 2/15/26 | 37.09 | 19.90 | 4.98% |
| 2/15/27 | 35.43 | 20.90 | 4.96% |
| 2/15/28 | 33.86 | 21.90 | 4.95% |

[5] The U.S. Treasury created a program called *Separate Trading of Registered Interest and Principal of Securities* (STRIPS) in February 1985 to promote liquidity in the zero-coupon bond market. For more information regarding STRIPS, see Fabozzi and Fleming (2005).

umn in the table contains the continuously compounded yield to maturity computed using equation (2.5) based on the reported ask price. The column shows that the *zero-coupon yield curve* (i.e., the relation between yield and term to maturity) is upward sloping for maturities up to about 12 years and then flattens at a level of about 5%.

## COUPON-BEARING BONDS

This section focuses on coupon-bearing bonds. A *coupon-bearing bond* or, simply, a *coupon bond* pays a stated rate of interest periodically throughout the bond's life, ending with an interest payment and repayment of the bond's par value. While the valuation and risk measurement of a coupon-bearing bond is seemingly more complicated than a discount bond, it is important and useful to recognize that a coupon bond is nothing more than a portfolio of discount bonds.[6]

### Valuation

The value of a coupon bond, $B_c$, is the sum of the values of its constituent discount bonds, that is,

$$B_c = \sum_{i=1}^{n} B_{d,i} = \sum_{i=1}^{n} CF_i e^{-r_i T_i} \tag{2.20}$$

where the subscript $i$ denotes the $i$th discount bond and the value of $i$th discount bond is now denoted, $B_{d,i}$. $CF_i$ is the amount of the cash flow received at the maturity of the $i$th discount bond, $r_i$ is the zero-coupon discount rate used to bring the cash flow to the present, and $T_i$ is the time until the cash flow $i$ occurs. Prior to maturity, the cash flow equals the coupon interest payment, $CF_i$ = COUP, as is shown in Figure 2.3. The amount of the interest payment, COUP, is the stated coupon interest rate times the par value of the bond, $F_n$. At maturity, the cash flow equals the coupon interest payment plus the repayment of the face value, $CF_i$ = COUP + $F_n$. The number of coupon payments is denoted $n$. Note that equation (2.20) uses maturity-specific discount rates for each cash flow. The relation between zero-coupon yields and their terms to maturity is called the *term structure of interest rates* or the *zero-coupon yield curve*. We discuss the yield curve shortly.

**FIGURE 2.3** Cash flows of a coupon-bearing bond.

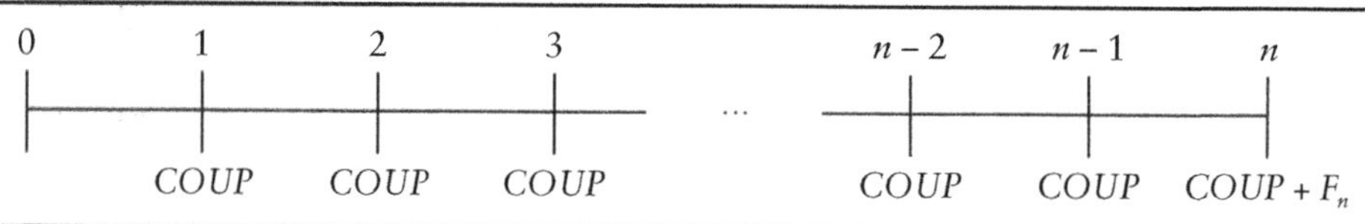


[6] This valuation principle is called *valuation by replication* and is key to understanding derivative contract valuation and risk management.

**ILLUSTRATION 2.4** Compute value of coupon-bearing bond given zero-coupon yield curve.

*Assume that the current zero-coupon yield curve is given by the function,*

$$r_i = 0.04 + 0.01\ln(1 + T_i)$$

*where $T_i$ is measured in years. Compute the value of a five-year semiannual coupon-bearing bond with a 7% coupon interest rate.*

To value the bond, you need the zero-coupon interest rates corresponding to each cash flow. To do so, you apply the given term structure formula. The zero-coupon yield rate corresponding to the first constituent discount bond maturity in 0.5 years, for example, is $r_i = 0.04 + 0.01 \ln(1 + 0.5) = 4.405\%$. The cash flow promised in 0.5 years is $0.07/2 \times 100 = 3.50$, so the value of the first discount bond is $3.50e^{-0.04405(0.5)} = 3.4237$. Applying this procedure recursively (i.e., coupon bond valuation formula (2.20)), the value of the five-year, 7% coupon bond is 105.0902, the individual discount bonds of which are summarized in the table below.

| Years to Maturity | Zero-Coupon Yield | Cash Flow | PV of Cash Flow |
|---|---|---|---|
| 0.5 | 4.405% | 3.50 | 3.4237 |
| 1.0 | 4.693% | 3.50 | 3.3395 |
| 1.5 | 4.916% | 3.50 | 3.2512 |
| 2.0 | 5.099% | 3.50 | 3.1607 |
| 2.5 | 5.253% | 3.50 | 3.0693 |
| 3.0 | 5.386% | 3.50 | 2.9778 |
| 3.5 | 5.504% | 3.50 | 2.8867 |
| 4.0 | 5.609% | 3.50 | 2.7965 |
| 4.5 | 5.705% | 3.50 | 2.7076 |
| 5.0 | 5.792% | 103.50 | 77.4772 |
| Total value | | | 105.0902 |

This value may be confirmed using the OPTVAL function,

OV_IR_FIXED_ZC(*coup*, *freq*, *face*, *tb*, *ncoupr*, *term*, *rate*, *vdc*)

where *coup* is the coupon interest rate expressed in decimal form (i.e., 0.07), *freq* is the frequency of coupons per year (i.e., two), *face* is the face value of the bond (i.e., 100), *tb* is the time until the first coupon payment expressed in years (i.e., 0.5), *ncoupr* is the number of coupons remaining (i.e., 10), *term* is the vector of times to maturity of the discount bonds (i.e., the numbers in the first column in the above table), and *rate* is the vector containing the corresponding zero-coupon rates (i.e., the numbers in the second column in the above table). The indicator variable *vdc* instructs the function to return the bond's value ("*v*" or "*V*"), duration ("*d*" or "*D*"), or convexity ("*c*" or "C"). The bond's value, for example, is

B8 =OV_IR_FIXED_ZC($B$1,$B$2,$B$3,$B$4,$B$5,$D$3:$D$12,$E$3:$E$12,"V")

| | A | B | C | D | E | F | G | H |
|---|---|---|---|---|---|---|---|---|
| 1 | Coupon rate: | 7.00% | | Zero-coupon yield curve | | | | |
| 2 | Frequency: | 2 | | Years to maturity | Yield | | | |
| 3 | Par value: | 100 | | 0.5 | 4.405% | | | |
| 4 | Years to first coupon: | 0.5 | | 1.0 | 4.693% | | | |
| 5 | No. of coupons remaining: | 10 | | 1.5 | 4.916% | | | |
| 6 | | | | 2.0 | 5.099% | | | |
| 7 | Fixed-rate bond | | | 2.5 | 5.253% | | | |
| 8 | Value | 105.0902 | | 3.0 | 5.386% | | | |
| 9 | Duration | 4.3174 | | 3.5 | 5.504% | | | |
| 10 | Convexity | 20.3825 | | 4.0 | 5.609% | | | |
| 11 | | | | 4.5 | 5.705% | | | |
| 12 | | | | 5.0 | 5.792% | | | |

## Risk Measurement

Like in the case of discount bonds, the two most commonly used interest rate risk measures for coupon bonds are duration and convexity. In both cases, they are weighted averages of the durations and convexities of the constituent discount bonds where the weights are the proportion of coupon bond value attributable to the $i$th discount bond. Letting $w_i$ represent the weight attributable to the $i$th discount bond, we have

$$\sum_{i=1}^{n} w_i = \frac{\sum_{i=1}^{n} B_{d,i}}{B_c} = 1 \tag{2.21}$$

**Duration** The duration of a coupon bond is

$$\text{DUR}_c = -\sum_{i=1}^{n} w_i \text{DUR}_{d,i} = -\sum_{i=1}^{n} w_i T_i \tag{2.22}$$

where the duration of the discount bond is given by (2.11), that is, $\text{DUR}_{d,i} = T_i$. Expression (2.22) shows that the duration of a coupon bond is a *weighted average term to maturity* of a coupon bond. Equation (2.22) also offers some important insights regarding the price risk or interest rate risk of a coupon bond. First, the longer the term to maturity of a bond, the greater the proportion of coupon bond value attributable to distant cash flows, the greater the duration, and, hence, the greater the interest rate risk. Second, the higher the coupon interest rate of a bond, the greater the proportion of the bond's value received earlier in the bond's life, the lower the duration, and, hence, the lower the interest rate risk. Third, the higher the level of interest rates, the lower importance of distant cash flows in the determination of bond value, the shorter the duration, and the lower the interest rate risk.

**Convexity** The convexity of a coupon bond is

$$\text{CVX}_c = \sum_{i=1}^{n} w_i \text{CVX}_{d,i} = \sum_{i=1}^{n} w_i T_i^2 \tag{2.23}$$

Like in the case of duration, the convexity of a coupon bond (2.23) is a weighted average of the convexities of the constituent discount bonds where the weights are the proportion of coupon bond value attributable to the *i*th discount bond, and the convexity of a discount bond is given by (2.15), that is, $\text{CVX}_{d,i} = T_i^2$. It is important to recognize that the duration and convexity measures (2.22) and (2.23) make the implicit assumption that the zero-coupon yield curve shifts in a parallel manner (e.g., all yields shift upward or downward by the same amount).[7]

**ILLUSTRATION 2.5** Compute duration and duration/convexity approximations for a coupon bond.

*Compute the actual percent change in the value of a five-year semiannual coupon-bearing bond with a 7% coupon interest rate assuming the zero-coupon yield curve changes from*

$$r_i = 0.04 + 0.01\ln(1 + T_i)$$

*to*

$$r_i = 0.05 + 0.01\ln(1 + T_i)$$

*Compare the actual percent value change with the value changes based on the duration and duration/convexity approximations.*

The first step is to compute the duration and the convexity of this coupon-bearing bond. The table below details the calculations. The present value of the cash flow represented in the first row constitutes 3.258% of the total value of the coupon bond, that is,

$$\frac{3.50e^{-0.04405(0.5)}}{105.0902} = \frac{3.4237}{105.0902} = 0.03258$$

The duration of this discount bond is 0.5, so its contribution to the duration of the coupon bond is 0.03258(0.5) = 0.01629. The convexity of this discount bond is $0.5^2 = 0.25$, so its contribution to the convexity of the coupon bond is 0.03258(0.25) = 0.00814. Repeating the computations for each row, and then summing shows that the duration of the coupon bond is 4.3714 and the convexity is 20.3825.

[7] It is, of course, possible to allow the yield curve to shift in other ways. Chapter 18 focuses on the valuation of fixed income securities under different assumptions regarding the movement of interest rates through time.

| Years to Maturity | Zero-Coupon Yield | Cash Flow | PV of Cash Flow | Proportion of Total | Components of | |
|---|---|---|---|---|---|---|
| | | | | | Duration | Convexity |
| 0.5 | 4.405% | 3.50 | 3.4237 | 0.03258 | 0.01629 | 0.00814 |
| 1.0 | 4.693% | 3.50 | 3.3395 | 0.03178 | 0.03178 | 0.03178 |
| 1.5 | 4.916% | 3.50 | 3.2512 | 0.03094 | 0.04641 | 0.06961 |
| 2.0 | 5.099% | 3.50 | 3.1607 | 0.03008 | 0.06015 | 0.12030 |
| 2.5 | 5.253% | 3.50 | 3.0693 | 0.02921 | 0.07302 | 0.18254 |
| 3.0 | 5.386% | 3.50 | 2.9778 | 0.02834 | 0.08501 | 0.25502 |
| 3.5 | 5.504% | 3.50 | 2.8867 | 0.02747 | 0.09614 | 0.33649 |
| 4.0 | 5.609% | 3.50 | 2.7965 | 0.02661 | 0.10644 | 0.42577 |
| 4.5 | 5.705% | 3.50 | 2.7076 | 0.02576 | 0.11594 | 0.52172 |
| 5.0 | 5.792% | 103.50 | 77.4772 | 0.73724 | 3.68622 | 18.43111 |
| Total | | | 105.0902 | 1.0000 | 4.3174 | 20.3825 |

These values may be confirmed using the OPTVAL function,

OV_IR_FIXED,ZC(*coup*, *freq*, *face*, *tb*, *ncoupr*, *term*, *rate*)

whose parameters are defined above. The duration function is invoked in the spreadsheet below.

B9 =OV_IR_FIXED_ZC($B$1,$B$2,$B$3,$B$4,$B$5,$D$3:$D$12,$E$3:$E$12,"D")

| | A | B | C | D | E | F | G | H |
|---|---|---|---|---|---|---|---|---|
| 1 | Coupon rate: | 7.00% | | Zero-coupon yield curve | | | | |
| 2 | Frequency: | 2 | | Years to maturity | Yield | | | |
| 3 | Par value: | 100 | | 0.5 | 4.405% | | | |
| 4 | Years to first coupon: | 0.5 | | 1.0 | 4.693% | | | |
| 5 | No. of coupons remaining: | 10 | | 1.5 | 4.916% | | | |
| 6 | | | | 2.0 | 5.099% | | | |
| 7 | Fixed-rate bond | | | 2.5 | 5.253% | | | |
| 8 | Value | 105.0902 | | 3.0 | 5.386% | | | |
| 9 | Duration | 4.3174 | | 3.5 | 5.504% | | | |
| 10 | Convexity | 20.3825 | | 4.0 | 5.609% | | | |
| 11 | | | | 4.5 | 5.705% | | | |
| 12 | | | | 5.0 | 5.792% | | | |

Next, compute the anticipated percentage changes in bond value based on the duration and duration/convexity approximations. Based solely on duration, the anticipated change is

$$-4.3174 \times 0.01 = -4.3174\%$$

while, based on duration and convexity, the anticipated change is

$$-4.3174(0.01) + \frac{1}{2}(20.3825)(0.0001) = -4.2155\%$$

If you simply shift the zero-coupon yield curve up by 100 basis points, you will find that the bond's value has changed from 105.0902 to 100.6585—an actual percent change of –4.2171%. Thus, you have measured the degree of approximation error for each method. The approximation based solely on duration overstates the percent movement by 0.1003%, and the approximation based on duration/convexity understates the percent movement by 0.0016%.

### Coupon Bond Conventions

As noted earlier, the duration and convexity measures (2.22) and (2.23) make the implicit assumption that the zero-coupon yield curve shifts in a parallel manner (e.g., all yields shift by the same amount). To simplify matters, it is not uncommon in practice to see a single discount rate called the *yield to maturity* used to discount all cash flows of a coupon bond.

**Yield to Maturity** Yield to maturity is a summary statistic that describes the bond's promised rate of return. The yield to maturity is computed by setting the current bond price equal to the present value of the cash flows and solving for $y$, that is,

$$B_c = \sum_{i=1}^{n} CF_i e^{-yT_i} \tag{2.24}$$

Under the assumption that there is a single discount rate, the duration of a coupon bond is given by

$$\text{DUR}'_c = -\sum_{i=1}^{n} \left( \frac{CF_i e^{-yT_i}}{B_c} \right) T_i \tag{2.25}$$

and its convexity is given by

$$\text{CVX}'_c = \sum_{i=1}^{n} \left( \frac{C_i e^{-yT_i}}{B_c} \right) T_i^2 \tag{2.26}$$

Note that the duration and convexity computed using (2.25) and (2.26) are only *approximations* of the correct values (2.22) and (2.23). The present value of the $i$th cash flow is not equal to the price of the $i$th discount bond, that is,

$$CF_i e^{-yT_i} \neq B_{d,i}$$

The OPTVAL Function library contains a function for computing the value, the duration, and the convexity of a fixed rate bond given its yield to maturity:

OV_IR_FIXED_YLD(*coup*, *freq*, *face*, *tb*, *ncoupr*, *yld*, *vdc*)

where *coup* is the coupon interest rate expressed in decimal form, *freq* is the frequency of coupons per year, *face* is the face value of the bond, *tb* is the time until the first coupon payment expressed in years, *ncoupr* is the number of coupons remaining, and *yld* is the bond's promised yield to maturity. The indicator variable *vdc* instructs the function to return the bond's value ("*v*" or "*V*"), duration ("*d*" or "*D*"), or convexity ("*c*" or "*C*").

**ILLUSTRATION 2.6** Compute yield to maturity of coupon-bearing bond given the yield curve.

*Assume that the current zero-coupon term structure of spot rates is given by the curve,*

$$r_i = 0.04 + 0.01\ln(1 + T_i)$$

*where $T_i$ is measured is years. Compute the value and the yield to maturity of a five-year semiannual coupon-bearing bond with a 7% coupon interest rate. If this coupon-bearing bond can be purchased for \$104, can you earn a costless arbitrage profit, and, if so, how?*

You know from Illustration 2.4 that the five-year, 7% bond is 105.0902. The yield to maturity of this bond is computed by setting the bond price equal to the present value of the cash flows and solving for a single discount rate. The discount rate that satisfies

$$105.0902 = \sum_{i=1}^{9} 3.50e^{-yT_i} + 103.50e^{-yT_{10}}$$

is 5.729% as is shown in the table below. The syntax for the OPTVAL function is

OV_IR_FIXED_YLD_YIELD(*coup*, *freq*, *face*, *tb*, *ncoupr*, *bprce*)

where all parameters are defined as above and *bprce* is the bond's price including accrued interest.

B7 =OV_IR_FIXED_YLD_YIELD($B$1,$B$2,$B$3,$B$4,$B$5,$B$6)

| | A | B | C | D | E | F |
|---|---|---|---|---|---|---|
| 1 | Coupon rate: | 7.00% | | | | |
| 2 | Frequency: | 2 | | | | |
| 3 | Par value: | 100 | | | | |
| 4 | Years to next payment: | 0.5 | | | | |
| 5 | No. of payments remaining: | 10 | | | | |
| 6 | Bond price: | 105.0902 | | | | |
| 7 | Implied yield to maturity: | 5.729% | | | | |

Note that this yield to maturity of the coupon bond is below the zero-coupon rate on a five-year zero-coupon bond, 5.792%, in Illustration 2.5. This is because a five-year coupon-bearing bond does not have five years to maturity from an economic standpoint. The intermediate payments made during the bond's life effectively shorten its overall maturity.

Assuming the coupon-bearing bond can be purchased for \$104, a costless arbitrage profit can be earned. To do so, you would buy the coupon bond and then sell zero-coupon bonds in the amount and maturity of each cash flow, that is, sell 3.50 in par value of zero-coupon bonds maturing in six months, and 3.50 in par value of zero-coupon bonds maturing in one year, and so on. In this way, the interest receipts of the coupon-bearing bond exactly match the payments you need to make to cover your short sale obligations. Since you know that you can buy the coupon bond for \$104 and sell the zero-coupon bond portfolio (using the zero-coupon yield curve) for \$105.0902, the present value of the costless arbitrage profit of \$1.0902.

**ILLUSTRATION 2.7** Compute duration and convexity of coupon bond using yield to maturity.

*Again, assume that the current zero-coupon yield curve is given by the function,*

$$r_i = 0.04 + 0.01\ln(1 + T_i)$$

*where $T_i$ is measured is years. Compute the duration and convexity of a five-year semiannual coupon-bearing bond with a 7% coupon interest rate using the single yield to maturity, 5.729%, from Illustration 2.6.*

The table below summarizes the computations from basic principles. First, you compute the present values of the cash flows using a constant yield to maturity. Naturally, the total of the values of the discount bonds computed using yield to maturity is 105.0902. Recall from Illustration 2.6, this is exactly how the yield to maturity was defined. Next, you compute the proportion of total coupon bond value that is attributable to each discount bond. The first row of the table shows

$$3.4012e^{-0.05729(0.5)}/105.0902 = 0.01618$$

Finally, compute the contributions of each discount bond to the duration and convexity of the coupon bond and sum as you did in Illustration 2.4. The yield-based duration is 4.3240, compared with 4.3174 using the zero-coupon yield curve approach, and the yield-based convexity is 20.4273, compared 20.3825 using the zero-coupon yield curve approach. While these differences are small in the illustration at hand, they will vary depending on factors such as the coupon rate of the bond, its term to maturity, and the slope of the yield curve.

| Years to Maturity | Cash Flow | PV of Cash Flow | Proportion of Total | Components of Duration | Components of Convexity |
|---|---|---|---|---|---|
| 0.5 | 3.50 | 3.4012 | 0.03236 | 0.01618 | 0.00809 |
| 1.0 | 3.50 | 3.3051 | 0.03145 | 0.03145 | 0.03145 |
| 1.5 | 3.50 | 3.2118 | 0.03056 | 0.04584 | 0.06876 |
| 2.0 | 3.50 | 3.1211 | 0.02970 | 0.05940 | 0.11880 |
| 2.5 | 3.50 | 3.0329 | 0.02886 | 0.07215 | 0.18038 |
| 3.0 | 3.50 | 2.9473 | 0.02805 | 0.08414 | 0.25241 |
| 3.5 | 3.50 | 2.8640 | 0.02725 | 0.09539 | 0.33385 |
| 4.0 | 3.50 | 2.7832 | 0.02648 | 0.10593 | 0.42374 |
| 4.5 | 3.50 | 2.7046 | 0.02574 | 0.11581 | 0.52115 |
| 5.0 | 103.50 | 77.7191 | 0.73955 | 3.69773 | 18.48867 |
| Total | | 105.0902 | 1.0000 | 4.3240 | 20.4273 |

## Risk Management

Risk management is the general theme of this book. Although the purpose of this chapter is to lay the foundation for risk management using derivatives, it is instructive to introduce the concept of hedging at this juncture to reinforce the use of the bond risk management tools of duration and convexity.

Risk has a number of definitions. For now, assume that risk refers to unanticipated changes in the value of an asset that we hold. *Hedging* refers to reducing the risk of our position by buying or selling other assets whose collective value changes by the same amount as the value of the asset we hold. In the context of bonds and interest rate risk measurement, a perfect hedge is one whose value changes in an equal and opposite direction, that is,

$$\frac{d\text{Value of unhedged position}}{dr} = \frac{d\text{Value of hedge instruments}}{dr} \tag{2.27}$$

Duration and convexity provide the means for measuring the value changes of your portfolio and the hedge instruments should interest rates change. To completely hedge interest rate risk exposure means finding the number of units of the hedge instrument to buy or sell such that the value of the overall hedged portfolio does not change if interest rates change, that is,

$$dB_P + n_H dB_H = 0 \tag{2.28}$$

where $B_P$ is the value of your bond position and $B_H$ is the value of one unit of the hedge instrument, where the expression $dr$ has been dropped because it is common to both sides of the equation. Duration-based hedging means approximating the changes of value with the product of duration and bond value. The number of units of the hedge instrument to buy or sell is therefore determined by solving

$$\text{DUR}_P B_P + n_H \text{DUR}_H B_H = 0 \tag{2.29}$$

where $\text{DUR}_P(\text{DUR}_H)$ is the duration of the unhedged bond portfolio (hedge instrument) and $B_P(B_H)$ is the market value of the unhedged bond portfolio (market value of the hedge instrument). Rearranging (2.29) to solve for the number of hedge bonds $n_H$, we get

$$n_H = -\frac{\text{DUR}_P B_P}{\text{DUR}_H B_H} \tag{2.30}$$

**ILLUSTRATION 2.8** Hedge interest rate risk of bond portfolio using duration.

*Suppose you own \$30 million in par value of a 10% coupon-bearing bond with 10 years to maturity. Its current yield to maturity is 8%. Suppose also that you expect that interest rates may increase over the next few days and want to hedge your interest rate risk exposure. Unfortunately, the bond you hold does not have a liquid market and selling quickly is impossible. You have the opportunity to sell a more liquid bond, however. Its coupon rate is 9%, term to maturity is 12 years, par value is \$100,000, and yield to maturity is 7%. How many bonds should you sell? Assume both bonds pay coupons semiannually with the first coupon being paid in exactly six months. Show how effective the hedge is by plotting the changes in the hedged portfolio value over a range of yield changes from –5% to +10%.*

The first step is to compute the value and the duration of the bonds. Since you have no information about the zero-coupon yield curve, you can use the yield-based computations (2.24) and (2.25). And, rather than go through the algebra, use the OPTVAL functions. The value and durations of the unhedged bond position and the hedge instrument are as follows:

C11 =OV_IR_FIXED_YLD($C$3,$C$4,$C$5,$C$6,$C$7,$C$8,"d")

| | A | B | C | D | E |
|---|---|---|---|---|---|
| 1 | | Bond | Hedge | | |
| 2 | | portfolio | instrument | | |
| 3 | Coupon rate | 10.00% | 9.00% | | |
| 4 | Frequency | 2 | 2 | | |
| 5 | Par value | 30,000,000 | 100,000 | | |
| 6 | Years to next payment | 0.5 | 0.5 | | |
| 7 | Number of payments | 20 | 24 | | |
| 8 | Yield to maturity | 8.00% | 7.00% | | |
| 9 | | | | | |
| 10 | Value | 33,719,782.77 | 114,965.65 | | |
| 11 | Duration | 6.7539 | 7.8916 | | |

The number of the hedge bonds to sell to immunize your portfolio from interest rate movements is therefore

$$n_H = -\frac{6.7539(33{,}719{,}782.77)}{7.8916(114{,}965.65)} = -251.019$$

To test the effectiveness of the hedge, compute (a) the change in value of the unhedged bond portfolio, and (b) the change in value of the hedged portfolio using a range of yield changes from –5% to +10%. These changes in value are shown in the figure below. As the figure shows, a yield increase produces a significant decline in the unhedged portfolio value. A yield increase of 200 basis points reduces bond portfolio value by more than $4,000,000. After the hedge is in place, however, a yield increase causes the hedged portfolio value to fall by about $63,000 (which cannot be detected on the figure because of the scale). The fact that the hedged portfolio value changes are not 0 across *all* levels of yield change means that the hedge is not fully effective. Recall that the duration-based hedge fails to account for the convexity of the bond valuation formula. Accounting for both duration and convexity will improve the hedging effectiveness.

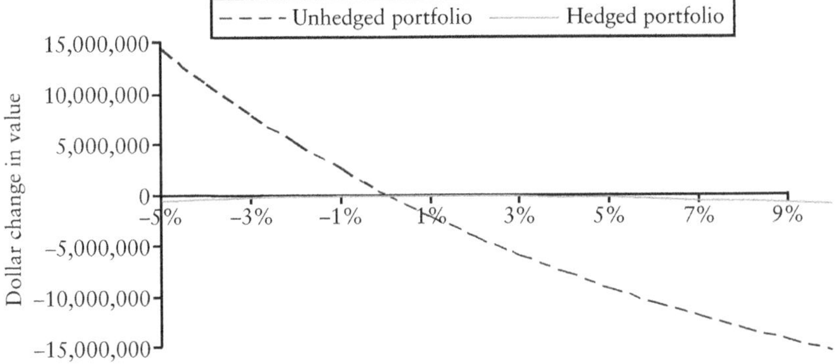


Hedging effectiveness can be improved by incorporating both duration and convexity components of bond value change. In order to do so, however, two hedge instruments will be required. To identify the appropriate number of hedge bonds to buy or sell, you will need to match the duration and the convexity of the bond portfolio that you want to hedge with the duration and convexity of the hedge instruments. To negate the duration risk of the portfolio, you must satisfy the duration constraint

$$\text{DUR}_P B_P + n_{H,1}\text{DUR}_{H,1}B_{H,1} + n_{H,2}\text{DUR}_{H,2}B_{H,2} = 0 \qquad (2.31)$$

Equation (2.31) is the counterpart to (2.29) in which only duration risk was considered. The constraint merely says that you do not have any duration risk exposure after setting $n_{H,1}$ and $n_{H,2}$. Simultaneously, you must also satisfy the convexity constraint,

$$\text{CVX}_P B_P + n_{H,1}\text{CVX}_{H,1}B_{H,1} + n_{H,2}\text{CVX}_{H,2}B_{H,2} = 0 \qquad (2.32)$$

where CVX refers to convexity of the different instruments and the subscripts 1 and 2 refer to the first and second hedge instruments. Since there are two equations (i.e., (2.31) and (2.32)) and two unknowns ($n_{H,1}$ and $n_{H,2}$), we can solve uniquely. The solution can be found algebraically or computationally using a iterative technique such as Microsoft Excel's SOLVER.

**ILLUSTRATION 2.9** Hedge interest rate risk of bond portfolio using duration/convexity.

*Use the same problem information as in Illustration 2.8. In addition, assume that a second hedge bond is available. Its coupon rate is 5%, term to maturity is 20 years, par value is \$100,000, and yield to maturity is 7.5%. How many of each hedge bonds should you sell if you want to hedge both the duration and convexity risk of your portfolio? Show how effective the duration/convexity hedge is relative to the duration-only hedge by plotting the changes in the hedged portfolio value over a range of yield changes from –5% to +10%.*

The first step is to compute the value, and convexity of the bonds. The information is summarized below.

D12 =OV_IR_FIXED_YLD(D\$3,D\$4,D\$5,D\$6,D\$7,D\$8,"c")

| | A | B | C | D |
|---|---|---|---|---|
| 1 | | Bond | Hedge | Hedge |
| 2 | | portfolio | instrument 1 | instrument 2 |
| 3 | Coupon rate | 10.00% | 9.00% | 5.00% |
| 4 | Frequency | 2 | 2 | 2 |
| 5 | Par value | 30,000,000 | 100,000 | 100,000 |
| 6 | Years to next payme | 0.5 | 0.5 | 0.5 |
| 7 | Number of payments | 20 | 24 | 40 |
| 8 | Yield to maturity | 8.00% | 7.00% | 7.50% |
| 9 | | | | |
| 10 | Value | 33,719,782.77 | 114,965.65 | 73,139.32 |
| 11 | Duration | 6.7539 | 7.8916 | 11.5501 |
| 12 | Convexity | 57.4665 | 79.6506 | 185.5095 |

The system of equations (2.31) and (2.32) are:

$$6.7539(33{,}719{,}782.77) + n_{H,1}(7.8916)(114{,}965.65) + n_{H,2}(11.5501)(73{,}139.32) = 0$$

and

$$57.4665(33{,}719{,}782.77) + n_{H,1}(79.6506)(114{,}965.65) + n_{H,2}(185.5095)(73{,}139.32) = 0$$

The solution for the risk-free hedge is $n_{H,1} = -317.661$ and $n_{H,2} = 71.572$. The effectiveness of the duration/convexity hedge vis-à-vis the duration-only hedge is shown in the figure below. For small changes in yield, the hedges perform about the same. For large changes in yield, however, the duration/convexity hedge clearly outperforms.

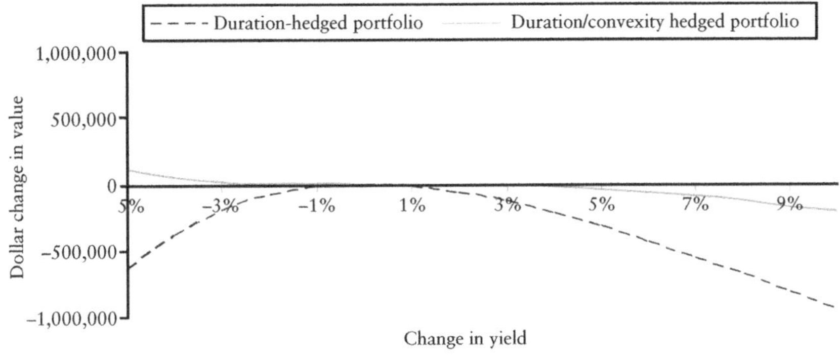


## Coupon Bonds Traded in the Marketplace

Probably the most widely known coupon bonds are the *T-bonds* and *T-notes* issued by the U.S. Treasury. Both are coupon bonds—the difference between them is that T-notes are originally issued with two to 10 years to maturity and T-bonds are originally issued with maturities longer than 10 years. On August 2001, the U.S. Treasury suspended the periodic auctioning of the 30-year bond. In August 2005, the Treasury announced its reintroduction. The first auction after the reintroduction was held on February 9, 2006. This issue is the 4½ Feb 2036 that appear in Table 2.3.

Table 2.3 contains U.S. Treasury bond and note prices on March 29, 2006. A number of reporting conventions appear. First, coupon bond prices are reported with a dash rather than a decimal. This is because the digits to the right of the dash represent the number of 32nds rather than the number of 100ths. A price of 99-16 implies 99.50% of par. Where the price has the suffix "+," an additional one-half 32nds is added to the price. A price of 99-16+ is, therefore, $99^{33}/_{64}$ or 99.515625% of par.

A second convention, although not stated in the panel of prices reported in the table, is that coupon payments are semiannual (i.e., occur each 6 months). The "6¼s of May 2030," for example, pay coupon interest of 3.125% of par on November 15 and May 15 each year through the bond's life. The last coupon and the face value are paid on May 15, 2030.

A third convention is that the *reported* or *quoted* price of the T-bond or T-note excludes *accrued interest* during the current coupon period. Accrued interest equals the amount of the semiannual coupon payment times the proportion of the current coupon period that has elapsed since the last coupon payment, that is,

$$AI = \text{COUP}\left(\frac{\text{Number of days since last coupon was paid}}{\text{Total number of days in current coupon period}}\right) \tag{2.33}$$

**TABLE 2.3** Selected U.S. Treasury bond and note prices drawn from Bloomberg on March 29, 2006.

| Rate | Maturity | Bid | Ask | Ask Yield | Notes |
|---|---|---|---|---|---|
| 2¾ | Jun 2006 | 99-16+ | 99-17 | 4.58 | |
| 2⅞ | Nov 2006 | 98-22 | 98-22+ | 4.86 | |
| 3¾ | Mar 2007 | 98-28+ | 98-29+ | 4.86 | |
| 4⅝ | Mar 2008 | 99-20 | 99-20+ | 4.82 | 2-year |
| 4½ | Feb 2009 | 99-05 | 99-05+ | 4.81 | 3-year |
| 4½ | Feb 2011 | 98-21+ | 98-22 | 4.80 | 5-year |
| 13⅞ | May 2006-11 | 101-03+ | 101 | 4.49 | callable |
| 4⅞ | Feb 2012 | 100-09 | 100-10 | 4.81 | |
| 11¾ | Nov 2009-14 | 122-20 | 122-28 | 8.02 | callable |
| 4¼ | Nov 2014 | 95-25 | 95-26 | 4.85 | |
| 4¼ | Aug 2015 | 95-19+ | 95-20+ | 4.83 | |
| 4½ | Nov 2015 | 97-12+ | 97-14 | 4.84 | |
| 4½ | Feb 2016 | 97-20 | 97-20+ | 4.80 | 10-year |
| 9⅛ | May 2018 | 137-20 | 137-22+ | 4.95 | |
| 8⅛ | Aug 2021 | 132-27+ | 132-28+ | 5.03 | |
| 7⅝ | Feb 2025 | 131-14 | 131-15+ | 5.02 | |
| 6⅛ | Nov 2027 | 114-15 | 114-17 | 5.02 | |
| 6¼ | May 2030 | 118-00 | 118-01+ | 4.96 | |
| 5⅜ | Feb 2031 | 106-11 | 106-13+ | 4.92 | |
| 4½ | Feb 2036 | 94-31+ | 95-00 | 4.82 | 30-year |

The quoted bond price is reported as its current price less accrued interest. Thus, if we purchase the bond today, we pay the reported price plus accrued interest. This practice seems silly. It is! But, it was instituted many decades ago, and traditions are sometimes hard to break. In the parlance of bond traders, the price excluding accrued interest is called the "clean price," and the price including accrued interest is called the "dirty price," "gross price," or "full price."[8,9]

A fourth convention is that Treasury bonds with hyphenated maturity dates are callable. Table 2.3 has two such issues. The notation "13⅞ May 2006-14" means that the U.S. Treasury has the right to call all bonds back at any of the coupon dates between May 15, 2006 and May 15, 2011. Given the high coupon of this issue, it should not be surprising to learn that, on January 13, 2006, the U.S. Treasury called for redemption of this issue at par on May 15, 2006. Consequently, it is being priced as if its term to maturity is about two months. Compare its promised yield to, say, the 2¾ Jun 2006 issue as opposed to the 4⅞ Feb

[8] This "actual/actual" definition of accrued interest applies only to Treasury notes and bonds. Accrued interest for corporate and municipal bonds is based on a 360-day year, with each month having 30 days, and is referred to as being on a "30/360" basis.

[9] Like Treasury bills, Treasury notes and bonds have a one business day settlement convention. Corporate bonds, on the other hand, generally have three-day settlement.

2012 issue. The 11½ Nov 2009-14 issue is also callable. Since this call option has value to the Treasury, its price (yield) will be less (greater) than comparable issues with no call feature. Note that the 11½ Nov 2009-14 have a higher promised yield to maturity than comparable maturity bonds in the table.

Finally, it is worth noting that, while the market for Treasuries is extremely active, the most recent issues, called *on-the-run securities*, have the highest trading volume. This can be seen in Table 2.3. The bonds and notes denoted by "*n*-year" in the last column are on-the-run issues. Note that the spreads between the bid and ask price quotes are smaller for these issues than for the off-the-run issues. Holding other factors constant, the higher the trading volume, the lower the bid/ask spread.

**ILLUSTRATION 2.10** Deduce price of coupon-stream.

*In Table 2.2, the strip bond maturing in February 2016 has a reported ask price of 61.88. In Table 2.3, the 4½ Feb 2016 issue has a reported ask price of 97.20+. Deduce the price of the coupons of the 4½ Feb 2016 without using the bond valuation formula.*

First, we need to compute the decimal price of the 4½ Feb 2016 coupon-bearing bond. The reported ask price in Table 2.3 is 97-20+, which translates to $97^{41}/_{64}$ or 97.6406% of par. The number of days that have elapsed in the current coupon period as of March 29, 2006 is 42, and the total number of days in the current coupon period is 184. The accrued interest is, therefore,

$$(4.50/2) \times (42/181) = 0.5221$$

and the full price of the bond is 97.6406 + 0.5221 = 98.1627. Second, by the law of one price, the present value of the principal of the coupon-bearing bond is 61.88% of par. Consequently, the price of the coupon stream is 36.2827. To summarize,

| | Price | |
|---|---|---|
| | In 32nds | In Decimal |
| **Coupon-bearing bond** | | |
| Quoted bond price: | 97.205 | 97.6406 |
| Accrued interest: | | 0.5221 |
| Market price of bond: | | 98.1627 |
| **Strip bond** | | |
| Quoted bond price: | | 61.8800 |
| PV of coupon payments: | | 36.2827 |

**ILLUSTRATION 2.11** Compute price of call feature in coupon-bearing bond.

*Suppose that you observe the following U.S. Treasury bond prices (quoted in 32nds):*

| Coupon Rate | Maturity | Price |
|---|---|---|
| 8¼% | May 15, 2010-15 | 103-19 |
| 12% | May 15, 2015 | 133-13 |
| 0% | May 15, 2015 | 47-14 |

*The 8¼% bond is callable at par on any May 15 in the years 2010 through 2015. Based on the reported prices, compute the value of the embedded call feature.*

The value of the call feature can be deduced by using the valuation by replication principle. From the problem information, you can create an 8¼% coupon-bearing, noncallable bond from the 12% coupon-bearing bond and the zero-coupon bond. To reproduce the 8¼% coupon payments, you need to buy

$$\frac{8.25}{12} = 0.6875 \text{ units}$$

of the 12% bond. While this purchase creates the desired coupon stream, the repayment of the principal in May 2015 will amount to only 68.75. To make up for the difference, 100 – 68.75 = 31.25, you need to buy 0.3125 units of the zero-coupon bond. Thus, in the absence of costless arbitrage opportunities, the price of an 8¼% coupon-bearing noncallable bond is

$$0.6875 \times 133.40625 + 0.3125 \times 47.43750 = 106.5410$$

The value of the call feature is, therefore, 106.5410 – 103.59375 = 2.9473.

**Bond Equivalent Yield** The continuously compounded yield to maturity of the 6¼s of May 2030 can be computed using equation (2.24) and is 5.5847%.[10] In Table 2.2, however, the yield to maturity of the 6¼s of May 2030 is reported as 5.66%. The reported rate is called a *bond equivalent yield.* While bond equivalents yield are not used is any of the subsequent chapters, it is useful to know the conventions that bond markets have adopted, if only to be able to reconcile market reporting with actual economic values.

The bond equivalent yield, $y_s$, is a nominal yield. It is determined by equating the market price of a bond to the present value of its cash flows and solving for $y_s$, that is,

$$B_c = (1 + y_s/2)^{-n_{dr}/n_{dcp}} \sum_{i=0}^{n-1} CF_i(1 + y_s/2)^{T_i} \tag{2.34}$$

where $n_{dr}$ is the number of days remaining in the current coupon period, and $n_{dcp}$ is the total number of days in the current coupon period.[11] In essence, what the right-hand side of (2.34) does is have you go forward until the date of the next coupon payment and value the bond, and then discount the value at the time of the next coupon using a discount factor that depends on the fraction of the current coupon period remaining. Note that when you compute the value of the bond at the time of the next coupon, the first coupon in the summation does not get discounted since it is being paid immediately. It is also worth noting that the reported bond equivalent yield is based on the ask price (rather than the bid

[10] The continuously compounded yield to maturity may be computed using OV_IR_FIXED_YIELD(*cdat, lcpn, ncpn, coup, mdat, bprce*), where *cdat* is the current date, *lcpn* is the last coupon date, *ncpn* is the next coupon date, *coup* is the coupon rate expressed in decimal, *mdat* is the maturity date of the bond, and *bprce* is the bond price including accrued interest.

[11] Again, this convention applies to Treasury bonds and notes only. Corporate and municipal bonds have a different day count convention.

price). The rationale is that, if you bought the bond, the bond equivalent yield is the approximate rate of return you would earn if you held it to maturity. The bond equivalent yield of the 6¼s of May 2030, for example, is determined by

$$110.2092 = (1 + y_s/2)^{-76/184} \sum_{i=0}^{60-1} CF_i(1 + y_s/2)^{T_i}$$

where $CF_i$ equals the coupon interest payment, 3.125, in each period but the last and is the coupon interest payment plus the repayment of principal at maturity, 103.125.

## TERM STRUCTURE OF INTEREST RATES

The rates reported for the discount bonds in Tables 2.1 and 2.2 reveal that the zero-coupon interest rate (or *spot* rate of interest[12]) varies with term to maturity. The relation between spot rates and term to maturity is called (interchangeably) the *term structure of interest rates*, the *term structure of spot rates*, and the *zero-coupon yield curve*. Depending on the economic environment, the nature of the relation may change.[13] Note that it is important that all bonds used in examining the term structure of interest rates must have a common degree of default risk. We do not want the relation between yield and term to maturity to be obfuscated by the fact that yields also vary with risk. In practice, the shape of the zero-coupon yield curve is determined using the rates from U.S. Treasury instruments like those reported in Tables 2.1 and 2.2. Treasury securities are all viewed as being free from default risk.

In applying the coupon bond valuation formula (2.20), it is necessary to know the zero-coupon rate for each cash flow. The cash flows of a coupon bond, however, may fall between the maturities of the zero-coupon rates observed in the marketplace. Suppose, for example, that the bond you are valuing has a cash flow occurring in four months, and you can find only zero-coupon rates with three months and six months to maturity. Somehow, you have to come up with a four-month zero-coupon rate. One method is *linear interpolation*. You would simply take a time-weighted average of the three-month and six-months rates, weighting the three-month rate with 2/3 and the six-month rate with 1/3. Another approach is to smooth the entire set of zero-coupon rates at once using techniques such as *ordinary least squares regression* or *cubic spline interpolation*. Such techniques are described in detail in Chapter 18.

For illustrative purposes, we assume that the entire term structure of observed rates has been smoothed and can be represented by a mathematical relation such as

$$r_i = 0.04 + 0.01 \ln(1 + T_i) \tag{2.35}$$

[12] It is called the *spot* rate of interest because it applies to a loan that begins today.

[13] Typically, the curve is upward sloping because lenders of funds prefer short maturities while borrowers prefer long.

where $r_i$ is the continuously compounded rate on a loan maturing in $T_i$ years. Where $T_i$ is 0, the rate is 4%. This is the rate of interest on an overnight loan. Where $T_i$ is 5, the rate of interest is 5.792%. Figure 2.1 shows the rates produced by (2.35) for different terms to maturity. As the figure shows, the term structure is upward sloping, with the rate of increase diminishing with term to maturity. Also plotted in Figure 2.1 are the discount factors corresponding to each zero-coupon rate. Many practitioners prefer working with discount factors rather than discount rates. Recall that a discount factor is today's price of $1 received at future time $T_i$, that is,

$$DF_i = e^{-r_i T_i}$$

### Implied Forward Rates of Interest

The zero-coupon yield curve represents the spot rates interest on loans of varying maturities. The loans begin *today* and extend until the end of the bond's life, $T$. The zero-coupon yield curve also embeds information about the rates of interest that may be earned on loans in the *future*. Such rates are called *forward rates of interest*. To deduce the forward rate on a loan that will begin at time $T_1$ and run until time $T_2$, we first go to the zero-coupon yield curve and find the spot rates corresponding to each maturity, that is, $r_1$ and $r_2$. Next, assume that we want to invest $1 for a period of time equal to $T_2$. One way we can do this is to buy a zero-coupon bond with maturity $T_2$. Another way is to buy a zero-coupon bond with maturity $T_1$, and then reinvest the terminal proceeds in a zero-coupon bond with maturity $T_2 - T_1$. The forward rate of interest from $T_1$ to $T_2$ can be deduced by equating the terminal values of the two investment alternatives, that is,

$$e^{r_2 T_2} = e^{r_1 T_1} e^{f_{1,2}(T_2 - T_1)} \tag{2.36}$$

Taking the natural logarithm of both sides of (2.36), replacing subscript 1 with the notation $i$ and 2 with $j$, and rearranging to isolate $f_{i,j}$, the *implied forward rate of interest* on a loan beginning at time $T_i$ and ending at time $T_j$ is

$$f_{i,j} = \frac{r_j T_j - r_i T_i}{T_j - T_i} \tag{2.37}$$

The zero-coupon yield curve can also be used to deduce *forward discount factors*. From (2.36), we know

$$\frac{1}{DF_2} = \frac{1}{DF_1} \times \frac{1}{FDF_{1,2}} \tag{2.38}$$

where $DF_i$ is the discount factor of the $i$th zero-coupon bond currently observed in the marketplace and $FDF_{i,j}$ is the *implied forward discount factor* beginning at time $T_i$ and ending at time $T_j$. Rearranging (2.38), we see that, in general, implied forward discount factors may be computed as

$$FDF_{i,j} = \frac{DF_j}{DF_i} \tag{2.39}$$

Consequently, implied forward rates may also be computed as

$$f_{i,j} = \frac{\ln(DF_i/DF_j)}{T_j - T_i} \tag{2.40}$$

**ILLUSTRATION 2.12** Compute forward rates and forward discount factors from zero-coupon yield curve.

*Assume that the current zero-coupon term structure of spot rates is given by the curve,*

$$r_i = 0.04 + 0.01\ln(1 + T_i)$$

*Compute the spot rates and discount factors on loans beginning now and ending in years 1 through 10, by increments of one year. Also, compute the one-year forward rates and one-year forward discount factors beginning at the end of years 1 through 9 by increments of one year.*

To compute the zero-coupon spot rates, apply the given term structure formula. The one-year spot rate, for example, is $r_1 = 0.04 + 0.01\ \ln(1 + 1) = 4.693\%$. The one-year discount factor is $DF_1 = e^{-0.04693(1)} = 0.9542$. The complete set of results is shown in the table below. To compute the forward rates and forward discount factors based on the zero-coupon spot rates, you apply the formula (2.37) and (2.39). The implied forward rate on a one-year loan beginning in 1 year is

$$f_{1,2} = \frac{0.05099(2) - 0.04693(1)}{2 - 1} = 5.504$$

The implied price of a one-year discount bond paying \$1 in year 2 is

$$FDF_{1,2} = \frac{DF_2}{DF_1} = \frac{0.9031}{0.9542} = 0.9464$$

Note also the relation between the implied forward rate and the implied discount factor, that is,

$$f_{1,2} = \frac{\ln(0.9464)}{2 - 1} = 5.504\%$$

The OPTVAL Function library includes a routine for computing implied forward rates:

OV_IR_TS_FORWARD_RATE($r1$, $r2$, $t1$, $t2$)

where $r1$ and $r2$ are the spot rates maturing at the beginning and at the end of the forward rate period, and $t1$ and $t2$ are the times to maturity of the respective rates. An application of the function is shown in the spreadsheet below.

| D5 | | fx =OV_IR_TS_FORWARD_RATE(B5,B6,A5,A6) | | | |
|---|---|---|---|---|---|
| | A | B | C | D | E | F |
| 1 | | | | One-year | Forward | |
| 2 | Years to | Spot | Discount | forward | discount | |
| 3 | maturity | rate | factor | rate | factor | |
| 4 | 0 | 4.000% | 1.0000 | | | |
| 5 | 1 | 4.693% | 0.9542 | 5.504% | 0.9464 | |
| 6 | 2 | 5.099% | 0.9031 | 5.962% | 0.9421 | |
| 7 | 3 | 5.386% | 0.8508 | 6.279% | 0.9391 | |
| 8 | 4 | 5.609% | 0.7990 | 6.521% | 0.9369 | |
| 9 | 5 | 5.792% | 0.7486 | 6.717% | 0.9350 | |
| 10 | 6 | 5.946% | 0.6999 | 6.881% | 0.9335 | |
| 11 | 7 | 6.079% | 0.6534 | 7.022% | 0.9322 | |
| 12 | 8 | 6.197% | 0.6091 | 7.145% | 0.9310 | |
| 13 | 9 | 6.303% | 0.5671 | 7.256% | 0.9300 | |
| 14 | 10 | 6.398% | 0.5274 | | | |

Note that the implied one-year forward rate starting at time 0 equals the one-year spot rate. This stands to reason since a forward rate loan beginning at time 0 is simply a spot rate loan. Note also that the implied forward rates can be significantly higher than the spot rates. The spot rates on 9-year and 10-year loans are 6.303% and 6.398%, respectively, and yet the implied one-year forward rate for a loan beginning at the end of year 9 is 7.256%.

**ILLUSTRATION 2.13** Lock-in interest rate on forward loan.

*Suppose that you go to your local bank and tell the manager that you want to borrow $50,000 in three months and want to repay the loan with a single balloon payment nine months later. Because you believe interest rates will rise over the next three months, you further request that the interest be locked-in today. The manager says that your credit risk is no problem, but that he cannot lock-in the interest rate because he has no idea what it will be in three months. You then ask about the current borrowing and lending rates at the bank, and he gives you the following table.*

| Term | Lending Rate | Borrowing Rate |
|---|---|---|
| 3 months | 3.00% | 3.50% |
| 6 months | 3.50% | 4.00% |
| 9 months | 4.00% | 4.50% |
| 1 year | 4.50% | 5.00% |

*Based on these quoted rates, what forward rate can you lock in today on a nine-month loan beginning in three months? Show how to structure the forward loan. What rate can you lock in today? (Assume all interest rates are continuously compounded.)*

In order to compute the forward rate, you must identify the two spot rates that straddle the forward period, that is, the spot rates that mature at the beginning and end of the forward loan period—three months and one year. Because you want to borrow money in the forward period, the longer term spot rate needs to be a borrowing rate, 5.00%. Since you do not need the loan over the first three months of the year, the shorter term spot rate is the lending rate, 3.00%. Thus, the implied forward rate of interest on a nine-month loan beginning loan beginning in three months is

$$f_{0.25,\,1} = \frac{0.05(1) - 0.03(0.25)}{1 - 0.25} = 5.667\%$$

In order to structure the forward loan, you must figure out how much to borrow. Recall that you need to borrow \$50,000 in three months and want to repay the loan nine months later. To provide for the \$50,000 cash inflow, you need to lend the present value of the \$50,000 in three months. The rate that you will earn on such a deposit is 3.00%. The present value of \$50,000 received at the end of three months is

$$50{,}000e^{-0.03(0.25)} = 49{,}626.40$$

But where do you get the needed deposit of \$49,626.40? The answer is that you borrow that amount for a year. By borrowing \$49,626.40 for one year and lending that same amount for three months, you have synthetically structured a nine-month forward loan beginning in three months. The net cash flows of the agreement are certain and are as follows:

| Action | Today | 3 Months | 1 Year |
|---|---|---|---|
| Borrow | 49,626.40 | | -52,170.80 |
| Lend | -49,626.40 | 50,000.00 | |

The rate on the forward loan is ln(52,170.80/50,000)/0.75 = 5.667%.

## STOCK VALUATION

Shares of stock are pieces of the ownership of a corporation. Shareholders derive value in two ways, through periodic cash dividend payments and through any price appreciation (or depreciation) that may occur while holding the stock. Valuing a stock is like valuing a coupon-bearing bond in the sense that both are present values of expected future cash flow streams. Unlike a bond, however, the expected periodic cash flows (i.e., dividend payments) are not specified in a contract. Moreover, absent bankruptcy, the life of a stock is infinite.

In the stock valuation problem, the expected future cash flows are cash dividends. We denote $D_i$ as the $i$th future cash dividend, where the dividend stream continues indefinitely, that is, $D_1$, $D_2$, $D_3$, . . . . The time from now until the $i$th dividend is received is denoted $t_i$. The current dividend, $D_0$, is assumed to have just been paid. The present value of all expected future cash dividends is

$$S = \sum_{i=1}^{\infty} D_i e^{-kt_i} \tag{2.41}$$

where $k$ is the required rate of return on the stock.[14]

Equation (2.41) is a *stock valuation formula*. On first appearance, it may seem appropriate only for those individuals who plan to hold the stock indefinitely, but

[14] For expositional convenience, the rate of return k is assumed to be the same for each cash dividend payment. There is no reason in principle, however, that the discount rate cannot be a function of time.

that is not the case. Even if our anticipated holding period is much shorter, (2.41) remains an appropriate model. To see this, consider the value that we would assign the stock if we anticipated selling it after the *n*th dividend is paid, that is,

$$S = \sum_{i=1}^{n} D_i e^{-kt_i} + S_n e^{-kt_n} \tag{2.42}$$

where $S_n$ is the expected share price at time $t_n$. To develop an expectation of the expected share price at time $t_n$, assume that we sell the stock to someone who plans to hold it indefinitely. The trade price will be

$$S_n = \sum_{i=n+1}^{n} D_i e^{-k(t_i - t_n)} \tag{2.43}$$

Substituting (2.43) into (2.42) and simplifying, we are back to (2.41).

### Constant Dividend Growth

As a practical matter, the valuation equation (2.41) is difficult to implement since it requires that we estimate the cash dividend amounts from next period through infinity. What is more common in practice is to estimate next period's cash dividend, $D_1$, and then assume that subsequent dividends grow at a constant rate. Assuming dividends grow at a continuous constant rate, $g$, we can rewrite (2.41) as

$$S = \sum_{i=1}^{\infty} D_i e^{-(k-g)t_i} \tag{2.44}$$

As it turns out, (2.44) is the sum of an infinite geometric progression whose value is easily computed, as is demonstrated in Appendix 2B. The common ratio, $b$, in Appendix 2B is $b = e^{-(k-g)}$, so $1/b = e^{k-g}$ and the per share value of the common stock[15] is

$$S = \frac{D_0}{e^{k-g} - 1} \tag{2.45}$$

**ILLUSTRATION 2.14** Value common stock with constant dividend growth.

*Suppose you are considering buying a particular stock at its current price of \$15 a share. The stock just paid a dividend of \$2 a share. Based upon your historical dividend analysis, you expect the stock's dividend to grow at a constant continuous rate of 1% a year indefinitely,*

$$D_t = 2e^{0.01t}, \text{ for } t = 1, 2, 3, \ldots$$

[15] This is one variation of what is often referred to as the Gordon (1962) constant growth model.

*where the dividends are paid annually. Based on your risk analysis, you believe the required rate of return for the stock is 12%. Should you buy the stock?*

Based on the parameters you have estimated, the stock's value is

$$S = \frac{D_0}{e^{k-g} - 1} = \frac{2}{e^{0.12-0.01} - 1} = 17.20$$

Consequently, the stock is under-priced and should be purchased.

## SUMMARY

Effective risk management requires precise risk measurement, and precise risk measurement requires a thorough understanding of security valuation. This chapter provides the foundations of security valuation. The first section discussed the two key assumptions underlying valuation—the absence of costless arbitrage opportunities and frictionless markets. The first assumption is predicated on the notion that individuals prefer more wealth to less. It is essential. The second assumption is one of convenience. It allows security valuation models to be developed in an unencumbered fashion. We relax this assumption in various ways as we proceed through the remaining chapters in the book.

The next five sections focus on the time value of money and its implications for security valuation. The mechanics of continuously compounded interest rates is provided first, and then the mechanics are applied to security valuation. The third section focuses on the valuation of, perhaps, the simplest type of security—a discount bond. The value of a discount bond is simply the present value of its promised payment at maturity. The fourth section focuses on coupon bonds and shows that they are simply portfolios of discount bonds. In both sections, the valuation formulas are used to develop the interest rate risk measures of duration and convexity. Since coupon bonds have multiple cash flows through time, the fifth section addresses the issue of maturity-specific interest rates. Zero-coupon interest rates are shown to imply forward rates of interest. Finally, the interest rate mechanics are applied to common stock valuation. The value of a share of stock is shown to be the present value of an infinite series of expected dividend payments.

## REFERENCES AND SUGGESTIONS FOR FURTHER READING

Fabozzi, Frank J., and Michael Fleming. 2005. U.S. Treasury and agency securities. Chapter 10 in *The Handbook of Fixed Income Securities*, edited by Frank J. Fabozzi. New York: McGraw-Hill.

Gordon, Myron J. 1962. *The Investment, Financing, and Valuation of the Corporation.* Homewood, IL: Irwin.

Macaulay, Frederick. 1938. *Some Theoretical Problems Suggested by the Movement of Interest Rates, Bond Yields, and Stock Prices in the U.S. Since 1856*. National Bureau of Economic Research.

Redington, F. M. 1952. Review of the principle of life office valuation. *Journal of the Institute of Actuaries* 78: 286–340.

Samuelson, Paul A. 1945. The effect of interest rate increases on the banking system. *American Economic Review* 35: 16–27.

## APPENDIX 2A: TAYLOR SERIES EXPANSION OF BOND VALUE

In using the duration and convexity to predict bond price movements, we implicitly used a *Taylor series expansion* of the bond valuation formula. From calculus, we know that most smooth functions $f(x)$ can be expanded in a *Taylor series* about the point $x_0$,[16] that is,

$$\begin{aligned} f(x) &= f(x_0) + \frac{f'(x_0)}{1}(x - x_0) + \frac{f''(x_0)}{1 \cdot 2}(x - x_0)^2 + \frac{f'''(x_0)}{1 \cdot 2 \cdot 3}(x - x_0)^3 + \cdots \\ &= \sum_{n=0}^{\infty} \frac{f^{(n)}(x_0)}{n!}(x - x_0)^n \end{aligned} \tag{2A.1}$$

In (2A.1), replace $x$ with the yield to maturity of the bond, $r$, and $f(x)$ with the bond valuation function, $B(r)$.

## APPENDIX 2B: SUM OF A GEOMETRIC PROGRESSION

A *geometric progression* is a sequence of numbers, $a_i$, $i = 1, \ldots, n$, whose adjacent terms satisfy the property that

$$\frac{a_{i+1}}{a_i} = b$$

where $b$ is called the *common ratio*. The sum of an $n$ element geometric series whose first element is 1 is

$$S_n = 1 + b + b^2 + \cdots + b^{n-3} + b^{n-2} + b^{n-1} \tag{2B.1}$$

While this sum may seem tedious to compute, it may be simplified considerably. First, multiply (2B.1) by $b$.

$$bS_n = b + b^2 + \cdots + b^{n-2} + b^{n-1} + b^n \tag{2B.2}$$

Now, subtract (2B.2) from (2B.1).

$$(1 - b)S_n = 1 - b^n$$

[16] For the special case where $x_0 = 0$, (A.1) is sometimes called the Maclaurin series of $f(x)$.

or

$$S_n = \frac{1 - b^n}{1 - b} \tag{2B.3}$$

Where the number of elements in the series is infinite (i.e., $n = \infty$) and $b < 1$, the sum of the geometric progression is

$$S_\infty = \frac{1}{1 - b} \tag{2B.4}$$

If the infinite series begins with $b$, the sum is

$$S_\infty = \frac{b}{1 - b} = \frac{1}{1/b - 1} \tag{2B.5}$$

CHAPTER 3

# Relation between Return and Risk

An important facet of valuation not yet discussed is the relation between expected return and risk. In the bond and stock valuation models discussed in Chapter 2, risk enters into the valuation formulas through the interest rate used to discount the expected cash flows to the present. In financial economics, the *capital asset pricing model* (CAPM)[1] provides the structural relation between expected return and risk. It relies on the assumption that individuals prefer more wealth to less wealth, but at a decreasing rate. Such individuals are risk averse, and risk aversion is the focus of the utility theory discussion in the first section. In the second section, we extend the discussion to show how such individuals allocate their wealth among securities. In the third section, we aggregate security demands across all individuals in the marketplace and identify the equilibrium expected return/risk relations for individual securities and security portfolios. Finally, in the fourth section, we apply the CAPM relations to evaluate portfolio performance.

## UTILITY THEORY

In most financial economic models, individuals are assumed to be *risk averse.* Investors do not like risk but are willing to bear it if paid an adequate risk premium. Risk premiums arise from the nature of how an individual's satisfaction varies with wealth. Called a *utility of wealth function*, $U(w)$ is the level of satisfaction (measured in units of utility) realized from having a level of wealth, $w$. An individual's marginal utility of wealth is assumed to be positive (i.e., $dU(w)/dw > 0$)—the more wealth, the more satisfaction. Indeed, this property is the driving force behind the absence of costless arbitrage opportunities in a rationally functioning marketplace. As wealth increases, however, the rate at which satisfaction increases falls (i.e., $d^2U(w)/dw^2 > 0$). The next dollar earned is not quite as satisfying as the last dollar earned.

[1] The central role that the CAPM plays in financial economics is attested to by the fact that five of the key players in its development—Harry Markowitz, James Tobin, William Sharpe, John Lintner, and Robert C. Merton—have received Nobel Prizes in Economics.

Figure 3.1 illustrates the shape of the utility function for an individual with diminishing positive marginal utility of wealth. Note that, as wealth increases, utility increases, but at a decreasing rate. To show that this individual is a risk averter, consider his behavior when presented with a fair bet. A *fair bet* is any bet whose expected outcome is 0. A 50-50 chance of winning or losing $X$, for example, constitutes a fair bet. Accepting a fair bet implies that there is no change in the individual's expected wealth level. If the individual's certain wealth level before the bet is $w_0$, his expected wealth level upon accepting the bet remains at $w_0$, that is,

$$E(\tilde{w}) = 0.5(w_0 + \tilde{X}) + 0.5(w_0 - \tilde{X}) = w_0$$

But, because the individual's expected wealth does not change, that does not mean he is indifferent about whether or not to accept the bet. He will not. The reason is that, after accepting the bet, his expected satisfaction level is

$$E[\tilde{U}(w)] = 0.5U(w_0 + \tilde{X}) + 0.5U(w_0 - \tilde{X})$$

Because his utility function is concave from below, as shown in Figure 3.2, the expected utility of wealth after taking the bet rests below the utility that he had to begin with, $E[\tilde{U}(w)] < U(w_0)$. Because taking a fair bet reduces the individual's expected utility, an individual with diminishing positive marginal utility of wealth is said to be a *risk averter*.

**FIGURE 3.1** Utility function of a risk averse individual.

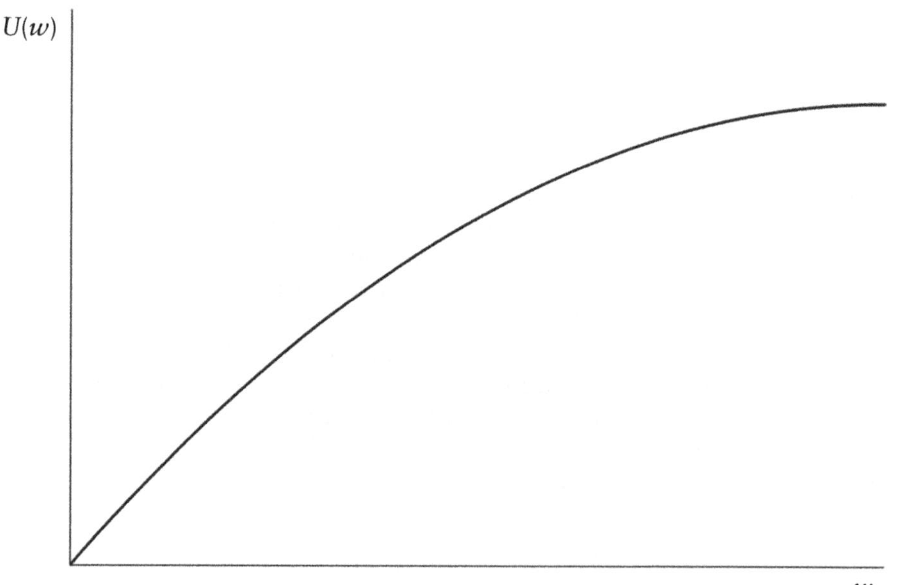

**FIGURE 3.2** Utility function of a risk averse individual when evaluating a fair bet.

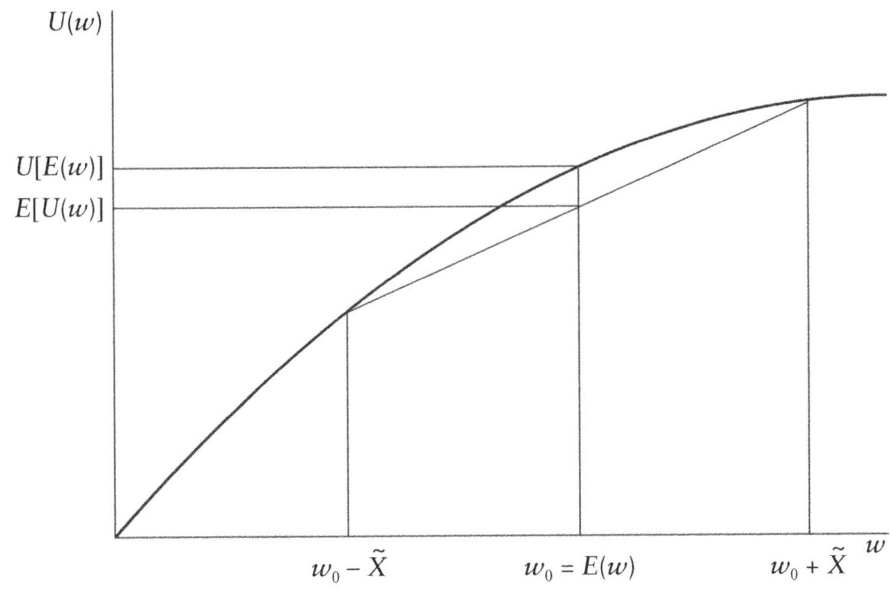


Utility theory is useful not only in demonstrating general behavioral principles but also in evaluating specific investment opportunities. In order to make specific decisions, however, the mathematical character of the utility function needs to be more precisely defined.[2] A logarithmic utility of wealth function, $U(w) = \ln w$, mimics the behavior of a risk-averter—$dU(w)/dw = 1/w > 0$ and $d^2U(w)/dw^2 = -1/w^2 < 0$. So does a square root utility of wealth function, $U(w) = \sqrt{w}$, since $dU(w)/dw = 0.5w^{-0.5} > 0$ and $d^2U(w)/dw^2 = -0.25w^{-1.5} < 0$. We use these utility of wealth functions in the illustrations that follow.

Aside from knowing the specific character of the utility function, a handful of definitions are also important. In the illustrations that follow, we assume that the individual holds two assets—a risk-free asset whose value is $R$ and a risky asset whose value in one period is either $\tilde{X}_1$ or $\tilde{X}_2$, with probabilities $p$ and $1 - p$, respectively. Assuming the risk-free interest rate is zero, the individual's *expected utility of terminal wealth* is

$$E[\tilde{U}(w)] = pU(R + \tilde{X}_1) + (1 - p)U(R + \tilde{X}_2) \tag{3.1}$$

Now, suppose someone approaches this individual and asks him to sell his risky asset. What is the least amount that the individual will take? To answer this question, we must first identify the cash equivalent of the individual's overall

[2] The four most commonly used utility of wealth functions used in financial economics are: (a) the logarithmic utility function $U(w) = \ln w$, (b) the quadratic utility function $U(w) = aw - bw^2$ where $a > 2bw$ and $b > 0$, (c) the exponential utility function $U(w) = -e^{-aw}$ where $a > 0$, and (d) the power utility function $U(w) = w^a$ where $0 < a < 1$.

position. The *cash equivalent* is that certain amount of cash, C, that the individual is willing to take for his entire position and is computed by setting the utility of the cash amount equal to the expected utility of terminal wealth, that is,

$$U(C) = E[\tilde{U}(w)] \tag{3.2}$$

With the amount of the cash equivalent, C, known, the *minimum selling price* of the risky asset equals $C - R$.

**ILLUSTRATION 3.1** Identify maximum insurance premium.

*Consider two individuals—A with a logarithmic utility function and B with a square root utility function. Both individuals have \$100,000 in cash and face the prospect of losing \$50,000, with a 5% probability. What is the maximum amount that each individual would be willing to pay for insurance?*

Individual A currently enjoys an expected satisfaction level,

$$E[\tilde{U}_A(w)] = 0.05\ln(100{,}000 - 50{,}000) + 0.95\ln(100{,}000) = 11.478$$

Holding expected utility constant, this implies that A is indifferent between staying in his current position (i.e., holding \$100,000 in cash and having the prospect of losing \$50,000) and having a certain amount of cash C as determined by

$$U_A(C) = \ln C = 11.478$$

Solving for C, you find $C = e^{11.478} = 96{,}593.63$. In other words, A is indifferent between having (a) \$100,000 in cash and running a 5% chance of losing \$50,000, and (b) \$96,593.63 in cash. Thus, the maximum amount A is willing to pay for insurance against loss is \$100,000 – 96,593.63 or \$3,406.37.

Individual B currently enjoys a satisfaction level,

$$E[\tilde{U}_B(w)] = 0.05\sqrt{100{,}000 - 50{,}000} + 0.95\sqrt{100{,}000} = 311.597$$

Individual B's cash equivalent wealth level is determined by

$$U_B(C) = \sqrt{C} = 311.597$$

Solving for C, $C = 311.597^2 = 97{,}092.51$, which means B is willing to pay up to \$2,907.49 for insurance against loss. Apparently an individual with logarithmic utility is more risk averse than an individual with square root utility.

**ILLUSTRATION 3.2** Are options really a zero-sum game?

*In Chapter 1, derivative trades are described as zero-sum games—what the buyer gains, the seller loses, and vice versa. This does* not *imply, however, that both the buyer and the seller cannot gain from trading. Assume Individual A has \$50 in cash and one share of a common stock. The stock, he believes, has a 60% chance of falling in price to \$80 and a 40% chance of increasing in price to \$120. Individual B has \$100 in cash and no other holdings. B, however, follows the stock held by A and is much more optimistic regarding its prospects. Specifically, B assigns only a 30% chance of the stock of falling in price to \$80 and a 70% chance of it increasing to \$120. Demonstrate that both A and B can both be made better of by trading a put option written on the stock. Assume the put has an* *exercise price of \$100 and costs \$10. Assume both individuals have square root utility functions. Ignore the time value of money.*

Assume Individual A wants to buy the put, considering his pessimistic outlook regarding the stock's prospects. A's current expected utility level is

$$E[\tilde{U}(w_A)] = 0.6\sqrt{50+80} + 0.4\sqrt{50+120} = 12.06$$

where the terminal wealth levels are 130 or 170, depending on the performance of the stock. On the other hand, if he buys the put, his terminal wealth level is 130 less the put price plus the payoff on the put if the stock price falls and is 170 less the put price is the stock price rises. Thus, if he buys the put, his expected utility is

$$E[\tilde{U}(w_A)] = 0.6\sqrt{130-10+(100-80)} + 0.4\sqrt{170-10+0} = 12.16$$

Thus, from an expected utility of terminal wealth standpoint, A is made better off by buying the put.

Individual B, on the other hand, is more optimistic regarding the stock's prospects and is considering selling the put. B currently enjoys a utility of wealth equal to

$$U(w_B) = \sqrt{100} = 10$$

If he sells the put, his terminal wealth will be either 100 plus the put price less the put payoff (that goes to A) if the stock price falls and 100 plus the put price if the stock price rises. Thus, after selling the put, his expected utility of wealth is

$$E[\tilde{U}(w_B)] = 0.3\sqrt{100+10-(100-80)} + 0.7\sqrt{100+10-0} = 10.09$$

Since selling the put provides B a portfolio with higher expected utility of wealth, B, too, is made better off by the trade.

The fact that both A and B are made better off by trading with each other does not negate the fact that the trade, in itself, is zero-sum. It is. If the stock price falls, A's net payoff equals the option payoff less the put price, that is, (100 – 80) – 10 = +10, and B's net payoff is the put price less the exercise proceeds 10 – (100 – 80) = –10. If the stock price rises, the put expires worthless, which means that A's net loss on the put, 10, is B's net gain.

## PORTFOLIO THEORY

The expected utility framework is useful in a number of decision-making contexts. A weakness of the framework, however, is that the individual's utility function must be specified. Exactly how one goes about identifying the mathematical structure of an individual's utility function is unclear. Fortunately, for the individual's portfolio allocation decision, a specific structure is not necessary. The reason is that Tobin (1958) shows that individuals with diminishing positive marginal utility have expected return ($E$)/risk ($\sigma$) indifference curves shaped like those shown in Figure 3.3,[3] where risk is measured by the standard deviation of return. Along each

[3] Technically speaking, Tobin (1958) proved this result in two general cases: (a) individuals have quadratic utility of wealth; and (b) the distribution of security returns is multivariate normal.

**FIGURE 3.3** Indifference curves of a risk-averse individual.

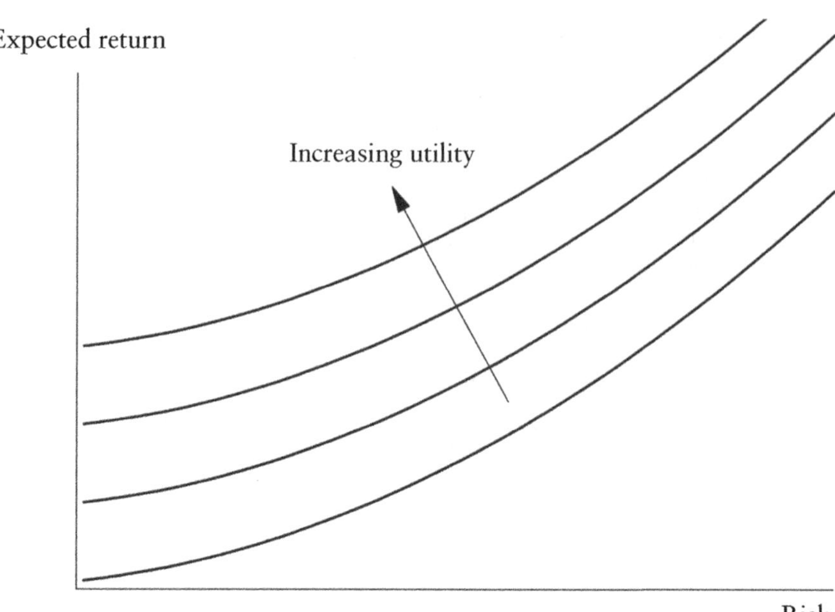


indifference curve, expected utility is held constant. The curves have the properties $dE/d\sigma > 0$ and $d^2E/d\sigma^2 > 0$. The first derivative says that an individual will demand a more return as risk increases. The second derivative says that the rate at which the individual demands more return grows faster and faster as risk increases. In Figure 3.3, note also that the higher the indifference curve, the greater the expected utility. That means individuals choose portfolios that have the highest expected return for a given level of risk and/or portfolios that have the lowest risk for a given level of expected return. Such portfolios are called *efficient portfolios*.

Prior to formulating the individual's portfolio allocation decision, it is worthwhile to note that how a risk-averter's indifference curves differ from those of an individual who is risk-neutral. Figure 3.4 illustrates the indifference curves of a risk-neutral individual. The fact that the curves are horizontal means that a risk-neutral individual does not care about risk. Such an individual chooses a portfolio that maximizes expected return. At the other behavioral extreme are indifference curves that are vertical, as shown in Figure 3.5. This individual is a *risk minimizer* and will choose a portfolio that minimizes portfolio risk.

### Portfolio Allocation with *n* Risky Securities

The focus now turns to identifying efficient portfolios, that is, portfolios with the highest expected return for a given level of risk and/or with the lowest risk for a given level of expected return. To do so, an individual must gather a considerable amount of information. Assuming *n* risky securities exist in the marketplace, an

**FIGURE 3.4** Indifference curves of a risk-neutral individual.

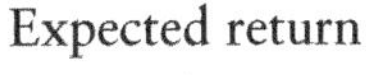


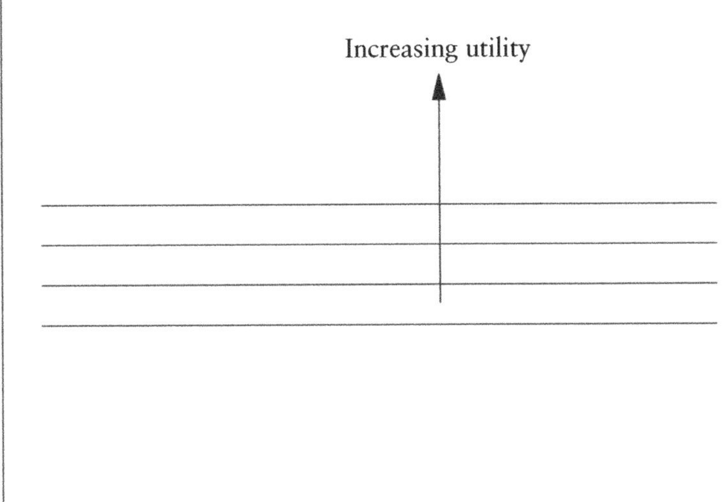


**FIGURE 3.5** Indifference curves of a risk minimizer.

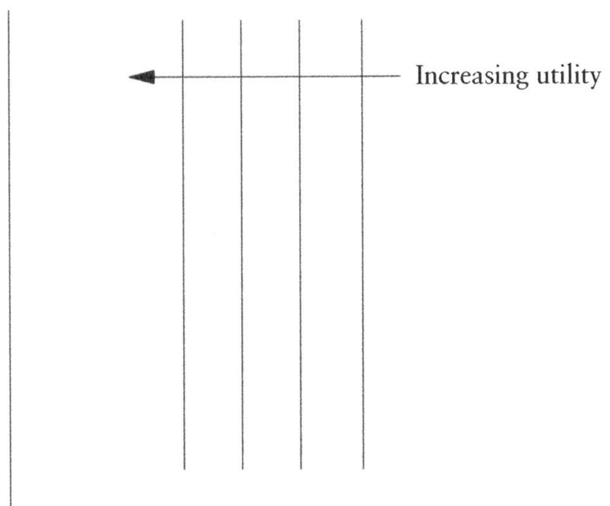

individual must estimate: (a) the expected return of each risky security, $E_i$, $i = 1, \ldots, n$, (b) the standard deviation of return of each risky security, $\sigma_i$, $i = 1, \ldots, n$ and (c) the correlation of returns for each pair of securities in the marketplace, $\rho_{ij}$, $i = 1, \ldots, n$ and $j = 1, \ldots, n$. At first blush, there seems to be a need to estimate $n^2$ different correlation coefficients. With respect to these correlations, however, we know that $\rho_{ij} = +1$ where $i = j$ and that $\rho_{ij} = \rho_{ji}$. This reduces the number of necessary estimates to $n(n - 1)/2$. For expositional convenience, covariances are used below. The covariance between the returns of securities $i$ and $j$ is defined as $\sigma_{ij} = \rho_{ij}\sigma_i\sigma_j$.

Certain definitions are required to set up the portfolio allocation problem. The expected return on portfolio $S$ is

$$E_S = \sum_{i=1}^{n} X_i E_i \tag{3.3}$$

where $X_i$ is the proportion on the individual's wealth invested in security $i$. Naturally the sum of the proportions equals 1, that is,

$$\sum_{i=1}^{n} X_i = 1$$

This is sometimes called the *wealth constraint*. The standard deviation of the portfolio return is

$$\sigma_S = \sqrt{\sum_{i=1}^{n} \sum_{j=1}^{n} X_i X_j \sigma_{ij}} \tag{3.4}$$

Now, to identify the individual's optimal allocation among the $n$ risky securities, we minimize portfolio risk,

$$\text{Minimize } \sigma_S^2 = \sum_{i=1}^{n} \sum_{j=1}^{n} X_i X_j \sigma_{ij} \tag{3.5}$$

subject to

$$\sum_{i=1}^{n} X_i E_i = E_S \tag{3.5a}$$

and

$$\sum_{i=1}^{n} X_i = 1 \tag{3.5b}$$

Constraint (3.5a) requires that the weights produce an expected portfolio return equal to the target level, $E_S$, and constraint (3.5b) requires that all risky security wealth is fully allocated. The objective function (3.5), together with the constraints (3.5a) and (3.5b), constitute a *nonlinear programming problem*. Some such problems can be solved analytically; other numerically. For current purposes, however, it is sufficient to know that, as long as no two risky securities have returns that are perfectly correlated, the solution to the problem is a unique set of allocations, $X_i^*$, $i = 1, \ldots, n$, that produce a minimum variance portfolio. If we solve this portfolio allocation problem for a range of levels of target expected portfolio return, $E_S$, we can trace out the minimum variance (or minimum risk) frontier shown in Figure 3.6. This frontier is sometimes referred to as the *Markowitz* (1952) *efficiency frontier*, in honor of Nobel laureate, Harry Markowitz, who originally developed the framework more than 50 years ago.

**FIGURE 3.6** Minimum variance (or Markowitz efficiency) frontier.

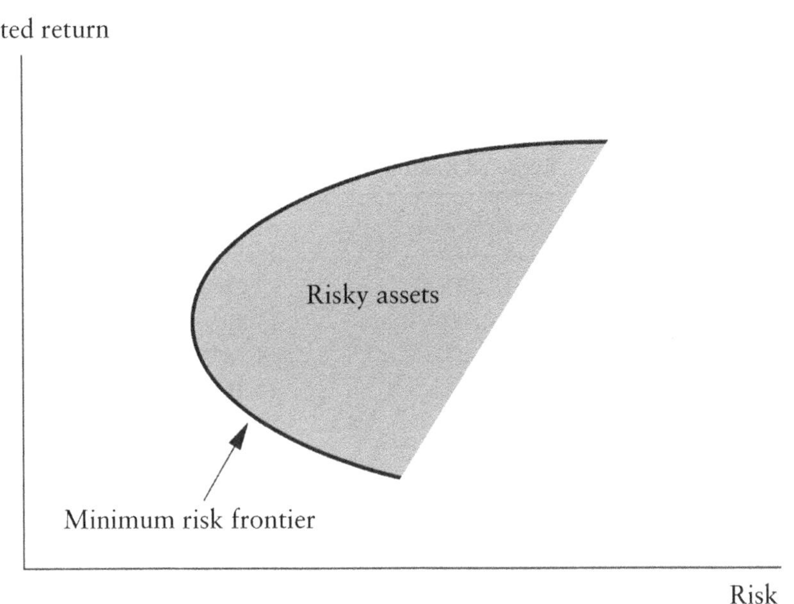


**ILLUSTRATION 3.3** Identify efficient portfolios comprised of two risky securities.

*Describe the range of efficient portfolio allocations when only two risky securities are available in the marketplace. The expected returns and standard deviations of returns of the two securities are shown below. Assume the correlation between the returns of security 1 and security 2 is 0.25.*

| Security | Expected Return | Standard Deviation |
|---|---|---|
| 1 | 18% | 20% |
| 2 | 12% | 16% |

In order to identify the set of efficient portfolios that can be generated by allocating your wealth between securities 1 and 2, you first need to identify what portfolios are *feasible*. The expected return and standard deviation of return of portfolios created by allocating wealth between security 1 and security 2 are given by (3.3) and (3.4), where the number of securities $n$ equals 2. Thus, the expected portfolio return is

$$\begin{aligned} E_S &= X_1E_1 + (1 - X_1)E_2 \\ &= X_1(0.18) + (1 - X_1)(0.12) \end{aligned}$$

and the standard deviation of portfolio return is

$$\begin{aligned} \sigma_S &= \sqrt{X_1^2\sigma_1^2 + 2X_1(1 - X_1)\rho_{12}\sigma_1\sigma_2 + (1 - X_1)^2\sigma_2^2} \\ &= \sqrt{X_1^2(0.20)^2 + 2X_1(1 - X_1)(0.25)(0.20)(0.16) + (1 - X_1)^2(0.16)^2} \end{aligned}$$

Note that since there are only two securities, the proportion of wealth invested in security 2 is $X_2 = 1 - X_1$. The rest of the exercise is a matter of computing $E_S$ and $\sigma_S$ for different levels of $X_1$. This can be easily accomplished in Microsoft Excel. The table below summarizes the results.

| Proportion of Wealth Invested in Security | | Portfolio Attributes | |
|---|---|---|---|
| 1 | 2 | Expected Return | Standard Deviation |
| 1.0 | 0.0 | 18.00% | 20.00% |
| 0.9 | 0.1 | 17.40% | 18.47% |
| 0.8 | 0.2 | 16.80% | 17.08% |
| 0.7 | 0.3 | 16.20% | 15.89% |
| 0.6 | 0.4 | 15.60% | 14.95% |
| 0.5 | 0.5 | 15.00% | 14.28% |
| 0.4 | 0.6 | 14.40% | 13.95% |
| 0.3 | 0.7 | 13.80% | 13.97% |
| 0.2 | 0.8 | 13.20% | 14.33% |
| 0.1 | 0.9 | 12.60% | 15.03% |
| 0.0 | 1.0 | 12.00% | 16.00% |

The table shows that the expected portfolio return falls from 18% to 12% as the proportion of wealth invested in security 1 goes from 1 to 0. The standard deviation of portfolio return, on the other hand, initially falls as $X_1$ is reduced, but then begins to rise again after $X_1$ passes the level 0.40 on its way to zero. The figure below summarizes the results. Exactly what allocation produces the minimum risk portfolio can be determined by taking the derivative of the portfolio standard deviation and setting it equal to 0. For the two-security portfolio, the minimum risk allocation is

$$X_1 = \frac{\sigma_2^2 - \rho_{12}\sigma_1\sigma_2}{\sigma_1^2 + \sigma_2^2 - 2\rho_{12}\sigma_1\sigma_2} \tag{3.6}$$

Substituting the problem parameters, we find that the risk-minimizing portfolio is created by allocating 0.355 of wealth to security 1 and 0.645 to security 2. This portfolio has an expected return equal to 14.13% and a standard deviation of return equal to 13.91%. Thus, while the above table shows the range of feasible portfolios that can be created by allocating one's wealth between security 1 and security 2, no risk-averse individual will hold a portfolio with less (more) than 0.355 (0.645) of his wealth allocated to security 1 (2). The range of allocations that produces *efficient portfolios* is $0.355 \leq X_1 \leq 1$.[4]

A short digression is important here. While we have identified the range of allocations that produces efficient portfolios, one efficient portfolio—the minimum risk portfolio—will *never* be held by a risk averter. The reason is that the slope of the expected return/risk frontier at the minimum risk portfolio is infinite. An individual whose indifference curves have the properties $dE/d\sigma > 0$ and $d^2E/d\sigma^2 > 0$ is not allowed to choose such a portfolio. Consequently, the range of portfolios from which a risk averter chooses his optimal portfolio is defined by $0.355 < X_1 \leq 1$.[5]

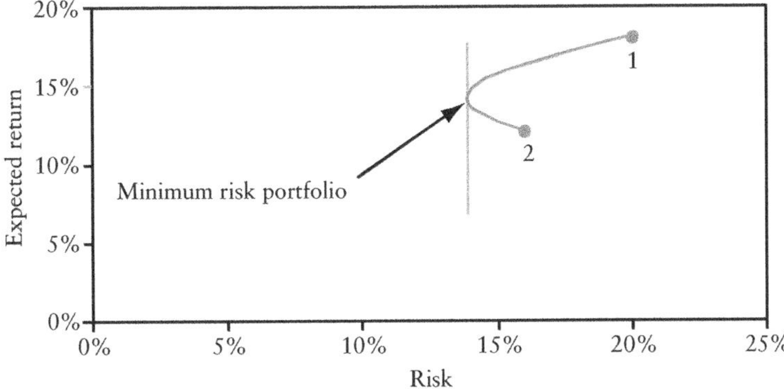


It is also worthwhile to note the Microsoft Excel has a powerful tool called *Solver* that is useful in nonlinear optimization problems such as this. You will find it in the Tool menu:

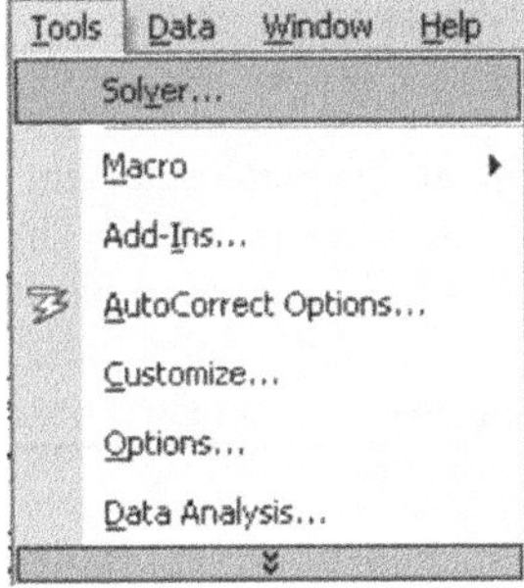


The Excel file, **Two-asset portfolio.xls,** contains the expected return/risk and correlation attributes of the two securities used in this illustration. It shows how Solver can be used to identify the risk-minimizing portfolio numerically. Note that in the worksheet below, the portfolio risk appears in cell C16. At the top of the Solver Parameters box, you tell Solver to find a minimum value for C16 by changing the cells C11 and C12. Just below, you tell Solver that the sum of the allocations to the risky securities, C13, must equal one. Click "Solve" and you are done. This solution, computed using a numerical search procedure, is equal to the risk-minimizing allocations that you solved for analytically using (3.6):

---

[4] Technically speaking, the range of efficient portfolios continues on to the right of security 1 since short sales of security 2 are permitted.

[5] This distinction becomes very important in the risk management strategies of Chapter 5.

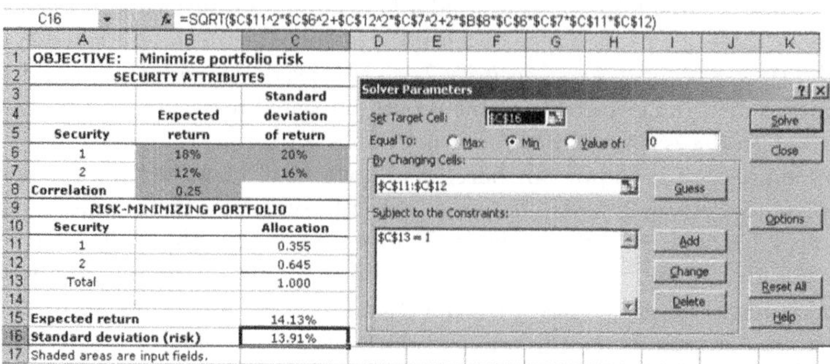

C16 =SQRT($C$11^2*$C$6^2+$C$12^2*$C$7^2+2*$B$8*$C$6*$C$7*$C$11*$C$12)

| | A | B | C |
|---|---|---|---|
| 1 | OBJECTIVE: | Minimize portfolio risk | |
| 2 | | SECURITY ATTRIBUTES | |
| 3 | | | Standard |
| 4 | | Expected | deviation |
| 5 | Security | return | of return |
| 6 | 1 | 18% | 20% |
| 7 | 2 | 12% | 16% |
| 8 | Correlation | 0.25 | |
| 9 | | RISK-MINIMIZING PORTFOLIO | |
| 10 | Security | | Allocation |
| 11 | 1 | | 0.355 |
| 12 | 2 | | 0.645 |
| 13 | Total | | 1.000 |
| 14 | | | |
| 15 | Expected return | | 14.13% |
| 16 | Standard deviation (risk) | | 13.91% |
| 17 | Shaded areas are input fields. | | |



To trace out the entire risky asset efficient frontier, you need to modify the instructions to the Solver tool. Instead of solving for the portfolio weights that unconditionally minimize the risk of the portfolio, suppose you minimize portfolio risk subject to the constraint that the "target" expected return on the portfolio equals, say, 15%. The modified instructions are as follows:

C17 =SQRT($C$11^2*$C$6^2+$C$12^2*$C$7^2+2*$B$8*$C$6*$C$7*$C$11*$C$12)

| | A | B | C |
|---|---|---|---|
| 1 | OBJECTIVE: | Minimize portfolio risk subject to target expected return | |
| 2 | | Security Attributes | |
| 3 | | | Standard |
| 4 | | Expected | deviation |
| 5 | Security | return | of return |
| 6 | 1 | 18% | 20% |
| 7 | 2 | 12% | 16% |
| 8 | Correlation | 0.25 | |
| 9 | | Risk-minimizing portfolio | |
| 10 | Security | | Allocation |
| 11 | 1 | | 0.500 |
| 12 | 2 | | 0.500 |
| 13 | Total | | 1.000 |
| 14 | | | |
| 15 | Target return | | 15.00% |
| 16 | Expected return | | 15.00% |
| 17 | Standard deviation (risk) | | 14.28% |
| 18 | Shaded areas are input fields. | | |

Solver Parameters
Set Target Cell: $C$17
Equal To: Max Min Value of: 0
By Changing Cells:
$C$11:$C$12
Subject to the Constraints:
$C$13 = 1
$C$16 = $C$15
Solve
Close
Guess
Options
Add
Change
Delete
Reset All
Help

Note that you need to impose the additional constraint that the expected return of the portfolio, C16, equals the target rate of return C15. The risk-minimizing portfolio with an expected return of 15% has equal allocations of wealth in assets 1 and 2.

**ILLUSTRATION 3.4** Identify efficient portfolios comprised of four risky securities.

*Assume you have four risky securities available for investment. Their expected returns, risks, and correlations are presented in the shaded areas of the table below. With four risky securities, the number of required parameter estimates is 14: (a) four expected security returns, (b) four standard deviations of security returns, and (c) $n(n-1)/2 = 4(4-1)/2 = 6$ correlations between pairs of security returns. Find the risk-minimizing portfolio with a target expected return of 19%. Do so first allowing short sales, and then disallowing short sales.*

Security Attributes

| Security | 1 | 2 | 3 | 4 |
|---|---|---|---|---|
| Expected return | 10% | 15% | 18% | 20% |
| Risk | 20% | 30% | 25% | 35% |

| | Security Attributes | | | |
|---|---|---|---|---|
| Correlations | 1 | 2 | 3 | 4 |
| 1 | 1 | 0.20 | 0.30 | 0.10 |
| 2 | 0.20 | 1 | 0.05 | 0.10 |
| 3 | 0.30 | 0.05 | 1 | 0.05 |
| 4 | 0.10 | 0.10 | 0.05 | 1 |

Solving this problem analytically is possible but cumbersome. Consequently, you may want to rely on Solver. The expressions for the expected return and risk of the four-asset portfolio are given by (3.3) and (3.4). These are programmed into cells B16 and B17 of the Excel file, **Four-asset portfolio.xls.** Verify that the computations are consistent with the formulas. To find the risk-minimizing portfolio with a target expected return of 19%, use Solver. The optimal allocations among the four risky securities are:

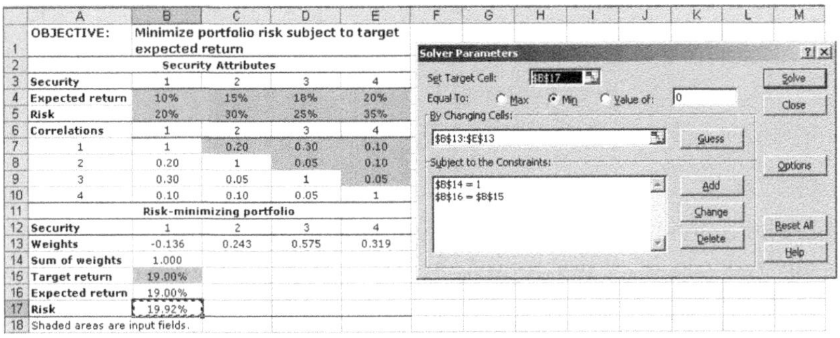

| | A | B | C | D | E |
|---|---|---|---|---|---|
| 1 | OBJECTIVE: | Minimize portfolio risk subject to target expected return | | | |
| 2 | | Security Attributes | | | |
| 3 | Security | 1 | 2 | 3 | 4 |
| 4 | Expected return | 10% | 15% | 18% | 20% |
| 5 | Risk | 20% | 30% | 25% | 35% |
| 6 | Correlations | 1 | 2 | 3 | 4 |
| 7 | 1 | 1 | 0.20 | 0.30 | 0.10 |
| 8 | 2 | 0.20 | 1 | 0.05 | 0.10 |
| 9 | 3 | 0.30 | 0.05 | 1 | 0.05 |
| 10 | 4 | 0.10 | 0.10 | 0.05 | 1 |
| 11 | | Risk-minimizing portfolio | | | |
| 12 | Security | 1 | 2 | 3 | 4 |
| 13 | Weights | -0.136 | 0.243 | 0.575 | 0.319 |
| 14 | Sum of weights | 1.000 | | | |
| 15 | Target return | 19.00% | | | |
| 16 | Expected return | 19.00% | | | |
| 17 | Risk | 19.92% | | | |
| 18 | Shaded areas are input fields. | | | | |

Solver Parameters
Set Target Cell: $B$17
Equal To: Max Min Value of: 0
By Changing Cells:
$B$13:$E$13
Subject to the Constraints:
$B$14 = 1
$B$16 = $B$15
Solve Close Guess Options Add Change Delete Reset All Help

Note that the problem setup is identical to the two-asset case—we minimize portfolio risk subject to the constraints that the portfolio has a particular expected return and that the portfolio weights sum to one. The risk-minimizing portfolio has a risk level of 19.92%. The security weights in the risk-minimizing portfolio are –0.136, 0.243, 0.575, and 0.319 for securities 1 through 4, respectively. The negative weight on security 1 implies that it is sold short. The proceeds from the short sale, together with initial wealth, are invested in securities 2 through 4. The sum across all weights equals 1.

In many real-world portfolio allocation decisions, short sales of particular securities are not possible. To find the risk-minimizing portfolio with no short sales permitted, we impose four additional constraints in the risk-minimization problem. The Solver instructions are shown below. The risk-minimizing portfolio now consists of only two securities—50% in security 3 and 50% in security 4. No money is invested in securities 1 and 2. Note that the portfolio risk level is now 22.01%, well above the 19.92% when short sales were allowed. This stands to reason. The more the portfolio allocation decision is constrained, the less effective it becomes at reducing risk.

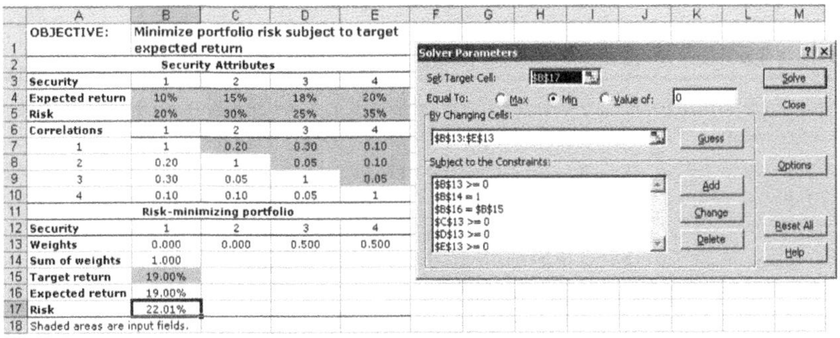

| | A | B | C | D | E |
|---|---|---|---|---|---|
| 1 | OBJECTIVE: | Minimize portfolio risk subject to target expected return | | | |
| 2 | | Security Attributes | | | |
| 3 | Security | 1 | 2 | 3 | 4 |
| 4 | Expected return | 10% | 15% | 18% | 20% |
| 5 | Risk | 20% | 30% | 25% | 35% |
| 6 | Correlations | 1 | 2 | 3 | 4 |
| 7 | 1 | 1 | 0.20 | 0.30 | 0.10 |
| 8 | 2 | 0.20 | 1 | 0.05 | 0.10 |
| 9 | 3 | 0.30 | 0.05 | 1 | 0.05 |
| 10 | 4 | 0.10 | 0.10 | 0.05 | 1 |
| 11 | | Risk-minimizing portfolio | | | |
| 12 | Security | 1 | 2 | 3 | 4 |
| 13 | Weights | 0.000 | 0.000 | 0.500 | 0.500 |
| 14 | Sum of weights | 1.000 | | | |
| 15 | Target return | 19.00% | | | |
| 16 | Expected return | 19.00% | | | |
| 17 | Risk | 22.01% | | | |
| 18 | Shaded areas are input fields. | | | | |

Solver Parameters
Set Target Cell: $B$17
Equal To: Max Min Value of: 0
By Changing Cells:
$B$13:$E$13
Subject to the Constraints:
$B$13 >= 0
$B$14 = 1
$B$16 = $B$15
$C$13 >= 0
$D$13 >= 0
$E$13 >= 0
Solve Close Guess Options Add Change Delete Reset All Help

### Portfolio Allocation with *n* Risky Securities and a Risk-Free Security

Tobin (1958) extended the Markowitz framework by introducing a risk-free security. To keep things simple at the outset, consider what happens when an individual created a two-security portfolio where one of the two securities is the risk-free security. The expected return on this portfolio is

$$E_P = X_1E_1 + (1 - X_1)r = r + (E_1 - r)X_1 \tag{3.7}$$

and the standard deviation of the portfolio return is

$$\sigma_P = \sqrt{X_1^2\sigma_1^2 + 2X_1(1 - X_1)\rho_{12}\sigma_1\sigma_2 + (1 - X_1)^2\sigma_2^2} = X_1\sigma_1 \tag{3.8}$$

Isolating $X_1$ in (3.8) and substituting into (3.7), we can generate any portfolio along the line

$$E_P = r + \left(\frac{E_1 - r}{\sigma_1}\right)\sigma_P \tag{3.9}$$

But since the individual can combine the risk-free security with any risky security or any risky security portfolio *S*, he will choose a portfolio that maximizes the slope of the line emanating from the risk-free rate in Figure 3.7, that is, he will borrow or lend with the risky security portfolio *S* that is tangent to the Markowitz efficiency frontier. Note that all other portfolios below the line have lower expected returns for a given level of risk. This line,

$$E_P = r + \left(\frac{E_S - r}{\sigma_S}\right)\sigma_P \tag{3.10}$$

now represents the individual's set of efficient portfolios. The individual's optimal portfolio is identified by mapping the individual's indifference curves on Figure 3.7. If his highest indifference curve is tangent to the left of *S*, his final portfolio will be a *lending* portfolio—some wealth invested in risky security portfolio *S* and some in the risk-free security. If it is tangent to the right of *S*, the individual not only has all of his wealth in *S*, but has also borrows additional funds, which are also invested in *S*.

**ILLUSTRATION 3.5** Identify composition of tangency risky-security portfolio.

*Using the problem information from Illustration 3.4, find the composition of risky asset tangency portfolio. Then find the compositions of (a) the risk-minimizing portfolio with a target return of 24%, and (b) the expected return-maximizing portfolio with a risk tolerance of 15%.*

The risky asset tangency portfolio is denoted *S* in Figure 3.7 and consists only of risky assets. To identify its composition, you must modify the objective function from Illustration 3.4. In place of minimizing portfolio risk subject to a given level of expected return, you maximize the ratio of the expected excess portfolio return to the standard deviation of portfolio return, that is,

$$\max\left(\frac{E_S - r}{\sigma_S}\right)$$

The necessary modifications are shown in the following illustration. The tangency portfolio has an expected return equal to 17.73% and a standard deviation of return equal to 17.90%. The weights invested in each of the risky assets are 0.017, 0.226, 0.487, and 0.270, and sum to one.

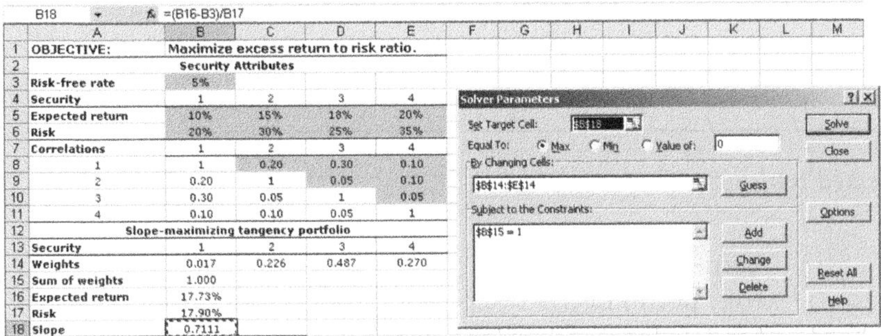
B18 = =(B16-B3)/B17

| | A | B | C | D | E |
|---|---|---|---|---|---|
| 1 | OBJECTIVE: | Maximize excess return to risk ratio. | | | |
| 2 | | Security Attributes | | | |
| 3 | Risk-free rate | 5% | | | |
| 4 | Security | 1 | 2 | 3 | 4 |
| 5 | Expected return | 10% | 15% | 18% | 20% |
| 6 | Risk | 20% | 30% | 25% | 35% |
| 7 | Correlations | 1 | 2 | 3 | 4 |
| 8 | 1 | 1 | 0.20 | 0.30 | 0.10 |
| 9 | 2 | 0.20 | 1 | 0.05 | 0.10 |
| 10 | 3 | 0.30 | 0.05 | 1 | 0.05 |
| 11 | 4 | 0.10 | 0.10 | 0.05 | 1 |
| 12 | Slope-maximizing tangency portfolio | | | | |
| 13 | Security | 1 | 2 | 3 | 4 |
| 14 | Weights | 0.017 | 0.226 | 0.487 | 0.270 |
| 15 | Sum of weights | 1.000 | | | |
| 16 | Expected return | 17.73% | | | |
| 17 | Risk | 17.90% | | | |
| 18 | Slope | 0.7111 | | | |



The next step in the portfolio allocation decision is compute the allocation between the risk-free asset and the risky asset portfolio, *S*. You can achieve this by specifying a target expected rate of return or a risk tolerance level. For a target expected return of 24%, for example, equation (3.7) says that

$$X_S = \frac{E_P - r}{E_S - r} = \frac{0.24 - 0.05}{0.1773 - 0.05} = 1.493$$

of your wealth should be allocated to risky portfolio *S*. In order to do this, of course, you must borrow 49.3% of your wealth at the risk-free rate of interest. *Risk tolerance* is usually defined as the maximum risk that you are willing to undertake and is specified as a standard deviation of return. For a risk tolerance of 15%, equation (3.8) says that

$$X_S = \frac{\sigma_P}{\sigma_S} = \frac{0.19}{0.1790} = 0.838$$

of your wealth should be allocated to risky portfolio *S* and 1 – 0.838 = 0.162 to risk-free bonds.

The figure that follows summarizes the results. All portfolios that lie on the straight line emanating from the risk-free rate of interest are efficient (i.e., maximize expected return for a given level of risk and/or minimize risk for a given level of expected return. All points on the line to the left of the point of tangency are *lending portfolios* in the sense that a positive amount is invested in risk-free bonds and a positive amount in risky portfolio *S*. The dot on the line immediately to the left of the tangency portfolio is the portfolio with a risk tolerance of 15%. All points on the line to the right of the tangency portfolio are *borrowing portfolios* in the sense that all initial wealth together with some risk-free borrowings is invested in the tangency portfolio *S*. The dot immediately to the right is the efficient portfolio with a target return of 24%.

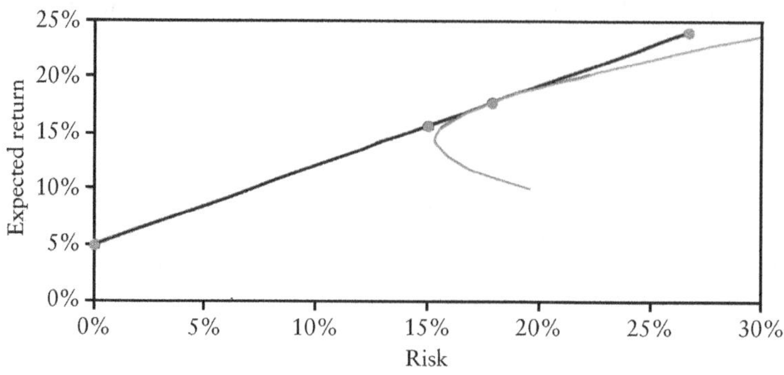


**FIGURE 3.7** Minimum variance frontier with risk-free borrowing and lending.

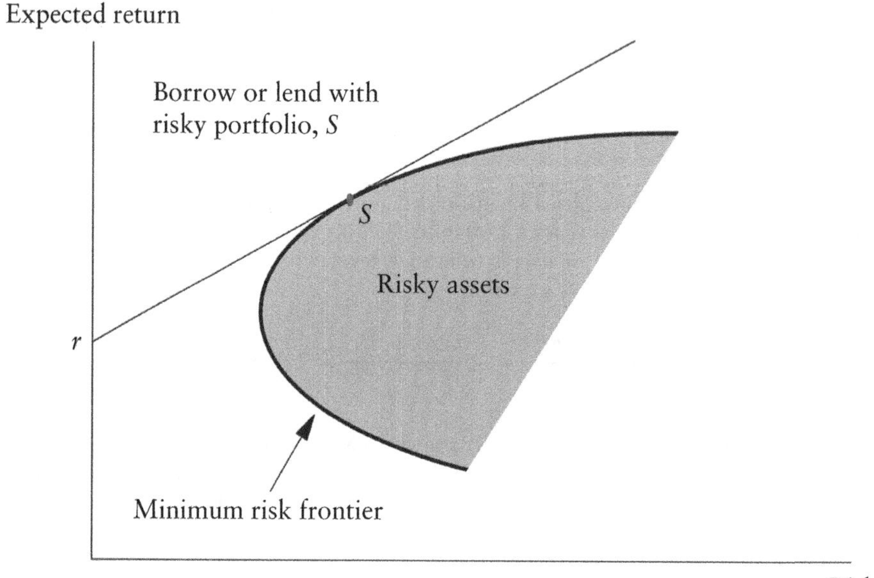


## CAPITAL ASSET PRICING MODEL

The capital asset pricing model (CAPM) specifies the formal relation between the expected rate of a security and its risk. Sharpe (1964) and Lintner (1965) independently developed this model by imposing two final assumptions on the Markowitz (1952)/Tobin (1958) framework,[6] that is, individuals share beliefs about the expected returns, standard deviations (variances), and correlations (covariances) of security returns, and individuals can all borrow and lend at the

[6] Jack L. Treynor independently developed the CAPM in a working paper dated 1962. Unfortunately, his paper was never published.

same risk-free rate of interest. The CAPM has three main results: (1) the capital market line, (2) the composition of the market portfolio, and (3) the security market line. We develop each in turn.

## Capital Market Line

The *capital market line* represents the relation between expected return and risk for efficient portfolios. With common expectations regarding the expected returns, standard deviations, and correlations for risky assets and with all individuals being able to borrow and lend at the same risk-free interest rate, all individuals have the same tangency portfolio $S$ in the Tobin framework. Since $S$ must contain all risky assets in the economy, we relabel it $M$ and call it the *market portfolio*. According to the model, all individuals will hold the market portfolio in combination with the risk-free asset. The relation between expected return and risk for these efficient portfolios is

$$E_P = r + \left(\frac{E_M - r}{\sigma_M}\right)\sigma_P \tag{3.11}$$

and is illustrated in Figure 3.8. An individual's allocation between the market portfolio and the risk-free asset will depend on his degree of risk aversion. A risk minimizer will invest all of his wealth in the risk-free asset. A risk-averse

**FIGURE 3.8** Minimum variance frontier with risk-free borrowing and lending and common expectations.

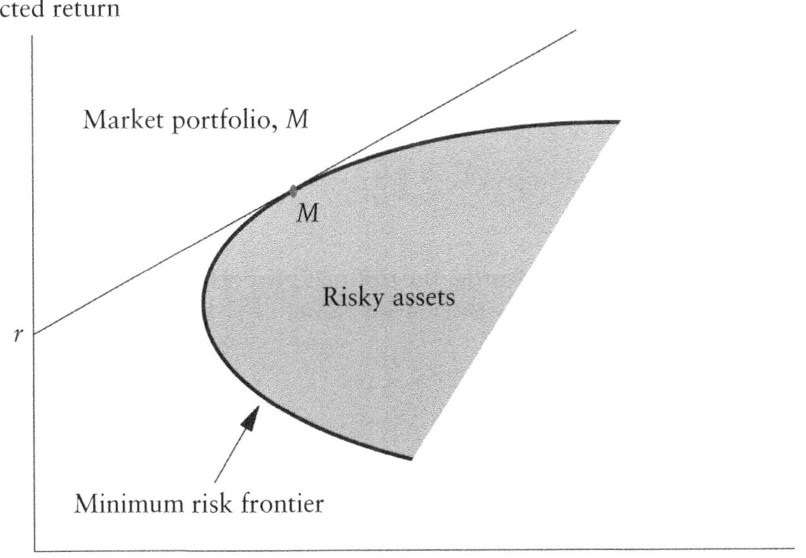

individual will choose a portfolio that lies along the *capital market line* (3.11). If his highest indifference curve is tangent to the left of $M$, the final portfolio will be a *lending* portfolio—some wealth invested in $M$ and some in the risk-free asset. If it is tangent to the right of $M$, the individual not only has all of his wealth in $M$, but has also borrows additional funds to invest in $M$.

### Composition of the Market Portfolio

The allocation among risky securities in creating $M$ can be established in a fairly intuitive fashion. We know that, if the market is in equilibrium, the total demand by individuals for risky asset $i$ must equal total supply of asset $i$, that is,

$$\sum_{k=1}^{m} X_i^k w^k = V_i \tag{3.12}$$

where $k$ represents the $k$th individual, $m$ represents the number of individuals in the market, $X_i^k$ is the proportion of $k$'s risky asset wealth, $w^k$, invested in asset $i$, and $V_i$ is the market value of asset $i$. We also know that, in equilibrium, total demand by individuals for risky assets must equal total supply, that is,

$$\sum_{k=1}^{m} w^k = \sum_{i=1}^{n} \sum_{k=1}^{m} X_i^k w^k = \sum_{i=1}^{n} V_i = V_M \tag{3.13}$$

where $n$ is the number of risky assets in the market, and $V_M$ is the market value of all risky assets. Finally, we know from the work of Markowitz that the allocation among risky securities in creating $M$ (or any portfolio along the Markowitz efficiency frontier) is unique, that is, all investors allocate their risky asset wealth in the same proportions, that is, $X_i^k = X_i$ for all $k$. Thus, from (3.12) and (3.13), we find that

$$X_i = \frac{V_i}{V_M} \tag{3.14}$$

for all risky assets. In other words, the optimal proportion of risky asset wealth invested in risky asset $i$ equals the market value of risky asset $i$ divided by the market value of all risky assets.

### Security Market Line

The security market line represents the equilibrium expected return/risk relation for risky assets. To identify this relation, we must identify asset $i$'s contribution to the expected excess return and risk of the market portfolio. The market portfolio expected excess return and risk are defined as

$$E_M - r = \sum_{i=1}^{n} X_i(E_i - r) \tag{3.15}$$

and

$$\sigma_M^2 = \sum_{i=1}^{n}\sum_{j=1}^{n} X_i X_j \sigma_{ij} \tag{3.16}$$

The marginal contribution of asset $i$ to the expected excess return of the market portfolio is

$$\frac{\partial E_M - r}{\partial X_i} = E_i - r \tag{3.17}$$

and the marginal contribution of asset $i$ to the risk of the market portfolio is

$$\frac{\partial \sigma_M^2}{\partial X_i} = \sum_{j=1}^{n} X_j \sigma_{ij} = \sigma_{iM} \tag{3.18}$$

In equilibrium, all risky assets must have the same expected excess return/risk tradeoff, therefore

$$\frac{E_i - r}{\sigma_{iM}} = \frac{E_M - r}{\sigma_M^2} \tag{3.19}$$

The term on the right-hand side of (3.19) is often referred to as the *market price of risk.*[7] Rearranging,

$$E_i = r + (E_M - r)\frac{\sigma_{iM}}{\sigma_M^2} = R + (E_M - r)\beta_i \tag{3.20}$$

Equation (3.20) is called the *security market line* (SML). The SML represents the equilibrium expected return/risk relation for all risky securities in the marketplace. This includes stocks, bonds, currencies, and commodities, as well as, we shall see later, all types of derivative contracts. The three key results of the CAPM are summarized in Table 3.1.

[7] In a later chapter, we will rely on the concept of the market price of risk when we value options whose underlying asset is not actively traded.

**TABLE 3.1** Summary of three key results from the Sharpe (1964)/Lintner (1965) capital asset pricing model.

**Capital market line (CML):**

The CML is the relation between expected return and risk for efficient portfolios, that is, portfolios with the highest level of expected return for a given level of risk or the lowest level of risk for a given level of expected return.

$$E_P = r + \left(\frac{E_M - r}{\sigma_M}\right)\sigma_P \tag{3.11}$$

where $r$ is the risk-free rate of return, $E_P$ and $E_M$ are the expected returns on efficient portfolio $P$ and the market portfolio $M$, respectively, and $\sigma_P$ and $\sigma_M$ are the standard deviation of the rate of return of efficient portfolio $P$ and the market portfolio $M$, respectively.

**Composition of market portfolio:**

$$X_i = \frac{V_i}{V_M} \text{ for all } i \tag{3.14}$$

where $X_i$ is the proportion of risky security wealth invested in the market portfolio, and $V_i$ and $V_M$ are the market values of risky security $i$ and the market portfolio, respectively.

**Security market line (SML):**

The SML is the relation between expected return and risk for all risky securities in the market.

$$E_i = r + (E_M - r)\beta_i \tag{3.20}$$

where $r$ is the risk-free rate of return, $E_i$ and $E_M$ are the expected returns of risky security $i$ and the market portfolio $M$, respectively, and $\beta_i$ is the relative systematic risk (i.e., "beta") of risky security $i$.

**ILLUSTRATION 3.6** Estimate total risk and relative systematic risk of individual stock.

*Estimate the total risk and relative systematic risk of IBM's stock using monthly stock returns. The historical data are provided in the Excel file,* ***IBM.xls****. The file contains 60 months of returns for IBM, a value-weighted stock market index (i.e., a market portfolio proxy), and one-month Eurodollar time deposits (i.e., the money market rate used as a proxy for the risk-free rate of interest) over the past 60 months. Estimate the total risk and relative systematic risk of the excess returns of IBM and the market portfolio over the period January 2000 through December 2004.*

To estimate total risk, we simply compute the standard deviations of the different return series. This can be accomplished using the AVERAGE() and STDEV() functions in Microsoft Excel as shown below. The total risk of IBM over the estimation period is 10.38%, compared with 4.92% for the market portfolio. These values are usually reported on an annualized basis, which means we must multiply each by $\sqrt{12}$. On an annualized basis, the values are 35.95% and 17.06%, respectively. Note that the standard deviations of the excess returns (i.e., monthly return less the money market rate) are approximately the same at 10.37% and 4.95%, respectively. This result is expected since the standard deviation (i.e., total risk) of the money market rate is near 0.

B67 =STDEV(B4:B63)

| | A | B | C | D | E | F |
|---|---|---|---|---|---|---|
| 1 | | **Monthly holding period returns (2000-2004)** | | | | |
| 2 | | Returns | | Risk-free | Excess returns | |
| 3 | Month | IBM | VW index | return | IBM | VW index |
| 4 | 20000131 | 0.0406 | -0.0398 | 0.0050 | 0.0356 | -0.0448 |
| 5 | 20000229 | -0.0836 | 0.0318 | 0.0047 | -0.0883 | 0.0271 |
| 6 | 20000331 | 0.1484 | 0.0535 | 0.0051 | 0.1433 | 0.0484 |
| 61 | 20041029 | 0.0468 | 0.0178 | 0.0014 | 0.0453 | 0.0164 |
| 62 | 20041130 | 0.0520 | 0.0483 | 0.0018 | 0.0503 | 0.0465 |
| 63 | 20041231 | 0.0461 | 0.0352 | 0.0020 | 0.0441 | 0.0332 |
| 64 | | | | | | |
| 65 | | Summary statistics | | | | |
| 66 | Mean | 0.0041 | 0.0002 | 0.0025 | 0.0016 | -0.0023 |
| 67 | StDev | 0.1038 | 0.0492 | 0.0018 | 0.1037 | 0.0495 |
| 68 | | | | | | |
| 69 | | OLS regression results | | | | |
| 70 | | alpha | t(alpha) | beta | t(beta) | R-squared |
| 71 | Returns | 0.0038 | 0.3881 | 1.4421 | 7.1439 | 0.4681 |
| 72 | Excess returns | 0.0049 | 0.4950 | 1.4279 | 7.1025 | 0.4652 |

To estimate beta, we perform the regression,

$$R_{IBM,\,t} = \alpha + \beta R_{Market,\,t} + \varepsilon_t$$

where $R_{IBM,t}$ and $R_{Market,t}$ are the daily returns for IBM and the market index. (Recall a review of ordinary least squares (OLS) regression is provided in Appendix B of the book.) To do so, we can use the OPTVAL function,

OV_STAT_OLS_SIMPLE(*y*, *x*, *intercept*, *out*)

where *y* is dependent variable (i.e., the vector of IBM returns), *x* is the independent variable, *intercept* is an indicator variable set equal to "Y" or "y" if the regression includes an intercept and "N" or "n" if the regression does not include an intercept, and *out* is an indicator variable set equal to "H" or "h" if the output array is to be returns horizontally and "V" or "v" if the output array is to be returned vertically. To use the function, we need to highlight five adjacent cells either horizontally or vertically, insert the function, fill in the menu information, and then press the <Shift><Ctrl><Enter> keys simultaneously. The output array contains five elements: the estimated intercept term, its *t*-ratio for the null hypothesis that the intercept is 0, the estimated slope term (i.e., the "beta"), its *t*-ratio for the null hypothesis that the slope is 0, and the *R*-squared of the regression. As shown below, the estimated beta is 1.4421. The *R*-squared is 46.81%, which means that about 46.81% of IBM's total risk is market-related and that about 53.19% is diversifiable.

The second line of the regression results corresponds to the regression using excess returns, that is,

$$R_{IBM,\,t} - R_{MM,\,t} = \alpha + \beta(R_{Market,\,t} - R_{MM,\,t}) + \varepsilon_t$$

The estimated beta coefficient is virtually identical to the returns regression. This second regression is preferred since, according to the security market line of the CAPM, the expected value of the intercept term equals 0. Thus, an intercept term significantly different from 0 implies that the stock performed significantly better (worse) the expected according to the CAPM. For the excess return regression the estimated intercept is 0.0049 and its *t*-ratio is 0.4950. That means that IBM performed better than expected (0.0049 is positive), but that it is not significantly different than what was expected.

B71 {=OV_STAT_OLS_SIMPLE(B4:B63,C4:C63,"Y","H")}

| | A | B | C | D | E | F |
|---|---|---|---|---|---|---|
| 1 | Monthly holding period returns (2000-2004) | | | | | |
| 2 | | Returns | | Risk-free | Excess returns | |
| 3 | Month | IBM | VW index | return | IBM | VW index |
| 4 | 20000131 | 0.0406 | -0.0398 | 0.0050 | 0.0356 | -0.0448 |
| 5 | 20000229 | -0.0836 | 0.0318 | 0.0047 | -0.0883 | 0.0271 |
| 6 | 20000331 | 0.1484 | 0.0535 | 0.0051 | 0.1433 | 0.0484 |
| 61 | 20041029 | 0.0468 | 0.0178 | 0.0014 | 0.0453 | 0.0164 |
| 62 | 20041130 | 0.0520 | 0.0483 | 0.0018 | 0.0503 | 0.0465 |
| 63 | 20041231 | 0.0461 | 0.0352 | 0.0020 | 0.0441 | 0.0332 |
| 64 | | | | | | |
| 65 | | Summary statistics | | | | |
| 66 | Mean | 0.0041 | 0.0002 | 0.0025 | 0.0016 | -0.0023 |
| 67 | StDev | 0.1038 | 0.0492 | 0.0018 | 0.1037 | 0.0495 |
| 68 | | | | | | |
| 69 | | OLS regression results | | | | |
| 70 | | alpha | t(alpha) | beta | t(beta) | R-squared |
| 71 | Returns | 0.0038 | 0.3881 | 1.4421 | 7.1439 | 0.4681 |
| 72 | Excess returns | 0.0049 | 0.4950 | 1.4279 | 7.1025 | 0.4652 |

## PORTFOLIO PERFORMANCE MEASUREMENT

One of the many useful applications of the CAPM is portfolio performance measurement, that is, evaluating the historical performance of security portfolios on a risk-adjusted basis. Sometimes this is done in the context of assessing the performance of a fund manager. At other times, the measures are used to choose among available funds. Whatever the application, the most commonly-applied measures are shown in Table 3.2 and include the Sharpe (1966) ratio, the Modigliani and Modigliani (1997) *M*-squared, the Treynor (1965) ratio, and the Jensen (1968) alpha. In this section, we explain each in turn, showing that each assumes that the market behaves as it should with the CAPM. We also introduce a risk measure called semistandard deviation.

### Total Risk Performance Measures

Two of the four performance measures—the Sharpe ratio and the $M^2$—are based on the total risk of the portfolio being evaluated. To understand the linkage between these measures and the CAPM, recall that, under the assumptions of the CAPM, all individuals hold efficient portfolios (i.e., portfolios that have the highest expected return for a given level of total risk). Recall also that all efficient portfolios lie along the capital market line (3.11).

The formula for computing the Sharpe ratio is given in Table 3.2. The notation on the right-hand side of the Sharpe ratio is different from the CAPM because to measure performance we rely on realized (ex post) returns rather than expected (ex ante) returns. Typically, monthly realized returns over the performance evaluation period are used. The length of the evaluation period ranges from as little as two years to more than a decade. It depends upon the objective. The parameters in the formulas are estimated from historical returns over the

**TABLE 3.2** Summary of CAPM-based portfolio performance measures. $\bar{R}_f$, $\bar{R}_M$, and $\bar{R}_P$ are the mean returns of a "risk-free" money market instrument, the market, and the portfolio under consideration over the evaluation period, $\hat{\sigma}_M$ and $\hat{\sigma}_P$ are the standard deviations of the returns ("total risk") of the market and the portfolio, and $\hat{\beta}_P$ is the portfolio's systematic risk ("beta").

**Total risk-based measures**

$$\text{Sharpe ratio} = \frac{\bar{R}_P - \bar{R}_f}{\hat{\sigma}_P}$$

$$M^2 = (\bar{R}_P - \bar{R}_f)\left(\frac{\hat{\sigma}_M}{\hat{\sigma}_P}\right) - (\bar{R}_M - \bar{R}_f)$$

**Systematic risk based measures**

$$\text{Treynor ratio} = \frac{\bar{R}_P - \bar{R}_f}{\hat{\beta}_P}$$

$$\text{Jensen's alpha} = \bar{R}_P - \bar{R}_f - \hat{\beta}_P(\bar{R}_M - \bar{R}_f)$$

evaluation period: $\bar{R}_f$, $\bar{R}_M$, and $\bar{R}_P$ are the mean monthly returns of a "risk-free" money market instrument, the market, and the portfolio under consideration over the evaluation period, and $\hat{\sigma}_M$ and $\hat{\sigma}_P$ are the standard deviations of the returns ("total risk") of the market and the portfolio. Now assume that the portfolio $P$ behaved exactly as predicted over the evaluation period (i.e., expectations are realized). Under this assumption, the Sharpe ratio may be written

$$\text{Sharpe ratio} = \frac{\bar{R}_P - \bar{R}_f}{\hat{\sigma}_P} = \frac{E_P - r}{\sigma_p} \tag{3.21}$$

But according to the CML (3.11), the expected excess return per unit of total risk for efficient portfolio $P$ equals the expected excess return per unit of total risk for the market portfolio $M$, and, with expectations being realized,

$$\text{Sharpe ratio} = \frac{\bar{R}_P - \bar{R}_f}{\hat{\sigma}_P} = \frac{E_P - r}{\sigma_p} = \frac{E_M - r}{\sigma_M} = \frac{\bar{R}_M - \bar{R}_f}{\hat{\sigma}_M} \tag{3.22}$$

In other words, the benchmark realized return/total risk ratio is that of the market portfolio, that is, the rightmost term in (3.22). If portfolio being evaluated performed as expected under the CAPM, its realized return/total risk ratio should be the same as the market portfolio,

$$\frac{\bar{R}_P - \bar{R}_f}{\hat{\sigma}_P} = \frac{\bar{R}_M - \bar{R}_f}{\hat{\sigma}_M} \tag{3.23}$$

If, on the other hand, we were able to identify underpriced securities in the selection of our portfolio and our portfolio outperformed the market, the portfolio's Sharpe ratio would exceed that of the market.

The $M^2$ measure of performance levers portfolio $P$ in such a way that its total risk equals that of the market portfolio, and then examines the difference between the excess returns of the portfolio and the market. The term, $\hat{\sigma}_M/\hat{\sigma}_P$, in the $M^2$ formula shown in Table 3.2 is the degree of leverage. If the portfolio's total risk was below (above) the market's during the evaluation period, the ratio will exceed (be below) one and the excess return of the portfolios will be levered up (down) in order to match the total risk of the market, that is,

$$\hat{\sigma}_P(\hat{\sigma}_M/\hat{\sigma}_P) = \hat{\sigma}_M$$

With equal risk levels, we can compare the levered portfolio's return with the market return directly. Assuming the portfolio behaved as expected under the CAPM and expectations were realized, the realized abnormal performance of the portfolio, as measured by $M^2$, is

$$M^2 = (\bar{R}_P - \bar{R}_f)\left(\frac{\hat{\sigma}_M}{\hat{\sigma}_P}\right) - (\bar{R}_M - \bar{R}_f) = (E_P - r)\left(\frac{\sigma_M}{\sigma_P}\right) - (E_M - r) = 0 \tag{3.24}$$

Where $M^2 > 0$, portfolio $P$ outperformed the market on a risk-adjusted basis, and vice versa.

### Systematic Risk Performance Measures

The remaining two performance measures—the Treynor ratio and the Jensen alpha—are based on systematic risk and are the counterparts to the Sharpe ratio and $M^2$, respectively. To understand the linkage between the systematic risk performance measures, recall that, under the assumptions of the CAPM, all risky securities lie along the security market line (3.20). Since a portfolio is nothing more than a weighted combination of securities, it is also the case that portfolios lie along the SML, that is,

$$E_P = r + (E_M - r)\beta_P \tag{3.25}$$

The formula for the Treynor ratio is given in Table 3.2. The portfolio's realized systematic risk or beta, $\hat{\beta}_P$ is estimated by an ordinary least squares, time-series regression of the excess returns of the portfolio on the excess returns of the market, that is,

$$R_{P,t} - R_{f,t} = \alpha + \beta_P(R_{M,t} - R_{f,t}) + \varepsilon_{P,t} \tag{3.26}$$

Like in the case of the Sharpe ratio, the realized excess return per unit of risk for the portfolio should, in equilibrium, be equal to the excess return of the market portfolio, however, since $\beta_M = 1$,

$$\text{Treynor ratio} = \frac{\bar{R}_P - \bar{R}_f}{\hat{\beta}_P} = \frac{E_P - r}{\beta_P} = \frac{E_M - r}{\beta_M} = E_M - r = \bar{R}_M - \bar{R}_f \tag{3.27}$$

If a portfolio outperformed the market on a risk-adjusted basis, its Treynor ratio will exceed the realized excess return of the market.

Jensen's alpha is essentially the intercept term in a regression of the excess returns of the portfolio on the excess returns of the market (3.26). If the market behaves according to the CAPM and expectation are realized,

$$\text{Jensen's alpha} = \bar{R}_P - \bar{R}_f - \hat{\beta}_P(\bar{R}_M - \bar{R}_f) = E_P - r - \beta_P(E_M - r) = 0 \tag{3.28}$$

If the estimated value of Jensen's alpha, $\hat{\alpha}_P$, is greater than zero, the portfolio outperformed the market on a risk-adjusted basis.

## Alternative Risk Measures

The performance measures in Table 3.2 are occasionally criticized because the Sharpe (1964)/Lintner (1965) mean/variance capital asset pricing model assumes investors measure total portfolio risk by the standard deviation of returns. Among other things, this implies that investors view an unexpectedly large positive return with the same distaste as an unexpectedly large negative return. Common sense dictates otherwise. Investors are willing to pay for the chance of a large positive return (i.e., positive skewness) holding other factors constant, but will want to be paid for taking on negative skewness. Since the standard performance measures do not recognize these premiums/discounts, portfolios with positive skewness will appear to underperform the market on a risk-adjusted basis, and portfolios with negative skewness will appear to overperform.

Ironically, while the Sharpe/Linter CAPM is based on the mean/variance portfolio theory of Markowitz (1952), it was Markowitz (1959) who first noted that using standard deviation to measure risk is too conservative since it regards all extreme returns, positive or negative, as undesirable. Markowitz (1959, Ch. 9) advocates the use of semivariance or semistandard deviation as a total risk measure.[8] To understand the relation between standard deviation and semistandard deviation, begin with total risk as measured traditionally using the standard deviation of excess returns, that is,

[8] Indeed, in his Nobel Prize acceptance speech, the Markowitz (1991) continues to argue semivariance seems more plausible than variance as a measure of risk.

$$\text{Standard deviation}_i = \sqrt{\frac{\sum_{t=1}^{T}(R_{i,t} - R_{f,t} - k)^2}{T}} \tag{3.29}$$

where $k$ is the mean realized excess return.[9] With no loss of generality, we can write (3.29) as

$$\text{Standard deviation}_i = \sqrt{\frac{\sum_{t=1}^{T}\min(R_{i,t} - R_{f,t} - k, 0)^2}{T} + \frac{\sum_{t=1}^{T}\max(R_{i,t} - R_{f,t} - k, 0)^2}{T}} \tag{3.30}$$

Under the square root sign, we now have two terms. The first is the sum of the squared deviations when the excess return is below $k$ and the second is the sum of the squared deviations when the excess return is above $k$. Suppose we are willing to conjecture that individuals care about risk only to the extent that their risky asset portfolio does not produce a rate of return as high as the risk-free rate of return. To create such a risk measure, we set $k = 0$ and drop the second term under the square root sign. In the context of performance measurement, semistandard deviation can be defined as the square root of the average of the squared deviations from the risk-free rate of interest, where positive deviations are set equal to zero, that is,

$$\text{Semistandard deviation}_i = \sqrt{\frac{\sum_{t=1}^{T}\min(R_{i,t} - R_{f,t}, 0)^2}{T}} \tag{3.31}$$

where $i = M,P$. Returns on risky assets, when they exceed the risk-free rate of interest, do not affect risk. To account for possible asymmetry of the portfolio return distribution, we recompute the total risk portfolio performance measures (1) and (2) using the estimated semideviations of the returns of the market and the portfolio are inserted for $\hat{\sigma}_M$ and $\hat{\sigma}_P$.[10]

The systematic risk-based portfolio performance measures (3) and (4) also have theoretical counterparts in a semivariance framework. The only difference lies in the estimate of systematic risk. To estimate the beta, a time-series regression *through the origin* is performed using the excess return series of the market and the portfolio. Where excess returns are positive, they are replaced with a zero value. The time-series regression specification is

$$\min(R_{P,t} - R_{f,t}, 0) = \beta_p \min(R_{M,t} - R_{f,t}, 0) + \varepsilon_{P,t} \tag{3.32}$$

[9] Technically speaking, the denominator should be $T - 1$ since we use up a degree of freedom when we estimate the mean excess return.

[10] The ratio of realized excess return relative to the semistandard deviation of return is commonly referred to as the Sortino ratio. See Sortino and Van der Meer (1991).

**ILLUSTRATION 3.7** Estimate performance of CBOE's buy-write index portfolio (BXM).

*The Excel file,* ***Performance measurement.xls****, contains monthly returns of the CBOE's BXM index, the S&P 500 index (i.e., the "market" index), and a 30-day money market instrument (i.e., 30-day Eurodollar time deposits) for the period January 1996 through December 2004. Based on the monthly returns, compute the performance of the BXM portfolio, and comment on the results.*

The usual way to compute the performance measures is to compute the mean and standard deviation (and semistandard deviation) of the monthly (excess) return series as well as each series "beta" and then substitute the estimated parameters in the formulas reported in Table 3.2.

The first step is to compute the means and standard deviations of the return variables. The second step is to estimate the beta of the BXM using OLS regression. The results are as follows:

B122 | fx =E112/B113

| | A | B | C | D | E | F |
|---|---|---|---|---|---|---|
| 1 | Month | Monthly returns | | | Excess returns | |
| 2 | end | BXM | SPX | MM | BXM | SPX |
| 3 | 19960131 | 0.00846 | 0.03404 | 0.00513 | 0.00333 | 0.02891 |
| 4 | 19960229 | -0.00229 | 0.00927 | 0.00428 | -0.00657 | 0.00499 |
| 5 | 19960329 | 0.01481 | 0.00963 | 0.00418 | 0.01063 | 0.00545 |
| 108 | 20041029 | 0.00913 | 0.01528 | 0.00145 | 0.00768 | 0.01383 |
| 109 | 20041130 | 0.00260 | 0.04046 | 0.00175 | 0.00084 | 0.03871 |
| 110 | 20041231 | 0.02559 | 0.03403 | 0.00195 | 0.02364 | 0.03208 |
| 111 | | | | | | |
| 112 | Mean | 0.00872 | 0.00873 | 0.00342 | 0.00530 | 0.00531 |
| 113 | StDev | 0.03311 | 0.04703 | 0.00170 | 0.03301 | 0.04693 |
| 114 | | | | | | |
| 115 | | OLS regression results | | | | |
| 116 | | alpha | t(alpha) | beta | t(beta) | R-squared |
| 117 | Returns | 0.00336 | 2.11009 | 0.61452 | 18.40195 | 0.76160 |
| 118 | Excess returns | 0.00204 | 1.29886 | 0.61343 | 18.35223 | 0.76062 |
| 119 | | | | | | |
| 120 | | | | | | |
| 121 | Measure | BXM | SPX | | | |
| 122 | Sharpe ratio | 0.16002 | 0.11293 | | | |
| 123 | M-squared | 0.221% | | | | |
| 124 | Treynor ratio | 0.00864 | 0.00531 | | | |
| 125 | Jensen's alpha | 0.204% | | | | |

The results are interesting in a number of respects. First, note that the mean monthly returns of the BXM and the S&P 500 are virtually identical—0.872% versus 0.873%—while the standard deviation of return for the BXM is about 2/3 of the S&P 500—3.311% versus 4.703%. This is the first indication that the BXM outperformed the market during the evaluation period. Second, note that the return regression produces virtually the same beta as the excess regression. This is, again, a reflection of the fact that the variance of the money market rate (i.e., the proxy for the risk-free rate) is small in relation to the variances of the BXM and the S&P 500 returns. Finally, all four performance measures indicate that the BXM outperformed the market on a risk-adjusted basis during the evaluation period, January 1996 through December 2004. The Sharpe ratio of the BXM is computed as the realized excess return on the BXM divided by its standard deviation. To evaluate performance, we must also compute the Sharpe ratio for the market portfolio. Since 0.16002 exceeds 0.11293, the BXM outperformed the market. The $M^2$ is 0.221%, which means that the BXM outperformed the market portfolio by 0.221% or 22 basis points per month. For this measure, as well as the Jensen alpha, no benchmark measure is necessary since they market performance is implicitly incorporated. The Treynor ratio as well as Jensen's alpha also show that the BXM produced a higher than expected return on a risk-adjusted basis.

Preprogrammed functions for the performance measures are also included in the OPTVAL Function Library. The syntax for the Sharpe Ratio function call, for example, is

OV_PERF_SR(*RetP, RetF, Measure*)

where *RetP* is the vector of portfolio returns whose performance is to be evaluated, *RetF* is the vector of money market rates, and *Measure* is an indicator variable whose value is 0 for total risk measured using the standard deviation of return and 1 for total risk measured as semistandard deviation. The panel below illustrates. The remaining function calls are:

OV_PERF_M2(*RetP, RetM, RetF, Measure*)
OV_PERF_TR(*RetP ,RetM, RetF, Measure*)
OV_PERF_JA(*RetP, RetM, RetF, Measure*)

where *RetM* is the vector of market returns and the remaining terms are defined as before.

C123 =OV_PERF_SR($B$3:$B$110,$D$3:$D$110,1)

| | A | B | C | D | E | F |
|---|---|---|---|---|---|---|
| 1 | Month | Monthly returns | | | Excess returns | |
| 2 | end | BXM | SPX | MM | BXM | SPX |
| 3 | 19960131 | 0.00846 | 0.03404 | 0.00513 | 0.00333 | 0.02891 |
| 4 | 19960229 | -0.00229 | 0.00927 | 0.00428 | -0.00657 | 0.00499 |
| 5 | 19960329 | 0.01481 | 0.00963 | 0.00418 | 0.01063 | 0.00545 |
| 108 | 20041029 | 0.00913 | 0.01528 | 0.00145 | 0.00768 | 0.01383 |
| 109 | 20041130 | 0.00260 | 0.04046 | 0.00175 | 0.00084 | 0.03871 |
| 110 | 20041231 | 0.02559 | 0.03403 | 0.00195 | 0.02364 | 0.03208 |
| 111 | | | | | | |
| 112 | Mean | 0.00872 | 0.00873 | 0.00342 | 0.00530 | 0.00531 |
| 113 | StDev | 0.03311 | 0.04703 | 0.00170 | 0.03301 | 0.04693 |
| 114 | | | | | | |
| 115 | | OLS regression results | | | | |
| 116 | | alpha | t(alpha) | beta | t(beta) | R-squared |
| 117 | Returns | 0.00336 | 2.11009 | 0.61452 | 18.40195 | 0.76160 |
| 118 | Excess returns | 0.00204 | 1.29886 | 0.61343 | 18.35223 | 0.76062 |
| 119 | | | | | | |
| 120 | | BXM | | SPX | | |
| 121 | | Mean- | Mean- | Mean- | Mean- | |
| 122 | Measure | stddev | semi-stddev | stddev | semi-stddev | |
| 123 | Sharpe ratio | 0.16002 | 0.22218 | 0.11293 | 0.16281 | |
| 124 | M-squared | 0.221% | 0.194% | | | |
| 125 | Treynor ratio | 0.00864 | 0.00815 | 0.00531 | 0.00531 | |
| 126 | Jensen's alpha | 0.204% | 0.185% | | | |

The performance results for the BXM and S&P 500 portfolios computed using the appropriate OPTVAL functions are as shown above. The numerical values under the column heading "Mean-stddev" are exactly the same as those computed by hand. The values under the column heading "Mean-semi-stddev" also show that the BXM performed better than the market on a risk-adjusted basis, however, the performance is not as high under the mean/semistandard deviation framework as the CAPM's mean/standard deviation framework. The reason is simple. The returns of the BXM (the lighter shaded bars) are more negatively skewed than those of the market (the darker shaded bars). Since the semistandard deviation focuses only on returns below the risk-free interest rate, the negative skewness relative to the market results in lower performance measures. A histogram of the BXM and S&P 500 returns over the evaluation period are shown below. But even after extracting a penalty for negative skewness, the BXM strategy appears to outperform the market (as proxied by the S&P 500 index portfolio).

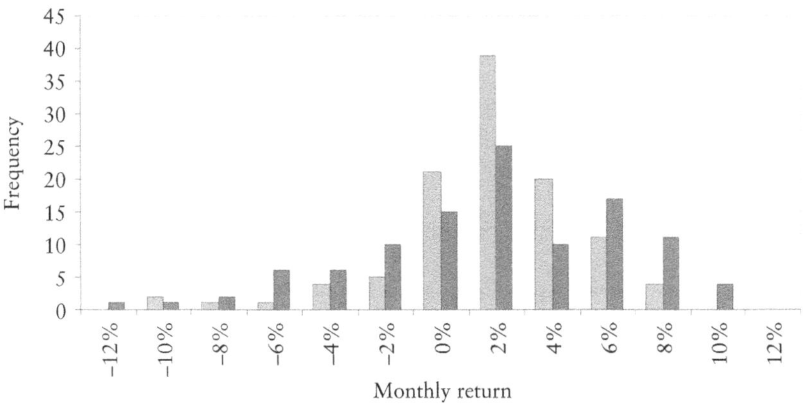


## SUMMARY

Effective risk management requires a thorough understanding of the tradeoff between expected return and risk. This chapter reviews expected return/risk mechanics. A risky security is characterized by its expected return, standard deviations of return, and the correlations of its returns with all other securities in the marketplace. Given this characterization, we show how a risk-averse individual allocates his wealth among securities under a variety of scenarios and constraints. Individual security demands are then aggregated across all individuals in the marketplace to create a market portfolio. The marginal contribution of each security to the expected excess return and risk of the market portfolio identifies the equilibrium expected return/risk relation for risky securities. The expected return/risk relations, known collectively as the capital asset pricing model, will be used again and again throughout the chapters of this book, as it guides us in analyzing and designing risk management strategies. We apply the relations in this chapter to examine historical portfolio performance.

## REFERENCES AND SUGGESTED READINGS

Arditti, Fred. 1971. Another look at mutual fund performance. *Journal of Financial and Quantitative Analysis* 6: 909–912.

Jensen, Michael C. 1968. The performance of mutual funds in the period 1945–64. *Journal of Finance* 23 (May): 389–416.

Leland, Hayne E. 1999. Beyond mean-variance: performance measurement in a nonsymmetrical world. *Financial Analysts Journal* (January/February): 27–36.

Lintner, John. 1965. The valuation of risk assets and the selection of risky investments in stock portfolios and capital budgets. *Review of Economics and Statistics* 47: 13–37.

Markowitz, Harry. 1991. Foundations of portfolio theory. *Journal of Finance* 46: 469–477.

Markowitz, Harry. 1952. Portfolio selection. *Journal of Finance* 12 (March): 77–91.

Markowitz, Harry. 1959. *Portfolio Selection*. New York: John Wiley and Sons.

Merton, Robert C. 1973. An intertemporal capital asset pricing model. *Econometrica* 41: 867–888.

Modigliani, Franco, and Merton H. Miller. 1958. The cost of capital, corporation finance and the theory of investment. *American Economic Review* 48 (June): 261–297.

Sharpe, William F. 1964. Capital asset prices: a theory of market equilibrium under conditions of risk. *Journal of Finance* 19: 425–442.

Sharpe, William F. 1966. Mutual fund performance. *Journal of Business* 39 (1): 119–138.

Sortino, Frank A., and Robert van der Meer. 1991. Downside risk. *Journal of Portfolio Management* (Summer): 27–31.

Stutzer, Michael. 2000. A portfolio performance index. *Financial Analysts Journal* 56: 52–60.

Tobin, James. 1958. Liquidity preference as behavior towards risk. *Review of Economic Studies* 25 (February): 65–86.

Treynor, Jack L. 1965. How to rate management of investment funds. *Harvard Business Review* 43 (1): 63–75.

PART
# Three

# Forwards/Futures/ Swap Valuation

# 4

# No-Arbitrage Price Relations: Forwards, Futures, Swaps

In Chapter 1, we described the nature of exchange-traded and OTC derivatives contracts traded worldwide. Of these, the lion's share is plain-vanilla forwards, futures, and swaps. The purpose of this chapter is to develop no-arbitrage price relations for forward, futures, and swap contracts. In doing so, we rely only on the assumption that two perfect substitutes *must* have the same price. The two substitutes, in this case, are a forward/futures contract and a levered position in the underlying asset. The key to understanding the forward/futures valuation lies in identifying the net cost of carrying (i.e., "buying and holding") an asset. We begin therefore with a discussion of carry costs/benefits. We then proceed by developing a number of important no-arbitrage relations governing forward and futures prices. Finally, we show that, since a swap contract is an exchange of future payments at a price agreed upon today, it can be valued as a portfolio of forward contracts. The chapter concludes with a brief summary.

## UNDERSTANDING CARRY COSTS/BENEFITS

Derivative contracts are written on four types of assets—stocks, bonds, foreign currencies and commodities. The derivatives literature contains seemingly independent developments of derivative valuation principles for each type of asset. Generally speaking, however, the valuation principles are not asset-specific. The only distinction among assets is how carry costs/benefits are modeled.

The *net cost of carry* refers to the difference between the costs and the benefits of holding an asset. Suppose a breakfast cereal producer needs 5,000 bushels of wheat for processing in two months. To lock in the price of the wheat today, he can buy it and carry it for two months. One carry cost common to all assets is the opportunity cost of funds. To come up with the purchase price, he must either borrow money or liquidate existing interest-bearing assets. In either case, an interest cost is incurred. We assume this cost is incurred at the risk-free rate of interest. Beyond interest cost, however, carry costs vary depending upon the nature of the asset. For a *physical asset* or *commodity* such as wheat, we incur storage costs (e.g., rent and insurance). At the same time, certain benefits may accrue. By storing wheat we may avoid some costs of possible running out of our regular inventory before two months are up and having to pay extra for emergency deliveries. This is called *convenience yield*. Thus, the net cost of carry for a commodity equals interest cost plus storage costs less convenience yield, that is,

$$\text{Net carry cost} = \text{Cost of funds} + \text{Storage cost} - \text{Convenience yield} \tag{4.1a}$$

For a *financial asset* or *security* such as a stock or a bond, the carry costs/benefits are different. While borrowing costs remain, securities do not require storage costs and do not have convenience yields. What they do have, however, is income (yield) that accrues in the form of quarterly cash dividends or semiannual coupon payments. Thus, the net cost of carry for a security is

$$\text{Net carry cost} = \text{Cost of funds} - \text{Income} \tag{4.1b}$$

Carry costs and benefits are modeled either as continuous rates or as discrete flows. Some costs/benefits such as the cost of funds (i.e., the risk-free interest rate) are best modeled as continuous rates. The dividend yield on a broadly based stock portfolio, the interest income on a foreign currency deposit, and the lease rate on gold also fall into this category. Other costs/benefits such as warehouse rent payments for holding an inventory of grain, quarterly cash dividends on individual common stocks, and semiannual coupon receipts on a bond are best modeled as discrete cash flows. Below we provide the continuous rate and discrete flow cost of carry assumptions. For ease of exposition, we first introduce some notation. The current price of the asset is denoted $S$. Its price at future time $T$ is $\tilde{S}_T$, where the tilde denotes the future asset price is uncertain. The opportunity cost of funds (i.e., the risk-free rate of interest) is assumed to be a constant, continuous rate and is denoted $r$. If we borrow to buy the asset today, we will owe $Se^{rT}$ at time $T$.

## Continuous Rates

The types of assets whose carry costs are typically modeled as constant, continuous rates include broadly based stock index portfolios, foreign currencies, and gold. Assume that we borrow at the risk-free rate of interest to buy a stock index portfolio that pays cash dividends at a constant continuous rate $i$. If we buy one unit of the index today and reinvest all dividends immediately as they are received in more shares of the index portfolio, the number of units of the index portfolio will grow to exactly $e^{iT}$ units at time $T$. Alternatively, if we want exactly one unit of the index on hand at time $T$, we buy only $e^{-iT}$ units today at a cost of $Se^{-iT}$. The terminal value of our investment in the index portfolio at time $T$ will be $\tilde{S}_T$.[1] The loan value has accrued from $Se^{-iT}$ to $Se^{-iT}e^{rT} = Se^{(r-i)T}$. After repaying the loan, the terminal portfolio value will be $\tilde{S}_T - Se^{(r-i)T}$. Within this continuous rate framework, the net cost of carry rate of an index portfolio equals the difference between the risk-free rate of interest $r$ and the dividend yield rate $i$. The situation for a foreign currency is identical. If we borrow at the domestic risk-free rate, buy a foreign currency, and then invest the currency at the prevailing foreign risk-free rate, the net cost of carry rate equals the difference between the domestic interest rate $r$ and the foreign interest rate $i$. Similarly, if we borrow at the risk-free rate, buy gold, and then lend it in the marketplace, the net cost of carry rate equals the difference between the interest rate $r$ and the lease rate on gold $i$. Within this framework, the total cost of carry paid at time $T$ is

$$\text{Net carry cost}_T = S[e^{(r-i)T} - 1] \tag{4.2}$$

**ILLUSTRATION 4.1** Lock in number of units of stock index portfolio in future.

*Assume that the S&P 500 index is currently at a level of 1,100 and pays dividends at the continuous rate of 3% annually. Assume also that "shares" of the S&P 500 index can be purchased and sold at the index level (i.e., one share currently costs $1,100). Suppose that you want exactly 3,000 shares of the S&P 500 index on hand in five days. How many shares of the S&P 500 index must you buy today if all dividends paid are reinvested in more shares of the index portfolio? Demonstrate that you will have exactly 3,000 shares at the end of five days, assuming that the S&P 500 index levels are 1,100, 1,160, 1,154, 1,145, 1,170, and 1,175 on days 0 through 5, respectively. Compute the total amount of dividends paid and reinvested.*

If you want 3,000 shares of the index on hand at in five days, you need to buy $3{,}000e^{-0.03(5/365)} = 2{,}998.77$ shares today. Over the first day, your number of shares will grow by a factor $e^{0.03(1/365)}$ due to the reinvestment of dividends, bringing the number of shares to $2{,}998.77e^{0.03(1/365)} = 2{,}999.01$. Over the second day, your number of shares will again grow by a factor $e^{0.03(1/365)}$ due to the reinvestment of dividends, bringing the number of shares to 2,999.26. Since the dividends are being paid at a constant, continuous rate, we know the original number of shares purchased will grow to exactly 3,000 shares by the end of day 5 (i.e., $3{,}000e^{0.03(5/365)}e^{-0.03(5)(1/365)} = 3{,}000$), as is shown in the table below.

| Day | Index Level | Units of Index | Value of Index Position |
|---|---|---|---|
| 0 | 1,100.00 | 2,998.77 | 3,298,644 |
| 1 | 1,160.00 | 2,999.01 | 3,478,856 |
| 2 | 1,154.00 | 2,999.26 | 3,461,146 |
| 3 | 1,145.00 | 2,999.51 | 3,434,435 |
| 4 | 1,170.00 | 2,999.75 | 3,509,712 |
| 5 | 1,175.00 | 3,000.00 | 3,525,000 |

## Discrete Flows

For most other types of assets including stocks with quarterly cash dividends and bonds with semiannual coupon payments, noninterest carry costs/benefits are best modeled as discrete flows. Suppose a stock promises to pay $n$ known cash dividends

[1] This result is demonstrated numerically using simulation in the Excel file, **Telescoping asset position.xls**. In the file's worksheet, the (random) price path of an asset over a 10-day period is considered. If the position starts with $e^{-iT}$ units on day 0 and increases by a factor of $e^{i}$ each day due to reinvestment of income, exactly one unit will be on hand at the end of day 10. Pressing the F9 key generates a new asset price path. As you will see, independent of the price path, the number of units on day 10, is 1.

in the amount $I_i$ at time $t_i$, $i = 1, \ldots, n$ between now and future time $T$. If we borrow $S$ to cover the purchase price of the stock and reinvest all cash dividends as they are received at the risk-free rate of interest, the terminal value of our position will be

$$\tilde{S}_T + \sum_{i=1}^{n} I_i e^{r(T-t_i)} - Se^{rT}$$

In this instance, the net cost of carry at time $T$ is

$$\text{Net carry cost}_T = S(e^{rT} - 1) - \sum_{i=1}^{n} I_i e^{r(T-t_i)} \tag{4.3}$$

For coupon-bearing bonds, the expressions are the same, however $S$ denotes the bond price and $I_i$ at time $t_i$, $i = 1, \ldots, n$ denote coupon payments.

**ILLUSTRATION 4.2** Compute future value of asset that pays discrete cash flow.

*Suppose that you buy 10,000 shares of ABC Corporation and carry your position for 90 days. ABC's current share price is \$50, and the stock promises to pay a \$4 dividend in exactly 30 days. What will be the value of your portfolio when you unwind in 90 days? Assume the risk-free rate of interest is 5%.*

As the table below shows, the initial investment in 10,000 shares of ABC costs \$500,000. You financed the entire purchase price with risk-free borrowings, hence your initial investment is \$0. In 90 days, you have three components to your portfolio. First, you own 10,000 shares valued at $\tilde{S}_T$ a share. Next, you must repay the \$500,000 in risk-free borrowings plus interest at a cost of \$506,202.54. Finally, you received cash dividends of \$4 a share or \$40,000 on day 30, which you invested immediately in risk-free discount bonds. Dividends plus accrued interest amount to \$40,330.12 on day $T$. Thus, the total value of the portfolio in 90 days is $10{,}000\tilde{S}_T - 506{,}202.54 + 40{,}330.12$.

| Trade | Initial Investment | Value on Day $T$ |
|---|---|---|
| Buy stock | –50(10,000) | $10{,}000\tilde{S}_T$ |
| Borrow funds | 500,000 | $-500{,}000e^{0.05(90/365)} = -506{,}202.54$ |
| Receive cash dividends on day $t$, and reinvest at risk-free rate until day $T$ | | $40{,}000e^{0.05(60/365)} = 40{,}330.12$ |
| Value of position | 0 | $10{,}000\tilde{S}_T - 506{,}202.54 + 40{,}330.12$ |

### Summary and Some Guidelines

Carry costs/benefits are the known costs/benefits associated with holding an asset over a fixed period of time. In general, they consist of two components—(1) interest and (2) income (in the case of a financial asset) or storage (in the case of a physical asset). The interest component is always expressed as a rate. If we buy an asset today with borrowed funds, we will owe $e^{rT}$ per unit of the asset on day $T$. Income and noninterest costs are expressed either as a continuous proportion of the asset price or as discrete cash flows, depending upon the nature of the underlying asset. Firms potentially have four different sources of price risk—equity risk, interest rate risk, foreign exchange risk, and commodity price risk. Table 4.1 presents terminal values of leveraged asset positions using the net cost of carry assumption appropriate to each asset category.

## VALUING FORWARDS

With the concept of net cost of carry in hand, we now turn to valuing forward contracts. A forward is a contract that requires its seller to deliver the underlying asset on future day $T$ at price agreed upon today. We denote today's forward price as $f$. Its price on day $T$ is denoted $\tilde{f}_T$. A forward with no time remaining to expiration must have the same price as the underlying asset, that is, $\tilde{f}_T = \tilde{S}_T$ as shown in Figure 4.1. Otherwise, a costless arbitrage profit is possible by buying the asset and selling the forward, or vice versa. The purpose of this section is to derive the value of a forward contract relative to its underlying asset price prior to time $T$ under the continuous and discrete net carry cost assumptions.

### Continuous Rates

To establish the price of a forward today, consider a U.S. corporation that needs to make a EUR 1,000,000 payment in $T$ days and wants to lock in the U.S. dollar value of this payment today. The firm can accomplish this goal in two ways. First, it

**FIGURE 4.1** Price paths of forward contract and its underlying asset through time. Price convergence occurs at expiration.

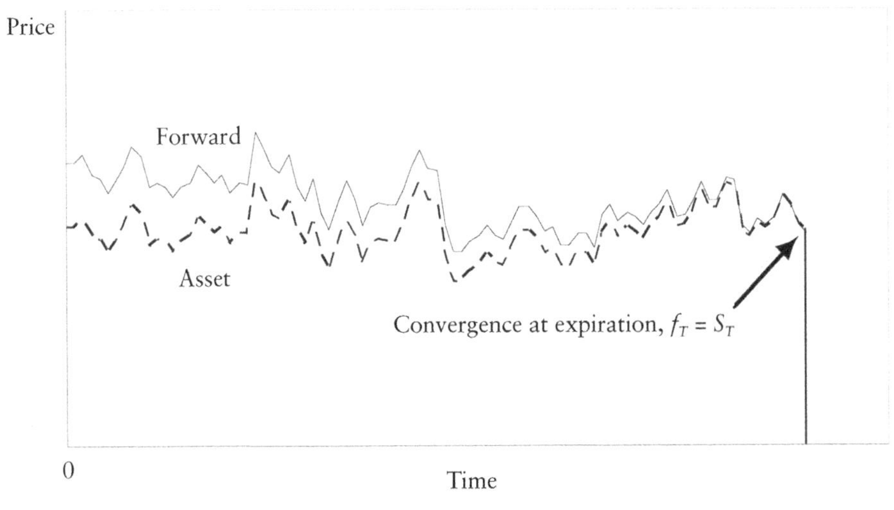

**TABLE 4.1** Future value at time $T$ of a leveraged asset position using continuous rate/discrete flow net cost of carry assumptions. All assets are assumed to incur interest cost at a constant continuous rate $r$.

| Asset Type | Recommended Model | Terminal Value | Explanation of Noninterest Carry Costs/Benefits |
|---|---|---|---|
| Equity | | | |
| Individual stock or narrowly-based stock portfolio | Discrete flow | $\tilde{S}_T - (Se^{rT} - FVI)$ | For individual common stocks or narrowly-based stock indexes, income accrues in the form of discrete cash dividends $I_i$ paid at time $t_i$, and the dividends are carried forward until time $T$ at the risk-free interest rate $r$, that is, $FVI = \sum_{i=1}^{n} I_i e^{r(T-i_i)}$ |
| Stock portfolio | Continuous rate | $\tilde{S}_T - Se^{(r-i)T}$ | For broadly based stock portfolios, income accrues at a constant, continuous dividend yield rate $i$. |
| Bonds | Discrete flow | $\tilde{S}_T - (Se^{rT} - FVI)$ | For coupon-bearing bonds, income accrues in the form of discrete coupon payments $I_i$ paid at time $t_i$, and the coupons are carried forward until time $T$ at the risk-free interest rate $r$, that is, $FVI = \sum_{i=1}^{n} I_i e^{r(T-i_i)}$ |
| Currency | Continuous rate | $\tilde{S}_T - Se^{(r-i)T}$ | For foreign currency deposits, income accrues at a constant, continuous foreign rate of interest $i$. |
| Commodity | Discrete flow | $\tilde{S}_T - (Se^{rT} - FVI)$ | For most physical commodities, storage costs (e.g., warehouse rent and insurance) are paid and convenience yield accrues. In this case, FVI is the future value of convenience yield less the future value of the discrete storage cost payments, that is, $FVI = FV(\text{Convenience yield}) - FV(\text{Storage costs})$ While storage costs can be modeled as discrete flows, convenience yield (e.g., the lease rate on gold) may be modeled as a rate. |

can borrow U.S. dollars and buy euros today at the spot exchange rate $S$, and then carry the position for $T$ days. To have one euro on hand in $T$ days, they need to buy $e^{-iT}$ units today where $i$ is the risk-free interest rate in Europe. To finance the entire purchase today, they need to borrow $Se^{-iT}$. The repayment of the loan will occur in $T$ days, and the principal plus interest will amount to $Se^{-iT}e^{rT}$ per euro where $r$ is the U.S. risk-free interest rate. Second, it can negotiate the price of a $T$-day forward contract with its bank. Under the terms of the forward contract, the firm will buy 1,000,000 euros in $T$ days at a cost of $f$ per euro. No money changes hands today. In making its decision about which strategy to take, the firm will compare the forward price with the future value had the euros been purchased today and carried until day $T$. If $f$ exceeds $Se^{(r-i)T}$, the firm will buy the euros in the spot market and carry them. If $f$ is less than $Se^{(r-i)T}$, the firm will buy the forward contract. Both alternatives provide the firm with EUR 1,000,000 in $T$ days at a price locked in today. Since they are perfect substitutes, they *must* have the same price. The value of a forward in a constant continuous net cost of carry framework is

$$f = Se^{(r-i)T} \tag{4.4}$$

The relation (4.4) is sometimes called the *net cost of carry relation.* When the prices of the forward and the asset are such that (4.4) holds exactly, the forward market is said to be *at full carry.* Unless costless arbitrage is somehow impeded, we can be assured that the forward market will always be at full carry. Suppose, for an instant in time, $f > Se^{(r-i)T}$. Such a condition implies that there is a costless arbitrage opportunity. We should immediately sell the forward and buy the asset, financing the purchase of the asset with risk-free borrowing. Table 4.2 shows the outcome. With no investment today, we earn a certain outcome of $f - Se^{(r-i)T} > 0$ on day $T$. Naturally, the market cannot be in equilibrium. The costless arbitrage activity would continue until the selling pressure on the forward price and the buying pressure on the asset price makes the arbitrage profit equal to 0. Where no arbitrage opportunity exists, the cost of carry relation (4.4) holds.

The net cost of carry relation (4.4) is written in future value form, since both sides of the equation are values on day $T$, as shown in Table 4.2. The relation can also be expressed in present value form. Multiplying both sides of (4.4) by the discount factor $e^{-rT}$, we get

$$fe^{-rT} = Se^{-iT} \tag{4.5}$$

What (4.5) says is that the *prepaid forward contract*, $fe^{-rT}$, equals the initial cost of the asset position, $Se^{-iT}$.

**TABLE 4.2** Costless arbitrage trades where $f > Se^{(r-i)T}$.

| Trades | Initial Investment | Value on Day $T$ |
|---|---|---|
| Buy $e^{-iT}$ units of asset | $-Se^{-iT}$ | $\tilde{S}_T$ |
| Borrow (sell risk-free bonds) | $Se^{-iT}$ | $-Se^{(r-i)T}$ |
| Sell forward contract | | $-(\tilde{S}_T - f)$ |
| Net portfolio value | 0 | $f - Se^{(r-i)T}$ |

### Discrete Flows

In the event that income or noninterest carry costs are more appropriately modeled as discrete cash flows, the net cost of carry relation is

$$f = Se^{rT} - FVI \tag{4.6}$$

where $FVI$ is the future value of the promised income receipts. If the underlying asset is a physical asset, the future value of the income, $FVI$, may be *negative* as a result of storage cost payments. The relation can also be written in its present value form,

$$fe^{-rT} = S - PVI \tag{4.7}$$

where $PVI$ is the present value of the promised income receipts, that is, $PVI = FVIe^{-rT}$. The prepaid forward price equals $S - PVI$, where the underlying asset distributes discrete known cash flows through time.

**ILLUSTRATION 4.3** Compute value of forward contract on dividend-paying stock.

*Compute the value of a six-month forward contract on 3,000 shares of HAL Company assuming that the current share price is \$120 and that a \$3 cash dividend will be paid in two months and then again in five months. Assume the risk-free rate of interest is 5%.*

Since the cash dividend payments are discrete cash inflows, the cost of carry relation (4.2) is the most appropriate. The future value of the first dividend payment is $3e^{0.05(4/12)}$ and the future value of the second dividend is $3e^{0.05(1/12)}$. The future value of all income received during the forward contract's life is therefore

$$FVI = 3e^{0.05(4/12)} + 3e^{0.05(1/12)} = 6.06$$

The value of the forward contract is therefore

$$f = 120e^{0.05(6/12)} - 6.06 = 116.97 \text{ per share}$$

or \$350,910 in total. This computation can be verified using the OPTVAL function,

OV_FORWARD_VALUE_DISCRETE($s$, $r$, $t$, *income*, *term*, *fp*)

where $s$ is the asset price, $r$ is the risk-free rate of interest, $t$ is the time to expiration of the forward, *income* is a vector of cash income receipts received during the life of the forward, *term* is a vector of the times to receipt of each of the income receipts, and *fp* is a indicator variable instructing the function to return the forward/futures price ("*f*" or "*F*") or the prepaid forward/futures price ("*p*" or "*P*"). The worksheet below illustrates.

B12 =OV_FORWARD_VALUE_DISCRETE($B$1,$B$2,$B$3,$B$7:$B$8,$C$7:$C$8,"f")

| | A | B | C | D | E | F | G | H | I | J |
|---|---|---|---|---|---|---|---|---|---|---|
| 1 | Stock price | 120.00 | | | | | | | | |
| 2 | Interest rate | 5.00% | | | | | | | | |
| 3 | Time to expiration | 0.50 | | | | | | | | |
| 4 | | | | | | | | | | |
| 5 | | | Time to | | | | | | | |
| 6 | Dividend | Amount | payment | | | | | | | |
| 7 | 1 | 3.00 | 0.1667 | | | | | | | |
| 8 | 2 | 3.00 | 0.4167 | | | | | | | |
| 9 | | | | | | | | | | |
| 10 | FVD | 6.0629 | | | | | | | | |
| 11 | | | | | | | | | | |
| 12 | Forward price | 116.97 | | | | | | | | |
| 13 | Prepaid forward price | 114.09 | | | | | | | | |

**TABLE 4.3** Hedging a stock portfolio using a forward contract.

| Trades | Initial Investment | Value on Day $T$ |
|---|---|---|
| Own stock portfolio. Reinvest all dividend income into more shares of stocks. | $-S$ | $\tilde{S}_T e^{iT}$ |
| Sell $e^{-iT}$ forward contract | 0 | $-(\tilde{S}_T - f)e^{iT}$ |
| Net portfolio value | 0 | $fe^{iT}$ |

## Hedging with Forwards

Before turning to futures contract valuation, it is worth considering the no-arbitrage portfolio in Table 4.2 more closely. It contains important intuition regarding hedging risk. Suppose that we hold a stock portfolio and fear that the market will decline over the next few months. To avoid the risk of a stock market decline, we can sell our stocks and buy risk-free bonds. Alternatively, we can sell a forward contract on our stock portfolio. These alternatives are *perfect substitutes*.

To see this, assume that our portfolio is sufficiently broad-based that it is reasonable to assume that the dividend yield is a constant continuous rate, $i$. If all dividend income is invested in more units of the stock portfolio, one unit in the stock portfolio today will grow to $e^{iT}$ units on day $T$, as we discussed earlier and illustrated in Table 4.3. To hedge the price risk exposure of $e^{iT}$ units of the stock portfolio on day $T$, we need to sell $e^{iT}$ forward contracts today. The value of this forward position will be $-(\tilde{S}_T - f)e^{iT}$ on day $T$. Once the positions are netted, the terminal value of the portfolio is $fe^{iT}$. Note that the value is certain. The forward price, the dividend yield rate, and the hedge period horizon (i.e., the life of the forward contract) are all known on day 0. To see that the return on the hedged portfolio equals the risk-free return, substitute the net cost of carry relation, $f = Se^{(r-i)T}$, in the expression for the terminal value of the portfolio in Table 4.3. The net terminal value is $fe^{iT} = Se^{(r-i)T}e^{iT} = Se^{rT}$, exactly the amount we would have had if the stock portfolio had been liquidated and invested in risk-free bonds at the outset.

## Summary

A long forward position is a perfect substitute for buying the asset using risk-free borrowings. Consequently, the price of a forward equals the price of the asset plus net carry costs. But, this is only one possible combination of positions in the asset, the forward, and risk-free bonds. Table 4.4 shows all possible pairings. Using the net cost of carry relation, we can demonstrate why Position 1 is a perfect substitute for Position 2 in all six rows of the table. A full understanding of each relation will prove invaluable in understanding the valuation and risk management problems that are addressed in subsequent chapters of the book.

**TABLE 4.4** Perfect substitutes implied by the net cost of carry relation.

| Position 1 | | Position 2 |
|---|---|---|
| Buy asset/sell forward | = | Buy risk-free bonds (lend) |
| Buy risk-free bonds (lend)/buy forward | = | Buy asset |
| Buy asset/sell risk-free bonds (borrow) | = | Buy forward |
| | | |
| Sell asset/buy forward | = | Sell risk-free bonds (borrow) |
| Sell risk-free bonds (borrow)/sell forward | = | Sell asset |
| Sell asset/buy risk-free bonds (lend) | = | Sell forward |

**TABLE 4.5** Cash flows of long futures positions through time.

| Day $t$ | Futures Price | Mark-to-Market Gain/Loss on Day $t$ | Value of Gain/Loss on Day $T$ |
|---|---|---|---|
| 0 | F | | |
| 1 | $\tilde{F}_1$ | $\tilde{F}_1 - F$ | $(\tilde{F}_1 - F)e^{r(T-1)}$ |
| 2 | $\tilde{F}_2$ | $\tilde{F}_2 - \tilde{F}_1$ | $(\tilde{F}_2 - \tilde{F}_1)e^{r(T-2)}$ |
| ... | | | ... |
| $t$ | $\tilde{F}_t$ | $\tilde{F}_t - \tilde{F}_{t-1}$ | $(\tilde{F}_t - \tilde{F}_{t-1})e^{r(T-t)}$ |
| ... | | | ... |
| $T-1$ | $\tilde{F}_{T-1}$ | $\tilde{F}_{T-1} - \tilde{F}_{T-2}$ | $(\tilde{F}_{T-1} - \tilde{F}_{T-2})e^{r}$ |
| $T$ | $\tilde{F}_T$ | $\tilde{F}_T - \tilde{F}_{T-1}$ | $\tilde{F}_T - \tilde{F}_{T-1}$ |
| Total | | $\tilde{F}_2 - \tilde{F}_1$ | $\sum_{t=1}^{T} (\tilde{F}_t - \tilde{F}_{t-1})e^{r(T-t)}$ |

## VALUING FUTURES

Futures contracts are like forward contracts, except that price movements are *marked-to-market* each day rather than waiting until contract expiration and having a single, once-and-for-all settlement. If the marking-to-market produces a gain during the futures contract's life, the gain can be reinvested in interest-bearing securities. Conversely, if the marking-to-market produces a loss, the loss must be covered with either existing interest-bearing assets or borrowing at the risk-free interest rate.

To distinguish between buying a forward and buying a futures, consider the futures position cash flows shown in Table 4.5. As we discussed earlier, a forward contract purchased today has a value $\tilde{S}_T - f$ on day $T$. In contrast, a futures contract is marked to market each day, and the daily gains/losses gather interest. If risk-free rate of interest is 0%, the terminal value of the futures position (i.e., the sum of the mark-to-market gain/loss column) is the same as the terminal value of the forward position. If risk-free rate of interest is greater than 0%, however, the value of the futures position on day $T$ may be greater or less than the terminal value of the forward position, depending on the path that futures prices follow over the life of the contract.

**ILLUSTRATION 4.4** Compare terminal values of long forward and long futures positions.

*Suppose that you need £1,000,000 in three days and want to lock in the price today. Suppose also that a three-day forward contract on British pounds is priced at \$1.60 per pound and that a British pound futures contract with three days remaining to expiration also has a price of \$1.60. Compare the terminal values of a long forward position with a long futures position at the end of three days assuming the domestic risk-free rate is 5%. Assume that the futures prices over the next three days are \$1.71, \$1.67, and \$1.70, respectively.*

The terminal value of a long forward position is simply the exchange rate on day 3, \$1.70, less the forward price, \$1.60, times one million, \$100,000, exactly equal to the sum of the mark-to-market gains/losses on the long futures position. The terminal value of the long futures position when the mark-to-market gains/losses are invested/financed at the risk-free rate of interest, however, is \$100,024.66, as is shown in the table below. In general, the terminal value of a long forward and a long futures will be different.

| Day *t* | Futures Price | Mark-to-Market Gain/Loss on day *t* | Value of Gain/Loss on Day *T* |
|---|---|---|---|
| 0 | 1.60 | | |
| 1 | 1.71 | 110,000.00 | 110,030.14 |
| 2 | 1.67 | –40,000.00 | –40,005.48 |
| 3 | 1.70 | 30,000.00 | 30,000.00 |
| Total | | 100,000.00 | 100,024.66 |

The reason that the terminal values are different is that the terminal value of the futures position depends on how the futures price evolves through time. Other futures price paths will produce different terminal values. If, for example, the futures price had been \$1.51 on day 1 rather than \$1.71, the terminal value of the futures position would have been \$99,997.26, below (not above) the \$100,000 terminal value of the long forward.

## Telescoping Futures Position

Interestingly, the fact that a long forward position does not have the same terminal value of a long futures position does not imply that the forward and futures prices are different. Indeed, as we will show shortly, they are equal. We can control the effect of the reinvestment of the mark-to-market proceeds by creating a "telescoping futures position."

A telescoping futures position is created as follows. We begin, on day 0, with $e^{-rT}$ futures contracts. Since we enter the position at the close of day 0, the marked-to-market gain for the day is 0. In preparation for day 1, we increase the size of the futures position by a factor $e^r$. At the end of day 1, the futures position is marked-to-market, generating proceeds of $e^{-r(T-1)}(\tilde{F}_1 - F)$. If this gain/loss is carried forward at the risk-free interest rate until day $T$, the terminal gain/loss will be $e^{-r(T-1)}(\tilde{F}_1 - F)\,e^{r(T-1)} = \tilde{F}_1 - F$, as shown in Table 4.6. On day 2, the position is again increased by a factor $e^r$ and is marked-to-market at $e^{-r(T-2)}(\tilde{F}_2 - \tilde{F}_1)$. Car-

**TABLE 4.6** Cash flows of telescoping futures position providing same terminal value as forward position on day $T$.

| Day $t$ | Futures Price | No. of Futures Contracts | Mark-to-Market Gain/Loss on Day $t$ | Value of Gain/Loss on Day $T$ |
|---|---|---|---|---|
| 0 | $F$ | $e^{-rT}$ | | |
| 1 | $\tilde{F}_1$ | $e^{-r(T-1)}$ | $e^{-r(T-1)}(\tilde{F}_1 - F)$ | $e^{-r(T-1)}(\tilde{F}_1 - F)e^{r(T-1)}$ $= (\tilde{F}_1 - F)$ |
| 2 | $\tilde{F}_2$ | $e^{-r(T-2)}$ | $e^{-r(T-2)}(\tilde{F}_2 - \tilde{F}_1)$ | $\tilde{F}_2 - \tilde{F}_1$ |
| ... | | | ... | |
| $t$ | $\tilde{F}_t$ | $e^{-r(T-t)}$ | $e^{-r(T-t)}(\tilde{F}_t - \tilde{F}_{t-1})$ | $\tilde{F}_t - \tilde{F}_{t-1}$ |
| ... | | | ... | |
| $T-1$ | $\tilde{F}_{T-1}$ | $e^{-r}$ | $e^{-r}(\tilde{F}_{T-1} - \tilde{F}_{T-2})$ | $\tilde{F}_{T-1} - \tilde{F}_{T-2}$ |
| $T$ | $\tilde{F}_T$ | 1 | $\tilde{F}_T - \tilde{F}_{T-1}$ | $\tilde{F}_T - \tilde{F}_{T-1}$ |
| Total | | | | $\tilde{F}_T - F = \tilde{S}_T - F$ |

rying this amount forward to day $T$, we have $e^{-r(T-2)}(\tilde{F}_2 - \tilde{F}_1)\, e^{r(T-2)} = (\tilde{F}_2 - \tilde{F}_1)$, and so on. Because the number of futures is chosen to exactly offset the accumulated interest factor on the daily mark-to-market gain/loss, there will be exactly one futures contract on hand on day $T$, and the value of the futures position will be $S_T - F$. Assuming that the futures and forward contracts expire at the same time, the telescoping futures position will have exactly the same terminal value as the long forward position.[2]

**ILLUSTRATION 4.5** Compare terminal values of long forward and long telescoping futures positions.

*Suppose that you need £1,000,000 in three days and want to lock in the price today. Suppose also that a three-day forward contract on British pounds is priced at \$1.60 per pound and that a British pound futures contract with three days remaining to expiration also has a price of \$1.60. Compare the terminal values of a long forward position with a long telescoping futures position at the end of three days assuming the domestic risk-free interest rate is 5%. Assume that the futures prices over the next three days are \$1.71, \$1.67, and \$1.70, respectively.*

As in the case of Illustration 4.4, the terminal value of a long forward position is the exchange rate on day 3, \$1.70 less the forward price, \$1.60, times on million, or \$100,000. Because the initial futures position has less than 1 million units, the total of the mark-to-market gains/losses column is less than \$100,000. The terminal value of the

[2] This result is demonstrated numerically using simulation in the Excel file, **Telescoping futures position.xls.** In the file's worksheet, 10-day forward and futures positions are considered. Pressing the F9 key generates new price paths for the asset and forward/futures over the life of the contracts. Independent of the price path, the gain/loss on the forward position over the 10-day life of the contract is identically equal to the gain/loss on telescoping futures position.

telescoping futures position when the mark-to-market gains/losses are invested/financed at the risk-free rate of interest is exactly $100,000, as is shown in the table below. The dynamic rebalancing of the futures position within the telescoping strategy assures that the outcome is exactly the same as a long forward position.

| Day | Futures Price | Number of Units | Mark-to-Market Gain/Loss on Day $t$ | Value of Gain/Loss on Day $T$ |
|---|---|---|---|---|
| 0 | 1.60 | | | |
| 1 | 1.71 | 999,726.06 | 109,969.87 | 110,000.00 |
| 2 | 1.67 | 999,863.02 | -39,994.52 | -40,000.00 |
| 3 | 1.70 | 1,000,000.00 | 30,000.00 | 30,000.00 |
| Total | | | 99,975.35 | 100,000.00 |

### Equivalence of Forward and Futures Prices

The fact that a long telescoping futures position has a terminal value of $\tilde{S}_T - F$ and that a long forward position has a terminal value of $\tilde{S}_T - F$ implies that the futures price and forward price must be equal to each other.[3] If they are not, a costless arbitrage profit would be possible by selling the forward and entering a long telescoping position in the futures (if $f > F$) or by buying the forward and entering a short telescoping position in the futures (if $f < F$). Given the equivalence of forward and futures prices, the valuation equations for a futures contract are the same as those of the forward, that is,

$$F = f = Se^{(r-i)T} \tag{4.8}$$

if all carry costs are constant continuous rates, and

$$F = f = Se^{rT} - FVI \tag{4.9}$$

if noninterest carry costs are discrete.

**ILLUSTRATION 4.6** Short sell stock synthetically using stock futures.

*Retail investors in the U.S. often find it costly to short sell shares of common stock. Consequently, stocks futures were recently launched. Assume that you want to short sell a particular stock over the next* T *days. Its current share price is* S, *and a cash dividend of* D *has been declared and will be paid in* t *days. Prove that selling a telescoping position in share futures is equivalent to short selling the stock.*

[3] Cox, Ingersoll, and Ross (1981) use no-arbitrage arguments to demonstrate the equivalence of forward and futures prices when future interest rates are known. They go on to show, however, that if interest rates are uncertain, the futures price will be greater than or less than the forward price, depending upon whether the correlation between futures price changes and interest rate changes is negative or positive. See also Jarrow and Oldfield (1981).

First, you need to identify the value in $T$ days of a short position in the stock. Short selling a share of the stock generates proceeds of $S$. You take the proceeds and invest them at the risk-free rate of interest. In addition, the stock pays a cash dividend of $D$ on day $t$. Because you shorted the stock, you are responsible for paying the cash dividend. On day $T$, the value of each security position in your portfolio is as reported in the table below. The net portfolio value on day $T$ is $Se^{rT} - De^{r(T-t)} - \tilde{S}_T$.

| Trades | Initial Investment | Value on Day $T$ |
|---|---|---|
| Short sell stock. Must pay cash dividends, if any. | $S$ | $-\tilde{S}_T - De^{r(T-t)}$ |
| Buy risk-free bonds | $-S$ | $Se^{rT}$ |
| Net portfolio value | 0 | $Se^{rT} - De^{r(T-t)} - \tilde{S}_T$ |

From the discussion above, you know that selling a telescoping position in the share futures has a terminal value of $F - \tilde{S}_T$. But, from valuation equation (4.9), you know that, in the absence of costless arbitrage opportunities, $F = Se^{rT} - De^{r(T-t)}$. Substituting, you find that the value of the short futures position on day $T$ is $Se^{rT} - De^{r(T-t)} - \tilde{S}_T$, an amount identical to that of the short stock position.

### Hedging with Futures

The telescoping futures position has implications in terms of hedging with futures contracts. For the hedge to be completely effective, the number of futures must equal the number of units of the underlying asset on day $T$. Under the continuous carry cost assumption, we know that one unit of the asset grows to $e^{iT}$ units on day $T$. We also know that telescoping futures positions that starts with $e^{-rT}$ futures contracts today has a single contract at time $T$. Consequently, to hedge the long asset position in Table 4.3, our futures hedge would start off with being short $e^{-(r-i)T}$ futures contract on day 0, and would scale up by a factor of $e^r$ contracts per day over the life of the hedge. Assuming the futures expires on day $T$, the terminal value of the short telescoping position would be $-(\tilde{S}_T - F)e^{iT}$ and the net terminal value of the hedged portfolio would be $Fe^{iT}$. Substituting the net cost of carry relation (4.8), the net terminal value of the hedged portfolio may be written $Se^{rT}$, which shows that hedging using a short telescoping futures position is equivalent to liquidating the asset position and buying risk-free bonds. The day-to-day increase in the size of the futures position by the interest factor $e^r$ undoes the effects of interest on the daily marking to market of the futures gains/losses. In practice, this dynamic, day-to-day adjustment is called *tailing the hedge*.

### Summary

Futures contracts are like forward contracts except that price movements are marked to market daily. Because these daily gains/losses are allowed to accrue interest until the end of the contract's life, a long futures position will not in general have the same terminal value as a long forward position. The effects of the interest accrual on the mark-to-market gains/losses can be undone, however, using a telescoping futures position. Each day $t$, the number of futures is set equal to $e^{-r(T-t)}$ for each unit of the underlying asset at the end of the hedging interval. Set in this way, the terminal value of a long telescoping position in the futures equals the terminal value of a long forward. From a costless arbitrage perspective, therefore, the following are perfect substitutes:

Long telescoping futures position = Long forward position

Short telescoping futures position = Short forward position

The telescoping futures strategy also has implications for hedging. To undo the effects of interest on the daily marking to market of the futures gains/losses when the life of the futures matches the hedging horizon $T$, the size of a futures hedge starts at a level equal to the present value of the number of terminal units of that asset, that is, $e^{-rT}$ for each unit of the asset and increases in size by a factor of $e^r$ each day.

## IMPLYING FORWARD NET CARRY RATES

Thus far, we have examined forward/futures contracts with a single maturity. A casual examination of the financial pages, however, shows multiple maturities for the same underlying asset. In these situations, we can use the net cost of carry relation (4.4) to deduce implied forward cost of carry rates.

**ILLUSTRATION 4.7** Compute implied forward interest rate in Britain.

*Suppose that the current USD/GBP exchange rate is 1.6830, and that the three-month and six-month forward exchange rates are 1.6755 and 1.6683, respectively.*[4] *If the three-month and six-month U.S. risk-free rates of interest are 5.163% and 5.103%, respectively, compute the implied forward risk-free rate of interest in Britain on a three-month loan beginning in three months.*

Based on the above information, your first job is to compute the three-month and six-month risk-free rates in Britain, $r_{f,3}$ and $r_{f,6}$, respectively. This can be done by solving for the foreign interest rates in the following two applications of the net cost of carry relation:

$$1.6755 = 1.6830e^{(0.05163 - r_{f,3})0.25}$$

and

$$1.6683 = 1.6830e^{(0.05103 - r_{f,6})0.5}$$

The three-month risk-free rate in Britain is 6.950% and the six-month rate is 6.858%. These values can be computed using the OPTVAL function,

OV_FORWARD_II($s$, $f$, $r$, $t$)

where $s$ is the asset price, $f$ is the forward price, $r$ is the domestic risk-free interest rate, and $t$ is the time to expiration of the forward. The panel below illustrates how the function can be used in the current illustration.

[4] For foreign currencies, the income rate equals the rate of interest on a foreign risk-free bond.

B12 fx =ov_forward_ii($B$3,$B$4,$B$8,$C$4)

| | A | B | C | D | E |
|---|---|---|---|---|---|
| 1 | | | Time to | | |
| 2 | | Rate | expir. | | |
| 3 | Spot exchange rate | 1.6830 | | | |
| 4 | 3-month forward price | 1.6755 | 0.250 | | |
| 5 | 6-month forward price | 1.6683 | 0.500 | | |
| 6 | | | | | |
| 7 | U.S. interest rates | *Rate* | | | |
| 8 | 3-month | 5.163% | | | |
| 9 | 6-month | 5.103% | | | |
| 10 | | | | | |
| 11 | British interest rates | | | | |
| 12 | 3-month | 6.950% | | | |
| 13 | 6-month | 6.858% | | | |
| 14 | | | | | |
| 15 | Implied forward rate | 6.766% | | | |

Next, you know from the discussion of implied forward interest rates in the last chapter that

$$e^{0.06858(6/12)} = e^{0.06950(3/12)}e^{f_3(3/12)}$$

or, alternatively,

$$0.06858(0.5) = 0.06950(0.25) + f_3(0.25)$$

Rearranging to isolate the forward rate, you get

$$f_3 = \frac{0.06858(0.5) - 0.06950(0.25)}{0.25} = 6.766 \text{ percent}$$

The implied three-month risk-free rate of interest in Britain on a loan beginning is three months is 6.766%.

## VALUING SWAPS

A swap contract is an agreement to exchange a set of future cash flows. A plain-vanilla swap is usually regarded to be an exchange of a fixed payment for a floating payment, where the floating payment is tied to some reference rate, index level, or price. Like a forward contract, the underlying asset can be anything from a financial asset such as a stock or a bond to a physical asset such as crude oil or gold. Also, like a forward contract, a swap involves no upfront payment.

The key information needed to value a swap contract is the *forward curve* of the underlying asset and the *zero-coupon yield curve* for risk-free bonds. The forward curve refers to the relation between the price of a forward contract on the underlying asset and its time to expiration or settlement. Where the time to expiration is 0, the forward price equals the prevailing spot price. Figure 4.2 shows two possible forward curve relations. Where the curve is upward sloping, the market is said to be in *contango*, and, where the curve is downward sloping, the market is said to be in *backwardation*. For financial assets, the slope will depend on the net difference between the risk-free rate and the income received

**FIGURE 4.2** Forward curve: Relation between forward price and its time to expiration. Where time to expiration is 0, forward price equals spot price.

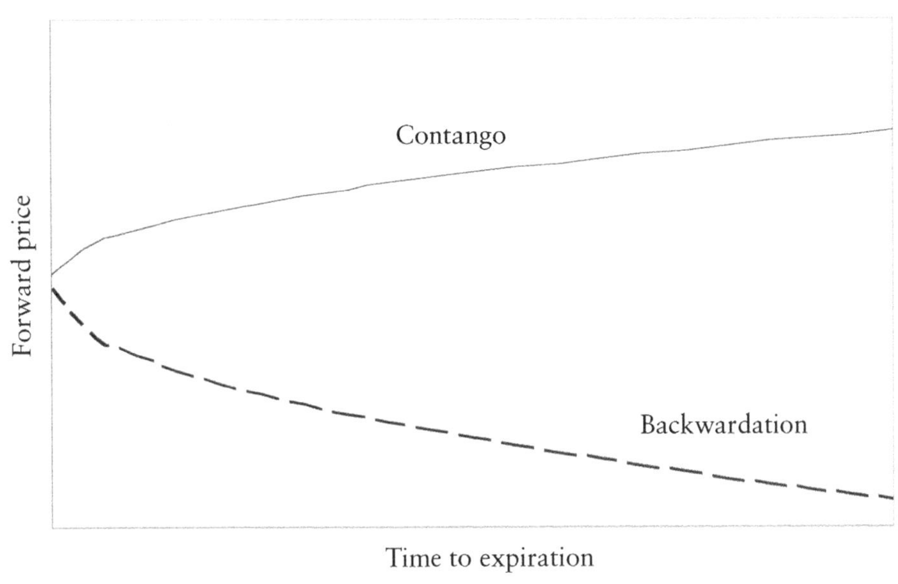


on the underlying asset. In markets where the interest rate is greater than the income rate, the market will be in contango, and, where the interest rate is less than the income rate, the market will be in backwardation. For physical assets or commodities, the nature of the forward curve depends also on the cost of storage and convenience yield. The zero-coupon yield curve refers to the relation between interest rates and term to maturity and was discussed in Chapter 2.

In terms of swap valuation, the nature of the forward curve is irrelevant as long as the forward prices represent tradable prices. To see this, consider a jeweler (i.e., long hedger) who needs 1,000 Troy ounces of gold each quarter over the next two years and wants to lock in his input cost today. One hedging alternative is to buy a *strip* of forward (or futures) contracts, one corresponding to each desired delivery date. The cost of the gold each quarter will be locked-in, however, the cost of the gold will be different each quarter unless the forward curve is a horizontal line. The gold market, however, is typically in contango, so the cost, although certain, will escalate through time. A second alternative is to buy a swap contract that provides for the delivery of 1,000 ounces of gold each quarter, where there is single fixed price for all deliveries.[5] In the absence of costless arbitrage opportunities, it must be the case that the present value of the

[5] As a practical matter, many swap agreements are cash-settled, so, instead of paying the fixed price per ounce and receiving 1,000 ounces in gold, we will receive in cash 1,000 times the difference between the prevailing (random) spot price of gold each quarter and the fixed price. If the spot price is greater than the fixed price, we receive a cash payment from our counterparty, and vice versa.

deliveries using the forward curve must be the same as the present value of the deliveries using the fixed price of the swap contract, that is,

$$\sum_{i=1}^{n} f_i e^{-r_i T_i} = \sum_{i=1}^{n} \bar{f} e^{-r_i T_i} \tag{4.10}$$

where $n$ is the number of delivery dates, $f_i$ is the price of a forward contract with time to expiration $T_i$, $r_i$ is the risk-free rate of interest corresponding to time to expiration $T_i$,[6] and $\bar{f}$ is the fixed price in the swap agreement.[7] In an instance where the right-hand side of (4.10) is greater (less) than the left-hand side, an arbitrageur would buy (sell) the swap and sell (buy) the strip of forward contracts, pocketing the difference. Because such free money opportunities do not exist, (4.10) must hold as an equality.

Equation (4.10) can be rearranged to isolate the fixed price of the swap agreement, that is,

$$\bar{f} = \frac{\sum_{i=1}^{n} f_i e^{-r_i T_i}}{\sum_{i=1}^{n} e^{-r_i T_i}} = \sum_{i=1}^{n} f_i \left( \frac{e^{-r_i T_i}}{\sum_{i=1}^{n} e^{-r_i T_i}} \right) \tag{4.11}$$

Expressed in this fashion, it becomes obvious that the fixed price of a swap is a weighted average of forward prices, one corresponding to each delivery date.

**ILLUSTRATION 4.8** Compute fixed rate of swap based on forward curve.

*Suppose that you produce gold watches and require 1,000 ounces each quarter. Fearing that the price of gold will rise, you decide to hedge your input costs over the next two years by buying a commodity swap, specifically a contract that provides a cash payment equal to the difference between the gold price and the fixed price of the swap on 1,000 ounces of gold each quarter. The swap dealer is quoting you a price of \$401.50 an ounce. Evaluate the fairness of this price assuming the forward curve is approximated by the function,*

$$f_i = 400 + \sqrt{T_i}$$

*and the zero-coupon yield curve for risk-free bonds is given by the function,*

$$r_i = 0.04 + 0.01 \ln(1 + T_i)$$

Based on the forward curve and the yield curve, you compute prepaid forward prices for each of the eight delivery dates. You then sum the prepaid forward prices, and divide by the sum of the discount factors to determine the fixed price. The intermediate computations are as follows.

[6] Note that we are allowing for the fact that the risk-free rate may be term-specific.
[7] The delivery quantity is irrelevant since it is the same on both sides of the equation. That is, equation (4.10) assumes that one unit is delivered on each delivery date.

| Time to Prepayment | Gold Forward Price | Risk-Free Rate | Discount Factor | Prepaid Forward Price |
|---|---|---|---|---|
| 0.25 | 400.50 | 4.22% | 0.9895 | 396.29 |
| 0.50 | 400.71 | 4.41% | 0.9782 | 391.98 |
| 0.75 | 400.87 | 4.56% | 0.9664 | 387.39 |
| 1.00 | 401.00 | 4.69% | 0.9542 | 382.62 |
| 1.25 | 401.12 | 4.81% | 0.9416 | 377.71 |
| 1.50 | 401.22 | 4.92% | 0.9289 | 372.70 |
| 1.75 | 401.32 | 5.01% | 0.9160 | 367.62 |
| 2.00 | 401.41 | 5.10% | 0.9031 | 362.50 |
| Total | | | 7.5779 | 3,038.81 |

Based on the forward curve, the fixed rate on the swap should be

$$\bar{f} = \frac{3{,}038.81}{7.5779} = 401.01 \text{ per ounce}$$

The difference between the dealer's quote and your computation of the fair price based on the forward curve is 49 cents an ounce, or \$3,920 across all promised deliveries. The fairness of the quote depends upon your ability and willingness to buy the strip the forward (or futures) contracts in lieu of the swap.

Finally, the OPTVAL Function Library contains a function that values a commodity swap with uniform quantities each period. The function is

$$\text{OV\_SWAP\_COMMODITY}(t, f, r, vr)$$

where $t$ is a vector containing the times to each delivery date, $f$ is a vector of forward/futures prices corresponding to each date, $r$ is a vector of zero-coupon risk-free rates corresponding to each delivery date, and $vr$ is an indicator variable instructing the function to compute (a) the sum of the present values of the prepaid forward contracts ("$v$" or "$V$"), (b) the sum of the discount factors ("$d$" or "$D$"), or (c) the breakeven fixed price of the swap based on the forward curve ("$r$" or "$R$"). The worksheet below illustrates.

E16 =OV_SWAP_COMMODITY($A$4:$A$11,$B$4:$B$11,$C$4:$C$11,$D$16)

| | A | B | C | D | E | F | G | H | I |
|---|---|---|---|---|---|---|---|---|---|
| 1 | | Gold | | | Prepaid | | | | |
| 2 | Time to | forward | Risk-free | Discount | forward | | | | |
| 3 | payment | price | rate | factor | price | | | | |
| 4 | 0.25 | 400.50 | 4.22% | 0.9895 | 396.29 | | | | |
| 5 | 0.50 | 400.71 | 4.41% | 0.9782 | 391.98 | | | | |
| 6 | 0.75 | 400.87 | 4.56% | 0.9664 | 387.39 | | | | |
| 7 | 1.00 | 401.00 | 4.69% | 0.9542 | 382.62 | | | | |
| 8 | 1.25 | 401.12 | 4.81% | 0.9416 | 377.71 | | | | |
| 9 | 1.50 | 401.22 | 4.92% | 0.9289 | 372.70 | | | | |
| 10 | 1.75 | 401.32 | 5.01% | 0.9160 | 367.62 | | | | |
| 11 | 2.00 | 401.41 | 5.10% | 0.9031 | 362.50 | | | | |
| 12 | Total | | | 7.5779 | 3,038.81 | | | | |
| 13 | | | | | | | | | |
| 14 | Fixed price of swap | | | | 401.0104 | | | | |
| 15 | | | | | | | | | |
| 16 | Present value of prepaid forwards | | | V | 3,038.81 | | | | |
| 17 | Present value of discount factors | | | D | 7.5779 | | | | |
| 18 | Break-even fixed price on swap | | | R | 401.0104 | | | | |

**ILLUSTRATION 4.9** Compute unwind price of swap based on forward curve.

*Suppose that three months have elapsed and spot price of gold has fallen to $390 an ounce. As a result, you had to make a net payment of $11.50 an ounce to your counterparty. Now, fearing a further decline in gold prices, you approach your counterparty and ask for an "unwind" price, that is, a price at which he is willing to tear up the existing swap agreement. The forward curve is now*

$$f_i = 390 + 0.9\sqrt{T_i}$$

*and the yield curve is*

$$r_i = 0.035 + 0.01\ln(1 + T_i)$$

The unwind price will equal the difference between the present value of the remaining fixed payments and the present value of the payments under the current forward curve. Based on the problem information, we must first generate the gold forward curve and the zero-coupon risk-free yield curve. Then, based on the curves, we can compute the present value of each leg of the swap using

OV_SWAP_COMMODITY($t$, $f$, $r$, $vr$)

The worksheet below illustrates. Under the current market environment and swap terms, you have promised to pay the dealer $401.01 per ounce of gold each quarter during the remaining seven quarters. The present value of the promised payments is $2,689.923 per ounce. In return, the swap dealer has promised to pay you the spot price of gold each quarter during the remaining seven quarters. The present value of his obligation is $2,621.84 per ounce. Thus, the least that the dealer will require for rescinding the agreement is $68,079.

D13 =OV_SWAP_COMMODITY($A$4:$A$10,$D$4:$D$10,$C$4:$C$10,$C$12)

| | A | B | C | D | E | F | G | H |
|---|---|---|---|---|---|---|---|---|
| 1 | | Gold | | | | | | |
| 2 | Time to | forward | Risk-free | Swap | | | | |
| 3 | payment | price | rate | payment | | | | |
| 4 | 0.25 | 390.45 | 3.72% | -401.01 | | | | |
| 5 | 0.50 | 390.64 | 3.91% | -401.01 | | | | |
| 6 | 0.75 | 390.78 | 4.06% | -401.01 | | | | |
| 7 | 1.00 | 390.90 | 4.19% | -401.01 | | | | |
| 8 | 1.25 | 391.01 | 4.31% | -401.01 | | | | |
| 9 | 1.50 | 391.10 | 4.42% | -401.01 | | | | |
| 10 | 1.75 | 391.19 | 4.51% | -401.01 | | | | |
| 11 | | | | | | | | |
| 12 | PV of prepaid forwards | | V | 2,621.843 | | | | |
| 13 | PV of fixed payments | | V | -2,689.923 | | | | |
| 14 | Net value per ounce | | | -68.079 | | | | |
| 15 | Total value of 1,000 ounces | | | -68,079 | | | | |

## SUMMARY

This chapter develops the price relations for forwards, futures, and swaps under a single assumption—two perfect substitutes must have the same price. We begin by developing the notion of the net cost of carry. The net cost of carry refers to the cost of holding an asset over a period of time. One component of the cost of carry for all assets is the opportunity cost of funds. In order to buy the asset, we must pay for it. Beyond interest cost, however, carry costs may be positive or negative, depending upon the nature of the underlying asset. If the asset is a *physical asset* or *commodity* such as grain, the asset holder must pay storage costs such as warehouse rent and insurance. If the underlying asset is a *financial asset* or *security* such as a stock, a bond, or a currency, on the other hand, there are no storage costs. Indeed, such assets produce a known income stream in the form of dividend payments or interest receipts, and this income can be used to subsidize the cost of borrowing. We model interest cost as a constant continuous rate and the noninterest costs/benefits as either continuous rates or discrete cash flows, depending on the nature of the underlying asset.

With the assumption and the cost of carry definition in hand, we develop pricing equations for forward and futures contracts. We show that the price of a forward equals the price of a futures and that both are equal to the asset price plus net carry costs. This stands to reason. If we need an asset on hand at some future date at a price "locked-in" today, we can buy a forward contract, buy a futures, or buy the underlying asset and carry it. Perfect substitutes must have the same price. The results in this chapter are general and apply to any underlying asset. In the applications chapters that follow, we rely on these powerful price relations in developing and analyzing risk management strategies.

Finally, we derive the relation between the forward curve and the fixed price of a swap. In the absence of costless arbitrage opportunities, the fixed price is a weighted average of the prices of the corresponding forward contracts, with the weights equal to discount factor of each flow in relation to the sum of all discount factors.

## REFERENCES AND SUGGESTED READINGS

Cox, John C., John E. Ingersoll, and Stephen A. Ross. 1981. The relation between forward and futures prices. *Journal of Financial Economics* 9: 321–346.

Jarrow, Robert A., and George S. Oldfield. 1981. Forward contracts and futures contracts. *Journal of Financial Economics* 9 (December): 373–382.

# 5

# Risk Management Strategies: Futures

This chapter builds on Chapters 3 and 4. In Chapter 3, we learned the mechanics of expected return and risk. In Chapter 4, we learned about the no-arbitrage price relation that links the price of a forward/futures to the price of its underlying asset. This chapter explores the role of forward/futures contracts in managing expected return and risk. In moving forward through the chapter, we will use only the term "futures" rather than "forward and futures" for expositional convenience. The risk management techniques apply to both contracts equally well. The decision to use "futures" rather than "forwards" is based on the fact that historical futures data are more broadly available for estimation purposes. Since the chapter deals with expected return and risk, the most natural place to begin is with a demonstration of how futures fit within the capital asset pricing model (CAPM). We then focus on using futures contracts to manage different types of risks. We begin with price risk and show how an airline can hedge the cost of jet fuel. Next we focus on revenue risk and show how a farmer can hedge the sales proceeds of his crop in an environment with both price and quantity risks. For other corporate risk managers, gross margin (i.e., uncertain revenue less uncertain costs) risk is often the primary risk management focus. Oil refiners, for example, are concerned about the difference between the revenue they realize through the sale of heating oil and unleaded gasoline and the cost of the crude oil they must acquire to produce these products. For fund managers, more than one risk factor may be affecting portfolio value. Someone managing a junk bond portfolio, for example, faces both interest rate and stock market risk exposures. We show how to incorporate multiple risk factors in setting the optimal hedge. The chapter concludes with a brief summary.

## EXPECTED RETURN AND RISK

Like other risky financial instruments, futures contracts have expected returns and risks that can be modeled within the CAPM. The key to understanding exactly how lies in the relation between the rate of price change of a futures and the rate of return of its underlying asset.

To begin, we recall the net cost of carry relation,

$$F_t = S_t e^{(r-i)(T-t)} \tag{5.1}$$

where the subscript $t$ has been added to denote a particular point in time prior to the contract's expiration. Taking the natural logarithm of both sides of (5.1) provides

$$\ln F_t = (r-i)(T-t) + \ln S_t \tag{5.2}$$

Now consider the transformed net cost of carry relation (5.2) an instant earlier in time at $t + 1$, that is,

$$\ln F_{t-1} = (r-i)(T-t+1) + \ln S_{t-1} \tag{5.3}$$

Subtracting (5.3) from (5.2), we find that the continuous rate price change of the futures is

$$R_F \equiv RA_F \equiv \ln(F_t/F_{t-1}) = -(r-i) + \ln(S_t/S_{t-1}) \tag{5.4}$$

In equation (5.4), $R_F$ denotes the rate of return on a futures contract and $RA_F$ is its rate of price appreciation. We make this distinction to underscore the fact that the only income arising from holding a futures contract is price change.[1] The rate of return from investment in the underlying asset, $R_S$, on the other hand, is the sum of two components—the continuous rate of price appreciation $RA_S \equiv \ln(S_t/S_{t-1})$ and the income rate $i$. The relation between the random returns of the futures and its underlying asset is therefore

$$\tilde{R}_F = \tilde{R}_S - r \tag{5.5}$$

where tildes have been added to distinguish between what is uncertain (i.e., the returns on the futures and its underlying asset) from what is certain (i.e., the risk-free rate of interest).

### Expected Return-Risk Relation

With the return relation (5.5) in hand, the role of futures contracts within the CAPM is easily uncovered. To do so, first note the expected return on a futures contract equals the expected return on the underlying asset less the risk-free rate of interest, that is,

[1] The distinction also serves to combat the criticism that, since the futures involves no net investment, the rate of return on a futures is undefined.

$$E_F = E_S - r \tag{5.6}$$

Next, note that total risk (as measured by return variance or its square root, standard deviation) and market risk (as measured by beta) of the futures contract equal the total risk and the market risk of the underlying asset. The variance of futures return equals the variance of the asset return,[2]

$$\text{Var}(\tilde{R}_F) = \text{Var}(\tilde{R}_S - r) = \text{Var}(\tilde{R}_S) \tag{5.7}$$

and the beta of the futures contract equals the beta of the underlying asset,

$$\beta_F \equiv \frac{\text{Cov}(\tilde{R}_F, \tilde{R}_M)}{\text{Var}(\tilde{R}_M)} = \frac{\text{Cov}(\tilde{R}_S - r, \tilde{R}_M)}{\text{Var}(\tilde{R}_M)} = \frac{\text{Cov}(\tilde{R}_S, \tilde{R}_M)}{\text{Var}(\tilde{R}_M)} \equiv \beta_S \tag{5.8}$$

Hence, while the risks of the futures contract are the same as those of the underlying asset, the expected return of the futures is below the expected return of the underlying asset by an amount equal to the risk-free rate of interest.

Now let us move to the CAPM. In Chapter 3, we showed that the expected return of the asset is

$$E_S = r + (E_M - r)\beta_S \tag{5.9}$$

Substituting (5.6) and (5.8) into (5.9), we find that the expected return on the futures is

$$E_F = (E_M - r)\beta_F = (E_M - r)\beta_S \tag{5.10}$$

While on first appearance the relation (5.10) may seem perplexing, it makes a good deal sense intuitively. In buying the asset, we actually buy two things—the risk-free asset and a risk premium. We are entitled to the rate of return on the risk-free asset, $r$, because we have funds tied up in the asset, independent of its risk level. In addition, we are entitled to the risk premium associated with holding the asset, $(E_M - r)\beta_S$, because we have put our investment at risk. In buying the futures, we have accepted only the risk and, therefore, are entitled to receive only the risk premium, $(E_M - r)\beta_S$. With no funds tied up, we have no right to any risk-free return.

### Relation to Net Cost of Carry

In Chapter 4, we discussed the net cost of carry relation and its implications. We showed that being long the asset and short a futures meant that we were implicitly long risk-free bonds. Equations (5.9) and (5.10) confirm this result. Being

[2] The rules of expectation operators are provided in Appendix A: Elementary Statistics at the end of the book.

**TABLE 5.1** Perfect substitutes implied by the capital asset pricing model.

| Position 1 | | Position 2 |
|---|---|---|
| Buy asset/sell forward | = | Buy risk-free bonds (lend) |
| Buy risk-free bonds (lend)/buy forward | = | Buy asset |
| Buy asset/sell risk-free bonds (borrow) | = | Buy forward |
| Sell asset/buy forward | = | Sell risk-free bonds (borrow) |
| Sell risk-free bonds (borrow)/sell forward | = | Sell asset |
| Sell asset/buy risk-free bonds (lend) | = | Sell forward |

long the asset means that we expect rate of return $E_S$ and being short the futures means that we expect rate of return $E_F$. Thus the net portfolio return from being long the asset and short the futures equals the risk-free rate of interest,

$$E_S - E_F = r + (E_M - r)\beta_S - (E_M - r)\beta_S = r \tag{5.11}$$

The risk premium associated with buying the asset is exactly offset by the risk premium associated with selling the futures.

Just as in Chapter 4, we can pair up any two instruments to create the other. Suppose, for example, we buy risk-free bonds and buy a futures. The expected portfolio return is exactly equal to that of the underlying asset, that is,

$$r + E_F = r + (E_M - r)\beta_S = E_S \tag{5.12}$$

Table 5.1 summarizes all possible pairings, and is the counterpart to Table 4.5 in Chapter 4. The intuition is simple. Buying or selling a futures is the same as buying or selling a risk premium. Buying and selling an asset, on the other hand, means buying and selling a portfolio that consists of the risk-free asset and a risk premium. Note that, if the risk premium of the asset happens to equal zero, the expected rate of price change in the futures is zero.

### Futures as Predictor of Expected Asset Price

The relation between expected return and risk of the asset and the futures also provides us with insight regarding the relation between the current futures price and the expected asset price when the futures expires at time $T$. To see this, consider committing to buy the asset at time $T$. The present value of the expected asset price is

$$S = E(\tilde{S}_T)e^{-E_S T}$$

where $E_S$ is the asset's expected risk-adjusted rate of return.[3] On the other hand, consider committing to buy the asset at time $T$ by buying a futures contract

[3] Recall that in Chapter 3 we used the CAPM to arrive at this value.

today at price $F$. Since $F$ is paid at time $T$ and is certain, the present value of this obligation is $Fe^{-rT}$. Since both quantities represent the same thing—the present value of one unit of the commodity at time $T$—they should be equal in value. Thus, the current futures price may be written

$$F = E(\tilde{S}_T)e^{-(E_S - r)T} \tag{5.13}$$

The structure of (5.13) says that the difference between the futures price and the expected asset price is nonzero. This means that the futures price is a biased predictor of the expected asset price. If the risk premium is positive, as is usually the case, the futures price is a downward biased predictor. The only instance in which the futures price is an unbiased predictor of the expected future asset price is where the risk premium of the asset equals 0.

### Hedging Assets Using Futures Contracts

With the CAPM framework in hand, we can now turn to the exercise of managing the expected return and risk of a position in the asset underlying the futures contract. To do so, consider a portfolio that consists of one unit of the asset and futures contracts. Its expected rate of return is equal to

$$E_H = E_S - n_F E_F = (1 + n_F)E_S - n_F r \tag{5.14}$$

To find its total risk, recognize that the rate of return relation (5.5) implies that the futures return and the asset return are perfectly positively correlated, that is, $\rho_{SF} = +1$. This means that a portfolio that consists of one unit of the asset and $n_F$ futures contracts has a standard deviation (i.e., total risk) equal to

$$\sigma_H = |\sigma_S + n_F \sigma_F| = |(1 + n_F)\sigma_S| \tag{5.15}$$

Managing expected return and risk of the portfolio therefore amounts to selecting a value for $n_F$.

Figure 5.1 summarizes some obvious choices of $n_F$. To make matters as a clear as possible, we use numerical values for the expected return and risk parameters. Specifically, we assume that the expected return and risk of the asset are 12% and 20%, respectively, and the risk-free rate of interest is 4%. This means that the expected return and risk of the futures contract are 8% and 20%. Where $n_F = 0$, the portfolio is unhedged. We hold only the asset, and the portfolio has an expected return of 12% and a risk of 20%. Selling futures against the long position in the asset reduces expected return and risk. At $n_F = -0.5$, we are implicitly selling one futures contract for every two units of the asset we hold. The risk level of this portfolio is below the risk level of the asset so we have "hedged." This particular hedge portfolio has an expected return of $0.5E_S + 0.5r$ or 8% and a risk of $0.5\sigma_S$ or 10%. Where we set $n_F = -1$, the hedge portfolio has an expected return of 4% and no risk. Since this is the lowest risk level possible, this particular hedge portfolio is called the "risk-minimizing hedge."

**FIGURE 5.1** Relation between expected return and risk for portfolio consisting of one unit of asset and $n_F$ futures contracts.

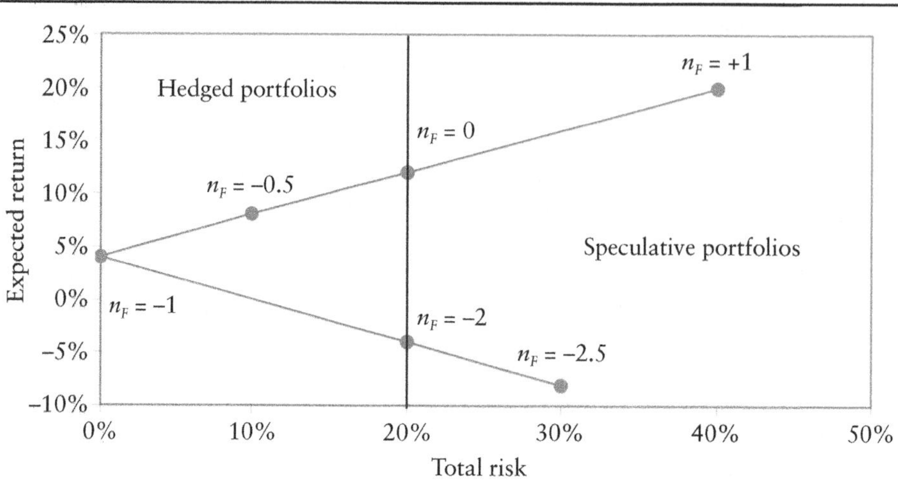


Note that, as we continue to sell more futures (i.e., $n_F < -1$), risk starts to increase, but, as long as $\sigma_H < \sigma_S$, we are hedging. Where $n_F < -2$, we are speculating in that the portfolio risk level exceeds the risk level of the asset held in isolation. The same applies where we buy futures (i.e., $n_F > 0$) rather than sell. Thus in Figure 5.1, where $-2 < n_F < 0$, we hold a hedged portfolio, and, where $n_F < -2$ and $n_F > 0$, we hold a speculative portfolio.

## HEDGING PRICE RISK

In general, identifying the set of viable hedge opportunities is more complicated than Figure 5.1 suggests. The reason is *basis risk*. Basis risk refers to the fact that the futures price movements and asset price movements are not perfectly correlated. To understand why, it is useful to think of basis risk as being the sum of two components, that is,

$$\text{Basis risk} = \text{Time basis risk} + \text{Grade basis risk} \tag{5.16}$$

*Time basis risk* refers to uncertainty in the difference between the futures price and the underlying asset price. In the first section, the time basis risk was equal to zero because we assumed the net cost of carry relation holds at all points in time. In order to arrive at that relation we assumed that markets are frictionless and that the risk-free rate of interest, $r$, and the income rate on the asset, $i$, are constant through time. As a practical matter, arbitrageurs incur trading costs, and short-term interest and income rates may have a modest amount of uncertainty. This means that the futures price movements and asset price movements will not be perfectly correlated, except in the special case where the length of the hedge horizon exactly matches the time to expiration of the futures and the convergence of the futures and asset prices is assured.

**FIGURE 5.2** Evolution of time and grade basis over the life of futures contract.

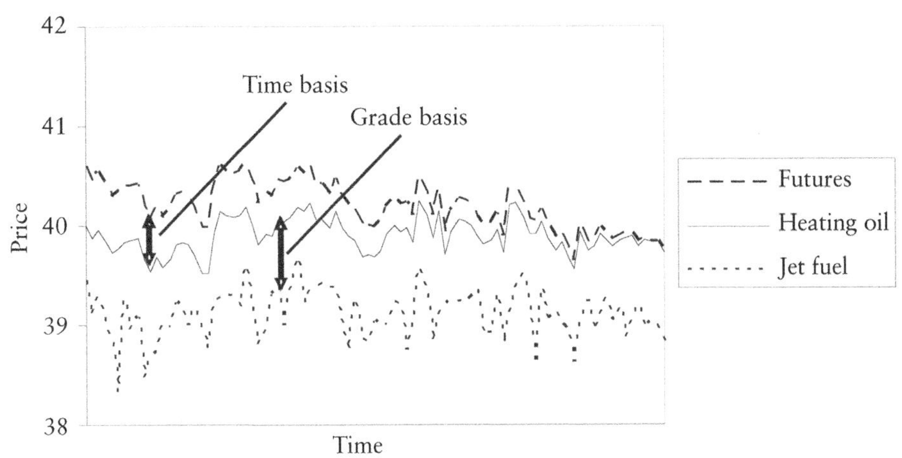


The second component is grade basis risk. Often we find situations in which futures contracts are not written on the asset whose price risk we want to manage. Many airlines, for example, want to hedge their jet fuel costs, however jet fuel futures contracts are not available. Fortunately, jet fuel and heating oil are very close substitutes, and heating oil futures can be used to cross-hedge. In this case, *grade basis risk* refers to the uncertainty in the difference between the price of heating oil and the price of jet fuel.[4] Figure 5.2 shows the evolution of time and grade basis over the life of the futures contract. The top line represents the heating oil futures prices, the middle line heating oil, and the bottom line jet fuel. The difference between the prices of the heating oil futures and heating oil is the time basis. As time passes, the time basis narrows. At expiration, the futures price equals the spot price of heating oil, and the time basis is zero. If the length of the hedging horizon is less than the life of the futures, a futures hedge must be unwound prior to expiration and time basis risk is incurred. The difference between the heating oil price and the jet fuel price (the lowest line) is the grade basis. It too varies through time. In this instance, however, convergence is not assured. Thus, in using heating oil futures to hedge the price of jet fuel, both time basis risk and grade basis risk are incurred. We now develop a framework for handling such a price risk management problem.

## Minimize Price Risk

To make the development of a price risk-minimizing hedge as an intuitive as possible, let us use the example of an airline that wants to minimize the price risk of jet fuel that it needs at time *T*. Assume, for the sake of simplicity, that the

[4] The term "grade" arose in the agricultural futures market. The wheat futures contract traded on the Chicago Board of Trade, for example, allows the short futures to deliver different "grades" of wheat.

airline has no ability to store jet fuel—it buys jet fuel as it is needed at the market price. Assume also that we are considering a single refueling at time $T$. The jet fuel price at time $T$ is denoted $\tilde{S}_T$. The current heating oil futures price is denoted $F$, and its price at time $T$ is denoted $\tilde{F}_T$. Assuming the airline buys $n_F$ futures contracts, its net cost of jet fuel at time $T$ is

$$\tilde{C}_T = \tilde{S}_T + n_F(\tilde{F}_T - F) \tag{5.17}$$

Naturally, where $n_F = 0$, the airline pays the market price for fuel at time $T$.

To find the risk-minimizing hedge, use (5.17) to help write the variance of the hedged cost of fuel, that is,

$$\begin{aligned} \text{Var}(\tilde{C}_T) &= \text{Var}(\tilde{S}_T + n_F\tilde{F}_T) \\ &= \text{Var}(\tilde{S}_T) + n_F^2\text{Var}(\tilde{F}_T) + 2n_F\text{Cov}(\tilde{S}_T, \tilde{F}_T) \end{aligned} \tag{5.18}$$

where $\text{Var}(\tilde{S}_T)$ and $\text{Var}(\tilde{F}_T)$ are the variances of the asset and futures prices, respectively, and $\text{Cov}(\tilde{S}_T, \tilde{F}_T)$ is the covariance of the asset and futures prices. To find the number of futures contracts necessary to minimize $\text{Var}(\tilde{C}_T)$, $n_F^*$, we take the derivative of (5.18) with respect to $n_F$, and set it equal to zero, that is,

$$\frac{d\text{Var}(\tilde{C}_T)}{dn_F} = 2n_F^*\text{Var}(\tilde{F}_T) + 2\text{Cov}(\tilde{S}_T, \tilde{F}_T) = 0 \tag{5.19}$$

Rearranging, we find that the risk-minimizing hedge is

$$n_F^* = -\frac{\text{Cov}(\tilde{S}_T, \tilde{F}_T)}{\text{Var}(\tilde{F}_T)} = -\rho(\tilde{S}_T, \tilde{F}_T)\frac{\sqrt{\text{Var}(\tilde{S}_T)}}{\sqrt{\text{Var}(\tilde{F}_T)}} \tag{5.20}$$

where $\rho(\tilde{S}_T, \tilde{F}_T)$ or, simply $\rho$, is the correlation between the asset and futures prices.

The "optimal" hedge, $n_F^*$, as shown by the expression (5.20), is interesting in a number of respects. First, and foremost, $n_F^*$ is negative since the variances are positive by definition and the correlation between the asset and futures prices is, presumably, positive. This means that, if the hedger is long the asset, he needs to sell futures, and vice versa. Second, if the futures is written on the specific asset being hedged, and the futures expires at the end of the hedge period, the end-of-period prices must be equal $\tilde{F}_T = \tilde{S}_T$. This implies that the variances of the asset and futures prices are equal, $\text{Var}(\tilde{S}_T) = \text{Var}(\tilde{F}_T)$, and that the correlation between the asset and futures prices is one, $\rho = +1$. The risk-minimizing futures hedge is therefore a one-to-one hedge against the asset, that is,

$$n_F^* = -\rho\frac{\sqrt{\text{Var}(\tilde{S}_T)}}{\sqrt{\text{Var}(\tilde{F}_T)}} = -\frac{\sqrt{\text{Var}(\tilde{S}_T)}}{\sqrt{\text{Var}(\tilde{F}_T)}} = -1$$

Third, the effectiveness of the hedge depends upon the correlation between the asset and futures prices. If $\rho = +1$, the hedge is perfect, and the optimal hedge is to sell one futures contract. If $\rho = -1$, the hedge is also perfect, and the optimal hedge is to buy one futures contract. If $-1 < \rho < +1$, the hedge will not be fully effective, with the effectiveness decreasing as the correlation approaches 0. At $\rho = 0$, the asset and futures prices are independent, so there is no point in taking a futures position.

### Estimating Variance/Covariance

Before applying the risk-minimizing hedge framework, we need to discuss how to estimate the variance and covariance expressions in (5.20). In deriving the risk-minimizing hedge, we formulated the problem as a one-period hedge, from time 0 to time $T$. The length of the hedge period is arbitrary. For the sake of illustration, assume its $T$ days. Now let us consider the variance of the asset price, $\text{Var}(\tilde{S}_T)$. Over the hedge horizon, we will observe a sequence of asset prices $S, \tilde{S}_1, \tilde{S}_2, \ldots, \tilde{S}_T$. To see how $\text{Var}(\tilde{S}_T)$ can be expressed in terms of the price sequence, note that

$$\text{Var}(\tilde{S}_T) = \text{Var}(\tilde{S}_T - S_0) = \text{Var}\left(\sum_{t=1}^{T} \tilde{S}_t - \tilde{S}_{t-1}\right) = \text{Var}\sum_{t=1}^{T} \Delta\tilde{S}_t \tag{5.21}$$

where $\Delta\tilde{S}_t = \tilde{S}_t - \tilde{S}_{t-1}$. Assuming that price changes are independent and identically distributed (i.i.d.), the variance of the end-of-period asset price is simply $T$ times the daily variance of the asset price change, that is,

$$\text{Var}(\tilde{S}_T) = T\text{Var}(\Delta\tilde{S}) \tag{5.22}$$

By the same logic, the variance the end-of-period futures price is

$$\text{Var}(\tilde{F}_T) = T\text{Var}(\Delta\tilde{F}) \tag{5.23}$$

and the covariance of the end-of-period asset price and futures price is

$$\text{Cov}(\tilde{S}_T, \tilde{F}_T) = T\text{Cov}(\Delta\tilde{S}, \Delta\tilde{F}) \tag{5.24}$$

Thus, the risk-minimizing hedge over the interval from 0 to $T$ (5.20) can be rewritten in terms of daily price changes

$$\begin{aligned} n_F^* &= -\frac{\text{Cov}(\tilde{S}_T, \tilde{F}_T)}{\text{Var}(\tilde{F}_T)} = -\frac{T\text{Cov}(\Delta\tilde{S}, \Delta\tilde{F})}{T\text{Var}(\Delta\tilde{F})} \\ &= -\frac{\text{Cov}(\Delta\tilde{S}, \Delta\tilde{F})}{\text{Var}(\Delta\tilde{F})} = -\rho_{\Delta S, \Delta F}\frac{\sigma_{\Delta S}}{\sigma_{\Delta F}} \end{aligned} \tag{5.25}$$

In the hedge illustrations developed through this chapter, we take advantage of this property.

### Setting Risk-Minimizing Hedge

We now show how to apply the risk-minimizing hedge framework. Assume that the airline needs 150,000 gallons of jet fuel in exactly 30 days and that it wants to minimize the variance of the cost of acquiring the fuel. Assume also that the airline has no ability to store jet fuel. Setting a risk-minimizing hedge has four steps.

**Step 1: Identify Appropriate Futures Contract** Choosing the appropriate futures contract involves at least two factors. First, the higher is the correlation between the futures price and the fuel price, the more effective is the hedge. Ideally this means using a jet fuel futures contract to hedge, if one is available. In this way, only time basis risk is incurred. As noted earlier, however, futures contracts on jet fuel are not traded. The closest substitute is heating oil futures. Second, given heating oil futures listed on the New York Mercantile Exchange (NYMEX)[5] have 18 different contract maturities, how do we choose among available contracts? The tradeoff here is contract liquidity versus the cost of "rolling" the futures position. In general, nearby contracts are the most liquid and, hence, have the lowest trading costs. Unfortunately, however, the nearest available contract may expire before the hedge horizon is complete, in which case we must roll into the next available maturity (i.e., the nearby futures position is closed and a second nearby futures position is entered). Given that the hedge horizon is only 30 days in our illustration, using the heating oil futures contract that expires just after the hedge horizon is compete probably makes the most sense.

**Step 2: Collect Historical Prices** With the futures contract selected, we must now estimate the standard deviations and correlation of the daily price changes on the right-hand side of (5.25). Note that, within the hedge framework, these values are expected *future* standard deviations and correlation. Since we have no means of observing these parameters, we usually rely on historical time-series data to develop estimates. For the problem at hand, we will have to collect historical time series data for the jet fuel and the heating oil futures contract. These data are provided in the Excel file, **Jet fuel.xls**.

**Step 3: Estimate Standard Deviation and Correlation Parameters** With the data in hand, we now compute the standard deviation of the jet fuel price change, the standard deviation of the heating oil futures contract price change, and the correlation between the price changes of jet fuel and the heating oil futures. The estimator of the standard deviation of the historical asset price change series is

$$\hat{\sigma}_{\Delta S} = \sqrt{\frac{1}{T-1}\sum_{t=1}^{T}(\Delta S_t - \overline{\Delta S})^2} \tag{5.26}$$

where the symbol "^" indicates a specific estimate based on a sample of prices and $T$ is the number of historical prices in the time series ($t = 1, \ldots, T$).[6] The

[5] The NYMEX is the dominant exchange in the U.S. listing futures contracts on petroleum and petroleum products.

[6] These formulas are taken from the review of elementary statistics provided in Appendix A of this book.

standard deviation of the historical future price change series is similar. The estimator of the correlation between two historical price change series of the asset and the futures is

$$\hat{\rho}_{\Delta S, \Delta F} = \frac{\sqrt{\sum_{t=1}^{T} (\Delta S_t - \overline{\Delta S})(\Delta F_t - \overline{\Delta F})}}{\sqrt{\sum_{t=1}^{T} (\Delta S_t - \overline{\Delta S})^2 \sum_{t=1}^{T} (\Delta F_t - \overline{\Delta F})^2}} \tag{5.27}$$

The estimates are: $\hat{\sigma}_{\Delta S} = 0.0422$, $\hat{\sigma}_{\Delta F} = 0.0357$, and $\hat{\rho}_{\Delta S, \Delta F} = 0.9320$.

**Step 4: Compute the Risk-Minimizing Hedge** The fourth and final step is to compute the optimal number of futures, which is done using (5.25), that is,

$$n_F^* = -\frac{0.9320(0.0422)}{0.0357} = -1.0997$$

The negative sign implies that we sell futures to create the risk-minimizing hedge. The optimal number of futures to sell is –1.0997 gallons for each gallon of jet fuel. Figure 5.3 shows the effect that changing the number of futures has on the standard deviation of cost per gallon.

Once the optimal hedge ratio is determined, finding the number of futures contracts to use is a matter of multiplying the hedge ratio by the quantity

**FIGURE 5.3** Relation between the number of futures contracts held (+ long; – short) and the risk (standard deviation) of hedged jet fuel cost. (Parameters: $\hat{\sigma}_{\Delta S} = 0.0422$, $\hat{\sigma}_{\Delta F} = 0.0357$, and $\hat{\rho}_{\Delta S, \Delta F} \rho_{\Delta S, \Delta F} = 0.9320$.)

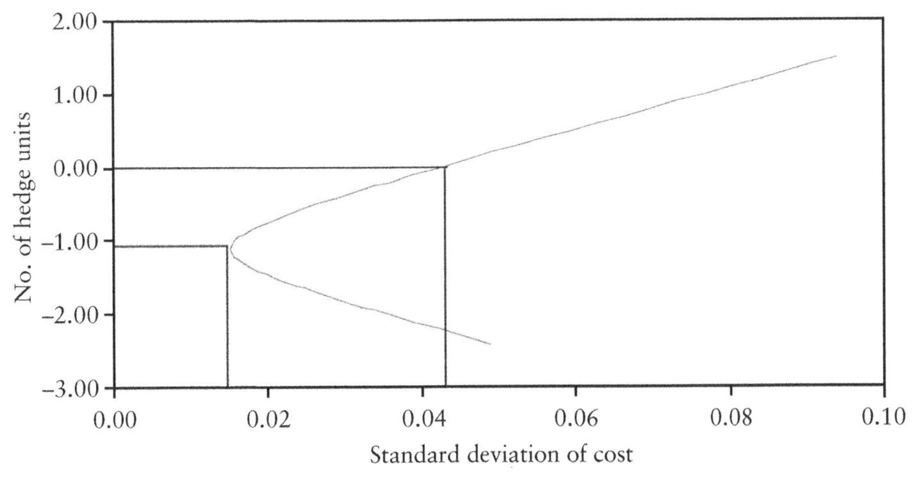

demanded and dividing by the futures contract denomination. A single heating oil futures has a 42,000 gallon denomination, so the number of futures to sell is

$$1.997\left(\frac{150{,}000}{42{,}000}\right) = 3.928$$

In practice, we would also "tail the hedge" by multiplying 3.928 by the discount factor $e^{-r(30/365)}$. One each subsequent day, the number of contracts would be increased a a factor of $e^{r(1/365)}$. For expositional convenience, we ignore this practice of tailing the hedge through the remainder of the chapter.

### Relation to OLS Regression

*Ordinary least squares* (OLS) regression offers a convenient direct means of estimating the risk-minimizing hedge. Once the necessary time-series price data ($t$ = 1, . . ., $T$) are collected, run the regression,

$$\Delta\tilde{S}_t = \alpha_0 + \alpha_1 \Delta\tilde{F}_T + \tilde{\varepsilon}_t \tag{5.28}$$

As it turns out, the value of the regression coefficient $\alpha_1$ under OLS regression is defined as[7]

$$\alpha_1 = \frac{\text{Cov}(\Delta\tilde{S}, \Delta\tilde{F})}{\text{Var}(\Delta\tilde{S})} \tag{5.29}$$

Thus the risk-minimizing number of futures contracts may be written as a function of the estimated slope coefficient, that is,

$$n_F^* = -\alpha_1 \tag{5.30}$$

Aside from eliminating the need to estimate directly the individual standard deviations and correlation in (5.25), the OLS regression's adjusted $R$-squared provides a measure of hedging effectiveness. The risk of the unhedged asset price risk is $\text{Var}(\tilde{S}_T)$. Of this amount, selling $\alpha_1$ futures explains $\alpha_1^2\text{Var}(\tilde{F}_T)$. The adjusted $R$-squared therefore tells us the percent of the total unhedged asset price change risk that is hedgable risk,

$$\begin{aligned}\bar{R}^2 &= \frac{\alpha_1^2\text{Var}(\tilde{F}_T)}{\text{Var}(\tilde{S}_T)} = \frac{\text{Hedgable risk}}{\text{Unhedged risk}} \\ &= 1 - \frac{\text{Var}(\tilde{\varepsilon}_T)}{\text{Var}(\tilde{S}_T)} = 1 - \frac{\text{Unhedgable risk}}{\text{Unhedged risk}}\end{aligned} \tag{5.31}$$

[7] See OLS regression review is Appendix B of this book.

An adjusted $R$-squared of 100% means that the asset price risk is fully hedgable, while an adjusted $R$-squared of 0% says that there is no point in hedging.

To verify that the ordinary least squares regression approach produces the same risk-minimizing hedge, apply the OPTVAL Library function,

OV_STAT_OLS_SIMPLE($y$, $x$, *intercept*, *out*)

where $y$ is the vector of jet fuel prices, $x$ is the vector of heating oil futures prices, *intercept* is an indicator variable whose value is "Y" is the regression includes an intercept term and is "N" is the intercept term is being suppressed, and *out* is an indicator variable instructing the function to display the results horizontally ("H" or "h") or vertically ("V" or "v"). This function returns a horizontal array of output of length 5. The array contains the estimate of the intercept terms, its standard error, the estimate of the slope coefficient, its standard error, and the adjusted R-squared. When calling this function, we must highlight five contiguous cells, enter the relevant data, and then press the Shift, Ctrl, and Enter keys simultaneously. The panel below demonstrates.

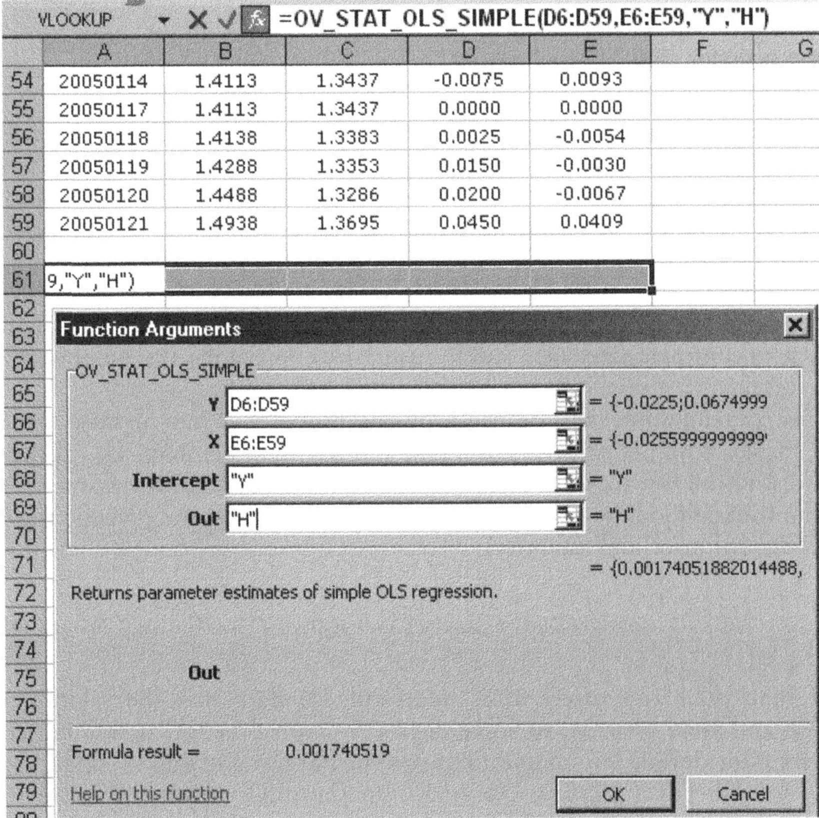


The estimated slope coefficient is 1.0997, exactly as before.

| Criterion | $\hat{\alpha}_0$ | $s(\hat{\alpha}_0)$ | $\hat{\alpha}_1$ | $s(\hat{\alpha}_1)$ | $\bar{R}^2$ |
|---|---|---|---|---|---|
| Minimize price risk | 0.0017 | 0.0021 | 1.0997 | 0.0593 | 0.8686 |

The focus on price changes (and returns) rather than prices in risk management becomes the norm from this point forward. Where the underlying asset is a physical asset or commodity like grain, we assume that price changes are independent and identically distributed (i.i.d.) through time. The reason is that most commodity prices tend to be mean-reverting. The reason is simple. If the price of a commodity becomes too low, producers of the commodity will slow or stop production, inventories will become depleted, and prices will rise. If the price of a commodity becomes too high, consumers will cut back on demand, and prices will fall. The prices of financial assets, however, are different. Consider a common stock. The company engages in a particular type of business activity and generates cash flow. This cash flow is used to expand operations, and the expanded operations generate proportionately more cash. For such an asset, price, it is more reasonable to assume that price is expected to grow at a constant rate and to have a constant variance rate. To model such behavior, it is most common to assume that the difference in the natural logarithm of asset prices or continuous returns (i.e., $\ln(S_t) - \ln(S_{t-1}) = \ln(S_t/S_{t-1}) = R_t$) are independent and identically distributed (i.i.d.) through time.

## HEDGING REVENUE RISK

The apparatus for managing price risk is the same independent of whether we are managing the risk of costs or income. A corn farmer, for example, may want to hedge the price at which he will sell his crop when he harvests in the fall. To identify the risk-minimizing hedge, he can run a regression of the price per bushel of the grade of corn that he has planted on the price per bushel of a corn futures contract.[8] He would then multiply the estimated slope coefficient (i.e., the risk-minimizing hedge per bushel) by his planned harvest size and divide by the futures contracts size (i.e., 5,000 bushels) to determine the number of contracts to sell.

This oversimplifies the farmer's problem, however. When he seeds his fields in the spring, both the price of corn, $\tilde{S}_T$, and the yield per acre, $\tilde{n}_T$, at the time of harvest in the fall are unknown. What is more germane to the farmer is revenue. In all likelihood, he is more interested in minimizing the revenue risk (i.e., the product of price and quantity),

$$\text{Var}(\tilde{R}_T) = \text{Var}(\tilde{n}_T\tilde{S}_T + n_F\tilde{F}_T) \tag{5.32}$$

rather than price risk alone. It is interesting to note that the relation price between and yield provide, to some degree, a *natural* hedge. If weather conditions are poor during the summer months, the harvest size will be small and the price per bushel will likely to be high. On the other hand, the fall brings a

[8] The corn futures contract traded at the Chicago Board of Trade calls for the delivery of No. 2 yellow corn at par, No. 1 yellow corn at 1½ cents per bushel over the contract price, or No. 3 yellow at 1½ cents per bushel under the contract price. Assuming the farmer has planted yet a different grade, he incurs both time and grade basis risk.

bumper crop, prices are likely to be low. The negative correlation between price and quantity tends to reduce the level of revenue risk, holding other factors constant.

Whether the correlation is negative or positive is irrelevant in estimating the revenue risk-minimizing hedge. To find the revenue risk-minimizing hedge, we simply replace the dependent variable in regression (5.28). In place of using the price change of corn, we use the change in revenue per acre.

**ILLUSTRATION 5.1** Hedging price risk versus revenue risk.

*Consider the case of a farmer who has just planted his 10,000 acres of land with wheat. Compare the number of futures contracts to sell if he decides to minimize revenue risk rather than price risk. The Excel file,* **Wheat.xls**, *contains historical data over the past 30 years. For the price risk-minimizing hedge, assume the farmer anticipates harvesting 60 bushels per acre.*

The first step is to summarize the data, and compute revenue per acre. The figures are shown in the table below. The average wheat price at harvest over the past 30 years was $3.00 per bushel, and the average yield per acre was 60 bushels. The "Revenue per acre" column with the subheading "Constant yield" is simply the harvest price times 60 bushels per acre (e.g., 2.469 × 60 = 148.15 per acre), and the "Revenue per acre" column with the subheading "Varying" is the harvest price times yield per acre in that year (e.g., 2.469 × 68.39 = 168.86 per acre).

| | | | | Revenue per Acre | | Change in Revenue per Acre | | |
|---|---|---|---|---|---|---|---|---|
| Month | Spot Price | Futures Price | Yield | Constant Yield | Varying Yield | Constant Yield | Varying Yield | Futures Price Change |
| 1 | 2.469 | 2.448 | 68.39 | 148.15 | 168.86 | | | |
| 2 | 2.664 | 2.638 | 64.76 | 159.82 | 172.50 | 11.67 | 3.64 | 0.191 |
| 3 | 2.176 | 2.123 | 70.32 | 130.56 | 153.02 | –29.26 | –19.48 | –0.515 |
| 4 | 2.481 | 2.501 | 69.08 | 148.88 | 171.41 | 18.32 | 18.40 | 0.378 |
| 5 | 2.737 | 2.686 | 65.20 | 164.24 | 178.47 | 15.36 | 7.06 | 0.185 |
| ... | ... | ... | ... | ... | ... | ... | ... | ... |
| 26 | 3.493 | 3.667 | 57.66 | 209.61 | 201.42 | 0.93 | 41.24 | –0.260 |
| 27 | 3.700 | 3.620 | 50.52 | 222.00 | 186.91 | 12.40 | –14.51 | –0.047 |
| 28 | 4.065 | 4.054 | 45.29 | 243.88 | 184.11 | 21.88 | –2.80 | 0.434 |
| 29 | 3.833 | 4.054 | 50.68 | 230.00 | 194.26 | –13.88 | 10.15 | 0.000 |
| 30 | 3.298 | 3.722 | 53.68 | 197.88 | 177.02 | –32.12 | –17.23 | –0.332 |
| Mean | 3.000 | 3.017 | 60.00 | 180.00 | 176.61 | 1.71 | 0.28 | |
| StDev | 0.480 | 0.557 | 7.887 | 28.77 | 11.00 | 17.70 | 15.20 | |

To find the price risk-minimizing hedge, we regress the "Change in revenue per acre—Constant yield" column on the "Futures price change" column, and, to find the revenue risk-minimizing hedge we regress the "Change in revenue per acre—Varying yield" column on the "Futures price change" column. The estimated slope coefficients, $\hat{\alpha}_1$, in the regressions are the number of bushels of wheat that need to be sold using the futures contract. The regression results are as follows:

| Criterion | $\hat{\alpha}_0$ | $s(\hat{\alpha}_0)$ | $\hat{\alpha}_1$ | $s(\hat{\alpha}_1)$ | $\bar{R}^2$ |
|---|---|---|---|---|---|
| Minimize price risk | −0.2765 | 1.7110 | 45.3321 | 5.1264 | 0.7433 |
| Minimize revenue risk | 0.1242 | 2.8909 | 3.5806 | 8.6616 | 0.0063 |

The regression results reveal that the two hedges are quite different from each other. If the farmer chooses to minimize price risk, he needs to sell 45.3321 bushels in futures per acre of land. With 10,000 acres, this means a total of 453,321 bushels. The wheat futures contracts traded on the Chicago Board of Trade have a denomination of 5,000 bushels, so a total of 90.664 contracts should be sold. On the other hand, if the farmer chooses to minimize revenue risk, he needs to sell only 3.5806 bushels per acre, or 7.161 futures contracts. Fewer contracts are required in the revenue risk-minimizing hedge because price and yield per care are inversely related. This negative correlation manifests itself in risk exposure. In the above table, the standard deviation of the revenue change with the fixed 60 bushels per acre (i.e., price risk) is 17.70, while the standard deviation of revenue change with varying yield (i.e., revenue risk) is 15.20. Because price and quantity are inversely related, the amount of risk that needs to be managed is less.

## HEDGING MARGIN RISK

Another type of risk that may be faced by a processor or producer is gross processing margin risk. *Gross processing margin* refers to the difference between total revenue from production and the total costs of production, that is,

$$\tilde{M}_T = \tilde{n}_O \tilde{S}_{O,T} - n_I \tilde{S}_{I,T} - \text{Fixed costs} \tag{5.33}$$

where $n_{O,T}$ is the quantity demanded at time $T$ when output price is $S_{O,T}$ per unit, $n_I$ is the number of input units required for production, and $\tilde{S}_{I,T}$ is input cost per unit.[9] Consider an oil refiner, for example. In the normal course of production, he buys crude oil, distills it, and sells heating oil and unleaded gasoline. If he is planning for production that will occur at time $T$, he faces both revenue and price risk. The revenue risk arises because the refiner knows neither the market price per gallon of product (e.g., unleaded gasoline) at time $T$ nor the number of gallons that will be demanded. The price risk arises because the price per barrel of crude oil at time $T$ will depend on supply and demand conditions at that time. Thus the refiner's risk management problem may be to minimize the variance of his margin risk,

$$\text{Var}(\tilde{n}_O \tilde{S}_{O,T} - n_I \tilde{S}_{I,T} + n_F \tilde{F}_T) \tag{5.34}$$

Like in the previous examples, this can be accomplished by regressing the change in the gross processing margin on the futures price change. The slope coefficient estimate realized from the regression in the risk-minimizing number of futures. It is

[9] We assume that production takes place instantaneously (i.e., products are produced as quickly as the inputs are acquired), and that unsold production cannot be carried over from one period to the next. Naturally, both of these assumptions can be relaxed.

important to recognize that, like a revenue hedge, a margin hedge implicitly accounts for the fact that input costs and output prices may be strongly correlated. Such a natural hedge reduces the number of necessary futures contracts.

**ILLUSTRATION 5.2** Hedging margin risk.

*Consider the case of a gold watch manufacturing firm. Over the past 67 months, they have produced and sold an average of 6,274 gold watches per month at an average sales price of $3,727. Month-by-month sales statistics are included in* ***Watch manufacturer.xls.*** *The key input cost of each watch is gold, and its price is uncertain from month to month. All the firm knows is that it takes four Troy ounces of gold to manufacture each watch. Their fixed monthly costs are $5,000,000. Find the optimal number of futures contract to enter to minimize the variance of the firm's end-of-month profit margin. Also, compute the minimum revenue risk and minimum cost risk hedges. The denomination of the gold futures contract is 100 Troy ounces.*

The data file contains a history of sales prices and quantity sold together with prices of gold and gold futures over a 67-month period. The format is as follows:

| | | Gold Watch Production | | | | |
|---|---|---|---|---|---|---|
| Month | Gold | Price | Quantity | Revenue | Gold Cost | Margin |
| 19990101 | 287.75 | 3,444.45 | 6,534 | 22,504,718 | −7,520,201 | 9,984,517 |
| 19990201 | 287.65 | 3,467.84 | 6,511 | 22,578,920 | −7,491,500 | 10,087,419 |
| 19990301 | 285.85 | 3,455.90 | 6,546 | 22,623,962 | −7,485,246 | 10,138,716 |
| 19990401 | 280.45 | 3,381.07 | 6,600 | 22,316,724 | −7,404,423 | 9,912,301 |
| ... | ... | ... | ... | ... | ... | ... |

| | | Changes in | | | |
|---|---|---|---|---|---|
| Month | Gold | Revenue | Gold Cost | Margin | Futures |
| 19990101 | 287.75 | | | | |
| 19990201 | 287.65 | 74,202 | 28,701 | 102,903 | −2.21 |
| 19990301 | 285.85 | 45,042 | 6,255 | 51,297 | −3.45 |
| 19990401 | 280.45 | −307,238 | 80,823 | −226,416 | −4.93 |
| ... | ... | ... | ... | ... | ... |

The column headings are largely self-explanatory. Revenue equals the watch price times the quantity of watches sold. The cost of the gold used in each watch is the spot price of gold per ounce times four ounces times the quantity of watches produced. The margin equals the revenue less the variable costs less the $5,000,000 in fixed costs. The final four columns are the monthly changes in each of the variables.

Based on the information in the file, you regress (a) revenue change on the futures price change, (b) cost change on the futures price change, and (c) margin change on the futures price change. The results are summarized in the table below. The estimated slope coefficients, $\hat{\alpha}_1$, are the number of ounces of futures contracts that you should sell to hedge the effects of the gold price. Recall that the gold futures contract denomination is 100 ounces, so these figures need to be divided by 100.

| Criterion | $\hat{\alpha}_0$ | $s(\hat{\alpha}_0)$ | $\hat{\alpha}_1$ | $s(\hat{\alpha}_1)$ | $\bar{R}^2$ |
|---|---|---|---|---|---|
| Minimize revenue risk | 19,314 | 28,729 | 24,462 | 2,028 | 0.6944 |
| Minimize price risk | –5,705 | 9,484 | –8,617 | 670 | 0.7213 |
| Minimize margin risk | 13,609 | 22,173 | 15,845 | 1,565 | 0.6155 |

To minimize the effect that gold price uncertainty has on revenue, you should sell 244.62 gold futures contracts. To minimize the effect that gold price uncertainty has on input costs, you should buy 86.17 contracts. Finally, to minimize the effect that gold price uncertainty has on profit margin, you should sell 158.45 gold futures. Note that the revenue risk hedge less the price risk hedge equals the margin hedge, 24,462 – 8,617 = 15,845. Apparently, the firm is able to pass along some the change in gold input cost by changing the price of its watches.

## HEDGING PORTFOLIO VALUE

Up to this point in the chapter, we have looked at expected return/risk management of commodity price risk exposures embedded within operating costs, revenue, and gross margin. The next series of applications focus on managing the risk of financial assets. Suppose that we hold a portfolio of AAA-rated corporate bonds, for example, and know that there will be a major announcement by the Federal Reserve next week. Given the impending announcement, we would like to hedge our long-term interest rate risk exposure. One possible action is to liquidate our bond position. This action may be expensive, however, because the bond markets are not particularly liquid and trading costs are high. Another is to hedge the portfolio value using long-term interest rate futures contracts. Such markets are very liquid and trading costs are low. This section examines the expected return/risk management of a portfolio of securities where security value has only one source of underlying financial uncertainty (e.g., long-term interest rate risk, stock market risk, or currency risk).

To begin, we assume that the fund manager's objective function is to minimize the variance of the value of his portfolio over a single period ending at time $T$. The expression that we use for portfolio value risk is

$$\text{Var}(\tilde{V}_T + n_F\tilde{F}_T) \tag{5.35}$$

where $V_T$ is the sum of the market values of all securities in the portfolio at time $T$, and $F_T$ is the price of the futures contract most closely tied to the portfolio's underlying source of risk (e.g., if $V_T$ is a well-diversified portfolio of stocks, $F_T$ would be a stock index futures contract).

Like in the previous risk-management problems of this chapter, we will focus initially on determining the risk-minimizing hedge. This approach to solving the problem needs to be modified slightly. The reason is that financial assets, unlike commodities, tend to grow in value through time. Consider a stock index portfolio, for example. Contributing to the growth in the value of this portfolio is the fact that not only do the individual stocks in the portfolio have prices that are expected to grow through time, but also any stocks that pay dividends will have those dividends reinvested in more shares of the stock portfolio. To manage this rate growth over the hedge horizon, we focus the natural logarithm of the portfolio value instead of the value itself. The sequence of the values over the hedge horizon is $\ln V, \ln \tilde{V}_1, \ln \tilde{V}_2, \ldots, \ln \tilde{V}_T$. Note that the end-of-hedge-period $\text{Var}(\ln \tilde{V}_T)$ can be expressed in terms of the day to day values through time, that is,

$$\begin{aligned}\text{Var}(\ln \tilde{V}_T) &= \text{Var}(\ln \tilde{V}_T - \ln V_0) \\ &= \text{Var}\left(\sum_{t=1}^{T} \ln \tilde{V}_t - \ln \tilde{V}_{t-1}\right) = \text{Var}\left(\sum_{t=1}^{T} \tilde{R}_{V,t}\right)\end{aligned} \tag{5.36}$$

where $\tilde{R}_{V,t} = \ln(\tilde{V}_t/\tilde{V}_{t-1})$ is the continuously compounded return on the portfolio. Assuming that returns are independent and identically distributed (i.i.d.), the variance of the end-of-period portfolio value is simply $T$ times the daily variance of the asset price change, that is,

$$\text{Var}(\ln \tilde{V}_T) = T\text{Var}(\tilde{R}_V) \tag{5.37}$$

By the same logic, the variance the end-of-period futures price is

$$\text{Var}(\ln \tilde{F}_T) = T\text{Var}(\tilde{R}_F) \tag{5.38}$$

and the covariance of the end-of-period asset price and futures price is

$$\text{Cov}(\ln \tilde{V}_T, \ln \tilde{F}_T) = T\text{Cov}(\tilde{R}_V, \tilde{R}_F) \tag{5.39}$$

Thus the risk-minimizing hedge over the interval from 0 to $T$ (5.20) can be rewritten in terms of daily price changes

$$\begin{aligned}n_F^* &= -\frac{\text{Cov}(\ln \tilde{V}_T, \ln \tilde{F}_T)}{\text{Var}(\ln \tilde{F}_T)} = -\frac{T\text{Cov}(\tilde{R}_V, \tilde{R}_F)}{T\text{Var}(\tilde{R}_F)} \\ &= -\frac{\text{Cov}(\tilde{R}_V, \tilde{R}_F)}{\text{Var}(\tilde{R}_F)} = -\rho_{V,F}\left(\frac{\sigma_V}{\sigma_F}\right)\end{aligned} \tag{5.40}$$

where $\sigma_V$ and $\sigma_F$ are the standard deviations of the continuously compounded returns of the portfolio and the futures, and $\rho_{V,F}$ is the correlation between the rates of return of the portfolio and the futures.

Just as was the case in the earlier risk-minimizing hedge problems, the number of futures contracts to sell can be determined by OLS regression. Consider the relation between the portfolio value and the futures at the end of the hedge period standing today, that is,

$$\ln \tilde{V}_T = \alpha_0 + \alpha_1 \ln \tilde{F}_T + \tilde{\varepsilon}_T \tag{5.41}$$

The slope coefficient in this relation, $\alpha_1$, is a price elasticity. It gives us the percentage change in the value of the portfolio for a given percentage change in the futures price. To hedge, however, we need to know *dV/dF*, that is, the change in the dollar value of the portfolio associated with a change in the futures price. In this way, we can sell exactly *dV/dF* futures contracts so that, if something unexpected happens and the value of the portfolio (and futures price) changes, the overall portfolio value change is zero, that is,

$$dV - n_F dF = dV - \left(\frac{dV}{dF}\right) dF = 0 \tag{5.42}$$

But the regression relation (5.41) provides only

$$\frac{d\ln V}{d\ln F} = \alpha_1$$

How can we get *dV/dF*? The answer in the chain rule:

$$\frac{dV}{dF} = \frac{dV}{d\ln V} \times \frac{d\ln V}{d\ln F} \times \frac{d\ln F}{dF} = V \times \alpha_1 \times \frac{1}{F} = \alpha_1\left(\frac{V}{F}\right) \tag{5.43}$$

We simply scale the regression coefficient $\alpha_1$ by the ratio of the portfolio value to the value of a single futures contract.

To estimate $\alpha_1$, we rely on the differenced form of (5.41), that is, the regression,

$$R_{V,t} = \alpha_0' + \alpha_1 R_{F,t} + \varepsilon_t' \tag{5.44}$$

where $\tilde{R}_{V,t} = \ln(\tilde{V}_t/\tilde{V}_{t-1})$ and $\tilde{R}_{F,t} = \ln(\tilde{F}_t/\tilde{F}_{t-1})$. We do this because the returns of the portfolio and the futures, $\tilde{R}_{V,t}$ and $\tilde{R}_{F,t}$, as well as the error term in the regression, $\varepsilon_t'$, are assumed to be i.i.d. While the intercept term in (5.44) is not the same as the intercept term in (5.41), the slope coefficient (and, hence, the hedge ratio) is identical.

**ILLUSTRATION 5.3** Hedging value.

*Consider the case of a life insurance company that holds a large portfolio of AAA-rated corporate bonds. Its daily values for the period January 1, 2004 through February 16, 2005 are reported in* ***Life insurance.xls****. Based on these values, the natural logarithm of value and portfolio return are computed. Also included in the file are the continuously-compounded returns of the Chicago Board of Trade's (CBT's) Treasury bond futures contract. The current (2/16/05) T-bond futures price is 1.1525 per dollar of face value, and the T-bond futures contract denomination is $100,000. Find the risk-minimizing hedge for the bond portfolio.*

The data included in the file are as follows:

| Date | AAA Portfolio Value | Natural Log of Value | Portfolio Return | Futures Return |
|---|---|---|---|---|
| 20040101 | 29,004,133 | 17.183 | | |
| 20040102 | 28,677,998 | 17.172 | –0.0113 | –0.01295 |
| 20040105 | 28,679,125 | 17.172 | 0.0000 | –0.00029 |
| 20040106 | 28,931,665 | 17.180 | 0.0088 | 0.01066 |
| 20040107 | 29,006,580 | 17.183 | 0.0026 | 0.00343 |
| ... | ... | ... | ... | ... |
| 20050210 | 32,858,283 | 17.308 | –0.0116 | –0.01018 |
| 20050211 | 32,802,473 | 17.306 | –0.0017 | –0.00189 |
| 20050214 | 32,955,513 | 17.311 | 0.0047 | 0.00350 |
| 20050215 | 32,821,210 | 17.307 | –0.0041 | –0.00323 |
| 20050216 | 32,671,455 | 17.302 | –0.0046 | –0.00514 |

Based on the data, we regress the portfolio return on the futures return. This can be handled using the OPTVAL function, OV_STAT_OLS_SIMPLE. The results are as follows:

| Criterion | $\hat{\alpha}_0$ | $s(\hat{\alpha}_0)$ | $\hat{\alpha}_1$ | $s(\hat{\alpha}_1)$ | $\bar{R}^2$ |
|---|---|---|---|---|---|
| Minimize value risk | 0.0001 | 0.0000 | 0.8935 | 0.0075 | 0.9797 |

The slope coefficient estimate, 0.8935, implies that, for a one percentage change in the futures price, the portfolio value will change by 0.8935%. To determine the hedge that minimizes the dollar value change of the portfolio, we must account for the current value of the portfolio as well as the price of the futures. Earlier in this illustration, we reported that the current portfolio value is \$32,671,455, and that the current futures price is 1.1525 times its \$100,000 denomination. Thus, the value risk-minimizing hedge is to sell 253.30 futures contracts:

$$n_F = -0.8935\left(\frac{32,671,455}{1.1525 \times 100,000}\right) = -253.30$$

With an adjusted $R$-squared of nearly 98%, you have good reason to believe that the futures hedge will be very effective.

## HEDGING MULTIPLE SOURCES OF RISK

Aside from its convenience, the regression approach to setting a risk-minimizing hedge is easily generalized to handle asset portfolios whose values are influenced by a number of risk factors. Suppose we are managing a fund that invests primarily in stocks from the oil refining industry. Since the portfolio is not well diversified due to its concentration in oil stocks, its value is vulnerable not only to unexpected stock market movements but also to unexpected changes in the price of oil. Suppose that, given the political situation in Iraq, we come to the conclusion that there is a substantial risk that the price of crude oil will spike upward in the near future. This places us in a conundrum. While an increase in the crude oil price will likely cause the stock market level to fall, it may well have a positive influence on the prices of the oil stocks in our portfolio. Thus selling the stocks and buying risk-free bonds is not an appropriate strategy since it would eliminate both the stock market and crude oil price risk exposures. Our objective is to negate the stock market risk of our portfolio without negating the crude oil price risk.

A straightforward approach to handling this risk management problem is to use the multiple regression model,

$$R_V = \alpha_0 + \alpha_1 R_{F,1} + \alpha_2 R_{F,2} + \ldots + \alpha_n R_{F,n} + \tilde{\varepsilon} \tag{5.45}$$

where all futures contracts whose returns are thought to influence the value of our portfolio are used. With respect to the illustration at hand, we might include only two risk factors: the S&P 500 futures contract to proxy for stock market risk, and an oil futures contract to proxy for the effects of oil price risk. Once the regression is estimated, we can hedge any of the risk exposures using the estimated slope coefficients.

**ILLUSTRATION 5.4** Hedging with two risk factors.

*Suppose you manage a fund that invests primarily in oil refining stocks. As such, you are exposed to both movements in oil prices and in the stock market. Given the current uneasiness in the stock market, you find yourself in a dilemma. On one hand, you believe that there is a strong chance that the market will fall over the next couple of weeks due to a rise in the price of crude oil, but, on the other, that your particular portfolio of oil stocks will appreciate in value relative to the stock market due to the rising price of crude. Consequently, you want to hedge your market risk exposure, but not your oil risk exposure. Compute the stock market risk-minimizing hedge using the return data provided in* **Oil hedge.xls**. *Use the S&P 500 futures contract traded on the Chicago Mercantile Exchange to represent the equity risk factor and the crude oil futures contract traded on the New York Mercantile Exchange to represent the oil risk factor. The contract denomination of the S&P 500 futures is 250 times the index level, and the denomination of the crude oil futures is 1,000 barrels.*

An important first step in an analysis of the hedge involving multiple risk factors is to understand the correlation among the returns series. The raw data in the file appears as follows:

| Date | Oil Stock Portfolio Value | Mar. 2005 S&P 500 Futures Price | Mar. 2005 Crude Futures Price | Oil Stock Portfolio Return | Mar. 2005 S&P 500 Futures Return | Mar. 2005 Crude Futures Return |
|---|---|---|---|---|---|---|
| 20040701 | 44,590,000 | 1128.50 | 37.00 | | | |
| 20040702 | 44,720,000 | 1127.30 | 36.64 | 0.00291 | −0.00106 | −0.00978 |
| 20040706 | 45,100,000 | 1116.70 | 37.63 | 0.00846 | −0.00945 | 0.02666 |
| 20040707 | 45,370,000 | 1119.70 | 37.11 | 0.00597 | 0.00268 | −0.01392 |
| ... | ... | ... | ... | ... | ... | ... |
| 20050216 | 58,480,000 | 1210.50 | 48.33 | 0.02704 | −0.00017 | 0.02239 |
| 20050217 | 58,130,000 | 1201.00 | 47.54 | −0.00600 | −0.00788 | −0.01648 |
| 20050218 | 59,410,000 | 1202.30 | 48.35 | 0.02178 | 0.00108 | 0.01689 |
| 20050222 | 58,250,000 | 1184.70 | 51.15 | −0.01972 | −0.01475 | 0.05630 |

In Excel, go to the "Tools" menu, choose "Data analysis," and then "Correlation." This tool will allow you to generate the following matrix of correlations.

| | Portfolio | S&P 500 | Crude |
|---|---|---|---|
| Portfolio | 1 | | |
| S&P 500 | 0.4641 | 1 | |
| Crude | 0.2738 | –0.2060 | 1 |

The portfolio returns are strongly positively correlated with both the S&P 500 index, 0.4641, and the return of crude oil, 0.2738. At the same time, the S&P 500 return is inversely correlated with the return of crude oil, –0.2060. In other words, where the stocks, in general, fall as the price of crude oil rises, your particular portfolio of oil stocks tends to rise as crude oil rises.

Your objective is to hedge the stock market risk of your portfolio over the short-term. In order to estimate the appropriate hedge, you need to regress your portfolio returns on the returns of *all* known risk factors—in this case, the S&P 500 return and the crude oil return. The estimation results are as follows:

| **Regression Statistics** | |
|---|---|
| Multiple *R* | 0.5982 |
| *R*-square | 0.3579 |
| Adjusted *R*-square | 0.3498 |
| Standard error | 0.0080 |
| Observations | 162 |

| | Coefficients | Std. Error | *t* Stat |
|---|---|---|---|
| Intercept | 0.0010 | 0.0006 | 1.6483 |
| S&P 500 | 0.8252 | 0.0986 | 8.3697 |
| Crude oil | 0.1792 | 0.0302 | 5.9395 |

The regression results, indeed, confirm that the value of your portfolio increases with the stock market and crude oil. The estimated coefficient on the S&P 500 is 0.8252, which means that for a 1% change in the price of the S&P 500 futures contract, your portfolio increases in value by 0.8252%, holding the effects of crude oil constant.[10] The number of S&P 500 futures to sell is determined by using the estimated slope coefficient, the market value of the portfolio, the market price of the futures, and the futures contract denomination is the following way:

$$n_F = -0.8252\left(\frac{58{,}250{,}000}{1184.70 \times 250}\right) = -162.30$$

[10] This is precisely why it is important to include all possible risk factors. Otherwise, it is impossible to disentangle the effects of the different factors, except in the unusual case where the risk factors are independent of one another. In OLS regression, this problem is referred to as *omitting relevant explanatory variables*, and its consequences are discussed in Appendix B to this book.

Finally, in the interest of completeness, suppose we set the stock market risk-minimizing hedge using the estimated slope coefficient from a simply regression of portfolio return on stock index futures return. The regression results are:

| Regression Statistics | |
|---|---|
| Multiple $R$ | 0.4641 |
| $R$-square | 0.2154 |
| Adjusted $R$-square | 0.2105 |
| Standard error | 0.0088 |
| Observations | 162 |

| | Coefficients | Std. Error | $t$ Stat |
|---|---|---|---|
| Intercept | 0.0014 | 0.0007 | 2.0722 |
| S&P 500 | 0.7046 | 0.1063 | 6.6272 |

With the estimated slope coefficient being 0.7046, the number of S&P 500 futures contracts to sell is now

$$n_F = -0.7046\left(\frac{58{,}250{,}000}{1184.70 \times 250}\right) = -138.57$$

Selling this "risk-minimizing" number of futures is *wrong*. This number of contracts is *downward biased* because we failed to account for the fact that the crude oil return and the S&P 500 return are negatively correlated. Without the crude oil return in the regression, the S&P 500 return is proxying for two factors—the stock market and crude oil. Since the crude oil and the stock market are negatively correlated, this means that the slope coefficient in the simple regression on the S&P 500 futures return is downward biased. If the correlation had been positive, the slope coefficient in the simple regression would have been upward biased.

Finally, with multiple risk factors, measuring the effectiveness of the hedge becomes slightly more complicated. The $R$-squared in the first regression, 0.3579, says that 35.79% of the variance of the return of the oil stock portfolio can be explained by the returns of the S&P 500 futures and the crude oil futures. But, what percentage of this risk remains after the S&P 500 futures hedge is in place?

To answer this question, we compute the standard deviation of the unhedged portfolio return, $\sigma(\tilde{R}_P)$, as well as the standard deviation of the hedged portfolio return, $\sigma(\tilde{R}_V - 0.8252 \times \tilde{R}_{S\&P500})$. They are 0.00993 and 0.00540, respectively. Thus the proportion of the unhedged portfolio return variance that remains after the hedge is put in place is

$$\frac{0.00883^2}{0.00993^2} = 79.09\%$$

## ESTIMATION ISSUES

There are some subtle regression estimation issues that worth noting at this juncture. An important one is the proper selection of the frequency of the price observations used in generating price changes or returns. The regression can be performed on daily, weekly, or monthly price changes or returns—given that price changes/returns are i.i.d., it should not matter. From a purely statistical standpoint, however, the higher is the frequency, the better. The greater is the number of observations for a given historical time period, the greater the amount of information that gets impounded in the estimate. From a practical perspective, however, there is a tradeoff. While greater frequency means more information, it also means more measurement error.

Measurement errors arise from a variety of sources. We will discuss three—bid/ask price bounce, nonsimultaneous price observations, and infrequent trading. Before addressing the effects of these potential sources of error, it is useful to think conceptually about the use of regression analysis for setting hedge ratios. Implicitly or explicitly, we made a number of assumptions. A critically important one was that the relation between asset returns (price changes) and futures returns (price changes) was *stationary* through time. Among other things, this allowed us to project expected *future* variances and covariances that go into setting the hedge ratio from *past* price data. Other assumptions are also critical. In using historical price data, we implicitly assume that we are measuring "true" prices[11] and that the asset and futures prices at a given time $t$ are observed at exactly the same instant in time. Both of these assumptions are normally violated. Indeed the magnitude of the errors induced by these considerations may be quite large.

### Bid/Ask Price Bounce

The problem here emanates from the fact that the daily prices recorded in historical data bases are usually last trade prices. A *last trade price* is the price recorded at the time of the last transaction of the day. In general, the last trade price will *not* be the security's true price. One reason for this is that, in all likelihood, the trade took place on one side of the market. If the last trade was seller-motivated, the trade was probably consummated at the prevailing bid price, and, if the trade was buyer-motivated, it probably took place at the ask. (See Figure 5.4.) A better proxy for the end-of-day true price is the midpoint of the prevailing bid/ask price quotes at the end of the day, however, histories of daily price quotes are not generally available.

Now consider how prices are used in the regression of asset return on futures return. For the asset, return is measure from close to close. The computed asset return, therefore, has two measurement errors, one for each price. The same is true for the futures. Thus, the number of measurement errors included in a regression using $T$ days of returns is $4 \times (T + 1)$. This *errors-in-the-*

[11] Here we are considering the "true" price of the security to be its price in a frictionless market.

**FIGURE 5.4** Relation between last trade price of the day and true price.

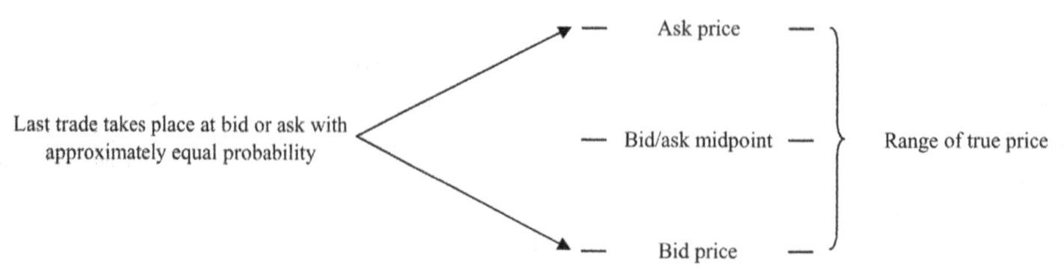


*variables* problem tends to bias the estimated slope coefficient downward.[12] Note that, if the spreads between the bid and ask prices in the asset and futures markets is zero, this problem disappears. Conversely, in markets that are not particularly liquid, bid/ask spreads will be high and the effects of this problem will be large. Note also that we can control for the bias induced by bid/ask price bounce somewhat by lengthening the period over which returns are measured. The reason is that we are reducing the sheer number of errors. In regressions based on true prices, daily data are expected to produce the same slope coefficient as weekly or monthly data. A regression involving weekly returns based on last trade prices, however, will have proportionately fewer errors than a daily return regression (with five trading days per week, about five times fewer errors), and, hence, will produce a slope coefficient that is less downward biased.

### Nonsimultaneous Price Observations

Another source of measurement error is that the price observations that are used in generating returns for the asset and the futures may not be simultaneous. Consider regressing the daily returns of a stock portfolio on the returns of the S&P 500 futures contract. If we use closing prices for each market, we have another errors-in the-variables problem because the stock market closes at 4:00 PM (EST), while the S&P 500 index futures market closes at 4:15 PM. This timing mismatch causes that the slope coefficient in the regression to be downward biased. Part of the observed futures return will not be reflected in the stock portfolio return until the following day.[13]

### Infrequent Trading

Yet another problem arises when the asset that we are trying to hedge is an amalgam of other asset prices that have varying degrees of trading frequency. Consider the closing index level of the S&P 500 portfolio each day, for example. The "true" S&P 500 index level at the close should be based on a weighted-average of the "true" prices of all 500 index stocks, where each and

[12] For a discussion of the errors-in-the-variables problem, see Appendix B of this book.

[13] In principle, this problem could be handled by including a lagged futures return in the regression model. The procedures for doing so are somewhat inexact, however.

every stock traded at exactly the close. But each stock did not trade at the close. While in a typical trading day stocks like General Electric and IBM trade almost continuously right up until the close, others trade fairly much less frequently. Indeed some stocks may not to have been traded during the last few hours of the day. For these stocks, the last trade price is a poor indicator of the true end-of-day price. Indeed, because the index is computed on the basis of last trade prices of the constituent stocks, the "observed" index will always lag its true level. Among other things, this means the observed index returns will be positively serially correlated, thereby violating the regression assumption that returns are i.i.d.

**ILLUSTRATION 5.5** Testing for robustness.

*The file* ***High yield.xls*** *contains the daily returns of the Merrill Lynch high-yield B bond index, the CBT's T-bond futures, and the CME's S&P 500 futures. Bonds rated below BBB are sometimes called "junk" bonds. Junk bond prices are usually sensitive to both long-term interest rate and stock market movements. Regress the daily return of the bond portfolio on the returns of the T-bond futures and S&P 500 futures as if you were attempting to hedge the bond portfolio risk factors. Now create Wednesday to Wednesday returns by summing the daily returns over the week, and run the same regression on weekly returns. Compare and comment on the regression results.*

The table below summarizes the regression results. The daily regression results indicate that the bond portfolio value is relatively insensitive to movements in the T-bond futures price (long-term interest rates) and in the S&P 500 index. For a 1% change in the T-bond futures price, the bond portfolio value changes by 0.0693%, and a 1% change in the S&P 500 futures price causes the bond portfolio value to change by 0.0138%. The hedging effectiveness appears to be very low, at 11.93%.

The weekly results are quite different. The coefficient estimate on the T-bond futures return is 0.1625 and on the S&P 500 futures return is 0.0440, both more than twice as high as in the daily regression. In addition, the hedging effectiveness is more than twice what it appeared in the daily regression. The biweekly results improve matters even further.

| | | $\alpha_0$ | $\alpha_1$ | $\alpha_2$ | $R^2$ |
|---|---|---|---|---|---|
| Daily | Coefficient | 0.0003 | 0.0693 | 0.0444 | 0.1193 |
| | Std. error | 0.0001 | 0.0138 | 0.0118 | |
| Weekly | Coefficient | 0.0014 | 0.1625 | 0.1401 | 0.2668 |
| | Std. error | 0.0006 | 0.0440 | 0.0416 | |
| Biweekly | Coefficient | 0.0026 | 0.1758 | 0.1725 | 0.3546 |
| | Std. error | 0.0012 | 0.0590 | 0.0563 | |

These results reveal the danger in blindly applying regression analysis. The nature of the data used in the regression needs to be carefully considered before the regression is performed. In this particular instance, the most likely culprit is the bond index. Corporate bonds with a high degree of credit risk trade infrequently. Indeed, it is not uncommon for some corporate bonds to be traded shortly after issuance and then never again. Consequently, it is highly likely that the bond index suffers from infrequent trading effects.

One way to test this possibility is to examine the autocorrelation function of the bond portfolio returns. This can be done using the OPTVAL Library function

OV_STAT_AUTOCORREL(*k*, *x*, *out*)

where *k* is the maximum number of lags, *x* is the time series vector, and *out* is an indictor variable controlling the output vector (0 = horizontal, and 1 = vertical).[14] With 294 daily returns in the time series, the standard error is $1/\sqrt{294} = 0.58$.

| Lag | 1 | 2 | 3 | 4 | 5 |
|---|---|---|---|---|---|
| Bond portfolio | 0.5578 | 0.3684 | 0.3232 | 0.2175 | 0.1772 |
| T-bond futures | 0.0206 | –0.0941 | 0.0492 | 0.0202 | 0.0201 |
| S&P 500 futures | 0.0287 | –0.0542 | –0.0147 | –0.0556 | 0.0349 |

As the results show, we can reject the hypothesis that the first-order autocorrelation of the daily bond portfolio returns is zero. At the same time, we cannot reject the hypotheses that the T-bond futures returns and the S&P 500 futures returns are uncorrelated.

Like the bid/ask price effects, the effects of infrequent trading begin to disappear as the distance between adjacent price observations used in the computation of returns becomes larger. The autocorrelation functions for the weekly and biweekly bond returns are as follows:

| Lag | 1 | 2 | 3 | 4 | 5 |
|---|---|---|---|---|---|
| Weekly | 0.3148 | –0.0804 | 0.0177 | –0.0411 | –0.1000 |
| Biweekly | 0.1219 | –0.1179 | 0.0759 | 0.0245 | –0.0528 |

where the standard error for the weekly correlations is 0.130, and the standard error for the biweekly correlations is 0.183. What the results indicate is that the first-order autocorrelation remains significant in the weekly returns but disappears for biweekly returns. Based on this analysis, it is safer to use the regression results from the biweekly regression in setting the risk-minimizing hedge.

## SUMMARY

This chapter explores the role of forward/futures contracts in managing expected return and risk. We begin by showing how futures contracts fit within the CAPM and develop the concept of hedging. We then focus on using futures to manage different types of risks. We start with price risk and consider the case in which an airline wants to hedge the cost of jet fuel. We then focus on revenue risk and show how a farmer can hedge the sales proceeds of his crop in an environment with both price and quantity risks. Next we consider gross margin (i.e., uncertain revenue less uncertain costs) risk. Oil refiners, for example, are concerned about the difference between the revenue they realize through the sale of heating oil and unleaded gasoline and the cost of the crude oil they must acquire

[14] The use of the autocorrelation function is described in greater detail in Appendix A of this book.

to produce these products. Finally, we consider risk management when the asset or portfolio has multiple risk factors. Someone managing a junk bond portfolio, for example, faces both interest rate and stock market risk exposures. For the most part, the illustrations discussed in this chapter are confined to risk-minimizing hedges. The principles can easily be extended to include the tradeoff between expected return and risk. For setting risk-minimizing hedges, OLS regression winds up being an indispensable tool. As important as the regression technique, however, is a thorough understanding of the data being used in the regression estimation.

## REFERENCES AND SUGGESTED READINGS

Anderson, Ronald W., and Jean-Pierre Danthine. 1980. Hedging and joint production: Theory and illustrations. *Journal of Finance* 35: 487–498.

Anderson, Ronald W., and Jean-Pierre Danthine. 1981. Cross hedging. *Journal of Political Economy* 89 (December): 1182–1196.

Black, Fischer. 1976. The pricing of commodity contracts. *Journal of Financial Economics* 3 (March): 167–179.

Dale, Charles. 1981. The hedging effectiveness of currency futures markets. *Journal of Futures Markets* 1: 77–88.

Eaker, Mark, and Dwight Grant. 1990. Currency hedging strategies for international diversified equity portfolios. *Journal of Portfolio Management* 17 (Fall): 30–32.

Ederington, Louis H. 1979. The hedging performance of the new futures markets. *Journal of Finance* 34 (March): 157–170.

Figlewski, Stephen. 1984. Hedging performance and basis risk in stock index futures. *Journal of Finance* 39 (July): 657–669.

Figlewski, Stephen, Yoram Landskroner, and William L. Silber. 1991. Tailing the hedge: Why and how. *Journal of Futures Markets* 11: 201–212.

Frankle, C. 1980. The hedging performance of the new futures markets: Comment. *Journal of Finance* 35: 1273–1279.

Grant, Dwight. 1985. Theory of the firm with joint price and output uncertainty and a forward market. *American Journal of Agricultural Economics* 67: 630–635.

Howard, Charles T., and Louis J. D'Antonio. 1994. The cost of hedging and the optimal hedge ratio. *Journal of Futures Markets* 14 (April): 237–258.

Park, T., and L. Switzer. 1995. Bivariate GARCH estimation of the optimal hedge ratios for stock index futures: A note. *Journal of Futures Markets* 15: 61–67.

Working, Holbrook. 1953. Futures trading and hedging. *American Economic Review* 48: 314–343.

# PART Four

# Option Valuation

# 6

# No-Arbitrage Price Relations: Options

The purpose of this chapter is to develop no-arbitrage price relations for option contracts. Unlike forwards and futures, options provide the right, but not the obligation, to buy or sell the underlying asset at a specified price. The right to buy is a *call* option, the right to sell is a *put*. The price at which the underlying asset is bought (in the case of a call) or sold (in the case of a put) is called the *exercise* price or *strike* price of the option.

In this chapter, the assumption that two perfect substitutes have the same price is again applied. In the absence of costless arbitrage opportunities, options have three types of no-arbitrage price relations—lower bounds, put-call parity relations, and intermarket relations.[1] Each type of relation is developed in turn, for both European- and American-style options[2] and under both the continuous rate and discrete flow net cost of carry assumptions. Before deriving the no-arbitrage price relations for options, however, we focus on clearly distinguishing between the characteristics of option and forward contracts.

## OPTIONS AND FORWARDS

Options differ from forwards in two key respects. First, the net cost of carry of a forward contract is zero since it involves no investment outlay. An option, on the other hand, involves investment. An option buyer pays the option premium for the right to buy or sell the underlying asset, and, like the buyer of any other asset, faces carry costs. For an option, however, the only carry cost is interest. Holding an option neither produces income like a dividend-paying stock nor requires storage costs like a commodity (i.e., a physical asset).

The effects of carry costs on the terminal profit functions of forward and option contracts are shown in Figures 6.1 through 6.3. The profit from a long forward position at expiration is

[1] Much of the material used in this chapter was drawn from Stoll and Whaley (1986).

[2] *European-style* options can be exercised only on expiration day, while *American-style* options can be exercised at any time up to and including the expiration day. Both types of options are traded on exchanges and in OTC markets.

**FIGURE 6.1** Terminal profit of long and short forward positions.

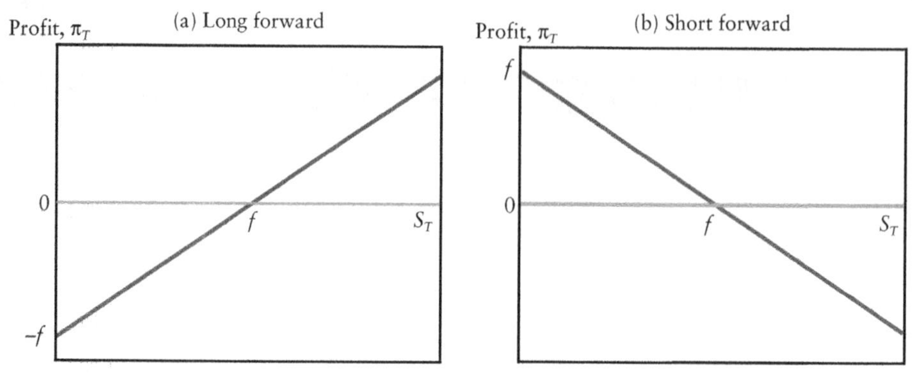


**FIGURE 6.2** Terminal profit of long and short call positions.

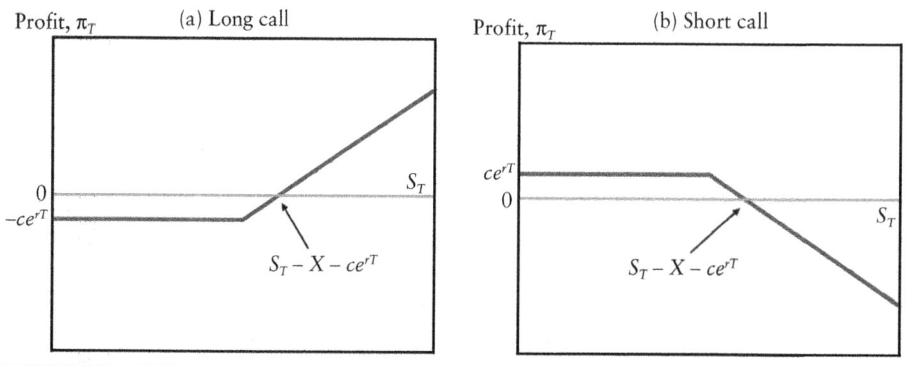


**FIGURE 6.3** Terminal profit of long and short put positions.

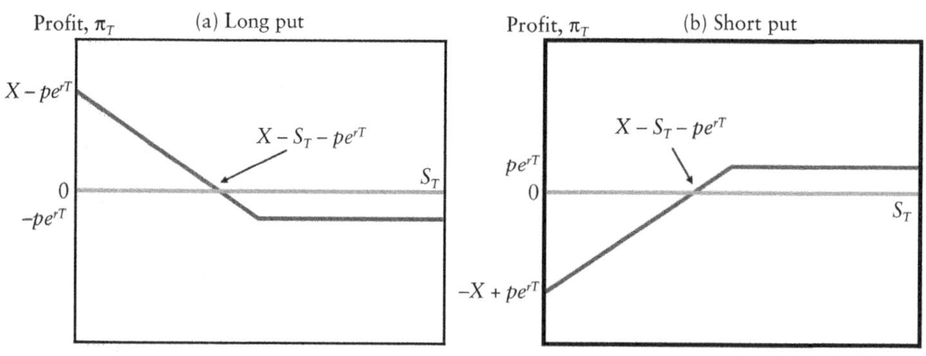


$$\pi_{\text{long forward}, T} = S_T - f \tag{6.1}$$

On the other hand, the profit from a long call position is

$$\pi_{\text{long call}, T} = \begin{cases} S_T - X - ce^{rT}, & \text{if } S_T \geq X \\ -ce^{rT}, & \text{if } S_T < X \end{cases} \tag{6.2}$$

and from a long put position is

$$\pi_{\text{long put}, T} = \begin{cases} -pe^{rT}, & \text{if } S_T \geq X \\ X - S_T - pe^{rT}, & \text{if } S_T < X \end{cases} \tag{6.3}$$

All notation used in (6.1) through (6.3) is as defined in Chapter 4, except $c$ and $p$, which are the prices of a European-style call and put, respectively, and $X$, which is the exercise price or strike price of the option. Note that the profit functions for the long call and the long put (6.2) and (6.3) reflect the fact that the initial option premiums, $c$ and $p$, are carried forward until the option's expiration at the risk-free interest rate. We have lost the opportunity cost of the funds we tied up in buying the option. Conversely, short call and short put positions (i.e., $\pi_{\text{short call},T} = -\pi_{\text{long call},T}$ and $\pi_{\text{short put},T} = -\pi_{\text{long put},T}$) reflect the fact that the option seller receives the premium payment and invests the cash at the risk-free interest rate. The profit function of a long forward position (6.1) has no interest component since the forward price is a promised payment on day $T$ rather than a cash outlay today.

The second key difference between forwards and options is that the buyer of a forward is obliged to buy the underlying asset at expiration, independent of whether or not the terminal asset price is greater than or less than the initial forward price. The buyer of an option, on the other hand, is not obliged to buy or sell the underlying asset, but will do so only when it is profitable. The profit function for the long call position (6.2), for example, shows that the option is exercised only when $S_T \geq X$. If $S_T < X$, the call option buyer chooses not to exercise, forfeiting only his original investment plus carry costs, $ce^{rT}$. The limited liability feature of the long call and long put positions are illustrated in Figures 6.2a and 6.3a, respectively. In the interest of completeness, the short positions in the respective instruments are illustrated in Figures 6.1b through 6.3b.

The profit functions of the call and the put show a certain complementarity to the profit function of a forward. Suppose we buy a call and sell a put at the same exercise price. The profit function for the overall position is

$$\pi_{c,T} - \pi_{p,T} = \begin{cases} S_T - X - ce^{rT} + pe^{rT}, & \text{if } S_T \geq X \\ S_T - X - ce^{rT} - pe^{rT}, & \text{if } S_T < X \end{cases}$$

$$= S_T - X - ce^{rT} - pe^{rT}$$

Now, suppose that we chose the exercise price of the options such that $X = f - ce^{rT} + pe^{rT}$. The profit functions of the option portfolio and the long forward position will be exactly the same. If we buy the option portfolio and sell the forward contract, the terminal value of the overall position must 0. In the absence of costless arbitrage opportunities, the current value of the position must also be equal to 0, and, therefore, the call and put prices must be equal. Buying the call and selling the put (with the exercise price defined as above) is a perfect substitute for buying a forward. Viewed in this way, we can see that we were slightly imprecise in Chapter 1 when we said that there are only *two* basic types of derivatives—a forward and an option. Fact of the matter is that we can construct virtually any derivatives contract from any of the following pairs of basic instruments (1) a forward and a call, (2) a forward and a put, and (3) a call and a put.

## CONTINUOUS RATES

In Chapter 4, the modeling of net carry costs was described in detail. Under the continuous rate assumption, both interest cost and noninterest costs/benefits are modeled as continuous rates. Under the discrete flow assumption, interest cost is modeled as a continuous rate but noninterest costs/benefits are modeled as discrete cash flows. This section relies on the continuous rate assumption. The interest carry cost rate is represented by the notation $r$, and the noninterest carry benefit/cost rate is $i$. If the asset holder receives income from holding the asset such as the dividend yield on a stock portfolio or interest on a foreign currency investment, the income rate is positive (i.e., $i > 0$). If the asset holder pays costs in addition to interest in order to hold the asset (e.g., storage costs of holding a physical commodity), the income rate is negative (i.e., $i < 0$). Where $i = 0$, the only cost of carry is interest. As noted earlier in this section, the net cost of carry of an option is simply the interest rate.

### Lower Price Bound of European-Style Call

Under the continuous rate assumption, the lower price bound of a European-style call option is

$$c \geq \max(0, Se^{-iT} - Xe^{-rT}) \tag{6.4}$$

The reason that the call price must be greater or equal to 0 is obvious—we do not have to be paid to take on a privilege. The reason the call price must exceed $Se^{-iT} - Xe^{-rT}$ is less obvious and is derived by means of an arbitrage portfolio. Suppose we form a portfolio by selling $e^{-iT}$ units of the underlying asset[3] and

[3] Recall that under the continuous cost of carry rate assumption, the continuously paid income received from holding the asset is immediately reinvested in more units of the asset, so that $e^{-iT}$ units on day 0 grows to one unit on day $T$. For a short asset position, the reverse applies in the sense that our liability (in terms of number of units owed) grows at rate $i$.

buying a European-style call. In addition, to make sure that we have enough cash on hand to exercise the call at expiration, we buy $Xe^{-rT}$ in risk-free bonds. The initial investment and terminal values of these positions are shown in Table 6.1. On day $T$, the net terminal value of the portfolio depends on whether the asset price is above or below the exercise price. If the asset price is less than the exercise price (i.e., $S_T < X$), we let the call expire worthless. We then use the risk-free bonds to buy one unit of the asset to cover the short sale obligation. What remains is $X - \tilde{S}_T$, which we know is greater than 0. If the asset price is greater than or equal to the exercise price (i.e., $S_T \geq X$), we exercise the call. This requires a cash payment of $X$. Fortunately we have exactly that amount on hand in the form of risk-free bonds. The unit of the asset that we receive upon exercising the call is used to retire the short sale obligation. In this case, the net terminal value is certain to be 0.

What are the implications of this strategy? Well, we have formed a portfolio that is *certain* to have a terminal value of at least 0. In the absence of costless arbitrage opportunities, this implies that the greatest initial value is 0. More simply, we cannot reasonably expect to collect money at the outset without risk of loss. In the absence of costless arbitrage opportunities, $Se^{-iT} - Xe^{-rT} - c \leq 0$. Hence, a lower price bound for the European-style call is $c \geq Se^{-iT} - Xe^{-rT}$.[4]

In general, the lower price bound of an option is called its *intrinsic value*, and the difference between the option's market value (price)[5] and its intrinsic value is called its *time value*. Thus a European-style call has an intrinsic value of $\max(0, Se^{-iT} - Xe^{-rT})$ and a time value of $c - \max(0, Se^{-iT} - Xe^{-rT})$. This chapter deals with identifying intrinsic values by virtue of no-arbitrage arguments. The next chapter uncovers the determinants of time value.

**TABLE 6.1** Arbitrage portfolio trades supporting lower price bound of European-style call option where the underlying asset has a continuous net carry rate, $c \geq Se^{-iT} - Xe^{-rT}$.

| Trades | Initial Investment | Value on Day T | |
|---|---|---|---|
| | | $S_T < X$ | $S_T \geq X$ |
| Sell asset | $Se^{-iT}$ | $-\tilde{S}_T$ | $-\tilde{S}_T$ |
| Buy call option | $-c$ | 0 | $\tilde{S}_T - X$ |
| Buy risk-free bonds | $-Xe^{-rT}$ | $X$ | $X$ |
| Net portfolio value | $Se^{-iT} - Xe^{-rT} - c$ | $X - \tilde{S}_T$ | 0 |

[4] It is also worthwhile to note that the lower price bound of the call can be reexpressed relative to the forward/futures prices. In Chapter 4, we developed the net cost of carry relation, $fe^{-rT} = Se^{-iT}$ (see equation (4.5)). Substituting the cost of carry relation into (6.4), $c \geq \max(0, fe^{-rt} - Xe^{-rT})$.

[5] The distinction between *value* and *price* is subtle, but important. A *price* is what we observe for the security in the marketplace; a *value* is what we believe a security is worth. If the value exceeds the price, the security is *underpriced*, and, if the value is less than the price, the security is *overpriced*.

**ILLUSTRATION 6.1** Examine lower price bound of European-style call option.

*Suppose a three-month European-style call option written on a stock index portfolio has an exercise price of 70 and a market price of 4.25. Suppose also the current index level is 75, the portfolio's dividend yield rate is 4%, and the risk-free rate of interest is 5%. Is a costless arbitrage profit possible?*

To test for the possibility of a costless arbitrage profit, substitute the problem parameters into the lower price bound (6.4), that is,

$$4.25 < \max[0, 75e^{-0.04(3/12)} - 70e^{-0.05(3/12)}] = 5.12$$

Since the lower bound relation is violated, a costless arbitrage profit of at least 5.12 – 4.25 = 0.87 is possible. Since the violation may result from either the call being *underpriced* or the asset being *overpriced*, the arbitrage requires *buying* the call and *selling* the asset.[6] The appropriate arbitrage trades are provided in Table 6.1. Substituting the prices and rates,

| Trades | Initial Investment | Value at Time $T$ | |
|---|---|---|---|
| | | $S_T < 70$ | $S_T \geq 70$ |
| Sell index portfolio | 74.25 | $-\tilde{S}_T$ | $-\tilde{S}_T$ |
| Buy call option | –4.25 | 0 | $\tilde{S}_T - 70$ |
| Buy risk-free bonds | –69.13 | 70 | 70 |
| Net portfolio value | 0.87 | $70 - \tilde{S}_T$ | 0 |

In examining the net portfolio value, note that you (a) earn an immediate profit of 0.87, and (b) have the potential of earning even more if the index level is below 70 at the option's expiration. If prices in the market were actually configured at such levels, you should expect that buying pressure on the call and selling pressure on the index portfolio would very quickly return the market to equilibrium. In the absence of costless arbitrage opportunities, $c \geq Se^{-iT} - Xe^{-rT}$.

## Lower Price Bound of American-Style Call

American-style options are like European-style options except that they can be exercised at any time up to and including the expiration day. Since this additional right cannot have a negative value, the relation between the prices of American-style and European-style call options is

$$C \geq c \tag{6.5}$$

where the upper case $C$ represents the price of an American-style call option with the same exercise price and time to expiration and on the same underlying

[6] Note that we are not making any judgment on whether the call price is too high or too low *per se*. We are saying only that the call is incorrectly priced (in this case it is priced too low) *relative* to the price of the underlying asset. To execute the arbitrage, we must trade both the call and the underlying asset, so that we make money when their prices come back into line relative to each other. In this example, the prices come back into line with each other for certain at the option's expiration.

asset as the European-style call. The lower price bound of an American-style call option is

$$C \geq \max(0, Se^{-iT} - Xe^{-rT}, S - X) \quad (6.6)$$

This is the same as the lower price bound of the European-style call (6.4), except that the term $S - X$ is added within the maximum value operator on the right-hand side. The reason is, of course, that the American-style call cannot sell for less than its immediate early exercise proceeds, $S - X$. If $C < S - X$, a costless arbitrage profit of $S - X - C$ can be earned by simultaneously buying the call (and exercising it) and selling the asset.

**ILLUSTRATION 6.2** Examine lower price bound of American-style call option.

*Suppose a three-month American-style call option written on a stock index portfolio has an exercise price of 70 and a market price of 4.25. Suppose also the current index level is 75, the portfolio's dividend yield rate is 4%, and the risk-free rate of interest is 5%. Is a costless arbitrage profit possible?*

To test for the possibility of a costless arbitrage profit, substitute the problem information into (6.6), that is,

$$4.25 < \max[0, 75e^{-0.04(3/12)} - 70e^{-0.05(3/12)}, 75 - 70] = \max(0, 5.12, 5) = 5.12$$

At the current call price of 4.25, two types of arbitrage are possible. A costless arbitrage profit of 5.00 – 4.25 = 0.75 is possible simply by buying the call, exercising it, and selling the asset. The amount of this arbitrage profit, however, is less than the arbitrage profit of at least 5.12 – 4.25 = 0.87 that can be earned by buying the call, selling the asset, buying risk-free bonds, and holding the portfolio until the call's expiration, as was shown in the arbitrage table of Illustration 6.1. Under this second alternative, you earn an immediate profit of 0.87, and have the potential of earning even more if the asset price is below 70 at the option's expiration.

## Early Exercise of American-Style Call Options

The structure of the lower price bound of the American-style call (6.6) can used to provide important insight regarding the possibility of early exercise. The second term in the squared brackets, $Se^{-iT} - Xe^{-rT}$, is the minimum price at which the call can be sold in the marketplace.[7] The third term is the value of the American-style if it is exercised immediately. If the value of the second term is greater than the third term (for a certain set of call options), the call's price in the marketplace will be always exceed its exercise proceeds so it will never be optimal to exercise the call early.

[7] To exit a long position in an American-style call option, we have three alternatives. First, we can hold it to expiration, at which time we will (a) let it expire worthless if it is out of the money or (b) exercise it if it is in the money. Second, we can exercise it immediately, receiving the difference between the current asset price and the exercise price. Third, we can sell it in the marketplace. There is, after all, an active secondary market for standard calls and puts.

To identify this set of calls, we must examine the conditions under which the relation

$$Se^{-iT} - Xe^{-rT} > S - X$$

holds. The job is easier if we rearrange the relation to read

$$S(e^{-iT} - 1) > -X(1 - e^{-rT}) \qquad (6.7)$$

Since the risk-free interest rate is positive, the expression of the right-hand side is negative. If the left-hand side is positive or zero, the call option holder can always get more by selling his option in the marketplace than by exercising it; so early exercise will never be optimal and the value of the American-style call is equal to the value of the European-style call, $C = c$. This condition is met for calls whose underlying asset has a negative or zero noninterest carry rate, $i \leq 0$.

The intuition for this result can be broken down into two components—interest cost, $r$, and noninterest benefit (i.e., $i > 0$) or cost (i.e., $i < 0$). With respect to interest cost, recognize that exercising the call today requires that we pay $X$ today. If we defer exercise until the call's expiration, on the other hand, we have the opportunity to earn interest (i.e., our liability is only the present value of the exercise cost, $Xe^{-rT}$). So, holding other factors constant, we always have an incentive to defer exercise.[8] With respect to the noninterest costs, recall that assets with $i < 0$ are typically physical assets that require storage. If we exercise a call written on such an asset, we must take delivery, whereupon we immediately begin to incur storage costs. If we defer exercise, on the other hand, and continue to hold the claim on the asset rather than the asset itself, we avoid paying storage costs. Thus, where $i < 0$, there are two reasons not to exercise early. But even if storage costs are zero (i.e., with $i = 0$), condition (6.7) holds since the interest cost incentive remains.

For American-style call options on assets with $i > 0$ (e.g., stock index portfolio with a nonzero dividend yield and foreign currencies with a nonzero foreign interest rate), on the other hand, early exercise *may* be optimal. The intuition is that, while there remains the incentive to defer exercise and earn interest on the exercise price, deferring exercise means forfeiting the income on the underlying asset (e.g., the dividend yield on a stock index portfolio). The only way to capture this income is by exercising the call and taking delivery of the asset. For American-style call options on assets with $i > 0$, early exercise may be optimal and, therefore, $C > c$.

### Lower Price Bound of European-Style Put

The lower price bound of a European-style put option is

[8] This point was first demonstrated by Merton (1973) for call options on nondividend-paying stocks. He refers to such options are being worth more "alive" than "dead."

**TABLE 6.2** Arbitrage portfolio trades supporting lower price bound of European-style put option where the underlying asset has a continuous net carry rate, $p \geq Xe^{-rT} - Se^{-iT}$.

| | | Value on Day $T$ | |
|---|---|---|---|
| Trades | Initial Investment | $S_T < X$ | $S_T \geq X$ |
| Buy asset | $-Se^{-iT}$ | $\tilde{S}_T$ | $\tilde{S}_T$ |
| Buy call option | $-p$ | $X - \tilde{S}_T$ | 0 |
| Sell risk-free bonds | $Xe^{-rT}$ | $-X$ | $-X$ |
| Net portfolio value | $Xe^{-rT} - Se^{-iT} - p$ | 0 | $\tilde{S}_T - X$ |

$$p \geq \max(0, Xe^{-rT} - Se^{-iT}) \tag{6.8}$$

Again, the reason that the option price must be greater or equal to 0 is obvious—we do not have to be paid to take on a privilege. The reason the put price must exceed the bound, $Xe^{-rT} - Se^{-iT}$, is given by the arbitrage trade portfolio in Table 6.2. If we buy $e^{-iT}$ units of the asset and a put, and sell $Xe^{-rT}$ risk-free bonds, the net terminal value of the portfolio is certain to be greater than or equal to 0. If the asset price is less than or equal to the exercise price at the option's expiration (i.e., $S_T \leq X$), we will exercise the put, delivering the asset and receiving $X$ in cash. We will then use the exercise proceeds $X$ to cover our risk-free borrowing obligation. In the event the asset price is greater than the exercise price (i.e., $S_T \leq X$), we will consider the put expire worthless. We still need to cover our risk-free borrowing, which we do by selling the asset. After repaying our debt, we have $\tilde{S}_T - X$ remaining.

**ILLUSTRATION 6.3** Examine lower price bound of European-style put option.

*Suppose a three-month European-style put option written on a stock index portfolio has an exercise price of 70 and a market price of 8.80. Suppose also the current index level is 61, the portfolio's dividend yield rate is 4%, and the risk-free rate of interest is 5%. Is a costless arbitrage profit possible?*

To test for the possibility of a costless arbitrage profit, substitute the problem parameters into the lower price bound (6.8),

$$8.80 > \max[0, 70e^{-0.05(3/12)} - 61e^{-0.04(3/12)}] = 8.74$$

At the current price of 8.80, the no-arbitrage condition (6.8) holds, so no costless arbitrage opportunity exists.

### Lower Price Bound for American-Style Put

An American-style put has an early exercise privilege, which means that the relation between the prices of American-style and European-style put options is

$$P \geq p \tag{6.9}$$

where upper case $P$ represents the price of an American-style put option with the same exercise price, time to expiration and underlying asset as the European-style put. The lower price bound of an American-style put option is

$$p \geq \max(0, Xe^{-rT} - Se^{-iT}, X - S) \tag{6.10}$$

This is the same as the lower price bound of the European-style put (6.8), except that, because the American-style put may be exercised at any time including now, the exercise proceeds, $X - S$, is added within the maximum value operator on the right-hand side. If $P < X - S$, a costless arbitrage profit of $X - S - P$ can be earned by simultaneously buying the put (and exercising it) and buying the asset.

**ILLUSTRATION 6.4** Examine lower price bound of American-style put option.

*Suppose a three-month American-style put option written on a stock index portfolio has an exercise price of 70 and a market price of 8.80. Suppose also the current index level is 61, the portfolio's dividend yield rate is 4%, and the risk-free rate of interest is 5%. Is a costless arbitrage profit possible?*

To test for the possibility of a costless arbitrage profit, substitute the problem information into (6.10), that is,

$$8.80 < \max[0, 70e^{-0.05(3/12)} - 61e^{-0.04(3/12)}, 70 - 61] = \max(0, 8.74, 9.00) = 9.00$$

At the current price of 8.80, the no-arbitrage relation (6.10) is violated, indicating the presence of a costless arbitrage opportunity. Since it is the early exercise condition (third term) on the right-hand-side that is violated, you should buy the put (and exercise it) and buy the index portfolio. You would pay 8.80 for the put and 61 for the index portfolio, and receive 70 when you deliver the index portfolio upon exercising the put. The amount of the arbitrage profit is 0.20 and is earned immediately.

### Early Exercise of American-Style Put Options

In the case of an American-style call, we found that if the underlying asset had carry costs or and above interest (e.g., storage), the call option holder would never (rationally) exercise early. In the case of an American-style put, no comparable condition exists.[9] There is always some prospect of early exercise, so the American-style put is always worth more than the European-style put, that is, $P > p$. The intuition is straightforward. Suppose, for whatever reason, the asset price falls to 0. The put option holder should exercise *immediately*. There is no chance that the asset price will fall further, so delaying exercise means forfeiting the interest income that can be earned on the exercise proceeds of the put, $X$. The interest-induced, early-exercise incentive works in exactly the opposite way for the put than it did for the call. For the put, we want to exercise early to get the cash and let it begin to earn interest. For the call, we want to defer exercise and let the cash continue to earn interest.

[9] In the expression on the right-hand side of (6.10), the third term is greater than the second term over some range for $S$, independent of the level of $i$.

### Put-Call Parity for European-Style Options

Perhaps the most important no-arbitrage price relation for options is put-call parity.[10] The put-call parity price relation arises from the simultaneous trades in the call, the put, and the asset. Put-call parity for European-style options is given by

$$c - p = Se^{-iT} - Xe^{-rT} \tag{6.11}$$

The composition of the put-call parity arbitrage portfolio is given in Table 6.3. A portfolio that consists of a long position of $e^{-iT}$ units of the asset, a long put, a short call, and a short position of $Xe^{-rT}$ in risk-free bonds is certain to have a net terminal value of 0. If the terminal asset price is less than or equal to the exercise price of the options (i.e., $S_T \leq X$), we exercise the put and deliver the asset. The cash proceeds from exercise are used to repay our debt. The call option is out-of-the-money, so the call option holder will let it expire worthless. On the other hand, if the terminal asset price exceeds the exercise price (i.e., $S_T > X$), we will let our put expire worthless. The call option holder will exercise, requiring that we deliver a unit of the asset, which we just happen to have.[11] The call option holder pays us X, which we use to retire our risk-free borrowings. Since the net terminal portfolio value is zero, the cost of entering into such a portfolio today must also be 0, otherwise costless arbitrage would be possible. If the initial investment is 0, the put-call parity relation (6.11) holds.

The set of arbitrage trades spelled out in Table 6.3 (i.e., buy the asset, buy the put, sell the call, and sell risk-free bonds) is called a *conversion*. If all of the trades are reversed (i.e., sell the asset, sell the put, buy the call, and buy risk-free bonds), it is called a *reverse conversion*. These names arise from the fact that we can create any position in the asset, options, or risk-free bonds by trading (or *converting*) the remaining securities, in the same manner we used a call and a

**TABLE 6.3** Arbitrage portfolio trades for European-style put-call parity where the underlying asset has a continuous net carry rate, $c - p = Se^{-iT} - Xe^{-rT}$.

| | | Value at Time $T$ | |
|---|---|---|---|
| Trades | Initial Investment | $S_T < X$ | $S_T \geq X$ |
| Buy asset | $-Se^{-iT}$ | $\tilde{S}_T$ | $\tilde{S}_T$ |
| Buy put option | $-p$ | $X - \tilde{S}_T$ | 0 |
| Sell call option | $c$ | 0 | $-(\tilde{S}_T - X)$ |
| Sell risk-free bonds | $Xe^{-rT}$ | $-X$ | $-X$ |
| Net portfolio value | $Xe^{-rT} - Se^{-iT} - p + c$ | 0 | 0 |

[10] The term, "put-call parity," was first coined by Stoll (1969) in the first academic study to develop and test the relation.

[11] If we buy a put option, we pay the premium today for the *right* to sell the underlying asset at the exercise price. If we sell the put, we collect the premium today but have the *obligation* to deliver the asset and receive the exercise price if the put option buyer chooses to exercise.

**TABLE 6.4** Perfect substitutes implied by European-style put-call parity.

| Position 1 | | Position 2 |
|---|---|---|
| Buy asset/buy put/sell call | = | Buy risk-free bonds (lend) |
| Buy asset/buy put/sell risk-free bonds | = | Buy call |
| Sell asset/buy call/buy risk-free bonds | = | Buy put |
| Sell put/buy call/buy risk-free bonds | = | Buy asset |
| Sell asset/sell put/buy call | = | Sell risk-free bonds (borrow) |
| Sell asset/sell put/buy risk-free bonds | = | Sell call |
| Buy asset/sell call/sell risk-free bonds | = | Sell put |
| Buy put/sell call/sell risk-free bonds | = | Sell asset |

put to create a forward contract at the beginning of the chapter. Table 6.4 provides a complete list of the conversions that are possible using the put-call parity relation for European-style options. The first row says that buying the asset, buying a put, and selling a call is equivalent to buying risk-free bonds. We can check this by creating an arbitrage trade table, or by simply working through it mentally. If the asset price is less than the exercise price at expiration, we will exercise our put and sell the asset. If the asset price is greater than the exercise price, the call option holder will exercise, requiring that we deliver the asset. In both cases, we are certain to have $X$ in cash when all is said and done. This is the same as the amount we would have had if we bought risk-free bonds.

**ILLUSTRATION 6.5** Examine put-call parity for European-style options.

*Suppose that a three-month call and put with an exercise price of 70 have prices of 5.00 and 4.50, respectively. Suppose also that the current level of the index portfolio underlying the options is 70, the index portfolio has a dividend yield rate of 3%, and the risk-free rate of interest is 5%. Is a costless arbitrage profit possible?*

To test for the possibility of a costless arbitrage profit, substitute the problem parameters into the put-call parity relation (6.11),

$$5.00 - 4.50 = 0.50 > 70e^{-0.03(3/12)} - 70e^{-0.05(3/12)} = 0.34$$

Since the equation does not hold, a costless arbitrage profit is possible. Since the violation may result from either the call being overpriced, the put being underpriced, or the asset being underpriced, the arbitrage will require all three trades: selling the call, buying the put, and buying the asset. Using the trades as set out in Table 6.3, you get:

| | | Value at Time $T$ | |
|---|---|---|---|
| Trades | Initial Investment | $S_T < 70$ | $S_T \geq 70$ |
| Buy asset | –69.48 | $\tilde{S}_T$ | $\tilde{S}_T$ |
| Buy put option | –4.50 | $\tilde{S}_T - 70$ | 0 |
| Sell call option | 5.00 | 0 | $-(\tilde{S}_T - 70)$ |
| Sell risk-free bonds | 69.13 | –70 | –70 |
| Net portfolio value | 0.16 | 0 | 0 |

By forming this portfolio, you generate a costless arbitrage profit of 0.16. The buying pressure on the index portfolio and the put will cause their prices to rise, and the selling pressure on the call will cause its price to fall. The arbitrage trading will stop when the initial value investment column sums to zero (i.e., the costless arbitrage opportunity ceases to exist), or where $c - p = Se^{-iT} - Xe^{-rT}$.

**ILLUSTRATION 6.6** A "Sage" entrepreneur.

*Russell Sage, one of the great railroad speculators of the 1800s, understood the concept of put-call parity all too well. He used it to circumvent usury laws in the United States.*[12] *Among other ventures, Sage was in the business of making loans. The structure of his "loans" had three key features. First, Sage required that the borrower post stock as collateral for the loan, with the maximum loan amount being equal to the prevailing stock price. Second, in order to protect himself from a drop in the stock price, Sage demanded that the borrower provide a written guarantee stating that Sage could sell the stock back to the borrower at the original stock price. Third, Sage insisted that the borrower pay a cash premium for the right to buy back the stock at its original price. On face appearance, the borrower has an interest-free loan (i.e., he borrows S and repays S). But, such is not the case. The call option that the borrower is required to buy embeds the interest cost. Conveniently for Sage, usury laws did not apply to implicit interest rates.*

*Impressed by Sage's clever scheme, you decide to engage in the same line of business. A borrower approaches you and asks for a six-month loan based on 50,000 shares of ABC, Inc. ABC currently trades at $120 a share, so you are willing to provide up to $6 million, conditional upon the borrower giving you temporary ownership of the shares. Also under the terms of the agreement, you have the right to sell back the shares to the borrower at the end of 6 months at the original share price of $120. This protects you in the event the share price falls. Finally, you insist that the borrower pay you for the right to buy back the shares at $120. Indeed, it must be the borrower's expectation that the share price will be above $120 at the end of 6 months, otherwise he would simply have sold the shares at the outset. For this privilege, you charge the borrower $10 a share. Compute the embedded interest rate on this loan arrangement.*

At the outset, you are out-of-pocket $110 a share (i.e., the share price less the call premium) on 50,000 shares or $5,500,000. At the end of the loan's life, the agreement's contingencies depend on whether the share price is less than or greater than $120. If it is less than $120, you will exercise your right to "put" the stock back to the borrower at $120 a share. The borrower pays $6,000,000, and you return the shares. If the share price is greater than $120, the borrower will exercise his call option. You deliver the 50,000 shares and receive exercise proceeds in the amount of $6,000,000. Either way, you get $6,000,000 in 6 months on an investment of $5,500,000 today. Your implied, continuously-compounded rate of return on investment is

$$\frac{\ln(6{,}000{,}000/5{,}500{,}000)}{0.5}$$

or 17.40%.

[12] This anecdote was drawn from Gastineau (1988, p.15).

### Put-Call Parity for American-Style Options

The early exercise feature of American-style options complicates the put-call parity relation. The nature of the relation depends on the level of noninterest costs/benefits, $i$. Specifically, the put-call parity relations are

$$S - X \leq C - P \leq Se^{-iT} - Xe^{-rT} \text{ if } i \leq 0 \tag{6.12a}$$

and

$$Se^{-iT} - X \leq C - P \leq S - Xe^{-rT} \text{ if } i > 0 \tag{6.12b}$$

Each inequality in (6.12a) and in (6.12b) has a separate set of arbitrage trades. To illustrate, consider (6.12b), the case in which the asset pays some form of income, say, a stock index portfolio with a constant dividend yield rate, or a foreign currency with a constant foreign risk-free rate of interest. To establish the left-hand side inequality of (6.12b), consider the arbitrage portfolio trades in Table 6.5. To generate the table entries, assume the left-hand side inequality of (6.12b) is reversed. This means the asset price is overpriced, the put is overpriced, and/or the call is underpriced. Thus, the arbitrage portfolio must account for all three possibilities. We should sell the asset, sell the put, buy the call, and buy some risk-free bonds. At the options' expiration, the portfolio is certain to have positive value $X(e^{rT} - 1)$. If $S_T < X$, the put option holder exercises, requiring that we pay $X$ in return for a unit of the underlying asset. We pay the exercise price using a portion of our risk-free bonds, and use the delivered asset to cover our short position. On the other hand, if $S_T \geq X$, we exercise the call and receive the asset. The asset delivered on the call is used to cover the short position. We use some of the risk-free bonds to pay for the exercise price of the call.

The early exercise feature of the American-style options requires that we consider one other contingency within the arbitrage table, that is, what happens if the put option holder decides to exercise early at some arbitrary time $t$ between now and expiration. Looking at Table 6.5, we see that our obligation

**TABLE 6.5** Arbitrage portfolio trades supporting American-style put-call parity where the underlying asset has a continuous net carry rate, $Se^{-iT} - X < C - P$.

| Trades | Initial Investment | Early Exercise at $t$ | Value on Day $T$: $S_T < X$ | Value on Day $T$: $S_T \geq X$ |
|---|---|---|---|---|
| Sell asset | $Se^{-iT}$ | $-\tilde{S}_t e^{-i(T-t)}$ | $-\tilde{S}_T$ | $-\tilde{S}_T$ |
| Sell put option | $P$ | $-(X - \tilde{S}_t)$ | $-(X - \tilde{S}_T)$ | 0 |
| Buy call option | $-C$ | $\tilde{C}_t$ | 0 | $\tilde{S}_T - X$ |
| Buy risk-free bonds | $-X$ | $Xe^{rT}$ | $Xe^{rT}$ | $Xe^{rT}$ |
| Net portfolio value | $Se^{-iT} + P - C - X$ | $\tilde{S}_t[1 - e^{-i(T-t)}] + \tilde{C}_t + X(e^{rT} - 1)$ | $X(e^{rT} - 1)$ | $X(e^{rT} - 1)$ |

should the put be exercised early is $-(X - \tilde{S}_t)$. But since we have $Xe^{rt}$ in risk-free bonds, we have more than enough to cover the payment of $X$ to the put option holder. In return, we receive $\tilde{S}_t$, which is more than enough to cover our short asset position in the asset that has value $-\tilde{S}_t e^{-i(T-t)}$. In addition, we have a long position in the call with value $\tilde{C}_t$. Because the net portfolio value is positive at expiration and also in the event the put is exercised early, the initial investment must be negative (since if it were zero or positive, there would be a certain arbitrage). And, if $Se^{-iT} - X - C + P < 0$, then $Se^{-iT} - X < C + P$.

To establish the right-hand side inequality of (6.12b), consider the arbitrage portfolio trades in Table 6.6. To generate the table entries, again assume the right-hand side inequality of (6.9b) is reversed. This means the asset price is underpriced, the put is underpriced, and/or the call is overpriced. The arbitrage portfolio trades must account for all possibilities. We should buy the asset, buy the put, sell the call, and sell some risk-free bonds. At the options' expiration, the portfolio is certain to have positive value $\tilde{S}_T(e^{iT} - 1)$. If $S_T < X$, we exercise the put and sell the asset. The long asset position has a value $\tilde{S}_T e^{iT}$, which is more than enough to pay for the unit of the asset owed on the put. The cash received from exercising the put is used to cover our risk-free bond obligation. On the other hand, if $S_T \geq X$, the call option holder exercises, implying that we receive $X$ in return for delivering one unit of the asset. We use the call received from the call option holder to retire the risk-free bond position. The value of our asset position, $\tilde{S}_T e^{iT}$, is more than we need to deliver on the put.

The early exercise feature of the American-style call must also be considered, that is, what happens if the call option holder decides to exercise early on day $t$? Looking at Table 6.6, we see that the call exercise obligation is $-(\tilde{S}_t - X)$. But, if we receive $X$, that is more than enough to cover the balance of $-Xe^{-r(T-t)}$ in risk-free bonds. We must pay $\tilde{S}_t$, but we have more than one unit of the asset, that is, $\tilde{S}_t e^{i(T-t)}$. In addition, we have a long position in the put with value $\tilde{P}_t$. Since the net portfolio value is positive at expiration and in the event the call is exercised early, the initial investment must be negative. And, if $-S + Xe^{-rT} + C - P < 0$, $C - P < S - Xe^{-rT}$.

**TABLE 6.6** Arbitrage portfolio trades supporting American-style put-call parity where the underlying asset has a continuous net carry rate, $C - P < S - Xe^{-rT}$.

| Trades | Initial Investment | Early Exercise at $t$ | Value on Day $T$ | |
|---|---|---|---|---|
| | | | $S_T < X$ | $S_T \geq X$ |
| Buy asset | $-S$ | $\tilde{S}_t e^{it}$ | $\tilde{S}_T e^{iT}$ | $\tilde{S}_T e^{iT}$ |
| Buy put option | $-P$ | $\tilde{P}_t$ | $X - \tilde{S}_T$ | 0 |
| Sell call option | $C$ | $-(\tilde{S}_t - X)$ | 0 | $-(\tilde{S}_T - X)$ |
| Sell risk-free bonds | $Xe^{rT}$ | $-Xe^{-r(T-t)}$ | $-X$ | $-X$ |
| Net portfolio value | $-S - P + Xe^{rT} + C$ | $\tilde{S}_t(e^{it} - 1) + \tilde{P}_t + X[1 - e^{-r(T-t)}]$ | $\tilde{S}_T(e^{iT} - 1)$ | $\tilde{S}_T(e^{iT} - 1)$ |

**TABLE 6.7** No-arbitrage price relations for European- and American-style options where the underlying asset has a continuous net carry rate.

| Description | European-Style Options | American-Style Options |
|---|---|---|
| Lower price bound for call | $c \geq \max(0, Se^{-iT} - Xe^{-rT})$ | $C \geq \max(0, Se^{-iT} - Xe^{-rT}, S - X)$ |
| Lower price bound for put | $p \geq \max(0, Xe^{-rT} - Se^{-iT})$ | $P \geq \max[0, Xe^{-rT} - Se^{-iT}, X - S]$ |
| Put-call parity relation | $c - p = Se^{-iT} - Xe^{-rT}$ | $S - X < C - P < Se^{-iT} - Xe^{-rT}$ if $i \leq 0$<br>$Se^{-iT} - X < C - P < S - Xe^{-rT}$ if $i > 0$ |

### Summary

This completes the derivations of no-arbitrage price relations for European-style and American-style options on assets with a continuous net carry rate. For convenience, a summary of the no-arbitrage relations is provided in Table 6.7.

## DISCRETE FLOWS

With the no-arbitrage price relations for an underlying asset with a continuous carry cost rate in hand, the focus now turns to developing the same set of relations for an asset that has interest cost modeled as a continuous rate but noninterest costs/benefits modeled as a discrete flow. If the noninterest flow is income such as in the case of a cash dividend payment on a share of stock or a coupon payment on a bond, the income is represented as a positive value, that is, $I_t > 0$. If the flow is a cost such as, say, warehouse rent from storing an inventory of wheat, the income is represented as a negative value, that is, $I_t < 0$. Again, since this book deals primarily with financial assets, most of the illustrations will have $I_t$ discussed as being a positive value. Although $I_t$ represents a cash payment on any type of asset, we will call $I_t$ a dividend payment throughout this section for expositional convenience.

### Lower Price Bound of European-Style Call

The lower price bound of a European-style call option on an asset that makes a single, discrete cash dividend payment during the option's life is

$$c \geq \max(0, S - I_t e^{-rt} - Xe^{-rT}) \tag{6.13}$$

In this relation, $I_t e^{-rt}$ is the present value of the promised dividend to be received at time $t$, where $t < T$. The arbitrage trading strategy that supports (6.13) is: sell the asset, buy a call, and buy risk-free bonds. The initial investment and terminal values are shown in Table 6.8. The first row in the table represents the short asset position. Today, we collect $S$, and, at the option's expiration, the short position must be covered at a cost of $\tilde{S}_t$. Shorting an asset, however, requires that we pay any dividends on the underlying asset. If we are short a stock and

**TABLE 6.8** Arbitrage portfolio trades supporting lower price bound of European-style call option where the underlying asset pays a discrete cash dividend, $C - P < S - Xe^{-rT}$.

| Trades | Initial Investment | Cash Flow at $t$ | Value on Day $T$ | |
|---|---|---|---|---|
| | | | $S_T < X$ | $S_T \geq X$ |
| Sell asset | $S$ | $-I_t$ | $-\tilde{S}_T$ | $-\tilde{S}_T$ |
| Buy call option | $-c$ | | 0 | $\tilde{S}_T - X$ |
| Buy risk-free bonds | $-Xe^{-rT} - I_t e^{-rt}$ | $I_t$ | $X$ | $X$ |
| Net portfolio value | $S - I_t e^{-rt} - Xe^{-rT} - c$ | 0 | $X - \tilde{S}_T$ | 0 |

the stock pays a dividend, for example, we are obliged to pay the dividend out of our own pocket. Since the dividend is made during the option's life (i.e., $t < T$), the first row has a cash outflow of $-I_t$ paid on day $t$. The second row shows the long call position. On day $t$, the call is worth nothing if $S_T < X$ and $\tilde{S}_T - X$ if $S_T \geq X$. Finally, we buy some risk-free bonds. The amount necessary must be sufficient to cover the payment of the exercise price, $X$, on day $T$ and the payment of the cash dividend, $I_t$, on day $t$, that is, $-Xe^{-rT} - I_t e^{-rt}$. Since the portfolio is certain to have a *nonnegative* net value on day $t$, the net portfolio value today must be less than or equal to 0, which implies $c \geq S - I_t e^{-rt} - Xe^{-rT}$.

### Lower Price Bound of American-Style Call

A discrete cash dividend payment on the underlying asset affects the early exercise behavior of American-style call options differently than in the continuous carry rate case. In the case of an American-style call written on a stock, it may be optimal to exercise either just prior to the ex-dividend date (when the stock price falls by $I_t$) or at expiration. Early exercise between today and the ex-dividend instant and between the ex-dividend instant and expiration are *not* optimal because the call is worth more alive than dead.[13] The lower price bound of an American-style call is therefore the lower bound of a call expiring at the ex-dividend instant, $\max(0, S - Xe^{-rt})$, and the lower bound of the call expiring at expiration, $\max(0, S - I_t e^{-rt} - Xe^{-rT})$. Combining these two results,

$$c \geq \max(0, S - Xe^{-rt}, S - I_t e^{-rt} - Xe^{-rT}) \tag{6.14}$$

### Early Exercise of American-Style Call Options

The last two terms on the right-hand side of (6.14) provide important guidance in deciding whether to exercise the American call option early, just prior to the

[13] By not exercising in the period prior to ex-dividend, the call option holder enjoys the benefits of implicitly earning interest on the dividend and the exercise price of the call. By not exercising after the ex-dividend date but before expiration, the call option holder enjoys the benefit of implicitly earning interest on the exercise price of the call.

ex-date. The second term in the parentheses is the present value of the early proceeds of the call. If this amount is less than the lower price bound of the call that expires normally, that is, if

$$S - Xe^{-rt} < S - I_t e^{-rt} - Xe^{-rT}$$

an American-style call will not be exercised early. To understand why, rewrite the expression as

$$I_t < X[1 - e^{-r(T-t)}] \quad (6.15)$$

The American-style call will not be exercised early if the cash flow (e.g., dividend or coupon payment) captured by exercising prior to the ex-date is less than the interest implicitly earned by deferring exercise from the ex-date until expiration.

The logic underlying the relation (6.15) also applies to the case where there are multiple known dividends paid during the call option's life. Take a stock option, for example. If the *i*th dividend is less than the present value of the interest income that can be implicitly earned as a result of deferring the payment of the exercise price until the next dividend payment, that is, if

$$I_i < X[1 - e^{-r(t_{i+1} - t_i)}] \quad (6.16)$$

exercising just prior to the ith dividend payment will not be optimal. This relation proves useful for simplifying the valuation of long-term stock options, as will be shown in Chapter 13. The following example shows that dividend-induced early exercise on a long-term American-style call is most likely to occur just prior to the last dividend payment during the option's life.

**ILLUSTRATION 6.7** Identify prospect of early exercise for American-style calls on dividend-paying stocks.

*Identify whether an American-style call option with an exercise price of 50 and one year remaining to expiration may be exercised early just prior to any of the dividend payments. Assume that the stock pays a quarterly dividend of 0.50 in 70 days, 161 days, 252 days, and 343 days. Assume the risk-free rate of interest is 5%.*

Whether or not the call may be exercised early depends on the amount of the dividend payment in relation to the present value of the interest income implicitly received by deferring the payment of the exercise price. For the first dividend, compute the values in expression (6.16) and find

$$0.50 < 50[1 - e^{-0.05(161/365 - 70/365)}] = 0.6194$$

Hence, the call will not optimally be exercised just prior to the first dividend payment. The same is true for the second and third dividend payments, as shown in the table below.

| Quarter | Cash Dividend | Days to Dividend Payment | Years to Dividend Payment | PV of Interest Income |
|---|---|---|---|---|
| 1 | 0.50 | 70 | 0.1918 | 0.6194 |
| 2 | 0.50 | 161 | 0.4411 | 0.6194 |
| 3 | 0.50 | 252 | 0.6904 | 0.6194 |
| 4 | 0.50 | 343 | 0.9397 | 0.1505 |

For the last dividend payment in 353 days, condition (6.13) is violated, that is,

$$0.50 > 50[1 - e^{-0.05(365 - 343)/365}] = 0.1505$$

This implies that exercise just prior to the last dividend payment during this option's life may be optimal.

### Lower Price Bound of European-Style Put

The lower price bound for the European-style put option is

$$p \geq \max(0, Xe^{-rT} - S + I_t e^{-rt}) \tag{6.17}$$

Again, the asset price is reduced by the present value of the promised cash dividend on the asset. Unlike the call, however, the dividend payment *increases* the lower price bound of the European-style put. Because the put option is the right to sell the underlying asset at a fixed price, a discrete drop in the asset price such as one induced by the payment of a dividend on a stock serves to increase the value of the option. The arbitrage trades driving this relation are buy a put, buy a share of stock, and sell $I_t e^{-rt} + Xe^{-rT}$ risk-free bonds.

### Lower Price Bound of American-Style Put

The lower price bound of the American-style put is

$$P \geq \max(0, Xe^{-rt} - S + I_t e^{-rt}, X - S) \tag{6.18}$$

The second term on the right-hand side is the present value of the exercise proceeds if the put is exercised just after the dividend payment. This lower price bound is supported by the arbitrage trades listed above for the European-style put. The third term on the right is the exercise proceeds if the put is exercised immediately. If $P < X - S$, a costless arbitrage profit can be earned by buying the put and the asset, and then exercising the put. The arbitrage profit is $X - S - P > 0$.

### Early Exercise of American-Style Put Options

The early exercise behavior induced by the discrete cash dividend on the asset is different for the American-style put that it was for the call. If the third term exceeds the second in (6.18), the put will not be exercised early prior to the payment date. In that period the interest earned on the exercise proceeds of the option is less than the drop in the stock price from the payment of the dividend. For the third term to be larger than the second, that is,

$$Xe^{-rt} - S + I_t e^{-rt} > X - S$$

it must be the case that

$$I_t > X(e^{rt} - 1) \tag{6.19}$$

In other words, if the amount of the dividend amount exceeds the interest income that will accrue on the cash received if the put is exercised immediately, the put will not optimally be exercised early.

As in the case of the call, this argument can be generalized to handle the multiple dividends during the life of an American-style put. Again, consider a stock option. If the *i*th dividend is greater than the interest that will accrue over the period,

$$I_i > X[e^{r(t_i - t_{i-1})} - 1] \tag{6.20}$$

the put will not be exercised before the dividend payment, as the illustration below shows.

**ILLUSTRATION 6.8** Identify prospect of early exercise for American-style puts on dividend-paying stocks.

*Identify whether an American-style put option with an exercise price of 50 and one year remaining to expiration may be exercised early just after any of the dividend payments. Assume that the stock pays a quarterly dividend of 0.50 in 70 days, 161 days, 252 days, and 343 days. Assume the risk-free rate of interest is 5%.*

Whether or not the put may be exercised early depends on the amount of the dividend payment in relation to the interest income that could be earned if the put were exercised immediately. For the first dividend, compute the values in expression (6.20), that is,

$$0.50 > 50[e^{0.05(70/365)} - 1] = 0.4818$$

This implies that the put will not be exercised before the first dividend payment in 70 days.

The computation for the second dividend is

$$0.50 > 50[e^{0.05(161/365 - 70/365)} - 1] = 0.6272$$

This implies that the put may be exercised in the period between the first and second dividends. The same is true between the second and third dividends, and the third and fourth dividends, as indicated below. Early exercise after the fourth dividend is paid may also be optimal since no more dividends are paid during the option's life.

| Quarter | Cash Dividend | Days to Dividend Payment | Years to Dividend Payment | Accrued Interest |
|---|---|---|---|---|
| 1 | 0.50 | 70 | 0.1918 | 0.4818 |
| 2 | 0.50 | 161 | 0.4411 | 0.6272 |
| 3 | 0.50 | 252 | 0.6904 | 0.6272 |
| 4 | 0.50 | 343 | 0.9397 | 0.6272 |

## Put-Call Parity for European-Style Options

Put-call parity for European-style options on assets with discrete noninterest cash flows is

$$c - p = S - I_t e^{-rt} - Xe^{-rT} \tag{6.21}$$

To see this, assume the left-hand side of (6.21) is less than the right-hand side. If such is the case, an arbitrage profit can be made by selling the asset, selling the put, buying the call, and buying some risk-free bonds. The arbitrage is shown in Table 6.9. On day $t$, the net portfolio value is certain to be 0. The same is true on day $t$, when the cash dividend is made. Thus the value at time 0, $S - I_t e^{-rt} - Xe^{-rT} + p - c$, represents the arbitrage profit and is *positive* if the left-hand side of (6.21) is less than the right-hand side. Since the market cannot be in equilibrium, arbitrage will continue until the net portfolio value goes to 0. When it does, the market is in equilibrium and (6.21) holds.

## Put-Call Parity for American-Style Options

The put-call parity for American-style options on assets with discrete cash dividends is

$$S - I_t e^{-rt} - X \le C - P \le S - I_t e^{-rt} - Xe^{-rT} \tag{6.22}$$

To understand why, we consider each inequality in (6.22) in turn. The inequality on the left can be derived by considering the values of a portfolio that consists

**TABLE 6.9** Arbitrage portfolio trades supporting European-style put-call parity where the underlying asset pays a discrete cash dividend, $c - p = S - I_t e^{-rt} - Xe^{-rT}$.

| Trades | Initial Investment | Cash Flow at $t$ | Value on day $T$ | |
|---|---|---|---|---|
| | | | $S_T < X$ | $S_T \ge X$ |
| Sell asset | $S$ | $-I_t$ | $-\tilde{S}_T$ | $-\tilde{S}_T$ |
| Sell put option | $p$ | | $-(X - \tilde{S}_T)$ | 0 |
| Buy call option | $-c$ | | 0 | $\tilde{S}_T - X$ |
| Buy risk-free bonds | $-Xe^{-rT} - I_t e^{-rt}$ | $I_t$ | $X$ | $X$ |
| Net portfolio value | $S - I_t e^{-rt} - Xe^{-rT} + p - c$ | 0 | 0 | 0 |

of buying a call, selling a put, selling the stock, and buying $X + I_t e^{-rt}$ in risk-free bonds. Table 6.10 contains these trades as well as the net portfolio value.

In Table 6.10, we see that, if all positions stay open until expiration, the net portfolio value is positive independent of whether the terminal asset price is above or below the exercise price of the options. If the terminal asset price is above the exercise price, the call option is exercised, and the asset acquired at exercise price X is used to deliver, in part, against the short asset position. If the terminal asset price is below the exercise price, the put is exercised. The asset received in the exercise of the put is used to cover the short stock position. In the event the put is exercised early at time $\tau$, the investment in the risk-free bonds is more than sufficient to cover the payment of the exercise price, and the asset received upon delivery can be used to cover the short asset position. In addition, the call position remains open and has a nonnegative value. In other words, the combination of securities described in Table 6.10 will never have a negative future value. And, if the future value is certain to be nonnegative, the sum of the initial investment column must be nonpositive. In the absence of costless arbitrage opportunities, the left-hand inequality of (6.22) must hold.

The right inequality of (6.19) may be derived using the same portfolio used to prove European-style put-call parity. Table 6.11 contains the arbitrage portfolio trades. In this case, the net portfolio value at expiration is certain to be 0 should the option positions stay open until that time. In the event the American call option holder decides to exercise early, the portfolio holder delivers his share of stock, receives cash in the amount of the exercise price, and then used the cash to retire his outstanding debt. After these actions are taken, the portfolio holder still has an open long put position and cash in the amount of $X[1 - e^{-r(T-\tau)}]$. Since the portfolio is certain to have non-negative outcomes, the initial value must be negative or the right-hand inequality of (6.22) must hold.

## Summary

This completes our derivations of arbitrage relations for European-style and American-style options on assets with discrete cash dividends. Options on divi-

**TABLE 6.10** Arbitrage trades supporting American-style put-call parity where the underlying asset pays a discrete cash dividend, $S - I_t e^{-rt} - X < C - P$.

| Trades | Initial Value | Ex-Day Value ($t$) | Put Exercised Early, Intermediate Value ($\tau$) | Put Exercised Normally, Terminal Value ($T$) | |
|---|---|---|---|---|---|
| | | | | $\tilde{S}_T \le X$ | $\tilde{S}_T > X$ |
| Buy call | $-C$ | | $\tilde{C}_\tau$ | 0 | $\tilde{S}_T - X$ |
| Sell put | $P$ | | $-(X - \tilde{S}_\tau)$ | $-(X - \tilde{S}_T)$ | 0 |
| Sell asset | $S$ | $-I_t$ | $-\tilde{S}_\tau$ | $-\tilde{S}_T$ | $-\tilde{S}_T$ |
| Buy risk-free bonds | $-I_t e^{-rt} - X$ | $I_t$ | $Xe^{r\tau}$ | $Xe^{rT}$ | $Xe^{rT}$ |
| Net portfolio value | $-C + P + S - I_t e^{-rt} - X$ | 0 | $\tilde{C}_\tau + X(e^{r\tau} - 1)$ | $X(e^{rT} - 1)$ | $X(e^{rT} - 1)$ |

**TABLE 6.11** Arbitrage trades supporting American-style put-call parity where the underlying asset pays a discrete cash dividend, $C - P < S - I_t e^{-rt} - Xe^{-rT}$.

| Trades | Initial Value | Ex-Day Value ($t$) | Call Exercised Early, Intermediate Value ($\tau$) | Call Exercised Normally, Terminal Value ($T$) | |
|---|---|---|---|---|---|
| | | | | $\tilde{S}_T \le X$ | $\tilde{S}_T > X$ |
| Sell call | C | | $-(\tilde{S}_\tau - X)$ | 0 | $-(\tilde{S}_T - X)$ |
| Buy put | $-P$ | | $\tilde{P}_\tau$ | $X - \tilde{S}_\tau$ | 0 |
| Buy stock | $-S$ | $I_t$ | $\tilde{S}_\tau$ | $\tilde{S}_T$ | $\tilde{S}_T$ |
| Sell risk-free bonds | $I_t e^{-rt} + Xe^{-rT}$ | $-I_t$ | $-Xe^{-r(T-\tau)}$ | $-X$ | $-X$ |
| Net portfolio value | $C - P - S + I_t e^{-rt} + X$ | 0 | $\tilde{P}_\tau + X(1 - e^{r(T-\tau)})$ | 0 | 0 |

**TABLE 6.12** No-arbitrage price relations for European- and American-style options on assets where the underlying asset pays a discrete cash dividend.

| Description | European-Style Options | American-Style Options |
|---|---|---|
| Lower price bound for call | $c \ge \max(0, S - I_t e^{-rt} - Xe^{-rT})$ | $c \ge \max[0, S - Xe^{-rt}, S - I_t e^{-rt} - X]$ |
| Lower price bound for put | $p \ge \max(0, Xe^{-rT} - S + I_t e^{-rt})$ | $P \ge \max(0, X - S, Xe^{-rt} - S + I_t e^{-rt})$ |
| Put-call parity relation | $c - p = S - I_t e^{-rt} - Xe^{-rT}$ | $S - I_t e^{-rt} - X \le C - P \le S - I_t e^{-rt} - Xe^{-rT}$ |

dend-paying stocks and on coupon-bearing bonds fall into this category. Before proceeding with a discussion of arbitrage relations for futures options, we summarize our results in Table 6.12.

## NO-ARBITRAGE FUTURES OPTIONS RELATIONS

A *futures option* is like an asset option, except that if the option is exercised, a futures position is entered. Exercising a call option on a futures contract, for example, means that the holder will receive a long position in the futures at a price equal to the exercise price of the call.

Developing the lower bounds and put-call parity for European- and American-style futures options follows directly from the previous discussions. All we need to do is recall the prepaid version of the net cost of carry relations for futures: $Fe^{-rT} = Se^{-iT}$ where noninterest costs are modeled as a continuous rate (i.e., equation (4.5) in Chapter 4), and $Fe^{-rT} = S - Ie^{-it}$ where noninterest costs are modeled as a discrete flow (i.e., equation (4.7) in Chapter 4). Substituting $Fe^{-rT} = Se^{-iT}$ into the no-arbitrage price relations summarized in Table 6.7 or $Fe^{-rT} = S - Ie^{-it}$ in the relations summarized in Table 6.12 produces the no-arbitrage price relations for futures options summarized in Table 6.13. The arbitrage portfolios supporting each of these relations are the same as those used to derive the relations for the asset throughout the chapter.

**TABLE 6.13** No-arbitrage price relations for European- and American-style options on futures contracts.

| Description | European-Style Options | American-Style Options |
|---|---|---|
| Lower price bound for call | $c \geq \max[0, e^{-rT}(F - X)]$ | $C \geq \max(0, F - X)$ |
| Lower price bound for put | $p \geq \max[0, e^{-rT}(X - F)]$ | $P \geq \max(0, X - F)$ |
| Put-call parity relation | $c - p = e^{-rT}(F - X)$ | $Fe^{-rT} - X < C - P < F - Xe^{-rT}$ |

## NO-ARBITRAGE INTER-MARKET RELATIONS

In many cases, both asset options and futures options trade concurrently. The Chicago Board Options Exchange, for example, lists options on the S&P 500 index, while the Chicago Mercantile Exchanges lists options on the S&P 500 futures (which, in turn, is written on the S&P 500 index). The prices of asset options are inextricably linked to the prices of futures options. Under the assumption that the futures and options expire simultaneously and that the exercise prices of the asset and futures options are the same, a number of no-arbitrage price relations may be derived. Next we present such relations for European-style and American-style options.

### European-Style Options

The price of a European-style asset option is equal to the price of the corresponding futures option, that is,

$$c(S) = c(F) \tag{6.23a}$$

and

$$p(S) = p(F) \tag{6.23b}$$

The reason is that at expiration the payoffs of the asset option and the futures option are identical. Suppose, for the sake of illustration, that the price of a call on a futures exceeds the price of a call on an asset. In such a situation, costless arbitrage profits may be earned by buying the asset call and selling the futures call, as is shown in Table 6.14 below. The long asset option position pays nothing at expiration if the terminal asset price is less than the exercise price and pays $\tilde{S}_T - X$ if the terminal asset price exceeds the exercise price. At the same time, the short futures option position expires worthless at expiration if the terminal futures (asset) price is less than the exercise price and costs $-(\tilde{F}_T - X)$ if the terminal futures (asset) price exceeds the exercise price. But, since $\tilde{F}_T = \tilde{S}_T$, the net portfolio value is certain to be zero. A portfolio that is certain to pay nothing on day $T$ must cost nothing. Hence, in the absence of costless arbitrage opportunities, European-style asset options and European-style futures options have the same price.

**TABLE 6.14** Arbitrage portfolio trades demonstrating the equivalence of prices of European-style call options on an asset and a futures, $c(F) = c(S)$.

| Trades | Initial Investment | Value on Day $T$ | |
|---|---|---|---|
| | | $S_T < X$ | $S_T \geq X$ |
| Buy call option on asset | $-c(S)$ | 0 | $\tilde{S}_T - X$ |
| Sell call option on futures | $c(F)$ | 0 | $-(\tilde{F}_T - X) = -(\tilde{S}_T - X)$ |
| Net portfolio value | $c(F) - c(S)$ | 0 | 0 |

**TABLE 6.15** No-arbitrage relations between the prices of asset options and futures options.

| Description | European-Style Options | American-Style Options |
|---|---|---|
| Call | $c(S) = c(F)$ | $C(S) < C(F)$ if $F > S$<br>$C(S) > C(F)$ if $F < S$ |
| Put | $p(S) = p(F)$ | $P(S) > P(F)$ if $F > S$<br>$P(S) < P(F)$ if $F < S$ |

## American-Style Options

The relation between the price of an American-style asset option and the price of the corresponding futures option depends on whether the futures price is greater than the asset price or not. If $F > S$,

$$C(S) < C(F) \tag{6.24a}$$

and

$$P(S) > P(F) \tag{6.24b}$$

To see this, consider the American-style call options. Since both the call on the futures and the call on the asset may be exercised early, we can compare the early exercise proceeds to establish which has greater value. The call on the asset has immediate early exercise proceeds of $S - X$ and the call on the futures has early exercise proceeds of $F - X > S - X$. Thus as long as there is some chance of early exercise, the call on the futures is worth more than the call on the asset and the put on the asset is worth more than the put on the futures.

For cases where futures price is less than the asset price, the opposite results hold, that is,

$$C(S) > C(F) \tag{6.25a}$$

and

$$P(S) < P(F) \tag{6.25b}$$

The above arbitrage argument is merely reversed. Table 6.15 summarizes the results.

## SUMMARY

This chapter develops no-arbitrage price relations for European- and American-style options under the assumption that no costless arbitrage (i.e., free money) opportunities available in the marketplace. The net cost of carry of the underlying asset again plays an important role. Consequently, we model interest cost as a constant continuous rate and the noninterest cost as a continuous rate or as a discrete flow, depending on the nature of the underlying asset. For options on stock indexes, currencies, and some commodities, the continuous rate assumption is most appropriate. For options on stocks, bonds, and other commodities, the discrete flow assumption is preferred. With the assumptions and net cost of carry definitions in hand, lower price bounds, put-call parity price relations, and intermarket price relations are derived for both European-style and American-style options on an asset and on a forward/futures. The results in this chapter are general and apply to any underlying asset. These price relations will prove to be important in the risk management strategies of later chapters.

## REFERENCES AND SUGGESTED READINGS

Gastineau, Gary. 1988. *The Options Manual*, 3rd ed. New York: McGraw-Hill.

Merton, Robert C. 1973. Theory of rational option pricing. *Bell Journal of Economics and Management Science* 4: 141–183.

Smith Jr., Clifford W. 1976. Option pricing: A review. *Journal of Financial Economics* 3 (January/March): 3–51.

Stoll, Hans R. 1969. The relationship between put and call prices. *Journal of Finance* 24: 802–824.

Stoll, Hans R., and Robert E. Whaley. 1986. New option instruments: Arbitrageable linkages and valuation. *Advances in Futures and Options Research* 1 (A): 25–62.

# 7

# Valuing Standard Options Analytically

In Chapter 6, we developed option price relations in the absence of costless arbitrage opportunities. While the no-arbitrage price relations have useful applications, they provide only bounds on prices, not exact option values. In this chapter, we develop valuation equations for European-style options and show how the equations can be used for risk measurement. We also describe how to estimate of the parameters of the valuation equation.

An option, like any other security, can be valued as the present value of its expected cash flows. For a European-style call option, the expected cash flow is at the option's expiration and equals the expected difference between the underlying asset price and the exercise price conditional upon the asset price being greater than the exercise price. Thus the call's expected cash flow depends on, among other things, the expected risk-adjusted rate of price appreciation on the underlying asset between now and expiration. Once the call's expected terminal value is established, it must be discounted to the present. The discount rate applied to the expected terminal option value is the expected risk-adjusted rate of return for the option. The problem with this "traditional" approach to valuation is that it is difficult, if not impossible, to estimate precisely the expected risk-adjusted return parameters.

A major theoretical breakthrough occurred in 1973, with the publication of research papers by Black and Scholes (1973) and Merton (1973) (hereafter, BSM). They showed that if we can form a risk-free hedge between an option and its underlying asset, option valuation will not depend on individual risk preferences and need not depend on estimating expected risk-adjusted returns.[1] Indeed, if option valuation does not depend on risk preferences, we are free to choose any type of individual risk behavior in valuing an option. An obvious choice is to assume individuals are risk-neutral. In a risk-neutral world, all assets are expected to have a rate of return equal to their risk-free rate of interest. Consequently, the need to estimate risk-adjusted rates of return is eliminated.

This chapter has five sections. The first section builds the intuition underlying risk-neutral valuation using a simple, one-period binomial model. We show that

[1] If a risk-free hedge can be formed between two risky securities, the securities are *redundant*, and each can be priced in relation to the other as investors are risk-neutral.

BSM option values are the same as those obtained using risk-neutral individuals and risk-averse individuals. With the irrelevance of risk preferences established, we turn to risk-neutral option valuation. The BSM model assumes that the price of the asset underlying the option is log-normally distributed. In the second section, we develop the expressions for the expected value of the asset price given estimates of the mean and the variance of the normally distributed return distribution. With the expected terminal price of the option in hand, we present the valuation equation of a European-style call option in the third section and a European-style put option in the fourth. The fifth section shows how the option valuation formulas can be used to measure an option's risk characteristics. The final section contains a summary.

## INTUITION OF RISK-NEUTRAL VALUATION

The key insight of the BSM option valuation model is that, if a risk-free hedge may be formed between the option and its underlying asset, an option can be valued without knowing anything about individual risk preferences. To develop the intuition for the risk-free hedge, we use a simple, one-period binomial model and value a European-style call option. We then show the value of the call is the same for individuals who are risk-neutral and risk-averse.

### Risk-Free Hedge Portfolio Using a Binomial Model

To illustrate the nature of the risk-free hedge portfolio, consider a European-style call option that allows its holder to buy one unit of an asset in three months at an exercise price of 40. Suppose that the asset's current price is 40 and that at the end of three months the asset price will be either 45 or 35. These asset prices are shown in Figure 7.1. Depending on whether the asset price is 45 or 35, a call will have a value of 5 or 0.

**FIGURE 7.1** Binomial lattice showing terminal asset prices and call option values.

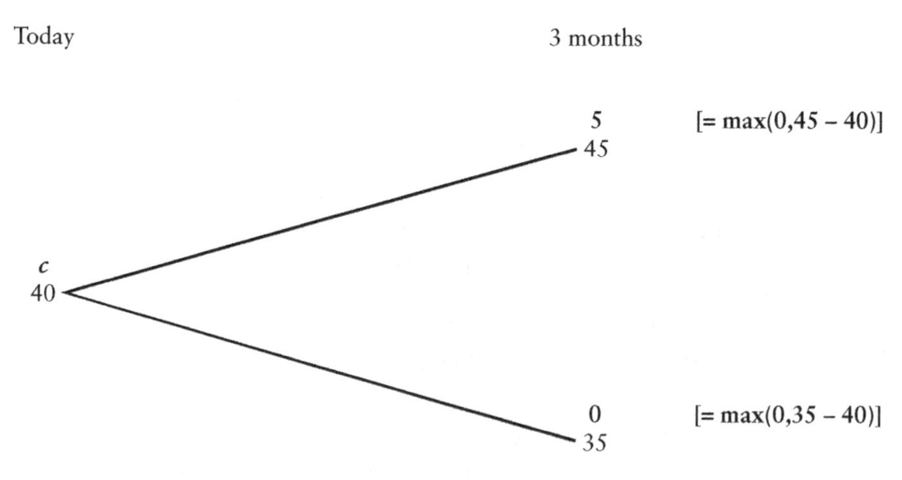

Now, consider buying one unit of the asset and selling $n$ call options. The terminal value of the portfolio will be $45 - 5n$ if the price of the asset rises and 35 if it falls. Now, if we set $n$ such that

$$45 - 5n = 35$$

we find that selling two call options (i.e., $n = 2$) eliminates all portfolio risk. In other words, if we buy one unit of the asset and sell two calls, the terminal value of the portfolio is certain to be 35—we have created a *risk-free hedge portfolio.*

The fact that the portfolio is risk-free means that in the absence of costless arbitrage opportunities the cost of forming this risk-free hedge portfolio today, $40 - 2c$, must be equal to the present value of the certain terminal value, 35, where the discount rate is the risk-free rate of interest. If the risk-free rate of interest is 2%, the call option can be valued by solving

$$40 - 2c = \frac{35}{1.02}$$

The value of the European-style call is 2.84.

**Costless Arbitrage Opportunity** To check that the value of the call is 2.84 for all individuals, independent of their attitudes toward risk, assume the call price is 3. What should we do? The answer is "Sell the call, buy a half unit of the asset, and borrow 17.16" (i.e., the present value of half of 35), as is shown in Table 7.1. This portfolio generates $3 - 0.5(40) + 17.16 = 0.16$ in cash. At the option's expiration in three months, the value of the portfolio is

$$-(45 - 40) + 0.5(35) - 17.50 = 0$$

if the asset price rises to 45, and is

$$0 + 0.5(35) - 17.50 = 0$$

if the asset price falls to 35. In other words, with this portfolio, we collect 16 cents up front and have no further obligation or risk. We have earned a *costless arbitrage profit.* Since everyone can engage in costless arbitrage if an opportunity arises,

**TABLE 7.1** Arbitrage portfolio trades.

| | | Value in 3 Months | |
|---|---|---|---|
| Trades | Initial Investment | $S_T = 35$ | $S_T = 45$ |
| Sell call | 3 | 0 | $-(45 - 40)$ |
| Buy asset | −20 | $0.5(35) = 17.50$ | $0.5(45) = 22.50$ |
| Sell risk-free bonds | 17.16 | −17.50 | −17.50 |
| Net portfolio value | 0.16 | 0 | 0 |

option valuation will not depend on individual risk preferences. In the absence of costless arbitrage opportunities (as should be the case in a rationally functioning marketplace), all individuals will agree that the fair value of the option is 2.84.

### Risk-Neutral Valuation Using a Binomial Model

In order to value the European-style call under the assumption that individuals are risk-neutral, we need to find the "risk-neutral" probabilities of an up-step and a down-step in our binomial model. Under risk-neutrality, the expected terminal price of the asset equals its current price times one plus the risk-free rate of interest, that is, 40(1.02). But the expected terminal asset price is also, by definition, equal to $45p + 35(1 - p)$, where $p$ is the probability of an up-step and $1 - p$ is the probability of a down-step. Equating these terms,

$$40(1.02) = 45p + 35(1 - p)$$

and solving, the risk-neutral probability of an up-step, $p$, equals 58%.

With the probabilities identified, the expected terminal value of the call may be computed as

$$\text{Expected terminal call value} = 5(0.58) + 0(0.42) = 2.90$$

The current value of the call is the present value of the expected terminal value. Normally, this would be the expected risk-adjusted rate of return on the call. Under the assumption of risk-neutrality, however, the expected rate of return on all risky assets is the risk-free rate of interest. The current call value is therefore

$$c = \frac{2.90}{1.02} = 2.84$$

exactly the value computed using the risk-free hedge portfolio approach.

### Risk-Averse Valuation Using a Binomial Model

In the interest of completeness, we will now value the European-style call in our illustration by assuming that individuals are risk-averse. This means we have to identify the expected risk-adjusted rate of return on the underlying asset in order to project the asset's expected terminal price, and the expected risk-adjusted rate of return on the call in order to discount the expected terminal value of the call to the present.[2]

[2] Recall that this was the state of the option valuation literature before the publication of the BSM model in 1973. Samuelson (1965) identified a formula for valuing a European-style call option eight years before Black-Scholes and Merton. His formula required the expected risk-adjusted rates of return for the call and the underlying asset. For a historical perspective on the development of modern-day option valuation theory, see Whaley (2003).

To identify the "risk-averse" probabilities of an up-step and a down-step, assume that the asset's expected rate of price appreciation over the three-month period is 4%—a 2% risk-free return plus a 2% premium arising from individual demands for bearing risk. Since the current asset price is 40 and its expected return is 4%, the "risk-averse" probabilities of an up-step, $p'$, and of a down-step, $1 - p'$, must be

$$40(1.04) = 45p' + 35(1 - p')$$

The risk-averse probability of an up-step, $p'$, is 66%. The up-step probability for a risk-averse individual is higher than it was for a risk-neutral individual (assuming that the terminal asset prices in the binomial model are the same) because the higher expected asset return in the risk-averse world must be reflected through a higher up-step probability given that the terminal asset prices are being held constant. With the probabilities in hand, we find the expected terminal value of the call, that is,

$$E(\tilde{c}_T) = 5(0.66) + 0(0.34) = 3.30$$

To determine the current value of the call, we now need to identify the expected risk-adjusted rate of return for the call. In a risk-neutral world, individuals are indifferent toward risk and therefore demand the risk-free rate of return on all assets—risky or risk-free. In a risk-averse world, however, individuals are averse to risk and demand proportionally higher expected rates of return as asset risk increases. Recall that we developed the relation between expected return and risk tradeoff in Chapter 3. It is called the capital asset pricing model (CAPM) and states that the expected rate of return of an asset is

$$E_S = r + (E_M - r)\beta_S \tag{7.1}$$

where $E_S$ and $E_M$ are the expected rates of return for the asset and the market portfolio, respectively, $r$ is the risk-free of return, and $\beta_S$ is the asset's "beta" risk.

In the expected return/risk tradeoff expressed in (7.1), the asset's beta, $\beta_S$, is the percent change in asset price with respect to a percent change in the level of the market. Since the CAPM applies to all risky assets including call options, the expected return for the call may be expressed as

$$E_c = r + (E_M - r)\beta_c \tag{7.2}$$

where the call's beta, $\beta_c$, is the percent change in call price with respect to a percent change in the level of the market. Recognizing that we can multiply $\beta_S$ by the percent change in call price with respect to the asset price to compute the call's beta, that is,

$$\beta_c = \beta_S\left(\frac{dc/c}{dS/S}\right)$$

hence, the expected risk-adjusted rate of return of the call is

$$E_c = r + (E_M - r)\beta_S\left(\frac{dc/c}{dS/S}\right) \tag{7.3}$$

Substituting the parameters from our illustration,

$$0.04 = 0.02 + (E_M - 0.02)\beta_S$$

This means that the "market risk premium" for the asset is

$$(E_M - 0.02)\beta_S = 0.02$$

We can also compute the percentage change in option price with respect to a percent change in asset price using the prices from our binomial model, that is,

$$\frac{dc/c}{dS/S} = \frac{dc}{dS} \times \frac{S}{c} = \frac{5-0}{45-35} \times \frac{40}{c} = \frac{20}{c}$$

Substituting 0.02 for $(E_M - 0.02)\beta$ and

$$\frac{20}{c} \text{ for } \frac{dc/c}{dS/S}$$

in (7.3), we get

$$E_c = 0.02 + 0.02\left(\frac{20}{c}\right)$$

Thus the present value of the expected terminal value of the call,

$$c = \frac{E(\tilde{c}_T)}{1 + E_c}$$

is

$$c = \frac{3.30}{1 + 0.02 + \dfrac{0.40}{c}}$$

or $c = 2.84$. Even risk-averse individuals agree that the call price should be 2.84.

## LOG-NORMAL PRICE DISTRIBUTION

The purpose of the illustration in the last section was to show the equivalence of valuing an option using a risk-free hedge, a risk-neutral world, and a risk-averse world. Since individual risk preferences are irrelevant, we are free to choose any type of risk preference structure we want without losing generality. We will proceed under the assumption that all individuals are risk-neutral. This simplifies matters considerably since all assets in a risk-neutral world are expected to have a rate of return equal to the risk-free rate.

The next major step in deriving an analytical model for valuing options is to introduce a more realistic distribution for the asset price at the option's expiration. In the last section we assumed that the asset price had one of two levels at the end of the option's life. In this section, we assume that the terminal asset price has a continuous distribution—specifically, a continuous log-normal distribution. This distribution follows from the BSM assumption that asset prices follow geometric Brownian motion.

### Geometric Brownian Motion

The BSM model assumes that the price of the asset underlying the option follows a geometric Brownian motion,[3]

$$dS = \alpha S dt + \sigma S dz \tag{7.4}$$

What (7.4) says is that, over the next infinitesimally small interval of time $dt$, the change in asset price, $dS$, equals an expected price increment (i.e., the product of the instantaneous expected rate of change in asset price, $\alpha$, times the current asset price, $S$, times the length of the interval) plus a random increment proportional to the instantaneous standard deviation of the rate of change in asset price, $\sigma$, times the asset price. The term, $dz$, denotes an increment to a Wiener process. For expositional convenience, we temporarily assume that the asset pays no income. In this way, we can refer to $\alpha$ as the expected return rather than the expected rate of price appreciation. At the end of this section, we generalize the results by allowing the asset to pay a known constant continuous income rate $i$, as we did in Chapters 4 and 6.

To gather more intuition about the assumed return process, rewrite the geometric Brownian motion (7.4) in discretized form, that is,

$$\Delta S = \alpha S \Delta t + \sigma S \sqrt{\Delta t}\varepsilon \tag{7.5}$$

where $\Delta t$ is a small discrete step in time and $\varepsilon$ is a random drawing from a normal distribution with a mean of zero and a standard deviation equal to one. Now, divide through by $S$:

[3] This assumption was first introduced by Boness (1964) and Samuelson (1965) and was later adopted in the work of Black-Scholes (1973) and Merton (1973).

$$\frac{\Delta S}{S} = \alpha\Delta t + \sigma\sqrt{\Delta t}\varepsilon \tag{7.6}$$

What (7.6) says is that, over a discrete interval of time, the asset's return is normally distributed with mean $\alpha\Delta t$ and standard deviation $\sigma\sqrt{\Delta t}$.

A problem with working with (7.6) is that asset returns, so defined, do not aggregate correctly through time. Suppose, for example, that we set $\Delta t$ equal to one month. Suppose that in the first month the asset price moves from its current level of 50 to 100, and then, in the second month, reverts back to 50. The rate of return over the first month is 100% and the second is –50%. The total return over the two-month period is therefore 50%. Obviously this is not true. Common sense dictates that the actual return on the asset over the 2-month interval is 0% (i.e., we started at 50 and ended at 50).

To circumvent this problem, we work with the logarithm of asset prices. If asset prices follow (7.4), it can be shown by Ito's lemma (see Appendix 7A of this chapter) that the logarithm of asset price follows

$$d\ln S = \mu dt + \sigma dz \tag{7.7}$$

or, in its discretized form,

$$\Delta \ln S = \mu\Delta t + \sigma\varepsilon\sqrt{\Delta t} \tag{7.8}$$

Now test the time aggregation property. The change in $\ln S$ (i.e., the *continuously compounded rate of return*) in the first month is

$$\ln 100 - \ln 50 = \ln\left(\frac{100}{50}\right) = 69.31\%$$

and the return in the second month is

$$\ln 50 - \ln 100 = \ln\left(\frac{50}{100}\right) = -69.31\%$$

Over the two-month period, the continuously compounded return is the sum of the two monthly returns or 0%, exactly the correct amount. The relation between $\alpha$, the continuously compounded mean return, and $\mu$, the mean continuously compounded return, is

$$\mu = \alpha - \frac{\sigma^2}{2}$$

(See Appendix 7B of this chapter.)

To flesh out this concept, consider a sequence of equally spaced asset prices beginning today and continuing through the option's expiration at time $T$, that is,

$$S_0, \tilde{S}_1, \tilde{S}_2, \ldots, \tilde{S}_T$$

There could be daily closing prices for the asset, for example. By (7.8), we know that the *continuously compounded daily return*, $\ln(\tilde{S}_t/\tilde{S}_{t-1})$, is normally distributed with mean $\mu$ and standard deviation $\sigma$, that is,

$$\ln(\tilde{S}_t/\tilde{S}_{t-1}) \sim \phi(\mu, \sigma)$$

where we have defined $\Delta t = t - (t-1) = 1$. The definitions of $\mu$ and $\sigma^2$ are

$$\mu = E[\ln(\tilde{S}_t/\tilde{S}_{t-1})]$$

and

$$\sigma^2 = Var[\ln(\tilde{S}_t/\tilde{S}_{t-1})]$$

respectively. The virtue of using continuously compounded returns, as discussed in Chapter 2 and illustrated in the numerical example above, is that $T$-day return is the sum of the $T$ different daily returns, that is,

$$\ln(\tilde{S}_T/S_0) = \sum_{t=1}^{T} \ln(\tilde{S}_t/\tilde{S}_{t-1})$$

Assuming that the mean and variance are constant through time (and that the daily returns are independent), the mean and the variance of the returns over the interval from 0 to $T$ are

$$E[\ln(\tilde{S}_T/S_0)] = \sum_{t=1}^{T} E[\ln(\tilde{S}_t/\tilde{S}_{t-1})] = \mu T \tag{7.9}$$

and

$$Var[\ln(\tilde{S}_T/S_0)] = \sum_{t=1}^{T} Var[\ln(\tilde{S}_t/\tilde{S}_{t-1})] = \sigma^2 T \tag{7.10}$$

### Log-Normal Asset Price Distribution

Thus far, we have established that, under the BSM assumption that asset prices follow geometric Brownian motion, the logarithmic asset return over the life of the option is normally distributed with mean $\mu T$ and standard deviation $\sigma\sqrt{T}$, that is,

$$\ln(\tilde{S}_T/S) = \ln\tilde{S}_T - \ln S \sim \phi(\mu T, \sigma\sqrt{T}) \tag{7.11}$$

Thus, the logarithm of the terminal asset price is normally distributed with mean $\ln S + \mu T$ and standard deviation $\sigma\sqrt{T}$, that is,

$$\ln\tilde{S}_T \sim \phi(\ln S + \mu T, \sigma\sqrt{T}) \tag{7.12}$$

Since $\ln\tilde{S}_T$ is normally distributed, it can be shown that $\tilde{S}_T$ is log-normally distributed with mean

$$E(\tilde{S}_T) = Se^{\alpha T} \tag{7.13}$$

and variance,

$$Var(\tilde{S}_T) = S^2 e^{2\alpha T}(e^{\sigma^2 T} - 1) \tag{7.14}$$

where $\alpha$ is the continuously compounded expected return of the asset.

Figure 7.2 illustrates the normal distribution of the continuously compounded returns, $\ln(S_T/S)$. The mean of the distribution is $\mu T$ and its standard deviation is $\sigma\sqrt{T}$. The returns range from $-\infty$ to $+\infty$ and are symmetric around the mean. Figure 7.3 illustrates the log-normal distribution of the terminal asset price, $S_T$. The mean of the distribution is $Se^{\alpha T}$ and its standard deviation is

$$\sqrt{S^2 e^{2\alpha T}(e^{\sigma^2 T} - 1)}$$

**FIGURE 7.2** Normal distribution of continuous asset returns.

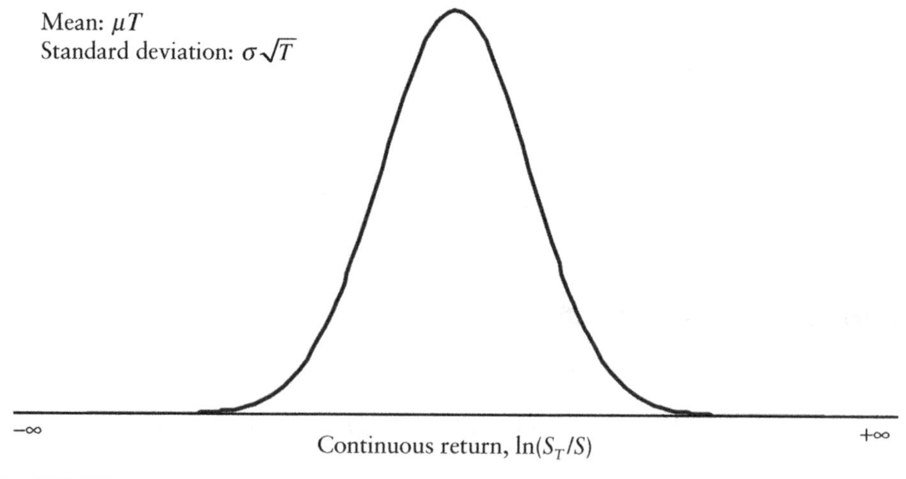

**FIGURE 7.3** Log-normal distribution of asset prices.

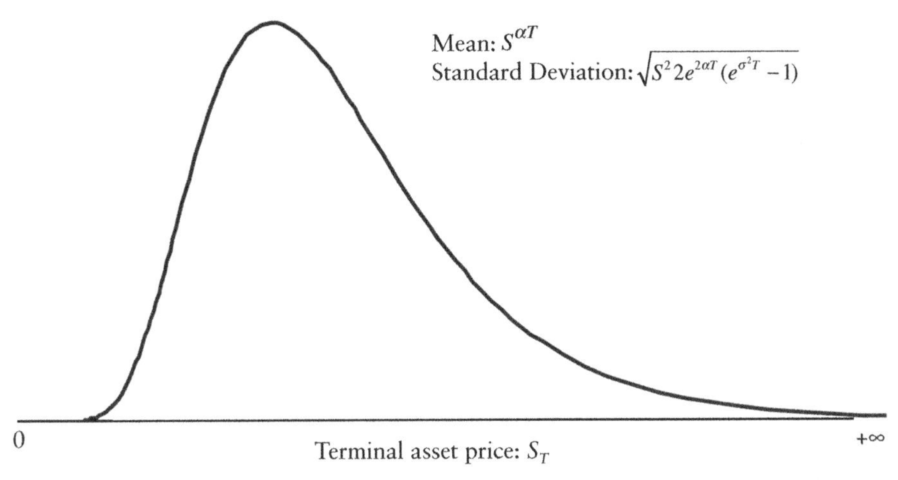


The log-normal price distribution is bounded from below by 0. This is an appealing characteristic since asset prices are always positive.[4] At the other end of the distribution, we see that asset prices can rise without limit. Finally, the relation between $\mu$ and $\sigma$ is sometimes confusing. To clearly distinguish between the two concepts, note that the former is the *mean of the continuously compounded return*,

$$\mu = \frac{E[\ln(\tilde{S}_T/S)]}{T}$$

while the latter is the *continuously compounded mean return*,

$$\alpha = \frac{\ln[E(\tilde{S}_T/S)]}{T}$$

The relation between the two quantities is $\mu = \alpha - \sigma^2/2$, as noted earlier. The only circumstance under which $\mu$ and $\alpha$ are equal is when the continuously compounded asset returns are the same each period, that is, there is no rate of return variability.

[4] In contrast, if we had assumed asset prices were normally distributed, there would be some chance that the asset price would go below zero.

**ILLUSTRATION 7.1** Compute expected asset price, variance of the asset price, and 95% confidence interval[5] on asset price in three months, given current asset price and mean and variance of the continuously compounded asset returns.

*Suppose that the current asset price is 50, and the mean and the standard deviation of the continuously compounded asset returns are 16% and 20%, respectively, on an annualized basis. Compute the expected asset price, $E(\tilde{S}_T)$, in three months. Also, compute a 95% confidence interval of the terminal asset price in three months.*

To compute the expected asset price, first compute the continuously compounded expected return of the asset. This is done as follows:

$$\alpha = \mu + \sigma^2/2 = 0.16 + 0.20^2/2 = 0.18$$

Next, we take the continuously compounded expected rate of return and the current asset price to find the expected asset price in three months, that is,

$$E(\tilde{S}_T) = Se^{\alpha T} = 50e^{0.18(3/12)} = 52.301$$

The variance of the asset price is computed as follows:

$$Var(\tilde{S}_T) = S^2e^{2\alpha T}(e^{\sigma^2 T} - 1) = 50^2e^{2(0.18)(3/12)}(e^{0.20^2(3/12)} - 1) = 27.492$$

Turning to the confidence interval, since the continuously compounded asset return is normally distributed, a 95% interval translates to plus or minus 1.96 standard deviations from the mean. The lower and upper bounds on the $\ln\tilde{S}_T$ are

$$\ln S + \mu T - 1.96\sigma\sqrt{T} < \ln\tilde{S}_T < \ln S + \mu T + 1.96\sigma\sqrt{T}$$

Substituting the problem parameters,

$$\ln 50 + 0.16(3/12) - 1.96(0.20)\sqrt{3/12} < \ln\tilde{S}_T < \ln 50 + 0.16(3/12) + 1.96(0.20)\sqrt{3/12}$$

or

$$3.756 < \ln\tilde{S}_T < 4.148$$

In turn, this is equivalent to

$$e^{3.756} = 42.778 < S_T < 63.309 = e^{4.148}$$

Note that the 95% confidence interval is not symmetric around the expected terminal asset price, 52.301. Since asset return is normally distributed, asset price is log-normally distributed.

### Computing Probabilities Given Threshold Asset Prices

With the relations between the parameters of the normally distributed continuously compounded asset returns and the log-normally distributed asset prices in hand, we now turn to applying the relations to answer important questions regarding terminal asset prices. Suppose, for example, we are interested in determining the probability that the asset price will exceed (or be below) a threshold

[5] Confidence intervals are discussed at length in Appendix A, "Elementary Statistics," of this book.

level, $X$, at time $T$ and are given the mean and the standard deviation of the continuously compounded returns. How can we use the mechanics that we have just developed to compute this probability?

To answer this question, we begin by rewriting (7.11) as

$$z = \frac{\ln(S_T/S) - \mu T}{\sigma\sqrt{T}} \tag{7.15}$$

where $z$ is normally distributed with mean 0 and variance 1, that is, $z \sim \phi(0,1)$. We know a great deal about the properties of $z$,[6] including the fact that its density function is

$$n(z) = \frac{1}{\sqrt{2\pi}}e^{-z^2/2} \tag{7.16}$$

The probability that a drawing from the unit normal distribution will produce a value less than the constant, $a$, may be obtained by integrating over the range of the density function from $-\infty$ to $a$, that is,

$$\begin{aligned} \Pr(\tilde{z} < a) &= \int_{-\infty}^{a} \frac{1}{\sqrt{2\pi}}e^{-z^2/2}dz \\ &= N(a) \end{aligned} \tag{7.17}$$

Given a value of $a$, the integration can be handled in a number of ways. First, it is common for statistics books to tabulate values of the probability $N(a)$. Such tables are provided in Tables C-1a and 1b in Appendix C, Statistical Tables, of this book. Algorithms have also been devised to approximate $N(a)$ with remarkable precision. Such an algorithm is provided in Appendix 7C of this chapter and the algorithm is programmed as function OV_PROB_PRUN in the OPTVAL Function Library. The function OV_PROB_PRUN_INV returns the inverse of the cumulative normal density function (i.e., the upper integral limit $a$ for a given probability.[7] These Excel spreadsheets illustrate this:

B2 fx =ov_prob_prun(B1)

| | A | B | C | D | E |
|---|---|---|---|---|---|
| 1 | a | 1.96 | | | |
| 2 | Pr(z<a) | 0.975 | | | |
| 3 | | | | | |
| 4 | Pr(z<a) | 0.025 | | | |
| 5 | a | -1.96 | | | |

[6] The properties of the normal distribution are provided in Appendix A, "Elementary Statistics," of this book.

[7] For those expert in Microsoft Excel, the statistical function NORMSDIST can be used to find $N(a)$ given $a$, and the function NORMSINV can be used to find $a$ given $N(a)$.

| B5 | | =OV_PROB_PRUN_INV(B4) | | |
|---|---|---|---|---|
| | A | B | C | D | E |

| | A | B | C | D | E |
|---|---|---|---|---|---|
| 1 | a | 1.96 | | | |
| 2 | Pr(z<a) | 0.975 | | | |
| 3 | | | | | |
| 4 | Pr(z<a) | 0.025 | | | |
| 5 | a | -1.96 | | | |
| 6 | | | | | |

Note that the function calls are not sensitive to the case of the letters.

Returning now to the problem of evaluating $\Pr(S_T > X)$, note that, if $S_T < X$,

$$\frac{\ln(S_T/S) - \mu T}{\sigma\sqrt{T}} < \frac{\ln(X/S) - \mu T}{\sigma\sqrt{T}}$$

since the same transformations are being applied to each side of the inequality. If we define $a$ as

$$a = \frac{\ln(X/S) - \mu T}{\sigma\sqrt{T}} = \frac{\ln(X/Se^{\mu T})}{\sigma\sqrt{T}} \tag{7.18}$$

and recall that the definition of $z$ is given by (7.15), it is apparent that the probability that the asset price will fall below $X$ at time $T$, that is, $\Pr(S_T < X) = \Pr(z < a) = N(a)$.

Unfortunately, we have answered the wrong question. What we wanted to know is the probability that the asset price will *exceed* $X$ at time $T$. Intuitively, we know the answer must be $1 - N(a)$. The probability that the asset price will exceed $X$ must be equal to one minus the probability that the asset price will fall below $X$. So, one useful property of the unit normally distributed variable $z$ is $\Pr(z \geq a) = 1 - \Pr(z < a)$. A second is that, since the unit normal distribution is symmetric around 0, the probability of drawing a value less than $a$ equals one minus the probability of drawing a value less than $-a$, that is,

$$N(a) = 1 - N(-a) \tag{7.19}$$

For reasons that will become readily apparent when we turn to call option valuation, it is more common to use an expression for the integral limit that captures the $\Pr(S_T > X)$ in a single step. To accomplish this task, we define the integral limit $d$ to be

$$d = -a = -\frac{\ln(X/Se^{\mu T})}{\sigma\sqrt{T}} = \frac{\ln(Se^{\mu T}/X)}{\sigma\sqrt{T}} \tag{7.20}$$

Under this definition,

$$\Pr(S_T > X) = N(d) \tag{7.21a}$$

and

$$\Pr(S_T < X) = N(-d) \tag{7.21b}$$

**ILLUSTRATION 7.2** Compute probability that asset price will exceed fixed level at future date.

*Suppose that the current asset price is 50, and the mean and the standard deviation of the continuously compounded asset returns are 16% and 20%, respectively, on an annualized basis. Compute the probability that the asset price will exceed 60 at the end of three months.*

First, transform the log-normal terminal price to a unit normal variable value using (7.20), that is,

$$d = \frac{\ln(Se^{\mu T}/S_T)}{\sigma\sqrt{T}} = \frac{\ln(50e^{0.16(0.25)}/60)}{0.20\sqrt{0.25}} = -1.423$$

Recall that, since the rates are quoted on an annualized basis, time must be measured in years.

Second, substitute the value of $d$ into the cumulative normal density function, $N(d)$, and compute the probability. Using the OV_PROB_PRUN function,

$$\Pr(S_T \geq 60) = \Pr(z < -1.423) = N(-1.423) = 0.077$$

In practice, it is more common to use the continuously compounded mean return, $\alpha$, in place of the mean of the continuously compounded return, $\mu$, when working with option valuation concepts. The necessary transformations to the integral limits when computing probabilities are straightforward. Recall that earlier in the chapter we showed that $\mu = \alpha - 0.5\sigma^2$. Substituting for $\mu$ in equation (7.20), the upper integral limit becomes

$$d = \frac{\ln(S/X) + (\alpha - 0.5\sigma^2)T}{\sigma\sqrt{T}} = \frac{\ln(Se^{\alpha T}/T) - 0.5\sigma^2 T}{\sigma\sqrt{T}} \tag{7.22}$$

and the probabilities that the asset price will exceed or be below the threshold level $X$ are

$$\Pr(S_T > X) = N(d) \tag{7.23a}$$

and

$$\Pr(S_T < X) = N(-d) \tag{7.23b}$$

respectively.

**ILLUSTRATION 7.3** Compute probability that asset price will exceed fixed level at future date.

*Suppose that an asset price has a current price of 50, an expected rate of return of 18%, and a volatility rate of 20%. (In practice, an asset's volatility rate refers to the standard deviation of the continuously compounded asset returns. Compute the probability that the asset price will exceed 60 at the end of three months.*

First, transform the log-normal terminal price to a unit normal variable value using (7.22), that is,

$$d = \frac{\ln(Se^{\alpha T}/T) - 0.5\sigma^2 T}{\sigma\sqrt{T}}$$

$$= \frac{\ln(50e^{0.18(0.25)}/60) - 0.5(0.20^2)0.25}{0.20\sqrt{0.25}} = -1.423$$

Second, substitute the value of $d$ into the cumulative normal density function, $N(d)$, and compute the probability. Using the OV_PROB_PRUN function

$$\Pr(S_T > 60) = N(z < -1.423) = 0.077$$

Alternatively, the OPTVAL Library has a function to compute the value of the probability directly. Its syntax is

OV_OPTION_ASSET_PROB(*s, x, t, alpha, v, ab*)

where *s* is the asset price, *x* is the threshold level, *t* is the time to the threshold level, *alpha* is the expected rate of appreciation in the asset price, *v* is the volatility rate, and *ab* is an indicator variable set equal to "a" if the asset price must be above the threshold price at the end of the period or "b" if the asset price must be below. The function is called in the following spreadsheet:

B12 =OV_OPTION_ASSET_PROB($B$3,$B$9,$B$8,$B$4,$B$5,"A")

| | A | B | C | D | E | F | G |
|---|---|---|---|---|---|---|---|
| 1 | **PROBABILITY COMPUTATION** | | | | | | |
| 2 | ***Asset*** | | | | | | |
| 3 | Price | 50 | | | | | |
| 4 | Expected return | 18.00% | | | | | |
| 5 | Volatility rate | 20.00% | | | | | |
| 6 | | | | | | | |
| 7 | ***Threshold*** | | | | | | |
| 8 | Time to expiration | 0.250 | | | | | |
| 9 | Threshold asset price | 60.000 | | | | | |
| 10 | | | | | | | |
| 11 | ***Probability*** | | | | | | |
| 12 | Exceeding threshold | 0.077 | | | | | |
| 13 | Below threshold | 0.923 | | | | | |

Thus far we have focused on assets whose only form of return is price appreciation. To generalize the results to handle assets that pay a known constant continuous rate of income $i$ (such as dividend yield), let $\alpha$ be the expected rate of price appreciation on the asset. Under this definition, the asset's total expected return equals $\alpha + i$. The upper integral limit $d$ remains as defined in

(7.22). The probability that the asset price will exceed the threshold level $X$ at time $T$ is (7.23a), and the probability that it will be less is (7.23b).

**ILLUSTRATION 7.4** Compute probability that asset price will exceed (be below) fixed level at future date where asset generates income at constant rate.

*Suppose that an asset has a current price of 50, an expected rate of return of 18%, an income rate of 4%, and a volatility rate of 20%. Compute the probability that the asset price will exceed 60 at the end of three months.*

First, note that the expected rate of price appreciation for the asset $\alpha$ equals its expected total return less the income rate, that is, 18 – 4 = 14%. This implies that the probability is less than that in Illustration 7.3 since the asset is not appreciating in value quite as quickly.

Second, transform the log-normal terminal price to a unit normal variable value using (7.21a), that is,

$$d = \frac{\ln(Se^{\alpha T}/X) - 0.5\sigma^2 T}{\sigma\sqrt{T}} = \frac{\ln(50e^{0.14(0.25)}/60) - 0.5(0.20^2)0.25}{0.20\sqrt{0.25}} = -1.523$$

Finally, substitute the value of $d$ into the cumulative normal density function, $N(d)$, and compute the probability. Using the OV_PROB_PRUN function,

$$\Pr(S_T > 60) = N(z < -1.523) = 0.064$$

As expected, the probability that the asset price will exceed 60 by the end of three months is reduced from 7.7% in Illustration 7.3 to 6.4% in this illustration. The following spreadsheet verifies the computations.

B13 =OV_OPTION_ASSET_PROB($B$3,$B$10,$B$9,$B$4-$B$5,$B$6,"A")

| | A | B | C | D | E | F | G |
|---|---|---|---|---|---|---|---|
| 1 | PROBABILITY COMPUTATION | | | | | | |
| 2 | ***Asset*** | | | | | | |
| 3 | Price | 50 | | | | | |
| 4 | Expected return | 18.00% | | | | | |
| 5 | Income rate | 4.00% | | | | | |
| 6 | Volatility rate | 20.00% | | | | | |
| 7 | | | | | | | |
| 8 | ***Threshold*** | | | | | | |
| 9 | Time to expiration | 0.250 | | | | | |
| 10 | Threshold asset price | 60.000 | | | | | |
| 11 | | | | | | | |
| 12 | ***Probability*** | | | | | | |
| 13 | Exceeding threshold | 0.064 | | | | | |
| 14 | Below threshold | 0.936 | | | | | |

**Value-at-Risk** Finally, in many finance applications, we are interested in determining a critical asset price for a given probability. One such application is *Value-at-Risk* or simply VAR. VAR measures the maximum dollar loss we can expect to incur over the given period of time at a particular confidence level.[8] VAR has two forms. The most common form is VAR is maximum dollar loss relative to the mean; that is, we want to compute the maximum dollar loss assum-

[8] Value-at-risk is discussed in greater detail in Appendix A, "Elementary Statistics," of this book.

ing the asset will appreciate at its expected rate. A less used, albeit informative, measure of VAR is compute maximum *absolute* dollar loss relative to the current asset value (i.e., relative to a mean appreciation rate of 0).

Assuming the asset or portfolio of assets has a log-normal price distribution, the mechanics of this section can be easily adapted to handle both of these VAR computations. The only subtlety is that in place of using OV_OPTION_ASSET_PROB to compute the probability that the asset price will be below a critical price at the end of a given period, we use OV_OPTION_ASSET_PROB_INV to compute a critical price below end-of-period asset price has a fixed probability of occurrence.

**ILLUSTRATION 7.5** Compute maximum dollar loss expected over given period of time at particular confidence level.

*Suppose you hold \$10 million worth of a security. It has a current price of 50, an expected rate of return of 18%, an income rate of 4%, and a volatility rate of 20%. Compute the value-at-risk over the week at the 5% level.*

To compute this value by hand, start by computing the inverse of the standard normal probability using OV_PROB_PRUN_INV and a probability of 0.05. Its value is –1.645.

Next, compute the level of $X$ that satisfies equation (7.21b), that is,

$$-1.645 = -\frac{\ln(Se^{\alpha T}/X) - 0.5\sigma^2 T}{\sigma\sqrt{T}}$$

$$= -\frac{\ln(50e^{0.14(0.25)}/X) - 0.5(0.20^2)(1/52)}{0.20\sqrt{0.25}}$$

The level of $X$ that satisfies the equation is $X = 47.881$. Thus, we are 95% confident that the asset price will be above 47.881 at the end of a week or, equivalently, the value of your portfolio holding will be above \$9,576,122. The VAR relative to the mean over a week at the 5% probability level is \$423,878.

The VAR relative to 0 is computed in a similar fashion, except that we set the expected rate of price appreciation to 0, that is, $\alpha = 0$. The value of $X$ that satisfies

$$-1.645 = -\frac{\ln(50/X) - 0.5(0.20^2)(1/52)}{0.20\sqrt{0.25}}$$

is 47.752 and the maximum absolute dollar loss over a week at the 5% probability level is \$449,625.

The OPTVAL Library has a function to compute the critical asset price given a level of probability. Its syntax is

OV_OPTION_ASSET_PROB_INV(*s*, *t*, *alpha*, *v*, *ab*, *prob*)

where *s* is the asset price, *t* is the time to the threshold level, *alpha* is the expected rate of appreciation in the asset price, *v* is the volatility rate, *ab* is an indicator variable set equal to “a” if the asset price must be above the threshold price at the end of the period or “b” if the asset price must be below, and *prob* is the assigned probability level. The function illustrated in the spreadsheet below computes the VAR relative to the mean. To compute VAR relative to 0, we simply set the expected return and the income rates equal to 0.

B17 =OV_OPTION_ASSET_PROB_INV($B$3,$B$11,$B$4-$B$5,$B$6,"b",$B$12)

| | A | B | C | D | E | F | G |
|---|---|---|---|---|---|---|---|
| 1 | VALUE-AT-RISK | | | | | | |
| 2 | ***Asset*** | | | | | | |
| 3 | Price | 50 | | | | | |
| 4 | Expected return | 18.00% | | | | | |
| 5 | Income rate | 4.00% | | | | | |
| 6 | Volatility rate | 20.00% | | | | | |
| 7 | | | | | | | |
| 8 | ***Portfolio*** | | | | | | |
| 9 | Value | 10,000,000 | | | | | |
| 10 | Number of shares | 200,000 | | | | | |
| 11 | Holding period (in years) | 0.019231 | | | | | |
| 12 | Probability level | 0.050 | | | | | |
| 13 | Critical price | 9,576,122 | | | | | |
| 14 | Maximum dollar loss | 423,878 | | | | | |
| 15 | | | | | | | |
| 16 | ***Critical asset prices*** | | | | | | |
| 17 | Lower bound | 47.881 | | | | | |
| 18 | Upper bound | 52.455 | | | | | |

## Computing Conditional Expected Asset Prices

The relations between the parameters of the normally distributed continuously compounded returns and the log-normally distributed asset prices also allow us to develop some convenient expressions for conditional expected asset prices. From (7.13), we know that the unconditional expected price of the asset at time $T$ is

$$E(\tilde{S}_T) = Se^{\alpha T}$$

But suppose that we are interested in knowing the expected asset price conditional upon the asset price being greater than a threshold level $X$.

Under the assumption that asset price is log-normally distributed at time $T$, it can be shown that the expected asset price conditional on the asset price being greater than the threshold level at time $T$ is

$$E(\tilde{S}_T | S_T > X) = Se^{\alpha T}\frac{N(d_1)}{N(d_2)} \tag{7.24}$$

where

$$d_1 = \frac{\ln(Se^{\alpha T}/X) + 0.5\sigma^2 T}{\sigma\sqrt{T}} \tag{7.24a}$$

and

$$d_2 = \frac{\ln(Se^{\alpha T}/X) - 0.5\sigma^2 T}{\sigma\sqrt{T}} = d_1 - \sigma\sqrt{T}^{9} \tag{7.24b}$$

The expected asset price conditional on the asset price being less than the threshold level at time $T$ is

$$E(\tilde{S}_T | S_T < X) = Se^{\alpha T}\frac{N(-d_1)}{N(-d_2)} \tag{7.25}$$

Finally, to reconcile that the difference between the conditional expected asset prices, $E(\tilde{S}_T|S_T > X)$ and $E(\tilde{S}_T|S_T < X)$, and the unconditional expected asset price, $E(\tilde{S}_T)$, recognize that, when evaluating the conditional expected values, the relevant probability distributions are the areas under the log-normal distribution above and below the threshold asset price, whereas, when evaluating an unconditional expected value, the relevant probability distribution is the entire area under the log-normal distribution. To compute the unconditional expected asset price from the conditional expected price expressions, we must weight each conditional expected price by the probability of its occurrence, that is,

$$\begin{aligned} E(\tilde{S}_T) &= E(\tilde{S}_T|S_T > X)\Pr(S_T > X) + E(\tilde{S}_T|S_T < X)\Pr(S_T < X) \\ &= Se^{\alpha T}\frac{N(d_1)}{N(d_2)}N(d_2) + Se^{\alpha T}\frac{N(-d_1)}{N(-d_2)}N(-d_2) \\ &= Se^{\alpha T}[N(d_1) + N(-d_1)] \\ &= Se^{\alpha T} \end{aligned} \tag{7.26}$$

Each expected conditional asset price weighted by its probability is called the *partial expectation* of the asset price being above or below $X$.

**ILLUSTRATION 7.6** Compute expected asset conditional on asset price being above or below threshold price at future date.

*Suppose that an asset has a current price of 50, an expected rate of return of 18%, and an income rate of 4%. Also, continue to assume that the standard deviation of the continuously compounded asset returns is 20%. Compute (1) the expected asset price at the end of three months; (2) the expected asset price conditional on the asset price exceed 60 at the end of three months; and (3) the expected asset price conditional on the asset price being below 60 at the end of three months. Using the probabilities computed in Illustration 7.4, show the numerical relation between the unconditional and conditional expected terminal asset prices.*

The expected asset price in three months can be computed straightforwardly:

[9] Note that there is a subtle difference in the definitions of $d_1$ and $d_2$. Note also that $d_2$ is the same as $d$ in (7.23a). Thus, $N(d_2) = \Pr(S_T > X)$.

$$E(\tilde{S}_T) = Se^{\alpha T} = 50e^{0.14(0.25)} = 51.781$$

The expected asset price conditional on the asset price exceeding 60 in three months is

$$E(\tilde{S}_T | S_T > 60) = 50e^{0.14(0.25)}\frac{N(d_1)}{N(d_2)} = 62.716$$

where

$$d_1 = \frac{\ln(50e^{0.14(0.25)}/60) + 0.5(0.20^2)0.25}{0.20\sqrt{0.25}} = -1.423$$

and

$$d_2 = -1.423 - 0.20\sqrt{0.25} = -1.523$$

and the expected asset price conditional on the asset price being below 60 in three months is

$$E(\tilde{S}_T | S_T < 60) = 50e^{0.14(0.25)}\frac{N(-d_1)}{N(-d_2)} = 51.035$$

These computations can be verified using the OPTVAL function,

OV_OPTION_ASSET_EV(*s, x, t, alpha, v, ab*),

where *s* is the asset price, *x* is the threshold level, *t* is the time to the threshold level, *alpha* is the expected rate of appreciation in the asset price, *v* is the volatility rate, and *ab* is an indicator variable set equal to “a” if the asset price must be above the threshold price at the end of the period or “b” if the asset price must be below. The function is called in the following spreadsheet:

B18 =OV_OPTION_ASSET_EV($B$3,$B$10,$B$9,$B$4-$B$5,$B$6,"A")

| | A | B | C | D | E | F | G |
|---|---|---|---|---|---|---|---|
| 1 | **CONDITIONAL EXPECTED VALUE** | | | | | | |
| 2 | ***Asset*** | | | | | | |
| 3 | Price | 50 | | | | | |
| 4 | Expected return | 18.00% | | | | | |
| 5 | Income rate | 4.00% | | | | | |
| 6 | Volatility rate | 20.00% | | | | | |
| 7 | | | | | | | |
| 8 | ***Threshold*** | | | | | | |
| 9 | Time to expiration | 0.250 | | | | | |
| 10 | Threshold asset price | 60.000 | | | | | |
| 11 | | | | | | | |
| 12 | ***Probability*** | | | | | | |
| 13 | Exceeding threshold | 0.064 | | | | | |
| 14 | Below threshold | 0.936 | | | | | |
| 15 | | | | | | | |
| 16 | ***Expected values*** | | | | | | |
| 17 | Unconditional | 51.781 | | | | | |
| 18 | Conditional on ST>60 | 62.716 | | | | | |
| 19 | Conditional on ST<60 | 51.035 | | | | | |
| 20 | Unconditional | 51.781 | | | | | |

The relation between the unconditional and conditional expected terminal asset prices is

$$\begin{aligned} E(\tilde{S}_T) &= \Pr(S_T > X)E(\tilde{S}_T | S_T > X) + \Pr(S_T < X)E(\tilde{S}_T | (S_T < X)) \\ &= 0.064(62.716) + 0.936(51.035) \\ &= 51.781 \end{aligned}$$

**Conditional Value-at-Risk** Conditional asset prices are often used in assessing the risk profiles of assets and portfolios of assets. *Conditional value-at-risk* (CVAR) or *tail* VAR is the expected loss conditional[10] on a particular level of asset price. In computing VAR, for example, we computed the critical price below which there was a 5% chance that the asset price at time $T$ was below the critical price. Suppose we ask the question, "Assuming the asset price is below the critical price at time $T$, what is the expected loss?" This is the definition of CVAR and, assuming the asset price is log-normally distributed, we can compute its value straightforwardly using (7.25) or (7.26).

**ILLUSTRATION 7.7** Compute tail value-at-risk of security position over planned horizon.

*Suppose you hold \$10 million worth of a security. It has a current price of 50, an expected rate of return of 18%, an income rate of 4%, and a volatility rate of 20%. Compute the 5% tail VAR (CVAR) of your portfolio over the next week.*

The first step in computing the tail VAR or CVAR is to compute the critical asset price. We did this in Illustration 7.5. At the 5% probability level, the maximum loss expected over the next at the 5% level is \$47.881.

Next, we compute the expected asset price conditional on the asset price being below 47.881 in a week. From (7.25), we know

$$E(\tilde{S}_T | S_T < 47.881) = 50e^{0.14(0.25)} = 47.332$$

where

$$-d_1 = -\frac{\ln(50e^{0.14(0.25)}/47.881) + 0.5(0.20^2)(1/52)}{0.20\sqrt{1/52}} = -1.672$$

and

$$-d_2 = -1.672 + 0.20\sqrt{1/52} = -1.645$$

These computations can be verified using the OPTVAL function,

OV_OPTION_ASSET_EV(*s, x, t, alpha, v, ab*)

The 5% tail VAR is computed as

$$\$10{,}000{,}000 - 47.332 \times 200{,}000 = \$533{,}653$$

[10] Conditional value-at-risk is also called *mean excess loss* and *mean shortfall*.

## Summary

This section contains the mechanics for working with an asset price distribution that is log-normally distributed at some future time $T$. The required parameters in the computation of the probabilities, unconditional and conditional expected values, and confidence intervals are the current asset price, the expected rate of asset price appreciation, and the standard deviation of the continuously compounded asset returns. Table 7.2 contains a summary of the important relations developed in this section. The two panels in the table correspond to risk-averse and risk-neutral investors. Depending upon the application in the remaining part of this chapter or a later chapter, we use one set of results or the other. Note that the structural form of the expressions for the different investors is the same, except for the rate of price appreciation. In a risk-averse world, the expected rate of price appreciation is $\alpha$, and the asset's total expected return is $\alpha + i$. In a risk-neutral world, the expected rate of price appreciation is $b$, and the asset's total expected return is $b + i = r - i + i = r$ or the risk-free interest rate.

**TABLE 7.2** Summary of expressions for evaluating probabilities and conditional expected values.

| | **Risk-Averse (or "Real World") Investors** <br> **($\alpha$ is expected rate of price appreciation on asset[a])** |
|---|---|
| Unconditional expected asset price | $E(\tilde{S}_T) = Se^{\alpha T}$ |
| Probability of asset price being above or below threshold level $X$ | $\Pr(S_T > X) = N(d_2)$ and $\Pr(S_T < X) = N(-d_2)$ |
| Expected asset price conditional on threshold price $X$ | $E(\tilde{S}_T \mid S_T > X) = Se^{\alpha T}\dfrac{N(d_1)}{N(d_2)}$ <br> and <br> $E(\tilde{S}_T \mid S_T < X) = Se^{\alpha T}\dfrac{N(-d_1)}{N(-d_2)}$ |
| 95% confidence interval for terminal asset price | $Se^{(\alpha - 0.5\sigma^2)T - 1.96\sigma\sqrt{T}} < \tilde{S}_T < Se^{(\alpha - 0.5\sigma^2)T + 1.96\sigma\sqrt{T}}$ |
| Integral limits | $d_1 = \dfrac{\ln(Se^{\alpha T}/X) + 0.5\sigma^2 T}{\sigma\sqrt{T}}$ <br> and <br> $d_2 = \dfrac{\ln(Se^{\alpha T}/X) - 0.5\sigma^2 T}{\sigma\sqrt{T}} = d_1 - \sigma\sqrt{T}$ |
| Unconditional expected asset price | $E(\tilde{S}_T) = Se^{bT} = F$ |
| Probability of asset price being above or below threshold level $X$ | $\Pr(S_T > X) = N(d_2)$ and $\Pr(S_T < X) = N(-d_2)$ |

**TABLE 7.2** (Continued)

| | Risk-Neutral Investors ($b$ is expected rate of price appreciation on asset[a]) |
|---|---|
| Expected asset price conditional on threshold price $X$ | $E(\tilde{S}_T \mid S_T > X) = Se^{bT}\frac{N(d_1)}{N(d_2)}$ and $E(\tilde{S}_T \mid S_T < X) = Se^{bT}\frac{N(-d_1)}{N(-d_2)}$ |
| 95% confidence interval for terminal asset price | $Se^{(b-0.5\sigma^2)T - 1.96\sigma\sqrt{T}} < \tilde{S}_T < Se^{(b-0.5\sigma^2)T + 1.96\sigma\sqrt{T}}$ |
| Integral limits | $d_1 = \frac{\ln(Se^{bT}/X) + 0.5\sigma^2 T}{\sigma\sqrt{T}}$ and $d_2 = \frac{\ln(Se^{bT}/X) - 0.5\sigma^2 T}{\sigma\sqrt{T}} = d_1 - \sigma\sqrt{T}$ |

[a] Note that all of the expressions in the table depend upon the asset expected rate of price appreciation not its expected return. If the asset pays a known constant income rate $i$, the asset's expected return is $\alpha + i$ in a risk-averse world and $b + i = r - i + i = r$ in a risk-neutral world.

## VALUING A EUROPEAN-STYLE CALL OPTION

We now turn to valuing European-style call options. The valuation approach is "traditional" in the sense that we compute the theoretical value of the call by taking the present value of its expected terminal value.[11] The first order of business is to value a call option under the assumption that investors are risk-averse. The resulting valuation equation, called the "Samuelson (1965) formula," proves to be tractable analytically but difficult to implement. Next we value the call under the assumption that investors are risk-neutral. The risk-neutral option valuation formula manages to circumvent the estimation problems of the Samuelson formula and has been dubbed the "Black-Scholes (1973)/Merton(1973) formula." It is general in its nature and contains a host of special cases.

### The Samuelson Formula

In a world with risk-averse investors, the value of a European-style call option is simply

$$c = e^{-\alpha_c T} E(\tilde{c}_T) \tag{7.27}$$

[11] Appendix 7D of this chapter contains the continuous-time, risk-free hedge development of the BSM model.

where $c$ is the value of the call, $\alpha_c$ is the expected risk-adjusted rate of return on the call over its life, and $E(\tilde{c}_T)$ is the expected terminal value of the call. To estimate $E(\tilde{c}_T)$, consider the call's terminal price distribution, that is,

$$\tilde{c}_T = \begin{cases} \tilde{S} - X & \text{if } S_T > X \\ 0 & \text{if } S_T \le X \end{cases} \tag{7.28}$$

Expression (7.28) shows that the terminal call price distribution is truncated from below. Based on this truncated distribution, the expected value of $\tilde{c}_T$ may be written

$$\begin{aligned} E(\tilde{c}_T) &= E(\tilde{S}_T - X | S_T \ge X)\Pr(S_T \ge X) + E(0|S_T < X)\Pr(S_T < X) \\ &= E(\tilde{S}_T - X | S_T \ge X)\Pr(S_T \ge X) \end{aligned} \tag{7.29}$$

Since the call expires worthless if the asset price is below the exercise price at expiration, the region of the asset price distribution in which the asset price is below the exercise price has no influence in the determination of $E(\tilde{c}_T)$. Instead, the expected terminal call value depends only on the product of the expected difference between the asset price and the exercise price conditional on the asset price exceeding the exercise price at the option's expiration, $E(\tilde{S}_T - X | S_T \ge X)$, and the probability that the asset price will exceed the exercise price at expiration, $\Pr(S_T \ge X)$.

Expression (7.29) is useful to the extent that it clearly identifies what drives the expected terminal value of the call. As it stands, however, it cannot be implemented. In order to develop a formula or valuation methodology for computing $E(\tilde{c}_T)$, we must invoke an assumption regarding the shape of the price distribution for the asset underlying the options. Here is where we insert the assumption that the asset price is log-normally distributed at the option's expiration. Substituting (7.24) and (7.23a) from the previous section into (7.29),

$$\begin{aligned} E(\tilde{c}_T) &= E(\tilde{S}_T - X | S_T > X)\Pr(S_T > X) \\ &= \left( Se^{\alpha_S T} \frac{N(d_1)}{N(d_2)} - X \right) N(d_2) \\ &= Se^{\alpha_S T} N(d_1) - XN(d_2) \end{aligned} \tag{7.30}$$

where

$$d_1 = \frac{\ln(Se^{\alpha_S T}/X) + 0.5\sigma^2 T}{\sigma\sqrt{T}} \tag{7.30a}$$

$$d_2 = d_1 - \sigma\sqrt{T} \tag{7.30b}$$

and the subscript "$S$" has been added to the expected rate of price appreciation of the underlying asset to clearly distinguish it from the expected rate of return on the call, $\alpha_c$. Substituting (7.30) into (7.27), the current value of a European-style call option is

$$\begin{aligned} c &= e^{-\alpha_c T}[Se^{\alpha_S T} N(d_1) - XN(d_2)] \\ &= Se^{(\alpha_S - \alpha_c)T} N(d_1) - Xe^{-\alpha_c T} N(d_2) \end{aligned} \tag{7.31}$$

Presented in this way, the intuition underlying the structure of the European-style call option formula is straightforward. The term

$$Se^{(\alpha_S - \alpha_c)T} N(d_1)$$

is the present value of the expected benefit of exercising the call option at expiration conditional on the terminal asset price being greater than the exercise price at the option's expiration times the probability that the option will be in the money. The term, $N(d_2)$, is the probability that the asset price will be greater than the exercise price at expiration. Therefore the term

$$Xe^{-\alpha_c T} N(d_2)$$

is the present value of the cost of exercising the call times the probability the option will be in the money.

As simple and elegant as the Samuelson formula (7.31) appears, it is not very useful. To implement the formula requires estimates of the risk-adjusted rates of price appreciation for both the asset and the call option. The estimation of these values is difficult. In the case of the call, estimation is particularly troublesome because the expected return of the call depends not only on the expected rate of price appreciation of the asset but also the passage of time.

### The Black-Scholes/Merton Formula

In the first section of this chapter, we showed that, because a risk-free hedge can be formed between an option and its underlying asset, the value of an option does not depend on risk preferences. An risk-averse investor will value an option at the same level as a risk-neutral investor. In a risk-neutral world, the expected return of all assets and options is the risk-free rate of interest. The expected rate of price appreciation on an asset that pays income at rate $i$ is therefore $\alpha = b(= r - i)$, and the expected rate of return on the call is $\alpha_c = r$. Making these substitutions into (7.31), we find that the value of a European-style call is

$$
\begin{aligned}
c &= e^{-rT}[Se^{bT}N(d_1) - XN(d_2)] \\
&= Se^{(b-r)T}N(d_1) - Xe^{-rT}N(d_2)
\end{aligned}
\tag{7.32}
$$

where

$$
d_1 = \frac{\ln(Se^{bT}/X) + 0.5\sigma^2 T}{\sigma\sqrt{T}}
\tag{7.32a}
$$

and

$$
d_2 = d_1 - \sigma\sqrt{T}
\tag{7.32b}
$$

This formula is commonly referred to as the BSM formula. Its terms may be interpreted in the same way as the terms of the Samuelson formula. We must be carefully to distinguish the nature of the probabilities, however. In the Samuelson formula, "risk-averse" (or so-called "real-world") probabilities are used. In the BSM, "risk-neutral" probabilities are used. It is also worthwhile to note that, because $b \equiv r - i$, the BSM formula is often written

$$
c = Se^{-iT}N(d_1) - Xe^{-rT}N(d_2)
\tag{7.33}
$$

where

$$
d_1 = \frac{\ln(Se^{(r-i)T}/X) + 0.5\sigma^2 T}{\sigma\sqrt{T}}
\tag{7.33a}
$$

and

$$
d_2 = d_1 - \sigma\sqrt{T}
\tag{7.33b}
$$

The European-style call formula (7.32), as we have presented it, is a generalized version of the BSM formula. It covers call option valuation for a broad range of underlying asset including nondividend-paying stocks, stock indexes, foreign currencies, and futures. The distinction between the different valuation problems rests only in the asset's risk-neutral price appreciation parameter, $b$.

**Nondividend-Paying Stock Options** The most well-known option valuation problem is that of valuing options on nondividend-paying stocks. This is, in fact, the valuation problem addressed by Black and Scholes (1973). With no dividends paid on the underlying stock, the expected risk-neutral rate of price appreciation of the stock equals the risk-free rate of interest (i.e., $b = r$) and the call option valuation equation becomes the familiar "Black/Scholes formula,"

$$c = SN(d_1) - Xe^{-rT}N(d_2) \tag{7.34}$$

where

$$d_1 = \frac{\ln(Se^{rT}/X) + 0.5\sigma^2 T}{\sigma\sqrt{T}} \text{ and } d_2 = d_1 - \sigma\sqrt{T}$$

**Constant-Dividend-Yield Stock Options** Merton (1973) generalizes stock option valuation by assuming that the underlying stock or stock index pays dividends at a constant, continuous rate, $\delta$. In such a case, the expected risk-neutral rate of price appreciation of the stock equals the risk-free rate of interest less the dividend yield rate (i.e., $b = r - \delta$). Substituting into (7.32), we get the "Merton model:"

$$c = Se^{-\delta T}N(d_1) - Xe^{-rT}N(d_2) \tag{7.35}$$

where

$$d_1 = \frac{\ln(Se^{(r-\delta)T}/X) + 0.5\sigma^2 T}{\sigma\sqrt{T}} \text{ and } d_2 = d_1 - \sigma\sqrt{T}$$

**Foreign Currency Options** Garman and Kohlhagen (1983) and Biger and Hull (1983) value European-style options on a foreign currency. The expected risk-neutral rate of price appreciation for a currency equals the domestic rate of interest less the foreign rate of interest (i.e., $b = r_d - r_f$). The valuation formula for a European-style call on a foreign currency is therefore

$$c = Se^{-r_f T}N(d_1) - Xe^{-r_d T}N(d_2) \tag{7.36}$$

where

$$d_1 = \frac{\ln(Se^{(r_d - r_f)T}/X) + 0.5\sigma^2 T}{\sigma\sqrt{T}} \text{ and } d_2 = d_1 - \sigma\sqrt{T}$$

**Futures Options** Black (1976) values options on futures. In a risk-neutral world, the expected rate of price appreciation on a futures contract is zero. Substituting $b = 0$ and $F = S$, we get what is commonly known in the futures industry as the "Black model."

$$c = e^{-rT}[FN(d_1) - XN(d_2)] \tag{7.37}$$

where

$$d_1 = \frac{\ln(F/X) + 0.5\sigma^2 T}{\sigma\sqrt{T}} \text{ and } d_2 = d_1 - \sigma\sqrt{T}$$

**Futures-Style Futures Options** Following the work of Black, Asay (1982) values futures-style futures options. Such options trade on a number of exchanges including London International Financial Futures Exchange (LIFFE) and the Sydney Futures Exchange (SFE) and have the distinguishing feature that the option premium is not paid up front. Instead, the option position is marked-to-market in the same manner as the underlying futures. To value this option in a risk-neutral world, we not only set $b = 0$ inside the squared brackets to reflect the zero expected rate of price appreciation on the futures but also set $r = 0$ outside the squared brackets because an option requiring zero investment up-front must have a zero expected rate of return. The resulting formula is called the "Asay model,"

$$c = FN(d_1) - XN(d_2) \tag{7.38}$$

where

$$d_1 = \frac{\ln(F/X) + 0.5\sigma^2 T}{\sigma\sqrt{T}} \text{ and } d_2 = d_1 - \sigma\sqrt{T}$$

**Equivalence of Alternative Expressions for $d_1$ and $d_2$** In the valuation equations starting at the BSM formula (7.32) and ending with the Asay formula (7.38), there appear to be different expressions for the integral limits $d_1$ and $d_2$. While these expressions appear different, they are *not*; they are exactly the same. We simply use different notation in each problem to emphasize the economic determinants of each different option valuation problem. The general expressions are

$$d_1 = \frac{\ln M + 0.5\sigma^2 T}{\sigma\sqrt{T}} \text{ and } d_2 = d_1 - \sigma\sqrt{T}$$

where $M$ is the degree to which the option is expected to be in or out of the money at expiration (i.e., the option's so-called *moneyness*). Thus $M$ equals the ratio of the forward price of the asset to the option's exercise price. But the forward price may, in turn, be expressed in terms of the asset price using net cost of carry relation, $F = Se^{bT}$. Thus we have

$$\ln M = \ln(F/X) = \ln(Se^{bT}/X)$$

In the above expression, the terms in parentheses are values at time $T$, when the option expires. It probably makes the most sense to use these expressions to remind ourselves that the option valuation probabilities are assess the likelihood that the asset price is above or below $X$ at time $T$. Nonetheless many people choose to write the option's moneyness in terms of present values. Since both $F$ and $X$ are terms known today, we can discount these future values to the present at the risk-free rate of interest. Thus we can add two more expressions for moneyness to the list—all of them equivalent,

$$\ln M = \ln(F/X) = \ln(Se^{bT}/X) = \ln(Fe^{-rT}/Xe^{-rT}) = \ln(Se^{(b-r)T}/Xe^{-rT})$$

It is also worthwhile to note that expression for $d_1$ is also sometimes written,

$$d_1 = \frac{\ln(S/X) + (b + 0.5\sigma^2)T}{\sigma\sqrt{T}}$$

This expression, too, is equivalent to the others. Note that we can rearrange terms in the numerator in the following manner:

$$d_1 = \frac{\ln(S/X) + (b + 0.5\sigma^2)T}{\sigma\sqrt{T}} = \frac{\ln(S/X) + bT + 0.5\sigma^2 T}{\sigma\sqrt{T}}$$

$$= \frac{\ln(Se^{bT}/X) + bT + 0.5\sigma^2 T}{\sigma\sqrt{T}} = \frac{\ln M + 0.5\sigma^2 T}{\sigma\sqrt{T}}$$

While all of these equivalent expressions may seem confusing, our discussion here is motivated by the fact that there appears to be no standard expressions across research publications and books on derivatives securities. Through the remainder of the book, we use either

$$d_1 = \frac{\ln(Se^{(r-i)T}/X) + 0.5\sigma^2 T}{\sigma\sqrt{T}} \text{ or } d_1 = \frac{\ln(Se^{-iT}/Xe^{-rT}) + 0.5\sigma^2 T}{\sigma\sqrt{T}}$$

depending of which expression provides the fewest numerical computations in valuing an option.

**ILLUSTRATION 7.8** Find value of European-style call written on stock index.

*Compute the value of a European-style call option written on a stock index, where the call has an exercise price of 50 and a time to expiration of three months. Assume the index has a level of 49, a dividend yield of 2%, and a volatility rate of 20%. The risk-free rate is 5%. Also compute the European-style call assuming that it is written on a futures contract on the stock index, and that the futures has three months remaining to expiration.*

To value the call on the index, let us use the prepaid version of moneyness in the computation of $d_1$ and $d_2$. First, compute the prepaid values of the forward and the exercise price, that is,

$$Fe^{-rT} = Se^{-iT} = 49e^{-0.02(0.25)} = 48.756 \text{ and } Xe^{-rT} = 50e^{-0.05(0.25)} = 49.379$$

Next, substitute these values into the expressions for the integral limits,

$$d_1 = \frac{\ln(48.756/49.379) + 0.5(0.20^2)0.25}{0.20\sqrt{0.25}} = -0.0770$$

$$d_2 = -0.0770 - 0.20\sqrt{0.25} = -0.1770$$

Next, compute the cumulative normal probabilities using the OV_PROB_PRUN function from the OPTVAL Function Library. The risk-neutral probabilities are

$$N(-0.0770) = 0.4693 \text{ and } N(-0.1770) = 0.4297$$

Finally, substitute into the call option valuation formula (7.35) and compute the option value,

$$c = 48.756(0.4693) - 49.379(0.4297) = 1.661$$

The OPTVAL Function Library contains a number of functions that can assist you with the European-style option valuation computations. To compute the integral limits, $d_1$ and $d_2$, for example, you can use

OV_OPTION_D(*s, x, t, r, i, v, n*)

where *s* is the underlying asset prices, *x* is the exercise price of option, *t* is the option's time remaining to expiration, *r* is the risk-free interest rate, *i* is the income rate, *v* is the volatility rate, and *n* is "1" or "2", depending on whether you want the value of $d_1$ or $d_2$, respectively. Substituting the problem parameters, you get

OV_OPTION_D(49, 50, 0.25, 0.05, 0.02, 0.20, 1) = –0.0770

and

OV_OPTION_D(49, 50, 0.25, 0.05, 0.02, 0.20, 2) = –0.1770

The Library also contains functions to perform the probability computations, that is,

OV_OPTION_ND(49, 50, 0.25, 0.05, 0.02, 0.20, 1) = 0.4693

and

OV_OPTION_ND(49, 50, 0.25, 0.05, 0.02, 0.20, 2) = 0.4297

Finally, the option value can be computed directly using

OV_OPTION_VALUE(*s, x, t, r, i, v, cp, ae*)

where all notation is defined above, except for *cp*, which is set "c" for call and "p" for put, and *ae*, which is set "a" for American-style option and "e" for European-style option. Thus

OV_OPTION_VALUE(49, 50, 0.25, 0.05, 0.02, 0.20, "c", "e") = 1.661

To compute the value of the call option written on the stock index futures, we follow the same steps.

To value the call on the index, let us use the forward price version of moneyness in the computation of $d_1$ and $d_2$. First, compute the forward price, that is,

$$F = Se^{(r-i)T} = 49e^{(0.05-0.02)0.25} = 49.369$$

Substitute these values into the expressions for the integral limits, $d_1$ and $d_2$, that is,

$$d_1 = \frac{\ln(49.369/50) + 0.5(0.20^2)0.25}{0.20\sqrt{0.25}} = -0.0770$$

$$d_2 = -0.0770 - 0.20\sqrt{0.25} = -0.1770$$

Because the integral limits are the same, so are the probabilities:

$$N(-0.0770) = 0.4693 \text{ and } N(-0.1770) = 0.4297$$

Finally, substitute into the call option valuation formula (7.37) and compute the option value,

$$\begin{aligned} c &= e^{-rT}[FN(d_1) - XN(d_2)] \\ &= e^{-0.05(0.25)}[49.369(0.4693) - 50(0.4297)] \\ &= 1.661 \end{aligned}$$

The OPTVAL Function Library contains parallel functions for the valuation of futures options. The value of the call option, for example, is

OV_FOPTION_VALUE(49, 50, 0.25, 0.05, 0.20, "c", "e") = 1.661

**All-or-Nothing Options** Interestingly, even through a standard European-style call option is considered to be the simplest of all options, it can be viewed as a portfolio of two more basic options—long an asset-or-nothing call option and short a cash-or-nothing call option. An *asset-or-nothing call* pays the asset price at time $T$ if the asset price exceeds some predefined level, call it $X$.[12] A *cash-or-nothing call* pays a fixed amount of cash, $CASH$, if the asset price exceeds $X$. Under the assumptions of risk-neutral individuals and log-normally distributed asset prices, the value of an asset-or-nothing call is

$$c_{AON} = E(\tilde{S}_T | S_T > X)\Pr(S_T > X) = Se^{-iT}\frac{N(d_1)}{N(d_2)}N(d_2) = Se^{-iT}N(d_1) \quad (7.39)$$

that is, the first term on the right-hand side of (7.33). Assuming $CASH = X$, the value of a cash-or-nothing call is

$$c_{CON} = Xe^{-rT}N(d_2) \quad (7.40)$$

that is, the second term on the right-hand side of (7.33). Therefore a standard European-style call is nothing more than a portfolio that consists of buying an asset-or-nothing call and selling a cash-or-nothing call.

## VALUING A EUROPEAN-STYLE PUT OPTION

Valuing a European-style put under risk-neutrality follows straightforwardly from valuing the call. In the absence of costless arbitrage opportunities in the marketplace, we know that

[12] Asset-or-nothing and cash-or-nothing options are commonly referred to as "binary" or "digital" options and, in spite of their simplicity, are generally categorized under the heading "nonstandard options." Nonstandard options are the primary focus of Chapter 8.

$$c - p = Se^{-iT} - Xe^{-rT} \tag{7.41}$$

by virtue of put-call parity price relation from Chapter 6. If we isolate $p$ and substitute the call option formula (7.33), we get

$$\begin{aligned} p &= Xe^{-rT} - Se^{-iT} + c \\ &= Xe^{-rT} - Se^{-iT} + Se^{-iT}N(d_1) - Xe^{-rT}N(d_2) \\ &= Xe^{-rT}N(-d_2) - Se^{-iT}N(-d_1) \end{aligned} \tag{7.42}$$

As in the case of the European-style call formula, the structure of the European-style put formula lends itself to straightforward interpretation. The term, $Xe^{-rT}N(-d_2)$, is the present value of the expected benefit of exercising the put option at expiration conditional upon the terminal asset price being less than the exercise price times the risk-neutral probability that the option will be in the money at expiration. Recall the put option provides the right to sell the asset so the benefit from holding the option is the cash we receive when we exercise the option, that is, $X$. $N(-d_2)$ is the risk-neutral probability that the asset price will be less than the exercise price at expiration. Note that it is the complement of $N(d_2)$, the risk-neutral probability that the terminal asset price will exceed the exercise price. The present value of the expected cost of exercising the put option conditional upon the put option being in-the-money at expiration is $Se^{-iT}N(-d_1)$. If we exercise the put, we must forfeit the asset as fulfillment of your obligation, so the present value of the expected terminal asset price conditional upon exercise times the probability that the option expires in the money is your cost today.

Also, as in the case of the standard European-style call, the value of a standard put may be considered to be the value of a portfolio of more basic options. This time the portfolio consists of buying a cash-or-nothing put and selling an asset-or-nothing put. A cash-or-nothing put pays a fixed amount of cash, $CASH$, if the asset price is below the pre-specified level $X$. Under the assumptions of risk-neutral individuals and log-normally distributed asset prices, the value of a cash-or-nothing put where $CASH = X$ is

$$p_{CON} = Xe^{-rT}N(-d_2) \tag{7.43}$$

The value of an asset-or-nothing put is

$$p_{AON} = Se^{-iT}N(-d_1) \tag{7.44}$$

Taking the difference in values, we get the put formula (7.42).

**ILLUSTRATION 7.9** Find value of European-style put written on stock index.

*Compute the value of a three-month European-style stock index put option with an exercise price of 50. Assume the index has a level of 49, a dividend yield of 2%, and a volatility rate of 20%. The risk-free rate is 5%.*

First, note that $d_1$ and $d_2$ are the same as in Illustration 7.4; $d_1 = -0.0770$, and $d_2 = -0.1770$. Second, compute the cumulative normal probabilities,

$$N(0.0770) = 0.5307 \text{ and } N(0.1770) = 0.5703$$

Finally, gather the terms and compute the option value.

$$p = 50e^{-0.05(0.25)}(0.5703) - 49e^{-0.02(0.25)}(0.5307) = 2.284$$

All computations can be verified using appropriate OPTVAL functions. The function call for the valuation of the index put, for example, is illustrated below.

F12 =OV_OPTION_VALUE($B$3,$B$8,$B$9,$B$12,$B$4,$B$5,"p","E")

| | A | B | C | D | E | F | G | H |
|---|---|---|---|---|---|---|---|---|
| 1 | **VALUATION OF EUROPEAN-STYLE OPTIONS** | | | | | | | |
| 2 | **Index** | | | | **Call** | **Put** | | |
| 3 | Level | 49 | | $d_1$/-$d_1$ | -0.0770 | 0.0770 | | |
| 4 | Dividend yield | 2% | | $d_2$/-$d_2$ | -0.1770 | 0.1770 | | |
| 5 | Volatility rate | 20% | | | | | | |
| 6 | | | | N($d_1$) | 0.4693 | 0.5307 | | |
| 7 | **Option parameters** | | | N($d_2$) | 0.4297 | 0.5703 | | |
| 8 | Exercise price | 50 | | | | | | |
| 9 | Time to expiration | 0.25 | | *S* exp(-*iT*) | 48.756 | 48.756 | | |
| 10 | | | | *X* exp(-*rT*) | 49.379 | 49.379 | | |
| 11 | **Market parameters** | | | | | | | |
| 12 | Interest rate | 5% | | **Index option** | 1.661 | 2.284 | | |
| 13 | | | | **Futures option** | 1.661 | 2.284 | | |
| 14 | **Index futures** | | | | | | | |
| 15 | Price, *F* | 49.369 | | | | | | |

## MEASURING RISK OF EUROPEAN-STYLE OPTIONS

"Greeks" is a term used in industry to characterize the risks of an option, that is, the option value's sensitivity to unexpected movements in its underlying determinants. The primary purpose of the Greeks is for dynamic risk management. Before examining some dynamic risk management problems, however, we develop formulas for the different risk measures.[13]

From the last section, we know that the European-style call and put formulas are

$$c = Se^{-iT}N(d_1) - Xe^{-rT}N(d_2) \tag{7.33}$$

and

$$p = Xe^{-rT}N(-d_2) - Se^{-iT}N(-d_1) \tag{7.42}$$

where

[13] Appendix 7E of this chapter derives the Greeks from basic principles. Only the final expression is shown in the text of this chapter.

$$d_1 = \frac{\ln(Se^{(r-i)T}/X) + 0.5\sigma^2 T}{\sigma\sqrt{T}} \text{ and } d_2 = d_1 - \sigma\sqrt{T}$$

On the right-hand side of the valuation equations are six underlying determinants (i.e., $S$, $X$, $r$, $i$, $s$, and $T$). The exercise price is constant. We are interested in knowing how the option value changes as each of the remaining five determinants changes. Because the European-style call and put values are expressed as formulas, we can take partial derivatives of the formulas to determine the Greeks. After showing the expression for each partial derivative, we give a numerical example.

All of the examples are for hypothetical stock index options. The current index level is 49, its dividend yield of 2%, and its volatility rate of 20%. The call and put option share a common exercise price, 50, and a common time to expiration, three months. The risk-free rate of interest is 5%.

### Delta: Change in Asset Price

The change in the call option value with respect to a change in the asset price is called the option's *delta*. The delta of a European-style call option is

$$\Delta_c = \frac{\partial c}{\partial S} = e^{-iT}N(d_1) > 0 \tag{7.45a}$$

The call's delta is positive in sign since both the discount factor and the probability are positive. The implication of the delta being positive is that an increase in asset price will cause the call price to rise. This makes sense since the call option is the right to buy the underlying asset at a fixed price. The higher the asset price, the higher the call value.

Figure 7.4 shows the change in European-style call value (i.e., the call's delta) as a function of the asset price. Notice that when the call option is out-of-

**FIGURE 7.4** Delta as a function of asset price.

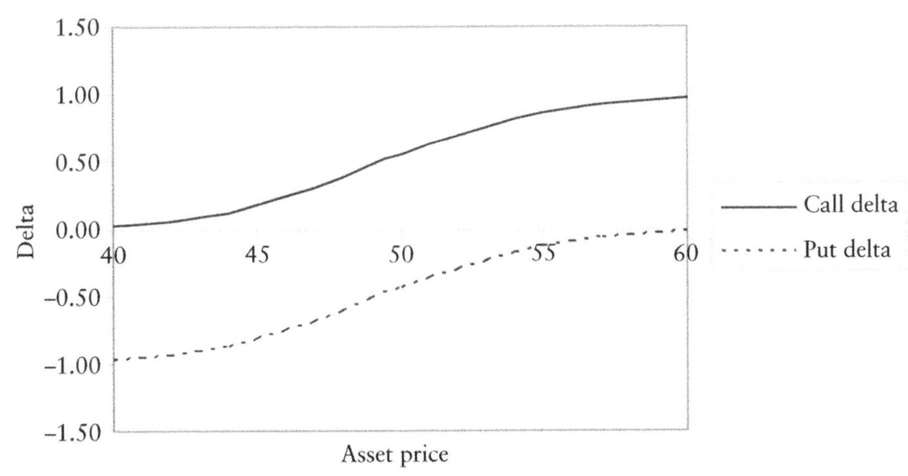

the-money, its slope is fairly flat. Out-of-the-money call options have very low delta values; that is, the call value does not respond very quickly to changes in the asset price. As the call moves into the money, the slope becomes steeper. Where the call is deep in-the-money, the delta value is nearly one, that is, the call value changes almost dollar for dollar with the asset price. Where the underlying asset distributes no cash (i.e., $i = 0$), the change is exactly one-to-one.

For the index call option, the delta is 0.467 for the parameters of the valuation problem. This means that, if the index level rises by one dollar from its level of 49, the call value will increase by about 46.7 cents. Knowing this quantity can be very useful in controlling asset price risk exposure. Suppose that we own the index call. If the index falls by a dollar, our option falls in value by 46.7 cents. To control this risk, we might want to sell 0.467 units of the index. If the index falls by a dollar, we lose 46.7 cents on the option but gain 46.7 cents on the index. On the other hand, if the index rises by a dollar, we gain 46.7 cents on the option but lose 46.7 cents on the short position in the index. This is called a "delta-neutral" hedge portfolio.

The delta of a European-style put is

$$\Delta_p = \frac{\partial p}{\partial S} = -e^{-iT}N(-d_1) < 0 \tag{7.45b}$$

The delta of a put is negative—an increase in asset price reduces the put value. Figure 7.4 also shows the put's delta as a function of the asset price. At low levels of asset price, the put is deep in-the-money and has a delta near –1. As the asset price rises, the delta becomes smaller. A deep out-of-the-money put has a delta near zero.

### Eta: Percent Change in Asset Price

The option's *eta* is the percentage change in the option value with respect to the percentage change in the asset price. Although eta is generally not used directly for risk management purposes, it is a useful metric for measuring an option's risk relative to the risk of the underlying asset. The call's eta is

$$\eta_c = \Delta_c\frac{S}{c} = e^{-iT}N(d_1)\frac{S}{c} > 1 \tag{7.46}$$

The call's eta is always greater than 1. To see this, substitute the call option formula for $c$ in the expression for eta. Since $c > 0$ and $Xe^{-rT}N(d_2) > 0$,

$$\eta_c = \frac{Se^{-iT}N(d_1)}{Se^{-iT}N(d_1) - Xe^{-rT}N(d_2)} > 1$$

The value of the eta can be quite large, as Figure 7.5 demonstrates. At an asset price level of 49, the call's eta is 13.78. This means that if the underlying asset

**FIGURE 7.5** Eta as a function of asset price.

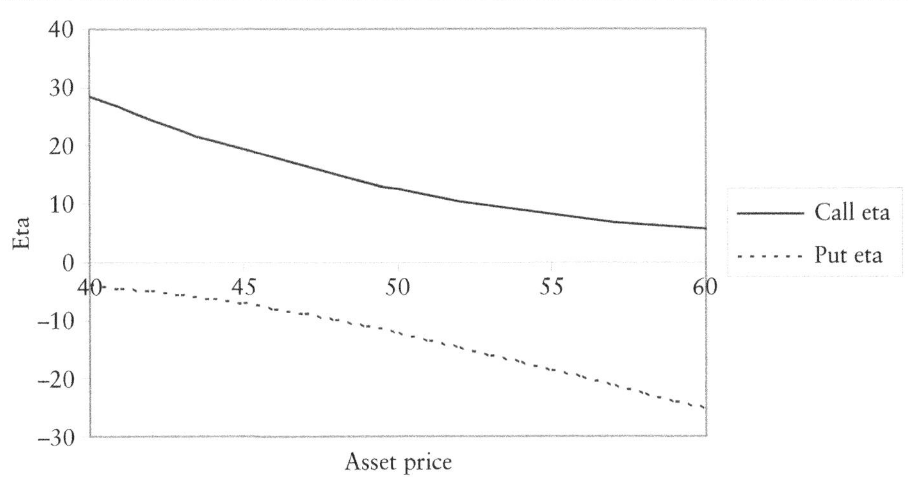


price rose by 1%, the call value would rise by about 13.78%. As the figure shows, the eta grows larger as the asset price falls and the call becomes out-of-the-money.

The eta of the put is

$$\eta_p = \Delta_p \frac{S}{p} = e^{-iT} N(d_1) \frac{S}{p} > 1 \tag{7.47b}$$

The put's eta is negative and will always have a value less than −1.

The values of eta are useful in the assessment of option risk within a capital asset pricing model framework. As we saw earlier in the chapter, the "beta" of an option equals the beta of the underlying asset times the option's eta, that is, $\beta_c = \eta_c \beta_S$ and $\beta_p = \eta_p \beta_S$. Options, being levered instruments, are much riskier in a rate of return sense than the underlying asset. In return for the additional risk, individuals can expect to get a higher return.

## Gamma: Change in Delta from a Change in Asset Price

An option's *gamma* is the change in delta as the asset price changes. The expressions for gamma for the European-style call and the European-style put are the same,

$$\gamma_c = \gamma_p = \frac{e^{-iT} n(d_1)}{S\sigma\sqrt{T}} > 0 \tag{7.47}$$

where, as noted earlier in the chapter, $n(d_1)$ is the univariate normal density at $d_1$, that is,

**FIGURE 7.6** Gamma as a function of asset price.

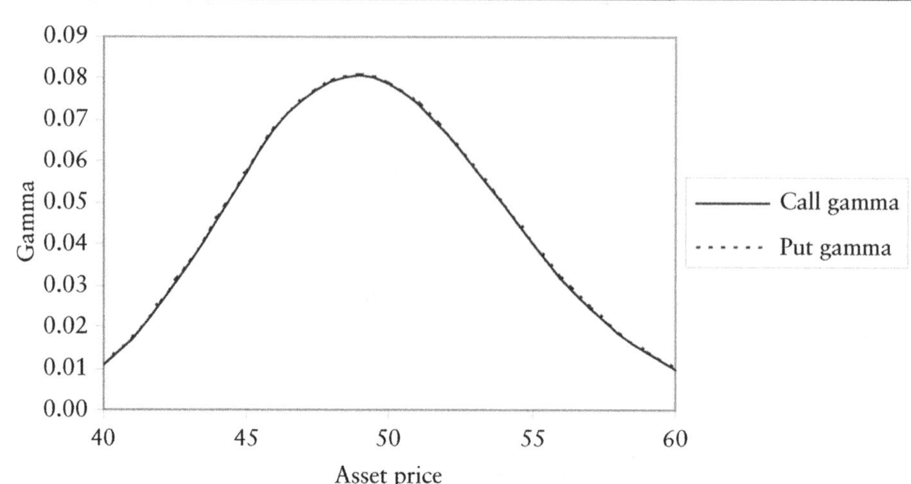


$$n(d_1) = \frac{1}{\sqrt{2\pi}} e^{-d_1^2/2}$$

The gamma tells us how quickly the delta changes as the asset price changes. Figure 7.6 shows gamma as a function of the underlying asset price. At an index level of 49, the gamma of the call is 0.081. Recall that the delta for this option is 0.467. The level of gamma tells us that if the index level rises by a dollar, the delta will increase from 0.467 to a level of about 0.541. The highest level of gamma occurs when the option is at the money. This means that at-the-money options are hardest to hedge. It also means that if we believe that the asset price is about move in one direction or another an at-the-money spread will maximize the portfolio's dollar response to underlying asset price movements.

### Rho$_r$: Change in Interest Rate

The change in the call value with respect to a change in the risk-free rate of interest is called the option's $rho_r$ and is expressed as

$$\rho_c^r = \frac{\partial c}{\partial r} = TXe^{-rT}N(d_2) > 0 \tag{7.48a}$$

The sign of the partial derivative indicates that call value increases as the interest rate increases. The reason is that the present value of the exercise price falls. The value of $rho_r$ in our illustration is 5.305. If the interest rate increases by 100 basis points, the call value will increase in value by about 5.3 cents.

The partial derivative of the put option price with respect to the risk-free rate of interest is

**FIGURE 7.7** Rho – r as a function of asset price.

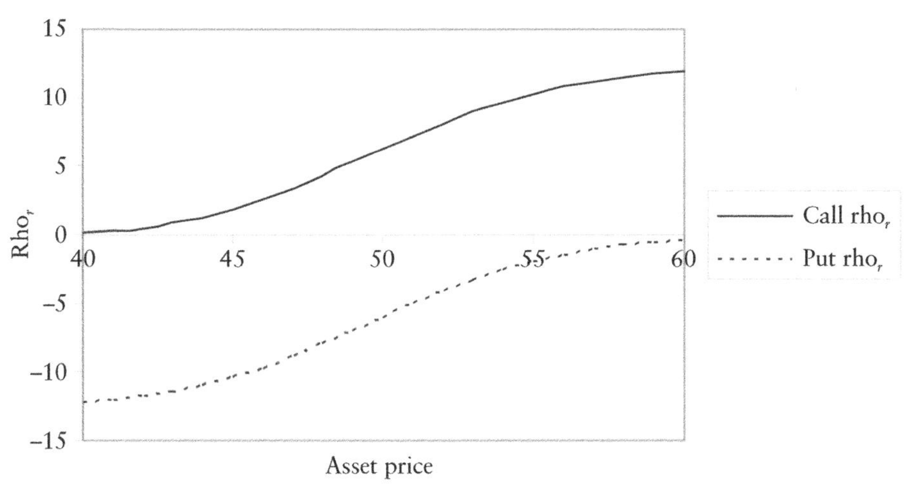


$$\rho_p^r = \frac{\partial p}{\partial r} = -TXe^{-rT}N(-d_2) < 0 \tag{7.48b}$$

For the put, the value of $rho_r$ is negative. As the risk-free rate of interest rises, the present value of the exercise price received upon exercising the option falls. The value of $rho_r$ for the put option in the illustration –7.040, implying that an increase in the interest rate of 100 basis points reduces the option value by about 7 cents. The levels of $rho_r$ for different levels asset price are illustrated in Figure 7.7.

### Rho$_i$: Change in Income Rate

The change in the call option price with respect to a change in the asset's income rate is called $rho_i$. The partial derivative of the call value with respect to a change in the income rate is

$$\rho_c^i = \frac{\partial c}{\partial i} = -TSe^{-iT}N(d_1) < 0 \tag{7.49a}$$

As the income rate increases, the call value falls, holding constant the asset price and the other variables. The higher the income rate of the asset, the lower the expected rate of price appreciation and the lower the call option value. The magnitude of the derivative is small, however. For the stock index call option in our illustration, the $rho_i$ value is –5.720. In other words, if the income rate on the index increases by 100 basis points, the call price will fall by approximately 6 cents. The call's $rho_i$ falls as the asset price increases, as is illustrated in Figure 7.8. The more the call is in the money, the greater is the effect that an increase in $rho_i$ will have on the option value.

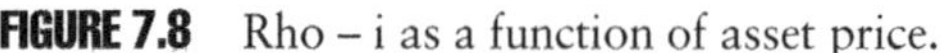

**FIGURE 7.8** Rho – i as a function of asset price.

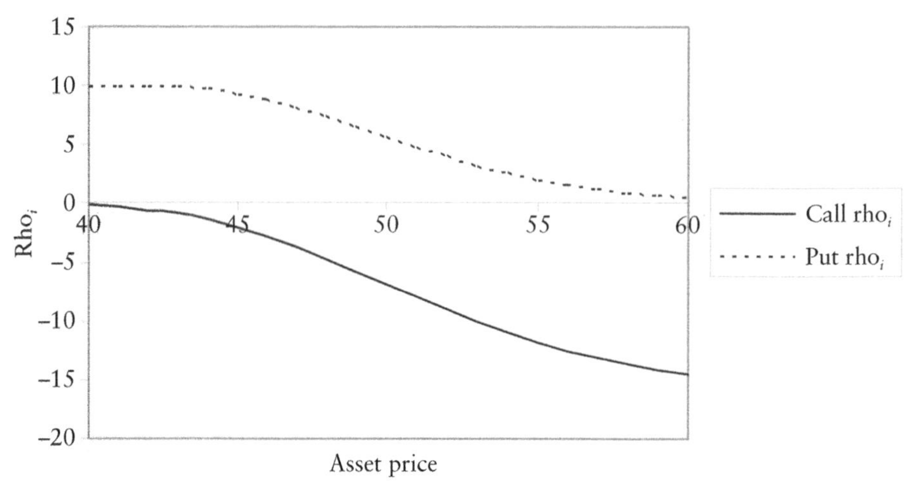


The partial derivative of the put option price with respect to the asset's income rate is

$$\rho_p^i = \frac{\partial p}{\partial i} = TSe^{-iT}N(-d_1) > 0 \tag{7.49b}$$

As the income rate increases, the expected rate of appreciation in the asset price falls and hence the value of the put option rises. The numerical value of $rho_i$ for the put option in our illustration is 6.469.

### Vega: Change in Volatility Rate

The change in the option price with respect to a change in the volatility is called "vega."[14] The vega of a European-style call option is

$$\text{Vega}_c = \frac{\partial c}{\partial \sigma} = Se^{-iT}n(d_1)\sqrt{T} > 0 \tag{7.50a}$$

The sign of the derivative is positive, indicating that as the volatility of the underlying asset return increases, the call option value increases. The intuition for this result is that an increase in the volatility rate increases the probability of large upward movements in the underlying asset price. The probability of large downward asset price movements also increases, however, it is of no consequence since the call option holder has limited liability.

[14] The fact that vega is not a Greek letter shows what happens when industry participants are allowed to assign names to concepts.

**FIGURE 7.9** Vega as a function of asset price.

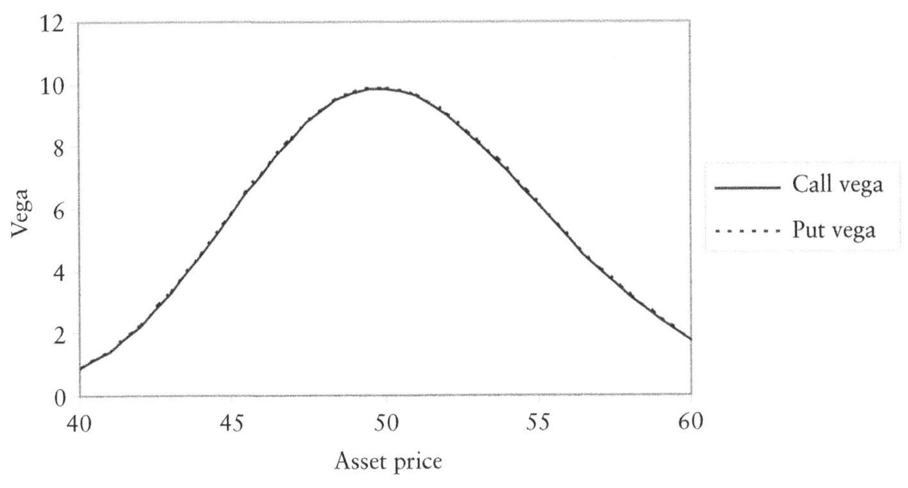


Figure 7.9 shows the option's vega as a function of the asset price. This pattern is very similar to that of the option gamma. The vega is highest where the option is approximately at-the-money, and falls as the call goes deeper in (out of) the money. The numerical value of the call option's vega implies that the option's price is more sensitive to volatility than it is to either the cost of carry rate or the interest rate. The call vega for the option in our illustration is 9.696. An increase in volatility of 100 basis points increases the call's value by nearly ten cents.

The put option's vega is the same as that of the call, that is,

$$\text{Vega}_p = \frac{\partial p}{\partial \sigma} = Se^{-iT}n(d_1)\sqrt{T} > 0 \tag{7.50b}$$

The put option value also increases with an increase in volatility since the probability of a large asset price decrease increases. The vega of the put is also 9.696.

### Theta: Change in Time to Expiration

The partial derivative of the option price with respect to the time to expiration parameter is called the option's *theta*. The theta of the European-style call is

$$\theta_c = \frac{\partial c}{\partial T} = Se^{-iT}n(d_1)\frac{\sigma}{2\sqrt{T}} - iSe^{-iT}N(d_1) + rXe^{-rT}N(d_2) \tag{7.51a}$$

The expression for theta makes it difficult to determine whether the call value will increase or decrease as the time to expiration falls. The theta is the sum of three components. The first term on the right-hand side is positive and reflects the increase in call value from an increase in the time to expiration increases the probability of upward price movements in the asset price and increases the value of the option. The second term may be positive or negative depending on whether the income rate $i$ is greater than or less than 0. If $i < 0$, the term is positive since as the time to expiration increases the present value of the expected terminal asset price grows large (recall that the underlying asset price grows at rate $r - i$ while the discount rate of the terminal value of the option is $r$). Finally, the third term is positive. As time to expiration increases, the present value of the exercise price grows small. Note that the only case where the overall value of theta is positive is where $i \leq 0$.

Figure 7.10 shows how the theta of the call changes as a function of the asset price. The theta takes its highest value for at-the-money calls. The theta for the call in our illustration, for example, is near-the-money and is 4.482. This means that if the option's time to expiration is reduced by one day (i.e., 1/365th of a year), the call will fall in value by about 1.2 cents. Over seven days, the expected *time decay* is 8.6 cents.

The theta of the European-style put option is

$$\theta_p = \frac{\partial p}{\partial T} = Se^{-iT}n(d_1)\frac{\sigma}{2\sqrt{T}} + iSe^{-iT}N(d_1) - rXe^{-rT}N(d_2) \tag{7.51b}$$

Like in the case of the call, the sign of the put's theta is ambiguous. The interpretation of the terms in the expression of the put option's theta parallels that of the call option. The first term is the increase in put value resulting from the prospect of larger asset price movements when the time to expiration is large. The second term is negative if $i \leq 0$. In the case of the put, option value increases where the cost of carry rate is below the interest rate. The third term is negative. It reflects the fact that an increase in the time to expiration delays the receipt of the exercise price and hence reduces the put option value. The value of the theta for the put option in our illustration is 2.988.

**FIGURE 7.10** Theta as a function of asset price.

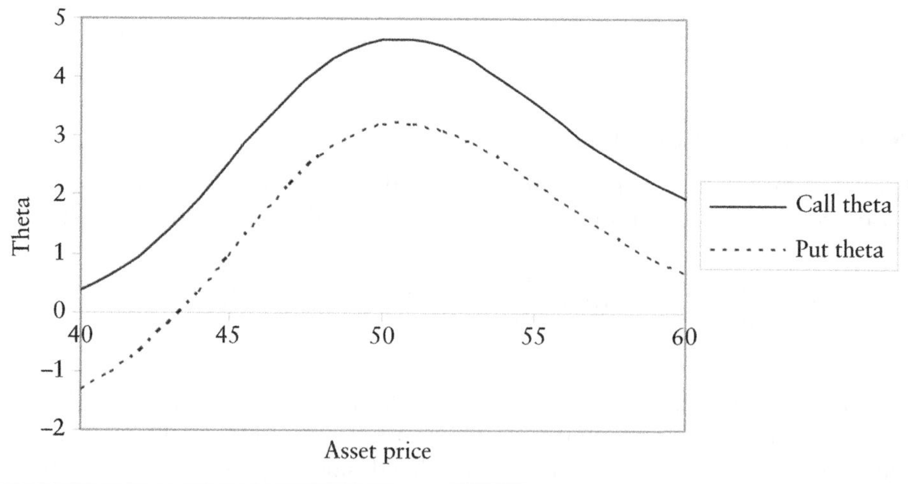

**FIGURE 7.11** Time decay of one-year out-of-the-money call option.

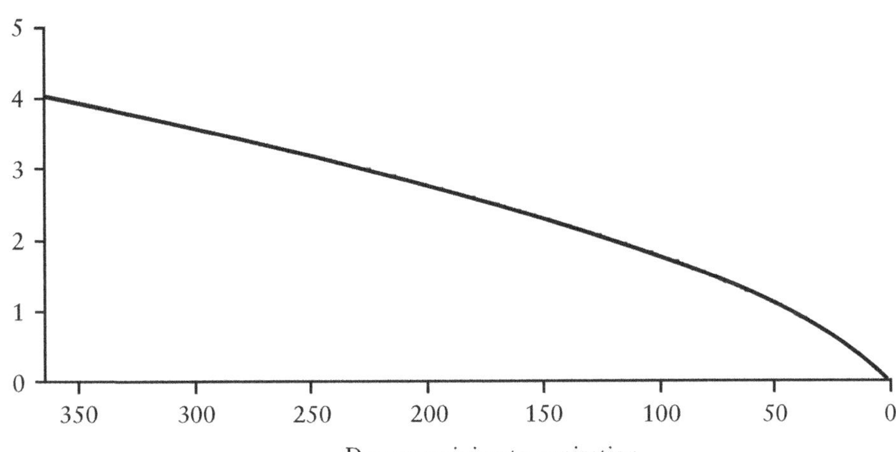


**Time Decay** An option is a *wasting asset* in the sense that its value generally falls as time passes. This must always be true for out-of-the-money options, for example, since their value at expiration is 0. It is worth noting the rate of time decay, however. Figure 7.11 shows the value of the index call in our illustration with times to expiration ranging from 365 days down to 1 day. For options with long times to expiration, option value decays at a reasonably steady daily rate. Once the option gets close to expiration, however, the rate of decrease increases.

### Summary

This section contains analytical expressions for measuring the risk characteristics of European-style options. In industry, these measures are called the "Greeks," because of the Greek letters to denoting each of the risk measurement. All the expressions are derived by taking the partial derivative of the option valuation formulas with respect to the parameter of interest. Table 7.3 summarizes the valuation equations as well as the formulas for the Greeks.

The summary in Table 7.3 can also be used for European-style options whose noninterest carry costs are best modeled as discrete flows. Only two minor adjustments are necessary. First, we must deflate the current asset price by the present value of promised income during the option's life, that is, set the asset price in all the expressions of Table 7.1 equal to $S - PVI$. Second, we must set the continuous income rate $i$ equal to 0.

Likewise Table 7.4 can be used for European-style futures options. Here, we must set the income rate equal to the risk-free rate so that the embedded cost of carry rate of the futures equals 0. For your convenience, Table 7.4 summarizes the valuation equations as well as the formulas for the Greeks for European-style futures options. Note that since the futures does not have an income rate, $rho_i$ does not appear.

**TABLE 7.3** Summary of valuation equations and risk measures for European-style options where the underlying asset has a continuous income rate $i$.[a]

| | Call Option | Put Option |
|---|---|---|
| Value | $c = Se^{-iT}N(d_1) - Xe^{-rT}N(d_2)$ | $p = Xe^{-rT}N(-d_2) - Se^{-iT}N(-d_1)$ |
| | $d_1 = \frac{\ln(Se^{(r-i)T}/X) + 0.5\sigma^2 T}{\sigma\sqrt{T}} = \frac{\ln(Se^{-iT}/Xe^{-rT}) + 0.5\sigma^2 T}{\sigma\sqrt{T}}$ | |
| | $d_2 = d_1 - \sigma\sqrt{T}$ | |
| Delta | $\Delta_c = e^{-iT}N(d_1)$ | $\Delta_p = -e^{-iT}N(-d_1)$ |
| Eta | $\eta_c = e^{-iT}N(d_1)\frac{S}{c}$ | $\eta_p = -e^{-iT}N(-d_1)\frac{S}{p}$ |
| Gamma | $\gamma_c = \gamma_p = \frac{e^{-iT}n(d_1)}{S\sigma\sqrt{T}}$ | |
| $\text{Rho}_r$ | $\rho_c^r = TXe^{-rT}N(d_2)$ | $\rho_p^r = -TXe^{-rT}N(-d_2)$ |
| $\text{Rho}_i$ | $\rho_c^i = -TSe^{-iT}N(d_1)$ | $\rho_p^i = TSe^{-iT}N(-d_1)$ |
| Vega | $\text{Vega}_c = \text{Vega}_p = Se^{-iT}n(d_1)\sqrt{T}$ | |
| Theta | $\theta_c = Se^{-iT}n(d_1)\frac{\sigma}{2\sqrt{T}} - iSe^{-iT}N(d_1) + rXe^{-rT}N(d_2)$ | $\theta_p = Se^{-iT}n(d_1)\frac{\sigma}{2\sqrt{T}} + iSe^{-iT}N(d_1) - rXe^{-rT}N(-d_2)$ |

[a] For the case where the asset pays income as discrete flows rather than as a continuous rate, two adjustments to the expressions in this table are necessary. First, set the income rate $i$ equal to 0. Second, wherever the asset price appears in an expression, substitute the asset price less the present value of the discrete income flows that are paid during the option's life, that is, $S - PVI$.

**TABLE 7.4** Summary of valuation equations and risk measures for European-style futures options.

| | Call Option | Put Option |
|---|---|---|
| Value | $c = e^{-rT}[FN(d_1) - XN(d_2)]$ | $p = e^{-rT}[XN(-d_2) - FN(-d_1)]$ |
| | $d_1 = \frac{\ln(F/X) + 0.5\sigma^2 T}{\sigma\sqrt{T}}, \; d_2 = d_1 - \sigma\sqrt{T}$ | |
| Delta | $\Delta_c = e^{-rT}N(d_1)$ | $\Delta_p = -e^{-rT}N(-d_1)$ |
| Eta | $\eta_c = e^{-rT}N(d_1)\frac{F}{c}$ | $\eta_p = -e^{-rT}N(-d_1)\frac{F}{p}$ |

**TABLE 7.4** (Continued)

| | Call Option | Put Option |
|---|---|---|
| Gamma | $\gamma_c = \gamma_p = \dfrac{e^{-rT}n(d_1)}{F\sigma\sqrt{T}}$ | |
| Rho$_r$ | $\rho_c^r = TXe^{-rT}N(d_2)$ | $\rho_p^r = -TXe^{-rT}N(-d_2)$ |
| Vega | $\text{Vega}_c = \text{Vega}_p = Fe^{-rT}n(d_1)\sqrt{T}$ | |
| Theta | $\theta_c = Fe^{-rT}n(d_1)\dfrac{\sigma}{2\sqrt{T}} - rc$ | $\theta_p = Fe^{-rT}n(d_1)\dfrac{\sigma}{2\sqrt{T}} - rp$ |

**ILLUSTRATION 7.10** Compute values of European-style call and European-style put written on a futures contract. Also report their "Greeks."

*Compute the values of a one-month European-style call and a one-month European-style put written on a wheat futures contract assuming the options have an exercise price of 500 cents per bushel. Also report the options' Greeks. Assume the underlying wheat futures has a price of 495 cents per bushel and a 12% volatility rate. Assume also that the risk-free rate of interest is 5%. The contract denomination is 5,000 bushels.*

The option values and Greeks can be computed straightforwardly using the formulas summarized in Table 7.3. The values and risk measures are:

| | In Cents per Bushel | | In Dollars per Contract | |
|---|---|---|---|---|
| | Call | Put | Call | Put |
| Value | 4.6429 | 9.6221 | 232.1453 | 481.11 |
| Delta | 0.3909 | -0.6050 | 19.5434 | -30.2487 |
| Eta | 41.6722 | -31.1222 | 41.6722 | -31.1222 |
| Gamma | 0.0223 | 0.0223 | 1.1161 | 1.1161 |
| Rho – r | 15.7364 | -25.7570 | 786.82 | -1,287.85 |
| Vega | 54.6958 | 54.6958 | 2,734.79 | 2,734.79 |
| Theta | 39.1488 | 38.8999 | 1,957.44 | 1,944.99 |

The values may also be computed using the OPTVAL functions with the prefix OV_FOPTION_*Greek*, where *Greek* is DELTA, ETA, GAMMA, and so on.

The pair of columns on the left is in cents per bushel. The pair on the right are total dollar values. The total dollar value is computed by multiplying by the contract size, 5,000 bushels, and dividing by 100 to convert from cents to dollars. The eta is not transformed in the same manner as the others because it is an elasticity, that is, a percent change in the option value with respect to a percent change in the underlying asset price. The value of the vega for the call is 1,957.44. This means that if the volatility rate increases from, say, 12 to 13%, the call option value will increases by approximately $1{,}957.44 \times 0.01 = 19.57$ dollars.

**ILLUSTRATION 7.11** Compute realized volatility and compare with volatility "implied" by option price.

*The Excel file, **RIMM.xls**, contains a history of daily closing stock prices for Research in Motion Limited (ticker symbol RIMM), manufacturer of the infamous "Blackberry" for the calendar year 2004. As of the close on December 31, 2004, RIMM's share price was 82.42. At the same time, a call option with an exercise price of 85 and an expiration date of June 18, 2005 had a closing price of 10.10. Determine whether this call option was fairly priced on December 31, 2004, assuming that the risk-free interest rate was 2.72%. RIMM is not expected to pay cash dividends over the next year.*

In order to determine whether the option is fairly priced, we must determine its theoretical value. The BSM call option pricing formula requires six parameters, five of which are known.[15] The stock price is 82.42, and the stock pays no cash dividends. The option's exercise price is 85, and its time to expiration is 169 days or 0.4630 years. The risk-free rate of interest is 2.72%. What remains to be estimated is futures volatility rate of the stock's return.

One way to develop an estimate of the future volatility rate is to estimate historical volatility. Based upon the daily price series in the Excel file, compute the standard deviation of the daily continuously compounded rates of return, $R_t = \ln(S_t/S_{t-1})$. If it is reasonable to assume that RIMM's immediate volatility will persist into the future, the historical estimate is a reasonable proxy for future volatility. Based upon the daily returns, the historical volatility is 3.10% per day. To annualize this volatility, we multiply by the square root of the number of trading days in the year (i.e., $\sqrt{252}$ ). The annual volatility rate, based on daily returns, is 49.17%.

Before proceeding to the next step of valuing the call option, it is useful to remind yourself of any implicit assumptions you are making in your estimation. You used daily rates of return in computing your estimate of volatility, for example. But, the rates of return may be for any length period—a day, a week, or a month. As a general rule in statistics, the more information (i.e., number of observations) that you use in estimation, the more accurate will be your estimator. Weekly returns will therefore provide a more reliable estimate than monthly returns, holding the overall length of the estimation period constant (in this case, one year).

Following the same logic, it would seem daily returns will provide a more reliable estimate than weekly returns. Unfortunately, this may not be the case. The reason is that each return is based on daily closing prices, and each daily closing price has error. What you want to measure at the close each day is the "true" price of the stock. What you have is the stock price at the time of the last trade. The last trade price did not occur at the true price, but rather at the bid price if the trade was seller-motivated or at the ask price if the trade was buyer-motivated. Since the true price is presumably in between, each day's return is computed with error. The observed volatility that you computed, therefore 3.10% per day, is the sum of two components—the true volatility of the stock and volatility of the error in measurement. Without knowing whether each trade was a buy or a sell, you cannot unwind the effects of this error in the daily prices.

What you can do instead is increase the length of time between price observations from, say, daily to weekly. In place of having 252 "errors" in your estimate, you will now have only 52. The Excel file, **RIMM.xls**, also contains a spreadsheet with weekly prices. Note that the prices are for Wednesday each week. As a practical matter, fewer holidays

[15] Even though exchange-traded stock options are American-style, we can use the BSM European-style option formula because, as we showed in Chapter 6, American-style options on nondividend-paying stocks will not optimally be exercised early.

fall on Wednesdays so that the time between observations is usually exactly seven days. Based on weekly returns, the volatility rate is 6.17% per week. To annualize this figure, we multiply by the square root of 52. Hence, based on weekly returns, the annualized volatility rate is 44.46%, well below the 49.17% computed based on daily returns. Based on these results, it is probably most sensible to use 44.46% as the estimate of expected future volatility.

Having all of the necessary parameters in hand, we can now compute call option value. Substituting the parameters in to the option valuation function, we get

OV_OPTION_VALUE(82.42, 85, 0.463, 0.0272, 0.0, 0.4446, "c", "e") = 9.26

The closing option price was 10.10, however, indicating that the call is overpriced by 84 cents.

Often traders prefer to talk about "implied volatilities" rather than prices when talking about different option series. An implied volatility is the level of expected future volatility that equates the price of the option to its theoretical value. You can do this using Excel's SOLVER. Simply find the level of volatility, $v$, that satisfies the constraint that

OV_OPTION_VALUE(82.42, 85, 0.463, 0.0272, 0.0, $v$, "c", "e") = 10.10

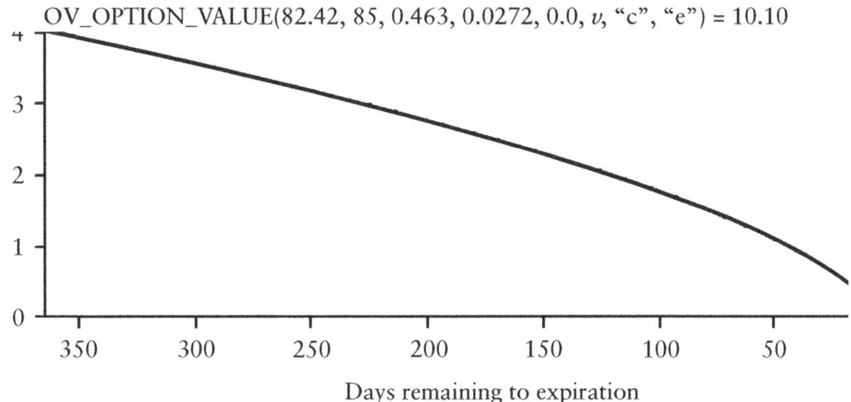


Given the observed option price of 10.10, the implied volatility is 48.23%. One interpretation of this volatility is as a "market consensus" estimate in the sense that both a buyer and a seller are presumably in the market and willing to trade at 10.10. For ease of computation, the OPTVAL Function Library contains an implied volatility function. To verify the SOLVER solution,

OV_OPTION_ISD(82.42, 85, 0.463, 0.0272, 0.0, 10.10, "c", "e") = 0.4823

## SUMMARY

This chapter focuses on valuing European-style options under the assumptions that individuals are risk-neutral and that asset prices are log-normally distributed at the option's expiration. At the outset, we establish that option values are the same regardless of whether individuals are risk-neutral or risk-averse. With the irrelevance of risk preferences established, we adopt a risk-neutral valuation framework. Assuming that the underlying asset price is log-normally distributed at the option's expiration, we value a European-style option by taking the present value of its expected future value. With an analytical expression of option value in hand, we examine the option's sensitivity of option value to changes in its underlying parameters. These risk measures are popularly referred to as the "Greeks." They will be used extensively in the risk management applications examined in later chapters of the book.

## REFERENCES AND SUGGESTED READINGS


Asay, Michael R. 1982. A note on the design of commodity option contracts. *Journal of Futures Markets* 2 (Spring): 1–8.

Biger, Nahum, and John Hull. 1983. The valuation of currency options. *Financial Management* 12 (Spring): 24–28.

Black, Fischer. 1976. The pricing of commodity contracts. *Journal of Financial Economics* 3 (March): 167–179.

Black, Fischer, and Myron Scholes. 1973. The pricing of options and corporate liabilities, *Journal of Political Economy* 81: 637–659.

Boness, A. James. 1964. Elements of a theory of stock option value. *Journal of Political Economy* 72: 163–75.

Cox, John C., and Stephen A. Ross. 1976. The valuation of options for alternative stochastic processes. *Journal of Financial Economics* 3: 145–166.

Garman, Mark B., and S. W. Kohlhagen. 1983. Foreign currency option values. *Journal of International Money and Finance* 2 (December): 231–237.

Ito, K. 1951. On stochastic differential equations. *Memoirs, American Mathematical Society* 4: 1–51.

Merton, Robert C. 1973. Theory of rational option pricing. *Bell Journal of Economics and Management Science* 4: 141–183.

Samuelson, Paul A. 1965. Rational theory of warrant pricing. *Industrial Management Review* 10 (Winter): 13–31.

Whaley, Robert E. 1997. Building on Black-Scholes. *Risk* (December): 149–156.

Whaley, Robert. E. 2003. Derivatives. in *Handbook of the Economics of Finance*, edited by in George Constantinides, Milton Harris, and Rene Stulz. Elsevier North-Holland, Amsterdam: 1129–1206.


## APPENDIX 7A: APPLICATIONS OF ITO'S LEMMA

*Ito's lemma* is an important mathematical result[16] that has found many applications in finance, particularly in the area of derivatives valuation. This appendix provides Ito's lemma, and then applies it in several ways.

### Ito's Lemma

A statement of Ito's lemma begins with the definition of an Ito process. A variable $x$ is said to follow an *Ito process* if it dynamics can be described in the form,

$$dx = a(x, t)dt + b(x, t)dz \tag{7A.1}$$

where $dz$ is an increment to a Wiener process, $z(t)$, and $a$ and $b$ are functions of $x$ and $t$. In (7A.1), the variable $x$ drifts at a rate of $a$ and has a variance rate of $b^2$.

[16] See Ito (1951).

Now suppose there exists a function $f$ that depends on $x$ and $t$. Under Ito's *lemma*, this function also follows an Ito process with a drift rate and variance rate as shown below,[17]

$$df = \left(\frac{\partial f}{\partial x}a + \frac{\partial f}{\partial t} + \frac{1}{2}\frac{\partial^2 f}{\partial x^2}b^2\right)dt + \frac{\partial f}{\partial x}b\,dz \tag{7A.2}$$

where the $dz$ is the same Wiener process as in (7A.1).

### Application 1: Derivatives Price Movements

The Black-Scholes/Merton (BSM) option valuation framework assumes that the asset prices follows the Geometric Brownian,

$$dS = \alpha S dt + \sigma S dz \tag{7A.3}$$

where $\alpha$ and $\sigma$ are constant. Comparing (7A.3) to (7A.1), we see that $a(x,t) = \alpha S$ and $b(x,t) = \sigma S$. It therefore follows that the price movements of a derivative contract written on the asset depends on $S$ and $t$, that is, $f(S,t)$, follows the dynamics,

$$df = \left(\frac{\partial f}{\partial S}\alpha S + \frac{\partial f}{\partial t} + \frac{1}{2}\frac{\partial^2 f}{\partial S^2}\sigma^2 S^2\right)dt + \frac{\partial f}{\partial S}\sigma S\,dz \tag{7A.4}$$

### Application 2: Forward Price Movements

Equation (7A.4) applies Ito's lemma to find the dynamics of derivatives prices given the dynamics of asset prices. We now turn to a specific derivative contract to further illustrate our results. From Chapter 3, we know the net cost of carry for a forward contract is

$$f = Se^{b(T-t)} \tag{7A.5}$$

where $t$ represents the evolution of time (i.e., the time to expiration of the forward contract rows short as time passes). Using (7A.5) to find the derivatives in (7A.4), we get

$$\frac{\partial f}{\partial S} = e^{b(T-t)}, \quad \frac{\partial^2 f}{\partial S^2} = 0, \quad \text{and} \quad \frac{\partial f}{\partial t} = -bSe^{b(T-t)}$$

The forward price, therefore, follows the dynamics

[17] The drift rate equals the term in the parentheses. The variance rate is $\left(\frac{\partial f}{\partial x}\right)^2 b^2$.

$$\begin{aligned} df &= [e^{b(T-t)}\alpha S - bSe^{b(T-t)}]dt + e^{b(T-t)}\sigma Sdz \\ &= (\alpha - b)fdt + \sigma fdz \end{aligned} \tag{7A.6}$$

where $dz$ is the same Wiener process as in (7A.3). In other words, the forward price, like the asset price, follows geometric Brownian motion, however, the drift rate of the forward is lower than the drift rate of the asset by the cost of carry rate, $b$.

### Application 3: Modeling the Logarithm of Asset Price

As noted in the text of the chapter, it is sometimes convenient to work with the logarithm of asset prices rather than asset prices directly. Since $\ln S$ qualifies as a function of $S$ and $t$, we can apply Ito's lemma to find the dynamics of $\ln S$. If $f = \ln S$, then

$$\frac{\partial f}{\partial S} = \frac{1}{S}, \quad \frac{\partial^2 f}{\partial S^2} = -\frac{1}{S^2}, \quad \text{and} \quad \frac{\partial f}{\partial t} = 0$$

Thus, the movements in the logarithm of stock price follow the geometric Brownian motion,

$$\begin{aligned} d\ln S &= \left(\alpha - \frac{\sigma^2}{2}\right)dt + \sigma dz \\ &= \mu dt + \sigma dz \end{aligned} \tag{7A.7}$$

where $\mu$ is the drift rate in the logarithm of asset price, as distinct from $\alpha$, which is the drift rate in asset price itself.

## APPENDIX 7B: RELATION BETWEEN THE CONTINUOUSLY COMPOUNDED MEAN RETURN AND THE MEAN CONTINUOUSLY COMPOUNDED RETURN

The continuously compounded mean return of the asset over the interval 0 to $T$ is defined as

$$E(\tilde{S}_T/S_0) = e^{\alpha T} = E(e^{\tilde{x}}) \tag{7B.1}$$

where $\tilde{x}$ is the normally distributed, continuously compounded rate of return from 0 to $T$. The rate of return, $\tilde{x}$, can be reexpressed in terms of a standardized unit normally distributed variable, $\tilde{z}$, that is,

$$\tilde{x} = \mu T + \sigma\sqrt{T}\tilde{z}$$

where $\mu$ and $\sigma$ are the mean and and the standard deviation of the continuously compounded rate of return on the asset. We can write the rate of price appreciation of the asset as

$$\tilde{S}_T/S_0 = e^{\tilde{x}} = e^{\mu T + \sigma\sqrt{T}\tilde{z}} \tag{7B.2}$$

and the mean expected rate of price appreciation as

$$\begin{aligned} e^{\alpha T} &= E(e^{\mu T + \sigma\sqrt{T}\tilde{z}}) \\ &= e^{\mu T} E(e^{\sigma\sqrt{T}\tilde{z}}) \end{aligned} \tag{7B.3}$$

Since $z$ is unit normally distributed, we may write (7B.3) as

$$E(e^{\sigma\sqrt{T}\tilde{z}}) = \int_{-\infty}^{+\infty} e^{\sigma\sqrt{T}z} e^{-z^2/2} \frac{1}{\sqrt{2\pi}} dz \tag{7B.4}$$

where

$$n(\tilde{z}) = \frac{1}{\sqrt{2\pi}} e^{-z^2/2}$$

is the normal density function. Now add and subtract an amount $\sigma^2 T/2$ in the exponent on the right-hand side of (7B.4). We get

$$\begin{aligned} E(e^{\sigma\sqrt{T}\tilde{z}}) &= \int_{-\infty}^{+\infty} e^{\sigma^2 T/2 - \sigma^2 T/2 + \sigma\sqrt{T}z - z^2/2} \frac{1}{\sqrt{2\pi}} dz \\ &= e^{\sigma^2 T/2} \int_{-\infty}^{+\infty} e^{-\sigma^2 T/2 + \sigma\sqrt{T}z - z^2/2} \frac{1}{\sqrt{2\pi}} dz \\ &= e^{\sigma^2 T/2} \int_{-\infty}^{+\infty} e^{-(\sigma\sqrt{T} - z)^2/2} \frac{1}{\sqrt{2\pi}} dz \end{aligned} \tag{7B.5}$$

Since integral expression on the right-hand side of (7B.5) is the area under the unit normal density function and equals one. Thus

$$E(e^{\sigma\sqrt{T}\tilde{z}}) = e^{\sigma^2 T/2} \tag{7B.6}$$

Substituting into (7B.3), we get

$$e^{\alpha T} = e^{\mu T + \sigma^2/2} \tag{7B.7}$$

or more simply

$$\alpha = \mu + \sigma^2/2 \tag{7B.8}$$

## APPENDIX 7C: APPROXIMATION OF THE UNIVARIATE NORMAL PROBABILITY

The probability that a random drawing from a unit normally distributed variable will be below $d$ is

$$\Pr(z < a) = \frac{1}{2\pi\sqrt{1-\rho^2}}\int_{-\infty}^{d}\frac{1}{\sqrt{2\pi}}\exp(-z^2/2)dz$$
$$= N_1(a)$$

The following polynomial provides an approximation of this probability that has a maximum absolute error of 0.000000075.

$$N_1(a) \approx 1 - a_0 e^{-d^2/2}(a_1 t + a_2 t^2 + a_3 t^3 + a_4 t^4 + a_5 t^5)$$

where

$$t = \frac{1}{1 + 0.2316419d},$$
$$a_0 = 0.3989423,\ a_1 = 0.319381530,\ a_2 = -0.356563782,$$
$$a_3 = 1.781477937,\ a_4 = -1.821255978, \text{ and } a_5 = 1.330274429$$

The value of $a$ must be greater than 0. To obtain the probability for a negative value of $a$, compute the probability for $-a$, $N_1(-a)$, and then subtract from one, that is, $N_1(a) = 1 - N_1(-a)$. This approximation appears as the function OV_PROB_PRUN in the OPTVAL Function Library. An illustration follows:

B2 fx =ov_prob_prun(B1)

| | A | B | C | D |
|---|---|---|---|---|
| 1 | a | 1.96 | | |
| 2 | Pr(z<a) | 0.975 | | |

## APPENDIX 7D: DERIVATION OF BLACK-SCHOLES/MERTON OPTION VALUATION FORMULA

The derivation of the Black-Scholes (1973)/Merton (1973) (BSM) formula follows directly from the Ito mechanics described in Appendix 7A. If the asset price movements follow the geometric Brownian motion,

$$dS = \alpha S dt + \sigma S dz \tag{7D.1}$$

derivatives written on this asset have price movements described by

$$df = \left(\frac{\partial f}{\partial S}\alpha S + \frac{\partial f}{\partial t} + \frac{1}{2}\frac{\partial^2 f}{\partial S^2}\sigma^2 S^2\right)dt + \frac{\partial f}{\partial S}\sigma S dz \tag{7D.2}$$

where the underlying source of uncertainty, $dz$, in (7D.1) and (7D.2) is the same.

The key insight of Black-Scholes and Merton option valuation model is that, if the underlying source of risk is the same for both the asset and derivative contracts written on the asset, it should be possible to create a risk-free hedge portfolio by buying the asset and selling the derivative contract or vice versa. To see this, suppose we sell one derivative contract and buy $\partial f/\partial S$ units of the underlying asset. The value of our portfolio will be

$$V = -f + \frac{\partial f}{\partial S}S \tag{7D.3}$$

Over the next instant in time, the portfolio value changes in response to changes in the prices of the derivative contract and the asset, as well as a result of collecting income on the asset at the constant, continuous rate, $i$. Algebraically,

$$dV = -df + \frac{\partial f}{\partial S}dS + \frac{\partial f}{\partial S}iSdt \tag{7D.4}$$

Substituting (7D.2) and (7D.1) for $df$ and $dS$,

$$\begin{aligned} dV &= -\left(\frac{\partial f}{\partial S}\alpha_S S + \frac{\partial f}{\partial t} + \frac{1}{2}\frac{\partial^2 f}{\partial S^2}\sigma^2 S^2\right)dt - \frac{\partial f}{\partial S}\sigma S dz + \frac{\partial f}{\partial S}(\alpha_S S dt + \sigma S dz) + \frac{\partial f}{\partial S}iSdt \\ &= -\left(\frac{\partial f}{\partial t} + \frac{1}{2}\frac{\partial^2 f}{\partial S^2}\sigma^2 S^2 - \frac{\partial f}{\partial S}iS\right)dt \end{aligned}$$

Note that by constructing the portfolio in this manner, the only source of risk, $dz$, has been eliminated. Since the portfolio is risk-free and perfect substitutes must have the same price, holding this portfolio is equivalent to holding an equal dollar investment in risk-free bonds, that is,

$$-\left(\frac{\partial f}{\partial t}+\frac{1}{2}\frac{\partial^2 f}{\partial S^2}\sigma^2 S^2-\frac{\partial f}{\partial S}iS\right)dt = r\left(-f+\frac{\partial f}{\partial S}S\right)dt \tag{7D.5}$$

By rearranging (7D.5), the BSM partial differential equation is identified,

$$\frac{\partial f}{\partial t}+(r-i)S\frac{\partial f}{\partial S}+\frac{1}{2}\sigma^2 S^2\frac{\partial^2 f}{\partial S^2} = rf \tag{7D.6}$$

Equation (7D.6) is the *Black-Scholes/Merton model*, and should not be confused with the *Black-Scholes/Merton formula*. The latter is a special case of the model to be discussed shortly. The BSM model (7D.6) applies to *all* derivatives written on $S$ including calls, puts, European-style options, American-style options, caps, floors, and collars—any derivative contract for which it is appropriate to assume the asset price dynamics follow geometric Brownian motion.[18] What distinguishes each derivative is the set of boundary equations applied to (7D.6). For a European-style call option, the boundary condition is $f = \max(0,S - X)$ at time $T$. For a European-style put option, the boundary condition is $f = \max(0,X - S)$ at time $T$. For American-style calls and puts, the respective boundary conditions apply at all times between the current time 0 and the expiration date $T$. Sometimes the partial differential equation subject to a boundary condition has a solution that can be expressed as an analytical formula. This is true for European-style options, for example. At other times, no analytical formula is possible and approximation methods must be used. Methods for approximating the value of derivatives contracts are the focus of Chapter 9.

To test whether the BSM call option formula, $f = Se^{-iT}N(d_1) - Xe^{-rT}N(d_2)$, satisfies (7D.6), substitute the formula as well as its partial derivatives,

$$\frac{\partial f}{\partial t} = Se^{-iT}n(d_1)\frac{\sigma}{2\sqrt{T}} - iSe^{-iT}N(d_1)+rXe^{-rT}N(d_2),$$

$$\frac{\partial f}{\partial S} = e^{-iT}N(d_1), \text{ and } \frac{\partial^2 f}{\partial S^2} = \frac{e^{-iT}n(d_1)}{S\sigma\sqrt{T}}$$

into the differential equation (7D.6) and get

[18] This eliminates many derivatives contracts written on interest rate instruments whose underlying asset price cannot rise above a certain level (e.g., an option on a Treasury bill). In these instances, it is more common to let the underlying source of uncertainty be the short-term interest rate.

$$-Se^{-iT}n(d_1)\frac{\sigma}{2\sqrt{T}} + iSe^{-iT}N(d_1) - rXe^{-rT}N(d_2) + (r-i)Se^{-iT}N(d_1)$$
$$+\frac{1}{2}\sigma^2 S^2 \frac{e^{-iT}n(d_1)}{S\sigma\sqrt{T}} = r[Se^{-iT}N(d_1) - Xe^{-rT}N(d_2)]$$

A little algebra shows that all terms cancel, implying that the BSM option valuation formula satisfies the BSM model (i.e., the partial differential equation (7D.6)).

## APPENDIX 7E: DERIVATION OF THE "GREEKS"

The "Greeks" for the BSM formula are provided in the chapter. Each of them is derived below by taking the partial derivative of the option with respect to each of its determinants.

The BSM formulas are:

$$c = Se^{-iT}N(d_1) - Xe^{-rT}N(d_2)$$
$$p = Xe^{-rT}N(-d_2) - Se^{-iT}N(-d_1)$$

where

$$d_1 = \frac{\ln(Se^{(r-i)T}/X) + 0.5\sigma^2 T}{\sigma\sqrt{T}} = \frac{\ln(Se^{-iT}/Xe^{-rT}) + 0.5\sigma^2 T}{\sigma\sqrt{T}} \text{ and } d_2 = d_1 - \sigma\sqrt{T}$$

### Useful Relations

To begin, it is useful to note the following relations. First, note that the partial derivatives of $d_1$ and $d_2$ with respect to $S$ are

$$\frac{\partial d_1}{\partial S} = \frac{1}{S\sigma\sqrt{T}} = \frac{\partial d_2}{\partial S} \tag{7E.1}$$

Next, from the relation between $d_1$ and $d_2$,

$$d_2 = d_1 - \sigma\sqrt{T}$$

we can develop the relation between $d_1^2$ and $d_2^2$, that is,

$$\begin{aligned} d_2^2 &= d_1^2 - 2d_1\sigma\sqrt{T} + \sigma^2 T \\ &= d_1^2 - 2[\ln(S/X) + (r-i)T + 0.5\sigma^2 T] + \sigma^2 T \\ &= d_1^2 - 2\ln[Se^{(r-i)T}/X] \end{aligned} \tag{7E.2}$$

From the definition of the normal density function,

$$n(d) = \frac{1}{\sqrt{2\pi}} e^{-d^2/2}$$

the relation between $n(d_1)$ and $n(d_2)$ can be derived,

$$\begin{aligned} n(d_2) &= \frac{1}{\sqrt{2\pi}} e^{-d_2^2/2} \\ &= \frac{1}{\sqrt{2\pi}} e^{-d_1^2/2 + \ln[Se^{(r-i)T}/X]} \\ &= n(d_1)\frac{Se^{(r-i)T}}{X} \end{aligned} \tag{7E.3a}$$

It follows that

$$n(d_1) = n(d_2)\frac{X}{Se^{(r-i)T}} \tag{7E.3b}$$

## Delta

Delta of call, $\Delta_c$:

$$\begin{aligned} \frac{\partial c}{\partial S} &= e^{-iT}N(d_1) + Se^{-iT}\frac{\partial N(d_1)}{\partial S} - Xe^{-rT}\frac{\partial N(d_2)}{\partial S} \\ &= e^{-iT}N(d_1) + Se^{-iT}\frac{\partial N(d_1)}{\partial S}\frac{\partial d_1}{\partial S} - Xe^{-rT}\frac{\partial N(d_2)}{\partial S}\frac{\partial d_2}{\partial S} \\ &= e^{-iT}N(d_1) + Se^{-iT}n(d_1)\frac{\partial d_1}{\partial S} - Xe^{-rT}n(d_2)\frac{\partial d_2}{\partial S} \\ &= e^{-iT}N(d_1) + Se^{-iT}n(d_1)\frac{\partial d_1}{\partial S} - Xe^{-rT}n(d_1)Se^{(r-i)T}/X\frac{\partial d_2}{\partial S} \\ &= e^{-iT}N(d_1) + Se^{-iT}n(d_1)\frac{\partial d_1}{\partial S} - Se^{-iT}n(d_1)\frac{\partial d_1}{\partial S} \\ &= e^{-iT}N(d_1) > 0 \end{aligned} \tag{7E.4a}$$

Delta of put, $\Delta_p$:

$$\frac{\partial p}{\partial S} = Xe^{-rT}\frac{\partial N(-d_2)}{\partial S} - e^{-iT}N(-d_1) - Se^{-iT}\frac{\partial N(-d_1)}{\partial S}$$

$$= e^{-iT}N(-d_1) - Xe^{-rT}n(-d_1)Se^{(r-i)T}/X\frac{\partial d_1}{\partial S} + Se^{-iT}n(-d_1)\frac{\partial d_1}{\partial S} \quad (7E.4b)$$

$$= e^{-iT}N(-d_1) < 0$$

## Eta

Eta of call, $\eta_c$:

$$\frac{\partial c/c}{\partial S/S} = \Delta_c\frac{S}{c} = e^{-iT}N(d_1)\frac{S}{c} > 1 \quad (7E.5a)$$

Eta of put, $\eta_p$:

$$\frac{\partial p/p}{\partial S/S} = \Delta_p\frac{S}{p} = -e^{-iT}N(-d_1)\frac{S}{p} < -1 \quad (7E.5b)$$

## Gamma

Gamma of call, $\gamma_c$:

$$\frac{\partial^2 c}{\partial S^2} = \frac{\partial \Delta_c}{\partial S} = \frac{\partial e^{-iT}N(d_1)}{\partial S} = e^{-iT}n(d_1)\frac{\partial d_1}{\partial S} = \frac{e^{-iT}n(d_1)}{S\sigma\sqrt{T}} > 0 \quad (7E.6a)$$

Gamma of put, $\gamma_p$:

$$\frac{\partial^2 p}{\partial S^2} = \frac{\partial \Delta_p}{\partial S} = \frac{\partial[-e^{-iT}N(-d_1)]}{\partial S} = \frac{e^{-iT}n(d_1)}{S\sigma\sqrt{T}} = \gamma_c > 0 \quad (7E.6b)$$

## Partial Derivative with Respect to Exercise Price

$$\frac{\partial c}{\partial X} = -e^{-rT}N(d_2) < 0 \quad (7E.7a)$$

$$\frac{\partial p}{\partial X} = e^{-rT}N(-d_2) > 0 \quad (7E.7b)$$

### Rho$_r$

Rho$_r$ of call, $\rho_c^r$:

$$\frac{\partial c}{\partial r} = TSe^{-iT}N(d_1) - TSe^{-iT}N(d_1) + Se^{-iT}\frac{\partial N(d_1)}{\partial r}$$

$$+ TXe^{-rT}N(d_2) - Xe^{-rT}\frac{\partial N(d_2)}{\partial r} \tag{7E.8a}$$

$$= TXe^{-rT}N(d_2) > 0$$

Rho$_r$ of call, $\rho_c^r$:

$$\frac{\partial p}{\partial r} = -TXe^{-rT}N(-d_2) + Xe^{-rT}\frac{\partial N(-d_2)}{\partial r} - TSe^{-iT}N(-d_1)$$

$$+ TSe^{-iT}N(-d_1) - Se^{-iT}\frac{\partial N(-d_1)}{\partial r} \tag{7E.8b}$$

$$= -TXe^{-rT}N(-d_2) < 0$$

### Rho$_i$

Rho$_i$ of call, $\rho_c^i$:

$$\frac{\partial c}{\partial i} = -TSe^{-iT}N(d_1) + Se^{-iT}\frac{\partial N(d_1)}{\partial i} - Xe^{-rT}\frac{\partial N(d_2)}{\partial i}$$

$$= -TSe^{-iT}N(d_1) > 0 \tag{7E.9a}$$

Rho$_i$ of put, $\rho_p^i$:

$$\frac{\partial p}{\partial i} = TSe^{-iT}N(-d_1) + Xe^{-rT}\frac{\partial N(-d_2)}{\partial i} - Se^{-iT}\frac{\partial N(-d_1)}{\partial i}$$

$$= TSe^{-iT}N(-d_1) < 0 \tag{7E.9b}$$

### Vega

Vega of call, Vega$_c$:

$$\begin{aligned}\frac{\partial c}{\partial \sigma} &= Se^{-iT}n(d_1)\frac{\partial d_1}{\partial \sigma} - Xe^{-rT}n(d_2)\frac{\partial d_2}{\partial \sigma} \\ &= Se^{-iT}n(d_1)\left[\frac{\partial d_1}{\partial \sigma} - \frac{\partial d_2}{\partial \sigma}\right] \\ &= Se^{-iT}n(d_1)\sqrt{T} > 0\end{aligned} \tag{7E.10a}$$

Vega of put, $\text{Vega}_p$:

$$\begin{aligned}\frac{\partial p}{\partial \sigma} &= -Xe^{-rT}n(-d_2)\frac{\partial d_2}{\partial \sigma} + Se^{-iT}n(-d_1)\frac{\partial d_1}{\partial \sigma} \\ &= Se^{-iT}n(d_1)\left[\frac{\partial d_1}{\partial \sigma} - \frac{\partial d_2}{\partial \sigma}\right] \\ &= Se^{-iT}n(d_1)\sqrt{T} = Vega_c > 0\end{aligned} \tag{7E.10b}$$

where

$$\frac{\partial d_1}{\partial \sigma} - \frac{\partial d_2}{\partial \sigma} = \left[-\frac{\ln(Se^{(r-i)T}/X)}{\sigma^2\sqrt{T}} + 0.5\sqrt{T}\right] - \left[-\frac{\ln(Se^{(r-i)T}/X)}{\sigma^2\sqrt{T}} - 0.5\sqrt{T}\right] = \sqrt{T}$$

## Theta

Theta of call, $\theta_c$:

$$\begin{aligned}\frac{\partial c}{\partial T} &= -iSe^{-iT}N(d_1) + Se^{-iT}n(d_1)\frac{\partial d_1}{\partial T} + rXe^{-rT}N(d_2) - Xe^{-rT}n(d_2)\frac{\partial d_2}{\partial T} \\ &= Se^{-iT}n(d_1)\left[\frac{\partial d_1}{\partial T} - \frac{\partial d_2}{\partial T}\right] - iSe^{-iT}N(d_1) + rXe^{-rT}N(d_2) \\ &= Se^{-iT}n(d_1)\frac{\sigma}{2\sqrt{T}} - iSe^{-iT}N(d_1) + rXe^{-rT}N(d_2) <> 0\end{aligned} \tag{7E.11a}$$

Theta of put, $\theta_p$:

$$\frac{\partial p}{\partial T} = -rXe^{-rT}N(-d_2) - Xe^{-rT}n(-d_2)\frac{\partial d_2}{\partial T} + iSe^{-iT}N(-d_1) + Se^{-iT}n(-d_1)\frac{\partial d_1}{\partial T}$$

$$= -rXe^{-rT}N(-d_2) + iSe^{-iT}N(-d_1) + Se^{-iT}n(d_1)\left[\frac{\partial d_1}{\partial T} - \frac{\partial d_2}{\partial T}\right] \qquad (7E.11b)$$

$$= Se^{-iT}n(d_1)\frac{\sigma}{2\sqrt{T}} + iSe^{-iT}N(-d_1) - rXe^{-rT}N(-d_2) <> 0$$

where

$$\frac{\partial d_1}{\partial T} - \frac{\partial d_2}{\partial T} = \left[-\frac{\ln(S/X)}{2\sigma T^{3/2}} + \frac{r-i}{2\sigma\sqrt{T}} + \frac{\sigma}{4\sqrt{T}}\right] - \left[-\frac{\ln(S/X)}{2\sigma T^{3/2}} + \frac{r-i}{2\sigma\sqrt{T}} - \frac{\sigma}{4\sqrt{T}}\right] = \frac{\sigma}{2\sqrt{T}}$$

CHAPTER 8

# Valuing Nonstandard Options Analytically

In Chapter 7, we valued standard European-style options analytically with the Black-Scholes (1973)/Merton (1973) option valuation framework. This chapter continues to focus on options that can be valued analytically within the BSM framework, however, the types of options that we examine are unusual or nonstandard.[1] While we discuss eleven different types of contracts, do not be misled. There are a virtually limitless number of variations of derivative contracts that have or can be structured. Some can be valued analytically. These are the focus of this chapter. Some require the use of numerical methods. These are the focus of the next chapter. As we proceed through this chapter describing the different types of contracts and their analytical valuation equations, it is important to try to imagine possible applications. In many instances, the contracts have sensible return/risk management properties. In other instances, the contracts seem only to be a cleverly structured bet.

## ALL-OR-NOTHING OPTIONS

In Chapter 5, we showed that the valuation equations for asset-or-nothing and cash-or-nothing call and put options were impounded within the BSM call and put formulas. Recall that an asset-or-nothing call that pays one unit of the asset at time $T$ if the asset price exceeds the exercise price $X$. The terminal profit from buying an asset-or-nothing call option is shown in Figure 8.1. Note that, for terminal asset prices below $X$, the option holder forfeits the premium that he paid for the option at the outset. For terminal prices above $X$, the option holder receives one unit of the asset, which at least partially covers the original cost of the option. Under the BSM assumptions, the value of a European-style asset-or-nothing option is

$$c_{AON}(X, T) = e^{-iT}N(d_1) \tag{8.1}$$

[1] The label "exotic" has often been applied to nonstandard options.

**FIGURE 8.1** Terminal profit from buying an asset-or-nothing call option.

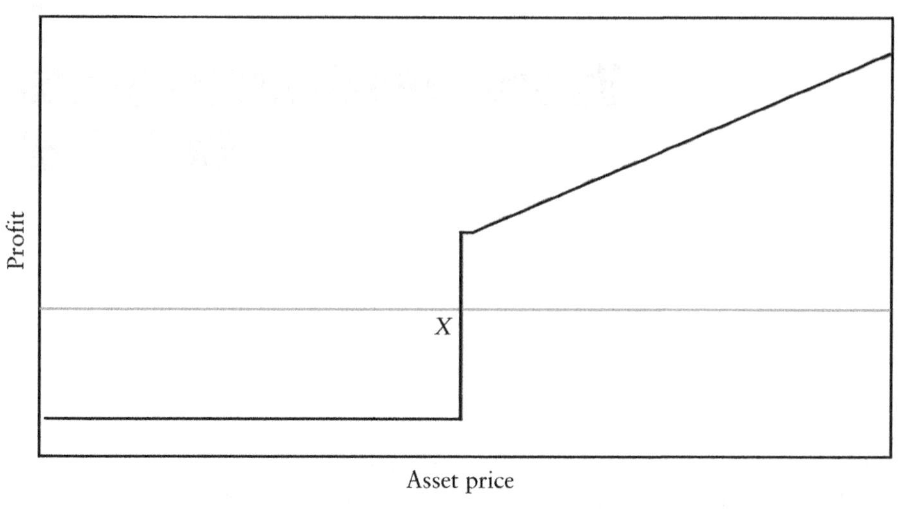


where[2]

$$d_1 = \frac{\ln(Se^{-iT}/Xe^{-rT}) + 0.5\sigma^2 T}{\sigma\sqrt{T}}$$

and

$$d_2 = d_1 - \sigma\sqrt{T}$$

The terminal profit from buying a cash-or-nothing call option is shown in Figure 8.2. For terminal asset prices below $X$, the option holder forfeits the original cash-or-nothing option premium. For terminal prices above $X$, the option holder receives one dollar. Under the BSM assumptions, the value of a European-style cash-or-nothing option is

$$c_{CON}(X, T) = e^{-rT}N(d_2) \tag{8.2}$$

where the fixed cash amount equals one dollar.

A standard European-style call option provides the right to buy the underlying asset whose current price is $S$ for amount of cash equal to $X$ at time $T$. To construct a standard call option, we buy $S$ units of an asset-or-nothing call and sell $X$ units of a cash-or-nothing call. Thus the valuation-by-replication principle says that the value of a standard European-style call option is

[2] As noted in Chapter 7, there are a number of different, albeit equivalent, expressions for $d_1$ in European-style option valuation problems. The prepaid forward version is used here to minimize the number of redundant computations.

**FIGURE 8.2** Terminal profit from buying a cash-or-nothing call option.

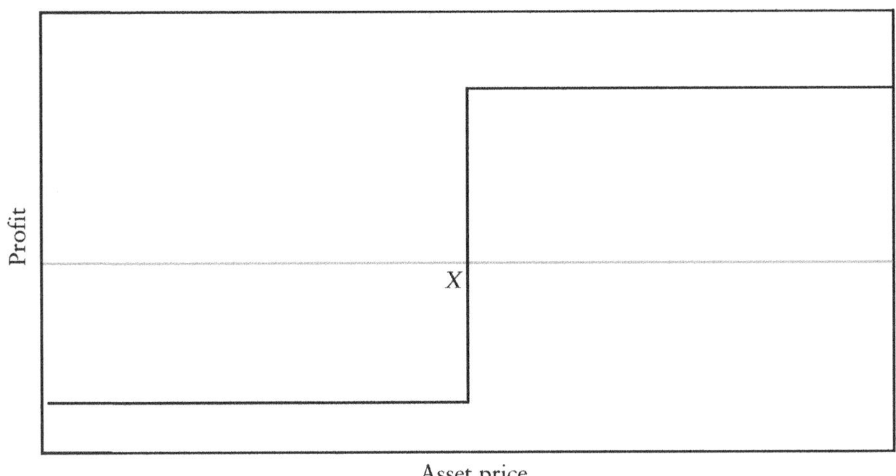


$$c_{BSM} = Se^{-iT}N(d_1) - Xe^{-rT}N(d_2) \tag{8.3}$$

In the interest of completeness, an asset-or-nothing put option pays one unit of the asset at time $T$ if the asset price is below the exercise price and is valued as

$$p_{AON}(X, T) = e^{-iT}N(-d_1) \tag{8.4}$$

A cash-or-nothing put pays one dollar in cash at time $T$ if the asset price is below the exercise price and is valued as

$$p_{CON}(X, T) = e^{-rT}N(-d_2) \tag{8.5}$$

A standard European-style put option provides the right to sell the underlying asset $S$ for amount of cash equal to $X$ at time $T$. To construct a standard put option, we sell $S$ units of an asset-or-nothing put and buy $X$ units of a cash-or-nothing put. Thus, the value of a standard European-style put option is

$$p_{BSM} = Xe^{-rT}N(-d_2) - Se^{-iT}N(-d_1) \tag{8.6}$$

**ILLUSTRATION 8.1** Value cash-or-nothing call option.

*Suppose your uncle tells you that he will give you \$100 if XYZ's stock price is greater than \$100 in six months time. XYZ's current stock price is \$90 a share, its dividend yield rate is 1%, and its volatility rate is 20%. The risk-free interest rate is 3%. What is the value of his gift to you?*

First, compute the prepaid forward prices for the underlying asset and risk-free bonds, that is, $Se^{-iT} = 90e^{-0.01(0.5)} = 89.551$ and $Xe^{-rT} = 100e^{-0.03(0.5)} = 98.511$. Next, compute the integral limit

$$d_2 = \frac{\ln(89.551/98.511) + 0.5(0.20^2)0.5}{0.20\sqrt{0.5}} = -0.7450$$

Finally, plug the information into formula (8.2), that is,

$$\begin{aligned} c_{CON} &= e^{-0.03(0.5)} N(-0.7450) \times 100 \\ &= 24.453 \end{aligned}$$

The values of asset-or-nothing and cash-or-nothing options where the underlying asset has a current price of one dollar can be computed using the OPTVAL library function

OV_NS_ALL_OR_NOTHING_OPTION(*s*, *x*, *t*, *r*, *i*, *v*, *cp*, *ac*)

where *s* is the asset price, *x* is the exercise price, *t* is the time to expiration expressed in years, *r* is the risk-free interest rate, *i* is the income rate of the asset, *v* is the asset return volatility rate, *cp* is a (c)all/(p)ut indicator, and *ac* is an (a)sset/(c)ash indicator. The value of the option in this illustration is

OV_NS_ALL_OR_NOTHING_OPTION(90,100,0.5,0.04,0.01,0.20, “c”, “c”) = 0.24453

## Measuring Risk of All-or-Nothing Options

All-or-nothing options are useful more as a pedagogic device than they are in practice. The reason is that they are expensive and difficult to hedge, particularly for short times to expiration. To address the hedging issue, let us consider the risk characteristics (i.e., the Greeks) of all-or-nothing options. Since we have analytical valuation formulas, we can compute analytically the Greeks of all-or-nothing options by taking the partial derivatives of the formulas with respect to each of the option formula's determinants (e.g., $S$, the asset price, $\sigma$, the volatility rate, and so on). But doing so necessarily involves developing more expressions in a chapter that will have no shortage of formulas.[3]

Instead, in this chapter, we measure risk characteristics numerically. The procedure is straightforward. Recall that the delta of an option is the change in option value with respect to a change in asset price. To obtain the delta of an option numerically, we can perturb the current asset price $S$ by a small amount $\phi$ in either direction, that is, $S + \phi$ and $S - \phi$, and value the option at each asset price, $OV(S + \phi)$ and $OV(S - \phi)$. Figure 8.3 illustrates. The valuation function $OV(.)$ can be any of the valuation methodologies discussed in this chapter, the last chapter, or the next. The values generated in Figure 8.3 were generated using the BSM formula for a European-style put. While what we would like to

[3] It is also important to recognize that many OTC derivative contracts that we will discuss in later chapters have American-style option features or multiple, interrelated contingencies. In many, if not the majority, of these cases, analytical valuation is not possible and numerical methods must be applied. With no analytical formulas, the risk characteristics of these agreements must, necessarily, be computed numerically.

**FIGURE 8.3** Numerical approximation for the delta of a put option.

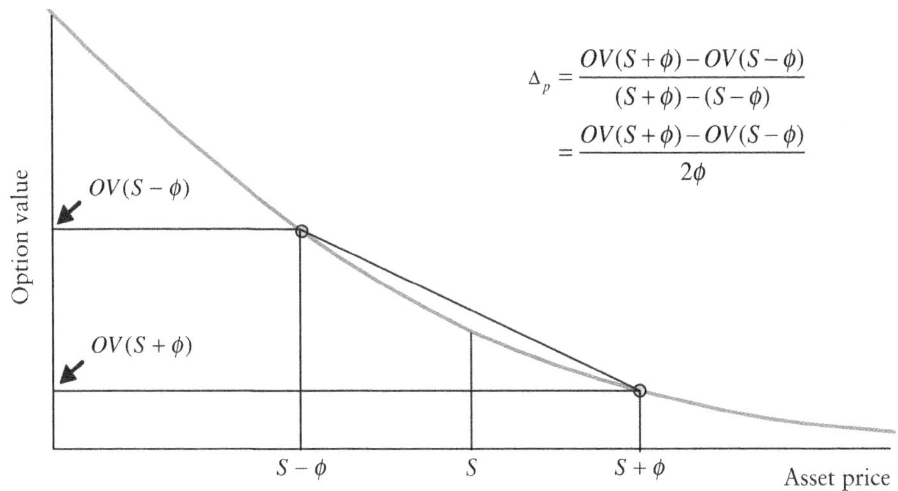


measure is the slope of the $OV$ function at the asset price $S$, we approximate the slope of the function by taking the ratio of the difference between the computed option values to the difference between the perturbed asset prices, that is,

$$\Delta_p = \frac{OV(S+\phi) - OV(S-\phi)}{(S+\phi) - (S-\phi)}$$

In general, all of the Greeks for options can be measured using the expression,

$$\text{Greek}_k = \frac{OV(k+\phi) - OV(k-\phi)}{2\phi} \tag{8.7}$$

where $OV$ represents any valuation method that we use in this book, $k$ is the option determinant of interest (e.g., $S$ for delta risk, $\sigma$ for vega risk, and so on), and $\phi$ is a small positive constant selected by the user. The gamma, that is, the change in the delta with respect to a change in the asset price, can be computed using

$$\text{Gamma} = \frac{OV(S+\phi) - 2 \times OV(S+\phi) + OV(S-\phi)}{\phi^2} \tag{8.8}$$

**ILLUSTRATION 8.2** Assess accuracy of risk measures computed numerically.

*Consider a six-month European-style put option whose exercise price is 50. Assume the underlying asset has a price of 49, a dividend yield of 1%, and a volatility rate of 20%, compute the delta, gamma, and vega of the put analytically and then numerically. Assume the risk-free rate of interest is 3%.*

First, compute the delta value of the European-style put analytically. From Chapter 5, we know that the delta value of the put is

$$\Delta_p = -e^{-0.01(0.5)}N(-d_1) = -0.4981$$

where

$$d_1 = \frac{\ln(49e^{-0.01(0.5)}/50e^{-0.03(0.5)}) + 0.5(0.20^2)(0.5)}{0.20\sqrt{0.5}} = -0.00143$$

and

$$N(0.00143) = 0.5006$$

Next compute the delta value of the put numerically by perturbing the asset price by, say, 0.1. Using the BSM put formula (8.6) for the function $OV$ in (8.8), the numerical value of delta is

$$\Delta_p = \frac{OV(40+0.1) - OV(40-0.1)}{(49+0.1)-(49-0.1)}$$
$$= \frac{2.9702 - 3.0698}{0.2} = -0.4981$$

In other words, the numerical (approximate) delta value of the put is accurate to four decimal places. The accuracy of the approximation is affected by the size of the perturbation parameter. To judge the appropriate size, experiment with an option whose Greeks are analytically tractable. Below is a summary of the results for delta, gamma, and vega of the put computed using (8.7) and (8.8). All of them are accurate to four decimal places for the perturbation amounts shown.

| Greek | Analytical Value of Greek | Perturbation Amount, $\phi$ | Numerical Value of Greek |
|---|---|---|---|
| Delta | –0.4981 | 0.1 | –0.4981 |
| Gamma | 0.0573 | 0.5 | 0.0573 |
| Vega | 13.7537 | 1.00% | 13.7537 |

Returning to risk characteristics of all-or-nothing options that are the focus of this section, consider in Figure 8.4, which shows the distribution of delta values of asset-or-nothing call options with three months, one month, and one day to expiration as a function of the underlying asset price. These values were computed numerically using one dollar increments in the asset price. Several observations about Figure 8.4 are noteworthy. First, note that for deep out-of-the-money options, the deltas are near zero. The reason is simple. With virtually no chance of ever being in the money at expiration, the asset-or-nothing option is insensitive to movements in asset price. Second, note that deep in-the-money options have deltas near one. With virtually no chance of ever being out of the money, the option price behaves just like the asset price. Third, and perhaps most importantly, the delta value of at-the-money, asset-or-nothing call options (unlike standard call options) can be well in excess of one and increases as the

**FIGURE 8.4** Delta values of asset-or-nothing call options with three months, one month, and one day to expiration. ($X = 50$, $r = 0.05$, $i = 0.00$, $\sigma = 0.50$).

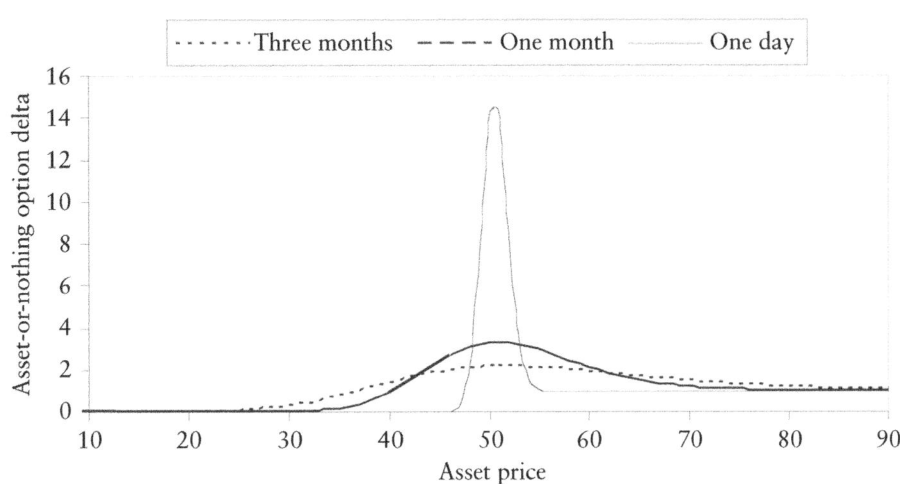


time to expiration grows short. The maximum delta value is, or course, equal to the asset price. With only a few minutes to expiration, an asset price movement from slightly out of the money to slightly in the money will cause the asset-or-nothing option value to go from 0 to $S$.

## GAP OPTIONS

A *gap option* is an option whose payoff is determined by the exercise price $X_1$, but another constant $X_2$ determines whether or not the payoff is made. Consider a gap call option for example. Suppose $X_1 = 45$ and $X_2 = 50$. Figure 8.5 shows the call's payoff at expiration. Note that, over the asset price interval between 45 and 50, the call's payoff is 0. This is because the trigger price $X_2 = 50$ has not been reached. Once the asset price goes beyond the trigger price, the call's payoff is the difference between the asset price and $X_1$.

With the asset-or-nothing and cash-or-nothing valuation equations in hand, valuing a gap call option is a straightforward task.[4] Consider a portfolio is long an asset-or-nothing call with exercise (trigger) price $X_2$ and is short $X_1$ cash-or-nothing calls with exercise (trigger) price $X_2$. This portfolio has payoffs identical to those shown in Figure 8.5. In the absence of costless arbitrage opportunities, therefore, the value of a gap call option can be identified using (8.1) and (8.2), that is,

$$c_{gap}(X_1, X_2) = Se^{-iT}N(d_1) - X_1e^{-rT}N(d_2) \tag{8.9}$$

[4] The construction of the gap option valuation formula from all-or-nothing options was first shown in Rubinstein and Reiner (1991b).

**FIGURE 8.5** Terminal payoff of a gap call option with $X_1 = 45$ and $X_2 = 50$.

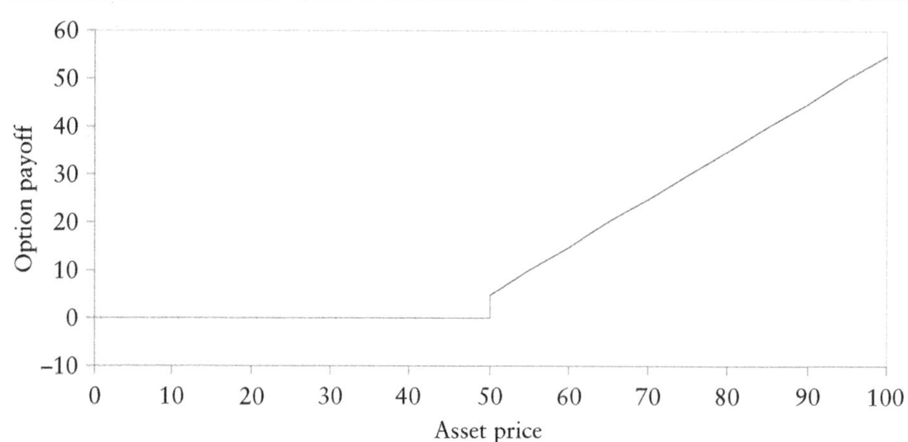


where

$$d_1 = \frac{\ln(Se^{-iT}/X_2e^{-rT}) + 0.5\sigma^2 T}{\sigma\sqrt{T}}$$

and $d_2 = d_1 - \sigma\sqrt{T}$. The value of a gap put option is

$$p_{gap}(X_1, X_2) = X_1e^{-rT}N(-d_2) - Se^{-iT}N(-d_1) \tag{8.10}$$

It is important to note that there is no restriction on whether the trigger price $X_2$ is greater than or less than the exercise price $X_1$. Figure 8.5 shows the payoffs of a gap call under the condition $X_1 < X_2$. Where $X_1 > X_2$, however, we get the unusual payoff structure shown in Figure 8.6. Because the trigger price is reached before the exercise price, the call option holder is forced to exercise even though it is not profitable to do so. In the asset price interval between 50 and 55, the option holder pays $S - 55$. Indeed, there is exercise price at which the gap call option premium (8.6) will be equal to 0.

**ILLUSTRATION 8.3** Value gap call option.

*Compute the value of a six-month European-style gap call option whose exercise price is 55 and whose trigger price is 50. Assume the underlying index has a level of 49, a dividend yield of 1%, and a volatility rate of 20%. The risk-free rate of interest is 3%.*

The values of the prepaid forward and exercise prices in the gap call option formula are:

$$Se^{-iT} = 49e^{-0.01(0.5)} = 48.756$$

$$X_1e^{-rT} = 55e^{-0.03(0.5)} = 54.181$$

$$X_2e^{-rT} = 50e^{-0.03(0.5)} = 49.256$$

The values of $d_1$ and $d_2$ are

$$d_1 = \frac{\ln(48.756/49.256) + 0.5(0.20^2)(0.5)}{0.20\sqrt{0.5}} = -0.0014$$

and $d_2 = -0.1429$. The value of the gap call is therefore

$$c_{gap}(55,50) = 48.756N(-0.0014) - 54.181N(54.181) = 0.3367$$

This value can also be obtained using the OPTVAL function

OV_NS_GAP_OPTION(*s, x1, x2, t, r, i, v, cp*)

where *x1* is the exercise price of the option and determines the payoff, *x2* is the price that triggers exercise, and all other function notation is as defined earlier in the chapter. Thus

OV_NS_GAP_OPTION(49, 55, 50, 0.5, 0.03, 0.01, 0.20, “c”) = 0.3367

One final aspect of gap options is worthwhile noting. As the difference (i.e., gap) between the exercise price and the trigger price grows large, the gap call (put) option value decreases (increases). Indeed, where the exercise price is 55.77 rather than 55 in this illustration, the gap call value is 0. Figure 8.7 shows gap call and put option values for a range of exercise prices where all other parameter values are as described above.

**FIGURE 8.6** Terminal payoff of a gap call option with $X_1 = 55$ and $X_2 = 50$.

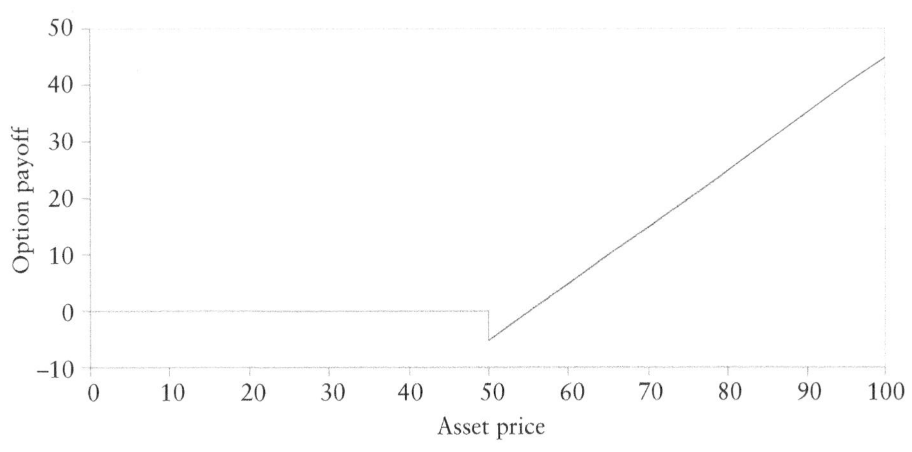


## CONTINGENT PAY OPTIONS

A *contingent pay option* is an option whose premium is set today but is paid at expiration contingent upon the option being in the money.[5] Naturally, such an option will be more expensive that a standard European-style option, however, you will pay for the option only in the event the option is in the money at expira-

[5] Contingent pay options are also referred to as *pay-later options* or *collect-on-delivery options.*

**FIGURE 8.7** Gap option values as a function of exercise price. Option parameters are: $S = 49$, $X_2 = 50$, $T = 0.5$, $r = 0.03$, $i = 0.01$, and $\sigma = 0.20$.

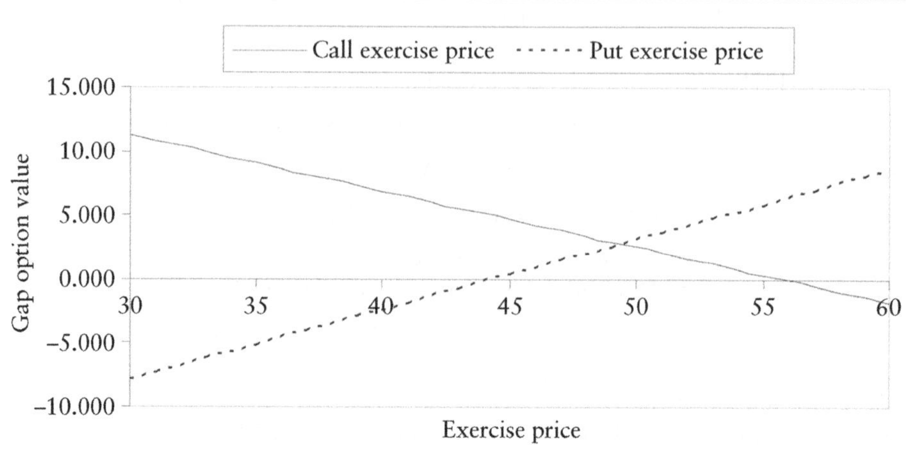


tion. Again, identifying the appropriate replicating portfolio is the key to solving for option value. To value a European-style contingent pay call option, consider the payoffs of a portfolio formed by buying a standard call option and selling a cash-or-nothing call with the cash amount being equal to the current value of the contingent pay option, $c_{\text{contingent pay}}$. At time $T$, the portfolio has a terminal value equal to (1) 0 if $S_T < X$ and (2) $S_T - X - c_{\text{contingent pay}}$ if $S_T \geq X$, exactly the required payoffs. The value of the portfolio at time 0 is $c_{BSM} - e^{-rT}N(d_2)c_{\text{contingent pay}}$, however, since this contract by its nature has no upfront premium, we must set the initial portfolio value equal to zero and solve for the contingent pay option premium. The value of a European-style contingent pay call option is

$$c_{\text{contingent pay}} = \frac{c_{BSM}}{e^{-rT}N(d_2)} = \frac{Se^{-iT}N(d_1) - X_1 e^{-rT}N(d_2)}{e^{-rT}N(d_2)} \tag{8.11}$$

where

$$d_1 = \frac{\ln(Se^{-iT}/Xe^{-rT}) + 0.5\sigma^2 T}{\sigma\sqrt{T}}$$

and $d_2 = d_1 - \sigma\sqrt{T}$. A similar derivation shows that the value of a European-style contingent pay put option is

$$p_{BSM} = \frac{p}{e^{-rT}N(-d_2)} = \frac{Xe^{-rT}N(-d_2) - Se^{-iT}N(-d_1)}{e^{-rT}N(-d_2)} \tag{8.12}$$

**ILLUSTRATION 8.4** Value contingent pay put option.

*Compute the value of a three-month European-style contingent pay stock index put option with an exercise price of 50. Assume the index has a level of 49, a dividend yield of 2%, and a volatility rate of 20%. The risk-free rate is 5%.*

First, the values of the prepaid forward and exercise prices in the contingent pay put option are

$$Se^{-iT} = 49e^{-0.02(0.25)} = 48.756$$

$$Xe^{-rT} = 50e^{-0.05(0.25)} = 49.379$$

compute the values of $d_1$ and $d_2$,

$$d_1 = \frac{\ln(48.756/49.379) + 0.5(0.20)^2(0.25)}{0.20\sqrt{0.25}} = -0.0770$$

$$d_2 = -0.0770 - 0.20\sqrt{0.25} = -0.1770$$

and identify the cumulative normal probabilities,

$$N(0.0770) = 0.5307 \quad \text{and} \quad N(0.1770) = 0.5703$$

Gather the terms and compute the standard European-style put option value, that is,

$$p = 49.379(0.5703) - 48.756(0.5307) = 2.284$$

The value of the contingent pay put option is

$$p_{\text{contingent pay}} = \frac{2.284}{e^{-0.05(0.25)}(0.5703)} = 4.056$$

The values of contingent pay calls and puts can be solved using the OPTVAL function,

OV_NS_CONTINGENT_PAY_OPTION(*s*, *x*, *t*, *r*, *i*, *v*, *cp*)

where all function parameter notation is as defined earlier. Thus

OV_NS_CONTINGENT_PAY_OPTION(49, 50, 0.25, 0.05, 0.02, 0.25, "c") = 3.913

and

OV_NS_CONTINGENT_PAY_OPTION(49, 50, 0.25, 0.05, 0.02, 0.25, "p") = 4.056

## FORWARD-START OPTIONS

A *forward-start option* is like a standard option with exercise price $X$ and time to expiration $T$, except that the option's life begins only after prespecified period $t$. Figure 8.8 illustrates. Buying a standard option means paying for the option today and having its life begin. Buying a forward-start option means paying for the option today but having its life begin at time $t$. Thus, at time 0, the forward-start option's time to expiration is $T$, and, at time $t$, it is $T - t$. Another distinction is that a forward-start option's exercise price is set at time $t$. By convention, the exercise price is set equal to some positive constant times $\alpha$ the prevailing

**FIGURE 8.8** Comparison of standard and forward-start option lives.

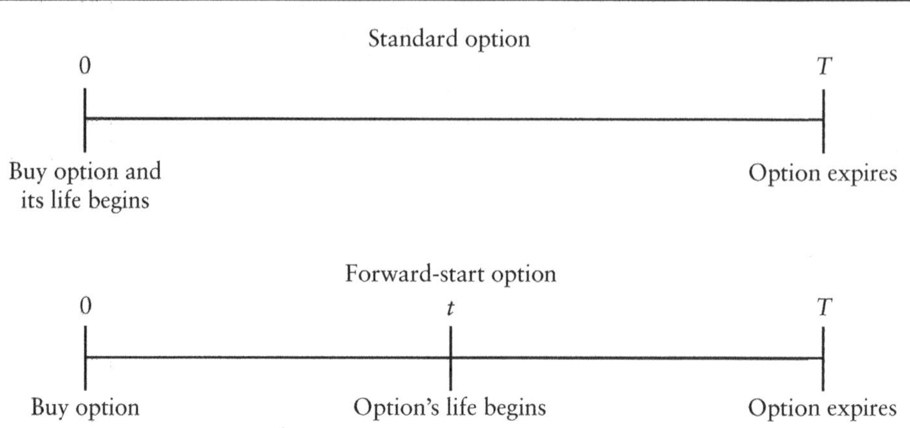


asset price at time $t$. Where $\alpha = 1$, the option will be at-the-money at time $t$. Where $\alpha > 1$, the call will be out of the money and the put will be in the money, and, where $\alpha < 1$, the call will be in the money and the put will be out of the money.

To value a forward-start option, we must account for the fact that the underlying asset price continues to appreciate over the time between now and when the option's life begins.[6] In a risk-neutral world, the expected asset price at time $t$ equals the forward price of the asset, that is, $E(\tilde{S}_t) = F = Se^{(r-i)t}$. The expected exercise price of the forward-start option is therefore $\alpha E(\tilde{S}_t) = \alpha Se^{(r-i)t}$. To value a forward-start call option, we replace the asset price $S$ and exercise price X in the BSM call option formula (8.3) with the prepaid forward price $Se^{-it}$ and prepaid exercise price $\alpha Se^{-it}$. The value of a European-style forward-start call option is

$$c_{\text{forward-start}} = Se^{-it}e^{-i(T-t)}N(d_1) - \alpha Se^{-it}e^{-i(T-t)}N(d_2) \tag{8.13}$$

where

$$d_1 = \frac{\ln(e^{-iT}/\alpha e^{-rT}) + 0.5\sigma^2(T-t)}{\sigma\sqrt{T-t}}$$

and $d_2 = d_1 - \sigma\sqrt{T-t}$. The value of a forward-start put option is

$$p_{\text{forward-start}} = Se^{-it}[\alpha e^{-r(T-t)}N(-d_2) - e^{-i(T-t)}N(-d_1)] \tag{8.14}$$

[6] Valuation equations for forward-start options are developed in Rubinstein (1991a).

**ILLUSTRATION 8.5** Value forward-start call option.

*Compute the value of a nine-month European-style call option that is 10% out-of-the-money and compare it to the value of a nine-month European-style call option that begins in three months. Assume the underlying asset has a price of 60, a dividend yield of 1%, and a volatility rate of 30%. The risk-free rate is 4%.*

The value of the forward-start call option may be computed as follows:

$$c_{\text{forward-start}} = 60e^{-0.01(0.25)}[e^{-0.01(0.5)}N(d_1) - 1.1e^{-0.04(0.5)}N(d_2)] = 3.120$$

where

$$d_1 = \frac{\ln(60e^{-0.01(0.5)}/60(1.1)e^{-0.04(0.5)}) + 0.5(0.30^2)0.5}{0.30\sqrt{0.5}} = -0.2725$$

$d_2 = -0.2725 - 0.30\sqrt{0.5} = -0.4847$, $N(d_1) = 0.3926$, and $N(d_2) = 0.3140$.
Its value can be confirmed using the OPTVAL function

OV_NS_FORWARD_START_OPTION(*s, alpha, td, t, r, i, v, cp*)

where *alpha* is a positive constant that sets the exercise price of the option relative to the asset price at the beginning of the forward-start period, *td* is the time until the beginning of the forward-start period, and all other function notation is as defined earlier. For the forward-start call in this illustration,

OV_ NS_FORWARD_START_OPTION (60, 1.1, 0.25, 0.75, 0.04, 0.01, 0.30, "c")
= 3.120

The value of an ordinary European-style call option with nine months to expiration is

$$c = 60[e^{-0.01(0.75)}N(d_1) - 1.1e^{-0.04(0.75)}N(d_2)] = 4.386$$

where

$$d_1 = \frac{\ln(e^{-0.01(0.75)}/1.1e^{-0.04(0.75)}) + 0.5(0.30^2)0.75}{0.30\sqrt{0.75}} = -0.1503$$

$$d_2 = -0.1503 - 0.30\sqrt{0.75} = -0.4102$$

$N(d_1) = 0.4402$, and $N(d_2) = 0.3408$. The forward-start European-style call has lower value because, although the underlying asset price is expected to be the same at the end of nine months, the range of possible option prices in nine months is smaller for the forward start call than the standard call.

## RATCHET OPTIONS

A *ratchet option* (also called a *cliquet option*) is a sequence of forward-start options. At the end of each option's life a new option is written at a strike price equal to the prevailing asset times the preset constant, $\alpha$. A one-year ratchet option with monthly payments will normally have 12 payments (exercise dates) equal to the maximum of the asset price less the exercise price or zero. The exercise price of each one month option is usually set at the beginning of each period. Thus the exercise price of the first option is known today and equals $\alpha S$. The overall value of the ratchet call option is the sum of the values of its forward-start call options, that is,

$$c_{\text{ratchet}} = \sum_{i=1}^{n} Se^{-it_i}[e^{-i(T_i - t_i)}N(d_{1,i}) - \alpha e^{-r(T_i - t_i)}N(d_{2,i})] \tag{8.15}$$

where $n$ is the number of settlements, $t_i$ is the time to the forward start of the $i$-th option when the exercise price is fixed, and $T_i$ is the time to maturity of the $i$-th. The upper integral limits are

$$d_{1,i} = \frac{\ln(e^{-iT_i}/\alpha e^{-rT_i}) + 0.5\sigma^2(T_i - t_i)}{\alpha\sqrt{T_i - t_i}}$$

and $d_{2,i} = d_{1,i} - \alpha\sqrt{T_i - t_i}$. The value of a ratchet put option is

$$p_{\text{ratchet}} = \sum_{i=1}^{n} Se^{-it_i}[\alpha e^{-r(T_i - t_i)}N(d_2) - e^{-i(T_i - t_i)}N(d_1)] \tag{8.16}$$

**ILLUSTRATION 8.6** Value ratchet call option.

*Compute the value of a 12-month European-style ratchet call option with monthly settlements. Assume the exercise price of each option is set at the beginning of the month. Assume the call is written on the S&P 500 index. The level of the index is 1,150, its dividend yield rate is 1%, and its volatility rate is 20%. The risk-free rate is 4%.*

The value of the first forward-start call in the series is

$$c_1 = 1{,}150e^{-0.01(1/12)}[e^{-0.01(1/12)}N(d_1) - e^{-0.04(1/12)}N(d_2)] = 27.888$$

where

$$d_1 = \frac{\ln(e^{-0.001(1/12)}/e^{-0.04(1/12)}) + 0.5(0.20^2)(1/12)}{0.20\sqrt{1/12}} = 0.0722$$

$d_2 = 0.0722 - 0.20\sqrt{1/12} = 0.0144$, $N(d_1) = 0.5288$, and $N(d_2) = 0.5058$. This can be confirmed using the OPTVAL function,

OV_NS_FORWARD_START_OPTION(1150, 1, 0, 1/12, 0.04, 0.01, 0.20, "c")
= 27.888

The value of the second forward-start call in the series is

$$c_2 = 1{,}150e^{-0.01(1/12)}[e^{-0.01(1/12)}N(d_1) - e^{-0.04(1/12)}N(d_2)] = 27.865$$

or

OV_NS_FORWARD_START_OPTION(1150, 1, 1/12, 2/12, 0.04, 0.01, 0.20, "c")
= 27.865

and so on. The value of the ratchet option in total can easily be computed in using Excel and the forward-start option valuation function as is illustrated in the table below.

| Month | $t_i$ | $T_i$ | Forward Start Option |
|---|---|---|---|
| 1 | 0.00000 | 0.08333 | 27.888 |
| 2 | 0.08333 | 0.16667 | 27.865 |
| 3 | 0.16667 | 0.25000 | 27.842 |
| 4 | 0.25000 | 0.33333 | 27.819 |
| 5 | 0.33333 | 0.41667 | 27.796 |
| 6 | 0.41667 | 0.50000 | 27.772 |
| 7 | 0.50000 | 0.58333 | 27.749 |
| 8 | 0.58333 | 0.66667 | 27.726 |
| 9 | 0.66667 | 0.75000 | 27.703 |
| 10 | 0.75000 | 0.83333 | 27.680 |
| 11 | 0.83333 | 0.91667 | 27.657 |
| 12 | 0.91667 | 1.00000 | 27.634 |
| Value of ratchet option | | | 333.132 |

The value of the ratchet option can also be computed using

OV_NS_RATCHET_OPTION(*s*, *alpha*, *td*, *tb*, *n*, *r*, *i*, *v*, *cp*),

where *s* is the current asset price, *alpha* is the exercise price expressed as a proportion of the prevailing asset price, *td* is the time until the first option expires, *tb* is the time between reset dates, *n* is the number of reset dates, *r* is the risk-free rate of interest, *i* is the income rate on the asset, *v* is the asset's volatility rates, and *cp* is a call/put indicator variable. Thus

OV_NS_RATCHET_OPTION(1150, 1, 1/12, 1/12, 12, 0.04, 0.01, ,20, "c") = 333.132

## CHOOSER OPTIONS

A *chooser option* is an option that gives its holder the right to choose whether the option is to be a standard call or put after time *t*, where the call and the put have the same exercise price X and time to maturity *T*.[7] Figure 8.9 compares the chooser option's life with that of a standard option. In buying a standard option, the option buyer makes an irrevocable decision to buy a call or a put. In buying a chooser option, the option buyer is allowed the additional privilege of being able to decide between the call and the put at prespecified date during the option's life.

[7] The valuation equation of a European-style chooser option first appeared in Rubinstein (1991b). Rubinstein also values a *complex chooser option* that provides its holder with the choice between a call and a put at time *t*, however, the call and put have different exercise prices and time to expiration.

**FIGURE 8.9** Comparison of standard and chooser option lives.

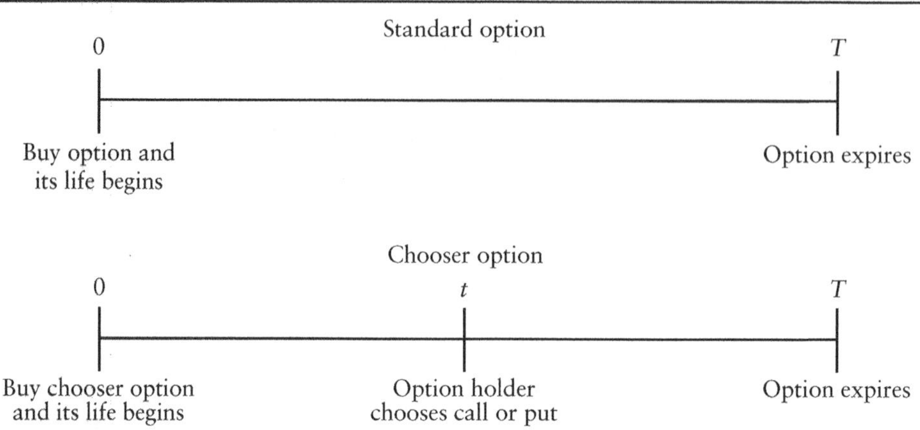


To value the chooser option, it is best to first focus on the value of the chooser option at time $t$, that is,

$$\max[c_{BSM}(S_t, X, T-t), p_{BSM}(S_t, X, T-t)] \tag{8.17}$$

where $c_{BSM}(S,X,T-t)$ and $p_{BSM}(S_t,X,T-t)$ are the BSM call and put valuation equations evaluated at time $t$ with uncertain asset price $S_t$. Note that, by virtue of put-call parity, expression (8.17) may be rewritten as

$$\begin{aligned} &\max[c_{BSM}(S_t, X, T-t), (c_{BSM}(S_t, X, T-t) - S_t e^{-i(T-t)} + Xe^{-r(T-t)})] \\ &= c_{BSM}(S_t, X, T-t) + \max[0, (Xe^{-r(T-t)} - S_t e^{-i(T-t)})] \end{aligned} \tag{8.18}$$

To value a chooser option, consider the value at time $t$ of a replicating portfolio that involves buying a standard European-style call with exercise price $X$ and time to expiration $T$, $c_{BSM}(S,X,T-t)$, and a standard European-style put option with an exercise price of $Xe^{-r(T-t)}$ and a time to expiration of $t$ whose underlying asset price is $Se^{-i(T-t)}$, $p_{BSM}(Se^{-i(T-t)},Xe^{-r(T-t)},t)$. At time $t$, the call option has a value of $c_{BSM}(S,X,T-t)$, and the put option has a value of (a) 0 if $Se^{-i(T-t)} \geq Xe^{-r(T-t)}$, and (b) $Xe^{-r(T-t)} - Se^{-i(T-t)}$ if $Se^{-i(T-t)} < Xe^{-r(T-t)}$. Thus, we have mimicked the payoffs in (8.18). The value of a European-style chooser option is therefore

$$\begin{aligned} c_{\text{chooser}}(S, X, t, T) &= Se^{-iT}N(d_1) - Xe^{-rT}N(d_2) \\ &\quad - Se^{-iT}N(-d') + Xe^{-rT}N(-d_2') \end{aligned} \tag{8.19}$$

where

$$d_1 = \frac{\ln(Se^{-iT}/Xe^{-rT}) + 0.5\sigma^2 T}{\sigma\sqrt{T}}, \quad d_2 = d_1 - \sigma\sqrt{T-t}$$

$$d_1' = \frac{\ln(Se^{-iT}/Xe^{-rT}) + 0.5\sigma^2 t}{\sigma\sqrt{t}}, \quad d_2' = d_1' - \sigma\sqrt{T-t}$$

Note that, where $t = T$, the chooser has the same value as a European-style straddle (i.e., equals the sum of the values of a standard European-style call and put with exercise price $X$ and time to expiration $T$). Note also that as $t \to 0$, the values of $N(-d_1')$ and $N(-d_2')$ approach 0 or 1, depending upon whether $Se^{-iT}$ is greater than or less than $Xe^{-rT}$. If $Se^{-iT} > Xe^{-rT}$, $N(-d_1')$ and $N(-d_2')$ are 0, in which case the last two terms in (8.19) disappear and the lower price bound of the chooser is the standard European-style call option value. If $Se^{-iT} < Xe^{-rT}$, $N(-d_1')$ and $N(-d_2')$ are 1, in which case the last two terms in (8.19) become $-Se^{-iT} + Xe^{-rT}$, and the lower price bound of the chooser is the standard European-style put option value, that is,

$$\begin{aligned} c_{\text{chooser}}(S, X, t, T) &\geq Se^{-iT}N(d_1) - Xe^{-rT}N(d_2) - Se^{-iT} + Xe^{-rT} \\ &= Xe^{-rT}N(-d_2) - Se^{-iT}N(-d_1) \end{aligned}$$

**ILLUSTRATION 8.7** Value chooser option.

*Compute the value of a one-year European-style chooser option that allows you to choose whether the option is a call or a put at the end of three months. Assume the option is written on the S&P 500 index portfolio, and that the S&P 500 index has a current level of 1,100, a dividend yield rate of 1%, and a volatility rate of 15%. Assume that the exercise price of the chooser is 1,150 and that risk-free rate of interest is 4%.*

First, compute the prepaid forward price of the stock index and the prepaid exercise price.

$$Se^{-iT} = 1{,}100e^{-0.01(1)} = 1{,}089.05$$

and

$$Xe^{-rT} = 1{,}150e^{-0.04(1)} = 1{,}104.91$$

Second, compute the upper integral limits.

$$d_1 = \frac{\ln(1{,}089.05/1{,}104.91) + 0.5(0.15^2)(1)}{0.15\sqrt{1}} = -0.0213$$

$$d_2 = -0.0213 - 0.15\sqrt{1} = -0.1713$$

$$d_1' = \frac{\ln(1{,}089.05/1{,}104.91) + 0.5(0.15^2)(0.25)}{0.15\sqrt{0.25}} = -0.1552$$

$$d_2' = -0.1552 - 0.15\sqrt{0.25} = -0.2302$$

Third, compute the respective risk-neutral probabilities.

$$N(d_1) = 0.4915, N(d_2) = 0.4320, N(-d_1) = 0.5617, \text{and } N(-d_2) = 0.5910$$

Finally, compute the chooser option value.

$$\begin{aligned} c_{\text{chooser}} &= 1{,}089.05(0.4915) - 1{,}104.91(0.4320) - 1{,}089.05(0.5617) + 1{,}104.91(0.5910) \\ &= 99.3086 \end{aligned}$$

To verify the computation, use the OPTVAL function

OV_NS_CHOOSER_OPTION($s, x, td, t, r, i, v$)

where $td$ is the time until the choice between the call and the put must be made, and all other notation has been defined. Thus

OV_NS_CHOOSER_OPTION(1100, 1150, 0.25, 1., 0.04, 0.01, 0.15) = 99.3086

Note that the values of standard call and put options with one year to expiration are 57.9604 and 73.8134, respectively. The chooser option is more valuable since it allows the holder to choose between the call and put after three months of asset price movement has elapsed rather than now. Since the put has the highest value of the standard options today, it serves as the lower value bound of the chooser option. When the time until the choose date is 0, $c_{\text{chooser}} = 73.8134$. When the time until the choose date equals one year, the chooser value equals the value of a straddle, that is, the sum of the standard call and put values, 131.7737. The value of the chooser option rises at a decreasing rate as the time until the choose date approached the option's time to expiration, as is shown in the following figure.

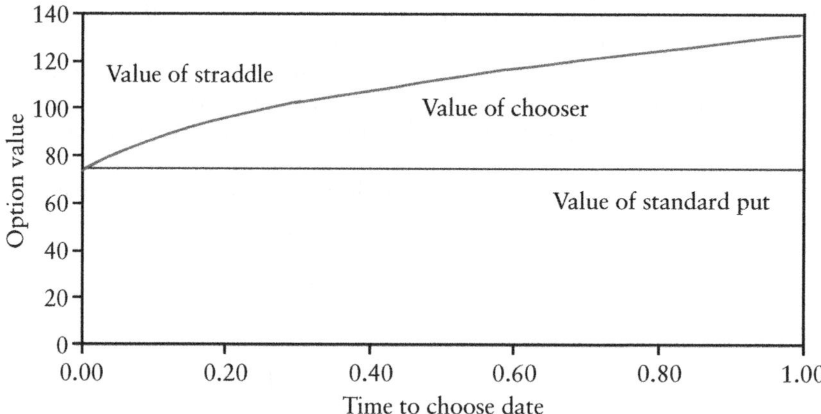


## EXCHANGE OPTIONS

An *exchange option*[8] is the right to exchange one asset for another. The value of the right to exchange asset 2 for asset 1 (i.e., a call option to buy conveying the right to buy asset 1 by paying asset 2 is

[8] The exchange option formula for the two-asset case where both assets have a cost of carry rate equal to the risk-free rate of interest was derived by Margrabe (1978). The formula presented here generalizes the Margrabe result to allow the assets to have different income rates. The $n$-asset exchange option was later developed by Margrabe (1982).

$$c_{exchange}(S_1, S_2) = S_1 e^{-i_1 T} N_1(d_1) - S_2 e^{-i_2 T} N_1(d_2) \tag{8.20}$$

where

$$d_1 = \frac{\ln(S_1 e^{-i_1 T} / S_2 e^{-i_2 T}) + 0.5\sigma^2 T}{\sigma\sqrt{T}}, \; d_2 = d_1 - \sigma\sqrt{T},$$

$$\sigma = \sqrt{\sigma_1^2 + \sigma_2^2 - 2\rho\sigma_1\sigma_2}$$

$S_1$ and $S_2$ are the underlying asset prices, $T$ is the time between now and the expiration date, $i_1$ and $i_2$ are the income rates (e.g., dividend yields) of asset 1 and asset 2, $\sigma_1$ and $\sigma_2$ are the expected future volatility rates of assets 1 and 2, and $\rho$ is the expected correlation between the returns of assets 1 and 2. The term $N(d_2)$ is the risk-neutral probability that the price of asset 1 will exceed the price of asset 2 at expiration. As noted in Chapter 3, the terms,

$$S_1 e^{-i_1 T} \text{ and } S_2 e^{-i_2 T}$$

are the prices of prepaid forward contracts on assets 1 and 2, respectively.

The exchange option formula (8.20) is interesting in a number of respects. First, it contains the BSM call option formula as a special case. In the BSM model, the prepaid forward price on the asset 2 is the present value of the exercise price, that is,

$$Se^{-i_2 T} = Xe^{-rT}$$

The expression for $d_1$ can be rearranged to yield the more familiar

$$d_1 = \frac{\ln(S_1 e^{-i_1 T} / Xe^{-rT}) + 0.5\sigma^2 T}{\sigma\sqrt{T}}$$

And, since asset 2 is risk-free, the volatility rate becomes

$$\sigma = \sqrt{\sigma_1^2 + \sigma_2^2 - 2\rho\sigma_1\sigma_2} = \sigma_1$$

Another interesting aspect of (8.20) is that the value of a call option to "buy" asset 1 with asset 2, $c_{exchange}(S_1,S_2)$, equals the value of a put option to "sell" asset 2 for asset 1, $p_{exchange}(S_2,S_1)$. In the case of the call, the option is exercised at expiration if the price of asset 1 exceeds the price of asset 2; otherwise, it expires worthless. In the case of the put, the option is exercised at expiration if the price of asset 2 is less than the price of asset 1; otherwise it expires worthless. Since the payoffs of these two options are identical, the value of the options must be the same, that is,

$$c_{\text{exchange}}(S_1,S_2) = p_{\text{exchange}}(S_2,S_1)$$

The value of a put option to "sell" asset 1 for asset 2, on the other hand, is

$$p_{\text{exchange}}(S_2, S_1) = S_2 e^{-i_2 T} N_1(-d_2) - S_1 e^{-i_1 T} N_1(-d_1) \tag{8.21}$$

where $d_1$ and $d_2$ are as defined below equation (8.20). It is equivalent in value to a call option to exchange asset 1 for asset 2.

Exchange options are traded primarily in the OTC market. The underlying assets can be virtually any financial or commodity. Exchange options are also often embedded in other financial contracts. The CBT's corn futures contract, for example, calls for the delivery of No. 2 yellow corn at par, but also permits the delivery of No. 3 yellow at a 1½ cent discount below the contract price. Thus, standing prior to the delivery day, an individual who is short the corn futures contract and holds No. 2 yellow has the right to deliver No. 3 yellow and will do so if the price difference between No. 2 yellow and No. 3 yellow is greater than 1½ cents. We will discuss this particular application in Chapter 20.

**ILLUSTRATION 8.8** Value exchange call option.

*Compute the value of a three-year European-style exchange call option that allows you to exchange one unit of the DJIA index level for ten units of the S&P 500 index level. Assume the S&P 500 portfolio has a current level of 1,150, a dividend yield rate of 1%, and a volatility rate of 20%. Assume the DJIA has a current level of 10,500, a dividend yield rate of 2%, and a volatility rate of 18%. Finally, assume the correlation between the returns of the two indexes is .85. Also, compute the value of a three-year European-style put option that allows you to sell 10 units of the S&P 500 index and receive one unit of the DJIA. Comment on the difference between the two option values.*

The values of the prepaid forwards that appear in the exchange option formula are

$$S_1 e^{-i_1 T} = 10 \times 1{,}150 \times e^{-0.01(3)} = 11{,}160.12$$

and

$$S_2 e^{-i_2 T} = 10{,}500 \times e^{-0.02(3)} = 9{,}888.53$$

Since the first prepaid forward has a higher value than the second, the call is currently in the money. The value of the exchange call option is

$$c_{\text{exchange}}(S_1, S_2) = 11{,}160.12 N_1(d_1) - 9{,}888.53 N_1(d_2) = 1{,}565.19$$

where

$$d_1 = \frac{\ln(11{,}160.12/9{,}888.53) + 0.5\sigma^2(3)}{\sigma\sqrt{3}}, \quad d_2 = d_1 - \sigma\sqrt{3}$$

$$\sigma = \sqrt{0.20^2 + 0.18^2 - 2(0.85)(0.20)(0.18)} = 0.106$$

Its value may be computed using the OPTVAL function

OV_NS_EXCHANGE_OPTION(*s1*, *s2*, *t*, *i1*, *i2*, *v1*, *v2*, *rho*, *cp*)

where *s1* and *s2* are the prices of assets 1 and 2, *t* is the time to expiration, *i1* and *i2* are the income rates of assets 1 and 2, *v1* and *v2* are the volatility rates of assets 1 and 2, rho is the correlation between the returns of assets 1 and 2, and *cp* is a (c)all/(p)ut indicator. Thus

OV_NS_EXCHANGE_OPTION(11500, 10500, 0.01, 0.02, 0.20, 0.18, 0.85, "c")
= 1,565.19

The value of the corresponding European-style exchange put option can be computed in the same manner:

OV_NS_EXCHANGE_OPTION(11500, 10500, 0.01, 0.02, 0.20, 0.18, 0.85, "p")
= 293.59

The difference between the prices is 1,565.19 – 293.59 = 1,271.60. Note that this is also the difference between the two prepaid forward contract prices, 11,160.12 – 9,888.53 = 1,271.60. The reason is, of course, put-call parity. For exchange options,

$$c_{\text{exchange}}(S_2, S_1) - p_{\text{exchange}}(S_2, S_1) = S_1 e^{-i_1 T} - S_2 e^{-i_2 T}$$

## OPTIONS ON THE MAXIMUM AND THE MINIMUM

Options on the maximum and minimum of two or more risky assets are closely related to exchange options.[9] In place of exchanging one asset for another, however, the option holder gets to choose between the two risky assets. A call option on the maximum of two risky assets, for example, provides its holder with the right to buy the more expensive of asset 1 and asset 2 for exercise price $X$ at the option's expiration date, $T$. In this section, we provide and interpret the valuation equations for (1) a call on the maximum of two risky assets; (2) a call on the minimum of two risky assets; (3) a put on the maximum of two risky asset; and (4) a put of the minimum of two risky assets.

### Call on Maximum

The payoff contingencies of a European-style call on the maximum are:

$$c_{\max, T} = \begin{cases} S_{1,T} - X, & \text{if } S_{1,T} \geq S_{2,T} \text{ and } S_{1,T} \geq X \\ S_{2,T} - X, & \text{if } S_{2,T} \geq S_{1,T} \text{ and } S_{2,T} \geq X \\ 0, & \text{if } S_{1,T} < X \text{ and } S_{2,T} < X \end{cases} \tag{8.22}$$

[9] Other names for the option on the maximum are "the better of two assets" or "outperformance options." The models presented here are on the maximum or the minimum of two risky assets, and the valuation equations are based on Stulz (1982). To generalize these models to consider three or more risky assets, see Johnson (1987).

The valuation equation for a call option on the maximum is

$$\begin{aligned} c_{\max}(S_1, S_2, X) = {} & S_1 e^{-i_1 T} N_2(d_{11}, d_1'; \rho') + S_2 e^{-i_2 T} N_2(d_{21}, d_2'; \rho_2') \\ & - X e^{-rT}[1 - N_2(-d_{12}, -d_{22}; \rho_{12})] \end{aligned} \tag{8.23}$$

where

$$d_{11} = \frac{\ln(S_1 e^{-i_1 T}/X e^{-rT}) + 0.5\sigma_1^2 T}{\sigma_1 \sqrt{T}}, \; d_{12} = d_{11} - \sigma_1 \sqrt{T}$$

$$d_{21} = \frac{\ln(S_2 e^{-i_2 T}/X e^{-rT}) + 0.5\sigma_2^2 T}{\sigma_2 \sqrt{T}}, \; d_{22} = d_{21} - \sigma_2 \sqrt{T}$$

$$\sigma^2 = \sigma_1^2 + \sigma_2^2 - 2\rho_{12}\sigma_1\sigma_2$$

$$d_1' = \frac{\ln(S_1 e^{-i_1 T}/S_2 e^{-i_2 T}) + 0.5\sigma^2 T}{\sigma \sqrt{T}}, \; d_2' = \frac{\ln(S_2 e^{-i_2 T}/S_1 e^{-i_1 T}) + 0.5\sigma^2 T}{\sigma \sqrt{T}}$$

$$\rho_1' = \frac{\sigma_1 - \rho_{12}\sigma_2}{\sigma}, \text{ and } \rho_2' = \frac{\sigma_2 - \rho_{12}\sigma_1}{\sigma}$$

In equation (8.23), the term, $N_2(-d_{12}, -d_{22}; \rho_{12})$ is the *compound* risk-neutral probability that both asset 1 and asset 2 will have prices below the exercise price at the option's expiration. It is called a compound probability because there are two sources of uncertainty. We want to know the probability that asset 1's price will be below the exercise *and* that asset 2's price will be below the exercise price. Recall $N(a)$ is the probability that a random drawing $x$ from a univariate normal distribution have a value below $a$, that is, $\Pr(x \leq a) = N(a)$. Here, $N_2(a,b;\rho)$ is the probability that random drawings $x$ and $y$ from a bivariate normal distribution will have values below $a$ and $b$, respectively, that is, $\Pr(x \leq a, y \leq b) = N_2(a,b;\rho)$, where $\rho$ is the correlation between the random variables $x$ and $y$. Where we have used the OPTVAL function OV_PROB_PRUN(*a*) to compute $N(a)$, we use OV_PROB_PRBN(*a,b,rho*) to $N_2(a,b;\rho)$. An algorithm for computing the bivariate normal probability is provided in Appendix 8.A. If $N_2(-d_{12}, -d_{22}; \rho_{12})$ is the compound risk-neutral probability that both asset 1 and asset 2 will have prices below the exercise price at the option's expiration, then $[1 - N_2(-d_{12}, -d_{22}; \rho_{12})]$ must be the risk-neutral probability that one of the two asset prices will exceed the exercise price $X$ at time $T$, and $Xe^{-rT}[1 - N_2(-d_{12}, -d_{22}; \rho_{12})]$ is the present value of the cost of exercising the option times the risk-neutral probability that the option will be exercised.

The two remaining terms on the right-hand side of (8.23) also have economic interpretations. The term

$$S_1e^{-i_1T}N_2(d_{11}, d_1'; \rho_1')$$

is the present value of the expected price of asset 1 at the option's expiration conditional upon asset 1 having a price greater than asset 2 and greater than the exercise price times the risk-neutral probability that the terminal price of asset 1 will exceed the terminal price of asset 2 and will exceed the exercise price. The term

$$S_2e^{-i_2T}N_2(d_{21}, d_2'; \rho_2')$$

has a similar interpretation but for asset 2.

**ILLUSTRATION 8.9** Value call on maximum.

*Consider a call option that provides its holder the right to buy $100,000 worth of the S&P 500 index portfolio at an exercise price of $1,200 or $100,000 worth of a particular T-bond at an exercise price of $100, whichever is worth more at the end of three months. The S&P 500 index is currently priced at $1,080, pays dividends at a rate of 1% annually and has a return volatility of 20%. The T-bond is currently priced at $98, pays a coupon yield of 6% and has a return volatility of 15%. The correlation between the rates of return of the S&P 500 and the T-bond is 0.5. The risk-free rate of interest is 4%. Compute the value of this call option on the maximum.*

Before applying the option on the maximum formula, it is important to recognize that there are two exercise prices in this problem: 1,200 for the S&P index portfolio and 100 for the T-bond. What this implies is that we can buy 100,000/1,200 = 83.333 units of the index portfolio or 100,000/100 = 1,000 units of T-bonds at the end of three months, depending on which is worth more. At this juncture, we must decide whether to work with the valuation equation (8.23) in units of the S&P 500 index portfolio, in which case we multiply the current T-bond price and its exercise price by 12 and then multiply the computed option price by 83.333, or to work with the valuation equation (8.20) in units of the T-bond, in which case we divide the current S&P 500 price and the option's S&P 500 exercise price by 12 and then multiply the computed option price by 1,000.[10]

Given the choice between methods is arbitrary and produces the same option value, we will proceed with the problem solution working in units of the S&P 500 index portfolio. We begin, therefore by adjusting the T-bond prices. The current T-bond price is assumed to be 1,176 and the T-bond exercise price is 1,200. With the units of the two underlying assets comparable, we now compute the prepaid forward prices of assets 1 and 2 as well as the prepaid exercise price, that is,

$$S_1e^{-i_1T} = 1{,}080e^{-0.01(0.25)} = 1{,}077.30$$

$$S_2e^{-i_2T} = 1{,}176e^{-0.06(0.25)} = 1{,}158.49$$

and

$$Xe^{-rT} = 1{,}200e^{-0.04(0.25)} = 1{,}188.06$$

[10] These types of adjustments can be made freely because the option price is linearly homogeneous in both the asset price and the exercise price. See Merton (1973).

Substituting the problem parameters into equation (8.23), we get

$$\begin{aligned} c_{max}(S_1, S_2, X) &= 1{,}077.30 \times N_2(d_{11}, d'_1; \rho'_1) + 1{,}158.49 \times N_2(d_{21}, d'_2; \rho'_2) \\ &\quad - 1{,}188.06 \times [1 - N_2(-d_{12}, -d'_{22}; \rho'_{12})] \\ &= 27.239 \end{aligned}$$

where

$$d_{11} = \frac{\ln(1{,}077.30/1{,}188.06) + 0.5(0.20^2)(0.25)}{0.20\sqrt{0.25}} = -0.9296$$

$$d_{12} = -0.9296 - 0.20\sqrt{0.25} = -0.2985$$

$$d_{21} = \frac{\ln(1{,}058.49/1{,}188.06) + 0.5(0.15^2)(0.25)}{0.15\sqrt{0.25}} = -1.0286$$

$$d_{22} = -1.0286 - 0.15\sqrt{0.25} = -0.3735$$

$$d'_1 = \frac{\ln(1{,}077.30/1{,}058.49) + 0.5\sigma^2(0.25)}{\sigma\sqrt{0.25}} = -0.7610$$

$$d'_2 = -(-0.7610 - \sigma\sqrt{0.25}) = 0.8511$$

$$\sigma = \sqrt{0.20^2 + 0.15^2 - 2(0.5)(0.20)(0.15)} = 0.1803$$

$$\rho'_1 = \frac{0.20 - 0.5(0.15)}{0.1803} = 0.6934$$

and

$$\rho'_2 = \frac{0.15 - 0.5(0.20)}{0.1803} = 0.2774$$

The risk-neutral probabilities are $N_2(d_{11}, d'_1; \rho'_1) = 0.1102$, $N_2(d_{21}, d'_2; \rho'_2) = 0.3355$, and $N_2(-d_{12}, -d_{22}; \rho_{12}) = 0.5958$. The computed option value is 27.239. This can be confirmed using the OPTVAL function

OV_NS_MAXMIN_OPTION(*s1, s2, x, t, r, i1, i2, v1, v2, rho, cp, mm*),

where *s1* and *s2* are the prices of assets 1 and 2, *x* is the exercise price of the option, *t* is the time to expiration, *i1* and *i2* are the income rates of assets 1 and 2, *v1* and *v2* are the volatility rates of assets 1 and 2, *rho* is the correlation between the returns of assets 1 and 2, *cp* is a (c)all/(p)ut indicator, and *mm* is a ma(x)imum/mi(n)imum indicator. Thus

OV_NS_MAXMIN_OPTION(1080, 1176, 1200, 0.25, 0.04, 0.01, 0.06, 0.20, 0.15, 0.5, "c", "x") = 27.239

which implies the total value of the option contract is 27.239 × 83.333 = 2,269.90. The probability that either or both the components of the option are in-the-money at expiration is $[1 - N_2(1.0286, 0.3735; 0.5)] = 0.4042$ or 40.42%.

Before turning to the call on the minimum, it is worthwhile to note that the formula for the call on the maximum becomes the exchange option formula when the exercise price of the option is zero. Where X = 0, equation (8.23) may be written

$$c_{max}(S_1, S_2, 0) = S_1 e^{-i_1 T} N_2(\infty, d_1'; \rho_1') + S_2 e^{-i_2 T} N_2(\infty, d_2'; \rho_2') \\ - 0e^{-rT}[1 - N_2(-\infty, -\infty; \rho_{12})] \\ = S_1 e^{-i_1 T} N_1(d_1') + S_2 e^{-i_2 T} N_1(d_2')$$

which is the exchange option formula (8.20) presented earlier.

### Call on Minimum

The payoff contingencies of a European-style call on the minimum are:

$$c_{min,T} = \begin{cases} S_{1,T} - X, & \text{if } S_{1,T} \le S_{2,T} \text{ and } S_{1,T} \ge X \\ S_{2,T} - X, & \text{if } S_{2,T} \le S_{1,T} \text{ and } S_{2,T} \ge X \\ 0, & \text{if } S_{1,T} < X \text{ or } S_{2,T} < X \end{cases} \tag{8.24}$$

Under the BSM assumptions, the value of a European-style call on the minimum is

$$c_{max}(S_1, S_2, X) = S_1 e^{-i_1 T} N_2(d_{11}, -d_1'; -\rho_1') + S_2 e^{-i_2 T} N_2(d_{21}, -d_2'; -\rho_2') \\ - Xe^{-rT} N_2(d_{12}, d_{22}; -\rho_{12}) \tag{8.25}$$

where all notation is as previously defined. Note that, unlike the call on the maximum of two risky assets, the risk-neutral probability in (8.25), $N_2(d_{12}, d_{22}; \rho_{12})$, requires that both asset prices exceed the exercise price $X$ at time $T$. If one of the terminal asset prices is below $X$ at time $T$, the call on the minimum expires worthless. It is also worthwhile to note that the sum of the payoffs of a call on the maximum and a call on the minimum are

$$c_{max,T} + c_{min,T} = \max[\max(S_{1,T}, S_{2,T}) - X, 0] + \max[\min(S_{1,T}, S_{2,T}) - X, 0] \\ = \max[S_{1,T} - X, 0] + \max[S_{2,T} - X, 0]$$

In absence of costless arbitrage opportunities, this means that the sum of the values a call on the maximum and a call on the minimum is equal to the sum of the values of standard call options written on the individual assets, that is,

$$c_{max}(S_1, S_2, X) + c_{min}(S_1, S_2, X) = c_{BSM}(S_1, X) + c_{BSM}(S_2, X) \tag{8.26}$$

**ILLUSTRATION 8.10** Value call options on maximum and minimum.

*Consider call options on the minimum and the maximum of one share of ABC and DEF shares. The options' exercise prices are 50, and their time to expiration is six months. ABC is currently priced at 51, pays dividends at a rate of 1% annually, and has a return volatility of 35%. DEF is currently priced at 49, pays a dividend yield of 3% and has a return volatility of 32%. The correlation between the rates of return of ABC and DEF is 0.75. The risk-free rate of interest is 4%. Compute the value of the call option on the minimum. Also, compute the value of a call option on the maximum, and the values of standard call options on the individual shares.*

Given that we showed all the underpinnings of an option on the minimum/maximum in Illustration 8.9, we will simply apply the appropriate OPTVAL functions to value the options. The call option on the minimum has a value,

OV_NS_MAXMIN_OPTION(51, 49, 50, 0.5, 0.04, 0.01, 0.03, 0.35, 0.32, .5, "c", "n")
= 2.932,

and the call option on the maximum is

OV_NS_MAXMIN_OPTION(51, 49, 50, 0.5, 0.04, 0.01, 0.03, 0.35, 0.32, 0.5, "c", "n")
= 6.917.

The sum of the values is 2.932 + 6.917 = 9.850. The values of standard call options written on the shares of ABC and DEF are

OV_OPTION_VALUE (51, 50, 0.5, 0.04, 0.01, 0.35, "c", "e") = 5.828

and

OV_OPTION_VALUE (49, 50, 0.5, 0.04, 0.03, 0.32, "c", "e") = 4.022

The sum of the values of the standard call options is also 9.850, verifying the no-arbitrage condition (8.26).

## Put on Maximum

The value of a European-style put on the maximum is

$$p_{\max}(S_1, S_2, X) = Xe^{-rT}N_2(-d_{12}, -d_{22}; \rho_{12}) - S_1e^{-i_1T}N_2(-d_{11}, -d_1'; -\rho_1') - S_2e^{-i_2T}N_2(-d_{21}, d_2'; -\rho') \quad (8.27)$$

Similar to the situation with the call on the minimum, $N_2(d_{12}, d_{22}; \rho_{12})$ is the risk-neutral probability that both asset prices are below the exercise price $X$ at time $T$. If one of the terminal asset prices is above $X$ at time $T$, the put on the maximum expires worthless.

## Put on Minimum

The value of a European-style put on the minimum is

$$p_{\min}(S_1, S_2, X) = Xe^{-rT}N_2(-d_{12}, -d_{22}; \rho_{12}) - S_1e^{-i_1T}N_2(-d_{11}, -d_1'; -\rho_1') - S_2e^{-i_2T}N_2(-d_{21}, d_2'; -\rho') \quad (8.28)$$

where all notation is as previously defined. In (8.28), the term, $[1 - N_2(d_{12},d_{22};\rho_{12})]$, is the risk-neutral probability that one of the two asset prices will be below the exercise price $X$ at time $T$ or, alternatively, one minus the probability that both asset prices will exceed the exercise price at the option's expiration. Like in the case of the call, the sum of the values of a put on the maximum and a put on the minimum equals the sum of the values of standard put options written on the individual assets, that is,

$$p_{\max}(S_1, S_2, X) + p_{\min}(S_1, S_2, X) = p_{BSM}(S_1, X) + p_{BSM}(S_2, X) \tag{8.29}$$

## COMPOUND OPTIONS

A *compound option* is an option on an option. It is like a standard option in the sense that it conveys the right to buy or sell an underlying asset at the contract's expiration. The only difference is that the underlying asset happens to be an option. Compound options are traded in the OTC market. The most common forms include calls on calls, puts on calls, calls on puts, and puts on puts. We will address each in turn.[11]

### Call on Call

A call on a call conveys the right to buy an underlying call option with exercise price $X$ and time to expiration $T$. The call on the call (i.e., the compound option) has exercise price $c^*$ and time to expiration $t$. Its value is denoted $c_{\text{call}}$. Under risk-neutral valuation, a call on a call may be written

$$c_{\text{call}}(c^*, t) = e^{-rt}E(\tilde{c}_t) \tag{8.30}$$

where $c_t$ is the value of the underlying call at time $t$,

$$c_{\text{call}}(c^*, t) = \begin{cases} c(S_t, T-t, X) & \text{if } c_t > c^* \\ 0 & \text{if } c_t \le c^* \end{cases}$$

$$c(S_t, T-t, X) = S_t e^{-i(T-t)}N_1(d_1) - Xe^{-r(T-t)}N_1(d_2) \tag{8.31}$$

$$d_1 = \frac{\ln(S_t e^{-i(T-t)}/Xe^{-r(T-t)}) + 0.5\sigma^2 T}{\sigma\sqrt{T}}, \text{ and } d_2 = d_1 - \sigma\sqrt{T}$$

[11] The formulas in this section are based on Geske (1979). Interestingly, he derived the formulas under the BSM assumptions before the instruments ever traded in the OTC market. His application arose from the observation that the equity of a firm can be viewed as a call option on the value of the firm with the exercise being equal to the value of the firm's bonds. Consequently, exchange-traded call and put options on the shares of the firm are actually a call on a call and a put on a call.

The first step in valuing a call on a call is determining the critical asset price at time $t$ above which you will exercise the compound option at time $t$. It can be determined by iteratively searching for the asset price $S_t^*$ that makes the value of the underlying call equal to the exercise price of the compound call, that is,

$$c(S_t^*, T-t, X) = c^* \tag{8.32}$$

With $S_t^*$ known, the value of a European-style call on a call is

$$c_{\text{call}}(c^*, t) = Se^{-iT}N_2(a_1, b_1; \rho) - Xe^{-rT}N_2(a_2, b_2; \rho) - e^{-rt}c^*N_1(b_2) \tag{8.33}$$

where

$$a_1 = \frac{\ln(Se^{-iT}/Xe^{-rT}) + 0.5\sigma^2 T}{\sigma\sqrt{T}}, \; a_2 = a_1 - \sigma\sqrt{T}$$

$$b_1 = \frac{\ln(Se^{-iT}/S_t^* e^{-rT}) + 0.5\sigma^2 T}{\sigma\sqrt{T}}, \; b_2 = b_1 - \sigma\sqrt{T}, \; \rho = \sqrt{\frac{t}{T}}$$

and $N_1(.)$ and $N_2(.)$ are the cumulative univariate and bivariate unit normal density functions.

Notice the similarity between the structure of (8.33) and the structure of the BSM call option formula (8.3). The first two terms of the right-hand side of (8.33) correspond to the BSM formula. Instead of getting the underlying asset upon exercising a standard call, you get a call option. The last term on the right-side is the present value of the exercise price of the compound option, $e^{-rt}c^*$, times the risk-neutral probability that the asset price will exceed the critical asset price at time $t$, $N_1(b_2)$, or the expected cost of exercising the compound call conditional upon it being in the money at time $t$. The term, $N_2(a_2,b_2;\rho)$, is the risk-neutral compound probability that the asset price will exceed $S_t^*$ at time $t$ and will exceed the exercise price $X$ at time $T$. The asset price must jump both hurdles to be in-the-money at time $T$. The sign of correlation coefficient, $\rho$, reflects whether asset price should move in the same or opposite direction in the interval between time 0 and time $t$ as in the interval between time $t$ and time $T$ in order for the underlying option to be in-the-money at time $T$. For a call on a call, the sign is positive because you want the asset price to increase in both intervals. For a put on a call, the sign will be negative because you want the asset price to be low enough for the compound option to be exercised at time $t$ and yet be high enough to exceed the exercise price of the underlying call at time $T$.

### Put on Call

A put on a call conveys the right to sell an underlying call option with exercise price $X$ and time to expiration $T$. The put has exercise price $c^*$ and time to expiration $t$. The simplest way to derive the valuation equation for a put on a call is to begin with a compound option version of put-call parity. From Chapter 5, we know that, for a nonincome producing asset,[12] the call price less the put price equals the asset price less the present value of the exercise price. The equivalent condition here is that the call on a call price, $c_{call}(c^*,t)$, less the put on a call price, $p_{call}(c^*,t)$, equals the underlying European-style call option price, $Se^{-iT}N_1(a_1) - Xe^{-rT}N_1(a_2)$, less the present value of the exercise price, $e^{-rt}c^*$, that is,

$$c_{call}(c^*, t) - p_{call}(c^*, t) = Se^{-iT}N_1(a_1) - Xe^{-rT}N_1(a_2) - e^{-rt}c^* \tag{8.34}$$

To value a put on a call, we isolate the value of the put on the call and get

$$p_{call}(c^*, t) = Xe^{-rT}N_2(a_2, -b_2; -\rho) - Se^{-iT}N_2(a_1, -b_1; -\rho) + e^{-rT}c^*N_1(-b_2) \tag{8.35}$$

where all notation is defined above.[13] In (8.35), $N_1(-b_2)$ is the risk-neutral probability that the asset price will be below the critical asset price at time $t$, $S_t^*$. In this region, the compound option will be exercised. The underlying call value, however, increases with the asset price. The correlation in the compound probability then is negative, and the term, $N_2(a_2,-b_2;-\rho)$, is the risk-neutral compound probability that the asset price will be below $S_t^*$ at time $t$ and will exceed the exercise price $X$ at time $T$.

### Put on Put

A put on a put conveys the right to sell an underlying put option with exercise price $X$ and time to expiration $T$. The put has exercise price of $p^*$ and time to expiration $t$. Under risk-neutral valuation, the value of a put on a put is

$$p_{put}(p^*, t) = e^{-rt}E(\tilde{p}_t) \tag{8.36}$$

where $p_t$ is the value of the underlying put at time $t$,

$$p_{put,t}(p^*, 0) = \begin{cases} p(S_t, T-t, X) & \text{if } p_t > p^* \\ 0 & \text{if } p_t \le p^* \end{cases}$$

$$p(S_t, T-t, X) = Xe^{-r(T-t)}N_1(-d_2) - S_te^{-iT}N_1(-d_1) \tag{8.37}$$

$$d_1 = \frac{\ln(S_te^{-i(T-t)}/Xe^{-r(T-t)}) + 0.5\sigma^2(T-t)}{\sigma\sqrt{T-t}}, \text{ and } d_2 = d_1 - \sigma\sqrt{T}$$

[12] Recall that in Chapter 5 we discussed the fact that the cost of carry rate for an option is the risk-free rate of interest.

[13] In deriving (8.32), we use some properties of the cumulative univariate and bivariate normal distributions. Specifically, $1-N_1(b) = N_1(-b)$ and $N_1(a) - N_2(a,b;-\rho)$. See Abramowitz and Stegum (1972, p. 936).

The first step in valuing a put on a put is determining the critical asset price at time $t$ above which you will exercise your option to sell the underlying put. It can be determined by iteratively searching for the value $S_t^*$ that satisfies

$$p(S_t^*, T-t, X) = p^* \tag{8.38}$$

With $S_t^*$ known, the value of a European-style put on a put is

$$p_{\text{put}}(p^*, t) = Se^{-iT}N_2(-a_1, b_1; -\rho) - Xe^{-rT}N_2(-a_2, b_2; -\rho) + e^{-rt}p^*N_1(b_2) \tag{8.39}$$

where all notation is defined above. The term, $N_1(b_2)$, is the risk-neutral probability that the asset price will be above the critical asset price at time $t$, $S_t^*$ (i.e., the put will be exercised), and the term, $N_2(-a_2,b_2;-\rho)$, is the risk-neutral probability that the asset price will be above $S_t^*$ at time $t$ and will be below the exercise price $X$ at time $T$.

### Call on Put

A call on a put conveys the right to buy an underlying put option with exercise price $X$ and time to expiration $T$. The call has exercise price $p^*$ and time to expiration $t$. Again, put-call parity can be used to arrive at the valuation formula. For a nonincome producing asset, the call price less the put price equals the asset price less the present value of the exercise price. The equivalent condition here is that the call on a put price, $c_{\text{put}}(p^*,t)$, less the put on a put price, $p_{\text{put}}(p^*,t)$, equals the underlying European-style put option price, $Xe^{-rT}N_1(-a_2) - Se^{-iT}N_1(-a_1)$, less the present value of the exercise price, $e^{-rT}p^*$, that is,

$$c_{\text{put}}(p^*, t) - p_{\text{put}}(p^*, t) = Xe^{-rT}N_1(-a_2) - Se^{-iT}N_1(-a_1) - e^{-rt}p^* \tag{8.40}$$

Rearranging to isolate the value of a European-style call on a put and simplifying,

$$c_{\text{put}}(p^*, t) = Xe^{-rT}N_2(-a_2, -b_2; \rho) - Se^{-iT}N_2(-a_1, -b_1; \rho) - e^{-rt}p^*N_1(-b_2) \tag{8.41}$$

where all other notation is as previously defined. The term, $N_1(-b_2)$, is the risk-neutral probability that the asset price will be above the critical asset price at time $t$, $S_t^*$ (i.e., the put will be exercised), and the term, $N_2(-a_2,-b_2;\rho)$, is the risk-neutral probability that the asset price will be below $S_t^*$ at time $t$ and will be below the exercise price $X$ at time $T$.

**ILLUSTRATION 8.11** Value call on put.

*Consider a call option that provides its holder with the right to buy a put option on the S&P 500 index portfolio. The put that underlies the call has an exercise price of 1,200 and a time to expiration of nine months. The call has an exercise price of 40 and a time to expiration of three months. The S&P 500 index is currently at 1,150, pays dividends at a constant rate of 1% annually, and has a volatility rate of 15%. The risk-free rate of interest is 3%.*

The first step is to compute the critical asset price below which the call will be exercised at time $t$ to take delivery of the put. This is done by solving $p(S_t^*, T-t, X) = 40.00$. The critical index level, $S_t^*$ is 1,210.72. The next step is to apply the valuation formula. Here, we get

$$\begin{aligned} c_{\text{put}} &= 1{,}200e^{-0.03(0.75)}N_2(-a_2, -b_2; \rho) - 1{,}150e^{0.01(0.75)}N_2(-a_1, -b_1; \rho) \\ &\quad - e^{-0.03(0.25)}(40)N_1(-b_2) \\ &= 41.6110 \end{aligned}$$

where

$$a_1 = \frac{\ln(1{,}150e^{-0.01(0.75)}/1{,}200e^{-0.03(0.75)}) + 0.5(0.15^2)(0.75)}{0.15\sqrt{0.75}} = -0.1472$$

$$a_2 = -0.1472 - 0.15\sqrt{0.75} = -0.2771$$

$$b_1 = \frac{\ln(1{,}150e^{-0.01(0.25)}/1{,}210.72e^{-0.03(0.25)}) + 0.5(0.15^2)(0.25)}{0.15\sqrt{0.25}} = -0.5818$$

$$b_2 = -0.5818 - 0.15\sqrt{0.25} = -0.6568$$

$$\rho = \sqrt{\frac{0.25}{0.75}} = 0.5774$$

The risk-neutral probability that the asset price will be below the critical asset price at time $t$, $N_1(0.6568)$ is 74.44%. The risk-neutral probability that the asset price will be below $S_t^*$ at time $t$ and below the exercise price $X$ at time $T$, $N_2(0.2771, 0.6568; 0.5774)$ is 53.16%. The value of a put on a put with the same terms as the call on the put is 4.0866.

The OPTVAL Function Library contains the compound option valuation function

OV_NS_COMPOUND_OPTION(*s, cp1, x1, tim1, cp2, x2, tim2, r, i, v*)

where *cp1* is (c)all/(p)ut indicator for the initial option, *x1* is the exercise price of the initial option, *tim1* is the time to expiration of the initial option, *cp2*, *x2*, and *tim2* have the same definitions as before except apply to the option delivered if the initial option is exercised, and all other notation is as defined earlier. Thus

OV_NS_COMPOUND_OPTION(1150, "c", 40, 0.25, "p", 1200, 0.75, 0.03, 0.01, 0.15) = 41.6110

## LOOKBACK OPTIONS

Aside from compound options and options on the maximum and the minimum, many other exotic options trade in OTC markets. Some of the options are backward looking. A *lookback call option*, for example, provides its holder with settlement proceeds equal to the difference between the terminal asset price and the lowest asset price observed during the life of the option, as is shown in Figure 8.10. A *lookback put option* provides its holder with settlement proceeds equal to the difference between the highest asset price during the life of the option and

**FIGURE 8.10** Terminal payoff of lookback call option with a floating exercise price.

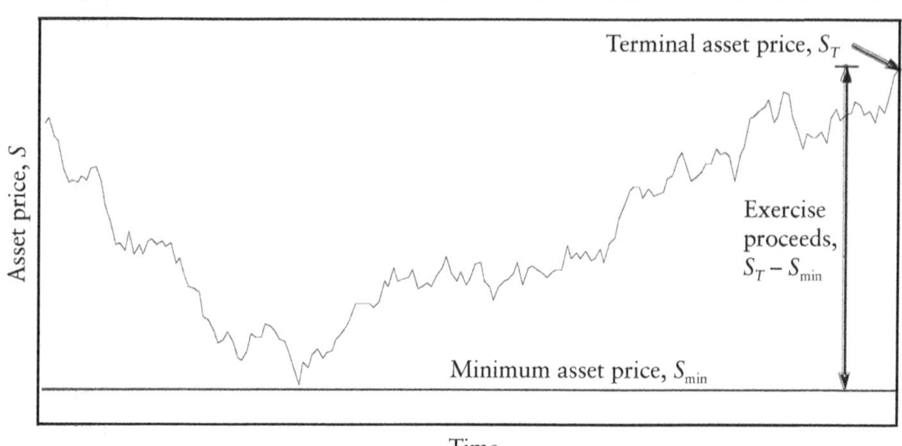


the terminal asset price.[14] It should come as no surprise, therefore, that these options are sometimes referred to as "no-regret options."

In a sense, lookback options are like American-style options because the option holder is guaranteed the most advantageous exercise price. Unlike American-style options, however, lookback options can be valued analytically using the BSM risk-neutral valuation mechanics. The reason for this is that it never pays to exercise a lookback option prior to expiration. Independent of how low the exercise price (asset price) has been set thus far during the call option's life, there is always some positive probability that it will fall further. For this reason, the call option holder will always defer early exercise in the hope of recognizing higher exercise proceeds in the future.

Under the assumptions of risk-neutral valuation and lognormally distributed future asset prices, the value of a lookback call may be written as

$$\begin{aligned} c_{\text{lookback}}(S, S_{\min}) &= Se^{-iT}N_1(d_1) - S_{\min}e^{-rT}N_1(d_2) \\ &\quad + \frac{S}{\lambda}\left[e^{-rT}\left(\frac{S}{S_{\min}}\right)^{-\lambda}N_1(d_3) - e^{-iT}N_1(-d_1)\right] \end{aligned} \tag{8.42}$$

where $S_{\min}$ is the current minimum asset price observed during the option's life,

[14] Many variations of lookback options exist. For a partial summary, see Haug (1998, pp. 61–69). The lookback options discussed in this section have a floating exercise price and were originally valued by Goldman, Sosin, and Gatto (1979). Other lookback options have a fixed exercise and have a terminal payoff equal to the difference between the maximum observed asset price during the option's life and the exercise price in the case of a call and the difference between the exercise price and the minimum observed asset price in the case of a put. These are valued in Conze and Viswanathan (1991).

$$\lambda = \frac{2(r-i)}{\sigma^2},\ d_1 = \frac{\ln(Se^{-iT}/S_{\min}e^{-rT}) + 0.5\sigma^2 T}{\sigma\sqrt{T}}$$

$$d_2 = d_1 - \sigma\sqrt{T}, \text{ and } d_3 = -d_1 + \frac{2(r-i)\sqrt{T}}{\sigma}$$

Note that the first two terms of the option are the value of a European-style call option whose exercise price is the current minimum value of the underlying asset. This is the least the lookback call can be worth since the asset price may fall below $X$, thereby driving the exercise price down further.

**ILLUSTRATION 8.12** Value lookback call.

*Compute the value at inception of a lookback call option that provides its holder with the right to buy the S&P 500 index at any time during the next three months. The S&P 500 index is currently at a level of 1,050, pays dividends at a constant rate of 1% annually, and has a volatility rate of 20%. The risk-free rate of interest is 3%.*

The value of the lookback call is therefore

$$\begin{aligned} c_{\text{lookback}}(1{,}050, 1{,}050) &= 1{,}050e^{-0.01(0.25)}N_1(d_1) - 1{,}050e^{-0.03(0.25)}N_1(d_2) \\ &\quad + \frac{1{,}050}{1.000}\left[e^{-0.03(0.25)}\left(\frac{1{,}050}{1{,}050}\right)^{-1.000}N_1(d_3)\right. \\ &\quad \left. - e^{-0.01(0.25)}N_1(-d_1)\right] \\ &= 84.871 \end{aligned}$$

where

$$\lambda = \frac{2(0.03-0.01)}{(0.20)^2} = 1.000,\ d_1 = \frac{\ln(1{,}050e^{-0.01(0.25)}/1{,}050e^{-0.03(0.25)})}{0.20\sqrt{0.25}} = 0.1000$$

$$d_2 = 0.1000 - 0.20\sqrt{0.25} = 0.0000, \text{ and}$$

$$d_3 = -0.1000 + \frac{2(0.03-0.01)\sqrt{0.25}}{0.20} = 0.0000$$

Note that the price of the lookback call is considerably higher than an at-the-money index call option. The value of a European-style call (i.e., the sum of the first two terms in the valuation equation) is only 44.327. The value of a lookback call option can be computed with the OPTVAL function

OV_NS_LOOKBACK_OPTION(*s, sm, t, r, i, v, cp*)

where *sm* is the current minimum asset price for a call (or current maximum price for a put), and the other notation is as defined as before. Thus

OV_NS_LOOKBACK_OPTION(1050, 1050, 0.25, 0.03, 0.01, 0.20, "c") = 84.430

The value of a lookback put option is

$$p_{LB} = Xe^{-rT}N_1(-d_2) - Se^{-iT}N_1(-d_1) + \frac{S}{\lambda}\left[e^{-iT}N_1(d_1) - e^{-rT}\left(\frac{S}{S_{\max}}\right)^{-\lambda}N_1(-d_3)\right] \quad (8.43)$$

where all notation is as defined for the lookback call except that $S_{\max}$, the current maximum asset price observed during the option's life, replaces $S_{\min}$ in the expression

$$d_1 = \frac{\ln(Se^{-iT}/S_{\max}e^{-rT}) + 0.5\sigma^2 T}{\sigma\sqrt{T}}$$

Note that a European-style put option is the lower bound for the price of the lookback put option. The third term is necessarily positive. Using the same parameters as in Illustration 8.12, the value of a lookback put option is 83.430, with the underlying standard European-style put being valued at 39.103.

Other backward-looking options are also traded. *Average price* or *Asian options* are based on the average (either arithmetic or geometric) asset price during the option's life. The average asset price may be used as the exercise price of the option, in which case the settlement value of the call will be the terminal asset price less the average price, or it may be used as the terminal asset price, in which case the settlement value will be the average price less the exercise price. Unfortunately, most traded Asian options do not have closed-form valuation equations, and valuation requires the use of numerical methods. Valuing options numerically is the focus of the next chapter.

## BARRIER OPTIONS

*Barrier options* are options that come into existence or terminate automatically when underlying asset price touches a prespecified level.[15] A *down-and-out call*, for example, is a call that expires if the asset price falls below a prespecified "out" barrier, $H$. At that time, the option buyer may receive a cash rebate, $R$. A *down-and-in call* is a call that comes into existence if the asset price falls below the "in" barrier, $H$, at any time during the option's life. For such options, the rebate is received if the option has not knocked in during its lifetime. Figure 8.11 shows a random price path of an asset over a 180-day. If the option has an exercise price of 100 and a barrier of 90, a down-and-out call would cease to exist and a down-and-in call would come into existence on day 39 when the asset price touches 90. Note that if we buy a down-and-out call and a down-and-in call with the same barrier price, $H$, exercise price, $X$, and time to expira-

[15] Double barrier options have an upper and lower barrier on the asset price. Their valuation is addressed in in Ikeda and Kunitoma (1992) and Geman and Yor (1996).

**FIGURE 8.11** Underlying asset price path for 180-day barrier option with an exercise price of 100 and a barrier of 90.

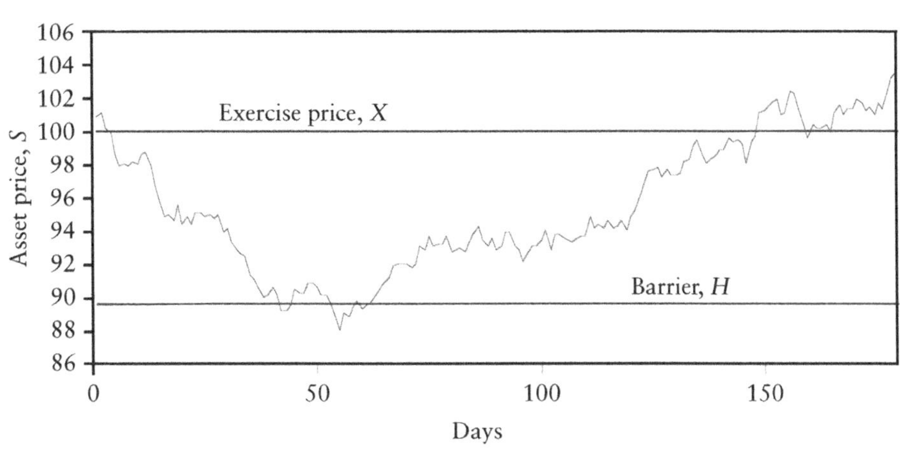


tion, $T$, and no rebate, the portfolio has the same payoff contingencies as a standard call option.

The valuation of barrier options is made tedious by the shear number of possible contract specifications.[16] For options with "out" barriers, there are both down-and-out calls and puts. While on face appearance, this would seem to indicate that the number of valuation equations is four. Unfortunately, the number is actually eight since there are two equations for each "out" option, depending on whether the barrier price, $H$, is above or below the exercise price, $X$. For options with "in" barriers, the same situation arises, so the total number of equations is 16. To make the presentation of these results as palatable as possible, we adopt the mechanics used in Rubinstein and Reiner (1991). Table 8.1 defines a number of expressions that are used in the valuation equations. Table 8.2 then assembles the valuation equation for each of the 16 different valuation problems.

To illustrate the mechanics, we will value a down-and-out call option whose barrier price, $H$, is less than the exercise price. As Table 8.2 shows, such an option has a value equal to the first equation in Table 8.1 less the third equation plus the sixth equation (i.e., [1] – [3] + [6]). Piecing things together, we get

$$\begin{aligned} c_{\text{do}} &= Se^{-iT}N(a_1) - Xe^{-rT}N(a_2) \\ &\quad - Se^{-iT}(H/S)^{2(\mu+1)}N(b_1) + Xe^{-rT}(H/S)^{2\mu}N(b_2) \\ &\quad + R[(H/S)^{\mu+\lambda}N(f_1) + (H/S)^{\mu-\lambda}N(f_2)] \end{aligned} \tag{8.44}$$

16 A number of authors have focused on barrier options. Merton (1973), for example, values a down-and-out call. Perhaps the most comprehensive treatment is in Rubinstein and Reiner (1991a). This section is based largely of their work. Haug (1998, pp. 65–85) provides valuation procedures for a variety of more complex barrier options.

**TABLE 8.1** Definitions required for valuing European-style barrier options. Option notation: $X$ is the exercise price, $T$ is the time to expiration, $H$ is the barrier level, and $R$ is the amount of the cash rebate. Asset notation: $S$ is the asset price, $i$ is the asset's income rate, and $\sigma$ is the asset's return volatility rate. Other notation: $r$ is the risk-free rate of interest.

$$[1] \equiv \phi S e^{-iT} N(\phi a_1) - \phi X e^{-rT} N(\phi a_2)$$

$$[2] \equiv \phi S e^{-iT} N(\phi b_1) - \phi X e^{-rT} N(\phi b_2)$$

$$[3] \equiv \phi S e^{-iT} (H/S)^{2(\mu+1)} N(\eta c_1) - \phi X e^{-rT} (H/S)^{2\mu} N(\eta c_2)$$

$$[4] \equiv \phi S e^{-iT} (H/S)^{2(\mu+1)} N(\eta d_1) - \phi X e^{-rT} (H/S)^{2\mu} N(\eta d_2)$$

$$[5] \equiv e^{-rT} R[N(\eta b_2) - (H/S)^{2\mu} N(\eta d_2)]$$

$$[6] \equiv R[(H/S)^{\mu+\lambda} N(\eta f_1) + (H/S)^{\mu-\lambda} N(\eta f_2)]$$

where

$$a_1 = \frac{\ln(S/X)}{\sigma\sqrt{T}} + (1+\mu)\sigma\sqrt{T},\ a_2 = a_1 - \sigma\sqrt{T}$$

$$b_1 = \frac{\ln(S/H)}{\sigma\sqrt{T}} + (1+\mu)\sigma\sqrt{T},\ b_2 = b_1 - \sigma\sqrt{T}$$

$$c_1 = \frac{\ln(H^2/SX)}{\sigma\sqrt{T}} + (1+\mu)\sigma\sqrt{T},\ c_2 = c_1 - \sigma\sqrt{T}$$

$$d_1 = \frac{\ln(H/S)}{\sigma\sqrt{T}} + (1+\mu)\sigma\sqrt{T},\ d_2 = d_1 - \sigma\sqrt{T}$$

$$f_1 = \frac{\ln(H/S)}{\sigma\sqrt{T}} + \lambda\sigma\sqrt{T},\ f_2 = f_1 - 2\lambda\sigma\sqrt{T}$$

$$\mu = \frac{r - i - \sigma^2/2}{\sigma^2},\ \lambda = \sqrt{\mu^2 + \frac{2r}{\sigma^2}}$$

where $H$ is the barrier asset price below which the call option life ends,

$$a_1 = \frac{\ln(S/X)}{\sigma\sqrt{T}} + (1+\mu)\sigma\sqrt{T},\ a_2 = a_1 - \sigma\sqrt{T}$$

$$c_1 = \frac{\ln(H^2/SX)}{\sigma\sqrt{T}} + (1+\mu)\sigma\sqrt{T},\ c_2 = c_1 - \sigma\sqrt{T}$$

**TABLE 8.2** Equations for valuing European-style barrier options. Option notation: $X$ is the exercise price, $T$ is the time to expiration, $H$ is the barrier level, and $R$ is the amount of the cash rebate. Asset notation: $S$ is the asset price.

| Description | Condition | Payoff | Valuation equation | Parameters $h$ | Parameters $f$ |
|---|---|---|---|---|---|
| Down-and-out call | $S > H$ | $\max(S - X, 0)$ if $S > H$ before $T$ else $R$ at hit | If $X > H$, [1] − [3] + [6] | 1 | 1 |
| | | | If $X < H$, [2] − [4] + [6] | 1 | 1 |
| Up-and-out call | $S < H$ | $\max(S - X, 0)$ if $S < H$ before $T$ else $R$ at hit | If $X > H$, [6] | −1 | 1 |
| | | | If $X < H$, [1] − [2] + [3] − [4] + [6] | −1 | 1 |
| Down-and-out put | $S > H$ | $\max(X - S, 0)$ if $S > H$ before $T$ else $R$ at hit | If $X > H$, [1] − [2] + [3] − [4] + [6] | 1 | −1 |
| | | | If $X < H$, [6] | 1 | −1 |
| Up-and-out put | $S < H$ | $\max(X - S, 0)$ if $S < H$ before $T$ else $R$ at hit | If $X > H$, [2] − [4] + [6] | −1 | −1 |
| | | | If $X < H$, [1] − [3] + [6] | −1 | −1 |
| Down-and-in call | $S > H$ | $\max(S - X, 0)$ if $S < H$ before $T$ else $R$ at expiry | If $X > H$, [3] + [5] | 1 | 1 |
| | | | If $X < H$, [1] − [2] + [4] + [5] | 1 | 1 |
| Up-and-in call | $S < H$ | $\max(S - X, 0)$ if $S > H$ before $T$ else $R$ at expiry | If $X > H$, [1] + [5] | −1 | 1 |
| | | | If $X < H$, [2] − [3] + [4] + [5] | −1 | 1 |
| Down-and-in put | $S > H$ | $\max(X - S, 0)$ if $S < H$ before $T$ else $R$ at expiry | If $X > H$, [2] − [3] + [4] + [5] | 1 | −1 |
| | | | If $X < H$, [1] + [5] | 1 | −1 |
| Up-and-in put | $S < H$ | $\max(X - S, 0)$ if $S > H$ before $T$ else $R$ at expiry | If $X > H$, [1] − [2] + [4] + [5] | −1 | −1 |
| | | | If $X < H$, [3] + [5] | −1 | −1 |

$$f_1 = \frac{\ln(H/S)}{\sigma\sqrt{T}} + \lambda\sigma\sqrt{T},\ f_2 = f_1 - 2\lambda\sigma\sqrt{T}$$

$$\text{and } \mu = \frac{r - i - 0.5\sigma^2}{\sigma^2}$$

Note that the sum of the first two terms on the right-hand side, (i.e., [1]), is a standard European-style call option. The value of the standard call is deflated then due to the fact that the option expires automatically when the barrier is touched (i.e., [3]). The last term reflects the potential of receiving a cash rebate (i.e., [6]).

**ILLUSTRATION 8.13** Value down-and-out call.

*Consider a down-and-out call option with an exercise price of 100, a barrier of 90, no rebate, and a time to expiration of six months. The option's underlying stock has a price of 100, a dividend yield rate of 2%, and a volatility rate of 35%. Compute the value of the down-and-out call assuming the risk-free interest rate is 4%.*

From Table 8.2, we know the value of the down-and-out call with no rebate is [1] – [3] and can be written

$$\begin{aligned} c_{do} &= 100e^{-0.02(0.5)}N(a_1) - 100e^{-0.04(0.5)}N(a_1 - 0.35\sqrt{0.5}) \\ &\quad - 100e^{-0.02(0.5)}(90/100)^{2(\mu+1)}N(b_1) \\ &\quad + 100e^{-0.04(0.5)}(90/100)^{2\mu}N(b_1 - 0.35\sqrt{0.5}) \\ &= 7.4378 \end{aligned}$$

where

$$a_1 = \frac{\ln(100/100)}{0.35\sqrt{0.5}} + (1 - 0.3367)0.35\sqrt{0.5} = 0.1641,$$

$$a_2 = 0.1641 - 0.35\sqrt{0.5} = -0.0833$$

$$c_1 = \frac{\ln(90^2/(100 \times 100))}{0.35\sqrt{0.5}} + (1 - 0.3367)0.35\sqrt{0.5} = -0.6873$$

$$c_2 = -0.6873 - 0.35\sqrt{0.5} = -0.9348$$

$$\text{and } \mu = \frac{0.04 - 0.02 - 0.5(0.35^2)}{0.35^2} = -0.3367$$

This value can be verified using the OPTVAL function,

OV_NS_BARRIER_OPTION(*s*, *x*, *h*, *t*, *rebate*, *r*, *i*, *v*, *TypeFlag*)

where *s* is the asset price, *x* is the exercise price, *h* is the barrier level, *t* is the time to expiration, *r* is the risk-free rate of interest, *i* is the income rate, and *v* is the volatility rate. The *TypeFlag* consists of three contiguous lower case letters. The first is a (c)all/(p)ut indicator, the second is a (d)own/(u) indicator, and the third is a (i)n/(o)ut indicator. For a down-and-out call, *TypeFlag* is "cdo." Hence, the value of a down-and-out call is

OV_NS_BARRIER_OPTION(100, 100, 90, 0.5, 0, 0.04, 0.02, 0.35, "cdo") = 7.4378

Hence, the value of a down-and-in call is

OV_NS_BARRIER_OPTION(100, 100, 90, 0.5, 0, 0.04, 0.02, 0.35, "cdi") = 2.7643

The sum of the values of the down-and-out call and the down-and-in call (with no rebate) equals the value of a standard European-style call option, that is,

OV_OPTION_VALUE (100, 100, 0.5, 0.04, 0.02, 0.35, "c", "e") = 10.2021

## SUMMARY

This chapter focuses on the valuation of some nonstandard option contracts traded in the OTC market. One characteristic shared by all of these options are that they are valued under the BSM risk-neutral, lognormal asset price distribution framework. Another is that they have analytical valuation equations. As such, the options included in this chapter are European-style. (The valuation of American-style nonstandard options requires the use of numerical methods, which is the focus of the next chapter.) Interestingly, most of the options can be valued using valuation-by-replication and the valuation results derived in Chapter 5. The options valued in this chapter include:

- All-or-nothing options
- Gap options
- Contingent pay options
- Forward-start options
- Ratchet options
- Chooser options
- Exchange options
- Options on the maximum and the minimum
- Compound options
- Lookback options
- Barrier options

While this list seems to cover a wide range of nonstandard option contracts, do not be misled—we have only discussed eleven of a countless number of option contract designs that exist in the OTC markets. Others will be discussed as the chapters progress in the chapters that follow. Whether an option is valued analytically or numerically is of no consequence to risk measurement. The risk characteristics of options can be measured numerically with a high degree of accuracy.

## REFERENCES AND SUGGESTED READINGS

Abramowitz, Milton, and Irene A. Stegum. 1972. *Handbook of Mathematical Functions*, 10th ed. Washington, DC: National Bureau of Standards.

Black, Fischer, and Myron Scholes. 1973. The pricing of options and corporate liabilities. *Journal of Political Economy* 81: 637–659.

Conze, A., and R. Viswanathan. 1991. Path dependent options: The case of lookback options. *Journal of Finance* 46: 1893–1907.

Drezner, Z. 1978. Computation of the bivariate normal integral. *Mathematics of Computation* 32: 277–279.

Geman, H., and M. Yor. 1996. Pricing and hedging double barrier options. *Mathematical Finance* 6: 365–378.

Geske, Robert. 1979. The valuation of compound options. *Journal of Financial Economics* 7: 63–81.

Goldman, B., H. Sosin, and M. A. Gatto. 1979. Path dependent options: Buy at the low, sell at the high. *Journal of Finance* 34 (December): 1111–1127.

Haug, Espen Gaarder. 1998. *The Complete Guide to Option Pricing Formulas*. New York: McGraw-Hill.

Ikeda, M., and N. Kunitomo. 1992. Pricing options with curved boundaries. *Mathematical Finance* 2: 275–298.

Johnson, Herbert E. 1987. Options on the minimum and maximum of several assets. *Journal of Financial and Quantitative Analysis* 22 (September): 277–283.

Margrabe, William. 1978. The value of an option to exchange one asset for another. *Journal of Finance* 33 (March): 177–186.

Margrabe, William. 1982. A theory of the price of a contingent claim on N asset prices. Working paper 8210 (September 1982), School of Government and Business Administration, George Washington University.

Merton, Robert C. 1973. Theory of rational option pricing. *Bell Journal of Economics and Management Science*: 141–183.

Rubinstein, Mark. 1991a. Pay now, choose later. *RISK* 4 (February): 13.

Rubinstein, Mark. 1991b. Options for the undecided. *RISK* 4 (April): 43.

Rubinstein, Mark, and Eric Reiner. 1991a. Breaking down the barriers. *RISK* 4 (September): 31–35.

Rubinstein, Mark, and Eric Reiner. 1991b. Unscrambling the binary code. *RISK* 4 (October): 75–83.

Stulz, Rene. 1982. Options on the minimum or maximum of two assets. *Journal of Financial Economics* 10: 161–185.


## APPENDIX 8A: APPROXIMATION OF THE BIVARIATE NORMAL PROBABILITY

The joint probability that $x$ is less than $a$ and $y$ is less than $b$ is

$$\begin{aligned}\Pr(x \le a, y < b) &= \frac{1}{2\pi\sqrt{1-\rho^2}} \int_{-\infty}^{a}\int_{-\infty}^{b} \exp\left[-\frac{x^2 - 2\rho xy + y^2}{2(1-\rho^2)}\right] dx\,dy \\ &= N_2(a, b, \rho)\end{aligned}$$

where $x$ and $y$ are random variables with unit normal distributions (i.e., mean 0 and variance 1) with correlation, $\rho$. The approximation method provided here relies on Gaussian quadratures,[17] and has a maximum absolute error of 0.00000055.

First, program a routine that evaluates the term $\phi(a,b;\rho)$.

$$\phi(a, b;\rho) \approx 0.31830989\sqrt{1-\rho^2}\sum_{i=1}^{5}\sum_{j=1}^{5} w_i w_j f(x_i, x_j)$$

where

$$f(x_i, x_j) = \exp[a_1(2x_i - a_1) + b_1(2x_j - b_1) + 2\rho(x_i - a_1)(x_j - b_1)]$$

the pairs of weights ($w$) and the corresponding abscissa values ($x$) are:

| *i,j* | $w$ | $x$ |
|---|---|---|
| 1 | 0.24840615 | 0.10024215 |
| 2 | 0.39233107 | 0.48281397 |
| 3 | 0.21141819 | 1.0609498 |
| 4 | 0.03324666 | 1.7797294 |
| 5 | 0.000824853 | 2.6697604 |

and the coefficients are computed using

$$a_1 = \frac{a}{\sqrt{2(1-\rho^2)}} \quad \text{and} \quad b_1 = \frac{b}{\sqrt{2(1-\rho^2)}}$$

Next, compute the product, $ab\rho = a \times b \times \rho$. If $ab\rho \leq 0$, compute the bivariate normal probability by applying one of the following rules:

| If | | | Then |
|---|---|---|---|
| $a \leq 0$ | $b \leq 0$ | $\rho \leq 0$ | $N_2(a,b;\rho) = \phi(a,b;\rho)$ |
| $a \leq 0$ | $b \geq 0$ | $\rho \geq 0$ | $N_2(a,b;\rho) = N_1(a) - \phi(a,-b;-\rho)$ |
| $a \geq 0$ | $b \leq 0$ | $\rho \geq 0$ | $N_2(a,b;\rho) = N_1(b) - \phi(-a,b;\rho)$ |
| $a \geq 0$ | $b \geq 0$ | $\rho \leq 0$ | $N_2(a,b;\rho) = N_1(a) + N_1(b) - 1 + \phi(-a,-b;\rho)$ |

where $N_1(d)$ is the cumulative univariate normal probability. (Recall that Appendix 7C in the previous chapter contains the approximation algorithm for the cumulative univariate normal probability $N_1(d)$. It is also available as the function OV_PROB_PRUN($a$) in the OPTVAL Function Library.) If $ab\rho > 0$, compute the bivariate normal probability as

$$N_2(a, b;\rho) = N_2(a, 0;\rho_{ab}) + N_2(b, 0;\rho_{ba}) - \delta$$

where the values of $N_2(\cdot)$ on the right-hand side are computed using the rules for $ab\rho \leq 0$,

[17] The Gaussian quadrature method for approximating the bivariate normal probability is from Drezner (1978).

$$\rho_{ab} = \frac{(\rho a - b)\text{Sgn}(a)}{\sqrt{a^2 - 2\rho ab + b^2}}, \quad \rho_{ba} = \frac{(\rho b - a)\text{Sgn}(b)}{\sqrt{a^2 - 2\rho ab + b^2}}$$

$$\delta = \frac{1 - \text{Sgn}(a) \times \text{Sgn}(b)}{4}, \text{ and}$$

$$\text{Sgn}(x) = \begin{cases} 1 & \text{if } x \geq 0 \\ -1 & \text{if } x < 0 \end{cases}$$

Applying this procedure provides the following probabilities:

| $a$ | $b$ | $\rho$ | $N_2(a,b;\rho)$ |
|---|---|---|---|
| –1 | –1 | –0.5 | 0.00378 |
| –1 | 1 | –0.5 | 0.09614 |
| 1 | –1 | –0.5 | 0.09614 |
| 1 | 1 | –0.5 | 0.68647 |
| –1 | –1 | 0.5 | 0.06251 |
| –1 | 1 | 0.5 | 0.15487 |
| 1 | –1 | 0.5 | 0.15487 |
| 1 | 1 | 0.5 | 0.74520 |
| 0 | 0 | 0.5 | 0.33333 |
| 0 | 0 | 0 | 0.25000 |
| 0 | 0 | –0.5 | 0.16667 |

To check these values, you may use OV_PROB_PRBN from the OPTVAL Function Library.

# 9

# Valuing Options Numerically

The last two chapters focused on valuing options analytically. Analytical valuation equations were possible because, in general, the options were European-style with only one exercise opportunity. For other types of options, the valuation problem is not so simple. With American-style options, for example, there are an infinite number of early exercise opportunities between now and the expiration date, and the decision to exercise early depends on a number of factors including all subsequent exercise opportunities. An analytical solution for the American-style option valuation problem (i.e., a valuation equation) has not been found.[1] The same is true for many Asian-style options (e.g., options written on an arithmetic average) and many European-style options with multiple sources of underlying price risk (e.g., spread options). In such cases, options must be valued numerically. Moreover, even in instances where analytical solutions to option contract values are possible (e.g., accrual options), numerical methods are often easier to apply.

The purpose of this chapter is to discuss numerical methods for valuing options. All of them are developed within the Black-Scholes/Merton (BSM) option valuation framework. The underlying asset's price is assumed to follow a geometric Brownian motion (i.e., to be log-normally distributed at any future instant in time), and a risk-free hedge between the option and its underlying asset(s) is possible. Three of the methods involve replacing the continuous Brownian diffusion with a process that involves discrete jumps. The *binomial method,* for example, assumes that the asset price moves to one of two levels over the next increment in time. The size of the move and its likelihood are chosen in a manner so as to be consistent with the log-normal asset price distribution. In a similar fashion, the *trinomial method,* described in the second section, allows the asset price to move to one of three levels over the next increment in time. The third section describes a *Monte Carlo simulation* technique, which uses a discretized version of geometric Brownian motion to enumerate every possible path that the asset's price may take over the life of the option. The *quadratic approximation method*, discussed in the fourth section, addresses the value of early exercise by modifying the BSM partial differential equation.[2] As important

[1] The exception is American-style call options on assets with zero or negative income rates.

as valuation, however, is risk measurement. The fifth section of the chapter describes how to compute the risk characteristics (i.e., the Greeks) of options using numerical methods. Finally, the sixth section contains a brief summary.

## BINOMIAL METHOD

The binomial method is the most popular approximation for valuing American-style options. It is easy to implement and flexible enough to handle a wide range of option valuation problems. Under the binomial method, the option's life is divided into fixed-length time steps, and, in each time step, the asset price is allowed to jump up or down. Defining $n$ as the number of time steps, each time increment has length $\Delta t = T/n$, where $T$ is the time remaining to expiration of the option.

The binomial distribution is characterized by the size of its price steps and their probabilities. We must choose the parameters in such a way that the mean and the variance of the discrete binomial distribution are consistent with the mean and the variance of the continuous log-normal distribution underlying the BSM model. To make matters simple as possible, we will focus on the logarithm of the asset price at the end of the time increment $\Delta t$, which, under the BSM assumptions is normally distributed with mean $\ln S + \mu\Delta t$ and variance $\sigma^2\Delta t$. First, we set the mean of the binomial distribution equal to the mean of the logarithm of asset price distribution, that is,

$$p(\ln S + v) + (1-p)(\ln S + w) = \ln S + \mu\Delta t \tag{9.1}$$

In (9.1), $p$ is the probability that the logarithm of asset price changes by $v$, and $1-p$ is the probability that the logarithm of asset price changes by $w$. Note that we have made no assumption yet regarding the sizes of $v$ and $w$, although we will do so shortly. The ln $S$ terms fall out of (9.1), and we are left with the mean constraint,

$$pv + (1-p)w = \mu\Delta t \tag{9.2}$$

Next we set the variance of the binomial distribution equal to the variance of the logarithm of asset price distribution, that is,

$$p(\ln S + v - (\ln S + \mu\Delta t))^2 + (1-p)(\ln S + w - (\ln S + \mu\Delta t))^2 = \sigma^2\Delta t \tag{9.3}$$

The ln$S$ terms are again irrelevant, and, with a little additional algebra, equation (9.3) becomes the variance constraint,

$$pv^2 + (1-p)w^2 = \sigma^2\Delta t + \mu^2\Delta t^2 \tag{9.4a}$$

Equation (9.4a) is a little unusual in the sense that it has a term that includes the time increment squared, $\Delta t^2$. In applying the binomial method to value options,

[2] Recall Appendix 7D in Chapter 7.

however, a large number of time steps is usually used, so $\Delta t$ is very small and terms with higher order values of $\Delta t$ can safely be ignored. Ignoring the higher order term, the variance constraint is

$$pv^2 + (1 - p)w^2 = \sigma^2 \Delta t \tag{9.4b}$$

Note that the terms on the right-hand side of (9.2) and (9.4), $\mu$ and $\sigma^2$, are known parameters of the normal distribution of the logarithm of asset prices. Our objective is to find the values of $v$, $w$, and $p$ that make the mean and variance of the binomial distribution consistent with the mean and the variance of the normal distribution of the logarithm of asset prices. With two equations (i.e., (9.2) and either (9.4a) or (9.4b)) and three unknowns, we cannot solve for the parameters $v$, $w$, and $p$ uniquely, so another constraint must be imposed. Below, we discuss the constraints used in two well-known implementations of the binomial method.

### Cox-Ross-Rubinstein (1979) Parameters

Cox, Ross and Rubinstein (1979) (hereafter CRR) impose the symmetry constraint, $w = -v$, where $v$ is a positive increment. This implies that, over the next increment in time $\Delta t$, the asset price will either rise to level, $\ln S + v$, or fall to level, $\ln S - v$. CRR use (9.4b) to tie the variance of the binomial distribution to the variance of the logarithm of asset prices. The value of $v$ that satisfies (9.4b) is

$$v = \sigma\sqrt{\Delta t} \tag{9.5}$$

With $v$ and $w$ known, we turn to finding the level of probability, $p$. Substituting (9.5) into the mean condition (9.2) and rearranging to isolate $p$, the probability of an up-step is

$$p = \frac{1}{2} + \frac{1}{2}\left(\frac{\mu}{\sigma}\right)\sqrt{\Delta t} \tag{9.6}$$

As in Chapter 7, we adopt the practice of using the continuously compounded mean rate of price appreciation, $\alpha$, rather than the mean continuously compounded rate, $\mu$. Substituting $\mu = \alpha - 0.5\sigma^2$ into (9.6), we get

$$p = \frac{1}{2} + \frac{1}{2}\left(\frac{\alpha - 0.5\sigma^2}{\sigma}\right)\sqrt{\Delta t} \tag{9.7}$$

Also recall that under the BSM option valuation framework, a risk-free hedge can be formed between the option and its underlying asset. This implies that option valuation is not sensitive to the risk preferences of an individual, so in the interest of mathematical tractability, we assume risk-neutrality, in which case the continuously compounded mean rate of price appreciation, $\alpha$, becomes the asset's cost of carry rate (i.e., $\alpha = b$) and the probability of an up-step is

$$p = \frac{1}{2} + \frac{1}{2}\left(\frac{b - 0.5\sigma^2}{\sigma}\right)\sqrt{\Delta t} \tag{9.8}$$

### Jarrow-Rudd (1983) Parameters

In another well-known implementation of the binomial method, Jarrow and Rudd (1983) (hereafter JR) impose the constraint that the up-step and down-step probabilities are both equal to $p = 1/2$. This means that the constraint that matches the mean of the binomial distribution with the mean of the change in the logarithm of prices (9.2) may be written

$$v + w = 2\mu\Delta t \tag{9.9}$$

To express the variance constraint, JR use (9.4a). With $p = 1/2$, the variance constraint can be rewritten as

$$v^2 + w^2 = 2\sigma^2\Delta t + \frac{1}{2}(4\mu^2\Delta t^2) \tag{9.10}$$

Substituting the square of (9.9) into the parentheses on the right-hand side of (9.10), rearranging, factoring, taking the square root and then simplifying, we get

$$v - w = 2\sigma\sqrt{\Delta t} \tag{9.11}$$

Equations (9.9) and (9.11) can now be used to identify $u$ and $v$. With the probability set equal to 1/2, the up-step coefficient is

$$v = \mu\Delta t + \sigma\sqrt{\Delta t} = (b - 0.5\sigma^2)\Delta t + \sigma\sqrt{\Delta t} \tag{9.12a}$$

and the down-step coefficient is

$$w = \mu\Delta t - \sigma\sqrt{\Delta t} = (b - 0.5\sigma^2)\Delta t - \sigma\sqrt{\Delta t} \tag{9.12b}$$

In going from the middle term to the last term in (9.12a) and (9.12b), we are, of course, invoking an assumption of risk-neutrality.

### Applying the Binomial Method

With the binomial distribution parameters now defined, we turn to applying the model. Applying the binomial method has three steps. To illustrate each step, we value a two-year American-style put option with an exercise price of 55. The'umed to be a foreign currency (FX rate) whose current price is 50 and whose volatility rate is 20%. The domestic rate of interest is assumed to be 5%, and the foreign rate of interest, 2%. The expected risk-neutral rate of price appreciation of the currency is therefore 3%. We apply the binomial method first using the CRR parameters and then, in the interest of comparison, using the JR parameters.

**Step 1: Create the Asset Price Lattice** The first step in the binomial method is to use the computed parameters of the binomial process to trace out every conceivable path that the asset price may take between now and the option's expiration. Thus far we have focused on movements in the logarithm of asset price. To generate a lattice for $\ln S$, we must set the number of time steps, $n$. The greater the number of time steps, the higher the accuracy of the approximation, but the higher the computational cost. The time increment is $\Delta t = T/n$, where $T$ is the time to expiration of the option. We set the number of time steps in our illustration to 2. The time increment $\Delta t$ is therefore one year.

Figure 9.1 shows the possible paths that the logarithm of asset price may take during the option's life. Four paths are possible: (1) up, up, (2) up, down, (3) down, up, and (4) down, down. Note that if the asset price goes up in the first year and down in the second (or vice versa), the logarithm of asset price is back where it started. This is the symmetry condition imposed by CRR. The size of the jump in the logarithm of asset price from period to period, $v$, is given by (9.5). From the problem information, we can compute the price increment, $v = 0.20\sqrt{1} = 0.20$. The logarithm of the current asset price is $\ln 50 = 3.912$. Applying the price increment to identify the values of the nodes of the lattice in year 1 and year 2, we can trace out all of the possible movements of the logarithm of asset prices over the life of the option. These movements are shown in Figure 9.2.

**FIGURE 9.1** Two-period lattice showing the logarithm of asset price at different times during the option's life.

| Year | 0 | 1 | 2 |
|---|---|---|---|
| | | | $\ln S + 2v$ |
| | | $\ln S + v$ | |
| | $\ln S$ | | $\ln S$ |
| | | $\ln S - v$ | |
| | | | $\ln S - 2v$ |

**FIGURE 9.2** Two-period lattice showing numerical values for the logarithm of asset price at different times during the option's life.

| Time | 0 | 1 | 2 |
|---|---|---|---|
| | | | 4.312 |
| | | 4.112 | |
| | 3.912 | | 3.912 |
| | | 3.712 | |
| | | | 3.512 |

**FIGURE 9.3** Two-period lattice showing the asset price at different times during the option's life.

| Year | 0 | 1 | 2 |
|---|---|---|---|
| | | | $uuS$ |
| | | $uS$ | |
| | $S$ | | $S$ |
| | | $dS$ | |
| | | | $ddS$ |

In general, individuals who apply the binomial method prefer to see the lattice expressed in asset price rather than the logarithm of asset price. To create such a lattice, we can raise the logarithm of the asset price shown in Figure 9.2 to the power of $e$. Alternatively, we can redefine the problem from one which uses absolute price changes to one which uses relative price changes. To do so, recognize that an additive jump of $v$ in the logarithm of asset price $S$, (i.e., $\ln S + v$), is equivalent to a multiplicative jump of $u$ in the asset price $S$, (i.e., $Su$), where

$$u = e^{v} = e^{\sigma\sqrt{\Delta t}}$$

and an additive jump of $-v$ in the logarithm of asset price $S$, (i.e., $\ln S - v$), is equivalent to a multiplicative jump of $d$ in the asset price $S$ (i.e., $Sd$), where $d = e^{-v} = 1/u$. Like before, successive up and down steps return the asset to its original price, as shown in Figure 9.3. At the end of one year, the possible asset prices are $uS$ and $dS$. At the end of year 2, the possibilities are that the asset price moves from $uS$ to $uuS$ or $S$ and from $dS$ to $S$ or $ddS$. In this two-period problem, all possible paths that the asset price may follow between and the option's expiration are shown in Figure 9.3. Since the volatility rate is 20% and the time increment is one year, the values of $u$ and $d$ are

$$u = e^{0.20\sqrt{1}} = 1.2214 \quad \text{and} \quad d = \frac{1}{u} = \frac{1}{1.2214} = 0.8187$$

Applying these coefficients to the current asset price of 50 produces Figure 9.4, and computing the numerical values in each cell of Figure 9.4 produces Figure 9.5. Note that the node values in Figure 9.5 are simply the values in Figure 9.2 raised to the power of $e$.

**Step 2: Value Option at Expiration** With all of the asset price nodes at the option's expiration computed, we turn to valuing the option. At this stage of the numerical procedure, the only option values that we can compute are those on the expiration date. The value of the option at expiration equals the maximum of its exercisable value and 0. The terminal values of the put in our illustration are shown in boldface in Figure 9.6.

**FIGURE 9.4** Two-period lattice showing numerical values for the asset price at different times during the option's life.

| Time | 0 | 1 | 2 |
|---|---|---|---|
| | | | 1.22142(50) |
| | | 1.2214(50) | |
| | 50 | | 1.2214(0.8187)50 |
| | | 0.8187(50) | |
| | | | 0.81872(50) |

**FIGURE 9.5** Two-period lattice showing numerical values for the asset price using the Cox-Ross-Rubinstein parameters.

| Time | 0 | 1 | 2 |
|---|---|---|---|
| | | | 74.59 |
| | | 61.07 | |
| | 50 | | 50.00 |
| | | 40.94 | |
| | | | 33.52 |

**FIGURE 9.6** Two-period lattice showing the terminal values of put option written on asset using the Cox-Ross-Rubinstein parameters.

| Time | 0 | 1 | | 2 |
|---|---|---|---|---|
| | | | max(0,55 – 74.59) = | 0.00<br>74.59 |
| | | 61.07 | | |
| | | | max(0,55 – 50) = | 5.00<br>50.00 |
| | 50 | | | |
| | | 40.94 | | |
| | | | max(0,55 – 33.52) = | 21.48<br>33.52 |

**Step 3: Value Option at Earlier Nodes by Taking the Present Value of the Expected Future Value** The next step is to value the option at earlier nodes. This is done recursively move one step back in time and valuing the option at each vertical node by taking the present value of the expected future value of the option based on the two nodes lying immediately to its right. This means that, in order to identify the value of the option at the upper node in year 1 of Figure 9.6, we need to know the probability that the asset price will move from 61.07 to 74.59 and the probability that the asset price will move from 61.07 to 50.

The expression used for computing the probability of an up-step in the CRR procedure is (9.8). Evaluating the probability,[3] we get

$$p = \frac{1}{2}+\frac{1}{2}\left(\frac{0.03-0.5(0.20^2)}{0.20}\right)\sqrt{1} = 0.525$$

The probability of a down-step in asset price is the complement of the probability of an up-step, that is, 1 – 0.525 = 0.475.

With the probabilities in hand, we can compute the expected future value of the put conditional upon being in year 1 with an asset price level 61.09. The *expected future value* (EFV) is

$$EFV = 0.525(0) + 0.475(5) = 2.375$$

Under risk-neutrality, the *present value of the expected future value* (PVEFV) is

$$PVEFV = e^{-r\Delta t}(2.375) = e^{-0.05(1)}(2.375) = 2.26$$

Thus we have identified the value of the put in year 1 conditional upon the asset price being 61.07, as shown in Figure 9.9. The year 1 value of the put conditional upon the asset price being 40.94 is obtained using the same procedure and equals 12.20. Taking the present value of the expected future value in year 0 reveals that the current value of the put is 6.64.

The computations supporting the option values shown in Figure 9.7 indicate that the current value of the put is 6.64. But what is the style of the put option we have valued? The answer is European-style. In computing the current value, we did not account for the prospect of early exercise. In applying the binomial method to value American-style options, we must check whether the put should have been exercised early at the beginning and any of the intermediate nodes of the lattice.

**FIGURE 9.7** Current and intermediate values of European-style put option written on asset using the Cox-Ross-Rubinstein parameters.

| Time | 0 | 1 | 2 |
|---|---|---|---|
| | | | 0.00<br>74.59 |
| | | 2.26<br>61.07 | |
| | 6.64<br>50.00 | | 5.00<br>50.00 |
| | | 12.20<br>40.94 | |
| | | | 21.48<br>33.52 |

[3] Occasionally, the probability for the CRR method is approximated using $p = (e^{b\Delta t} - t)/(u - d)$. We refer to this practice as the *simple method*.

**Step 3a: Check for Optimal Early Exercise** In our two-period illustration, the only opportunities for early exercise occur in year 0 and year 1. The early exercise checks are made, starting in year 1, each time a new present value is computed. Consider the year 1 node in which the asset price is 61.07. The present value of the expected future value is 2.26 and represents the value of the option if left alive. The early exercise proceeds at this node are max(0,55 – 61.07) = max(0,–6.07) = 0. Clearly the put is worth more alive than dead. Now, consider the year 1 node where the asset price is 40.94. The put if left alive is 12.20, while the early exercise proceeds are max(0,55 – 40.94) = 14.06. Obviously, we are better off exercising. At such nodes, we replace the value of the option left alive with the early exercise proceeds. Applying this procedure each time a present value in computed in year 1, and then again in year 0, we find that the current value of the American-style put option is 7.48. The American-style put option values at each node are shown in Figure 9.8. Note that the European-style put option value in Figure 9.7 is 6.64, and the American-style option value in Figure 9.8 is 7.48. The value of the privilege of being able to exercise this option early (i.e., the *early exercise premium*) appears to be about 84 cents.

We now use the JR parameters to determine the value of the put and isolate any differences. The up-step and down-step coefficients are given by (9.12a) and (9.12b). Substituting the problem information and raising the values to the exponent of $e$, we get the up-step and down-step coefficients of the asset price, that is,

$$u = e^v = e^{(b - 0.5\sigma^2)\Delta t + \sigma\sqrt{\Delta t}} = e^{(0.03 - 0.5(0.20^2))1 + 0.20\sqrt{1}} = 1.2337$$

and

$$d = e^w = e^{(b - 0.5\sigma^2)\Delta t - \sigma\sqrt{\Delta t}} = e^{(0.03 - 0.5(0.20^2))1 - 0.20\sqrt{1}} = 0.8270$$

**FIGURE 9.8** Valuing an American-style put option using the Cox-Ross-Rubinstein parameters.

| Time | 0 | 1 | 2 |
|---|---|---|---|
| | | | 0.00 |
| | | | 74.59 |
| | | 2.26 | |
| | | 61.07 | |
| | 7.48 | | 5.00 |
| | 50.00 | | 50.00 |
| | | 14.06 | |
| | | 40.94 | |
| | | | 21.48 |
| | | | 33.52 |

**FIGURE 9.9** Valuing an American-style put option using the Jarrow-Rudd parameters.

| Year | 0 | 1 | 2 |
|---|---|---|---|
| | | | 0.00<br>76.10 |
| | | 1.90<br>61.68 | |
| | 7.40<br>50.00 | | 3.99<br>51.01 |
| | | 13.65<br>41.35 | |
| | | | 20.81<br>34.19 |

Applying these coefficients to the current price of 50 generates the asset price lattice shown in Figure 9.9. Note that when the asset has an up-step followed by a down-step, it does not return to its original level. This is because JR set the up-step and down-step probabilities equal to 1/2. Consequently, any expected drift in the asset price through time must be handled through a lattice that drifts upward or downward. In contrast, the CRR procedure had an up-step followed by a down-step that returned the asset to its original price. Thus, the expected drift in asset price must be handled through the up-step and down-step probabilities. Recall that (9.8) shows that the probability of an up-step is greater than 1/2 as long as the asset price is expected to drift upward.

Figure 9.9 also contains the American-style put option values. They are computed using the same three-step procedure that we applied earlier. The only difference, as already noted, is in the definition of the values of $u$, $d$, and $p$. Note that the current value of the put is 7.40, where its value under the CRR parameters is 7.48. The difference is attributable to approximation error, and will tend to disappear as the number of time steps is increased.

The steps in the binomial method are summarized in Table 9.1. The main intuition underlying the procedure is that we can construct a discrete binomial asset price distribution whose jump sizes ($u$ and $d$) and probabilities ($p$ and $1 - p$) generate a mean and a variance equal to the mean and variance of the BSM continuous log-normal asset price distribution over the time increment, $\Delta t$. The combinations of jump sizes and probabilities are not unique. Table 9.1 also contains three different, commonly used parameter possibilities.[4]

### Valuing a Barrier Option

The binomial method not only is straightforward to apply but also is very flexible in terms of the numbers and types of options that it can value. In Chapter 6, we introduced barrier options. Barrier options are of two types—"knock-out" and "knock-in." A knockout option is like a standard option except that the

[4] Yet another possibility is given in Rendleman and Bartter (1979).

**TABLE 9.1** Three steps in applying the binomial approximation method.

1. *Create asset price lattice.* Divide the option's time to expiration $T$ into $n$ increments of length $\Delta t$, that is, $\Delta t = T/n$. Start at the current level of asset price, $S$, and generate an asset price lattice by allowing the asset price jump up (down) by proportion $u(d)$. At the end of the first time increment, there will be two asset price nodes, $Su$ and $Sd$. At the end of two time increments, there will be three asset price nodes, and so on. The final column in the lattice will have $n + 1$ nodes. The lattice is meant to capture all possible paths that the asset price may travel through the life of the option. The number of paths increases with $n$.
2. *Value option at expiration.* Value the option at expiration for each asset price node. The option value is 0 or the exercise proceeds, whichever is greater.
3. *Value option at earlier nodes by taking the present value of the expected future value.* Work your way back through time, one increment $\Delta t$ at a time, by taking the present value of the expected future value of the option based on the two option nodes directly to the right of the valuation node. The expected values are computed using $p$, the probability of an up-step, and $1 - p$, the probability of a down-step. With each present value computation, check for any "boundary" violations (e.g., the early exercise boundary of an American-style option). When the recursive procedure is arrives back at time 0, the current value of the option is found.

The application of the binomial method requires values for the parameters $u$, $d$, and $p$. These are found by equating the mean and the variance of the discrete binomial distribution to the mean and the variance of the continuous log-normal distribution. Many combinations of parameters are possible. Three possibilities follow:

| Method | $u$ | $d$ | $p$ |
|---|---|---|---|
| Cox-Ross-Rubinstein (1979) | $e^{\sigma\sqrt{\Delta t}}$ | $e^{-\sigma\sqrt{\Delta t}}$ | $\frac{1}{2}+\frac{1}{2}\left(\frac{b-0.5\sigma^2}{\sigma}\right)\sqrt{\Delta t}$ |
| Jarrow-Rudd (1983) | $e^{(b-\sigma^2/2)\Delta t+\sigma\sqrt{\Delta t}}$ | $e^{(b-\sigma^2/2)\Delta t-\sigma\sqrt{\Delta t}}$ | 1/2 |
| Simple | $e^{\sigma\sqrt{\Delta t}}$ | $e^{-\sigma\sqrt{\Delta t}}$ | $\frac{e^{b\Delta t}-d}{u-d}$ |

option terminates if the asset price goes below or above some prespecified knock-out level. A knock-in option, on the other hand, is like a standard option except that it becomes "alive" only if the asset price goes below or above the knock-in barrier.

To illustrate the valuation of a barrier option, we modify the terms of the American-style FX put. Instead of assuming that the option is a *standard* American-style put, we assume that it is an *up-and-out* American-style put with a knock-out barrier of 60. In other words, this put terminates (i.e., expires worthless) if the asset price rises above 60 at any time during the option's life.

The steps of the binomial valuation are exactly as outlined above, except for Step 3(a). In addition to checking each node in year 1 for early exercise, we check if the knock-out condition applies. The upper node in year 1 has an asset price of 61.07, so the put is "knocked out" and its value is set equal to 0, as

**FIGURE 9.10** Valuing an American-style "knock-out" FX put option using the binomial method.

| Time | 0 | 1 | 2 |
|---|---|---|---|
| | | | 0.00 |
| | | | 74.59 |
| | | 0.00 | |
| | | 61.07 | |
| | 6.35 | | 5.00 |
| | 50.00 | | 50.00 |
| | | 14.06 | |
| | | 40.94 | |
| | | | 21.48 |
| | | | 33.52 |

shown in Figure 9.10. The lower node in year 1 has an asset price of 40.94, so the knock-out condition does not apply. Taking the present value of the expected future value standing in year 0 then tells us that the value of this American-style, knock-out put is 6.34. Note that adding the knock-out feature reduces the value of the put by 1.13. This may help explain their popularity. If you are completely entirely convinced that the currency price will not rise, why pay for the extra insurance?

### Assessing the Degree of Accuracy

The decision to use two time steps in the above illustrations was made only for expositional convenience. Fact of the matter is that such a crude grid provides a poor approximation of the option value. The procedure as outlined above, however, is perfectly general. We can set the number of time steps equal to any number we like. As the number of time steps is increased, the asset price lattice becomes more dense, with exponentially more price paths being considered. The number of price paths in the binomial model is $2^n$. At two time steps, it was easy to see that the number of asset price paths over the life of the option is four. At 20 time steps, the number of paths is well over a million.

The decision regarding the appropriate number of time steps to use in the binomial method is therefore a cost/benefit analysis. The cost is computational time; the benefit is increased precision in valuation and risk measurement.[5] To gauge the degree of approximation error in the binomial method for a particular application, we can compare its results to the results of an option valuation problem whose valuation equation is known. Assume, for example, that the FX put

[5] The need for frequent time steps is particularly acute in the valuation of American-style barrier options. If the barrier price does not happen to coincide with nodes in the asset lattice, the monitoring of the barrier and, hence, option valuation will be inaccurate. Boyle and Lau (1994) show how to adjust the number of time steps in the binomial method so that the barrier price falls exactly on or very close to node values.

option in our illustration is European-style. Its value using the BSM option valuation formula (5.32) is 6.41. This is the true value and serves as our benchmark. Now, we apply the binomial method again and again increasing the number of time steps from 1 to, say, 100. At one time step, the value is 7.28, which represents a valuation error of 87 cents—13.67% of the true option value. At two time steps, the value is 6.64, as we established earlier in the chapter. This represents a valuation error of 23 cents[6]—3.70% of the true option value. As we increase the number of time steps, valuation precision increases albeit not monotonically. Figure 9.11 shows the pattern. The valuation error is –6 cents (–1.10%) at five time steps, 12 cents (1.89%) at 10 time steps, and so on. By 50 time steps, the absolute relative valuation error generally stays below 0.25%.[7]

The cost of increasing the number of time steps is computational time. From the description of the computational procedure, which is summarized in Table 9.1, it is fairly obvious that computational cost increases in direct proportion to the number of nodes in the lattice (i.e., the same set of computations is performed at each node prior to the option's expiration date). The number of nodes

**FIGURE 9.11** Percent valuation error of the CRR binomial method as a function of the number of time steps.

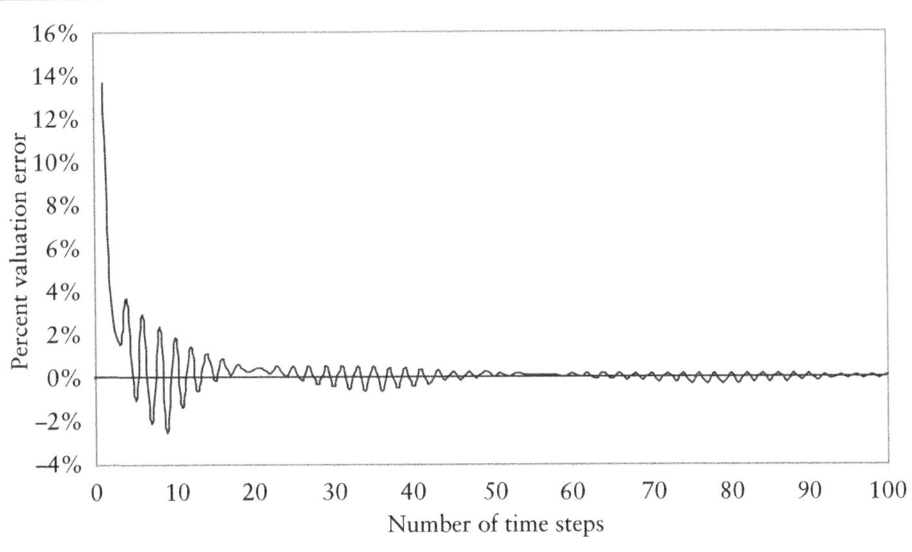


[6] The reader can verify these figures using the OPTVAL Excel Function Library—OV_OPTION_VALUE provides the BSM model values and OV_APPROX_STD_OPT_BIN, provides the CRR and JR binomial method values.

[7] The fact that the valuation error oscillates from even to odd numbers of times steps is useful in designing more computationally efficient valuation procedures. With 30 time steps, for example, the number of nodes is 496 and the valuation error is –0.38%, and, with 31 time steps, the number of nodes is 528 and the valuation error is 0.58%. Thus, in this illustration, it is computationally cheaper and more accurate to average the values of the option obtained using 30 and 31 time steps (i.e., valuation error of 0.10%) than to use 50 times steps, where the number of nodes is 1,326 and the valuation error is about 0.25%.

in the lattice, on the other hand, increases at an increasing rate with the number of time steps, that is,

$$\text{Number of nodes} = \frac{(n+1)(n+2)}{2}$$

With two time steps, the number of nodes is six, with three time steps 10, with four time steps 15, and so on, as is illustrated in Figure 9.11. The question is where to set $n$. At 20 time steps, for example, the number of nodes is 231 and the relative pricing error falls in the range of ±0.5%. At 50 time steps, the number of nodes is 1,326 and the relative pricing error falls in the range of ±0.25%. Thus, to achieve increased relative valuation precision of 0.25%, we incurred 5.75 times the computational cost. Was it worth it?

There is no one answer to the question. It depends on the nature of the available computational resources and the importance of accuracy. The cost issue has become less important through time thanks to *Moore's law.* In April 1965, Gordon Moore, an engineer and cofounder of Intel, predicted that integrated circuit complexity would double every two years. His prediction has been surprisingly accurate. Today, the processing speed of a typical PC is more than 1,000 times faster than 20 years ago, while the cost of the PC is about a third. The accuracy issue is largely one of contract size. In terms of our European-style put illustration, a 0.25% valuation error amounts to less than 2 pennies (i.e., $6.41 \times 0.0025 = 0.0160$), hardly an amount worthy of concern. But, if the number of units of the underlying currency in the contract is 100 million rather than 1 (which has been implicitly assumed all along), however, the error is \$1.6 million, an amount large enough to buy a supercomputer.

**ILLUSTRATION 9.1** Assess degree of accuracy of competing valuation methods.

*Consider a two-year European-style put option with an exercise price of 55. The underlying asset is assumed to be a foreign currency whose current price is 50 and whose volatility rate is 20%. The domestic rate of interest is assumed to be 5%, and the foreign rate of interest is 2%. Compare the performance of the binomial method using the CRR parameters with the binomial method using the JR parameters. Which is more accurate, holding the number of time steps constant, and why?*

To make this assessment, we will first value the put analytically using the BSM formula. From the OPTVAL Library, we know

OV_OPTION_VALUE(50, 55, 2, 0.05, 0.02, 0.20, "p", "e") = 6.41

Because the put is European-style, we know that the analytical value is correct.

To assess the degree of accuracy of the competing binomial methods, we will use the OPTVAL function,

OV _APPROX_STD_OPT_BIN(50, 55, 2, 0.05, 0.02, 0.20, *n*, "p","e", *mthd*)

In using the function, we will vary the number of time steps $n$ from 1 to 100. The binomial method algorithm uses the CRR parameters where *mthd* is set equal to 1 and the JR parameters where *mthd* is set equal to 2. The percent valuation error (relative to the analytical value) is then computed and plotted as a function of the number of time steps. The results are as shown below. The JR parameters appear to perform better than the CRR parameters. The oscillations in the percent valuation error are smaller, particularly for small numbers of time steps, and disappear almost completely for high numbers of time steps. The reason that the JR parameters produce a more accurate value is that they are based on the correct variance constraint in linking the means and the variances of the binomial distribution with the normal distribution of the logarithm of asset prices, that is, equation (9.4a). The CRR method uses only an approximation (9.4b). The valuation difference disappears as the number of time steps is increased (i.e., $\Delta t \to 0$).

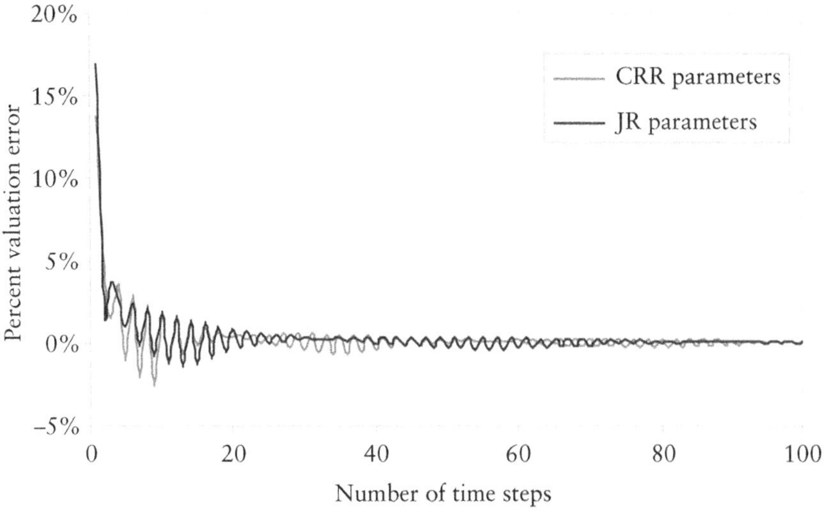


## Incorporating Discrete Flows

Thus far, we have addressed American-style option valuation when all of the carry costs of the asset underlying the option can be modeled as continuous rates. Recall that this assumption is most appropriate for foreign currencies and widely diversified stock portfolios. For common stock options or bond options, however, the dividend and coupon payments are best modeled as discrete cash flows. In such cases, the binomial method must be modified to account for these costs. The changes to the methodology are relatively minor, however. The intuition is that, if the amount and the timing of the discrete cash flows are known, the uncertainty regarding asset price is the uncertainty of the asset price net of the present value of the known cash flows. The steps in the binomial method are modified as follows.

In Step 1, create a lattice in terms of the asset price net of the present value of the income payments, that is, $S_0^x = S_0 - PVI_0$. This entails replacing the current asset price $S_0$ with $S_0^x$, since all subsequent values of the asset price are determined by applying the factors $u$ and $d$ to the current price. Note that the up-step and down-step coefficient $u$ and $d$ are computed using $b = r$, since the only *continuous* carry cost is the interest rate.

Step 2 remains unaltered. At time $T$, all of the income payments on the underlying asset made during the option's life have been made, and the lattice prices represent actual asset prices.

In Step 3, we compute the present value of the expected future values as before. The only distinction here is that we must adjust the early exercise bound to reflect the present value of any dividends paid between the valuation date at which we stand and the expiration date. For an American-style call, the early exercise proceeds are $\max(0, S^x_{i,j} + PVD_i - X)$, where $S^x_{i,j}$ is the lattice price at node (*i*,*j*), that is, at time *i* and asset price *j*, and $PVD_i$ is the present value of all income payments between time *i* and expiration at time *T*. Note that at time 0, the early exercise proceeds of the call for the single remaining node are $\max(0, S^x_0 + PVD_0 - X)$, where $S^x_0 + PVD_0$ equals the current asset price *S* by the way we constructed the lattice.

**ILLUSTRATION 9.2** Value American-style call option on dividend-paying stock.

*Suppose that you own an American-style call option on a dividend-paying-stock. The call has 14 days remaining to expiration and an exercise price of \$55. The current stock price is \$60, and the volatility rate is 40%. The stock promises to pay a \$1 cash dividend in seven days. The risk-free rate of interest is 5%. Compute the value of the call using the binomial method with CRR parameters. Use two time steps.*

First, identify the parameters of the binomial method implementation. The up-step and down-step coefficients are

$$u = e^{0.40\sqrt{7/365}} = 1.0570 \quad \text{and} \quad d = \frac{1}{u} = \frac{1}{1.0570} = 0.9461$$

the up-step probability is

$$p = \frac{1}{2} + \frac{1}{2}\left(\frac{0.05 - 0.5(0.40)^2}{0.40}\right)\sqrt{7/365} = 0.4948$$

and the down-step probability is 0.5052.

Second, compute the stock price net of the present value of the promised dividend, and create the stock price grid. The stock price net of the present value of the dividend is $60 - 1e^{-0.05(7/365)} = 59.001$. The stock price after two up-steps, for example, is $59.001(1.0570)^2 = 65.913$.

Third, compute the European-style call price by recursively taking the present value of the expected future value. The value of the European-style call is 4.66, as demonstrated in the lattice below. To illustrate the recursive computations, the value of the call at the upper node on day 7 is computed as

$$PVEFV = e^{-r\Delta t}EFV = e^{-0.05(7/365)}[0.4948(10.913) + 0.5052(4.001)] = 7.414$$

| Days | 0 | 7 | 14 |
|---|---|---|---|
| | | | **10.913** |
| | | | 65.913 |
| | | **7.414** | |
| | | 62.361 | |
| | **4.663** | | **4.001** |
| | 59.001 | | 59.001 |
| | | **1.978** | |
| | | 55.822 | |
| | | | **0.000** |
| | | | 52.813 |

Finally, to compute the value of the American-style call option, we must consider the effects of possible early exercise at the upper and lower nodes on day 7. At the upper node, compare the computed value, 7.414, with the value if exercised, 62.361 + 1 – 55 = 8.361. Since the early exercise proceeds are higher, replace the computed option value at this node with the early exercise proceeds.[8] At the lower node the, computed value, 1.978, exceeds the early exercise proceeds, 55.822 + 1 – 55 = 1.822, so no replacement is made. The value of the American-style call is as shown below. The value of the American-style call is 5.132, hence the value of the early exercise premium is 0.469.

| Days | 0 | 7 | 14 |
|---|---|---|---|
| | | | **10.913** |
| | | | 65.913 |
| | | **8.361** | |
| | | 62.361 | |
| | **5.132** | | **4.001** |
| | 59.001 | | 59.001 |
| | | **1.978** | |
| | | 55.822 | |
| | | | **0.000** |
| | | | 52.813 |

## Two Underlying Sources of Risk

The binomial method can also be extended to handle multiple sources of risk. As discussed in Chapter 6, options on the minimum and the maximum of two risky assets qualify. A call option on the maximum, for example, has a payoff $\max[0, \max(\tilde{S}_{1,T}, \tilde{S}_{2,T}) - X]$ at the option's expiration. Stulz (1982) shows that if options on the minimum and maximum of two risky assets are European-style, they can be valued analytically.[9] If they are American-style, however, they must be valued numerically. Similarly, both European- and American-style spread options must be valued numerically. A European-style call option on a spread, for example, has a payoff $\max[0, \tilde{S}_{1,T} - \tilde{S}_{2,T} - X]$ at the option's expiration. Since asset prices are log-normally distributed under the BSM assumptions, the price difference, $\tilde{S}_{1,T} - \tilde{S}_{2,T}$, is not log-normally distributed and, hence, the usual BSM valuation mechanics cannot be applied.

Boyle, Evnine, and Gibbs (1989) modify the CRR binomial method to handle multiple sources of risk. We consider only the two-asset case. Like in the CRR framework, each asset's price is allowed to jump up or down. Hence, at any given instant, four jumps are possible—up-up, up-down, down-up and down-down, where the first move in each pair of movements is for asset 1 and the second is for asset 2. The probabilities of each pair of movements are $p_1$ through $p_4$, respectively. The proportionate jumps in asset price are the same as those for the CRR formulation, that is,

[8] The motivation for early exercise is being driven by the fact, if the call option holder waits until expiration to exercise, he will have forfeit the opportunity to receive the dividend.

[9] Johnson (1987) shows how the Stulz (1982) results can be extended to the case of multiple underlying assets.

$$u_i = e^{\sigma_i\sqrt{\Delta t}} \text{ and } d_i = 1/u_i, \text{ for } i = 1, 2 \tag{9.13}$$

The probabilities of the different pairings are

$$p_1 = \frac{1}{4}\left[1 + \rho + \sqrt{\Delta t}\left(\frac{\mu_1}{\sigma_1} + \frac{\mu_2}{\sigma_2}\right)\right] \tag{9.14a}$$

$$p_2 = \frac{1}{4}\left[1 - \rho + \sqrt{\Delta t}\left(\frac{\mu_1}{\sigma_1} - \frac{\mu_2}{\sigma_2}\right)\right] \tag{9.14b}$$

$$p_3 = \frac{1}{4}\left[1 - \rho + \sqrt{\Delta t}\left(-\frac{\mu_1}{\sigma_1} + \frac{\mu_2}{\sigma_2}\right)\right] \tag{9.14c}$$

and

$$p_4 = \frac{1}{4}\left[1 + \rho + \sqrt{\Delta t}\left(-\frac{\mu_1}{\sigma_1} - \frac{\mu_2}{\sigma_2}\right)\right] \tag{9.14d}$$

Under the assumption of risk-neutrality, the mean continuously compounded rate of price appreciation equals the asset's risk-neutral cost of carry rate, that is, $\mu_i = b_i - 0.5\sigma_i^2$, for $i = 1, 2$.

**ILLUSTRATION 9.3** Value spread option using binomial method.

*Compute the value of a American-style call option on the "crack" spread between the prices of an unleaded gasoline futures and a crude oil futures*[10] *using the binomial method. Assume the gasoline futures has a price of \$22 per barrel and a volatility rate of 30% annually, and the crude oil futures has a price of \$20 per barrel and a volatility rate of 20%. The correlation between the rates of price appreciation for the two futures contracts is 0.85. The option has an exercise price of \$2 and a time to expiration of three months. The risk-free rate of interest is 5%.*

The three steps of the binomial method are summarized in Table 9.1. Since the mechanics of setting up a two-dimensional price lattice are cumbersome, we will simply apply the appropriate valuation approximation from the OPTVAL function library. The syntax of the function call is

OV_APPROX_SPRD_OPT_BIN(*s1*, *s2*, *x*, *t*, *r*, *i1*, *i2*, *v1*, *v2*, *rho*, *n*, *cp*, *ae*),

where *s1* and *s2* are the underlying asset prices (with the spread defined as *s1* – *s2*), *x* is the exercise price of option, *t* is the option's time remaining to expiration, *r* is the risk-free interest rate, *i1* and *i2* are the income rates of assets 1 and 2, *v1* and *v2* are the volatility rates of

[10] Crack spread futures options trade on the New York Mercantile Exchange (NYMEX). The parameters for this illustration are drawn from Whaley (1996).

assets 1 and 2, *rho* is the correlation between asset returns, *n* is the number of time steps, *cp* is a call/put indicator ("C" or "c" for call and "P" or "p" for put), and *ae* is an American- or European-style option indicator ("A" or "a" for American-style and "E" or "e" for European-style). Using 25 time steps, the value of the call is

OV_APPROX_SPRD_OPT_BIN(22, 20, 2, 0.25, 0.05, 0.05, 0.05, 0.30, 0.20, 0.85, 25, "c","e") = 0.7519.

Note that the risk-free interest rate is used as the income rate for both assets. We tricked the valuation algorithm into thinking the underlying assets are futures contracts by implicitly setting the net cost of carry rate to zero.[11] Like in the univariate case, the accuracy of the bivariate binomial method improves with the number of times steps. For the valuation parameters in this illustration, little variation in value remains after 20 time steps.

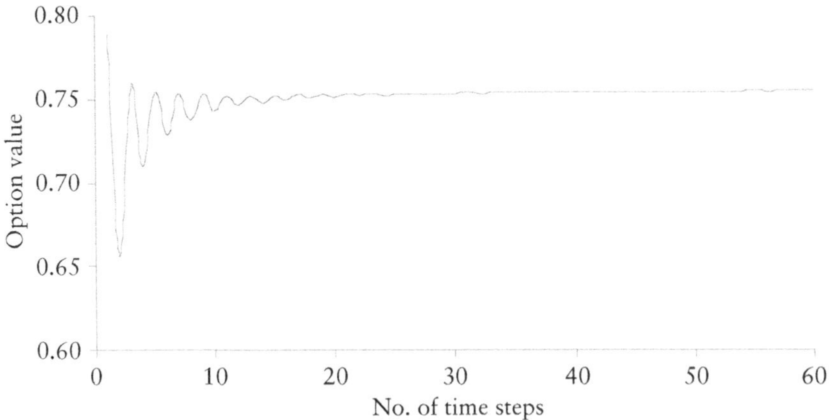


## TRINOMIAL METHOD

The trinomial method has the same three steps as the binomial method. The only difference is that in place of allowing the asset price to go only up or down from its current price, the asset price can go up, down, or stay the same. The definitions of the up-step and down-step coefficients change, as do the definitions of the probabilities.

Under the trinomial method, we set the mean and the variance of a discrete trinomial distribution for the logarithm of asset price equal to the corresponding mean and variance of the continuous normal distribution of the logarithm of asset price. The mean constraint is

$$p_u v + p_d(-v) = \mu \Delta t \tag{9.15}$$

where $p_u$ is the probability of an up-step, and $p_d$ is the probability of a down-step. Condition (9.15) is the trinomial method's counterpart to the mean constraint (9.2) in the development of the binomial method. Note that we are assuming that

[11] Recall that the Black (1976) futures option valuation formula in Chapter 7 was a special cash of the BSM formula (7.32) where the cost of carry rate *b* was set equal to zero.

the absolute size of the up-step and the down-step are the same. In this sense, we have imposed the CRR symmetry restriction. The probability of no change in the asset price is $p_m = 1 - p_u - p_d$ and does not enter (9.15) since the price change is zero. In our implementation of the trinomial method, the variance constraint is

$$v^2(p_u + p_d) = \sigma^2 \Delta t \tag{9.16}$$

This is the counterpart to the binomial method's variance constraint (9.4b) in which the higher order terms of $\Delta t$ are ignored. While ignoring higher order terms simplifies matters, a further restriction on the parameters is necessary in order to make the model usable since we have three unknowns—$p_u$, $p_d$, and $v$, and only two equations—(9.15) and (9.16).

The final restriction is drawn from the work of Boyle (1988a) and Kamrad and Ritchken (1991) (hereafter, "KR"). They assume the up-step coefficient has the functional form, $v = \lambda\sigma\sqrt{\Delta t}$, where $\lambda \geq 1$. Substituting into (9.16), we find that the sum of the probabilities of an up-step and a down-step is

$$p_u + p_d = 1/\lambda^2 \tag{9.17}$$

The probability of no change in price is therefore

$$p_m = 1 - 1/\lambda^2 \tag{9.18a}$$

Isolating the probability of a down-step in (9.17) and then substituting into (9.15), shows that

$$\begin{aligned} p_u &= \frac{1}{2\lambda^2} + \frac{\mu\Delta t}{2\lambda\sigma\sqrt{\Delta t}} \\ &= \frac{1}{2\lambda^2} + \frac{1}{2\lambda}\left(\frac{b - 0.5\sigma^2}{\sigma}\right)\sqrt{\Delta t} \end{aligned} \tag{9.18b}$$

and therefore

$$\begin{aligned} p_d &= \frac{1}{2\lambda^2} - \frac{\mu\Delta t}{2\lambda\sigma\sqrt{\Delta t}} \\ &= \frac{1}{2\lambda^2} - \frac{1}{2\lambda}\left(\frac{b - 0.5\sigma^2}{\sigma}\right)\sqrt{\Delta t} \end{aligned} \tag{9.18c}$$

Where $\lambda = 1$, note that the trinomial model collapses to the CRR binomial model. The probability of a zero price change is 0, so the middle node drops out. The up-step coefficient in asset price is

$$u = e^{v} = e^{\lambda\sigma\sqrt{\Delta t}} = e^{\sigma\sqrt{\Delta t}}$$

exactly as in CRR, and the probability of an up-step within the trinomial framework (9.18b) equals the probability of an up-step in the binomial framework (9.6).[12]

The choice of an appropriate value of $\lambda$ is left to the user. The higher the value of $\lambda$, the greater is the probability that the asset price will move sideways rather than up or down. In the application below, we set $\lambda$ equal to the square root of 2. At $\lambda = \sqrt{2}$, the probability of the middle step is $p_m = 1 - 1/\lambda^2 = 1/2$.

### Applying the Trinomial Method

Applying the trinomial method has the same three steps as the binomial method. To illustrate its use, we will value a two-year, American-style FX put option with an exercise price of 55. The current exchange rate is 50, and its volatility rate is 20%. The domestic rate of interest is assumed to be 5%, and the foreign rate of interest, 2%. The expected risk-neutral rate of price appreciation of the currency is 3%.

**Step 1: Create the Asset Price Lattice** Like in the case of the binomial method, the first step in the trinomial method is to set up the asset price lattice. If the current asset price is $S$, the asset price may jump only up to a level of $uS$ (where $u > 1$), down to a level of $dS$ (where $d < 1$), or horizontally to the level $S$. The CRR restriction $ud = 1$ has been assumed. Setting $\lambda = \sqrt{2}$, the value of $u$ is

$$u = e^{\sigma\sqrt{2\Delta t}} = e^{0.20\sqrt{2}} = 1.3269$$

and the value of $d$ is $d = 1/u = 0.7536$. Applying these coefficients to the current asset price generates the two-period lattice shown in Figure 9.12. Note that the tree is denser than the binomial tree. This stands to reason since the number of branches from each node is three instead of two. The range of terminal asset prices at the option's expiration is also greater.

**FIGURE 9.12** Two-period trinomial asset price lattice for valuing an option.

| Time | 0 | 1 | 2 |
|---|---|---|---|
| | | | 88.03 |
| | | 66.34 | 66.34 |
| | 50.00 | 50.00 | 50.00 |
| | | 37.68 | 37.68 |
| | | | 28.40 |

[12] Rubinstein (2000) discusses the relation between the binomial and trinomial option pricing models.

**FIGURE 9.13** Valuing an American-style put option using a two-period trinomial method.

| Year | 0 | 1 | 2 |
|---|---|---|---|
| | | | 0.00 |
| | | | 88.03 |
| | | 1.10 | 0.00 |
| | | 66.34 | 66.34 |
| | 7.06 | 6.21 | 5.00 |
| | 50.00 | 50.00 | 50.00 |
| | | 17.32 | 17.32 |
| | | 37.68 | 37.68 |
| | | | 26.60 |
| | | | 28.40 |

**Step 2: Value the Option at Expiration** The second step also parallels the binomial method, that is, we value the option at expiration. At expiration (i.e., where $i = T$), the value of the option at node $j$ is $\max(0, X - S_{i,j})$. The numerical values of the put at expiration are shown in Figure 9.13.

**Step 3: Value Option at Earlier Nodes by Taking the Present Value of the Expected Future Value** The next step is again similar to the binomial method in that we take the present value of the expected future value in an iterative fashion. The probability of the middle step is 1/2, as was noted earlier. The probabilities of an up-step and a down-step are computed using (9.18b) and (9.18c), that is,

$$p_u = \frac{1}{2} + \frac{1}{2}\left(\frac{0.03 - 0.5(0.20^2)}{0.20}\right) = 0.2677$$

and

$$p_u = \frac{1}{2} - \frac{1}{2}\left(\frac{0.03 - 0.5(0.20^2)}{0.20}\right) = 0.2323$$

We now compute the present value of the expected future value at each node in the tree. Consider the asset price at the highest node in year 1, 66.34. The present value of the expected future value of the put is

$$PVEFV = e^{-0.05\sqrt{1}}[0.2677(0.00) + 0.5000(0.00) + 0.2323(5.00)] = 1.10$$

Before proceeding to the next node, we check the early exercise condition. Since the put is out of the money at this node, we leave it alive. At the year 1 asset price node of 50,

$$PVEFV = e^{-0.05\sqrt{1}}[0.2677(0.00) + 0.5000(5.00) + 0.2323(17.32)] = 6.21$$

At an asset price of 50, the put has exercise proceeds of 5. Since its value if left alive is 6.21, early exercise is not optimal and we do not replace the *PVEFV* with the exercise proceeds. At the year 1 asset price node of 37.68,

$$PVEFV = e^{-0.05\sqrt{1}}[0.2677(5.00) + 0.5000(17.32) + 0.2323(26.60)] = 15.39$$

Here, the put has exercise proceeds of 17.32, which exceed the value of the put if left alive. Thus, we replace the present value, 15.39, with the exercise proceeds, 17.32, and move to the next time step. The value of the American-style put option using the trinomial lattice with two time steps is 7.06. The value of the European-style put is 6.63.

### Assessing the Degree of Accuracy

Like the binomial method, the accuracy of the trinomial method improves with the number of time steps. Indeed, it does so at a much quicker rate, as Figure 9.14 shows. At ten time steps, the trinomial method appears to produce option values as accurate as the binomial method at 20. This should not be surprising. Recall that the binomial method produces $(n + 1)(n + 2)/2$ nodes and considers

**FIGURE 9.14** Approximation error of the binomial and trinomial approximation methods as a function of the number of time steps.

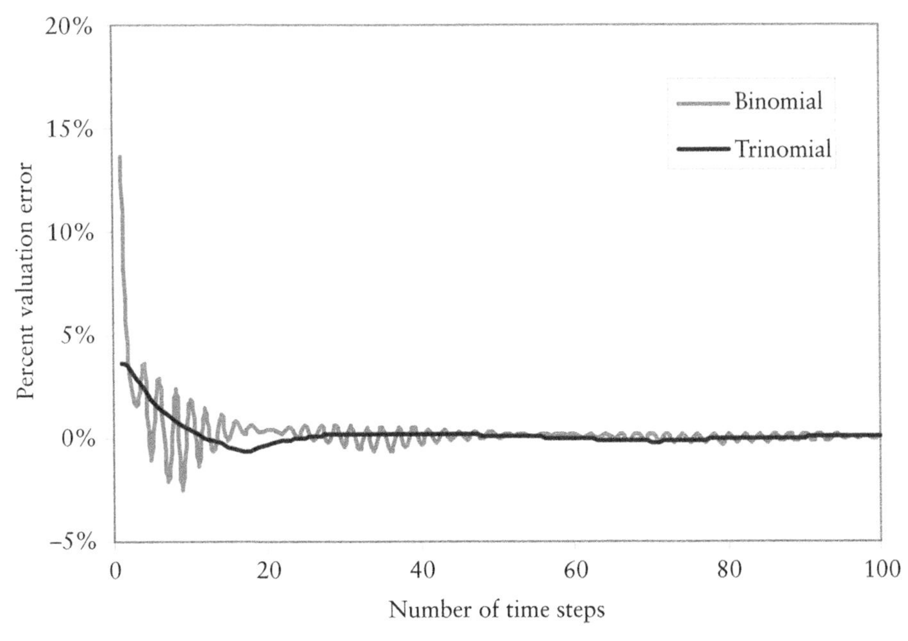

$2^n$ asset price paths over the life of the option. For the same number of time steps, the trinomial method produces $(n + 1)^2$ nodes and considers $3^n$ price paths. At 10 time steps, the binomial method has 66 nodes and incorporates 1,024 possible asset price paths. The trinomial method, on the other hand, has 121 nodes and incorporates 59,049 price paths. But the increased accuracy of the trinomial method comes at a cost. Recall that computational cost varies directly with the number of nodes computed. For the 10-time step example, the trinomial method costs roughly double the binomial method.

## MONTE CARLO SIMULATION

Monte Carlo simulation techniques are also used to value derivative contracts.[13] Like the lattice-based procedures, the technique involves simulating possible paths that the asset price may take over the life of the option. Unlike the lattice-based procedures that trace out all possible asset price paths at the outset, the Monte Carlo technique produces a price path adding up a series of randomly drawn price increments over the life of the option. Each drawing corresponds to the time increment $\Delta t$, and a series of $n$ drawings produces a *simulation run* (i.e., an asset price path). The Monte Carlo technique involves repeated simulation runs or trials. To value a European-style put option, for example, each trial produces a terminal asset price, which, in turn, is used to determine the terminal option value. After, say, 10,000 trials, the terminal options values are averaged arithmetically to obtain the expected terminal option value, $E(\tilde{p}_T)$, and then the expected value is discounted to the present at the risk-free interest rate, $p = e^{-rT}E(\tilde{p}_T)$.

### Geometric Brownian Motion

What remains is the description of how each asset price path is generated. Under the BSM model, the asset price follows a continuous Brownian diffusion process. Like in the case of the lattice-based procedures, we must replace this continuous process with movements over discrete intervals. By setting the number of time intervals during the life of the option, $n$, the time increment becomes $\Delta t = T/n$. To generate a movement over the interval, we draw a random number, $\varepsilon$, from a unit normal distribution.[14] This number is used to update the asset price at the beginning on the time interval. Recall that under the BSM assumptions, the change in the logarithm of asset price is normally distributed with mean, $(b - \sigma^2/2)\Delta t$, and

---

[13] Boyle (1988b) was the first to apply Monte Carlo simulation techniques to option valuation.

[14] Methods for generating univariate normal deviates (i.e., random numbers drawn from a normal distribution with mean 0 and variance 1) are available in most computer programming languages. In Excel, the task can be accomplished using the command, =NORMSINV(RAND()). The logic is as follows. NORMSINV is the inverse of the function NORMSDIST. Recall that we used NORMSDIST in Chapter 7 to measure the probability that a random number drawn from a unit normal distribution has a value below $d$. Thus if we have a random number drawn from a uniform distribution over the range from zero to one, we can insert it into the NORMSINV function to generate a random drawing from a unit normal distribution. The function, RAND() generates a random number from a uniform distribution whose range is zero to one.

standard deviation, $\sigma\sqrt{\Delta t}$.[15] To update the logarithm of asset price, therefore, we (a) scale the random drawing $\varepsilon$ (which has a standard deviation of 1) by the standard deviation of the logarithm of asset price change, $\sigma\sqrt{\Delta t}$, (b) add it to the expected movement, $(b - \sigma^2/2)\Delta t$, and (c) add the sum to the beginning of period logarithm of asset price, $\ln S_t$, that is,

$$\ln S_{t+\Delta t} = \ln S_t + (b - \sigma^2/2)\Delta t + \sigma\sqrt{\Delta t}\varepsilon \tag{9.19}$$

Like in the case of the lattice-based procedures, individuals working with the Monte Carlo technique may prefer to see the sequence of asset prices in the simulation run rather than the sequence of the logarithm of asset prices. In this case, the updating is accomplished using an equation created by raising both sides of (9.19) to the power of $e$, that is,

$$S_{t+\Delta t} = S_t e^{(b - \sigma^2/2)\Delta t + \sigma\sqrt{\Delta t}\varepsilon} \tag{9.20}$$

Equation (9.20) transforms the unit normally distributed random variable $\varepsilon$ into a log-normally distributed asset price.

Table 9.2 uses the parameters of our two-year put option illustration to show some of the computations performed in the first simulation run. We arbitrarily set the number of time steps to be equal to the number of days to expiration, 730. The first drawing from the unit normal distribution produced a value of –0.8369. Substituting into (9.20), we find that the asset price at the end of the first day is

**TABLE 9.2** First simulation run in valuing a two-year European-style put option written on a currency price using Monte Carlo simulation.

| Number of Time Step | Random Drawing from a Unit Normal Distribution, $\varepsilon$ | Asset Price, $S_{t+\Delta t}$ |
|---|---|---|
| 0 | | 50.0000 |
| 1 | –0.8369 | 49.5652 |
| 2 | –0.1723 | 49.4773 |
| 3 | 0.1871 | 49.5757 |
| ... | ... | ... |
| 728 | –0.9772 | 66.5649 |
| 729 | 0.1087 | 66.6425 |
| 730 | –0.1798 | 66.5190 |

[15] Under the BSM assumptions, the change in the log of asset price, $\ln S_{t+\Delta t} - \ln S_t$, is normally distributed with mean $(b - \sigma^2/2)\Delta t$ and standard deviation, $\sigma\sqrt{\Delta t}$. Thus it follows that

$$\varepsilon = \frac{(\ln S_{t+\Delta t} - \ln S_t) - (b - \sigma^2/2)\Delta t}{\sigma\sqrt{\Delta t}}$$

has a unit normal distribution.

$$S_1 = 50e^{(0.03-0.20^2/2)(1/730)+0.20\sqrt{1/730}(-0.8369)} = 49.5652$$

The drawing on the second day, –0.1723, produces an asset price of

$$S_2 = 49.5652e^{(0.03-0.20^2/2)(1/730)+0.20\sqrt{1/730}(-0.1723)} = 49.4773$$

as so on. After the 730th drawing in the simulation run, the asset price is 66.5190. Since the put option has an exercise price of 55, the put finishes out-of-the-money and has a terminal value of 0. This completes the first trial.

The simulation run procedure is repeated 9,999 more times. Each time, the terminal value of the put is recorded. Table 9.3 summarizes the results across the 10,000 runs. The average terminal asset price is 53.1144. This closely corresponds, but is not exactly equal, to the expected terminal asset price computed based on the cost of carry rate, that is, $50e^{0.03(1)} = 53.0918$. The difference is attributable to sampling error in the simulation. Across the 10,000 trials, the terminal asset price ranged from 18.2019 to 139.7387, and the standard deviation of the terminal asset price was 15.4352. To measure the degree of potential error, we can compute the standard error of the estimate as

**TABLE 9.3** Terminal asset price and terminal put option value in each of the 10,000 simulation runs performed for the European-style put option written on a currency price using Monte Carlo simulation.

| Simulation Run | Terminal Asset Price | Terminal Put Value |
|---|---|---|
| 1 | 66.5190 | 0.0000 |
| 2 | 40.8806 | 14.1194 |
| 3 | 59.5425 | 0.0000 |
| ... | ... | ... |
| 9,998 | 50.4133 | 4.5867 |
| 9,999 | 30.7052 | 24.2948 |
| 10,000 | 51.8364 | 3.1636 |
| **Summary statistics** | | |
| Average | 53.1144 | 7.1274 |
| Std. deviation | 15.4352 | 8.1269 |
| Std. error | 0.1544 | 1.1288 |
| Minimum | 18.2019 | 0.0000 |
| Maximum | 139.7387 | 36.7981 |
| **95% confidence interval** | | |
| Lower bound | 52.8119 | 4.9150 |
| Upper bound | 53.4169 | 9.3398 |
| **Current values** | | |
| Present value of expected value | 50.0213 | 6.4492 |

$$\begin{aligned}\text{Standard error of estimate} &= \frac{\text{Standard deviation of terminal values}}{\sqrt{\text{Number of trials}}} \\ &= \frac{15.4352}{\sqrt{10{,}000}} \\ &= 0.1544\end{aligned} \tag{9.21}$$

Thus, the 95% confidence interval for the estimate is

$$53.1144 - 1.96(0.1544) = 52.8119 \leq S_T \leq 53.4156 = 53.1144 + 1.96(0.1544)$$

Although the Monte Carlo procedure is imprecise, we are 95% confident that the terminal asset price will lie between 52.8119 and 53.4169.

The average terminal value of our European-style put is 7.1274, and its 95% confidence interval is 4.9157 to 9.3406. This range of terminal put option values is quite large. While increasing the number of trials increases the precision of the estimate of option value, the increased precision increases only with the square root of the number of trials, as is shown in the formula for the standard error of the estimate (9.21). Note that the current value of the option using 10,000 Monte Carlo simulation runs, 6.4492, is reasonably close to the value of the BSM European-style put option valuation equation, that is, 6.41.

A key advantage of the Monte Carlo method is that we can measure the degree of valuation error directly using the standard error of the estimate. Another advantage of the Monte Carlo technique is its flexibility. Since the path of the asset price beginning at time 0 and continuing through the life of the option is observed, the technique is well suited for handling a variety of nonstandard options whose payoff contingencies are well defined through time (e.g., European barrier options, and accrual options) and for simulating the performance of possible trading strategies. Yet another advantage is that it can be adapted easily to handle multiple sources of price uncertainty. The Monte Carlo technique's chief disadvantage is that it can be applied only when the option payout does not depend on the option's value at future points in time. This eliminates the possibility of valuing American-style options since the decision to exercise early depends on the value of the option that will be forfeit.

**ILLUSTRATION 9.4** Using Monte Carlo simulation to capture effects of dynamic hedging.

*Suppose that you own 2 million shares of ABC's stock and have just entered a costless collar agreement on your shares with an OTC options dealer. In the collar agreement, you are long a European-style put with an exercise price of $30 a share, and you are short a European-style call with an exercise price of $60 a share. Both of the options have one-year to expiration, and the agreement was consummated with no upfront payment. Compute the amount of the fee embedded in this OTC agreement, and use Monte Carlo simulation to demonstrate how the OTC dealer earns the fee. Set the time step equal to one month. Assume the risk-free rate of interest is 5%. Also assume that ABC's stock has an expected rate of return of 15%, a share price of $45, a volatility rate is 40%, and no expected cash dividends.*

The embedded cost of the collar may be computed using the European-style option valuation formulas from Chapter 7. Using the problem parameters, the values of the call and put are \$3.415 and \$0.899, respectively. Since you are short the call and long the put, you have implicitly paid a fee of \$2.516 per share on 2 million shares or \$5,032,042 in total. Assuming this amount is invested at the risk-free rate of interest, its value at the end of one year is \$5,290,040.

| Collar Valuation | |
|---|---|
| Stock pricce | 45.00 |
| Put exercise price | 30.00 |
| Call exercise price | 60.00 |
| Time to expiration in years | 1.00 |
| Interest rate | 5.00% |
| Expected stock return | 15.00% |
| Volatility rate | 40.00% |
| Put value | 0.899 |
| Call value | 3.415 |
| Call less put value | 2.516 |
| Number of shares | 2,000,000 |
| PV of embedded fee | 5,032,042 |
| FV of embedded fee | 5,290,040 |

Under a costless collar agreement, no money changes hands at the outset. But, as your computations show, you have paid an implicit fee of \$5,032,042. Your counterparty, the OTC options dealer, has received this fee in the form of a long call/short put position valued at \$5,032,042. To lock-in this gain (i.e., to "monetize" the value of this trade), the dealer must dynamically hedge his option position. Since holding a long call and a short put is equivalent to holding the underlying stock, the dealer can hedge by shorting stocks so that any change in the value of the option position is offset by the change in the short stock position. The number of shares to short is determined by the collar's delta. The delta of the put is –0.0903 and the delta of the call is 0.3467. Thus, the dealer needs to sell 0.4371 shares of stock for each share in the agreement. The total number of shares that he will sell to hedge the collar agreement is 874,110. This generates \$39,334,962 in cash, which he promptly puts in risk-free bonds. The value of these bonds at the end of the year is \$41,351,708.

As you are aware, the initial hedge is risk-free only for the next instant in time and for infinitesimal movements in the stock price. Rebalancing continuously, however, is not practical since trading costs would be infinite. Here, we assume rebalancing takes place on a monthly basis. At the end of the first month, the dealer will rebalance his position to again make it delta-neutral. To simulate the value/risk of his position, he draws a unit normally distributed random variable and computes an end-of-month stock price.

$$S_1 = 45e^{(0.15-0.20^2/2)(1/12)+0.40\sqrt{1/12}(-0.836854)} = 41.0941$$

He then computes the new deltas for the call and the put. Because the net delta of the position has fallen, he now needs fewer shares to hedge. He buys back 118,481 shares in the market at the prevailing price of \$41.0941, which costs \$4,868,864. He then carries that cost for 11 months, producing a terminal cash outflow of \$5,097,213.

At the end of the second month, he will rebalance his portfolio yet once again. To simulate the value/risk of his position, he draws another random variable, –0.172280, and updates the stock price,

$$S_2 = 41.0941e^{(0.15-0.20^2/2)(1/12)+0.40\sqrt{1/12}(-0.172280)} = 40.5204$$

He again computes the new deltas, and he finds that he needs yet fewer shares in his delta-hedge. He buys back another 56,512 shares at the prevailing market price of \$40.5204. The cost is \$2,289,905 at the end of month two, or \$2,387,334 at the end of the options' lives.

The simulation is repeated again and again through month 12, and a summary is provided below. Note that at expiration, the amount of money in the cash account is \$125,617,428. But, the market maker has 2 million shares shorted, which he has to cover. He buys the shares at the prevailing market price, \$70.0197, which costs \$140,039,368 in total. He then exercises his calls. Each call is in-the-money by \$10.0197, so he earns \$20,039,368 in total. The net terminal value across all of these values is \$5,617,428. Based on the prices when the position was entered, the terminal value was expected to be \$5,290,040. The difference, \$327,388, is attributable to the fact that we performed only a single simulation run. The Excel file, **Delta hedge.xls**, contains the worksheet used to generate the table below. You will not get exactly the same values because your set of random drawings will be different. Nonetheless, it will help to reinforce the mechanics of the computations. Note that this spreadsheet may perform very slowly given the number of trials being executed:

| Period | Random Draw | Closing Price | Years to Expiration | Put Delta | Call Delta | Net Delta | Aggregate Delta | Change in Delta | Shares Sold | Cash Paid/ Received | Terminal Value of Cash |
|---|---|---|---|---|---|---|---|---|---|---|---|
| 0 | | 45.0000 | 1.0000 | –0.0903 | 0.3467 | 0.4371 | 874,110 | | –874,110 | 39,334,962 | 41,351,708 |
| 1 | –0.836854 | 41.0941 | 0.9167 | –0.1286 | 0.2492 | 0.3778 | 755,629 | –118,481 | 118,481 | –4,868,864 | –5,097,213 |
| 2 | –0.172280 | 40.5204 | 0.8333 | –0.1314 | 0.2182 | 0.3496 | 699,117 | –56,512 | 56,512 | –2,289,905 | –2,387,334 |
| 3 | 0.187117 | 41.6476 | 0.7500 | –0.1096 | 0.2199 | 0.3295 | 659,100 | –40,017 | 40,017 | –1,666,620 | –1,730,304 |
| 4 | 1.615440 | 50.4818 | 0.6667 | –0.0315 | 0.3961 | 0.4276 | 855,205 | 196,105 | –196,105 | 9,899,729 | 10,235,281 |
| 5 | –0.176774 | 49.7512 | 0.5833 | –0.0285 | 0.3576 | 0.3861 | 772,104 | –83,100 | 83,100 | –4,134,343 | –4,256,703 |
| 6 | 0.653145 | 53.9623 | 0.5000 | –0.0106 | 0.4423 | 0.4529 | 905,720 | 133,616 | –133,616 | 7,210,216 | 7,392,744 |
| 7 | –0.546364 | 50.9595 | 0.4167 | –0.0119 | 0.3362 | 0.3481 | 696,203 | –209,517 | 209,517 | –10,676,871 | –10,901,639 |
| 8 | 0.194146 | 52.4197 | 0.3333 | –0.0046 | 0.3456 | 0.3502 | 700,428 | 4,225 | –4,225 | 221,481 | 225,204 |
| 9 | 0.925709 | 58.6746 | 0.2500 | –0.0002 | 0.5203 | 0.5205 | 1,040,961 | 340,533 | –340,533 | 19,980,621 | 20,231,947 |
| 10 | 1.204321 | 67.8231 | 0.1667 | 0.0000 | 0.8114 | 0.8114 | 1,622,870 | 581,908 | –581,908 | 39,466,841 | 39,797,106 |
| 11 | 1.530555 | 81.4077 | 0.0833 | 0.0000 | 0.9969 | 0.9969 | 1,993,786 | 370,917 | –370,917 | 30,195,459 | 30,321,536 |
| 12 | –1.355560 | 70.0197 | 0.0000 | 0.000 | 1.000 | 1.0000 | 2,000,000 | 6,214 | –6,214 | 435,096 | 435,096 |
| Totals | | | | | | | | | –2,000,000 | | 125,617,428 |

| | Shares Outstanding | Share Price Change | Terminal Value |
|---|---|---|---|
| Terminal value of cash account | | | 125,617,428 |
| Cover remaining shares outstanding | –2,000,000 | 70.020 | –140,039,368 |
| Bank exercises call option | | | 20,039,368 |
| Customer exercises put option | | | 0 |
| Net proceeds from selling collar | | | 5,617,428 |

To determine the effectiveness of delta-hedging on a monthly basis on average, the simulation experiment as outlined above would be run again and again. In the table below, the simulation results are reported. With 1,000 simulation runs, the average terminal value is \$5,191,907, much close to the expected terminal value of \$5,290,040. The range of terminal values is incredibly large, however, from –\$10,008,845 to \$26,521,463. In all likelihood, the OTC dealer would find this level of risk unacceptable, and would rebalance more frequently:

| | Mean | Standard Deviation | Minimum | Maximum | Average Number of Shares Traded | After Trading Cost Profit | Profit per Unit of Risk |
|---|---|---|---|---|---|---|---|
| Monthly | 5,191,907 | 4,108,591 | –10,008,845 | 26,521,463 | 3,135,707 | 4,878,336 | 1.187 |
| Weekly | 5,343,014 | 2,002,836 | –631,657 | 13,943,237 | 5,192,995 | 4,823,714 | 2.408 |
| Daily | 5,285,976 | 786,634 | 2,174,783 | 8,786,527 | 12,085,420 | 4,077,434 | 5.183 |
| Hourly (6) | 5,290,299 | 301,906 | 4,316,409 | 6,852,635 | 27,957,722 | 2,494,527 | 8.263 |
| Hourly (12) | 5,296,894 | 214,420 | 4,418,705 | 6,416,575 | 38,567,903 | 1,440,104 | 6.716 |
| Hourly (24) | 5,304,550 | 151,603 | 4,646,940 | 6,116,745 | 54,896,398 | –185,089 | –1.221 |

With weekly rebalancing, the average terminal value across the 1,000 simulation runs is \$5,343,014, even closer to the expected value of \$5,290,040. Note also that the standard deviation of the terminal values across the 1,000 runs for weekly rebalancing is less than half the standard deviation for monthly rebalancing. With the monthly rebalancing, the average number of shares traded to hedge the collar over its life was 3,135,707. With weekly rebalancing, the average number was 5,192,995. Assuming trading costs of \$.10 a share, the expected profit for weekly rebalancing remains higher. To gauge the performance on a risk-adjusted basis, expected after-trading cost value can be divided by the standard deviation of terminal value. The ratio for monthly rebalancing is 1.187 and the ratio for weekly rebalancing is 2.408, indicating the dominance of the weekly strategy.

The table also includes daily rebalancing as well as hourly rebalancing (assuming 6, 12 and 24 hours in the day). The more frequent the rebalancing, the lower the standard deviation of terminal values, however, the greater the trading costs. The maximum ratio of expected after-trading cost profit to risk is 8.263 and occurs for the simulation in which the hedge is rebalanced six times a day. Any risk reduction benefit from rebalancing more frequently is offset by incremental trading costs. Indeed, rebalancing each hour, 24 hours a day, produces an expected after-trading cost of –\$185,089.

**ILLUSTRATION 9.5** Value average rate option.

*An average rate option (sometimes referred to as an Asian-style option) is an option whose payoff is based on an arithmetic average*[16] *of the underlying asset price during the option's life. In some instances, the exercise price is fixed, and the average asset price is used as the terminal asset price. In other instances, the average asset price is used as the exercise price and is compared to the terminal asset price to determine the option's payoff.*[17] *Monte Carlo simulation is a useful tool in valuing these path dependent options.*

[16] Less frequently, Asian options are based on a geometric average. While using a geometric average makes the valuation problem more tractable (see Kemna and Vorst (1990)), the option payoffs are less effective from a hedging standpoint.

[17] Asian options are particularly useful when the underlying is thinly traded and subject to manipulation. The markets for commodities and some currencies qualify. They have lower premiums than standard European-style options and offer general protection in situations where regular cash flows need to be hedged. Occasionally, the average rate period applies for a short period at the end of the option's life. This period is referred to as the *Asian tail.*

*Compute the value of an average rate call option with one year to expiration and an exercise price of \$50. Assume that the average is computed using end-of-month asset prices, the asset's current price is \$50, its income rate is 1%, and its volatility rate is 40%. The risk-free interest rate is 5%.*

The steps of the Monte Carlo simulation, as applied to the valuation of average rate options, are pre-programmed in the OPTVAL function,

OV_APPROX_ASIAN_OPT_MC(*s, x, t, r, i, v, n, ntrial, cp, sx, ag*)

The first six parameters are already known. The parameter *n* is the number of observations used in computing the average. If the option's life is one year and *n* is set equal to 12, the average is computed based on monthly asset prices. The parameter *ntrial* is the number of simulation runs. The parameter *cp* is either "C" or "P," depending upon whether you are valuing a call or a put. The parameter *sx* is either "S" or "X," depending upon whether you are averaging the asset price to replace the asset price or the exercise price of the average rate option. Finally, the parameter *ag* is either "A" or "G," depending upon whether the average rate of the option is arithmetic or geometric. For the illustration at hand,

OV_APPROX_ASIAN_OPT_MC(50, 50, 1, 0.05, 0.01, 0.40, 12, 10000, "C", "S", "A") = 5.2812

In applying the OPTVAL function, you will not get exactly the same answer since the random drawings from the normal distribution will not be exactly the same. It is also worthwhile to note that if quarter observations are used in the computation of the average, the value of the option increases, that is,

OV_APPROX_ASIAN_OPT_MC (50, 50, 1, 0.05, 0.01, 0.40, 4, 10000, "C", "S", "A") = 5.9598

The reason is, of course, that variance of the average asset price and the option's value shrink as the number of observations increases. In the extreme case where the number of observations going into the computation of the average is one, the average rate option value is

OV_APPROX_ASIAN_OPT_MC (50, 50, 1, 0.05, 0.01, 0.40, 1, 10000, "C", "S", "A") = 8.7833

and should be identically equal to the BSM value of a European-style option,

OV_OPTION_VALUE(50, 50, 1, 0.05, 0.01, 0.40, "C", "E") = 8.7017

The small difference arises because Monte Carlo simulation is an approximation method.

## Two Underlying Sources of Risk

The Monte Carlo simulation can be extended to handle multiple sources of risk. Consider a European-style put option on the minimum, for example. Since the option is written on the minimum of two risky assets, the option has two underlying sources of price risk. At expiration, the option holder receives

$$\max[X - \min(\tilde{S}_{1,T}, \tilde{S}_{2,T})]$$

If both asset prices follow geometric Brownian motions, the option can be valued analytically, as was noted earlier in the chapter. Nonetheless, we will value the option numerically using Monte Carlo simulation. In order to do so, we must explicitly account for the fact that movements in the asset prices are likely to be correlated with one another.

To handle the correlation between movements in asset prices, we make one small change to the Monte Carlo simulation procedure. First, we draw a unit normal random deviate for asset 1. Label it $\varepsilon_1$. Next, we draw a second unit normal random deviate for asset 2. Label it $\varepsilon_2$. Naturally $\varepsilon_1$ is uncorrelated with $\varepsilon_2$ since they are independent drawings. To induce correlation between the deviates, we apply the following transformation to the second deviate,

$$\varepsilon_2' = \rho\varepsilon_1 + \sqrt{1-\rho^2}\varepsilon_2 \tag{9.22}$$

where $\rho$ is the correlation between the variables in the bivariate distribution. Note that this new variable $\varepsilon_2'$ remains unit normal. Its mean is

$$E(\varepsilon_2') = \rho E(\varepsilon_1) + \sqrt{1-\rho^2}E(\varepsilon_2) = 0$$

and its variance is

$$\mathrm{Var}(\varepsilon_2') = \rho^2\mathrm{Var}(\varepsilon_1) + (1-\rho^2)\mathrm{Var}(\varepsilon_2) = 1$$

Note also that the covariance (correlation) between $\varepsilon_1$ and $\varepsilon_2'$ is

$$\begin{aligned}\mathrm{Cov}(\varepsilon_1, \varepsilon_2') &= \mathrm{Cov}(\varepsilon_1, \rho\varepsilon_1 + \sqrt{1-\rho^2}\varepsilon_2)\\ &= \rho\mathrm{Var}(\varepsilon_1) + \mathrm{Cov}(\varepsilon_1, \sqrt{1-\rho^2}\varepsilon_2)\\ &= \rho\end{aligned}$$

We then generate prices for asset 1 and asset 2 using $\varepsilon_1$ and $\varepsilon_2'$

$$S_{1,t+\Delta t} = S_{1,t}e^{(b_1-\sigma_1^2/2)\Delta t + \sigma_1\sqrt{\Delta t}\varepsilon_1} \tag{9.23}$$

and

$$S_{2,t+\Delta t} = S_{2,t}e^{(b_2-\sigma_2^2/2)\Delta t + \sigma_{21}\sqrt{\Delta t}\varepsilon_2'} \tag{9.24}$$

With the prices at each time step identified, we value the option.

**ILLUSTRATION 9.6** Find value of European-style call on maximum of two risky assets.

*Consider a call option that provides its holder the right to buy \$100,000 worth of the S&P 500 index portfolio at an exercise price of \$1000 or \$100,000 worth of a particular T-bond at an exercise price of \$100, whichever is worth more at the end of three months. The S&P 500 index is currently priced at \$1075, pays dividends at a rate of 1% annually and has a return volatility of 18%. The T-bond is currently priced at \$105, pays a cou-*

*pon yield of 6% and has a return volatility of 8%. The correlation between the rates of return of the S&P 500 and the T-bond is 0.5. The risk-free rate of interest is 3%.*

Before applying the Monte Carlo simulation technique, it is important to recognize that there are two exercise prices in this problem: $1,000 for the S&P index portfolio and $100 for the T-bond. What this implies is that we can buy 100,000/1,000 = 100 units of the index portfolio or 100,000/100 = 1,000 units of T-bonds at the end of three months, depending on which is worth more. At this juncture, we must decide whether to value the call option on the maximum in units of the S&P 500 index portfolio, in which case we multiply the current T-bond price and its exercise price by 10 and then multiply the computed option price by 100, or to value the option in units of the T-bond, in which case we divide the current S&P 500 price and the option's S&P 500 exercise price by 10 and then multiply the computed option price by 1,000.[18] We choose to work in units of the S&P 500 index portfolio, so we adjust the T-bond prices: the current T-bond price is assumed to be 10,500 and the T-bond exercise price is 1,000. With the units of the two underlying assets comparable, we apply the OPTVAL function,

OV_APPROX_MAXMIN_OPT_MC(s1,s2,x,t,r,i1,i2,v1,v2,rho,n,ntrial,cp,mm)

to find

OV_APPROX_MAXMIN_OPT_MC(1100,980,1000,0.25,0.03,0.01,0.06,0.18,0.08,0.5,10, 10000,"C", "X") = 98.671

The computed option value is 98.671 per $1,000 or $98.671 × 1,000 = $9,867.10 in total.

## Mean Reversion

Another advantage in using Monte Carlo simulation is that other processes for asset price movements can be introduced seamlessly. While an assumption geometric Brownian motion may be sensible for movements in the price of underlying assets such as stocks and stock indexes which tend to grow through time, the prices of assets such as gold and oil as well as interest rates on bonds tend to revert back to mean levels.[19] A simple mean reversion process is

$$dS = \kappa(\theta - S)dt + \sigma dz \tag{9.25}$$

where $\kappa$ is the continuous-time speed of mean reversion or pull rate, $\theta$ is the mean reversion level, and $\sigma$ is the continuous-time standard deviation of the price changes.[20] Under this assumption, discrete movements in asset price through time are described by

---

[18] These types of adjustments can be made freely because the option price is linearly homogeneous in both the asset price and the exercise price. See Merton (1973).

[19] Schwartz and Smith (1999), for example, model the short-term movements of commodity prices as a mean-reverting process and model movements in the long-term equilibrium price as a Brownian motion. asicek (1977) models movements in short-term interest rate as a mean-reverting process.

[20] This process is commonly referred to as an Ornstein-Uhlenbeck process or, alternatively, a Gauss-Markov process.

$$S_{t+\Delta t} - S_t = \theta k - kS_t + \sigma_{\Delta t}\varepsilon \tag{9.26}$$

where $k = 1 - e^{-\kappa\Delta t}$ is the discrete-time reversion rate over the interval $\Delta t$,

$$\sigma_{\Delta t} = \sqrt{\frac{1 - e^{-2\kappa\Delta t}}{2\kappa\Delta t}}\sigma$$

is the discrete-time volatility, and where $\varepsilon$ is a drawing from a unit normal distribution. Figure 9.15, Panels A and B, show simulated price movements of an

**FIGURE 9.15** Simulated asset price path for mean reversion process.
Panel A: Mean reversion rate of 0.05.

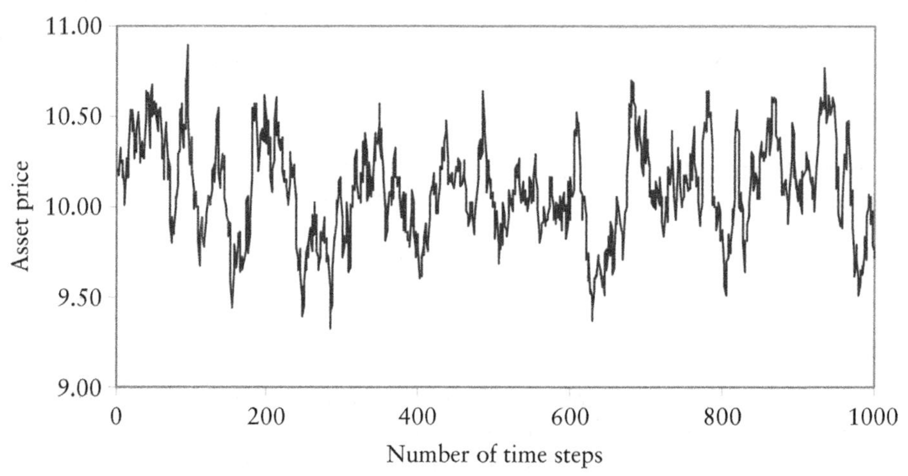


Panel B: Mean reversion rate of 0.20.

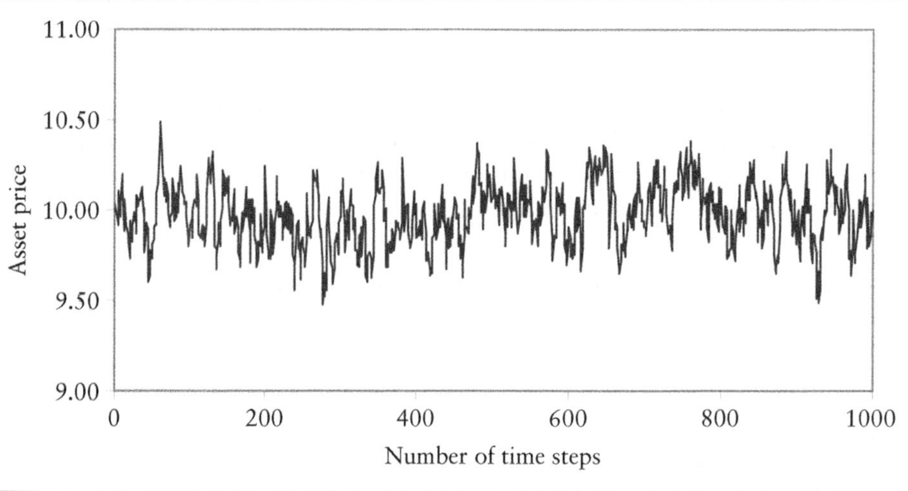

asset that follows a mean reversion process. The processes include 1,000 time steps, with each time step $\Delta t = 1$. The mean reversion level is 10, and the continuous-time volatility rate is 0.10 (i.e., discrete-time volatility rate of 0.09755). Panel A has a continuous-time reversion rate of 0.05 (i.e., a discrete-time reversion rate of 0.04877), while Panel B has a reversion rate of 0.20 (i.e., a discrete-time reversion rate of 0.018127). As the figures show, the higher the rate of mean reversion, the quicker price is pulled back toward the mean, and the less the variation in price. To value options on an asset whose price is mean-reverting, we simply generate the asset price path using (9.26) rather than (9.20). All other steps in the Monte Carlo valuation procedure are the same.[21]

## QUADRATIC APPROXIMATION

The quadratic approximation, developed by MacMillan (1986) and Barone-Adesi and Whaley (1987),[22] is based on the simple notion that an American-style option can be thought of as the sum of an otherwise similar European-style option and an early exercise premium, that is,

$$C = c + \varepsilon_C \tag{9.27}$$

and

$$P = p + \varepsilon_P \tag{9.28}$$

where $\varepsilon_C$ and $\varepsilon_P$ are the early exercise premiums on the American-style call and put, respectively. The virtue in doing so is that the European-style options have analytical valuation equations. In the last chapter, the European-style option valuation formulas were presented as

$$c = Se^{-iT}N(d_1) - Xe^{-rT}N(d_2) \tag{9.29}$$

and

$$p = Xe^{-rT}N(-d_2) - Se^{-iT}N(-d_1) \tag{9.30}$$

where

$$d_1 = \frac{\ln(Se^{-iT}/Xe^{-rT}) + 0.5\sigma^2 T}{\sigma\sqrt{T}}, \text{ and } d_2 = d_1 - \sigma\sqrt{T}$$

[21] In order to apply the risk-neutral option valuation principles, we must adjust the rate of drift by the market price of risk—a discussion which we defer to a later chapter.

[22] The quadratic approximation is also applied to futures options in Whaley (1986).

The term $N(d)$ is the cumulative normal density function, as defined in the last chapter.

Under the quadratic approximation, the value of an American-style call on an asset with a constant, continuous carry rate is

$$C = \begin{cases} c + A_2(S/S^*)^{q_2} & \text{if } S < S^* \\ S - X & \text{if } S \geq S^* \end{cases} \tag{9.31}$$

where

$$A_2 = \frac{S^*\{1 - e^{-iT}N[d_1(S^*)]\}}{q_2}, \quad d_1(S) = \frac{\ln(Se^{-iT}/Xe^{-rT}) + 0.5\sigma^2 T}{\sigma\sqrt{T}},$$

$$q_2 = \frac{1 - n + \sqrt{(n-1)^2 + 4k}}{2}, \quad n = \frac{2(r-i)}{\sigma^2}, \quad k = \frac{2r}{\sigma^2(1 - e^{-rT})}$$

$c$ is the value of the corresponding European-style call option using (9.29), and $S^*$ is the critical asset price above which the American-style call should be exercised immediately and is the solution to

$$S^* - X = c(S^*) + \{1 - e^{-iT}N[d_1(S^*)]\}S^*/q_2 \tag{9.32}$$

Figure 9.16, Panels A and B, provide some intuition for how the quadratic approximation works. Before valuing the call option using (9.31), it is necessary to identify the critical asset price above which the call will be exercised immediately. This is done using (9.32). The critical price, $S^*$, is that unique asset price at which (9.32) holds as an equality and does not depend on the current asset price. Panel A shows where this price lies. Below $S^*$, the call is valued using the first line on the right-hand side of (9.31). Above $S^*$, the call value is simply the difference between the asset price and the exercise price (i.e., the second line on the right-hand side of (9.31)). With $S^*$ in hand, we can then generate call option values over a range of asset prices. This is done in Panel B of Figure 9.16. Note that the early exercise premium—the difference between the American-style and the European-style call option values—grows large as the asset price rises.

The quadratic approximation for an American-style put on an asset with a constant, continuous carry rate is

$$P = \begin{cases} p + A_1(S/S^{**})^{q_1} & \text{if } S > S^{**} \\ X - S & \text{if } S \leq S^{**} \end{cases} \tag{9.33}$$

where

**FIGURE 9.16** Illustration of the components of the quadratic approximation method.
Panel A: Determination of critical asset price, $S^*$.

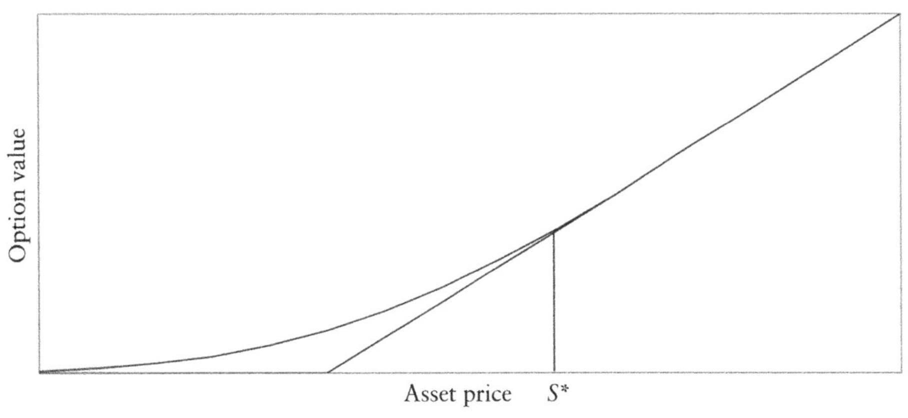


Panel B: Early exercise premium.

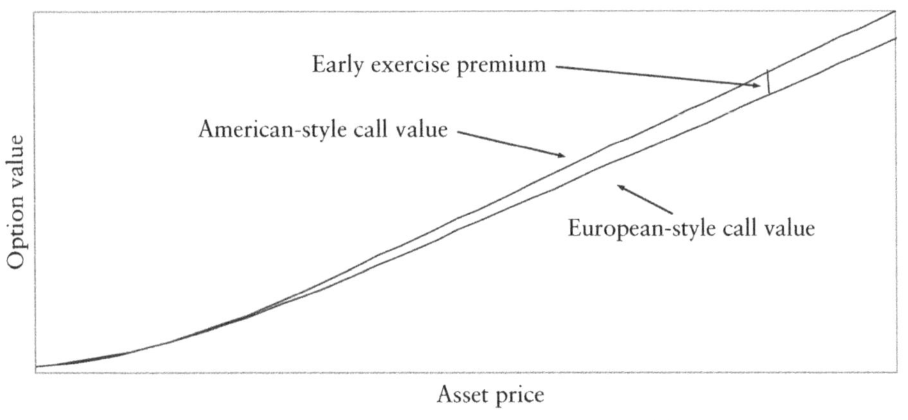


$$A_1 = -\frac{S^{**}\{1 - e^{-iT}N[-d_1(S^{**})]\}}{q_1}$$

$$q_1 = \frac{1 - n - \sqrt{(n-1)^2 + 4k}}{2}$$

$p$ is the value of the corresponding European-style put option using (9.32), and $S^{**}$ is the critical asset price below which the American-style put should be exercised immediately and is the solution to

$$X - S^{**} = p(S^{**}) - \{1 - e^{-iT}N[-d_1(S^{**})]\}S^{**}/q_1 \tag{9.34}$$

**ILLUSTRATION 9.7** Compute value of American-style option using quadratic method.

*Compute the value of a two-year American-style put option with an exercise price of 55. Use the quadratic approximation. Assume the underlying asset is a foreign currency whose current price is 50 and whose volatility rate is 20%. Assume the domestic rate of interest is 5%, and the foreign rate of interest, 2%. Use the quadratic approximation, and show intermediate computations.*

To begin, use the domestic and foreign interest rates to identify the expected rate of price appreciation of the currency, that is,

$$b = r_d - r_f = 0.05 - 0.02 = 0.03$$

Next compute the values of $n$ and $k$. Using the problem parameters, these are

$$n = \frac{2b}{\sigma^2} = \frac{2(0.03)}{0.20^2} = 1.5$$

and

$$k = \frac{2r}{\sigma^2(1 - e^{-rT})} = \frac{2(0.05)}{0.20^2(1 - e^{-0.05(2)})} = 26.2708$$

With the values of $n$ and $k$, can compute the value of $q_1$, that is,

$$q_1 = \frac{1 - 1.5 - \sqrt{(1.5 - 1)^2 + 4(26.2708)}}{2} = -5.3816$$

Now the critical asset price below which you would exercise the American-style put immediately, $S^{**}$, must be identified by solving

$$55 - S^{**} = (p(S^{**}) + \{1 - e^{-(0.03 - 0.05)2}N[-d_1(S^{**})]\}S^{**})/5.3816$$

The value $S^{**}$ of that satisfies the equation is 41.1776. This means the value of $A_1$ is

$$A_1 = \frac{41.1776\{1 - e^{-(0.03 - 0.05)2}N[-d_1(41.1776)]\}}{5.3816} = 2.1490$$

With all of the parameters identified, put valuation becomes a matter of applying

$$P = \begin{cases} p + 2.1490(S/41.1776)^{-5.3816} & \text{if } S > 41.1776 \\ 55 - S & \text{if } S \leq 41.1776 \end{cases}$$

where $p$ is the value of a European-style put with the same parameters. At the currency of 50, the value of the European-style put is 6.41, and the value of the American-style put is 7.16. This implies that the early exercise premium has a value of approximately 75 cents.

The quadratic approximation technique is not as flexible as lattice-based methods for valuing options with nonstandard features. For standard options on assets with a constant continuous carry rate (e.g., foreign currency options, stock index options, futures options), however, the quadratic approximation is faster and more accurate than competing methods.

## MEASURING RISK NUMERICALLY

Just as the options studied in this chapter must valued numerically, the risk characteristics of these options must be computed numerically. The procedure is straightforward. Recall that the delta of an option is the change in option value with respect to a change in asset price. To obtain the delta of an option numerically, perturb the current asset price $S$ by a small amount $\phi$ in either direction, that is, $S + \phi$ and $S - \phi$, and value the option at each asset price, $OV(S + \phi)$ and $OV(S - \phi)$. Figure 9.17 illustrates. The valuation function $OV(.)$ can be any of the valuation methodologies discussed in this chapter. In the figure, the quadratic approximation was used to generate the values of an American-style FX put option for different levels of the exchange rate. Ideally, we would like to know the slope of the $OV$ function at the current exchange rate $S$. We cannot do so by taking the partial derivative of $OV$ with respect to $S$ because we do not have an analytical expression for $OV$. To approximate the delta, therefore, we take the ratio of the difference between the computed option values to the difference between the perturbed asset prices, that is,

$$\Delta_p = \frac{OV(S + \phi) - OV(S - \phi)}{(S + \phi) - (S - \phi)}$$

**FIGURE 9.17** Numerical approximation for the delta of a FX put option.

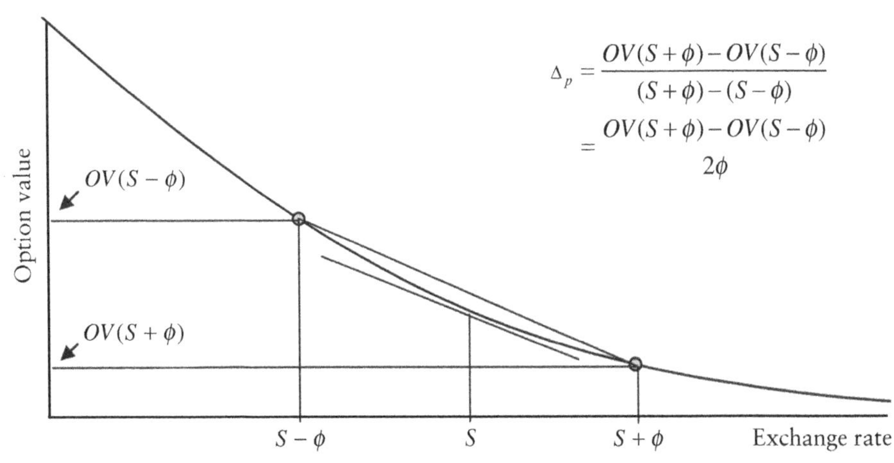

To assess the accuracy of this numerical procedure, consider the two-year put option that we have used as an illustration throughout the chapter, but assume, for the moment, that put is European-style. The *analytical* option value is 6.406 and, using the formula from the last chapter, its *analytical* delta is –0.474. Now suppose that there is no formula for computing the delta, and, instead, it must be computed using the numerically. First, perturb the asset price up by, say, 25 cents to a level of 50.25, and compute the put value. Using the BSM formula, the put value is 6.288. Next perturb the asset price downward by the same amount. The put option value at an asset price of 49.75 is 6.525. The numerical delta for this put is therefore

$$\Delta_p = \frac{6.288 - 6.525}{(50 + 0.25) - (50 - 0.25)} = \frac{-0.237}{0.50} = -0.474$$

Not surprisingly, the *analytical* delta and the *numerical* delta values are very close. At three decimal places the difference is not apparent. At six decimal places, the analytical delta is –0.474039 and the numerical delta is –0.474038.

In general, all of the Greeks for options can be measured using the expression

$$\text{Greek}_k = \frac{OV(k + \phi) - OV(k - \phi)}{2\phi} \tag{9.35}$$

where $OV$ represents one of the numerical valuation methods that we described earlier in the chapter (e.g., the binomial method, the trinomial method, Monte Carlo simulation, and the quadratic approximation), $k$ is the option determinant of interest (e.g., $S$ for delta risk, $\sigma$ for vega risk, and so on), and $\phi$ is a small positive constant selected by the user. The gamma, that is, the change in the delta with respect to a change in the asset price, may be computed using

$$\text{Gamma} = \frac{OV(S + \phi) - 2 \times OV(S + \phi) + OV(S - \phi)}{\phi^2} \tag{9.36}$$

It is also worth noting that, if the delta and theta of the option have already been computed, the gamma can be solved for analytically.[23] Recall that the Black-Scholes/Merton partial differential equation for valuing options (i.e., equation (7D.6) from Appendix 7D in Chapter 7) may be written

$$-\theta + bS\Delta + \frac{1}{2}\sigma^2 S^2 \gamma = rOV \tag{9.37}$$

where $OV$ is the option value. Rearranging to isolate gamma,

[23] This idea was first suggested by Carr (2001).

$$\gamma = \frac{rOV + \theta - bS\Delta}{0.5\sigma^2 S^2} \tag{9.38}$$

The formulas (9.35) and (9.36) provide the means for calculating the Greeks numerically and can be applied to obtain any risk measures detailed in Table 9.4. The numerical values of the Greeks for the American-style put illustration maintained throughout the chapter are reported in Table 9.5. The quadratic approximation is used to value the put. The values reported in the table are identical to those that would be obtained by using the OV_OPTION_VALUE function from the OPTVAL Library. Note that condition (9.38) is satisfied.

## SUMMARY

Numerical methods are an indispensable tool in option valuation and risk measurement. The reasons are that numerical methods: (1) are required in instances where the option valuation problem is intractable from a mathematical standpoint (i.e., American-style options); (2) are more convenient than analytical methods in situations where the option valuation problem has large numbers of

**TABLE 9.4** Details of formula use for evaluating option risk measures numerically.

| Change in option value with respect to a change in: | Determinant, $k$ | Greek$_y$ | Symbol |
|---|---|---|---|
| Asset price | $S$ | Delta | $\Delta$ |
| Interest rate | $r$ | Rho$_r$ | $\rho^r$ |
| Income rate | $i$ | Rho$_i$ | $\rho^i$ |
| Volatility rate | $\sigma$ | Vega | Vega |
| Time to expiration | $T$ | Theta | $\theta$ |
| | | | |
| Change in delta with respect to a change in: | | | |
| Asset price | $S$ | Gamma | $\gamma$ |

**TABLE 9.5** Summary of risk characteristics of the American-style put written on a currency evaluated numerically using the quadratic approximation.

| Partial Derivative with Respect to | Greek Symbol | Perturbation Amount, $\phi$ | Numerical Value of Greek |
|---|---|---|---|
| $S$ | $\Delta$ | 0.25 | –0.555 |
| $\Delta$ | $\gamma$ | 0.25 | 0.037 |
| $r$ | $\rho^r$ | 0.05% | –35.384 |
| $i$ | $\rho^i$ | 0.05% | 30.416 |
| $\sigma$ | Vega | 0.05% | 25.736 |
| $T$ | $\theta$ | 0.01 | 0.706 |

contingencies (e.g., accrual options); and (3) can be extremely accurate if applied properly. This chapter examines three different numerical methods—the binomial method, the trinomial, method and Monte Carlo simulation. All three methods involve replacing the BSM assumption that the underlying asset price has continuous geometric Brownian diffusion with an assumption that underlying asset price jumps over small discrete time intervals during the option's life. The *binomial method,* for example, assumes that the asset price moves to one of two levels over the next increment in time. The size of the move and its likelihood are chosen in a manner so as to be consistent with the log-normal asset price distribution. In a similar fashion, the *trinomial method* allows the asset price to move to one of three levels over the next increment in time, and *Monte Carlo simulation* uses a discretized version of geometric Brownian motion to enumerate every possible path that the asset's price may take over the life of the option. Each of these three numerical methods is illustrated using a variety of derivatives contracts including standard American-style options, spread options, Asian-style options, and options on the minimum and maximum. For valuing standard American-style options, the *quadratic approximation method* is also discussed. It addresses the value of early exercise by modifying the BSM partial differential equation.

## REFERENCES AND SUGGESTED READINGS

Barone-Adesi, Giovanni, and Robert E. Whaley. 1987. Efficient analytic approximation of american option values. *Journal of Finance* 42 (June): 301–320.

Black, Fischer, and Myron Scholes. 1973. The pricing of options and corporate liabilities. *Journal of Political Economy* 81: 637–659.

Boyle, Phelim P. 1988. A lattice framework for option pricing with two state variables. *Journal of Financial and Quantitative Analysis* 23 (March): 1–12.

Boyle, Phelim P. 1977. Options: A Monte Carlo approach. *Journal of Financial Economics* 4: 323–338.

Boyle, Phelim P., J. Evnine, and S. Gibbs. 1989. Numerical evaluation of multivariate contingent claims. *Review of Financial Studies* 2: 241–250.

Boyle, Phelim P. and S. H. Lau. 1994. Bumping up against the barrier with the binomial method. *Journal of Derivatives* 1 (Summer): 6–14.

Carr, Peter. 2001. Deriving derivatives of derivative securities. *Journal of Computational Finance* 4: 5–30.

Cox, John C., Stephen A. Ross, and Mark Rubinstein. 1979. Option pricing: A simplified approach. *Journal of Financial Economics* 7 (September): 229–264.

Figlewski, Stephen, and Bin Gao. 1999. The adaptive mesh model: A new approach to efficient option pricing. *Journal of Financial Economics* 53: 313–351.

Jarrow, Robert A., and Andrew Rudd. 1983. *Option Pricing.* Homewood, IL: Irwin.

Johnson, Herbert E. 1987. Options on the minimum and maximum of several assets. *Journal of Financial and Quantitative Analysis* 22 (September): 277–283.

Kamrad, Bardia, and Peter Ritchken. 1991. Multinomial approximating models for options with k state variables. *Management Science* 37 (12): 1640–1652.

Kemna, A., and A. Vorst. 1990. A pricing method for options based on average asset values. *Journal of Banking and Finance* 14 (March): 113–129.

MacMillan, Lionel W. 1986. Analytic approximation for the american put option. *Advances in Futures and Options Research* 1: 119–139.

Merton, Robert C. 1973. Theory of rational option pricing. *Bell Journal of Economics and Management Science*: 141–183.

Rendleman Jr., Richard J., and Brit J. Bartter. 1979. Two-state option pricing. *Journal of Finance* 34 (December): 1093–1110.

Rubinstein, Mark. 2000. On the relation between binomial and trinomial option pricing models. *Journal of Derivatives* 8 (Winter): 47–50.

Stulz, Rene. 1982. Options on the minimum or maximum of two assets. *Journal of Financial Economics* 10: 161–185.

Whaley, Robert E. 1986. Valuation of American futures options: Theory and empirical tests. *Journal of Finance* 41 (March): 127–150.

Whaley, Robert E. 1996. Valuing spreads options. *Energy in the News* (Summer): 42–45.

# 10

# Risk Management Strategies: Options

Chapters 7 through 9 deal with option valuation. Knowing how to value options, in turn, provides a means for measuring risk. The focus now turns to option trading strategies. Two major categories exist—dynamic strategies and passive strategies. Dynamic strategies are those that focus on value changes over the next instant in time. Dynamic expected return/risk management, for example, attempts to manage changes in portfolio value caused by unexpected changes in the asset price, volatility, and interest rates, as well as the natural erosion of option's time value as it approaches expiration. These strategies are of particular importance to exchange-traded option market makers or OTC option dealers who, in the normal course of business, acquire option positions with risks that need to be managed on a day-to-day (minute-to-minute) basis. The first two sections of the chapter are devoted to dynamic strategies. In the first, we tie the expected return/risk characteristics of options and option portfolios to the CAPM. In the second, we consider the dynamic risk management problem faced by an option market maker.

Passive strategies, on the other hand, are those that involve holding an option over some discrete interval of time such as a week, a month, or even held to expiration. In this instance, the rates of return of the option and the asset are not perfectly correlated and the mechanics for analyzing the position are somewhat different. The third section of the chapter is devoted to analyzing passive strategies. Specifically, we assess the expected return/risk characteristics of portfolios that are entered and then held to expiration. We begin first with a review of the profit functions for basic option/futures/asset positions. Next, we discuss how to compute expected profits and expected returns under the assumption that the underlying asset price is log-normally distributed at the options' expiration.[1] In particular, we show how to compute the probability that a particular option trading strategy will be profitable at the options' expiration as well as the level of its expected profit. Finally, we simulate the performance of trading strategies using Monte Carlo simulation.

[1] Recall that this assumption was first introduced in Chapter 7.

## EXPECTED RETURN AND RISK

### Individual Options

The key to understanding how options fit within the mean-variance CAPM is in the recognition of how an option's expected return and risk are tied to the expected return and risk of the underlying asset.[2] The CAPM states that the expected rate of return on the asset is

$$E_S = r + (E_M - r)\beta_S \tag{10.1a}$$

where $E_S$ and $E_M$ are the expected rates of return for the asset and the market portfolio, respectively, $r$ is the risk-free of return, and $\beta_S$ is the asset's beta risk. Since the CAPM applies to all risky assets, its also applies to options. The expected rate of return of a call option written on the asset, for example, may be written

$$E_c = r + (E_M - r)\beta_c \tag{10.1b}$$

Since a risk-free hedge can be formed between the call and the asset, the rates of return of the call and the asset are perfectly positively correlated. Consequently, the variance of the call return is $\text{Var}(R_c) = \eta_c^2 \text{Var}(R_S)$, where $\eta_c$ is the call option's eta or price elasticity.[3] Total risk, which we have defined as the standard deviation of return, is therefore

$$\sigma_c = |\eta_c|\sigma_c \tag{10.2a}$$

and

$$\sigma_p = |\eta_p|\sigma_S \tag{10.2b}$$

for the call and the put, respectively, and the absolute value operator has been applied to ensure that the standard deviation is positive. Similarly, the option's beta is defined as the covariance of the option's return with the market return divided by the variance of the market return. Thus the relation between the beta for an option and the beta for the underlying asset is

$$\beta_c = \frac{\text{Cov}(R_c, R_M)}{\text{Var}(R_M)} = \frac{\eta_c \text{Cov}(R_S, R_M)}{\text{Var}(R_M)} = \eta_c \beta_S \tag{10.3a}$$

[2] It is important to recognize that in this section we are focusing on dynamic risk management and instantaneous rates of return in the manner of Merton (1973). Over discrete intervals of time, the rates of return for the option and its underlying asset will not be perfectly correlated (as we discuss later in this chapter).

[3] Recall the elasticity of option price with respect to the asset price is $\eta_c = \Delta_c(S/c)$ and $\eta_p = \Delta_p(S/p)$, where $\Delta$ is the option's delta.

and

$$\beta_p = \frac{\text{Cov}(R_p, R_M)}{\text{Var}(R_M)} = \frac{\eta_p \text{Cov}(R_S, R_M)}{\text{Var}(R_M)} = \eta_p \beta_S \tag{10.3b}$$

Note that, since $\eta_p < 0$, the beta for a put option is negative. The value of the put falls as the market rises, and vice versa.

To better understand the expected return/risk characteristics of options, consider the following stock option illustration. Assume that the current stock price is 50, the expected stock return is 16%, the stock's beta is 1.20, the volatility of the stock return is 40%, and the stock pays no dividends. Also assume that there exist three-month European-style call and put options with exercise prices of 45, 50, and 55, and that all of these options have prices equal to their European-style formula values from Chapter 5. The risk-free interest rate is assumed to be 4%. Using the risk relations (10.2) and (10.3) as well as the security market relation,

$$E_i = r + (E_M - r)\beta_i \tag{10.4}$$

from Chapter 3, the expected returns and risks of the different options can be computed and are summarized in Table 10.1. Note that we can use the security market line relation (10.4) to find the implied expected return on the market, assuming the capital market is in equilibrium, that is, $0.16 = 0.04 + (E_M - 0.04)1.20$, or $E_M = 14\%$.

The results in Table 10.1 are interesting in variety of respects. First, note the startling high values of the risk measures. The in-the-money call, for example, has a beta equal to 6.347 and a total volatility rate of 211.58%. This should not be surprising in the sense that calls are nothing more than leveraged positions in the underlying asset. The implicit degree of leverage is given by the call's eta. Owning the 45-call is like borrowing 428.95% of your current wealth, and investing all of your wealth as well as the borrowings in stock (i.e., 528.95% of

**TABLE 10.1** Expected returns and risks of European-style options written on a stock. Stock price is 50, expected stock return is 16%, stock beta is 1.20, volatility rate is 40%, and dividend yield is zero. Interest rate is 4%, and expected return on market is 14%. Options have three months remaining to expiration.

| Money-ness | Exercise Price | (C)all/ (P)ut | Value | Delta | Eta | Expected Return | Beta | Total Risk |
|---|---|---|---|---|---|---|---|---|
| ITM | 45 | c | 7.0965 | 0.7507 | 5.2895 | 67.47% | 6.347 | 211.58% |
| ATM | 50 | c | 4.2167 | 0.5596 | 6.6358 | 83.63% | 7.963 | 265.43% |
| OTM | 55 | c | 2.3051 | 0.3720 | 8.0693 | 100.83% | 9.683 | 322.77% |
| | | | | | | | | |
| OTM | 45 | p | 1.6487 | -0.2493 | -7.5594 | -86.71% | -9.071 | 302.38% |
| ATM | 50 | p | 3.7192 | -0.4404 | -5.9205 | -67.05% | -7.105 | 236.82% |
| ITM | 55 | p | 6.7578 | -0.6280 | -4.6465 | -51.76% | -5.576 | 185.86% |

your wealth is invested in the stock). As we go from in-the-money calls to out-of-the-money calls, the degree of leverage increases and the risk measures go up. Figure 10.1 illustrates the expected return/beta tradeoff. Figure 10.2 shows the relation between expected return and volatility.

A second noteworthy observation about the values reported in Table 10.2 (as well as Figures 10.1 and 10.2) is that put options have large negative expected returns. These, too, are leveraged positions, but this time the leverage goes the other way, that is, we are implicitly short selling stocks and placing the proceeds in the risk-free asset. The out-of-the-money put in Table 10.1, for example, has an eta equal to –7.5594. This means that short selling an amount of stock equal to 755.94% of your wealth and using the proceeds, together with your initial wealth, to buy the risk-free asset has an expected return equal to the expected return of the OTM put,

$$-7.5594(0.16) + 8.5594(0.04) = -86.71\%$$

### Option Portfolios

The CAPM expected return/risk mechanics can also be applied to portfolios in order to analyze different trading strategies. A covered call strategy involves selling a call option for each unit of the underlying asset held. A protective put strategy involves buying a put for each unit of the asset held. To analyze these portfolios, expressions for the expected return and risks of the portfolio are

**FIGURE 10.1** Expected return/beta relation of European-style options written on a stock. Stock price is 50, expected stock return is 16%, stock beta is 1.20, volatility rate is 40%, and dividend yield is zero. Interest rate is 4%, and expected return on market is 14%. Options have three months remaining to expiration.

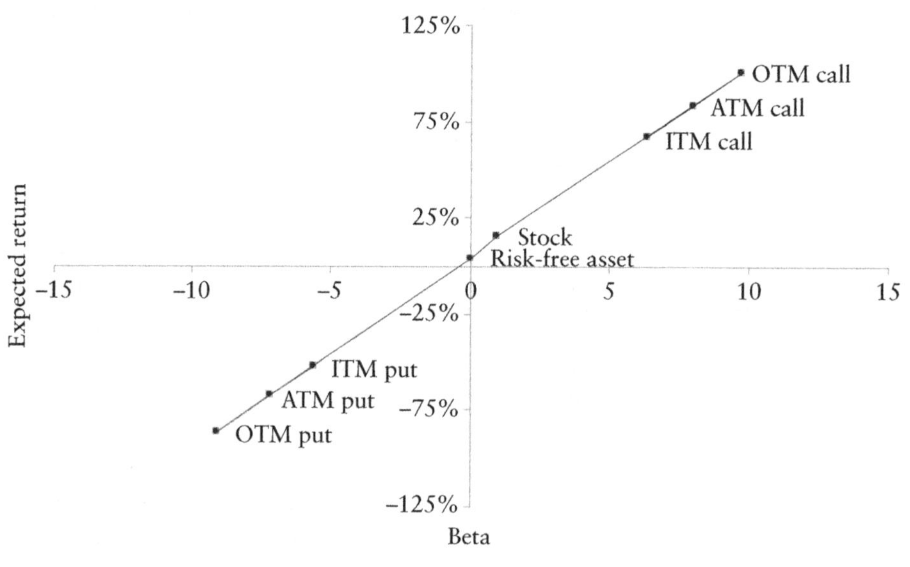

**FIGURE 10.2** Expected return/volatility relation of European-style options written on a stock. Stock price is 50, expected stock return is 16%, stock beta is 1.20, volatility rate is 40%, and dividend yield is zero. Interest rate is 4%, and expected return on market is 14%. Options have three months remaining to expiration.

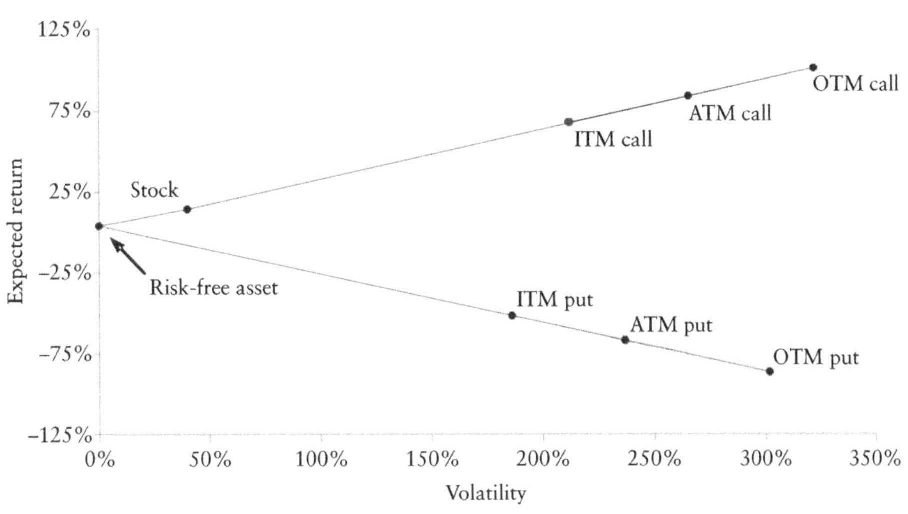


**TABLE 10.2** Expected returns and risks of covered call and protective put trading strategies. Stock price is 50, expected stock return is 16%, stock beta is 1.20, volatility rate is 40%, and dividend yield is zero. Interest rate is 4%, and expected return on market is 14%. Options have three months remaining to expiration.

| Moneyness | Exercise Price | (C)all/ (P)ut | X | Expected Return | Beta | Total Risk |
|---|---|---|---|---|---|---|
| ITM | 45 | c | 1.165 | 7.49% | 0.349 | 11.62% |
| ATM | 50 | c | 1.092 | 9.77% | 0.577 | 19.24% |
| OTM | 55 | c | 1.048 | 11.90% | 0.790 | 26.33% |
| OTM | 45 | p | 0.968 | 12.72% | 0.872 | 29.07% |
| ATM | 50 | p | 0.931 | 10.25% | 0.625 | 20.83% |
| ITM | 55 | p | 0.881 | 7.93% | 0.393 | 13.11% |

needed. For portfolio consisting of the asset and an option, the expected portfolio return is

$$E_{\text{portfolio}} = XE_S + (1 - X)E_o \tag{10.5}$$

the beta of the portfolio is

$$\beta_{\text{portfolio}} = X\beta_S + (1 - X)\beta_o \tag{10.6}$$

and the volatility of the portfolio is

$$\sigma_{\text{portfolio}} = X\sigma_S + (1-X)\sigma_c \tag{10.7a}$$

for calls, and

$$\sigma_{\text{portfolio}} = X\sigma_S + (1-X)\sigma_p \tag{10.7b}$$

for puts.[4] The proportion of wealth invested in the asset for the covered call strategy is

$$X = \frac{S}{S-c} \tag{10.8}$$

Note that in the denominator of (10.8) the proceeds from writing the call are assumed to be used to subsidize the cost of buying the asset. The proportion of wealth invested in the asset for the protective put strategy is

$$X = \frac{S}{S+p} \tag{10.9}$$

Since both the put and the asset are purchased, the sum of the prices appears in the denominator as the cost of the portfolio.

The first panel of Table 10.2 contains the expected return/risk properties of the covered call strategies created from the call options listed in the first panel of Table 10.1. To illustrate the computations, consider the ITM call. The expected return of the covered call strategy using the 45-call is

$$E_{\text{portfolio}} = \left(\frac{50}{50-7.0965}\right)0.16 + \left(\frac{-7.0965}{50-70.965}\right)0.6747 = 7.49\%$$

The beta of the covered call is

$$\beta_{\text{portfolio}} = \left(\frac{50}{50-7.0965}\right)1.20 + \left(\frac{-7.0965}{50-70.965}\right)6.347 = 0.349$$

and the volatility rate is

$$\sigma_{\text{portfolio}} = \left(\frac{50}{50-7.0965}\right)0.40 + \left(\frac{-7.0965}{50-70.965}\right)2.1158 = 11.62\%$$

[4] The expressions for portfolio for the call and put are different because, while both the returns of the call and put are perfectly correlated with the asset, the call returns are positively correlated and the put returns are negatively correlated.

**FIGURE 10.3** Expected return/volatility relation of covered call strategies. Stock price is 50, expected stock return is 16%, stock beta is 1.20, volatility rate is 40%, and dividend yield is zero. Interest rate is 4%, and expected return on market is 14%. Options have three months remaining to expiration.

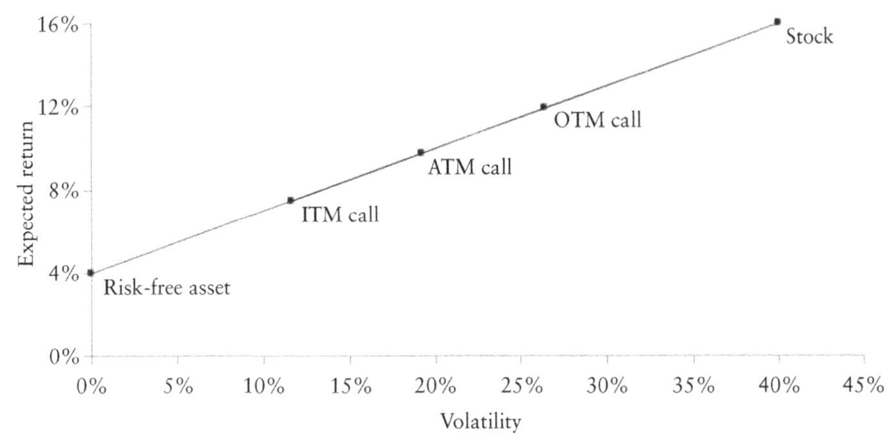


In other words, writing a call option against a long position is a hedge. The further the call is in-the-money, the greater is the risk reduction, and the lower is this strategy's expected return. Figure 10.3 shows the expected return/risk coordinates of the covered call portfolios using each of the calls in Table 10.1.

The second panel of Table 10.2 summarizes the expected return/risk properties of the protective put trading strategies. Like writing calls against the stock, buying puts hedges the long stock position. The higher the put's exercise price, the greater the risk reduction, and the lower the expected return. Figure 10.4 shows the expected return/risk attributes of the protective put strategies using each of the puts in the second panel of Table 10.1.

## MANAGING UNEXPECTED CHANGES

This section deals with the dynamic risk management of a portfolio of options. The most natural way to think about this process is to consider an option market maker on an exchange floor or an OTC option dealer at a desk in a bank who, in the course of business, winds up with a portfolio of different option positions. While these positions are open, they may change in value with unexpected changes in asset price, the volatility rate, and/or the interest rate. To immunize the value of the overall position from these risks, the market maker uses dynamic hedging techniques. This section deals with the dynamic risk management problem.

### The General Framework

In general, an options dealer may have as many as four types of instruments in his portfolio—options, the underlying asset, futures, and cash (bonds). The value of his portfolio is

**FIGURE 10.4** Expected return/volatility relation of protective put strategies. Stock price is 50, expected stock return is 16%, stock beta is 1.20, volatility rate is 40%, and dividend yield is zero. Interest rate is 4%, and expected return on market is 14%. Options have three months remaining to expiration.

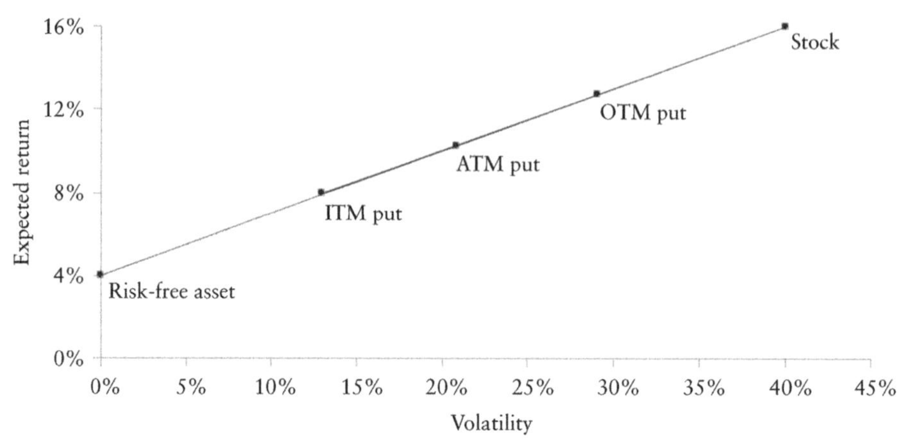


$$V = \sum_{i=1}^{N} n_i O_i + n_S S + B \tag{10.10}$$

where $O_i$ is the price of option $i$, where there are $N$ option series in his portfolio,[5] $S$ is the current asset price, and $B$ is the value of the risk-free bonds. Note that, while futures contracts are in the portfolio, they involve no investment and, hence, do not contribute to the initial value of your portfolio.

To identify the change in value of the portfolio if risk attribute $k$ changes,[6] take the partial derivative of (10.10) with respect to $k$, that is,

$$\frac{\partial V}{\partial k} = \sum_{i=1}^{N} n_i \frac{\partial O_i}{\partial k} + n_S \frac{\partial S}{\partial k} + n_F \frac{\partial F}{\partial k} + \frac{\partial B}{\partial k} \tag{10.11}$$

where the futures price now appears because it may affect the change in the value of the portfolio. To find the change in portfolio value resulting from a change in risk attribute $k$, compute how each option value changes from a change in $k$, multiply by the number of contracts, and sum across all option positions. The asset price, the futures price and risk-free bond may also be affected by a change in $k$. Where $k$ is the asset price, the delta of the portfolio is being measured. In this case, all of the deltas on the right-hand side of (10.11) are nonzero except for $\partial B/\partial S$. The asset's delta is $\partial S/\partial S = \Delta_S = 1$, and the futures delta is $\partial F/\partial S = \Delta_F = e^{(r-i)T}$. The value of risk-free bonds is not a function of the asset price so its delta is zero.

[5] Recall an *option series* has three identifying characteristics: (a) exercise price, (b) expiration date, and (c) call or put.

[6] The risk attribute $k$ of an option portfolio refers to the change in portfolio value resulting from a change in the asset price, the interest rate, the income rate, or the volatility rate.

Where $k$ is the risk-free rate of interest, the rho of the portfolio is being measured and all derivatives are nonzero. Where $k$ is the volatility rate, the portfolio vega is being computed, and all partial derivatives on the right-hand side of (10.11) except $\partial O_i / \partial \sigma$ are assumed to be equal to zero.[7] Finally, equation (10.11) can be used to measure how the portfolio value will change as time passes. Chapter 7 contains expressions for the thetas of European-style call and put options. The prices of the futures and the risk-free bonds also change as time passes.

Often second-order effects like gamma are also actively managed through time. The second derivative of (10.10) with respect to risk attribute $k$ is, likewise, a weighted average of the individual components, that is,

$$\frac{\partial^2 V}{\partial k^2} = \sum_{i=1}^{N} n_i \frac{\partial^2 O_i}{\partial k^2} + n_S \frac{\partial^2 S}{\partial k^2} + n_F \frac{\partial^2 F}{\partial k^2} + \frac{\partial^2 B}{\partial k^2} \tag{10.12}$$

Where $k$ is the asset price, the portfolio's gamma is being measured. The gammas of the asset and the futures are zero since their deltas are not a function of the asset price. Likewise, the gamma of a risk-free bond is also zero.

Once the risk measurements have been made, setting up a dynamic, risk-minimizing hedge is straightforward—decide which risk attributes of the *unhedged portfolio* should be negated and then identify a portfolio of hedge instruments (called the *hedge portfolio*) that has exactly the opposite risk attributes.[8] When the two portfolios are combined, the *hedged portfolio* is risk-neutral. In general, one hedge security will be needed for each risk attribute. Hedging delta and gamma, for example, requires two hedge instruments. Hedging delta, gamma, and vega requires three.

**ILLUSTRATION 10.1** Hedge asset price risk.

*Suppose a market maker in S&P 500 index options, as a result of accommodating customer orders to buy and sell, ends the day with the following positions:*

| Option Series | | | No. of Contracts |
|---|---|---|---|
| Exercise Price | (C)all/(P)ut | Days to Expiration | (+ long/– short) |
| 900 | c | 30 | –100 |
| 950 | c | 30 | –200 |
| 1000 | c | 90 | –150 |
| 900 | p | 90 | 50 |
| 950 | p | 360 | –100 |
| 1000 | p | 720 | –200 |
| 1100 | c | 720 | –100 |

[7] This assumption is made largely for convenience. In principal, a change in the volatility rate will affect the asset price and also the futures price. The mechanism for identifying the vegas of the asset price and the futures is the CAPM.

[8] Hedging need not involve completely negating the risk exposure. Depending on his appetite for risk, the market maker may want to retain some proportion of the exposure depending upon his directional view about the potential movement in the risk attribute.

*Suppose also that, before the market closes, the market maker wants to completely hedge the delta risk of his position. He is considering two alternatives—buying S&P 500 futures and buying 975-call options. The S&P 500 futures has 90 days to expiration, is currently priced at full carry, 1004.94, and has a delta of 1.0049.*[9] *The 975-call has 90 days to expiration and is currently priced at 55.432 and its delta is 0.635. Identify the number of contracts to sell in each case. Assume also that the S&P 500 index level is currently at 1,000, its dividend yield is 2%, and its volatility rate is 20%. The risk-free interest rate is 4%.*

The first step is to compute the overall risk characteristics of the portfolio. We confine ourselves to delta, gamma, vega, and rho. The OPTVAL Function Library contains the necessary functions for computing the Greeks of each futures and option series. Equations (10.11) and (10.12) are used to determine the aggregate exposures. The results are:

| Option Series | | | No. of Contracts | | | | | |
|---|---|---|---|---|---|---|---|---|
| Exercise Price | (C)all/ (P)ut | Days to Expiration | (+ long/ – short) | Value | Delta | Gamma | Vega | Rho |
| 900 | c | 30 | –100 | 10,196.59 | –96.94 | –0.1154 | –1,896.45 | –7,129.19 |
| 950 | c | 30 | –200 | 11,367.74 | –165.61 | –0.8831 | –14,516.94 | –12,677.73 |
| 1000 | c | 90 | –150 | 6,271.21 | –80.54 | –0.5966 | –29,423.39 | –18,311.65 |
| 900 | p | 90 | 50 | –313.98 | –6.12 | 0.1020 | 5,028.22 | –1,586.17 |
| 950 | p | 360 | –100 | 4,601.73 | 31.76 | –0.1774 | –34,996.41 | 35,859.39 |
| 1000 | p | 720 | –200 | 17,546.70 | 74.87 | –0.2625 | –103,560.06 | 182,293.85 |
| 1100 | c | 720 | –100 | 8,500.74 | –45.83 | –0.1363 | –53,771.90 | –73,630.18 |
| Portfolio value/risk exposures | | | | 58,170.73 | –288.41 | –2.07 | –233,136.93 | 104,818.32 |

The value of the portfolio is $58,170.73. The aggregate delta is –288.41, which means that for every point increase in the S&P 500 index, the portfolio will fall in value by 288.41. The aggregate gamma is –2.07, which means that, if the S&P 500 index moves up by one point, the delta of the option portfolio will fall by about 2.07. The aggregate vega is –233,136.93, which means that the market maker is *short volatility.*[10] If the volatility rate moves up by 100 basis points, the portfolio value will fall by 2,331.37. The aggregate rho is 104,818.32.

To hedge the delta exposure, futures can be purchased. Each futures has a delta of 1.0049, so the number of futures needed to eliminate the delta risk is

$$n_F = \frac{288.41}{1.0049} = 286.99 \text{ contracts}$$

As the table below shows, the hedged portfolio delta is now equal to 0. Note that the value of the portfolio does not change because the futures requires no cash outlay. Likewise, neither the gamma- or vega-risk attributes change. The futures price is sensitive to movements in the interest rate, that is,

[9] Recall that the futures delta is $\Delta_F = e^{(r-i)T}$. Since the futures delta is not a function of asset price, the futures gamma is equal to zero, $\gamma_F = 0$, and, since the futures price is not a function of the underlying asset's return volatility, the futures vega is zero, $xega_F = 0$. Finally, the futures price is a function of the risk-free rate of interest, and $\rho_F^r = TSe^{(r-i)T}$.

[10] In practice, it is commonplace to find market makers short volatility because the trading public tends to prefer to buy, rather than sell, options.

$$\rho_F^r = TSe^{(r-i)T} = (90/365)1{,}000e^{(0.04-0.02)(90/365)} = 247.79$$

The interest rate risk exposure has therefore increased to a level of 175,932.54. An unexpected increase in the interest rate of 10 basis points, the portfolio value will rise by about

$$175{,}932.54 \times 0.001 = 175.93$$

| Option Series | | | No. of Contracts | | | | | |
|---|---|---|---|---|---|---|---|---|
| Exercise Price | (C)all/ (P)ut | Days to Expiration | (+ long/ – short) | Value | Delta | Gamma | Vega | Rho |
| Unhedged portfolio | | | | 58,170.73 | –288.41 | –2.07 | –233,136.93 | 104,818.32 |
| Hedge instruments: | | | | | | | | |
| | F | 90 | 286.99 | 0.00 | 288.41 | 0.00 | 0.00 | 71,114.22 |
| Hedged portfolio | | | | 58,170.73 | 0.00 | –2.07 | –233,136.93 | 175,932.54 |

A different delta hedge is possible using the 975-call with 90 days to expiration. Its delta is 0.635, so the hedge will require

$$n_{975\text{ call}} = \frac{288.41}{0.635} = 453.98 \text{ contracts}$$

After the hedge is in place, the hedged portfolio delta is again 0, as is shown below. Note that using the 975-calls to hedge requires a payment of $25,165.31 to buy the options. In addition, buying the calls has affected the portfolio's other risk attributes. Specifically, gamma and vega have fallen, and rho has increased.

| Option Series | | | No. of Contracts | | | | | |
|---|---|---|---|---|---|---|---|---|
| Exercise Price | (C)all/ (P)ut | Days to Expiration | (+ long/ – short) | Value | Delta | Gamma | Vega | Rho |
| Unhedged portfolio | | | | 58,170.73 | –288.41 | –2.07 | –233,136.93 | 104,818.32 |
| Hedge instruments: | | | | | | | | |
| 975 | c | 90 | 453.98 | –25,165.31 | 288.41 | 1.7043 | 84,049.44 | 64,909.08 |
| Hedged portfolio | | | | 33,005.43 | 0.00 | –0.37 | –149,087.49 | 169,727.40 |

To understand how effective these hedges will be, consider the figure below, which shows the change in the value of the unhedged and hedged portfolios as the asset price moves in one direction of the other. The unhedged portfolio obviously has a negative delta. As the index level increase, portfolio value falls. For the hedged portfolios, this is not the case. As the index level moves by a small amount in either direction from its current level of 1,000, portfolio value does not change. For large moves, however, the value of the portfolio falls. This is the effect of the negative gamma of both hedged portfolio positions. The fact that the hedged portfolio value changes by less using the 975-calls to hedge rather than the futures is due to the fact that the 975-calls incidently reduced the portfolio's gamma exposure.

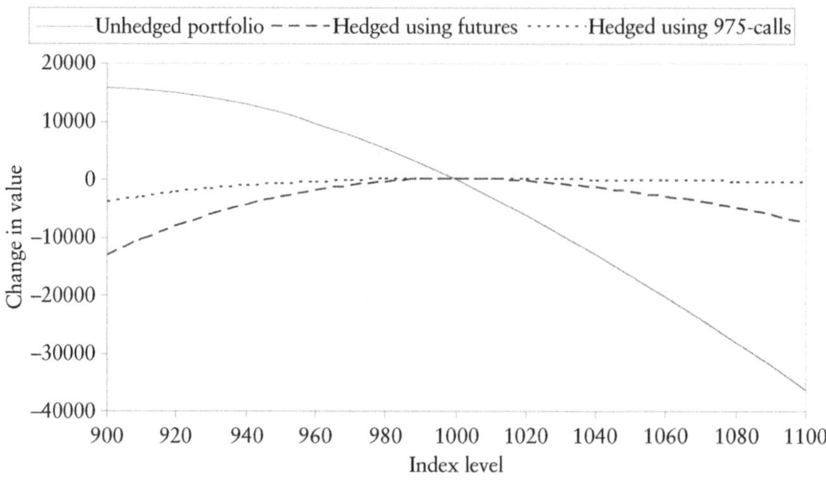


**ILLUSTRATION 10.2** Hedge delta and vega risk.

*Suppose the market maker's end-of-day position is as described in Illustration 10.1, and that, before the market closes he wants to hedge completely both the delta and vega risks of his position. To do so, he will use the S&P 500 futures and the 975-call options. Identify the number of each contract to buy or sell.*

The optimal numbers of contracts to enter is identified by setting the number of contracts in the hedge portfolio in such a way that it has risk attributes equal in magnitude but opposite in sign as the unhedged portfolio. This means solving simultaneously the follow system of equations:

$$n_F(1.0049) + n_{975\text{ call}}(0.635) = 288.41$$
$$n_F(0) + n_{975\text{ call}}(185.14) = 233{,}136.93$$

Since the vega of the futures is assumed to be 0, only the call can be used to negate the unhedged portfolio's vega-risk. The optimal number of calls to buy is

$$n_{975\text{ call}} = \frac{233{,}136.27}{185.14} = 1{,}259.27$$

The number of futures is then determined by

$$n_F = \frac{288.41 - 1{,}259.27(0.635)}{1.0049} = -509.06$$

The hedged portfolio risk exposures are now

| Option services | | | No. of Contracts | | | | | |
|---|---|---|---|---|---|---|---|---|
| Exercise Price | (C)all/ (P)ut | Days to Expiration | (+ long/ – short) | Value | Delta | Gamma | Vega | Rho |
| Unhedged portfolio | | | | 58,170.73 | –288.41 | –2.07 | –233,136.93 | 104,818.32 |
| Hedge instruments | | | | | | | | |
| | F | 90 | –509.06 | 0.00 | –511.58 | 0.00 | 0.00 | –126,142.89 |
| 975 | c | 90 | 1,259.27 | –69,803.70 | 799.99 | 4.7275 | 233,136.93 | 180,045.24 |
| Hedged portfolio | | | | –11,632.97 | 0.00 | 2.66 | 0.00 | 158,720.67 |

To understand how the delta- and vega-risk of the portfolio have changed, consider the figures below. In the first, the gains/losses of the unhedged portfolio are shown. The unhedged portfolio is short the index and net short volatility. As the index level and volatility rate rise, the unhedged portfolio value falls. The effectiveness of the hedge instruments at controlling for delta and vega risk is shown in the second figure. For small changes in the index and/or the volatility rate, the hedged portfolio value does not change. Interestingly, portfolio value increases for large moves in the index in one direction or the other. The large position in the 975-calls has given the hedged portfolio positive gamma. Note also that, with large index moves, the hedged portfolio again becomes sensitive to vega risk, that is, it gains a short volatility exposure.

Unhedged portfolio

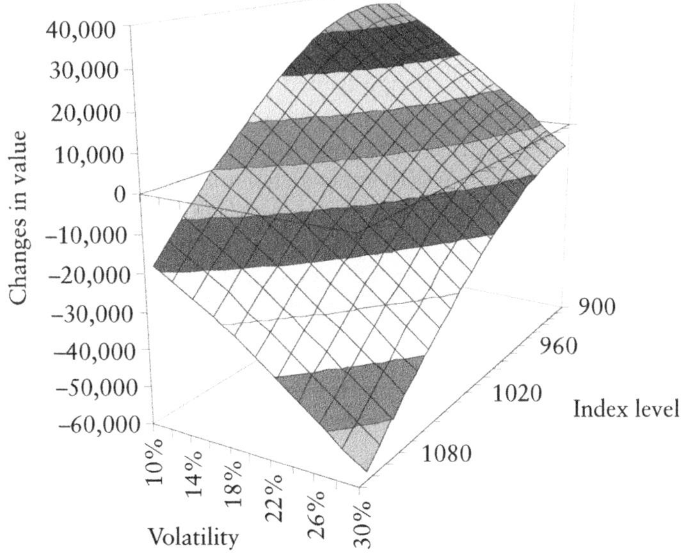

Hedged portfolio

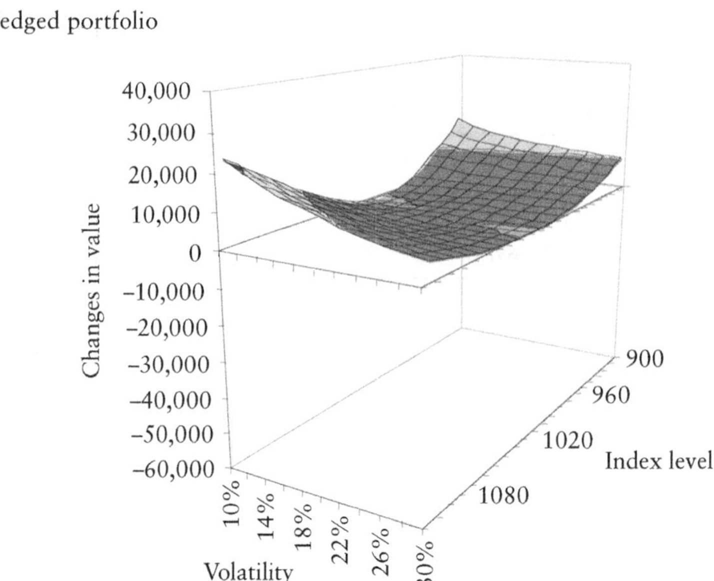


### Practical Considerations

Normally the market maker will have a variety of hedge instruments from which to choose. Presumably, in setting the hedge, he will want to minimize costs. One cost will be the trading costs associated with buying/selling the hedge instruments. Trading costs in exchange-traded futures and options markets are usually incurred on a per contract basis. Another cost is the opportunity cost of the funds tied up in the hedge instruments. In Illustration 10.2, for example, the 975-call options were purchased, which means that interest must be paid on the option premiums. Finally, options in the hedge portfolio erode in value as time passes.[11] Depending on whether the market maker is short or long options, this may be a benefit or a cost. All of these benefits/costs can be measured, and the composition of the "least-cost," risk-minimizing hedge portfolio can be identified.

**ILLUSTRATION 10.3** Hedge delta and vega risk for one day.

*Reconsider the market maker's problem in Illustration 10.2. Suppose that the available hedge instruments are as follows:*

| Potential Hedge Instruments | | | |
|---|---|---|---|
| Exercise Price | (F)utures/(C)all/(P)ut | Days to Expiration | Price |
| | F | 90 | 1,004.94 |
| 975 | c | 90 | 25.78 |
| 975 | p | 90 | 55.43 |
| 1025 | c | 90 | 50.52 |
| 1025 | p | 90 | 30.66 |

[11] Options in the unhedged portfolio also erode in value, but that cost is sunk.

*Assume the market maker pays a \$5 per contract in trading costs and his borrowing/lending rate is 4%. Identify the least-cost, risk-minimizing hedge portfolio assuming his hedging horizon is one day. First, use as many hedge instruments as you would like, and then use only two.*

The market faces three costs over the hedge horizon. If trading costs were the only consideration, the market maker would simply find the delta/vega-neutral portfolio that minimized the number of contract. But here, he also needs to consider the opportunity cost of the funds in the portfolio as well as the erosion in time premium.

To begin, we need to identify the cost structure for each potential hedge instrument. The total commissions are simple—number of contracts times the \$5 commission per contract. The interest cost is also straightforward. If options are sold, the market maker collects interest, and, if they are purchased, interest is paid. To adjust for the interest income/expense, the option premiums (i.e., the number of contracts times the option price) are multiplied by $e^{rT} - 1 = e^{0.04(1/365)} - 1$. Finally, to adjust for the time erosion in option premiums, we compute the thetas of each hedge instrument.[12] Since the interpretation of theta is the change in price as time to expiration increases, we must affix a minus sign in front. Also, since the rates are on annualized basis, we multiply the theta by 1/365 to determine the erosion in option value over a single day.

The table below identifies the set of hedge instruments that minimizes the market maker's costs while negating his delta and vega risk exposures. The use of Excel's SOLVER greatly facilitates finding the solution quickly. The minimum cost hedge portfolio appears to contain only three instruments— the 975-call, the 1025-call, and the 1025-put. Virtually no futures or 975-puts appear. Note that, since the option positions in the hedge portfolio are all long positions, interest is paid on the hedge portfolio value, and the hedge portfolio value decays with time. The total cost of the hedge for one day appears to be approximately \$6,265.89.

| Option Series | | | No. of Contracts | | | | | | | |
|---|---|---|---|---|---|---|---|---|---|---|
| Exercise Price | (C)all/ (P)ut | Days to Expiration | (+ long/ – short) | Value | Delta | Vega | Theta | Trading Costs | Interest Cost | Time Erosion |
| Unhedged portfolio | | | | 58,170.73 | -288.41 | -233,136.93 | 122.82 | | | |
| Hedge instruments: | | | | | | | | | | |
| | F | 90 | 2.32 | 0.00 | 2.33 | 0.00 | 46.60 | -11.59 | | 0.13 |
| 975 | c | 90 | 0.00 | 0.00 | 0.00 | 0.00 | 0.00 | 0.00 | 0.00 | 0.00 |
| 975 | p | 90 | 0.00 | 0.00 | 0.00 | 0.01 | 0.00 | 0.00 | 0.00 | 0.00 |
| 1025 | c | 90 | 956.44 | -29,321.68 | 419.38 | 186,448.92 | -82,830.17 | -4,782.21 | -3.21 | -226.93 |
| 1025 | p | 90 | 239.50 | -12,098.66 | -133.30 | 46,688.00 | -15,784.53 | -1,197.50 | -1.33 | -43.25 |
| Hedged portfolio | | | | 16,750.39 | 0.00 | 0.00 | -98,445.29 | -5,991.30 | -4.54 | -270.05 |
| Total costs | | 6,265.89 | | | | | | | | |

The SOLVER solution is imprecise, however. We asked it to perform an incredibly difficult search procedure, and eventually many minutes it produced the above results. We could have imposed more information about the structure of the problem, however. Since we are interested in hedging only two risk factors, the minimum cost hedge portfolio will consist of only two hedge instruments, that is, there is only one pair of the five hedge instruments that will produce the minimum cost portfolio. To be certain which two, *total costs should be computed for the 10 different pairings of the five instruments.* Since it is unlikely that the futures or the 975-options are included in the least-cost port-

[12] Recall that the theta of the futures is $\theta_F = (r - i)Se^{(r-i)T}$.

folio, we them from the set of feasible hedge instruments and rerun SOLVER. The minimum costs hedge has total hedge costs are about \$10 less than the previous solution.

| Option Series | | | No. of Contracts | | | | | | | |
|---|---|---|---|---|---|---|---|---|---|---|
| Exercise Price | (C)all/ (P)ut | Days to Expiration | (+ long/ – short) | Value | Delta | Vega | Theta | Trading Costs | Interest Cost | Time Erosion |
| Unhedged portfolio | | | | 58,170.73 | –288.41 | –233,136.93 | 122.82 | | | |
| Hedge instruments | | | | | | | | | | |
| 1025 | c | 90 | 958.78 | –29,393.47 | 420.41 | 186,905.42 | –83,032.98 | –4,793.92 | –3.22 | –227.49 |
| 1025 | p | 90 | 237.16 | –11,980.36 | –132.00 | 46,231.51 | –15,630.20 | –1,185.79 | –1.31 | –42.82 |
| Hedged portfolio | | | | 16,796.90 | 0.00 | 0.00 | –98,540.36 | –5,979.70 | –4.53 | –270.31 |
| Total costs | | 6,254.55 | | | | | | | | |

## PROFIT FUNCTIONS

To analyze the profitability of option portfolios, we need to define the profit function for each type of security/derivatives position. There are eight profit functions that will serve as the basis for our analysis: long and short the asset underlying the derivatives contracts, long and short the futures, long and short a call option, and long and short a put option.

### Asset

The profit function for a long asset position is

$$\pi_{\text{long asset}, T} = S_T - Se^{(r-i)T} \tag{10.13a}$$

and is shown in Figure 10.5, Panel A. As the figure shows, the terminal profit on a long position in the asset varies directly with the level of the asset price at time $T$. Setting (10.13a) equal to 0, the breakeven terminal asset price is identified as $S_T^* = Se^{(r-i)T}$. In the event the terminal asset price exceeds the sum of the initial asset price and carry costs, the position makes money. As the asset price rises without limit, the profit from this position does also. If the terminal asset price is below the initial asset price plus carry costs, the position loses money. The maximum possible loss is the initial asset price plus carry costs.

A short asset position has the opposite profit function of the long asset position,

$$\pi_{\text{short asset}, T} = -[S_T - Se^{(r-i)T}] \tag{10.13b}$$

and is shown in Figure 10.5, Panel B. The largest potential profit $Se^{(r-i)T}$ is where the terminal asset price is 0. In this instance, $e^{-iT}$ units of the asset were sold short at time 0, and the proceeds were invested in risk-free bonds. If the terminal asset price is 0, the short seller of the asset covers his short sale obligation at no cost and keeps the proceeds from the short sale. Figure 10.5, Panel B also shows the potential liability of this strategy. As the terminal asset price rises, profit falls. Indeed, assuming the asset price can rise without limit, the potential loss from a short asset position is unlimited.

**FIGURE 10.5** Terminal profit diagrams for long and short asset positions.
Panel A. Long asset

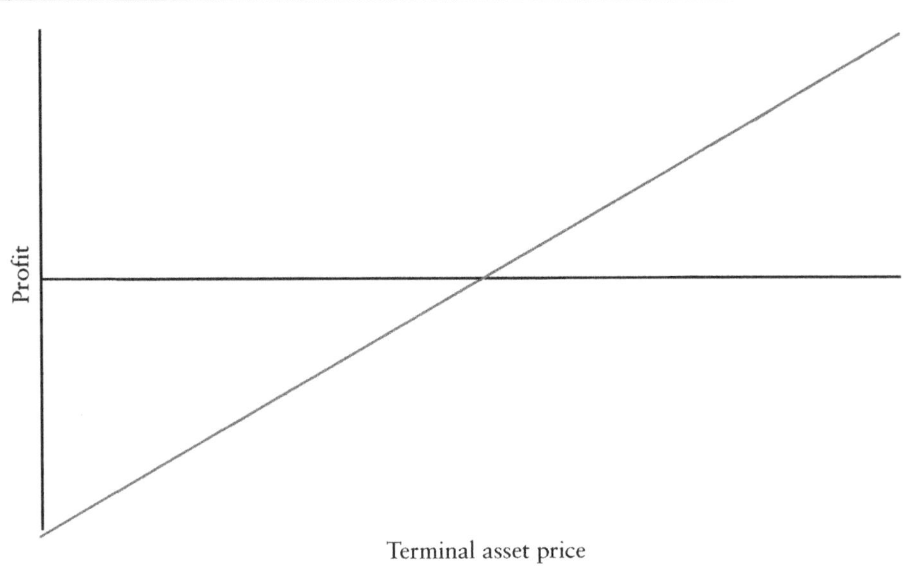


Panel B. Short asset

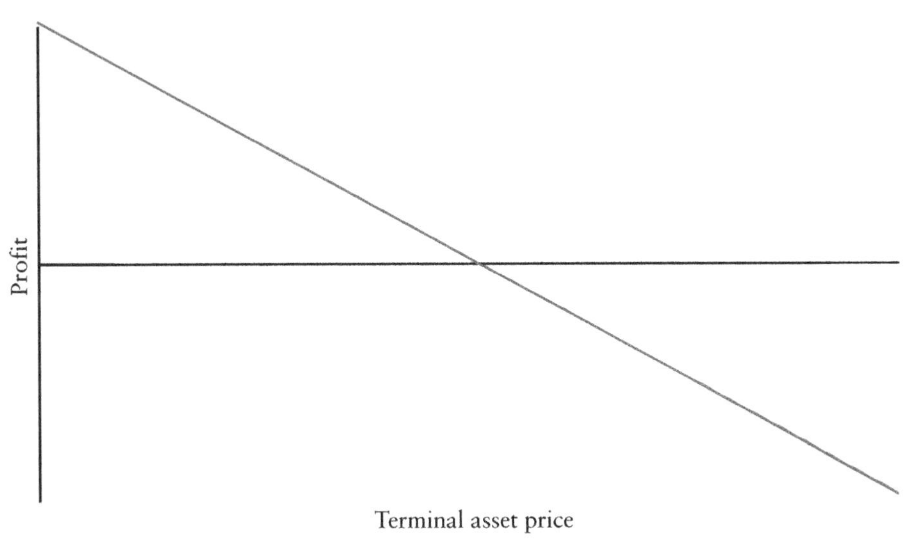

### Futures

The profit functions for a long and a short futures position are virtually identical to a long and a short asset position, respectively. The only difference in the profit functions is that the initial asset price plus carry costs is replaced by the futures price. This should not be surprising considering that in Chapter 3 we demonstrated that $F = Se^{(r-i)T}$ in the absence of costless arbitrage opportunities. The profit function of a long futures position is

$$\pi_{\text{long futures}, T} = S_T - F \tag{10.14a}$$

and is shown in Figure 10.6, Panel A. Given the zero-sum nature of derivatives contracts, a short futures position has the profit function,

$$\pi_{\text{short futures}, T} = -(S_T - F) \tag{10.14b}$$

and is shown in Figure 10.6, Panel B. The breakeven terminal asset price is where $S_T^* = F$.

### Call Option

The profit function of a long call position is

$$\pi_{\text{long call}, T} = \begin{cases} S_T - X - ce^{rT} & \text{if } S_T > X \\ -ce^{rT} & \text{if } S_T \leq X \end{cases} \tag{10.15a}$$

**FIGURE 10.6** Terminal profit diagrams for long and short futures positions.
Panel A. Long futures

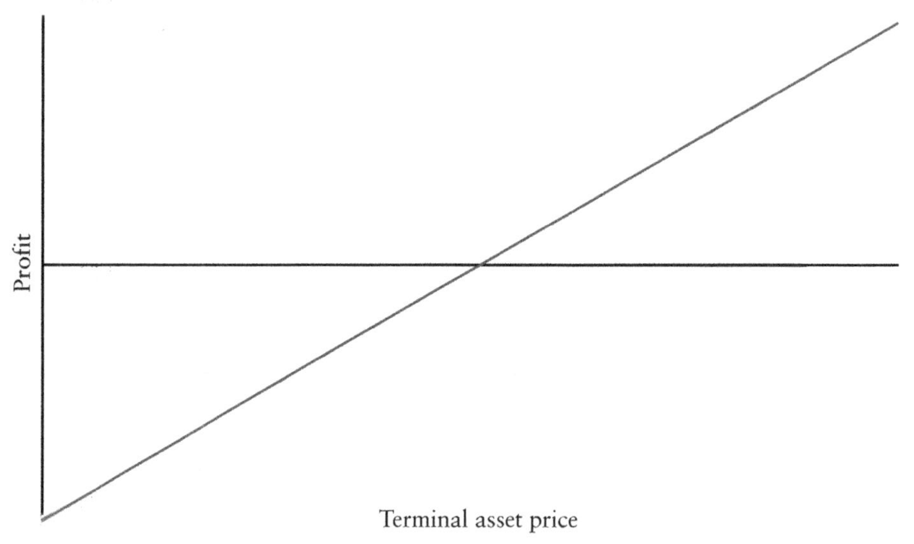

**FIGURE 10.6** (Continued)
Panel B. Short asset

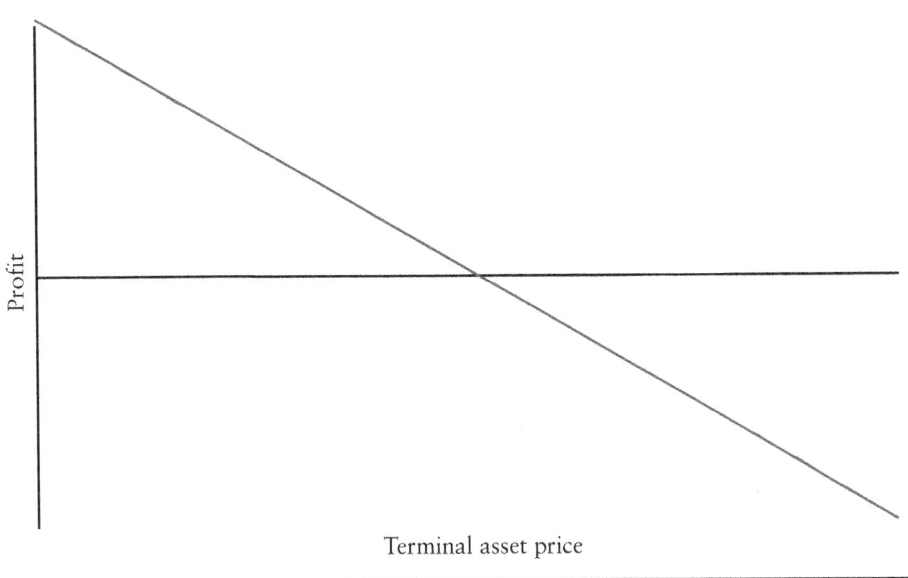


and is shown in Figure 10.7, Panel A. Note that the profit function depends on whether the asset price exceeds the exercise price at the option's expiration. If it does not, the call option buyer forfeits his initial investment (i.e., the call price) plus carry costs (i.e., the cost of financing the call option position over the interval from 0 to $T$). If the asset price exceeds the exercise price, the call will be exercised. If the asset price exceeds the breakeven price $S_T^*$, where $S_T^* = X + ce^{rT}$, the call option buyer makes money. The potential gain is unlimited.

The profit function for a short call position is

$$\pi_{\text{short call}, T} = \begin{cases} -(S_T - X - ce^{rT}) & \text{if } S_T > X \\ ce^{rT} & \text{if } S_T \leq X \end{cases} \tag{10.15b}$$

and is shown in Figure 10.7, Panel B. The call option seller's potential profit is limited to the option premium $c$ collected at time 0 plus the interest income that accrues on $c$ from time 0 to time $T$, and occurs in the event the call finishes out of the money. In the event the call is in the money at expiration, the option seller is obliged to deliver the underlying asset for a cash payment of $X$. If the asset price exceeds the breakeven price $S_T^*$, the seller loses money. The potential liability of the option seller rises without limit as the asset price rises.

**FIGURE 10.7** Terminal profit diagrams for long and short call positions.

Panel A. Long call

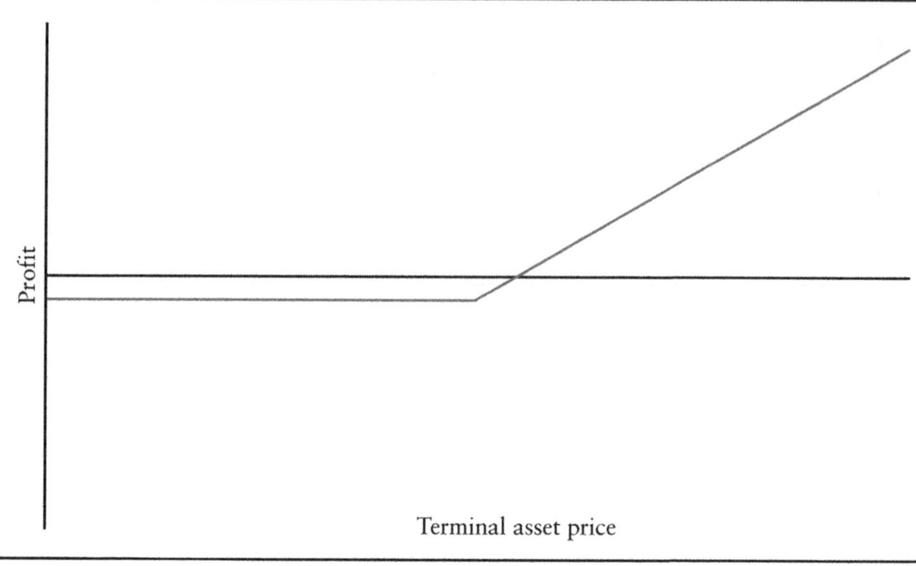


Panel B. Short call

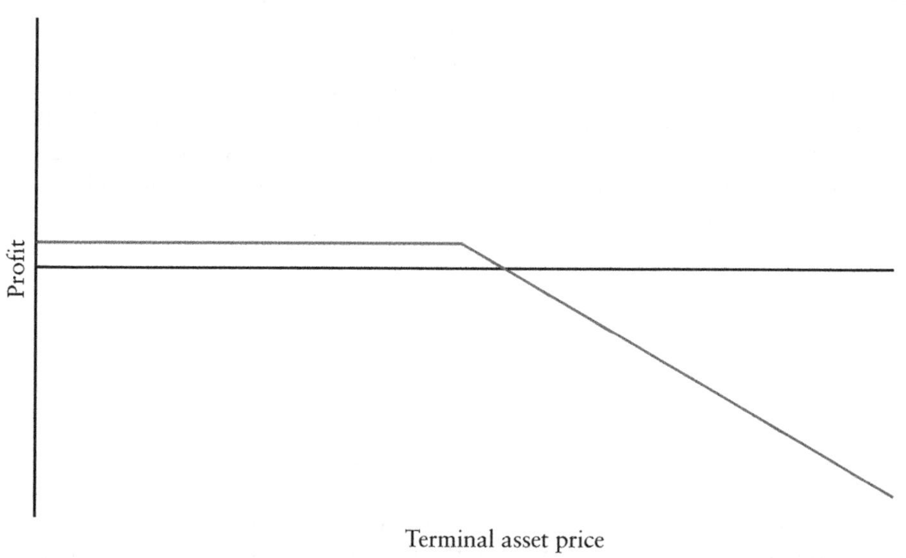

### Put Option

The profit function for a long put position is

$$\pi_{\text{long put}, T} = \begin{cases} -pe^{rT} & \text{if } S_T > X \\ X - S_T - pe^{rT} & \text{if } S_T \le X \end{cases} \tag{10.16a}$$

and is shown in Figure 10.8, Panel A. The put option buyer forfeits the put plus carry costs if the asset price exceeds the option's exercise price at expiration. If the asset price is below the exercise price, the put option holder will exercise her right to sell the underlying asset for a cash price $X$. Where the amount by which the asset price is below the exercise price exceeds the initial value of the put plus financing costs (i.e., the asset price is below the breakeven price $S_T^* = X - pe^{rT}$), the put option holder makes money.

The profit function for a short put position is

$$\pi_{\text{short put}, T} = \begin{cases} pe^{rT} & \text{if } S_T > X \\ -(X - S_T - pe^{rT}) & \text{if } S_T \le X \end{cases} \tag{10.16b}$$

**FIGURE 10.8** Terminal profit diagrams for long and short put positions.
Panel A. Long put

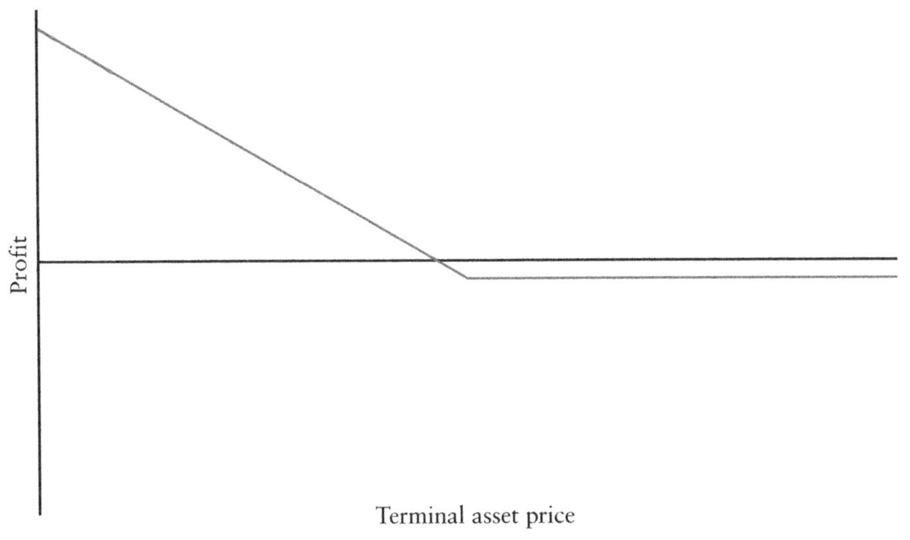

**FIGURE 10.8** (Continued)
Panel B. Short put

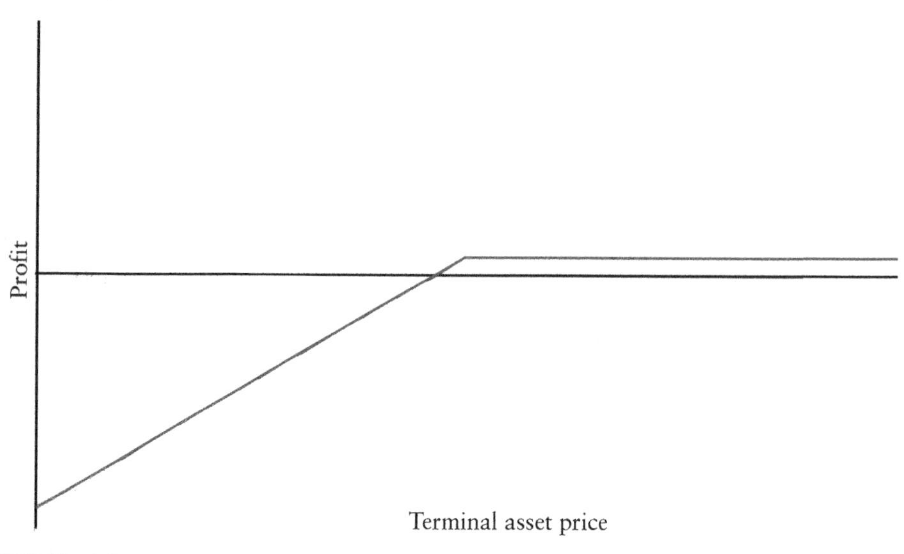


and is shown in Figure 10.8, Panel B. The maximum gain from selling a put is $pe^{rT}$, and is received when the put expires out of the money (i.e., $S_T > X$). If the terminal asset price is below the breakeven asset price $S_T^* = X - pe^{rT}$, the put option seller begins to lose money. The maximum loss on a short put position, $-(X - pe^{rT})$, occurs when the terminal asset price falls to zero, in which case the put option buyer exercises his right to sell the underlying asset at $X$. Since the asset is worthless, the put option seller pays the buyer $X$, and, in return, receives a worthless unit of the asset. The payment of $X$ by the put option seller is offset, in some degree, by the proceeds from the sale of the put option at time 0 plus accumulated interest, $pe^{rT}$.

## Portfolio Profit Functions

With the eight different profit functions listed above, a limitless number of option portfolios can be analyzed. To compute the profit function of a particular strategy, we simply sum the profit functions of the individual positions within the portfolio. One popular option strategy is the *buy-write* or *covered call.* This strategy consists of buying the asset and selling a call option. The profit function for this strategy is

$$\begin{aligned}\pi_{\text{buy-write},\,T} &= \pi_{\text{long asset},\,T} + \pi_{\text{short call},\,T}\\ &= \begin{cases} S_T - Se^{(r-i)T} + ce^{rT} & \text{if } S_T < X \\ S_T - Se^{(r-i)T} - (S_T - X) + ce^{rT} & \text{if } S_T \geq X \end{cases}\\ &= \begin{cases} S_T - Se^{(r-i)T} + ce^{rT} & \text{if } S_T < X \\ X - Se^{(r-i)T} + ce^{rT} & \text{if } S_T \geq X \end{cases}\end{aligned} \tag{10.17}$$

and is shown in Figure 10.9. As the figure shows, selling a call option against a long position creates a profit function that is identical to selling a put. If the terminal asset price exceeds the exercise price, the gain on the buy-write position is $X - Se^{(r-i)T} + ce^{rT}$. By virtue of the put-call parity relation developed in Chapter 4, this value equals $pe^{rT}$. As the terminal asset price falls below the exercise price, the buy-write strategy begins to lose money. The maximum loss is $-Se^{(r-i)T} + ce^{rT}$. Not surprisingly, by virtue of put-call parity, this is also the maximum loss on a short put position, that is, $-Se^{(r-i)T} + ce^{rT} = -X + pe^{rT}$.

Another popular option trading strategy is called a *protective put*. In this strategy, the investor is long the underlying asset and buys a put to insure against downward movements in the asset price. The profit function for this strategy is

**FIGURE 10.9** Terminal profit diagram of a buy-write or covered call strategy (i.e., long the asset and short a call option).

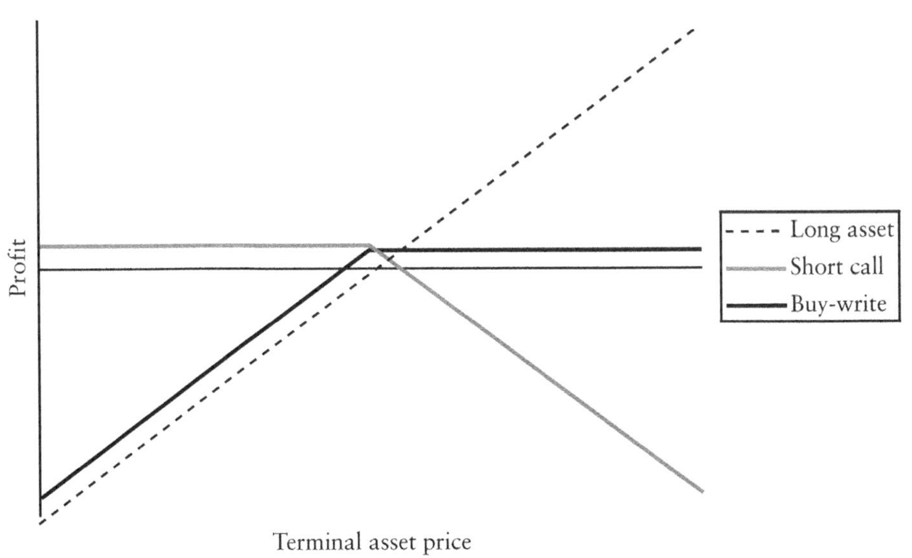

$$\pi_{\text{protective put}, T} = \pi_{\text{long asset}, T} + \pi_{\text{long put}, T}$$

$$= \begin{cases} S_T - Se^{(r-i)T} + (X - S_T) - pe^{rT} & \text{if } S_T < X \\ S_T - Se^{(r-i)T} - pe^{rT} & \text{if } S_T \geq X \end{cases} \tag{10.18}$$

$$= \begin{cases} X - Se^{(r-i)T} - pe^{rT} & \text{if } S_T < X \\ S_T - Se^{(r-i)T} - pe^{rT} & \text{if } S_T \geq X \end{cases}$$

as is illustrated in Figure 10.10. The protective put strategy appears to be nothing more that a synthetic long call position. As (10.18) shows, the lowest profit from holding the protective put position is $X - Se^{(r-i)T} - pe^{rT}$. By put-call parity, this amount equals $-ce^{rT}$. If the terminal asset price exceeds the exercise price, the profit is $S_T - Se^{(r-i)T} - pe^{rT}$. Substituting the put-call parity relation, we see that, when the terminal asset price exceeds the exercise price, the profit from the protective put strategy equals the profit from a long call position, $S_T - X - ce^{rT}$.

In general, we do not add up the profit functions analytically as we did in (10.17) and (10.18). It is much simpler to handle them numerically. The functions OV_PROFIT_ASSET and OV_PROFIT_OPTION in the OPTVAL Function Library were designed to facilitate such analyses. These functions compute the terminal profit of the eight asset/futures and option positions described by (10.13a) through (10.16b). OV_PROFIT_ASSET handles long and short asset and futures positions, and OV_PROFIT_OPTION handles long and short call and put option positions.

**FIGURE 10.10** Terminal profit diagrams of a protective put strategy (i.e., long the asset and long a put option).

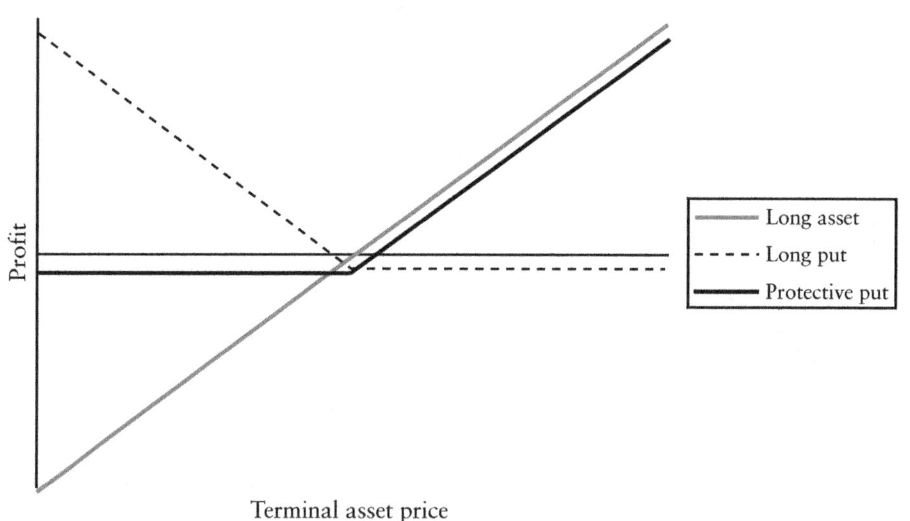

**ILLUSTRATION 10.4** Plot profit function of straddle.

*Assume that the current asset price is 50 and that the prices of at-the-money, three-month options are 4.196 for the call and 3.701 for the put. Assume that the risk-free rate of interest is 6%, and the asset has an income rate of 2%. Plot the profit functions for (1) a portfolio that consists of one long call and one long put, and (2) two long calls and two long puts. Keep the axes on the same scale so that you can compare the results.*

A portfolio that consists of a long call and a long put at the same exercise price is called a *straddle* or a *volatility spread.* The profit function of a straddle that consists of $n_c$ calls and $n_p$ puts is

$$\pi_{\text{straddle},\,T} = n_c \pi_{\text{long call},\,T} + n_p \pi_{\text{long put},\,T}$$

To see the terminal profit diagram for this strategy, we simply set up a terminal asset price column in a spreadsheet in Excel. For expositional convenience, let the grid run from 0 to 100 by increments of 10.[13] Next, compute the terminal values of the call and the put conditional on each terminal asset price. The syntax of the OV_PROFIT_OPTION function is

OV_PROFIT_OPTION(*st, op, x, t, r, np, cp*)

where *st* is the terminal asset price, *op* is the current option price, *x* is the exercise price of the option, *t* is its time to expiration, *r* is the risk-free interest rate, *np* is the number of option contracts (positive for a long position and negative for a short), and a call/put indicator *cp* ("C" or "c" for call, and "P" or "p" for put). Finally, sum the call and put values for each level of asset price. The profit diagram for the first volatility spread is

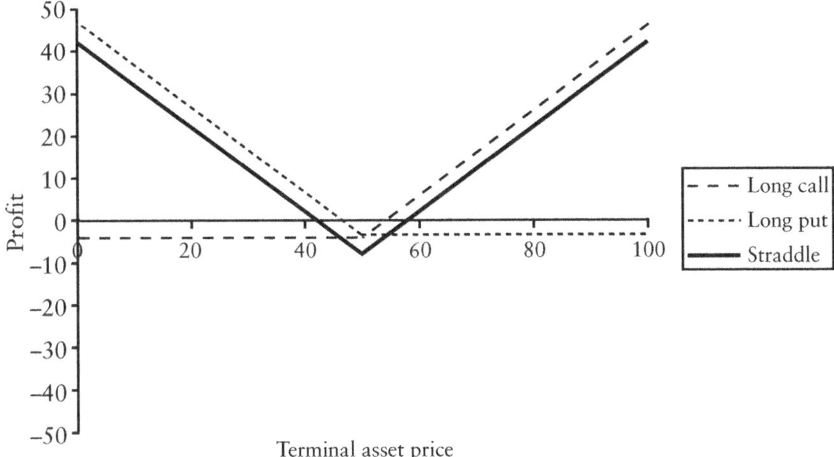


Next, repeat the procedure, except increase the number of option contracts in the function call from 1 to 2. This new volatility spread has a profit function that appears as

[13] In practice, a finer increment should be used. Our purpose here is only to illustrate the technique.

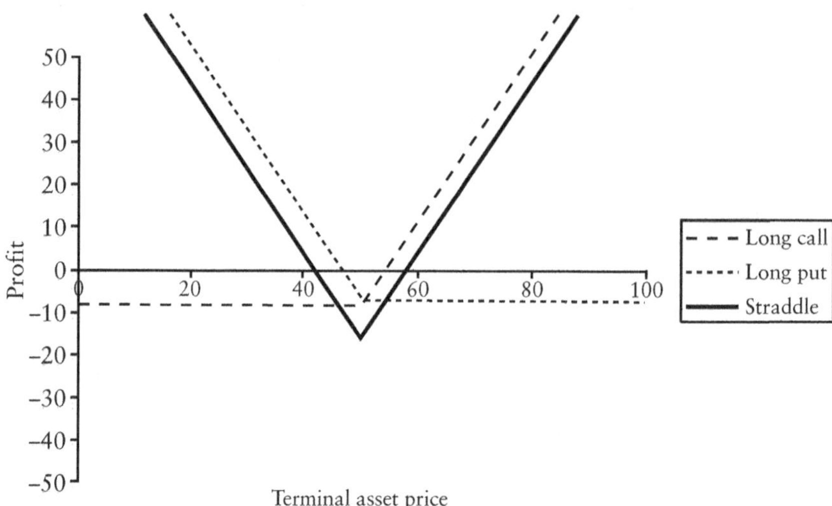


Comparing the two figures, we see that the breakeven prices are the same. The cost of the second strategy is double the first. The rate at which profits are realized should the asset price rise or fall also doubles.

## BREAKEVEN PROBABILITIES

Computing the probability that a particular strategy will be profitable at expiration depends upon the assumption regarding the distribution of asset price at time *T*. Assuming the distribution is lognormal, the mechanics were furnished in Chapter 7. Prior to applying those mechanics, however, it is necessary to compute the breakeven asset prices for the strategy at hand. Sometimes, the breakeven asset prices are most easily computed analytically. At other times, it is simpler to search numerically for the points at which the terminal portfolio profit is 0. Below we illustrate the former approach.

**ILLUSTRATION 10.5** Compute risk-neutral and risk-averse probabilities of straddle being profitable.

*Assume that the current asset price is 50 and that the prices of at-the-money, 3-month options are 4.196 for the call and 3.701 for the put. Assume that the risk-free rate of interest is 6%, and that the asset has an expected rate of return of 8% and an income rate of 2%. Compute the risk-neutral and risk-averse probabilities of the straddle being profitable at expiration.*

The first step is to compute the breakeven asset prices. For a long straddle position, for example, two breakeven points exist. One breakeven point exists where the terminal asset price $S_T$ equals the value $BE_l = X - (c + p)e^{rT}$, and the other where $S_T$ equals the value $BE_u = X + (c + p)e^{rT}$. This long straddle position makes money where $S_T < BE_l$ and where $S_T > BE_u$. For the problem at hand, the lower breakeven asset price is $BE_l = 50 - (4.196 + 3.701)e^{0.06(0.25)} = 41.984$ and the upper breakeven asset price is $BE_u = 50 + (4.196 + 3.701)e^{0.06(0.25)} = 58.016$.

Assuming that the asset price is log-normally distributed at the options' expiration, the risk-neutral probability that the straddle will be profitable at expiration can be found by using the cumulative standard normal distribution function, that is,

$$Pr(S_T < BE_l \text{ or } S_T > BE_u) = N(-d_1) + N(d_u)$$

where

$$d_l = \frac{\ln(Se^{bT}/BE_l) - 0.5\sigma^2 T}{\sigma\sqrt{T}}$$

and

$$d_u = \frac{\ln(Se^{bT}/BE_u) - 0.5\sigma^2 T}{\sigma\sqrt{T}}$$

The problem information appears incomplete, however, in that we know all of the parameters in $d_l$ and $d_u$ except $\sigma$. Since we know the initial option prices, this problem is not insurmountable. We simply set the option prices equal to the BSM option valuation formula and solve for the implied volatility. The OPTVAL Library function OV_OPTION_ISD may prove useful here. The implied volatility of both the call and the put is 40%.

With the volatility parameter in hand, the rest is computation. Here the OPTVAL Library function OV_OPTION_ASSET_PROB may prove useful. The syntax of the function is

OV_OPTION_ASSET_PROB(*s, x, t, alpha, v, ab*)

where $s$ is the current asset price, $x$ is the breakeven price, $t$ is the time to expiration, *alpha* is the asset's expected rate of price appreciation (equals the risk-free rate less the income rate in a risk-neutral world and the expected rate of return less the income rate is a risk-averse world), $v$ is the asset's return volatility rate, and *ab* is an indicator variable ("A" or "a" for the probability that the asset price will be above the break-even price $x$ and "B" or "b" for the probability that the asset price will be below the break-even price, $x$). Using this function, the risk-neutral probabilities are

$$\Pr(S_T < 41.984) = 20.51\% \quad \text{and} \quad \Pr(S_T > 58.016) = 21.38\%$$

for a total probability of 41.88%. The risk-averse probabilities are

$$\Pr(S_T < 41.984) = 19.80\% \quad \text{and} \quad \Pr(S_T > 58.016) = 22.11\%$$

for a total of 41.92%. The difference between the risk-averse and risk-neutral probabilities is driven by the fact that in a risk-averse world the asset is expected to appreciate at a rate of 6%, while in a risk-neutral world the expected rate of price appreciation is 4%.

## EXPECTED TERMINAL PROFIT/RETURN

Computing the expected profit/return for an option trading strategy is difficult to do analytically. The reason is that option profit is a nonlinear function of the underlying asset price. The expected terminal value of the call is simply the expected terminal value of the asset less the exercise price. To get a handle on these issues, Monte Carlo simulation is often used.

To understand how to use Monte Carlo simulation in this context, recall that, in Chapter 9, we showed that under the BSM assumptions the evolution of the asset price through time can be modeled as

$$S_{t+\Delta t} = S_t e^{(\alpha - \sigma^2/2)\Delta t + \sigma\sqrt{\Delta t}\varepsilon} \tag{10.19}$$

where $\alpha$ is the expected rate of price appreciation on the underlying asset, $\sigma$ is the standard deviation of the asset's return, $\Delta t$ is a fixed interval of time (e.g., a day, a week, or a month), and $\varepsilon$ is a normally distributed random variable with zero mean and unit standard deviation. In this initial discussion, we assume that $\Delta t$ is the life of the option $T$. Thus, for clarity, we write (10.20) as

$$S_T = Se^{(\alpha - \sigma^2/2)\Delta t + \sigma\sqrt{T}\varepsilon} \tag{10.20}$$

where $S$ is the current asset price. Generating a distribution of terminal asset distribution is a matter of drawing numbers from a univariate standard normal distribution (as we did in Chapter 9) and running them through (10.21), recording each terminal asset price as it is generated. Then, for each terminal asset price, we compute the option portfolio profit using the profit functions provided earlier in the chapter. We then average across all terminal portfolio profits to get an estimate of the expected terminal profit.

The main problem with using the Monte Carlo simulation is that a great number of runs are necessary. Even with as many as 10,000 drawings, the results can be quite misleading. An alternative, yet surprisingly accurate, means of computing the expected profit of a trading strategy numerically involves replacing the continuous lognormal asset price distribution with a discrete log of asset price distribution. Specifically, we (1) divide the continuous log of asset price distribution into bins; (2) identify the expected terminal log of asset price within each bin; (3) compute the expected strategy profit for each bin based on the expected terminal asset price; (4) compute the probability that the terminal asset price falls in each bin; and (5) sum the products of the expected profit and probability within each bin to get the expected terminal profit of the trading strategy.

To be more specific regarding how the procedure works, start by setting up the bins. Define the range of possible future asset prices as, say, four standard deviations from the expected asset price, $Se^{\alpha T}$. Under the BSM assumptions, this should account for 99.994% of the asset price distribution. To set up the grid in asset price, work initially with the natural logarithm of asset price. We know that $\ln(S_T/S_0)$ is normally distributed with mean $(\alpha - 0.5\sigma^2)T$ and standard deviation $\sigma\sqrt{T}$. Thus, define the range of the logarithm of asset price to go from

$$\ln(S_{min}) = \ln(S_0) + (\alpha - 0.5\sigma^2)T - 4\sigma\sqrt{T} \tag{10.21}$$

to

$$\ln(S_{max}) = \ln(S_0) + (\alpha - 0.5\sigma^2)T + 4\sigma\sqrt{T} \tag{10.22}$$

Next divide the range into $n$ equal sized increments. The increment width is defined as

$$\ln S_{inc} \equiv \frac{\ln S_{\max} - \ln S_{\min}}{n-1} \tag{10.23}$$

Define the first terminal asset price bin to be $\ln S_{\min} - 0.5 \ln S_{inc}$ to $\ln S_{\min} + 0.5 \ln S_{inc}$. For that bin, assume the terminal asset price is the average of the lower and upper bounds to the bin, that is, set the asset price to $\ln S_{\min}$. Proceed through the range of terminal asset prices. In general, the asset price is assumed to be $\ln S_i$ over the $i$th interval, which has range $\ln S_i \pm 0.5 \ln S_{inc}$, where

$$\ln S_i = \ln S_{\min} + (i-1)\ln S_{inc} \tag{10.24}$$

The probability that the terminal asset price will fall in this range is

$$\Pr(S_{l,i} < S_T < S_{u,i}) = N(-d_{u,i}) - N(-d_{l,i}) \tag{10.25}$$

where

$$d_{u,i} = \frac{\ln(Se^{\alpha T}/S_{u,i}) - 0.5\sigma^2 T}{\sigma\sqrt{T}} \tag{10.25a}$$

and

$$d_{l,i} = \frac{\ln(Se^{\alpha T}/S_{l,i}) - 0.5\sigma^2 T}{\sigma\sqrt{T}} \tag{10.25b}$$

The expected terminal asset price may, therefore, be computed as

$$E(S_T) = \sum_{i=1}^{n} [N(-d_{u,i}) - N(-d_{l,i})] S_{i,T} \tag{10.26}$$

The continuously compounded expected rate of price appreciation on the asset is

$$\alpha = \frac{\ln[E(S_T)/S]}{T} \tag{10.27}$$

(The expected rate of return on the asset equals the expected rate of price appreciation plus the income rate, $\alpha + i$.) Figure 10.11 illustrates the nature of the discrete log of asset price distribution. In Panel A, only 11 intervals are used, while in Panel B 101 intervals are used. Obviously, the degree of precision depends on the number of intervals $n$—the higher is $n$, the more precise is the approximation. The cost is, of course, computational time.

**ILLUSTRATION 10.6** Compute expected asset price.

*Compute the expected asset price in three months, assuming the current asset price is 50, its expected return is 8%, its income rate is 2%, and its volatility rate is 40%. The risk-free rate of interest is 5%. Compute the expected terminal asset price and the expected asset return under the assumption of risk-neutrality. Recompute the expected terminal profit/return assuming investors are risk averse.*

The first step is to compute the range of asset prices in three months. The expected rate of price appreciation under risk-neutrality is 0.05 – 0.02 = 0.03. The minimum of the asset price range is determined by

$$\ln(S_{\min}) = \ln(50) + (0.03 - 0.5(0.40^2))(0.25) - 4(0.40)\sqrt{0.25} = 3.100$$

and the maximum is

$$\ln(S_{\max}) = \ln(50) + (0.03 - 0.5(0.40^2))(0.25) + 4(0.40)\sqrt{0.25} = 4.700$$

For illustrative purposes, the number of intervals is set equal to 11, so that the width of each interval is

$$\ln S_{inc} = \frac{4.700 - 3.100}{10} = 0.160$$

The values of $\ln S_i$ are shown in the table below.

| | | Log of Asset Price | | Asset Price | | | | |
|---|---|---|---|---|---|---|---|---|
| Price Interval | $\ln S_i$ | Lower Bound | Upper Bound | Lower Bound | Upper Bound | Prob. in Interval | Asset Price $S_{i,T}$ | Prob. Times $H_{i,T}$ |
| 1 | 3.100 | 3.020 | 3.180 | 20.482 | 24.035 | 0.00015 | 22.187 | 0.0034 |
| 2 | 3.260 | 3.180 | 3.340 | 24.035 | 28.206 | 0.00240 | 26.037 | 0.0624 |
| 3 | 3.420 | 3.340 | 3.500 | 28.206 | 33.100 | 0.02019 | 30.555 | 0.6171 |
| 4 | 3.580 | 3.500 | 3.660 | 33.100 | 38.843 | 0.09232 | 35.856 | 3.3103 |
| 5 | 3.740 | 3.660 | 3.820 | 38.843 | 45.582 | 0.22951 | 42.078 | 9.6572 |
| 6 | 3.900 | 3.820 | 3.980 | 45.582 | 53.492 | 0.31084 | 49.379 | 15.3491 |
| 7 | 4.060 | 3.980 | 4.140 | 53.492 | 62.773 | 0.22951 | 57.947 | 13.2993 |
| 8 | 4.220 | 4.140 | 4.300 | 62.773 | 73.665 | 0.09232 | 68.001 | 6.2778 |
| 9 | 4.380 | 4.300 | 4.460 | 73.665 | 86.446 | 0.02019 | 79.800 | 1.6115 |
| 10 | 4.540 | 4.460 | 4.620 | 86.446 | 101.446 | 0.00240 | 93.646 | 0.2244 |
| 11 | 4.700 | 4.620 | 4.780 | 101.446 | 119.048 | 0.00015 | 109.895 | 0.0169 |
| | | | | | | | $E(S_T)$ | 50.4294 |

The lower and upper bounds of the interval are shown in the columns to the right of $\ln S_i$. The values reported in the first row are 3.100 – 0.5(0.16) and 3.100 + 0.5(0.16). The probability of being between these two levels of $\ln S_i$ is essentially zero.[14] The asset price for this interval is $e^{3.100} = 22.187$.

Multiplying the probability and asset price in each row and then summing across rows produces a value of 50.4294. This is the expected terminal asset price under the assumption that investors are risk neutral. According to the parameters of the problem,

[14] Note that the probabilities are symmetric about the middle row in the table. This is because the logarithm of asset prices is normally distributed.

however, the expected terminal asset price is $E(S_T) = Se^{bT} = 50e^{0.03(0.25)} = 50.3764$. The difference of 0.0529 is approximation error. This difference will disappear as the number of intervals is increased. With 101 intervals, expected terminal price is 50.3733, a difference of only −0.0031. The asset's expected rate of price appreciation is

$$\alpha = \frac{\ln(50.3733/50)}{0.25} = 2.975\%$$

very close to the 3% used in the construction of the illustration.[15] The expected rate of return of the asset using this computational procedure is 0.02975 + 0.02 = 4.975%.

The expected profit is greater than zero in a world where investors are risk-averse. They demand a risk premium for holding risky assets. Repeating our computations in the table above, but setting the expected rate of price appreciation to 6% instead of 3%, the expected terminal asset price in our example is 50.8090. With 101 intervals, it is 50.7525. Its value based on the expected rate of price appreciation is $50e^{0.06(0.25)} = 50.7557$. The expected rate of price appreciation is

$$\alpha = \frac{\ln(50.7557/50)}{0.25} = 5.975\%$$

The expected rate of return on the asset using this computational procedure is 7.975%, very close to the 8% assumed in this illustration.

**FIGURE 10.11** Discrete asset price distributions based on continuous log-normal asset price distribution. Panel A contains 11 intervals, and Panel B contains 101 intervals.
Panel A. 11 intervals

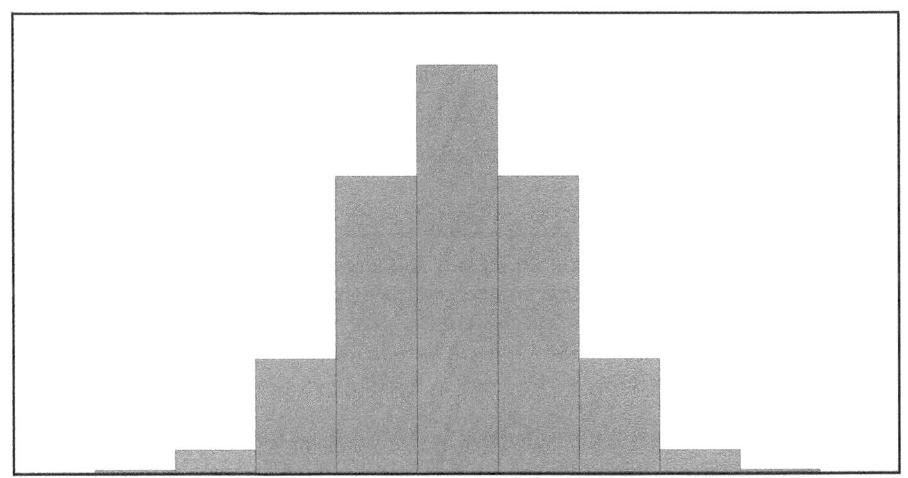

[15] Computing the expected terminal price and expected rate of price appreciation for the asset in this illustration is, of course, superfluous. We engage in these computations only to gauge the degree of error that is present in our computational procedure.

**FIGURE 10.11** (Continued)
Panel B. 101 intervals

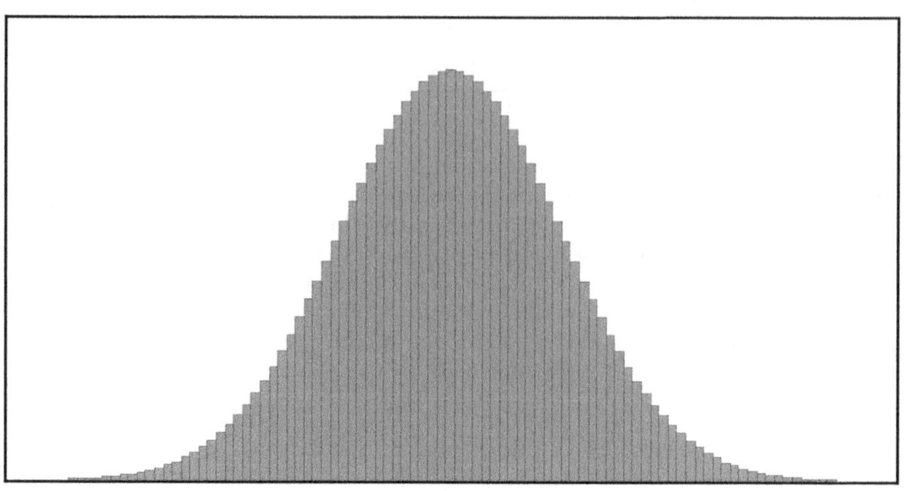

With the asset price bins and probabilities computed, computing the profit from an option trading strategy is straightforward. In each bin, we compute the profit based on the asset price in the bin and multiply by the probability of being in the bin. Then, sum across all bins, that is,

$$E(\pi_T) = \sum_{i=1}^{n} [N(-d_{u,i}) - N(-d_{l,i})]\pi_{i,T} \tag{10.28}$$

where $\pi_{i,T}$ is the strategy profit in bin $i$ conditional on asset price $S_{i,T}$

**ILLUSTRATION 10.7** Compute expected profit from straddle.

*Assume that the asset in Illustration 10.6 has a call and a put written on it. Both options have an exercise price of 50 and three months remaining to expiration. The price of the call is 4.1368 and the price of the put is 3.7650. (Note that the option values were computed using the BSM formula.) Compute the expected profit/return from a straddle formed using these options. Assume investors are risk-neutral, and then assume they are risk-averse.*

Illustration 10.6 takes you through the steps of setting up the asset price intervals. The only step that remains is computing the straddle's profit in each of the bins. The column labeled "Straddle Profit" contains the profit in each bin conditional on the terminal asset price for that bin. Each profit entry is multiplied by its respective probability to generate the last column. The last column is summed to find the expected profit from the strategy. In a risk-neutral world, the expected profit should be equal to zero. Using 11 intervals, the expected profit in our illustration is –0.0284. This profit would go to zero as the number of intervals in the procedure is increased. At 101 intervals, the expected profit is 0.0002.

| Price Interval | $\ln S_i$ | Log of Asset Price Lower Bound | Log of Asset Price Upper Bound | Asset Price Lower Bound | Asset Price Upper Bound | Prob. in Interval | Asset Price $S_{i,T}$ | Straddle Profit $\pi_{i,T}$ | Prob. Times $\pi_{i,T}$ |
|---|---|---|---|---|---|---|---|---|---|
| 1 | 3.107 | 3.027 | 3.187 | 20.636 | 24.216 | 0.00015 | 22.354 | 19.644 | 0.0030 |
| 2 | 3.267 | 3.187 | 3.347 | 24.216 | 28.418 | 0.00240 | 26.233 | 15.766 | 0.0378 |
| 3 | 3.427 | 3.347 | 3.507 | 28.418 | 33.349 | 0.02019 | 30.785 | 11.214 | 0.2265 |
| 4 | 3.587 | 3.507 | 3.667 | 33.349 | 39.135 | 0.09232 | 36.126 | 5.872 | 0.5421 |
| 5 | 3.747 | 3.667 | 3.827 | 39.135 | 45.926 | 0.22951 | 42.395 | –0.396 | –0.0909 |
| 6 | 3.907 | 3.827 | 3.987 | 45.926 | 53.894 | 0.31084 | 49.751 | –7.752 | –2.4096 |
| 7 | 4.067 | 3.987 | 4.147 | 53.894 | 63.245 | 0.22951 | 58.383 | 0.382 | 0.0876 |
| 8 | 4.227 | 4.147 | 4.307 | 63.245 | 74.219 | 0.09232 | 68.513 | 10.512 | 0.9704 |
| 9 | 4.387 | 4.307 | 4.467 | 74.219 | 87.097 | 0.02019 | 80.401 | 22.400 | 0.4524 |
| 10 | 4.547 | 4.467 | 4.627 | 87.097 | 102.209 | 0.00240 | 94.351 | 36.350 | 0.0871 |
| 11 | 4.707 | 4.627 | 4.787 | 102.209 | 119.944 | 0.00015 | 110.722 | 52.721 | 0.0081 |
| | | | | | | | | $E(\pi_T)$ | –0.0854 |

Like in the case of the underlying asset, the expected rate of return on this strategy may be computed by taking the expected terminal value of the position, dividing it by the initial value, and annualizing. The initial value of the portfolio is 4.1368 + 3.7650 = 7.9018. The expected terminal value equals the initial value carried until time $T$ at the risk-free rate, $7.9018e^{0.05(0.25)} = 8.0012$, plus the expected profit, 0.0002, or 8.0014. The expected rate of return on the strategy is

$$\frac{\ln(8.0014/7.9018)}{0.25} = 5.008\%$$

almost exactly equal to the risk-free rate of interest, as it should be in a risk-neutral world.

The expected profit is greater than zero in a world where investors are risk-averse. They demand a risk premium for holding risky assets. Repeating our computations in the table above, but setting the expected rate of price appreciation to 6% instead of 3%, the expected profit with 11 intervals is –0.0854. This result is driven by the fact that too few intervals were used. At 101 intervals, the expected profit becomes 0.0484. The expected terminal value equals the initial value carried until time $T$ at the risk-free rate, $7.9018e^{0.05(0.25)} = 8.0012$, plus the expected profit, 0.0484, or 8.0496. The expected rate of return on the strategy is

$$\frac{\ln(8.0496/7.9018)}{0.25} = 7.412\%$$

## SUMMARY

This chapter focuses on the two main categories of option trading strategies—dynamic and passive. Dynamic strategies are those that focus on expected return/risk management over the next short interval of time. For these strategies, we show the expected return/risk tradeoff and develop a set of dynamic risk management tools. These tools account for unexpected short-term movements in the asset price, volatility, and interest rates, as well as the natural erosion of option's time value as it approaches expiration. Passive strategies involve buying or selling a portfolio that includes options, and then holding the position unchanged over a discrete interval such as the option's time remaining until expiration. To analyze these strategies, we develop terminal profit functions for each of the eight basic security positions (i.e., long or short the asset, the futures, and call and the put), and then show how to combine these functions to analyze the terminal profits of a particular trading strategy. The lognormal asset price mechanics introduced in Chapter 5 is brought back into the discussion to allow us to make probabilistic statements regarding the trading strategy profitability as well as expected profitability and expected rate of return.

## REFERENCES AND SUGGESTED READINGS

Black, Fischer, and Myron Scholes. 1973. The pricing of options and corporate liabilities. *Journal of Political Economy* 81: 637–659.

Merton, Robert C. 1973. Theory of rational option pricing. *Bell Journal of Economics and Management Science* 4: 141–183.

# PART Five

# Stock Derivatives

# CHAPTER 11

# Stock Products

Options on common stocks have been traded in the United States since the 1790s. Originally, trading took place in the over-the-counter market. Put/call dealers would advertise their prices in the financial press, and interested buyers would call a dealer. These contracts were not standardized with respect to exercise prices or expiration dates. Without standardization, option positions were often difficult to unwind prior to expiration. An investor wanting to reverse his option position was forced to negotiate with the dealer with whom the original trade was made.

On April 26, 1973, the Chicago Board Options Exchange (CBOE) became the world's first organized secondary market for stock options. The beginnings were modest. The "exchange" was in a small smokers' lounge off the main floor of the Chicago Board of Trade. The only options traded were calls,[1] and calls were available only on 16 New York Stock Exchange (NYSE) stocks. The market was an immediate success. By 1975, the American Stock Exchange (AMEX) and the Philadelphia Stock Exchange (PHLX) began listing stock options, followed shortly thereafter by the Pacific Coast Exchange (PCE) and the NYSE. Today, calls and puts trade in the United States on over 2,200 hundred different stocks and on five exchanges. Worldwide, stock options trade on over 50 exchanges in 38 different countries. Futures contracts on individual stocks also trade on a handful of exchanges worldwide, but their popularity pales by comparison. Due to a regulatory dispute, stock futures did not begin trading in the United States until November 2002.[2]

This chapter has three sections. In the first section, the trading activity of the major stock derivatives markets worldwide is presented. U.S. stock option mar-

[1] The decision by the CBT to apply to the SEC for the trading of calls rather than calls and puts was a political one. At the time, short selling of stocks was regarded with suspicion. Rather than jeopardize its chances of having *any* stock option trading approved, the CBT's application was confined to options whose value increased as the stock price goes up.

[2] Until late 2000, trading in single stock futures was prohibited in the United States by virtue of the Johnson-Shad Accord (1984). In December 2000, Congress passed the Commodity Futures Modernization Act that, among other things, repealed the ban on single-stock futures, clearing the path for trading in the U.S. stock futures began trading in the OneChicago and NQLX markets on November 8, 2002.

kets are discussed in detail. Stock option contract specifications are also provided. In the second section, valuation principles based on the materials of Chapters 3 through 7 are summarized. For derivatives on common stocks, the discrete flow valuation framework is most appropriate. In the United States, cash dividend payments are made quarterly. The third section contains a discussion of stock option trading and risk management strategies. Dividend spread strategies, stock price collars, and variable prepaid forward contracts are considered. Also considered are strategies involving corporations buying and selling exchange-traded and OTC options on their own shares. The chapter concludes with a brief summary.

## MARKETS

Derivative contracts on individual common stocks trade both on exchanges and in the OTC market. Of the two contract markets, the stock option market is by far the most active in the United States. For the calendar year 2003, stock options accounted for 99.7% of all single stock futures and option trading.[3]

Stock futures trade on two exchanges in the United States—the OneChicago Exchange (ONE) and NQLX.[4] Both exchanges are fully electronic. OneChicago is a joint venture of the Chicago Board Options Exchange, the Chicago Mercantile Exchange, and the Chicago Board of Trade. During 2003, it had trading volume surpassing 1.6 million contracts. The NQLX is a wholly-owned company of Euronext.liffe, which, in turn, is a wholly-owned subsidiary of Euronext NV. Its trading volume during 2003 was approximately 60% of that of OneChicago.

Stock options trade on five exchanges in the United States—the Chicago Board Options Exchange (CBOE), the American Stock Exchange (AMEX), the Pacific Exchange (PCE), the Philadelphia Exchange (PHLX), and the International Securities Exchange (ISE).[5] The ISE is fully electronic. Figure 11.1 provides a breakdown of contract volume by exchange for the year 2003. The ISE had the greatest trading volume with 30% of all U.S. stock option trading volume. The CBOE was next with 26%. The AMEX had 21%, the PHLX 13%, and the PCX 10%.

As of December 2003, 2,227 stocks had options listed on exchanges in the United States. The decision about whether to list options on a particular stock rests only with the exchange. The firm/stock must satisfy certain listing criteria. The CBOE, for example, requires that the firm has:

[3] Historical statistics for single stock futures and options trading in the United States are available on the website of the Options Clearing Corporation (www.optionsclearing.com).

[4] U.S. stock futures and stock option trades clear through the Option Clearing Corporation or OCC. Founded in 1973, the OCC is the largest clearing organization in the world for single stock options and futures and was the first clearing house to receive an AAA credit rating from Standard & Poor's Corporation. Operating under the jurisdiction of the Securities and Exchange Commission and the Commodity Futures Trading Commission, OCC is jointly owned by the American Stock Exchange, Chicago Board Options Exchange, International Securities Exchange, Pacific Exchange and Philadelphia Stock Exchange.

[5] The New York Stock Exchange (NYSE) made markets in stock options until April 1997 when it sold its market to the CBOE and reduced the number of U.S. markets from five to four. With the ISE launching trading of stock options on May 26, 2000, the number of exchanges returned to five.

**FIGURE 11.1** Share of total U.S. stock option trading volume accounted for by each option exchange during the calendar year 2003.

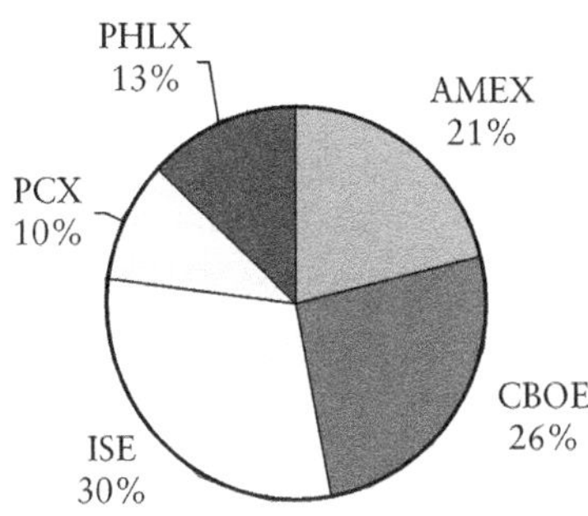


*Source:* www.optionsclearing.com.

1. A minimum of seven million shares outstanding not including those held by insiders.
2. A minimum of 2,000 shareholders.

In addition, it requires that stock be:

3. Traded at least 2,400,000 shares in the last 12 months.
4. Closed at a market price of at least $7.50 per share for the majority of the business days during the last three months.[6]

To identify new stock options, the CBOE monitors the trading activity of all stocks satisfying the listing criteria. Among the factors considered in gauging the market's potential interest are the stock's trading volume and return volatility.[7] The higher the trading volume and the greater the volatility, the greater the potential interest. Once the CBOE decides list options on a particular stock, it registers with the SEC. Trading begins a few days later. As a matter of courtesy, the CBOE sends a letter informing the firm of its decision.

### Stock Futures

Stock futures trade in a number of countries worldwide, with the U.S. markets being the most active. Table 11.1 provides the specifications of the single-stock futures contracts traded on the OneChicago Exchange. Each futures is written on 100 shares of stock, with prices quoted in pennies per share. They trade from 8:15AM to 3PM CST. Futures contracts on a particular stock are on the quarterly expiration cycles Mar/Jun/Sep/Dec. At any time the next two quarterly

[6] Chicago Board Options Exchange *Constitution and Rules* (May 2002), Paragraph 2113.
[7] Mayhew and Mihov (2004) provide empirical support for the proposition that volume and volatility in the underlying stock market are important in a stock option exchange's listing decision.

expirations as well as the next two monthly serial expirations are listed. The contracts expire on the third Friday on the contract month. Physical delivery of the underlying shares takes places three business days after contract expiration.

**TABLE 11.1** Selected terms of single stock futures contract traded on OneChicago Exchange.

| | |
|---|---|
| Contract size | 100 shares of underlying stock |
| Minimum price fluctuation (tick size) | $0.01 × 100 shares = $1.00 |
| Regular trading hours | 9:15 AM–4:02 PM Eastern Time |
| Position limits | None prior to the last five trading days prior to expiration. During the last five trading days, either 13,500 net contracts or 22,500 net contracts (long or short) as per CFTC requirements. |
| Daily price limits | None |
| Reportable position limit | 200 contracts |
| Contract months | Two quarterly expirations and two serial months trade at all times for a total of four expirations per product class. OneChicago follows the quarterly cycle of March (H), June (M), September (U), and December (Z). The serial months traded are the two nearby non-quarterly contract months. |
| Expiration date/last trading day | Third Friday of contract month or, if such Friday is not a business day, the immediately preceding business day. |
| Settlement/delivery | Physical delivery of underlying security on third business day following the last trading day. |
| **Additional Information** | |
| Margin requirements | Initial and maintenance margin requirement of 20% of the cash value of the contract. Certain offsets may apply. |
| Short sale advantages | No uptick required to initiate a short position. No stock borrowing costs or risks. |
| Clearing and settlement | Trades executed at OneChicago are cleared and settled by the Options Clearing Corporation (OCC) or by Chicago Mercantile Exchange Inc. (CME). |
| U.S. Government regulator | OneChicago is jointly regulated by the Commodity Futures Trading Commission (CFTC) and the Securities and Exchange Commission (SEC). |

## Stock Options

The stock options traded in the United States are also, for the most part, standardized products. Each stock option contract is written on 100 shares of stock, has its price reported in pennies per share,[8] expires on the Saturday after the third Friday of the contract month, and is American-style. For stocks with a share price in excess of $25, exercise price increments are usually in $5 increments, and, for share prices less than $25, exercise prices are in $2.50 increments. Options on a particular stock are on one of three quarterly expiration cycles (Jan/Apr/Jul/Oct, Feb/May/Aug/Nov, or Mar/Jun/Sep/Dec), and the two nearest contract months on the quarterly cycle are listed at any time. In addition, there will be options listed on the two nearby months, and, in the event that one of the two nearest months is on the quarterly cycle, the next quarterly expiration will also be traded. Dell's options, for example, are on the Feb/May/Aug/Nov cycle. This means that, if we are standing at the end of December (after the December options have expired), January, February, May, and August option expirations will be traded. Under these rules, stock options are short-term, with times to expiration less than nine months. That is not to say that longer term options do not exist. In the 1980s, the CBOE, in response to investor demand, began trading "Long-term Equity Anticipation Securities," more popularly known as "Leaps." Leaps, by convention, expire in the month of January, and have times to expiration up to three years.

Stock options are normally "unprotected" from cash dividend payments on the underlying stock. Dividend payments during the option's life reduce the price of the stock and hence reduce (increase) the value of the call (put). In the event of extraordinarily large cash dividend distributions (i.e., 5% of the prevailing stock price); however, the Options Clearing Corporation (OCC) "protects" the value of option contracts by adjusting the exercise prices of outstanding option series downward by the amount of the cash dividend payment.[9] Such an adjustment largely preserves the value of the option. Stock options are "protected" from the effects of stock splits and stock dividends. When a firm splits its shares or pays a stock dividend, the option's exercise price and open interest are adjusted accordingly. A 5-for-4 stock split (or a 25% stock dividend), for example, reduces a $50 exercise price to $40 and increases the number of options outstanding by 25%. In the event of the stock split/stock dividend produces a non-integer exercise price, the exercise price is rounded to the nearest 1/8.

The terms of stock option contracts are also adjusted in the event of a corporate restructuring or acquisition. On April 30, 2004, for example, Abbott Laboratories ("ABT") distributed the shares of Hospira, Inc. ("HSP") to ABT shareholders. The underlying deliverable security for outstanding ABT option

[8] Under current exchange rules, the minimum tick size for options trading up to $3 is five cents and for options trading above $3 is 10 cents.

[9] On July 20, 2004, Microsoft Corporation ("MSFT") announced a special cash dividend of $3 per share. At the time, the MSFT share price closed at $28.32, so the distribution amounted to 10.6% of the prevailing share price. On November 9, 2004, Microsoft shareholders approved a $3 special cash dividend payable on December 2, 2004, to shareholders of record on November 17, 2004. Therefore, as of November 15, 2004 (i.e., the ex-dividend date of Microsoft's shares), the exercise prices of all MSFT option series were reduced by $3.

series became 100 shares of ABT and 10 shares of HSP. For mergers and acquisitions, the shares of the target firm are adjusted, with the nature of the adjustment depending on how the bidding firm pays for the shares of the target firm. If the bidding firm acquires the shares of the target using its own shares to pay for the shares of the target firm, an adjustment is made to the number of deliverable shares. On April 26, 2004, for example, AngloGold Limited acquired Ashanti Goldfields Company Limited, paying 0.29 shares of the newly formed AngloGold Ashanti Limited (AU). Hence, the deliverable security on outstanding Ashanti option series became 29 shares of AU. If the bidding firm pays cash for the target firm, the adjustment is severe in the sense that the target firm's share price becomes the cash offer price. On March 29, 2004, for example, Henkel KGaA acquired the shares of Dial Corporation (DL) for $28.75 in cash. The deliverable security on outstanding DL option series therefore became $28.75 in cash. While the outstanding option contracts expire at their normal time, in-the-money options should be exercised immediately since there is no prospect of earning more money (i.e., the security price is fixed). Out-of-the-money option prices immediately go to 0. These three adjustments are only examples of what may occur. Many restructurings and acquisitions have more complicated terms, and, consequently, the revisions to the terms of stock option contracts become more complicated. A panel from the OCC's Securities Committee[10] attempts to make each of these adjustments in an equitable fashion for all parties concerned. Details of all contract adjustments can be found on the OCC's website, www.optionsclearing.com.

Table 11.2A (11.2B) contains a summary of trading of Dell stock options (leaps) midday on Tuesday, January 2004. The row in Table 11.2A is for the January 2004 call and put with an exercise price of 5. The expiration month and the exercise price are reported in the columns headed "Calls" and "Puts." Dell has four expiration months listed—January 2004, February 2004, May 2004, and August 2004. Dell's options are on the Feb/May/Aug/Nov quarterly expiration cycle. According to the rules described earlier, this means the January, February, May, and August options should be traded. The first five characters of the term in parenthesis is the option series ticker symbol. The call's ticker symbol, for example, is "DLYAA." Note that each ticker symbol in the table is unique. This is its identifier for trading purposes. The table shows that neither the call nor the put traded on January 6, at least as of the time the prices were downloaded (i.e., their volumes of trading are 0). Both options have traded at some time in the past, however, since the call has open interest of 580 and the put has open interest of 245. The call has a bid/ask price quote of 30.00/30.10. Since the current stock price quotes are 35.05/35.06, there is no arbitrage price violation. The last trade price, 28.60, lies outside the option's prevailing bid/ask quotes. This merely indicates that the market price of the option has moved since the time of the last trade. When the last trade occurred cannot be inferred from the information in the table. All that can be inferred is that the trade did not occur on January 6, 2004.

[10] The panel consists of two representatives from the exchanges on which the affected option is traded.

**TABLE 11.2A** Summary of price, volume, and open interest information for Dell stock options drawn from www.cboe.com at 1:53 PM on January 6, 2004. Underlying stock has contemporaneous bid (ask) price of 35.05 (35.06).

| Calls | Last Sale | Bid | Ask | Vol | Open Int |
|---|---|---|---|---|---|
| 04 Jan 5.00 (DLY AA-E) | 28.60 | 30.00 | 30.10 | 0 | 580 |
| 04 Jan 7.50 (DLY AU-E) | 27.40 | 27.50 | 27.60 | 0 | 935 |
| 04 Jan 10.00 (DLY AB-E) | 25.60 | 25.00 | 25.10 | 0 | 2,554 |
| 04 Jan 12.50 (DLY AV-E) | 22.30 | 22.50 | 22.60 | 0 | 1,872 |
| 04 Jan 15.00 (DLY AC-E) | 19.90 | 20.00 | 20.10 | 0 | 2,886 |
| 04 Jan 17.50 (DLY AW-E) | 17.30 | 17.50 | 17.60 | 0 | 2,554 |
| 04 Jan 20.00 (DLY AD-E) | 14.50 | 15.00 | 15.10 | 0 | 10,362 |
| 04 Jan 22.50 (DLQ AX-E) | 11.70 | 12.50 | 12.60 | 0 | 4,120 |
| 04 Jan 25.00 (DLQ AE-E) | 10.20 | 10.00 | 10.10 | 2 | 22,611 |
| 04 Jan 27.50 (DLQ AY-E) | 7.70 | 7.50 | 7.60 | 0 | 32,333 |
| 04 Jan 30.00 (DLQ AF-E) | 5.10 | 5.00 | 5.10 | 2 | 42,340 |
| 04 Jan 32.50 (DLQ AZ-E) | 2.65 | 2.55 | 2.65 | 140 | 47,599 |
| 04 Jan 35.00 (DLQ AG-E) | 0.55 | 0.55 | 0.65 | 1,490 | 126,530 |
| 04 Jan 37.50 (DLQ AT-E) | 0.05 | 0.00 | 0.05 | 0 | 49,257 |
| 04 Jan 40.00 (DLQ AH-E) | 0.05 | 0.00 | 0.05 | 0 | 42,460 |
| 04 Jan 42.50 (DLQ AS-E) | 0.05 | 0.00 | 0.05 | 0 | 255 |
| 04 Jan 45.00 (DLQ AI-E) | 0.05 | 0.00 | 0.05 | 0 | 8,573 |
| 04 Jan 50.00 (DLQ AJ-E) | 0.10 | 0.00 | 0.05 | 0 | 9,076 |
| 04 Feb 20.00 (DLY BD-E) | 14.90 | 15.00 | 15.20 | 0 | 1,313 |
| 04 Feb 22.50 (DLQ BX-E) | 12.30 | 12.50 | 12.70 | 0 | 1,165 |
| 04 Feb 25.00 (DLQ BE-E) | 8.50 | 10.00 | 10.20 | 0 | 1,954 |
| 04 Feb 27.50 (DLQ BY-E) | 6.80 | 7.60 | 7.70 | 0 | 1,657 |
| 04 Feb 30.00 (DLQ BF-E) | 5.40 | 5.20 | 5.30 | 0 | 2,477 |
| 04 Feb 32.50 (DLQ BZ-E) | 3.20 | 3.00 | 3.10 | 438 | 15,854 |
| 04 Feb 35.00 (DLQ BG-E) | 1.45 | 1.30 | 1.40 | 88 | 32,620 |
| 04 Feb 37.50 (DLQ BT-E) | 0.40 | 0.35 | 0.45 | 3,784 | 23,799 |
| 04 Feb 40.00 (DLQ BH-E) | 0.10 | 0.05 | 0.10 | 0 | 8,146 |
| 04 Feb 42.50 (DLQ BS-E) | 0.05 | 0.00 | 0.05 | 0 | 1,285 |
| 04 Feb 45.00 (DLQ BI-E) | 0.05 | 0.00 | 0.05 | 0 | 1,318 |
| 04 May 20.00 (DLY ED-E) | 15.00 | 15.10 | 15.20 | 0 | 2,194 |
| 04 May 22.50 (DLQ EX-E) | 12.40 | 12.60 | 12.80 | 0 | 1,066 |
| 04 May 25.00 (DLQ EE-E) | 9.50 | 10.20 | 10.40 | 0 | 862 |
| 04 May 27.50 (DLQ EY-E) | 7.40 | 7.90 | 8.00 | 0 | 695 |
| 04 May 30.00 (DLQ EF-E) | 5.30 | 5.70 | 5.80 | 0 | 1,981 |
| 04 May 32.50 (DLQ EZ-E) | 3.90 | 3.70 | 3.90 | 0 | 2,664 |
| 04 May 35.00 (DLQ EG-E) | 2.25 | 2.20 | 2.30 | 84 | 16,581 |
| 04 May 37.50 (DLQ ET-E) | 1.15 | 1.15 | 1.20 | 54 | 11,003 |
| 04 May 40.00 (DLQ EH-E) | 0.55 | 0.50 | 0.60 | 8 | 11,819 |
| 04 May 42.50 (DLQ ES-E) | 0.15 | 0.20 | 0.25 | 0 | 3,187 |
| 04 May 45.00 (DLQ EI-E) | 0.10 | 0.05 | 0.10 | 0 | 183 |
| 04 Aug 20.00 (DLY HD-E) | 0.00 | 15.20 | 15.30 | 0 | 0 |
| 04 Aug 22.50 (DLQ HX-E) | 0.00 | 12.80 | 12.90 | 0 | 10 |
| 04 Aug 25.00 (DLQ HE-E) | 10.10 | 10.40 | 10.60 | 0 | 18 |
| 04 Aug 27.50 (DLQ HY-E) | 7.60 | 8.20 | 8.30 | 0 | 110 |
| 04 Aug 30.00 (DLQ HF-E) | 6.30 | 6.20 | 6.30 | 0 | 71 |
| 04 Aug 32.50 (DLQ HZ-E) | 4.40 | 4.40 | 4.50 | 0 | 221 |
| 04 Aug 35.00 (DLQ HG-E) | 2.95 | 2.90 | 3.00 | 8 | 823 |
| 04 Aug 37.50 (DLQ HT-E) | 1.70 | 1.75 | 1.85 | 104 | 365 |
| 04 Aug 40.00 (DLQ HH-E) | 1.00 | 1.00 | 1.05 | 38 | 213 |
| 04 Aug 42.50 (DLQ HS-E) | 0.00 | 0.50 | 0.60 | 0 | 207 |
| 04 Aug 45.00 (DLQ HI-E) | 0.00 | 0.25 | 0.30 | 0 | 6 |
| Total | | | | 6,240 | 552,764 |

**TABLE 11.2A** (Continued)

| Puts | Last Sale | Bid | Ask | Vol | Open Int |
|---|---|---|---|---|---|
| 04 Jan 5.00 (DLY MA-E) | 0.05 | 0.00 | 0.05 | 0 | 245 |
| 04 Jan 7.50 (DLY MU-E) | 0.45 | 0.00 | 0.05 | 0 | 1,012 |
| 04 Jan 10.00 (DLY MB-E) | 0.05 | 0.00 | 0.05 | 0 | 12,981 |
| 04 Jan 12.50 (DLY MV-E) | 0.05 | 0.00 | 0.05 | 0 | 1,209 |
| 04 Jan 15.00 (DLY MC-E) | 0.05 | 0.00 | 0.05 | 0 | 7,190 |
| 04 Jan 17.50 (DLY MW-E) | 0.10 | 0.00 | 0.05 | 0 | 9,807 |
| 04 Jan 20.00 (DLY MD-E) | 0.05 | 0.00 | 0.05 | 0 | 27,524 |
| 04 Jan 22.50 (DLQ MX-E) | 0.05 | 0.00 | 0.05 | 0 | 7,753 |
| 04 Jan 25.00 (DLQ ME-E) | 0.05 | 0.00 | 0.05 | 0 | 23,350 |
| 04 Jan 27.50 (DLQ MY-E) | 0.05 | 0.00 | 0.05 | 0 | 21,488 |
| 04 Jan 30.00 (DLQ MF-E) | 0.05 | 0.00 | 0.05 | 0 | 39,133 |
| 04 Jan 32.50 (DLQ MZ-E) | 0.05 | 0.00 | 0.10 | 70 | 34,591 |
| 04 Jan 35.00 (DLQ MG-E) | 0.55 | 0.45 | 0.55 | 485 | 39,290 |
| 04 Jan 37.50 (DLQ MT-E) | 2.55 | 2.40 | 2.50 | 10 | 4,404 |
| 04 Jan 40.00 (DLQ MH-E) | 5.10 | 4.90 | 5.00 | 0 | 6,914 |
| 04 Jan 42.50 (DLQ MS-E) | 0.00 | 7.40 | 7.50 | 0 | 147 |
| 04 Jan 45.00 (DLQ MI-E) | 10.50 | 9.90 | 10.00 | 0 | 149 |
| 04 Jan 50.00 (DLQ MJ-E) | 14.20 | 14.90 | 15.00 | 0 | 168 |
| 04 Feb 20.00 (DLY ND-E) | 0.05 | 0.00 | 0.05 | 0 | 45 |
| 04 Feb 22.50 (DLQ NX-E) | 0.05 | 0.00 | 0.05 | 0 | 620 |
| 04 Feb 25.00 (DLQ NE-E) | 0.05 | 0.00 | 0.05 | 0 | 3,275 |
| 04 Feb 27.50 (DLQ NY-E) | 0.10 | 0.05 | 0.10 | 0 | 3,721 |
| 04 Feb 30.00 (DLQ NF-E) | 0.15 | 0.10 | 0.20 | 200 | 7,054 |
| 04 Feb 32.50 (DLQ NZ-E) | 0.50 | 0.40 | 0.45 | 15 | 18,014 |
| 04 Feb 35.00 (DLQ NG-E) | 1.25 | 1.20 | 1.30 | 265 | 10,863 |
| 04 Feb 37.50 (DLQ NT-E) | 3.00 | 2.75 | 2.85 | 20 | 2,117 |
| 04 Feb 40.00 (DLQ NH-E) | 5.80 | 4.90 | 5.10 | 0 | 1,051 |
| 04 Feb 42.50 (DLQ NS-E) | 7.90 | 7.40 | 7.50 | 0 | 32 |
| 04 Feb 45.00 (DLQ NI-E) | 10.50 | 9.90 | 10.00 | 0 | 97 |
| 04 May 20.00 (DLY QD-E) | 0.00 | 0.00 | 0.05 | 0 | 0 |
| 04 May 22.50 (DLQ QX-E) | 0.15 | 0.05 | 0.10 | 0 | 670 |
| 04 May 25.00 (DLQ QE-E) | 0.20 | 0.10 | 0.15 | 0 | 1,252 |
| 04 May 27.50 (DLQ QY-E) | 0.35 | 0.25 | 0.30 | 0 | 1,959 |
| 04 May 30.00 (DLQ QF-E) | 0.55 | 0.50 | 0.60 | 0 | 11,585 |
| 04 May 32.50 (DLQ QZ-E) | 1.10 | 1.05 | 1.15 | 50 | 7,858 |
| 04 May 35.00 (DLQ QG-E) | 2.10 | 2.00 | 2.05 | 0 | 6,313 |
| 04 May 37.50 (DLQ QT-E) | 3.20 | 3.40 | 3.50 | 40 | 893 |
| 04 May 40.00 (DLQ QH-E) | 5.70 | 5.30 | 5.40 | 0 | 910 |
| 04 May 42.50 (DLQ QS-E) | 0.00 | 7.50 | 7.60 | 0 | 1,155 |
| 04 May 45.00 (DLQ QI-E) | 0.00 | 9.90 | 10.00 | 0 | 380 |
| 04 Aug 20.00 (DLY TD-E) | 0.00 | 0.05 | 0.10 | 0 | 0 |
| 04 Aug 22.50 (DLQ TX-E) | 0.00 | 0.10 | 0.20 | 0 | 0 |
| 04 Aug 25.00 (DLQ TE-E) | 0.00 | 0.25 | 0.35 | 0 | 29 |
| 04 Aug 27.50 (DLQ TY-E) | 0.65 | 0.50 | 0.60 | 0 | 55 |
| 04 Aug 30.00 (DLQ TF-E) | 1.00 | 0.90 | 1.05 | 0 | 339 |
| 04 Aug 32.50 (DLQ TZ-E) | 1.60 | 1.60 | 1.70 | 100 | 611 |
| 04 Aug 35.00 (DLQ TG-E) | 2.70 | 2.60 | 2.70 | 0 | 1,153 |
| 04 Aug 37.50 (DLQ TT-E) | 4.20 | 4.00 | 4.10 | 110 | 141 |
| 04 Aug 40.00 (DLQ TH-E) | 0.00 | 5.70 | 5.80 | 0 | 121 |
| 04 Aug 42.50 (DLQ TS-E) | 0.00 | 7.70 | 7.90 | 0 | 1 |
| 04 Aug 45.00 (DLQ TI-E) | 0.00 | 10.00 | 10.10 | 0 | 0 |
| Total | | | | 1,365 | 319,669 |

**TABLE 11.2B** Summary of price, volume, and open interest information for Dell leaps drawn from www.cboe.com at 1:53 PM on January 6, 2004. Underlying stock has contemporaneous bid (ask) price of 35.05 (35.06).

| Calls | Last Sale | Bid | Ask | Vol | Open Int | Puts | Last Sale | Bid | Ask | Vol | Open Int |
|---|---|---|---|---|---|---|---|---|---|---|---|
| 05 Jan 5.00 (ZDE AA-E) | 29.30 | 30.00 | 30.20 | 0 | 237 | 05 Jan 5.00 (ZDE MA-E) | 0.00 | 0.00 | 0.15 | 0 | 0 |
| 05 Jan 10.00 (ZDE AB-E) | 25.30 | 25.10 | 25.30 | 0 | 1,000 | 05 Jan 10.00 (ZDE MB-E) | 0.05 | 0.00 | 0.15 | 0 | 1,316 |
| 05 Jan 15.00 (ZDE AC-E) | 17.90 | 20.20 | 20.40 | 0 | 1,464 | 05 Jan 15.00 (ZDE MC-E) | 0.10 | 0.00 | 0.15 | 0 | 4,597 |
| 05 Jan 17.50 (ZDE AW-E) | 18.70 | 17.80 | 18.00 | 0 | 570 | 05 Jan 17.50 (ZDE MW-E) | 0.20 | 0.05 | 0.15 | 0 | 1,044 |
| 05 Jan 20.00 (ZDE AD-E) | 13.70 | 15.40 | 15.60 | 0 | 5,759 | 05 Jan 20.00 (ZDE MD-E) | 0.25 | 0.15 | 0.25 | 0 | 4,618 |
| 05 Jan 22.50 (ZDE AX-E) | 11.90 | 13.10 | 13.30 | 0 | 3,021 | 05 Jan 22.50 (ZDE MX-E) | 0.60 | 0.30 | 0.40 | 0 | 6,358 |
| 05 Jan 25.00 (ZDE AE-E) | 11.00 | 10.90 | 11.10 | 0 | 6,291 | 05 Jan 25.00 (ZDE ME-E) | 0.65 | 0.60 | 0.70 | 50 | 7,969 |
| 05 Jan 27.50 (ZDE AY-E) | 8.20 | 8.90 | 9.00 | 0 | 11,869 | 05 Jan 27.50 (ZDE MY-E) | 1.00 | 1.00 | 1.10 | 0 | 4,784 |
| 05 Jan 30.00 (ZDE AF-E) | 6.40 | 7.00 | 7.20 | 0 | 18,903 | 05 Jan 30.00 (ZDE MF-E) | 1.75 | 1.60 | 1.70 | 0 | 7,978 |
| 05 Jan 32.50 (ZDE AZ-E) | 5.50 | 5.30 | 5.50 | 6 | 9,914 | 05 Jan 32.50 (ZDE MZ-E) | 2.65 | 2.35 | 2.50 | 0 | 6,032 |
| 05 Jan 35.00 (ZDE AG-E) | 4.00 | 3.90 | 4.10 | 13 | 47,104 | 05 Jan 35.00 (ZDE MG-E) | 3.60 | 3.40 | 3.60 | 0 | 16,575 |
| 05 Jan 37.50 (ZDE AT-E) | 2.90 | 2.80 | 2.90 | 76 | 8,299 | 05 Jan 37.50 (ZDE MT-E) | 5.10 | 4.80 | 5.00 | 0 | 1,605 |
| 05 Jan 40.00 (ZDE AH-E) | 1.90 | 1.90 | 2.00 | 72 | 19,980 | 05 Jan 40.00 (ZDE MH-E) | 6.50 | 6.40 | 6.60 | 0 | 3,127 |
| 05 Jan 42.50 (ZDE AS-E) | 1.35 | 1.25 | 1.35 | 50 | 2,990 | 05 Jan 42.50 (ZDE MS-E) | 8.90 | 8.20 | 8.40 | 0 | 1,418 |
| 05 Jan 45.00 (ZDE AI-E) | 0.75 | 0.80 | 0.90 | 0 | 7,157 | 05 Jan 45.00 (ZDE MI-E) | 12.30 | 10.30 | 10.50 | 0 | 1,132 |
| 05 Jan 50.00 (ZDE AJ-E) | 0.35 | 0.30 | 0.40 | 150 | 4,766 | 05 Jan 50.00 (ZDE MJ-E) | 15.60 | 14.90 | 15.00 | 0 | 2,833 |
| 06 Jan 20.00 (WDQ AD-E) | 16.40 | 16.20 | 16.40 | 0 | 1,078 | 06 Jan 20.00 (WDQ MD-E) | 0.55 | 0.55 | 0.65 | 0 | 426 |
| 06 Jan 22.50 (WDQ AX-E) | 0.00 | 14.10 | 14.40 | 0 | 220 | 06 Jan 22.50 (WDQ MX-E) | 0.95 | 0.90 | 1.00 | 0 | 391 |
| 06 Jan 25.00 (WDQ AE-E) | 12.30 | 12.20 | 12.40 | 10 | 543 | 06 Jan 25.00 (WDQ ME-E) | 1.50 | 1.35 | 1.45 | 0 | 311 |
| 06 Jan 27.50 (WDQ AY-E) | 10.80 | 10.40 | 10.60 | 0 | 642 | 06 Jan 27.50 (WDQ MY-E) | 2.40 | 1.95 | 2.05 | 0 | 476 |
| 06 Jan 30.00 (WDQ AF-E) | 8.50 | 8.70 | 9.00 | 0 | 1,310 | 06 Jan 30.00 (WDQ MF-E) | 2.80 | 2.70 | 2.80 | 20 | 1,249 |
| 06 Jan 32.50 (WDQ AZ-E) | 6.70 | 7.20 | 7.50 | 0 | 674 | 06 Jan 32.50 (WDQ MZ-E) | 3.80 | 3.60 | 3.80 | 0 | 5,498 |
| 06 Jan 35.00 (WDQ AG-E) | 5.50 | 5.90 | 6.10 | 0 | 7,414 | 06 Jan 35.00 (WDQ MG-E) | 5.40 | 4.80 | 4.90 | 0 | 8,683 |
| 06 Jan 37.50 (WDQ AT-E) | 4.40 | 4.80 | 5.00 | 0 | 369 | 06 Jan 37.50 (WDQ MT-E) | 7.10 | 6.10 | 6.20 | 0 | 4,621 |
| 06 Jan 40.00 (WDQ AH-E) | 3.40 | 3.80 | 4.00 | 0 | 3,826 | 06 Jan 40.00 (WDQ MH-E) | 9.40 | 7.50 | 7.80 | 0 | 834 |
| 06 Jan 42.50 (WDQ AS-E) | 2.55 | 2.95 | 3.10 | 0 | 801 | 06 Jan 42.50 (WDQ MS-E) | 0.00 | 9.20 | 9.50 | 0 | 695 |
| 06 Jan 45.00 (WDQ AI-E) | 2.10 | 2.30 | 2.45 | 0 | 1,642 | 06 Jan 45.00 (WDQ MI-E) | 11.10 | 11.10 | 11.30 | 0 | 1,911 |
| 06 Jan 50.00 (WDQ AJ-E) | 1.35 | 1.30 | 1.50 | 0 | 1,387 | 06 Jan 50.00 (WDQ MJ-E) | 15.10 | 15.20 | 15.40 | 0 | 1,188 |
| Total | | | | 377 | 169,230 | | | | | 70 | 97,669 |

In Table 11.2A, Dell stock options have exercise prices ranging up to 45. As a matter of policy, the exchange lists options with at least two exercise prices on each side of the current stock price. With the current stock price about $35, this means that exercise prices of 25, 30, 40 and 45 should appear, and they do. Where a wider range of exercise prices appear (such as in the case for Dell options on January 6, 2004), it may be (1) a reflection of a large stock price move during the life of the option or (2) that a specific exercise price was requested by a customer.

Table 11.2A reveals two interesting characteristics about stock option markets. First, at-the-money options tend to be the most active. Table 11.2A shows that more than 99% of call option trading volume and 85% of put option trading volume on January 6, 2004 was in option series with exercise prices between 32.50 and 37.50 (i.e., at-the-money options). Second, the total open interest for calls, 552,764, exceeds that of puts, 319,669. In stock option markets, there seems to be greater interest in speculating that the stock price will rise rather than fall. In the next chapter, we find the opposite pattern for stock index options. In that market, the demand for portfolio interest causes the open interest of puts to be significantly greater than for calls.

Table 11.2B has the same columns as Table 11.2A. The only difference is that Table 11.2B contains leaps written on Dell's stock. As noted earlier, leaps have January expirations. As of January 6, 2004, Dell had leaps expiring in January 2005 and January 2006. When Dell's January 2004 stock options expire on January 17, 2004, leaps with a January 2007 expiration will be introduced. Note that there is significant open interest in long-term options. Apparently a large number of traders have long-term directional views on Dell's stock price.

**Equity FLEX Options** The stock option exchanges also facilitate trading of stock options with nonstandard terms. Called "FLEX options," these contracts are tailor-made to suit a customer's needs. The contract can be a call or a put, American-style or European-style, and as long as three years to expiration. For puts, exercise prices may be set in 1/8 increments. For calls, exercise prices are limited to the minimum strike price intervals that are available for the non-FLEX stock options. Like standard stock options, FLEX options call for the delivery of the underlying stocks on expiration day.

## VALUATION

Valuing derivatives contracts written on common stocks follows the principles developed for the case where the underlying asset has discrete cash disbursements (i.e., cash dividends) during the life of the contract. All of the valuation principles are summarized in Table 11.3. Before applying these principles, however, the procedural aspects of cash dividend payments for U.S. firms are discussed. In addition, we provide a general sense for the number of U.S. firms that pay dividends vis-à-vis the firms that do not.

**TABLE 11.3** Summary of arbitrage price relations and valuation equations/methods for derivatives on common stocks.

**Arbitrage Relations**

**Forward/Futures**

$$f = F = Se^{rT} - FVD \text{ or } fe^{-rT} = Fe^{-rT} = S - PVD$$

where

$$FVD = \sum_{i=1}^{n} D_i e^{r(T-t_i)} \text{ and } PVD = e^{-rT} FVD = \sum_{i=1}^{n} D_i e^{-rt_i}$$

| **European-Style:** | **Options** | **Futures Options** |
|---|---|---|
| Lower bound for call | $c \geq \max(0, S - PVD - Xe^{-rT})$ | $c \geq \max[0, e^{-rT}(F - X)]$ |
| Lower bound for put | $p \geq \max(0, Xe^{-rT} - S + PVD)$ | $p \geq \max[0, e^{-rT}(X - F)]$ |
| Put-call parity | $c - p = S - PVD - Xe^{-rT}$ | $c - p = e^{-rT}(F - X)$ |
| **American-Style:** | **Options** | **Futures Options** |
| Lower bound for call | $C \geq \max(0, S - PVD - Xe^{-rT}, S - X)$ | $C \geq \max(0, F - X)$ |
| Lower bound for put | $P \geq \max(0, Xe^{-rT} - S + PVD, X - S)$ | $P \geq \max(0, X - F)$ |
| Put-call parity | $S - PVD - X \leq C - P \leq S - PVD - Xe^{-rT}$ | $Fe^{-rT} - X \leq C - P \leq F - Xe^{-rT}$ |

**Valuation Equations/Methods**

| **European-Style:** | **Options** | **Futures Options** |
|---|---|---|
| Call value | $c = S^x N(d_1) - Xe^{-rT} N(d_2)$ | $c = e^{-rT}[FN(d_1) - XN(d_2)]$ |
| Put value | $p = Xe^{-rT} N(-d_2) - S^x N(-d_1)$ where $S_x = S - PVD$ $d_1 = \frac{\ln(S^x/X) + (r + 0.5\sigma^2)T}{\sigma\sqrt{T}}$ and $d_2 = d_1 - \sigma\sqrt{T}$ | $p = e^{-rT}[XN(-d_2) - FN(-d_1)]$ where $d_1 = \frac{\ln(F/X) + 0.5\sigma^2 T}{\sigma\sqrt{T}}$ and $d_2 = d_1 - \sigma\sqrt{T}$ |
| **American-Style:** | **Options** | **Futures Options** |
| Call and put values | Numerical valuation: binomial and trinomial methods | Numerical valuation: quadratic approximation, binomial method, and trinomial method |

## Discrete Cash Dividend Payments

Cash dividends on U.S. stocks are generally paid on a quarterly basis. A firm's board of directors meets each quarter and makes the announcement. The announcement date is called the *dividend declaration date*. The announcement identifies: (1) who will get the dividend; (2) how much the dividend will be; and (3) when the dividend will be paid (i.e., the *dividend payment date*). The shareholders to receive the dividend are those holding shares on a particular date called the *shareholder record date*. Because stocks have delayed settlement, you must buy the stock prior to the record date in order to receive the dividend. Settlement is three business days. The *ex-dividend date* is the day the stock first begins trading without the escrowed dividend embedded in its price. If you buy the stock on the ex-dividend date or later, you will not be a shareholder of record by the shareholder record date and hence will not receive dividend.

The number of days between these dates varies across stocks. Figure 11.2 gives a sense of what might be typical. The figure contains the median number of days between (1) the declaration date and the ex-dividend date, (2) the ex-dividend date and the shareholder record date, and (3) the shareholder record date and the dividend payment date for all NYSE/AMEX and NASDAQ stocks paying quarterly dividends in the years 1996 through 2000. The stocks included are only those that had options listed on the CBOE during that period. As the figure shows, the amount of the cash dividend and the dividend payment date are typically known at least 32 days beforehand. For the valuation of short-term term stock options, this means that assuming that the amount and the timing of the dividend payment are *known* is literally true.

For longer-term options with multiple expected dividends paid during the option's life, cash dividend estimation becomes necessary. A casual inspection of cash dividend histories, however, will show that firms tend to: (1) pay the same cash dividend each quarter throughout the year; (2) pay the quarterly dividends at the same times each year; and (3) increase the annual total cash dividends at a constant rate through time. Even in the case of valuing longer-term stock options, therefore, using an assumption that the amount and timing of cash dividend payments are known is reasonable. The amount of the *i*th cash dividend will be denoted $D_i$ and the time to the payment of the *i*th dividend is $t_i$, where the relevant dividends for option valuation purposes are those prior to the option's expiration, $t_i < T$ for all $i$. We drop the subscript $i$ for cases in which only one dividend is paid during the option's life.

Finally, it is useful to have some general understanding of the number of stocks that pay dividends. Table 11.4 summarizes the number of U.S. stocks that pay dividends vis-à-vis those that do not. The numbers were generated from a listing of all stocks that had options listed on the CBOE during the five-year period 1996 through 2000. The total number of stocks is 2,387. Of these, less than 25% pay dividends. NYSE/AMEX stocks have a higher rate of dividend payment (about 47% of all stocks) than NASDAQ (less than 6% of all stocks). In other words, for the vast majority of stocks with options traded on a U.S. exchange, the underlying stock pays no dividends.

**FIGURE 11.2** Median number of calendar days between quarterly dividend dates for NYSE/AMEX and NASDAQ stocks during the calendar year 2003.

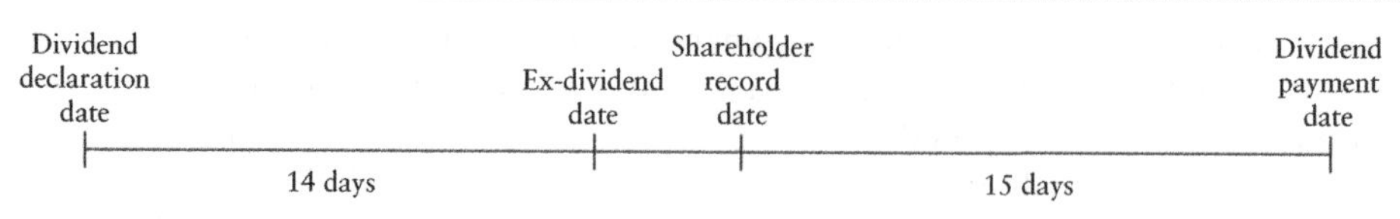

**TABLE 11.4** Number of dividend-paying/nondividend-paying stocks with listed options during calendar year 2003.

**Number of Stocks**

| | NYSE/AMEX | NASDAQ | Both |
|---|---|---|---|
| Pays dividends | 693 | 104 | 797 |
| No dividends | 717 | 981 | 1,698 |
| Total | 1,410 | 1,085 | 2,495 |

**Proportion of Total**

| | NYSE/AMEX | NASDAQ | Both |
|---|---|---|---|
| Pays dividends | 27.8% | 4.2% | 31.9% |
| No dividends | 28.7% | 39.3% | 68.1% |
| Total | 56.5% | 43.5% | 100.0% |

## Forwards/Futures

The net cost of carry relation for a futures contract written on a common stock is

$$F = Se^{rT} - FVD \tag{11.1a}$$

or

$$Fe^{-rT} = S - PVD \tag{11.1b}$$

where

$$FVD = \sum_{i=1}^{n} D_i e^{r(T-t_i)}$$

is the future value of the cash dividends paid during the futures life and

$$PVD = FVDe^{-rT} = \sum_{i=1}^{n} D_i e^{-rt_i}$$

is the present value of the cash dividends. The relation arises from the absence of costless arbitrage opportunities in the marketplace. The intuition for this relation is that there are two ways to have the stock on hand at time $T$ at a price known today. The first, represented by the left-hand side of (11.1a), is to buy a futures contract with maturity $T$. At time $T$, you pay $F$ and receive the stock. The second, represented by the right-hand side of (11.1a), is to borrow at a rate $r$ to buy the stock today, and then carry it until $T$ has elapsed. At time $T$, you must repay your borrowings plus interest, $Se^{rT}$, which is partially offset by the quarterly cash dividends (plus accrued interest) you received while holding the stock, *FVD*. Since you are indifferent between the two alternatives, the two sides of (11.1a) must be equal.

**ILLUSTRATION 11.1** Value of stock futures contract.

*Futures contracts on Australian stocks are listed on the Sydney Futures Exchange (SFE). Compute the value of a four-month futures contract on the shares of Foster Brewing. Assume the current share price is AD 27, the risk-free rate of interest is 5.75%, and the Foster's will pay a cash dividend of AD 0.25/share in exactly three months. The denomination of the SFE stock futures is 1,000 shares.*

Substituting into the cost of carry relation, you get

$$F = 27e^{(0.0575)(4/12)} - 0.25e^{0.0575(4/12-3/12)} = 27.271$$

The value of the futures contract is AD 27.271.

### Options: No-Arbitrage Price Relations

The arbitrage relations for common stock options are also summarized in the first panel of Table 11.3. For the options written directly on the stock (rather than on a stock futures), the relation usually involves reducing the current stock price, *S*, by the present value of the dividends paid during the option's life, *PVD*. The arbitrage transactions supporting each of these relations were described in detail in Chapter 4. Consequently, they are not rederived here. Instead, two of the relations are illustrated numerically.

**ILLUSTRATION 11.2** Compute lower price bound of leap.

*Compute the lower price bound of a three-year, European-style call option with an exercise price of 100. The current share price is 90. The stock is expected to pay quarterly cash dividend of \$.50 per share in three months, with each subsequent dividend growing at a continuous rate of 2% annually. The risk-free rate of interest on a three-year discount bond is 5.90%. The denomination of the leap contract is 100 shares.*

The present value of the cash dividends paid during the option's life is

$$PVD = \sum_{i=1}^{12} 0.50e^{-0.0590(i/4)}e^{0.02(i-1)/4} = 5.6066$$

The easiest way to compute this value is to use a spreadsheet such as that shown below. The lower price bound of the call is therefore

$$S - PVD - Xe^{-rT} = 90 - 5.6066 - 83.7780 = 0.6154$$

so the lower price bound on the leap contract is \$61.54.

| Lower Price Bound for European-Style Call on a Common Stock | | | | | |
|---|---|---|---|---|---|
| | | Quarterly Dividends | | | |
| Stock Price ($S$) | 90 | $i$ | $t_i$ | $D_i$ | $PV(D_i)$ |
| Interest rate ($r$) | 5.90% | 1 | 0.25 | 0.5000 | 0.4927 |
| Current dividend ($D$) | 0.5000 | 2 | 0.50 | 0.5025 | 0.4879 |
| Dividend growth ($g$) | 2.00% | 3 | 0.75 | 0.5050 | 0.4832 |
| | | 4 | 1.00 | 0.5076 | 0.4785 |
| Exercise price ($X$) | 100 | 5 | 1.25 | 0.5101 | 0.4738 |
| Years to expiration ($T$) | 3.00 | 6 | 1.50 | 0.5127 | 0.4692 |
| Denomination ($N$) | 100 | 7 | 1.75 | 0.5152 | 0.4647 |
| | | 8 | 2.00 | 0.5178 | 0.4602 |
| $PVD$ | 5.6066 | 9 | 2.25 | 0.5204 | 0.4557 |
| $Xe^{-rT}$ | 83.7780 | 10 | 2.50 | 0.5230 | 0.4513 |
| $S - PVD - Xe^{-rT}$ | 0.6154 | 11 | 2.75 | 0.5256 | 0.4469 |
| $(S - PVD - Xe^{-rT})N$ | 61.54 | 12 | 3.00 | 0.5283 | 0.4426 |

## Options: Valuation Equations/Methods

The valuation equations/methods for common stock options are summarized in the second panel of Table 11.3. Below are two illustrations, one for European-style option valuation and one for American-style option valuation.

**European-Style Option Valuation** As was noted earlier in the chapter, all exchange-traded stock options listed in the United States are American-style. Where the underlying stock pays no dividends during the option's life, the American-style call will not optimally be exercised prior to expiration, and, hence, can be valued using the European-style valuation equation.

**ILLUSTRATION 11.3** Compute implied volatilities from call option prices.

*Compute the implied volatilities of the Feb-04 Dell call options with exercise prices 32.50, 35, and 37.50 using the bid and ask price quotes reported in Table 11.2a. Assume Dell's share price is \$35.055. Dell does not pay cash dividends, and the risk-free interest rate is 0.82%.*

To compute the implied volatilities, you need all terms of the option valuation formula except $\sigma$. The stock price midpoint is 35.055, the exercise prices are given in the table, and the risk-free rate is 0.82%. The option contract month is February 2004. Stock options, by convention, expire the Saturday after the third Friday of the contract month, so, looking at a calendar, this means that the effective expiration date is the close of trading on Friday, February 20, 2004 (the option market is not open on Saturday). The times to expiration of the Feb-04 options are, therefore, 45 days.

Using the bid price quote, the implied volatility for the call with an exercise price of 32.50 may be computed by solving

$$3.00 = 35.055N(d_1) - 32.50e^{-0.0082(45/365)}N(d_2)$$

where

$$d_1 = \frac{\ln(35.055e^{0.0082(45/365)}/32.50) + 0.5\sigma^2(45/365)}{\sigma\sqrt{45/365}}$$

and $d_2 = d_1 - \sigma\sqrt{45/365}$.

The solution is found iteratively and is 27.99%.[11] For the remaining calls and price quotes, the implied volatilities are:

**DELL Call Option-Implied Volatilities**

| | |
|---|---|
| Valuation date | 1/6/2004 |
| Expiration date | 2/20/2004 |
| Days to expiration | 45 |
| Interest rate | 0.820% |
| Stock price midpoint | 35.055 |

| | Quotes | | Implied Volatilities | |
|---|---|---|---|---|
| Exercise Price | Bid | Ask | Bid | Ask |
| 32.50 | 3.00 | 3.10 | 27.99% | 30.78% |
| 35.00 | 1.30 | 1.40 | 25.59% | 27.63% |
| 37.50 | 0.35 | 0.45 | 23.33% | 25.98% |

Note that the bid/ask spread, when translated into an implied volatility spread is quite large. For the call option with the 32.50 exercise price, for example, the spread is 2.79%. Also, note that the implied volatilities at the bid (or at the ask) are not the same across exercise prices. There may be a variety of reasons for this. First, price quotes are rounded to the nearest $.05. As already noted, small differences in price translate into large differences in implied volatility. Second, computing implied volatilities using the BSM model presumes that Dell's share price is log-normally distributed at the options' expiration. To the extent that it is not, you can expect to see systematic variation in implied volatilities. Third, to the extent that traders focus on particular option series, prices (and hence implied volatilities) may be affected by supply/demand imbalances. In order to bring the implied volatilities into alignment, a dynamic hedge would be necessary. The costs of such a hedge over the life of the option may exceed the profit from an apparent arbitrage opportunity.

**American-Style Option Valuation** Table 11.3 summarizes the recommended methods for valuing American-style stock options. For options written on stock futures, all of the techniques described in Chapter 9 work well. For options written on dividend-paying stocks directly, however, using a lattice-based procedure is best. This section uses modifying the binomial method to value both American-style calls and puts on stocks with multiple known dividends during the option's life.

Generally speaking, the most expedient methods for valuing American-style options on dividend-paying stocks are the binomial and trinomial methods. The

[11] The function, OV_OPTION_ISD, from the OPTVAL Function Library can be used to compute implied volatility.

mechanics of these procedures are contained in Chapter 9. There are two exceptions, however. The first is where the stock's dividends are "small." If all the anticipated dividends paid during the call's life satisfy (6.16) in Chapter 6, for example, there is no chance that the American-style call will be exercised early, so the value of the call can be computed exactly using the European-style call formula. The second is where only a single dividend is paid during the call's life. In this case, an analytical valuation formula exists,[12] and it is provided in Appendix 11.A to this chapter. This formula can also be extended to cases where two or more dividends are paid during the option's life, however, the formula becomes cumbersome and difficult to evaluate, and the lattice-based methods wind up being more computationally efficient.[13]

**ILLUSTRATION 11.4** Compute value of American-style put option.

*Compute the value of an American-style put option with an exercise price of \$50 and a time to expiration of 90 days. Assume that the risk-free rate of interest is 5% annually, that the stock price is \$50, that the volatility rate of the stock is 36% per year, and that the stock pays a dividend of \$2 in exactly 75 days.*

For pedagogic reasons, perform three different valuations.

1. Compute the European-style put option value using the analytical valuation equation in Table 11.3.
2. Compute the European-style put option value using the JR binomial method outlined in Chapter 9.
3. Compute the American-style put option value using the JR binomial method.

By doing so, you not only value the American-style put option but also identify the degree of error that we might expect in our binomial approximation.

1. In applying the European-style put formula, it is first necessary to compute the current stock price net of the present value of the promised dividend, that is,

$$S^x = 50 - 2e^{-0.05(75/365)} = 48.020$$

With the adjusted stock price in hand, we apply the valuation formula from Table 11.3, that is,

$$p = 50e^{-0.05(90/365)}N(-d_2) - 48.020N(-d_1)$$

where

$$d_1 = \frac{\ln(48.020e^{0.05(90/365)}/50) + 0.5(0.36^2)(90/365)}{0.36\sqrt{90/365}} = -0.0677$$

The probabilities $N(0.0677)$ and $N(0.2464)$ are 0.5270 and 0.5973, respectively, so the European-style put value is

$$p = 49.387(0.5973) - 48.020(0.5270) = 4.195$$

[12] See Roll (1977), Geske (1979), and Whaley (1981).

[13] See Stephan and Whaley (1990).

This computation can be verified using the OPTVAL function

OV_ OPTION_VALUE (48.020, 50,90/365, 0.05, 0.36, "C", "E") = 4.195

2. The value of the European-style put is also computed using the binomial method. Apply the three-step procedure outlined in Chapter 9. The number of time steps is set equal to 90, so the time increment $\Delta t$ is one day or 0.00274 years. Under the JR binomial method, the values of the up-step and down-step coefficients are computed as

$$u = e^{(b - 0.5\sigma^2)\Delta t + 0.36\sqrt{\Delta t}} = e^{(0.05 - 0.5(0.36)^2)(1/365) + 0.36\sqrt{1/365}} = 1.01898$$

and

$$d = e^{(0.05 - 0.5(0.36)^2)(1/365) - 0.36\sqrt{1/365}} = 0.98129$$

and there are equal probabilities of an up-step and a down-step.[14] Applying the up-step and down-step coefficients to the current stock price net of the present value of the escrowed dividend provides a range of stock prices at the option's expiration from 8.776 to 260.828. Applying the binomial procedure without checking the early exercise bounds produces an option value of 4.195, the same as the value obtained using the analytical formula. Apparently, the binomial method works well at 90 times step.

The OPTVAL Function Library contains binomial and trinomial routines for valuing European- and American-style options on dividend-paying stocks. The syntax of the function call for the binomial method is

OV_STOCK_OPTION_VALUE_BIN(*s, x, t, r, v, n, cp, ae, mthd, dvd, tdvd*)

where $s$ is the current stock price, $x$ is the exercise price, $t$ is the time to expiration, $r$ is the risk-free interest rate, $v$ is the stock's volatility rate, $cp$ is a (c)all/(p)ut indicator, $ae$ is an (A)merican/(E)uropean-style option indicator, *mthd* is the choice of binomial coefficients (2 is JR coefficients),[15] *dvd* is a cash dividend vector, and *tdvd* is a vector containing the time to the dividend payments. For the information in the problem:

D15 =OV_STOCK_OPTION_VALUE_BIN($B$3,$B$11,$B$13,$B$16,$B$4,$D$11,"p","e",2,$B$5,$B$7)

| | A | B | C | D |
|---|---|---|---|---|
| 1 | **Stock option valuation using the binomial method** | | | |
| 2 | **Stock** | | ***Intermediate computations*** | |
| 3 | Price (*S*) | 50.00 | Time to expiration in years (*T*) | 0.2466 |
| 4 | Volatility rate (*σ*) | 36.00% | Time to ex-dividend in years (*t*) | 0.2055 |
| 5 | Amount (*D*) | 2.00 | *PVD* | 1.980 |
| 6 | Time to ex-dividend in days | 75 | *S-PVD* | 48.020 |
| 7 | Years to ex-dividend | 0.2055 | | |
| 8 | | | | |
| 9 | ***Option*** | | | |
| 10 | Call (*C*) or put (*P*) | *P* | ***Binomial parameters*** | |
| 11 | Exercise price (*X*) | 50 | No. of time steps (*n*) | 90 |
| 12 | Days to expiration | 90 | | |
| 13 | Years to expiration | 0.2466 | ***Option value*** | |
| 14 | | | European, analytic | 4.195 |
| 15 | ***Market*** | | European, binomial | 4.195 |
| 16 | Interest rate (*r*) | 5.00% | American, binomial | 4.234 |

[14] In this application, the risk-neutral net cost of carry rate, $b$, in (9.12a) and (9.12a) of Chapter 9 equals the risk-free rate of interest.

[15] Chapter 9 contains a description of three sets of coefficients that may be used in the binomial method.

3. The binomial procedure applied to value the European-style put is reapplied, this time checking the early exercise bounds at each node within the lattice. The value of the American-style put is computed to be 4.234. Hence the value of the early exercise feature of this American-style put is 4.234 – 4.195 or about 3.9 cents. The previous table summarizes the results.

### Options: Implied Volatilities in Days Surrounding Merger Events

Implied volatilities were introduced in Chapter 7. By setting an option's observed price equal to its model value, we can deduce the market's perception of expected future volatility in the same manner as setting a bond's price equal to its formula value allows us to deduce the expected yield to maturity. In the context of the stock option valuation models described earlier in this section, the implied volatilities of options on a particular stock should be approximately the same across exercise prices and constant through time. In certain instances, however, such is not the case. One such instance is when a firm becomes a target in a takeover attempt. Below we describe the behavior of stock prices, trading volumes, and volatilities in the days surrounding Lucent Technologies' acquisition of Octel Communications in 1997.

Just before the market open on Thursday, July 17, 1997, Lucent Technologies, Inc. (LU) announced that it would acquire Octel Communications Corp. (OCTL) in order to strengthen its voice mail, fax, and messaging technology business. Under the terms of the offer, Lucent agreed to pay $31 per share in cash. The LU/OCTL merger was less complicated than most in the sense that it was a cash deal, with both boards approving the deal before its announcement.[16] To examine the market's reaction to the news of the merger, we focus on share price, trading volume, and BSM implied volatility behavior in the 60 days before the announcement and the 60 days after the announcement became effective.

**Share Price Behavior** Figure 11.3 shows the share prices of LU and OCTL in the days surrounding the merger. The prices of both stocks meandered in an upward direction in the days leading up to the announcement day (with the vertical bar representing the announcement day). An explanation for this behavior is that the firms' merger negotiations were being conducted during June 1997, and the market was beginning to anticipate the news. On July 16, 1997, the day before the announcement, OCTL closed at 26.75, a 14.1% gain from the previous day's close, 23.4375. The strength of the gain suggests that some traders were confident about the terms of the potential acquisition and its likelihood of success and were willing to take a directional bet by buying the shares of OCTL. The merger announcement was made just before the market open on July 17, and the price of OCTL's shares reacted accordingly. OCTL's shares closed at 30.125, a gain of another 12.6%. Subsequent to the announcement, OCTL shares hovered at slightly below the offer price of $31 per share. The lack of variability in OCTL's share price during this period suggests that the market believed that the merger would be consummated at the $31 level. The slight drop in OCTL's share price on September 11, 1997 was as a result of an

[16] See "Lucent to buy Octel for $1.8 billion," *Reuters News*, 17 July 1997.

**FIGURE 11.3** Daily stock price behavior of Lucent Technologies, Inc. (LU) and Octel Communications, Inc. (OCTL) from April 23 (60 days before merger announcement date) to December 22, 1997 (60 days after merger effective date). Merger announcement date was July 17, 1997, and merger effective date was September 26, 1997.

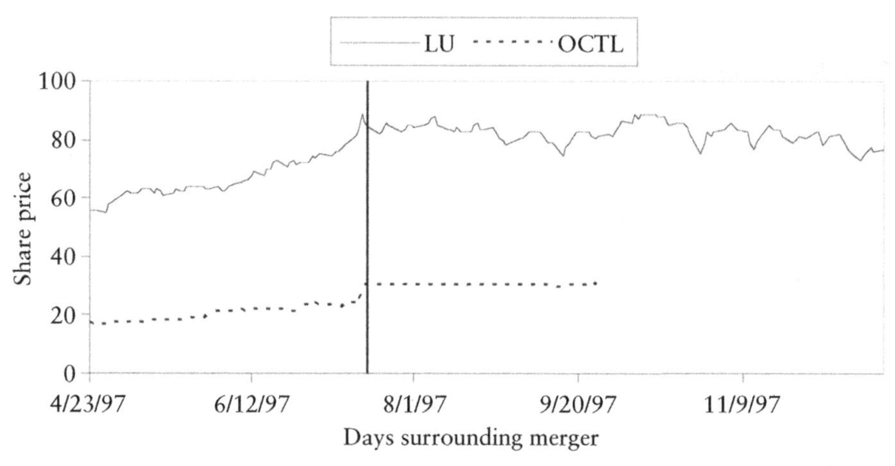


announcement that the antitrust division of U.S. Justice Department requested more information about the terms of the merger from Lucent. Included with this announcement, however, was language indicating that both companies were confident that the acquisition would be completed, as it indeed was.[17] The last day of public trading for OCTL's shares was September 26, 1997.

**Abnormal Share Price Behavior** The share price behavior in Figure 11.3 can be somewhat misleading to the extent that the stock prices have different scales, and the movement of the market during the period is ignored. Consequently, we standardize both price series to a beginning level of 100, and then update each price series by the daily relative stock price movement net of the corresponding market movement, using the S&P 500 index as a proxy for the market. Figure 11.4 shows the results. Relative to the S&P 500, both stocks performed well relative to the S&P 500 in the pre-announcement period, with each an posting abnormal gain of 25% or so in the 60 trading days leading up to the announcement. Again, this may have been as a result of information leakage regarding the merger negotiations. But, these abnormal gains were small relative to those experienced on the day before and the day of the announcement, 13.0% and 13.1%, respectively. Immediately after the announcement, the shares of LU or OCTL behaved similarly to the market, with both declining in the aftermath. The declines, however, were as a result of the S&P 500 index rising rather than share prices falling. (See Figure 11.3.)

[17] See "Lucent Extends Octel Tender Offer," *Newsbytes News Network*, 11 September 1997.

**FIGURE 11.4** Abnormal stock price behavior of Lucent Technologies, Inc. (LU) and Octel Communications, Inc. (OCTL) from April 23 (60 days before merger announcement date) to December 22, 1997 (60 days after merger effective date). Daily abnormal stock price movements are computed by subtracting the movement of the S&P 500 index each day, and both stock price series are normalized to a level of 100 on April 23, 1997.

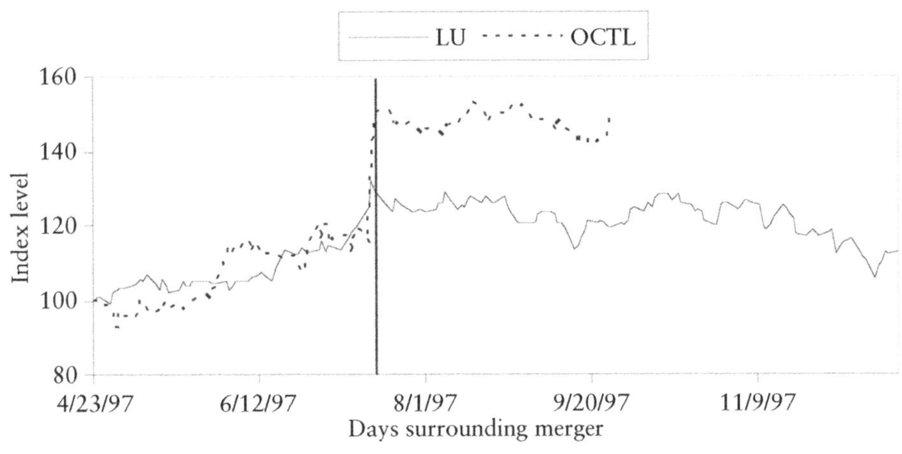


**Trading Volume** The market reaction of LU and OCTL shares to the news of the merger is also shown in trading volume. Figure 11.5 shows that in the period before the announcement, daily trading volume was about two million shares a day for LU and one million shares for OCTL. In the days leading up to the announcement, OCTL's share volume appears to have a slight increase, however, on the day before the announcement, 2.7 million shares traded, and, on the day of the announcement, a whopping 16.3 million shares traded. Similarly, LU experienced trading volume of 4.7 million shares on the day before the announcement and 4.2 million shares on the announcement day. Trading volumes remained above normal for both firms for a few days after the announcement, and then returned to preannouncement levels or below. Like price, trading volume confirms abnormal market behavior on the day before and the day of the announcement.

**Implied Volatility** Perhaps, the most intriguing information regarding the potential acquisition appeared in the stock option market. To do so, we examine the implied volatilities[18] of LU and OCTL stock options in the 60 days before the merger announcement and the 60 days after the merger became effective. We begin by examining OCTL volatilities. Figure 11.6 shows that, prior to July 1997, the implied volatility of two-month, at-the-money options on OCTL's stock averaged about 48%, only twice crossing the 50% level. On June 27, however, it crossed the 50% level, and then rose as high as 70% on the day

[18] The implied volatility in this case is for a hypothetical 60-day, at-the-money option. This implied volatility is computed on the basis of eight option series—the nearby and second nearby options (calls and puts) whose exercise prices are just in- and out-of-the-money.

**FIGURE 11.5** Daily trading volume is shares of Lucent Technologies, Inc. (LU) and Octel Communications, Inc. (OCTL) from April 23 (60 days before merger announcement date) to December 22, 1997 (60 days after merger effective date).

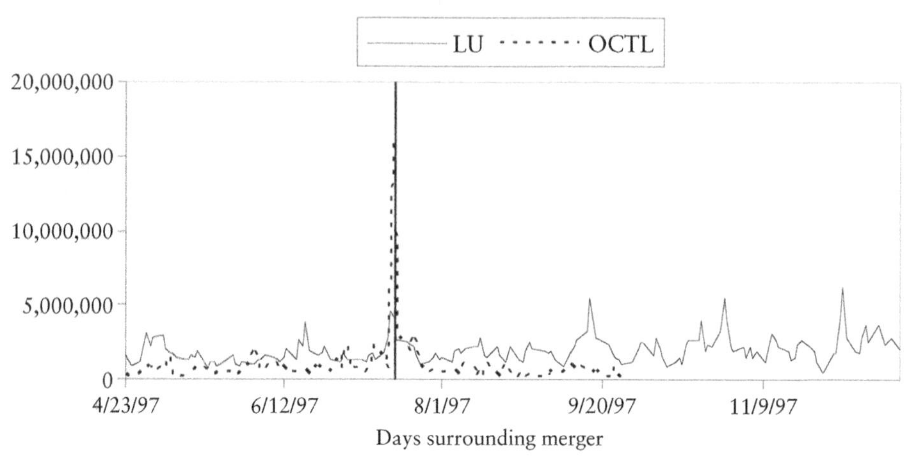


**FIGURE 11.6** Average BSM implied volatilities of stock options on Lucent Technologies, Inc. (LU) and Octel Communications, Inc. (OCTL) from April 23 (60 days before merger announcement date) to December 22, 1997 (60 days after merger effective date).

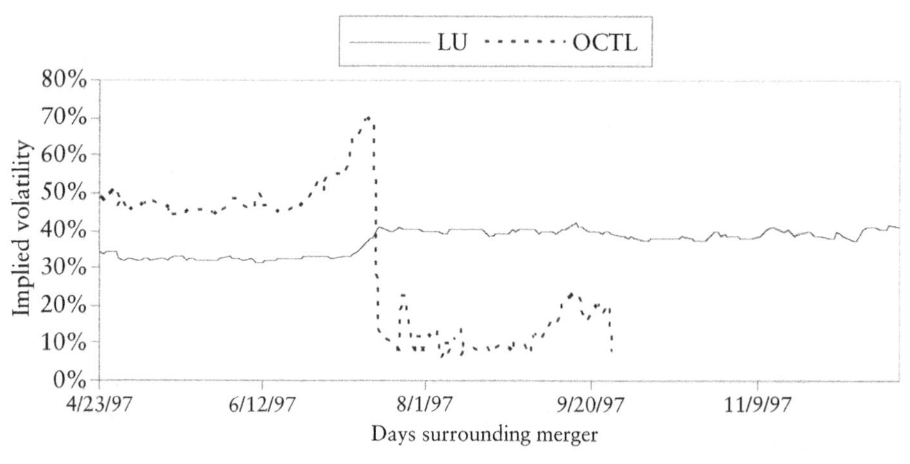


before the announcement. On the announcement day, OCTL volatility plummeted from its high to a level of 13.8%. OCTL's implied volatility bottomed out in the days following, hovering around 10%. But on September 3, eight days before the announcement that more information had been requested, OCTL's implied volatility rose to 12.3%. By the close on September 11, the implied volatility rose to 20.3%, and, by the close on September 15, 23.6%.

Taken together, this evidence suggests that the stock option market anticipated news about OCTL and its impending merger before the stock market. First, almost *two weeks* before the announcement day, OCTL's implied volatility began to increase monotonically, reaching levels nearly 46% higher (70% versus 48%) than had been observed in the recent past.[19] This is in contrast to OCTL's stock price behavior, which seemed to indicate that, at best, the information leaked out the day before the announcement. Second, in the postannouncement period, OCTL's implied volatility began to rise inexplicably eight days before the announcement that the antitrust department had requested more information regarding the impending merger. The stock market did not appear to react until the day of the announcement, September 11.

On first appearance, the dramatic drop in OCTL's implied volatility on the announcement day may seem perplexing. Upon further reflection, the mystery is resolved. The OCTL option prices in the days after the announcement can be thought of as an amalgam of two prices—one if the merger falls through and one if the merger is successful, that is,

$$O_{\text{observed}} = (1 - p)O_{\text{fall}} + pO_{\text{success}} \tag{11.2}$$

where $p$ is the probability that the merger will succeed. The option price conditional on failure, $O_{\text{fall}}$, may be computed using the BSM model. The option price conditional on success, $O_{\text{success}}$, equals the floor value of the option since, as noted earlier, the options will be settled in cash and should be exercised immediately when the merger is consummated. The dramatic reduction in OCTL's implied volatility (based on the observed option price) is therefore merely a reflection that the market anticipated that the probability of the merger succeeding was very high. It is also interesting to note that the probability that the merger will fail never completely disappears. Even on the day before the merger becoming effective, the OCTL implied volatility is nearly 8%, which implies that $p < 1$ in (11.2).

The behavior of the implied volatility of LU's shares is also intriguing. Up until a week before the merger announcement, its level was about 32%. On July 10, it began to rise, and, on July 17, it appears to have reached a new steady level of about 40%. These results are interesting in at least two respects. First, again the stock option market appears to have anticipated the news about the merger before the stock market—implied volatilities move before stock prices. One possibility is that "informed" investors choose the option market rather than the stock market to place directional bets. Another is the number of informed traders in each market before the announcement is the same, but, since the stock option market is less liquid, the same size stock equivalent trade has greater price impact (and is more detectible) in the option market than the stock market. Second, the market appears to digest the news about the merger very quickly in that the implied volatility embedded in LU's options rises to its new steady-state level on the announcement day. In other words, the option market incorporated the effect

[19] It is important to recognize that the implied volatility is based on call and put prices. An increase in implied volatility is not based on the call price rising faster than the stock price (i.e., the stock price being too low) but rather on the prices of the call and put rising relative to the stock price.

of the change LU's asset structure (replacing $1.8 billion in cash with OCTL's assets) on LU's return volatility well before the merger became effective.

## TRADING AND RISK MANAGEMENT STRATEGIES

Stock derivatives contracts can be used in a variety of trading/risk management strategies, many of which were discussed in Chapter 10. The purpose of this section is to describe the motivation for and execution of four commonly used strategies involving stock derivatives. The first strategy is a speculative trading strategy called a dividend spread and is designed to capture abnormal profit when American-style call option holders do not exercise early when it is in their best interests to do so. The second and third are risk management strategies used by individuals with concentrated positions in particular stocks. We examine both stock price collars and variable prepaid forward contracts. The fourth and final strategy, used by corporations, involves writing puts (and selling calls) to subsidize the cost of stock buyback programs.

### Dividend Spreads

In spite of the fact that it is straightforward to decide if and when an American-style option should be exercised early, many are not. In markets where such behavior is observed, it is possible to design a speculative trading strategy that captures the lost exercise proceeds. One such case is with an exchange-traded, American-style call option written on a stock that pays a dividend during its life.

The so-called *dividend capture* or *dividend spread* strategy involves identifying an in-the-money call option that should be exercised just prior to ex-dividend day. This is done by computing the call option value using the stock price net of the dividend amount (i.e., the ex-dividend stock price) and comparing it with the immediate exercise proceeds, $S_t - X$, where $t$ represents the time just prior to ex-dividend. If the computed value is less than the call's immediate exercise proceeds, we sell the call just prior to the market close and simultaneously buy the underlying stock. The net cost of the position is the stock price less the call option price, that is, $S_t - C_t$.

Two things can occur at the open on the following morning. First, we may find that the call option holder has exercised his option, in which case we must deliver underlying stock. We receive the exercise price in cash, and deliver the stock. Our profit equals the exercise price less the net cost of the strategy on the day before the stock goes ex-dividend, that is, $X - (S_t - C_t)$. Since the call must have been trading at its floor value before the dividend was paid, that is, $C_t = S_t - X$, our profit equals zero. Second, we may find that the call option holder has forgotten to exercise his call or simply failed to recognize that it was optimal to do so. In this situation, we immediately buy back the call at its price after the dividend is paid, $C_{t+\varepsilon}$, and sell the stock at its ex-dividend price, $S_{t+\varepsilon} \equiv S_t - D$.[20] Since we were long the stock at the ex-dividend instant, we receive the dividend payment, $D$. Our profit, therefore, equals the dividend plus the proceeds from the liquida-

[20] At the ex-dividend instant, the stock price is assumed to fall by an amount exactly equal to the dividend payment.

tion of the position, $D + (S_{t+\varepsilon} - C_{t+\varepsilon})$, less the net cost at inception, $S_t - C_t$, or, equivalently, the drop in the call option value resulting from the dividend payment, that is, $\pi_t = D + (S_{t+\varepsilon} - C_{t+\varepsilon}) - (S_t - C_t) = C_t - C_{t+\varepsilon}$. Some refer to this strategy as a dividend capture strategy, although only part of the dividend is being captured. A more appropriate name is a dividend spread.

**ILLUSTRATION 11.5** Identify and engage in dividend spread opportunity.

*Consider a call option on a stock on the day prior to a stock going ex-dividend. The call has an exercise price of 25 and three months remaining to expiration. Its current price is 4. The stock price is 29, its volatility rate is 25% annually, and the amount of the cash dividend is 2. The risk-free rate of interest is 5%. Identify whether a dividend spread opportunity exists, and, if so, how to profit.*

First compute the proceeds from exercising the option immediately. They are equal to the stock price less the exercise price, that is, 29 – 25 = 4. The fact that the call price is trading at or near its immediate exercise proceeds is the first indication that a dividend spread strategy may be profitable.

Next compute the value of the call immediately after the stock goes ex-dividend. Assuming no more dividends are paid during the call's life, the value of the call after the stock goes ex-dividend is

$$c = (29-2)N(d_1) - 25e^{-0.05(0.25)}N(d_2) = 2.76$$

where

$$d_1 = \frac{\ln(27e^{0.05(0.25)}/25) + 0.5(0.25^2)0.25}{0.25\sqrt{0.25}} = 0.7782$$

$$d_2 = 0.7782 - 0.25\sqrt{0.25} = 0.6532$$

$$N(0.7782) = 0.7818, \text{ and}$$

$$N(0.6532) = 0.7432$$

What this means is that it is optimal for the call option holder to exercise immediately, prior to the ex-dividend date. In doing so, he will receive exercise proceeds of 4. If he fails to do so, his option will decline in value to 2.76 after the dividend is paid. By choosing not to exercise, he implicitly loses 1.24.

Given that you know that early exercise is optimal and that not all call option holders exercise when they should, you can engage in a dividend spread by selling the call and buying the stock just prior to the dividend payment. This costs 25 (i.e., 29 – 4). If, on the following morning, you find that the call option holder has exercised, you deliver your stock against the call and receive 25 (i.e., the payment of the exercise price). Ignoring trading costs, you have neither made nor lost money. If, for some reason, the call option holder did not exercise, you should buy the call and sell the stock. The net proceeds are or 24.24. In addition, you receive the dividend from holding the stock, 2, bringing total proceeds to 26.24. Hence your profit is 1.24.

The profitability of engaging dividend spreads depends on the likelihood that the call option holder will exercise when he should. Naturally, trading costs should be factored into the decision about whether to engage in this type of speculative strategy.

### Collar Agreements

Individuals such as chief executive officers of a firm often find themselves in a position in which a significant portion of their wealth is tied to the firm's share price. Such an undiversified (and, sometimes, illiquid) position is risky. One alternative is to sell the shares or, at least, a large portion of their shares. This strategy is usually not viable, however, because shareholders and analysts generally regard the liquidation of shares by corporate insiders as bad news about the prospects of the firm. Moreover, the gains from selling shares would be recognized immediately for tax purposes.[21]

To circumvent these problems, many CEOs use *stock price collars*. Specifically, they buy out-of-the-money puts, financing their purchase with the sale of out-of-the-money calls. The puts eliminate some of the downside price risk of the stock. At the same time, they continue to hold the stock, thereby participating in its upside, collecting its dividends, preserving its voting rights, and deferring taxes. The cost is, of course, that if the share price rises above the exercise price on the call, the shares may be called away. Alternatively, the executive can choose to cash settle the contract, in which case they continue to retain ownership of the stock and defer tax payment.

Collar agreements are generally consummated in the OTC market. The reason is that the put and call options tend to be long-term and deep out-of-the-money. Such options are thinly traded on exchanges, and, indeed, may not trade at all. In addition, OTC agreements allow the exercise prices to be adjusted so that the collar has no upfront cost.

**ILLUSTRATION 11.6** Structure collar agreement.

*Suppose the CEO of ABC Corporation has approached an OTC derivatives firm about structuring a collar on his shares. The CEO wants to be protected against the share price being below \$36 per share in three years time. To pay for the insurance, he is willing to forfeit any share price gains beyond \$X per share in three years. What is the maximum value of X that the OTC derivatives dealer will allow assuming the stock currently has a share price of \$45 and a volatility rate of 35% annually, and pays no dividends? The risk-free rate of interest is 6%.*

The CEO wants to be protected against "... the share price being below 36 in three years time ...", so we need to determine the fair value of a *European-style* put. Using the function, OV_OPTION_VALUE, from the OPTVAL Function Library, the value of the three-year European-style put is 3.294.

The next step is to find the exercise price of a three-year call option whose price is 3.294 so that the collar is costless. The exercise price must be solved for iteratively using a routine such as SOLVER in Excel. As this table shows, a call option with an exercise price of 95.187 has a value of 3.294:

---

[21] Prior to the Taxpayer Relief Act of 1997, individuals could borrow against a large stock position and defer taxes by "shorting-against-the-box." By short selling shares, the individual could lock in the price of the underlying stock and borrow up to 95% of the locked-in value for reinvestment. The Taxpayer Relief Act of 1997 targeted such trades and earmarked them as "constructive sales;" that is, transactions considered to be sales for tax purposes, even if no shares are exchanged.

**Without Market Maker Fee**

| Stock | |
|---|---|
| Price ($S$) | 45.00 |
| Volatility rate ($s$) | 35.00% |
| Interest rate ($r$) | 6.00% |

| Put Option | | Call Option | |
|---|---|---|---|
| Exercise price ($X$) | 36 | Exercise price ($X$) | 95.187 |
| Years to expiration ($T$) | 3 | Years to expiration ($T$) | 3 |
| Value ($P$) | 3.294 | Value (C) | 3.294 |
| Difference in premiums | 0.000 | | |

In computing the maximum value of $X$, we assumed that the OTC firm charges nothing for its service. Instead, suppose that it embeds a one dollar per share fee to compensate for its costs of structuring and managing the risk of the assumed option position. What exercise price for the call will create a collar agreement with an upfront cost equal to zero?

The objective is now to find the exercise price of a three-year call option whose price is 4.294 (i.e. 3.294 goes to paying for the put; 1 towards the OTC firm's embedded fee). A call with an exercise price of 81.373 has a value of 4.294, as the following table shows.

**With Market Maker Fee**

| Stock | |
|---|---|
| Price ($S$) | 45.00 |
| Volatility rate ($s$) | 35.00% |
| Interest rate ($r$) | 6.00% |

| Put Option | | Call Option | |
|---|---|---|---|
| Exercise price ($X$) | 36 | Exercise price ($X$) | 85.551 |
| Years to expiration ($T$) | 3 | Years to expiration ($T$) | 3 |
| Value ($P$) | 3.294 | Value (C) | 4.294 |
| Difference in premiums | 1.000 | | |

## Variable Prepaid Forward Contracts

*Variable prepaid forward* (VPF) contracts are relatively new stock products. They arose from the fact that, while individuals can borrow against collared stock positions, banks will limit the amount that they can borrow to 50% of the market value of the stock if the individuals plan on investing in other equities.[22] VPFs circumvent this problem. A VPF is not regarded as a loan but rather as a

[22] For a lucid description of variable prepaid forwards, see "Having You Cake and Eating It, Too," *Bloomberg Wealth Manager*, April 2001, pp. 59–66.

sale of a contingent number of shares, which will be delivered at some future date, in exchange for a cash advance today. Since the number of shares, and thus their exact cash value, is not determined until maturity (based on the stock's price at the time), a VPF does not trip the constructive sale rule. It allows the individual to delay paying taxes while, at the same time, to hedge his stock price risk exposure and free up capital to invest in other securities.

The key elements of a VPF are as follows:

1. **Minimum share price.** The minimum share price is the least amount that the buyer of the VPF will receive for his shares to be delivered at time *T*. The minimum share price can be as much as 100% of the current price of the shares, but is often less.
2. **Cash advance.** At inception, the buyer of the VPF will receive a cash advance against the minimum share value, and the amount of the cash advance is the present value of the minimum share price. Thus the difference between the minimum share price and the cash advance is sometimes considered to be the implied financing cost of the trade.
3. **Maximum share price.** The maximum share price is the largest amount that the buyer will receive for his shares delivered at time *T*. The difference between the maximum and minimum shares prices will be at least 20 percentage points to avoid the constructive sale rule[23] and potential tax liability.
4. **Shares are pledged as collateral.** The shares are pledged as collateral with the seller of the contract.
5. **Optional sharing rule.** Some, but not all, VPFs have a sharing rule whereby the stock price appreciation above the maximum share price is shared by the buyer and seller of the contract (e.g., the buyer receives 10% while the seller receives 90%).
6. **Optional cash settlement.** The buyer, as his discretion can elect to settle the contract is cash rather than by delivery.

Perhaps the easiest way to understand the valuation of a variable prepaid forward is to examine its construction using the valuation-by-replication principle. Table 11.5 contains the four basic securities that comprise the VPF. First, the individual who buys the VPF is long stock, which he posts as collateral on the agreement. This trade is represented in the first row of the table. Ignoring dividends, the value of each share of stock at time $T$ is $\tilde{S}_T$. The second row shows the cash advance. The VPF buyer is guaranteed a minimum share price of $X_p$ at time $T$. The cash advance is received today and equals the present value of the minimum share price of the agreement, $X_p e^{-rT}$. By receiving the cash advance, the buyer has an implicit obligation to repay $X_p$ at time $T$. To provide for this repayment, he buys a European-style put option with exercise price $X_p$. The cost of the put is $p(X_p)$ today. At time $T$, it pays $X_p - \tilde{S}_T$ if the put is in the money and 0 otherwise. Finally, to subsidize the cost of the put, the VPF buyer forfeits all share price gains above the maximum share price. Thus, he is also implicitly short a European-style call option whose exercise price equals the

[23] If the minimum and maximum share prices are equal, the VPF is tantamount to short selling the stock.

**TABLE 11.5** **Construction of variable prepaid forward transaction.** Investor owns stock and posts it as collateral on risk-bond whose face value is $X_p$ at time $T$. In addition, investor buys a collar with a downside protection price (i.e., a floor value) of $X_p$ and a threshold appreciation price of $X_c$.

| Trades | Initial Investment | Value on Day $T$ | | |
|---|---|---|---|---|
| | | $S_T < X_p$ | $X_p \le S_T < X_c$ | $S_T \ge X_c$ |
| Long stock | $-S$ | $\tilde{S}_T$ | $\tilde{S}_T$ | $\tilde{S}_T$ |
| Cash advance (i.e., borrow present value of $X_p$) | $X_p e^{-rT}$ | $-X_p$ | $-X_p$ | $-X_p$ |
| Buy put with exercise price $X_p$ | $-p(X_p)$ | $X_p - \tilde{S}_T$ | 0 | 0 |
| Sell call with exercise price $X_c$ | $c(X_c)$ | 0 | 0 | $-(\tilde{S}_T - X_c)$ |
| Net portfolio value | $-S + X_p e^{-rT} - p(X_p) + c(X_c)$ | 0 | $\tilde{S}_T - X_p$ | $X_c - X_p$ |

maximum share price, denoted $X_c$. The value of the call today is $c(X_c)$. Its value at expiration is $-(\tilde{S}_T - X_c)$ if the call is in the money and is 0 otherwise. Thus, the value of a VPF may be written

$$VPF = -S + X_p e^{-rT} - p(X_p) + c(X_c) \tag{11.3}$$

Alternatively, the terminal values in Table 11.5 can be generated by buying a call with exercise price $X_p$ and selling a call with exercise price $X_c$. Thus, in the absence costless arbitrage opportunities, it must also be the case that

$$VPF = -c(X_p) + c(X_c) \tag{11.4}$$

With the valuation tools in hand, let us examine the terms of a specific contract. On July 25, 2003, a living trust created by Mr. Roy E. Disney bought a VPF for 7,500,000 shares of Walt Disney common stock from Credit Suisse First Boston Capital LLC.[24] The settlement date of the contract was August 18, 2008 (or has a time to expiration of 5.0712 years). On that date, Mr. Disney, on behalf of the trust, nominally agreed to sell the 7.5 million shares of Disney for $27.510 per share (i.e., 100% of the prevailing stock price at the time was entered).

At the time the VPF was entered, the trust received a cash advance of $124,959.495 or $16.66127 per share. At settlement, the trust is required to deliver a number of shares (or cash equivalent) as follows:

(a) all 7,500,000 shares if $S_T < 21.571$,

(b) $\left(\dfrac{21.571}{S_T}\right) \times 7{,}500{,}000$ shares if $21.571 \le S_T \le 32.6265$, and

(c) $\left(1 - \dfrac{10.8755}{S_T}\right) \times 7{,}500{,}000$ shares shares if $S_T > 32.6265$,

where $S_T$ is the settlement price of the contract.[25] Note that the number of shares delivered depends on the stock price at time $T$, hence the use of the term "variable" in the security's name. Indeed, it is this feature that allows the contract buyer to avoid the constructive sale rule.

Now, consider the key elements of this VPF. The difference between the minimum share price 27.510 and the cash advance 16.66127 is usually labeled the

[24] The terms of this contract were drawn from the SEC Form 4, Statement of Changes in Beneficial Ownership filed by Mr. Roy E. Disney on August 20, 2003. Such documents are a matter of public record and can be obtained from the SEC's website, www.sec.gov, under Filings and Forms (EDGAR).

[25] For simplicity, you may want to consider the settlement price of the contract to be the closing price on the settlement date. For this particular contract, however, the settlement price is actually the volume-weighted average of the common stock for the 20 trading days preceding and including the settlement date.

*implied financing cost.*[26] The implied interest rate may be computed by solving $16.66127e^{r(5.0712)} = 21.571$ and is 5.0927%. Thus if the settlement price is below 21.571 at expiration, Mr. Disney can deliver the shares, in which case he has no further obligation. Alternatively, he can pay Credit Suisse the cash equivalent of the shares, $S_T$ times 7.5 million.

The remaining contingencies are as follows. Under contingency (b), Mr. Disney receives all gains on the shares above 21.571 but below 32.6265. To provide Credit Suisse with its implicit loan repayment, Mr. Disney can deliver

$$\left(\frac{21.571}{S_T}\right) \times 7{,}500{,}000$$

shares of stock. Note that the number of shares is variable and depends on the share price. Recall that this is a requirement in order to avoid the constructive sale rule. Mr. Disney need not deliver the shares, however. Instead, he can pay the cash equivalent of the shares, that is,

$$S_T \times \left(\frac{21.571}{S_T}\right) \times 7{,}500{,}000$$

or $163,132,500. Under contingency (c), Mr. Disney must deliver

$$\left(1 - \frac{10.8755}{S_T}\right) \times 7{,}500{,}000$$

shares of stock if the stock price exceeds 32.6265 at the contract's expiration. Again, note that the number of shares depends on the prevailing share. The cash equivalent in this range is

$$S_T \times \left(1 - \frac{10.8755}{S_T}\right) \times 7{,}500{,}000$$

In summary, by entering a VPF contract rather than selling the shares of Disney outright, Mr. Disney generated more money up front than he would in after-tax proceeds of a sale, deferred the payment of the capital gains tax for at least the life of the contract, and did not lock himself into the sell decision, because at maturity he can make a cash settlement and keep his shares, or, alternatively, roll them into a new contract.

---

[26] Others refer to this discount as the *haircut* on the VPF.

### Option Trading by Corporations

During the mid-1990s, a number of U.S. corporations, particularly high-tech firms, bought and sold options on their own stock. Typically, the trading involved either selling at-the-money puts in isolation or selling at-the-money puts and buying at-the-money calls (i.e., an option collar). The corporate option trading was usually linked to share-buyback programs, however, many firms were simply using options to profit from expected stock price increases.

Under the put writing strategy, the firm collects the put premium. In a rising market such as that experienced in the bull market of the mid-1990s, the strategy can be quite profitable since the puts expire out of the money and the firm gets to keep the cash. This cash can be used to buy back shares or held in reserve.[27] If the share price falls, however, the firm must buy back its shares at an above-market price. The bear market in the late 1990s proved disastrous, particularly for high tech stocks such as Microsoft and Dell.

For buyback programs, "cashless" collars can be more effective. A cashless collar involves buying a call of the firm's shares and selling a put in such a way that no money changes hands at inception. It differs from the put writing strategy in that the proceeds of the put are used to buy a call rather than generate a cash premium. Consequently, if the firm's share price rises, the firm has the opportunity to buy back its shares at a predetermined below-market price by exercising its call. Under the put strategy, the shares are bought back at the prevailing market price and are subsidized only by the cash premium collected at the outset. If the share price falls, however, the firm must buy back its shares at an above-market price, just as it did in the put writing-only strategy.

## SUMMARY

This chapter focuses on derivative contracts written on common stocks. Although markets for both stock futures and stock options are active, stock option markets are the most active, with by far the largest amount of trading taking place in the United States. Cash dividends paid on the stock during the option's life may have an important impact on option value. The stock futures and option valuation results are summarized in Table 11.3.

Four stock option trading/risk management strategies are discussed. The first is a dividend spread and is speculative in nature. It is a trading strategy that is designed to profit from the fact that not all call option holders exercise when it is optimal to do so. The strategy involves selling an in-the-money call and buying the underlying stock just prior to the stock going ex-dividend. The second and third strategies are tailored to an individual with a large concentration in the shares of a single stock. A stock price collar, for example, is an OTC agreement that provides "costless" (or, perhaps more appropriately, "cashless") insurance against a stock price decline. The insurance is created by buying an out-of-the-money put and provides the individual with a guaranteed minimum price for the

[27] The cash is not taxable since a company does not recognize a gain or a loss when it deals in its own stock.

stock in the event of a price decline. Rather than paying for the put directly, however, the individual sells an out-of-the-money call. In the event of a large stock price increase, the individual forfeits gains above the call's exercise price. A variable prepaid forward strategy is similar to a stock option collar except that the hedger receives a cash advance in the amount of the present value of the put's exercise price upon entering the contract. The fourth and final strategy examines the practice of many firms to sell puts and/or buy calls on their own shares.

## REFERENCES AND SUGGESTED READINGS


Black, Fischer, and Myron Scholes. 1973. The pricing of options and corporate liabilities. *Journal of Political Economy* 81: 637–659.

Bollen, Nicolas P. B., and Robert E. Whaley. 2004. Does net buying pressure affect the shape of implied volatility functions? *Journal of Finance* 59: 711–754.

Geske, Robert. 1979. A note on an analytical formula for unprotected American call options on stocks with known dividends. *Journal of Financial Economics* 7 (October): 375–380.

Mayhew, Stewart, and Vassil Mihov. 2004. How do exchanges select stocks for option listing? *Journal of Finance* 59 (1): 447–471.

Merton, Robert C. 1973. Theory of rational option pricing. *Bell Journal of Economics and Management Science* 4: 141–183.

Roll, Richard. 1977. An analytic valuation formula for unprotected American call options on stocks with known dividends. *Journal of Financial Economics* 5 (November): 251–258.

Rubinstein, Mark. 1995. On the accounting valuation of employee stock options. *Journal of Derivatives* 3 (1): 8–24.

Smith Jr., Clifford W. 1977. Alternative methods for raising capital: Rights versus underwritten offerings. *Journal of Financial Economics* 5: 273–307.

Whaley, Robert E. 1981. On the valuation of American call options on stocks with known dividends. *Journal of Financial Economics* 9 (June): 207–211.

Whaley, Robert E. 1982. Valuation of American call options on dividend-paying stocks: Empirical tests. *Journal of Financial Economics* 10: 29–58.


## APPENDIX 11A: EXACT VALUATION OF AMERICAN-STYLE CALL OPTION ON A DIVIDEND-PAYING STOCK

An American-style call option on a dividend-paying stock can be valued exactly. This is possible because there are only a finite number of rational exercise opportunities—one prior to each dividend payment and one at expiration. This appendix provides the valuation equation for an American-style call option whose underlying stock pays one dividend during the option's life. A compound option valuation approach is used.[28]

As discussed in earlier in this chapter, an American-style call option may be exercised just prior to when the stock goes ex-dividend because the stock price will fall by the amount of the dividend. Assuming that future stock price net of the present value of the promised dividend is log-normally distributed, the value of an American-style call option on a dividend-paying stock is

[28] Recall that European-style compound options were valued in Chapter 8.

$$C = S^x[N_1(b_1) + N_2(a_1, -b_1; -\sqrt{t/T})] \\ - Xe^{-rT}[N_1(b_2)e^{r(T-t)} + N_2(a_2, -b_2; -\sqrt{t/T})] + De^{-rt}N_1(b_2)$$

where

$$a_1 = \frac{\ln(S^x e^{rT}/X) + 0.5\sigma^2 T}{\sigma\sqrt{T}}, \; a_2 = a_1 - \sigma\sqrt{T}$$

$$b_1 = \frac{\ln(S^x e^{rt}/S_t^*) + 0.5\sigma^2 t}{\sigma\sqrt{t}}, \; b_2 = b_1 - \sigma\sqrt{t}$$

$N_1(b)$ is the cumulative univariate normal density function with upper integral limit $b$[29] and $N_2(a,b;\rho)$ is the cumulative bivariate normal density function with upper integral limits, $a$ and $b$, and correlation coefficient, $\rho$.[30] As before, $S$ is the current stock price, and $\sigma$ is the stock's volatility rate. The stock is assumed to pay a dividend in the amount $D$ at time $t$. The exercise price of the call is denoted $X$, and $T$ is its time remaining to expiration. $S^x = S - De^{-rt}$ is the stock price net of the present value of the escrowed dividend. $S_t^*$ is the ex-dividend stock price that satisfies

$$c(S_t^*, T-t; X) = S_t^* + D - X$$

The valuation equation shows that the American-style call option formula is the sum of the present values of two conditional expected values—the present value of the expected call value conditional on early exercise, $S^xN_1(b_1) - (X - D)e^{-rt}N_1(b_2)$, and the present value of the expected terminal call conditional on no early exercise,

$$S^xN_2(a_1, -b_1; -\sqrt{t/T}) - Xe^{-rT}N_2(a_2, -b_2; -\sqrt{t/T})$$

The term $N_1(b_2)$ is the risk-neutral probability that the call will be exercised early and the term $N_2(a_2, -b_2; -\sqrt{t/T})$ is the risk-neutral probability that the call will not be exercised early and will be in-the-money at expiration.

Note that as the amount of the dividend approaches the present value of the interest income that would be earned by deferring exercise until expiration, the value of the critical ex-dividend stock price, $S_t^*$ approaches positive infinity, the values of $N_1(b_1)$ and $N_1(b_2)$ approach 0, the values of $N_2(a_1, -b_1; -\sqrt{t/T})$ and $N_2(a_2, -b_2; -\sqrt{t/T})$ approach $N_1(a_1)$ and $N_1(a_2)$, respectively, and the Ameri-

[29] We have added a subscript so as to distinguish the univariate normal from the bivariate normal.

[30] Details regarding the computation of the bivariate normal probability are contained in Appendix 8A of Chapter 8.

can call option formula becomes the dividend-adjusted BSM European-style call option formula shown in Table 11.5.

**ILLUSTRATION 11A.1** Compute value of American-style call.

*Compute the value of an American-style call option with an exercise price of 50 and a time to expiration of 90 days. Assume the stock is currently priced at \$50 a share, has a volatility rate of 36%, and pays a \$2 per share cash dividend in exactly 75 days.*

First, check if the dividend is so small that early exercise will never be optimal. This is done using (3.16) from Chapter 3.

$$2 > 50[1 - e^{-0.05(90/365 - 75/365)}] = 0.103$$

Since early exercise is possible, you must now proceed with determining the critical ex-dividend stock price by solving

$$c(S_t^*, T - t; 50) = S_t^* + 2 - 50$$

The critical stock price is 49.060.

Next, compute the stock price net of the present value of the promised dividend.

$$S^x = 50 - 2e^{-0.05(75/365)} = 48.020$$

The value of the American call is now computed as

$$C = 48.020[N_1(b_1) + N_2(a_1, -b_1; -\sqrt{t/T})]$$
$$- 50e^{-0.05(90/365)}[N_1(b_2) + N_2(a_2, -b_2; -\sqrt{t/T})] + 2e^{-rt}N_1(b_2)$$

where

$$t = 75/365, T = 90/365$$
$$\sqrt{t/T} = 0.9129$$

$$a_1 = \frac{\ln(48.020/50e^{0.05T}) + 0.5(0.36)^2T}{0.36\sqrt{T}} = -0.0676$$

$$a_2 = -0.0676 - 0.36\sqrt{T} = -0.2464$$

$$b_1 = \frac{\ln(48.020e^{0.05t}/49.059) + 0.5(0.36)^2t}{0.36\sqrt{t}} = 0.0134$$

$$b_2 = 0.0134 - 0.36\sqrt{t} = -0.1498$$

The bivariate normal probabilities are

$$N_2(a_1, -b_1; -\sqrt{t/T}) = 0.0520$$

and

$$N_2(a_2, -b_2; -\sqrt{t/T}) = 0.0484$$

and the univariate normal probabilities $N_1(b_1) = 0.5053$ and $N_1(b_2) = 0.4405$. The value of the American-style call is 3.445. The value of this call computed using the binomial method outlined in this chapter is 3.433. In other words, the binomial method has a 1.2 cent valuation error. The valuation computations for this illustration were performed using the OV_OPTION_VALUE_SO and OV_STOCK_OPTION_VALUE_BIN functions from the OPTVAL Function Library. A summary is shown here:

**Stock Option Valuation Using Analytical Method**

| **Stock** | | **Intermediate Computations** | |
|---|---|---|---|
| Price ($S$) | 50 | Years to expiration ($T$) | 0.2466 |
| Volatility rate ($s$) | 36.00% | Time to ex-dividend in years ($t$) | 0.2055 |
| Dividend ($D$) | 2.00 | $PVD$ | 1.980 |
| Time to ex-dividend in days | 75 | $S - PVD$ | 48.020 |
| | | $X[1 - e^{-r(T-t)}]$ | 0.103 |

| **Call Option** | | **Call Option Valuation (C)** | |
|---|---|---|---|
| Exercise price ($X$) | 50 | European | 2.828 |
| Days to expiration | 90 | American (analytical) | 3.445 |
| | | American (binomial) | 3.434 |
| **Market** | | No. of time steps | 90 |
| Interest rate ($r$) | 5.00% | | |

# 12
# Corporate Securities

Firms issue different types of securities to finance the assets of the firm—common stock preferred stock, discount bonds, coupon bonds, convertible bonds, warrants, convertible bonds, and so on. Some are issued to the public and are actively traded in the secondary markets. Others are placed publicly, but trade infrequently. Yet others are privately placed, and trade seldom if at all. The purpose of this chapter is to show how all of the firm's securities outstanding can be valued using only information regarding the firm's common stock price and volatility rate. This is possible because all of the firm's securities have the same source of uncertainty—the overall market value of the firm's assets. Consequently, all of the firm's securities have price movements that are perfectly correlated with one another over short periods of time. With such being the case, all corporate securities can be valued using information about the price and volatility rate of any *one* of the firm's outstanding securities. We choose to use the common stock of the firm because, of all the firm's securities, it has the deepest and most active secondary market. In this sense, all corporate securities may be considered common stock derivatives.

To develop the corporate security valuation framework, we rely on the BSM option valuation results from Chapter 7. The underlying source of uncertainty is the firm's overall market value, which we assume is log-normally distributed in the future. We also assume that a risk-free hedge may be formed between each of the firm's securities and the firm's overall value. As a practical matter, the firm's overall value (i.e., the sum of the market values of all of the firm's constituent securities) does not trade as a single asset, however, small changes in the value of the firm are perfectly correlated with the changes in the value of its stock. This means that, as long as the firm's common stock is actively traded, we can apply risk-neutral valuation with no loss in generality.

The chapter proceeds as follows. First, we address the valuation of corporate bonds assuming that the firm that has two securities outstanding—zero-coupon bonds and common stock. Second, we extend the framework to include multiple bond issues with varying degrees of seniority. Third, we value rights and warrants. Rights and warrants are call option-like securities written by the firm on its own stock. But because the firm issues these securities, option exercise implies that the value of existing shareholder equity is diluted, and the effects of dilution can have significant value. The same is true of convertible bonds, which are a hybrid security with bond and warrant-like features. Convertible bonds are the focus of the last section of the chapter.

## VALUING CORPORATE BONDS[1]

The first security that we consider is a corporate bond. Unlike bonds issued by the U.S. Treasury, corporate bonds have default risk. There is always some possibility, however remote, that a firm will be unable to make a promised payment to bondholders. The effect of default risk on corporate bond valuation is shown in three different ways. First, the bond value is modeled as the value of the firm less the value of the stock, where the stock is modeled as a call option on the value of the firm. Next we use put-call parity to reformulate the value of a corporate bond as the difference between the value of a risk-free bond and the value of a put option that allows the managers of the firm to put the firm's assets to bondholders if the firm value is less than the bond's face value when they mature. Finally, we show that the value of a corporate bond is equivalent to the value of a portfolio that consists of a long position in the risk-free bonds and a long position in the firm's stock. As was noted in the introduction, all corporate securities may be formulated in this way.

### Stock as Call Option on Firm

The bond valuation model assumes that the firm has two securities outstanding—a zero-coupon bond and stock. The bond's current value is denoted $B$, its face value is $F$, and its term to maturity is $T$. The market value of the firm's stock is denoted $S$, and the market value of the firm is $V \equiv S + B$. Since the bond has no coupons, bond default can be triggered only at bond maturity, when the value of the firm's assets is less than the face value of the bond.[2]

Under the above assumptions, the value of the firm's bond equals the total value of the firm less the value of the firm's stock, that is,

$$B = V - S \tag{12.1}$$

The firm's stock, in turn, can be thought of as a call option on the value of the firm. In the event that the market value of the firm is greater than the face value of the bond at the bond's expiration, the shareholders receive the value of the firm less the payment of the face value to bondholders; otherwise, they receive nothing, that is,

$$\tilde{S}_T = \max(\tilde{V}_T - F, 0) \tag{12.2}$$

Assuming the firm's value is log-normally distributed at the end of the bond's life, the current value of the firm's stock is given by the BSM call option valuation formula,

[1] The model developed in this section is frequently referred to as the "Merton model." Merton (1974) was the first to use the BSM framework to value corporate securities.

[2] With coupon-bearing bonds, default may also occur when the firm cannot meet a coupon interest payment.

$$S = VN(d_1) - Fe^{-rT}N(d_2) \tag{12.3}$$

where

$$d_1 = \frac{\ln(Ve^{rT}/F) + 0.5\sigma_V^2 T}{\sigma_V\sqrt{T}}, \quad d_2 = d_1 - \sigma_V\sqrt{T}$$

and the volatility rate is the volatility rate of the firm rather than the stock. From (12.1) and (12.3), the value of the risky bond may be written

$$B = V - [VN(d_1) + Fe^{-rT}N(d_2)] \tag{12.4}$$

The stock valuation equation (12.3) and the bond valuation equation (12.4) are useful in developing intuition regarding the relative values of the claims held by shareholders and bondholders. Suppose that the firm experiences an unexpected labor strike and now believes its earnings will be significantly below normal during the next few quarters. Naturally, the firm's value drops immediately. At first blush, one might think the shareholders of the firm are the only security holders to suffer since they are the residual claimants of the firm. The valuation equations (12.3) and (12.4) tell us otherwise, however. The stock's delta, that is, the change in stock value with respect to a change in firm value, may be derived from (12.3)[3] and has the form,

$$\Delta_S = N(d_1) \tag{12.5}$$

The bond's delta may be derived from (12.4) and is

$$\Delta_B = 1 - N(d_1) = N(-d_1) \tag{12.6}$$

Thus an unexpected drop in the firm value is split between the shareholders and the bondholders. The shareholders absorb $\Delta_S$ per dollar of firm value change, and the bondholders absorb $\Delta_B$. Naturally, the sum of the changes in value is one, that is, $\Delta_S + \Delta_B = 1$. The only instance in which the shareholders absorb the full amount of the change is when the value of the firm is considerably greater than the face value of the bonds, making the bonds are essentially default-free.

**ILLUSTRATION 12.1** Value corporate bond as firm value less call option.

*Assume that the firm has a current value of 25, and its annual volatility rate is 20%. The firm has two securities outstanding—a zero-coupon bond and common stock. The bond matures in five years and has a face value of 20. The stock pays no dividends, and the risk-free rate of interest is 5%. Compute the values and volatility rates of the firm's stock and bonds.*

[3] The partial derivatives of the BSM call option formula with respect to changes in the formula's determinants are given in Chapter 7, Appendix 7E.

To compute the value of the stock, we use the BSM call option valuation formula (12.3), that is,

$$S = 25N(d_1) - 20e^{-0.05(5)}N(d_2)$$

where

$$d_1 = \frac{\ln(25e^{0.05(5)}/20) + 0.5(0.20^2)5}{0.20\sqrt{5}} = 1.2816 \text{ and } d_2 = 1.2816 - 0.20\sqrt{5} = 0.8344$$

The risk-neutral probabilities are $N(d_1) = 0.9000$ and $N(d_2) = 0.7980$, and the call option value is 10.071.

The OPTVAL function library contains a number of valuation routines for corporate securities. They all have the prefix OV_CORP_. The valuation function for the firm's stock given the value of the firm is

OV_CORP_STOCK_FIRM(*firm, face, t, r, vf, vind*)

where *firm* is the value of the firm, *face* is the face value of the firm's zero-coupon bonds, *t* is the term to maturity of the bond's in years, *r* is the risk-free interest rate, and *vf* is the volatility rate of the firm. The term, *vind*, is an indicator variable whose value is set equal to 1 if the function is to return the stock's value and 2 if the function is to return the volatility rate. For the illustration at hand,

$S$ = OV_CORP_STOCK_FIRM(25, 20, 5, 0.05, 0.20, 1) = 10.071

To compute the stock's rate of return volatility, we use the elasticity (eta) of the stock value with respect to the firm value. Recall from the early discussion on dynamic strategies in Chapter 10 that, because the option's (stock's) rate of return is perfectly correlated with the asset's (firm's) rate of return, the stock's volatility rate may be written as a function of the firm's volatility rate, that is,

$$\sigma_S = \eta_S \sigma_V$$

where $\eta_S$ is the elasticity (eta) of the value with respect to the firm value. The eta, in turn, is

$$\eta_S = \Delta_S\left(\frac{V}{S}\right)$$

where $\Delta_S$ is the stock's delta. From the above results, we know $\Delta_S = N(d_1) = 0.9000$, so the stock's rate of return volatility is

$$\sigma_S = N(d_1)\left(\frac{V}{S}\right)\sigma_V = 0.9000\left(\frac{25}{10.071}\right)0.20 = 44.68\%$$

This value can be verified using the OPTVAL function

OV_CORP_STOCK_FIRM(*firm, face, t, r, vf, vind*)

The function value is

$\sigma_S$ = OV_CORP_STOCK_FIRM(25, 20, 5, 0.05, 0.20, 2) = 44.68%

With the stock value known, the bond value can be computed using (12.4), that is,

$$B = 25 - 10.071 = 14.929$$

Since the stock's delta is 0.9000, the bond's delta is 0.1000 (i.e., the delta of the firm is 1), the bond's eta is

$$\eta_B = \Delta_B\left(\frac{V}{B}\right) = 0.1000\left(\frac{25}{14.929}\right) = 16.74\%$$

and the bond's rate of return volatility is $\sigma_B = 0.1674(0.20) = 3.35\%$. These values can be verified using the functions

$$B = \text{OV\_CORP\_BOND\_FIRM}(25, 20, 5, 0.05, 0.20, 1) = 14.929$$

and

$$\sigma_S = \text{OV\_CORP\_BOND\_FIRM}(25, 20, 5, 0.05, 0.20, 2) = 3.35\%$$

Note that since both the rate of return of the bond and the rate of return of the stock are perfectly correlated, the volatility rate of the firm is a market value-weighted average of the volatility rates of the bond and the stock, that is,

$$\sigma_V = 0.0335\left(\frac{14.929}{25}\right) + 0.4468\left(\frac{10.071}{25}\right) = 20.00\%$$

Under the assumptions of the model, all corporate securities can be written is this way, albeit with different weights.

Figure 12.1 helps us develop the intuition for corporate bond valuation. It illustrates the tradeoff between shareholder and bondholder values as the value of the overall firm changes. All other parameters in the valuation equations are held constant. At very low levels of firm value, the probability of default is extremely high. Since the shareholders are unlikely to receive anything after bondholders are paid, the value of the bonds is simply the firm value. As firm value rises, the probability of default falls. Bond value rises, but at a decreasing rate, since the bondholders never receive more than the face value of their bonds. Share value, however, increases at an increasing rate. Once the bondholders are paid off, all of the firm's value goes to shareholders.

**FIGURE 12.1** Values of bond and stock as a function of the value of the firm.

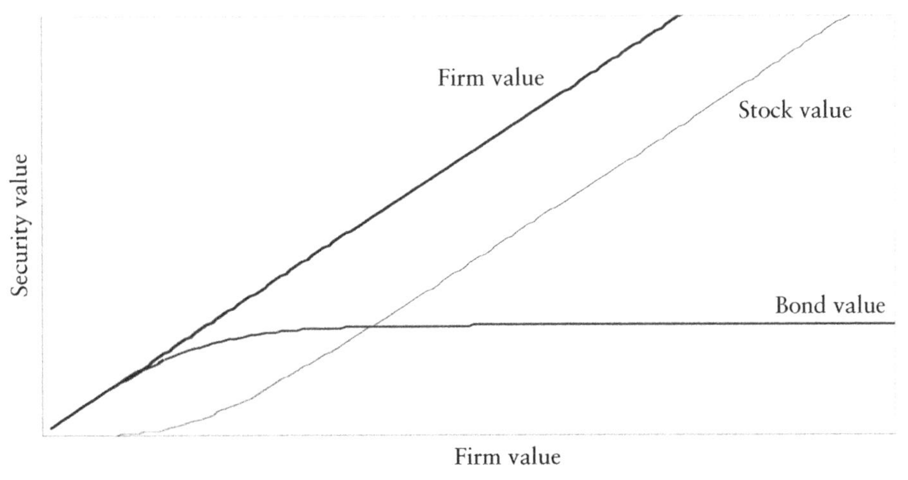

**FIGURE 12.2** Values of bond and stock as a function of the firm's volatility rate.

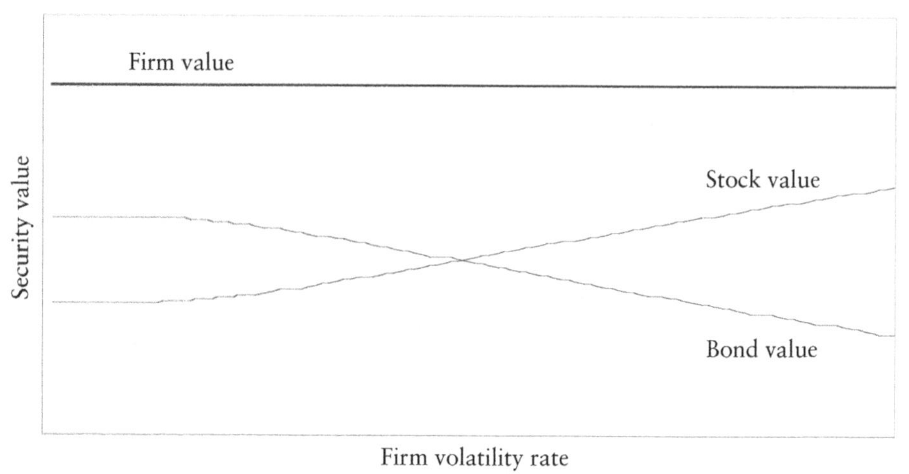


Another interesting feature of (12.3) is that the value of the firm's stock increases with an increase in the firm's volatility rate, as is shown in Figure 12.2. The intuition for this result is that, the higher the volatility, the greater the chance that the firm's value exceeds the face value of the bonds by a large amount at the bond's maturity. Higher volatility also increases the chance that the firm's value is below the bond's face value by a large amount. Since the shareholders do not face any liability from this shortfall, however, the value of stock is unaffected.

The bondholder, on the other hand, is affected by the shortfall. Recall that, in the bond valuation formula (12.4), the bondholder owns the firm but is short a call option. With an increase in the firm's volatility rate, the value of the call rises. Holding other factors constant, the bondholders suffer. Figure 12.2 also shows the zero-sum nature of the effects of volatility rate changes on the values of the bonds and the stock of the firm. As firm's volatility rate rises, the value of the bonds falls and the value of stock rises.

### Risky Bond Equals Risk-Free Bond Less Present Value of Expected Loss

Valuing a corporate bond as the difference between the firm value and the value of a call option provides several useful economic insights. But, this is only one possible formulation. By applying put-call parity to (12.4), we can derive an alternate specification that further enhances our understanding of bond valuation. In the context of valuing corporate securities, put-call parity[4] may be written

$$V - c = Fe^{-rT} - p \tag{12.7}$$

where $c$ is the value of a call option written on the firm, that is, $c \equiv VN(d_1) - Fe^{-rT}N(d_2)$, and $p$ is the value of the corresponding put option, that is, $p \equiv Fe^{-rT}N(-d_2) - VN(-d_1)$. Thus, the corporate bond value may also be written

[4] The European-style put-call parity was developed in Chapter 6.

$$B = Fe^{-rT} - [Fe^{-rT}N(-d_2) - VN(-d_1)] \tag{12.8}$$

Equation (12.8) says that the value of a corporate bond equals the difference between the value of a risk-free zero-coupon bond with face value $F$ and the value of a put that allows the managers of the firm to put the firm's assets to the bondholders if firm value falls below the bonds' face value at maturity. To understand the economic intuition underlying the put, recall that in Chapter 7 we show that the value of a put option may be written

$$e^{-rT}\left[F - Ve^{rT}\frac{N(-d_1)}{N(-d_2)}\right]N(-d_2) \tag{12.9}$$

In (12.9), the term,

$$Ve^{rT}\frac{N(-d_1)}{N(-d_2)}$$

is the expected firm value at time $T$ conditional on the value of the firm being less than the face value of the bonds, that is, $E(\tilde{V}_T | V_T < F)$. From a corporate bond perspective, this is called the bond's *expected recovery value*—what bondholders expect to receive in the event of default. If we subtract the expected recovery value conditional upon default from the bond's face value, we get the *expected loss* of the bond at time $T$ conditional upon default, that is, $F - E(\tilde{V}_T | V_T < F)$, which may be calculated using the term in squared brackets of (12.9). The full expression (12.9) is, therefore, the *present value of the expected loss* on the bond conditional on the value of the firm being less than the bond's face value at time $T$ times the *probability of default*, $\Pr(V_T < F) = N(-d_2)$. Hence, equation (12.9) provides another perspective on why bond value falls as the volatility rate rises (see Figure 12.2). As volatility rises, the expected loss conditional on default rises as does the probability of default.

**ILLUSTRATION 12.2** Compute present value of expected loss on corporate bond.

*Assume that the firm has a current value of 25, and its annual volatility rate is 20%. The firm has two securities outstanding—zero-coupon bonds and common stock. The bonds mature in five years and have a face value of 20. The stock pays no dividends, and the risk-free rate of interest is 5%. Compute the risk-neutral probability of default, the present value of the expected loss conditional upon default, the value of the firm's bonds, and the value of the firm's stock.*

The value of a risk-free bond with five years remaining to maturity is

$$Fe^{-0.05(5)} = 20e^{-0.05(5)} = 15.576$$

The risk-neutral probability of default is

$$N(-d_2) = 1 - N(d_2) = 1 - 0.7980 = 0.2020$$

which can be verified using the OPTVAL function,

OV_CORP_PROB_DEFAULT(*firm, face, t, alpha, vf*)

where *firm* is the value of the firm, *face* is the face value of the firm's zero-coupon bonds, *t* is the term to maturity of the bond's in years, *alpha* is the expected rate of appreciation in the value of the firm, and *vf* is the volatility rate of the firm. In a risk-neutral world, *alpha* is set equal to the risk-free rate of interest:

$$\Pr(V_T < F) = \text{OV\_CORP\_PROB\_DEFAULT}(25, 20, 5, 0.05, 0.20) = 0.2020$$

The expected recovery value conditional upon default is

$$25e^{0.05(5)}\left(\frac{0.1000}{0.2020}\right) = 15.888$$

and may be computed using

OV_CORP_RECOVERY_VALUE(*firm, face, t, alpha, vf*)

where all of the function arguments are as defined above. Substituting the problem parameters, we find

OV_CORP_RECOVERY_VALUE (25, 20, 5, 0.05, 0.20) = 15.888

The expected loss conditional upon default is. Alternatively, we can use the function

OV_CORP_EXPECTED_LOSS (25, 20, 5, 0.05, 0.20) = 4.112

The present value of the expected loss conditional upon default times the probability default is

$$e^{-0.05(5)}(4.112)(0.2020) = 0.647$$[5]

The value of the corporate bond is therefore

$$B = 15.576 - 0.647 = 14.929$$

and the value of the common stock is

$$S = V - B = 25 - 14.929 = 10.071$$

Note that the bond and stock values are consistent with Illustration 12.1.

### Risky Bond as Portfolio of Risk-Free Bond and Stock

The bond valuation (12.8), in turn, can be rearranged to provide further economic insight. To see this, first gather terms on $Fe^{-rT}$ and substitute $S + B$ for $V$, that is,

$$B = Fe^{-rT}N(d_2) + (S + B)N(-d_1) \tag{12.10}$$

Next rearrange terms to isolate $B$ and then divide through by $N(d_1)$. The resulting equation for the corporate bond value is

$$B = Fe^{-rT}\left(\frac{N(d_2)}{N(d_1)}\right) + S\left(\frac{N(-d_1)}{N(d_1)}\right) \tag{12.11}$$

[5] To check this computation, compute the value of the put option on the right-hand side of (12.8) using OV_OPTION_VALUE(25, 20, 5, 0.05, 0.0, 0.20, "p", "e") = 0.647.

Equation (12.11) says that any corporate bond may be written as a portfolio consisting of a long position in risk-free bonds and a long position in the firm's stock. The number of units of the risk-free bond is

$$\frac{N(d_2)}{N(d_1)}$$

and the number of units of the firm's stock is

$$\frac{N(-d_1)}{N(d_1)}$$ [6]

**ILLUSTRATION 12.3** Write firm's bond value as portfolio consisting of risk-free bonds and stock.

*Assume that the firm has a current value of 25, and its annual volatility rate is 20%. The firm has two securities outstanding—a zero-coupon bond and common stock. The bond matures in five years and has a face value of 20. The stock pays no dividends, and the risk-free rate of interest is 5%. Write the value of the bond as a portfolio consisting of a risk-free bond and the firm's stock.*

From Illustration 12.1, we know that the stock's value is 10.071, $N(d_1) = 0.9000$, and $N(d_2) = 0.7980$. From Illustration 12.2, we know that the value of the risk-free bond is $20e^{-0.02(5)} = 15.576$, and $N(-d_1) = 0.1000$. The value of the firm's bond is therefore

$$B = Fe^{-rT}\left(\frac{N(d_2)}{N(d_1)}\right) + S\left(\frac{N(-d_1)}{N(d_1)}\right)$$

$$= 20e^{-0.05(5)}\left(\frac{0.7980}{0.9000}\right) + 10.071\left(\frac{0.1000}{0.9000}\right) = 14.929$$

The number of units of risk-free bonds and stock may also be computed using the OPTVAL function

OV_CORP_RFBOND_STOCK_SPLIT(*firm, face, t, r, vf, sind*)

where *sind* is an indicator variable whose value is set equal to 1 to find the number of units of risk-free bonds, and 2 to find the number of units of stock. All other function arguments are as defined above. For example,

OV_CORP_RFBOND_STOCK_SPLIT(25, 20, 5, 0.05, 0.20, 1) = 0.887

and

OV_CORP_RFBOND_STOCK_SPLIT(25, 20, 5, 0.05, 0.20, 2) = 0.111.

Figures 12.3A and 12.3B illustrate the dynamics of increased leverage on the values of the firm's bonds and stock as well as on the numbers of units of risk-free bonds and stock to hold in order to synthetically create a corporate bond.

[6] Note that the weights do not sum to one. There is no reason that they should.

**FIGURE 12.3** Replication of corporate bond value using risk-free bonds and common stock. Parameters: $V = 25$, $T = 5$, $r = 0.05$, and $\sigma_V = 0.20$. The face value of the corporate bonds ($F$) varies from 1 to 85.

Panel A: Security value as a function of face value of bonds

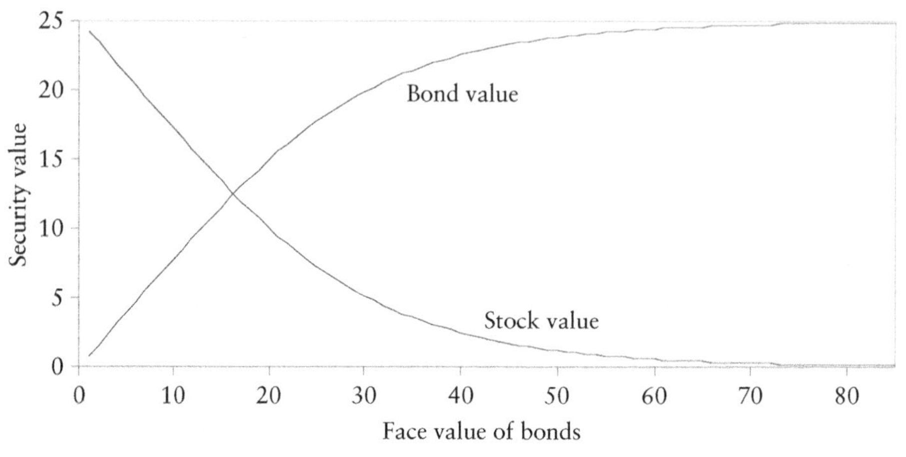


Panel B: Units of risk-free bonds and stock as a function of probability of default

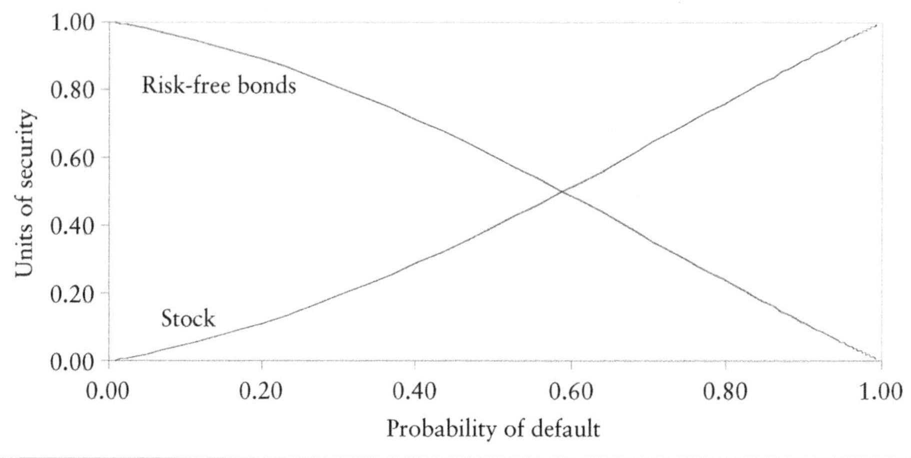


All of the parameters are the same as in the previous illustrations except that the face value of the bonds ($F$) is allowed to vary from 1 to 85. In Panel A, the bond and stock values are plotted. As the face value of the bonds increases, the value of the bonds rises and the value of the stock falls. This stands to reason. As the face value of the bonds increases, the present value of the face amount (i.e., the first term in (12.8)) increases proportionately, however, the value of the put option (i.e., the second term in (12.8)) increases at an increasing rate. Even though the face value of the value of the bonds is allowed to rise beyond the value of the firm (i.e., $V = 25$), the market value of the bonds converges to the value of the firm since the bondholders' claim cannot exceed the value of the firm's assets. In Panel B, the horizontal axis is the probability of default, which can be computed using $N(-d_2)$. The vertical axis is the numbers of units of risk-free bonds and stock that are necessary to replicate the bond value. At a default probability of zero, the portfolio consists almost entirely of risk-free bonds. This stands to reason since the firm's bonds are essentially risk-free. As the default probability increases, less units of risk-free bonds are held and more money is invested in stock. At high levels of default, the number of units of stock is high, however, the value of the stock is negligible.

### Estimating Bond Value Using Stock Price Information

The bond valuation formulas, (12.4), (12.8), and (12.10), are useful in developing economic intuition about the relation between bond value and the value of the firm. From a practical standpoint, however, these bond valuation formulas are not particularly useful. One reason is that we do not know the value of the firm. For most U.S. corporations, the only corporate security that is actively traded is the common stock. Corporate bonds trade largely in the over-the-counter market.[7] Because such trades are private negotiations, there is no mandated reporting of trade prices and quantities. Without knowing the price of the bonds, we cannot compute the value of the firm.[8] Another reason is that we have no means of estimating the firm's expected future volatility rate from historical data. Corporate bonds trade relatively infrequently, and the time between trades may vary from minutes apart to months apart. Indeed, it not uncommon for newly-issued corporate bonds to trade only in the first few days following issuance and never again. Thus, even if the current price of the bond can be observed, the lack of historical bond price data undermines our ability to compute historical firm prices and, hence, the firm's historical volatility rate. In sum, the bond valuation formulas, (12.4), (12.8), and (12.10), are difficult to implement because we cannot reliably identify the firm's current value, $V$, or its expected future volatility rate, $\sigma_V$.

As it turns out, both of these problems can be circumvented. To understand how, consider the bond valuation equation (12.4), and assume, for the moment, that we know the firm's volatility rate $\sigma_V$. Since all parameters on the right hand-side of the valuation equation (12.4) are known, except for $V$, we can solve for $V$ iteratively using a numerical search procedure such as Microsoft Excel's SOLVER function. With the firm value known, we compute the bond value as $B = V - S$.

Unfortunately, we do not know $\sigma_V$, so we are left with one equation and two unknowns. One way to solve for this somewhat perplexing problem is to find a second equation that is also a function of $\sigma_V$ and $V$, and then to solve for $\sigma_V$ and $V$ simultaneously. Since stock return volatility can be estimated using an available stock price history, a reasonable starting point is to look for some relation between stock return volatility $\sigma_S$ and firm return volatility $\sigma_V$. In Illustration

[7] This assumes, of course, that the bonds were publicly issued. Many bond issues are private placements.

[8] One possibility for estimating the value of the firm is to use the value of the firm's assets. The book value of assets, however, is seldom a good proxy for the firm's market value.

12.1, we relied upon the mechanics of Chapter 10 to demonstrate that, since the stock return and the firm return are perfectly correlated, the relation between stock return volatility and firm return volatility of the firm may be expressed as $\sigma_S = \eta_S\sigma_V$, where $\eta_S$ is the elasticity of the stock value with respect to the firm value. The elasticity measure, in turn, equals the stock's delta times the ratio of the firm's value to the value of the stock, that is,

$$\sigma_S = N(d_1)\frac{V}{S}\sigma_V \tag{12.12}$$

Isolating the known from the unknown parameters, we get

$$S\sigma_S = N(d_1)V\sigma_V \tag{12.13}$$

Since we can observe the value of the stock $S$ and can estimate the stock return volatility $\sigma_S$ from historical price data, we have two equations, (12.3) and (12.13), and two unknowns—the value of the firm, $V$, and the volatility rate of the firm, $\sigma_V$. Thus we can solve for the unknown parameters uniquely. With $V$ identified, the value of the corporate bond may be computed as $B = V - S$.

**ILLUSTRATION 12.4** Value corporate bond form stock price information.

*Assume that the firm's stock pays no dividends, has a value of 8, and has a volatility rate of 50%. Also assume the firm has a single zero-coupon bond. The bond promises to be redeemed at its face value of 20 at the end of five years. Finally, the five-year, zero-coupon, risk-free interest rate is 5%. Compute the value of the bond.*

To compute the value of the bond, insert the problem information into equations (12.3) and (12.13), that is,

$$8 = VN(d_1) - 20e^{-0.05(5)}N(d_2)$$

and

$$8(0.50) = 4 = N(d_1)V\sigma_V$$

where

$$d_1 = \frac{\ln(Ve^{0.05(5)}/20) + 0.5\sigma_V^2(5)}{\sigma_V\sqrt{5}} \text{ and } d_2 = d_1 - \sigma_V\sqrt{5}$$

With two equations and two unknowns, we can solve uniquely for $V$ and $\sigma_V$ using Excel's SOLVER function. The firm value is 22.503, and the firm's volatility rate is 21.02%. The bond value is $B = 22.503 - 8 = 14.503$.

The OPTVAL library contains a function that solves for the firm's value and volatility rate given information about the stock, that is,

OV_CORP_FIRM_STOCK(*stock, face, t, r, vs, vind*)

where *stock* is the value of the stock, *face* is the face value of the bonds, *t* is the bonds' term to maturity in years, and *vs* is the volatility rate of the stock. The argument *vind* is an indicator variable whose value is set equal to 1 if the function is to return the firm's value and 2 if the function is to return the firm's volatility rate. Applying the function, the value of the firm is

$$V = \text{OV\_CORP\_FIRM\_STOCK}(8, 20, 5, 0.05, 0.50, 1) = 22.503$$

and the firm's volatility rate is

$$\sigma_V = \text{OV\_CORP\_FIRM\_STOCK}(8, 20, 5, 0.05, 0.50, 2) = 21.02\%$$

### Estimating Bond Value Using Stock and Stock Option Price Information

Estimating the stock's volatility rate using historical price data presents a subtle theoretical inconsistency. If we assume the firm's volatility rate is constant, the stock's volatility rate is not and will change as the firm's value moves and time passes. This means that estimating the stock return volatility from a time-series of stock price data is error-prone. An alternative means of estimating stock return volatility is to compute implied volatility based on exchange-traded option prices. We cannot use the BSM model to compute implied volatility of the stock return, however, since the BSM model assumes that stock price (not the firm's value) is log-normal.

Again, these problems can be circumvented. An exchange-traded call option written on the firm's stock is a call on a call since the firm's stock is a call on the firm's value. Similarly, an exchange-traded put option written on the firm's stock is a put on a call. In other words, we can now apply the compound option valuation mechanics from Chapter 8 to the corporate security valuation problem at hand. Specifically, we use exchange-traded option prices to infer the value of the firm and its volatility rate. First, we model the value of a call option, and then we turn to the put option value.

To value a call on the firm's stock, first recall the valuation equation that we developed for the equity of the firm (12.3), that is,

$$S = VN(d_1) - Fe^{-rT}N(d_2) \tag{12.3}$$

where

$$d_1 = \frac{\ln(Ve^{rT}/F) + 0.5\sigma_V^2 T}{\sigma_V\sqrt{T}}, \text{ and } d_2 = d_1 - \sigma_V\sqrt{T}$$

The exchange-traded call on the firm's stock is assumed to have an exercise price of $X$ and a time to expiration of $t$, where $t < T$. In this corporate finance context, a European-style call on a call formula may be written

$$c = VN_2(d_1, a_1; \rho) - Fe^{-rT}N_2(d_2, a_1; \rho) - Xe^{-rt}N_1(a_2) \tag{12.14}$$

where

$$a_1 = \frac{\ln(Ve^{rt}/V^*) + 0.5\sigma_V^2 T}{\sigma\sqrt{t}}, \ a_2 = a_1 - \sigma_V\sqrt{t}, \text{ and } \rho = \sqrt{\frac{t}{T}}$$

Like in Chapter 8, we adopt the subscript "1" to indicate the univariate normal probability $N_1(d)$ and "2" to indicate the bivariate normal probability, $N_2(a,b;\rho)$.

The first step in valuing the call using (12.14) is to determine the critical value of the firm at time $t$ above which the call will be exercised. It can be determined by iteratively searching for the firm value $V^*$ that makes the value of the stock (i.e., the underlying call) equal to the exercise price of the call, that is,

$$V^* N_1(d_1^*) - Fe^{-r(T-t)} N_1(d_2^*) = X \tag{12.15}$$

With $V^*$ known, the call option value can be computed using (12.14).

Notice the similarity between the structure of (12.14) and the structure of (12.3). The first two terms of the right-hand side of (12.14) correspond to the formula (12.3). Upon exercising the call, we receive the stock, which can be valued using the BSM formula. The last term on the right-side is the present value of the call's exercise price, $e^{-rt}X$, times the risk-neutral probability that the firm value will exceed the critical firm value at time $t$, $N_1(a_2)$. This is the expected cost of exercising the compound call conditional upon it being in the money at time $t$. The term, $N_2(d_2,a_2;\rho)$, is the risk-neutral compound probability that the asset price exceeds $V_t^*$ at time $t$ and exceeds the face value of the bonds $F$ at time $T$. In other words, the firm value must jump both hurdles for the stock to be in the money at time $T$. The sign of the correlation coefficient reflects whether the firm value should move in the same or opposite direction in the interval between time 0 and time $t$ as in the interval between time $t$ and time $T$ in order for the stock to be in-the-money at time $T$. For a call on a call, the sign is positive because the firm value must increase in both intervals. For a put on a call, the sign is negative because the firm value must be low enough for the compound option to be exercised at time $t$ and yet high enough to exceed the face value of the bonds at time $T$.

A European-style put option on the shares of the firm has a similar valuation equation. The value of the put is

$$p = Fe^{-rT} N_2(d_2,-a_1;-\rho) - VN_2(d_1,-a_1;-\rho) + Xe^{-rt} N_1(-a_2) \tag{12.16}$$

where all notation is defined above. In (12.16), $N_1(-a_2)$ is the risk-neutral probability that the asset price is below the critical firm value at time $t$, $V^*$. In this region, the compound option is exercised. The stock (i.e., underlying call) value, however, increases with the value of the firm. The correlation in the compound probability that is negative and the term, $N_2(d_2,-a_2;-\rho)$, is the risk-neutral compound probability that the firm value is below $V^*$ at time $t$ and exceeds the face value of the bonds $F$ at time $T$.

**ILLUSTRATION 12.5** Value corporate bond using stock and stock option price information.

*Assume that the firm's stock pays no dividends, has a price of 8, and has a volatility rate of 50%. Assume also there exists a six-month call option written on the stock, with an exercise price of 10 and a market price of 0.5312. The firm has a single issue of zero-coupon bonds outstanding. The face value of the bonds is 20, and their term to maturity is five years. Finally, the five-year zero-coupon interest rate on risk-free debt is 5%. Compute the value of the bonds.*

To compute the value of the bonds, we need to identify the value of the firm and the firm's volatility rate. To do so, we use information regarding the stock's price and its volatility rate with valuation equation (10.3) and the call's price with valuation equation (10.14). Our two equations are

$$8 = VN(d_1) - 20e^{-0.05(5)}N(d_2)$$

where

$$d_1 = \frac{\ln(Ve^{0.05(5)}/20) + 0.5\sigma_V^2 5}{\sigma_V\sqrt{5}} \text{ and } d_2 = d_1 - \sigma_V\sqrt{5}$$

and

$$0.5312 = VN_2(d_1, a_1; \rho) - 20e^{-0.05(5)}N_2(d_2, a_1; \rho) - 10e^{-0.05(5)}N_1(a_2)$$

where

$$a_1 = \frac{\ln(Ve^{0.05(5)}/V^*) + 0.5\sigma_V^2(0.5)}{\sigma\sqrt{0.5}}, \ a_2 = a_1 - \sigma_V\sqrt{0.5}, \text{ and } \rho = \sqrt{\frac{0.5}{5}}$$

Rather than compute these formula values by hand, we will use the OPTVAL functions

OV_CORP_STOCK_FIRM(*firm, face, t, r, vf, vind*)

which solves for the value of the firm's stock, and

OV_CORP_OPTION_FIRM(*firm, face, t, r, vf, cp, x, topt*)

which solves for the value of an option written on the firm's stock. The parameters of the functions are as before: *firm* is the value of the firm, *face* is the face value of the firm's zero-coupon bonds, *t* is the term to maturity of the bond's in years, *r* is the risk-free interest rate, and *vf* is the volatility rate of the firm. The term, *vind*, is an indicator variable whose value is set equal to 1 if the function is to return the stock's value and 2 if the function is to return the volatility rate. The additional parameters of the option valuation function are as follows: *cp* is a call/put indicator variable ("c" or "p"), *x* is option's exercise price, and *topt* is the time to expiration of the option. Using the problem information, the appropriate function calls are

8 = OV_CORP_STOCK_FIRM(*firm*, 20, 5, 0.05, *vf*,1)

and

0.5312 = OV_CORP_OPTION_FIRM(*firm*, 20, 5, 0.05, *vf*, "c",10, 0.5)

The Excel function SOLVER can be used to identify the values of *firm* and *vf* that allow the above expressions to hold exactly. The solution values for the value of the firm and its volatility rate are 22.503 and 21.02%. The value of the bonds is therefore 22.503 – 8.00 or 14.503.

## Computing Expected Returns on Corporate Securities

The mechanics used to value corporate securities can also be used to determine the relation between the expected rate of return and risk of different corporate securities. From Chapter 10, we know that if a risk-free hedge can be formed between each of the securities of the firm and the underlying value of the firm, the expected rate of return of security $i$ may be expressed as

$$E_i = r + (E_V - r)\eta_i \tag{12.17}$$

where $E_i$ is the expected rate of return of security $i$, $E_V$ is the expected rate of return of the firm, $r$ is the risk-free rate of interest, and $\eta_i$ is the security $i$'s eta (i.e., its price elasticity with respect to the firm value). As noted earlier in the chapter, the eta may be expressed as a function of delta, that is,

$$E_i = r + (E_V - r)\Delta_i\left(\frac{V}{V_i}\right) \tag{12.18}$$

where $V_i$ is the value of security $i$, and

$$\sum_{i=1}^{n} V_i = V$$

where $n$ is the number of securities of the firm. In the above illustrations, $n = 2$ since the firm has only two types of corporate securities—a zero-coupon bond and common stock.

**ILLUSTRATION 12.6** Compute expected returns for corporate bond and stock.

*Assume that the firm has a current value of 25, an expected rate of return of 12%, and a volatility rate of 20%. It has two securities outstanding—a zero-coupon bond and common stock. The bond matures in five years and has a face value of 20. The stock pays no dividends, and the risk-free rate of interest is 5%. Compute the expected rates of return and the volatility rates of the firm's bond and stock, and plot them in a figure showing expected return on the vertical axis and return volatility on the horizontal axis.*

The volatility rates of the bond and the stock may be computed using the OPTVAL functions

$\sigma_B$ = OV_CORP_BOND_FIRM(25, 20, 5, 0.05, 0.20, 2) = 3.35%

and

$\sigma_S$ = OV_CORP_STOCK_FIRM(25, 20, 5, 0.05, 0.20, 2) = 44.68%

which were introduced earlier in the chapter. The OPTVAL Function Library also contains functions for computing the deltas and etas of the bond and the stock. The syntax of the functions are

OV_CORP_BONDDELTA_FIRM(*firm, face, t, r, vf, gind*)

and

OV_CORP_STOCKDELTA_FIRM(*firm, face, t, r, vf, gind*),

where *firm* is the value of the firm, *face* is the face value of the firm's zero-coupon bonds, *t* is the term to maturity of the bond's in years, *r* is the risk-free interest rate, and *vf* is the volatility rate of the firm. The term, *gind*, is an indicator variable whose value is set equal to "d" or "D" if the function is to return the delta and "e" or "E" if the function is to return the volatility rate. For the illustration at hand,

$$\eta_B = \text{OV\_CORP\_BONDDELTA\_FIRM}(25, 20, 5, 0.05, 0.20, \text{"e"}) = 16.74\%$$

and

$$\eta_S = \text{OV\_CORP\_STOCKDELTA\_FIRM}(25, 20, 5, 0.05, 0.20, \text{"e"}) = 223.41\%$$

The expected returns for the bond and the stock are, therefore,

$$E_B = 0.05 + (0.12 - 0.05)0.1674 = 6.17\%$$

and

$$E_S = 0.05 + (0.12 - 0.05)2.2341 = 44.68\%$$

For the problem parameters, the expected return/risk attributes of the firm's securities fall on a straight line emanating from the risk-free interest rate:

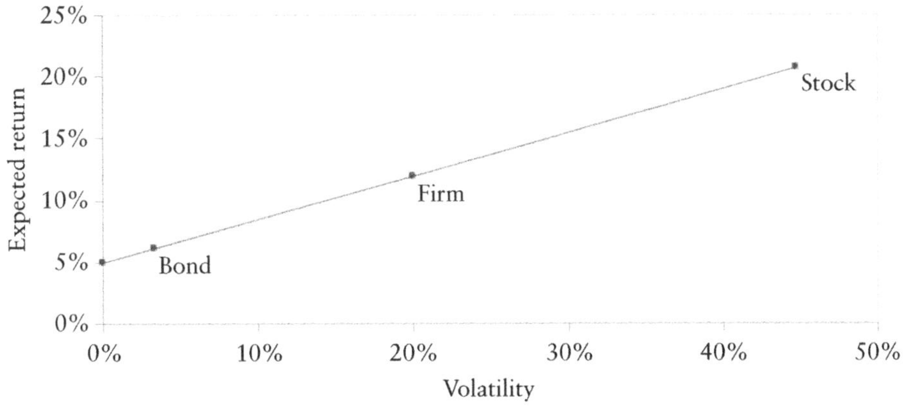


## VALUING SUBORDINATED DEBT

Subordinated debt refers to bonds of different seniority. Interest payments to bondholders follow a pecking order. The most senior bondholders are paid first, followed by the next most senior, and so on. In the event of bankruptcy, some tranches may be paid while others may not.

To value subordinated bond issues, we again begin with a framework in which we know the firm's value and volatility rate. Three bond issues are considered. They are labeled 1 through 3 in descending order of seniority. Their market values are denoted $B_1$, $B_2$, and $B_3$, and their respective face values are $F_1$, $F_2$, and $F_3$. All bonds are zero-coupon bonds and mature at time $T$. The notation $c(V,F)$ denotes the BSM call option formula value where the underlying asset price is $V$ and the option has an exercise price of $F$. To value each of the bond issues, we apply the valuation-by-replication technique.

The value of the most senior bond issue can be obtained using (12.4), that is,

$$B_1 = V - c(V,F_1) \tag{12.19}$$

In spirit, the most senior bondholders hold a portfolio in which they are long the value of the firm and short a call option whose exercise price equals the face value of the bonds. In other words, the senior bondholders own the firm but are not entitled to any firm value that goes beyond the face value of their bonds. The residual value goes to the remaining stakeholders of the firm.

Now, consider the bondholders with intermediate seniority. Again, bond valuation equation (12.4) applies in spirit. The intermediate bondholders are the firm value net of the value of the senior bonds, $V - B_1$, and are short a call option whose exercise price equals the sum of the face values of the senior and intermediate claims, $c(V, F_1 + F_2)$. The value of the intermediate bonds is therefore

$$B_2 = V - B_1 - c(V, F_1 + F_2) \tag{12.20}$$

The call option value in (12.20) represents the aggregate value of the remaining stakeholders of the firm—junior bondholders as well as the stockholders.

Finally, consider the most junior bondholders. The junior bondholders are long the firm value net of the senior and intermediate bondholder values, $V - B_1 - B_2$, and are short a call option whose exercise price equals the sum of the face amounts of all bond issues, $F_1 + F_2 + F_3$. This call is the value of the shareholders' claim since they receive the value of the firm's assets at the bonds' maturity net of the bondholder claims. The value of the junior bonds may be written

$$B_3 = V - B_1 - B_2 - c(V, F_1 + F_2 + F_3) \tag{12.21}$$

**ILLUSTRATION 12.7** Value subordinated bonds.

*Assume that the firm's value is 90, its expected return is 12%, and its volatility rate is 30%. Assume also that there are three issues of five-year, zero-coupon bonds outstanding. In decreasing order of seniority, they have face values of 50, 30, and 20. The risk-free interest rate is 4%. Compute the value of each bond issue, its expected rate of return, and its volatility rate.*

To value the bond issues, we begin with the most senior bonds and apply the valuation-by-replication principle. Holding the senior bonds is like being long the firm and short a call option with an exercise price of 50 and a time to expiration of five years. Using the BSM call option valuation formula, the call value is

OV_CORP_STOCK_FIRM(90, 50, 5, 0.04, 0.30, 1) = 51.382

Applying (12.19), the value of the most senior bond issue is 90 – 51.382 = 38.618. As noted earlier in the chapter, the expected rate of return of security $i$, is

$$E_i = r + (E_V - r)\Delta_i\left(\frac{V}{V_i}\right)$$

where $V_i$ is the value of security $i$, and

$$\sum_{i=1}^{n} V_i = V$$

where $n$ is the number of securities of the firm. In this illustration, $n$ = 4 since there are three bonds issues plus the common stock. The delta value for the most senior bonds equals one less the delta of a call on the firm with an exercise price of 50. The delta of the call may be computed using

OV_CORP_STOCKDELTA_FIRM(90, 50, 5, 0.04, 0.30, "D") = 0.9344

The delta of the senior bonds is, therefore, 1 – 0.9344 = 0.0656, and the expected rate of return of the senior bonds is

$$E_{B_1} = r + (E_V - r)\Delta_{B_1}\left(\frac{V}{B_1}\right)$$
$$= 0.04 + (0.12 - 0.04)(0.0656)\left(\frac{90}{36.618}\right) = 5.222\%$$

Finally, since the senior bond's eta equals

$$\eta_{B_1} = 0.0656\left(\frac{90}{36.618}\right) = 15.277\%$$

the volatility rate of the senior bond is $\sigma_{B_1} = \eta_{B_1}\sigma_V = 0.15277(0.30) = 4.583\%$.

To value the second most senior tranche, we apply the valuation-by-replication technique yet once again. Holding the intermediate bond is like being long the residual value of the firm after the most senior bondholders have been paid and being short a call option with an exercise price of 80 (i.e., the sum of the face values of the senior and intermediate bonds). Again, the BSM call option valuation formula can be applied. The call option value is

OV_CORP_STOCK_FIRM(90, 80, 5, 0.04, 0.30, 1) = 34.818

Thus the value of the intermediate bonds is 51.382 – 34.818 or 16.563. The combined delta of the senior and intermediate bonds equals one less the delta of a call on the firm with an exercise price of 80. The delta of the call may be computed using

OV_CORP_STOCKDELTA_FIRM(90, 80, 5, 0.04, 0.30, "D") = 0.7908

The delta of the intermediate bonds is therefore 1 – 0.7908 – 0.0636 = 0.1437. Consequently, its expected rate of return is

$$E_{B_2} = r + (E_V - r)\Delta_{B_2}\left(\frac{V}{B_2}\right)$$
$$= 0.04 + (0.12 - 0.04)(0.1437)\left(\frac{90}{16.563}\right) = 10.245\%$$

Finally, since the intermediate bond's eta equals

$$\eta_{B_1} = 0.0656\left(\frac{90}{36.618}\right) = 15.277\%$$

the volatility rate of the bond is $\sigma_{B_2} = 0.78065(0.30) = 23.419\%$.

Finally, holding the most junior bonds is like being long the residual value of the firm after the senior and intermediate bondholders have been paid and being short a call option with an exercise price of 100 and a time to expiration of 100. The BSM value of the call is

OV_CORP_STOCK_FIRM(90, 100, 5, 0.04, 0.30, 1) = 26.853

With only the junior bonds included with the stock, the value of the stock is 26.853. The value of the junior bonds, therefore, is the residual value less the stock value, 34.818 – 26.853, or 7.965. Similarly, the stock's delta is

OV_CORP_STOCKDELTA_FIRM(90, 100, 5, 0.04, 0.30, "D") = 0.6831

so the junior bond's delta must be 1 – 0.0656 – 0.1437 – 0.6831 = 0.1076. The junior bond's eta is 121.631%, its expected return is 13.371%, and its volatility rate is 36.489%.

As noted above, holding the stock of a firm is like holding a call option on the firm's value with the exercise price being equal to the sum of the face values of all bond issues. In this illustration, the stock value is 26.853, its delta is 0.6831, and its eta is 228.955%. Its expected rate of return is 22.316%, and its volatility rate is 68.687%. The table below summarizes all of the computations:

| Bond Issues | Face Value | Firm Value Before Claim | Call Value | Bond Value | Market Weight | Delta | Eta | Expected Return | Volatility Rate |
|---|---|---|---|---|---|---|---|---|---|
| Senior | 50 | 90.000 | 51.382 | 38.618 | 0.4291 | 0.0656 | 15.277% | 5.222% | 4.583% |
| Intermediate | 30 | 51.382 | 34.818 | 16.563 | 0.1840 | 0.1437 | 78.065% | 10.245% | 23.419% |
| Junior | 20 | 34.818 | 26.853 | 7.965 | 0.0885 | 0.1076 | 121.631% | 13.731% | 36.489% |
| Total bonds | | | | 63.147 | 0.7016 | 0.3169 | | | |
| Stock | | 26.853 | | 26.853 | 0.2984 | 0.6831 | 228.955% | 22.316% | 68.687% |
| Total | | | | 90.000 | 1.000 | 1.000 | | | |
| Market value weighted average | | | | | | | | 12.000% | 30.000% |

Note that a market-value, weighted averages of the expected rates of return and volatility rates of the individual corporate securities equals the assumed expected rate of return of the firm, 12%, and the assumed volatility rate of the firm, 30%. The following figure summarizes the expected return/risk relation for the bonds and the stock in this illustration.

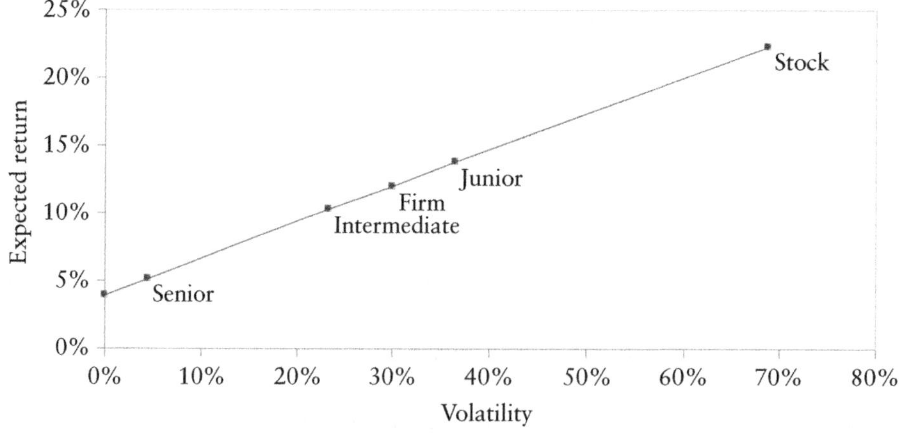

As was the case for the corporate bond discussed in the first section, the values of the securities other than the common stock are usually unknown. Consequently, the value of the firm, $V$, is unknown. In addition, since the price histories of the bonds are generally not available, it is impossible to develop a historical estimate the volatility rate of the firm, $\sigma_V$. Assuming the value of the stock and its volatility are known, we can solve for $V$ and $\sigma_V$ based on $S$ and $\sigma_S$ using the same iterative procedure as we used earlier. Assuming the value of the stock is observed in the marketplace is 26.583 and the stock's historical volatility rate is (coincidently)

$$0.6831\left(\frac{90}{26.583}\right)(0.30) = 68.69\%$$

(i.e., the assumed parameters in Illustration 12.7), the value of the firm is

OV_CORP_FIRM_STOCK(26.583, 100, 5, 0.04, 0.6869, 1) = 90

and the firm's volatility rate is

OV_CORP_FIRM_STOCK(26.583, 100, 5, 0.04, 0.6869, 2) = 0.30

Note that the exercise price in the above computations is the sum of the face values of all three bond issues in Illustration 12.7 (i.e., we treat all three bond issues as if they were one issue). Thus, we can perform the valuation of all three bond issues in Illustration 12.7 based on only on the knowledge of the current stock value and its volatility rate.

## VALUING WARRANTS

*Rights* and *warrants* are option-like securities issued by the firm. Usually they are attached to bond or preferred stock offerings by the firm in order to entice the buyers of the securities to accept lower coupon interest or dividend payments. Rights tend to be short-term and at-the-money when they are issued, and warrants tend to be long-term and out-of-the-money. Since there is little distinction between rights and warrants from a valuation standpoint, only the term, "warrants" is used in the remainder of this section.

Like call options, warrants provide holders with the right to buy the underlying stock at a predetermined price within a specified period of time. Unlike call options, however, warrants are issued by the firm. Since the exercise of the warrants creates more shareholders and the firm has a fixed amount of assets, exercising an in-the-money warrant dilutes the value of existing shares. This section focuses on warrant valuation in a manner that explicitly considers the effects of dilution induced by the prospect of warrant exercise.[9]

[9] The approach used here is based on Smith (1976).

To understand the effects of dilution on warrant (and stock) valuation, the BSM option valuation framework developed in Chapter 7 is again applied. The notation is as follows. The aggregate market value of the shares of the common stock currently outstanding is denoted $S$, and $n_S$ is the number of shares outstanding. The current share price is therefore $S/n_S$. Similarly, $W$ is the aggregate market value of the warrants currently outstanding, $n_W$ is the number of shares of stock sold to warrant holders if the warrants are exercised (for simplicity, one warrant is assumed to provide the right to buy one share), and $W/n_W$ is the current warrant price per share. The firm is assumed to have only two sources of financing, stock and warrants, so the aggregate market value of the firm is $V = S + B$. The total market value of the firm is assumed to be log-normally distributed at the warrants' expiration. The rate of return of the firm, $\ln(\tilde{V}_T/V)$, is therefore normally distributed and its variance is denoted $\sigma_V^2$. The stock is assumed to pay no dividends during the warrant's life. Finally, the warrant contract parameters are $T$, the time to expiration of warrants, and $X$, the aggregate exercise price of the warrants. The exercise price per share of stock is $X/n_W$. The proportion of the firm owned by warrant holders if they exercise their warrants is called the *dilution factor* and is denoted

$$\gamma = \frac{n_W}{n_S + n_W}$$

As usual, $r$ is the risk-free rate of interest.

To understand how to value warrants, first consider their value at expiration. At time $T$, the value of the firm's existing assets is $\tilde{V}_T$. If the warrants are in-the-money, the warrant holders will exercise, paying the firm $X$ is cash and driving the firm value to $\tilde{V}_T + X$. In return for paying $X$, the warrant holders receive proportion $\gamma$ of the value of the overall firm, that is, $\gamma(\tilde{V}_T + X)$. Thus the terminal value of the warrants may be written

$$\tilde{W}_T = \max[\gamma(\tilde{V}_T + X) - X, 0] \qquad (12.22)$$

Separating known from unknown values in (12.22),

$$\tilde{W}_T = \max[\gamma\tilde{V}_T - (1-\gamma)X, 0] \qquad (12.23)$$

Note the structure of the warrant value at expiration (12.23) is similar to the terminal value of a European-style call. The underlying asset price at expiration is $\gamma\tilde{V}_T$, which is log-normally distributed by assumption, and the exercise price is $(1 - \gamma)X$. It follows, therefore, that the current value of the warrants is

$$W = \gamma V N(d_1) - e^{-rT}(1 - \gamma)XN(d_2) \qquad (12.24)$$

where

$$d_1 = \frac{\ln\left[\frac{\gamma V e^{rT}}{(1-\gamma)X}\right] + 0.5\sigma_V^2 T}{\sigma\sqrt{T}} \text{ and } d_2 = d_1 - \sigma\sqrt{T}$$

The *market value per warrant* is simply $W$ from (12.24) divided by $n_W$.

Like in the case of corporate bond valuation, the warrant valuation equation (12.24) seems somewhat circular in the sense that the warrant value, $W$, appears on both sides of the equation—directly on the left-hand side of (12.24) and indirectly through $V$ (i.e., $W$ is embedded in $V$) on the right-hand side. This does not undermine the use of the formula, however. With all of the other valuation parameters known, we can find the value of $W$ that satisfies the equation using a numerical search procedure such as SOLVER in Excel. A pre-programmed function for valuing warrants, OV_CORP_WARRANT_STOCK, is also provided in the OPTVAL Function Library.

**ILLUSTRATION 12.8** Value warrant.

*Suppose that you have been hired by an internet firm to determine the worth of warrants written on the firm. In an initial public offering a few months ago, the firm sold 5 million shares of stock in the marketplace, while giving the employees of the firm 7 million shares with seven-year European-style warrants with an exercise price of \$35 per share on 7 million additional shares.*[10] *Compute the value of each warrant assuming the current stock price is \$40 per share, and the stock pays no dividends. The stock and the warrants are the firm's only two sources of financing. One warrant entitles its holder to one share of common stock. Assume that the risk-free rate of interest is 4%, and that the standard deviation of the rate of return of the firm is 30%. In the interest of completeness, compute the expected returns and volatility rates of the firm's stock and warrants assuming that the firm's expected return is 12%.*

In the event the warrants are exercised, the dilution factor is

$$\gamma = \frac{7{,}000{,}000}{12{,}000{,}000 + 7{,}000{,}000} = 36.84\%$$

That is, the warrant holders receive 36.84% of the firm value. The remaining shareholders are the investment public, with 26.32%, and the employees, with 36.84%. Prior to the exercise of the warrants, the investment public held 41.67% and the employees held 58.33%. The aggregate exercise proceeds from the exercise of the warrants are

$$X = 7{,}000{,}000 \times 35 = 245{,}000{,}000$$

and the current market value of the firm is

$$V = 12{,}000{,}000 \times 40 + W = 480{,}000{,}000 + W$$

The aggregate market value of the warrants is computed by solving

[10] Warrants are sometimes issued to provide incentives. For example, warrants may be issued to employees as an incentive to work hard. In doing so, they gather a greater share of the firm if it becomes successful.

$$W = 0.3684VN(d_1) - e^{-0.04(7)}0.6316(245{,}000{,}000)N(d_2)$$

where

$$d_1 = \frac{\ln\left[\frac{0.3684\,Ve^{0.04(7)}}{0.6316(245{,}000{,}000)}\right] + 0.5(0.30^2)(7)}{0.30\sqrt{7}} \quad \text{and } d_2 = d_1 - 0.30\sqrt{7}$$

The solution to this problem can be obtained using SOLVER in Excel. The aggregate warrant value is \$118,066,271 or \$16.867 per share. The intermediate computations for the final solution value are: $d_1 = 1.1949$, $d_2 = 0.4012$, $N(1.1949) = 0.8839$, and $N(0.4012) = 0.6559$. Alternatively, the warrant value can be computed using the OPTVAL function

OV_CORP_WARRANT_STOCK(*s, ns, nw, x, t, r, v, vfs, vind*)

where *s* is the current stock price, *ns* is the number of shares outstanding, *nw* is the number of warrants outstanding, *x* is the exercise price per share, *t* is the warrant's time to expiration in years, r is the risk-free interest rate, *v* is the volatility rate, *vfs* is either "V" or "S," depending upon whether the volatility rate is the volatility rate of the firm or of the stock, respectively, and *vind* is an indicator variable whose value is set equal to 1 if the function is to return the firm's value and 2 if the function is to return the firm's volatility rate. For the problem information at hand, the warrant value per share is

OV_CORP_WARRANT_STOCK(40, 12000000, 7000000, 35, 7, 0.04, 0.30, "V", 1)
= 16.867

and its volatility rate is

OV_CORP_WARRANT_STOCK(40, 12000000, 7000000, 35, 7, 0.04, 0.30, "V", 2)
= 0.4949

In order to compute the warrant's expected return, we need its eta. The warrant's delta is

OV_CORP_WARRANTDELTA_STOCK(40, 12000000, 7000000, 35, 7, 0.04, 0.30, "V", 1)
= 0.326

which means its eta is

$$0.326\left(\frac{598{,}066{,}271}{118{,}066{,}271}\right) = 164.97\%$$

and its expected return is

$$E_W = 0.04 + (0.12 - 0.04)1.6497 = 17.20\%$$

Since the warrant's delta is 0.326, the stock's delta is 0.674. The stock's eta is therefore,

$$0.674\left(\frac{598{,}066{,}271}{480{,}000{,}000}\right) = 0.8402$$

its expected return is

$$E_S = 0.04 + (0.12 - 0.04)0.8402 = 10.72\%$$

and its volatility rate is

$$\sigma_S = 0.8402(0.30) = 25.21\%$$

The expected return/volatility rate for each security is plotted in the figure below. The figure is unusual to the extent that the stock's return/risk parameters are below that of the firm. This arises because the firm has no securities more junior than stock.

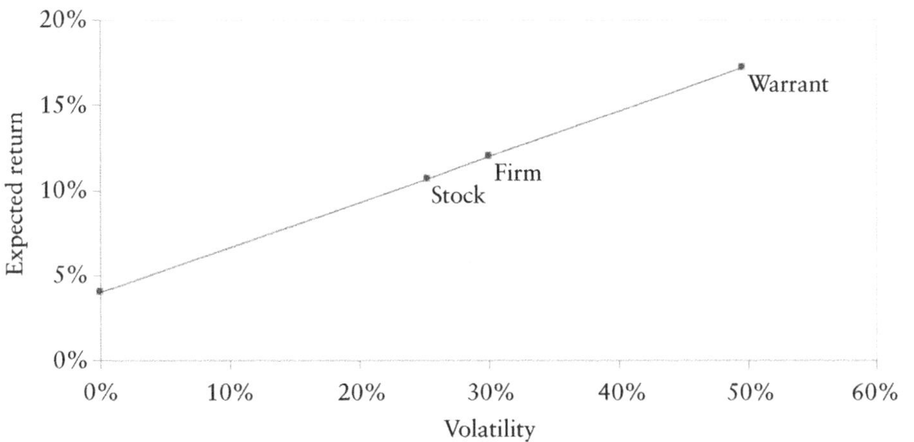


Illustration 12.8 assumes we can estimate the volatility rate of the firm, $\sigma_V$. Like corporate bonds, warrants are not actively traded. Without historical price series for both the stock and the warrant, we cannot obtain a history of firm values from which to estimate the historical rate of return volatility, $\sigma_V$. Fortunately, if we know the current value of the stock and the stock's volatility rate, we can solve for $V$ and $\sigma_V$ based on $S$ and $\sigma_S$ using the same iterative procedure as we used earlier. In Illustration 12.8, we know the current value of the stock is \$40 per share. Suppose we collect a history of stock prices and find that $\sigma_S = 25.21\%$. From discussions earlier in the chapter, we know that the return volatility of the stock may be expressed as a function of the return volatility of the firm, that is,

$$\sigma_S = N(d_1)\left(\frac{V}{S}\right)\sigma_V \tag{12.25}$$

Equation (12.25), together with (12.24), can be used to solve for $V$ and $\sigma_V$ uniquely. The OPTVAL function that performs this computation is

OV_CORP_WARRANT_STOCK(40, 12000000, 7000000, 35, 7, 0.04, 0.2521, "S", 1) = 16.867

Again, like in the case of corporate bonds, we can value warrants in a manner so as to incorporate the effects of dilution based on only on the knowledge of the current stock value and its volatility rate.

Before proceeding with the valuation of convertible bonds, it is worthwhile to assess the approximate magnitude of the effects of dilution. As noted earlier, it is not uncommon for individuals to value warrants using the BSM call option valuation formula with no adjustment for the effects of dilution. This practice overstates the warrant. The degree of bias is related to a number of the war-

**TABLE 12.1** Assessing the effects of potential dilution on warrant valuation for at-the-money warrants.

| Market/Warrant Parameters | | Dilution Factor | Warrant Value | Call Option Value | Percent Difference |
|---|---|---|---|---|---|
| *Stock* | | | | | |
| Price | 40.00 | 5.00% | 23.028 | 23.065 | 0.161% |
| No. of shares | 10,000,000 | 10.00% | 22.987 | 23.065 | 0.338% |
| Volatility type | S | 15.00% | 22.943 | 23.065 | 0.533% |
| Volatility rate | 40.00% | 20.00% | 22.894 | 23.065 | 0.748% |
| | | 25.00% | 22.840 | 23.065 | 0.986% |
| Warrant | | 30.00% | 22.780 | 23.065 | 1.251% |
| Exercise price | 40.00 | 35.00% | 22.713 | 23.065 | 1.548% |
| Years to expiration | 10 | 40.00% | 22.639 | 23.065 | 1.882% |
| | | 45.00% | 22.555 | 23.065 | 2.263% |
| Market | | 50.00% | 22.461 | 23.065 | 2.691% |
| Interest rate ($r$) | 4.00% | 55.00% | 22.352 | 23.065 | 3.188% |
| | | 60.00% | 22.227 | 23.065 | 3.768% |
| | | 65.00% | 22.082 | 23.065 | 4.454% |
| | | 70.00% | 21.908 | 23.065 | 5.281% |
| | | 75.00% | 21.697 | 23.065 | 6.304% |

rant's underlying parameters, particularly the dilution factor. For Illustration 12.8, the BSM value is

OV_OPTION_VALUE(40, 35, 7, 0.04, 0.00, 0.2521, "c", "e") = 16.983

which means that using the BSM formula overstates value by 11.6 cents. Table 12.1 shows the effects of the dilution factor on warrant valuation in more detail. For the assumed warrant valuation parameters, the degree of bias is only 0.161% when the dilution factor is 5%, however, the degree of bias is more than 2.5% when the dilution factor is 50%.

## VALUING CONVERTIBLE BONDS

A *convertible bond* is a hybrid security with bond-like and option-like features. Like a corporate bond, it promises to make periodic coupon interest payments throughout its life and then to repay the principal at some fixed maturity date. Also, like a corporate bond, there is a risk of default if the firm fails to make an interest payment or repay the principal at maturity. Aside from the bond features, however, a convertible bond allows its holder to exchange the bond for shares of the firm's stock. On first appearance, it may seem to be the case that a convertible bond may be valued by replication as the sum of the values of a corporate bond and a warrant, both of which we have already valued. Unfortunately, this is not the case because the bond must be forfeit in order to receive the shares. In this sense, it is like an exchange option of one risky asset for another.[11]

To value convertible bonds, we use the same approach that we used for corporate bonds and warrants. We assume that the firm has two sources of financing—common stock and convertible bonds. The market value of all shares outstanding is $S$, and the market value of the convertible bonds is $CV$. Thus, the value of the firm is $V = S + CV$. For convenience, the convertible bonds are assumed to be discount bonds. The market value of the overall firm is assumed to be log-normally distributed when the bond's mature. The number of shares outstanding is $n_S$, the number of shares underlying the convertible bonds $n_{CV}$, and $F$ is the face value of the bonds. The firm's volatility rate is $\sigma_V$, and $r$ is the risk-free rate of interest.

The bondholder's decision to convert at the bond's expiration depends on whether the per share market value of the stock exceeds the implicit exercise price of the embedded option, that is,

$$\frac{\tilde{V}_T}{n_S + n_{CV}} - \frac{F}{n_{CV}} > 0 \tag{12.26}$$

The first term on the left hand-side is the per share value of the stock if the convertibility option is exercised. The second term on the left-hand side is the exercise price per share being paid by the bond holder if he chooses to exercise. This is not a cash exercise price; the bond holder merely forfeits the face value (principal repayment) of the bond in return for shares of higher value.

To express things at an aggregate level, multiply the left-hand side of (12.26) by $n_{CV}$ and substitute the dilution factor,

$$\gamma = \frac{n_{CV}}{n_S + n_{CV}}$$

Like in the case of warrants, the exercise of in-the-money convertible bonds dilutes the value of the existing shareholders' equity. The convertibility option has a terminal value of $\max(\gamma V_T - X, 0)$ at time $T$, that is, the convertible bondholder will elect to exchange his bond for stock if it is profitable to do so. Applying the BSM call option valuation formula, we find that the value of the convertibility option is

$$c(\gamma V, F) = \gamma V N(d_1) - Fe^{-rT} N(d_2) \tag{12.27}$$

where

[11] Recall that exchange options were valued in Chapter 8. That framework is not directly applicable here since there is only one source of uncertainty (i.e., the firm's value) and dilution must be considered.

$$d_1 = \frac{\ln[\gamma V e^{rT}/F] + 0.5\sigma_V^2 T}{\sigma_V\sqrt{T}} \text{ and } d_2 = d_1 - \sigma_V\sqrt{T}$$

Applying the corporate bond valuation equation (12.8), the current value of the convertible bonds is therefore

$$CV = Fe^{-rT} - p(V,F) + c(\gamma V,F) \tag{12.28}$$

where $p(V,F)$ is the BSM put option value for a put written on $V$ with exercise price $F$. In other words, the value of the convertible bonds equals the value of risk-free bond with the same face amount and maturity date as the convertible bond less the value of the put option providing the firm with the right to put the assets of the firm to the bondholders in the event of default plus the value of the option to convert the bond into shares if it profitable to do so.

**ILLUSTRATION 12.9** Value convertible bonds.

*Assume that the firm's value is 12,000 and its volatility rate is 30%. Assume also that the stock pays no dividends, and there are currently 400 shares outstanding. The firm's convertible bond has a face value of 4,000, has five years to maturity, and may be exchanged into 100 shares of stock. The risk-free rate of interest is 4%. Compute the convertible bond value, the share price, and the aggregate value of stocks and bonds outstanding. Also, compute and plot the expected rates of return and volatility rates of all securities.*

First, compute the value of the risk-free bonds, that is,

$$Fe^{-rT} = 4{,}000e^{-0.04(5)} = 3{,}274.92$$

Next compute the value of the firm's put option to default. Since the face value of the bonds is 4,000 and the value of the firm is 12,000, the bonds are close to risk-free and the put option is worth only 40.52, and the value of the corporate bond without the convertibility feature is 3,274.92 – 40.52 = 3,234.41. This computation can be performed using the OPTVAL function

OV_CORP_BOND_FIRM(12000, 4000, 5, 0.04, 0.30, 1) = 3,234.41

Finally, we compute the value of the option to convert. The dilution factor is

$$\gamma = \frac{100}{400 + 100} = 20\%$$

The aggregate value of the call option to convert is 382.85; therefore the current value of the convertible bond is

$$3{,}274.92 - 40.52 + 382.85 = 3{,}617.26$$

A convertible bond valuation function is included in the OPTVAL library. The function is

OV_CORP_CVBOND_FIRM(*firm, ns, ncb, face, t, r, vf, vind*)

where *firm* is the firm value, *ns* is the number of shares of stock outstanding, *ncb* is the number of shares underlying the convertible bonds, *face* is the face value of the convertible bonds, *t* is the term to maturity of the bonds in years, *r* is the risk-free interest rate, and $vf$ is the volatility rate of the firm. The term $vind$ is an indicator variable. A value of 1 returns the convertible bond value and 2 returns the convertible bond volatility rate. For the problem at hand,

$$\text{OV\_CORP\_CVBOND\_FIRM}(12000, 400, 100, 4000, 5, 0.04, 0.30, 1) = 3{,}617.26$$

With the convertible bond value being 3,617.26, the value of the firm's common stock is

$$S = V - B = 12{,}000 - 3{,}617.26 = 8{,}382.74$$

and the firm's share price is

$$\frac{8{,}382.74}{400} = 20.96$$

The expected rate of return and volatility rate for each of the firm's securities can be computed in the same manner as previous illustrations. For convenience, the expected return and volatility rate of a straight bond with the same face value and maturity as the convertible bond are also computed. The results are as follows:

| Security | Expected Return | Volatility |
|---|---|---|
| Risk-free | 4.00% | 0.00% |
| Bond | 4.34% | 1.29% |
| Stock | 10.18% | 23.16% |
| Firm | 12.00% | 30.00% |
| Convertible bond | 16.23% | 45.85% |

The figure below shows that all securities fall on a line emanating from the risk-free rate of interest. The straight bond is nearly risk-free and lies at the extreme left of the figure. The convertible bond, on the other hand, is more risky than the stock given its embedded option. For the parameters of this problem, the expected return/risk characteristics of the stock are below those of the firm.

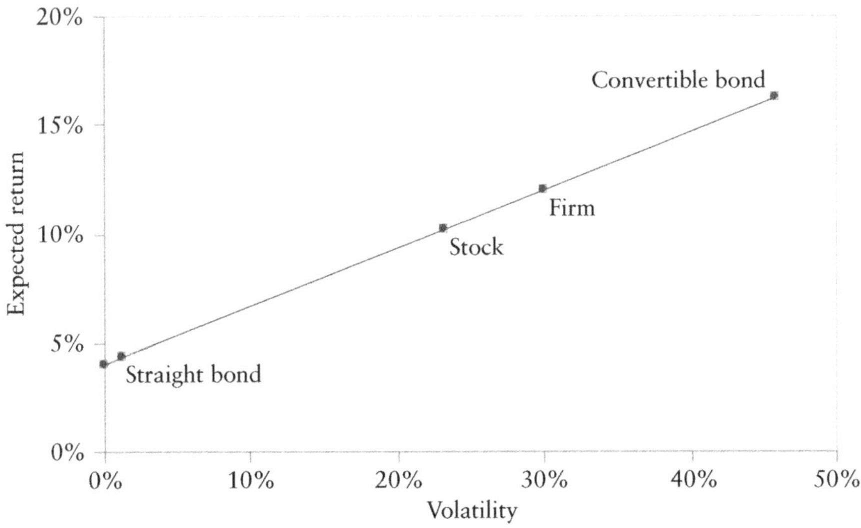

Illustration 12.9 is intended only to illustrate the convertible bond valuation mechanics. Like in the previous valuation problems of this chapter, it is generally the case that the value of the firm, $V$, and the volatility rate of the firm, $\sigma_V$, are not known. But again we can circumvent the problem by using the value of the stock, $S$, and the volatility rate of the stock, $\sigma_S$. To understand how to do this, note that equation (12.28) is incomplete. If we know the value of the stock, we can write the value of the firm as the sum of the values of the stock and the convertible bonds, that is,

$$V = S + Fe^{-rT} - p(V,F) + c(\gamma V,F) \tag{12.29}$$

We also know that the relation between the volatility of the stock and the volatility of the firm is

$$\sigma_S = \eta_S \sigma_V \tag{12.30}$$

Assuming the value of the stock $S$ and its volatility $\sigma_S$ are known, we can solve uniquely for $V$ and $\sigma_V$. For the sake of illustration, assume that the current value of the common shares of the firm is 8,382.74. Also, assume that a history of stock prices was collected and that the estimate of the historical stock return volatility is 23.16% (which just happens to equal the

$$0.5393\left(\frac{12{,}000}{8{,}382.74}\right)(0.30) = 0.2316$$

in Illustration 12.9. With two equations, (12.29) and (12.30), and two unknowns, we can solve uniquely for $V$ and $\sigma_V$ using Excel's SOLVER function. Alternatively, OPTVAL includes the function

OV_CORP_CV_FIRM_STOCK(*stock, ns, ncb, face, t, r, vs, vind*)

where *stock* is the value of the stock, *ns* is the number of shares of stock, *ncb* is the number of shares underlying the convertible bonds, *face*, is the face value of the bonds, *t* is the term to maturity of the bonds in years, *r* is the risk-free interest rate, and *vs* is the volatility rate of the stock. The argument *vind* is an indicator telling the function to return the firm value 1 or the firm volatility rate 2. Applying the function

OV_CORP_CV_FIRM_STOCK(8382.74, 400, 100, 4000, 5, 0.04, 0.2316, 1) = 12,000

and

OV_CORP_CV_FIRM_STOCK(8382.74, 400, 100, 4000, 5, 0.04, 0.2316, 2) = 0.50

We can then value the convertible bonds of the firm using market information for only the common shares, that is, the current stock value and its volatility rate.

## SUMMARY

In this chapter, we show how to value an array of different types of corporate securities using only information about the firm's common stock price and the stock's volatility rate. This is possible because we assume that there is a single source of uncertainty—the firm's value. With a single source of uncertainty, all of the firm's securities have price movements that are perfectly correlated with one another over short periods of time. Thus, under the BSM assumptions, all corporate securities can be valued using information about the price and volatility rate of any *one* of the firm's outstanding securities. We use the firm's common stock because, of all the firm's securities, it has the deepest and most active secondary market.

In the model's development, we simplify the firm's securities in order to focus on the economic intuition underlying valuation. Initially, we assume that the firm has two sources of financing—common stock and bonds. The common stock pays no dividends, and bonds pay no coupons. Under these assumptions, the firm's common stock is a European-style call option written on the value of the firm, where the exercise price and time to expiration of the option equal the face value and term to maturity of the firm's zero-coupon bonds, respectively. The firm's bond value, in turn, equals the firm value less the value of the stock. Due to European-style put-call parity, it also equals the value of a risk-free bond less the value of a European-style put option that allows the managers of the firm to put the firm's assets to the bondholders if asset value falls below the face value of the bonds. While the model becomes more complicated when bonds pay coupons and stocks pay dividends and valuation requires using the lattice-based procedures such as those described in Chapter 9, the economic intuition remains intact.

We then extend the model to include other types of corporate securities such as warrants and convertible bonds. For expositional convenience, we assume that the (embedded) options in these securities are European-style. In this way, we can apply the BSM formula directly and use it to develop the economic intuition regarding the valuation problem. In practice, both warrants and convertible bonds may be exercised at any time during the option's life, and convertible bonds are often callable by the firm. These valuation considerations can be handled using lattice-based procedures (as opposed to analytical formulas).

Finally, while it is beyond the scope of the chapter, the model can be generalized to handle multiple sources of uncertainty. Corporate bond prices, for example, may change for reasons other than firm value changes (e.g., changes in the level of interest rates). Again, numerical methods are used to address such valuation problems. The lattice-based procedures (e.g., the binomial and trinomial methods) and Monte Carlo simulation techniques described in Chapter 9 can be modified to handle multiple sources of underlying risk.

## REFERENCES AND SUGGESTED READINGS

Black, Fischer, and Myron Scholes. 1973. The pricing of options and corporate liabilities. *Journal of Political Economy* 81: 637–659.

Campbell, John Y., and Glen B. Taksler. 2003. Equity volatility and corporate bond yields. *Journal of Finance* 58: 2321–2349.

Duffee, Gregory R. 1999. Estimating the price of default risk. *Review of Financial Studies* 12: 197–226.

Galai, Dan, and Ronald W. Masulis. 1976. The option pricing model and the risk factor of stock. *Journal of Financial Economics* 3: 53–81.

Geske, Robert. 1979. The valuation of compound options. *Journal of Financial Economics* 7: 63–81.

Kwan, Simon. 1996. Firm-specific information and the correlation between individual stocks and bonds. *Journal of Financial Economics* 40: 63–80.

Longstaff, Francis A., and Eduardo S. Schwartz. 1995. Valuing risky debt: A new approach. *Journal of Finance* 50: 789–820.

Merton, Robert C. 1974. On the pricing of corporate debt: The risk structure of interest rates. *Journal of Finance* 29: 449–470.

Merton, Robert C. 1973. Theory of rational option pricing. *Bell Journal of Economics and Management Science* 4: 141–183.

Smith Jr., Clifford W. 1977. Alternative methods for raising capital: Rights versus underwritten offerings. *Journal of Financial Economics* 5: 273–307.

Vassalou, Maria, and Yuhang Xing. 2004. Default risk in equity returns. *Journal of Finance* 59 (April): 831–868.

# 13 Compensation Agreements

Firms often struggle with identifying appropriate compensation packages for their employees. One important ingredient in designing such a package is stock ownership. By providing employees with the shares of the firm, or claims on the shares of the firm, management aligns the interests of employees with those of owners (i.e., the shareholders). Two common contracts used in this context are an *employee stock option* (ESO) and an *employee stock purchase plan* (ESPP). Like a warrant, an ESO is a call option contract issued by the firm. Typically, ESOs are at-the-money at the time of issuance (i.e., the exercise price is set equal to the stock price) and have terms to expiration of ten years. Over the first few (usually three) years, the options cannot be exercised. This is called the *vesting period*. If the employee leaves the firm during the vesting period, the options are forfeit. After the vesting date, the options can be exercised at any time but are *nontransferable*. Because they are nontransferable, the only way for the employee to capitalize on its value is to exercise the option. An ESPP allows the employee to buy the company's stock at a discount, usually 15%, within a certain period of time, typically six months. Some the ESPP includes a lookback provision that allows its holder to apply the discount to either the end-of-period or the beginning-of-period stock price, whichever is less.

The purpose of this chapter is to describe how to value some of the different types of stock compensation contracts that exist in practice. The first section shows that standard ESOs can be valued as call options, even though they have longer terms to expiration, greater dividend uncertainty, and vesting considerations. The second section addresses the valuation effects of the vesting period. As it turns out, unless the employee leaves the firm before the vesting period is up, being precluded from exercising the option has little effect on ESO value. The third section examines the consequences of the practice of using a constant dividend yield model to value ESOs. The resulting valuation errors may be quite large. The fourth section focuses on ESO valuation in circumstances where employees are known to exercise their options early, even though it is suboptimal to do so. We then turn to valuing two important, albeit more specialized, employee stock options—ESOs with indexed exercise prices in the fifth section and ESOs with reload features in the sixth. The last section of the chapter focuses on the valuation of ESPPs.

## STANDARD EMPLOYEE STOCK OPTIONS

Like warrants and convertible bonds, the exercise of employee stock options (ESOs) dilutes the value of existing shares. For most employee stock option plans, however, the existing shareholder base is so large that the dilution factor and the effect on ESO valuation are small. Consequently, the BSM call option valuation equations/ methods that we applied to exchanged-traded stock options in Chapter 11 can also be applied here. All that is needed are estimates of the interest rate, the expected dividend stream, and the expected volatility rate.

Given the long-term nature of ESOs, we need to be especially careful in estimating the parameters that go into determining option value. Small changes in the parameter values can produce large changes in value. Probably the best estimate for the risk-free interest rate is the continuously compounded yield on a U.S. Treasury strip bond with the same maturity date as the ESO. Recall from Chapter 2 that this rate is computed using the transformation,

$$r = \frac{\ln(100/B)}{T}$$

where $B$ is the price of the strip bond as a percentage of par, and $T$ is the term to maturity of the bond expressed in years. The expected dividend stream for the underlying stock should account for the discrete nature of quarterly cash dividend payments. In Chapter 11, we discussed dividend payment practices by U.S. firms. In that discussion, we noted that firms tend to (1) pay the same cash dividend each quarter throughout the year; (2) pay the quarterly dividends at the same times each year; and (3) increase the annual total cash dividends at a constant rate through time. Consequently, projecting the amount and timing of quarterly cash dividends over the ESO's life is not as difficult as it might seem at first blush.[1] Finally, to estimate the volatility parameter, historical return data should be used.[2] It is probably a good idea to use weekly returns rather than daily returns to mitigate the effects of measurement errors in prices.[3] The length of the return history needs to be at least as long as the ESO's life to so that we can be comfortable that we are seeing the firm's share price across of the range of business cycles that it might face over such a long period. Where the firm is newly-listed and does not have a long price history, all available price data should be used. Then, it would then be wise to compare the estimate against the historical volatility estimates of the stocks in the firm's peer group.

[1] Naturally, more thought must be given to situations in which the firm does not currently pay dividends but may do so during the life of the option. One potentially useful source of information is the dividend yield levels of firms in a comparable peer group.

[2] The best estimate of volatility is the implied volatility from exchange-traded options on the firm's stock. But, this is true only if the exchange-traded options have the same time to expiration as the ESOs. In general, this is not the case—exchange-traded stock options have much shorter times to expiration than ESOs. Consequently, implied volatility from short-term options is a very noisy predictor of expected long-term volatility.

[3] Recall that the effects of measurement errors were discussed at the end of Chapter 7.

In valuing employee stock options, the effects of discrete cash dividend payments need to be recognized explicitly. Using a constant dividend yield assumption can produce significant errors, as we will show later in the chapter. Discrete dividends have a distinctly different effect on early exercise than continuous dividends. Recall that, in Chapter 6, it was shown that an American-style call will not optimally be exercised just prior to a dividend payment if the amount of the dividend is less than the present value of the interest that can be earned implicitly on the exercise price by holding the option,[4] that is,

$$D_i < X(1 - e^{-r(t_{i+1} - t_i)}) \tag{13.1}$$

A quick check of the projected cash dividends will tell us if early exercise is likely or not. Suppose that we are valuing a 10-year, at-the-money stock option. The stock price is 100, and the stock's volatility rate is 36%. The firm's next quarterly dividend is to be paid in 20 days and will be 1.00 per share. The same dividend is expected to be paid for the next three quarters. The quarterly dividends (the same each quarter) are expected to grow by 5% annually. The quarterly dividends in the second year, therefore, are projected to be 1.0513 (= $1.00e^{0.05}$). In the final year, the quarterly dividends are 1.568. Now, compare these dividend amounts to the present value of the interest income that will be earned implicitly by deferring exercise. The amount for all quarters except for the last is

$$PVInt_i = X(1 - e^{-r(t_{i+1} - t_i)}) = 100(1 - e^{-0.07(91/365)}) = 1.730$$

as is shown in Table 13.1. Comparing each quarterly dividend with this amount shows that early exercise will not be optimal until the very last quarter of the option's life, if at all. In the last quarter, the present value of the interest income is

$$PVInt_{40} = 100(1 - e^{-0.07(81/365)}) = 1.541$$

which means that early exercise just prior to the last dividend payment *may* be optimal. The maximum amount of the early exercise premium, however, is small. The maximum gain from exercising just prior to the last dividend is 1.568 – 1.541 = 0.027. The maximum gain is the present value of this amount or 0.014, as indicated in the table. Indeed, the actual early exercise premium is trivial. The OPTVAL Function Library contains binomial and trinomial routines for valuing European- and American-style options on dividend-paying stocks. The syntax of the function call for the binomial method is

OV_STOCK_OPTION_VALUE_BIN(*s, x, t, r, v, n, cp, ae, mthd, dvd, tdvd*)

where *s* is the current stock price, *x* is the exercise price, *t* is the time to expiration, *r* is the risk-free interest rate, *v* is the stock's volatility rate, *cp* is a (c)all/(p)ut indicator, *ae* is an (A)merican/(E)uropean-style option indicator, *mthd* is

[4] This was condition (6.16) in Chapter 6.

**TABLE 13.1** Evaluating the optimality of early exercise for a long-term employee stock option.

| Stock | |
|---|---|
| Price ($S$) | 100 |
| Current dividend ($D_1$) | 1.0000 |
| Dividend growth ($g$) | 5.00% |
| No. of days to 1st divd. | 20 |
| Volatility rate ($\sigma$) | 36.00% |
| **Market** | |
| Interest rate ($r$) | 7.00% |
| **Option parameters** | |
| Exercise price ($X$) | 100 |
| Years to expiration ($T$) | 10.00 |
| **Discrete dividend assumption:** | |
| *PVD* | 35.571 |
| *S-PVD* | 64.429 |
| Call option value | |
| European-style, analytical ($c$) | 32.529 |
| European-style, binomial ($c$) | 32.523 |
| American-style, binomial ($C$) | 32.523 |
| Final dividend | 1.568 |
| Days remaining | 81 |
| Present value of interest | 1.541 |
| Maximum gain from exercise | 0.027 |
| Maximum exercise premium | 0.014 |
| **Continuous dividend yield assumption:** | |
| Implied dividend yield | 4.396% |
| Call option value (yield) | |
| European-style, analytical ($c$) | 32.529 |
| European-style, binomial ($c$) | 32.522 |
| American-style, binomial ($C$) | 37.271 |
| Difference | 4.748 |
| Percent error | 14.60% |
| No. of time steps | 1,000 |
| Method | 2 |

| Quarterly Dividends | | | | | |
|---|---|---|---|---|---|
| $i$ | Days | $t_i$ | $D_i$ | $PVInt_i$ | $PV(D_i)$ |
| 1 | 20 | 0.0548 | 1.0000 | 1.730 | 0.9962 |
| 2 | 111 | 0.3041 | 1.0000 | 1.730 | 0.9789 |
| 3 | 202 | 0.5534 | 1.0000 | 1.730 | 0.9620 |
| 4 | 293 | 0.8027 | 1.0000 | 1.730 | 0.9454 |
| 5 | 384 | 1.0521 | 1.0513 | 1.730 | 0.9766 |
| 6 | 475 | 1.3014 | 1.0513 | 1.730 | 0.9597 |
| 7 | 566 | 1.5507 | 1.0513 | 1.730 | 0.9431 |
| 8 | 657 | 1.8000 | 1.0513 | 1.730 | 0.9268 |
| 9 | 748 | 2.0493 | 1.1052 | 1.730 | 0.9575 |
| 10 | 839 | 2.2986 | 1.1052 | 1.730 | 0.9409 |
| 11 | 930 | 2.5479 | 1.1052 | 1.730 | 0.9246 |
| 12 | 1,021 | 2.7973 | 1.1052 | 1.730 | 0.9086 |
| 13 | 1,112 | 3.0466 | 1.1618 | 1.730 | 0.9387 |
| 14 | 1,203 | 3.2959 | 1.1618 | 1.730 | 0.9225 |
| 15 | 1,294 | 3.5452 | 1.1618 | 1.730 | 0.9065 |
| 16 | 1,385 | 3.7945 | 1.1618 | 1.730 | 0.8908 |
| 17 | 1,476 | 4.0438 | 1.2214 | 1.730 | 0.9203 |
| 18 | 1,567 | 4.2932 | 1.2214 | 1.730 | 0.9044 |
| 19 | 1,658 | 4.5425 | 1.2214 | 1.730 | 0.8887 |
| 20 | 1,749 | 4.7918 | 1.2214 | 1.730 | 0.8733 |
| 21 | 1,840 | 5.0411 | 1.2840 | 1.730 | 0.9022 |
| 22 | 1,931 | 5.2904 | 1.2840 | 1.730 | 0.8866 |
| 23 | 2,022 | 5.5397 | 1.2840 | 1.730 | 0.8713 |
| 24 | 2,113 | 5.7890 | 1.2840 | 1.730 | 0.8562 |
| 25 | 2,204 | 6.0384 | 1.3499 | 1.730 | 0.8845 |
| 26 | 2,295 | 6.2877 | 1.3499 | 1.730 | 0.8692 |
| 27 | 2,386 | 6.5370 | 1.3499 | 1.730 | 0.8542 |
| 28 | 2,477 | 6.7863 | 1.3499 | 1.730 | 0.8394 |
| 29 | 2,568 | 7.0356 | 1.4191 | 1.730 | 0.8672 |
| 30 | 2,659 | 7.2849 | 1.4191 | 1.730 | 0.8522 |
| 31 | 2,750 | 7.5342 | 1.4191 | 1.730 | 0.8374 |
| 32 | 2,841 | 7.7836 | 1.4191 | 1.730 | 0.8230 |
| 33 | 2,932 | 8.0329 | 1.4918 | 1.730 | 0.8502 |
| 34 | 3,023 | 8.2822 | 1.4918 | 1.730 | 0.8355 |
| 35 | 3,114 | 8.5315 | 1.4918 | 1.730 | 0.8210 |
| 36 | 3,205 | 8.7808 | 1.4918 | 1.730 | 0.8068 |
| 37 | 3,296 | 9.0301 | 1.5683 | 1.730 | 0.8335 |
| 38 | 3,387 | 9.2795 | 1.5683 | 1.730 | 0.8191 |
| 39 | 3,478 | 9.5288 | 1.5683 | 1.730 | 0.8049 |
| 40 | 3,569 | 9.7781 | 1.5683 | 1.541 | 0.7910 |

the choice of binomial coefficients (2 is JR coefficients),[5] *dvd* is a cash dividend vector, and *tdvd* is a vector containing the time to the dividend payments. Using this function, the values of European-style and American-style calls are both 32.523. In other words, the early exercise premium is less than 1/10 of one penny. It is also worth noting that the values obtained using the binomial model are slightly less than that obtained using the BSM European-style option valuation formula. This amount, less than a penny, is approximation error.

One last caveat—by most accounts, the assumed dividend payment stream is extremely generous. The implicit dividend yield exceeds 4% annually. This is high by U.S. standards. With smaller dividends, the probability of early exercise becomes even smaller. What this means is that little is lost by valuing the American-style employee stock option using the European-style valuation equation. Simply subtract the present value of the promised dividends over the option's life from the current stock price and apply the BSM formula. The formula value, 32.529, is also reported in Table 13.1.

## VESTING PERIOD

Most employee stock options have a vesting period just after they are issued during which time option exercise is prohibited. Typically, the vesting period runs three years. While, intuitively, one might think that prohibiting the exercise of the ESO during the vesting period reduces the ESO value, it does not. In the ESO valuation problem shown in Table 13.1 and discussed above, we demonstrated that early exercise is seldom optimal. Indeed, using the binomial method, the value of the American-style call was identically equal to the value of the European-style call, so the early exercise premium was, for all practical purposes, valueless. Thus, for the valuation problem at hand, prohibiting exercise during the vesting period, or at any time during the ESO's life for that matter, has no economic value holding other factors constant. If early exercise may be optimal, the effects of vesting can be handled within the binomial framework by not checking the early exercise boundaries during the vesting period.

## EARLY EXERCISE

Based on the discussion in the preceding sections, using a cash-dividend-adjusted version of the BSM call option valuation formula seems entirely appropriate for valuing ESOs. Some argue that this practice overstates the true value of the ESO because its assumes that the option holder will never exercise early since it is not optimal to do so. As a practical matter, this is not the case. If an employee voluntarily or involuntarily leaves the firm in the postvesting period, he must exercise the ESO since it is not transferable. This makes the BSM value using the stated expiration of the ESO too high. A quick-and-dirty fix to this

[5] Chapter 9 contains a description of three sets of coefficients that may be used in the binomial method.

problem is to replace the stated time for expiration with an expected time to expiration based on the historical employment records of the firm.[6]

Perhaps, more important, however, is that, for many ESO holders, the value of the options represents a significant portion of their wealth. Exercising early offers the employee the opportunity to cash-in and diversify a relatively undiversified portfolio. On this matter, there is empirical evidence to suggest that employees tend to exercise ESOs when the stock price reaches certain multiples of the option's exercise price. As it turns out, this type of behavior can be accommodated easily with lattice-based valuation procedures like the binomial method. We simply impose a barrier on the stock price lattice, and, where the stock price at a particular node in the lattice exceeds the barrier, we replace the option value at that node with the option's exercise proceeds.

**ILLUSTRATION 13.1** Value ESO with maximum stock price.

*Compute the value of a 10-year, at-the-money ESO where the holder plans to exercise when the stock price is twice as high as the option's exercise price. Assume that the underlying stock has a price of 50, a volatility rate of 40%, and pays no dividends. The risk-free rate of interest is 7%. Use the binomial method with the CRR coefficients and two time steps.*

The first step in the binomial method is to compute the stock price lattice. To do so, we compute the up-step and down-step coefficients, $u$ and $d$, for the CRR method outlined in Chapter 9. Using the problem parameters, the numerical values are

$$u = e^{0.40\sqrt{5}} = 2.4459 \quad \text{and} \quad d = \frac{1}{u} = \frac{1}{2.4459} = 0.4088$$

Starting at time 0 with a stock price of 50, the stock price lattice becomes

**Stock Price Lattice**

| Time | 0 | 1 | 2 |
|---|---|---|---|
| | | | 299.130 |
| | | 122.297 | |
| | 50.000 | | 50.000 |
| | | 20.442 | |
| | | | 8.358 |

The second step in the binomial method is to value the option at expiration at each stock price node. For a call, the value is the maximum of 0 and the difference between the stock price and the exercise price, $\max(0, S_{i,j} - X)$. The bold values at time 2 in the table below are the terminal option values.

[6] This adjustment is inexact because the BSM option value is a nonlinear function to time to expiration.

**Option/Stock Price Lattice for European-Style Option**

| Time | 0 | 1 | 2 |
|---|---|---|---|
| | | | 249.130<br>299.130 |
| | | 82.872<br>122.297 | |
| | 27.567<br>50.000 | | 0.000<br>50.000 |
| | | 0.000<br>20.442 | |
| | | | 0.000<br>8.358 |

The third step is to value the option at earlier nodes by taking the present value of the expected future value at each node. To compute the expected value, it is necessary to know the probabilities of an up-step and a down-step. The probability of an up-step is given by (9.8) in Chapter 9. The numerical value for the problem at hand is

$$p = \frac{1}{2} + \frac{1}{2}\left(\frac{0.07 - 0.5(0.40^2)}{0.40}\right)\sqrt{.5} = 0.4720$$

The complementary probability of a down-step is 0.5280. The present value of the expected future value at the top stock price node at time 1 is therefore

$$e^{-0.07(5)}[0.4720(249.13) + 0.5280(0)] = 82.872$$

Similar computations can be performed to fill in the remaining option value nodes. Using two time steps, the value of a European-style call option is 27.567.

To incorporate the effects of the option holder's desire to exercise the option should the stock price exceed the exercise price by a factor of two, you need to impose boundary restrictions. Each time the stock price exceeds 100 in the lattice, you need to replace the computed option value with the option's immediate exercise proceeds. If you impose this constraint on the option values in the lattice, you obtain the following lattice:

**Option/Stock Price Lattice for ESO with Early Exercise Constraint**

| Time | 0 | 1 | 2 |
|---|---|---|---|
| | | | 50.000<br>299.130 |
| | | 50.000<br>122.297 | |
| | 16.632<br>50.000 | | 0.000<br>50.000 |
| | | 0.000<br>20.442 | |
| | | | 0.000<br>8.358 |

In other words, if we impose the constraint that the ESO will be exercised if the stock price exceeds 100, the ESO value drops from 27.567 to 16.632. The cost of exercising early can be quite significant. At 1,000 time steps, the value of the ESO with no early exercise constraint is 32.464, while the ESO value with the early exercise constraint is 22.375. Thus the value of transferability is 10.089.

## CONSTANT DIVIDEND YIELD MODELS

Employee stock options are often valued under the assumption that the common stock pays a constant dividend yield over the life of the option. The only reason for doing this is convenience. Estimating the amount and timing of quarterly dividend payments is cumbersome. Assuming a single dividend yield for the underlying stock is easy. Unfortunately, although valuing options under a constant dividend yield assumption is easy, it is also prone to make serious errors.

Under the constant dividend yield assumption, the firm pays out dividends as a constant, continuous proportion of stock price. This means that dividends are paid continuously (not quarterly). It also means that, if the stock price goes up, dividend income goes up, and, if the stock price goes down, dividend income goes down. Clearly these attributes are inconsistent with actual dividend payment behavior. But more seriously, when this assumption is used for ESO valuation, the results can be misleading.

To illustrate, use the example summarized in Table 13.1. To apply the constant dividend yield model, we are first faced with the problem of estimating the constant dividend yield. How should this be done? The answer is not simple. The problem is that with the constant dividend yield model you do not know the dollar amount of dividends earned. While the dividend rate is constant, the dividend payments are random. Since we know the value of the European-style call under the assumption of discrete dividends, 32.529, we can set it equal to the formula for European-style call under a continuous dividend yield assumption and solve for dividend yield. Using the parameters from the above example,

$$32.5286 = 100e^{-i(10)}N(d_1) - 100e^{-0.07(10)}N(d_2)$$

where

$$d_1 = \frac{\ln(100e^{(0.07-i)10}/100) + 0.5(0.36^2)10}{0.36\sqrt{10}} \quad \text{and} \quad d_2 = d_1 - 0.36\sqrt{10}$$

and the implied dividend yield is 4.396% annually.

Now recall that the objective is to value the ESO and the ESO is American-style. If we use the binomial method for valuing the call under the assumption of a 4.396% dividend yield and the use of 1,000 time steps, the ESO value is 37.271—nearly 15% greater than the value you obtained by addressing the problem more realistically. The constant dividend yield approach says that the value of the early exercise premium in this ESO is about 4.742, when it is, in fact worthless. Using a constant dividend yield assumption in valuing American-style options on discrete dividend-paying stocks is a practice that should be avoided.

## ESOs WITH INDEXED EXERCISE PRICES

Some employee options have exercise prices that vary with an index of stock prices of firms within the same industry. This type of contract makes a good deal of sense from the firm's perspective. With standard employee stock options, option values increase as the market rises even if the firm is not doing as well as its competitors. With an indexed exercise price, employees benefit based on stock price performance. If the stock price rises relative to the index, option value increases, independent of whether the market rises or falls.

Valuing options with an indexed exercise price can be handled using standard techniques, as we saw in Chapter 8. An exchange option is like a standard option except in place of paying (receiving) the exercise price in cash at expiration, we pay (receive) a second risky asset. For an indexed ESO, the second asset is the index. The value of the ESO with an indexed exercise price is

$$c = S_1^x N(d_1) - S_2^x N(d_2) \tag{13.2}$$

where

$$d_1 = \frac{\ln(S_1^x / S_2^x) + 0.5\sigma^2 \sqrt{T}}{\sigma\sqrt{T}} \quad \text{and} \quad d_2 = d_1 - \sigma\sqrt{T}$$

In the valuation formula (13.7), $S_1^x$ is the current share price net of the present value of dividends paid during the option's life and $S_2^x$ is the index level net of dividends.[7] The volatility rate, $\sigma$, is defined as

$$\sigma = \sqrt{\sigma_1^2 + \sigma_2^2 - 2\rho_{12}\sigma_1\sigma_2}$$

where $\sigma_1$ and $\sigma_2$ are the return volatilities of the stock and the index, respectively, and $\rho_{12}$ is the correlation between the return of the stock and the return of the index.

**ILLUSTRATION 13.2** Value indexed employee stock option.

*(1) Suppose that a firm decides to award employee stock options based on performance. More specifically, assume, that instead of awarding standard 10-year, at-the-money stock options, they award 10-year, at-the-money indexed stock options, where the index is created as a value-weighted average of the firm's competitors' stock prices standardized to the firm's current stock price. The firm's current stock price is 50 per share, it pays no divi-*

[7] Another way to think of $S_1^x$ and $S_2^x$ is as the prices of prepaid forward contracts on assets 1 and 2.

*dends, and its volatility rate is 40%. The index's current value is 50, it pays no dividends, and its volatility rate is 25%. Assume also that the correlation between the firm's returns and the index returns is 0.75. Compute the values of standard employee stock options and indexed stock options assuming both are European-style. Assume the interest rate is 7%.*

The value of the standard employee stock option can be computed using the BSM model.

OV_OPTION_VALUE(50, 50, 10, .07, 0.00, 0.40, "c", "e") = 32.476

The value of the indexed employee stock option is

OV_NS_EXCHANGE_OPTION(50, 50, 10, 0.00, 0.00, 0.40, 0.25, 0.75) = 16.485

*(2) Suppose that at the end of the first year, the market has fallen—the firm's share price is now at 45, and the index level is at 35. Compute the rate of return on the standard employee stock options vis-à-vis the indexed options. Assume that all other problem information remains the same.*

The new option values are as follows:

OV_OPTION_VALUE(45, 50, 9, .07, .00, .40, "c", "e") = 26.665

and

OV_NS_EXCHANGE_OPTION(45, 35, 9, .00, .00, .40, .25, .75) = 18.115

The decline in stock price caused the standard ESO to drop in value by 17.89%. The indexed ESO, on the other hand, increased in value by 9.89%. Even though stock prices fell, the firm did well relative to the index, and the indexed options rewarded the employees accordingly.

*(3) Alternatively, suppose that at the end of the first year, the market has risen—the firm's share price is now at 55, and the index level is at 60. Compute the rate of return on the standard employee stock options vis-à-vis the indexed options. Assume that all other problem information remains the same.*

The new option values are as follows:

OV_OPTION_VALUE(55, 60, 9, 0.07, 0.00, 0.40, "c", "e") = 35.356

and

OV_NS_EXCHANGE_OPTION(55, 60, 9, 0.00, 0.00, 0.40, 0.25, 0.75) = 15.637

The rise in stock price caused the standard ESO to rise in value by 8.87%. The indexed ESO, on the other hand, fell by 5.14%. Again, the indexed option provided an appropriate reward. Even though the stock price rose, the firm did relatively less well than the index, and the indexed options rewarded the employees accordingly.

## ESOs WITH RELOAD FEATURES

Reload options are like standard employee stock options, except that the holder has the right to exercise the option periodically, locking in the exercise proceeds from the original option issue and receiving new at-the-money stock options in their place. More specifically, upon the exercise of a reload option, the holder receives (1) cash proceeds equal to the difference between the stock price and the exercise price, $S - X$, for each original option owned, plus (2) $X/S$ new at-the-money options with the same expiration date as the original options.[8] This reload feature adds significant value to a standard ESO.

To value a reload option, a binomial lattice framework can be used. To simplify the problem, assume the stock pays no dividends and that the option holder has a single opportunity to "reload" his option. With no dividends, the value of a standard employee stock option (with no reload feature) can be computed using the BSM formula from Table 13.3. To value the ESO with a reload feature, compute the stock price lattice for the binomial method in the usual fashion. With the computed stock price lattice in hand, start at the end of the option's life and work backward to the present. At the end of the option's life, the option value at each stock price node is the maximum of 0 and the exercise proceeds. With the expiration values computed, the procedure steps back one time increment, $\Delta t$, to time $n - 1$ and values the option at each node by taking the present value of the expected future value. Then, for each node, in place of checking for early exercise, we check whether any of the computed option values are less than the reload proceeds, $S_{i,j} - X + (X/S_{i,j})c_{i,j}$, where $S_{i,j}$ is the stock price at node $j$ and time $i$, $c_{i,j}$ is the value of a European-style call, and $X/S_{i,j}$ is the new number of calls, as per the contract design. If so, replace the computed option value with the reload proceeds. The procedure is repeatedly recursively until time 0.

**ILLUSTRATION 13.3** Value employee stock option with reload feature.

*Compute the value of a ten-year, at-the-money employee stock option with a single opportunity to reload. Assume that the underlying stock has a price of 50, a volatility rate of 40%, and pays no dividends. The risk-free rate of interest is 7%. Use two time steps and the CRR method.*

The first step in the binomial method is the same as in Illustration 11.1. Starting at time 0 with a stock price of 50, the stock price lattice becomes

**Stock Price Lattice Underlying Reload Option**

| Time | 0 | 1 | 2 |
|---|---|---|---|
| | | | 299.130 |
| | | 122.297 | |
| | 50.000 | | 50.000 |
| | | 20.442 | |
| | | | 8.358 |

[8] Presumably, the reason that fewer options (i.e., $X/S$) are awarded at the time of reload is that the option has "cashed-in" a value of $S - X$ for each option. If the option had no time remaining to expiration, the option holder would receive $S - X$ for each underlying share and the $X/S$ new, at-the-money options would be valueless. This would leave the shareholders of the firm indifferent about the reload feature. But, if the options have any time remaining to expiration, the option holder receives a windfall gain (and the shareholders a windfall loss) equal to the time value (i.e., the option value less its intrinsic value) of the newly issued options. The optimal reload exercise behavior for the option holder is therefore to exercise at every available opportunity should the option be in the money. Indeed, it may be beneficial to exercise when the option is slightly out of the money, particularly, if the time to expiration is long.

The second step in the binomial method is to value the option at expiration at each stock price node. For a call, the value is the maximum of 0 and the difference between the stock price and the exercise price, $\max(0,S_{i,j} - X)$. The bold values at time 2 in the following table are the terminal option values:

**Option/Stock Price Lattice with No Reload**

| Time | 0 | 1 | 2 |
|---|---|---|---|
| | | | **249.130** |
| | | | 299.130 |
| | | 82.872 | |
| | | 122.297 | |
| | 27.567 | | **0.000** |
| | 50.000 | | 50.000 |
| | | 0.000 | |
| | | 20.442 | |
| | | | **0.000** |
| | | | 8.358 |

The third step is to value the option at earlier nodes by taking the present value of the expected future value at each node. Using two time steps, the value of a European-style call option with no reload feature is 27.567.

To incorporate the reload feature, you need to check for the possibility of reloading at each node. Again, illustrating by focusing on the top node at time 1, you know that the value of the option in the absence of reloading is 82.872. If the option is reloaded, however, the holder receives cash proceeds equal to the difference between the stock price and the exercise price, $S_{i,j} - X$ plus $X/S_{i,j}$ new, at-the-money call options with no remaining opportunity to reload. The numerical value is therefore

$$122.297 - 50 + (50/122.297)56.562 = 95.422$$

where 56.562 is the value of an at-the-money European-style call with an exercise price of 122.297 and a five-year time to expiration. Similar checks are performed for the remaining nodes. The value of the ESO with the reload feature is 31.742, compared with the value of the ESO with no reload feature, 27.567. The opportunity to reload can have significant value:

**Option/Stock Price Lattice with Reload**

| Time | 0 | 1 | 2 |
|---|---|---|---|
| | | | 249.130 |
| | | | 299.130 |
| | | 95.422 | |
| | | 122.297 | |
| | 31.742 | | 0.000 |
| | 50.000 | | 50.000 |
| | | 0.000 | |
| | | 20.442 | |
| | | | 0.000 |
| | | | 8.358 |

From Chapter 9, you know that the binomial method is not particularly accurate with only two time steps. To increase the precision, you need to increase the number of time steps and revalue the ESO. The table below reports the results where the number of time steps is 200. Even with 200 time steps, however, the binomial method remains imprecise. With no reloads, the ESO value can be computed using the BSM formula. Its value is 32.476. The binomial method with 200 time steps produces a value of 32.417—about a six-cent error. Second, the value of the reload feature is 2.265 or about 6.5% of the ESO value. For the problem at hand, the reload feature is quite valuable:

**Valuation of Employee Stock Options with Reload Feature**

| **Stock** | | **Binomial parameters** | |
|---|---|---|---|
| Price ($S$) | 50 | No. of time steps | 200 |
| Volatility rate | 40.00% | Method | 1 |
| **Option** | | **Option valuation** | |
| Exercise price ($X$) | 50 | Analytical with no reload | 32.476 |
| Years to expitation ($T$) | 10 | Binomial with no reload | 32.417 |
| | | Binomial with one reload | 34.682 |
| **Market** | | Reload value | 2.265 |
| Interest rate ($r$) | 7.00% | | |

## EMPLOYEE STOCK PURCHASE PLANS

A typical employee stock purchase plan (ESPP) allows its holder to buy the company's stock at a discount within a certain period of time. The discount is usually 15%, and the investment period is typically six months. Many ESPPs also have an embedded lookback option that allows the holder to apply the discount to either the end-of-period stock price or the beginning-of-period price, whichever is less. To see how to value an ESPP, consider its value upon expiration. Assume that $k$ is the discount, expressed as a proportion of the stock price (e.g., $k$ = 15%) and that the investment period ends at time $T$. The terminal value of the ESPP may be expressed as

$$ESPP_T = \begin{cases} \tilde{S}_T - (1-k)S & \text{if } S_T > S \\ \tilde{S}_T - (1-k)\tilde{S}_T & \text{if } S_T \leq S \end{cases} \tag{13.3}$$

If the end-of-period stock price $S_T$ exceeds the beginning-of-period price $S$, the employee will choose to buy the shares at (1 – $k$) times the beginning-of-period price, and, if the end-of-period stock price $S_T$ is less than the beginning-of-period price $S$, the employee will choose to buy the shares at (1 – $k$) times the end-of-period price.

With the payoff contingencies in hand, we will value the ESPP using *valuation-by-replication.* Recall that valuation-by-replication involves finding a portfolio of securities whose values we know has payoff contingencies identical to those of the instrument we wish to value. In the absence of costless arbitrage opportunities, the value of the instrument must equal the value of the portfolio. Consider a portfolio in which we (a) buy the stock, (b) borrow $(1 - k)Se^{-rT}$, and (c) buy $(1 - k)$ put options with an exercise price of $S$ and a time until expiration of $T$. The terminal value of this portfolio is

$$\text{Portfolio}_T = \begin{cases} \tilde{S}_T - (1-k)S + 0 & \text{if } S_T > S \\ \tilde{S}_T - (1-k)S + (1-k)(S - \tilde{S}_T) & \text{if } S_T \leq S \end{cases} \tag{13.4}$$

With a little simplification, it becomes obvious that (13.4) is the same as (13.3). The value of the ESPP, therefore, must equal the sum of the values of the securities in the portfolio, that is,

$$\begin{aligned} ESPP &= S - (1-k)Se^{-rT} + (1-k)[Se^{-rT}N(-d_2) - SN(-d_1)] \\ &= S - (1-k)Se^{-rT} + (1-k)Se^{-rT}N(-d_2) - (1-k)SN(-d_1) \\ &= S - (1-k)S[1 - N(d_1)] - (1-k)Se^{-rT}N(d_2) \\ &= kS + (1-k)[SN(d_1) - Se^{-rT}N(d_2)] \end{aligned} \tag{13.5}$$

where

$$d_1 = \frac{\ln(Se^{rT}/S) + 0.5\sigma^2\sqrt{T}}{\sigma\sqrt{T}} \quad \text{and} \quad d_2 = d_1 - \sigma\sqrt{T}$$

Interestingly enough, the reworking of equation (13.5) has produced another possible replicating portfolio. The value of an ESPP equals the value of a portfolio that consists of $k$ shares of stock and $(1 - k)$ at-the-money call options.[9] To verify this conclusion, write the terminal value contingencies for this replicating portfolio:

$$\text{Portfolio}_T = \begin{cases} k\tilde{S}_T - (1-k)(\tilde{S}_T - S) & \text{if } S_T > S \\ k\tilde{S}_T + 0 & \text{if } S_T \leq S \end{cases} \tag{13.6}$$

A little algebra shows (13.6) is the same as (13.4). The intuition is that the *ESPP* provides its holder with an award of $k$ percent of the stock price at the end of

[9] To verify this assertion, write the payoff contingencies of this two-security portfolio.

the investment period plus a "kicker" equal to $(1 - k)$ times the difference between the beginning- and ending-of-period stock prices if $S_T > S$ (i.e., the *ESPP* holder buys at the lower of $S$ and $S_T$).

**ILLUSTRATION 13.4** Value ESPP.

*Suppose your employer provides gives you an ESPP that allows you to buy 10,000 shares of the firm's stock at a 15% discount at today's price or at the market price in six months. The current stock price is 50, the stock's volatility rate is 40%, and the risk-free interest rate is 5%. What is the value of the ESPP?*

To determine the value of the ESPP, you can simply apply (13.3). Substituting the problem parameters, you get

$$ESPP = 0.15(50) + (1 - 0.15)[50N(d_1) - 50e^{-0.05(0.5)}N(d_2)] = 12.764$$

where

$$d_1 = \frac{\ln(50e^{0.05(0.5)}/50) + 0.5(0.40^2)0.5}{0.40\sqrt{0.5}} \quad \text{and} \quad d_2 = d_1 - 0.40\sqrt{0.5}$$

This value can also be computed using the OPTVAL Library function,

OV_STOCK_OPTION_ESPP(*s*, *k*, *t*, *r*, *v*)

where $s$ is the stock price, $k$ is the discount rate, $t$ is the length of the investment period, $r$ is the risk-free rate of interest, and $v$ is the volatility rate.

## SUMMARY

Designing appropriate employee compensation schemes is no easy task. One important ingredient in the mixture, however, is tying compensation to stock price performance. Employee stock options (ESOs) and employee stock purchase plans (EESPs) are such devices. This chapter examines the valuation of ESOs and ESPPs. The effects of vesting, early exercise, and discrete and continuous cash dividends are considered. In addition, two important new types of ESOs—ESOs with indexed exercise prices and ESOs with reload features—are valued.

## REFERENCES AND SUGGESTED READINGS

Black, Fischer, and Myron Scholes. 1973. The pricing of options and corporate liabilities. *Journal of Political Economy* 81: 637–659.

Financial Accounting Standards Board. 1995. *Statement of Financial Accounting Standards No. 123*. Norwalk, CT: F.A.S.B.

Heath, Chip, Steven Huddart, and Mark Lang. 1999. Psychological factors and stock option exercise. *Quarterly Journal of Economics* 26: 601–627.

Huddart, Steven, and Mark Lang. 1996. Employee stock option exercises: An empirical analysis. *Journal of Accounting and Economics* 21: 5–43.

Merton, Robert C. 1973. Theory of rational option pricing. *Bell Journal of Economics and Management Science* 4: 141–183.

Rubinstein, Mark. 2004. Employee stock options: Getting the accounting right. Working paper, Haas School of Business, University of California, Berkeley.

Rubinstein, Mark. 1995. On the accounting valuation of employee stock options. *Journal of Derivatives* (Fall): 2–24.

# PART Six

# Stock Index Derivatives

# CHAPTER 14

# Stock Index Products: Futures and Options

Arguably the most exciting financial innovation of the 1980s was the development of stock index derivative contracts. Although derivatives on the Dow were contemplated by the Chicago Board of Trade (CBT) as early as the late 1960s, it was not until the early 1980s that index derivatives began trading. The Kansas City Board of Trade (KCBT) was the first by introducing the Value Line index futures in February 1982, and the Chicago Mercantile Exchange (CME) followed two months later with the S&P 500 index futures. On the options side, the CME launched trading in S&P 500 index futures options in January 1983, and the Chicago Board Options Exchange (CBOE) in S&P 100 index options in March 1983. Within a few years, stock index products began to appear on other major exchanges worldwide. The Sydney Futures Exchange (SFE) introduced the All Ordinaries index futures (options) in February 1983 (June 1985), the London International Financial Futures Exchange (LIFFE) the FT-SE 100 index futures (options) in May 1984 (October 1992), and the Hong Kong Futures Exchange (HKFE) introduced Hang Seng index futures (options) in May 1986 (March 1993). In spite of their relatively short history, the contracts have been a phenomonal success. Billions of dollars in equities change hands every day through index derivatives trading in nearly 30 different countries.

This chapter and the next focus on stock index derivatives product markets and portfolio return/risk management strategies. In this chapter, the primary focus is exchange-traded derivatives. We begin by describing the U.S. markets for stock index futures and options as well as providing the specifications of some popular index contracts. The second section focuses on the construction of stock indexes. In most cases, the underlying index is a market value-weighted combination of stocks, with the notable exception being the price-weighted Dow Jones Industrial Average (DJIA). The third section summarizes the no-arbitrage price relations and valuation principles for index derivatives. For the most part, these are the same as those of individual stocks since stock indexes are nothing more than portfolios of stocks. Occasionally, however, traders choose to model the dividend income on the index portfolio as a continuous rate rather than discrete flows. For completeness, we provide the no-arbitrage prices relations and valuation principles for derivatives written on an index with a continuous dividend yield rate. The fourth section contains two important return/risk management strategies using index derivatives. First, stock index futures are used to tailor the expected return-risk characteristics of a stock portfolio for purposes of market timing and asset allocation. Second, protected equity notes are analyzed. A protected equity note is an investment that allows individuals to protect the principal value of their investment, while, at the same time, share in the upside of a market index. Although these products are traded primarily in the OTC market, they can be created synthetically using risk-free bonds and exchange-traded index call options. Chapter 15 follows with descriptions of some advanced strategies/products including passive and dynamic portfolio insurance, buy-write ETFs, and market volatility derivatives.

## MARKETS

Like stock derivatives, stock index derivatives trade both on exchanges and in the OTC market. Index futures and options have traded on exchanges for more than two decades. In addition, exchange-traded funds (ETFs) have recently attracted significant trading volume. ETFs are an effective, albeit indirect, means of trading stock portfolios. Each ETF is a basket of securities but trades like a single security. Forwards, options, and a wide variety of structured products are offered in the OTC market. The purpose of this section is to provide a broad overview of stock index products. We begin first with a brief history of the evolution of index products.

### Evolution of Index Products

The idea of trading stock index derivatives contracts was contemplated as early as 1968. At the time, grain surpluses had driven grain prices down to governmental support levels. Without price volatility, trading activity in the futures market was substantially reduced. Rather than wait for the situation to recover, members of the CBT began to explore the possibility of creating futures contracts on assets other than physical commodities—assets with less cyclical price behavior. Their original notion was a cash-settled futures contract on the DJIA. Fears of running afoul with the SEC and the Illinois State gambling laws, however, caused the CBT to abandon the idea in favor of creating a market for stock options.[1] Subsequently, the idea of trading a stock index futures contract lay dormant for more than a decade. It was not until February 1982 (14 years later) that the first futures contract on a stock index was launched—the Kansas City Board of Trade's ill-fated Value Line Composite Index futures contract.

A brief digression on the "first-mover" advantage is probably worthwhile, as it pertains to the failure of the Value Line futures contract. As a rule of thumb, history has shown that the first exchange to launch futures trading in a new asset category captures the lion's share of trading volume, holding other factors constant. Similar products introduced later by other exchanges have difficulty gather-

[1] For a historical recount of the events surrounding the CBT's decision, see Falloon (1998).

ing market share because the primary means of exchanges competing is the size of market makers' bid/ask spread. In a competitive environment such as an exchange's futures pit, bid/ask spreads vary inversely with trading volume. The higher the volume, the lower the market maker's fixed cost per trade. Since the first-mover initially monopolizes trading activity, any new product offered by a competing exchange must either provide lower trading costs (i.e., lower bid/ask spreads) or change the contract specifications in such a way that attracts new market participants. In the case of the Value Index futures contract, the KCBT was the first-mover. The product was aimed at the institutional need to hedge stock market risk. The index underlying the futures contract could have been the level of any broad-based, well-diversified stock portfolio. From the discussion of the CAPM in Chapter 3, we know that well-diversified stock portfolios have returns that are highly correlated with one another. All futures contracts written on well-diversified portfolios will therefore be very close substitutes. But therein lies the reason for the failure of the Value Line futures contract market. While the Value Line index had in excess of 1,500 stocks and, by all accounts, should have been well-diversified, its construction was atypical in that it did not represent the value of a stock portfolio. Instead of taking a value-weighted arithmetic sum of the constituent stock prices (like the value of any well-diversified portfolio), the Value Line index was calculated by taking an equal-weighted geometric product of stock prices.[2] This has two unfortunate consequences. First, it means that the Value Line index returns will not be highly correlated with the returns of a well-diversified stock portfolio. Second, it means that it is impossible for the Value Line futures price and the Value Line index level to be linked by arbitrage because the index, itself, cannot be traded.[3] Without strong correlation between the returns of the futures and the underlying index and strong correlation between the returns of the index and well-diversified portfolios, the Value Line futures was an ineffective means of hedging stock market risk[4] and contract volume waned. Eventually, the index was redesigned as a value-weighted arithmetic sum, but, unfortunately it was too late. The first-mover advantage had been relinquished to the CME.

The first viable futures contract on a broad-based (arithmetic) index portfolio was the S&P 500 futures, launched by Chicago Mercantile Exchange in April 1982. Consistent with the first-mover principle, it remains by far the most active index futures contract today. Table 14.1 summarizes the trading volume of the eight most active index futures contracts on U.S. exchanges during the calendar year 2003. While a total of 35 index futures traded across U.S. exchanges, the eight most active accounted for 92.43% of total contract volume.[5] Measuring

[2] More specifically, the Value Index was computed by taking the product of the price of all of the stocks in the index and adjusting by a divisor.

[3] This is true only for the Value Line index. In general, the movements in a stock index can be replicated by trading the basket of underlying stocks. Because the Value Line index is generally weighted, replication is not possible.

[4] For an early evaluation of the properties of the Value Line Index futures, see Modest and Sundaresan (1983).

[5] Contract volumes for the calendar year 2003 were drawn from *Futures Industry Association Monthly Report* (December 2003). The total trading volume across all stock index futures listed on U.S. exchanges during 2003 was 296,694,711 contracts.

**TABLE 14.1** Market value of the eight most active index futures contracts traded in the United States during the calendar year 2003.

| Contract | Exchange | Underlying Index | Contract Mulitplier | Closing Level 12/31/2003 | Contract Volume in 2003 | Dollar Contract Volume in 2003 |
|---|---|---|---|---|---|---|
| E-Mini S&P 500 | CME | S&P 500 | 50 | 1111.92 | 161,176,639 | 8,960,776,421,844 |
| S&P 500 | CME | S&P 500 | 250 | 1111.92 | 20,175,462 | 5,608,374,926,760 |
| E-Mini NASDAQ 100 | CME | NASDAQ 100 | 20 | 1467.92 | 67,888,938 | 1,993,110,597,379 |
| NASDAQ 100 Index | CME | NASDAQ 100 | 100 | 1467.92 | 4,421,221 | 648,999,873,032 |
| Mini ($5) Dow Jones Industrial Index | CBT | DJIA | 5 | 10453.9 | 10,859,690 | 567,630,566,455 |
| Dow Jones Industrial Index | CBT | DJIA | 10 | 10453.9 | 4,416,302 | 461,675,794,778 |
| E-Mini Russell 2000 | CME | Russell 2000 | 100 | 556.91 | 3,878,935 | 216,021,769,085 |
| E-Mini S&P Midap 400 Index | CME | S&P Midcap 400 | 100 | 576.01 | 1,417,513 | 81,650,166,313 |
| Total | | | | | 274,234,700 | 18,538,240,115,646 |

*Source:* Data compiled from *Futures Industry Association Monthly Report* (December 2003) and *Datastream*.

the importance of trading activity in terms of numbers of contracts can be misleading, however, since different contracts have different contract multipliers and index levels. To accurately measure the economic significance of the trading volume for each contract, dollar contract volume (i.e., number of contracts traded times the contract multiplier times the index level) was computed and is reported in the last column of Table 14.1. The CME's S&P 500 contracts accounted for about 79% of the dollar contract volume in 2003.

To further elaborate on the evolution of exchange-traded stock index derivatives and the first-mover advantage, consider Table 14.2, which reports the correlation coefficients computed from the daily returns of the major stock market indexes in the U.S. during the calendar years 2002 and 2003. By way of history, the New York Futures Exchange (NYSE) was created in 1982 by the New York Stock Exchange (NYSE) for the exclusive purpose of trading futures contracts on the NYSE Composite index. In May 1982, a month after the launch of S&P 500 futures trading, the NYSE Composite index futures began trading. Other than having a different well-diversified portfolio serving as the underlying index, the contract specifications (e.g., contract size and expiration cycle) were very much like those of the S&P 500 index futures. Table 14.2 shows that the correlation between the returns of the S&P 500 and NYSE Composite indexes is 0.979. With virtually perfect correlation between the returns of the two indexes, futures contracts written on these indexes are nearly perfect substitutes.[6] It should not be surprising, therefore, to find that, while the NYSE Composite futures continues to trade, its contract volume is less than one percent of the S&P 500 contract volume. In a similar vein, the correlation between the S&P 500 and the S&P 100 is 0.994, again indicating that having futures contracts written on both indexes is redundant. Anecdotally, the CME launched S&P 100 futures contracts in the mid-1980s. The contract failed to attract significant trading volume and was delisted shortly thereafter.

The Chicago Board of Trade was late to step into the stock index futures market competition. The CBT's plans were to create index futures on the Dow Jones Industrial Average. At the same time, the American Exchange (AMEX) was planning to launch trading in index option contracts on the Dow. Unfortu-

**TABLE 14.2** Correlation between daily index returns of major U.S. stock market indexes using data from the calendar years 2002 and 2003.

| Index | DJIA | S&P500 | NYSE | S&P 100 | S&P 400 | NASD 100 |
|---|---|---|---|---|---|---|
| S&P 500 | 0.980 | | | | | |
| NYSE | 0.966 | 0.979 | | | | |
| S&P 100 | 0.980 | 0.994 | 0.969 | | | |
| S&P 400 | 0.892 | 0.925 | 0.925 | 0.897 | | |
| NASD 100 | 0.857 | 0.905 | 0.853 | 0.894 | 0.883 | |
| Russell 2000 | 0.809 | 0.854 | 0.850 | 0.825 | 0.946 | 0.861 |

[6] This presumes that there is the same amount of basis risk between each futures and its underlying index.

nately, Dow Jones refused to allow either exchange to proceed. In a retaliatory move, the AMEX created the Major Market Index (MMI)—an index designed to look like the DJIA. It was a price-weighted index (like the DJIA) and consisted of 20 "blue chip" stocks, 15 of which happened to be in the DJIA at the time. The CBT licensed the rights for trading futures and futures option contracts on the MMI from AMEX and began trading MMI futures in July 1984. The contract floundered and was later delisted.

In a reversal of its longstanding policy not to allow derivatives traded on its indexes, Dow Jones began to consider proposals to license its DJIA to serve as the index underlying index derivatives contracts in 1997. The CBT and the CME competed for the right to trade futures and futures option contracts, and the AMEX and the CBOE competed for the right to trade options. Dow Jones awarded the license for futures and futures option contracts to the CBT and the option contracts to the CBOE. On October 6, 1997, Dow options began trading on the CBOE and Dow futures and futures options on the CBT. The success of the Dow derivatives contracts, however, has been modest. In part, this is attributable to the high degree of correlation between the DJIA and the S&P 500 index. Table 14.2 shows that the correlation between the two indexes is 0.980. To maximize the probability of success, however, the CBT, in discussions with Dow Jones, attempted to differentiate the Dow contract from other index futures by making it considerably smaller. In this way, they aspired to attract retail (i.e., small investor) rather institutional (i.e., large investor) business. Unfortunately, the CME was quick to respond to this initiative. When Dow Jones awarded the license for DJIA futures contracts to the CBT, the CME immediately countered by creating a miniaturized version of its successful S&P 500 futures. The "E-mini S&P 500" contract is 1/5 the size of its big brother (and about half the size of the Dow contract) and began trading on September 9, 1997, about a month before the CBT was able to unveil the Dow futures. Judging by the contract volume figures reported in Table 14.1, there was pent up demand for a smaller index futures contract. Indeed, the E-mini S&P 500 futures contract now has greater dollar volume than its big brother. The E-mini S&P 500 futures also appears to have had a first-mover advantage in the sense that its dollar contract volume in 2003 was nearly ten times higher than the two futures contracts list on the DJIA.

Table 14.1 also shows that the NASDAQ 100 futures contracts have been quite successful, with trading volume in excess of 1.6 billion contracts in 2003. One reason for their success may be given in Table 14.2. The correlation between the returns of the S&P 500 index and the NASDAQ 100 index is only 0.905. Thus the S&P 500 index and NASDAQ 100 index are not perfect substitutes. Another reason may be that the NASDAQ contracts are about half the size of their S&P 500 counterparts and may be attracting more retail business. These cannot be the only reasons, however, since the Russell 2000 index has even lower correlation with the S&P 500 index, and the E-mini Russell 2000 futures is a very small contract. The remaining reason is that index arbitrage is more easily and cheaply executed using an index portfolio of 100 highly liquid stocks than with an index portfolio with 2,000 stock with varying degress of liquidity. The greater the arbitrage activity between the futures and its underlying index, the higher the correlation between the return of the futures and its underlying index and the more effective the futures is as a return/risk management tool.

The trading volumes of index options and index futures options traded on U.S. exchanges during the calendar year 2003 are reported in Table 14.3. Under the stock index options panel, the contract volume is greatest for exchange-traded funds. But this is aggregate trading volume across a number of different ETF option classes. By far the most active index option class is the S&P 500 index options traded on the CBOE. Excluding options on ETFs, S&P 500 options account for 47.6% of all index option trading. The second most active contract is the S&P 100 index options.

**TABLE 14.3** Contract volume for stock index option and stock index futures option contracts in the United States during the calendar year 2003.

| Contract | Exchange | Contract Volume | Percent of Total | Percent of Total (excl.) |
|---|---|---|---|---|
| **Stock index options:** | | | | |
| Exchange Traded Funds | CBOE | 41,146,233 | 34.8% | |
| S&P 500 Index Options (SPX) | CBOE | 36,754,720 | 31.1% | 47.6% |
| S&P 100 Index Options (OEX) | CBOE | 14,343,992 | 12.1% | 18.6% |
| Dow Jones Industrial Index (DJX) | CBOE | 10,193,708 | 8.6% | 13.2% |
| NASDAQ 100 Mini (MNX) | CBOE | 4,034,201 | 3.4% | 5.2% |
| Mini NASDAQ Non-Financial 100 Index (MNX) | AMEX | 2,436,756 | 2.1% | 3.2% |
| S&P 100 European Exercise (XEO) | CBOE | 1,933,355 | 1.6% | 2.5% |
| NASDAQ 100 (NDXCBO) | CBOE | 1,622,687 | 1.4% | 2.1% |
| Gold/Silver Index (XA U) | PHLX | 1,130,430 | 1.0% | 1.5% |
| Oil Service Sector (OSX) | PHLX | 1,006,718 | 0.9% | 1.3% |
| Other | | 3,713,816 | 3.1% | 4.8% |
| TOTAL | | 118,316,616 | | |
| TOTAL (excluding ETFs) | | 77,170,383 | | |
| **Stock index futures options:** | | | | |
| S&P 500 Index | CME | 4,986,456 | 90.1% | |
| Dow Jones Industrial Index | CBT | 263,629 | 4.8% | |
| E-Mini S&P 500 | CME | 112,864 | 2.0% | |
| Russell 1000 | NYBOT | 61,264 | 1.1% | |
| NASDAQ 100 Index | CME | 50,439 | 0.9% | |
| NYSE Composite Index | NYBOT | 25,320 | 0.5% | |
| Revised NYSE Composite | NYBOT | 18,912 | 0.3% | |
| Other | | 16,062 | 0.3% | |
| TOTAL | | 5,534,946 | | |

*Source:* Data compiled from *Futures Industry Association Monthly Report* (December 2003).

Interestingly, the first options on a stock index were the CME's S&P 500 futures options, which began trading in January 1983. Compared with other futures options activity, the S&P 500 contracts account for 90.1% of total index futures option trading volume in 2003. Compared with the S&P 500 index options traded on the CBOE, however, their volume is about 12.1%. Adjusting for contract size, the relative trading volume is 30.3%. One reason for the dominance of index options over index futures options is that many institutional investors can trade in securities markets but not futures markets. Another is that longer-term contracts are available in the index option market.

Security and futures exchanges tend to develop reputations as leaders in particular styles of contracts based on their relative trading volumes. Table 14.4 summarizes trading volume by U.S. exchange for the calendar year 2003. In terms of the reputation, the CME is the market leader in the stock index futures and the stock index futures options markets in the U.S. Table 14.5 shows that they account for 94.6% of stock index futures trading and 93.3% of stock index futures options trading in the U.S. The CBOE is the leader in index options trading, with 93.7% of the total index option contracts traded.

**TABLE 14.4** Number of contracts listed and contract volume for stock index products traded on U.S. exchanges during the calendar year 2003.

| Exchange | Symbol | No. of Contracts | Contract Volume | Percent of Total |
|---|---|---|---|---|
| **Stock index futures:** | | | | |
| Chicago Mercantile Exchange | CME | 22 | 280,649,663 | 94.6% |
| Chicago Board of Trade | CBT | 3 | 15,319,313 | 5.2% |
| New York Board of Trade | NYBOT | 7 | 720,147 | 0.2% |
| OneChicago | ONE | 1 | 3,197 | 0.0% |
| Kansas City Board of Trade | KCBT | 1 | 2,391 | 0.0% |
| TOTAL | | 34 | 296,694,711 | |
| **Stock index options:** | | | | |
| Chicago Board Options Exchange | CBOE | 15 | 110,822,092 | 93.7% |
| American Exchange | AMEX | 25 | 4,272,740 | 3.6% |
| Philadelphia Exchange | PHLX | 16 | 3,221,784 | 2.7% |
| TOTAL | | 56 | 118,316,616 | |
| **Stock index futures options:** | | | | |
| Chicago Mercantile Exchange | CME | 6 | 5,163,151 | 93.3% |
| Chicago Board of Trade | CBT | 1 | 263,629 | 4.8% |
| New York Board of Trade | NYBOT | 6 | 108,166 | 2.0% |
| TOTAL | | 13 | 5,534,946 | |

*Source:* Data compiled from *Futures Industry Association Monthly Report* (December 2003).

**TABLE 14.5** Selected terms of S&P 500 index futures contract.

| | |
|---|---|
| Exchange | Chicago Mercantile Exchange (CME) |
| Contract unit | \$250 times S&P 500 index |
| Tick size | 0.10 |
| Tick value | \$25 |
| Contract months | Nearest eight months in the March quarterly expiration cycle (i.e., Mar./Jun./Sep./Dec.). |
| Trading hours | FLOOR trading: 8:30 AM to 3:15 PM CST. All contract months are traded.<br>GLOBEX trading: 3:30 PM to 8:15 AM (the following morning) Monday through Thursday, and 5:30 PM to 8:15 AM (the following morning) Sundays and holidays. Shutdown period from 4:30 PM to 5:00 PM nightly. Only nearby contract month is traded. |
| Expiration day | Third Friday of the contract month. |
| Last day of trading | Business day immediately preceding the day of the determination of the final settlement price. |
| Final settlement price | Cash-settled at a special quotation of the index based on the opening prices of the index stocks on the expiration day. |

### Stock Index Futures

Index futures are standardized contracts, with a number of conventions regarding denomination, expiration, and method of settlement. Table 14.1, for example, shows the contract multiplier of the eight most active index futures traded in the U.S. The contract multiplier for the S&P 500 contract is 250 times the index futures price. A futures price of 1,110 implies that trading a single contract is like trading \$275,000 in the S&P 500 index portfolio. The 250-multiplier has not been in effect for too long. From inception on April 21, 1982 through October 31, 1997, the multiplier was 500. The redenomination of the contract was an attempt by the CME to make the contract more accessible for investors.[7]

The contract specifications of the S&P 500 futures are presented in Table 14.5. As noted earlier, the contract multiplier is \$250. Since the tick size is 0.10 index points, the minimum price movement in the contract is \$25 (i.e., 0.10 × \$250). The S&P 500 futures contract is on the March quarterly expiration cycle, which means that March, June, September, and December contracts are available. On any given date, eight contract months are listed. Hence, as of April 2004, June 2004 through March 2006 contract months are available. The last trading day of the S&P 500 futures contract is the third Thursday of the contract month. Cash settlement of the contract takes place at a special settlement quotation based on opening prices of the index stocks on Friday.

The S&P 500 futures trades on the floor of the exchange during regular trading hours as well electronically during the rest of the day. The floor trading

[7] For an analysis of the effect of the CME's re-denomination of the S&P 500 futures contract, see Bollen, Smith, and Whaley (2003).

hours of the S&P 500 futures are from 8:30 AM to 3:15 PM Central Standard Time (CST) Monday through Friday. All eight contract months are traded. Note that the hours of trading for the index futures are usually chosen to coincide with trading in the stock market, with the possibility of a short window before or after the stock market is opened or closed. For the S&P 500 futures, regular trading extends fifteen minutes beyond the close of the market, that is, trading on the NYSE is from 9:30 AM to 4:00 PM Eastern Standard Time (EST). Outside the floor trading hours, the nearby S&P 500 futures contract trades electronically on GLOBEX.[8] The electronic trading hours are from 3:30 PM (CST) until 8:15 AM (CST) the following morning Monday through Thursday, and 5:00 PM (CST) until 8:15 AM (CST) the following morning on Sundays and holidays.

The contract specifications of the E-mini S&P 500 futures are virtually identical to those of the S&P 500 futures. The only notable exception is that the contract multiplier is 50 instead of 250. The E-mini S&P 500 futures trades electronically virtually twenty-four hours a day—from 3:30 PM to 3:15 PM CST (on the following day) on Monday through Thursday and from 5:30 PM to 5:15 PM CST (on the following day) on Sunday and holidays Only the two nearby contract months are traded.

### Stock Index Options

Stock index options are written on both stock index futures and the stock index. There are subtle differences in the contract designs, as discussed below.

**Index Futures Options** The first stock index futures option contracts to trade in the U.S. were the Chicago Mercantile Exchange's S&P 500 and the New York Futures Exchange's NYSE Composite futures option contracts. They began trading on January 28, 1983. Trading in index futures options is less active than index futures. Indeed, for the U.S. index futures contracts listed in Table 14.3, the only futures option contract to have trading volume greater than 500,000 contracts during 2003 was the S&P 500 futures option.

Table 14.6 contains the product specifications of the S&P 500 futures option contract. Each futures option is written on a single S&P 500 futures contract. Tick size, tick value, and trading hours conventions are the same as those of the underlying futures. S&P 500 futures options, like all futures options traded in the United States, are American-style. In the event of early exercise, the underlying futures contract is delivered. Exercising a long call position, for example, means that a long position in the underlying futures is delivered. A seller of the call, selected randomly from the outstanding short positions, would receive the offsetting short futures position. Both futures positions are marked-to-market at the exercise price of the call at the end of day.

[8] GLOBEX is an electronic trading system developed by the CME (and Reuters) and began live trading June 25, 1992. On the first day of operation, 2,063 futures and futures option contracts on Deutsche marks and Japanese yen were traded. Today nearly all CME products are traded on GLOBEX, and trading activity averages more than one million contracts per day—a staggering 44% of total CME volume!

**TABLE 14.6** Selected terms of S&P 500 index futures option contract.

| | |
|---|---|
| Exchange | Chicago Mercantile Exchange (CME) |
| Contract unit | One S&P 500 futures contract |
| Tick size | 0.10 |
| Tick value | $25 |
| Contract months | Four expirations on the quarterly cycle Mar./Jun./Sep./Dec. Also, two nearby contract months such that a total of six contract months are listed. |
| Trading hours | FLOOR trading: 8:30 AM to 3:15 PM CST. All contract months are traded.<br>GLOBEX trading: 3:30 PM to 8:15 AM (the following morning) Monday through Thursday, and 5:30 PM to 8:15 AM (the following morning) Sundays and holidays. Shutdown period from 4:30 PM to 5:00 PM nightly. Only nearby contract month is traded. |
| Exercise style | American |
| Expiration day | Third Friday of the contract month. |
| Last day of trading | The same date and time as the underlying futures contract for the quarterly cycle and on the third Friday of the contract month for the other months. |
| Final settlement price | Quarterly expirations are cash-settled at a special quotation of the index based on the opening prices of the index stocks on the expiration day. Nonquarterly expirations call for the delivery of the underlying futures contract. |

To illustrate the mechanics of exercising an American-style futures option, suppose you hold the June 2004 call with an exercise price 1050 listed in Table 14.7. On the morning of April 14, 2004, you decide to exercise the option. To do so, you must call your broker and tell him that you want to exercise your call. At the end of the day, what would appear in your futures account would include a long position in the June 2004 futures plus mark-to-market cash proceeds in the amount of $19,925 (i.e., the futures settlement price, 1,129.70, less the exercise price, 1050, times the contract denomination, $250).

Note that in the above illustration the exercise proceeds equal the difference between the settlement price and the exercise price at the end of the day even though you tendered exercise early in the day. Locking in the exercise proceeds earlier in the day is also possible. Suppose, for example, that the price of the June 2004 futures was at 1150 in the morning of April 14. To lock in the exercise proceeds at that futures price level, you call your broker and instruct him to (1) exercise the call and (2) sell the futures. Assuming the futures order is executed at 1150, your end-of-day settlement would include a mark-to-market gain of 1150 – 1129.70 times $250 on your short futures position, and a mark-to-market gain of 1129.70 – 1050 times $250 on the long futures position obtained when exercising the call. The total gain is $25,000, and the futures position is closed.

Table 14.6 describes both quarterly and nonquarterly expiration cycles. The quarterly expiration cycle patterns the futures—March, June, September, and December. The S&P 500 futures options with these contract months are written

**TABLE 14.7** Settlement prices of selected S&P 500 index futures options drawn from www.cme.com on April 14, 2004. Settlement price of June 2004 S&P 500 futures was 1129.70.

| Exercise Price | Call Options | | | Put Options | | |
|---|---|---|---|---|---|---|
| | Apr/04 | May/04 | Jun/04 | Apr/04 | May/04 | Jun/04 |
| 1000 | | | 134.20 | | 1.70 | 4.90 |
| 1025 | 104.70 | 107.10 | 111.20 | 0.05 | 2.60 | 6.80 |
| 1050 | 79.80 | 83.80 | 89.10 | 0.10 | 4.20 | 9.60 |
| 1075 | 54.90 | 61.40 | 68.00 | 0.20 | 6.80 | 13.50 |
| 1100 | 30.20 | 41.00 | 48.90 | 0.55 | 11.40 | 19.30 |
| 1125 | 8.10 | 23.70 | 32.40 | 3.40 | 19.00 | 27.70 |
| 1150 | 0.30 | 11.10 | 19.20 | 20.60 | 31.40 | 39.40 |
| 1175 | 0.05 | 4.00 | 10.10 | 45.30 | 49.20 | 55.30 |
| 1200 | | 1.00 | 4.60 | 70.30 | 71.20 | 74.70 |
| 1225 | | 0.30 | 1.90 | 95.30 | | 97.00 |
| 1250 | | 0.15 | 0.80 | 120.30 | | 120.80 |
| 1275 | | 0.05 | 0.30 | | | |
| 1300 | | | 0.20 | | | 170.30 |

on the corresponding futures. Table 14.7, however, shows April and May contract months, where no April and May S&P 500 futures are traded. These are called serial months and are written on the June 2004 futures. Upon exercising a serial option, the option holder receives a position in the nearby futures contract, in this case the June 2004 futures, and is marked-to-market at the exercise price. If serial options are carried to their expiration on the third Friday of the contract month, they are automatically exercised if in the money. On the other hand, S&P 500 futures options expiring on the quarterly cycle are cash-settled at expiration—the June 2004 futures option expires at the same instant as the June 2000 futures.

**Index Options** The first stock index option contract to trade in the United States was the Chicago Board Options Exchange's S&P 100 index option.[9] They began trading on March 11, 1983. The CBOE launched trading in S&P 500 index options on July 1, 1983. Since the early 1980s, options on a number of narrowly-based industry indexes have also been introduced. Few have managed to generate significant trading volume. Nonetheless, options on more than fifty different stock indexes trade in the U.S. alone.

[9] Although the S&P 100 index is less well-known than the S&P 500 index, S&P 100 options had the greatest trading volume until only recently. By way of history, when the CBOE was initially considering introducing an index option contract in the early 1980's, it decided upon a value-weighted index of the one hundred largest stocks for which CBOE listed stock options. Originally, the index was called the "CBOE 100." Later, the CBOE reached an agreement for Standard & Poors' to track the portfolio composition, at which time, the index was renamed the S&P 100.

Table 14.3 summarized the trading volume of index options in the calendar year 2003. Most of their volume is concentrated in the broad-based indexes. The S&P 500 contract, for example, has 47.6% of the total non-ETF index option volume, and the S&P 100 contract has 18.6%. The only narrow-based index option to have significant volume is the Dow Jones index options, with 13.2% of total volume. To some degree, this is surprising considering that the market was launched on October 6, 1997—less than eight years ago. Part of this phenomenon, however, may be attributable to the fact that the Dow options have a smaller contract denomination. Finally, NASDAQ 100 index options account for about 7.3% of total trading volume.

All active index option contracts, except those on the S&P 100, are European-style. The S&P 100 index options are American-style. If an S&P 100 index option buyer exercises early, he or she receives the difference between the closing index level on that day and the exercise price of the option. The offsetting option seller, who is obliged to make the cash payment to the buyer, is randomly chosen from all of the open short positions in that option.

Table 14.8 contains selected terms of the S&P 500 option contract. In many ways, the terms of stock index options parallel those of stock options. The contract unit is $100 times the index level, mimicking the fact the stock options are written on 100 shares of stock. The tick size convention is also consistent with stock options. Option premiums at $3 and below have a minimum tick size of $.05 while options with premiums above $3 have a minimum tick size of $.10. The available contract months include the three near-term months followed by three additional months from the quarterly expiration cycle.[10] Leaps extending out three years are also offered. Also like stock options, the contracts expire on the Saturday after the third Friday of the contract month. Unlike stock options, however, stock index options are cash settlement rather than delivery contracts.

**TABLE 14.8** Selected terms of S&P 100 index option contract.

| | |
|---|---|
| Exchange | Chicago Board Options Exchange (CBOE) |
| Ticker symbol | SPX |
| Contract unit | $100 times the S&P 500 index |
| Tick size | 0.05 point up to $3 premiums; 0.10 point over $3 |
| Tick value | $5; $10 |
| Contract months | Three near-term months followed by three additional months from the March quarterly cycle. |
| Trading hours | 8:30 to 3:15 PM CST |
| Exercise style | American |
| Expiration day | Saturday following the third Friday of the contract month |
| Last day of trading | Business day (usually a Thursday) preceding the day on which the final settlement price is computed. |
| Final settlement price | Cash-settled at a special quotation of the index based on the opening prices of the index stocks on the expiration day. |

[10] On October 28, 2005, the CBOE launched trading in one-week options on the S&P 500. The so-called "weeklys" are listed each Friday, and expire the following Friday.

Like the S&P 500 index futures, the S&P 500 index option is settled on the expiration day at a special morning settlement quotation based on opening prices of the index stocks on Friday.[11]

### Exchange Traded Funds[12]

An *exchange traded fund* (ETF) is a hybrid security that behaves like an index portfolio but trades like a stock. To understand the popularity of ETFs, a brief review of the history of fund indexing is useful. The origin of fund indexing rests in the Sharpe (1964)/Lintner (1965) capital asset pricing model (CAPM), The CAPM says that investors should hold well-diversified portfolios that consist of all risky securities in the marketplace, with the proportion of wealth invested in each security equal to that security's market value relative to the total market value of all risky securities. Active portfolio management is unnecessary. Cash dividends are simply reinvested in the proportions dictated by the current market value weights. Other than that, investors "buy-and-hold."

Out of what seemed an esoteric theory in the early 1960s grew the practice of fund indexing. Early on, the most widely known, market value weighted index in the United States was the S&P 500.[13] Consequently, index funds began pegging their holdings to the S&P 500 portfolio, and the practice was born. The growth in the S&P 500 funds has been incredible. Perhaps the most well-known S&P 500 fund is the *Vanguard Index Trust—500 Portfolio*. The net asset value of the *500 Portfolio* was $14 million in 1976. At the end of December 2003, the amount was $64,368 million—an increase of nearly 460,000%! But this is only a single fund pegged to the S&P 500 portfolio. The total wealth invested in the S&P 500 index portfolio must account for Vanguard's other S&P 500 funds, other publicly traded S&P 500 funds managed by other investment companies, and privately held funds pegged to the S&P 500. In its 2003 *U.S. Indexed Assets Survey*, Standard & Poor's reported that assets tied to the S&P 500 exceeded the $1 trillion market, nearly 10% of the total market capitalization of the index.

Aside from the built-in diversification, index funds offer significant cost savings. Because the portfolio is passive, excessive trading costs (e.g., brokerage commissions and bid/ask spreads) associated with frequent turnover in actively managed portfolios are avoided. In addition, management fees are small. Since the portfolio composition is dictated by some third party (e.g., Standard and Poor's), index fund management *per se* is only a matter of taking new cash inflows (e.g., cash dividends) and allocating them across the index's constituent stocks. The only real disadvantage of traditional index funds is that they cannot be bought and sold on a real-time basis. Purchases and sales of the index fund occur only at

[11] For the quarterly expiration cycle, the settlement quotation is the same for S&P 500 futures, S&P 500 futures options, and S&P 500 index options. The financial press sometimes refers to this as a "triple-witching" hour.

[12] For a lucid review of all aspects of exchange traded funds, see Gastineau (2002). The materials in this section are drawn from the source, as well as information and data from the American Stock Exchange.

[13] The earliest public advocate of fund indexing was John Bogle of the Vanguard Group. For his reflections of fund indexing and the mutual fund industry, see Bogle (1994).

end-of-day closing values. In addition, many important trading strategies require a short position in the market. Short selling index funds is not possible.

The basic idea underlying an ETF is trading an entire portfolio as if it were a stock. The first foray into this arena was in 1989 when the Philadelphia Stock Exchange (PHLX) and the American Stock Exchange (AMEX) launched the Index Participation Shares (IPS). While IPS on a number of indexes were available, the IPS on the S&P 500 were by far the most popular. The market showed significant promise, however, not without controversy. The Chicago Mercantile Exchange (CME) and the Commodity Futures and Trading Commission (CFTC) filed a lawsuit charging that IPS were futures contracts and must be traded on a futures exchange, not a securities exchange.[14] IPS were cleared by the Options Clearing Corporation and fell under the regulatory jurisdiction of the Securities and Exchange Commission (SEC). Unfortunately, from the securities exchanges' perspective, the IPS were like futures contracts in the sense that there was a zero net supply. For every long, there was a short, and vice versa. A federal court in Chicago ruled that the IPS were illegal futures contracts, and PHLX and AMEX were required to close down IPS trading.

The next significant event in the history of ETFs in the United States was AMEX's launch of Standard and Poor's Depository Receipts (SPDRs) on January 29, 1993. These receipts represent an interest in the S&P 500 index stocks held by a unit investment trust, and trade like shares of a common stock. They can be bought on margin, and can be sold short, even on a downtick. The key features that earmark SPDRs as a security rather than a futures are (1) they are both created from the securities of an underlying portfolio; and (2) they can be redeemed into the securities of an underlying portfolio during any trading day.[15] Because of the substitutability of SPDRs with S&P 500 index stocks, price discrepancies will be few.[16] Otherwise, arbitrageurs will quickly move in to profit.[17] ETF holders are eligible to receive their pro rata share of dividends, if any, accumulated on the stocks held in the portfolio.

Figure 14.1 shows the annual trading volume of the AMEX SPDRs since inception. While the initial pace of trading was modest, with less than an average of 100 million shares traded annually in the period 1993 through 1995, volume has grown to over 10.3 billion shares in 2003—a phenomenal success by most standards. The wealth invested in SPDRs now exceeds all S&P 500 index funds other than the Vanguard Group's *Index Trust—500 Portfolio*. The dollar trading volume of SPDRs still lags behind S&P 500 futures. The dollar value of

---

[14] Recall the discussion of competing regulatory authorities in Chapter 1.

[15] The AMEX was not the first securities exchange to adopt a unit trust style of ETF. Toronto Stock Exchange Index Participations or TIPS had introduced such an ETF in Canada a number of years earlier.

[16] AMEX has a webpage (that can be accessed from www.amex.com) for calculating summary statistics of the size of the premium/discount over the recent past. As of April 19, 2004, the mean (standard deviation) of the premium of the bid/ask midpoint over the net asset value of the fund over all trading days during the most recent 12 months was –0.01 (0.04). The minimum value observed over the period was –0.27, and the maximum was 0.14.

[17] ETF creations and redemptions are restricted to large transactions, typically in multiples of 50,000 shares but ranging from 25,000 to 600,000 shares, usually transacted by large investors and institutions.

**FIGURE 14.1** Number of shares traded and dollar value of shares traded by year for AMEX SPDRs during the period January 1993 through December 2003.

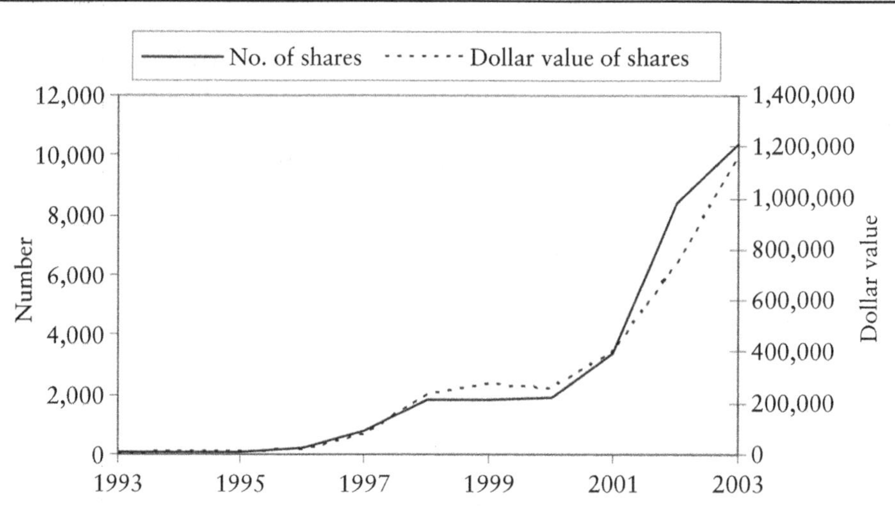


the SPDRs traded in 2003 was $1.15 trillion, compared to $14.57 trillion for the S&P 500 futures (about 7.91%). But SPDRs are aimed at a retail customer market. S&P 500 futures are largely used by institutional customers.

SPDRs are not the only successful ETF. Table 14.9 shows that the daily dollar volume of the most ETFs traded on the AMEX as of the close on April 13, 2004. Although the trading volume of the SPDRs was nearly double that of the NASDAQ 100 QQQQs, the so-called "quadruple Qs" volume was respectable at $3.66 billion. Indeed, the dollar value of shares outstanding in the form of unit trusts is greater for the QQQs than the SPDRs. The table also shows that the AMEX now has 122 ETFs on a variety of indexes including broad-based stock portfolios, stock industry sectors, international stock portfolio, and bond indexes. The DIAMONDS are shares of the Dow Jones Industrial Average (DJIA). The iShares are a family of ETFs based created by Barclay Global Investors on a variety of different indexes.

## COMPOSITION OF STOCK INDEXES

Before discussing no-arbitrage price relations and valuation equations for stock index derivatives, it is important to have a clear understanding of index construction and its implications for modeling dividend income. Generally speaking, stock indexes underlying derivative contracts are either (1) value-weighted or (2) price-weighted. With a value-weighted index, each stock is weighted by its market capitalization, while, with a price-weighted index, each stock is weighted by its price. In this section, the details of index construction are provided. Value-weighted indexes are discussed first, followed by price-weighted indexes. The section also examines the daily cash dividend payments of the S&P 500 and Dow Jones Industrial Average indexes in order to ascertain the most

**TABLE 14.9** Summary of trading activity on April 13, 2004 for all AMEX ETFs with shares outstanding in excess of 1 billion dollars.

| Name | Ticker Symbol | Last Trade | In Dollars | | In Shares | |
|---|---|---|---|---|---|---|
| | | | Daily Volume | Shares Outstanding | Daily Volume | Shares Outstanding |
| NASDAQ-100 Index Tracking Stock | QQQQ | 36.63 | 99,984,200 | 729,800,000 | 3,662,421,246 | 26,732,574,000 |
| Vanguard Total Stock Market VIPERs | VTI | 109.51 | 365,800 | 222,506,000 | 40,058,758 | 24,366,632,060 |
| SPDRS | SPY | 113.21 | 55,791,200 | 168,873,000 | 6,316,121,752 | 19,118,112,330 |
| MidCap SPDRS | MDY | 110.07 | 1,935,200 | 72,431,000 | 213,007,464 | 7,972,480,170 |
| DIAMONDS | DIA | 103.84 | 6,793,000 | 61,008,000 | 705,385,120 | 6,335,070,720 |
| iShares MSCI-EAFE | EFA | 142.45 | 324,300 | 35,800,000 | 46,196,535 | 5,099,710,000 |
| iShares Russell 2000 | IWM | 116.64 | 8,225,000 | 38,800,000 | 959,364,000 | 4,525,632,000 |
| iShares S&P 500 | IVV | 113.34 | 217,900 | 36,600,000 | 24,696,786 | 4,148,244,000 |
| iShares Russell 1000 Value | IWD | 59.41 | 181,900 | 44,400,000 | 10,806,679 | 2,637,804,000 |
| iShares GS $ InvesTop Corp Bond Fn | LQD | 110.31 | 91,200 | 22,200,000 | 10,060,272 | 2,448,882,000 |
| iShares MSCI-Japan | EWJ | 10.94 | 10,457,700 | 208,200,000 | 114,407,238 | 2,277,708,000 |
| iShares Russell 1000 | IWB | 60.69 | 72,300 | 30,900,000 | 4,387,887 | 1,875,321,000 |
| iShares S&P MidCap 400 | IJH | 120.48 | 113,800 | 14,150,000 | 13,710,624 | 1,704,792,000 |
| iShares Lehman 1-3 Year Treasury B | SHY | 82.31 | 181,500 | 18,700,000 | 14,939,265 | 1,539,197,000 |
| iShares Russell 2000 Growth | IWO | 62.72 | 1,825,600 | 24,450,000 | 114,501,632 | 1,533,504,000 |
| iShares Russell 1000 Growth | IWF | 47.58 | 191,900 | 31,750,000 | 9,130,602 | 1,510,665,000 |
| iShares MSCI-Mexico | EWW | 20.74 | 257,300 | 67,292,000 | 5,336,402 | 1,395,636,080 |
| iShares Russell 3000 | IWV | 64.27 | 75,700 | 21,300,000 | 4,865,239 | 1,368,951,000 |
| iShares S&P SmallCap 600 | IJR | 141.69 | 352,000 | 9,150,000 | 49,874,880 | 1,296,463,500 |
| Select Sector SPDR-Technology | XLK | 20.54 | 501,400 | 58,201,000 | 10,298,756 | 1,195,448,540 |
| iShares Russell 2000 Value | IWN | 168.10 | 385,900 | 5,950,000 | 64,869,790 | 1,000,195,000 |
| Others | | | 523,500 | 5,600,000 | 997,893,020 | 19,032,796,250 |
| TOTAL | | | 7,316,500 | 66,608,000 | 13,392,333,947 | 139,115,818,650 |
| No. of funds | | 122 | | | | |

*Source:* Data compiled from www.amex.com.

realistic way to model the dividend income of the index portfolio (i.e., as a discrete flow or as a continuous rate).

### Value-Weighted Indexes[18]

The "value" of the common stocks in a value-weighted index refers to the total market capitalization of the firm's outstanding shares, that is, the number of shares outstanding, $n_{i,t}$, times the current price per share, $p_{i,t}$. The total market value of the index at time $t$ is therefore

$$\text{Total market value of index}_t = \sum_{i=1}^{N} n_{i,t} p_{i,t} \tag{14.1}$$

where $N$ is the number of stocks in the index. This market value is then scaled by a divisor so that the index in period $t$ is

$$S_t = \frac{\sum_{i=1}^{N} n_{i,t} p_{i,t}}{\text{Divisor}_t} \tag{14.2}$$

The divisor represents what the stocks currently in the index would have been worth in the base period. In the base period the divisor is the market value of the stocks in the index,

$$\text{Divisor}_t = \sum_{i=1}^{N} n_{i,0} p_{i,0} \tag{14.3}$$

Note that stock splits and stock dividends have no effect on the index level because the increase in shares outstanding is proportionately offset by a reduction in share price.

Over time, the numerator of (14.2) changes because stocks enter or leave the index or because certain corporate actions such as restructurings, spinoffs, share issuance or repurchase affect the market value of a stock and hence the value of the index. Because such changes do not reflect market movements, an adjustment to the divisor is made on the day that a change occurs.[19] The new divisor on day $t$ is just the old divisor on day $t$ adjusted by the ratio of the market value of the new index composition on day $t$ divided by the market value of the old index composition on day $t$,

---

[18] A value-weighted index is an inherently better measure of market performance. When the market is in equilibrium, the supply of stocks equals demand. The contribution of stock $i$ to the performance of the market, therefore, equals the performance of stock $i$ times the market value of all of $i$'s shares outstanding as a proportion of the total market value of all stocks.

$$\text{New divisor}_t = \frac{\text{Market value of new index}_t}{\text{Market value of old index}_t} \times \text{Old divisor}_t \qquad (14.4)$$

The best known value-weighted index in the United States is the S&P 500. The S&P 500 consists of 500 common stocks, 423 of which traded on the NYSE as of March 1, 2004 and 77 of which traded NASDAQ. The index was designed by Standard & Poors' to contain stocks from a broad variety of industry groupings. The market value for the base period of the S&P 500 is the average market values of the component stocks during the years 1941 through 1943. At that time, the index was set equal to 10. The S&P 500 index level at the close of trading on March 1, 2004 was 1,155.96. This is based on a total S&P 500 index market capitalization of $10,715,550,195,285 and a divisor of $9,269,805,842.

Value-weighted indexes can be heavily swayed by only a few stocks. Table 14.10 contains a list of the largest 50 stocks in the S&P 500 index as of the close of trading on March 1, 2004. Note that the largest 50 stocks account for nearly 52% of the total market capitalization of the index. The largest 10 stocks account for over 23%. To see the effect that a single large stock may have, consider the shares of General Electric, which accounted for 3.07% of the index on March 1, 2004. Using the information in Table 14.10 together with the above information about the total market capitalization and the divisor of the index, it is possible to show that a $1 move in the share price of General Electric will move the S&P 500 index by 1.08 points.

It is also worth noting that the stock indexes underlying derivatives contracts traded in non-U.S. countries are, in general, value-weighted indexes. These include Germany's DAX-30, France's CAC-40, the U.K.'s FT-SE 100, Australia's All Ordinaries Share Price index, Hong Kong's Hang Seng index, and Canada's TSE-35.

### Price-Weighted Indexes

A *price-weighted index* is like a value-weighted index, except that the number of shares outstanding does not play a role. The price-weighted index is computed as

$$S_t = \frac{\sum_{i=1}^{N} p_{i,t}}{\text{Divisor}_t} \qquad (14.5)$$

[19] An interesting phenomenon in its own right is the behavior of the price of the stock when it is added to or deleted from the S&P 500 index. Because about 10% of the market capitalization of the S&P 500 index portfolio is held as passive index mutual funds (e.g., The Vanguard Group's *500 Portfolio*) or exchange-traded funds (e.g., AMEX's SPDRs), an addition to (deletion from) implies that 10% of a stock's outstanding shares must be purchased (sold) on the day of the change. Such order imbalances generate abnormal price movements in the stock market. The early evidence indicated abnormal returns on order of two percent, See, for example, Harris and Gurel (1986) and Shliefer (1986). Because of substantial growth in indexing to the S&P 500 in recent years, the effect has become much larger. See, for example, Beneish and Whaley (1997, 2002).

**TABLE 14.10** Fifty highest market value stocks in the S&P 500 index portfolio as of the close of trading on March 1, 2004.

| Ticker | Company | Closing Price | No. of Shares | Market Value | Relative Weight | Cumulative Weight |
|---|---|---|---|---|---|---|
| GE | General Electric | 32.79 | 10,041 | 329,240 | 3.07% | 3.07% |
| MSFT | Microsoft Corp. | v26.70 | 10,812 | 288,693 | 2.69% | 5.77% |
| PFE | Pfizer, Inc. | 36.90 | 7,632 | 281,603 | 2.63% | 8.39% |
| XOM | Exxon Mobil Corp. | 42.52 | 6,610 | 281,049 | 2.62% | 11.02% |
| WMT | Wal-Mart Stores | 60.45 | 4,328 | 261,614 | 2.44% | 13.46% |
| C | Citigroup Inc. | 50.46 | 5,159 | 260,307 | 2.43% | 15.89% |
| INTC | Intel Corp. | 29.72 | 6,532 | 194,131 | 1.81% | 17.70% |
| AIG | American Int'l. Group | 74.09 | 2,608 | 193,223 | 1.80% | 19.50% |
| IBM | International Bus. Machines | 97.04 | 1,720 | 166,950 | 1.56% | 21.06% |
| CSCO | Cisco Systems | 23.54 | 6,903 | 162,505 | 1.52% | 22.58% |
| JNJ | Johnson & Johnson | 53.76 | 2,968 | 159,567 | 1.49% | 24.07% |
| PG | Procter & Gamble | 103.86 | 1,297 | 134,678 | 1.26% | 25.32% |
| BAC | Bank of America Corp. | 82.13 | 1,486 | 122,029 | 1.14% | 26.46% |
| KO | Coca Cola Co. | 49.62 | 2,452 | 121,644 | 1.14% | 27.60% |
| MO | Altria Group, Inc. | 58.18 | 2,031 | 118,174 | 1.10% | 28.70% |
| MRK | Merck & Co. | 48.45 | 2,225 | 107,801 | 1.01% | 29.71% |
| VZ | Verizon Communications | 38.70 | 2,762 | 106,872 | 1.00% | 30.70% |
| WFC | Wells Fargo | 57.63 | 1,692 | 97,512 | 0.91% | 31.61% |
| CVX | ChevronTexaco Corp. | 90.27 | 1,069 | 96,495 | 0.90% | 32.51% |
| PEP | PepsiCo Inc. | 52.16 | 1,717 | 89,546 | 0.84% | 33.35% |
| DELL | Dell Inc. | 33.52 | 2,560 | 85,825 | 0.80% | 34.15% |
| JPM | J.P. Morgan Chase & Co. | 41.53 | 2,040 | 84,732 | 0.79% | 34.94% |
| HD | Home Depot | 36.84 | 2,275 | 83,819 | 0.78% | 35.72% |
| AMGN | Amgen | 64.19 | 1,290 | 82,802 | 0.77% | 36.50% |
| LLY | Lilly (Eli) & Co. | 73.44 | 1,123 | 82,466 | 0.77% | 37.27% |
| SBC | SBC Communications Inc. | 24.25 | 3,311 | 80,284 | 0.75% | 38.02% |
| UPS | United Parcel Service | 69.85 | 1,124 | 78,528 | 0.73% | 38.75% |
| TWX | Time Warner Inc. | 17.23 | 4,522 | 77,910 | 0.73% | 39.48% |
| FNM | Fannie Mae | 77.25 | 972 | 75,061 | 0.70% | 40.18% |
| HPQ | Hewlett-Packard | 23.00 | 3,049 | 70,130 | 0.65% | 40.83% |
| AXP | American Express | 53.65 | 1,286 | 69,009 | 0.64% | 41.47% |
| ORCL | Oracle Corp. | 13.07 | 5,227 | 68,312 | 0.64% | 42.11% |
| CMCSA | Comcast Corp. | 30.33 | 2,251 | 68,271 | 0.64% | 42.75% |
| ABT | Abbott Labs | 43.40 | 1,563 | 67,850 | 0.63% | 43.38% |
| VIA.B | Viacom Inc. | 38.74 | 1,749 | 67,766 | 0.63% | 44.01% |
| MWD | Morgan Stanley | 60.75 | 1,083 | 65,795 | 0.61% | 44.63% |
| WB | Wachovia Corp. (New) | 48.66 | 1,324 | 64,414 | 0.60% | 45.23% |
| MMM | 3M Company | 78.78 | 785 | 61,833 | 0.58% | 45.81% |
| ONE | Bank One Corp. | 54.44 | 1,118 | 60,860 | 0.57% | 46.37% |
| MER | Merrill Lynch | 62.29 | 945 | 58,883 | 0.55% | 46.92% |
| TYC | Tyco International | 29.11 | 1,999 | 58,194 | 0.54% | 47.47% |
| MDT | Medtronic Inc. | 47.25 | 1,212 | 57,270 | 0.53% | 48.00% |
| USB | U.S. Bancorp | 28.71 | 1,929 | 55,374 | 0.52% | 48.52% |
| DIS | Walt Disney Co. | 26.87 | 2,045 | 54,959 | 0.51% | 49.03% |
| BMY | Bristol-Myers Squibb | 28.24 | 1,939 | 54,765 | 0.51% | 49.54% |
| TXN | Texas Instruments | 31.02 | 1,731 | 53,684 | 0.50% | 50.04% |
| WYE | Wyeth | 39.64 | 1,332 | 52,793 | 0.49% | 50.54% |
| BLS | BellSouth | 27.68 | 1,848 | 51,156 | 0.48% | 51.01% |
| GS | Goldman Sachs Group | 107.35 | 473 | 50,827 | 0.47% | 51.49% |
| QCOM | QUALCOMM Inc. | 62.75 | 800 | 50,204 | 0.47% | 51.96% |

In a price-weighted index, the divisor in the base period equals the sum of the prices of the stocks in the base period, that is,

$$\text{Divisor}_0 = \sum_{i=1}^{N} p_{i,0} \tag{14.6}$$

Like a value-weighted index, the divisor of a price-weighted index is adjusted to reflect changes in composition, stock splits, stock dividends and spin-offs so that the index level remains unchanged. Unlike the value-weighted index, however, the divisor of the price-weighted index is not adjusted for new stock issues or share repurchases.

The best known price-weighted is the Dow Jones Industrial Average or DJIA or, simply, the Dow, in honor of Charles H. Dow who unveiled this average of industrial stock prices on May 26, 1896. The mechanics of the index had to be simple since, at the time, the index had to be computed by hand. The index was therefore a simple average of the prices of the constituent stocks. At inception, the Dow had only 12 stocks and a level of 40.94. In 1916, the number of stocks was increased to 20, and, in 1928, to 30, where it remains today. It was in 1928 that the Dow initiated the use of a divisor to handle changes in composition and corporate actions including stock splits, stock dividends, restructurings and spin-offs. Its level as of March 1, 2004 was 10,678.14. Of the 30 stocks in the Dow, 28 trade on the NYSE and 2 trade on NASDAQ.

The composition of the DJIA on March 1, 2004 is given in Table 14.11. Only one of the original 12 Dow stocks remains, General Electric. Note the implied weights of the stocks in the Dow. Proctor & Gamble has the most weight, followed by IBM. The last three columns of Table 14.11 construct the weights for each Dow stock if the index was value-weighted. Proctor & Gamble constitutes only 4.13% of the value-weighted Dow, considerably less than its 7.20% price-weight. General Electric's value-weighted contribution, on the other hand, is 10.11%, considerably more than its price-weighted contribution of 2.27%. Overall, the correlation between the price-weights and value-weights is only 0.41. The market value of the Dow is \$3.258 trillion, about 30% of the market value of the S&P 500.

To illustrate the computation of the DJIA, consider the values reported at the bottom on Table 14.11. The sum of the prices of the Dow stocks on March 1, 2004 was \$1,441.58. On the same day, the divisor was 0.13500289. The closing level of the Dow on March 1, 2004 was therefore 10,678.14.

### Discrete or Continuous Dividend Income?

The decision about whether to model the dividend income of an index portfolio as discrete cash payments or as a continuous dividend yield must be based on an analysis of the actual dividend payments. Here, such an analysis is conducted for the S&P 500 and DJIA indexes, as they have two of the most active derivative contract markets.

**TABLE 14.11** Thirty Dow Jones Industrial Average stocks as of the close of trading on March 1, 2004.

| Ticker | Company | Closing Price | Price Weight | No. of Shares | Market Value | Value Weight |
|---|---|---|---|---|---|---|
| PG | Procter & Gamble Co. | 103.86 | 7.20% | 1,297 | 134,678 | 4.13% |
| IBM | International Business Machines Corp. | 97.04 | 6.73% | 1,720 | 166,950 | 5.12% |
| UTX | United Technologies Corp. | 92.20 | 6.40% | 515 | 47,517 | 1.46% |
| MMM | 3M Co. | 78.78 | 5.46% | 785 | 61,833 | 1.90% |
| CAT | Caterpillar Inc. | 76.84 | 5.33% | 347 | 26,682 | 0.82% |
| WMT | Wal-Mart Stores Inc. | 60.45 | 4.19% | 4,328 | 261,614 | 8.03% |
| MO | Altria Group Inc. | 58.18 | 4.04% | 2,031 | 118,174 | 3.63% |
| JNJ | Johnson & Johnson | 53.76 | 3.73% | 2,968 | 159,567 | 4.90% |
| AXP | American Express Co. | 53.65 | 3.72% | 1,286 | 69,009 | 2.12% |
| C | Citigroup Inc. | 50.46 | 3.50% | 5,159 | 260,307 | 7.99% |
| KO | Coca-Cola Co. | 49.62 | 3.44% | 2,452 | 121,644 | 3.73% |
| GM | General Motors Corp. | 48.65 | 3.37% | 561 | 27,281 | 0.84% |
| MRK | Merck & Co. Inc. | 48.45 | 3.36% | 2,225 | 107,801 | 3.31% |
| DD | E.I. DuPont de Nemours & Co. | 45.63 | 3.17% | 997 | 45,483 | 1.40% |
| IP | International Paper Co. | 44.50 | 3.09% | 480 | 21,381 | 0.66% |
| BA | Boeing Co. | 43.77 | 3.04% | 841 | 36,821 | 1.13% |
| XOM | Exxon Mobil Corp. | 42.52 | 2.95% | 6,610 | 281,049 | 8.63% |
| JPM | J.P. Morgan Chase & Co. | 41.53 | 2.88% | 2,040 | 84,732 | 2.60% |
| AA | Alcoa Inc. | 38.40 | 2.66% | 865 | 33,230 | 1.02% |
| HD | Home Depot Inc. | 36.84 | 2.56% | 2,275 | 83,819 | 2.57% |
| HON | Honeywell International Inc. | 35.31 | 2.45% | 862 | 30,439 | 0.93% |
| GE | General Electric Co. | 32.79 | 2.27% | 10,041 | 329,240 | 10.11% |
| INTC | Intel Corp. | 29.72 | 2.06% | 6,532 | 194,131 | 5.96% |
| EK | Eastman Kodak Co. | 29.03 | 2.01% | 287 | 8,319 | 0.26% |
| MCD | McDonald's Corp. | 28.41 | 1.97% | 1,269 | 36,057 | 1.11% |
| DIS | Walt Disney Co. | 26.87 | 1.86% | 2,045 | 54,959 | 1.69% |
| MSFT | Microsoft Corp. | 26.70 | 1.85% | 10,812 | 288,693 | 8.86% |
| SBC | SBC Communications Inc. | 24.25 | 1.68% | 3,311 | 80,284 | 2.46% |
| HPQ | Hewlett-Packard Co. | 23.00 | 1.60% | 3,049 | 70,130 | 2.15% |
| T | AT&T Corp. | 20.37 | 1.41% | 790 | 16,090 | 0.49% |
| | Sum across closing prices on 3/1/4 | 1,441.58 | 100.00% | | 3,257,913 | 100.00% |
| | Divisor on 3/1/4 | 0.13500289 | | | | |
| | Closing DJIA 3/1/4 | 10,678.14 | | | | |

In Chapter 8, cash dividends of individual U.S. stocks were shown to be paid on a quarterly cycle. Since a stock index is nothing more than a portfolio of stocks, the dividend income of a value-weighted index is simply the sum of the value-weighted dividends of the index stocks, that is,

$$d_{VW,t} = \frac{\sum_{i=1}^{N} n_{i,t} d_{i,t}}{\text{Divisor}_t} \tag{14.7}$$

and the dividend income of a price-weighted index is the sum of the equal-weighted dividends of the index stocks, that is,

$$d_{PW,t} = \frac{\sum_{i=1}^{N} d_{i,t}}{\text{Divisor}_t} \tag{14.8}$$

If the quarterly dividend payment cycles of the stocks comprising the index are randomly distributed throughout the year and if the number of stocks in the index is large, the dividend stream of the index will be reasonably smooth, and modeling the index dividends as a continuous yield would be appropriate. On the other hand, if the cash dividend payment cycles tend to cluster at different times during the year or if the number of stocks is small, modeling the index dividends as discrete cash payments is better.

**S&P 500 Dividends** Figure 14.2 shows the average daily cash dividends of the S&P 500 index by calendar month during the period 1989 through 2003. Note the prominence of the cash dividends in the Feb./May/Aug./Nov. cycle. The amount of the dividends paid during these four months is nearly as much as the other eight months combined. This seasonal pattern induces considerable variation in the index's dividend yield rate. Based on Figure 14.2, the dividend yield rate in the month of January is about half that of February. Depending on which calendar months the life of the derivatives contract spans, the dividend yield rate on the S&P 500 index will vary. This is not very comforting if you want to apply the constant dividend yield valuation framework.

**FIGURE 14.2** Average daily cash dividends of the S&P 500 index by month of year during the period January 1989 through December 2003.

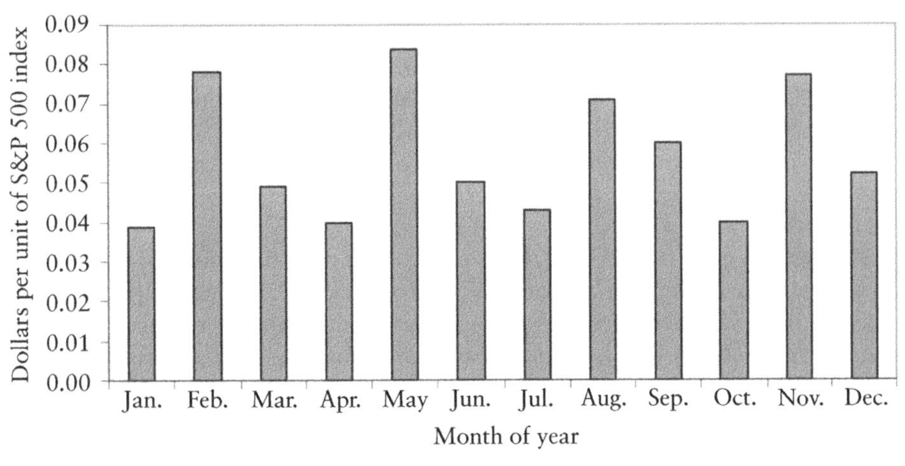

**FIGURE 14.3** Average daily cash dividends of the S&P 500 index by day of week during the period January 1989 through December 2003.

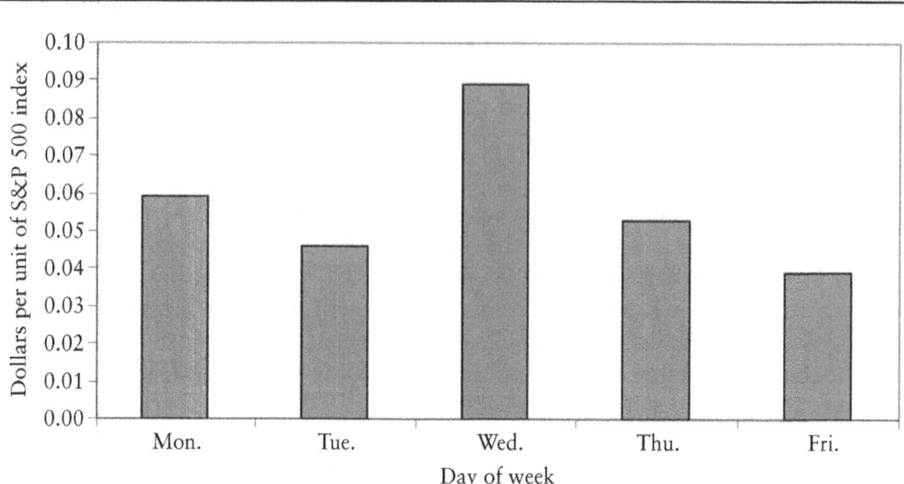


The quarterly payment cycle is not the only pattern that appears in the S&P 500 index cash dividends. Figure 14.3 shows the average daily cash dividends of the S&P 500 index by day of week. More dividends are paid on Mondays and Wednesdays than other days of the week. For short-term derivative contracts, this variation in dividend payments can have a pronounced effect on valuation. Put differently, the dividend yield rate of the index will vary during the derivative contract's life. Taken together, the evidence showing monthly and daily variation in cash dividends supports the application of the discrete flow cost of carry framework.

One final note regarding the S&P 500 cash dividends is warranted. Over the period 1989 through 2003, the total cash dividends paid on the S&P 500 index has grown by about 58%, as is shown in Figure 14.4. The growth in the index itself, however, has been about 285%. Consequently, the annual dividend yield rate has fallen dramatically over the period, from 3.89% annually in 1989 to only 1.96% in 2003.[20] The smaller are the dividends relative to the index level, the less important modeling dividends accurately becomes. Hence, using the constant dividend yield model to value S&P 500 derivatives is not completely without merit.

**DJIA Dividends** Figure 14.5 shows the average daily cash dividends of the DJIA by calendar month during the period 1963 through 2003. For the DJIA, the cash dividends in the Feb./May/Aug./Nov. cycle are even more pronounced than they were for the S&P 500. The amount of the dividends paid during these four months easily exceeds the other eight months combined. Figure 14.6 shows the average daily cash dividends of the DJIA by day of week. Considerably more

[20] The reported dividend yield of the S&P 500 is a continuous rate computed as $\ln[(S + DVDS)/S]$, where $DVDS$ is the sum of the cash dividends paid during the year and $S$ is the closing level of the index on the last day of trading of the previous year.

**FIGURE 14.4** Total cash dividends and dividend yield of the S&P 500 index by year during the period January 1989 through December 2003.

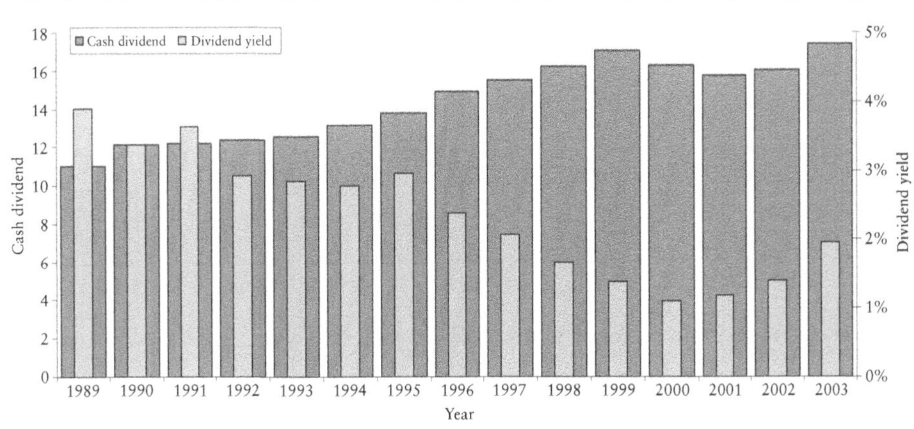


**FIGURE 14.5** Average daily cash dividends of the DJIA index by month of year during the period January 1963 through December 2002.

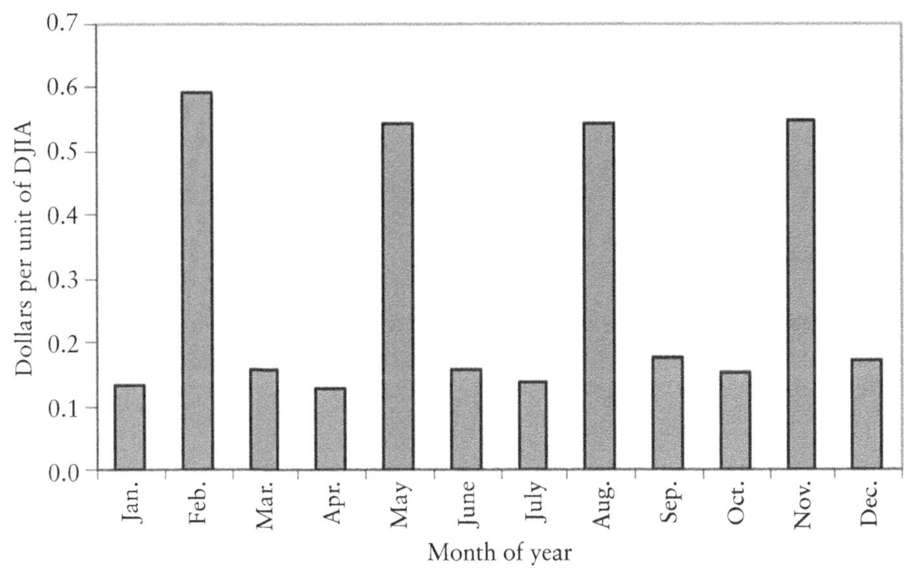


dividends are paid on Mondays than other days of the week. For the DJIA, it is clearly inappropriate to apply a valuation framework that assumes the dividend yield rate is constant through time. The evidence clearly supports the application of the discrete flow valuation results.

**FIGURE 14.6** Average daily cash dividends of the DJIA index by day of week during the period January 1963 through December 2002.

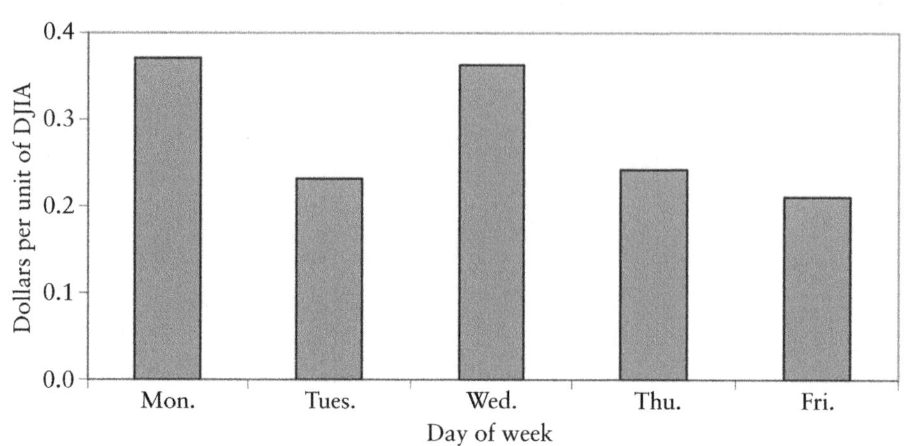


## NO-ARBITRAGE RELATIONS AND VALUATION

Under the assumption of discrete dividend payments on the underlying index, the no-arbitrage price relations and valuation methods for stock index derivatives are summarized in Table 14.12. For completeness, the valuation results for an index with a continuous dividend yield rate are provided in Table 14.13. Below, the focus is primarily on the former.

### Stock Index Futures

**Index Arbitrage** The cost of carry relation between the stock index futures price and the level of the underlying index under the assumption of known discrete dividends in future value form is

$$F = Se^{rT} - FVD \tag{14.9}$$

and, expressed as a prepaid forward contract, is

$$Fe^{-rT} = S - PVD \tag{14.10}$$

where

$$FVD = \sum_{i=1}^{n} D_i e^{r(T-t_i)}$$

is the future value of the cash dividends paid during the futures life and

**TABLE 14.12** Summary of no-arbitrage price relations and valuation equations/ methods for derivatives on stock indexes with discrete dividends.

| No-Arbitrage Price Relations | | |
|---|---|---|
| **Forward/Futures** | $f = F = Se^{rT} - FVD$ or $fe^{-rT} = Fe^{-rT} = S - PVD$ | |
| | where $FVD = \sum_{i=1}^{n} D_i e^{r(T-t_i)}$ and $PVD = e^{-rT}FVD = \sum_{i=1}^{n} D_i e^{-rt_i}$ | |
| **European-Style:** | **Options** | **Futures Options** |
| Lower bound for call | $c \geq \max(0, S - PVD - Xe^{-rT})$ | $c \geq \max[0, e^{-rT}(F - X)]$ |
| Lower bound for put | $p \geq \max(0, Xe^{-rT} - S + PVD)$ | $p \geq \max[0, e^{-rT}(X - F)]$ |
| Put-call parity | $c - p = S - PVD - Xe^{-rT}$ | $c - p = e^{-rT}(F - X)$ |
| **American-Style:** | | |
| Lower bound for call | $C \geq \max(0, S - PVD - Xe^{-rT}, S - X)$ | $C \geq \max(0, F - X)$ |
| Lower bound for put | $P \geq \max(0, Xe^{-rT} - S + PVD, X - S)$ | $P \geq \max(0, X - F)]$ |
| Put-call parity | $S - PVD - X \leq C - P \leq S - Xe^{-rT}$ | $Fe^{-rT} - X \leq C - P \leq F - Xe^{-rT}$ |
| **Valuation Equations/Methods** | | |
| **European-Style:** | **Options** | **Futures Options** |
| Call value | $c = S^x N(d_1) - Xe^{-rT}N(d_2)$ | $c = e^{-rT}[FN(d_1) - XN(d_2)]$ |
| Put value | $p = Xe^{-rT}N(-d_2) - S^x N(-d_1)$ | $p = e^{-rT}[XN(-d_2) - FN(-d_2)]$ |
| | where $S^x = S - PVD$, | where |
| | $d_1 = \frac{\ln(S^x / Xe^{-rT}) + 0.5\sigma^2 T}{\sigma\sqrt{T}}$ and $d_2 = d_1 - \sigma\sqrt{T}$ | $d_1 = \frac{\ln(F/X) + 0.5\sigma^2 T}{\sigma\sqrt{T}}$ and $d_2 = d_1 - \sigma\sqrt{T}$ |
| **American-Style:** | | |
| Call and put values | Numerical valuation: binomial method and trinomial method. | Numerical valuation: quadratic approximation, binomial method, and trinomial method. |

**TABLE 14.13** Summary of arbitrage price relations and valuation equations for derivatives on stock indexes with continuous dividend yields.

| **No-Arbitrage Price Relations** | | |
|---|---|---|
| **Forward/Futures** | Future value: $f = F = Se^{(r-\delta)T}$ Present value: $fe^{-rT} = Fe^{-rT} = Se^{-dT}$ | |
| **European-Style:** | **Options** | **Futures Options** |
| Lower bound for call | $c \geq \max(0, Se^{-\delta T} - Xe^{-rT})$ | $c \geq \max[0, e^{-rT}(F - X)]$ |
| Lower bound for put | $p \geq \max(0, Xe^{-rT} - Se^{-\delta T})$ | $p \geq \max[0, e^{-rT}(X - F)]$ |
| Put-call parity | $c - p = Se^{-\delta T} - Xe^{-rT}$ | $c - p = e^{-rT}(F - X)$ |
| **American-Style:** | | |
| Lower bound for call | $C \geq \max(0, Se^{-\delta T} - Xe^{-rT}, S - X)$ | $C \geq \max(0, F - X)$ |
| Lower bound for put | $P \geq \max(0, Xe^{-rT} - Se^{-\delta T}, X - S)$ | $P \geq \max(0, X - F)]$ |
| Put-call parity | $Se^{-\delta T} - X \leq C - P \leq S - Xe^{-rT}$ | $Fe^{-rT} - X \leq C - P \leq F - Xe^{-rT}$ |
| **Valuation Equations/Methods** | | |
| **European-Style:** | **Options** | **Futures Options** |
| Call value | $c = Se^{-\delta T}N(d_1) - Xe^{-rT}N(d_2)$ | $c = e^{-rT}[FN(d_1) - XN(d_2)]$ |
| Put value | $p = Xe^{-rT}N(-d_2) - Se^{-\delta T}N(-d_1)$ | $p = e^{-rT}[XN(-d_2) - FN(-d_2)]$ |
| | where $S^x = S - PVD$, | where |
| | $d_1 = \frac{\ln(Se^{-\delta T}/Xe^{-rT}) + 0.5\sigma^2 T}{\sigma\sqrt{T}}$ and $d_2 = d_1 - \sigma\sqrt{T}$ | $d_1 = \frac{\ln(F/X) + 0.5\sigma^2 T}{\sigma\sqrt{T}}$ and $d_2 = d_1 - \sigma\sqrt{T}$ |
| **American-Style:** | | |
| Call and put values | Numerical valuation: quadratic approximation, binomial method, and trinomial method. | Numerical valuation: quadratic approximation, binomial method, and trinomial method. |

$$PVD = FVDe^{-rT} = \sum_{i=1}^{n} D_i e^{-rt_i}$$

is the present value of the cash dividends. The relation arises from the absence of costless arbitrage opportunities in the marketplace. The intuition for this relation is that we have two ways to have a stock portfolio on hand at time $T$ at a price we know today. The first, represented by the left-hand side of (14.8), is to buy a futures contract with maturity $T$. At time $T$, we pay $F$ and receive the stock portfolio. The second, represented by the right-hand side of (14.8), is to borrow at a rate $r$ to buy the stock portfolio today at $S$, and then carry it until $T$ has elapsed. At time $T$, we must repay our borrowings plus interest, $Se^{rT}$, which is partially offset by the accumulated cash dividends (plus accrued interest) received while holding the stock portfolio, $FVD$. Since the two alternatives are perfect substitutes, the two sides of (14.8) must be equal. The second formulation (14.9) is the same as (14.8), except that it is expressed in present value terms.

**Fair Value** The term *fair value* is often used in conjunction with stock index arbitrage. Unfortunately, it is not always used in a consistent manner, and this often leads to confusion. To some, the definition of fair value is the theoretical futures price given the current index level, the cash dividends promised during the futures' life, and the risk-free rate of interest. In the interest of clarity, we will call this definition the *fair value of the futures*. By virtue of the cost of carry relation (14.8), we know that

$$\text{Fair value of futures} = Se^{rT} - FVD \tag{14.11}$$

To others, fair value is the theoretical futures price less the current index level. We will call this definition the *fair value of the basis*. Subtracting the current index level from (14.10), we get

$$\text{Fair value of basis} = S(e^{rT} - 1) - FVD \tag{14.12}$$

It is important to recognize that fair values are theoretical values and may not correspond to *actual* prices reported in the marketplace. The *premium* (or *spread*) refers to the difference between the current prices of the futures and the index assuming both markets are open. Thus, if the premium is above the fair value of the basis, index arbitrageurs will sell futures and buy the underlying stocks, driving the price of the futures down and the prices of stocks up. The arbitrage will continue until where the premium equals fair value. On the other hand, if the premium is below fair value, index arbitrageurs will buy the futures and sell the underlying stocks, driving the price of the futures up and the prices of stocks down.

Figure 14.7 shows the difference between the premium and the fair value (i.e., the *basis mispricing*) for the S&P 500 index and index futures on a minute-to-minute basis throughout the trading day on August 29, 2003. The vertical axis is in index points. The solid horizontal lines at 1.5 and –1.5 represent trading cost

**FIGURE 14.7** Intraday basis mispricing of the September 2003 S&P 500 futures on August 29, 2003.

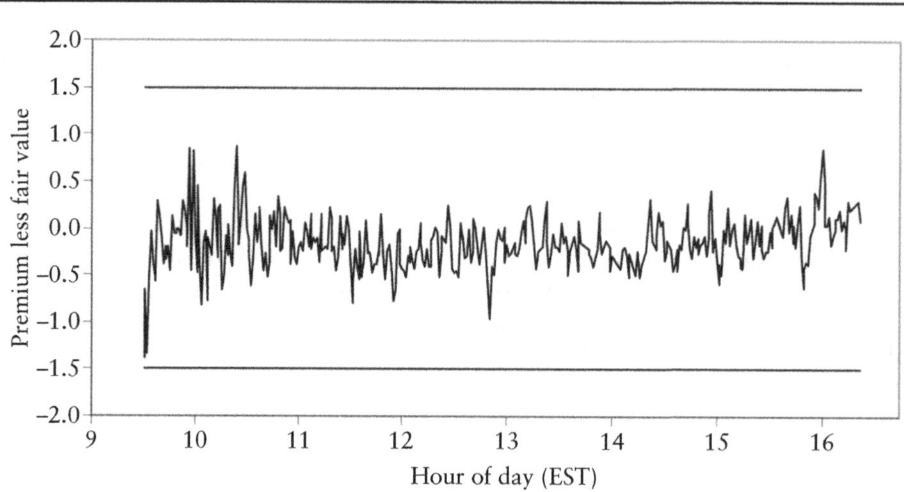


bands. Index arbitrageurs look for differences between the premium and fair value of at least 1.5 index points in order to cover the trading costs of index arbitrage. Note that the premium seldom violated the trading costs bands during the day. This should not be surprising in the sense that a number of index arbitrageurs monitor the basis mispricing continuously throughout the day and trade quickly each time there is a profitable arbitrage opportunity appears. The large deviations that appear at the beginning of the day are illusory. The S&P 500 index is based on last trade prices, and, when the index begins getting computed each morning (9:30 AM EST), it is based largely on the closing prices of the previous trading day. A few minutes after the open, when all stocks have traded (and incorporated overnight news), the premium is back near fair value.

**Program Trading** Stock index arbitrage is unlike typical basis arbitrage in the sense that buying and selling the underlying asset means buying and selling a precisely weighted *portfolio* of common stocks. Engaging in index arbitrage with the S&P 500 index, for example, requires a mechanism for buying or selling quickly and simultaneously all 500 stocks in the S&P 500 index portfolio. Since the simultaneous purchase or sale of the stocks in a precisely weighted and timely fashion is cumbersome, computers and computer programs are usually used to place transaction orders as well as to assist in the execution of those orders. For this reason, trading of portfolios of stocks is called *program trading*.

**Pre-Open Stock Market Predictions** Financial news programs such as Squawk Box on CNBC use the fair value of the basis to generate predictions regarding the level at which the stock will open (relative to the previous day's close) based on the fair value of the basis. The arithmetic is simple. They report two numbers. The first is the change in the futures price expected due to the fact that the stock market and the futures market close at different times during the day (4:00 versus 4:15 PM EST). This gets reported with the caption "Fair value." For the sake of illustration, suppose that what appears on the screen is "Fair value ▲5.00." The second is the change in the futures price from its previous day's close at 4:15 PM EST. The index futures contract trades electronically virtually 24 hours a day. Suppose that as of 8:30 AM EST (one hour before the stock market opens), the futures price change is reported as "Futures ▲2.00." Based of these two values reported on the screen, the commentator might say, "Even with the futures up 2, they are well below fair value and are a negative for the opening. We need to get to plus 5 in order to be at fair value." The implicit arithmetic is simply the difference between the second number and the first, that is, 2.00 − 5.00 = −3.00. The stock market is expected to open 3 points lower.

The mechanics of their computation is this. First, they compute the fair value of the basis using (14.9b), where $T$ is the time to expiration (expressed in years) of the futures contract and the index level is the previous day's close, $S_{4:00\text{ PM}}$.[21] Assume, for the sake of argument, fair value is 6.00. Next they compute the difference between the closing futures price and the closing index level. When both markets are open, we would expect the difference between the two prices to hover around fair value due the presence of index arbitrageurs in the marketplace (e.g., see Figure 14.7). The stock market closes at 4:00 PM EST, however, and the index futures market closes at 4:15 PM EST. The futures price may move up or down during this 15-minute interval of time as new market information arrives, and the closing premium may be quite different from fair value. Suppose, for the sake of argument, the futures price closes at a 1.00 premium to the closing index while fair value is 6.00. What would appear on the television screen is "Fair value ▲5.00," which means, based on the closing index level and the computed fair value, the futures price should be five points higher. If the early morning futures price is only 2.00 points higher than its close ("Futures ▲2.00"), the stock market is expected to open 3.00 points lower than the previous day's close. If the futures price is 9.00 points higher ("Futures ▲9.00"), the stock market is expected to open 4.00 points higher, and, if the futures price is 7.00 points lower ("Futures ▼7.00"), the stock market is expected to open 12.00 points lower.

### Special Settlement Quotation

S&P 500 index products use a special cash settlement quotation based on the opening prices of index stocks. As this number plays a key role in the profitability and risk of stock index arbitrage strategies, some discussion of the settlement procedure is warranted.

Probably the first question that arises in considering the settlement of the index derivatives contracts is why use the opening price rather than the closing price? After all, stock option contracts had expired at the close since they began trading a decade before index products were introduced.[22] The answer to the

[21] By this definition the fair value of the basis will be constant throughout the trading day.

[22] There is the subtle, but important, distinction that stock options settle through the delivery of the underlying stock, however.

question is that exchange-traded index products *were*, indeed, cash settled at the close when they were first introduced in the early 1980s. After about four years of closing settlements, the financial press and other market commentators uncovered the fact that stock indexes moved "abnormally" during the last hour of trading on the quarterly expiration of index futures, index futures options, and index options (the notorious "triple-witching hour"). Regulators quickly jumped into the fray, charging that index derivatives had become a destabilizing influence on the stock market and should be banned.

The key to understanding the controversy lies in the mechanics of index arbitrage and the cash settlement of index derivatives. Consider stock index futures arbitrage, for example. During the life of the futures contract, arbitrageurs tend to build up large positions in index futures and the stocks of the underlying index portfolio. If the premium tended to be above the fair value on average during the futures contract's life, arbitrageurs are likely be short index futures and long the index portfolio's stocks going into contract expiration, and vice versa. (Keep in mind that all index arbitrageurs see the same set of signals during the futures contract's life and are therefore likely to have similar positions.) Now consider the actions of the arbitrageurs at contract expiration. Because the index futures is cash-settled at the closing index level, arbitrageurs must unwind their stock portfolios at the same prices that go into the closing index level computation. To accomplish this, they place market-on-close orders.[23] If arbitrageurs are long stocks, they place market-on-close orders to sell and the excess selling pressure causes stock prices to fall at the close. If arbitrageurs are short stocks, the excess buying pressure causes stock prices to rise. Since the net positions of index arbitrageurs on the expiration day are not known, the direction of the price movement is not predictable. It is these uncertain price movements on the quarterly expiration cycle that are at the center of the triple-witching hour controversy.

Claims that index derivatives contract expirations destabilize the stock market have been refuted, however.[24] Stoll and Whaley (1987) examined movements in the S&P 500 index on the ten quarterly expirations (September 1983 through December 1985) and found they are roughly the same size as one would expect given trading costs in the marketplace. Indeed most of the observed index movement in the last hour of trading is not a real movement in stock prices. Consider the nature of the reported index level at any point in time during the day. The S&P 500 index, for example, is based on the last trade prices for each of the stocks within the index portfolio. The last trade price of a stock, in turn, may be at the bid or at the ask, depending on whether the trader sold or bought. Assuming the last trades of the 500 stocks in the index are approximately evenly balanced between buys and sells, the reported index level at any point in time can be thought of as being at a midpoint between the bid and ask

[23] A market-on-close (MOC) order is an order that is executed at the closing price of the day. Under current NYSE rules, a MOC order is assured of execution at the closing price if it is entered by a certain time during the trading day. There is no such mechanism to provide such assurance for NASDAQ trades, however.

[24] In this discussion, we focus primarily on U.S. stock markets, however, expiration-day effects have been analyzed empirically for Japan (see Karolyi (1996)), Australia (see Stoll and Whaley (1997)), and Hong Kong (see Bollen and Whaley (1999)).

levels of its constituent stocks. Now consider what happens when index arbitrageurs unwind their positions at the close on expiration day. Assuming they are long (short) stocks, they place MOC order to sell (buy). With all 500 stocks traded at bid (ask) prices, the reported index level moves, not because of selling pressure moving prices but only because the reported index level at this one instant in time is based entirely on bid (ask) prices.

Even though the evidence indicated that the price movements during the triple-witching hour were not abnormal, the Chicago Mercantile Exchange (CME) adopted a suggestion by the Securities and Exchange Commission (SEC) to move its S&P 500 futures and futures options expiration from the close of the trading day to the open beginning with the June 1987 contract expiration. The rationale was that at the open the NYSE specialists have the opportunity to disseminate information about large order imbalances to off-floor market participants, thereby minimizing price impact. The Chicago Board Options Exchange (CBOE) continued to settle its index options at the close. Put differently, as of June 1987, the triple-witching hour at the close of trading on the quarterly contract expiration cycle ceased to exist, and was replaced with a double-witching hour at the open and a single witching hour at the close.

Stoll and Whaley (1991) assessed the effect of the change in procedure and found that the absolute size of the price movement at the open was slightly smaller than it was under the previous regime. One possible explanation for this result is that expiration-day trading was split between the open and the close. Another is that the change in settlement procedure accomplished its goal of reducing price impact. Over time, a consensus seemed to develop that the opening settlement worked best, and the CBOE adopted the practice for its S&P 500 index options. Now all contracts are settled at the special opening quotation, and the triple-witching hour has reemerged, albeit at the open of the trading day.

Index arbitrageurs do not care whether they have close or open settlement. As long as they can liquidate their stocks at the same prices that are used to compute the settlement index level of the futures, they can exit their arbitrage positions risklessly. But the special opening settlement quotation has introduced an interesting anomaly. Since the settlement quotation is computed on the basis of the opening trade prices and opening trades occur at different times in the morning, the settlement quotation may be quite different from *any* reported index level during the trading day. Figure 14.8 shows the reported levels of the S&P 500 index on September 21, 2001—the expiration day of the September 2001 S&P 500 futures, futures options, and index options. The special settlement quotation for the S&P 500 contracts, based on the opening trade prices of the index stocks, was 939.57. During the trading day, however, the reported S&P 500 index level, based on last trade prices, never fell below 944.75, 5.18 points higher than the settlement quotation. Imagine the confusion of someone holding a September 2001 call with an exercise price of 940!

### Stock Index Options

The valuation equations/methods for index options are also provided in Tables 14.11 and 14.12. Most index options traded in the United States are European-

**FIGURE 14.8** Reported intraday S&P 500 index levels on September 21, 2001 in relation to previous day's close and the special opening quotation for the S&P 500 index (SET).

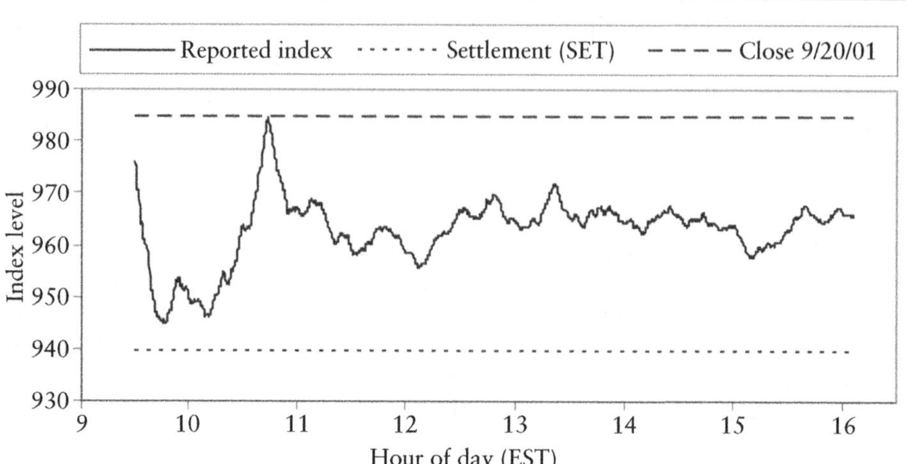


style. The most notable exception is the S&P 100 index options, which are American-style. All of the index futures options traded in the U.S. are American-style.

**ILLUSTRATION 14.1** Compute implied volatilities from at-the-money S&P 500 index option prices.

*Assume that the S&P 500 index level is 1,100, the three-month S&P 500 futures price is 1,103, and the three-month S&P 500 at-the-money call and puts options have prices of 48.50 and 45.60, respectively. The risk-free rate of interest is 2.5%. Compute the market's perception of expected stock market volatility over the next three months.*

The valuation formulas for European-style call and put options are given in Table 14.11. Since the present value of the cash dividends promised during the options' lives is not provided, you must find a way to deduce the amount. Since you are given the futures price, you can use the cost of carry relation (14.8a) to compute the future value of the dividends paid during the options' lives as

$$FVD = Se^{rT} - F = 1{,}100e^{0.025(3/12)} - 1{,}103 = 3.897$$

Based on the value of $FVD$, $PVD = 3.897e^{0.025(3/12)} = 3.872$.

With the present value of dividends computed, you can compute the index level net of the present value of the dividends paid during the options' life, that is, $S^x = 1{,}100 - 3.872 = 1{,}096.128$. Now you have all the information you need to solve for the implied standard deviations of the call and the put. Using the OV_OPTION_ISD function from the OPTVAL Library, the implied volatility of the call is 21.53% and the implied volatility of the put is 21.57%. Given put-call parity, the implied volatility figures should be exactly equal to one another. Their values are slightly different because reported prices are discrete (option prices above $3 are reported in dimes). To mitigate part of this error, you may want to average the call and put implied volatilities to arrive at your estimate of expected future volatility, 21.55%.

**ILLUSTRATION 14.2** Plot relation between implied volatility and exercise price.

*Under the BSM assumptions, the prices of all options written on the same underlying asset or futures should have the same implied volatility. In practice, however, they are not. Based on the settlement prices of the S&P 500 futures options reported in Table 14.7, compute the implied volatilities for all June 2004 put options and plot them as a function of exercise price. The closing Jun/04 S&P 500 futures prices was 1129.70, and the risk-free rate of interest was 0.8879%. The options have 65 days remaining to expiration.*

Futures options traded in the U.S. are American-style. To compute the implied volatilities for each option series, we use the OPTVAL function OV_FOPTION_ISD. Setting the option style argument in the function to "A" (for American-style) means that option valuation occurs using the quadratic approximation. The implied volatilities of the Jun/04 put option series are as shown:

| Exercise Price | Jun/04 Put Prices | Implied Volatility |
|---|---|---|
| 1000 | 4.90 | 22.71% |
| 1025 | 6.80 | 21.24% |
| 1050 | 9.60 | 19.85% |
| 1075 | 13.50 | 18.39% |
| 1100 | 19.30 | 17.06% |
| 1125 | 27.70 | 15.83% |
| 1150 | 39.40 | 14.67% |
| 1175 | 55.30 | 13.85% |
| 1200 | 74.70 | 13.12% |
| 1225 | 97.00 | 12.72% |
| 1250 | 120.80 | 12.38% |
| 1300 | 170.30 | 12.70% |

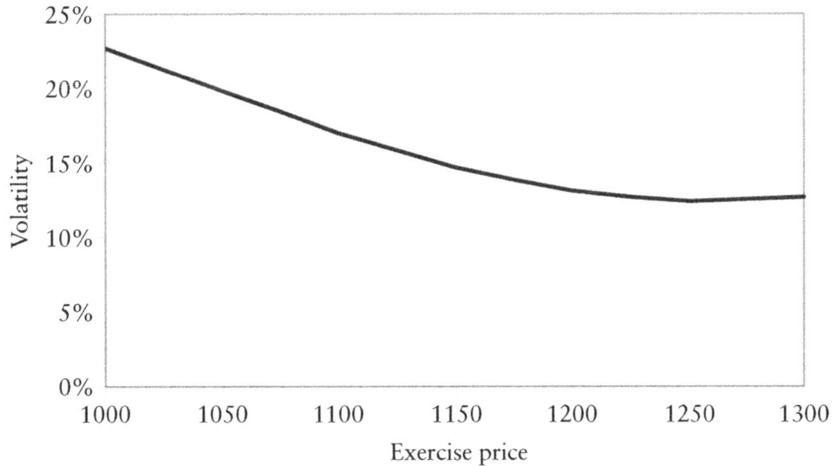

**Implied Volatility Function (IVF)** The relation between implied volatility and exercise price for index options shown in the above illustration is popularly referred to as the implied volatility "smile" or "sneer." Where this relation should be a horizontal line under the assumptions of the BSM model, implied volatility of S&P 500 futures options declines monotonically as exercise price rises. Most attempts to explain the shape of the IVF focus on relaxing the BSM assumption of constant volatility by allowing the local volatility rate of underlying security returns to evolve either deterministically or stochastically through time. Emanuel and MacBeth (1982) examine the power of the deterministic Cox and Ross (1976) constant elasticity of variance (CEV) model to explain the cross-sectional distribution of stock option prices. With its additional degree of freedom, the CEV model (necessarily) fits the observed structure of option prices better than the BSM constant volatility model. Out of sample, however, Emanuel and MacBeth conclude that the CEV model does no better than the BSM model. Similarly, the implied binomial tree framework of Dupire (1994), Derman and Kani (1994), and Rubinstein (1994) offers a deterministic local volatility structure so flexible that, in sample, it can describe the cross-section of options prices exactly at any point in time. Empirical tests by Dumas, Fleming, and Whaley (1998), however, show that a model based on a simple deterministic volatility structure has parameters that are highly unstable through time. Taken together, this evidence suggests that deterministic volatility models cannot explain the time-series variation in option prices or, equivalently, in the shape of the IVF.

Option valuation models based on stochastic volatility assumptions also have the potential to explain the shape of the IVF. In particular, a stochastic volatility model can generate the observed downward sloping IVF if innovations to volatility are negatively correlated with underlying asset returns. A negative relation between volatility and returns has been documented empirically by Black (1976) for individual stocks and Nelson (1991) for the index. Chernov et al. (2003) study a two-factor stochastic volatility model and find that it achieves a good fit to daily Dow Jones Industrial Average returns. Studies by Jorion (1989) and Anderson, Benzoni, and Lund (2002) report that randomly arriving jumps in security price in addition to stochastic volatility are required to capture the time-series dynamics of index returns.

Recent examinations of the performance of stochastic volatility option valuation models indicate that, at best, they can provide only a partial explanation of the shape of the index IVF. Bakshi, Cao, and Chen (1997), for example, advocate the use of a stochastic volatility model with jumps for valuing S&P 500 index options. While their model appears to perform better than the BSM formula, some of the implied parameter estimates, including the volatility of volatility coefficient, differ significantly from the ones estimated directly from returns. Similarly, Bates (2000) examines the ability of a stochastic volatility model, with and without jumps, to generate the negative skewness consistent with a steep IVF. He finds that the inclusion of a jump process can improve the model's ability to generate IVFs consistent with market prices, but in order to do so parameters must be set to unreasonable values. Along a similar line, Jackwerth attempts to recover risk aversion functions from S&P 500 index option prices and concludes that they are "irreconcilable with a representative investor" (2000, p. 450).

Another avenue of investigation that seems to lead to a better understanding of the IVF is the study of option market participants' supply and demand for different option series in different option markets. One way to think of the IVF is as a series of market clearing option prices quoted in terms of BSM implied volatilities. Under dynamic replication, the supply curve for each option series is a horizontal line. No matter how large the demand for buying a particular option, its price and implied volatility are unaffected. In reality, however, there are limits to arbitrage. Shleifer and Vishny (1997) describe how the ability of professional arbitrageurs to exploit mis-priced securities is limited by the responsiveness of investors to intermediate losses. Liu and Longstaff (2000) show that it is often optimal for a risk-averse investor to take a smaller position in a profitable arbitrage than his margin constraints allow, since intermediate mark-to-market losses may force liquidation of his position prior to convergence. In the same way, a market maker will not stand ready to sell an unlimited number of contracts in a particular option series. As his position grows large and imbalanced, his hedging costs and/or volatility risk exposure also increase, and he is forced to charge a higher price. With an upward sloping supply curve, differently shaped IVFs in different markets can be expected. The result of these limits to arbitrage is that market prices can diverge from model values, and that the divergence can persist. In effect, the no-arbitrage band within which prices can fluctuate can be quite wide, allowing price to be affected by supply and demand considerations.

Interacting with the market maker's willingness to supply options is investor demand. The level of implied volatility will be higher or lower depending upon whether net public demand for a particular option series is to buy or to sell. In the S&P 500 index option market, for example, it is well known that institutional investors buy index puts as portfolio insurance. Unfortunately, there are no natural counterparties to these trades, and market makers must step in to absorb the imbalance. With an upward sloping supply curve, implied volatility will exceed actual return volatility, with the difference being the market maker's compensation for hedging costs and/or exposure to volatility risk.[25] If institutional demand tends to be focused in a particular option series, such as out-of-the-money puts, the IVF will be downward sloping.

Bollen and Whaley (2004) investigate the role of supply and demand in the options market by exploring the possibility that market makers set option prices with a model not radically different from BSM and that the shape of the IVF is attributable to the buying pressure of specific option series and a limited ability of arbitrageurs to bring prices back into alignment. In particular, they document that daily changes in the implied volatility of an option series are significantly related to net buying pressure and that the changes are transitory, as market makers are gradually able to rebalance their portfolios. Buying pressure on index put options appears to drive the permanently downward sloping shape of the S&P 500 index option IVF, consistent with hedgers seeking portfolio insurance. In contrast, buying pressure on call options appears to drive the shape of stock option IVFs. A simulated trading strategy that sells options, and then delta-hedges the positions using the underlying security, generates significant paper profits for the index but

[25] In contrast, the ability to dynamically replicate option positions in the idealized (frictionless) BSM world ensures that the market maker earns the risk-free rate of return.

not for individual stocks. For index options, they find that profits are highest for the category of options that contain the OTM puts, which corresponds to the institutional demand for portfolio insurance. While the prices of these options are considerably higher than is suggested by the BSM formula and the actual level of volatility in the marketplace, they do not represent profitable arbitrage opportunities for the market maker once the costs of hedging volatility risk are considered.

## RISK MANAGEMENT LESSONS: BARINGS BANK PLC

The collapse of Barings Bank PLC in 1995 has been described as one of the worst "derivatives disasters" in history.[26] Disaster to be sure. Unsanctioned index futures and options trading bankrupted Britain's oldest, most venerable, bank—a bank that had financed both the Louisiana Purchase in 1803 and the Napoleonic Wars. But, is it fair to characterize Barings Bank as a derivatives disaster? Not really. The exchange-traded futures and options contracts/markets behaved exactly as they should. The main problem was that senior management of Barings Bank allowed a single trader, Nick Leeson, to place huge, unauthorized bets on the direction of the Japanese stock market over a period of more than two years. By the time that Barings' senior management came to grips with the illicit trading activity, the bank had lost $1.2 billion and was essentially worthless.

The key player in the Barings Bank controversy was Nicholas William Leeson, a man of humble beginnings. He was born in Watford, Hertfordshire in England, the son of a self-employed plasterer. Upon completing high school, Leeson opted for finance career and took a job as a bank clerk at Coutts & Co. In June 1987, about two years later, he moved on to Morgan Stanley as a futures and options settlement clerk. In June 1989, he joined the settlements department of Barings Securities at an annual salary of £12,000.

Leeson's big break came in 1990 when he was assigned to the back-office operations[27] of the Indonesian branch of Barings Securities to sort out a large number of unreconciled stock trades that had stacked up in the bank's error account (the infamous "88888 account"). The bank's use of an error account was not uncommon. By isolating trade discrepancies, a bank can proceed with its remaining back office activities in an unencumbered and timely fashion. What was uncommon, however, is that the trade discrepancies were not reconciled and closed out within a day. In spite of its own internal guidelines, Barings allowed them to accumulate through time.

Over a period of many months, Leeson managed to clean up the back-office problems in Jakarta. Indeed, he was so successful in executing his duties that, in

[26] The story of Nick Leeson and the demise of Barings Bank has been reported in a number of venues including the HBO movie, *Rogue Trader*. Two particularly insightful recounts are Rawnsley (1995) and Marthinsen (2005, Ch. 7). Brown and Steenbeek (2001) analyze Leeson's trading strategy. Many of the details provided in this section are drawn from these sources.

[27] The back office handles the administrative functions of the bank such as trade confirmation, settlement, regulatory compliance, reconciling, and clearing. The front office, on the other hand, handles brokerage business (i.e., direct interface with customers and the execution of their orders) and proprietary trading (i.e., trading for the bank's own accounts).

April 1992, he was promoted and assigned to Barings Futures (Singapore) (hereafter BFS), a new indirect subsidiary of Barings Securities Limited, to set up accounting and settlement functions. Only July 1, 1992, BFS started trading on the SIMEX, with Leeson in charge of operations, including *both* the trading (front office) and the accounting and settlement (back office) activities. Apparently, the bank believed that it was unnecessary to separate the front-office and back-office operations because Leeson's trading was merely executing orders on behalf of clients. In the ensuing months, the brokerage business waned as Japanese clients began set up their own trading operations. To compensate for the loss in line of business, Barings turned to proprietary trading. By early 1993, Leeson was actively involved in stock index arbitrage—not between the futures and the underlying basket of stocks but rather between the Nikkei 225 futures contracts traded simultaneously on the Singapore International Monetary Exchange (SIMEX) and the Osaka Stock Exchange (OSE). Since the contract specifications are virtually identical, arbitraging between the two markets means profiting from (minor) contract price discrepancies between the two markets, selling the more expensive and buying cheaper. Being long and short the same contract, this trading activity is virtually riskless.[28] Curiously, Leeson quickly began reporting extraordinary profits. So large were the reported profits during 1993, BFS accounted for 20% of Barings' worldwide profits. His bonus for the year was £130,000.

The extraordinary profits reported by Leeson should have set off alarms. The strategy is relatively mindless and can be executed mechanically using a PC, real-time pricing information, and electronic links to the trading floors. Since the barriers to entry for engaging in this strategy are small, competition would quickly drive the revenue from this strategy down to a level at which it equals marginal costs of trading. Common sense dictates that reported abnormal profits from this strategy should have been a "red herring."

In truth, Leeson had been placing directional bets all along. The bets were relatively modest at the outset. Some paid off, others did not. As it turns out, Leeson had created the ability to hide losses early. On July 2, 1992, just a day after BFS commenced trading on SIMEX, Leeson gave specific instructions to change the back-office software to exclude the 88888 account from all market activity reports. Its only use was to be for determining futures/options margins. By reporting winning trades to management and hiding losing trades in the 88888 account, Leeson was able to convince the bank's management that he was a brilliant trader. His credibility became beyond reproach. Senior management (from his direct supervisor through the board of directors) turned a "blind eye" to virtually all of his activities. During the first half of 1994, Leeson's reported profits accounted for about 50% of Barings' worldwide profit. All the while, Leeson was *doubling*[29] his bets trying to recover the mounting losses. The charade continued through 1994. At yearend, his reported profits were 500% greater than expected, and his bonus for the year was £450,000. Hidden in the background, however, were accumulated losses of $835 million.

[28] The only risk is "legging into" the transactions. You must buy and sell the contracts in different markets at exactly the same time.

[29] *Doubling* refers to the gambling strategy of doubling the bet each time there is a loss. See Brown and Steenbeek (2001).

Leeson's fundamental bet was that the Japanese stock market would rise. From mid-1994 through the end of the year, the Nikkei 225 was on a steady path downward, as shown in Figure 14.9. The futures contracts were, of course, marked-to-market each day, requiring that variation margin be paid. Leeson requested funding from Barings Securities London and, to his surprise, they wired the money. They apparently beleived his stories that the transfers were needed mostly to meet the needs of BFS customers who operated in different time zones and had difficulty in clearing checks in time and that large margin calls were to be expected in his index arbitrage trading activity. Neither story was, in fact, true. The funding from Barings was not adequate to cover margin calls. Consequently, Leeson decided to write Nikkei 225 option straddles to generate additional cash.[30] At the same time, he also began to record fictitious trades and falsified internal transfer records to lower the size of margin calls by lowering his exposures.

In the first two weeks of January 1995, as the market declined, Leeson began to bet more and more heavily that the Nikkei 225 would not fall below a level of 19,000. Unfortunately, the Kobe earthquake hit on January 17, 1995, disrupting markets throughout Japan. The market fell through the 19,000 level on Friday, January 20. In an attempt to bid up the stock market to restore the profitability of his short straddles and long futures positions, Leeson bought more and more index futures. But, to no avail. Over the weekend, the Nikkei 225 dropped by more than 1,000 points, substantially worsening Leeson's plight. Although he had managed to recover his losses since the earthquake by January 30, he bought even more futures because of his belief that the market would recover further. In the early days of February, the market, again, turned against him. The stress became too much. On Thursday, February 23, Leeson attended work as usual,

**FIGURE 14.9** Nikkei 225 during the Barings Bank scandal.

joined colleagues for drinks at a local bar after the market close, went home,

[30] From Chapter 10, we know that straddles generate cash and are profitable as long as the market does not move dramatically in one direction or the other.

packed his bags, and flew to Borneo for a vacation with his wife. At the time of his departure, his open long index futures position alone was 61,039 contracts.

To illustrate the scope of the risk of the position that Leeson had amassed as of the close of trading on February 23, we can compute the 5% value-at-risk (VAR) and conditional value-at-risk (CVAR) measures over one day.[31] The historical volatility rate of the Nikkei 255 over the most recent 30 days leading up to and including February 23 was 23.3% on an annualized basis. At an assumed index futures price of 17,830.02 and an assumed futures price appreciation rate of 0%, the critical level below which the index level may be within one day at 5% probability is

OV_OPTION_ASSET_PROB_INV(17830.02,1/365,0,0.233,"b",0.05) = 17,474.61

The futures contract denomination is JPY 2,500, and the size of the SIMEX position was 61,039 contracts. Hence the 5% VAR over one day was

$$(17{,}830.02 - 17{,}474.61) \times \text{JPY } 2{,}500 \times 61{,}039 = \text{JPY } 54.2 \text{ billion}$$

or USD 560.9 million.[32] In other words, standing at the close on February 23, 1995, there was a 5% chance that the open index futures position could lose about USD 561 million by the close the next day. The 5% tail VAR or CVAR was USD 700.7 million. That is, conditional upon a loss in the 5% tail, the expected loss is about USD 701 million.

In retrospect, Leeson was a rogue trader whose massive, unauthorized, speculation in the futures and options went unmonitored by his employer, Britain's oldest and most venerable bank. Could the situation have been avoided? Absolutely! Like in most derivatives fiascos, the main culprits were:

1. *Rogue trader.* Leeson became addicted to his own fame. In order to protect his reputation as a brilliant trader and keep reporting extraordinary profits for the bank (and earning extraordinary bonuses for himself), he accelerated his trading activity. Since the bank had placed him in a position in which he was responsible for trading and compliance, alarms did not go off early in 1993 when they should have. If the trading had stopped at that time, losses would have been miniscule by comparison.
2. *Lack of understanding by senior management.* The fact that the index arbitrage activity was producing extraordinary profits in early 1993 should have alarmed Barings' senior management, from Leeson's direct supervisor through the board of directors. Apparently, they did not have a basic understanding of the law of one price—two perfect substitutes must have the same price.[33] Simultaneously buying and selling the same futures contract on different exchanges is a virtually riskless activity. At best, the strategy should produce only small returns.

[31] Recall the these measures were developed in Chapter 7 under the assumption that the underlying security has a lognormal price distribution. See Illustrations 7.5 and 7.7.

[32] The exchange rate at the time was JPY 96.7/USD.

[33] Recall that this assumption was introduced in Chapter 2 and is the foundational assumption of derivatives valuation and risk management.

3. *Lack of meaningful supervision by senior management.* Judging by their actions, Barings' senior management did not supervise Leeson's trading activities in any meaningful way. Indeed, because they had continued to allow Leeson to be responsible for proprietary trading and compliance, they were "allowing the fox to guard the henhouse." Effective risk management demands a clear separation of these two activities for obvious reasons.

From Borneo, Leeson then traveled to Frankfurt, where he had hoped to find safe haven. He was apprehended and extradited back to Singapore, where he pleaded guilty to fraud and spent three and a half years of a six and a half year sentence in a Singapore jail. Upon completing his sentence, he returned to England.

## RETURN/RISK MANAGEMENT STRATEGIES

Exchange-traded stock index derivatives can be used in a variety of important trading strategies including market timing, asset allocation, and protected equity notes. The purpose of this section is to elaborate on each of these strategies, showing precisely what trades need to be executed.

### Alter Market Risk of a Stock Portfolio Using Index Futures

The key to effective market timing and asset allocation is the ability to modify the expected return/risk characteristics of your portfolio quickly and efficiently. Stock index futures are ideally suited for this purpose. To understand exactly how to use them, we need to recall some of the principles from earlier chapters. First, in Chapter 5, we demonstrated that a stock portfolio's beta can be used to determine the optimal number of index futures to sell in order to minimize portfolio risk. The optimal hedge was

$$n_F = -\beta_P\left(\frac{P}{S}\right) \tag{14.13}$$

where $\beta_P$ and $P$ are the beta and the market value of the stock portfolio, and $S$ is the market value of an index unit (i.e., the index level times the denomination of the futures). Second, in Chapter 4, we learned that the net cost of carry relation implies the return of the futures equals the return on the underlying index portfolio less the risk-free rate of interest, that is,

$$R_F = R_S - r \tag{14.14}$$

Third, by virtue of the CAPM, we know that the expected return of a risky asset (e.g., your portfolio $P$) equals the risk-free rate of return plus a market risk premium equal to the product of the difference between the expected rate of return on the market and the risk-free rate and the asset's beta, that is,

$$E_P = r + (E_S - r)\beta_P \tag{14.15}$$

With these tools in hand, we can now address the market timing/asset allocation problem.

First use (14.13) and (14.14) to verify that the optimal hedge ratio (14.12) is correct. You want to set the hedge so that the expected return on your hedge portfolio equals the risk-free rate of return, that is,

$$E_P + n_F E_F = r \tag{14.16}$$

But from (14.14) and (14.13) you know that $E_P = r + (E_S - r)\beta_P = r + E_F\beta_P$, so the left hand side of expected return of the hedge portfolio (14.15) becomes

$$r + \beta_P E_F + n_F E_F = r \tag{14.17}$$

We immediately see that the optimal number of futures is $n_F = -\beta_P$, which we then scale by the ratio of the market value of our portfolio relative to the market value of a unit of the index portfolio underlying the futures to arrive at (14.12). Thus we have verified a result from an earlier chapter using a different, albeit equivalent, approach.

Next, rather than set the expected return on your hedged portfolio equal to the risk-free rate as we did in (14.15), we set it equal to the expected return on a portfolio with our desired risk level, $\beta^*$, that is,

$$r + (E_S - r)\beta_P + n_F^* E_F = r + (E_S - r)\beta^* \tag{14.18}$$

Substituting (14.13) and simplifying, we find that the number of futures contracts to buy or sell in order to adjust our market risk exposure to $\beta^*$ is $n_F^* = \beta^* - \beta_P$. Adjusting for the difference in size of our portfolio relative to an index portfolio unit, the general result is

$$n_F^* = (\beta^* - \beta_P)\left(\frac{P}{S}\right) \tag{14.19}$$

If our desired risk level is 0, we get the minimum variance hedge (14.12). If we want to increase our risk exposure (i.e., $\beta^* > \beta_P$), we buy futures rather than sell.

**ILLUSTRATION 14.3** Alter risk of stock portfolio.

*Suppose you manage a \$30 million stock portfolio with a beta of 1.50. The current level of the S&P 500 is 1,200, and the three-month S&P 500 futures price is 1,218.14. The risk-free interest rate is 6%. Find the appropriate number of the index futures to buy to bring the portfolio's risk exposure up to a level of $\beta^* = 2.50$.*

To find the number of index futures to buy today, substitute the problem information into (14.18), that is,

$$n_F = (2.50 - 1.50)\left(\frac{30{,}000{,}000}{1{,}200(250)}\right) = 100$$

### Creating Protected Equity Notes

A *protected equity note* (PEN) is a discount bond-like contract structured to provide a guaranteed rate of return on the principal invested plus a fraction of the any upside relative price appreciation (or total return) on an underlying equity security such as a stock index. PENs were introduced by the over-the-counter market in the late 1980s, and are known by a variety of other names including *principal-protected notes, capital-guarantee notes, safe-return certificates, equity-linked notes,* and *index-linked bonds.*

To value a PEN, we, again, apply the valuation by replication. We begin by describing the notation. Let $V$ be the principal amount of the PEN, $g$ be its guaranteed investment return, $k$ be the proportion of price appreciation earned if the market rises (i.e., the "participation rate"), and $T$ be the time remaining to expiration. Let the underlying index have a current price of $S$, a dividend yield rate of $\delta$, and a volatility rate of $\sigma$. For the sake of convenience, we initially assume $S = V$.[34] The risk-free interest rate is denoted $r$.

Under the assumed notation, the terminal value of the PEN may be expressed as

$$PEN_T = \begin{cases} Ve^{gT} + k(\tilde{S}_T - Ve^{gT}) & \text{if } S_T > Ve^{gT} \\ Ve^{gT} & \text{if } S_T \leq Ve^{gT} \end{cases} \tag{14.20}$$

As (14.34) shows, the protected equity note guarantees a minimum terminal value of $Ve^{gT}$. The only way to guarantee this minimum future value is to include risk-free bonds in the replicating portfolio. To provide a floor level of $Ve^{gT}$ at time $T$, we need to buy $Ve^{-(r-g)T}$ in risk-free bonds. Next, in the event the equity index appreciates more than rate $g$ over the life of the PEN, the protected equity note also pays $k$ percent of any excess appreciation, $S_T - Ve^{gT}$. Obviously, this is nothing more than a European-style call option with an exercise price of $Ve^{gT}$ and a time to expiration of $T$. Using the BSM model, the value of the call is

$$c = Se^{-\delta T}N(d_1) - Ve^{(g-r)T}N(d_2) \tag{14.21}$$

where

$$d_1 = \frac{\ln(Se^{-\delta T}/Ve^{(g-r)T}) + 0.5\sigma^2 T}{\sigma\sqrt{T}} \tag{14.21a}$$

and

$$d_2 = d_1 - \sigma\sqrt{T} \tag{14.21b}$$

[34] We relax this assumption in the illustrations that follow.

Since the replicating portfolio has terminal value contingencies exactly equal to those of the PEN, the value of the PEN must be

$$PEN = Ve^{-(r-g)T} + kc \tag{14.22}$$

In the event that the PEN is linked to the total return of the index rather than its price appreciation, we set the dividend yield rate equal to 0 in (14.20) even though the index, itself, may pay dividends. Naturally, such call will be more expensive and, hence, we can expect to receive a lower participation rate on the PEN, other factors being held constant.

**ILLUSTRATION 14.4** Value protected equity note.

*Suppose your bank offers protected equity notes to its customers. Under the terms of the agreement, you invest \$100,000 for one year. At the end of the year, you receive a guaranteed return of 2% and 30% of any price appreciation of the S&P 500 index over and above the guaranteed return. Value the PEN assuming that the S&P has a current level of 1,250, a dividend yield rate of 1.5%, and a volatility rate of 16%. Assume the risk-free rate of interest is 6%.*

First, compute the guaranteed floor value of the investment at the end of one year, that is,

$$Ve^{gT} = 100{,}000e^{0.02(1)} = 102{,}020.13$$

The present value of the risk-free bonds necessary to provide a guaranteed return of 2% (i.e., the first term on the right hand-side of (14.36)) is

$$Ve^{-(r-g)T} = e^{-0.06(1)}(102{,}020.13) = 96{,}078.94$$

Second, recognize that the principal amount of the PEN and the index are at different levels—100,000 versus 1,250. This problem is overcome simply by scaling the current level of the index by a factor of 80. Now, compute the value of the call option embedded in the agreement. Using the BSM formula, the call value is

$$c = 100{,}000e^{-0.015(1)}N(d_1) - 100{,}000e^{(0.02-0.06)1}N(d_2) = 7{,}495.32$$

where

$$d_1 = \frac{\ln(100{,}000e^{-0.015(1)}/102{,}020.13e^{-0.06(1)}) + 0.16^2(1)}{0.16\sqrt{1}} = 0.2363$$

$$d_2 = d_1 - 0.16\sqrt{1} = 0.0763,$$
$$N(d_1) = 0.5934, \text{ and } N(d_2) = 0.5304$$

Finally, compute the value of the PEN as the sum of the value of the risk-free bonds and $k$ times the value of the call option, that is,

$$PEN = 96{,}078.94 + 0.30 \times 7{,}495.32 = 98{,}327.54$$

Had the PEN be written on the total return of the index, the call option value is 8,405.68 and the value of the PEN is 98,600.65.

The computations can be verified using the OPTVAL Function Library. The function (and its syntax) that values a protected equity note is

OV_NS_PROTECTED_EQUITY_NOTE(*princ*, *g*, *k*, *t*, *r*, *i*, *v*, *rp$*)

where *princ* is the amount of principal of the PEN, *g* is the minimum guaranteed rate of return, *k* is the participation rate, *t* is the time to expiration, *r* is the risk-free interest rate, *i* is income rate of the underlying index, *v* is the index's volatility rate, and *rp$* is a (r)eturn/(p)rice indicator. If the PEN provides a share of the total return on the index, *rp$* = "r", and, the PEN provides a share of the price appreciation of the index, *rp$* = "p". An example of the function call is provided here:

B18 = OV_NS_PROTECTED_EQUITY_NOTE(B3,B4,B7,B5,B15,B11,B12,B6)

| | A | B | C | D | E | F |
|---|---|---|---|---|---|---|
| 1 | **PROTECTED EQUITY NOTE ANALYSIS** | | | | | |
| 2 | ***Equity note description*** | | | | | |
| 3 | Principal (*V*) | 100,000 | | | | |
| 4 | Minimum growth rate (*g*) | 2.00% | | | | |
| 5 | Years to expiration (*T*) | 1.00 | | | | |
| 6 | (R)eturn/(P)rice appreciation | P | | | | |
| 7 | Rate of participation | 30.00% | | | | |
| 8 | | | | | | |
| 9 | ***Underlying index/stock:*** | | | | | |
| 10 | Level (*S*) | 1250.00 | | | | |
| 11 | Dividend yield (*d*) | 1.50% | | | | |
| 12 | Volatility ($\sigma$) | 16.00% | | | | |
| 13 | | | | | | |
| 14 | ***Market parameters*** | | | | | |
| 15 | Interest rate (*r*) | 6.00% | | | | |
| 16 | | | | | | |
| 17 | ***Protected equity note*** | | | | | |
| 18 | Value | 98,327.54 | | | | |

Financial institutions that offer products such as PENs demand a fee for the contract that they are structuring for you. To deduce the size of the fee, you simply compare the principal of the note, *V*, with its economic value as determined by (14.36). In order to do so, you will have to estimate the dividend yield rate and volatility rate of the index and identify the risk-free interest rate on a discount bond of comparable. But these are tasks about which we are familiar. It is also important to note that the reason is that these products are popular is that many individuals are unfamiliar with index option markets and do not understand that they can form a portfolio with exactly the same payoff contingencies on their own.

## SUMMARY

This chapter discusses exchange-traded stock index products. The first section is devoted to describing stock index derivatives markets worldwide. Contract specifications of selected index products are provided. The framework for valuing index derivatives depends critically on how the cash dividends of the index portfolio are paid through time. In the second section, the dividend payment patterns of the S&P 500 and DJIA stocks indexes are presented. The patterns indicate that accurate modeling of stock index derivatives requires using a discrete cash dividend framework. The third section provides the valuation principles under the discrete dividend (as well as the continuous dividend yield rate) frameworks.

The fourth section discusses two important index derivatives trading strategies. The first is tailoring the expected return/risk characteristics of a stock portfolio using index futures. Such adjustments can be made using the stock portfolio's current beta in relation to the desired level of risk exposure. Where the desired exposure is 0, the optimal number of futures to sell matches that of the minimum variance hedge developed in Chapter 2. Increasing the risk exposure of the portfolio in response to a prediction of a bull market (i.e., a market timing strategy) or to a desire to have more of the portfolio wealth invested in stocks (i.e., an asset allocation strategy) means buying rather than selling index futures contracts. The second return/risk management strategy discussion focuses on a structured product called a protected equity note in which the buyer is provided a guaranteed minimum rate of return on investment plus a share of the return (or price appreciation) in an index portfolio. Valuation by replication is used to demonstrate that this instrument is nothing more than risk-free bonds plus an index call option.

## REFERENCES AND SUGGESTED READINGS


Anderson, Torben, Luca Benzoni, and Jesper Lund. 2002. An empirical investigation of continuous-time equity return models. *Journal of Finance* 57: 1239–1284.

Bakshi, Gurdip, Charles Cao, and Zhiwu Chen. 1997. Empirical performance of alternative option pricing models. *Journal of Finance* 52: 2003–2049.

Bates, David S. 2000. Post-'87 crash fears in the S&P 500 futures options market. *Journal of Econometrics* 94: 181–238.

Beneish, Messod D., and Robert E. Whaley. 1997. A scorecard from the S&P game. *Journal of Portfolio Management* 23 (Winter): 16–23.

Beneish, Messod D., and Robert E. Whaley. 2002. S&P 500 index replacements: A new game in town. *Journal of Portfolio Management* 28 (Fall): 51–60.

Black, Fischer. 1976. Studies of stock price volatility changes. *Proceedings of the 1976 Meetings of the Business and Economics Section, American Statistical Association*: 177–181.

Black, Fischer, and Myron Scholes. 1973. The pricing of options and corporate liabilities. *Journal of Political Economy* 81: 637–659.

Bogle, John C. 1994. *Bogle on Mutual Funds: New Perspectives for Intelligent Investors.* Barr Ridge, IL: Irwin Professional Publishing.

Bollen, Nicolas P. B., Tom Smith, and Robert E. Whaley. 2003. Optimal contract design: For whom? *Journal of Futures Markets* 23 (August): 719–750.

Bollen, Nicolas P. B., and Robert E. Whaley. 1999. Do expirations of Hang Seng index derivatives affect stock market volatility? *Pacific-Basin Finance Journal* 7: 453–470.

Bollen, Nicolas P. B., and Robert E. Whaley. 2004. Does net buying pressure affect the shape of implied volatility functions? *Journal of Finance* 59: 711–754.

Brown, Stephen J., and Onno. W. Steenbeek. 2001. Doubling: Nick Leeson's trading strategy. *Pacific-Basin Finance Journal* 9: 83–99.

Chernov, Mikhail, Ron Gallant, Eric Ghysels, and George Tauchen. 2003. Alternative models of stock price dynamics. *Journal of Econometrics* 116: 225–257.

Cox, John C., and Stephen A. Ross. 1976. The valuation of options for alternative stochastic processes. *Journal of Financial Economics* 3: 145–166.

Derman, Emanuel, and Iraj Kani. 1994. Riding on the smile. *Risk* 7: 32–39.

Dumas, Bernard, Jeff Fleming, and Robert E. Whaley. 1998. Implied volatility functions: Empirical tests. *Journal of Finance* 53: 2059–2106.

Dupire, Bruno. 1994. Pricing with a smile. *Risk* 7: 18–20.

Emanuel, David C., and James D. MacBeth. 1982. Further results on the constant elasticity of variance call option pricing model. *Journal of Financial and Quantitative Analysis* 4: 533–554.

Fallon, William D. 1998. *Market Maker: A Sesquicentennial Look at the Chicago Board of Trade.* Chicago: Chicago Board of Trade.

Gastineau, Gary L. 2002. *The Exchange-Traded Funds Manual.* New York: John Wiley & Sons, Inc.

Harris, Lawrence, and Eitan Gurel. 1986. Price and volume effects associated with changes in the S&P 500 list: New evidence for the existence of price pressures. *Journal of Finance* 41: 815–829.

Jackwerth, Jens C. 2000. Recovering risk aversion from option prices and realized returns. *Review of Financial Studies* 13: 433–451.

Jorion, Phillippe. 1989. On jumps in the foreign exchange and stock market. *Review of Financial Studies* 4: 427–445.

Karolyi, G. Andrew. 1996. Stock market volatility around expiration days in Japan. *Journal of Derivatives* 4 (Winter): 23–43.

Lintner, John. 1965. The valuation of risk assets and the selection of risky investments in stock portfolios and capital budgets. *Review of Economics and Statistics* 47: 13–37.

Liu, Jun, and Francis A. Longstaff. 2000. Losing money on arbitrages: Optimal dynamic portfolio choice in markets with arbitrage opportunities, Working paper, UCLA.

Marthinsen, John E. 2005. *Risk Takers: Uses and Abuses of Financial Derivatives.* Boston: Pearson Addison-Wesley.

Merton, Robert C. 1973. Theory of rational option pricing. *Bell Journal of Economics and Management Science* 4: 141–183.

Modest, David M., and Mahedevan Sundaresan. 1983. The relationship between spot and futures prices in stock index futures markets: Some preliminary evidence. *Journal of Futures Markets* 3: 15–41.

Nelson, Daniel B. 1991. Conditional heteroskedasticity in asset returns: A new approach. *Econometrica* 59: 347–370.

Rawnsley, Judith H. 1995. *Total Risk: Nick Lesson and the Fall of Barings Bank.* New York: HarperCollins.

Rubinstein, Mark. 1994. Implied binomial trees. *Journal of Finance* 49: 771–818.

Sharpe, William F. 1964. Capital asset prices: A theory of market equilibrium under conditions of risk. *Journal of Finance* 19: 425–442.

Shleifer, Andrei. 1986. Do demand curves for stocks slope down? *Journal of Finance* 41: 579–590.

Shleifer, Andrei, and Robert Vishny. 1997. The limits of arbitrage. *Journal of Finance* 52: 35–55.

Stoll, Hans R. 1995. Lost Barings: A tale in three parts concluding with a lesson. *The Journal of Derivatives* (Fall) 3: 109–115.

Stoll, Hans R., and Robert E. Whaley. 1987. Program trading and expiration-day effects. *Financial Analysts Journal* 43: 16–28.

Stoll, Hans R., and Robert E. Whaley. 1991. Expiration-day effects: What has changed? *Financial Analysts Journal* 47: 58–72.

Stoll, Hans R., and Robert E. Whaley. 1997. Expiration-day effects of the All Ordinaries Share Price Futures: Empirical evidence and alternative settlement procedures. *Australian Journal of Management* 22 (December): 139–174.

# CHAPTER 15

# Stock Index Products: Strategy Based

Many stock index products are inextricably linked to particular index derivative trading strategies. This chapter focuses on such products. The first is portfolio insurance. Portfolio insurance is a means of protecting a stock portfolio against the prospect of declining prices. Like any insurance policy, the face amount of the insurance is prespecified as is the life of the policy. The insurance is purchased by buying a put, either directly or synthetically, with an exercise price equal to the face amount of the insurance and a time to expiration equal to the term of the policy. Buying the put directly is called *passive portfolio insurance*; creating it synthetically, *dynamic portfolio insurance*. The first section describes a variety of portfolio insurance trading strategies.

The second group of products are funds based on an index/option trading strategy. The first such product to appear in the marketplace was based on the CBOE's Buy-Write Index (BXM). The BXM buy-write strategy involves buying the S&P 500 index portfolio and selling one-month, at-the-money call options. While such a strategy should theoretically perform the same as the S&P 500 portfolio on a risk-adjusted basis (as we demonstrated in Chapter 10), it has performed better over the last 16 years. The reason is that index options appear to have been overpriced (i.e., their implied volatility has been too high relative to realized volatility) and converge to their correct values over time. The second section describes the BXM trading strategy in detail and shows its historical performance.

The final group of index products that we discuss is market volatility derivatives. Essentially two types exist—contracts on realized volatility and contracts on volatility implied by index option prices. In the third section, we describe different volatility contract specifications and show how the CBOE's Market Volatility Index (VIX) can be constructed from a portfolio of S&P 500 index options. We then illustrate how volatility derivatives can be used as an alternative investment in an asset allocation framework.

## INSURING STOCK PORTFOLIOS

Portfolio insurance is a means of protecting your portfolio against the prospect of declining prices. Like any insurance policy, the face amount of the insurance as well as the term of the policy are specified. The insurance is created by buying a put, either directly or synthetically. The put's exercise price is the face amount of the policy and its time to expiration is the term. Buying the put directly is called *passive portfolio insurance*; creating it synthetically, *dynamic portfolio insurance*.

The history of portfolio insurance in the United States is an interesting story in financial innovation.[1] It began in the mid-1970s when Hayne Leland, a Berkeley finance professor, dreamed up the concept of dynamic portfolio insurance. The easiest way to create portfolio insurance is to buy a put option written on the stocks in the portfolio, but, at the time, neither put options in general nor index put options in particular were traded. Leland's idea, further refined with Mark Rubinstein, was to mimic the payoffs of an insured portfolio by continuously rebalancing a portfolio of stock and T-bills or a portfolio of stocks. As the market rose, risk-free bonds would be liquidated and more stocks purchased. As the market fell, stocks would be sold and risk-free bonds purchased. The two academics enlisted the help of a professional marketer named John O'Brien, formed an advisory firm called "Leland-O'Brien-Rubinstein" (LOR) and began marketing portfolio insurance. Their service was to provide clients with instructions on how to rebalance their portfolios as the market moved. They landed their first client in the fall of 1980.

An early problem in implementing the strategy was that it was difficult and costly for many clients to buy and sell simultaneously the stocks in their portfolio. Program trading was in its infancy. Another problem was that active portfolio managers did not take kindly to outsiders giving them orders to buy or sell stocks in their portfolio with little or no warning. Consequently, the birth of S&P 500 index futures in March 1982 was a godsend. Index futures allowed managers to tailor their market risk exposures quickly and inexpensively, without touching the stocks in their portfolios. The market for portfolio insurance flourished. By 1987, more than $60 billion in stock portfolios were covered by dynamic portfolio insurance.

The end came with the market crash on Monday, October 19, 1987. On Friday, October 16, 1987, there was a nervousness in the market. The S&P 500 index fell by more than 5% during the trading day. Figure 15.1 shows that the December 1987 futures price was at a discount relative to the index several times during the day including at the close. The nervousness grew over the weekend, and, by Monday morning, there was outright panic. The December 1987 futures price opened about 19 points lower than its Friday close and at an 18 point discount to the index. See Figure 15.2. With the decline in the market, dynamic portfolio insurances triggers were hit, and futures contracts were sold. But, the success of LOR dynamic portfolio insurance depends on the futures price being at its theoretical level, and the futures contract stays at its theoretical level only when index arbitrageurs are at work. On the morning of October 19, the trading of stocks on the NYSE was hopelessly congested. And, without

[1] See Bernstein (1996, pp. 316–320).

**FIGURE 15.1** Intraday prices for the December 1987 S&P 500 futures and S&P 500 index on Friday, October 16, 1987.

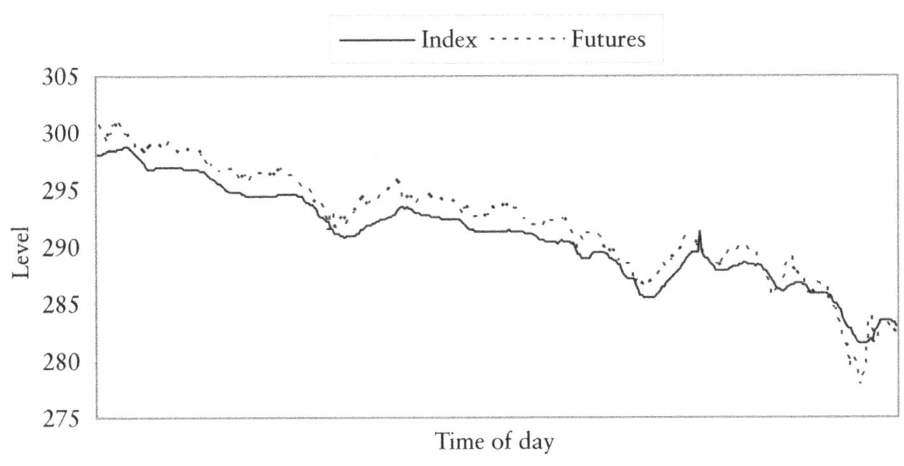


**FIGURE 15.2** Intraday prices for the December 1987 S&P 500 futures and S&P 500 index on Monday, October 19, 1987.

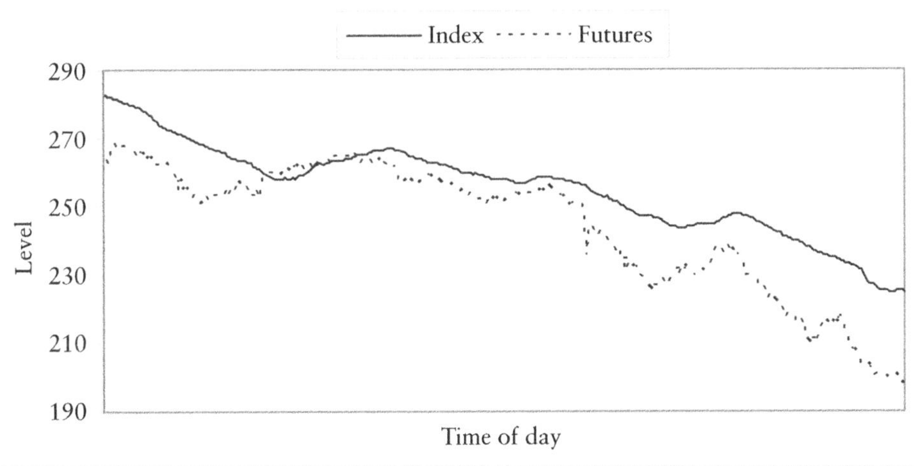


the ability to sell shares, index arbitrageurs were unwilling to buy the futures. Consequently, the futures price went into a freefall, reaching levels as high as 30 points below the reported index level.

The failure of dynamic portfolio insurance during the October 1987 crash spurred interest in passive portfolio insurance. While index put options had been launched by the CBOE in March 1983, their trading volume was modest. After the crash, trading volume exploded. With such strong demand, the OTC markets took notice. Since exchange-traded products are standardized, portfolio managers have limited degrees of freedom in setting floor values and insurance horizons. In addition, OTC option dealers have the flexibility to write puts on any basket of stocks that the customer wants as opposed to the handful of indexes offered by the exchanges.[2]

This section focuses first on the passive portfolio insurance created by buying index puts. It then uses the mechanics of a passively insured portfolio and the Black-Scholes/Merton (BSM) option valuation formula to develop many of the dynamic portfolio insurance trading strategies that have been used in the marketplace.

## Passive Portfolio Insurance

Passive portfolio insurance involves buying an index put option. To start, assume that the underlying stock portfolio is an index like the S&P 500 and that the put is written directly on the index. The level of the S&P 500 index is denoted $S$, $\delta$ is its dividend yield rate,[3] and $\sigma$ is its volatility rate. The price of a European-style index put with exercise price $X$ and time to expiration $T$ is $p$. To insure the value of the index portfolio, we buy one put for each $e^{-\delta T}$ units in the index portfolio.[4] Since the continuous dividend yield assumption involves immediately reinvesting all dividends in the index portfolio, $e^{-\delta T}$ units grow to exactly 1 unit at expiration. The initial and terminal values of this portfolio are shown in Table 15.1. If the index level at expiration closes below the floor value of the insurance, gains on the put will offset exactly any losses on the stocks. If the index level closes above the floor value, the investor earns the gains.

**TABLE 15.1** Insuring an index portfolio using an index put.

| Position | Initial Value | Terminal Value ($T$) | |
|---|---|---|---|
| | | $S_T \leq X$ | $S_T > X$ |
| Buy index portfolio | $-Se^{-\delta T}$ | $\tilde{S}_T$ | $\tilde{S}_T$ |
| Buy index put | $-p$ | $X - \tilde{S}_T$ | 0 |
| Net portfolio value | $Se^{-\delta T} + p$ | X | $\tilde{S}_T$ |

**ILLUSTRATION 15.1** Create static portfolio insurance by buying index puts.

*Suppose you are an index fund manager with a \$50 million position in the S&P 500 portfolio, and want to buy insurance that the portfolio value will not fall below a level of \$50 million by the end of next year. The current level of the S&P 500 is 1,500, its dividend yield rate is 1.5%, and its volatility rate is 20%. The current risk-free interest rate is 6%.*

---

[2] Responding to customer demand for more flexible contracts, the CBOE introduced FLEX options in which the customer is allowed to choose the exercise price, expiration date, the style of option, and the means of settlement. The underlying index, however, must be the same as the index options already trading at the CBOE.

[3] The constant dividend yield rate assumption is the more difficult case. Adjusting for discrete dividend payments means only subtracting the present value of the promised portfolio dividends from the value of the portfolio being insured.

[4] If the stock portfolio is not the index but rather a stock portfolio with risk level $\beta_P$ relative to the index, we scale the number of puts by a factor of $\beta_P$.

*Find the appropriate number (and exercise price) of the index puts needed to provide for the $50 million floor value in one year. Show the initial and terminal values of the insured portfolio for a range of index levels between 500 and 2,500 in increments of 100. The denomination of the S&P 500 index option is 100 times the index level.*

**Compute number of puts and exercise price**

To find the number of index puts to buy today, you need to find the number of units of the index portfolio that we will have in one year. With $50 million in the index portfolio and each unit worth 1,500, you currently have

$$n = \frac{50{,}000{,}000}{1{,}500(100)} = 333.333$$

units, where the 100 in the denominator is the contract multiplier of the S&P 500 index option contract. As a result of the S&P 500 index paying dividends, however, the number of index units will grow to $n = 333.33e^{0.015(1)} = 338.371$ by the end of one year. The required number of index puts is therefore 338.371. With the number of index puts computed, you now must compute the exercise price of each put. With the floor value of the portfolio set at $50 million in one year, the exercise price of each put should be

$$X = \frac{50{,}000{,}000}{338.371(100)} = 1{,}477.67$$

**Compute terminal values**

At an exercise price of 1,477.67, each put costs $76.3363 (according to the BSM formula), that is,

OV_OPTION_VALUE(1500,1477.67,1,0.06,0.015,0.20,"P","E") = 76.3363

The total cost of the portfolio insurance is therefore

$$\$76.3363 \times 100 \times 338.371 = \$2{,}583{,}000$$

With this level of insurance, the values of the insured portfolio in one year for index levels ranging between 500 and 2,500 are as follows:

| Terminal Values | | | |
|---|---|---|---|
| Index Level | Stock Portfolio Value | Value of Puts | Insured Portfolio Value |
| 500 | 16,918,551 | 33,081,449 | 50,000,000 |
| 600 | 20,302,261 | 29,697,739 | 50,000,000 |
| 700 | 23,685,972 | 26,314,028 | 50,000,000 |
| 800 | 27,069,682 | 22,930,318 | 50,000,000 |
| 900 | 30,453,392 | 19,546,608 | 50,000,000 |
| 1,000 | 33,837,102 | 16,162,898 | 50,000,000 |
| 1,100 | 37,220,812 | 12,779,188 | 50,000,000 |
| 1,200 | 40,604,523 | 9,395,477 | 50,000,000 |
| 1,300 | 43,988,233 | 6,011,767 | 50,000,000 |
| 1,400 | 47,371,943 | 2,628,057 | 50,000,000 |
| 1,500 | 50,755,653 | 0 | 50,755,653 |

| Terminal Values | | | |
|---|---|---|---|
| Index Level | Stock Portfolio Value | Value of Puts | Insured Portfolio Value |
| 1,600 | 54,139,363 | 0 | 54,139,363 |
| 1,700 | 57,523,074 | 0 | 57,523,074 |
| 1,800 | 60,906,784 | 0 | 60,906,784 |
| 1,900 | 64,290,494 | 0 | 64,290,494 |
| 2,000 | 67,674,204 | 0 | 67,674,204 |
| 2,100 | 71,057,915 | 0 | 71,057,915 |
| 2,200 | 74,441,625 | 0 | 74,441,625 |
| 2,300 | 77,825,335 | 0 | 77,825,335 |
| 2,400 | 81,209,045 | 0 | 81,209,045 |
| 2,500 | 84,592,755 | 0 | 84,592,755 |

**Compute initial values**

The tables that follow show the initial values of the portfolio assuming you purchased the required number of puts and the index level immediately changes to a different level. Note that, before the put's expiration, the portfolio value may be substantially less than the floor value of $50 million. At an index level of 500, for example, the insured portfolio value is only $47,088,238, well short of the $50 million required. The reason is, of course, that you bought European-style puts, that is, you bought an insurance policy to guarantee at least $50 million in one year. The portfolio value, $47,088,238, is simply the present value of the $50 million, that is, $\$47,088,238 = \$50,000,000e^{-0.06(1)}$. In one year, if the index level remains at 500, the stock portfolio value will have grown to $16,918,551 due to the re-investment of dividends (i.e., $\$16,666,667e^{0.015(1)} = \$16,918,551$) and the terminal value of the puts is their exercise value, $30,081,449 (i.e., 338.371(100)(1,477.67 – 500)).

| Portfolio Values with One Year to Expiration | | | |
|---|---|---|---|
| Index Level | Stock Portfolio Value | Value of Puts | Insured Portfolio Value |
| 500 | 16,666,667 | 30,421,560 | 47,088,227 |
| 600 | 20,000,000 | 27,088,239 | 47,088,239 |
| 700 | 23,333,333 | 23,755,263 | 47,088,596 |
| 800 | 26,666,667 | 20,426,203 | 47,092,869 |
| 900 | 30,000,000 | 17,119,553 | 47,119,553 |
| 1,000 | 33,333,333 | 13,889,916 | 47,223,250 |
| 1,100 | 36,666,667 | 10,839,846 | 47,506,513 |
| 1,200 | 40,000,000 | 8,100,014 | 48,100,014 |
| 1,300 | 43,333,333 | 5,783,980 | 49,117,313 |
| 1,400 | 46,666,667 | 3,948,601 | 50,615,267 |
| 1,500 | 50,000,000 | 2,583,000 | 52,583,000 |
| 1,600 | 53,333,333 | 1,624,612 | 54,957,946 |
| 1,700 | 56,666,667 | 986,331 | 57,652,998 |

| Portfolio Values with One Year to Expiration | | | |
|---|---|---|---|
| Index Level | Stock Portfolio Value | Value of Puts | Insured Portfolio Value |
| 1,800 | 60,000,000 | 580,381 | 60,580,381 |
| 1,900 | 63,333,333 | 332,300 | 63,665,633 |
| 2,000 | 66,666,667 | 185,807 | 66,852,474 |
| 2,100 | 70,000,000 | 101,801 | 70,101,801 |
| 2,200 | 73,333,333 | 54,814 | 73,388,147 |
| 2,300 | 76,666,667 | 29,082 | 76,695,749 |
| 2,400 | 80,000,000 | 15,240 | 80,015,240 |
| 2,500 | 83,333,333 | 7,904 | 83,341,237 |

### Dynamic Insurance Using Stocks and Risk-Free Bonds

Dynamic portfolio insurance does the same thing as the passive portfolio insurance, except that a put option is not purchased directly. Instead the fund manager dynamically rebalances a portfolio consisting of stocks and risk-free bonds (or a portfolio of stocks and stock index futures or a portfolio of stocks, index futures and risk-free bonds) in such a way that the payoff contingencies of the portfolio exactly match the payoff contingencies of the passively insured portfolio. Dynamic portfolio insurance using a mix of the stock portfolio and risk-free bonds is discussed first, followed by dynamic insurance using the stock portfolio and stock index futures and then by the stock portfolio together with index futures and risk-free bonds. Recall that this is the order that LOR followed in providing their portfolio insurance advisory service.

To create a dynamic portfolio insurance portfolio, you need to create a portfolio of stocks and risk-free bonds in such a way that the portfolio has (1) the same value as the passive portfolio insurance portfolio; and (2) the same change in value as the passive portfolio insurance portfolio with respect to a change in the level of the index $S$. The *value constraint* is

$$V' = Se^{-\delta T} + p = w_S Se^{-\delta T} + w_B Xe^{-rT} \tag{15.1}$$

where $w_S$ is the number of units of the index portfolio, $w_B$ is the number of risk-free bonds, and $X$ is the floor value of the portfolio insurance at time $T$ (i.e., the exercise price of the dynamically created put option). To identify the *delta constraint*, first substitute the European-style put option valuation equation from Table 14.13 in Chapter 14 into equation (15.1) and then take the partial derivative of (15.1) with respect to a change in the index level $S$, that is,

$$\frac{\partial V}{\partial S} = e^{-\delta T} - e^{-\delta T}N(-d_1) = w_S e^{-\delta T} + w_B \frac{\partial Xe^{-rT}}{\partial S} = w_S e^{-\delta T} \tag{15.2}$$

Note that since the value of the risk-free bonds with respect to a change in the index level is 0, the appropriate number of units of the stock portfolio to buy can be identified by factoring $e^{-\delta T}$ from (15.2), that is,

$$w_S = 1 - N(-d_1) = N(d_1) \tag{15.3}$$

Substituting (15.3) back into the value constraint (15.1), the appropriate number of bonds can be identified by solving

$$Se^{-\delta T} + Xe^{-rT}N(-d_2) - Se^{-\delta T}N(-d_1) = Se^{-\delta T}N(d_1) + w_B Xe^{-rT} \tag{15.4}$$

Since $Se^{-\delta T} = Se^{-\delta T}N(-d_1) + Se^{-\delta T}N(d_1)$, the appropriate number of bonds to sell is

$$w_B = N(-d_2) \tag{15.5}$$

**Asset-or-Nothing and Cash-or-Nothing Options** Before returning to the illustration, it is worthwhile to note that you can identify the appropriate number of index portfolio units and bond portfolio units by using the values of two more primitive options. The payoffs of portfolio insurance can be replicated by buying an asset-or-nothing call and a cash-or-nothing put with the same exercise price. The asset-or-nothing call provides the upside. If the index portfolio value rises, you will exercise the call and take delivery of the stock portfolio. If the index portfolio value falls, you will exercise the put and take delivery of the cash. Summing the option values, you get $Se^{-\delta T}N(d_1) + Xe^{-rT}N(-d_2)$. Note how the probability terms in this expression correspond to the values of $w_S$ and $w_B$, respectively.

**ILLUSTRATION 15.2** Create dynamic portfolio insurance using stock portfolio and risk-free bonds.

*Assume that you face the same insurance situation as in Illustration 15.1, except that you want to use a dynamic portfolio insurance strategy with stocks and risk-free bonds. Find the appropriate weights of the index portfolio and risk-free bonds. Show the initial values of the insured portfolio for a range of index levels between 500 and 2,500 in increments of 100.*

**Compute portfolio weights**

The values of $w_S$ and $w_B$ are obtained using (15.3) and (15.5). At the current index level of 1,500, the weights are 0.6554 and 0.4207, respectively. Multiplying each weight by the value of the stock and bond portfolios and then summing, you get \$52,583,000, exactly the figure you started with using passive portfolio insurance.

**Compute initial values**

The table below shows the portfolio weights for different levels of the index. As the index level rises, you sell bonds and buy more stocks according to the new values of $w_S$ and $w_B$. Conversely, as the index falls, you sell stocks and buy bonds. The insured portfolio behaves exactly like the passively insured portfolio described earlier. Assuming the index level falls to 500, for example, you will be entirely in bonds. If the index level stays at that level for the entire year, the terminal value of the bonds will be \$50 million (i.e., the current value plus risk-free interest, $\$47,088,238e^{0.06(1)}$), exactly the desired result.

Portfolio Values with One Year to Expiration

| Index Level | Stock Portfolio Value | Value Bonds | $w_S$ | $w_B$ | Insured Portfolio Value |
|---|---|---|---|---|---|
| 500 | 16,666,667 | 47,088,227 | 0.0000 | 1.0000 | 47,088,227 |
| 600 | 20,000,000 | 47,088,227 | 0.0000 | 1.0000 | 47,088,239 |
| 700 | 23,333,333 | 47,088,227 | 0.0003 | 0.9998 | 47,088,596 |
| 800 | 26,666,667 | 47,088,227 | 0.0030 | 0.9984 | 47,092,869 |
| 900 | 30,000,000 | 47,088,227 | 0.0156 | 0.9907 | 47,119,553 |
| 1,000 | 33,333,333 | 47,088,227 | 0.0518 | 0.9662 | 47,223,250 |
| 1,100 | 36,666,667 | 47,088,227 | 0.1249 | 0.9116 | 47,506,513 |
| 1,200 | 40,000,000 | 47,088,227 | 0.2371 | 0.8201 | 48,100,014 |
| 1,300 | 43,333,333 | 47,088,227 | 0.3762 | 0.6969 | 49,117,313 |
| 1,400 | 46,666,667 | 47,088,227 | 0.5219 | 0.5576 | 50,615,267 |
| 1,500 | 50,000,000 | 47,088,227 | 0.6554 | 0.4207 | 52,583,000 |
| 1,600 | 53,333,333 | 47,088,227 | 0.7651 | 0.3006 | 54,957,946 |
| 1,700 | 56,666,667 | 47,088,227 | 0.8475 | 0.2045 | 57,652,998 |
| 1,800 | 60,000,000 | 47,088,227 | 0.9052 | 0.1332 | 60,580,381 |
| 1,900 | 63,333,333 | 47,088,227 | 0.9432 | 0.0835 | 63,665,633 |
| 2,000 | 66,666,667 | 47,088,227 | 0.9670 | 0.0507 | 66,852,474 |
| 2,100 | 70,000,000 | 47,088,227 | 0.9813 | 0.0299 | 70,101,801 |
| 2,200 | 73,333,333 | 47,088,227 | 0.9897 | 0.0172 | 73,388,147 |
| 2,300 | 76,666,667 | 47,088,227 | 0.9944 | 0.0097 | 76,695,749 |
| 2,400 | 80,000,000 | 47,088,227 | 0.9970 | 0.0054 | 80,015,240 |
| 2,500 | 83,333,333 | 47,088,227 | 0.9984 | 0.0029 | 83,341,237 |

### Dynamic Insurance Using Stocks and Index Futures

Rebalancing the portfolio that consists of stocks and risk-free bonds is not the only means of dynamically insuring a stock portfolio. In practice, dynamic portfolio insurance can also be created with a trading strategy that involves a portfolio of stocks and stock index futures. To identify the appropriate number of units of the stock portfolio and the index futures to use in creating an insured portfolio, use the value and delta constraints. Starting with the value constraint,

$$V = Se^{-\delta T} + p = w_S Se^{-\delta T} + w_F F = w_S Se^{-\delta T} \tag{15.6}$$

Note that since the futures involves no initial outlay, the number of units of the stock portfolio to buy is simply

$$w_S = 1 + \frac{p}{Se^{-\delta T}} \tag{15.7}$$

Substituting the European-style put option valuation equation from Table 14.13 in Chapter 14 into equation (15.6) and then taking the partial derivative of (15.6) with respect to a change in the index level $S$, the delta constraint is

$$\frac{\partial V}{\partial S} = e^{-\delta T} - e^{-\delta T}N(-d_1) = w_S e^{-\delta T} + w_F \frac{\partial F}{\partial S} \tag{15.8}$$

The cost of carry relation is $F = Se^{(r-\delta)T}$, which implies

$$\frac{\partial F}{\partial S} = e^{(r-\delta)T}$$

Substituting into (15.8),

$$\frac{\partial V}{\partial S} = e^{-\delta T} - e^{-\delta T}N(-d_1) = w_S e^{-\delta T} + w_F e^{(r-\delta)T} \tag{15.9}$$

Factoring $e^{-\delta T}$ and rearranging,

$$w_F = e^{-rT}[N(d_1) - w_S] \tag{15.10}$$

**ILLUSTRATION 15.3** Create dynamic portfolio insurance using stock portfolio and stock index futures.

*Assume that you face the same insurance that you did in Illustration 15.1, except that you want to use a dynamic portfolio insurance strategy with stocks and index futures. Find the appropriate weights of the index portfolio and index futures. Show the initial values of the insured portfolio for a range of index levels between 500 and 2,500 in increments of 100.*

**Compute portfolio weights**

The values of $w_S$ and $w_F$ are obtained using (15.7) and (15.10). At the current index level of 1,500, the weights are 1.0517 and –0.3732, respectively. Multiplying $w_S$ by the value of the stock portfolio (i.e., the futures position has no value), you get \$52,583,000, exactly the figure you started with using passive portfolio insurance. Note that you have more units of the stock than before since you took the money needed to buy the put under the passive insurance scheme and invested it in stocks.

| Portfolio Values with One Year to Expiration | | | | | |
|---|---|---|---|---|---|
| Index Level | Futures Price | Stock Portfolio Value | $w_S$ | Insured Portfolio Value | $w_F$ |
| 500 | 523.01 | 16,666,667 | 2.8253 | 47,088,227 | -2.6608 |
| 600 | 627.62 | 20,000,000 | 2.3544 | 47,088,239 | -2.2173 |
| 700 | 732.22 | 23,333,333 | 2.0181 | 47,088,596 | -1.9003 |
| 800 | 836.82 | 26,666,667 | 1.7660 | 47,092,869 | -1.6603 |
| 900 | 941.43 | 30,000,000 | 1.5707 | 47,119,553 | -1.4645 |
| 1,000 | 1046.03 | 33,333,333 | 1.4167 | 47,223,250 | -1.2854 |
| 1,100 | 1150.63 | 36,666,667 | 1.2956 | 47,506,513 | -1.1025 |
| 1,200 | 1255.23 | 40,000,000 | 1.2025 | 48,100,014 | -0.9092 |
| 1,300 | 1359.84 | 43,333,333 | 1.1335 | 49,117,313 | -0.7132 |
| 1,400 | 1464.44 | 46,666,667 | 1.0846 | 50,615,267 | -0.5299 |
| 1,500 | 1569.04 | 50,000,000 | 1.0517 | 52,583,000 | -0.3732 |
| 1,600 | 1673.64 | 53,333,333 | 1.0305 | 54,957,946 | -0.2499 |
| 1,700 | 1778.25 | 56,666,667 | 1.0174 | 57,652,998 | -0.1600 |
| 1,800 | 1882.85 | 60,000,000 | 1.0097 | 60,580,381 | -0.0984 |
| 1,900 | 1987.45 | 63,333,333 | 1.0052 | 63,665,633 | -0.0585 |
| 2,000 | 2092.06 | 66,666,667 | 1.0028 | 66,852,474 | -0.0337 |
| 2,100 | 2196.66 | 70,000,000 | 1.0015 | 70,101,801 | -0.0189 |
| 2,200 | 2301.26 | 73,333,333 | 1.0007 | 73,388,147 | -0.0104 |
| 2,300 | 2405.86 | 76,666,667 | 1.0004 | 76,695,749 | -0.0056 |
| 2,400 | 2510.47 | 80,000,000 | 1.0002 | 80,015,240 | -0.0030 |
| 2,500 | 2615.07 | 83,333,333 | 1.0001 | 83,341,237 | -0.0016 |

### Dynamic Insurance Using Stock Portfolio and Dynamic Adjustment of Index Futures and Risk-Free Bonds

As was noted earlier, stock portfolio managers may be reluctant to change the composition of their stock holdings as the market moves. In addition, transaction costs in the stock market are generally higher than in the index futures and risk-free bond markets. Consequently, we now focus on a dynamic portfolio insurance strategy that allows the stock portfolio manager to leave his equity holdings untouched.

Again start with the portfolio value constraint. In this case, it is written

$$V = Se^{-\delta T} + p = Se^{-\delta T} + w_F F + w_B X e^{-rT} \tag{15.11}$$

Since the futures involves no initial outlay, the number of units of risk-free bonds equals

$$w_B = \frac{p}{Xe^{-rT}} \tag{15.12}$$

Substituting the European-style put option valuation equation from Table 14.13 in Chapter 14 into equation (15.11) and then taking the partial derivative of (15.11) with respect to a change in the index level $S$, the delta constraint is

$$\frac{\partial V}{\partial S} = e^{-\delta T} - e^{-\delta T}N(-d_1) = e^{-\delta T} + w_F\frac{\partial F}{\partial S} \quad (15.13)$$

The cost of carry relation is $F = Se^{(r-\delta)T}$, which implies

$$\frac{\partial F}{\partial S} = e^{(r-\delta)T}$$

Substituting into (15.13),

$$\frac{\partial V}{\partial S} = -e^{-\delta T}N(-d_1) = w_F e^{(r-\delta)T} \quad (15.14)$$

Factoring $e^{-\delta T}$ and rearranging,

$$w_F = e^{-rT}N(-d_1) \quad (15.15)$$

**ILLUSTRATION 15.4** Create dynamic portfolio insurance using stock portfolio and dynamic adjustment of stock index futures and risk-free bonds.

*Assume that you want the same insurance as in Illustration 15.1. In this instance, however, leave the number of units in the stock portfolio untouched and dynamically insure your portfolio using stock index futures and risk-free bonds. Determine the appropriate number of risk-free bonds and index futures to execute this strategy. Show the initial values of the insured portfolio for a range of index levels between 500 and 2,500 in increments of 100.*

**Compute portfolio weights**

The values of $w_B$ and $w_F$ are obtained using (15.12) and (15.13). At the current index level of 1,500, the number of risk-free bonds is 0.0549 and the number of index futures is −0.3245. Multiplying $w_B$ by the value of the risk-free bond, and adding the value of the stock portfolio the stock portfolio, you get $52,583,000, exactly the figure you started with using passive portfolio insurance (recall the futures position has no initial value).

Note that, under this scheme, the dynamic adjustment has to do with risk-free bonds and index futures. As the market falls, the short futures position generates cash, which is used, in turn, to buy more units of risk-free bonds. As the market rises, the sale of risk-free bonds is used to cover the losses on the short position in the index futures. All the while, the number of units invested in the stock portfolio remains intact, and the insured portfolio values are the same as under the previous alternatives.

| Portfolio Values with One Year to Expiration | | | | | | |
|---|---|---|---|---|---|---|
| Index Level | Futures Price | Stock Portfolio Value | Bond Value | $w_B$ | $w_F$ | Insured Portfolio Value |
| 500 | 523.01 | 16,666,667 | 47,088,227 | 0.6461 | −0.9418 | 47,088,227 |
| 600 | 627.62 | 20,000,000 | 47,088,227 | 0.5753 | −0.9418 | 47,088,239 |
| 700 | 732.22 | 23,333,333 | 47,088,227 | 0.5045 | −0.9415 | 47,088,596 |
| 800 | 836.82 | 26,666,667 | 47,088,227 | 0.4338 | −0.9389 | 47,092,869 |
| 900 | 941.43 | 30,000,000 | 47,088,227 | 0.3636 | −0.9271 | 47,119,553 |
| 1,000 | 1046.03 | 33,333,333 | 47,088,227 | 0.2950 | −0.8929 | 47,223,250 |
| 1,100 | 1150.63 | 36,666,667 | 47,088,227 | 0.2302 | −0.8241 | 47,506,513 |
| 1,200 | 1255.23 | 40,000,000 | 47,088,227 | 0.1720 | −0.7185 | 48,100,014 |
| 1,300 | 1359.84 | 43,333,333 | 47,088,227 | 0.1228 | −0.5875 | 49,117,313 |
| 1,400 | 1464.44 | 46,666,667 | 47,088,227 | 0.0839 | −0.4502 | 50,615,267 |
| 1,500 | 1569.04 | 50,000,000 | 47,088,227 | 0.0549 | −0.3245 | 52,583,000 |
| 1,600 | 1673.64 | 53,333,333 | 47,088,227 | 0.0345 | −0.2213 | 54,957,946 |
| 1,700 | 1778.25 | 56,666,667 | 47,088,227 | 0.0209 | −0.1436 | 57,652,998 |
| 1,800 | 1882.85 | 60,000,000 | 47,088,227 | 0.0123 | −0.0893 | 60,580,381 |
| 1,900 | 1987.45 | 63,333,333 | 47,088,227 | 0.0071 | −0.0535 | 63,665,633 |
| 2,000 | 2092.06 | 66,666,667 | 47,088,227 | 0.0039 | −0.0311 | 66,852,474 |
| 2,100 | 2196.66 | 70,000,000 | 47,088,227 | 0.0022 | −0.0176 | 70,101,801 |
| 2,200 | 2301.26 | 73,333,333 | 47,088,227 | 0.0012 | −0.0097 | 73,388,147 |
| 2,300 | 2405.86 | 76,666,667 | 47,088,227 | 0.0006 | −0.0053 | 76,695,749 |
| 2,400 | 2510.47 | 80,000,000 | 47,088,227 | 0.0003 | −0.0028 | 80,015,240 |
| 2,500 | 2615.07 | 83,333,333 | 47,088,227 | 0.0002 | −0.0015 | 83,341,237 |

### Practical Considerations in Choosing Between Passive and Dynamic Portfolio Insurance

The mechanics of the above illustrations show that dynamic portfolio insurance must be more expensive than passive portfolio insurance. As the market moves and time passes, the portfolio manager is left readjusting his portfolio weights, incurring transaction costs with each adjustment. For this reason, portfolio managers often set trigger levels whereby portfolio adjustments are not made until the market moves by, say, 5%. The effect of not making continuous and instantaneous adjustments is that the insurance scheme will have a lower floor value and less upside potential. One may question the reason for the existence of dynamic portfolio. The reason, as alluded to earlier, is that index put options did not exist when portfolio insurance was first introduced into the marketplace.

Another distinction between passive and dynamic portfolio insurance is worthy of note. When a portfolio manager buys an index put, he locks in the amount he will pay for expected future volatility (i.e., the price he pays for the put implies the level of volatility). If subsequently realized volatility is lower than expected, the passive portfolio insurer will have overpaid for insurance.

Under the dynamic scheme, this would not have been the case. On the other hand, if subsequently realized volatility is higher than expected, the dynamic portfolio insurer will pay more for insurance, akin to buying fire insurance on your home after the fire has started.

## INDEX OPTION BUY-WRITE STRATEGIES

Option trading strategies are becoming an increasingly important part of the investment landscape. Indeed, since mid-2004, more than 42 new buy-write investment products (closed-end funds or structured products) alone have been launched with more than $18 billion in assets. Many of these are index products, and, currently, the most popular buy-write index is the Chicago Board Options Exchange's Buy-Write Index (BXM).

The BXM is based on a buy-write trading strategy using the S&P 500 index portfolio and index call options. In Chapter 10, we defined a buy-write strategy as buying an asset and selling a call option against it. Such a strategy contributes incremental return over and above the asset return conditional on the underlying asset price staying with in a tight range during the life of the call. Unconditionally, however, the buy-write strategy is risk-reducing (relative to holding the asset alone) and, hence, should lead to lower returns. In this section, we describe the BXM trading strategy, and examine and discuss its historical performance.

### Buy-Write Return Distributions and the Central Limit Theorem

Evaluating the performance of trading strategies involving options can be difficult because the nonlinear payoff structure of an option can dramatically affect the skewness of the return distibution. Recall, from Chapter 3, commonly used portfolio performance evaluation techniques assume the portfolio's return distibution is normal or, at least, symmetric. To analyze this problem, we focus on the BXM index.

The BXM index is a total return index based on writing the nearby, just out-of-the-money S&P 500 call option against the S&P 500 index portfolio each month on the day the previous nearby contract expires, which is usually the third Friday of the month.[5] Assuming for the moment that the S&P 500 portfolio pays no dividends, its continuously compounded return over the one-month holding period is

$$R_S = \ln\left(\frac{S_T}{S_0}\right) \tag{15.16}$$

[5] Since expirations occur monthly and there are 52 weeks in the calendar year, some "one-month" options have 28 days to expiration at the time they are written and others have 35 days.

where $S_0$ and $S_T$ are the index levels on adjacent option expiration days. Over the same period, the continuously compounded return on the BXM buy-write strategy over the month is

$$R_{BXM} = \ln\left(\frac{S_T - \max(S_T - X, 0)}{S_0 - C_0}\right) \tag{15.17}$$

where $C_0$ is price of the call when it is sold and $\max(S_T - X,0)$ is the price of the call when it expires. Note that the the buy-write return over the month has a truncated distribution, that is,

$$R_{BXM} = \begin{cases} \ln\left(\dfrac{X}{S_0 - C_0}\right) & \text{if } S_T > X \\ \ln\left(\dfrac{S_T}{S_0 - C_0}\right) & \text{if } S_T \leq X \end{cases} \tag{15.18}$$

In other words, when the call expires in the money, the buy-write return is capped at

$$\ln\left(\frac{X}{S_0 - C_0}\right)$$

When the call finishes out of the money, the buy-write return is higher than index return as a result of the sales proceeds of the call.

To illustrate the implications of (15.18) with respect to the shape of the buy-write return distibution, we perform a Monte Carlo simulation.[6] In the simulation, the continuously compounded index returns are assumed to be normally distributed with a mean ($\mu$) of 12% and a volatility rate ($\sigma$) of 20% annually. In each simulation run, a single monthly index return is generated. Based on this index return, the monthly return of a buy-write strategy is computed using (15.18). The price of the one-month, at-the-money call at the beginning of the month is set equal to its BSM value. The assumed risk-free rate of interest is 6%. The call's price at the end of the month is set equal to its exercise proceeds. The simulation is repeated 1,000 times. Figure 15.3 shows a histogram the results. In the figure, the lighter bars represent index returns. Not surprisingly, the returns appear symmetrically distributed around the mean monthly return of 1%. This merely tells us that the simulation procedure is working. The darker bars represent the reutrns of the buy-write index. Note the large spike at about 3%.[7] More than 50% of the time, the call option finishes in the-money and the buy-write strategy realizes its maximum monthly return. This makes sense

[6] The Monte Carlo simulation procedure is described at length in Chapter 9.

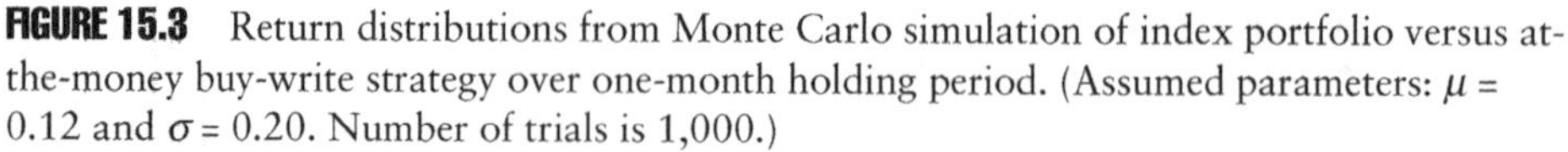

**FIGURE 15.3** Return distributions from Monte Carlo simulation of index portfolio versus at-the-money buy-write strategy over one-month holding period. (Assumed parameters: $\mu = 0.12$ and $\sigma = 0.20$. Number of trials is 1,000.)

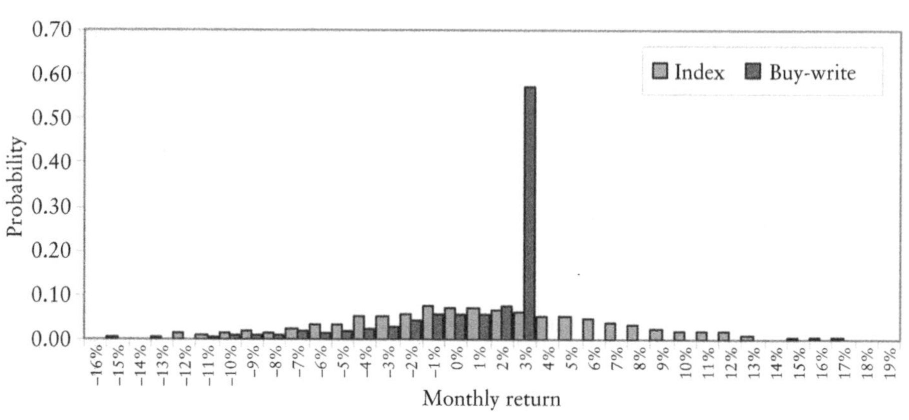


because the index is expected to appreciate in value (i.e., $\mu > 0$), and a call option that is currently at the money is therefore expected to be in the money at expiration. Note that if the call option finishes out of the money, the probability of a particular negative buy-write return is less then the probability of the index return. This is merely another way of saying that, if the option finishes out of the money, the buy-write return will exceed the index return. The negative skewness of the buy-write strategy implies that the portfolio performance measures in Chapter 3.

The histogram in Figure 15.3 represents the return distibution of the buy-write strategy if it is used only once. A buy-write strategy program, however, involves selling call options again and again over a long period of time, say, 10 or 20 years. In Appendix A: Elementary Statistics, we discussed the Central Limit Theorem. In the context of the buy-write strategy, the Central Limit Theorem says that even though the monthly return distribution is highly negatively skewed, the distribution of the mean of monthly returns over time becomes approximately normal with mean $\mu$ and variance $\sigma^2/n$, where $n$ is the number of months over which the buy-write strategy is repeated. Figures 15.4 and 15.5 show the shape of the return distibutions if the monthly buy-write strategy is repeated over a 10-year and 20-year horizons, respectively. For the 10-year horizon the buy-write return distribution remains negatively skewed, however, the degress of skewness is trivial in relation to Figure 15.3. For the 20-year horizon, the buy-write strategy has approximately a normal distribution. Indeed, if we apply the Jarque-Bera test of normality (see Appendix A at the end of the book), the null hypothesis that the buy-write return distibution is normal is not rejected. In other words, depending on the trading strategy and the number of times the strategy is repeated in the trading program, it may or may not be

[7] Given the simulation parameters, the maximum monthly return of the buy-write strategy is 2.59%.

**FIGURE 15.4** Return distributions from Monte Carlo simulation of index portfolio versus at-the-money buy-write strategy over 120-month holding period. (Assumed parameters: $\mu$ = 0.12 and $\sigma$ = 0.20. Number of trials is 1,000.)

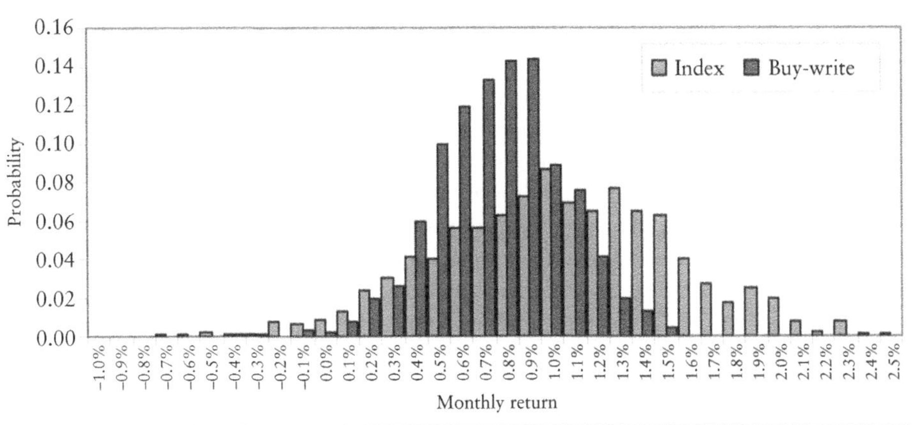


**FIGURE 15.5** Return distributions from Monte Carlo simulation of index portfolio versus at-the-money buy-write strategy over 240-month holding period. (Assumed parameters: $\mu$ = 0.12 and $\sigma$ = 0.20. Number of trials is 1,000.)

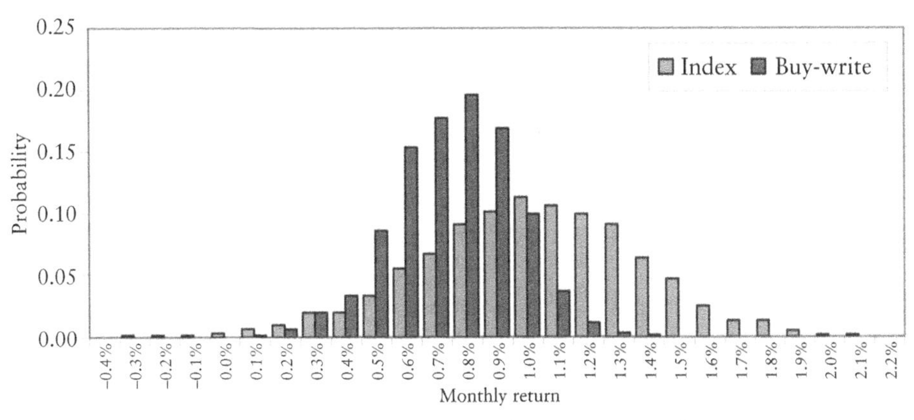


appropriate to apply the mean-variance portfolio perfromance measures from Chapter 3. Before applying any of these techniques, it is a good idea to examine the return distibution, compute its skewness, and, perhaps, perform a test for normality. In the event that skewness is a problem, applying performance measures based on mean/semivariance may provide a more accurate assessment.[8]

[8] While using semivariance as a risk measure is intuitively appealing, it is somewhat *ad hoc* in nature. Stutzer (2000) offers an alternative approach that is more rigorous from a theoretical standpoint.

### Historical Performance of BXM

In this section, we examine the hsitorical performance of the BXM over the 211-month period June 1988 through December 2005. The data history is available on the CBOE's website[9] and is contained in the Excel file **BXM history.xls**. The first two series in the file are the total return index levels of the BXM and the S&P 500 (SPTR), and the second two are continuously compounded monthly returns. The monthly money market rates in the final column are the continuously compounded rates of return of a 30-day Eurodollar time deposit whose number of days to maturity matches the number of days in the month. The Eurodollar rates were downloaded from Datastream.

Table 15.2 shows that the average monthly return of the one-month money market instruments over the 211-month period was 0.398%. Over the same period, the S&P 500 index portfolio generated an average monthly return of 0.920%, while the BXM generated an average monthly return of 0.926%. Surprisingly, the monthly average monthly return of the BXM was 0.6 basis points *higher* than the S&P 500 even though the BXM risk, as measured by the standard deviation of return, was substantially lower. For the BXM, the standard deviation of monthly returns was 2.747%, while, for the S&P 500, the standard deviation was 4.071%. In other words, BXM produced a monthly return approximately equal to the S&P 500 index portfolio, but at about 67% of the S&P 500's risk (i.e., 2.747% versus 4.071%), where risk is measured in the usual way.

The realized returns and risks of the BXM, the S&P 500, and the 30-day money market instrument are summarized in Figure 15.6. For purposes of comparison, we assume a 100 investment in each instrument on June 1, 1988, and then watch how the investment value moves through time. As the figure shows, the BXM tracked the S&P 500 index closely at the outset. Then, starting in 1992, the BXM began to rise faster than the S&P 500, but, by mid-1995, the level of the S&P 500 total return index surpassed the BXM. Beginning in 1997, the S&P 500 index charged upward in a fast but volatile fashion. The BXM

**TABLE 15.2** Summary statistics for monthly returns of CBOE's BXM index, the S&P 500 index, and money market deposits during the period June 1988 through December 2005.

| | BXM | SPTR | MM |
|---|---|---|---|
| No. of months | 211 | 211 | 211 |
| Mean | 0.926% | 0.920% | 0.407% |
| Median | 1.236% | 1.280% | 0.443% |
| Standard deviation | 2.747% | 4.071% | 0.191% |
| Skewness | –1.420 | –0.597 | 0.133 |
| Excess kurtosis | 5.006 | 1.120 | –0.576 |
| Jarque-Bera test statistic | 291.187 | 23.583 | 3.543 |
| Probability or normal | 0.000 | 0.000 | 0.170 |

[9] The CBOE's BXM webpage is at http://www.cboe.com/micro/bxm/introduction.aspx.

**FIGURE 15.6** Month-end total return indexes for BXM index, S&P 500 total return index (SPTR), and 30-day money market index (MM) for the period June 1988 through December 2005.

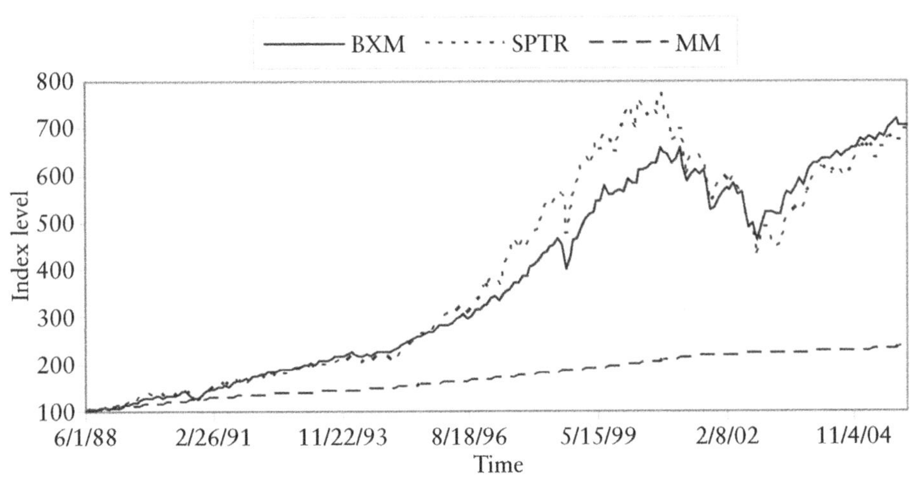


lagged behind, as should be expected. When the market reversed in mid-2000, the BXM again moved ahead of the S&P 500. The steadier path taken by the BXM reflects the fact that it has lower risk than the S&P 500.

Table 15.2 also reports the skewness and excess kurtosis of the monthly return distributions as well as the Jarque-Bera statistic for testing the hypothesis that the return distribution is normal. It is interesting to note that both the S&P 500 portfolio and the BXM have negative skewness. For the BXM, negative skewness should not be surprising in the sense that a buy-write strategy truncates the upper end of the index return distribution. But, the Jarque-Bera statistic rejects the hypothesis that returns are normal for the BXM and S&P 500 but not for the money market rates. The negative skewness for the BXM and S&P 500 does not appear to be severe, however. Figure 15.5 shows the standardized monthly returns of the S&P 500 and BXM in relation to the normal distribution. The S&P 500 and BXM return distributions appear more negatively skewed than the normal, but only slightly. What stands out in the figure is that both the S&P 500 and the BXM return distributions have greater kurtosis than the normal distribution. This is reassuring in the sense that most portfolio performance measures work well for symmetric distributions but not asymmetric ones.

To evaluate the historical performance of the BXM, we use the Sharpe ratio and $M$-squared performance measures from Chapter 3. Risk is measured using the standard deviation and the semi-standard deviation of portfolio returns. To the extent that BXM returns are skewed, the measures derived from the two different models will differ. Since the standardized BXM return distribution show slight negative skewness, the performance measures based on semi-standard deviation should be less than their standard deviation counterparts, but not by much. The portfolio performance results over the period June 1988 through December are reported in Table 15.3.

**TABLE 15.3** Estimated performance measures based on monthly returns of CBOE's BXM index and the S&P 500 index during the period June 1988 through December 2005.

| Performance Measure | Total Risk Measure | BXM | SPTR |
|---|---|---|---|
| Sharpe ratio | Standard deviation | 0.18901 | 0.12596 |
| | Semistandard deviation | 0.26144 | 0.18203 |
| *M*-squared | Standard deviation | 0.257% | |
| | Semistandard deviation | 0.224% | |

The results of Table 15.3 support two main conclusions. First, the BXM has outperformed the S&P 500 index on a risk-adjusted basis over the BXM's history. Both the Sharpe ratio and *M*-squared performance measures support this conclusion, independent of whether total risk is measured using standard deviation or semistandard deviation. The outperformance using standard deviation as the total risk measure, for example, is 25.7 basis points per month. Second, the performance measures using mean/semistandard deviation are slightly lower than their counterparts using mean/standard deviation. The reason is, of course, that the BXM returns are negatively skewed, as was indicated in Table 15.2 and Figure 15.6. The effect of skewness is impounded through the risk measure. The skewness "penalty" is about 3.3 basis points per month.

In an efficiently functioning capital market, the risk-adjusted return of a buy-write strategy using S&P 500 index options should be no different than the S&P 500 portfolio. Yet, the BXM has provided an abnormally high return relative to the S&P 500 index portfolio over the period June 1988 through December 2005. What could cause such an aberration? One possible explanation, suggested by Stux and Fanelli (1990), Schneeweis and Spurgin (2001), and others, is that the volatilities implied by option prices are too high relative to realized volatility. Indeed, Bollen and Whaley (2004) argue that there is excess buying pressure on S&P 500 index puts by portfolio insurers. Since there are no natural counterparties to these trades, market makers must step in to absorb the imbalance. As the market maker's inventory becomes large, implied volatility will rise relative to actual return volatility, with the difference being the market maker's compensation for hedging costs and/or exposure to volatility risk.[10] The implied volatilities of the corresponding calls also rise from the reverse conversion arbitrage supporting put-call parity.

To examine whether this explanation is consistent with the observed performance of the BXM, Whaley (2004) compares the average implied volatility[11] of the calls written in the BXM strategy to the average realized volatility over the call's life. Figure 15.8 shows that the difference has not been constant through time, perhaps indicating variation in the demand for portfolio insurance. The

[10] Bollen and Whaley (2004) also show that the same phenomenon does not exist for options on high market capitalization stocks whose empirical return distributions are shaped similarly to the S&P 500 returns.

[11] The implied volatility was computed by setting the observed call price equal to the Black-Scholes (1973)/Merton (1973) call option formula.

difference is persistently positive, however, with the mean (median) difference between the ATM call implied volatility and realized volatility being about 167 (234) basis points on average.[12]

**FIGURE 15.7** Distribution of standardized monthly returns for the BXM index and S&P 500 total return index (SPTR) indexes during the period June 1988 through December 2005. Normally distributed standard returns are also included.

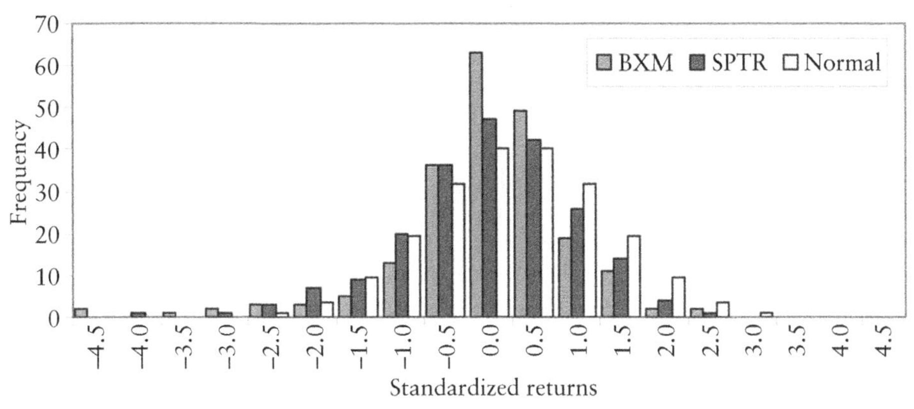


**FIGURE 15.8** Average implied and realized volatility for S&P 500 index options in each year 1988 through 2001.

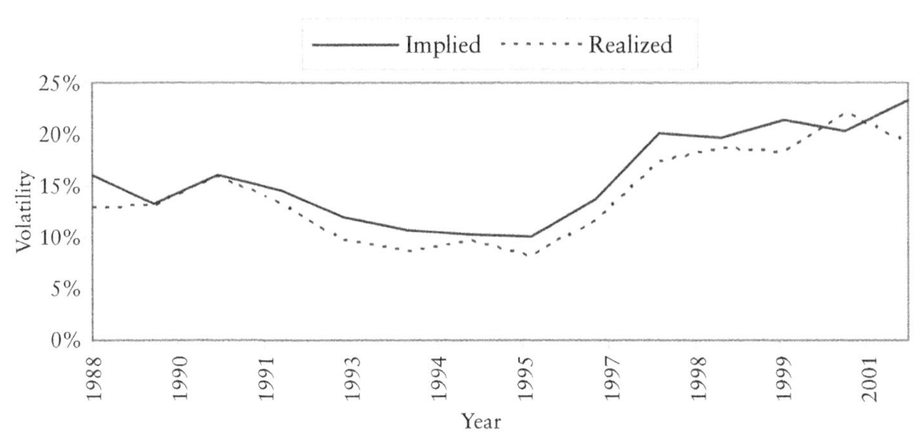


[12] Indeed, Whaley (2004) recreates the BXM where the one-month calls are traded at their BSM values using the standard deviation of the returns actually earned over the option's life rather that at their bid/ask quotes for the calls observed in the marketplace as the volatility parameter, and finds that the buy-write strategy performs no differently than the S&P 500 index portfolio on a risk-adjusted basis.

## VOLATILITY DERIVATIVES

Another relatively new stock index product are *volatility derivatives*. Although such instruments had been contemplated since the early 1990s,[13] it was not until the Long-Term Capital Management (LTCM) fiasco in late 1998 that the market finally began to recognize the value of trading stock market volatility as a separate asset class. LTCM lost $1.3 billion from being short implied stock index volatility through the sale of long-term index call and put options on stock market indexes in the United States and Europe.[14] Assuming the aggregate delta values of the calls and puts were approximately equal, the overall position would be relatively immune to movements in the underlying indexes. Unfortunately, however, being short index options implies having significant vega-risk. Indeed, LTCM had written so many index options with volatilities in the range of 19% that their net vega exposure was –$40 million in the U.S. alone. Market volatility rose significantly during the last months before LTCM's collapse—to a level of nearly 45% by mid-September 1998 as Figure 15.9 shows. With these option positions being marked-to-market on a daily basis, the cash drain was enormous. It is exactly this type of risk exposure that volatility derivatives are intended to address.

**FIGURE 15.9** Implied volatility of S&P 500 index options prior to the collapse of Long-Term Capital Management.

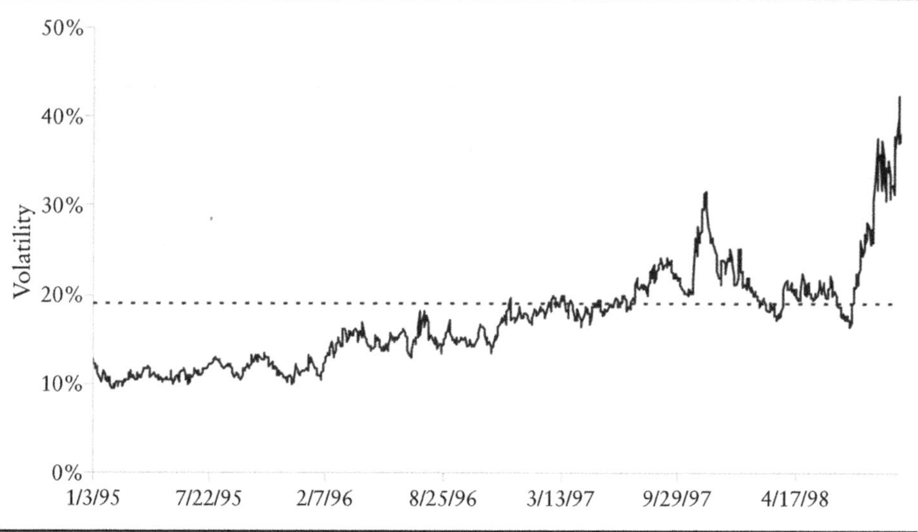


[13] The Chicago Board Options Exchange (CBOE) contemplated launching trading volatility options as early as 1993. See Whaley (1993). On January 19, 1998, the Deutsche Terminborse (DTB) became the first exchange in the world to list volatility futures. The CBOE launched trading of VIX futures on its CBOE Futures Exchange on March 26, 2004, with contracts on three-month realized variance being launched on May 18, 2004. The CBOE launched VIX options on February 24, 2006.

[14] Lowenstein (2000) provides a brief account of LTCM's trading strategies. The sale of stock index options accounted for nearly 30% of the $4.5 billion in firm losses.

Today volatility derivative contracts are written not only on stock indexes, but also interest rates, currencies, and commodities like crude oil. Prior to the advent of volatility derivatives, stock market volatility risk was managed using options written on the underlying index. The problem with doing so is that it is expensive. Options have two sources of price risk—risk associated with movements in the underlying index level and risk associated with movements in the market's perception of expected future volatility rate. The only way to isolate the volatility exposure is by trading the options and delta-hedging using the underlying index, index futures, and other index options.

This section describes volatility derivative contracts and their uses. We focus primarily on stock market volatility since stock market volatility contracts are the most actively traded. The discussion has two parts. First, we discuss realized volatility contracts and their applications, and then we turn to implied volatility contracts.

### Realized Volatility Derivative Contracts

At the outset, we need to correct a misnomer. Industry has come to refer to realized volatility contracts as volatility swaps. A *volatility swap* is not a swap; it is a forward contract. They have traded in OTC markets for more than five years, and are now also exchange-traded. A volatility forward (or swap) is written on the *realized future volatility* of an asset (say, the S&P 500 index). At expiration, its payoff is based on the statistical formula for the annualized standard deviation of index return, that is,

$$\sigma_{\text{realized}} = \sqrt{\frac{\sum_{t=2}^{n_T}\left[\ln\left(\frac{S_t}{S_{t-1}}\right) - \text{mean}\right]^2}{n_T - 2}} \times \sqrt{\text{no. of time intervals in a year}} \qquad (15.19)$$

where $n_T$ is the number of price observations used in the computation,[15] and $S_t$ is the index level. Volatility forwards are usually based on daily closing prices, however, since they are traded primarily in the OTC market, any frequency (e.g., hourly, weekly) is possible. The contract also specifies the source from which for the prices will be obtained. Volatility forwards are sometimes based on squared returns, and sometimes on squared deviations. Formula (15.19) shows squared deviations. The formula for squared returns is the special case where the mean term in the squared brackets of (15.19) is set equal to zero and the adjustment in the numerator is increased to $n_T - 1$. Finally, the volatility is annualized. For daily prices, the last term on the right-hand side is usually $\sqrt{252}$, that is, the square root of the typical number of business days in a year. For weekly prices, the last term is $\sqrt{52}$.

The value represented by formula (15.19) is the price of the asset underlying the forward contract at expiration. The only difference is the underlying asset is

[15] Note that $n_T$ prices produce $n_T - 1$ returns. Since we lose one degree of freedom from estimating the mean (see Appendix A, "Elementary Statistics," of this book), the appropriate divisor is $n_T - 2$.

not tradable; it is simply a computation of realized volatility. At inception, the buyer and seller agree to a fixed delivery price (quoted as an annualized volatility), $\sigma_X$, on the expiration date, $T$. As expiration approaches, the forward's settlement price becomes more and more certain because some of the prices used in (15.19) have been realized already. On the last day before expiration, only the index level on expiration day remains unknown. Upon settlement, the buyer receives

$$\text{Notional} \times (\sigma_{\text{realized}} - \sigma_X) \tag{15.20}$$

that is, the notional amount of the swap times the difference between the realized and contracted volatility. The seller receives the opposite amount. Sometimes the volatility derivatives are written on the square of volatility, or variance. The buyer of a *variance swap* receives the payoff,

$$\text{Notional} \times (\sigma^2_{\text{realized}} - \sigma^2_X) \tag{15.21}$$

**ILLUSTRATION 15.5** Compute settlement price of realized volatility swap.

*Suppose that on Friday, August 1, 2003, you bought a 13-week volatility forward from an OTC derivatives dealer. Its price was 0.12, and its notional amount was \$100 million. Compute the settlement price and the settlement proceeds using squared weekly returns. Recompute the values using squared deviations. Comment on the difference. The Friday closing index levels over the period were as follows:*

| Friday Close | S&P 500 Index |
|---|---|
| 20030801 | 980.15 |
| 20030808 | 977.59 |
| 20030815 | 990.67 |
| 20030822 | 993.06 |
| 20030829 | 1008.01 |
| 20030905 | 1021.39 |
| 20030912 | 1018.63 |
| 20030919 | 1036.30 |
| 20030926 | 996.85 |
| 20031003 | 1029.85 |
| 20031010 | 1038.06 |
| 20031017 | 1039.32 |
| 20031024 | 1028.91 |
| 20031031 | 1050.71 |

The first step is to compute the weekly returns. Next compute the mean weekly return, and the squared returns and deviations. Compute the sum of squares and the annualized volatility. To annualize weekly returns, use the factor, $\sqrt{52}$. The cash settlement proceeds are \$1.27 million for the squared returns contract and \$.65 million for squared deviations. The difference is unusually large because the S&P 500 index level rose abnormally during this 13-week period, at least relative to historical standards. The rate of return of the S&P 500 index was about 7.2%—nearly 30% on an annualized basis.

| Friday Close | S&P 500 Index | S&P 500 Return | Squared Returns | Squared Deviations |
|---|---|---|---|---|
| 20030801 | 980.15 | | | |
| 20030808 | 977.59 | –0.00262 | 0.00000684 | 0.00006340 |
| 20030815 | 990.67 | 0.01329 | 0.00017665 | 0.00006310 |
| 20030822 | 993.06 | 0.00241 | 0.00000581 | 0.00000863 |
| 20030829 | 1008.01 | 0.01494 | 0.00022327 | 0.00009206 |
| 20030905 | 1021.39 | 0.01319 | 0.00017388 | 0.00006145 |
| 20030912 | 1018.63 | –0.00271 | 0.00000732 | 0.00006485 |
| 20030919 | 1036.30 | 0.01720 | 0.00029577 | 0.00014044 |
| 20030926 | 996.85 | –0.03881 | 0.00150634 | 0.00195002 |
| 20031003 | 1029.85 | 0.03257 | 0.00106068 | 0.00074097 |
| 20031010 | 1038.06 | 0.00794 | 0.00006305 | 0.00000672 |
| 20031017 | 1039.32 | 0.00121 | 0.00000147 | 0.00001709 |
| 20031024 | 1028.91 | –0.01007 | 0.00010134 | 0.00023759 |
| 20031031 | 1050.71 | 0.02097 | 0.00043958 | 0.00024395 |
| | Mean | 0.00535 | | |
| | Total | | 0.00033850 | 0.00030752 |
| | Annualized volatility | | 0.13267 | 0.12646 |
| | Notional amount | | 100,000,000 | 100,000,000 |
| | Forward price | | 0.120 | 0.120 |
| | Cash settlement value | | 1,267,275 | 645,649 |

The CBOE Futures Exchange (CFE) launched its three-month realized volatility futures contract on May 18, 2004. The CFE is an all-electronic exchange that was created by the Chicago Board Options Exchange (CBOE) in March 2004. The CFE's realized volatility contract is based on S&P 500 return variance rather than return standard deviation, and its product specifications are provided in Table 15.4. The contract denomination is \$50 per variance point. A price quotation of 633.50, for example, means the contract value is \$31,675. Up to four contracts may trade simultaneously. The contracts are on the March quarterly expiration cycle (March, June, September, December). The final settlement date is the third Friday of the contract month. Trading stops at the close on the preceding business day.

The final settlement price is a variance number and assumes the mean return is zero. Hence, the realized volatility formula (15.19) becomes

$$\sigma^2_{\text{realized}} = \frac{\sum_{t=1}^{n_a}\left[\ln\left(\frac{S_t}{S_{t-1}}\right)\right]^2}{n_e - 1} \times 252 \tag{15.22}$$

**TABLE 15.4** Selected terms of S&P 500 three-month variance futures contract.

| | |
|---|---|
| Exchange | CBOE Futures Exchange (CFE) |
| Ticker symbol | VT |
| Contract unit | \$50 per variance point |
| Tick size | 0.5 of one variance point |
| Tick value | \$25 |
| Trading hours | 8:30 AM to 3:15 PM CST |
| Contract months | Up to four contract months on the March cycle (Mar., Jun., Sep., Dec.) |
| Last day of trading | Close of trading on business day before final settlement date. |
| Final settlement date | Third Friday of contract month. |
| Final settlement price | Final settlement price is based on the standardized calculation of the realized variance of the S&P 500. This calculation uses continuously compounded daily returns for a three-month period assuming a mean daily return of zero. The calculated variance is then annualized assuming 252 business days per year. The final settlement price is this annualized, calculated variance multiplied by 10,000. |

where $n_a$ is the actual number of trading days in the three-month interval, and $n_e$ is the expected number of days in the three-month interval. Normally, $n_a$ and $n_e$ are equal. In the event of a market disruption during the contract's life, however, $n_a$ will be less than $n_e$. Generally speaking, a "market disruption event," as determined by the CFE, occurs when trading on the primary exchanges of a significant number of S&P 500 stocks is suspended or limited in some way or when the primary exchange on which index stocks unexpectedly closes early (or does not open) on a particular day. For each market disruption event, the value of $n_a$ is reduced by one.

**Volatility versus Variance Contracts** Industry has come to define volatility as the standard deviation of the natural logarithm of the price ratios.[16] If the forward is defined in terms of variance (i.e., volatility squared) rather than volatility, the payoff structure is quite different. Consider Figures 15.10 and 15.11, which plot the payoffs of a volatility forward contract versus a variance forward contract for long and short positions. Since the horizontal axis is defined in terms of volatility, its terminal payoffs are a linear function of volatility. The variance forward, on the other hand, is nonlinear. The long variance position (the dotted line in Figure 15.10) has convexity. As volatility falls, the terminal payoff of the long variance position decreases, but at a decreasing rate. At the same time, as volatility increases, the terminal payoff of the long variance forward increases at an increasing rate. Indeed, the variance payoffs loosely resemble a long call position, while the variance payoffs of the short variance futures resemble a short call position.

[16] Recall that this is consistent with the BSM model's use of continuously compounded returns.

**FIGURE 15.10** Payoff structure of volatility and variance forward contracts: Long positions.

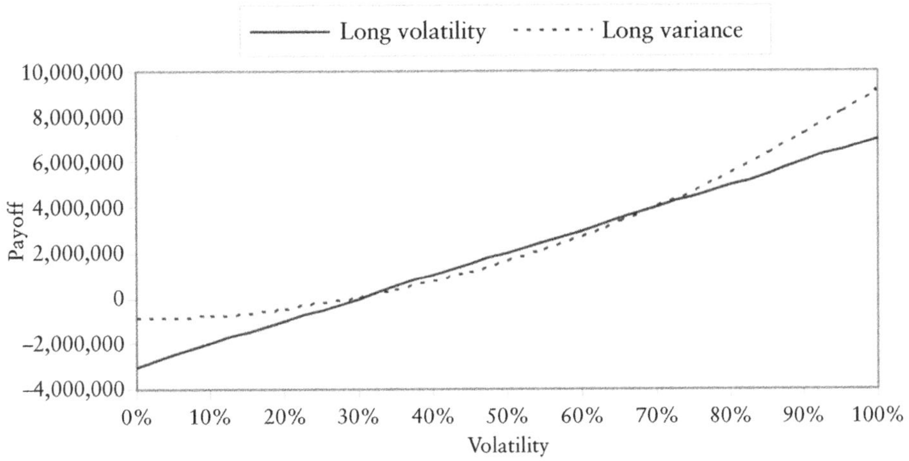

Long volatility
Long variance
10,000,000
8,000,000
6,000,000
4,000,000
2,000,000
0
–2,000,000
–4,000,000
Payoff
0%
10%
20%
30%
40%
50%
60%
70%
80%
90%
100%
Volatility

**FIGURE 15.11** Payoff structure of volatility and variance forward contracts: Short positions.

Short volatility
Short variance
4,000,000
2,000,000
0
–2,000,000
–4,000,000
–6,000,000
–8,000,000
–10,000,000
Payoff
0%
10%
20%
30%
40%
50%
60%
70%
80%
90%
100%
Volatility

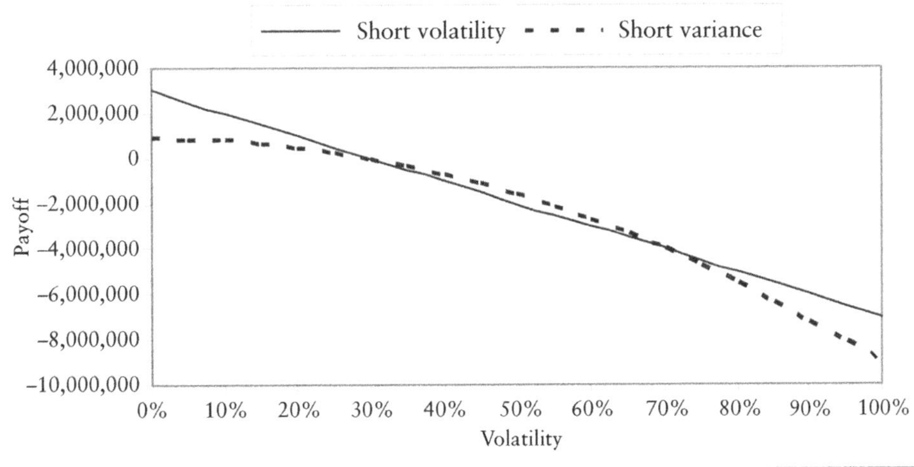

**Expected Return/Risk Management Applications** At first blush, the volatility forward contract seems to be purely a speculative instrument. Traders who believe future volatility will be high relative to the forward price will go long the swap, and those who believe that the market will be very calm will go short. But, the hedging possibilities using realized volatility forwards are many. In the normal course of operation, for example, some market participants become inherently short volatility. Consider LTCM's ill-fated index option strategy. Because index option implied volatilities were as high as they had been anytime since the October 1987 market crash, LTCM sold both index calls and puts with the belief that implied volatility would return to normal levels. Unfortunately, a problem arose when implied volatility continued to rise and their positions were marked-to-market. The cash drain was enormous. Buying realized volatility forwards would have hedged this exposure, at least in part. The same is true for index option market makers who are short market volatility as a result of selling index puts to portfolio insurers.[17]

Another hedging possibility is for risk arbitrageurs. Immediately after a merger is announced, risk arbitrageurs step in and buy shares of a target firm and sell the shares of bidder. Because the probability that the merger will be successful is not known, the prices of the target and the bidder will not fully reflect the terms of the offer. If the merger is successful, the spread between the prices will converge. Before the deal is consummated, however, market volatility may increase, making the merger less likely, thereby causing the spread to widen. Buying a realized volatility forward contract can hedge this type of risk exposure.

Yet another application is for individuals or portfolio managers who attempt to track some sort of benchmark index. During periods of high volatility, the portfolio may require more frequent rebalancing and greater transaction cost expenses. Again, buying a realized forward contract on volatility can hedge this exposure.

### Implied Volatility Derivatives Contracts

The CFE also lists a futures contract written on the implied return volatility of the S&P 500 index. The CBOE Market Volatility Index or VIX is constructed in such a way that it represents the implied volatility of an at-the-money S&P 500 index option with exactly thirty calendar days to expiration. It is sometimes called the "investor fear gauge" because it is set by *investors* and expresses their consensus view about *expected future stock market volatility.* The specific details of its construction are contained in Appendix 15A of this chapter. What is interesting about its construction is that the index can be created using a static portfolio of SPX options. This is important since arbitrage between the VIX futures and the underlying VIX index promotes liquidity in both markets.

The relation between the movements of the VIX and the movements of the S&P 500 index are important to understand. Figure 15.12 shows the daily levels of the S&P 500 index and the VIX during the period January 1990 through December 2004. A number of interesting patterns appear. First, note that the VIX level (i.e., the dark line) is more jagged than the S&P 500 index level. What this means is that the volatility of the volatility of the S&P 500 index is greater than the volatility of the index itself.[18] Second, there tends to be an inverse rela-

[17] On a typical day, S&P 500 put option volume (and open interest) is nearly double that of S&P 500 calls.

[18] Time-series variation in the expected volatility of stock indexes has been documented in a number of studies. Day and Lewis (1992), for example, demonstrate that the expected variance of the S&P 100 index follows a mean-reverting process. They also show that implied volatilities from S&P 100 index options (OEX) explain a significant amount of the changes in expected variance. In a related paper, Fleming (1998) finds that OEX implied volatilities are good (but not perfect) forecasts of future volatility.

**FIGURE 15.12** Daily levels of the S&P 500 index and the VIX during the period January 1990 through December 2004.

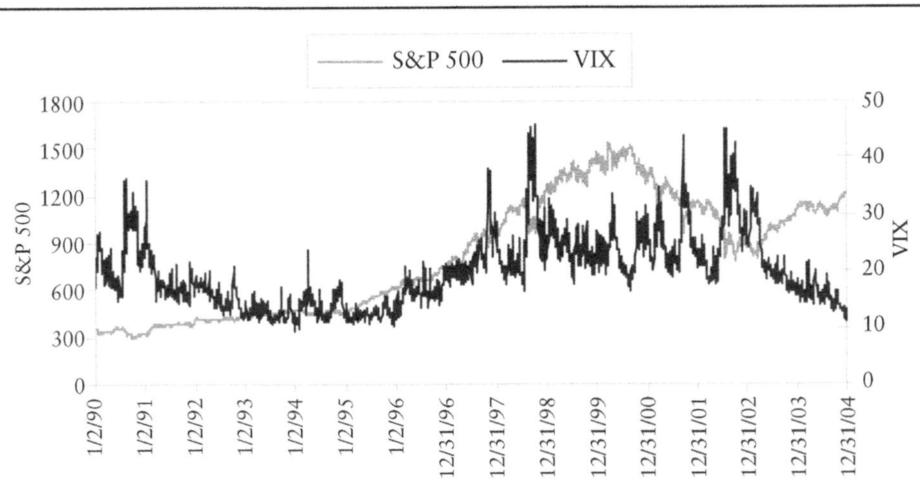


tion between the level of VIX and the level of the S&P 500 index—as the stock market goes up, volatility tends to fall. During 2003 and 2004, for example, the S&P 500 is systematically increasing while the level of VIX falls. Third, the inverse correlation is not perfect. During 1996 and 1997, for example, the level of market volatility is increasing while the stock market is also increasing. All of these phenomenon contribute to making futures contracts on the VIX a potentially new and useful expected return/risk management tool, as we will see in the illustration that follows.

The CFE VIX futures contract has, as its underlying, the VIX. The futures contract specifications are given in Table 15.5. Its denomination is \$100 times the increased-value VIX. The "increased-value VIX" (ticker symbol VBI) is simply the level observed in the marketplace times ten ($VBI = VIX \times 10$). The tick size of the contract is 0.1 of one VBI point or \$10. The available contract months include the two near-term contract months plus two contract months on the February quarterly cycle (February, May, August, and November). The expiration day is the third Friday of the contract month, although trading stops on the preceding Tuesday. The contract is cash-settled on the Wednesday preceding the third Friday, at a special opening quotation (SOQ).

To understand the distinction between the VIX and the VIX futures, consider Figure 15.13. The figure assumes that we traded the February 2005 VIX futures on June 21, 2004. At the close on June 21, the VIX level was 15.26, and the Feb/05 VIX was at 200.50. Recall that the futures is scaled by 10, so the futures price represents a volatility rate of 20.05%. As the figure illustrates, the level of VIX reflects the market's expected future volatility over the next thirty calendar days (from June 21 to July 21, 2004), while the VIX futures reflects the expected future market volatility during a 30-calendar day period beginning when the Feb/05 futures contract expires and ending thirty calendar days later (February 15 to March 17, 2005). In other words, the VIX futures is a one-month forward volatil-

**TABLE 15.5** Selected terms of Market Volatility Index (VIX) futures contract.

| | |
|---|---|
| Exchange | CBOE Futures Exchange (CFE) |
| Ticker symbol | VX |
| Contract unit | $100 times Increased-Value VIX[a] |
| Tick size | 0.1 of one VBI point |
| Tick value | $10 |
| Trading hours | 8:30 AM to 3:15 PM CST |
| Contract months | Two near-term contract months plus two contract months on the February quarterly cycle (Feb., May, Aug., and Nov.) |
| Expiration day | Third Friday of the contract month. |
| Last day of trading | Tuesday prior to the third Friday of the expiring month. |
| Final settlement date | Wednesday prior to the third Friday of the expiring month. |
| Final settlement price | Cash settled. Final settlement price for VIX futures shall be 10 times a Special Opening Quotation (SOQ) of VIX calculated from the options used to calculate the index on the settlement date. The opening price for any series in which there is no trade shall be the average of that option's bid price and ask price as determined at the opening of trading. The final settlement price will be rounded to the nearest 0.10. |

[a] Increased-Value VIX (VBI) is 10 times the VIX index level.

**FIGURE 15.13** VIX index and February 2005 VIX futures assuming futures was traded on June 21, 2004.

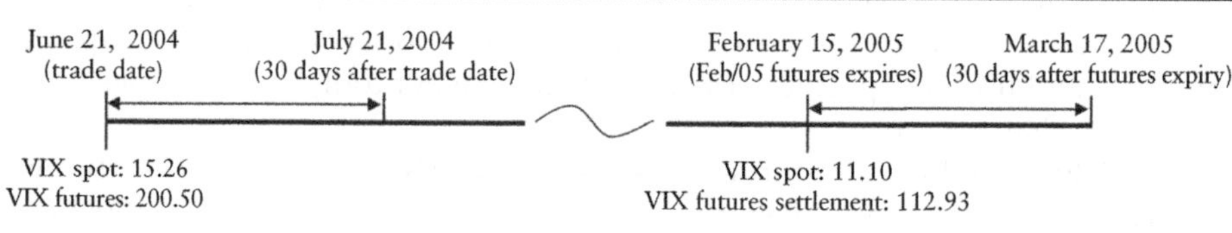


ity rate that begins some time in the future. As it turns out, on February 15, 2005, the Feb/05 VIX was cash settled in the morning at ten times the spot level of VIX, 112.93. By the end of the day, the level of VIX had fallen to 11.10.

The convergence of the Feb/05 VIX futures to the VIX index over the period June 21, 2004 through February 15, 2005 is shown in Figure 15.14. The VIX is multiplied by 10 to put it on the same scale as the futures price. Where the two prices were about 50 points apart in June 2004, they slowly and steadily converged to the same level at expiration. Figure 15.15 shows the open interest of the Feb/05 VIX futures contract. In June 2004, the Feb/05 futures was a distant contract maturity and did not have much open interest. Through time, as the shorter contract maturities expired, the open interest in the Feb/05 contract rose, reaching a peak above 6,000 contracts in January 2005. Like most cash-settled futures, open interest remained high until contract settlement.[19]

[19] Recall that, in Chapter 1, we discussed the fact that futures contracts with physical delivery are generally unwound before contract maturity to avoid the costs of transportation. With cash settlement, no such costs exist.

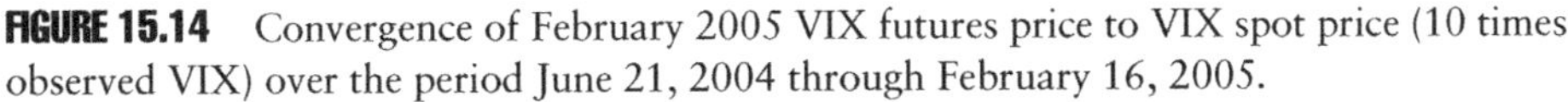

**FIGURE 15.14** Convergence of February 2005 VIX futures price to VIX spot price (10 times observed VIX) over the period June 21, 2004 through February 16, 2005.

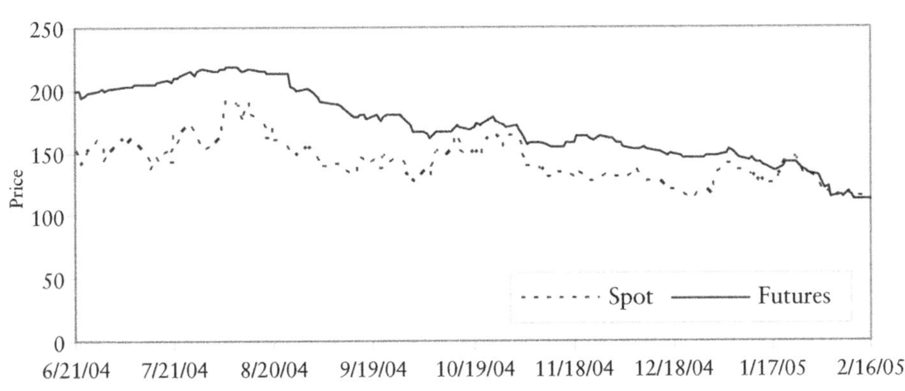


**FIGURE 15.15** Open interest of February 2005 VIX futures over its life (June 21, 2004 through February 16, 2005).

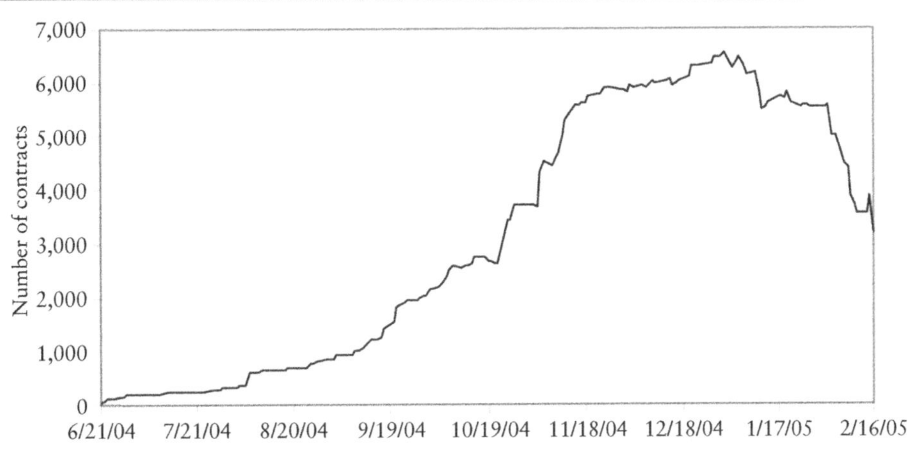


To get a sense for how VIX futures contracts are priced, let us assume that we are considering the variance of S&P 500 index returns over the next 60 calendar days (i.e., two months). If the returns of the index are independent through time, we can write

$$\bar{\sigma}^2_{1\text{-}60}\left(\frac{60}{365}\right) = \bar{\sigma}^2_{1\text{-}30}\left(\frac{30}{365}\right) + \bar{\sigma}^2_{31\text{-}60}\left(\frac{60-30}{365}\right) \tag{15.23}$$

In (15.23), $\bar{\sigma}^2_{1\text{-}60}$ and $\bar{\sigma}^2_{1\text{-}60}$ can be considered spot rates of variance, that is, the expected variance rates over the next 30 calendar days and 60 calendar days, respectively. The term,

$$\bar{\sigma}^2_{31\text{-}60}\left(\frac{30}{365}\right)$$

however, is a forward variance, that is, the average variance rate that we can expect to observe over a 30-day period beginning 30 days from now. To determine the forward volatility rate, we can rearrange (5.23) to yield

$$\bar{\sigma}_{31\text{-}60} = \sqrt{\frac{\bar{\sigma}^2_{1\text{-}60}\left(\frac{60}{365}\right) - \bar{\sigma}^2_{1\text{-}30}\left(\frac{30}{365}\right)}{\frac{60-30}{365}}} \tag{15.24}$$

Equation (15.24) provides us with the insight we need in understanding how to value the VIX futures. The rate on the left-hand side of (15.24) can be thought of as the VIX futures price. In order to estimate its value, we need to know the two variance rates in the numerator on the right-hand side. One way to get these values is to request quotes on 30-day and a 60-day variance forwards from an OTC swap dealer. Another is to use S&P 500 index options to imply the variance rates of 30- and 60-day intervals.[20] Note that, in this particular instance, the rate $\bar{\sigma}_{1\text{-}30}$ is also the current level of the VIX because the forward period begins in exactly 30 calendar days. Whether the forward price exceeds the current spot price, as it did for the Feb/05 VIX futures, depends upon whether the term structure of realized variance swaps is upward- or downward-sloping. In an upward-sloping environment, the forward price will exceed the spot price, and vice versa. Given that volatility tends to follow a mean-reverting process, the forward rate will be equal to the spot rate on average.

**ILLUSTRATION 15.6** Estimate VIX futures price.

*Suppose that you are given the assignment of determining the fair value of the VIX futures where the contract expires in exactly 15 days. You have contacted an OTC derivatives dealer, and he quoted you rates of 400 and 420 on 15-day and 45-day realized variance swaps.*

The quoted realized variance swap rates straddle the forward period corresponding to the VIX futures. Hence, the fair value of the VIX futures can be determined by

$$VIX \text{ futures} = \sqrt{\frac{420\left(\frac{45}{365}\right) - 400\left(\frac{15}{365}\right)}{\frac{45-15}{365}}} = 20.74$$

expressed in VIX points, or 207.40 expressed in VBI points.

[20] The procedure in Appendix 15A of this chapter can be adapted to handle this exercise.

**Expected Return/Risk Management Applications** Exchange-traded futures on volatility also offer a number of new expected return/risk management strategies. In the illustration below, we show that VIX futures can be regarded as a new asset class and can potentially improve the expected return/risk opportunity set. Indeed, because the returns of the S&P 500 portfolio and the returns of the VIX are inversely correlated, the diversification effects can well surpass other strategies such as diversifying across countries.[21] VIX futures can also be used to manage individual stock volatility. Individual stock volatility can be thought of as the sum of two components: stock market volatility and firm-specific volatility. Market volatility products allow investors to hedge the stock market volatility component to develop selected exposures in the idiosyncratic risk of individual stocks.[22]

One caveat is necessary, however. Many stock market volatility hedging needs are long-term. The VIX futures contract, on the other hand, is on the stock market volatility rate in a thirty-day forward period. Consequently, in order to effectively hedge a short volatility position over a long period of time, it may be necessary to buy a strip of VIX futures so that the volatility rate over the entire hedge interval may be captured.

**ILLUSTRATION 15.7** Using VIX futures as alternative investment.

*Suppose that you are a pension fund manager and have just finished your stock portfolio allocation decisions for the year. The expected return of the stock portfolio is 12%, and its standard deviation of return is 16%. The risk-free interest rate is 4%. Since the pension fund has a stated risk tolerance level of 14%, you place 12.5% of the portfolio's funds in risk-free bonds and 87.5% in the stock portfolio. The expected overall portfolio return is therefore*

$$E_P = 0.125(0.04) + 0.875(0.12) = 0.04 + (0.12 - 0.04)(0.14/0.16) = 11\%^{23}$$

*Now suppose that you have just become aware of VIX futures contract. Since stock market volatility tends to follow a mean-reverting process, you believe that the expected rate of price appreciation in the VIX futures is 0%. After some statistical analysis, you assess the volatility of the rate of price appreciation in the VIX futures to be 80%, and the correlation between the VIX futures return and your stock portfolio return to be –0.6. Can you benefit by buying or selling VIX futures?*

To answer the question, you need to recall from Chapter 5 that the expected return and risk of a portfolio that consists of a long position in the asset and $n_F$ futures contracts may be written

$$E_P = E_S + n_F E_F$$

and

[21] Stock returns in different countries tend to be positively correlated. A major economic shock in one market is usually felt across markets.

[22] Whaley (1993) demonstrates that, for large market capitalization firms, nearly 50% of movement in individual stock volatility rate is explained by movements in the market volatility rate.

[23] The expected return/risk mechanics is drawn directly from Chapter 3. Risk tolerance is the maximum return volatility (expressed in standard deviation of return) that the portfolio is willing to sustain.

$$\sigma_P = \sqrt{\sigma_S^2 + n_F^2\sigma_F^2 + 2n_F\rho_{SF}\sigma_S\sigma_F}$$

where $E$ is expected rate of return, $\sigma$ is the standard deviation of return, and $\rho$ is the correlation between rates of return. With the current allocation, the expected excess return-to-risk ratio (i.e., the Sharpe ratio) is

$$\text{Sharpe ratio} = \frac{E_S - r}{\sigma_S} = \frac{0.12 - 0.04}{0.16} = 0.5$$

Can you arrive at a higher Sharpe ratio by buying/selling VIX futures?

To answer this question, you can use Excel's SOLVER to find the value of $n_F$ that maximizes

$$\frac{E_P - r}{\sigma_P} = \frac{0.12 - 0.04}{\sqrt{0.16^2 + n_F^2(0.80^2) + 2n_F(-0.6)(0.16)(0.80)}}$$

where, because the expected return on the VIX futures is zero, it does not appear in the numerator of the portfolio's excess return-to-risk ratio. For the problem information at hand, the optimal value of $n_F$ is 0.12. At $n_F = 0.12$, the expected portfolio return ($E_P$) stays at 12% (since the expected return on the VIX futures is 0), however, the standard deviation of portfolio return ($\sigma_P$) is only 12.8% and the expected excess return/risk ratio is 0.625. If the pension fund does permit borrowing, the final portfolio should consist of only the stock portfolio and a long position the VIX futures, and no money in risk-free bonds. If the pension fund allows for borrowing and wants to maintain its stated risk tolerance of 14%, it must lever up the portfolio by 14/12.8 – 1 = 0.09375. Thus, the optimal allocation is to borrow 9.375% of the portfolio's value, invest 109.375% of the portfolio's value in the stock portfolio, and buy 1.09375(0.12) VIX futures. The expected return of the overall portfolio is now 12.75% at a 14% risk tolerance, well above the 11% expected when the VIX futures are not considered. The figure shown below summarizes the results of this illustration. Without the VIX futures, the pension fund is expected to reside at point A with an expected return of 11%. With the VIX futures as part of the portfolio, the fund has a higher expected return, 12.75%, at the same level of risk and resides at point B.

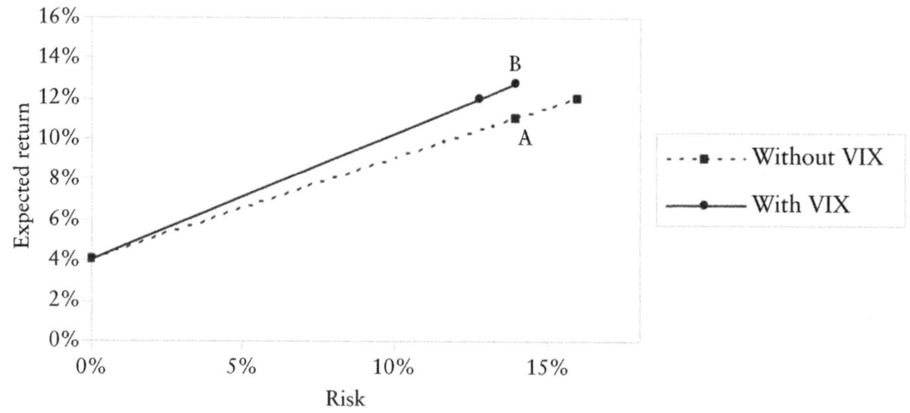

**TABLE 15.6** Selected terms of Market Volatility Index (VIX) option contract.

| | |
|---|---|
| Exchange | Chicago Board Options Exchange (CBOE) |
| Ticker symbol | VIX |
| Contract unit | 100 times CBOE Market Volatility index |
| Exercise price increments | 2-1/2 point increments |
| Exercise style | European |
| Tick size | 0.05 point up to $3 premiums; .10 point over $3 |
| Tick value | $5; $10 |
| Trading hours | 8:30 AM to 15:15 PM CST |
| Contract months | Two near-term contract months plus two contract months on the February quaterly cycle (Feb., May, Aug., and Nov.) |
| Expiration day | Wednesday that is 30 days prior to the third Friday of the calendar month immediately following the expiring month. |
| Last day of trading | Tuesday prior to expiration date each month. |
| Final settlement price | Cash settled. Exercise settlement value shall be a Special Opening Quotation (SOQ) of VIX calculated from the sequence of opening prices of options used to calculate the index on the settlement date. The opening price for any series in which there is no trade shall be the average of that option's bid price and ask price as determined at the opening of trading. Exercise will result in the delivery of cash on the business day following expiration. The exercise settlement amount is equal to the difference between the exercise-settlement value and the exercise price of the option times $100. |

The Chicago Board Options Exchange (CBOE) launched VIX option contracts on Friday, February 24, 2006. Like the VIX futures, the CBOE's VIX options contract has, as its underlying, the VIX. The option contract specifications are given in Table 15.6. Its ticker symbol is "VIX," and its denomination is $100 times the level of the CBOE's Market Volatility index. The tick size (value) of the contract is 0.05 ($5) for option premiums below $3.00 ($300), and 0.10 ($100) for premiums greater than $3 ($300). The available contract months include the two near-term contract months plus two contract months on the February quarterly cycle (February, May, August, and November). The expiration day is the Wednesday that is 30 days before the third Friday of the calendar month following the expiring month. Trading stops on the Tuesday before the expiration day. The contract is cash-settled on the day after the expiration at at a special opening quotation (SOQ). The exercise settlement amount equals the difference between the exercise-settlement value and the exercise price times $100.

## SUMMARY

Many stock index products are inextricably linked to particular index derivative trading strategies. This chapter focuses on such products. The first is portfolio insurance. After examining a brief history on how the strategy evolved, a detailed analysis of passive and dynamic portfolio insurance schemes is provided. Passive insurance means buying an appropriate number of index puts. Dynamic insurance implies that the portfolio consists of either stocks and risk-free bonds or stocks and index futures and is rebalanced continuously through time and as the market moves in such a way that the portfolio payoffs mimic the payoffs of an insured portfolio. The second group of products are funds based on an index/option trading strategy. Including options in an investment portfolio can dramatically affect the shape of the portfolio's rate of return distribution, undermining the usefulness of commonly applied portfolio performance evaluation techniques. We examine this problem using the history of buy-write returns for the CBOE's Buy-Write Index (BXM). The final group of index products that we discuss is market volatility derivatives. Essentially two types exist—contracts on realized volatility and contracts on volatility implied by index option prices. We describe different volatility contract specifications and show how the CBOE's Market Volatility Index (VIX) can be constructed from a portfolio of S&P 500 index options. We also illustrate how volatility derivatives can be used as an alternative investment in an asset allocation framework.

## REFERENCES AND SUGGESTED READINGS


Bernstein, Peter L. 1996. *Against the Gods: The Remarkable Story of Risk*. New York: John Wiley & Sons.

Black, Fischer, and Myron Scholes. 1973. The pricing of options and corporate liabilities. *Journal of Political Economy* 81: 637–659.

Bollen, Nicolas P. B., and Robert E. Whaley. 2004. Does net buying pressure affect the shape of implied volatility functions? *Journal of Finance* 59: 711–754.

Breeden, Douglas T., and Robert H. Litzenberger. 1978. Prices of state-contingent claims implicit in option prices. *Journal of Buisness* 51: 621–651.

Chicago Board Options Exchange. 2003. VIX: CBOE volatility Index. Working paper.

Day, Theodore E., and Craig M. Lewis. 1992. Stock market volatility and the information content of stock index options. *Journal of Econometrics* 52 (April–May): 267–287.

Demeterfi, Kresimir, Emanuel Derman, Michael Kamal, and Joseph Zou. 1999. More than you ever wanted to know about volatility swaps. Working paper, Quantitative Strategies Research Notes, Goldman Sachs.

Dunbar, Nicholas. 2000. *Inventing Money: The Story of Long-Term Capital Management and the Legends Behind It*. Chichester: John Wiley & Sons.

Fleming, Jeff. 1998. The quality of market volatility forecasts implied by S&P 100 index option prices. *Journal of Empirical Finance* 5 (October): 317–345.

Grossman, Sanford. 1988. An analysis of the implications for stock and futures price volatility of program trading and dynamic hedging strategies. *Journal of Business* 61: 275–298.

Heston, Steven L., and Saikat Nandi. 2000. Derivatives on volatility: Some simple solutions based on obsrvables. Working paper, Federal Reserve Bank of Atlanta.

Javaheri, Alivreza, Paul Wilmott, and Espen G. Haug. 2002. GARCH and volatility swaps. Working paper, Royal Bank of Canada.

Lintner, John. 1965. The valuation of risk assets and the selection of risky investments in stock portfolios and capital budgets. *Review of Economics and Statistics* 47: 13–37.

Lowenstein, Roger C. 2000. *When Genius Failed: The Rise and Fall of Long-Term Capital Management*. New York: Random House.

Markowitz, Harry. 1952. Portfolio selection. *Journal of Finance* 12 (March): 77–91.
Markowitz, Harry. 1959. *Portfolio Selection.* New York: John Wiley & Sons.
Markowitz, Harry. 1991. Foundations of portfolio theory. *Journal of Finance* 46: 469–477.
Merton, Robert C. 1973. Theory of rational option pricing. *Bell Journal of Economics and Management Science* 4: 141–183.
Modigliani, Franco, and Leah Modigliani. 1997. Risk-adjusted performance. *Journal of Portfolio Management* (Winter): 45–54.
Schneeweis, Thomas, and Richard Spurgin. 2001. The benefits of index option-based strategies for institutional portfolios. *Journal of Alternative Investments* (Spring): 44–52.
Sharpe, William F. 1964. Capital asset prices: A theory of market equilibrium under conditions of risk. *Journal of Finance* 19: 425–442.
Sharpe, William F. 1966. Mutual fund performance. *Journal of Business* 39 (1): 119–138.
Stutzer, Michael. 2000. A portfolio performance index. *Financial Analysts Journal* 56: 52–60.
Stux, Ivan E., and Peter R. Fanelli. 1990. Hedged equities as an asset class. Working paper. Morgan Stanley Equities Analytical Research.
Sulima, Cheryl L. 2001. Volatility and variance swaps. *Capital Market News Federal Reserve Bank of Chicago* (March): 1–4.
Theoret, Raymod, Lyide Zabre, and Pierre Rostan. 2002. Pricing volatility swaps: Empirical testing with Canadian data. Working paper. School of Business, University of Quebec, Montreal.
Whaley, Robert E. 1993. Derivatives on market volatility: Hedging tools long overdue. *Journal of Derivatives* 1: 71–84.
Whaley, Robert E. 2002. Return and risk of CBOE buy-write monthly index. *Journal of Derivatives* 10 (2): 35–42.
Whaley, Robert E. 2000. The investor fear gauge. *Journal of Portfolio Management* 26 (3): 12–17.

## APPENDIX 15A: CONSTRUCTION OF THE CBOE'S MARKET VOLATILITY INDEX (VIX)

The purpose of this appendix is to describe the algorithm with which the CBOE's Market Volatility Index (VIX) is computed.[24] The VIX is the expected future volatility of the S&P 500 index over the next thirty days. It is an *implied* volatility in that it is based on S&P 500 index option prices. Unlike the implied volatilities from the BSM option valuation model, however, the VIX does not depend on a particular return distribution.[25]

To compute the VIX, an eight-step procedure is used.

**Step 1: Collect relevant information.** The information needed to compute the VIX is (1) the bid/ask price quotes of all nearby and second nearby call and put options

[24] The procedure for calculating VIX is described in CBOE (2003). The theory underlying the procedure is based on the Breeden and Litzenberger (1978) result that the probability density function of asset price can be inferred from the prices of options written on that asset, where the options have a common expiration date and continuum of exercise prices. Demeterfi, Derman, Kamal, and Zou (1999) apply this result in a discretized form to arrive at an equation for the volatility of asset price.

[25] Recall that the BSM model assumes a log-normal asset price distribution at the option's expiration.

traded on the S&P 500 index; and (2) the risk-free interest rate corresponding to each expiration date. For each option series, the bid/ask midpoint is computed. The difference between the call midpoint and put midpoint at each exercise price is computed.

**Step 2: Compute the time to expiration in minutes and then years from the current time until option expiration.** The time to expiration in minutes is the sum of three components.[26] First, we must compute the number of minutes from the current time until midnight on the same day. We next compute the number of minutes from midnight today until midnight on the day before expiration. Finally, we must compute the number of minutes from midnight on the day before expiration until cash settlement at the open on expiration day. The last number is, of course, a constant. The time of cash settlement is at 8:30 AM on expiration day. The number of minutes from midnight on the day before expiration until the time of expiration is therefore

$$8.5 \text{ hours} \times 60 \text{ minutes per hour} = 510 \text{ minutes}$$

The first and second components depend upon the time of day and the number of days to expiration, respectively.

To illustrate, assume that we are computing the level of VIX at 8:38 AM (CST) on October 6, 2003. The number of minutes to midnight on October 6 is

$$22 \text{ minutes} + 15 \text{ hours} \times 60 \text{ minutes per hour} = 922 \text{ minutes}$$

On October 6, 2003, the nearby and second expirations of the S&P 500 index options are the October 17, 2003 and November 21, 2003, respectively, and the number of days to expiration are 12 and 47 days inclusive of the current date and the expiration date. The current date and expiration date are already incorporated, however. The number of minutes until midnight on the current date is 922, and the number of minutes from midnight on the day before expiration until time of expiration on the expiration day is 510. Thus we reduce the number of days to expiration for the nearby and second nearby expirations to 10 and 45 and compute the number of minutes. With 1,440 minutes in each 24-hour day, the number of minutes for the second component of the nearby contract is

$$10 \text{ days} \times 1{,}440 \text{ minutes per day} = 14{,}400$$

and the number of minutes for the second component of the second nearby contract is

$$45 \text{ days} \times 1{,}440 \text{ minutes per day} = 64{,}800$$

The total numbers of minutes for the two contract expirations are therefore

$$\text{Nearby contract: } 922 + 14{,}400 + 510 = 15{,}832$$

and

[26] Time to expiration is computed in minutes to conform to industry practice.

Second nearby contract: 922 + 64,800 + 510 = 66,232

The times to expiration in years are then computed as

$$T_1 = 15{,}832/525{,}600 = 0.0301217656$$

and

$$T_2 = 66{,}232/525{,}600 = 0.1260121766$$

where 525,600 in the number of minutes in a calendar year (i.e., 1,440 minutes per day times 365 days).

**Step 3: Compute the interest accumulation factor for each option expiration.** The interest accumulation factor is defined as the terminal amount that $1 will accumulate to by the option's expiration if invested at the risk-free rate of interest. On October 6, 2003, the risk-free rate corresponding to the nearby expiration was 0.920% on an annualized basis, and the risk-free rate corresponding to the second nearby expiration was 0.850%.[27] The accumulation factors for the nearby and second nearby contracts were

$$e^{r_1 T_1} = e^{0.00920(0.03012177)} = 1.0002772$$

and

$$e^{r_2 T_2} = e^{0.00850(0.12601218)} = 1.0010717$$

respectively.

**Step 4: Identify the at-the-money options for each option expiration.** To identify the at-the-money options for each expiration, we must first compute the bid/ask midpoints for all calls and puts with the nearby and second nearby contract expirations. This is shown in Tables 15A.1 and 15A.2. For each exercise price for which a call price and put price are available, compute the absolute difference between the call price and put price. Note that the calls and puts with zero bid prices are excluded for consideration. Such options appear in bold face. The exercise price with the lowest absolute difference is defined as the at-the-money option. On October 6, 2003, the nearby at-the-money exercise price is 1030 (as is shown in Table 15A.1), and the second nearby exercise price is 1035 (as is shown in Table 15A.2).

**Step 5: Compute the forward index level for each contract expiration.** With the identity of the at-the-money options known, we compute the implied forward index level using the forward value version of put-call parity, that is,

$$F_i = X_i + e^{r_i T_i}(C_i - P_i)$$

[27] On this particular day, the yield curve of the risk-free rate was inverted at short maturities.

**TABLE 15A.1** Nearby S&P 500 index option prices used in the computation of the VIX on October 6, 2003 at 8:38 AM (CST).

Nearby Contract Expiration: 20031017

| Exercise Price | Call Price Quotes | | | Put Price Quotes | | | Absolute Difference |
|---|---|---|---|---|---|---|---|
| | Bid | Ask | Midpoint | Bid | Ask | Midpoint | |
| 725 | 304.10 | 307.10 | 305.600 | 0.00 | 0.50 | | |
| 750 | 279.10 | 282.10 | 280.600 | 0.00 | 0.50 | | |
| 775 | 254.10 | 257.10 | 255.600 | 0.00 | 0.50 | | |
| 800 | 229.10 | 232.10 | 230.600 | 0.00 | 0.40 | | |
| 825 | 204.10 | 207.10 | 205.600 | 0.00 | 0.25 | | |
| 850 | 179.10 | 182.10 | 180.600 | 0.05 | 0.20 | 0.125 | 180.475 |
| 875 | 154.20 | 157.20 | 155.700 | 0.10 | 0.20 | 0.150 | 155.550 |
| 890 | 139.20 | 142.20 | 140.700 | 0.00 | 0.50 | | |
| 900 | 129.30 | 132.30 | 130.800 | 0.20 | 0.40 | 0.300 | 130.500 |
| 910 | 119.40 | 122.40 | 120.900 | 0.00 | 0.50 | | |
| 915 | 114.40 | 117.40 | 115.900 | 0.05 | 0.50 | 0.275 | 115.625 |
| 925 | 104.50 | 107.50 | 106.000 | 0.25 | 0.60 | 0.425 | 105.575 |
| 930 | 100.00 | 102.60 | 101.300 | 0.30 | 0.70 | 0.500 | 100.800 |
| 935 | 95.10 | 97.10 | 96.100 | 0.50 | 0.60 | 0.550 | 95.550 |
| 940 | 90.20 | 92.20 | 91.200 | 0.45 | 0.90 | 0.675 | 90.525 |
| 945 | 85.30 | 87.30 | 86.300 | 0.40 | 0.90 | 0.650 | 85.650 |
| 950 | 80.40 | 82.40 | 81.400 | 0.65 | 1.00 | 0.825 | 80.575 |
| 955 | 75.80 | 77.80 | 76.800 | 0.75 | 1.10 | 0.925 | 75.875 |
| 960 | 70.90 | 72.90 | 71.900 | 0.80 | 1.30 | 1.050 | 70.850 |
| 970 | 61.30 | 63.30 | 62.300 | 1.10 | 1.60 | 1.350 | 60.950 |
| 975 | 56.50 | 58.50 | 57.500 | 1.50 | 1.90 | 1.700 | 55.800 |
| 980 | 51.80 | 53.80 | 52.800 | 1.70 | 2.20 | 1.950 | 50.850 |
| 985 | 47.20 | 49.20 | 48.200 | 2.00 | 2.50 | 2.250 | 45.950 |
| 990 | 42.60 | 44.60 | 43.600 | 2.30 | 3.10 | 2.700 | 40.900 |
| 995 | 38.20 | 40.20 | 39.200 | 3.00 | 3.70 | 3.350 | 35.850 |
| 1005 | 29.50 | 31.50 | 30.500 | 4.40 | 5.20 | 4.800 | 25.700 |
| 1010 | 25.50 | 27.50 | 26.500 | 5.40 | 6.40 | 5.900 | 20.600 |
| 1015 | 21.80 | 23.80 | 22.800 | 6.60 | 7.60 | 7.100 | 15.700 |
| 1020 | 18.50 | 19.50 | 19.000 | 8.00 | 9.00 | 8.500 | 10.500 |
| 1025 | 16.00 | 16.90 | 16.450 | 9.90 | 10.90 | 10.400 | 6.050 |
| 1030 | 13.00 | 14.00 | 13.500 | 11.60 | 13.20 | 12.400 | 1.100 |
| 1035 | 10.10 | 11.50 | 10.800 | 14.00 | 15.60 | 14.800 | 4.000 |
| 1040 | 8.00 | 9.00 | 8.500 | 16.80 | 18.40 | 17.600 | 9.100 |
| 1045 | 6.10 | 7.00 | 6.550 | 19.90 | 21.50 | 20.700 | 14.150 |
| 1050 | 4.70 | 5.50 | 5.100 | 23.20 | 25.20 | 24.200 | 19.100 |
| 1055 | 3.40 | 4.20 | 3.800 | 26.90 | 28.90 | 27.900 | 24.100 |
| 1060 | 2.50 | 3.30 | 2.900 | 30.90 | 32.90 | 31.900 | 29.000 |
| 1065 | 1.90 | 2.40 | 2.150 | 35.20 | 37.20 | 36.200 | 34.050 |

**TABLE 15A.1** (Continued)

| Exercise Price | Call Price Quotes | | | Put Price Quotes | | | Absolute Difference |
|---|---|---|---|---|---|---|---|
| | Bid | Ask | Midpoint | Bid | Ask | Midpoint | |
| 1070 | 1.30 | 1.80 | 1.550 | 39.60 | 41.60 | 40.600 | 39.050 |
| 1075 | 0.90 | 1.40 | 1.150 | 44.20 | 46.20 | 45.200 | 44.050 |
| 1100 | 0.10 | 0.20 | 0.150 | 68.60 | 70.60 | 69.600 | 69.450 |
| 1115 | 0.00 | 0.50 | | 83.40 | 85.40 | 84.400 | 84.400 |
| 1125 | 0.00 | 0.15 | | 93.40 | 95.40 | 94.400 | 94.400 |
| 1135 | 0.00 | 0.50 | | 102.90 | 105.90 | 104.400 | 104.400 |
| 1150 | 0.00 | 0.10 | | 117.80 | 120.80 | 119.300 | 119.300 |
| 1175 | 0.00 | 0.50 | | 142.80 | 145.80 | 144.300 | 144.300 |
| 1200 | 0.00 | 0.50 | | 167.80 | 170.80 | 169.300 | 169.300 |
| 1225 | 0.00 | 0.50 | | 192.80 | 195.80 | 194.300 | 194.300 |
| 1250 | 0.00 | 0.50 | | 217.80 | 220.80 | 219.300 | 219.300 |
| 1275 | 0.00 | 0.50 | | 242.80 | 245.80 | 244.300 | 244.300 |
| 1300 | 0.00 | 0.50 | | 267.80 | 270.80 | 269.300 | 269.300 |
| 1325 | 0.00 | 0.50 | | 292.80 | 295.80 | 294.300 | 294.300 |
| 1350 | 0.00 | 0.50 | | 317.70 | 320.70 | 319.200 | 319.200 |
| 1375 | 0.00 | 0.50 | | 342.70 | 345.70 | 344.200 | 344.200 |

**TABLE 15A.2** Second nearby S&P 500 index option prices used in the computation of the VIX on October 6, 2003 at 8:38 AM (CST).

| Second Nearby Contract Expiration: | | | | 20031121 | | | |
|---|---|---|---|---|---|---|---|
| Exercise Price | Call Price Quotes | | | Put Price Quotes | | | Absolute Difference |
| | Bid | Ask | Midpoint | Bid | Ask | Midpoint | |
| 600 | 427.70 | 430.70 | 429.200 | 0.00 | 0.30 | | |
| 625 | 402.70 | 405.70 | 404.200 | 0.00 | 0.50 | | |
| 650 | 377.80 | 380.80 | 379.300 | 0.00 | 0.50 | | |
| 675 | 352.80 | 355.80 | 354.300 | 0.00 | 0.50 | | |
| 700 | 327.90 | 330.90 | 329.400 | 0.00 | 0.50 | | |
| 725 | 303.00 | 306.00 | 304.500 | 0.00 | 0.50 | | |
| 750 | 278.10 | 281.10 | 279.600 | 0.00 | 0.50 | | |
| 775 | 253.30 | 256.30 | 254.800 | 0.10 | 0.60 | 0.350 | 254.450 |
| 800 | 228.50 | 231.50 | 230.000 | 0.30 | 0.80 | 0.550 | 229.450 |
| 825 | 203.90 | 206.90 | 205.400 | 0.60 | 1.10 | 0.850 | 204.550 |
| 850 | 179.40 | 182.40 | 180.900 | 1.10 | 1.60 | 1.350 | 179.550 |
| 875 | 155.00 | 158.00 | 156.500 | 1.70 | 2.20 | 1.950 | 154.550 |
| 895 | 135.80 | 138.80 | 137.300 | 2.30 | 3.10 | 2.700 | 134.600 |
| 900 | 131.20 | 134.20 | 132.700 | 2.60 | 3.30 | 2.950 | 129.750 |
| 925 | 107.70 | 110.70 | 109.200 | 3.90 | 4.70 | 4.300 | 104.900 |
| 950 | 85.40 | 87.40 | 86.400 | 6.00 | 7.00 | 6.500 | 79.900 |
| 975 | 64.00 | 66.00 | 65.000 | 9.50 | 10.50 | 10.000 | 55.000 |
| 980 | 60.00 | 62.00 | 61.000 | 10.20 | 11.80 | 11.000 | 50.000 |

**TABLE 15A.1** (Continued)

| Second Nearby Contract Expiration: | | | 20031121 | | | | |
|---|---|---|---|---|---|---|---|
| Exercise Price | Call Price Quotes Bid | Ask | Midpoint | Put Price Quotes Bid | Ask | Midpoint | Absolute Difference |
| 985 | 56.00 | 58.00 | 57.000 | 11.20 | 12.80 | 12.000 | 45.000 |
| 990 | 52.10 | 54.10 | 53.100 | 12.30 | 13.90 | 13.100 | 40.000 |
| 995 | 48.30 | 50.30 | 49.300 | 13.50 | 15.10 | 14.300 | 35.000 |
| 1005 | 41.20 | 43.20 | 42.200 | 16.80 | 17.90 | 17.350 | 24.850 |
| 1010 | 37.80 | 39.80 | 38.800 | 17.90 | 19.50 | 18.700 | 20.100 |
| 1015 | 34.50 | 36.50 | 35.500 | 19.70 | 21.30 | 20.500 | 15.000 |
| 1020 | 31.40 | 33.40 | 32.400 | 21.30 | 23.30 | 22.300 | 10.100 |
| 1025 | 28.40 | 30.40 | 29.400 | 23.30 | 25.30 | 24.300 | 5.100 |
| 1035 | 22.90 | 24.90 | 23.900 | 27.90 | 29.90 | 28.900 | 5.000 |
| 1050 | 16.20 | 17.80 | 17.000 | 35.90 | 37.90 | 36.900 | 19.900 |
| 1060 | 12.40 | 14.00 | 13.200 | 42.10 | 44.10 | 43.100 | 29.900 |
| 1065 | 10.70 | 12.30 | 11.500 | 45.40 | 47.40 | 46.400 | 34.900 |
| 1070 | 9.50 | 10.00 | 9.750 | 48.90 | 50.90 | 49.900 | 40.150 |
| 1075 | 8.20 | 9.20 | 8.700 | 52.50 | 54.50 | 53.500 | 44.800 |
| 1080 | 7.00 | 8.00 | 7.500 | 56.30 | 58.30 | 57.300 | 49.800 |
| 1100 | 3.50 | 4.30 | 3.900 | 73.00 | 75.00 | 74.000 | 70.100 |
| 1125 | 1.40 | 1.90 | 1.650 | 95.70 | 97.70 | 96.700 | 95.050 |
| 1150 | 0.60 | 0.90 | 0.750 | 119.20 | 122.20 | 120.700 | 119.950 |
| 1175 | 0.00 | 0.50 | | 143.80 | 146.80 | 145.300 | 145.300 |
| 1200 | 0.00 | 0.50 | | 168.60 | 171.60 | 170.100 | 170.100 |
| 1225 | 0.00 | 0.50 | | 193.50 | 196.50 | 195.000 | 195.000 |
| 1250 | 0.00 | 0.50 | | 218.40 | 221.40 | 219.900 | 219.900 |
| 1275 | 0.00 | 0.50 | | 243.40 | 246.40 | 244.900 | 244.900 |

For the nearby at-the-money options, the forward price is

$$F_1 = 1030 + 1.0002771586449(13.500 - 12.400) = 1031.10$$

For the second nearby at-the-money options, the forward price is

$$F_2 = 1025 + 1.0010716773370(29.400 - 26.600) = 1029.99$$

**Step 6: Identify the option series used in the computation of the VIX.** In computing the VIX, only the prices of out-of-the-money calls and puts are used. To distinguish between in-the-money and out-of-the-money options, the exercise price just below the implied forward price ($X_{i,0}$) is used. The out-of-the-money calls are those with exercise prices greater than or equal $X_{i,0}$, and the out-of-the-money puts are those with exercise prices less than or equal to $X_{i,0}$. If any of these option series have a bid price equal to zero, they are eliminated from consideration.[28] For the nearby and second nearby option series in the illustration, the exercise prices just below the forward index levels are $X_{1,0} = 1030$ and $X_{2,0}$

= 1035. Since this procedure identifies two options (a call and a put) at exercise price $X_{i,0}$, the arithmetic average of the call and put prices is used.

**Step 7: Compute the implied variance for each contract expiration.** The formula for computing the implied variance for the nearby contract is

$$\sigma_1^2 = \frac{2}{T_1}\sum_{i=1}^{n_1}\frac{\Delta X_{1,i}}{X_{1,i}^2}e^{r_1T_1}O(X_{1,i}) - \frac{1}{T_1}\left(\frac{F_1}{X_{1,0}} - 1\right)^2 \tag{15A.1}$$

where $T_1$ is the nearby contract month's time to expiration expressed in years, $n_1$ is the number of out-of-the-money option series for the nearby contract month, $X_{1,i}$ is the exercise price of the $i$-th option, $r_1$ is the interest rate corresponding to option's expiration date, $F_1$ is the forward index level implied by the at-the-money call and put prices, $O(X_{1,i})$ is the bid/ask price midpoint of the nearby option with an exercise price of $X_{1,i}$, and $X_{1,0}$ is the exercise price just below the implied nearby forward price. The summation term also includes the at-the-money options. For the at-the-money options, the average of the call and put midpoints is used as $O(X_{1,i})$. Finally, the term $\Delta X_{1,i}$ is the average of the exercise prices that straddle option $i$'s exercise price. At the highest and lowest exercise prices, $\Delta X_{1,i}$, is the absolute difference between option $i$'s exercise price and the adjacent exercise price. The last term on the right-hand side is called the displacement factor.

The same procedure is used to compute the second nearby implied variance,

$$\sigma_2^2 = \frac{2}{T_2}\sum_{i=1}^{n_1}\frac{\Delta X_{2,i}}{X_{2,i}^2}e^{r_2T_2}O(X_{2,i}) - \frac{1}{T_2}\left(\frac{F_2}{X_{2,0}} - 1\right)^2 \tag{15A.2}$$

To illustrate the mechanics of these computations, first compute the values of the last term on the right-hand side (i.e., the displacement factors) of the nearby and second nearby contracts. For the nearby contract,

$$\frac{1}{T_1}\left(\frac{F_1}{X_{1,0}} - 1\right)^2 = \frac{1}{0.03012177}\left(\frac{1031.10}{1030} - 1\right)^2 = 0.3789\times10^{-4}$$

and, for the second nearby contract,

$$\frac{1}{T_2}\left(\frac{F_2}{X_{2,0}} - 1\right)^2 = \frac{1}{0.12601218}\left(\frac{1027.80}{1035} - 1\right)^2 = 0.00018843$$

[28] In the event that the bid prices of two calls (puts) at adjacent exercise prices are equal to zero, all call (put) option series with higher (lower) exercise prices are eliminated even though they may have nonzero bid prices.

Next take the sum in the first term on the right-hand side. Table 15A.3 shows the values of each of the $n_1$ terms for the nearby contract, and Table 15A.4 shows the values of each of the $n_2$ terms of the second nearby contract. The first term in the nearby contract's summation is

$$\frac{\Delta X_{1,1}}{X_{1,1}^2} e^{r_1 T_1} O(X_{1,1}) = \frac{25}{850^2} \times 1.0002772 \times 0.125 = 0.433 \times 10^{-5}$$

as is shown in Table 15A.3. Note that the option price used in the expression is the forward price (i.e., the current price carried forward until the end of the contract's life). The sum of the weighted average of the forward option prices is 0.0005943786 for the nearby contract and 0.0025376773 for the second nearby contract. The variance of the nearby contract is therefore

$$\sigma_1^2 = \frac{2}{0.03012177} \times 0.00059438 - 0.3789 \times 10^{-4} = 0.03942717$$

and the variance of the second nearby contract is

$$\sigma_2^2 = \frac{2}{0.12601218} \times 0.00253768 - 0.00018843 = 0.04008827$$

**Step 8: Compute the annualized volatility over the next 30 calendar days.** The variances of the nearby and second nearby contracts correspond to times to expiration of $T_1$ years and $T_2$ years, respectively. VIX, however, maintains a constant time to expiration of 30 days or 30/365 = 0.0821917808 years. To find the variance over the 30 calendar-day interval, we must interpolate between the variances of the nearby and second nearby contracts, that is,

$$\begin{aligned}\sigma_{30\text{-day}}^2 &= \left(\frac{T_2 - T_{30\text{-day}}}{T_2 - T_1}\right)\sigma_1^2 T_1 + \left(\frac{T_{30\text{-day}} - T_1}{T_2 - T_1}\right)\sigma_2^2 T_2 \\ &= 0.00328583\end{aligned}$$

To compute the level of VIX, we annualize the 30-day variance and take the square root, that is,

$$VIX = \sqrt{\sigma_{30\text{-day}}^2\left(\frac{1}{T_{30\text{-day}}}\right)} = \sqrt{0.03997755\left(\frac{1}{0.08219178}\right)} = 19.99\%$$

This is precisely the level of VIX reported by the CBOE at 8:38 AM (CST) on October 6, 2003. The Excel file, **VIX computation.xls**, contains the background computations used in this illustration.

**TABLE 15A.3** Nearby S&P 500 index option prices contribution to the computation of the VIX on October 6, 2003 at 8:38 AM (CST).

Nearby Contract Expiration: 10/17/2003

| C/P | Exercise Price | Price Midpoint | $\Delta X_i$ | Weight | Weight Times Forward Option Price |
|---|---|---|---|---|---|
| P | 850 | 0.125 | 25 | 0.0000346021 | 0.0000043265 |
| P | 875 | 0.150 | 25 | 0.0000326531 | 0.0000048993 |
| P | 900 | 0.300 | 20 | 0.0000246914 | 0.0000074095 |
| P | 915 | 0.275 | 12.5 | 0.0000149303 | 0.0000041070 |
| P | 925 | 0.425 | 7.5 | 0.0000087655 | 0.0000037264 |
| P | 930 | 0.500 | 5 | 0.0000057810 | 0.0000028913 |
| P | 935 | 0.550 | 5 | 0.0000057194 | 0.0000031465 |
| P | 940 | 0.675 | 5 | 0.0000056587 | 0.0000038207 |
| P | 945 | 0.650 | 5 | 0.0000055989 | 0.0000036403 |
| P | 950 | 0.825 | 5 | 0.0000055402 | 0.0000045719 |
| P | 955 | 0.925 | 5 | 0.0000054823 | 0.0000050725 |
| P | 960 | 1.050 | 7.5 | 0.0000081380 | 0.0000085473 |
| P | 970 | 1.350 | 7.5 | 0.0000079711 | 0.0000107640 |
| P | 975 | 1.700 | 5 | 0.0000052597 | 0.0000089440 |
| P | 980 | 1.950 | 5 | 0.0000052062 | 0.0000101548 |
| P | 985 | 2.250 | 5 | 0.0000051534 | 0.0000115985 |
| P | 990 | 2.700 | 5 | 0.0000051015 | 0.0000137779 |
| P | 995 | 3.350 | 7.5 | 0.0000075756 | 0.0000253852 |
| P | 1005 | 4.800 | 7.5 | 0.0000074256 | 0.0000356526 |
| P | 1010 | 5.900 | 5 | 0.0000049015 | 0.0000289267 |
| P | 1015 | 7.100 | 5 | 0.0000048533 | 0.0000344680 |
| P | 1020 | 8.500 | 5 | 0.0000048058 | 0.0000408610 |
| P | 1025 | 10.400 | 5 | 0.0000047591 | 0.0000495081 |
| $X_0$ | 1030 | 12.950 | 5 | 0.0000047130 | 0.0000610500 |
| C | 1035 | 10.800 | 5 | 0.0000046676 | 0.0000504235 |
| C | 1040 | 8.500 | 5 | 0.0000046228 | 0.0000393045 |
| C | 1045 | 6.550 | 5 | 0.0000045786 | 0.0000299985 |
| C | 1050 | 5.100 | 5 | 0.0000045351 | 0.0000231357 |
| C | 1055 | 3.800 | 5 | 0.0000044923 | 0.0000170753 |
| C | 1060 | 2.900 | 5 | 0.0000044500 | 0.0000129085 |
| C | 1065 | 2.150 | 5 | 0.0000044083 | 0.0000094805 |
| C | 1070 | 1.550 | 5 | 0.0000043672 | 0.0000067710 |
| C | 1075 | 1.150 | 15 | 0.0000129800 | 0.0000149311 |
| C | 1100 | 0.150 | 25 | 0.0000206612 | 0.0000031000 |
| | | | | Sum | 0.0005943786 |

**TABLE 15A.4** Second nearby S&P 500 index option prices contribution to the computation of the VIX on October 6, 2003 at 8:38 AM (CST).

Second Nearby Contract Expiration: 11/21/2003

| C/P | Exercise Price | Price Midpoint | $\Delta X_i$ | Weight | Weight Times Forward Option Price |
|---|---|---|---|---|---|
| P | 775 | 0.350 | 25 | 0.0000416233 | 0.0000145838 |
| P | 800 | 0.550 | 25 | 0.0000390625 | 0.0000215074 |
| P | 825 | 0.850 | 25 | 0.0000367309 | 0.0000312548 |
| P | 850 | 1.350 | 25 | 0.0000346021 | 0.0000467629 |
| P | 875 | 1.950 | 22.5 | 0.0000293878 | 0.0000573675 |
| P | 895 | 2.700 | 12.5 | 0.0000156050 | 0.0000421787 |
| P | 900 | 2.950 | 15 | 0.0000185185 | 0.0000546882 |
| P | 925 | 4.300 | 25 | 0.0000292184 | 0.0001257738 |
| P | 950 | 6.500 | 25 | 0.0000277008 | 0.0001802484 |
| P | 975 | 10.000 | 15 | 0.0000157791 | 0.0001579600 |
| P | 980 | 11.000 | 5 | 0.0000052062 | 0.0000573292 |
| P | 985 | 12.000 | 5 | 0.0000051534 | 0.0000619076 |
| P | 990 | 13.100 | 5 | 0.0000051015 | 0.0000669015 |
| P | 995 | 14.300 | 7.5 | 0.0000075756 | 0.0001084467 |
| P | 1005 | 17.350 | 7.5 | 0.0000074256 | 0.0001289715 |
| P | 1010 | 18.700 | 5 | 0.0000049015 | 0.0000917559 |
| P | 1015 | 20.500 | 5 | 0.0000048533 | 0.0000995995 |
| P | 1020 | 22.300 | 5 | 0.0000048058 | 0.0001072852 |
| $X_0$ | 1025 | 26.850 | 7.5 | 0.0000071386 | 0.0001918770 |
| C | 1035 | 23.900 | 12.5 | 0.0000116689 | 0.0002791852 |
| C | 1050 | 17.000 | 12.5 | 0.0000113379 | 0.0001929503 |
| C | 1060 | 13.200 | 7.5 | 0.0000066750 | 0.0000882041 |
| C | 1065 | 11.500 | 5 | 0.0000044083 | 0.0000507497 |
| C | 1070 | 9.750 | 5 | 0.0000043672 | 0.0000426258 |
| C | 1075 | 8.700 | 5 | 0.0000043267 | 0.0000376823 |
| C | 1080 | 7.500 | 12.5 | 0.0000107167 | 0.0000804617 |
| C | 1100 | 3.900 | 22.5 | 0.0000185950 | 0.0000725984 |
| C | 1125 | 1.650 | 25 | 0.0000197531 | 0.0000326275 |
| C | 1150 | 0.750 | 25 | 0.0000189036 | 0.0000141929 |
| | | | | Sum | 0.0025376773 |

# PART Seven

# Currency Derivatives

# 16
# Currency Products

Futures on *foreign exchange* (FX) rates were the first financial futures contract introduced by an exchange. On May 16, 1972, the Chicago Mercantile Exchange launched trading futures on three currencies—the British pound, the Deutschemark, and the Japanese yen. Before that time there was little need for derivatives markets on currencies. Exchange rates were essentially fixed as a result of the Bretton Woods Agreement, which required each country to fix the price of its currency in relation to gold. With the failure of the Bretton Woods Agreement and the removal of the gold standard in 1971, exchange rates began to fluctuate more freely, motivating a need for exchange rate risk management tools. FX options and futures options did not appear until about 10 years later, being introduced by the Philadelphia Stock Exchange and the Chicago Mercantile Exchange in 1982. While exchange-traded derivatives are not nearly as active as stock index and interest rate derivatives, currency derivatives today account for about 12% of the notional amount of all OTC derivatives trading worldwide.[1]

This chapter has four sections. In the first section, exchange-traded and OTC FX derivative markets are discussed. In the second section, arbitrage relations and valuation methods for FX forward, futures, option, and swap contracts are provided. For currencies, the continuous net cost of carry no-arbitrage relations and valuation methods apply. The third section illustrates a number of important currency risk management strategies. Among them are using a currency swap or a strip of currency forwards to redenominate fixed rate debt in one currency into another, using forward/options to manage the price risks of single and multiple transactions, and using forward/options to manage balance sheet risk.

## MARKETS

By far the largest market in currencies is the *interbank* market. Major banks around the world trade both spot and forward currencies on a 24-hour basis. Spot transactions call for delivery and payment within two days. Forward trans-

[1] *Bank for International Settlements* (June 2004).

actions call for delivery and payment at the time specified in the forward contract. Table 16.1 contains quoted spot and forward currency rates on Monday, March 27, 2006. These rates are indicative of what might be charged by major New York banks on large purchases/sales (greater than USD 1 million) of the various currencies. According to the table, buying U.S. dollars with Canadian dollars in the spot market costs CAD 1.1696/USD. On the other hand, selling U.S. dollars for Canadian dollars generates CAD 1.1693/USD. It is also worth noting that an important inverse relation exists between the purchases and sales of different currencies. Buying U.S. dollars with Canadian dollars is the same as selling Canadian dollars for U.S. dollars. For each Canadian dollar sold, we generate 1/1.1696 or 0.85499 U.S. dollars. Similarly, selling U.S. dollars for Canadian dollars is the same as buying Canadian dollars with U.S. dollars. The exchange rate in this case is 1/1.1693 or USD 0.85521/CAD. This inverse relation will prove useful throughout the remaining pages of the chapter.

The forward exchange rates quoted in Table 16.1 have times to expiration up to five years. These particular standard maturities are reported to give a sense for the relation between forward exchange rates and their terms to maturity, that is, the *term structure of forward exchange rates*. Banks are generally willing to quote a forward rate on any maturity that a customer requests. Shorter-term contracts are generally more active and competitively-traded, as is reflected by the fact that the spread between the quoted bid and ask rates is narrower for short maturities than long maturities. Since the CAD/USD forward rates are lower than the spot rate, the U.S. dollar is selling at a *forward discount* (relative to the Canadian dollar), or, alternatively, the Canadian dollar is said to be selling at a *forward premium* (relative to the U.S. dollar).

**TABLE 16.1** Bid and ask spot and forward exchange rates drawn from Bloomberg on Monday, March 27, 2006.

| | USD/GBP | | CHF/USD | | CAD/USD | | USD/EUR | | JPY/USD | |
|---|---|---|---|---|---|---|---|---|---|---|
| Term | Bid Rate | Ask Rate | Bid Rate | Ask Rate | Bid Rate | Ask Rate | Bid Rate | Ask Rate | Bid Rate | Ask Rate |
| Spot | 1.7475 | 1.7478 | 1.3095 | 1.3097 | 1.1693 | 1.1696 | 1.2009 | 1.2011 | 116.67 | 116.69 |
| 1 week | 1.7476 | 1.7479 | 1.3086 | 1.3088 | 1.1690 | 1.1694 | 1.2014 | 1.2016 | 116.56 | 116.58 |
| 1 month | 1.7480 | 1.7483 | 1.3055 | 1.3057 | 1.1683 | 1.1686 | 1.2031 | 1.2033 | 116.21 | 116.23 |
| 2 month | 1.7487 | 1.7490 | 1.3011 | 1.3014 | 1.1673 | 1.1676 | 1.2054 | 1.2056 | 115.71 | 115.73 |
| 3 month | 1.7494 | 1.7497 | 1.2971 | 1.2973 | 1.1662 | 1.1667 | 1.2076 | 1.2078 | 115.24 | 115.26 |
| 4 month | 1.7503 | 1.7506 | 1.2928 | 1.2931 | 1.1653 | 1.1657 | 1.2099 | 1.2101 | 114.74 | 114.76 |
| 5 month | 1.7510 | 1.7514 | 1.2891 | 1.2895 | 1.1643 | 1.1647 | 1.2118 | 1.2121 | 114.29 | 114.32 |
| 6 month | 1.7519 | 1.7522 | 1.2853 | 1.2856 | 1.1633 | 1.1637 | 1.2139 | 1.2142 | 113.82 | 113.84 |
| 9 month | 1.7543 | 1.7547 | 1.2746 | 1.2750 | 1.1605 | 1.1610 | 1.2197 | 1.2200 | 112.48 | 112.51 |
| 1 year | 1.7562 | 1.7567 | 1.2648 | 1.2654 | 1.1582 | 1.1587 | 1.2249 | 1.2252 | 111.23 | 111.26 |
| 2 year | 1.7602 | 1.7615 | 1.2297 | 1.2309 | 1.1495 | 1.1503 | 1.2438 | 1.2444 | 106.78 | 106.84 |
| 3 year | 1.7645 | 1.7688 | 1.1981 | 1.2013 | 1.1413 | 1.1436 | 1.2617 | 1.2629 | 103.10 | 103.21 |
| 4 year | 1.7685 | 1.7763 | 1.1685 | 1.1737 | 1.1315 | 1.1348 | 1.2785 | 1.2807 | 99.87 | 100.04 |
| 5 year | 1.7760 | 1.7853 | 1.1395 | 1.1620 | 1.1272 | 1.1333 | 1.2958 | 1.2989 | 96.78 | 97.05 |

**TABLE 16.2** Conversion rates between euro and national currencies when irrevocably fixed on December 31, 1998.

| Country | Currency | 1 euro = |
|---|---|---|
| Austria | ATS | 13.7603 |
| Belgium | BEF | 40.3399 |
| Finland | FIM | 5.94573 |
| France | FRF | 6.55957 |
| Germany | DEM | 1.95583 |
| Ireland | IEP | 0.787564 |
| Italy | ITL | 1936.27 |
| Luxembourg | LUF | 40.3399 |
| NLG | NLG | 2.20371 |
| Portugal | PTE | 200.482 |
| Spain | ESP | 166.386 |

Exchange-traded FX futures and options markets are also active worldwide. In recent years, contract volume has waned. One reason is that, on December 31, 1998, 11 European countries irrevocably fixed their currencies to the Euro. The countries who are members of the European Union (EU), their former currencies, and the fixed exchange rates are reported in Table 16.2. With all of these countries adopting the euro as the common currency, the need to hedge currency risk across EU countries is eliminated. A second reason is that the OTC currency derivatives market has usurped some of the trading volume from the derivatives exchanges. The OTC market is more well suited to tailor FX derivatives contracts to meet customer risk management needs.

## Futures

In the United States, the most active FX futures contracts are traded on the Chicago Mercantile Exchange's International Monetary Market division. Figure 16.1 shows the breakdown of the CME's FX futures by number of contracts traded during the calendar year 2003. The total contract volume during this period was 31,873,938 contracts. The euro futures contract is the most active, with about 36% of the total contract volume. The Japanese yen futures was second at 19%, followed by the Canadian dollar futures and the Swiss franc futures with 13% and 11% of contract volume, respectively. All of the aforementioned contracts are USD denominated (quoted in USD per unit of the underlying currency). The CME also lists cross-rate futures contracts, however, the trading volume is slight and is included with less active USD denominated contracts with the category heading "All others."

Each of the exchange's contracts has preset terms. Contract specifications of the CME's euro futures are listed in Table 16.3. The contract requires EUR 125,000 to be delivered on the third Wednesday of the contract month. The price of the euro futures contract is quoted in USD/EUR. The minimum price

**FIGURE 16.1** Relative trading volumes of FX futures contracts traded on the Chicago Mercantile Exchange during the calendar year 2003. Total contract volume was 31,873,938 contracts.

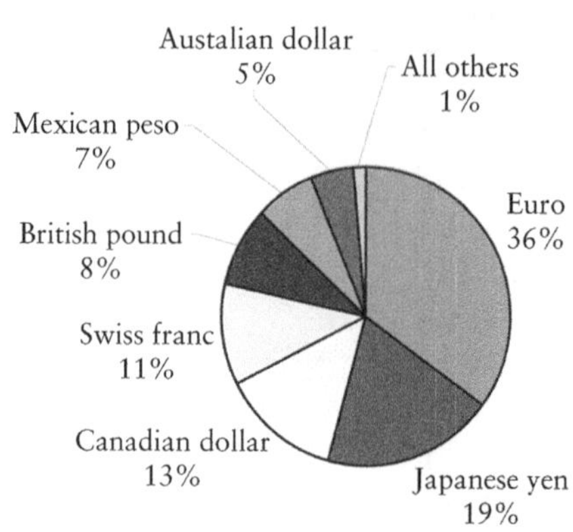


*Source:* Data compiled from www.cme.com.

**TABLE 16.3** Selected terms of euro futures contract.

| | |
|---|---|
| Exchange | Chicago Mercantile Exchange (International Monetary Market Division) |
| Contract unit | 125,000 euro |
| Tick size | $0.0001 per euro |
| Tick value | $12.50 per contract |
| Trading hours | 7:20 AM to 2:00 PM (CST) |
| | GLOBEX: Monday through Thursday, 5 PM to 4 PM; Sundays and holidays, 5 PM to 4 PM. |
| Contract months | Six months in March quarterly expiration cycle (Mar., Jun., Sep., Dec.). |
| Last day of trading | 9:16 AM on second business day immediately preceding third Wednesday of contract month. |
| Final settlement | Physical delivery on third Wednesday of contract month. |

*Source:* www.cme.com.

movement (i.e., tick size) is USD 0.0001. Such a movement implies a change in contract value of USD 12.50. Six contract months on the March quarterly expiration cycle (March, June, September, December) are available on any given time. The contracts trade virtually 24 hours a day—from 7:20 AM to 2:00 PM (CST) in an open outcry format in the trading pits of Chicago but from 5:00 PM to 4:00 PM the following afternoon on GLOBEX.

## Options

In the United States, FX options take two forms: options on FX futures and options on FX spot currencies. The CME's futures options are the most active,

**FIGURE 16.2** Relative trading volumes of FX futures option contracts traded on the Chicago Mercantile Exchange during the calendar year 2003. Total contract volume was 2,142,684 contracts.

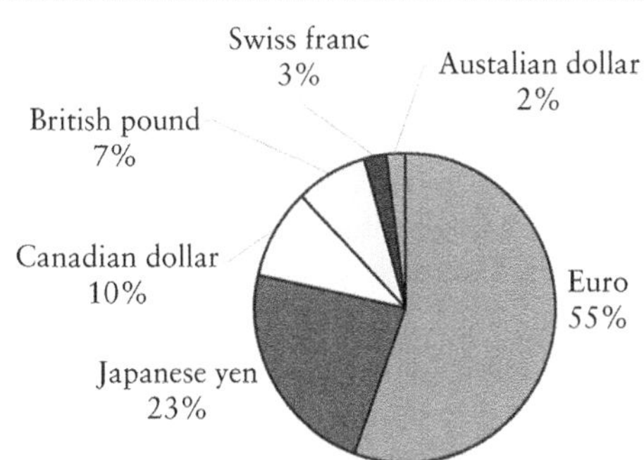


*Source:* Data complied from www.cme.com.

followed by the Philadelphia Stock Exchange's (PHLX) spot currency options. Figure 16.2 shows the breakdown of trading volume for the CME's FX futures option contracts by underlying currency during the calendar year 2003. The total contract volume was 2,142,684, approximately 6.7% of the FX futures volume. Euro FX futures option contracts were the most active, with 55% of the total contract volume. The Japanese yen and Canadian dollar contracts followed, with 23% and 10% of the total volume, respectively. Like in the case of currency futures, the USD denominated option contracts are the most active. Cross-rate futures account for little contract volume.

The CME's futures options and the PHLX's spot currency options are very similar in nature, however, there are some minor distinctions. The contract specifications of the CME's EUR futures option contract and the PHLX's EUR option contract are provided in Tables 16.4 and 16.5, respectively. The EUR futures options require the delivery of the underlying futures; so they have a contract denomination of EUR 125,000. The tick size and tick value are the same as the underlying futures, as are the trading hours. The CME's most active futures options are American-style, although they also offer European-style contracts. The American-style contracts can be exercised at any time to gain a position in the underlying futures. When a call is exercised, the option holder receives a long position in the underlying futures and is marked-to-market at the difference between the futures price and the exercise price of the option. Available contract months include the next four months in the March quarterly expiration cycle plus two that are not. Standing on March 30, 2005, this means that June, September, and December 2005 as well as the March 2006 contracts are traded as well as April and May 2005. Because the underlying futures are on a quarterly expiration cycle, the April and May futures options are written on the June 2005 futures. The futures options expire at the close of trading on the second Thursday preceding the third Wednesday of the contract month.

The currency options traded on the PHLX are half the size of the CME's futures option, EUR 62,500. The tick size is the same, and a one tick movement is worth $6.25. The PHLX offers both American-style and European-style

**TABLE 16.4** Selected terms of euro futures option contract.

| | |
|---|---|
| Exchange | Chicago Mercantile Exchange (International Monetary Market Division) |
| Contract unit | One euro futures contract |
| Tick size | $0.0001 per euro |
| Tick value | $12.50 per contract |
| Trading hours | 7:20 AM to 2:00 PM (CST) |
| | GLOBEX: Monday through Thursday, 5 PM to 4 PM; Sundays and holidays, 5 PM to 4 PM. |
| Exercise style | American |
| Contract months | Four contract months in March quarterly cycle and two serial months, not in the March quarterly cycle, plus four weekly expirations. |
| Last day of trading | Quarterly and serial options: Close of trading on second Thursday preceding third Wednesday of contract month. Weekly options: Close of trading on Thursday of contract month that is not also termination for quarterly and serial European-style options. |
| Final settlement | Physical delivery of the underlying futures. |

**TABLE 16.5** Selected terms of euro option contract.

| | |
|---|---|
| Exchange | Philadelphia Stock Exchange |
| Contract unit | 62,500 euro |
| Tick size | $0.0001 per euro |
| Tick value | $6.25 per contract |
| Trading hours | 2:30 AM to 2:30 PM (EST) Monday through Friday |
| Exercise style | American- and European-styles available. |
| Contract months | Four months in March quarterly cycle (Mar., Jun., Sep., Dec.) plus two-near months. |
| Last day of trading/ contract expiry | Friday before third Wednesday of expiring month provided it is a business day (otherwise day immediately prior). |
| Final settlement | Physical delivery of euro currency on day after expiry. |

options for its FX options as well as several expiration months. On any given date, four contracts on the March quarterly expiration cycle (March, June, September, December) and two near-months are available for trade. The options expire on the Friday preceding the third Wednesday of the contract month. All of the PHLX's FX options require the delivery of the underlying currency.

Interestingly, the most active FX options traded on the PHLX are its *customized currency options*. These options allow users to set most of the terms of the option contract including exercise price, expiration date (up to two years), and premium quotation as either units of the currency or percent of underlying value. The contract denominations are preset according to the underlying currency. For more information, go the PHLX's website at www.phlx.com.

## VALUATION

The values of currency derivatives are best modeled under the continuous net carry cost assumption. The net cost of carry rate of a foreign currency is the difference between the domestic and foreign interest rates, that is, $b = r_d - r_f$. Substituting this definition into the valuation results of Chapters 4 through 9, we get the FX valuation principles summarized in Table 16.6. This section focuses on developing intuition for these results.

### Forwards/Futures

To value foreign currency forwards and futures, we use the net cost of carry relation,

$$F = Se^{(r_d - r_f)T} \tag{16.1}$$

Unless otherwise stated, we assume that $F$ and $S$ are the forward and spot prices of the currency in USD per unit of foreign currency for ease of exposition. Thus $r_d$ is the domestic (U.S.) risk-free interest rate and $r_f$ is the risk-free rate of interest in the foreign market. The net cost of carry relation (16.1) arises from the absence of costless arbitrage opportunities in the marketplace. The intuition underlying the relation is that we have two ways to have one unit of the foreign currency on hand at time $T$ at a price we know today. The first is represented on the left-hand side of the net carry relation (16.1), that is, we can buy a forward contract with maturity $T$ today, and pay $F$ at time $T$. The second is represented by the right-hand side of (16.1), that is, we can borrow domestically at a rate $r_d$ to buy one unit of the foreign currency today at a cost of $S$, and then invest the currency at the prevailing foreign interest rate $r_f$ until time, $T$. Under this second arrangement, the terminal cost is

$$S \times e^{r_d T} \times e^{-r_f T} = Se^{(r_d - r_f)T}$$

Since the two alternatives are perfect substitutes, the two sides of (16.1) must be equal.

**ILLUSTRATION 16.1** Compute implied risk-free rate in Canada given spot rate, forward rate, and U.S. risk-free rate.

*Compute the implied six-month risk-free rate in Canada given a spot exchange rate of USD 0.85510/CAD, and a six-month forward rate of USD 0.85948/CAD. (Note that these are the mid-rates implied by the bid/ask quotes from Table 16.1.) The six-month LIBOR rate is 4.90%.*

First, you need to compute the continuously-compounded domestic risk-free rate of interest. The LIBOR rate is a nominal rate over a 180-day period. To transform it to a continuous six-month rate on an annualized basis, we solve

$$e^{r_d(0.5)} = 1 + 0.0490\left(\frac{180}{360}\right)$$

**TABLE 16.6** Summary of no-arbitrage price relations and valuation equations for options on foreign currencies.

| **No-Arbitrage Price Relations** | | |
|---|---|---|
| Forward/Futures | $f = F = Se^{(r_d - r_f)T}$ | |
| **European-Style:** | **Options** | **Futures Options** |
| Lower bound for call | $c \geq \max(0, Se^{-r_f T} - Xe^{-r_d T})$ | $c \geq \max[0, e^{-r_d T}(F - X)]$ |
| Lower bound for put | $p \geq \max(0, Xe^{-r_d T} - Se^{-r_f T})$ | $p \geq \max[0, e^{-r_d T}(X - F)]$ |
| Put-call parity | $c - p = Se^{-r_f T} - Xe^{-r_d T}$ | $c - p = e^{-r_d T}(F - X)$ |
| **American-Style:** | | |
| Lower bound for call | $c \geq \max(0, Se^{-r_f T} - Xe^{-r_d T}, S - X)$ | $c \geq \max(0, F - X)$ |
| Lower bound for put | $p \geq \max(0, Xe^{-r_d T} - Se^{-r_f T}, X - S)$ | $p \geq \max(0, X - F)$ |
| Put-call parity | $Se^{-r_f T} - X \leq C - P \leq S - Xe^{-r_d T}$ | $Fe^{-r_d T} - X \leq C - P \leq F - Xe^{-r_d T}$ |

| **Valuation Equations/Methods** | | |
|---|---|---|
| **European-Style:** | **Options** | **Futures Options** |
| Call value | $c = Se^{-r_f T}N(d_1) - Xe^{-r_d T}N(d_2)$ | $c = e^{-r_d T}[FN(d_1) - XN(d_2)]$ |
| Put value | $p = Xe^{-r_d T}N(-d_2) - Se^{-r_f T}N(-d_1)$ | $p = e^{-r_d T}[XN(-d_2) - FN(-d_1)]$ |
| | where $d_1 = \dfrac{\ln(Se^{-r_f T}/Xe^{-r_d T}) + 0.5\sigma^2 T}{\sigma\sqrt{T}}$ and $d_2 = d_1 - \sigma\sqrt{T}$ | where $d_1 = \dfrac{\ln(F/X) + 0.5\sigma^2 T}{\sigma\sqrt{T}}$ and $d_2 = d_1 - \sigma\sqrt{T}$ |
| **American-Style:** | Numerical valuation: quadratic approximation, and binomial and trinomial methods. | Numerical valuation: quadratic approximation, and binomial and trinomial methods. |

to find that $r_d$ is 4.908%. Next, substitute the problem information into the net cost of carry relation, that is,

$$0.85948 = 0.85510e^{(0.04908 - r_f)0.5}$$

which can be rearranged to yield

$$r_f = 0.04908 - 2\ln\left(\frac{0.85948}{0.85510}\right) = 3.888\%$$

The six-month risk-free rate of interest in Canada is about 102 basis points lower than in the United States.

This computation can be verified using the forward pricing functions contained in the OPTVAL Function Library. To compute the implied income rate in the continuous version of the net cost of carry relation, use the function,

OV_FORWARD_II($s$, $f$, $r$, $t$)

where $s$ is the spot price, $f$ is the forward price, $r$ is the risk-free (domestic) interest rate, and $t$ is time to expiration of the forward contract.

B11 =OV_FORWARD_II($B$2,$B$3,$B$9,$B$4)

| | A | B | C | D |
|---|---|---|---|---|
| 1 | **Currency** | USD/CAD | CAD/USD | |
| 2 | Spot exchange rate | 0.85510 | 1.16945 | |
| 3 | Forward exchange rate | 0.85948 | 1.16350 | |
| 4 | Time to forward expiration | 0.5000 | | |
| 5 | | | | |
| 6 | **LIBOR rate** | | | |
| 7 | No. of days to maturity | 180 | | |
| 8 | Quoted LIBOR rate | 4.900% | | |
| 9 | Continuous compounded rate | 4.908% | | |
| 10 | | | | |
| 11 | **Implied risk-free rate in Canada** | 3.888% | | |

## Interest Rate Parity

In international finance literature, the relation (16.1) is sometimes called *interest rate parity* (IRP). The intuition underlying the IRP relation is developed as follows. Consider an investor who has one USD to invest. If the money is invested domestically at the risk-free rate, the value at time $T$ is $e^{r_d T}$. On the other hand, the dollar can be used to buy a foreign currency, and then that currency can be invested at the foreign risk-free rate. At the same time, we can write a contract to convert the proceeds of the foreign investment back into dollars at maturity, using the FX forward market. At time $T$, the dollar cash proceeds of this hedged foreign investment are

$$\frac{1}{S} \times e^{r_f T} \times F$$

Since both investments provide a risk-free return in the domestic currency, their terminal values must be equal. Setting $e^{r_d T}$ equal to $1/S \times e^{r_f T} \times F$ and rearranging provides the net cost of carry relation (16.1).

Sometimes interest rate parity is expressed in relative terms, that is,

$$\frac{F-S}{S} = e^{(r_d - r_f)T} - 1 \tag{16.2}$$

The left-hand side of (16.2) goes by a variety of names including the *forward premium* or *swap rate*. The term *swap rate* comes from the fact that investors frequently buy a foreign currency and agree to swap it back for dollars at some future date. The swap rate specifies the percentage gain or loss on such a transaction. The right-hand side is the interest differential between the two countries.

### Cross Rates and Triangular Arbitrage

The *cross-rate relation* is an arbitrage relation that involves three currencies. Suppose we buy (1) Canadian dollars using U.S. dollars, (2) euros using the Canadian dollars, and then (3) U.S. dollars using euros. In the absence of trading costs and costless arbitrage opportunities, we must be back exactly where we started, that is,

$$\left(\frac{\text{USD}}{\text{CAD}}\right)\left(\frac{\text{CAD}}{\text{EUR}}\right)\left(\frac{\text{EUR}}{\text{USD}}\right) = 1$$

Another way of thinking about it is the U.S. dollar cost of euros should be the same if we (1) used U.S. dollars to purchase Canadian dollars and then used the Canadian dollars to buy euros or (2) used U.S. dollars to buy euros directly, that is,

$$\left(\frac{\text{USD}}{\text{EUR}}\right) = \left(\frac{\text{USD}}{\text{CAD}}\right)\left(\frac{\text{CAD}}{\text{EUR}}\right)$$

To illustrate that the market is well aware of this cross-rate relation, consider the cross-rate relations reported in Table 16.7. The USD/EUR rate is reported as 1.2010. The USD/CAD rate is 0.85510, and the CAD/EUR rate is 1.4045. The product of 0.85510 and 1.4045 is 1.2010, exactly as expected. If the two methods gave different answers an opportunity for *triangular arbitrage* would exist. In the absence of triangular arbitrage opportunities, the following relation must hold for all triplets of currencies:

$$S_{i,j} = S_{i,k} S_{k,j} \tag{16.3}$$

where $S_{i,j}$ is the number of units of the $i$-th currency required to purchase one unit of the $j$-th currency.

**TABLE 16.7** Key currency cross rates on Monday, March 27, 2006.

| | USD | JPY | EUR | CAD | CHF | GBP |
|---|---|---|---|---|---|---|
| GBP | 0.57220 | 0.0049040 | 0.68721 | 0.48929 | 0.43692 | |
| CHF | 1.3096 | 0.0112 | 1.5728 | 1.1198 | | 2.2887 |
| CAD | 1.1695 | 0.010023 | 1.4045 | | 0.89298 | 2.0438 |
| EUR | 0.83264 | 0.0071361 | | 0.71199 | 0.63580 | 1.4552 |
| JPY | 116.68 | | 140.13 | 99.773 | 89.096 | 203.92 |
| USD | | 0.0085704 | 1.2010 | 0.85510 | 0.76359 | 1.7477 |

**ILLUSTRATION 16.2** Compute profit from triangular arbitrage opportunity.

*Suppose you observe the following exchange rates:*

*USD/EUR* *1.3500*
*CAD/EUR* *1.6200*
*USD/CAD* *0.8200*

*Is a costless arbitrage profit possible?*

To examine whether a costless arbitrage opportunity exists, take any two rates, multiply them appropriately, and see if the product equals the other rate. Given the way the problem information is presented, it is easiest to check whether

$$\left(\frac{\text{USD}}{\text{EUR}}\right) = \left(\frac{\text{USD}}{\text{CAD}}\right)\left(\frac{\text{CAD}}{\text{EUR}}\right)$$

Substituting the problem information, you find that

$$1.3500 > (0.82)(1.62) = 1.3284$$

hence, a costless arbitrage profit is possible. The trades that you need to place are as follows:

(1) Buy Canadian dollars with U.S. dollars at a rate of 0.82.
(2) Buy euros with the Canadian dollars from part (a) at a rate of 1.62.
(3) Sell euros from part (b) for U.S. dollars at a rate of 1.3500.

Assuming a trade size of USD 100,000, your risk-free profit is computed as follows:

(1) pay USD 100,000 for CDN 121,951.22
(2) pay CDN 121,951.22 for EUR 75,278.53
(3) deliver EUR 75,278.53 for USD 101,626.02.

The risk-free profit is USD 1,626.02 per USD 100,000 of arbitrage activity.

## RISK MANAGEMENT LESSON: AWA LTD.

Triangular arbitrage was nominally at the heart of the first modern-day derivatives "scandal." Amalgamated Wireless Australasia Ltd. (now AWA Ltd.) manufactured, imported and exported electronic and electrical products. In order to hedge its foreign currency risk exposure from contracts it had in place for the goods it imported, AWA decided in 1985 to buy currency contracts against actual or anticipated import requirements. At the time, however, the market between foreign currencies and Australia dollars was thin. Only the AD/USD forward market was liquid. To circumvent this problem, the firm decided to execute the hedge in two legs. In the first leg, AWA would go long in the foreign currency (e.g., Japanese yen) and short U.S. dollars, and, in the second, they would go long U.S. dollars and short Australian dollars. By virtue of the absence of triangular arbitrage opportunities, the risk management strategy was perfectly sensible.

So, how did AWA go about losing nearly AD 49.8 million? The answer is with the help of Andy Koval, a commerce graduate from the University of New South Wales. In 1984, Koval was hired as a trainee management accountant on AD 14,000 a year to help set up a money market operation for AWA. At the time, AWA's foreign currency (FX) operation was modest and, for the fiscal year ending June 30, 1985, they reported a pretax gain of only AD 282,000. During 1985, Andy was put in charge of FX operations. Things changed quickly. For the fiscal year ending June 30, 1986, the pretax FX gains rose to AD 7.5 million. Indeed, so successful was the program that, by September 1986, the firm had made its FX operation a profit center of the firm. The next year started off the same way. For the six-month period ending December 31, 1986, the FX operation posted a pretax profit of AD 10 million.

The amazing success of AWA's hedging program was well publicized. On March 10, 1987, the *Sydney Morning Herald* talked about "unprecedented returns from the foreign exchange operations" for AWA.[2] In the article, Mr. John Hooke, Chairman of AWA is reported as saying that "the forex profit had risen as the company had begun trading in currency futures, which it initially had taken out to hedge itself against movements in the Australian dollar against the yen." Two days later, the same newspaper featured an article titled "Andy Koval, AWA'S Forex Whiz-kid."[3] Among other things, the article says that the "unassuming Andy appears to have discovered trading techniques the rest of the Forex market is clamouring for." Andy, himself is quoted as saying, "Our success is to remain covered and make money out of a trend, rather than punting. There is none of this cowboy stuff." The article goes on to say, "Asked whether he feels it is somewhat unusual for one so young to be responsible for such a huge chunk of one of Australia's larger, albeit somewhat sleepy, public companies, Andy Kovel says: 'Yeah, sometimes. It's a bit funny with the board of directors. My parents think it's pretty amazing, too.'"

The public comments made by Hooke and Koval seemed to indicate that AWA was, in fact, hedging. Hooke's comment suggests that AWA had taken the hedges since it imported most of its components from Japan, while Koval clearly indicates that AWA's FX exposure "remains covered." But if hedges are in place, how can the firm be earning such extraordinary profits if they are hedging? As it turns out, they were not. The house of cards came tumbling down only a few months later when the Australian Stock Exchange discovered irregularities in AWA's reporting and determined that AWA had sustained substantial losses. After many months of investigation, a truer picture of Koval's actual trading activity emerged.

---

[2] *Sydney Morning Herald,* 10 March 1987, p. 21.

[3] *Sydney Morning Herald,* 12 March 1987, p. 23.

1. *Koval was not hedging.* Apparently, Koval had a strong directional view that the USD would fall, so he entered only the first leg of the hedge—he bought Japanese yen and sold U.S. dollars. Unfortunately, he was wrong in his view, very wrong. As the figure below shows, the JPY depreciated steady in value relative to the USD during the period Koval managed FX operations, and thereby had to have incurred significant speculative losses.

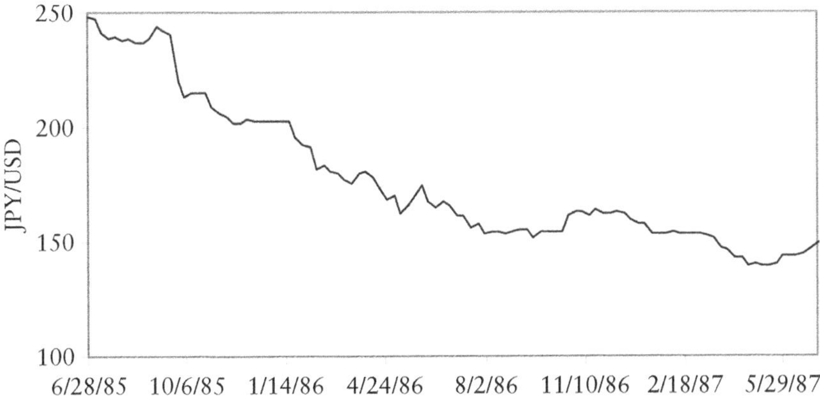


2. *Koval disregarded trading limits and took positions well beyond hedging needs.* Even if Koval had executed both legs of the hedge (i.e., buying JPY with USD, and buying USD with AD), there were other telltale signs that he was speculating. At the end of December 1986, for example, AWA's hedge requirement for Japanese yen over the next year was estimated to be about JPY 10 billion. At the time, however, AWA records show that actual open positions exceeded JPY 75 billion.
3. *Koval entered the second leg of the hedge in reverse.* Another telltale sign that Koval was speculating came on the occasions in which he appeared to execute the second leg of the hedge. Recall that buying JPY with AD can be accomplished by buying JPY with USD, and then buying USD with AD. What appeared in AWA's books, however, were trades in which Koval was buying AD with USD, exactly the reverse of what should be done. In other words, Koval was betting not only that the USD was going to tank relative to the yen but also that the USD was going to tank relative to the AD. In both cases, he was wrong.

Could the situation have been avoided? Absolutely! While the hedge strategy was entirely appropriate for a company needing to manage its foreign currency risk exposure on the costs of imports whose prices were fixed, no one monitored whether the strategy was being implemented properly. The primary factors driving the extraordinary losses were:

1. *Lack of meaningful supervision:* Koval was permitted by AWA management to operate without effective control and supervision.
2. *Absence of a proper system of books and records and other internal controls.* Koval had generally disclosed only the contracts showing a profit. Loss-making contracts were disclosed either by rolling them over at historical rates or by

paying the losses out of what were claimed to be unauthorized borrowings by Koval from a number of different banks, the existence of these loans were also concealed from AWA.

3. *Managers and boards of directors did not understand risk management strategy.* The hedge strategy developed by AWA was perfectly sensible in light of the liquidity of available hedge instruments. But given the simplicity of this hedge strategy (i.e., buying forwards/futures to hedge the currency risk exposure of input costs), extraordinary profits should have been the first sign that something was amiss. Did they choose to turn a blind eye to the matter of how the money was being earned? After all, the FX profits were huge in a company that was not otherwise performing well. Or was the board incapable of understanding the nature of the FX hedge operations? After all, it was the board that approved a budget which treated FX trading as a major profit center.
4. *Hubris.* The quotes in the *Sydney Morning Herald* in March 1987 support the view that both Hooke and Koval were almost giddy in their optimism about future FX trading profits. When asked about the amazing feat of earning nearly AD 20 million in pretax profits over 18 months, Koval stated that it was "No fluke."[4] He went on to say "I thought about going out on my own, but am fairly happy here at the moment." In the same article, Hooke is reported as saying that FX profits in the first half of 1987 "will be in line" with the AD 10 million earned in the last half of 1986."

In the end, AWA lost slightly less than AD 50 million. As is typical when such events occur, litigation ensued. What makes this story different is that the Australian courts held AWA's auditors liable for 80% of the damages because "they were negligent in their duties in failing to draw the attention of AWA's board and senior management to the absence of sufficient internal controls." They also held that "AWA was liable for contributory negligence and Hooke liable to contribute to the damages.

## Swaps

No-arbitrage price relations for swaps were also developed in Chapter 4. A currency swap contract is an agreement to exchange a set of future cash flows with no cash flow occurring at inception. A plain-vanilla currency swap is usually regarded to be an exchange of a fixed payment for a floating payment, where the floating payment is tied to an exchange rate. The key information needed to value a swap contract is the *forward curve* for the underlying currency and the *zero-coupon yield curve* for domestic risk-free bonds. All rates on both curves are assumed to be tied to the prices of tradable securities.

To make currency swap valuation as clear as possible, assume that we import goods from the United Kingdom in a uniform manner throughout the year and sell them in the United States. At the beginning of each year, we negotiate a fixed price for each unit we import during the year, and the price is quoted in British pounds. The goods we import, however, are sold in U.S. dollars. If the British pound appre-

[4] *Sydney Morning Herald*, 12 March 1987.

ciates in value relative to the dollar during the year and we cannot pass on the cost increase to our U.S. customers, our profit margin will fall. To manage this risk exposure, we may want to buy British pounds in the forward market. One alternative is to buy a *strip* of forward (or futures) contracts, one corresponding to each desired delivery date. Unfortunately, while the cost of the monthly delivery will be locked-in, it will be different each month, except in the special case in which the forward curve happens to be a horizontal line. If our customers' demands are uniform throughout the year, this means that our profit margin will vary from month to month, albeit in a deterministic way. A second alternative is to buy a swap contract that provides for a fixed delivery amount each month at a single fixed price for all deliveries. In the absence of costless arbitrage opportunities, the present value of the deliveries using the forward curve must be the same as the present value of the deliveries using the fixed price of the swap contract, that is,

$$\sum_{i=1}^{n} f_i e^{-r_i T_i} = \sum_{i=1}^{n} \bar{f} e^{-r_i T_i} \tag{16.4}$$

where $n$ is the number of delivery dates, $f_i$ is the price of a forward contract with time to expiration $T_i$, $r_i$ is the risk-free rate of interest corresponding to time to expiration $T_i$,[5] and $\bar{f}$ is the fixed price in the swap agreement.[6] In an instance where the right-hand side of (16.4) is greater (less) than the left-hand side, an arbitrageur would buy (sell) the swap and sell (buy) the strip of forward contracts, pocketing the difference. Because such free money opportunities do not exist, (16.4) must hold as an equality.

Equation (16.4) can be rearranged to isolate the fixed price of the swap agreement, that is,

$$\bar{f} = \frac{\sum_{i=1}^{n} f_i e^{-r_i T_i}}{\sum_{i=1}^{n} e^{-r_i T_i}} = \sum_{i=1}^{n} f_i \left( \frac{e^{-r_i T_i}}{\sum_{i=1}^{n} e^{-r_i T_i}} \right) \tag{16.5}$$

Expressed in this fashion, it becomes obvious that the fixed price of a swap is a weighted average of forward prices, one corresponding to each delivery date.

**ILLUSTRATION 16.3** Compute fixed exchange rate of swap based on forward exchange rate curve.

*Suppose that you own a chain of Irish pubs in Boston. Your customers' favorite brew is, of course, Guinness Irish Stout. Your supplier is a distributor in the United Kingdom, and you have negotiated a fixed price of £50 per keg, delivered in Boston, for all deliveries during the next year. Based upon consumption over the past few years, you anticipate*

[5] Note that we are allowing for the fact that the risk-free rate may be term-specific.

[6] The delivery quantity is irrelevant since it is the same on both sides of the equation. That is, equation (4.10) assumes that one unit is delivered on each delivery date.

*that the average consumption rate will be 10,000 kegs per month. Your customers are accustomed to paying USD 5.00 per pint. If the British pound appreciates relative to the USD, you will not be able to pass on the price increase to your customers. They will simply switch over to a less expensive domestic brand whose margins are much lower. Consequently, you are considering different hedging alternatives. Currently, the forward curve for the USD/GBP exchange rate is*

$$f_i = 1.92 - 0.035\ln(1 + T_i)$$

*and the zero-coupon yield curve for risk-free U.S. bonds is*

$$r_i = 0.03 + 0.01\ln(1 + T_i)$$

*Determine the fixed forward exchange rate on a 12-month currency swap with uniform monthly deliveries.*

Based on the forward curve and the yield curve, you can compute prepaid forward prices for each of the 12 delivery dates. You then sum the prepaid forward prices, and divide by the sum of the discount factors to determine the fixed price. The intermediate computations are as follows.

| Time to Payment | USD/GBP Forward Rate | Risk-Free Rate | Discount Factor | Prepaid Forward Price |
|---|---|---|---|---|
| 0.0833 | 1.9171 | 3.08% | 0.9974 | 1.9122 |
| 0.1667 | 1.9142 | 3.15% | 0.9948 | 1.9041 |
| 0.2500 | 1.9113 | 3.22% | 0.9920 | 1.8959 |
| 0.3333 | 1.9083 | 3.29% | 0.9891 | 1.8875 |
| 0.4167 | 1.9054 | 3.35% | 0.9861 | 1.8790 |
| 0.5000 | 1.9025 | 3.41% | 0.9831 | 1.8704 |
| 0.5833 | 1.8996 | 3.46% | 0.9800 | 1.8616 |
| 0.6667 | 1.8967 | 3.51% | 0.9769 | 1.8528 |
| 0.7500 | 1.8938 | 3.56% | 0.9737 | 1.8439 |
| 0.8333 | 1.8908 | 3.61% | 0.9704 | 1.8349 |
| 0.9167 | 1.8879 | 3.65% | 0.9671 | 1.8258 |
| 1.0000 | 1.8850 | 3.69% | 0.9637 | 1.8167 |
| | | | 11.7743 | 22.3847 |
| Fixed price of swap | | | | 1.9012 |

Based on the forward curve, the fixed rate on the swap should be

$$\bar{f} = \frac{22.3847}{11.7743} = 1.9012 \text{ USD per GBP}$$

The OPTVAL Function Library contains a function that values a currency swap with uniform quantities each period. The function is

OV_SWAP_CURRENCY(*t*, *f*, *r*, *vr*)

where *t* is a vector containing the times to each delivery date, *f* is a vector of forward/futures prices corresponding to each date, *r* is a vector of zero-coupon risk-free rates corresponding to each delivery date, and *vr* is an indicator variable instructing the function to compute (1) the sum of the present values of the prepaid forward contracts ($v$ or $V$), (2) the sum of the discount factors ($d$ or $D$), or (3) the break-even fixed price of the swap based on the forward curve ($r$ or $R$). For the illustration at hand,

E22 =OV_SWAP_CURRENCY($A$4:$A$15,$B$4:$B$15,$C$4:$C$15,$D$22)

| | A | B | C | D | E | F | G | H |
|---|---|---|---|---|---|---|---|---|
| 1 | | USD/GBP | | | Prepaid | | | |
| 2 | Time to | forward | Risk-free | Discount | forward | | | |
| 3 | payment | rate | rate | factor | price | | | |
| 4 | 0.0833 | 1.9171 | 3.08% | 0.9974 | 1.9122 | | | |
| 5 | 0.1667 | 1.9142 | 3.15% | 0.9948 | 1.9041 | | | |
| 6 | 0.2500 | 1.9113 | 3.22% | 0.9920 | 1.8959 | | | |
| 7 | 0.3333 | 1.9083 | 3.29% | 0.9891 | 1.8875 | | | |
| 8 | 0.4167 | 1.9054 | 3.35% | 0.9861 | 1.8790 | | | |
| 9 | 0.5000 | 1.9025 | 3.41% | 0.9831 | 1.8704 | | | |
| 10 | 0.5833 | 1.8996 | 3.46% | 0.9800 | 1.8616 | | | |
| 11 | 0.6667 | 1.8967 | 3.51% | 0.9769 | 1.8528 | | | |
| 12 | 0.7500 | 1.8938 | 3.56% | 0.9737 | 1.8439 | | | |
| 13 | 0.8333 | 1.8908 | 3.61% | 0.9704 | 1.8349 | | | |
| 14 | 0.9167 | 1.8879 | 3.65% | 0.9671 | 1.8258 | | | |
| 15 | 1.0000 | 1.8850 | 3.69% | 0.9637 | 1.8167 | | | |
| 16 | | | | 11.7743 | 22.3847 | | | |
| 17 | | | | | | | | |
| 18 | Fixed price of swap | | | | 1.9012 | | | |
| 19 | | | | | | | | |
| 20 | Present value of prepaid forwards | | | V | 22.3847 | | | |
| 21 | Present value of discount factors | | | D | 11.7743 | | | |
| 22 | Break-even fixed price on swap | | | R | 1.9012 | | | |

The swap valuation framework provided above makes the assumption that the number of units of currency needed each period is the same throughout the life of the swap. There are many instances in which this is not the case, however. Suppose we let quantity, $Q_i$, vary from period to period. To determine a single fixed exchange rate for all periods, we again equate the present value of the deliveries using the forward curve to the present value of the deliveries using the fixed price of the swap contract, that is,

$$\sum_{i=1}^{n} Q_i f_i e^{-r_i T_i} = \sum_{i=1}^{n} Q_i \bar{f} e^{-r_i T_i} \tag{16.6}$$

Equation (16.6) can be rearranged to isolate the fixed price of the swap agreement, that is,

$$\bar{f} = \frac{\sum_{i=1}^{n} Q_i f_i e^{-r_i T_i}}{\sum_{i=1}^{n} Q_i e^{-r_i T_i}} = \sum_{i=1}^{n} Q_i f_i \left( \frac{e^{-r_i T_i}}{\sum_{i=1}^{n} e^{-r_i T_i}} \right) \tag{16.7}$$

Expressed in this fashion, it becomes obvious that the fixed price of a swap is based on a weighted average of forward payments, one corresponding to each delivery date. Note that the forward payment explicitly accounts for the delivery amount.

**ILLUSTRATION 16.4** Compute fixed exchange rate of swap with time-varying quantities.

*Based upon your computations in 16.3, you feel prepared to negotiate with an OTC derivatives dealer with respect to the fixed rate on a currency swap. Based on your computations, you believe the fair fixed rate is 1.9012 USD/GBP. Nonetheless, you are perfectly prepared to pay as much as 1.9020 for the convenience of having a single-hedge contract (rather than a portfolio of contracts). The dealer earns this fee. Considering you need to buy GBP 6 million over the next year, the total fee is on order $5,000 (i.e., $0.0008 times GBP 6 million).*

*You describe your commitment to buy 120,000 kegs of Guinness over the next year at £50 a keg and your need to hedge the currency exposure on a monthly basis. The dealer quotes you a fixed rate of 1.9052 USD/BP for GBP 6 million that you need over the next year. He says he is giving the swap to you at cost because he is Irish, visits your pubs frequently, and is impressed by your altruistic spirit in trying to keep the price of a pint of Guinness stable. You tell him that you were not born yesterday and that he is demanding five times the fee that you were prepared to pay. He denies your allegations (at least the second one), and shows you his computations.*

*Upon looking at his work, you see that in the third month of the year, the quantity of Guinness delivered is 54,000 kegs, but is only 6,000 in the remaining months of the year. You ask why, and he says it should be obvious. Total demand is 120,000 kegs per year. Everyone knows that as a result of St. Patrick's Day's celebrations, consumption of Guinness is nine times higher in March than any other month of the year. You realize, of course, that he is absolutely right. Accounting for the quantity delivered each month, what is the fair fixed rate on the currency swap?*

To answer this question, you must weight the discount factors and prepaid forward prices by the monthly quantities. The computations are shown below. Based on the forward curve, the fair fixed rate is, indeed, 1.9052 USD/GBP. Note that the OPTVAL Function library has a quantity weighted swap valuation routine. The vector of monthly quantities in column G are used as an input to the function.

E22 =OV_SWAP_CURRENCY_QUANTITY($A$4:$A$15,$B$4:$B$15,$C$4:$C$15,$G$4:$G$15,D22)

| | A | B | C | D | E | F | G | H | I | J |
|---|---|---|---|---|---|---|---|---|---|---|
| 1 | | USD/GBP | | | Prepaid | Monthly | Monthly | Weighted | Weighted | |
| 2 | Time to | forward | Risk-free | Discount | forward | demand | demand | discount | prepaid | |
| 3 | payment | rate | rate | factor | price | (kegs) | (pounds) | factor | forward | |
| 4 | 0.0833 | 1.9171 | 3.08% | 0.9974 | 1.9122 | 6,000 | 300,000 | 299,231 | 573,651 | |
| 5 | 0.1667 | 1.9142 | 3.15% | 0.9948 | 1.9041 | 6,000 | 300,000 | 298,427 | 571,239 | |
| 6 | 0.2500 | 1.9113 | 3.22% | 0.9920 | 1.8959 | 54,000 | 2,700,000 | 2,678,331 | 5,118,961 | |
| 7 | 0.3333 | 1.9083 | 3.29% | 0.9891 | 1.8875 | 6,000 | 300,000 | 296,730 | 566,260 | |
| 8 | 0.4167 | 1.9054 | 3.35% | 0.9861 | 1.8790 | 6,000 | 300,000 | 295,844 | 563,705 | |
| 9 | 0.5000 | 1.9025 | 3.41% | 0.9831 | 1.8704 | 6,000 | 300,000 | 294,935 | 561,114 | |
| 10 | 0.5833 | 1.8996 | 3.46% | 0.9800 | 1.8616 | 6,000 | 300,000 | 294,006 | 558,490 | |
| 11 | 0.6667 | 1.8967 | 3.51% | 0.9769 | 1.8528 | 6,000 | 300,000 | 293,060 | 555,837 | |
| 12 | 0.7500 | 1.8938 | 3.56% | 0.9737 | 1.8439 | 6,000 | 300,000 | 292,097 | 553,158 | |
| 13 | 0.8333 | 1.8908 | 3.61% | 0.9704 | 1.8349 | 6,000 | 300,000 | 291,119 | 550,457 | |
| 14 | 0.9167 | 1.8879 | 3.65% | 0.9671 | 1.8258 | 6,000 | 300,000 | 290,127 | 547,736 | |
| 15 | 1.0000 | 1.8850 | 3.69% | 0.9637 | 1.8167 | 6,000 | 300,000 | 289,123 | 544,996 | |
| 16 | | | | 11.7743 | 22.3847 | 120,000 | 6,000,000 | 5,913,030 | 11,265,604 | |
| 17 | | | | | | | | | | |
| 18 | Fixed price of swap | | | | | | | | 1.9052 | |
| 19 | | | | | | | | | | |
| 20 | Present value of prepaid forwards | | | V | 11,265,604 | | | | | |
| 21 | Present value of discount factors | | | D | 5,913,030 | | | | | |
| 22 | Break-even fixed price on swap | | | R | 1.9052 | | | | | |

## Purchasing Power Parity

Another important currency-related arbitrage relation ties together the prices of a particular commodity in two different countries. *Purchasing power parity*

(PPP) says that the prices of a commodity in two different countries must be the same after adjustment for the exchange rate, that is,

$$\text{Price}_{i,d} = S_{d,f}\text{Price}_{i,f} \tag{16.8}$$

where $\text{Price}_{i,d}$ and $\text{Price}_{i,f}$ are the domestic and foreign prices of commodity $i$, and $S_{d,f}$ is the spot exchange rate expressed as number of units of the domestic currency per unit of the foreign currency. The intuition underlying this relation is straightforward. In perfect markets, if the USD price of a Sony television in the United States (i.e., $\text{Price}_{i,USD}$) is more than the USD price in Japan (i.e., USD/JPY × $\text{Price}_{i,JPY}$), arbitragers will buy televisions in Japan, and import and sell them in the United States, earning a costless arbitrage profit.

Naturally, the PPP relation is not expected to hold nearly as tightly as it does for interest rate parity or, for that matter, parity in the prices of any financial asset in two countries. The reason is that executing the arbitrage with physical assets may be cumbersome and costly. Transportation costs can be prohibitive. Shipping bulking goods such as televisions, for example, is expensive. In addition, governments may restrict trade to certain countries or impose import duties. Moreover, services such as labor are simply not traded as assets. The hourly rate of a car mechanic can only be "traded" by moving the mechanic from one country to another. Thus, restrictions on international migration may prevent arbitrage of services.

Nonetheless, PPP can provide important guidance in designing appropriate risk management strategies. Consider, for example, a U.S. firm that sells widgets in Ireland. If the U.S. firm fears that the euro will fall relative to the U.S. dollar and competes, in Ireland, with an Irish firm that also produces widgets, using forward contracts to hedge exchange rate risk will ensure that the U.S. firm can remain competitive. On the other hand, if widgets are unavailable elsewhere in Ireland, the U.S. firm may have the ability to simply increase price in accordance with the movement in the spot exchange rate to eliminate exchange rate risk exposure without using derivatives. In both cases, the PPP relation provides guidance.

## Options

The arbitrage relations and valuation equations/methods for FX options are also summarized in Table 16.6. Before applying some of the valuation results, it is worth noting that there are a certain complementary relations that exist among FX options. Consider, for example, an individual who holds a call option to buy 60,000 euros at USD 1.250/EUR. If the spot exchange rate is USD 1.500/EUR at the option's expiration, the call option holder earns USD 15,000 (i.e., EUR 60,000 times USD 0.25/EUR). At the same time, consider an individual in a EU member state who holds a put option to sell 75,000 (i.e., USD 1.250/EUR times EUR 60,000) USD at EUR 0.800/USD. If the spot exchange rate is EUR 0.6667/USD at expiration, the put option holder also earns EUR 10,000 or USD 15,000 (i.e., USD 75,000 times EUR 0.1333/USD times USD 1.500/EUR). Thus, a call option to buy currency A with currency B is nothing more than a put option to sell currency B for currency A.

**ILLUSTRATION 16.5** Compute values of European-style USD/GBP and GBP/USD options on spot currency and on futures.

*Suppose the USD/GBP exchange rate is 1.4912, the six-month USD/GBP futures price is 1.4968, the volatility rate of USD/GBP exchange rate is 10%, and the six-month U.S. risk-free rate of interest is 5.178%. Now do the following:*

*(1) Compute the value of a European-style call to buy British pounds using U.S. dollars, assuming the option's time to expiration is six months, the option's exercise price is USD 1.40/GBP, and the denomination of the option contract is GBP 1,000,000.*

*(2) Compute the value of a European-style put to sell U.S. dollars for British pounds, assuming the option's time to expiration is six months, the option's exercise price is GBP 0.7143/USD, and the denomination of the option contract is USD 1,400,000 (i.e., GBP 1,000,000 times USD 1.40/GBP since the contract sizes should be the same).*

*(3) Compute the value of the European-style options in parts (1) and (2) assuming they are written on the futures price rather than the spot exchange rate.*

*Part (1):* From Table 16.6, the valuation equation for a European-style call on a currency is

$$c = Se^{-r_f T}N(d_1) - Xe^{-r_d T}N(d_2)$$

where

$$d_1 = \frac{\ln(Se^{-r_f T}/Xe^{-r_d T}) + 0.5\sigma^2 T}{\sigma\sqrt{T}} \text{ and } d_2 = d_1 - \sigma\sqrt{T}$$

The problem information, however, does not include the foreign risk-free rate of interest. Fortunately, however, you know that six-month USD/GBP futures price is 1.4968. In the absence of costless arbitrage opportunities, the net cost of carry relation,

$$F = Se^{(r_d - r_f)T}$$

holds at all points in time. Substituting the problem information into the cost of carry relation and rearranging, you find that the risk-free interest rate in Britain is 4.428%, that is,

$$r_f = 0.05178 - \frac{\ln(1.4968/1.4912)}{0.5} = 4.428\%$$

Alternatively, you could have computed the integral limit directly as

$$d_1 = \frac{\ln(F/X) + 0.5\sigma^2 T}{\sigma\sqrt{T}}$$

Now that you have the risk-free rate on interest in Britain, you can compute the value of the call using the formula. Substituting into the formula, you get

$$c = 1.4912e^{-0.04428(0.5)}N(d_1) - 1.4000e^{-0.05178(0.5)}N(d_2)$$

where

$$d_1 = \frac{\ln(1.4912e^{-0.04428(0.5)}/1.4000e^{-0.05178(0.5)}) + 0.5(0.10^2)0.5}{0.10\sqrt{0.5}} = 0.9809$$

and

$$d_2 = 0.9809 - 0.10\sqrt{0.5} = 0.9101$$

The probability values are

$$N(d_1) = N(0.9809) = 0.8367 \quad \text{and} \quad N(d_2) = N(0.9101) = 0.8186$$

Thus, the value of the European-style call is

$$c = 1.4912e^{-0.04428(0.5)}(0.8367) - 1.4000e^{-0.05178(0.5)}(0.8186) = 0.10353 \text{ USD/GBP}$$

The contract denomination is GBP 1,000,000, so the value of the overall contract is USD 103,531, as summarized in the table below. The value of the corresponding European-style put is also provided, that is, USD 9,205.

The option value can be verified using the function OV_OPTION_VALUE from the OPTVAL Function library, that is,

OV_OPTION_VALUE(1.4912, 1.4000, 0.5, 0.05178, 0.04428, 0.10, "c", "e") = 0.10353

Note that, since you know the forward price, you could have also valued this European-style call as a forward option, that is,

OV_FOPTION_VALUE(1.4968, 1.4000, 0.5, 0.05178, 0.10, "c", "e") = 0.10353

*Part (2):* The valuation equation of a European-style put is given in Table 16.6. Note the domestic currency is now British pounds and the foreign currency is U.S. dollars. The value of a European-style put option to sell U.S. dollars for British pounds is

$$p = 0.7143e^{-0.04288(0.5)}N(-d_2) - 0.6706e^{-0.05178(0.5)}N(-d_1)$$

where

$$d_1 = \frac{\ln(0.6706e^{-0.05178(0.5)}/0.7143e^{-0.04428(0.5)}) + 0.5(0.10^2)0.5}{0.10\sqrt{0.5}} = -0.9101$$

and

$$d_2 = -0.9101 - 0.10\sqrt{0.5} = -0.9809$$

The probabilities are

$$N(-d_1) = N(0.9101) = 0.8186 \quad \text{and} \quad N(-d_2) = N(0.9811) = 0.8367$$

Thus, the value of the European-style put is

$$p = 0.7143e^{-0.04428(0.5)}(0.8367) - 0.6706e^{-0.05178(0.5)}(0.8186) = 0.04959 \text{ GBP/USD}$$

The OV_OPTION_VALUE function can be used to verify this result, that is,

OV_OPTION_VALUE(0.6706, 0.7143, 0.5, 0.04428, 0.05178,0.10, "p", "e") = 0.04959

The contract denomination is USD 1,400,000, so the value of the overall contract is GBP 69,429, as shown in the table below. Converting this value to USD using the current exchange rate, the USD value of this European-style put to sell British pounds for U.S.

dollars is USD 103,530 (i.e., USD 1.4912/GBP times GBP 69,429), exactly the same value as the European-style call to buy British pounds using U.S. dollars. In the interest of completeness, the value of the corresponding European-style call is USD 9,205, exactly the same value as the European-style put to buy British pounds for U.S. dollars.

*Part (3):* The values may again be computed using the formulas in Table 16.6. You should be able to reproduce the following values:

**European-Style Futures Option Values**

| | U.S. | Britain |
|---|---|---|
| Spot price | 1.4912 | 0.6706 |
| Futures prices | 1.4968 | 0.6681 |
| Volatility rate | 10.00% | 10.00% |
| Exercise price | 1.4000 | 0.7143 |
| Time to expiration | 0.5000 | 0.5000 |
| Interest rate | 5.178% | 4.428% |
| Value of call | 0.10353 | 0.00441 |
| Value of put | 0.00921 | 0.04959 |

These values are exactly the same as when the options were written directly on the spot currency, as we proved in Chapter 6.

The table below summarizes the results of this illustration.

| | USD/GBP | BP/USD |
|---|---|---|
| Spot rate | 1.4912 | 0.6706 |
| 6-month forward rate | 1.4968 | 0.6681 |
| Time to expiration | 0.5000 | |

| | USD | GBP |
|---|---|---|
| Interest rates | 5.178% | 4.428% |
| Exercise price | 1.4000 | 0.7143 |
| Volatility rate | 10.00% | |

**Buy USD Option to Buy/Sell GBP**

| | Call | Put |
|---|---|---|
| Option value (USD/GBP) | 0.103531 | 0.009205 |
| Quantity (BP) | 1,000,000 | 1,000,000 |
| Total value (USD) | 103,531 | 9,205 |

**Buy GBP Option to Buy/Sell USD**

| | Call | Put |
|---|---|---|
| Option value (GBP/USD) | 0.004409 | 0.049592 |
| Quantity (USD) | 1,400,000 | 1,400,000 |
| Total value (GBP) | 6,173 | 69,428 |
| Total value (USD) | 9,205 | 103,531 |

**Buy USD Futures Option to Buy/Sell GBP**

| | Call | Put |
|---|---|---|
| Option value (USD/GBP) | 0.103531 | 0.009205 |
| Quantity (GBP) | 1,000,000 | 1,000,000 |
| Total value (USD) | 103,531 | 9,205 |

**Buy GBP Futures Option to Buy/Sell USD**

| | Call | Put |
|---|---|---|
| Option value (GBP/USD) | 0.004409 | 0.049592 |
| Quantity (USD) | 1,400,000 | 1,400,000 |
| Total value (BP) | 6,173 | 69,428 |
| Total value (USD) | 9,205 | 103,531 |

**ILLUSTRATION 16.6** Compute values and early exercise premiums of American-style USD/GBP options on spot and forward exchange rates.

*Using the USD/GBP options and their parameters from Illustration 16.5, compute the values and early exercise premiums of the corresponding American-style options, and explain why there are differences between the values of the currency options and the futures options. Use the quadratic approximation method to handle the computations.*

The values of American-style FX options can be computed using the quadratic approximation method by calling the function OV_OPTION_VALUE from the OPTVAL function library.[7] The value of an American-style call option to buy British pounds using U.S. dollars is, for example,

OV_OPTION_VALUE(1.4912, 1.4000, 0.5, 0.05178, 0.04428, 0.10, “c”, “a”) = 0.10364

Applying the function for the remaining American-style FX options, we get:

| | European-Style Value | American-Style Value | Early Exercise Premium |
|---|---|---|---|
| **USD/BP options on currency** | | | |
| Call | 0.10353 | 0.10364 | 0.00011 |
| Put | 0.00921 | 0.00937 | 0.00017 |
| **USD/BP options on futures** | | | |
| Call | 0.10353 | 0.10453 | 0.000995 |
| Put | 0.00921 | 0.00927 | 0.000068 |
| **Difference** | | | |
| Call | 0.00000 | –0.00089 | –0.00089 |
| Put | 0.00000 | 0.00010 | 0.00010 |

In reviewing these figures, we see that the values of the American-style options exceed the values of the corresponding European-style options for both the options on the currency and the options on the futures. This is expected, since the American-style options have the same terms as the European-style option but provide the additional benefit of early exercise. Interestingly, the American-style call on the currency has a lower value than the American-style option on the futures. The reason for this is that the futures price, USD 1.4968/GBP, is above the spot currency rate, USD 1.4912/GBP. If the futures price is higher than the currency rate, then exercising the call on the futures early will provide greater proceeds than exercising the call on the spot currency early. The opposite is true for the put.

## RISK MANAGEMENT

Currency derivatives provide an effective means of managing different types of currency risk exposures. In the previous section, we reviewed the valuation of forward, futures, and options contracts as they apply to currencies. In this section, we

[7] A detailed example of all the computations embedded in the quadratic approximation method was provided in Chapter 6.

illustrate how these valuation/risk measurement tools can be used to manage currency risk exposures. In the first illustration, we show how to use a currency swap to redenominate the currency of a bond issue and potentially generate interest savings. We also show how to compare its cost effectiveness with buying a strip of forward contracts. The second illustration focuses on managing the risk of a large foreign currency transaction that is known to occur in the future. We compare the expected return/risk attributes of hedging using forward, options, and money market instruments. We also consider the effects when the transaction, itself, is uncertain. The third illustration considers the case where there are multiple transactions to be hedged. Here we consider not only currency swaps but also a nonstandard product—an average rate option. The fourth illustration focuses on the risk management of balance sheet risk, that is, the uncertainty of having certain assets and liabilities on the balance sheet being denominated in foreign currencies.

### Using Currency Swaps to Obtain Foreign Financing

In the first chapter of the book, we described a *plain-vanilla interest rate swap* as being a convenient means of "swapping" out of fixed rate debt into floating rate debt and vice versa. A *currency swap* is also a convenient means of restructuring debt—in this case swapping out of debt (interest payments and repayment of principal) denominated in one currency into debt denominated in another. Such swaps may be useful, for example, to a multinational firm that finds it comparatively less expensive to borrow domestically even though its financing need is in a foreign country.

To illustrate, suppose Canuck Brewing Inc., a small microbrewery in Canada, is looking to expand internationally by setting up breweries in other countries. Market research in different regions of the United States indicates that Canuck's products will be most popular in the Southeast region of the United States. Canuck therefore decides to build a new brewery in North Carolina and requires USD 5 million to acquire the land.

Canuck is currently evaluating different financing proposals. All else being equal, a USD-denominated loan would be best since the interest payments will be made from U.S. sales. In this way, Canuck avoids currency risk on the interest payments. The problem is that Canuck is not well known in the U.S. The lowest available coupon interest rate that it can obtain on a three-year, fixed rate USD 5 million bond is 7.5%. In Canada, where Canuck's credit is first rate and its products are well known, it can issue three-year, fixed rate bonds at 6.0%. Given the current exchange rate of CAD 1.40/USD, the par value of the Canadian bonds will be CAD 7.0 million.

**USD Bonds** The two alternative bond issues have different currency exposures. The first is denominated in U.S. dollars and therefore has no currency risk. The semiannual cash flows are contained in the following table. The continuously compounded implied yield to maturity of the loan is 7.36%.[8]

[8] The implied yield to maturity is the continuously compounded discount rate that equates the present value of the promised bond payments to the par value of the bond.

| U.S. Bonds | | | Year | | | | | | |
|---|---|---|---|---|---|---|---|---|---|
| Par value (USD) | 5,000,000 | | 0 | 0.5 | 1 | 1.5 | 2 | 2.5 | 3 |
| Coupon rate | 7.50% | Cash flows (USD) | | −187,500 | −187,500 | −187,500 | −187,500 | −187,500 | −5,187,500 |
| PV (cash flows) | −5,000,000 | PV (cash flows) | | −180,723 | −174,191 | −167,895 | −161,826 | −155,977 | −4,159,388 |
| Implied yield | 7.36% | | | | | | | | |

**CAD Bonds Plus Currency Swap** The second alternative is denominated in Canadian dollars. Consequently, Canuck faces currency risk when its U.S. dollar sales are used to cover the Canadian dollar interest payments and principal repayment. To undo the currency risk exposure, Canuck considers entering a currency swap. After some negotiation with an OTC swap dealer in Canada, Canuck finds that it can enter into a fixed-for-fixed currency swap in which it will receive interest at a rate of 6% on a CAD 7 million par amount and will pay interest at a rate of 7.25% on USD 5 million par. Payments will be made semiannually. Thus, if Canuck issues the Canadian bonds and enters the currency swap, it will have locked in a U.S. dollar denominated loan at a coupon interest rate of 7.25%, 25 basis points lower than it would have had it issued the U.S. bonds directly. The following table shows the combined cash flows of the Canadian dollar bond and the currency swap. Note that, unlike a plain-vanilla interest rate swap, the currency swap *requires* an exchange of principal. The continuously compounded implied yield to maturity of this alternative is 7.12%.

| Canadian Bonds | | | Year | | | | | | |
|---|---|---|---|---|---|---|---|---|---|
| Par value (CAD) | 7,000,000 | | 0 | 0.5 | 1 | 1.5 | 2 | 2.5 | 3 |
| Coupon rate | 6.00% | Cash flows (CAD) | | −210,000 | −210,000 | −210,000 | −210,000 | −210,000 | −7,210,000 |
| **Swap Agreement** | | | | | | | | | |
| Receive leg (CAD) | | | | | | | | | |
| Par value (CAD) | 7,000,000 | Cash flows (CAD) | | 210,000 | 210,000 | 210,000 | 210,000 | 210,000 | 7,210,000 |
| Coupon rate | 6.00% | | | | | | | | |
| **Pay Leg (US)** | | | | | | | | | |
| Par value (USD) | 5,000,000 | Cash flows (US) | | −181,250 | −181,250 | −181,250 | −181,250 | −181,250 | −5,181,250 |
| Coupon rate | 7.25% | | | | | | | | |
| **Net Payments (USD)** | | Cash flows (US) | | −181,250 | −181,250 | −181,250 | −181,250 | −181,250 | −5,181,250 |
| PV (cash flows) | −5,000,000 | PV (cash flows) | | −174,910 | −168,791 | −162,886 | −157,188 | −151,689 | −4,184,536 |
| Implied yield | 7.12% | | | | | | | | |

By issuing Canadian bonds and engaging in a currency swap, Canuck has managed to reduce the effective cost of financing from 7.36% to 7.12%. How does this saving arise? One possibility is that the terms of the swap were favorable to Canuck. To examine this explanation, we need to value the swap at inception. For simplicity, assume the risk-free term structure of interest rates is flat in both Canada and the United States, and the rates are 4.25% and 5.00%, respectively. Using these risk-free interest rates to discount the flows of each leg of the swap, we get the following:

| Risk-Free Rates | | | Year | | | | | | |
|---|---|---|---|---|---|---|---|---|---|
| CAD rate | 4.25% | | 0 | 0.5 | 1 | 1.5 | 2 | 2.5 | 3 |
| USD rate | 5.00% | | | | | | | | |
| **Swap Agreement** | | | | | | | | | |
| Receive leg (CAD) | | Cash flows (CAD) | | 210,000 | 210,000 | 210,000 | 210,000 | 210,000 | 7,210,000 |
| PV (receive) | 7,332,512 | PV (cash flows) | | 205,585 | 201,262 | 197,030 | 192,888 | 188,832 | 6,346,916 |
| Pay leg (US) | | Cash flows (USD) | | –181,250 | –181,250 | –181,250 | –181,250 | –181,250 | –5,181,250 |
| PV (pay) | –5,300,836 | PV (cash flows) (USD) | | –176,775 | –172,410 | –168,154 | –164,002 | –159,953 | –4,459,543 |
| PV (pay) (CAD) | –7,421,171 | | | | | | | | |
| Swap value | –88,659 | | | | | | | | |

The value of the currency swap at origination from Canuck's perspective is

$$V = B_d - SB_f$$

where $B_d$ is the present value of what Canuck receives (in Canadian dollars), $B_f$ is the present value of what Canuck pays in U.S. dollars, and $S$ is the CAD/USD exchange rate. Using the numbers in the table above, the present value of the receive leg is CAD 7,332,512, and the present value of the pay leg is USD 5,300,836 or CAD 7,421,171. The value of the swap is therefore –CAD 88,659. The figure represents a trading cost implicitly paid by Canuck to the swap dealer. Clearly, the terms of the swap are not driving the cost savings.

**CAD Bonds Plus Forward Strip** Is there an alternative to the currency swap that Canuck can consider to avoid the swap dealer's margin? The answer is yes. We know all swaps can be decomposed into portfolios of forwards and/or options. The current exchange rate is CAD 1.40/USD, and the Canadian and U.S. risk-free interest rates are 4.25% and 5.00%, respectively. By interest rate parity, the six-month forward exchange rate (i.e., CAD/USD) must be $1.4000e^{(0.0425-0.0500)0.05} = 1.3948$, the one-year forward rate $1.4000e^{(0.0425-0.0500)0.05} = 1.3895$, and so on. These CAD/USD forward rates can be inverted to get USD/CAD forward rates of 0.7143, 0.7170, and so on. Canuck can buy a strip of USD/CAD forwards, each with a contracted amount and time to delivery corresponding to the Canadian dollar payments to bondholders. These trades would commit Canuck to a stream of USD payments beginning with USD 150,564 in six months, USD 151,129 in 1 year, and so on. In return, Canuck would receive Canadian dollar payments in the amounts it needs to service the Canadian bondholders, as is shown in the next table. The implied yield to maturity under this arrangement is only 6.66%.

| Exchange Rates | | | Year 0 | 0.5 | 1 | 1.5 | 2 | 2.5 | 3 |
|---|---|---|---|---|---|---|---|---|---|
| Spot rate | 1.4000 | CAD/USD | 1.4000 | 1.3948 | 1.3895 | 1.3843 | 1.3792 | 1.3740 | 1.3689 |
| CAD risk-free rate | 4.25% | USD/CAD | 0.7143 | 0.7170 | 0.7197 | 0.7224 | 0.7251 | 0.7278 | 0.7305 |
| USD risk-free rate | 5.00% | | | | | | | | |
| Canadian bonds | | | | | | | | | |
| Par value (CAD) | 7,000,000 | Coupon payments (CAD) | | −210,000 | −210,000 | −210,000 | −210,000 | −210,000 | −7,210,000 |
| Interest rate | 6.00% | Received on forward (CAD) | | 210,000 | 210,000 | 210,000 | 210,000 | 210,000 | 7,210,000 |
| Par value (USD) | 5,000,000 | Paid of forward (USD) | | −150,564 | −151,129 | −151,697 | −152,267 | −152,839 | −5,267,188 |
| Implied yield | 6.66% | PV (cash flows) (USD) | | −145,631 | −141,389 | −137,271 | −133,273 | −129,391 | −4,313,044 |

## Using FX Futures and Options to Manage Transaction Risk—Single Flow

*Transaction risk* refers to the currency risk of a particular future transaction denominated in a foreign currency. Suppose, for example, Jetmaker, Inc., a U.S. jet manufacturer, receives an order for its new X626 plane from Alps Air, Inc., a Swiss airline. Payment for the new X626 is specified in Swiss francs and is to be made when the plane is delivered in six months. Jetmaker is exposed to significant currency risk. The Swiss franc may depreciate relative to the U.S. dollar over the next six months (i.e., the value of a Swiss franc, USD/SF, may fall), driving the U.S. dollar proceeds from the Swiss franc payment downward. Consider the following short hedging strategies will allow Jetmaker to reduce its transaction risk exposure.

**Short-Hedging Using a Forward Contract[9]** Suppose the cost of the X626 is SF 750 million. Assume also that the current exchange rate is USD 0.66/SF and that the six-month forward rate is USD 0.66667/SF. If Jetmaker chooses not to hedge, the USD value of the contract is subject to fluctuations in the exchange rate. If the Swiss franc depreciates relative to the U.S. dollar and the exchange rate is USD 0.60/SF in six months, Jetmaker receives USD 450 million (i.e., USD 0.60 times SF 750 million). On the other hand, if the Swiss franc appreciates to, say, USD 0.70/SF in six months, the firm receives USD 525 million. Jetmaker wants to eliminate this risk exposure.

To do so, Jetmaker can hedge by selling the SF 750 million exposure in the forward market. The current six-month forward rate is USD 0.66667. Selling the forward implies that Jetmaker will receive exactly USD 500 million in six months. If the exchange rate falls to USD 0.60/SF, for example, the net proceeds are USD 500 million—USD 450 million from the sale of the plane plus USD 50

[9] Futures contracts could also be used, but the size and maturity of a futures contract may not match the hedging need exactly.

million (i.e., USD 0.06667/SF times SF 750 million) from the short forward position. If the exchange rate rises to USD 0.70/SF, the net proceeds remain at USD 500 million—USD 525 million from the sale of the plane and –USD 25 million (i.e., –USD 0.03333/SF times SF 750 million) from the short forward position.

The following figure summarizes the net proceeds in six months over a wider range of USD/SF exchange rates. As the Swiss franc appreciates (depreciates) relative to the U.S. dollar, Jetmaker's unhedged sales proceeds increase (decrease). The proceeds from the short forward position, however, fall (rise) by an equal amount. The combination of the unhedged and forward positions, therefore, creates a certain net proceeds of USD 500 million in six months.

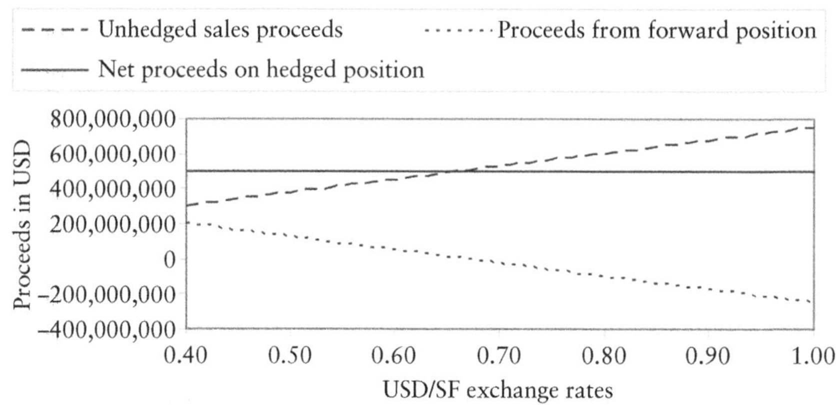


**Short-Hedging in the Money Market** By the cost of carry relation (or, in this case, interest rate parity), an equivalent hedge can be executed in the money market. Assume the U.S. risk-free rate of interest is 5.25%. The current exchange rate is USD 0.66/SF and the six-month forward exchange rate is USD 0.66667/SF. By interest rate parity, therefore, the six-month risk-free rate in Switzerland must be 3.24%.

Under a *money market hedge*, Jetmaker borrows against the SF 750 million payment that it will receive in six months. The amount of the loan is SF 737,947,886 (i.e., SF 750,000,000$e^{-0.0324(0.5)}$). Jetmaker then converts the Swiss franc proceeds into U.S. dollars at the current exchange rate and gets USD 487,045,605 (i.e., USD 0.66/SF times SF 737,947,886). The U.S. dollars are then invested at the U.S. risk-free rate. In six months, Jetmaker uses the Alps Air payment of SF 750 million to retire its loan and enjoys a USD 500 million (i.e., USD 487,045,768$e^{0.0525(0.5)}$) balance in its U.S. account.

**Short-Hedging Using an Option** Yet another alternative is to hedge by buying a European-style USD/SF put option. The benefit of doing so is that, if the Swiss franc appreciates relative to the U.S. dollar (i.e., USD/SF rises), Jetmaker receives the gain. On the other hand, if the Swiss franc depreciates relative to the U.S. dollar (i.e., USD/SF falls), Jetmaker's reduced sales proceeds are offset by the exercise proceeds of the put. Nothing is free, however. Jetmaker must pay for the put.

To illustrate, suppose that a six-month put with an exercise price of USD 0.66667/SF and a denomination of SF 750 million costs USD 0.01465/SF or

USD 10,990,032 in total. The cost of the put carried forward six months is USD $10{,}990{,}032e^{0.0525(0.5)}$, which must be paid regardless of the movement in the exchange rate. If the spot exchange rate is USD 0.60/SF in six months, Jetmaker receives USD 450 million from Alps Air and USD 50 million on its put position, thereby netting USD 488,717,660. On the other hand, if the spot exchange rate is USD0.70/SF in six months, Jetmaker receives USD 525 million from the sale of the X626, lets the put expire out of the money, and thereby nets USD 513,717,660, as shown in this table:

| | Spot Rate in 6 Months | |
|---|---|---|
| | 0.60000 | 0.70000 |
| Cost of put carried forward 6 months | −11,282,340 | −11,282,340 |
| Sales proceeds in USD | 450,000,000 | 525,000,000 |
| Proceeds from exercising put | 50,000,000 | 0 |
| Net proceeds | 488,717,660 | 513,717,660 |

The next figure summarizes the net proceeds from the put option hedge for a wider range of exchange rates. As the USD/SF exchange rate rises, the net proceeds from the sale of the jet increase. At the same time, the put option expires worthless allowing Jetmaker to enjoy the gain (net of the cost of the put). On the other hand, if the USD/SF rate falls, the unhedged proceeds of the X626 sale fall, however, they are exactly offset by the exercise proceeds from the put. The maximum loss is USD 11,282,340—the purchase price of the at-the-money put.

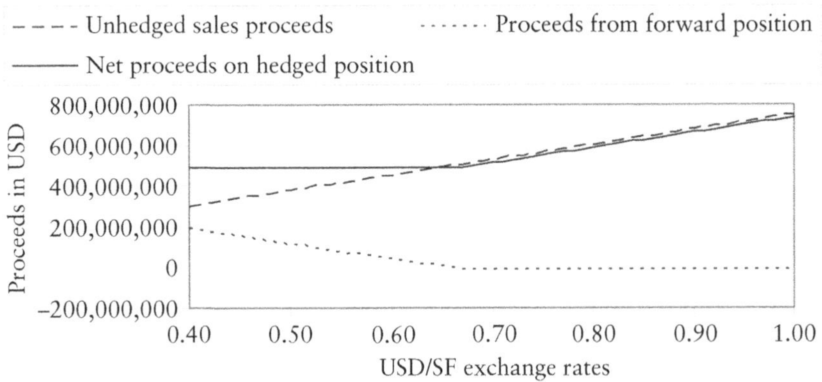


**Long-Hedging Using a Forward** Managing the transaction risk befalls Alps Air if the cost of the plane had been quoted in U.S. dollars. Suppose that all of the parameters in our illustration remain the same, except the cost of the X626 is USD 500 million payable in six months at the time of delivery. Alps Air faces the risk that the Swiss franc will depreciate relative to the U.S. dollar over the next six months, which means paying more Swiss francs to buy the plane. One long-hedging strategy is to buy a six-month forward contract on U.S. dollars. Since the current six-month forward rate to buy Swiss francs with U.S dollars is USD 0.66667/SF, the current six-month forward rate to buy U.S. dollars with Swiss francs must be SF 1.50/USD. By buying a forward contract at SF 1.50/USD, the cost of the plane is locked in at SF 750 million. If the Swiss franc depreciates relative to the U.S. dollar (i.e., USD/SF falls and SF/USD rises) and the spot exchange rate is, say, SF 1.66667/USD (i.e., USD0.60/SF) in six months, Alps Air pays SF 833,333,333 million to buy the plane but has earned SF 83,333,333 from its long forward position. Alps Air's net payment is, of course, SF 750 million. On the other hand, if the Swiss franc appreciates relative to the U.S. dollar (i.e., USD/SF rises and SF/USD falls) to, say, SF 1.42857/ USD (i.e., USD 0.70/SF) in six months, the firm must pay SF 714,285,714 to buy the plane and SF 35,714,286 to cover its forward obligation. The net payment is again SF 750 million. Thus Alps Air can eliminate all of its transaction risk by buying forward, as is shown in the following figure. By interest rate parity, we know that risk elimination can also be accomplished using a money market hedge.

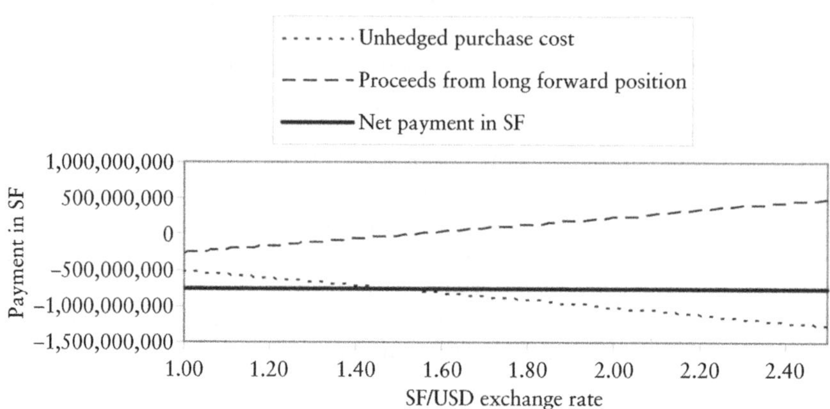


**Long-Hedging Using an Option** Alps Air can also long hedge by buying a European-style call option. The benefits are twofold. First, if the U.S. dollar appreciates relative to the Swiss franc (i.e., the SF/USD rate increases), Alps Air receives a subsidy in the form of the exercise proceeds on call. Second, if the U.S. dollar falls, the Swiss franc payment is reduced and the call expires out of the money. The cost of the hedge is, of course, that the firm must pay for the call.

To illustrate, suppose that a six-month call with an exercise price of SF 1.50/ USD and a denomination of USD 500 million costs SF 0.03330/USD or SF 16,651,563 in total. Carrying this forward six months implies a terminal cost of the call of SF 16,923,510 (i.e., SF $16{,}651{,}563e^{0.0324(0.5)}$), as is indicated in the first row of the table below. If the exchange rate falls to SF 1.42857, the net payment is SF 731,209,224—the purchase price of USD 500 million times SF 1.42857 or SF 714,285,714, plus the cost of the call carried forward, SF 16,923,510. The call expires worthless. On the other hand, if the exchange rate rises to, say, SF 1.66667/USD, the net payment is SF 766,923,510—the cost of the call carried forward, SF 16,923,510, plus purchase price of SF 833,333,333, less the exercise proceeds of the call, SF 83,333,333. Note that the exercise proceeds of the call always reduce the purchase price of the X626 to SF 750 million. The maximum that Alps Air will pay for the acquisition of the plane is SF 750 million plus the cost of the call carried forward, SF 16,923,510, as is shown in this next figure.

| | Spot Rate in 6 Months | |
|---|---|---|
| | 1.42857 | 1.66667 |
| Cost of call carried forward 6 months | −16,923,510 | −16,923,510 |
| Purchase price in SF | −714,285,714 | −833,333,333 |
| Exercise proceeds from call in SF | 0 | 83,333,333 |
| Net payment | −731,209,224 | −766,923,510 |

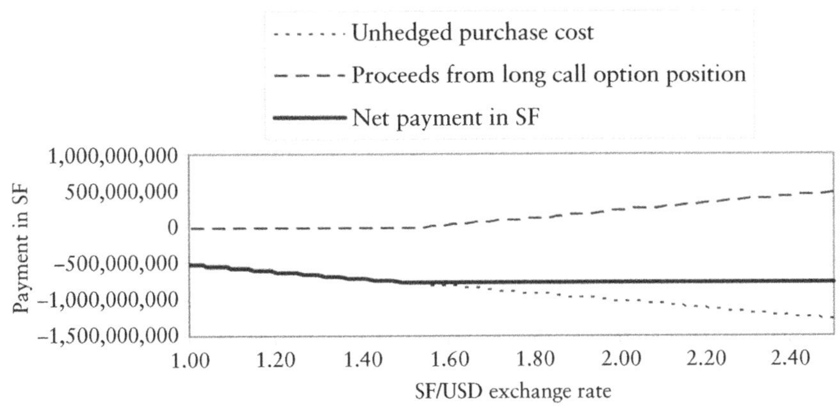


**Hedging an Uncertain Transaction** The hedging strategies discussed above presume that the purchase/sale of the plane will take place in six months. Hedging using a forward contract eliminates all transaction price risk, and hedging using an option contract, while costly, eliminates the downside transaction price risk and retains the upside transaction price risk. In many instances, however, the transaction may be uncertain. Suppose, for example, Alps Air has the right to cancel the agreement with Jetmaker at any time during the next six months. Jetmaker faces the risk that the Swiss franc will depreciate in value (i.e., USD/SF falls and SF/USD rises), but, if it sells forward to short hedge the foreign exchange risk, and the agreement is cancelled, it is left with an open currency forward position that may have to be liquidated at a loss as indicated in the following figure. Jetmaker's losses are unlimited as the Swiss franc depreciates without limit.

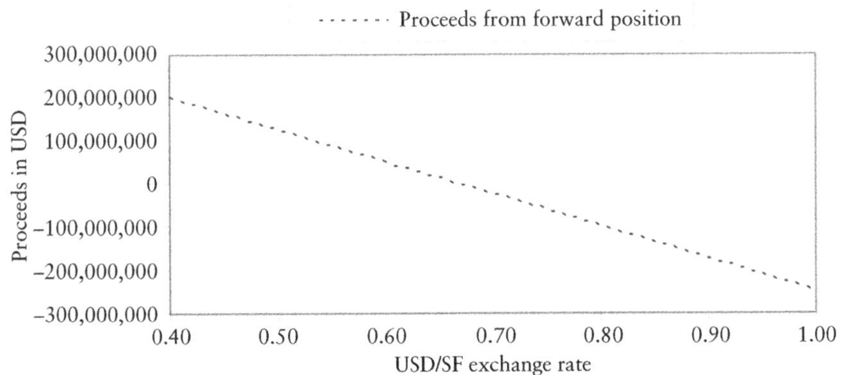

Under put option short-hedging strategy, however, Jetmaker locks in its maximum exposure at the cost of the put option, USD 11,282,340. If the sale is consummated, the least that Jetmaker will receive is USD 488,717,660. If the Swiss franc appreciates in value (i.e., USD/SF rises and SF/USD falls), Jetmaker receives more. On the other hand, if the sales agreement is cancelled, Jetmaker's loss is limited to the cost of the put. In the event that the Swiss franc appreciates, Jetmaker may even gain, as shown in the figure that follows. In effect, Jetmaker is buying a put option to hedge the cancellation option they have given Alps Air. Jetmaker has implicitly given Alps Air a put option to sell SF 750 million in return for the X626. Jetmaster hedges that risk by buying a put.

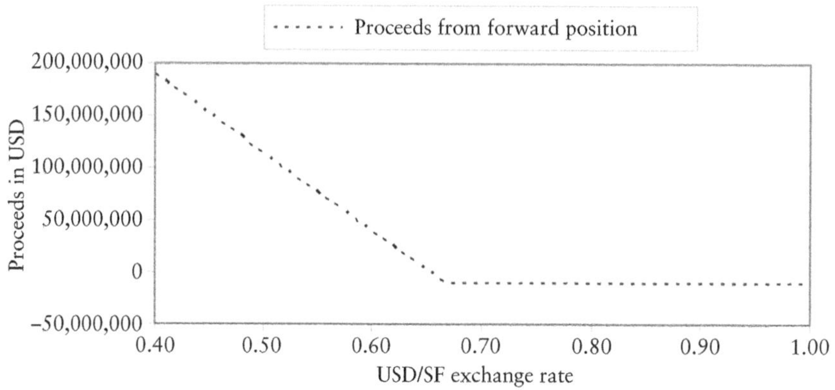


## Using FX Futures and Options to Manage Transaction Risk—Multiple Flows

Multinational firms often wish to create a package of hedges to manage the price risk of its inputs or outputs. Consider an Australian firm that produces goods to sell in Australia but imports its raw materials from Japan. Assuming that the Australian firm has negotiated the sales price of its production over the next 12 months, it may want to hedge the currency risk of its Japanese input costs. If its production input needs are predictable, fixed rate swaps and average rate option contracts may be added to the risk management arsenal.

**ILLUSTRATION 16.7** Comparing option alternatives.

*Suppose a U.S. firm wants to hedge its foreign input costs by buying insurance. More specifically, the firm has entered into a contract to buy 100,000 widgets per month over the next two years at EUR 0.50 per widget. The current exchange rate is USD 1.20/EUR, and its volatility rate is 10%. The risk-free rate of interest in the U.S. is 5%, and the rate in Europe is 6%. Compare the costs of (1) buying a portfolio of at-the-money call options expiring at the end of each month through the two-year period, (2) buying a single two-year at-the-money call option for the contract amount, and (3) buying an arithmetic average-rate at-the-money call option where the underlying exchange rate is an average of the month-end exchanges rates over the life of the contract.*

The firm has entered an agreement to buy widgets at a fixed price of EUR 0.50 per widget and at the rate of 100,000 per month for 24 months. This means that the firm will make annuity payments of EUR 50,000 each month, or EUR 120,000 in total over the life of the agreement. To hedge against a depreciating USD, it is considering different call option alternatives.

The first alternative is to buy a strip of at-the-money call options, one expiring each month. In the event the exchange rate rises to, say, USD 1.30/EUR by the end of the first month, for example, the option will pay USD 1.30 – 1.20 = 0.10. The net cost of buying euros at the end of the first month is therefore USD 1.30 – 0.10 = 1.20/EUR, or 50,000 times USD 1.20 or USD 60,000 in total. The value of the one-month call per euro is

OV_OPTION_VALUE(1.20, 1.20, 1/12, 0.05, 0.06, 0.10, "C", "E") = 0.05450

or USD 0.05450/EUR times 50,000 euros or USD 2,725 in total. If we repeat this computation 23 more times, once for each monthly cash flow, the total value of all option premiums is USD 199,853.

The second alternative is to buy a single 24-month at-the-money call option. The value of this option per euro is

OV_OPTION_VALUE(1.20, 1.20, 2, 0.05, 0.06, 0.10, "C", "E") = 0.2288

or USD 0.2288/EUR times 1,200,000 euros or USD 274,575 in total.

The final alternative is to buy an at-the-money average rate call option. The option's time to expiration is two years, and the final cash settlement price is the difference between the arithmetic average month-end exchange rate and the exercise price of the option, that is,

$$\max\left(\frac{1}{24}\sum_{t=1}^{24} S_t - 1.20\right)$$

where $S_t$ is the USD/EUR exchange rate at the end of each month. To value an at-the-money, arithmetic average rate option, an approximation method is necessary. In Chapter 7, we showed how Monte Carlo simulation can be used to value so-called "Asian-style options," one of which is an option on an average-rate. The OPTVAL function

OV_APPROX_ASIAN_OPT_MC(*s, x, t, r, i, v, n, ntrial, cp, sx, ag*)

can be used. The first six parameters were defined earlier. The parameter $n$ is the total number of observations used in computing the average. If the option's life is two years and monthly observations are used, $n$ is set equal to 24.[10] The parameter *ntrial* is the number of simulation runs. The parameter *cp* is either "C" or "P," depending upon whether you are valuing a call or a put. The parameter *sx* is either "S" or "X," depending upon whether you are averaging the asset price to replace the asset price or the exercise price of the average rate option. Finally, the parameter *ag* is either "A" or "G," depending upon whether the average rate of the option is arithmetic or geometric. For the illustration at hand,

OV_APPROX_ASIAN_OPT_MC(1.20, 1.20, 2, 0.05, 0.06, 0.10, 24, 10000, "C", "S", "A")
= 0.1370

This means that the cost of the average-rate option alternative is USD 0.1370/EUR, or 0.1370 times 1,200,000 or USD 164,459 in total.

[10] If $n$ is set equal to one, the value of an average rate option should equal the value of a European-style option. They will not be exactly the same, however, since the Monte Carlo simulation is an approximation method.

### Using FX Futures and Options to Manage Balance Sheet Risk

In many cases, a firm faces currency risk that is not tied to a particular transaction but rather to a particular asset or liability on the firm's balance sheet. A firm exporting to Ireland, for example, is likely to have both significant accounts receivable and inventory denominated in euros. Indeed, a firm's balance sheet may have both assets and liabilities denominated in various foreign currencies.

Managing *balance sheet risk* depends on whether the foreign currency obligation is contractual or not. A *contractual* obligation denominated in a foreign currency is subject to exchange rate risk because the contract price is set and cannot be changed. If the value of the currency falls, the foreign currency price cannot be adjusted. On the other hand, a *noncontractual* business operation is less subject to exchange risk because changes in exchange rates may be partially offset by price changes in the foreign currency. A U.S. widget manufacturer with an Irish subsidiary, for example, may find it possible to offset declines in the value of the euro by increasing the price of widgets sold in Ireland.

The nature of the balance sheet hedge depends on the nature of the underlying asset/liability. In the normal course of operation, a U.S. firm operating an Irish subsidiary might find it necessary to have a large euro balance in the subsidiary's cash account. Worried about a possible decline in the euro, the parent can hedge the cash position by selling futures. If the USD/EUR exchange rate falls, the decline in the U.S. dollar value of the cash will be offset by the profit on the short futures position. This hedge is analogous to the transaction risk hedge in the sense that both are contractual. This balance sheet hedge will not be as effective, however. The mismatch in the terms to maturity of the cash balance (term to maturity = 0) and futures contracts (term to maturity > 0) means that slippage will be incurred due to basis risk.[11] In addition, unlike a fixed transaction price agreement, the cash balance changes day to day from normal business operations.

An example of a balance sheet hedge of a noncontractual asset is hedging finished goods inventory denominated in euros. This hedge may be more complicated because a decline in the USD/EUR exchange rate will reduce the U.S. dollar value of the inventory. This, however, might be offset by an increase in the price of the finished goods in Ireland. Indeed, under purchasing power parity, a full price adjustment is expected. But the subsidiary may not have the freedom to change prices in a dramatic way. To illustrate, suppose prices may be increased by only 50% of the amount they should increase under PPP. Since the ability to re-price provides a partial (50%) natural hedge of the finished goods inventory, only half the inventory balance needs to be hedged in the futures market.

## SUMMARY

This chapter focuses on the management of currency risk using derivatives contracts. In the first section, currency derivative markets are discussed. The lion's

[11] Deciding the appropriate term to maturity of the futures contract is not straightforward. The shorter the term to maturity of the futures, the less the basis risk but the greater the trading costs associated with frequent rollovers in the futures position.

share of currency derivatives trading takes place in the OTC market, although the trading volumes on futures and options exchanges are respectable. In the second section, the principles of currency derivatives valuation and risk measurement are provided. No-arbitrage price relations and valuation equations/methods are provided for currency forwards, futures, options, and swaps. All of them are on the continuous net cost of carry results developed in Chapters 4 through 9. The continuous net cost of carry rate for currencies is the domestic risk-free interest rate less the foreign risk-free interest rate. The third section illustrates a number of important currency risk management strategies. Among them are using a currency swap or a strip of currency forwards to re-denominate fixed-rate debt in one currency into another, using forward/options to manage the price risks of single and multiple transactions, and using forward/options to manage balance sheet risk.

## REFERENCES AND SUGGESTED READINGS

Barone-Adesi, Giovanni, and Robert E. Whaley. 1987. Efficient analytic approximation of American option values. *Journal of Finance* 42 (June): 301–320.

Bates, David S. 1996. Jumps and stochastic volatility: Exchange rate processes implicit in PHLX Deuschemark options. *Review of Financial Studies* 9: 69–108.

Biger, Nahum, and John Hull. 1983. The valuation of currency options. *Financial Management* 12 (Spring): 24–28.

Black, Fischer. 1976. The pricing of commodity contracts. *Journal of Financial Economics* 3 (March): 167–179.

Chesney, Marc, and Scott, Louis. 1989. Pricing European currency options: A comparison of the modified Black-Scholes model and a random variance model. *Journal of Financial and Quantitative Analysis* 24 (3): 267–284.

Cornell, Bradford, and Mark R. Reinganum. 1981. Forward and futures prices: Evidence from the foreign exchange market. *Journal of Finance* 36: 1035–1045.

Garman, Mark B., and S. W. Kohlhagen. 1983. Foreign currency option values. *Journal of International Money and Finance* 2 (December): 231–237.

Grabbe, J. Orlin. 1983. The pricing of call and put options on foreign exchange. *Journal of International Money and Finance* 2 (December): 239–253.

Jorion, Philippe. 1995. Predicting volatility in the foreign exchange market. *Journal of Finance* 50: 507–528.

Jorion, Phillippe. 1989. On jumps in the foreign exchange and stock market. *Review of Financial Studies* 4: 427–445.

Shastri, Kuldeep, and Kishore Tandon. 1985. Arbitrage tests of the efficiency of the foreign currency options market. *Journal of International Money and Finance* 4 (December): 455–468.

Shastri, Kuldeep, and Kishore Tandon. 1986. On the use of European models to price American options on foreign currency. *Journal of Futures Markets* 6: 93–108.

Taylor, S. J., and X. Xu. 1993. The magnitude of implied volatility smiles: Theory and empirical evidence for exchange rates. *Review of Futures Markets* 13: 355–380.

# PART Eight

# Interest Rate Derivatives

# 17

# Interest Rate Products: Futures and Options

Interest rate derivative contracts seem less in the spotlight than are derivatives on stocks and stock indexes. One reason is that the markets for bonds are less active than the market for stocks. Do not be misled, however. The bond markets in the United States are, in fact, larger than stock markets. Of the $34.34 trillion in market value of stocks and bonds outstanding in the United States at the end of 2003, about 56% was bonds. It should not be surprising, therefore, that interest rate risk management is a primary concern for corporations, agencies, municipalities, and governments. Indeed, more than two-thirds of all OTC derivatives traded worldwide are written on interest rate instruments.

The first interest rate derivative contract on an exchange appeared 30 years ago, when the CBT introduced futures contracts on GNMA pass-through certificates. Futures contracts on U.S. Treasury bonds, notes, and bills quickly followed. Options on interest rate instruments were launched in late 1982. Even though many of these markets have become incredibly active by exchange standards, the greatest success story is the OTC interest rate swap market. The first interest rate swap was consummated in 1981. Today, about 20 years later, interest rate swaps account for more than half the notional amount of *all* derivatives outstanding worldwide. The interest rate products discussion is divided into two chapters. This chapter focuses on futures and options contracts, that is, contracts with a single future cash flow. The next chapter focuses on contracts with multiple future cash flows. In it, we discuss interest rate swaps, caps, collars, floors, and swaptions.

Our discussion of exchange-traded products in this chapter has three sections. In the first, details of selected exchange-traded contracts and contract markets are provided. Section two provides the principles of interest rate derivatives valuation. For the most part, the principles and valuation methods of Chapters 4 through 9 can be applied directly, with two notable exceptions. First, the no-arbitrage price relation for the CBT's T-bond futures must be modified to account for the fact that the seller has an option to deliver any one of a number of eligible bond issues. Second, for options on short-term debt instruments, the log-normal price distribution assumption is inappropriate. The price of a T-bill, for example, can never exceed its par value. Consequently, we are required to develop a new methodology for valuing interest rate options. To do so, we invoke the assumption that the short-term interest rate is log-normally distributed, and then modify the valuation methods of Chapters 7 through 9. Section three illustrates three important interest rate derviatives risk management strategies—a short-term long hedge, a long-term short hedge, and asset allocation.

## MARKETS

To place the development of interest rate derivatives markets in context, it is useful to get a sense for the underlying asset market. Unlike stocks, bonds are not actively traded on exchanges. They trade in over-the-counter markets, which do not have the transparency of stock markets. As a consequence, the public often perceives the bond market to be smaller and less important than the stock market. Nothing is further from the truth, however. Figure 17.1 shows the market value of stocks and bonds traded in the United States as of December 31, 2003. Of the \$34.34 trillion in outstanding securities, 56% are bonds and 44% are stocks. Corporate bonds are the single largest bond market, accounting for 20% of security value. Agencies are the second largest group at 18%, Treasuries account for 12%, and municipalities account for 6%. Below the evolution of interest rate derivatives is discussed. While exchange-traded interest rate derivatives markets are active, the trading volume now pales by comparison to the OTC market.

### Evolution of Interest Rate Derivatives

Derivatives contracts on interest rate instruments began trading in the mid-1970s. The first interest rate futures contract, introduced in the fall of 1975, was the Chicago Board of Trade's (CBTs) futures on GNMA Collaterialized

**FIGURE 17.1** Market values of bonds and stocks outstanding in the United States as of December 31, 2003. Total market value of all securities is \$34.34 trillion.

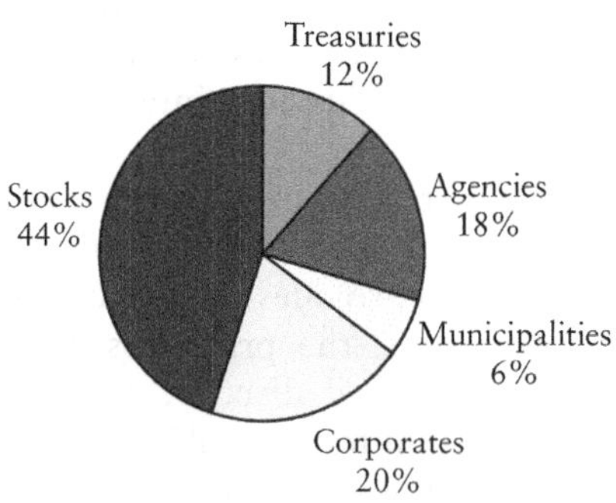


*Source:* Information compiled from *Flow of Fund Accounts of the United States* (fourth quarter 2003), www.federalreserve.gov.

Despositary Receipts (CDRs). The CDRs are pools of mortgages whose payments are insured by the Government National Mortgage Association (GNMA), a U.S. governmental agency. They are sometimes referred to as "pass-through" certificates because the payments of the mortgage holders passthrough to the holders of the certificates in the form of coupon interest payments. Prepayments by mortgagors, and prepayments by insurers in the case of default, also passthrough. The coupon rates on the certificates are 0.5% below the rate on the mortgages to cover the 0.44% retained by the servicer who collects and distributes the mortgage payments and the 0.06% paid to GNMA for insuring the pool against default. Different pools of mortgages, even ones with the same coupon rate, behave quite differently from one another due to different rates of prepayment. The futures contract permitted different coupon rates to be delivered, and had an imperfect system for translating these eligible bonds into an 8% coupon bond issue. Without a well-defined underlying asset, arbitrage between the futures and cash market is impeded, and the correlation between the futures and mortgage-backed securities is low, undermining the contract's effectiveness as a hedging vehicle. The contract was delisted in the late 1980s.[1]

The next interest rate futures contracts to be introduced were the Chicago Mercantile Exchange's (CMEs) T-bill futures contract in January 1976 and the CBT's U.S. Treasury bond futures in August 1977. Spurred by success of these contract markets, interest rate futures began to appear on other exchanges worldwide. The Sydney Futures Exchange, for example, introduced futures on 90-day Bank Accepted bills in October 1979, and the London International Financial Futures Exchange introduced trading on long gilt[2] futures in November 1982. Back in the United States, another important innovation occurred in December 1981 when the CME introduced the Eurodollar futures contract. This marked the first time an interest rate futures specified cash-settlement rather than physical delivery.

Options on interest rate instruments first appeared in late 1982. On October 1, 1982, the CBT and the CME simultaneously launched trading of option contracts on T-bond futures and Eurodollar futures, respectively. The Chicago Board Options Exchange (CBOE) introduced options on Treasury bonds and the American Stock Exchange (AMEX) introduced options on Treasury notes and bills on October 22, 1982. Interestingly, options written on interest rates futures are far more actively traded on exchanges than are options on debt instruments directly. One possible reason for this phenomenon is that there are just too many debt issues (for the U.S. Treasury alone) for each to have an actively traded market on an exchange. OTC option dealers, on the other hand, stand ready and willing to create an option on any bond issue that a customer wants.

The last noteworthy event in terms of the evolution of interest rate derivatives markets is the development of the swap market in the early 1980s. An *interest rate swap* is an agreement between two parties to exchange or "swap" a series of periodic interest payments. The most common interest rate swap is to exchange payments on fixed rate debt for floating rate debt. Such a swap is called

[1] Johnston and McConnell (1989) provide an interesting retrospective on the rise and fall of the CBT's GNMA contract market.

[2] A *gilt* (or gilt-edged stock) is a bond issued and guaranteed by the British government.

a *plain-vanilla interest rate swap*. An early example occurred in 1982, when Sallie Mae swapped the interest payments on intermediate-term fixed rate debt for floating rate payments indexed to the three-month T-bill yield. In the same year, a USD 300 million seven-year Deutsche Bank bond issue was swapped into USD LIBOR. While today, OTC swaps are written on a number of different types of underlying assets, interest rate swaps are far and away the largest asset category. As of yearend 2003, interest rate derivatives accounted for 72% of the notional amount of all OTC derivatives outstanding. (See Figure 17.2.) Of this amount, more than 76% of interest rate derivatives were swaps, with the remaining 24% being between split options (14.7%) and forwards (10.3%). (See Figure 17.3.) We return to OTC interst rate products in the next chapter.

### Interest Rate Futures

In the case of stock, stock index, and foreign currency products discussed in the last three chapters, there is a single source of risk underlying the derivatives contracts (i.e., the price risks of a stock, stock index, or foreign currency). Interest rate derivatives, on the other hand, are more intriguing in the sense that interest rate risk is often categorized by whether it is short-term, intermediate-term, or long-term, with the behavior of each interest rate being quite different. By far the most active short-term interest rate contract is the CME's three-month Eurodollar futures. The CBT's T-bond futures captures most of the trading in the long-term arena, and the CBT's 10-year and five-year contracts capture the intermediate term. All other interest rate futures contract trading volumes of the other contracts pale by comparison.

**FIGURE 17.2** Percentage of total notional amount of derivatives outstanding worldwide on December 2003 by underlying asset category. Total notional amount of derivatives is USD 197.2 trillion.

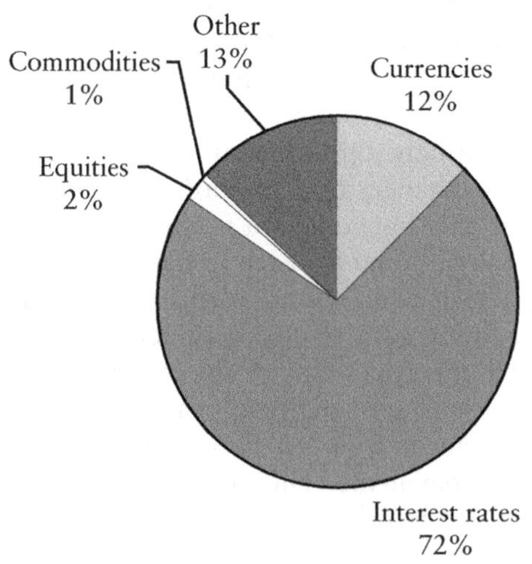


*Source:* Information compiled from Bank for International Settlements (www.bis.org), *BIS Quarterly Review*, June 2004.

**FIGURE 17.3** Percentage of total notional amount of single-currency, interest rate derivatives outstanding worldwide on December 2003 by contract type. Total notional amount of interest rate derivatives is USD 141.99 trillion.

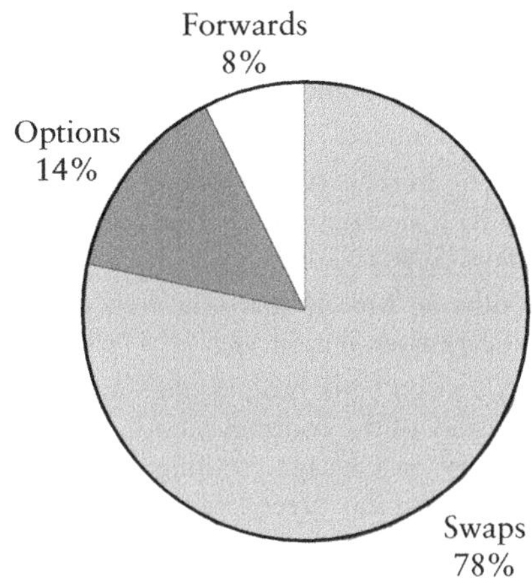


*Source:* Information compiled from Bank for International Settlements (www.bis.org), *BIS Quarterly Review*, June 2004.

**Eurodollar Futures** The contract specifications for the CME's Eurodollar futures are given in Table 17.1. The underlying instrument is a USD 1,000,000 Eurodollar deposit with three months to maturity. Its price is quoted as an index level and is created by subtracting the Eurodollar rate from 100. A price of 94.50, therefore, means that the contract buyer is willing to lend USD 1,000,000 at 5.50% for a three-month period beginning on the date the futures contract expires. Unlike many other interest rate futures, the Eurodollar futures is cash settled at expiration, which is set as the second London business day immediately preceding the third Wednesday of the contract month. The cash settlement price is the British Bankers Association (BBA) Interest Settlement Rate. At 11 AM London time, 16 BBA designated banks provide quotes that reflect their perception of the rate at which U.S. dollar deposits are generally available in the marketplace. The highest four and the lowest four are eliminated. The average of the remaining eight quotes (rounded to the fifth decimal place) is the fixing of the day.

Table 17.2 contains a summary of Eurodollar futures trading on Thursday, March 30, 2006. The June 2006 futures has a reported settlement price of 94.975. This means the promised rate on a three-month Eurodollar time deposit beginning on June 19, 2006 (second London business day immediately preceding the third Wednesday of the contract month) is 5.025%. As noted in Chapter 2, this nominal Eurodollar interest rate is a simple interest rate based on a 360-day year. To find the continuously compounded rate of return, we must undo the nominal rates and the 360-day banker's year converntion. Since

$$e^{r(92/365)} = 1 + 0.05025\left(\frac{92}{360}\right)$$

**TABLE 17.1** Selected terms of CME's Eurodollar futures contract.

| | |
|---|---|
| Exchange | Chicago Mercantile Exchange |
| Contract unit | $1,000,000 Eurodollar time deposit |
| Price quote | An index created by subtracting the Eurodollar rate from 100. (e.g., 94.50 implies a 5.50% Eurodollar interest rate.) |
| Tick size | 0.005 (1/2 basis point) |
| Tick value | $12.50 per contract |
| Trading hours | 7:20 AM to 2:00 PM (CT) Monday through Friday. GLOBEX: Monday through Thursday, 5 PM to 4 PM; Sundays and holidays, 5 PM to 4 PM. |
| Contract months | 40 months on March quarterly cycle (Mar., Jun., Sep., Dec.) plus four nearest serial months. |
| Last day of trading | Second London bank business day immediately preceding the third Wednesday of the contract month. If it is a bank holiday in New York City or Chicago, trading terminates on the first London bank business day preceding the third Wednesday of the contract month. If an Exchange holiday, trading terminates on the next preceding business day common to London banks and the Exchange. |
| Settlement | Cash settlement price determined by the British Bankers Association (BBA) Interest Settlement Rate. At 11 AM London time, 16 BBA designated banks provide quotes which reflect their perception of the rate at which U.S. dollar deposits are generally available in the market place. The four highest and the four lowest are eliminated. The average of the remaining eight quotes (rounded out to the fifth decimal place) is the fixing for the day. |

the continuous rate is

$$r = \frac{\ln(1 + 0.05025(92/360))}{92/365} = 5.2425\%$$

The function, OV_IR_CONV_ED_YIELD(*rate,days*), performs this transformation, where *rate* is the nominal Eurodollar interest rate and *days* is the number of days to maturity. In the present context,

$$\text{OV\_IR\_CONV\_ED\_YIELD}(0.05025,92) = 0.052425$$

Table 17.2 also shows a phenomenon that is uncommon to most exchange-traded derivatives, that is, contract months extend out into the future 10 years. For most exchange-traded derivatives with the March quarterly expiration (March, June, September, December), the nearby contract has the greatest trading volume, with the second nearby contract having only a small fraction of that of the nearby. For the Eurodollar contracts, even the June 2011 futures has 2,002 contracts outstanding. At a contract denomination of USD 1,000,000, this represents over USD 2 billion. The reason for the activity ranging out so far is that this is the primary market that OTC market makers use to hedge their floating rate

**TABLE 17.2** Summary of trading activity of Chicago Mercantile Exchange's Eurodollar futures on March 30, 2006.

| Month | Open | High | Low | Last | Settlement | Point Change | Estimated Volume | Open Interest |
|---|---|---|---|---|---|---|---|---|
| Apr-06 | 94.96 | 94.96 | 94.945 | 94.9475B | 94.95 | −1.25 | 5,693 | 44,588 |
| May-06 | 94.87 | 94.96B | 94.86A | 94.865A | 94.86 | −2 | 65 | 10,112 |
| Jun-06 | 94.825 | 94.84 | 94.79 | 94.795 | 94.795 | −3 | 327K | 1365K |
| Jul-06 | 94.785 | 94.79 | 94.765A | 94.77A | 94.765 | −3 | 748 | 1,043 |
| Aug-06 | — | — | 94.745A | 94.76A | 94.745 | −3 | 493 | |
| Sep-06 | 94.77 | 94.79 | 94.715 | 94.72 | 94.725 | −4 | 467K | 1340K |
| Dec-06 | 94.785 | 94.81 | 94.725 | 94.74 | 94.74 | −4 | 431K | 1388K |
| Mar-07 | 94.845 | 94.865 | 94.775 | 94.785 | 94.79 | −5 | 382K | 1098K |
| Jun-07 | 94.885 | 94.91 | 94.815 | 94.83 | 94.83 | −5 | 322K | 898,819 |
| Sep-07 | 94.905 | 94.93 | 94.835 | 94.85 | 94.855 | −4.5 | 188K | 786,126 |
| Dec-07 | 94.9 | 94.925 | 94.84 | 94.85 | 94.855 | −4.5 | 124K | 549,025 |
| Mar-08 | 94.905 | 94.92 | 94.83 | 94.845 | 94.85 | −4.5 | 78K | 356,216 |
| Jun-08 | 94.88 | 94.9 | 94.81 | 94.835B | 94.83 | −4.5 | 27K | 253,736 |
| Sep-08 | 94.86 | 94.88 | 94.79 | 94.815B | 94.81 | −4.5 | 21K | 213,770 |
| Dec-08 | 94.81 | 94.84 | 94.755A | 94.775B | 94.77 | −4.5 | 19K | 179,193 |
| Mar-09 | 94.82 | 94.82 | 94.74 | 94.76 | 94.755 | −4.5 | 13K | 129,372 |
| Jun-09 | 94.79 | 94.79 | 94.70A | 94.73 | 94.73 | −4.5 | 10K | 116,373 |
| Sep-09 | 94.765 | 94.765 | 94.67A | 94.7 | 94.7 | −5 | 7,654 | 107,602 |
| Dec-09 | 94.685 | 94.72B | 94.63A | 94.66 | 94.66 | −5 | 8,744 | 95,764 |
| Mar-10 | 94.675 | 94.71B | 94.615A | 94.645 | 94.645 | −5.5 | 6,926 | 78,810 |
| Jun-10 | 94.63 | 94.69B | 94.59A | 94.625A | 94.625 | −5.5 | 5,255 | 60,504 |
| Sep-10 | 94.615 | 94.665B | 94.565A | 94.6 | 94.595 | −6 | 3,842 | 54,679 |
| Dec-10 | 94.635 | 94.635 | 94.52 | 94.565 | 94.56 | −6 | 2,859 | 54,141 |
| Mar-11 | 94.625 | 94.625 | 94.52A | 94.555 | 94.55 | −6 | 3,712 | 23,939 |
| Jun-11 | — | — | 94.50A | 94.525B | 94.53 | −6 | 2,002 | 11,926 |
| Sep-11 | — | — | 94.48A | 94.505B | 94.505 | −6.5 | 202 | 16,176 |
| Dec-11 | — | — | 94.45A | 94.475B | 94.475 | −6.5 | 202 | 12,631 |
| Mar-12 | — | — | 94.445A | 94.47B | 94.47 | −6.5 | 202 | 9,374 |
| Jun-12 | 94.49 | 94.49 | 94.42A | 94.44B | 94.445 | −6.5 | 12 | 5,904 |
| Sep-12 | 94.47 | 94.47 | 94.40A | 94.42B | 94.42 | −7 | 11 | 7,659 |
| Dec-12 | 94.44 | 94.44 | 94.37A | 94.39B | 94.39 | −7 | 5 | 5,927 |
| Mar-13 | — | — | 94.365A | 94.385B | 94.385 | −7 | 2 | 2,883 |
| Jun-13 | — | — | 94.34A | 94.355B | 94.36 | −7 | 2 | 2,069 |
| Sep-13 | — | — | 94.315A | 94.335B | 94.335 | −7 | 2 | 1,336 |
| Dec-13 | — | — | 94.285A | 94.30B | 94.305 | −7 | 2 | 1,220 |
| Mar-14 | — | — | 94.28A | 94.295B | 94.3 | −7 | 2 | 1,400 |
| Jun-14 | — | — | 94.255A | 94.27B | 94.275 | −7 | 2 | 466 |
| Sep-14 | — | — | 94.23A | 94.245B | 94.25 | −7 | 2 | 641 |
| Dec-14 | — | — | 94.20A | 94.215B | 94.22 | −7 | 2 | 1,198 |
| Mar-15 | — | — | 94.195A | 94.21B | 94.215 | −7 | 2 | 392 |
| Jun-15 | — | — | 94.175A | 94.19B | 94.19 | −7.5 | 2 | 488 |
| Sep-15 | — | — | 94.155A | 94.17A | 94.165 | −8 | 2 | 565 |
| Dec-15 | — | — | 94.125A | 94.14A | 94.135 | −8 | 2 | 260 |
| Mar-16 | — | — | 94.12A | 94.135A | 94.13 | −8 | 2 | 230 |

*Source:* Data drawn from www.cme.com.

risk exposure on interest rate swaps. We discuss the linkage between these markets in the interest rate swap valuation section later in the next chapter.

**U.S. T-Bond and T-Note Futures** The contract specifications of the CBT's T-bond and 10-year T-note contracts are shown in Tables 17.3 and 17.4, respectively. Both requires the delivery of a $100,000 U.S. Treasury coupon-bearing instrument, however, in the case of the T-bond futures it is a T-bond with at least 15 years to maturity or, if the bond is callable, to first call date,[3] and in the case of the 10-year T-note futures it is a T-note with at least 6½ years but less than 10 years to maturity. Both contracts follow a quarterly expiration cycle. Delivery may take place at any time during the delivery month at the discretion of the short. The last day of trading of the futures contract is the eighth last business day of the contract month. Table 17.5 shows the prices of the T-bond and T-notes futures as of the close of trading on March 30, 2006. Note that like their underlying instruments, T-bond and T-note futures have their prices quoted in 32nds. The June 2006 T-bond futures settlement price of 109-06 means that the price is 109.1875% of par.

**TABLE 17.3** Selected terms of CBT's U.S. Treasury bond futures contract.

| | |
|---|---|
| Exchange | Chicago Board of Trade |
| Contract unit | One U.S. T-bond with a face value of $100,000 |
| Deliverable grades | Any U.S. T-bond with at least 15 years to maturity or to first call date from the first day of the delivery month. Invoice price equals settlement price times a conversion factor plus accrued interest. The conversion factor is the price of the delivered bond to yield 6%. |
| Price quote | Points ($1,000) and 1/32 of a point. E.g., 80-16 equals 80 16/32. |
| Tick size | 1/32 of a point |
| Tick value | $31.25 per contract |
| Trading hours | Open outcry: 7:20 AM to 2:00 PM CT, Monday through Friday<br>Electronic: 7:00 PM to 4:00 PM CT, Sunday through Friday |
| Contract months | Four contract months on March quarterly expiration cycle (Mar., Jun., Sep., Dec.) |
| Last day of trading | Seventh last day preceding the last business day of the delivery month. |
| Settlement | Physical delivery |
| First delivery day | First day of the contract month |
| Last delivery day | Last day of contract month |

[3] The U.S. Treasury stopped issuing 30-year bonds in November 2001, an era when the government was running budget surpluses—not deficits—and financing the government's debt was easier. Consequently, the deliverable supply of long-term U.S. Treasury bonds had been declining. In August 2005, the U.S. Treasury announced that it would once again issue 30-year bonds beginning February 2006.

For decades, the 30-year bond served as a closely followed benchmark for the entire fixed-income market. But Treasury stopped issuing the long bond in 2001, in an era when the government was finally running budget surpluses—not deficits—and financing the government's debt was easier.

**TABLE 17.4** Selected terms of CBT's 10-year U.S. Treasury note futures contract.

| | |
|---|---|
| Exchange | Chicago Board of Trade |
| Contract unit | One U.S. T-note with a face value of $100,000 |
| Deliverable grades | Any U.S. T-note with at least 6-1/2 years but not more than 10 years to maturity from the first day of the delivery month. Invoice price equals settlement price times a conversion factor plus accrued interest. The conversion factor is the price of the delivered bond to yield 6%. |
| Price quote | Points ($1,000) and one-half of 1/32 of a point. E.g., 80-165 equals 80 16.5/32. |
| Tick size | One-half of 1/32 of a point |
| Tick value | $15.625 per contract |
| Trading hours | Open outcry: 7:20 AM to 2:00 PM CT, Monday through Friday<br>Electronic: 7:00 PM to 4:00 PM CT, Sunday through Friday |
| Contract months | Four contract months on March Quarterly expiration cycle (Mar., Jun., Sep., Dec.) |
| Last day of trading | Seventh last day preceding the last business day of the delivery month. |
| Settlement | Physical delivery |
| First delivery day | First day of the contract month |
| Last delivery day | Last day of contract month |

**TABLE 17.5** Summary of trading activity of Chicago Board of Trade's Treasury bond and 10-year Treasury note futures on Thursday, March 30, 2006.

| Contract month | Open | High | Low | Settle | Chg | Open Interest |
|---|---|---|---|---|---|---|
| **Treasury Bonds (CBT)** | | | | | | |
| Jun-06 | 109-19 | 109-21 | 108-26 | 109-06 | –16 | 642,750 |
| Sep-06 | 109-16 | 109-16 | 108-29 | 109-07 | –16 | 3,429 |
| Dec-06 | | | | 109-19 | –16 | 588 |
| Mar-07 | | | | 109-14 | –16 | 1 |
| **10-Year Treasury Notes (CBT)** | | | | | | |
| Jun-06 | 106-200 | 106-200 | 106-040 | 106-100 | –0-095 | 2,045,545 |
| Sep-06 | 106-210 | 106-210 | 106-065 | 106-110 | –0-105 | 666,465 |
| Dec-06 | | | | 106-100 | –0-115 | 148 |
| Mar-07 | | | | 106-100 | –0-115 | 1 |

*Source:* Data drawn from www.cbot.com.

**Conversion Factor** The CBT's Treasury contracts call for the delivery of any Treasury instrument satisfying a particular maturity constraint. As noted, above, the T-bond futures contract calls for the delivery of any $100,000 U.S. Treasury bond with at least 15 years to maturity or to first call date. Different T-bonds, however, have different coupons and therefore different prices. If no other restriction is applied, the individuals who are short the futures would deliver zero-coupon bonds since, holding other factors constant, they have the lowest value.

The CBT's system of conversion is designed to make the short futures indifferent about which one of the eligible bonds to deliver. It does so by converting every bond to a common hypothetical 6% coupon-bearing bond.[4] To illustrate the principle underlying the CBT's system of conversion, consider the price of a 6%, semiannual coupon-bearing bond with 15 years to maturity. If the yield to maturity is 6%, the bond's price may be written

$$B = \sum_{t=1}^{30} \frac{3}{1.03^t} + \frac{100}{1.03^{30}} = 100.00$$

where the coupon rate and yield have been halved to account for the semiannual coupon payment convention. Now consider the price of a 9%, 15-year bond at a 6% yield to maturity, that is

$$B = \sum_{t=1}^{30} \frac{4.5}{1.03^t} + \frac{100}{1.03^{30}} = 129.40$$

Since the only difference between these bonds is their coupon payment, it must be the case that owning the 9% coupon-bearing bond is like owning 1.2940 6% bonds. Since the futures price is based on a 6% coupon bond, the futures price is multiplied by a conversion factor of 1.2940 to compute the amount paid (delivery price) by the long to the short if the short delivers the 9% coupon issue.

The actual formula for computing the CBT's conversion factor is more complicated than what is demonstrated in the above example because coupons are paid on a semiannual basis, and, in general, the next coupon payment is made in less than six months (i.e., we are part of the way through the current coupon period). The actual formula is

$$CF = (1+y/2)^{-X/6}\left\{\frac{C}{2} + \left[\frac{C}{y}(1-(1+y/2)^{-2n}) + (1+y/2)^{-2n}\right]\right\} - \frac{C}{2}\frac{(6-X)}{6} \quad (17.1)$$

where $CF$ is the conversion factor, C is the annual coupon rate of the bond in decimal form, $y$ equals 0.06, $n$ is the number of whole years to first call if the

[4] The reason that the CBT allows T-bonds with different coupons to be delivered is to prevent the possibility of market manipulation. Each T-bond has limited supply. If the futures contract were written on a single T-bond issue, it would be possible for a single individual or firm to corner the market in the underlying bond and attempt a short squeeze. See Chapter 1.

bond is callable or the number of years to maturity if the bond is not callable, and $X$ is the number of months that the maturity exceeds $n$, rounded down to the nearest quarter (e.g., $X = 0,3,6,9$). Note that if $X = 0,3,6$, the formula (17.1) is used directly. If $X = 9$, set $2n = 2n + 1$, $X = 3$, and calculate as above. The CBT and others publish and distribute conversion factor tables like those shown in Table 17.6. Note that in Table 17.6 the conversion factor of a 9% bond maturing in exactly 15 years is 1.2940, just as we computed earlier.

To illustrate the use of the conversion factor system, assume that we are considering delivering the 9½s of November 2021 on the June 2006 T-bond futures contract. This bond is eligible for delivery because, as of June 1, 2006 (i.e., the first possible delivery date), it has more than 15 years to maturity. In point of fact, on June 1, 2006, the 9½s of November 2021 have 15 years and five months to maturity (i.e., $n = 15$ and $X = 5$). When rounded down to the nearest quarter, we have $X = 3$. Thus, the CBT deems this bond to have 15 years to maturity for delivery purposes. Using Table 17.6, we see that the conversion factor of this bond is 1.3464. In other words, in place of delivering the hypothetical 6% bond underlying the June 2006 futures, we can deliver the 9½s of November 2021, and the buyer is going to have to pay 1.3464 times the prevailing futures price. The conversion factor may also be determined using the OPTVAL function,

OV_IR_CONV_TBOND_CONVFAC(*ncoup*,*nyrs*,*coup*)

where *ncoup* is nominal (annualized) coupon rate (in decimal) specified by the exchange, *nyrs* is the number of years to maturity of the T-bond being delivered, and *coup* is the coupon rate (in decimal) of the T-bond being delivered. Consequently,

OV_IR_CONV_TBOND_CONVFAC (0.06,15.41667,0.0950) = 1.3464

**Invoice Price** On the delivery date, the seller of the T-bond futures delivers an eligible T-bond to the buyer of the T-bond futures contract. In return, the buyer must pay an amount of money called the *invoice price*. The amount of the invoice price equals the sum of the futures price times the conversion factor of the delivered bond and the accrued interest on the delivered bond. Suppose that on June 1, 2006 (i.e., the first day of the delivery month), for example, the June 2006 futures is priced at 100-17. Like the underlying bonds, the digits to the right of the dash represent 32nds, so the futures price is actually 100.53125. If we sell the futures and then promptly deliver the 9½s of November 2021 to the futures contract buyer, we would receive the invoice price, which equals 100.53125 times 1,000 (the denomination of the futures contract) times 1.3464 (the conversion factor of the 9½s of November 2021 as of June 1, 2006), that is,

$$100.53125 \times \$1{,}000 \times 1.3464 = \$135{,}355.28$$

plus the accrued interest on the 9½s of November 2021 as of June 1, 2006,[5] that is,

[5] As of June 1, 2006, 15 days have elapsed in the current coupon period for the 9½s of November 2021 (from May 15 to June 1), where the current coupon period is 184 days in length (from May 15, 2006 to November 15, 2006).

**TABLE 17.6** Sample of CBT conversion factors for T-bonds eligible for delivery on T-bond futures.

| Years to Maturity | Coupon Interest Rate | | | | | | | | |
|---|---|---|---|---|---|---|---|---|---|
| | 9.000% | 9.125% | 9.250% | 9.375% | 9.500% | 9.625% | 9.750% | 9.875% | 10.000% |
| 15.00 | 1.2940 | 1.3063 | 1.3185 | 1.3308 | 1.3430 | 1.3553 | 1.3675 | 1.3798 | 1.3920 |
| 15.25 | 1.2969 | 1.3092 | 1.3216 | 1.3340 | 1.3464 | 1.3587 | 1.3711 | 1.3835 | 1.3959 |
| 15.50 | 1.3000 | 1.3125 | 1.3250 | 1.3375 | 1.3500 | 1.3625 | 1.3750 | 1.3875 | 1.4000 |
| 15.75 | 1.3028 | 1.3154 | 1.3280 | 1.3406 | 1.3533 | 1.3659 | 1.3785 | 1.3911 | 1.4037 |
| 16.00 | 1.3058 | 1.3186 | 1.3313 | 1.3441 | 1.3568 | 1.3695 | 1.3823 | 1.3950 | 1.4078 |
| 16.25 | 1.3085 | 1.3214 | 1.3342 | 1.3471 | 1.3600 | 1.3728 | 1.3857 | 1.3985 | 1.4114 |
| 16.50 | 1.3115 | 1.3245 | 1.3374 | 1.3504 | 1.3634 | 1.3764 | 1.3894 | 1.4023 | 1.4153 |
| 16.75 | 1.3141 | 1.3272 | 1.3403 | 1.3534 | 1.3665 | 1.3795 | 1.3926 | 1.4057 | 1.4188 |

$$(9.50/2) \times \$1{,}000 \times (15/184) = \$387.23$$

The total invoice price is $135,355.28 + 387.23 = $135,742.51.

The conversion factor mechanics are more tedious than they are difficult to understand. As noted earlier, the motivation for making a number of different T-bonds eligible for delivery is to ensure that no single individual or bank can attempt to corner the market in the bond underlying the futures. The system of conversion does not work exactly, however, and one of the eligible bonds winds up being "cheapest-to-deliver" in practice. We will show how to identify this bond and modify the futures pricing relation in the next section of the chapter.

### Interest Rate Options

The most active exchange-traded interest rate options are those written on the CME's Eurodollar futures, and the CBT's five-year T-note, 10-year T-note, and T-bond futures. All of these contracts are futures options. Although some exchanges such as the CBOE and the AMEX have tried to develop options on specific bond issues, none of the markets have been particularly successful. That is not say that bond option markets are inactive. They are, but not on exchanges. Recall that Figure 17.3 showed that the notional amount of interest rate options outstanding in the OTC market was about USD 20 trillion at the end of 2003.

**Eurodollar Futures Options** The contract specifications of the CME's Eurodollar futures options are given in Table 17.7. The options are American-style, and expire together with the underlying futures on the second London business day before the third Wednesday of the contract month. Exercise of a Eurodollar option before expiration results in the delivery of the underlying futures. Thus, if we hold a June 2006 call option written on a Eurodollar futures and exercise it, we will receive a long position in the June 2006 Eurodollar futures at the end of the day and will receive cash proceeds equal to the difference between the futures settlement price and the exercise price of the call.

Eurodollar futures options follow a quarterly expiration cycle like the futures. In addition, there are two serial months. If we are standing at the end of March 2006, for example, the nearby Eurodollar futures will be the June 2006 contract. Eurodollar futures options with April 2006, May 2006, and June 2006 expirations will appear—the April and May contracts being the serial months and the June contract being the quarterly expiration. In this case, the April and May options contracts, like the June contract, are written on the June 2006 Eurodollar futures. Unlike the June contract, which, if carried to expiration is cash-settled, the April and May contracts have delivery settlement.

**U.S. T-Bond Futures Options** The contract specifications of the CBT's option contracts on the T-bond and T-note futures are similar, so we present only the T-bond futures' contract specifications in Table 17.8. Like the Eurodollar futures options, early exercise results in receiving a position in the underlying futures. Exercising a call, for example, results in a long futures position, and exercising a put results in a short futures position. Unlike the Eurodollar futures options, however, the last

**TABLE 17.7** Selected terms of CME's Eurodollar futures options contract.

| | |
|---|---|
| Exchange | Chicago Mercantile Exchange |
| Contract unit | $1,000,000 Eurodollar time deposit |
| Price quote | An index created by subtracting the Eurodollar rate from 100. (e.g., 94.50 implies a 5.50% Eurodollar interest rate.) |
| Tick size | 0.01 (1 basis point) |
| Tick value | $25.00 per contract |
| Exercise prices | At 0.25 intervals for the nearest listed expiration in the quarterly cycle, and the serial month expirations with the same underlying futures. |
| Trading hours | 7:20 AM to 2:00 PM (CT), Monday through Friday. GLOBEX: Monday through Thursday 5 PM to 6:50 AM; Sundays and holidays, 5 PM to 6:50 AM. |
| Contract months | Eight months in March quaterly cycle (Mar., Jun., Sep., Dec.) cycle plus two serial months. |
| Last day of trading | Quarterly: Options trading shall terminate at 11:00 AM (London Time) 5:00 AM (Chicago Time) on the second London bank business day before the third Wednesday of the contract month. Serial Eurodollar options trading shall terminate on the Friday immediately preceding the third Wednesday of the contract month. If the foregoing date for termination is an Exchange holiday, options trading shall terminate on the immediately preceding business day. |
| Settlement | Cash settlement price determined by the British Bankers Association (BBA) Interest Settlement Rate. At 11 AM London time, 16 BBA designated banks provide quotes which reflect their perception of the rate at which U.S. dollar deposits are generally available. |
| Style | American-style |
| Settlement | The quarterly contracts are cash settled in the same manner as the futures. Early exercise or exercise of serial contracts requires the delivery of the underlying futures position. |

day of trading is the first Friday preceding, by *at least* two business days, the first notice day for the corresponding T-bond futures contract. In general, the first notice day of the futures is the first business day of the contract month. Thus although the June 2006 option contract is written on the June 2006 futures, it expires in May 2006, on the first Friday preceding, by *at least* two business days, June 1, 2006. The CBT also lists a "front month" contract, if the front month is not a quarterly expiration. This means that standing at the end of June 2006, there will be a July 2006 T-bond futures option contract, however, it is written on the September 2006 T-bond futures.

## NO-ARBITRAGE RELATIONS AND VALUATION

Like common stocks and stock indexes, the no-arbitrage price relations and valuation methods are best modeled using a discrete flow carry cost assumption.

**TABLE 17.8** Selected terms of CBT's U.S. Treasury bond futures options contract.

| | |
|---|---|
| Exchange | Chicago Board of Trade |
| Ticker symbol | CG for calls/PG for puts |
| Contract unit | One U.S. T-bond futures (of a specified maturity) having a face value of $100,000 |
| Tick size | 1/64 of a point |
| Tick value | $15.625 per contract |
| Exercise prices | |
| | 1-point strikes for the nearby contract month in a band consisting of the at-the-money, 4 above, and 4 below; 2-point strikes are listed outside this band. Back months are also listed in 2-point strike price intervals. |
| Trading hours | Open outcry: 7:20 AM to 2:00 PM CT, Monday through Friday<br>Electronic: 7:02 PM to 4:00 PM CT, Sunday through Friday |
| Contract months | First three consecutive contract months (two serial expirations and one quarterly expiration) plus the next two months in March quarterly cycle (Mar., Jun., Sep., Dec.). There will always be five months available for trading. Monthlies will exercise into the first nearby quarterly futures contract. Quarterlies will exercise into futures contracts of the same delivery period. |
| Last day of trading | Options cease trading on the last Friday, preceding by at least two business days, the last business day of the month preceding the contract month. |
| Style | American-style. Options that expire in-the-money are automatically exercised. |
| Settlement | Physical delivery of futures position |
| Trading hours | Open outcry: 7:20 AM to 2:00 PM CST, Monday through Friday |

The U.S. Treasury bonds underlying long-term bond futures and options, for example, pay coupons on a semiannual basis, with the amount of the coupon interest payment date as well as the payment date known. The debt instruments underlying short-term bond futures and options (e.g., T-bill and Eurodollar futures and options) make no intermediate coupon payments, in which case the only carry cost is the interest rate.

This section provides a summary of the no-arbitrage price relations and valuation equations of exchange-traded interest rate derivatives. Most of the results are straightforward extensions of the materials developed in Chapters 4 through 9. There are two notable exceptions, however. First, under the no-arbitrage price relations discussion, we are forced to consider the implications of the T-bond futures having eligible for delivery a number of different T-bond issues. Because the CBT's system of conversion does not work exactly as it should, one of the eligible T-bonds winds up being cheapest to deliver, and the cheapest to deliver bond may change through time. We examine how this contract idiosyncracy affects the structure of the net cost of carry relation. Second, the valuation results of Chapters 7 through 9 were based on the assumption that the underlying asset price was log-normally distributed at the option's expiration. While this assumption may be reasonable for options on long-term bonds, it becomes less and less palatable as the term to maturity of the bond becomes short. A T-bill, for example, cannot have a price that exceeds its par value at expiration. To circumvent this problem, we assume interest rates are log-normally distributed at the option's expiration.

### Net Cost of Carry Relation for CBT's T-Bond Futures

Table 17.9 summarizes the no-arbitrage price relations for futures and options written on coupon-bearing bonds. The relations are no different than they were for derivatives on stocks and stocks indexes. In place of the present value of cash dividends, we use the present value of coupons paid during the life of the derivative contract. The cost of carry relation of a bond futures is shown in Table 17.9 as being

$$F = Be^{rT} - FVC \tag{17.2}$$

where $F$ is the futures price, $B$ is the underlying coupon-bearing bond price, $r$ is the continuously compounded risk-free interest rate, $T$ is the time to expiration of the futures, and $FVC$ is the future value of the coupons paid on the bond (if any) during the futures' life. What (17.2) says is that we should be indifferent between (1) buying a coupon-bearing bond futures contract for delivery of the bond at time $T$, and (2) buying the coupon-bearing bond and carrying it with short-term, risk-free borrowings to time $T$. Neither investment alternative involves a cash outlay today. Yet, both alternatives provide the bond at time $T$ at a price known today. Note that $FVC$ is subtracted from the future value of the bond investment on the right-hand side of (17.2) since any coupons paid prior to $T$ are not included in the value of the bond at time $T$.

The net cost of carry relation (17.2) assumes that there is a single asset underlying the futures contract. Such is not the case for the CBT's T-bond futures contract—a number of bonds are eligible for delivery. Since the CBT's T-bond futures is the most active long-term interest rate futures traded in the United States, it is important that we develop an understanding of the cost of carry relation when multiple assets are eligible for delivery.

Before turning to the CBT's T-bond futures contract, it is helpful to be reminded about the bond price reporting conventions described in Chapter 2. In Chapter 2, we define $B$ as the market price of a coupon-bearing bond, that is, the amount that we would pay if we decided to buy the bond. In market parlance, $B$ is called the "gross price," the "full price," and/or the "dirty price" of the bond. What gets reported in the financial pages and displayed on pricing screens, however, is the "quoted price" or the "clean price," $B^-$. The quoted price $B^-$ is the full bond price, $B$, less the accrued interest in the current coupon period, $AI$, that is, $B^- = S - AI$. Since we have to reconcile the T-bond futures pricing relation with observed market prices later in the chapter, it is important to recognize the reporting conventions upfront.

**TABLE 17.9** Summary of no-arbitrage price relations and valuation equations/ methods for derivatives on interest rate products. Valuation equations/ methods are based on the assumption that bond/futures prices are log-normally distributed.

| Arbitrage Relations | | |
|---|---|---|
| **Forward/Futures** | $f = F = Be^{rT} - FVC$ or $fe^{-rT} = Fe^{-rT} = B - PVC$ where $FVC = \sum_{i=1}^{n} C_i e^{(T-t_i)}$ and $PVC = e^{-rT}FVC$ | |
| **European-Style:** | **Options** | **Futures Options** |
| Lower bound for call | $c \geq \max(0, B - PVC - Xe^{-rT})$ | $c \geq \max[0, e^{-rT}(F - X)]$ |
| Lower bound for put | $p \geq \max(0, Xe^{-rT} - B + PVC)$ | $p \geq \max[0, e^{-rT}(X - F)]$ |
| Put-call parity | $c - p = B - PVC - Xe^{-rT}$ | $c - p = e^{-rT}(F - X)$ |
| **American-Style:** | | |
| Lower bound for call | $C \geq \max(0, B - PVC - Xe^{-rT}, B - X)$ | $C \geq \max(0, F - X)$ |
| Lower bound for put | $P \geq \max(0, Xe^{-rT} - B + PVC, X - B)$ | $P \geq \max(0, X - F)$ |
| Put-call parity | $B - PVC - X \leq C - P \leq B - Xe^{-rT}$ | $Fe^{-rT} - X \leq C - P \leq F - Xe^{-rT}$ |
| **Valuation Equations/Methods** | | |
| **European-Style:** | **Options** | **Futures Options** |
| Call value | $c = B^x N(d_1) - Xe^{-rT}N(d_2)$ | $c = e^{-rT}[FN(d_1) - XN(d_2)]$ |
| Put value | $p = Xe^{-rT}N(-d_2) - B^x N(-d_1)$<br>where $B^x = B - PVC$<br>$d_1 = \frac{\ln(B^x/Xe^{-rT}) + 0.5\sigma^2 T}{\sigma\sqrt{T}}$ and $d_2 = d_1 - \sigma\sqrt{T}$ | $p = e^{-rT}[XN(-d_2) - FN(-d_1)]$<br>where $d_1 = \frac{\ln(F/X) + 0.5\sigma^2 T}{\sigma\sqrt{T}}$ and $d_2 = d_1 - \sigma\sqrt{T}$ |
| **American-Style:** | | |
| Call and put values | Numerical valuation: binomial and trinomial methods. | Numerical valuation: quadratic approximation, and binomial and trinomial methods. |

**Cheapest-to-Deliver at Futures Expiration** To see how the CBT's system *should* work, suppose we are standing on the expiration day of the futures contract $T$ and consider the profit from selling the futures and buying and delivering eligible bond $i$. In the absence of costless arbitrage opportunities, all bonds should have a realized profit of 0, that is,

$$\pi_{i,T} = F_T(CF_i) + AI_{i,T} - \bar{B}_{i,T} - AI_{i,T} = 0 \quad (17.3)$$

for all eligible bonds, where $F_T(CF_i) + AI_{i,T}$ is the invoice price received from delivering bond $i$ and $\bar{B}_{i,T} + AI_{i,T}$ is the price paid for the purchase of bond $i$. In practice, however, each bond will have a different value of $\pi_{i,T}$ because the CBT's system of conversion factors for the T-bond futures is not exact. All of the values of $\pi_{i,T}$ will be less than or equal to zero. The bond with the highest value of $\pi_{i,T}$ is called the "cheapest to deliver," and its $\pi_{i,T}$ will be equal to zero. The other bonds are said to be "more expensive to deliver" because the proceeds from the sale of the bond, $F_T(CF_i) + AI_{i,T}$, are less than the price paid for the bond that we are delivering, $\bar{B}_{i,T} + AI_{i,T}$. Instinctively, we might think that an arbitrage profit is possible by reversing the trades (i.e., buying the futures and selling the bond) when $\pi_{i,T} < 0$. That intuition does not apply here since it is the individual who is short the futures that has the right to decide which bond to deliver. The individual who is long the futures contract has no say. None of the bonds will have $\pi_{i,T} > 0$ because that would imply that a costless arbitrage profit could be earned by buying the bond, selling the futures, and then delivering the bond on the futures commitment.

The technical reason why a single T-bond will be cheapest to deliver bond is that the CBT's conversion factors are computed assuming the zero-coupon yield curve is a flat 6% (i.e., $y = 0.06$ in (17.1)). Such a valuation procedure implicitly assumes that all coupon payments are reinvested as they are received at 6% yield until the end of the bond's life. If the current zero-coupon yield curve implies that the reinvestment rates for coupon payments are higher than 6%, the CBT's conversion factor will be too low for high-coupon bonds relative to low coupon bonds, hence low coupon bonds will be the preferred bonds to deliver. On the other hand, if the current zero-coupon yield curve implies that the reinvestment rates for coupon payments are lower than 6%, high-coupon bonds will be delivered.

**ILLUSTRATION 17.1** Identify cheapest to deliver bond at futures expiration.

*Suppose that three bonds with 15 years to maturity are eligible for delivery on the CBT's T-bond futures contract. They have coupon rates of 3%, 6%, and 9%, respectively. The conversion factors of the bonds are 0.7060, 1.000, and 1.2940, respectively. Identify the cheapest to deliver bond assuming the zero-coupon yield curve is a flat 6%. Then, assume the current zero-coupon yield curve is a flat 8% and identify the cheapest to deliver bond. Explain the results.*

*6% yield curve.* With a 6% yield curve, the value of the 3%, 6% and 9% coupon bonds are

$$B_{3\%} = \sum_{t=1}^{30} \frac{1.5}{1.03^t} + \frac{100}{1.03^{30}} = 70.60$$

$$B_{6\%} = \sum_{t=1}^{30} \frac{3.0}{1.03^t} + \frac{100}{1.03^{30}} = 100.00$$

and

$$B_{9\%} = \sum_{t=1}^{30} \frac{4.5}{1.03^t} + \frac{100}{1.03^{30}} = 129.40$$

The CBT's system of conversion attempts to put all of these bonds on an equal footing with respect to being delivered on its T-bond futures contract. To translate each of these coupon-bearing bonds to a 6% coupon bond, we divide their values by the CBT's conversion factors to identify their implied values had they had 6% coupon rates. The results are shown in the table that follows. At a flat 6% yield to maturity, we are indifferent about which of the three bonds to deliver. All bonds have implied values equal to 100. In this case, the CBT's conversion factors work precisely as they should.

| Bond | Bond Value at Yield of 6% | CBT Conversion Factor | Implied Value if 6% Coupon |
|---|---|---|---|
| 3% | 70.60 | 0.7060 | 100.00 |
| 6% | 100.00 | 1.0000 | 100.00 |
| 9% | 129.40 | 1.2940 | 100.00 |

*8% yield curve.* With an 8% yield curve, the bond values and implied values are shown in the table below. The 3% coupon-bearing bond, for example, has a value of 56.77, that is,

$$B_{9\%} = \sum_{t=1}^{30} \frac{1.5}{1.04^t} + \frac{100}{1.04^{30}} = 56.77$$

and an implied value of 80.41, that is,

$$56.77/0.7060 = 80.41$$

The implied values of the 6% and 9% coupon bonds are 82.71 and 83.96. Obviously, we would prefer to deliver the 3% bonds, since they have the lowest value.

| Bond | Bond Value at Yield of 6% | CBT Conversion Factor | Implied Value if 6% Coupon | Modified Conversion Factor | Modified Value if 6% Coupon |
|---|---|---|---|---|---|
| 3% | 56.77 | 0.7060 | 80.41 | 0.6864 | 82.708 |
| 6% | 82.71 | 1.0000 | 82.71 | 1.0000 | 82.708 |
| 9% | 108.65 | 1.2940 | 83.96 | 1.3136 | 82.708 |

The last two columns in the previous table identify the problem. When the yield to maturity was 6%, the value of the 3% bond relative to the value of the 6% bond was 70.60/100.00 = 0.7060, exactly equal to the CBT's conversion factor. When the yield rises to 8%, the values of the bonds change relative to the 6% issue. At an 8% yield, holding a 3% coupon bond is like holding only 0.6864 6% bonds, and, holding a 9% is like holding 1.3136 6% bonds. If these "modified conversion factors" were used, all bonds would again be put on an equal footing for delivery purposes.

**Cheapest-to-Deliver Prior to Futures Expiration** Before maturity, as at maturity, the futures price is based on the price of the cheapest to deliver, and the cheapest to deliver is determined by finding the bond with the highest "cash-and-carry" portfolio[6] profit $\pi_{i,T}$,

$$\pi_{i,T} = F_0(CF_i) + AI_{i,T} + C_{i,t}e^{r(T-t)} - (B_{i,0}^- + AI_{i,0})e^{rT} \tag{17.4}$$

Note that (17.3) and (17.4) differ in some subtle ways. First, the futures price has a time subscript 0 to indicate that we are talking about today's price. The term $F_0(CF_i) + AI_{i,T}$ is the invoice price of the bond or the cash proceeds that we will receive from the sale of bond $i$ when the futures contract expires. The term $(B_{i,0}^- + AI_{i,0})e^{rT}$ is the price that we paid for the bond at time 0 carried forward until time $T$ at the risk-free rate of interest $r$. Finally, assuming a coupon interest payment was made at time $t$ before the futures expiration (i.e., $t < T$), we invest the coupon at the risk-free rate of interest until time $T$ and its contribution to the cash-and-carry portfolio profit is $C_{i,t}e^{r(T-t)}$. If no coupon is paid on bond $i$ before futures expiration, this term disappears. If we calculate the cash-and-carry profit for all bonds eligible for delivery, we will get an array of values less than 0. The cheapest-to-deliver bond is the one with the highest cash-and-carry profit, and its value will be near zero.

**Net Cost of Carry Relation** The cash-and-carry profit equation (17.4) allows us to specify the net cost of carry relation for the T-bond futures contract. With a single T-bond $i$ eligible for delivery, the relation can be obtained by setting the cash-and-carry profit equation (17.4) equal to 0 and solving for $F_0$, that is,

$$F_0 = \frac{(B_{i,0}^- + AI_{i,0})e^{rT} - AI_{i,T} - C_{i,t}e^{r(T-t)}}{CF_i} \tag{17.5}$$

But, many T-bonds are eligible for delivery and (17.4) is less than 0, even for the T-bond that is currently cheapest to deliver since there is no assurance that this bond will also be cheapest to deliver when the futures contract expires on day $T$. Consequently, the net cost of carry relation for the T-bond futures contract must be expressed as the inequality,

$$F_0 < \frac{(B_{i,0}^- + AI_{i,0})e^{rT} - AI_{i,T} - C_{i,t}e^{r(T-t)}}{CF_i} \tag{17.6}$$

The net cost of carry relation may also be written in a manner that explicitly recognizes the value of the *quality option*. The term "quality option" arose in the context of grain futures contracts, which allow the individual who is short the futures to deliver one of a number of different grades of a particular grain. The CBT's corn futures contract, for example, calls for the delivery of No. 2 yel-

[6] In this context, a cash-and-carry portfolio refers to buying the underlying T-bond, financing its purchase at the risk-free rate of interest, and selling the T-bond futures contract.

low corn at par, but also permits the delivery of No. 1 yellow at a 1½ cent premium over the futures contract price, and No. 3 yellow at a 1½ cent discount below the contract price. Come delivery day, the individual who is short the futures will be naturally choose to deliver the grade that is "cheapest."

The same situation arises with the T-bond futures contract. While the short may have entered a cash-and-carry position when bond $i$ was cheapest to deliver, he will deliver bond $j$ at maturity if its conversion price is below bond $i$'s, thereby earning a profit equal to the difference between the two prices. Thus the net cost of carry relation is

$$F_0 = \frac{(B_{i,0}^{-} + AI_{i,0})e^{rT} - AI_{i,T} - C_{i,t}e^{r(T-t)}}{CF_i} - \text{Quality option}_i \tag{17.7}$$

where bond $i$ is the current cheapest to deliver.[7]

**ILLUSTRATION 17.2** Value quality option embedded in T-bond futures.

*Suppose that there exist two bonds that are eligible for delivery on the T-bonds futures contract. Bond A has a 6% coupon rate, one month remaining until the next coupon payment is made, a full price of 95, a conversion factor of 1.0000, and a volatility rate of 12%. Bond B has an 8% coupon rate, four months remaining until the next coupon payment is made, a full price of 107, a conversion factor of 1.2311, and a volatility rate of 15%. The correlation between rates of return of the two bonds is 0.9. The T-bond futures has a time to expiration of three months, and the risk-free interest rate is 4%. Find the cheapest-to-deliver bond as well as the value of the quality option when the T-bond futures is priced off the cheapest-to-deliver.*

To identify the cheapest-to-deliver bond, we need to compute the implied futures price for each bond the first term on the right-hand side of (17.7). Bond A has an implied futures price of

$$IF_A = \frac{95e^{0.04(0.25)} - (6/2)e^{0.04(0.25-0.08333)}}{1.0000} = 92.935$$

Bond B has an implied futures price of

$$IF_B = \frac{107e^{0.04(0.25)}}{1.2311} = 87.874$$

Since bond B has the lowest implied futures price, it is currently the cheapest to deliver.

The individual who is short the futures contract currently plans to deliver the 8% coupon bond at the futures' expiration. There is some possibility, however, that the 6% coupon bond will become cheapest to deliver by the end of three months. If it does, the short futures will deliver the 6% bond. This "right-to-switch" or "quality option" can be valued using the exchange option valuation formula (8.20) from Chapter 8. In this particular case, the quality option is a put option that allows the short futures to deliver the first bond instead of the second if its implied futures price is less at the futures expiration.

---

[7] The value of the quality option can be computed using the exchange option valuation framework of Margrabe (1978) model. Recall that we applied the same framework in valuing call options with an indexed exercise price in Chapter 8.

To value this option, we need to recognize the fact that the value of a call option to buy asset 1 with asset 2 equals the value of a put option to sell asset 2 for asset 1. Under the first case, the option holder exercises the call if the price of asset 1 exceeds asset 2 at expiration. Under the second case, the option holder exercises the put if the price of asset 2 is below the price of asset 1 at expiration. The value of the quality option is therefore

$$p = 87.784e^{-0.04(0.25)}N(d_1) - 92.935e^{-0.04(0.25)}N(d_2) = 0.055$$

where

$$d_1 = \frac{\ln(87.784/92.935) + 0.5(0.0671^2)0.25}{0.0671\sqrt{0.25}}, \quad d_2 = d_1 - 0.0671\sqrt{0.25}$$

$$\sqrt{0.12^2 + 0.15^2 - 2(0.90)(0.12)(0.15)} = 0.0671$$

This value can be verified using the OPTVAL Library function,

OV_FOPTION_VALUE_EXCHANGE(92.935,87.784,0.25,0.04,0.12,0.15,0.9, “p”) = 0.055

The short futures also has a *timing option* that gives a choice about when during the contract month to deliver. The most valuable element in the timing option is called the *wildcard option.* In the delivery month the futures price at which delivery is made is the settlement price established at 2:00 PM when the market closes. The short has until 8:00 PM to declare delivery. Obviously, if news arrives that justifies a decline in bond prices, the short will choose to make delivery at the already established settlement price.

**Repurchase Agreements**[8] In discussing the net cost of carry relation for the T-bond futures contract, we used a risk-free rate of interest $r$. For T-bonds, it is important to digress and describe the most common form of financing the purchase of T-bonds, that is, a *sale repurchase agreement* (also known as a *repurchase agreement* or, simply, a *repo*).[9] A repo agreement is a single transaction with two separate trade confirmations: the first is the *sale* of the bond for immediate settlement, and the second is the *repurchase* of the bond for settlement at some future date. The repurchase price is known at the time the agreement is entered, and the difference between the repurchase price and the sales price is the interest on the loan. Specifically,

[8] More detailed discussions of repurchase and reverse repurchase agreements are provided in Stigum (1990, pp. 576-79), Fabozzi (1996, 131–135), and Tuckman (2002, pp. 303–10).

[9] Originally, just after World War II, repurchase agreements were used only for the purchase and sale of highly creditworthy and liquid debt securities such as U.S. Treasuries. Over time, the range of credits expanded to include collateral such as agency bonds and even investment grade corporate bonds. By the mid- to late 1990s, even speculative corporate bonds were being reversed out by hedge funds. The practice of reversing out “junk” bonds came to a screeching halt in the aftermath of the collapse of Long-Term Capital Management and the Asian debt crisis in 1997.

$$\text{Repurchase price} = \text{Sales price} \times \left[1 + \text{Repo rate}\left(\frac{n}{360}\right)\right] \tag{17.8}$$

where $n$ is the number of days the repo is outstanding.[10] Thus the *repo rate* is the implicit rate of interest paid by the borrower to the lender. A repo with a term of one day is called an *overnight repo* and carries an interest rate called the *overnight repo rate*. Repos (rates on repos) with more than one day to maturity are called *term repos* (*term repo rates*). Repo rates are negotiated on a transaction by transaction basis and vary depending on such factors as the term of the repo and the credit-quality of the underlying collateral.

Why would a borrower choose to finance the purchase of the bond with a repo agreement rather than simply borrowing the money from the bank? The answer is that it is cheaper. From an economic perspective, a repurchase agreement is a collateralized loan.[11] The borrower posts his bond to the lender as collateral during the life of the agreement, and, in the event of default, the lender has the right to immediately sell the bond in the marketplace to cover his losses. By attaching specific collateral to the loan, the borrower garners a lower rate of interest. Why would a lender choose to enter a repo agreement rather than buy T-bills or money market instruments? The answer is that repo rates are generally higher than comparable term instruments and yet remain highly liquid, secured investments.[12]

The repo market carries with it a goodly amount of Wall Street jargon. In the interest of completeness, we will consider some of it. While the borrower is said to enter a *repurchase agreement,* the lender is said to enter a *reverse repurchase agreement* (also known as a *reverse repo* or, simply, a *reverse*). By lending his securities to provide collateral for the loan, the borrower is said to be *reversing out* securities or *selling collateral*. On the other hand, in accepting the collateral on the loan, the lender is said to be *reversing in* securities or *buying collateral*. The borrower is said *to repo securities*; the lender is said *to do a repo*.

Despite the fact that the collateral underlying repo agreements is generally high quality, repos are carefully structured to reduce credit risk. One way of controlling credit risk is to apply a *haircut* to the purchase price of the security to

[10] Like T-bills and Eurodollar time deposits, repo rate quotes adopt the banker's convention of a 360-day year

[11] The term *collateralized loan* is not meant to have any legal interpretation. Indeed, it is unclear whether a repo agreement is collateralized borrowing or a sequence of securities trades. If it were collateralized borrowing, the lender's right to sell the borrower's collateral immediately in the event of default may be restricted to protect the borrower's other creditors.

[12] Municipalities are frequent lenders in the repo market to manage their cash flows. Tax revenue is collected only periodically during the year. At the time of tax collection, the municipality has no immediate need for the cash. Repo agreements offer the municipality the ability to earn interest at competitive short-term rates with the safety of being secured loans until the cash needs to be disbursed. In addition, although the Federal Reserve removed interest rate ceilings on term deposits at commercial banks on March 31, 1986, it maintained the requirement that no interest be paid on demand deposits. (For a historical recount of the phase-out of Regulation Q, see Gilbert (1986).) Overnight repos are a convenient way to earn interest on what amounts to a demand deposit.

protect the lender from adverse market movements. A 5% haircut means that only 95% of the price of the bond is borrowed, with the bond held as collateral. The size of the haircut (i.e., the *amount of the margin*) will depend on the level of creditworthiness of the borrower, as well as the price risk, default risk, and liquidity of the collateral. Another way to control credit risk for term repos is to *mark-to-market* the collateral on a periodic (e.g., daily) basis. Suppose that a bond dealer has a haircut provision of 5% and securities with a market value of $100 million. By reversing out securities in the repo market, he can effectively borrow $95 million. Now, suppose that the market value of the securities drops to $99 million on the next day. Clearly, the lender is in a more precarious position given that the worth of the collateral has fallen. When this happens, the repo agreement may specify that there will be a *margin call*, in which case the borrower will be required to post additional $1 million in market value of collateral to bring the level back up to $100 million. Alternatively, the repo agreement may *reprice* the repo, in which case the principal amount of the repo is reduced from $100 million to $99 million and the borrower pays the lender $950,000 (i.e., 95% of $1 million). For ease of exposition, we ignore haircuts and the marketing-to-market features that may appear in repurchase agreements in this section. We also transform the repo rate to a continuously-compounded rate of interest, that is,

$$r = \frac{\ln\left[1 + \text{Repo rate}\left(\frac{n}{360}\right)\right]}{(n/365)}$$

To perform this computation, the OPTVAL library contains the function,

OV_IR_CONV_REPO_YIELD(*rate, days*)

where *rate* is the repo rate, and *days* is the term of the repo agreement in days.

**Duration of the CBT's T-Bond Futures** The duration of a futures contract is closely tied to the duration of the cheapest-to-deliver T-bond. To develop a formal relation, assume, for simplicity, that no coupons are paid during the futures' life and that the value of the quality option equals zero. Under these simplifying assumptions, the net cost-of-carry relation (17.7) may be rewritten as

$$F = \frac{Be^{rT}}{CF} \tag{17.9}$$

where $B$ and $CF$ are the price and the conversion factor of the cheapest-to-deliver bond. The change in the futures price with respect to a change in the level of interest rates $r$ is

$$\frac{dF}{dr} = \frac{dBe^{rT}}{dr\,CF} + \frac{BTe^{rT}}{CF} \tag{17.10}$$

Dividing the left-hand side by $F$ and the right-hand side by $Be^{rT}/CF$, and simplifying, we get

$$\frac{dF/F}{dr} = \frac{dB/B}{dr} + T \tag{17.11}$$

In other words, the duration of the futures equals the duration of the cheapest-to-deliver bonds plus the term to maturity of the futures. The futures provides the underlying bond, but with deferred delivery.

### Option Valuation Equations Under Log-Normal Bond Prices

The valuation methods derived in Chapters 7 through 9 assume that the asset underlying the option has a log-normal price distribution at the option's expiration. For options on long-term bonds or long-term bond futures, the assumption is reasonable. Such is the case for many traders in the CBT's T-bond futures option pit, who use the BSM model to make markets in options.[13]

**ILLUSTRATION 17.3** Compute implied volatility from T-bond futures option price.

*The CBT's options on T-bond futures are American-style, and expire the Friday, preceding by at least two business days, the last business day of the month preceding the contract month. (See Table 17.9.) At the close on Friday, October 11, 2002, the December 2002 futures price was 112-10, and the December 2002 options on the December 2002 futures have prices as follows:*

| Exercise Prices | Prices (in 64ths) Call | Put |
|---|---|---|
| 110 | 3-26 | 1-06 |
| 111 | 2-49 | 1-29 |
| 112 | 2-13 | 1-57 |
| 113 | 1-46 | 2-26 |
| 114 | 1-20 | 3-00 |
| 115 | 0-63 | 3-43 |

*The risk-free interest rate is 1.772%. Compute the implied volatility for each reported option price using the quadratic approximation. Comment on the nature of the "implied volatility smile."*

The first step is to translate prices to decimal form. The futures price is reported in (32nds), so 112-10 becomes 112.3125. The option prices are reported in 64ths, so the values shown in the previous table are:

[13] Recall that the BSM formula reduces to the Black (1976) formula for valuating European-style futures options. A popular way of valuing American-style futures options is the quadratic approximation provided in Whaley (1986).

| Exercise Prices | Prices (in 64ths) | | Prices (in decimal) | |
|---|---|---|---|---|
| | Call | Put | Call | Put |
| 110 | 3-26 | 1-06 | 3.406250 | 1.093750 |
| 111 | 2-49 | 1-29 | 2.765625 | 1.453125 |
| 112 | 2-13 | 1-57 | 2.203125 | 1.890625 |
| 113 | 1-46 | 2-26 | 1.718750 | 2.406250 |
| 114 | 1-20 | 3-00 | 1.312500 | 3.000000 |
| 115 | 0-63 | 3-43 | 0.984375 | 3.671875 |

The next step is to deduce the number of days to expiration. The last Friday, preceding by at least two business days the last business day of the month preceding the contract month is November 22, 2002, and the number of days to expiration is therefore 42.

Finally, we use the OV_OPTION_ISD function to compute the implied volatilities.[14] The results are as shown in the following table and figure. Note that the implied volatilities for calls and puts are approximately equal and that implied volatilities decrease modestly with exercise price.

| Exercise Prices | Prices (in 64ths) | | Prices (in decimal) | | Implied Volatility | |
|---|---|---|---|---|---|---|
| | Call | Put | Call | Put | Call | Put |
| 110 | 3-26 | 1-06 | 3.406250 | 1.093750 | 0.1365 | 0.1362 |
| 111 | 2-49 | 1-29 | 2.765625 | 1.453125 | 0.1355 | 0.1354 |
| 112 | 2-13 | 1-57 | 2.203125 | 1.890625 | 0.1349 | 0.1348 |
| 113 | 1-46 | 2-26 | 1.718750 | 2.406250 | 0.1343 | 0.1344 |
| 114 | 1-20 | 3-00 | 1.312500 | 3.000000 | 0.1338 | 0.1340 |
| 115 | 0-63 | 3-43 | 0.984375 | 3.671875 | 0.1338 | 0.1341 |

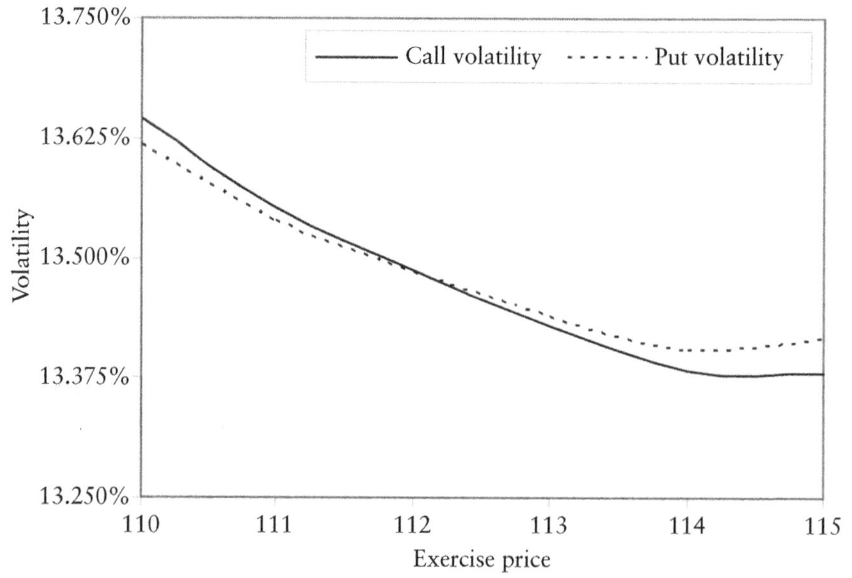


[14] OV_OPTION_ISD uses the quadratic approximation for American-style options.

### Option Valuation Equations Under Log-Normal Interest Rates

For most assets, the assumption that the underlying asset has a lognormal price distribution at the option's expiration works well. For options on short-term debt instruments such as T-bill or Eurodollar futures, it does not. The log-normal price distribution is inappropriate because it allows prices to become infinitely high. T-bills and Eurodollar futures prices cannot exceed 100. To circumvent this problem, we assume that the yield, rather than the price, of the short-term debt instrument is log-normally distributed at the option's expiration. Under this assumption, the yield can fall to zero, in which case the market price of the short-term debt instrument becomes its predetermined maturity value. On the other hand, if the yield rises without limit, the market price of the debt instrument converges to zero.

To illustrate this option valuation approach, we focus on the CME's Eurodollar futures options. Although these options are American-style, we will assume that they are European-style for expositional convenience. Aside from the assumption that the forward Eurodollar rate is log-normally distributed at the end of the option's life, we invoke the same assumptions that we used in Chapters 7 through 9. In particular, since both the futures and futures options are actively traded, we adopt risk-neutral valuation.

Under risk-neutral valuation, the current value of a European-style Eurodollar futures option today is the present value of the expected future terminal value, that is,

$$c = e^{-rT}E(\tilde{c}_T) \tag{17.12}$$

where the expected terminal value is discounted to the present at the zero-coupon rate corresponding to the expiration of the option. The terminal value of the option is, in turn, a function of the Eurodollar futures index level, $F_T$, that is,

$$\tilde{c}_T = \begin{cases} \tilde{F}_T - X & \text{if } F_T > X \\ 0 & \text{if } F_T > X \end{cases} \tag{17.13}$$

If the terminal futures price is log-normally distributed, we would evaluate $E(\tilde{c}_T)$ in the same manner as we did in Chapter 7. With the forward Eurodollar rate, $R$, being log-normally distributed, however, we must rewrite the option's payoff function as

$$\tilde{c}_T = \begin{cases} (100 - X) - \tilde{R}_T & \text{if } R_T < 100 - X \\ 0 & \text{if } R_T \geq 100 - X \end{cases} \tag{17.14}$$

where we have merely substituted the fact that the Eurodollar futures price is an index level created by subtracting the Eurodollar rate from 100, that is, $F = 100 - R$. But, equation (17.14) looks surprisingly familiar. It is the terminal value function of a European put option where $\tilde{R}_T$ has replaced $\tilde{S}_T$ and where $100 - X$ has replaced

$X$. Since $R_T$ is log-normally distributed, the BSM European-style put option formula from Chapter 5 can be applied directly. The expected terminal call price is

$$E(\tilde{c}_T) = (100 - X)N(-d_2) - (100 - F)N(-d_1) \tag{17.15}$$

where

$$d_1 = \frac{\ln[(100 - F)/(100 - X)] + 0.5\sigma_R^2 T}{\sigma_R \sqrt{T}} \text{ and } d_2 = d_1 - \sigma_R \sqrt{T}$$

where $\sigma_R$ is the standard deviation of the logarithm of the yield ratios, $\ln(R_t/R_{t-1})$. Substituting (17.15) into (17.12), we find that the value of a European-style call option on a Eurodollar futures contract is

$$c = e^{-rT}[(100 - X)N(-d_2) - (100 - F)N(-d_1)] \tag{17.16}$$

By virtue of put-call parity for European-style futures options, the value of a European-style put option on a Eurodollar futures contract is

$$p = e^{-rT}[(100 - F)N(-d_1) - (100 - X)N(-d_2)] \tag{17.17}$$

**ILLUSTRATION 17.4** Compute implied volatility from Eurodollar futures option price.

*The CME's options on Eurodollar futures are American-style, and expire the second London business day before the third Wednesday of the contract month. At the close on Friday, October 11, 2002, the December 2002 futures price was 98.30, and the December 2002 options on the December 2002 futures have prices as follows:*

| | Prices (in decimal) | |
|---|---|---|
| Exercise Prices | Call | Put |
| 9775 | 0.5575 | 0.0075 |
| 9800 | 0.3175 | 0.0175 |
| 9825 | 0.1450 | 0.0950 |
| 9850 | 0.0650 | 0.2650 |
| 9875 | 0.0250 | 0.4750 |
| 9900 | 0.0125 | 0.7100 |

*The risk-free interest rate is 1.771%. Compute the implied volatility for each reported option price using the European-style option valuation formula. Comment on the nature of the "implied volatility smile."*

The first step in this illustration is to deduce the number of days to expiration. The second London business day before the third Wednesday of the contract month is December 16, 2002, and the number of days to expiration is therefore 66.

Using the OV_OPTION_ISD function to compute the implied volatilities, we find:

| | Prices (in decimal) | | Implied Volatility | |
|---|---|---|---|---|
| Exercise Prices | Call | Put | Call | Put |
| 9775 | 0.5575 | 0.0075 | 0.4260 | 0.4074 |
| 9800 | 0.3175 | 0.0175 | 0.3466 | 0.3409 |
| 9825 | 0.1450 | 0.0950 | 0.4065 | 0.4059 |
| 9850 | 0.0650 | 0.2650 | 0.5309 | 0.5337 |
| 9875 | 0.0250 | 0.4750 | 0.6368 | 0.6479 |
| 9900 | 0.0125 | 0.7100 | 0.8200 | 0.8162 |

As the figure that follows shows, the implied volatilities for calls and puts are approximately the same even though the options are American-style. At very low exercise prices, however, there is a slight difference. At these exercise prices, the call is in the money, and the implied volatility is higher because the early exercise premium of the option is being ignored. Interestingly, a similar pattern does not appear for puts at high exercise prices.

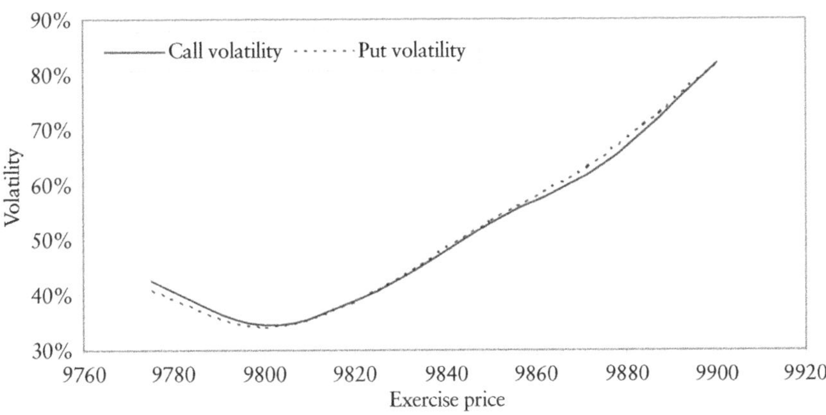


## RISK MANAGEMENT APPLICATIONS

This section focuses on some straightforward interest rate risk management problems using exchange-traded interest rate products. Many other interest rate strategies are discussed in Chapters 18 and 19.

### Short-Term, Long Hedge

Interest rate futures can be used to lock in forward interest rates. Suppose, for example, that on August 31, 2000 a company anticipates a cash inflow of $5,000,000 the following September 18, 2000. The cash, when it is received will be placed in a three-month certificate of deposit until December when it will be used to partially finance a major capital expenditure that the firm plans. Suppose also that the company's financial analyst expects short-term three-month CD rates to fall to a level of 5.5% by December, while the current implied three-month forward rate of the September 2000 Eurodollar futures based on its reported price of 93.32 is 6.68%. What can the company do to lock in the higher rate of interest?

Buying and selling Eurodollar futures contracts are a cost-efficient means of locking-in forward rates of interest. The solution to this problem is to buy five September 2000 Eurodollar futures at 93.32. To see how we have locked-in the 6.68% rate, consider what happens on September 18 when the Eurodollar futures expires. If the three-month rate is 5% at that time, the September 2000 futures will be priced at 95.00. That means we will have posted a gain of (9500 – 9332) × \$25 = \$21,000. We take this gain as well as the \$5 million cash payment and deposit them at the 5% interest rate. At the end of three months, the terminal value of our deposit is

$$\$5{,}021{,}000[1 + 0.05(91/360)] = \$5{,}084{,}459.86$$

Thus the simple rate of return on the \$5 million cash flow over the three-month period is

$$\$5{,}084{,}459.86/\$5{,}000{,}000 = 1.6892\%$$

and the nominal interest rate on an annualized basis is

$$1.6892\%\left(\frac{360}{91}\right) \approx 6.68\%$$

as promised.

### Long-Term, Short Hedge

In Chapter 2, we discussed hedging long-term interest rate risk exposure using duration-based techniques. We now modify these techniques to use futures contracts as the hedge instrument. Hedging means finding the number of futures to buy or sell such that the value of the overall hedged portfolio does not change if interest rates change, that is,

$$\Delta B_P + n_F \Delta F = 0$$

where $\Delta B_P$ and $\Delta F$ are the changes in value of your bond position and the futures resulting from a change in interest rates, $\Delta y$. Duration-based hedging means approximating the change the changes of value with the product of duration and bond value, that is,

$$D_P B_P + n_F D_F F = 0$$

where $D_P$ and $D_F$ are durations of the bond portfolio and the futures contract, respectively. The number of units of the hedge instrument to buy or sell is therefore given by

$$n_F = -\frac{D_P B_P}{D_F B_F}$$

**ILLUSTRATION 17.5** Short hedge bond portfolio with long-term interest rate risk.

*Suppose we currently manage a \$50 million bond portfolio with a duration of 10.00. Suppose also that the T-bond futures contract has a duration of 12.50 and a price of 99⁷⁄₃₂. Find the futures hedge that completely negates the long-term interest rate risk exposure.*

The optimal number of futures contracts to sell is

$$n_F = -\frac{10 \times 50{,}000{,}000}{12.50 \times 99.21875 \times 1{,}000} = -411.44$$

Once the hedge is in place, the combination of long bonds and short futures should behave as if it were \$50 million invested in T-bills.

**Equivalence of Duration-Based and OLS Regression Approaches** The duration-based approach to hedging formula derived above shows the optimal number of futures to sell against a long position in bonds is

$$h^* = -\frac{D_B B}{D_F F}$$

Yet, in the minimum variance hedging discussion of Chapter 5, we argued that the optimal hedge ratio is $-\alpha_1$ in an OLS regression of the changes in bond portfolio value on the changes in the value of the T-bond futures, that is,

$$\Delta B = \alpha_0 + \alpha_1 \Delta F + \varepsilon$$

Can these seemingly disparate results be reconciled?

To understand that these results are essentially the same, rewrite the duration-based optimal hedge ratio as follows:

$$h^* = -\frac{D_B B}{D_F F} = \frac{-\frac{\Delta B/B}{\Delta y}B}{-\frac{\Delta F/F}{\Delta y}F} = -\frac{\Delta B}{\Delta F}$$

where the slope coefficient in the regression is also

$$\alpha_1 = \frac{\Delta B}{\Delta F}$$

Thus from an analytical perspective, the results are the same. There will be slight differences in implementation, however, since they use different sources of information.

### Asset Allocation

The *asset allocation* decision refers to the allocation of fund wealth among various asset categories including stocks, bonds (government and corporate), real estate, and so on. Deep and liquid futures markets on the different asset categories provide cost-efficient vehicles for altering temporarily the asset mix or helping unwind or create large asset positions without incurring significant market impact costs.

**ILLUSTRATION 17.6** Adjust asset allocation using futures.

*Suppose that we currently manage a $100 million portfolio consisting of $50 million in stocks and $50 million in long-term government bonds. The stock portfolio is well diversified and has a beta of 1.5. The bond portfolio has a duration of 12. Change the asset allocation of this portfolio from 50% stocks and 50% bonds to 100% stocks using T-bond futures and S&P 500 index futures. Assume the T-bond futures has a duration of 9 and a price of 96. Assume that current S&P 500 index level is 1,500.*

First, we neutralize the long-term interest rate risk exposure. To do so, we sell T-bond futures, the exact number determined by

$$h_{TBF} = -\frac{50{,}000{,}000(12.00)}{9 \times 96.00 \times 1{,}000} = -694.44$$

By selling this number of futures, we eliminate the long-term interest rate risk exposure of the government bonds. What we have done, in essence, is transform the $50 million long-term government bond portfolio into $50 million in T-bills. Hence, as of this moment, the overall portfolio contains $50 million in cash and $50 million in stocks.

The next step is to create $50 million more in stock. We do this using the $50 million in cash and by buying S&P 500 index futures. The number of futures is given by

$$n_F^* = (\beta^* - \beta_P)\left(\frac{P}{S}\right)$$

where $\beta_P$, in this context, is the beta of the T-bills, $\beta^*$ is the desired beta of the portfolio (i.e., 1.5), $P$ is the desired investment in stocks, and $S$ is the market value of one index unit (i.e., the index level times the futures denomination). The number of futures contracts to buy is therefore

$$n_F^* = 1.50\left(\frac{50{,}000{,}000}{1{,}500(250)}\right) = 200$$

The 200 S&P 500 futures together with the $50 million in T-bills creates a $50 million stock portfolio with a beta of 1.50. Together with the $50 million invested in a stock portfolio with a beta of 1.50, we now have $100 million invested in stocks.

## SUMMARY

This chapter discusses exchange-traded interest rate products. Interest rate derivatives are by far the largest derivatives product category, although it may not seem so considering that most of the trading is conducted in the OTC market. The first section of this chapter reviews key contracts in exchange-traded markets. The second section deals with valuation. For the most part, the principles and valuation methods of Chapters 5 through 9 can be applied directly, with two notable exceptions. First, the no-arbitrage price relation for the CBT's T-bond futures must be modified to account for the fact that the seller has an option to deliver any one of a number of eligible bond issues. Second, for options on short-term debt instruments, the log-normal price distribution assumption is clearly inappropriate. The price of a T-bill, for example, can never exceed its par value. Consequently, a new methodology for valuing interest rate options is developed. We rely on an assumption that the short-term interest rate is log-normally distributed. Section three contains three important risk management applications using interest rate derivatives—a short-term long hedge, a long-term short hedge, and asset allocation.

## REFERENCES AND SUGGESTED READINGS

Black, Fischer. 1976. The pricing of commodity contracts. *Journal of Financial Economics* 3 (March): 167–179.

Chance, Donald M., and Michael L. Hemler. 1993. The impact of delivery options on futures prices: A survey. *Journal of Futures Markets* 13 (April): 127–155.

Fabozzi, Frank J., 1996. *Bond Markets, Analysis and Strategies*, 3rd ed. Upper Saddle River NJ: Prentice-Hall.

Gilbert, R. Alton. 1986. Requiem for Regulation Q: What it did and why it passed away. *Federal Reserve Bank of St. Louis* (February): 22–37.

Johnston, Elizabeth T., and John J. McConnell. 1989. Requiem for a market: An analysis of the rise and fall of a financial futures contract. *Review of Financial Studies* 2 (1): 1–23.

Margrabe, William. 1978. The value of an option to exchange one asset for another. *Journal of Finance* 33 (March): 177–186.

Stigum, Marcia. 1990. *The Money Market*, 3rd ed. Homewood, IL: Dow Jones-Irwin.

Stulz, Rene M. 1982. Options on the minimum or maximum of two assets. *Journal of Financial Economics* 10: 161–185.

# 18

# Interest Rate Products: Swaps

The first interest rate swap market originated in the early 1980s. An *interest rate swap* is an agreement between two parties to exchange or "swap" a series of periodic interest payments. The most common interest rate swap, a *plain-vanilla interest rate swap*, is an agreement to exchange payments on fixed rate debt for floating rate debt. An early example occurred in 1982 when Sallie Mae swapped the interest payments on intermediate-term fixed rate debt for floating rate payments indexed to the three-month T-bill yield. In the same year, a USD 300 million seven-year Deutsche Bank bond issue was swapped into USD LIBOR. While we discussed swaps on other types of assets in earlier chapters, interest rate swaps are far and away the largest asset category. As of yearend 2003, interest rate derivatives accounted for 72% of the notional amount of all OTC derivatives outstanding. Of this amount, more than 78% of interest rate derivatives were swaps, with the remaining 22% being split between options (14%) and forwards (8%) as is shown in Figure 18.1.

**FIGURE 18.1** Percentage of total notional amount of single-currency interest-rate derivatives outstanding worldwide on December 2003 by contract type. Total notional amount of interest-rate derivatives is USD 141.99 trillion.

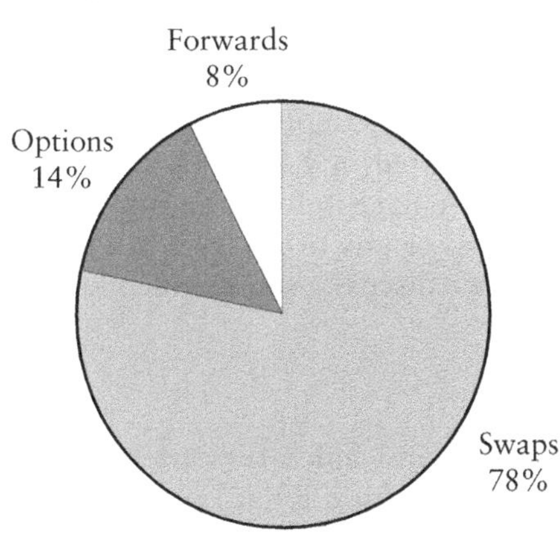


*Source:* The table was constructed from information contained in Bank for International Settlements (www.bis.org), *BIS Quarterly Review*, June 2004.

In general, this chapter deals with OTC interest rate products that have multiple cash flows through time. While plain-vanilla swaps is certainly the largest category within this group, there are also a variety of other instruments including caps, collars, floors, and swaptions. We will address each in turn. Before doing so, however, it is important to develop a thorough understanding of the zero-coupon yield curve and how it is estimated. This is the focus of the first section of this chapter. The second section describes the nature of interest rates swaps and how they are valued. The third and fourth sections focus on caps, collars, and floors, and swaptions, respectively.

## ESTIMATING THE ZERO-COUPON YIELD CURVE

In Chapter 2, we defined the term structure of interest rates (or the zero-coupon yield curve) as the relation between yield and term to maturity for zero-coupon bonds with a common degree of default risk. At the time, we used U.S. Treasury bills and strip bonds to illustrate the shape of the term structure. In the illustrations of the chapters that followed, we assumed that we knew the structure of the zero-coupon yield curve and usually expressed it as some form of mathematical function such as, for example, $r_i = 0.03 + 0.01\ln(1 + T_i)$. The assumption was motivated by the need to have a risk-free, zero-coupon interest rate for all future dates on which there was a cash flow.[1] In this section, we face the problem of determining the zero-coupon yield curve head on.

Estimating the zero-coupon yield curve has two steps. First, we must collect prices of instruments with varying times to maturity but the same degree of default risk. These are usually either U.S. Treasury rates or Eurodollar rates. Within each of these categories, we must choose among available instruments. For U.S. Treasuries, for example, the zero-coupon rates can be estimated using any combination of T-bills, strips, coupon-bearing notes and bonds, and constant maturity Treasury (CMT) rates. For Eurodollars, time-deposit rates, futures prices, and swap rates can all be used. The choice depends on the application at hand and the liquidity of the markets whose rates/prices are being used. From the prices of these instruments, we determine zero-coupon yields for terms to maturity, as is illustrated in Figure 18.2.

The second step involves "smoothing the yield curve." More specifically, we must decide how to estimate zero-coupon rates for cash flows that occur at times other than those represented in Figure 18.2. Consider a cash flow that occurs four years from now. We have only a zero-rate for year three and one for year five. Based on these rates, or any other rates in the figure, what is the best guess of the four-year rate? We discuss two possible methods.

### Identify Zero-Coupon Rates

As was noted earlier, zero-coupon yield curves are most commonly constructed using either U.S. Treasury rates or Eurodollar rates. Below we focus first on estimating the yield curve for Treasuries and then for Eurodollars.

[1] Put differently, we need to know today's prices of one dollar received at all future cash flow dates. These, of course, are the discount factors implied by the zero-coupon yield curve.

**FIGURE 18.2** Zero-coupon rates determined from available interest rate securities and derivative contracts.

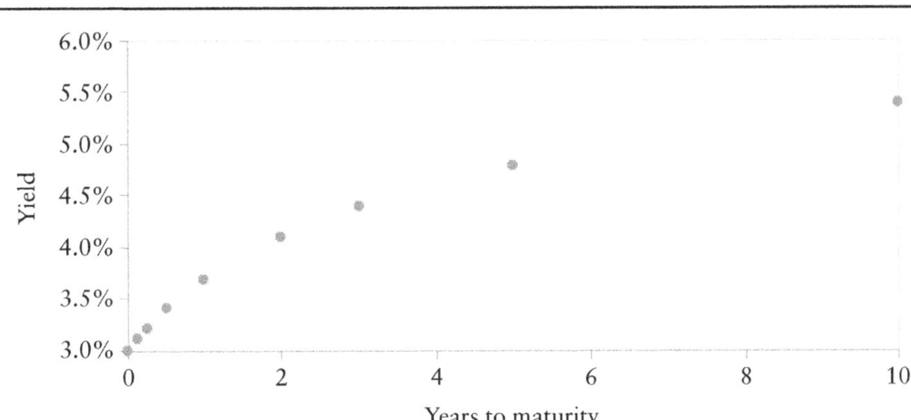


**Treasury Instruments** U.S. Treasury instruments come in a variety of forms. First, at the short-end, there are T-bills. T-bills are discount instruments and therefore have no intermediate interest payments. Each week the U.S. Treasury issues 28-day, 91-day, and 182- T-bills. As noted in Chapter 2, T-bill rates are quoted as a discount from par and use a 360-day banker's year. To compute the continuously-compounded yield to maturity of these discount instruments, we use the formula,

$$r_i = \frac{\ln(100/B_i)}{T_i} \tag{18.1}$$

where $B_i$ is the price of the T-bill, which is determined by taking the bill's quoted discount, $D_i$, and adjusting it by the number of days to maturity, $n_i$, in the following way,

$$B_i = 100 - D_i(n_i/360) \tag{18.2}$$

and $T_i$ is the actual number of years to maturity (i.e., $T_i = n_i/365$). Thus, based on quoted T-bill discount rates, we can identify the dots in Figure 18.2 up until 182 days to maturity.

To go beyond six months, however, we have a variety of alternatives. Strip bonds would be ideal since they have no intermediate coupon payments and their prices can be transformed to zero-coupon interest rates quite easily using (18.1), where $B_i$ represents the strip bond price quote. Unfortunately, the market for strip bonds is not particularly active, so the quote prices are sometimes unreliable. The same is true for most coupon-bearing notes and bonds. Most Treasuries trade actively for a short period of time just after they are issued (called *on-the-run* issues), and then infrequently thereafter (*off-the-run* issues).

In practice, the zero-coupon yield curve for Treasuries is usually constructed from "Constant Maturity Treasury" rates, or CMTs. CMT yields are computed each day by the U.S. Treasury and are intended to represent the yields to maturity of par bonds[2] with 1, 3 and 6 months and 1, 2, 3, 5, 7, 10, and 20 years to maturity. To estimate these rates, the Treasury gathers the closing market bid yields on on-the-run Treasury securities. These market yields are calculated from composites of over-the-counter market quotations obtained by the Federal Reserve Bank of New York each day. Based on these market yields, the Treasury then smoothes the relation between yield and term to maturity,[3] thereby allowing it to estimate rates at the standard maturities listed above. Thus a yield for a 10-year maturity can be computed even if no outstanding security has exactly 10 years remaining to maturity. To generate the zero-coupon yields for all maturities, we "reverse engineer" the CMTs using a technique called "bootstrapping."

In estimating the zero-rates from CMT rates, we must first separate CMTs into two groups—those with maturities of less than a year and those with maturities one year or greater. The reason is that short-term CMTs have no coupon interest payments while the long-term ones do. The following table shows the rates observed as of the close of trading on March 17, 2005. They were obtained from the U.S. Treasury's website at http://www.ustreas.gov/offices/domestic-finance/debt-management/interest-rate/yield.html. These rates will serve as the basis for illustrating the bootstrapping technique as we proceed with its description.

CMT Rates

| Type | Term | Yield |
|---|---|---|
| Months | 1 | 2.68 |
| | 3 | 2.79 |
| | 6 | 3.08 |
| Years | 1 | 3.29 |
| | 2 | 3.70 |
| | 3 | 3.89 |
| | 5 | 4.14 |
| | 7 | 4.30 |
| | 10 | 4.47 |
| | 20 | 4.87 |

To begin, we find the zero-coupon rates corresponding to the 1, 3, and 6 month CMT rates. As was noted above, these are not coupon bonds. There is one payment at the end of the bond's life that includes coupon interest as well as the repayment of principal. The continuously compounded zero-coupon yield to maturity for each of these three CMTs can be computed using

$$r_i = \frac{\ln(1 + (y_i/100)(m_i/12))}{m_i/12} \tag{18.3}$$

[2] A par bond is one whose price equals its face value. For such a bond, the coupon interest rate equals its yield to maturity compounded on a semiannual basis.
[3] The Treasury uses a cubic spline model to smooth the yield curve.

where $y_i$ is the annualized nominal yield to maturity of $CMT_i$, and $m_i$ is its number of months to maturity. For the one-month maturity, for example, the zero-coupon rate is

$$r_i = \frac{\ln(1 + (2.68/100)(1/12))}{1/12} = 2.677\%$$

The rates for three months and six months, together with the one-month rate, are summarized as follows:

**CMT Rates**

| Type | Term | Yield | Zero-Rate |
|---|---|---|---|
| Months | 1 | 2.68 | 2.677% |
| | 2 | 2.79 | 2.780% |
| | 3 | 3.08 | 3.057% |

Now we turn to the coupon-bearing CMT rates. Matters get slightly more complicated. For maturities of one year and greater, the CMT rates are yields on par bonds with semiannual coupon payments. A par bond is one whose price equals its face value. For such a bond, the coupon interest rate equals its yield to maturity compounded on a semiannual basis. This means that each CMT bond may be written as

$$100 = \sum_{i=1}^{n-1} e^{-r_i T_i}\left(\frac{COUP}{2}\right) + e^{r_n T_n}\left(100 + \frac{COUP}{2}\right) \tag{18.4}$$

where $r_i$ is the zero-coupon rate of a bond maturing at time $T_i$, $COUP$ is the annualized coupon rate (i.e., the CMT rate) of the bond under consideration, and $n$ is its number of semiannual coupons. What the bootstrapping technique does is start with the zero-coupon rate at the shortest maturity, and then solve for each new maturity recursively one at a time. Consider the one-year CMT rate. A one-year semiannual coupon CMT reported in the panel above has a yield of 3.29%. Substituting into (18.4), we get

$$100 = \sum_{i=1}^{2-1} e^{-0.03057(0.5)}\left(\frac{3.29}{2}\right) + e^{r_2(1)}\left(100 + \frac{3.29}{2}\right)$$

In this expression, the first term on the right-hand side is the present value of the first semiannual coupon which we can compute because we have already determined that the six-month continuously compounded zero-rate is 3.057%. Since we have one equation and one unknown, we can solve for the one-year zero-coupon rate by rearranging the expression to isolate $r_2$. Its value is 3.265%.

The next available CMT rate has two years to maturity. Substituting into (18.4) we get

$$100 = e^{-0.03057(0.5)}\left(\frac{3.70}{2}\right) + e^{-0.03265(1)}\left(\frac{3.70}{2}\right) + e^{-r_3(1.5)}\left(\frac{3.70}{2}\right) + e^{r_4(2)}\left(100 + \frac{3.70}{2}\right)$$

Now we are in a pickle. We have one equation and need to solve for the 1.5-year and two-year zero-coupon rates. To manage this particular conundrum, we assume that the 1.5 year rate equals the average of the one-year rate and the two-year rate, that is,

$$r_3 = \frac{r_2 + r_4}{2} = \frac{0.03265 + r_4}{2}$$

By imposing this restriction, we can compute $r_4$ and, hence, $r_3$. The two-year zero-rate is 3.676%, and the 1.5-year zero-rate is 3.470%.

From a practical perspective, it is best to go ahead and compute the CMT rates at half year interval from the outset. With the one-year CMT rate at 3.29% and the two-year CMT rate at 3.70%, the 1.5-year CMT rate, computed using linear interpolation, is 3.495%. With the three-year CMT rate at 3.89% and the five-year CMT rate at 4.14%, the 3.5-year CMT rate, computed using linear interpolation, is 3.9525%, and so on. Now, the zero-coupon rates at half-year intervals from one year to 20 years can be determined recursively (i.e., "bootstrapped") one at a time using a re-arranged version of equation (18.4), that is,

$$r_n = \frac{\ln\left(\dfrac{100 - \sum_{i=1}^{n-1} e^{-r_i T_i} COUP/2}{100 + COUP/2}\right)}{T_n} \tag{18.5}$$

The last rate we are able to compute has the same term to maturity as the longest CMT rate.

The bootstrap procedure for deducing zero-coupon rates from CMT rates is programmed as a function in the OPTVAL Function library. Its syntax is

OV_IR_TS_ZERO_FROM_CMT(*months*, *cmtm*, *years*, *cmty*, *rt*)

where *months* is the vector of months to maturity of the CMT rates less than a year, *cmtm* is the vector of rates of the CMT rates less than a year, *years* is the vector of years to maturity of the CMT rates one year or greater, *cmty* is the vector of rates of the CMT rates one year or greater, and *rt* is an indicator variable set to *r* or *R* if the function is to return an array of zero-coupon rates or *t* or *T* if the function is to return an array of the years to maturity of the zeros.[4] To use the function, we highlight cells F3:F14, call the function OV_IR_TS_ZERO_FROM_CMT and insert the necessary inputs, and then press Shift, Ctrl, and Enter simultaneously. The high-

[4] The function returns rates/terms corresponding to the maturities of the monthly input rates and then at half year intervals thereafter.

lighted region will then fill with the zero-coupon rates. Note that the 1.5-year and two-year rates correspond to our computations above.

F3 {=OV_IR_TS_ZERO_FROM_CMT(B3:B5,C3:C5,B6:B9,C6:C9,"R")}

| | A | B | C | D | E | F | G | H | I |
|---|---|---|---|---|---|---|---|---|---|
| 1 | | CMT rates | | | | Zero- | | | |
| 2 | Type | Term | Yield | | Years | rate | | | |
| 3 | Months | 1 | 2.68 | | 0.0833 | 0.02677 | | | |
| 4 | | 3 | 2.79 | | 0.2500 | 0.02780 | | | |
| 5 | | 6 | 3.08 | | 0.5000 | 0.03057 | | | |
| 6 | Years | 1 | 3.29 | | 1.00 | 0.03265 | | | |
| 7 | | 2 | 3.70 | | 1.50 | 0.03470 | | | |
| 8 | | 3 | 3.89 | | 2.00 | 0.03676 | | | |
| 9 | | 5 | 4.14 | | 2.50 | 0.03771 | | | |
| 10 | | | | | 3.00 | 0.03867 | | | |
| 11 | | | | | 3.50 | 0.03930 | | | |
| 12 | | | | | 4.00 | 0.03994 | | | |
| 13 | | | | | 4.50 | 0.04059 | | | |
| 14 | | | | | 5.00 | 0.04124 | | | |

**Eurodollars** For Eurodollars, zero-coupon rates are usually estimated using either (1) Eurodollar time-deposit rates for maturities less than one year and Eurodollar swap rates for one year and beyond; or (2) Eurodollar time-deposit rates for maturities to three months and Eurodollar futures prices beyond three months. If a combination of time-deposit and swap rates is used (approach (1)), the bootstrapping technique described for the CMT rates can be applied once again. Time-deposit rates are nominal interest rates on short-term deposits where interest is paid only at maturity, and swaps rates are essentially the coupon rates of semiannual coupon par bonds. On March 17, 2005, Eurodollar time deposit and swap rates were as follows:

| Eurodollar Time Deposits | | Eurodollar Swap Rates | |
|---|---|---|---|
| Months | Rate | Years | Rate |
| 1 | 2.8281 | 1 | 3.6900 |
| 3 | 3.0156 | 2 | 4.0800 |
| 6 | 3.2656 | 3 | 4.2950 |
| | | 4 | 4.4400 |
| | | 5 | 4.5550 |
| | | 6 | 4.6400 |
| | | 7 | 4.7150 |
| | | 8 | 4.7850 |
| | | 9 | 4.8500 |
| | | 10 | 4.9050 |
| | | 12 | 5.0000 |
| | | 15 | 5.1050 |
| | | 20 | 5.2000 |
| | | 25 | 5.2350 |
| | | 30 | 5.2500 |

The bootstrap procedure for deducing zero-coupon rates from Eurodollar time deposit/swap rates is programmed as a function in the OPTVAL Function library. Its syntax is

OV_IR_TS_ZERO_FROM_SWAP(*months*, *spot*, *years*, *swap*, *rt*)

where *months* is the vector of months to maturity of the time-deposit rates with maturities less than a year, *spot* is the vector of time-deposit rates, *years* is the vector of years to maturity of the swap rates of one year or greater, *swap* is the vector of swap rates, and and *rt* is an indicator variable set to *r* or *R* if the function is to return an array of zero-coupon rates or *t* or *T* if the function is to return an array of the years to maturity of the zeros.[5] To use the function, we highlight cells H3:H14, call the function OV_IR_TS_ZERO_FROM_SWAP and insert the necessary inputs, and then press Shif, Ctrl, and Enter simultaneously. The highlighted region will then fill with the zero-coupon rates.

H3 {=OV_IR_TS_ZERO_FROM_SWAP(A3:A5,B3:B5,D3:D7,E3:E7,"R")}

| | A | B | C | D | E | F | G | H | I |
|---|---|---|---|---|---|---|---|---|---|
| 1 | Eurodollar time deposits | | | Eurodollar swap rates | | | | Zero- | |
| 2 | Months | Rate | | Years | Rate | | Years | rate | |
| 3 | 1 | 2.8281 | | 1 | 3.6900 | | 0.0833 | 2.825% | |
| 4 | 3 | 3.0156 | | 2 | 4.0800 | | 0.25 | 3.004% | |
| 5 | 6 | 3.2656 | | 3 | 4.2950 | | 0.50 | 3.239% | |
| 6 | | | | 4 | 4.4400 | | 1.00 | 3.660% | |
| 7 | | | | 5 | 4.5550 | | 1.50 | 3.854% | |
| 8 | | | | | | | 2.00 | 4.050% | |
| 9 | | | | | | | 2.50 | 4.158% | |
| 10 | | | | | | | 3.00 | 4.267% | |
| 11 | | | | | | | 3.50 | 4.341% | |
| 12 | | | | | | | 4.00 | 4.415% | |
| 13 | | | | | | | 4.50 | 4.474% | |
| 14 | | | | | | | 5.00 | 4.534% | |

Note that we have computed continuously-compounded, zero-coupon rates for Treasuries and Eurodollars with comparable maturities and that the Eurodollar rates are uniformly higher. This reason is simple—credit risk. While both are rates of return on U.S. dollar deposits, Treasury rates are backed by the resources of the U.S. government. Eurodollar rates, on the other hand, are banked by the resources of the British bank where the deposit is held. Note also that the credit risk premium grows larger with term to maturity. This reflects the fact that the probability of default increases with time. While there may be little chance that the bank will default during the next year, there may be a significantly larger risk that it will default over the next 30 years.

[5] This function also returns rates/terms corresponding to the maturities of the monthly input rates and then at half year intervals thereafter.

| | Zero-Coupon Rates | | |
|---|---|---|---|
| Years | Treasuries | Eurodollars | Risk Premium |
| 0.0833 | 2.677% | 2.825% | 0.148% |
| 0.25 | 2.780% | 3.004% | 0.224% |
| 0.50 | 3.057% | 3.239% | 0.183% |
| 1.00 | 3.265% | 3.660% | 0.395% |
| 1.50 | 3.470% | 3.854% | 0.385% |
| 2.00 | 3.676% | 4.050% | 0.374% |
| 2.50 | 3.771% | 4.158% | 0.387% |
| 3.00 | 3.867% | 4.267% | 0.400% |
| 3.50 | 3.930% | 4.341% | 0.410% |
| 4.00 | 3.994% | 4.415% | 0.421% |
| 4.50 | 4.059% | 4.474% | 0.415% |
| 5.00 | 4.124% | 4.534% | 0.410% |

In the Eurodollar market, zero-coupon yields are also often computed using a combination of Eurodollar time-deposit rates and Eurodollar futures prices. The procedure is not unlike the bootstrapping procedure using with CMT and swap rates in the sense that we start with the shortest term to maturity and then add longer maturities, one at a time.[6] First, we identify the rate of interest on a Eurodollar time deposit that matures when the nearby quarterly Eurodollar futures contract settles. Standing on March 17, 2005, the nearby quarterly June futures expires June 15, 2005—in 90 days. The three-month Eurodollar time deposit rate was given earlier in this section and is 3.1056%. The continuously compounded, zero-coupon rate for this maturity is therefore

$$r_{90} = \frac{\ln\left(1 + 0.031056\left(\frac{90}{360}\right)\right)}{90/365} = 3.0460\%$$

Next, we use the settlement price of the June 2005 Eurodollar futures contract, 96.1510 to compute the forward rate on a Eurodollar time deposit that begins on June 15, 2005 and ends when the September 2005 settles on September 21, 2005. The forward rate expressed as a nominal rate is 100 − 96.5150 = 3.4850%. Expressed as a continuously compounded rate, the implied forward rate on a 98-day time deposit beginning in 90 days is

$$r_{98,90} = \frac{\ln\left(1 + 0.034850\left(\frac{98}{360}\right)\right)}{98/365} = 3.5167\%$$

[6] The procedure described here is intended to be illustrative only. We ignore considerations such as two-day settlement, three-month time intervals with varying numbers of days, and convexity.

The 188-day continuously compounded, zero-coupon rate is therefore determined by

$$r_{188}\left(\frac{188}{365}\right) = 0.03460\left(\frac{90}{365}\right) + 0.03517\left(\frac{98}{365}\right)$$

and is 3.2914%. The panel below summarizes the computations out to five years to maturity. The syntax of the OPTVAL function is

OV_IR_TS_ZERO_FROM_EDFUT(*ndt, srate, nexp, fp, rt*)

where *ndt* is today's date, *srate* is the rate of interest on the time deposit maturing when the nearby futures contract settles, *nexp* is the vector of settlement dates for the Eurodollar futures, *fp* is the corresponding vector of futures prices, and *rt* is an indicator variable instructing the function to return the term of maturity, *T*, or the zero-coupon rate, *R*.

F3 fx {=OV_IR_TS_ZERO_FROM_EDFUT(A3,C3,B8:B27,D8:D27,"T")}

| | A | B | C | D | E | F | G | H |
|---|---|---|---|---|---|---|---|---|
| 1 | Eurodollar time deposit | | | | | | Zero- | |
| 2 | | Days | Rate | | | Years | rate | |
| 3 | 3/17/2005 | 90 | 3.0156 | | | 0.2466 | 3.0460% | |
| 4 | | | | | | 0.5151 | 3.2914% | |
| 5 | Eurodollar futures prices | | | | | 0.7644 | 3.4931% | |
| 6 | Contract | Settlement | Days until | Settlement | | 1.0137 | 3.6585% | |
| 7 | month | date | next | price | | 1.2630 | 3.7873% | |
| 8 | Jun-05 | 6/15/2005 | 98 | 96.5150 | | 1.5123 | 3.8927% | |
| 9 | Sep-05 | 9/21/2005 | 91 | 96.1250 | | 1.7616 | 3.9810% | |
| 10 | Dec-05 | 12/21/2005 | 91 | 95.8700 | | 2.0110 | 4.0574% | |
| 11 | Mar-06 | 3/22/2006 | 91 | 95.7250 | | 2.2603 | 4.1218% | |
| 12 | Jun-06 | 6/21/2006 | 91 | 95.6100 | | 2.5096 | 4.1785% | |
| 13 | Sep-06 | 9/20/2006 | 91 | 95.5200 | | 2.7589 | 4.2299% | |
| 14 | Dec-06 | 12/20/2006 | 91 | 95.4400 | | 3.0082 | 4.2777% | |
| 15 | Mar-07 | 3/21/2007 | 91 | 95.3950 | | 3.2575 | 4.3210% | |
| 16 | Jun-07 | 6/20/2007 | 91 | 95.3450 | | 3.5068 | 4.3612% | |
| 17 | Sep-07 | 9/19/2007 | 91 | 95.2900 | | 3.7562 | 4.3992% | |
| 18 | Dec-07 | 12/19/2007 | 91 | 95.2300 | | 4.0055 | 4.4361% | |
| 19 | Mar-08 | 3/19/2008 | 91 | 95.1950 | | 4.2548 | 4.4710% | |
| 20 | Jun-08 | 6/18/2008 | 91 | 95.1500 | | 4.5041 | 4.5044% | |
| 21 | Sep-08 | 9/17/2008 | 91 | 95.1050 | | 4.7534 | 4.5365% | |
| 22 | Dec-08 | 12/17/2008 | 91 | 95.0450 | | 5.0027 | 4.5682% | |
| 23 | Mar-09 | 3/18/2009 | 91 | 95.0050 | | | | |
| 24 | Jun-09 | 6/17/2009 | 91 | 94.9650 | | | | |
| 25 | Sep-09 | 9/16/2009 | 91 | 94.9200 | | | | |
| 26 | Dec-09 | 12/16/2009 | 91 | 94.8650 | | | | |
| 27 | Mar-10 | 3/17/2010 | | 94.8350 | | | | |

**Smoothing the Yield Curve**

Thus far we have performed the first step in identifying the zero-coupon yield curve, that is, we have identified a series of zero-coupon spot rates at specific maturities (i.e., we have identified the location of the dots in Figure 18.2). The next step in building the zero-coupon yield curve involves deciding how to a zero-coupon rate at a maturity that falls between the dots in Figure 18.2. Suppose, for example, a cash flow that occurs four years from now. We have only a zero-rate for year three and one for year five. What is the best guess of the four-year rate? We discuss two possible methods.

Perhaps, the most popular method for handling this problem is called *linear interpolation*.[7] In essence, it involves drawing a straight line between the two rates on the term structure that straddle the desired maturity, and then reading the rate from the line. Algebraically, this amounts to the time-weighted average,

$$r_k = r_i\left(\frac{T_j - T_k}{T_j - T_i}\right) + r_j\left(\frac{T_k - T_i}{T_j - T_i}\right) \tag{18.6}$$

where $i$ and $j$ are the rates on either side of the desired maturity $k$, $T_m$ is the time to maturity of the $m$th rate (measured in days or years), and $T_i \leq T_k \leq T_j$. Suppose we would like to determine the six-month zero-coupon rate based on the zero-coupon rates we computed from futures prices. Applying the formula (18.6), we get

$$r_k = 0.030460\left(\frac{0.5000 - 0.2466}{0.5151 - 0.2466}\right) + 0.032914\left(\frac{0.5151 - 0.5000}{0.5151 - 0.2466}\right) = 3.278\%$$

In the event $T_k$ is less (greater than) $T_i(T_j)$, $r_k$ is set equal to $r_i(r_j)$. Linear interpolation can be performed using the function,

OV_IR_TS_INTERPOLATE(*sterm,term,rate*)

where *sterm* is the term to maturity of the desired rate, *term* is a vector of the terms to maturity of the available rates, and *rate* is the vector of available rates.

Another smoothing technique involves fitting a regression line through the available zero-coupon points. Suppose, for example, we fit the regression

$$r_i = \alpha_0 + \alpha_1 \ln(1 + T_i) + \varepsilon_i$$

through the zero-coupon rates deduced from Eurodollar futures prices. The fitted regression line is

$$\hat{r}_i = 0.02976 + 0.00922 \ln(1 + T_i)$$

As the figure below show, the regression does reasonably well at smoothing the points, with a tendency to overestimate very short-term rates and underestimate

[7] Other smoothing methods include multivariate regression and cubic splines. For a detailed description of different curve-fitting methods, see Tuckman (2002, Ch. 4).

intermediate term rates. The regression estimate for the six-month, zero-coupon rate is 3.438%.

Using a more elaborate regression model structure would improve matters. Two simple alternatives are to express the zero-coupon rate as a quadratic or cubic function of time to maturity. Regardless, however, the regression approach is somewhat troublesome in the sense that it will generally produces predicted zero-coupon rates that are different from the rates that are used as inputs in the regression. Put differently, the line does not go through the points in the figure below. Under linear interpolation, this would never happen.

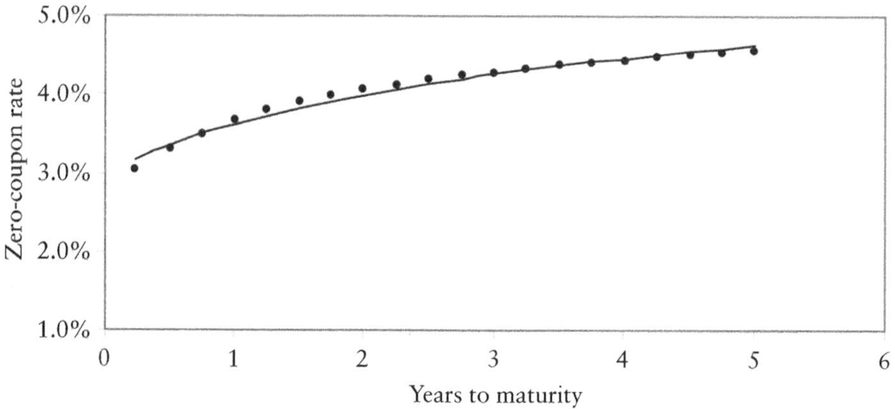


## INTEREST RATE SWAPS

The specifications of OTC interest rate swap contracts are much less transparent than for interest rate futures and options traded on exchanges. The reason is simple. The contracts are privately negotiated between counterparties, with neither having any obligation to report the terms publicly. Thanks to trade organizations such as the International Swaps and Derivatives Association (or *ISDA*), certain standard practices have emerged. Documents such as *2000 ISDA Definitions* and *Annex to the 2000 ISDA Definitions*[8] lay out the industry's "language" for communicating the terms of derivatives transactions. Other documents such as the *ISDA Master Agreement (Local Currency – Single Jurisdiction)* and the *ISDA Master Agreement (Multicurrency – Cross Border)* provide the text for actual contracts.

In this chapter, we focus primarily on plain-vanilla interest rate swaps. In these swaps, one leg requires the payment of interest based on a fixed rate, and the other leg requires payment of interest based on a floating rate. These swaps have become so active that their rates are quoted widely, and the spread between bid and ask rates is as little as four basis points. Table 18.1 contains midmarket fixed-for-floating swap rates as of the close of trading on Friday January 28, 2005. These rates are for "generic" interest rate swaps. Specifically, for these swaps, (1) no money changes hand at inception; (2) no exchange of principal

[8] See International Swap and Derivatives Association's (ISDA's) website at www.isda.org.

**TABLE 18.1** Fixed-for-floating swap rates reported by Bloomberg on Friday, January 28, 2005. By convention, the rates represent the fixed rate on a swap with semiannual interest payments and a floating rate based on six-month LIBOR. A swap to receive fixed and pay floating will be based on the bid rate, and a swap to pay fixed and receive floating will be based on the ask rate.

| Term in Years | Bid | Ask |
|---|---|---|
| 2 | 3.557 | 3.589 |
| 3 | 3.753 | 3.784 |
| 4 | 3.906 | 3.938 |
| 5 | 4.052 | 4.060 |
| 6 | 4.152 | 4.186 |
| 7 | 4.250 | 4.285 |
| 8 | 4.341 | 4.376 |
| 9 | 4.422 | 4.458 |
| 10 | 4.493 | 4.529 |
| 15 | 4.761 | 4.796 |
| 20 | 4.888 | 4.926 |
| 30 | 4.961 | 4.999 |

occurs; (3) interest payments are made semiannually and are netted (i.e., the party owing the largest payment pays the difference between the amount he owes and the amount he is supposed to receive); and (4) the floating rate is based on the six-month LIBOR rate.[9] With the contractual terms in mind, we can now interpret Table 18.1. The table contains the fixed rate on a fixed-for-floating swap. Thus, for a two-year fixed-for-floating swap, the fixed rate payer pays 3.589/2 or 1.7945% and receives six-month LIBOR rate each six months.

Fixed-for-floating interest rate swaps are just that—one party agrees to pay a fixed rate of interest and receive a floating rate, and the other party receives a fixed rate of interest and pays a floating rate. Interest rate swaps are usually consummated by a confirmation sheet faxed between the counterparties in the OTC market. Table 18.2 shows selected terms from a confirmation sheet of a plain-vanilla interest rate swap. The sheet is divided into three panels of information. The first panel provides the calculation amount, trade date, and termination date. The *calculation amount* is the notional amount upon which interest payments are computed. The *trade date* is the day on which the parties enter

[9] In some swaps, the interest rate on the floating rate leg gets reset more frequently than the payments (e.g., the floating-rate gets reset each month based on one-month LIBOR while interest payments are made semiannually). In these instances, the one-month reset rates observed during the payment interval are averaged to determine the floating rate payment. In general, the swap agreement will specify the method of averaging as "unweighted" or "weighted." Unweighted means a simple arithmetic average of all rates during the payment interval, and weighted means a time-weighted arithmetic average (i.e., each set rate is weighted by the proportion of the total number of days that the rate prevailed during the payment period). If the term sheet does not specify the method of averaging, unweighted averaging is assumed. See International Swaps and Derivatives Association (2000b, p.9).

**TABLE 18.2** Selected terms from the confirmation of an OTC interest rate swap

| | |
|---|---|
| The terms of the particular swap transaction to which this confirmation relates are as follows: | |
| Calculation amount | USD 30,000,000.00 |
| Trade date | May 28, 2004 |
| Effective date | June 1, 2004 |
| Termination date | June 1, 2009 |
| The fixed rate payer pays on each payment date an amount determined in accordance with the following: | |
| Fixed rate payer | Bank A |
| Payment dates | Commencing on December 1, 2004 and semiannually thereafter on the first calendar day of each calendar day of June and December up to and including the termination date. |
| Fixed rate | 4.238% |
| Fixed rate, day-count fraction | 30/360 |
| The floating rate payer pays on each payment date an amount determined in accordance with the following: | |
| Floating rate payer | Company B |
| Payment dates | Commencing on December 1, 2004 and semiannually thereafter on the first calendar day of each calendar day of June and December up to and including the termination date. |
| Floating rate option | USD-LIBOR-LIBO |
| Designated maturity | 6 months |
| Reset dates | The first day of the relevant calculation period |
| Rounding factor | One hundred-thousandth of 1% |
| Floating rate, day-count fraction | Actual/360 |

into the agreement, the *effective date* is the first day of the term of the agreement, and the *termination date* is the last day of the agreement.

The second and third panels of information specify obligations of the fixed-rate and floating rate payers, respectively. The fixed rate payer, in this case, is Bank A, which promises to make semiannual, fixed-interest payments at a rate of 4.238%. The "30/360" fixed rate, day-count fraction implies that each month (year) is assumed to have 30 (360) days. Thus Bank A is obliged to pay Company B an amount equal to

$$\$30{,}000{,}000 \times 0.04238 \times \frac{180}{360} = \$635{,}700$$

every six months for five years, with the first payment commencing on December 1, 2004.

At the same time, the floating rate payer, Company B, is obliged to make semiannual interest payments on the same dates. The *floating rate option* is specified to be "USD-LIBOR-LIBO" and the *designated maturity* is six months. The term, *USD-LIBOR-LIBO*, is defined in the *Annex to the 2000 ISDA Definitions*[10] and means the offered rate on U.S. dollar deposits for the period of the designated maturity as they appear on the Reuters Screen LIBO Page. Since the *reset date* is the first day of the calculation period, the first floating rate payment becomes known as of the effective date of the swap. If the rate is 1.5625% on June 1, 2004, the floating rate interest payment on December 1, 2004 will be computed as follows. First, you compute the actual number of days between June 1, 2004 and December 1, 2004. The actual number of days is 183. Next we compute the semiannual interest rate by taking the annual interest rate, 1.5625, multiplying it by the *floating rate, day-count fraction*, 183/360, and rounding it to 0.79427% (by virtue of the stated *rounding factor*). The floating rate payment that Company B is obliged to make on December 1, 2004 is $238,281. The fixed rate and floating rate payments are then *netted* so that only one party pays on a particular payment date. In our illustration, this means Bank A, the fixed rate payer, will pay Company B, the floating rate payer, $397,419 on December 1, 2004. Who pays and the amount of subsequent payments will depend on the level of the floating rates on the remaining reset dates.

In general, the terms of interest rate swaps are not available in financial publications such as the *Wall Street Journal*. Indeed, since OTC derivatives are privately negotiated and have wide-ranging terms, there are no means to systematically collect and report such information. One way to obtain indicative prices or rates of certain "generic" OTC derivatives deals is to subscribe to a service such as Bloomberg, Reuters, and Telerate that provides such quotes on a real-time basis. Essentially, what these services provide is access to a number of pages (computer screens), each page containing the current market quotes of generic types of trades. The fixed-for-floating swap rates shown in Table 18.1 are bid/ask quotes rates[11] from a real-time financial data service called *Bloomberg*. While interest rate swaps can have a wide variety of terms, the terms of these swaps are "standardized." The periodic payments of all these swaps are made semiannually, with the first payment occurring in six months. All of the rates are set in such a manner that the swaps have a zero upfront payment. The floating rate interest payment is indexed to the six-month LIBOR rate with an "actual/360" day-count fraction convention, and the fixed rate interest payment is based on the quotes appearing in the table and is calculated using a "30/360" day-count fraction convention. So, given these standard practices, the terms of the entire swap are summarized by the term and by the fixed rate. For real-time data services such as Bloomberg, bid and ask rates are displayed. These represent the highest bid rate and the lowest ask rate of all OTC dealers supplying Bloomberg with intraday quotes. If you buy the swap, you will pay the ask rate and receive LIBOR. If you sell the swap, you will receive the bid rate and pay LIBOR. The difference between the bid and ask rates is the dealer's

[10] See International Swaps and Derivatives Association (2000b, p.41).

[11] A midmarket rate is the average of the best bid rate and best ask rate prevailing in the marketplace at a given point in time.

spread. Competition among interest rate swap dealers has driven spreads in the plain-vanilla interest rate market to incredibly small levels—less than 4 basis points on average.

The reasons for entering a fixed-for-floating interest rate swap vary. Because the term structure of interest rates is usually upward sloping, the interest rate on long-term debt is usually higher than short-term debt. Assuming a firm has long-term financing needs, it may want to issue long-term, fixed rate debt so that there is no uncertainty regarding the level of future interest rate payments. On the other hand, a firm may decide to issue floating rate debt because it believes that the average level of interest payments over time will be less than those of a fixed rate loan. A problem with the floating rate alternative, however, is that, while there is good reason to believe that short-term rates will provide lower interest payments on average, it is not guaranteed. An unexpected spike in the short-term rate can have dramatic consequences, particularly when the firm finances much its capital expenditures using internally generated funds. Interest rate swaps are an inexpensive and convenient means of moving back and forth between the two alternative forms of financing. If a firm has fixed rate debt and is willing to incur the risk of floating rate debt in hopes of reducing interest payments, it can enter a fixed-for-floating swap in which it receives fixed rate payment (to offset in whole or in part its payment obligation to its bondholders) and pays floating. If a firm has floating-rate debt and wants to gain the certainty of fixed rate payments, it can enter a fixed-for-floating swap in which it receives floating (to offset in whole or in part its payment obligation to its bondholders) and pays fixed.

The terms of generic interest rate swaps are set such that (1) no money changes hand at inception; (2) no exchange of principal occurs; (3) interest payments are made semiannually and are netted (i.e., the party owing the largest payment pays the difference between the amount he owes and the amount he is supposed to receive); and (4) the floating rate interest payments are based on the six-month LIBOR rate.

The cash flows of a two-year fixed-for-floating swap are summarized in Table 18.3. In the table, the party is assumed to pay fixed and receive floating. The fixed rate is 8%, and is paid semiannually. Note that this implies that 4% of par is paid each period (six months). The floating leg is also paid each six months. The rate is based on the six-month LIBOR rate and is set at the begin-

**TABLE 18.3** Hypothetical cash flows of an interest rate swap in which the holder pays fixed and receives floating.

| | Time | 0 | 1 | 2 | 3 | 4 |
|---|---|---|---|---|---|---|
| Fixed rate leg | Interest | | –4.00 | –4.00 | –4.00 | –4.00 |
| | Principal | | | | | –100.00 |
| Floating rate leg | Interest | | 3.50 | 4.00 | 4.50 | 5.00 |
| | Principal | | | | | 100.00 |
| Net cash flows | Interest | | –0.50 | 0.00 | 0.50 | 1.00 |
| | Principal | | | | | 0.00 |

ning of each payment period. In the table, the six-month LIBOR rate is 7% at inception, implying that the interest receipt at the end of the first period is already known. The remaining interest receipts are not known at inception. The 4.00, 4.50, and 5.00 receipts are entered only to show the *netting* process, that is, the payments are netted each period, with the party owing the net amount paying the counterparty. Thus in period 1, the fixed rate payer pays –0.50. In period 2, no payment is made, and in periods 3 and 4, the fixed rate payer receives 0.50 and 1.00, respectively. The notional amount of the swap also appears on the terminal date. The net of the notional amounts is zero, implying that the notional amount has no bearing on the valuation of the swap.

**ILLUSTRATION 18.1** Transfer risk of floating rate payments.

*Suppose that, on July 1, 2004, ABC Company issued $100 million in six-year floating-rate debt at a rate of 100 basis points over six-month LIBOR. Suppose also that over the next year short-term interest rates rise precipitously and ABC becomes concerned that any further increase in short-term rates will take the firm's cash flows to a level that they will not be able to sustain their desired growth rate in investment. What alternatives are available to ABC?*

*Alternative 1: Take the "Ostrich" strategy.* Under this alternative, ABC does nothing. In leaving its short-term interest rate exposure unhedged, the firm is making a bet that short-term rates will stay the same or fall. If they rise, the firm is in trouble.

*Alternative 2: Issue fixed rate debt.* ABC may have the alternative to retire its floating-rate debt with a fixed rate bond issue. Such an action would lock in interest rate payments and alleviate the firm's short-term interest rate exposure. The main problem with this alternative is that the costs of issuing fixed rate debt may be as high as 250 basis points or more. This means that for every dollar raised, the underwriting firm takes 2.5%.

*Alternative 3: Enter a fixed-for-floating swap.* Under this scenario, ABC enters a five-year fixed-for-floating swap in which it pays fixed and receives floating (i.e., six-month LIBOR). It checks the current quotes in the OTC market and finds that five-year plain vanilla interest rate swaps are quoted at 4.22-4.26%. Since ABC will pay fixed, the ask rate, 4.26%, is the relevant rate. Assuming it can execute the swap at the prevailing rate, ABC's interest cash flows will appear as follows:

| | Payment |
|---|---|
| Current interest payment | –(LIBOR/2 + 0.50)% |
| Receive LIBOR | (LIBOR/2)% |
| Pay fixed | –(4.26/2)% = –2.13% |
| Net cash flow | 2.63% |

Note that ABC's floating rate interest payment has not disappeared. Its risk, however, has disappeared since ABC receives LIBOR as part of the swap. ABC's net cash flow each six-month payment period is fixed at 2.63%.

### Interest Rate Swap Valuation

As the above description indicates, an interest rate swap is like being long (short) a fixed rate bond and short (long) a floating rate bond. Applying the valuation-by-replication technique, the value of an interest rate swap is the difference between the values of a fixed rate bond and a floating rate bond.

A fixed rate bond is a coupon-bearing bond. It pays a stated rate of interest periodically throughout the bond's life, ending with an interest payment and repayment of the bond's par value or notional amount. To value a fixed rate bond, we take the present value of the promised fixed rate interest payments, that is,

$$PV_{fixed} = \sum_{i=1}^{n} e^{-r_i T_i} FIXED_i + e^{-r_n T_n} NOTIONAL \tag{18.7}$$

where $FIXED_i$ is the amount of the of the fixed rate payment (i.e., the fixed rate times the notional amount, $NOTIONAL$), $r_i$ is the annualized zero-coupon discount rate used to bring the cash flow to the present, $T_i$ is the number of years until the cash flow $i$ occurs, and $n$ is the number of interest payments.

Like a fixed rate bond, a floating rate bond pays interest periodically throughout the bond's life and then repays the principal at the bond's maturity. The difference is that, with a floating rate bond, the periodic interest rate "floats" from period to period. The interest rate is linked to a short-term reference rate such as LIBOR, T-bills, prime, and the Fed Funds rate and is set at the beginning of each payment period (i.e., on the *reset date*). The tenor of the reference rate is typically less than a year. Generic interest rate swaps, for example, are linked to six-month LIBOR.

Conceptually, valuing a floating rate bond may seem more difficult than valuing a fixed rate bond since the amounts of floating rate payments, except for the first, are unknown. To determine the value of a floating rate bond, we must first forecast the expected interest payments, $E(FLOAT_i)$, and then discount the expected interest payments to the present, that is,

$$PV_{floating} = e^{-r_1 T_1} FIXED_1 + \sum_{i=2}^{n} e^{-r_i T_i} E(FLOAT_i) + e^{-r_n T_n} NOTIONAL \tag{18.8}$$

The first payment, $FLOAT_1$, is treated separately to reflect the fact that the amount of the first interest payment is already set. The remaining interest payments are estimated using the forward rates implied by the zero-coupon yield curve.

Fortunately, (18.8) is not the only way to value a floating rate bond. A much simpler approach is possible. To understand this approach, note first that, on a reset date, the six-month LIBOR rate determines the amount of the interest payment in six months. Hence, the value of the floating rate bond in six months is $100(1 + LIBOR)$. Note also that the six-month LIBOR rate is the discount rate we would use to bring a future value occurring six months back to the present. Thus standing on each reset date, the value of a floating rate bond is

$$\frac{100(1 + LIBOR)}{1 + LIBOR} = 100$$

The only time the floating rate leg deviates in value from 100 is in the current period when interest rate payment has been set and the zero-coupon yield curve changes. On the next reset date, the value of the floating-rate bond again reverts to 100. Between reset dates, the value of the floating-rate bond is

$$PV_{floating} = e^{-r_1 T_1}(FLOAT_1 + NOTIONAL) \tag{18.9}$$

With valuation formulas for the fixed rate (18.7) and floating rate (18.9) legs of the interest rate swap, we can now value the swap itself. The value of an interest rate swap from the perspective of someone receiving fixed and paying floating is the difference,

$$V_{swap} = PV_{fixed} - PV_{floating} \tag{18.10}$$

**ILLUSTRATION 18.2** Find value of floating rate bond given zero-coupon yield curve.

*Suppose that the current zero-coupon yield curve is*

$$r_i = 0.04 + 0.01\ln(1 + T_i)$$

*Find the value of a five-year floating rate bond with semiannual interest rate payments.*

Like any other security, the valuation of the floating rate bond of an interest rate swap is a matter of identifying the amount and the timing of expected future cash flows and then discounting them to the present. To identify expected future cash flows, we use the current zero-coupon yield curve to identify forward rates, and then use forward rates to determine expected interest payments.

*Step 1:* Find the discount rate (factor) for each cash flow by substituting into the term structure equation. The spot rates and discount factors are shown in the following table. Recall the discount factor is today's price of \$1 received at time $T_i$, that is, $DF_i = e^{-r_i t_i}$.

| Years to Maturity | Spot Rate | Discount Factor | Implied Forward Rate |
|---|---|---|---|
| 0.00 | 4.000% | 1.00000 | |
| 0.50 | 4.405% | 0.97821 | 4.405% |
| 1.00 | 4.693% | 0.95415 | 4.981% |
| 1.50 | 4.916% | 0.92891 | 5.363% |
| 2.00 | 5.099% | 0.90305 | 5.646% |
| 2.50 | 5.253% | 0.87694 | 5.869% |
| 3.00 | 5.386% | 0.85079 | 6.054% |
| 3.50 | 5.504% | 0.82478 | 6.211% |
| 4.00 | 5.609% | 0.79901 | 6.347% |
| 4.50 | 5.705% | 0.77359 | 6.467% |
| 5.00 | 5.792% | 0.74857 | 6.575% |

*Step 2:* Find the implied forward rates between adjacent periods. This can be done using the forward rate formula from Chapter 2, that is,

$$f_{i,j} = \frac{r_j T_j - r_i T_i}{T_j - T_i}$$

where $f_{i,j}$ is the *implied forward rate of interest* on a loan beginning at time $T_i$ and ending at time $T_j$. The implied forward rate on a six-month loan, for example, is

$$f_{0.5,1} = \frac{0.04693(1) - 0.04405(0.5)}{1 - 0.5} = 4.981\%$$

The discount factors in the above table are also inextricably linked to forward rates. The price of a six-month discount bond with a par value of one dollar is 0.97821, and the price of a one-year discount bond is 0.95415. That means that the implied price of a six-month discount bond in six months is 0.95415/.97821 or 0.97540. Its forward rate of return is

$$f_{0.5,1} = \frac{\ln(0.97540)}{0.5} = 4.981\%$$

on an annualized basis.

| Years to Maturity | Spot Rate | Discount Factor | Implied Forward Rate | Implied Forward Discount Factor |
|---|---|---|---|---|
| 0.00 | 4.000% | 1.00000 | | |
| 0.50 | 4.405% | 0.97821 | 4.405% | 0.97821 |
| 1.00 | 4.693% | 0.95415 | 4.981% | 0.97540 |
| 1.50 | 4.916% | 0.92891 | 5.363% | 0.97354 |
| 2.00 | 5.099% | 0.90305 | 5.646% | 0.97217 |
| 2.50 | 5.253% | 0.87694 | 5.869% | 0.97108 |
| 3.00 | 5.386% | 0.85079 | 6.054% | 0.97018 |
| 3.50 | 5.504% | 0.82478 | 6.211% | 0.96942 |
| 4.00 | 5.609% | 0.79901 | 6.347% | 0.96876 |
| 4.50 | 5.705% | 0.77359 | 6.467% | 0.96818 |
| 5.00 | 5.792% | 0.74857 | 6.575% | 0.96766 |

*Step 3:* Find the expected floating rate interest payments. Recall that the floating rate used to determine the amount of the floating rate payment is the one prevailing at the beginning of the period. The first floating rate payment is therefore known today and is $100(e^{0.04405(0.5)} - 1) = 2.2272$. The amount of the second floating rate payment is an expected value based on the six-month forward rate starting in six months, that is, $100(e^{0.04981(0.5)} - 1) = 2.5217$. The remaining expected floating rate payments are as shown in the table below.

| Years to Maturity | Spot Rate | Discount Factor | Implied Forward Rate | Expected Cash Flow |
|---|---|---|---|---|
| 0.00 | 4.000% | 1.00000 | | |
| 0.50 | 4.405% | 0.97821 | 4.405% | 2.2272 |
| 1.00 | 4.693% | 0.95415 | 4.981% | 2.5217 |
| 1.50 | 4.916% | 0.92891 | 5.363% | 2.7176 |
| 2.00 | 5.099% | 0.90305 | 5.646% | 2.8630 |
| 2.50 | 5.253% | 0.87694 | 5.869% | 2.9782 |
| 3.00 | 5.386% | 0.85079 | 6.054% | 3.0733 |
| 3.50 | 5.504% | 0.82478 | 6.211% | 3.1541 |
| 4.00 | 5.609% | 0.79901 | 6.347% | 3.2244 |
| 4.50 | 5.705% | 0.77359 | 6.467% | 3.2865 |
| 5.00 | 5.792% | 0.74857 | 6.575% | 103.3421 |

*Step 4:* Take the present value of the expected floating rate payments by multiplying each expected payment by the corresponding discount factor. This table summarizes the results:

| Years to Maturity | Spot Rate | Discount Factor | Implied Forward Rate | Expected Cash Flow | PV of Expected Cash Flow |
|---|---|---|---|---|---|
| 0.00 | 4.000% | 1.00000 | | | |
| 0.50 | 4.405% | 0.97821 | 4.405% | 2.2272 | 2.1786 |
| 1.00 | 4.693% | 0.95415 | 4.981% | 2.5217 | 2.4061 |
| 1.50 | 4.916% | 0.92891 | 5.363% | 2.7176 | 2.5244 |
| 2.00 | 5.099% | 0.90305 | 5.646% | 2.8630 | 2.5855 |
| 2.50 | 5.253% | 0.87694 | 5.869% | 2.9782 | 2.6117 |
| 3.00 | 5.386% | 0.85079 | 6.054% | 3.0733 | 2.6147 |
| 3.50 | 5.504% | 0.82478 | 6.211% | 3.1541 | 2.6014 |
| 4.00 | 5.609% | 0.79901 | 6.347% | 3.2244 | 2.5763 |
| 4.50 | 5.705% | 0.77359 | 6.467% | 3.2865 | 2.5424 |
| 5.00 | 5.792% | 0.74857 | 6.575% | 103.3421 | 77.3590 |
| Total | | | | | 100.00 |

Surprisingly, or perhaps not so surprisingly, the present value of the floating rate bond equals 100. The intuition for this result is simple. Since the expected floating rate payment is determined from the forward rates of the zero-coupon yield curve and the zero-coupon yield curve contains the discount factors used to bring the cash flows back to the present, their effects outset each other, making the present value of the loan equal to its par value.

**ILLUSTRATION 18.3** Find fixed rate on plain-vanilla interest rate swap given zero-coupon yield curve.

*Suppose that the current zero-coupon yield curve is*

$$r_i = 0.04 + 0.01\ln(1 + T_i)$$

*Find the fixed rate on a five-year, fixed-for-floating, plain-vanilla interest rate swap.*

At inception, the value of a swap is 0. Since the present value of the floating rate leg is 100 on a reset date, this means that the fixed rate on a fixed-for-floating swap is that rate that makes the present value of the fixed rate leg equal to 100. This rate cannot be computed directly, and must be determined iteratively using the present value formula (18.7). At a 7% fixed rate, the present value of the fixed rate is too high, as shown below.

| **Fixed Rate:** | **7.0000%** | | |
|---|---|---|---|
| **Years to Maturity** | **Spot Rate** | **Promised Cash Flow** | **PV of Promised Cash Flow** |
| 0.00 | 4.000% | | |
| 0.50 | 4.405% | 3.5000 | 3.4237 |
| 1.00 | 4.693% | 3.5000 | 3.3395 |
| 1.50 | 4.916% | 3.5000 | 3.2512 |
| 2.00 | 5.099% | 3.5000 | 3.1607 |
| 2.50 | 5.253% | 3.5000 | 3.0693 |
| 3.00 | 5.386% | 3.5000 | 2.9778 |
| 3.50 | 5.504% | 3.5000 | 2.8867 |
| 4.00 | 5.609% | 3.5000 | 2.7965 |
| 4.50 | 5.705% | 3.5000 | 2.7076 |
| 5.00 | 5.792% | 103.5000 | 77.4772 |
| Total | | | 105.0900 |
| Value of swap | | | 5.0900 |

Since the present value is higher than 100, we must lower the fixed rate. If our next guess is 5.8124%, we will find that the present value of the fixed rate leg is 100. Alternatively, we can use the Microsoft Excel SOLVER function to assist us in our work.

| **Fixed Rate:** | **5.8214%** | | |
|---|---|---|---|
| **Years to Maturity** | **Spot Rate** | **Promised Cash Flow** | **PV of Promised Cash Flow** |
| 0.00 | 4.000% | | |
| 0.50 | 4.405% | 2.9107 | 2.8473 |
| 1.00 | 4.693% | 2.9107 | 2.7773 |
| 1.50 | 4.916% | 2.9107 | 2.7038 |
| 2.00 | 5.099% | 2.9107 | 2.6285 |
| 2.50 | 5.253% | 2.9107 | 2.5525 |
| 3.00 | 5.386% | 2.9107 | 2.4764 |
| 3.50 | 5.504% | 2.9107 | 2.4007 |
| 4.00 | 5.609% | 2.9107 | 2.3257 |
| 4.50 | 5.705% | 2.9107 | 2.2517 |
| 5.00 | 5.792% | 102.9107 | 77.0361 |
| Total | | | 100.0000 |
| Value of swap | | | 0.0000 |

The OTC swap dealer will set his bid-ask quotes surrounding this fixed rate. Assuming the bid/ask spread is four basis points, the dealer might quote a bid rate of 5.80% (i.e., the fixed rate the counterparty would receive while paying floating) and an ask rate of 5.84% (i.e., the fixed rate the counterparty would pay while receiving floating).

**ILLUSTRATION 18.4** Value of swap between interest payments.

*Suppose that we entered the swap in Illustration 18.3, and are receiving fixed at a rate of 5.8214% and paying floating. Two months has elapsed, and the new zero-coupon yield curve is*

$$r_i = 0.05 + 0.01\ln(1 + T_i)$$

*Compute the current value of the swap.*

The current value of the swap, from our perspective, is the present value of the fixed-rate payments (i.e., what we receive) less the present value of the floating rate payments (i.e., what we pay). The first step is to find the discount rate (factor) for each cash flow by substituting into the term structure equation. We next take the present value of the fixed rate payments (equation (18.7)), and, finally, we take the present value of the expected floating rate payments using equation (18.9). The table that follows summarizes the computations. Note that the first payment on the floating rate leg, 2.2272, was set two months earlier.

| Fixed Rate Leg | | | |
|---|---|---|---|
| Fixed Rate: | 5.8214% | | |
| Years to Maturity | Spot Rate | Promised Cash Flow | PV of Promised Cash Flow |
| 0.00 | | | |
| 0.33 | 5.288% | 2.9107 | 2.8599 |
| 0.83 | 5.606% | 2.9107 | 2.7779 |
| 1.33 | 5.847% | 2.9107 | 2.6924 |
| 1.83 | 6.041% | 2.9107 | 2.6055 |
| 2.33 | 6.204% | 2.9107 | 2.5184 |
| 2.83 | 6.344% | 2.9107 | 2.4319 |
| 3.33 | 6.466% | 2.9107 | 2.3463 |
| 3.83 | 6.576% | 2.9107 | 2.2622 |
| 4.33 | 6.674% | 2.9107 | 2.1797 |
| 4.83 | 6.764% | 102.9107 | 74.2142 |
| Total | | | 96.8884 |
| Value of swap | | -3.5527 | |

| Floating Rate Leg | | | | | |
|---|---|---|---|---|---|
| Years to Maturity | Spot Rate | Discount Factor | Implied Forward Rate | Expected Cash Flow | PV of Expected Cash Flow |
| 0.00 | 5.000% | 1.0000 | | | |
| 0.33 | 5.288% | 0.9825 | 5.288% | 2.2272 | 2.1883 |
| 0.83 | 5.606% | 0.9544 | 5.818% | 2.9520 | 2.8172 |
| 1.33 | 5.847% | 0.9250 | 6.249% | 3.1739 | 2.9359 |
| 1.83 | 6.041% | 0.8952 | 6.559% | 3.3340 | 2.9844 |
| 2.33 | 6.204% | 0.8652 | 6.800% | 3.4584 | 2.9923 |
| 2.83 | 6.344% | 0.8355 | 6.996% | 3.5599 | 2.9742 |
| 3.33 | 6.466% | 0.8061 | 7.161% | 3.6454 | 2.9386 |
| 3.83 | 6.576% | 0.7772 | 7.304% | 3.7193 | 2.8906 |
| 4.33 | 6.674% | 0.7489 | 7.429% | 3.7842 | 2.8338 |
| 4.83 | 6.764% | 0.7212 | 7.540% | 103.8421 | 74.8858 |
| Total | | | | | 100.4411 |

Note also that the present value of the floating rate leg was determined using the full set of computations performed in Illustration 18.3. This was unnecessary, since we have already shown that the present value of the floating rate leg is simply the present value of the sum of the next floating rate payment and the notional amount, that is,

$$PV_{floating} = e^{-0.05288(0.333)}(2.2272 + 100) = 100.4411$$

As the table shows, the value of the swap is now –\$3.5527, that is,

$$\begin{aligned}\text{Value of swap} &= PV_{fixed} - PV_{floating}\\ &= 96.8884 - 100.4411\\ &= -3.5527\end{aligned}$$

The fact that the swap has fallen in value from 0 should not be surprising—the duration of the fixed rate leg is higher than the duration of the floating rate leg. Interest rates rose over the past two months, hence the fixed rate leg fell in value by more than the floating rate leg. To unwind the swap, we would have to pay \$3.5527.

### Valuation of an Inverse Floater

An *inverse floater* is like a floating rate bond in the sense that its interest payments are based on a reference (i.e., floating) rate.[12] The only difference is that instead of receiving the prevailing floating rate each period, we receive a constant fixed rate less the reference rate (e.g., 10% less six-month LIBOR), that is,

$$\text{Rate on inverse} = \text{Fixed rate} - \text{Reference rate} \tag{18.11}$$

Occasionally the inverse floater will be *leveraged* or *supercharged*, in which case the reference rate is multiplied by a factor $\lambda$, where $\lambda > 1$. The rate on a *leveraged inverse floater* is

$$\text{Rate on inverse} = \text{Fixed rate} - \lambda \times \text{Reference rate} \tag{18.12}$$

Occasionally the rate on the inverse will have a cap or a floor too. For ease of exposition, we ignore both of these cases in the valuation and risk measurement discussions below. Since the generic reference rates are either quarterly or semiannual, generic inverse floaters have either quarterly or semiannual interest payments.

In order to value an inverse floater, we must first forecast the expected interest payments $E(INVFLOAT_i)$, and then discount the expected interest payments to the present. The valuation formula is

$$\begin{aligned}PV_{invfloater} &= e^{-r_1 T_1} INVFLOAT_1\\ &\quad + \sum_{i=2}^{n} e^{-r_i T_i} E(INVFLOAT_i) + e^{-r_n T_n} NOTIONAL\end{aligned} \tag{18.13}$$

[12] Inverse floaters first appeared in early 1986, after a period of sustained decreases in interest rates. Investor floaters are well suited for investors who anticipate interest rates to fall. For a detailed discussion of inverse floating rate swap structures, see Das (1994, pp. 428–453).

where , the first payment, is treated separately to reflect the fact that the amount of the first interest payment was set at the beginning of the period and is already known. By definition, the payment on an inverse floater equals a fixed rate less the reference floating rate, that is,

$$INVFLOAT = FIXED - FLOAT \tag{18.14}$$

Thus, given the expected cash flows of a floating rate bond, we can identify the expected cash flows and value of an inverse floater.

**ILLUSTRATION 18.5** Value of inverse floater given zero-coupon yield curve.

*Suppose that the current zero-coupon yield curve is*

$$r_i = 0.04 + 0.01\ln(1 + T_i)$$

*Find the value of a five-year, inverse floating rate bond whose payments are 10% less six-month LIBOR.*

The steps in the valuation of the inverse floater parallel those used for the floating rate bond in Illustration 18.4.

*Step 1:* Find the discount rate (factor) for each cash flow by substituting into the term structure equation.

*Step 2:* Find the implied forward rates between adjacent periods. This can be done using the forward rate formula from Chapter 2, that is,

$$f_{i,j} = \frac{r_j T_j - r_i T_i}{T_j - T_i}$$

where $f_{i,j}$ is the *implied forward rate of interest* on a loan beginning at time $T_i$ and ending at time $T_j$.

*Step 3:* Find the expected floating rate interest payments. Recall that the floating rate used to determine the amount of the floating rate payment is the one prevailing at the beginning of the period. The first floating rate payment is therefore known today and is $100(e^{0.04405(0.5)} - 1) = 2.2272$. The first inverse floater payment is, therefore, $10/2 - 2.2272 = 2.7728$. The expected of the second floating rate payment is an expected value based on the six-month forward rate starting in six months, that is, $100(e^{0.04981(0.5)} - 1) = 2.5217$. The expected amount of the second inverse floater payment is therefore $10/2 - 2.5217 = 2.4783$. The remaining expected floating rate and inverse floating rate payments are as shown in the following table. Note that the last payment of the floating rate loan, 103.3421, is the sum of the interest payment, 3.3421, and principal, 100. Likewise, the last payment of the inverse floater, 101.16579, is the sum of interest, $10/2 - 3.3421 = 1.6579$, and principal, 100.

| Years to Maturity | Spot Rate | Implied Forward Rate | Expected Forward Discount Factor | Expected Inverse Floater Payment |
|---|---|---|---|---|
| 0.00 | 4.000% | | | |
| 0.50 | 4.405% | 4.405% | 2.2272 | 2.7728 |
| 1.00 | 4.693% | 4.981% | 2.5217 | 2.4783 |
| 1.50 | 4.916% | 5.363% | 2.7176 | 2.2824 |
| 2.00 | 5.099% | 5.646% | 2.8630 | 2.1370 |
| 2.50 | 5.253% | 5.869% | 2.9782 | 2.0218 |
| 3.00 | 5.386% | 6.054% | 3.0733 | 1.9267 |
| 3.50 | 5.504% | 6.211% | 3.1541 | 1.8459 |
| 4.00 | 5.609% | 6.347% | 3.2244 | 1.7756 |
| 4.50 | 5.705% | 6.467% | 3.2865 | 1.7135 |
| 5.00 | 5.792% | 6.575% | 103.3421 | 101.6579 |

*Step 4:* Take the present value of the expected floating rate payments by discounting each expected payment by the corresponding zero-coupon spot rate. The table below summarizes the results.

| | | | | | PV of Expected Cash Flows | |
|---|---|---|---|---|---|---|
| Years to Maturity | Spot Rate | Implied Forward Rate | Expected Forward Discount Factor | Expected Inverse Floater Payment | Floater | Inverse Floater |
| 0.00 | 4.000% | | | | | |
| 0.50 | 4.405% | 4.405% | 2.2272 | 2.7728 | 2.1786 | 2.7124 |
| 1.00 | 4.693% | 4.981% | 2.5217 | 2.4783 | 2.4061 | 2.3647 |
| 1.50 | 4.916% | 5.363% | 2.7176 | 2.2824 | 2.5244 | 2.1202 |
| 2.00 | 5.099% | 5.646% | 2.8630 | 2.1370 | 2.5855 | 1.9298 |
| 2.50 | 5.253% | 5.869% | 2.9782 | 2.0218 | 2.6117 | 1.7730 |
| 3.00 | 5.386% | 6.054% | 3.0733 | 1.9267 | 2.6147 | 1.6393 |
| 3.50 | 5.504% | 6.211% | 3.1541 | 1.8459 | 2.6014 | 1.5224 |
| 4.00 | 5.609% | 6.347% | 3.2244 | 1.7756 | 2.5763 | 1.4188 |
| 4.50 | 5.705% | 6.467% | 3.2865 | 1.7135 | 2.5424 | 1.3256 |
| 5.00 | 5.792% | 6.575% | 103.3421 | 101.6579 | 77.3590 | 76.0983 |
| Total | | | | | 100.0000 | 92.9044 |

As before, the present value of the floating rate bond equals 100. Since the expected floating rate payment is determined from the forward rates of the zero-coupon yield curve and the zero-coupon yield curve contains the discount factors used to bring the cash flows back to the present, their effects outset each other, making the present value of the loan equal to its par value. The present value of the inverse floater's expected cash flows is 92.9044, with no obvious interpretation.

The valuation of an inverse floater can also be addressed in a different manner. Consider the value of the fixed rate bond (18.7) where the fixed rate is one-half the fixed rate in the inverse floater, that is,

$$PV_{fixed/2} = \sum_{i=1}^{n-1} e^{-r_i t_i} FIXED/2 + e^{-r_n t_n}(FIXED/2 + NOTIONAL) \qquad (18.15)$$

Suppose we buy two of the fixed rate bonds valued using (18.7) and sell a floating rate bond valued using (18.9). The portfolio value equals the value of an inverse floater, that is,

$$\begin{aligned} & 2 \times PV_{fixed/2} - PV_{floating} \\ &= \sum_{i=1}^{n-1} e^{-r_i t_i} FIXED + e^{-r_n t_n}(FIXED + 2 \times NOTIONAL) \\ &\quad - e^{-r_1 t_1} FLOAT_1 - \sum_{i=2}^{n} e^{-r_i t_i} E(FLOAT_i) - e^{-r_n t_n} NOTIONAL \\ &= e^{-r_1 t_1}(FIXED - FLOAT_1) + \sum_{i=2}^{n} e^{-r_i t_i}[FIXED - E(FLOAT_i)] \\ &\quad + e^{-r_n t_n} NOTIONAL \\ &= e^{-r_1 t_1}(INVFLOAT_1) + \sum_{i=2}^{n} e^{-r_i t_i}[E(INVFLOAT_i)] + e^{-r_n t_n} NOTIONAL \\ &= PV_{invfloater} \end{aligned} \qquad (18.16)$$

Since the floating rate loan can be valued succinctly as (18.9) and the fixed rate loan can be valued as (18.7), it is simplest to value the inverse floater as

$$PV_{invfloater} = 2 \times PV_{fixed/2} - PV_{floating} \qquad (18.17)$$

**ILLUSTRATION 18.6** Value of inverse floater as difference between two fixed rate bonds and floating rate bond.

*Suppose that the current zero-coupon yield curve is*

$$r_i = 0.04 + 0.01\ln(1 + T_i)$$

*Find the value of a five-year, inverse floating rate bond whose payments are 10% less six-month LIBOR.*

Consider the steps in the valuation of the inverse floater in Illustration 18.5, but add the expected cash flows and present value of expected cash flows of the two fixed-rate bonds with 5% (annualized) interest payments.

| Years to Maturity | Spot Rate | Implied Forward Rate | Expected Floating Rate Payment | Expected Inverse Floater Payment | Fixed-Rate Payment 5% | PV of Expected Cash Flows | | |
|---|---|---|---|---|---|---|---|---|
| | | | | | | Floater | Inverse Floater | Fixed Rate |
| 0.00 | 4.000% | | | | | | | |
| 0.50 | 4.405% | 4.405% | 2.2272 | 2.7728 | 5.0000 | 2.1786 | 2.7124 | 4.8911 |
| 1.00 | 4.693% | 4.981% | 2.5217 | 2.4783 | 5.0000 | 2.4061 | 2.3647 | 4.7708 |
| 1.50 | 4.916% | 5.363% | 2.7176 | 2.2824 | 5.0000 | 2.5244 | 2.1202 | 4.6445 |
| 2.00 | 5.099% | 5.646% | 2.8630 | 2.1370 | 5.0000 | 2.5855 | 1.9298 | 4.5153 |
| 2.50 | 5.253% | 5.869% | 2.9782 | 2.0218 | 5.0000 | 2.6117 | 1.7730 | 4.3847 |
| 3.00 | 5.386% | 6.054% | 3.0733 | 1.9267 | 5.0000 | 2.6147 | 1.6393 | 4.2540 |
| 3.50 | 5.504% | 6.211% | 3.1541 | 1.8459 | 5.0000 | 2.6014 | 1.5224 | 4.1239 |
| 4.00 | 5.609% | 6.347% | 3.2244 | 1.7756 | 5.0000 | 2.5763 | 1.4188 | 3.9951 |
| 4.50 | 5.705% | 6.467% | 3.2865 | 1.7135 | 5.0000 | 2.5424 | 1.3256 | 3.8679 |
| 5.00 | 5.792% | 6.575% | 103.3421 | 101.6579 | 205.0000 | 77.3590 | 76.0983 | 153.4572 |
| Total | | | | | | 100.0000 | 92.9044 | 192.9044 |

Note that the difference in the values of the two fixed rate bonds and the floating rate bond equals the value of the inverse floater, that is,

$$192.0044 - 100 = 92.0044$$

The function,

OV_IR_FLOAT_INVERSE(*reset, fixed, npaytr, freq, nxtim, face, term, rate, vd*)

can be used to value an inverse floater. The arguments of the function are: *reset*, the annualized interest rate set at the last reset date (i.e., the rate used at the time of the next payment); *fixed*, the fixed rate; *ncoupr*, the number of coupons remaining; *freq*, the number of coupons per year; *nxtim*, the time to the next coupon payment expressed in years; *face*, the notional amount of the inverse floater; *term*, a vector of times to maturity of zero-coupon rates; *rate*, a vector of zero-coupon rates; and, *vd*, an indicator variable set equal to *v* or *V* to return the value of the inverse floater, or *d* or *D* to return the duration of the inverse floater.

## Duration of an Inverse Floater

An unusual feature of an inverse floater is that its value is extremely sensitive to interest rate movements. To compute the duration of an inverse floater, we rearrange (18.16) as

$$2 \times PV_{fixed/2} = PV_{floating} + PV_{invfloat} \tag{18.18}$$

For an additive shift in the zero-coupon yield curve, this means that

$$2 \times D_{fixed/2} = \left(\frac{PV_{floating}}{PV_{fixed/2}}\right) D_{floating} + \left(\frac{PV_{invfloat}}{PV_{fixed/2}}\right) D_{invfloat} \tag{18.19}$$

where $D$ is duration or the percentage change in bond value for a given shift in the yield curve. Rearranging to isolate $D_{invfloat}$, we get

$$D_{invfloat} = \frac{2 \times D_{fixed/2} - \left(\dfrac{PV_{floating}}{PV_{fixed/2}}\right) D_{floating}}{\dfrac{PV_{invfloat}}{PV_{fixed/2}}} \tag{18.20}$$

Keeping in mind that the duration of the floating-rate bond is the time until the next interest payment (i.e., a maximum of six months for the six-month LIBOR rate), (18.20) shows that the duration of the inverse floater is about four times the duration of the fixed rate bond (two times the duration of the fixed rate bond in the numerator divided by a quantity approximately equal to 0.5).

**ILLUSTRATION 18.7** Find duration of inverse floater.

*Suppose that the current zero-coupon yield curve is*

$$r_i = 0.04 + 0.01\ln(1 + T_i)$$

*Find the duration of a five-year inverse floating-rate bond whose payments are 10% less six-month LIBOR.*

First, compute the duration of the two fixed-rate bonds. The individual contributions of the durations of each of the cash flows are summarized below.

| Years to Maturity | Spot Rate | Fixed Rate Payment 5% | PV of Fixed Rate Payment | Proportion of Total | Contribution to Total Duration |
|---|---|---|---|---|---|
| 0.00 | 4.000% | | | | |
| 0.50 | 4.405% | 5.0000 | 4.8911 | 0.02535 | 0.01268 |
| 1.00 | 4.693% | 5.0000 | 4.7708 | 0.02473 | 0.02473 |
| 1.50 | 4.916% | 5.0000 | 4.6445 | 0.02408 | 0.03612 |
| 2.00 | 5.099% | 5.0000 | 4.5153 | 0.02341 | 0.04681 |
| 2.50 | 5.253% | 5.0000 | 4.3847 | 0.02273 | 0.05682 |
| 3.00 | 5.386% | 5.0000 | 4.2540 | 0.02205 | 0.06616 |
| 3.50 | 5.504% | 5.0000 | 4.1239 | 0.02138 | 0.07482 |
| 4.00 | 5.609% | 5.0000 | 3.9951 | 0.02071 | 0.08284 |
| 4.50 | 5.705% | 5.0000 | 3.8679 | 0.02005 | 0.09023 |
| 5.00 | 5.792% | 205.0000 | 153.4572 | 0.79551 | 3.97755 |
| Total | | | 192.9044 | 1.0000 | 4.4688 |

The duration of the inverse floater is therefore

$$D_{invfloat} = \frac{4.4688 - \left(\dfrac{100}{192.0044}\right)0.5}{\dfrac{92.0044}{192.0044}} = 8.7411$$

## RISK MANAGEMENT LESSON: ORANGE COUNTY INVESTMENT POOL

The collapse of the Orange County Investment Pool (OCIP) in 1994 has been described as one of the worst "derivatives disasters" in history. Disaster to be sure—the taxpayers of Orange County reportedly lost $1.7 billion, about the same amount as the market capitalization of Bethlehem Steel, a DJIA component, at the time.[13] But was Orange County a derivatives disaster? No, not really. It was an enormous bet on interest rates that went awry.

The key player in the Orange County controversy was Robert L. Citron, Orange Country's Treasurer. As Treasurer, he supervised tax collection and the investment of funds. Like any other municipality, its problem is cash management. Tax revenue is collected a few times during the year, while cash disbursements are made over the entire year. To ensure that cash disbursements are unencumbered, municipalities generally invest tax revenue in highly liquid, short-term money market instruments (or, as noted Chapter 17, reverse repurchase agreements). In this way, funds in the investment pool generate additional revenue but can be withdrawn quickly and without loss as they are needed. But, Citron's strategy was different. In place of investing in short-term instruments, he invested in intermediate-term U.S. Treasuries, agency notes, corporate notes, and certificates of deposit with average maturities of about four years. From a historical standpoint, the yield curve is usually upward sloping. This means that the rates of return on intermediate-term bonds will generally be higher than short-term instruments. If interest rates do not change, a strategy such as Citron's will typically produce returns higher than money-market rates. If interest rates change, however, the situation is less clear. Since the duration of the intermediate-term bonds is higher than the duration of money market instruments, an unexpected increase in rates will cause the prices of the intermediate-term bonds to fall at a much quicker rate than the short-term rates, and vice versa. This is particularly dangerous for a municipality whose cash disbursement needs may require that the intermediate-term bonds be sold at a loss. Thus, at its most basic level, Citron's strategy was speculative. He was placing a bet that interest rates would be stable or fall.

The next twist in Citron's strategy was that he used repo agreements to increase the leverage (and, hence, duration) of the investment portfolio. In June 1990, for example, the investment pool had a leverage ratio of 1.5. A leverage ratio of one implies that the pool has no borrowed funds. A leverage ratio of 1.5 means that Citron had entered repurchase agreements with half the notes in the investment portfolio, and then used the cash proceeds to buy more notes.[14] Although OCIP used term repos, their maturities were six months or less so their effective duration was near zero. Consequently, if the duration of the original asset portfolio was 4, the increased leverage through repo agreements

[13] For a very readable and entertaining recount of the Orange County disaster and its chief instigator, County Treasurer Robert L. Citron, see Jorion (1995). Much of the material used in this vignette was drawn from this source. Miller and Ross (1997) argue that, in December 1994, OCIP was neither insolvent nor illiquid and its financial condition did not mandate bankruptcy.

[14] In industry parlance, the interest rate strategy of borrowing short-term and buying long-term is called "riding the yield curve."

increases the fund's duration exposure to 6. In a stable or declining interest rate environment, the strategy could be immensely profitable. And, it was. From the beginning of June 1990 until the end of December 1993, the Federal Reserve lowered the fed funds rate[15] no less than 18 times, taking it from a level of 8.25% to a level of 3% as shown in the figure below. Six-month money market rates (Eurodollar time deposits) fell accordingly, from 8.3125% in June 1990 to 3.4375% in December 1993. At the same time, the yield curve steepened (i.e., the spread between the five-year swap rate and six-month LIBOR widened).

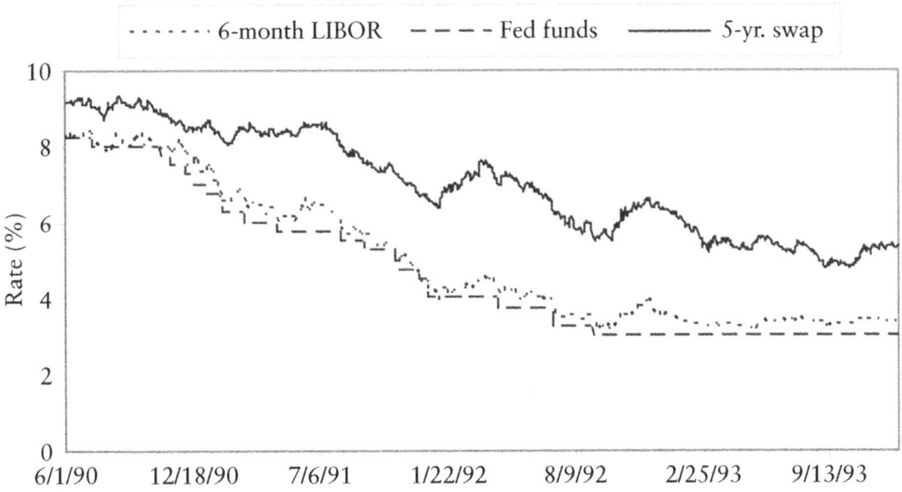


What was Citron's response? Increase leverage, of course. If the bet worked well in the past, why not double up? And, double up he did. By the end of April 1994, the leverage ratio stood at 2.71. Not only had he reversed out of the securities he owned, but he reversed out of the securities he bought with the cash proceeds he received from the original repos. Assuming the intermediate-term bonds in the original portfolio had a duration of 4, the duration of the overall portfolio now stood at a whopping 10.84! In other words, a 100 basis point upward shift in the yield curve would cause the overall portfolio value to fall by nearly 11%.

The table below summarizes the OCIP portfolio as of the end of April 1994. The data were drawn from Jorion (1995, p. 92, Table 10.2). Note that, while the total face value of the securities in the portfolio was \$19.86 billion, \$12.53 billion of the securities were financed using repo agreements, leaving a net portfolio value of the OCIP of only \$7.33 billion. The leverage ratio was \$19.86/\$7.33 or 2.71. As noted earlier, the lion's share of the portfolio was invested in intermediate-term Treasury notes, agency notes, corporate notes, and certificates of deposit. The last column contains the average maturity of the securities

[15] The fed funds rate is set by the Federal Reserve and is a target for the interest rate at which banks lend to each other overnight. While the rates on interbank loans are market-determined, the Fed can influence rates by supplying as much liquidity as there is for demand at the target rate. As the U.S. short-term benchmark, the Fed funds rate influences market interest rates throughout the world.

in each category. For the fixed rate notes, the average maturity of the securities in the category is a rough approximation for the category's duration. For the floating rate agency issues, however, this is not the case. While floating rate agency notes have a duration near zero, the face value of the floating rate notes was less than 10% of the $5.69 billion face value of the "Agency floating rate notes" category. More than two-thirds consisted of about 40 inverse floaters with a weighted average time to maturity of about four years and a weighted average fixed rate of about 11.64% versus six-month LIBOR. Using these average parameters and the zero-coupon yield curve on April 29, 1994, the duration of these inverse floaters was approximately 11.1. With $4 billion in inverse floaters, a one hundred basis point increase in the yield curve would result in a reduction in value of $444 million. Put simply, by the beginning of 1994, OCIP had placed an extraordinarily large bet that interest rates would remain steady or fall.

| Asset | Face Value (in millions) | Average Maturity |
|---|---|---|
| Treasury notes | 582 | 5 |
| Agency fixed rate notes | 8,480 | 4 |
| Agency floating rate notes | 5,693 | 4 |
| Corporate notes | 1,912 | 4 |
| Mortgage-backed securities | 127 | 10 |
| Certificates of deposit | 1,609 | 4 |
| Mutual funds | 421 | n/a |
| Discount notes | 686 | 0 |
| Commerical paper | 350 | 0 |
| Total portfolio value | 19,860 | |
| | | |
| Repos | –12,529 | |
| Net portfolio value | 7,331 | |
| | | |
| Leverage | 2.71 | |

Interest rates in 1994 were anything but steady. The Federal Reserve increased the fed funds rate six times during 1994, as is shown in the figure below. Money-market rates and intermediate-term bond rates also rose. What were the consequences? OCIP suffered extraordinary losses from (1) the decline in value of their leveraged fixed-rate bond position; (2) the decline in value of their inverse floater position; and (3) increased financing costs on the repos.[16] By December 1994, OCIP had reportedly lost $1.7 billion. The positions in the highly leveraged intermediate-term bonds were liquidated, and reinvested in money-market instruments.

[16] In using short-term borrowings to finance the purchase of long-term, fixed rate bonds, one faces risk of the short-term rate rising above the fixed coupon rate.

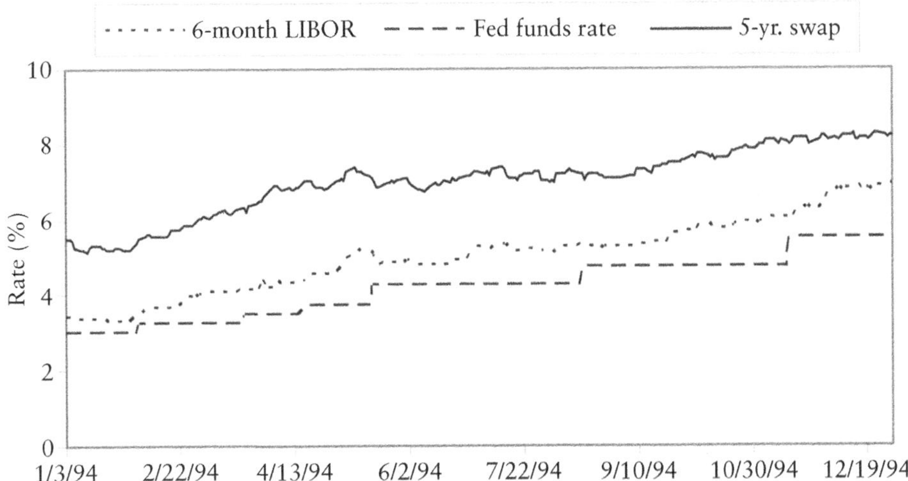


Clearly, Citron's investment strategy is not difficult to understand. It was a leveraged bet that interest rates would remain steady or fall. The strategy had been profitable in the years prior to 1994 because interest rates fell. When interest rates reversed direction at the beginning of 1994, Citron's fortunes changed for the worse.

Could the situation have been avoided? Absolutely! The investment strategy was entirely inappropriate for a municipality in managing its cash flows. Like controversies discussed in earlier chapters, the culprits are:

1. **Hubris.** Citron's astonishing performance in early years instilled overconfidence, as reflected by the fact that he dramatically increased the leverage of the investment pool through the use of repurchase agreements and inverse floaters. The overconfidence later turned to arrogance when he ignored the warnings of investment banks such as Goldman Sachs and Merrill Lynch about the possible consequences of interest rate advances.
2. **Lack of meaningful supervision.** Nominally, Citron had five elected supervisors. Unfortunately, by most accounts, none of them had a meaningful understanding of OCIP's investment strategy and/or how it was being executed. This situation is particularly egregious for OCIP since no one appeared to question what led to the abnormal performance of the pool. Municipalities aimed at managing cash flows should produce small, safe returns using money market instruments. But Citron's returns were much higher. This should have been the supervisors' red flag. Instead they left him alone to conduct his wizardry.

## INTEREST RATE CAPS, FLOORS, AND COLLARS

Interest rate caps and floors are OTC agreements that protect buyers and sellers of floating rate notes against adverse movements in interest rates. A firm with a floating rate loan, for example, faces the risk that its periodic interest payment will jump to a level too high to manage given the firm's current cash flow. By buying an *interest rate cap*, the firm can eliminate its interest rate risk exposure above a specified level. Conversely, an individual holding a floating rate note may want to limit his exposure to rates falling below a certain level. Buying an *interest rate floor* protects the floating rate receiver from such movements.

An *interest rate collar* involves buying an interest rate cap and selling an interest rate floor. The purchase of the cap offers protection from unexpected increases in the floating rate. The sale of the floor subsidizes the cost of the cap through a willingness to forfeit any interest savings if the floating rate falls. Interest rate collars are also marketed as OTC agreements.

There exists a put-call parity relation between the floating rate, a cap, and a floor. If you borrow at a floating rate, buy an interest rate cap with a cap rate of $R_X$, and sell an interest rate floor with a floor rate of $R_X$, you have transformed your floating rate loan into a fixed rate loan at $R_X$.

An important element in valuing caps and floors is contained in the reset mechanics of floating rate loans. Recall that floating rate loans generally have the interest rate set at the beginning of the payment period. Suppose you borrow \$100 million for five years at three-month LIBOR. Recall that on such loans, the interest rate is set at the beginning of the period (i.e., on the *reset date*) and interest payment is made at the end. If the current three-month LIBOR rate is 7%, the payment made in three months will be

$$\$100{,}000{,}000 \times (0.075/4) = \$1{,}875{,}000$$

In three months, the interest rate is reset. Suppose, at that time, the three-month LIBOR rate is 8%. The interest payment in six months will be

$$\$100{,}000{,}000 \times (0.08/4) = \$2{,}000{,}000$$

Suppose at the time you borrowed the money, you also bought a 7%, five-year interest rate cap based on three-month LIBOR. By convention, there is no protection on the first interest payment, since its amount is already known. The second payment is protected, however. On the first reset date in three months, the prevailing three-month LIBOR rate (8% in this illustration) is compared with the cap rate, 7%, and the difference in the rates is paid three months later. Thus, although you must make a \$2 million interest payment in six months, you will receive a payment of

$$\$100{,}000{,}000 \times [(0.08 - 0.07)/4] = \$250{,}000$$

on the interest rate cap agreement. The net interest payment of \$1,750,000 implies an annualized interest rate of 7%, exactly equal to the cap rate.

### Valuation of Caps, Floors, and Collars

To value an interest rate cap, we use a portfolio of European-style call options, with each option's expiration corresponding to a reset date of the underlying floating-rate bond. Assuming the forward three-month LIBOR rate at time $i$, $F_i$, is lognormally distributed and $R_X$ is the known interest rate cap (i.e., exercise price), the value of the first reset option (called a *caplet*) and $R_X$ is the interest rate cap,

$$c_i = e^{-r_{i+1}t_{i+1}}[F_i N(d_1) - R_X N(d_2)] \tag{18.21}$$

where

$$d_1 = \frac{\ln(F_i/R_X) + 0.5\sigma_i^2 t_i}{\sigma_i\sqrt{t_i}}, \quad d_2 = d_1 - \sigma_i\sqrt{t_i}$$

$t_i$ represents the time until the reset date, and $t_{i+1}$ represents the time until the payment date for the $i$-th reset. Two different times appear in (18.21) because the interest rate is set at the beginning of the reset period while the interest payment is made at the end of the period. Note that the volatility rate, $\sigma_i$, is specific to the time to the $i$-th reset date. (We will discuss the term structure of volatility later in this section.) The overall value of the interest rate cap is the sum of the $n$ caplets in the interest rate cap agreement, that is,

$$\text{Cap value} = \sum_{i=1}^{n} c_i \tag{18.22}$$

An interest rate floor agreement can be developed in a similar manner. Since the interest rate floor provides protection against downward movements in the floating rate, each *floorlet* is valued using a put option formula, that is,

$$p_i = e^{-r_{i+1}t_{i+1}}[R_X N(-d_2) - F_i N(-d_1)] \tag{18.23}$$

and the overall value of an interest rate floor is

$$\text{Floor value} = \sum_{i=1}^{n} p_i \tag{18.24}$$

If you buy a cap and sell a floor with the same terms, the value of each combined caplet and floorlet is

$$\begin{aligned} c_i - p_i &= e^{-r_{i+1}t_{i+1}}[F_i N(d_1) - R_X N(d_2)] - e^{-r_{i+1}t_{i+1}}[R_X N(-d_2) - F_i N(-d_1)] \\ &= e^{-r_i t_{i+1}}(F_i - R_X) \end{aligned} \tag{18.25}$$

Summing the values across the $n$ payments produces the value of an interest rate swap in which you pay fixed at rate $R_X$ and receive floating.

As noted earlier, the above valuation procedure uses a separate volatility for each period. These volatilities are called *forward forward volatilities* because they are the expected future volatility of the forward rate of interest. That is, each volatility rate is the forward volatility of a one-period forward rate that will exist in the future. It is not surprising, therefore, that some refer to this curve as the *forward volatility curve*. It is more common in practice, however, to see a single volatility used for all of the caplets (floorlets) in the cap (floor) for reporting purposes. These are called *flat volatilities*. If the flat volatilities for caps or floors for a number of maturities are available, you can deduce the spot volatility term structure by using a bootstrapping technique. Bootstrapping is analogous to computing the implied forward rate from the zero-coupon yield curve. If the one-period and two-period flat volatilities are known, we can infer the expected one-period volatility in one period.

**ILLUSTRATION 18.8** Value interest rate cap given zero-coupon yield curve and a flat volatility rate curve.

*Suppose that the current zero-coupon yield curve is*

$$r_i = 0.05 + 0.01\ln(1 + T_i)$$

*and that the flat volatility rate on a one-year cap is 30%. Compute the value of a one-year, 6% interest rate cap where the underlying floating rate loan has quarterly payments. Assume that the notional amount of the loan is $100,000.*

The first step is to generate the zero-coupon yield curve and deduce the implied forward rates. The spot rates in the table below are computed directly from the zero-coupon yield curve given above. The continuously componded forward rates are computed in the usual fashion, that is,

$$f_{i,j} = \frac{r_j T_j - r_i T_i}{T_j - T_i}$$

where $f_{i,j}$ is the implied forward rate of interest on a loan beginning at time $T_i$ and ending at time $T_j$. To convert the continuously compounded forward rate to a quarterly-compounded rate (i.e., the standard manner in which Eurodollar rates are quoted), we use

$$f^Q_{i,j} = \frac{e^{f_{i,j}(T_j - T_i)} - 1}{T_j - T_i}$$

The three-month forward rate in six months, for example, is

$$f^Q_{i,j} = \frac{e^{0.05588(0.5 - 0.25)} - 1}{0.5 - 0.25} = 0.05627$$

| Years to Maturity | Spot Rate | Discount Factor | Implied Forward Rate | |
|---|---|---|---|---|
| | | | Continuous | Quarterly |
| 0.00 | 5.000% | 1.00000 | | |
| 0.25 | 5.223% | 0.98703 | 5.223% | 5.257% |
| 0.50 | 5.405% | 0.97333 | 5.588% | 5.627% |
| 0.75 | 5.560% | 0.95916 | 5.868% | 5.911% |
| 1.00 | 5.693% | 0.94466 | 6.094% | 6.140% |

The next step is to value each of the caplets with the cap. Since the interest rate payment in three months has already been set, there is no caplet corresponding to the interest rate payment in three months. The value of the caplet corresponding to the payment in six months is

$$c_i = 100{,}000e^{-0.05405(0.5)}[(0.05257/4)N(d_1) - (0.06/4)N(d_2)] = 21.285$$

where

$$d_1 = \frac{\ln(0.05257/0.06) + 0.5(0.30)^2(0.25)}{0.30\sqrt{0.25}} \quad \text{and} \quad d_2 = d_1 - 0.30\sqrt{0.25}$$

Note that the forward rate and cap rate have been divided by four because the rates are annualized and the payments are quarterly. The value of each caplet is multiplied by 100,000 to account for the notional amount of the floating rate loan. For convenience, the value of each caplet can be computed using the function

OV_TS_VALUE_CAPLET(*f*,*rx*,*t1*,*t2*,*r2*,*v1*)

where *f* is the forward rate, *rx* is the cap rate, *t1* is the time until the reset date, *t2* is the time until the reset date payment, and *v1* is the volatility rate corresponding to time *t1*. For the caplet whose payment occurs in six months, the function produces a numerical value of

OV_TS_VALUE_CAPLET(0.05257/4,0.06/4,0.25,0.5,0.05405,0.30) = 0.00021285

Multiplying by the notional amount of the loan, the caplet value is 21.285.

The remaining caplets are computed in a similar fashion. The value of the cap is 234.675, as is shown in this table:

| Years to Maturity | Spot Rate | Discount Factor | Implied Forward Rate | | Value of Caplet |
|---|---|---|---|---|---|
| | | | Continuous | Quarterly | |
| 0.00 | 5.000% | 1.00000 | | | |
| 0.25 | 5.223% | 0.98703 | 5.223% | 5.257% | |
| 0.50 | 5.405% | 0.97333 | 5.588% | 5.627% | 21.285 |
| 0.75 | 5.560% | 0.95916 | 5.868% | 5.911% | 78.359 |
| 1.00 | 5.693% | 0.94466 | 6.094% | 6.140% | 135.121 |
| | | | | Cap value | 234.765 |

## VALUATION OF SWAPTIONS

A *swaption* is an option on an interest rate swap. It gives its holder the right to enter into a certain interest rate swap at a certain time in the future. A firm may know, for example, that in six months it will need to enter into a five-year floating-rate loan agreement and will want to swap the floating rate interest payments for fixed rate interest payments. By buying a swaption, the firm receives the right to receive six-month LIBOR and pay a fixed certain rate for a five-year period beginning in six months. The specified fixed rate of the swaption is its exercise price. If the rate on a five-year fixed versus floating interest rate swap is less than the exercise price in six months, the firm will exercise the swaption. If it is greater, the firm will choose not to exercise and will enter a swap in the marketplace. Because the firm has the right, but not the obligation, to enter the swap underlying the swaption, it must pay for the privilege. Naturally, the firm also has the alternative of entering a *forward* or *deferred swap* with no up-front cost. Like all forward contracts, however, the firm is obligated to enter into the swap agreement whether or not the terms are favorable relative to the then-prevailing market rates.

An interest rate swap is an agreement to exchange a fixed rate bond for a floating rate bond. At the start of the swap, the value of a floating rate bond always equals the principal amount of the swap. A swaption can therefore be regarded as an option to exchange a fixed rate bond for the principal amount of the swap. If a swaption gives the holder the right to pay fixed and receive floating, it is a put option on the fixed rate bond with an exercise price equal to the principal. If a swaption gives the holder the right to pay floating and receive fixed, it is a call option on the fixed rate bond with an exercise price equal to the principal.

### Valuation of Swaptions

Like in the valuation of caps and floors, the valuation of a swaption assumes that the underlying forward (swap) rate is distributed log-normally at the option's expiration. The volatility of the forward rate, therefore, is the volatility of a forward fixed rate on a fixed-for-floating swap. Suppose that at the swaption's expiration, the rate on an $n$-year swap is $R$. By comparing the cash flows on a swap where the fixed rate is $R$ to the cash flows on a swap where the fixed rate is $R_X$, we see that the payoff from the swaption consists of a series of cash flows equal to

$$\frac{L}{m}\max(R - R_X, 0) \tag{18.26}$$

where $L$ is the principal amount of the swap, and both and are expressed with a compounding frequency of $m$ times per year.

The cash flows are received $m$ times per year for the $n$ years of the life of the swap. Suppose that the payment dates are $t_1, t_2, \ldots, t_m$ measured in years. Each cash flow is the payoff from a call on $R$ with strike price $R_X$. In other words, you do not need a separate option value for each cash flow as you did for caps and floors. One will suffice. The value of the cash flow at time $t_i$ (where $t_i = T + i/m$) is

$$\frac{L}{m}e^{-r_i t_i}[FN(d_1) - R_X N(d_2)] \tag{18.27}$$

where

$$d_1 = \frac{\ln(F/R_X) + 0.5\sigma^2 T}{\sigma_i\sqrt{T}}, \quad d_2 = d_1 - \sigma_i\sqrt{t_i}$$

is the forward rate on an $n$-year swap that begins at time $T$, and $r_i$ is the continuously compounded zero-coupon interest rate for maturity $t_i$. The *swaption value* is therefore

$$\sum_{i=1}^{mn} \frac{L}{m} e^{-r_i t_i} [FN(d_1) - R_X N(d_2)] \tag{18.28}$$

Some of you will recognize that this formula is the present value of an annuity, that is,

$$\frac{L}{m}[FN(d_1) - R_X N(d_2)] \sum_{i=1}^{mn} e^{-r_i t_i} \tag{18.29}$$

The value of a put option is

$$\frac{L}{m} e^{-r_i t_i} [R_X N(-d_2) - FN(-d_1)] \tag{18.30}$$

Finally, it is worth noting that both caps/floors and swaptions are quoted in terms of the Black (1976) model in the marketplace even though it is theoretically inconsistent to do so. The cap/floor market uses the short-term LIBOR rate as the underlying source of uncertainty, while the swaptions market uses longer-term forward rates. Since forward swap rates are nearly linear in the individual forward rates, the log-normality assumption implicit in the Black model cannot hold simultaneously for both individual forward rates and forward swap rates (i.e., a linear combination of log-normal variates is not log-normal). Among other things, this means that direct comparisons between quoted implied volatilities for caps/floors and swaptions are improper. A general, all-encompassing (albeit more computationally intensive) framework for valuing interest rate products is provided in the next chapter.

**ILLUSTRATION 18.9** Value swaption.

*Suppose that the zero-coupon yield curve based on LIBOR is flat at 4% compounded continuously. Compute the value of a three-year option on a five-year swap assuming the swaption gives the holder the right to receive 4.2% fixed. Assume payments are made semiannually and principal is 100. Assume also that the volatility of the forward rate on five-year swaps in three years is 30%.*

The right to receive fixed is a put option. You will exercise only when the fixed rate on the five-year swap in three years is below 4.2%.

The put option swaption formula is

$$\text{Put on swap} = \frac{L}{m}[R_X N(-d_2) - FN(-d_1)] \sum_{i=1}^{mn} e^{-r_i t_i}$$

The sum of the discount factors is

| Years to Maturity | Continuous Rate | Discount Factor | Sum of Discount Factors |
|---|---|---|---|
| 0.00 | 4.000% | 1.000000 | |
| 0.50 | 4.000% | 0.980199 | |
| 1.00 | 4.000% | 0.960789 | |
| 1.50 | 4.000% | 0.941765 | |
| 2.00 | 4.000% | 0.923116 | |
| 2.50 | 4.000% | 0.904837 | |
| 3.00 | 4.000% | 0.886920 | |
| 3.50 | 4.000% | 0.869358 | 0.869358 |
| 4.00 | 4.000% | 0.852144 | 0.852144 |
| 4.50 | 4.000% | 0.835270 | 0.835270 |
| 5.00 | 4.000% | 0.818731 | 0.818731 |
| 5.50 | 4.000% | 0.802519 | 0.802519 |
| 6.00 | 4.000% | 0.786628 | 0.786628 |
| 6.50 | 4.000% | 0.771052 | 0.771052 |
| 7.00 | 4.000% | 0.755784 | 0.755784 |
| 7.50 | 4.000% | 0.740818 | 0.740818 |
| 8.00 | 4.000% | 0.726149 | 0.726149 |
| Total | | | 7.958452 |

The value of the put in the squared brackets is

$$[R_X N(-d_2) - FN(-d_1)] = 0.042N(0.3537) - 0.040N(-0.1659) = 0.009441$$

The value of the swaption is

$$\text{Put on swap} = \frac{100}{2}[0.009441]7.958452 = 3.7567$$

## SUMMARY

This chapter deals with OTC interest rate products which have multiple cash flows through time. A critical component in accurately valuing such derivative contracts is knowing how to measure the zero-coupon yield curve. The first section describes some commonly used data sources and estimation procedures. With the zero-coupon curve in hand, we then focus on the valuation of fixed-for-floating interest rate swaps and how they are used for risk management purposes. We then turn to the valuation of interest rate caps, collars, and floors, as well as swaptions.

## REFERENCES AND SUGGESTED READINGS

Black, Fischer. 1976. The pricing of commodity contracts. *Journal of Financial Economics* 3 (March): 167–179.

Das, Satyajit. 1994. *Swap and Derivative Financing: The Global Reference to Products, Pricing, Applications and Markets*, revised ed. Chicago, IL: Probus.

International Swaps and Derivatives Association. 2000a. *2000 ISDA Definitions*. New York: International Swaps and Derivatives Association.

International Swaps and Derivatives Association. 2000b. *Annex to the 2000 ISDA Definitions*, June 2000 version. New York: International Swaps and Derivatives Association.

Jorion, Philippe. 1995. *Big Bets Gone Bad*. San Diego, CA: Academic Press.

Miller, Merton H., and David J. Ross. 1997. The Orange County bankruptcy and its aftermath: Some new evidence. *Journal of Derivatives* (Summer): 51–60.

Tuckman, Bruce. 2002. *Fixed Income Securities*. 2nd ed. Hoboken, NJ: John Wiley & Sons.

# 19

# Credit Products

Perhaps the fastest growing area within the derivatives industry is credit derivatives. Simply defined, a *credit derivative* is an agreement that transfers the credit risk of an asset from one party (the *protection buyer*) to another (the *protection seller*). The oldest form of a credit derivative is a guarantee. A *guarantee* is a contract in which the seller accepts responsibility of the buyer's payment obligation(s) in the event of default. While guarantees have been arranged for thousands of years, two new and different classes of credit derivative contracts began to appear in the early 1990s—credit default products and credit spread products. *Credit default products* are those whose payoffs are triggered by a "credit event." A *credit event* need not be default and can be defined in any way that the two counterparties agree. Some common credit risk realizations are bankruptcy, failure to pay a coupon or to repay the full amount of the bond's principal, an invocation of a cross-default clause such as a more junior bond issue within the firm defaulting, a corporate restructuring that leaves bondholders worse off, and credit deterioration in the form of a downgrade in bond rating.[1] In contrast, *credit spread products* are those whose payoffs are linked to a *credit spread*, that is, the difference between the yield to maturity on a corporate bond and the yield to maturity of a risk-free bond (e.g., U.S. Treasury bond) with same coupon rate and maturity date. Naturally, credit spreads depend on all credit risk realizations to varying degrees.

The purpose of this chapter is to describe the different types of credit derivatives that are now traded in the OTC market and how they are used.[2,3] In the first

[1] Credit event definitions are contained in International Swaps and Derivatives Association (2003).

[2] No exchange-traded credit risk futures and options listed. In November 1998, the Chicago Mercantile Exchange (CME) launched trading of futures and options on the Quarterly Bankruptcy Index (QBI). The QBI is reported quarterly and is the total number of bankruptcy filings (in 000s) in U.S. courts over the previous quarter. Since most bankruptcy filings are by individuals, this contract was intended to be a credit risk management vehicle for those holding portfolios with a significant amount of consumer debt (e.g., credit card debt). Unfortunately, the product was a resounding failure. In five years after the product launch, the QBI futures and options have never traded. The CME's Board of Directors approved delisting all contract months on September 3, 2003.

[3] This chapter is intended to be only a primer on credit derivatives. For more details regarding the intricacies of the different contracts and their uses, see Tavakoli (1998) and Meissner (2005).

section, we discuss the evolution, growth and current size of OTC credit derivatives markets. In the second, we discuss one of the first modern-day credit derivative contracts—a total rate of return swap. In a total return swap, the buyer transfers all of the risks of the asset (e.g., the market risk and default risk of a corporate bond) to the seller in return for a risk-free interest payment. We then turn, in the third section, to credit default products, the most prominent of which is credit default swaps. In a credit default swap, the protection seller agrees, for an upfront or a continuing premium, to compensate the protection buyer upon a defined credit event. Since the buyer retains ownership of the underlying asset, a credit default swap isolates the credit risk inherent in the asset (e.g., the default risk of a corporate bond) from market risk (e.g., the interest rate risk of a corporate bond). Credit default swaps are used in structuring two other types of credit risk products—credit-linked notes (CLNs) and collateralized debt obligations (CDOs). A *credit-linked note*, described in the fourth section, is a bond-like security structured by a bank to behave like a particular corporate or sovereign bond. This is done by buying a risk-free bond and selling a credit default swap. The success of this market is driven by the fact that corporate bond markets are relatively illiquid and that many firms and institutions do not have authorization to trade derivative contracts or to engage in off-balance sheet transactions. A synthetic *collateralized debt obligation*, described in the fifth section, is like a CLN, except that the CDO sells a portfolio of different credit default swaps and issues bonds of varying degrees of seniority. Credit spread products are discussed last. These products have payoff structures that depend on the credit spread.

## CREDIT PRODUCT MARKETS

Like in most OTC markets, finding detailed information regarding credit derivative contract specifications and trading activity is difficult. The contracts are private negotiations and mandatory reporting is not required. Again, the International Swaps and Derivatives Association (ISDA) plays a significant role in the standardization of contract terms. More than 98% of all credit default swaps traded during 2003, for example, were based on ISDA documentation.[4]

Probably the most detailed information regarding the credit derivatives market is collected by the British Bankers' Association (BBA). Each year, the BBA surveys institutions regarding credit derivatives use. Most of the respondents are significant players in the international credit derivatives market. For the 2003/2004 survey, 30 institutions participated. More than a third had outstanding transactions in excess of USD 100 billion.

One important fact emerging from the 2003/2004 most recent BBA survey is that the size of the credit derivatives market is growing exponentially. Figure 19.1 shows the notional amount of credit derivatives at yearend during the period 1997 through 2003. Where only USD 180 billion were outstanding in 1997, the number had grown to 3,548 in 2003, nearly a 20-fold increase. The rate of increase from 2002 to 2003 was over 41% alone! Among the reasons cited for the rapid growth are increased market liquidity, a wider array of products, improved standardiza-

[4] See British Bankers' Association (2004, p. 27).

**FIGURE 19.1** Notional amount of global credit derivatives outstanding (excluding asset swaps) by year in USD billions.

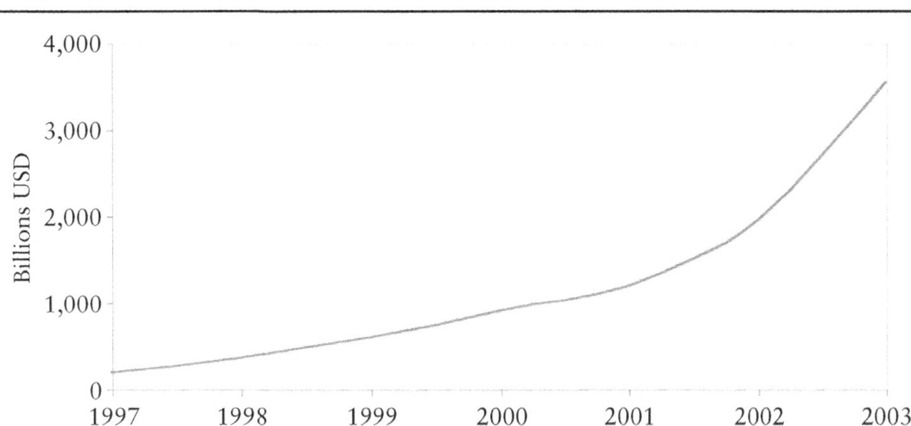


*Source:* The figure is based on information compiled from British Bankers' Association (2004, p. 11).

tion, and greater market understanding. While the growth in the credit derivatives market is unmistakable, with estimates tipping USD 8.2 trillion for the year ending 2006, the market remains small relative to other types of OTC products. The total notional amount of OTC derivatives outstanding was over USD 197 trillion for the year ending 2003. Thus, credit derivatives accounted for about 1.8%.

In general, a credit derivative is any financial contract that is designed to permit someone to change (increase or reduce) credit risk. The BBA's definition of credit derivatives, for survey purposes, includes:

> Any instrument that enables the trading or management of credit risk in isolation from other types of risks associated with an underlying asset. The instruments may include: single-name credit default swaps, credit spread products, total return products, basket products, credit linked notes, synthetic CDOs, equity linked credit products, index products and asset swaps. They include both single-name and portfolio transactions.[5]

Single-name *credit default swaps* (CDSs) are by far the largest category. Figure 19.2 shows that 51% of the notional amount of credit derivatives outstanding at the end of 2003 was accounted for by single-name CDSs. The descriptor, "single-name," in the name arises from the fact that these agreements specify a single corporate bond or loan, a sovereign bond, or an asset-backed security as the reference obligation[6] in contrast with a portfolio, basket, or index. The second largest category is collateralized debt obligations (CDOs) at 16%, followed by index trades at 11%, and *credit-linked notes* (CLNs) at 6%. Total return

[5] See British Bankers' Association (2004, p. 10).

[6] A *reference entity* (or *reference issuer*) is the issuer of the security underlying the credit derivative (e.g., Ford Motor Co.). A *reference obligation* (or *reference asset*) is one of the issuer's outstanding securities (e.g., a specific Ford Motor Co. bond).

**FIGURE 19.2** Proportional of notional value of credit derivatives outstanding at yearend 2003 accounted for by product category.

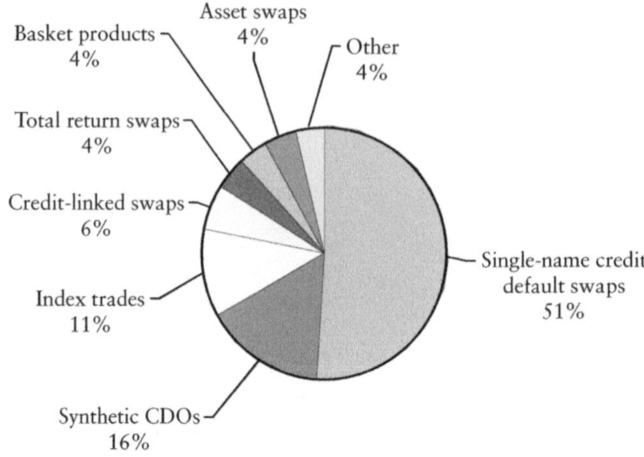


*Source:* Information compiled from British Bankers' Association (2004, p. 21).

**FIGURE 19.3** Types of institutions using credit derivatives to buy credit protection for the year ending December 2003.

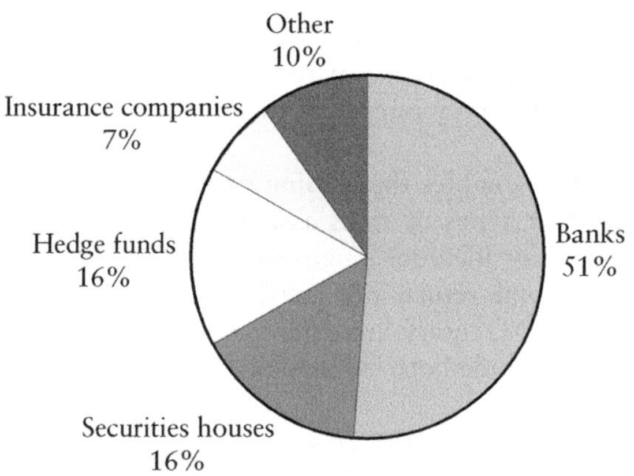


*Source:* Information compiled from British Bankers' Association (2004, p. 17).

swaps, basket products, and asset swaps account for 4% each, with the remaining credit products accounting for 4%.

Figures 19.3 and 19.4 give a flavor for who uses credit derivatives. The types of institutions using credit derivatives to *buy* credit protection are summarized in Figure 19.3. Like in previous years, banks buying credit protection accounted for the largest proportion of the total notional amount outstanding at the end of 2003—51%. Similarly, securities houses and insurance companies are large users,

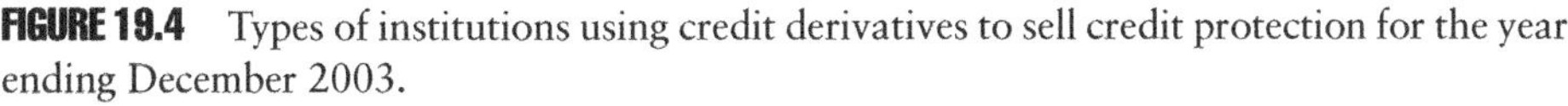

**FIGURE 19.4** Types of institutions using credit derivatives to sell credit protection for the year ending December 2003.

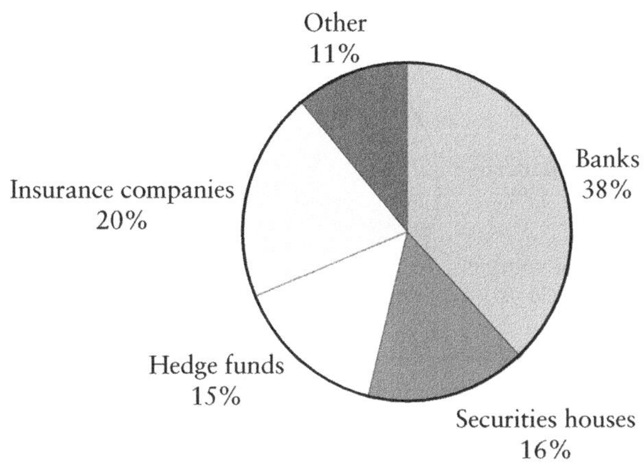


*Source:* Information compiled from British Bankers' Association (2004, p. 18).

accounting for another 23%. Interestingly, hedge funds accounted for 16% of total, up from 5% for the year ending 2001. The "Other" category includes entities such corporations, mutual funds, and pension funds. The types of institutions using credit derivatives to *sell* credit protection are summarized in Figure 19.4. Again banks are the single largest player, with 38% of total. Insurance companies are next with 20%. Comparing Figures 19.3 and 19.4, we find that banks are net buyers of protection, while insurance companies are net sellers.

Another useful source of information about the credit derivatives market is provided by FitchRatings (2004). Among the most interesting findings contained in their report are the tables and figures that break down credit derivatives by reference entity. Figure 19.5, for example, summarizes the FitchRating results for the end of year 2003 by reference entity type. Nonfinancial corporate exposures account for 65% of the notional amount of contracts outstanding, with financial corporate exposures accounting for another 17%. Sovereign risk[7] accounts for 6%, and asset-back securities, 5%. Table 19.1 summarizes the FitchRating information by gross value of protection sold and gross value purchased. Consistent with Figure 19.5, the most active reference entities are single names—either corporate or sovereign—with corporates taking the lion's share. At the top of the list are automobile and telecom companies, which should not be surprising considering the turbulent markets for these industries in recent years. The fact that company names appear in both columns simply reflects the fact the each agreement needs a counterparty. A little further down the list, sovereign debt begins to appear. Japan is the most used sovereign reference entity for both protection sales and purchases.

[7] *Sovereign risk* refers to the risk of default arising from changes in a country's foreign-exchange policies and/or regulations.

**FIGURE 19.5** Global credit derivatives exposures by reference entity type for year ending December 2003.

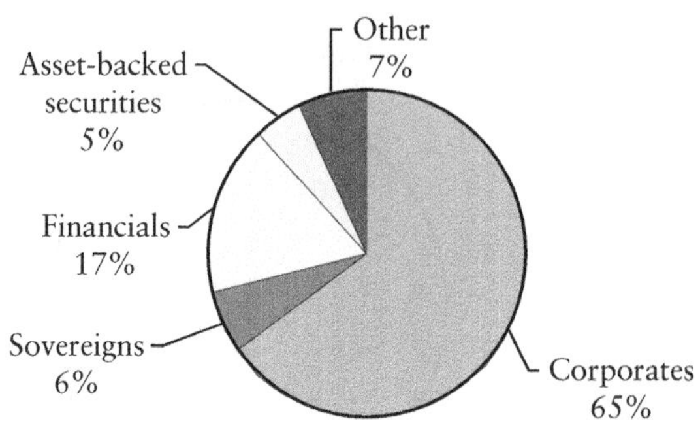


*Source:* Information drawn from FitchRating (2004, p. 8).

**TABLE 19.1** Top 25 reference entities appearing in credit derivative contracts in 2003 by gross dollars sold and gross dollars purchased.

| | Protection Sold | Protection Bought |
|---|---|---|
| 1 | Ford Motor Corp./Ford Motor Credit Co. | Ford Motor Corp./Ford Motor Credit Co. |
| 2 | General Motors/GMAC | DaimlerChrysler |
| 3 | France Telecom | General Motors/GMAC |
| 4 | DaimlerChrysler | France Telecom |
| 5 | Deutsche Telekom | Deutsche Telekom |
| 6 | General Electric/GECC | General Electric/GECC |
| 7 | Altria Group | Telecom Italia |
| 8 | Telecom Italia | Verizon |
| 9 | Japan | Altria Group |
| 10 | France | Japan |
| 11 | Italy | Merrill Lynch |
| 12 | Portugal | Volkswagen |
| 13 | Fannie Mae | Bayerische Hypo-und Vereinsbank |
| 14 | Verizon | Bayer |
| 15 | Allianz | Brazil |
| 16 | Merrill Lynch | BT |
| 17 | Volkswagen | Citigroup |
| 18 | AIG | Credit Suisse First Boston |
| 19 | Citigroup | JP Morgan Chase |
| 20 | Germany | Lehman Brothers |
| 21 | Spain | MBIA |
| 22 | BNP Paribas | Parmalat |
| 23 | Eastman Kodak | Repsol |
| 24 | Time Warner | Time Warner |
| 25 | ABN Amro | American Express |

*Source:* Information drawn from FitchRatings (2004, p. 8).

**FIGURE 19.6** Global credit derivatives exposures by bond rating for year ending December 2003.

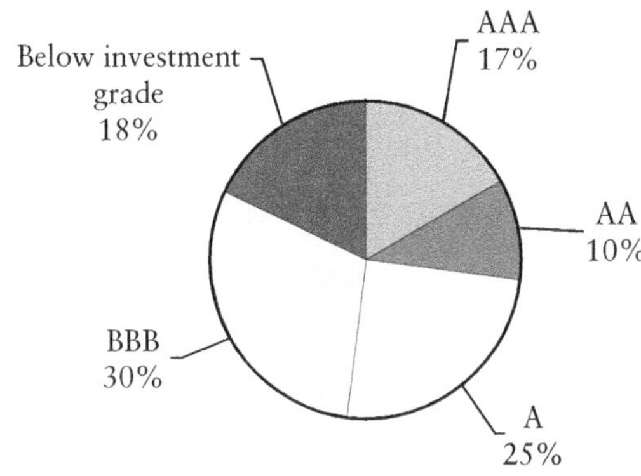


*Source:* Information drawn from FitchRating (2004, p. 9).

Finally, Figure 19.6 summarizes the notional amount of credit derivatives outstanding by bond rating. Interestingly, the size of the market for protection does not increase monotonically as the bond rating falls as one might expect—the lower the bond rating, the greater the credit risk and therefore the greater the need for credit protection. Noninvestment grade bonds, for example, account for only 18%, compared with 30% for the lowest-rated investment grade bonds BBB, and 25% for the second lowest rated investment grade bonds A. The most likely explanation for this phenomenon is that many institutions are barred from trading noninvestment grade issues. This has two consequences. First, it means that the size of the market for noninvestment grade bonds is smaller than investment grade bonds, hence the absolute demand for credit protection is lower. Second, it means that the market for protection in the BBB category will be highest. A rating downgrade from BBB means that the credit spread will rise not only from increased default risk but also from increased selling pressure brought about by institutions liquidating their holdings in bonds that have become noninvestment grade.

## TOTAL RETURN SWAP

A *total rate of return swap* (TRORS) is frequently lumped into the category of credit derivatives, although, technically, it is more than that. The total return on a reference obligation such as a corporate bond is affected by both interest rate risk (i.e., the risk associated with movements in the level of risk-free interest rates) and credit risk (i.e., the risk associated with default and/or the spread between the corporate bond and Treasury bond yields). Figure 19.7 shows the general nature of a total return swap. The protection buyer A (also called "total return payer") owns the reference asset and pays its total return (e.g., coupon interest and price change) to the protection seller B (also called "total return receiver") In return, A receives the risk-free return (e.g., six-month LIBOR plus

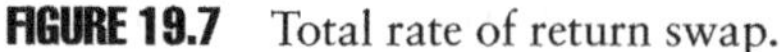

**FIGURE 19.7** Total rate of return swap.

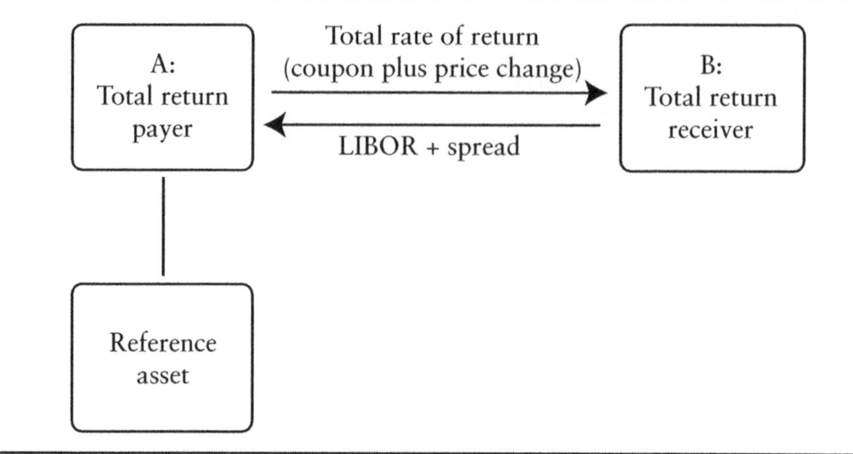


a premium of, say, 30 basis points). In the absence of default, A passes on any dividends or coupon interest on the reference asset during the life of the agreement on to the TRORS receiver. In addition, A pays B the price change on the reference asset over the life of the contract. If the reference asset price is \$75 at the beginning of the swap's life and \$100 at the end, for example, A pays B \$25. If the reference asset price is \$75 at the beginning of the swap's life and \$60 at the end, B pays A \$15.

In the event of default of the reference obligation before the expiration date of the swap, B makes A "whole" for both the market risk and the default risk of the reference asset. Under cash settlement, this means B will pay A the difference between the reference asset's price at the beginning of the swap agreement and its price at the time of default. Occasionally, finding a reliable bond price quote to use for settlement purposes will be difficult to find due to market illiquidity. In such cases, B may agree to take delivery of the reference asset from A and pay A the reference price set at the swap's inception. Once settlement occurs, the swap is terminated.

For purposes of illustration, consider the total return swap confirmation that appears in Table 19.2. The terms of the swap say that A pays B "All cash flows of the reference obligation on the same day as the cash flows are received." This means that, as A receives the semiannual coupon payments on its Northrop bond, they must be immediately paid to B. In return, A receives from B six-month LIBOR plus 30 basis points. Finally, at the agreement's termination, any unpaid interest by either party is paid. In addition, if the market price of the Northrop bond is less than its initial price of 100% of par, B pays A the difference, and vice versa. The credit events are bankruptcy or payment failure.

To understand the benefits of using a total return swap in which the investor receives the total return and pays floating, compare it "cash-and-carry" T-bond position discussed in Chapter 17. In essence, the TRORS is nothing more than a long position in a corporate bond financed by short-term borrowing. It should not be surprising, therefore, to learn that hedge funds frequently use total returns

**TABLE 19.2** Selected terms from the confirmation of a total return swap.

| | |
|---|---|
| Transaction | Total return swap |
| Trade date | January 6, 2005 |
| Effective date | January 7, 2005 |
| Termination date | March 20, 2008 or the "early redemption date" |
| Total return payer | Party A |
| Total return receiver | Party B |
| Reference entity | Northrop Gruman Corporation |
| Reference obligation | Guarantor: Northrop Gruman Corporation<br>Maturity: February 15, 2011<br>Coupon: 7.125%<br>CUSIP/ISIN: US666807AT91 |
| Calculation amount | USD 20,000,000 |
| A pays | All cash flows of the reference obligation on the same day as the cash flows are received. |
| B pays | Six-month LIBOR + 30 basis points |
| Termination payment | On the termination date, any accrued interest payments due A or B will be paid. In addition, the following termination payment amount will be made:<br>Calculation amount × (Initial price − Market value)<br>If positive, B pays A.<br>If negative, A pays B. |
| Initial price | 100% |
| Market value | The market value of the reference obligation, including accrued interest, on the termination date. A dealer panel will determine the market value using the market bid price. |
| Credit event(s) | The following credit event(s) shall apply to this transaction:<br>Bankruptcy<br>Failure to pay |

swaps as a means of financing credit exposures. In addition, TRORSs are frequently written on indexes. Like the index products discussed in Chapter 14, this offers the advantage of executing one swap transaction to implicitly buy or sell a basket of underlying securities. The TRORS is simple, efficient, and cost effective. Finally, for certain securities, a short sale of the security may be expensive or impossible to execute. Like selling a forward contract, entering a TRORS in which we pay the total return and receive floating is equivalent to shorting the security.

## CREDIT DEFAULT SWAP

Single-named credit default swaps are the largest category of credit derivatives, accounting for more than one-half of the notional amount of all credit derivatives contracts outstanding at the end of 2003. A "single-name" product, as noted earlier, means that there is one reference obligation underlying the swap.

Basket credit default swaps are less popular (i.e., about 4% in Figure 19.2). With basket products, the reference obligation is a basket or portfolio of obligations (e.g., a corporate bond from each of 20 different issuers). The most important attribute of a credit default swap (CDS) is that it isolates the credit risk of the underlying reference asset. The term "swap," however, is a misnomer. More or less, it is a put option whose premium is paid upfront or amortized over the life of the agreement.

Figure 19.4 shows the general nature of a credit default swap. In the figure, the default swap buyer, A, is buying protection from the default swap seller, B. To do so, A pays to B either an upfront or a periodic premium (i.e., fee). For a standard CDS, the premium is amortized and paid quarterly. For a cash settlement contract, B pays A the difference between the *reference price* set at the inception of the CDS (typically, the par value of 100) and the *final price* (also called the *recovery rate*) in the event of default (or other credit event).[8] With physical settlement, A delivers the defaulted bond to B, and receives the reference price. In most default swaps, the buyer has the right to deliver one bond of a number of prespecified bonds. This protects the protection buyer from getting squeezed in the event he does not own the reference bond. In the event default does not occur, the contract terminates with no further payments/obligations.

To further clarify the terms of a CDS, consider Table 19.3, which contains selected terms from the confirmation of an actual credit default swap.[9] The format is similar to other swaps. At the top are the trade date, effective date, and termination date, as well as the identities of the two parties to the swap. Next is the reference entity, Northrop Gruman Corporation. The reference obligation is the Northrop Gruman Corporation bond with a 7.125% coupon and a February 15, 2011 maturity date. The bond's CUSIP number is also specified so there is no ambiguity regarding the identity of the bond.

In this particular agreement, A is the protection buyer and B is the protection seller. Each quarter, A pays

$$0.0017 \times \left(\frac{Actual}{360}\right) \times \text{USD}5{,}000{,}000$$

**FIGURE 19.8** Credit default swap.

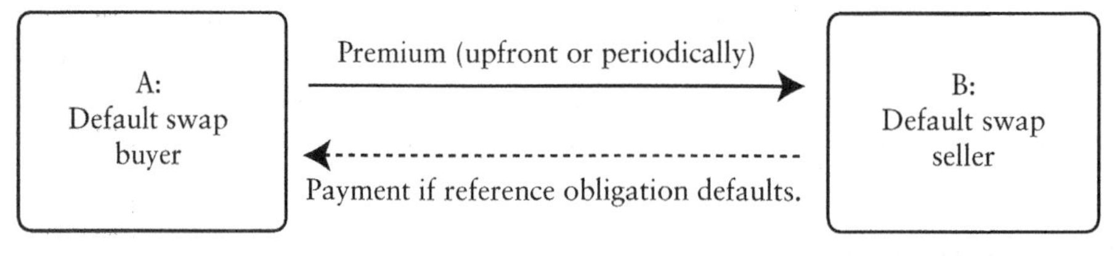


[8] Since the market for the bond may be illiquid, the settlement price is sometimes determined by a poll of several bond dealers.

[9] An ISDA Word document file containing all of the possible terms of a credit default swap confirmation can be downloaded at www.isda.org.

**TABLE 19.3** Selected terms from the confirmation of a credit default swap.

| | | |
|---|---|---|
| Transaction | Credit default swap | |
| Trade date | January 6, 2005 | |
| Effective date | January 7, 2005 | |
| Termination date | March 20, 2008 | |
| Fixed rate payer | Party A | |
| Floating rate payer | Party B | |
| Reference entity | Northrop Gruman Corporation | |
| Reference obligation | Guarantor: | Northrop Gruman Corporation |
| | Maturity: | February 15, 2011 |
| | Coupon: | 7.125% |
| | CUSIP/ISIN: | US666807AT91 |
| Reference price | 100% | |
| **Fixed payments** | | |
| Fixed rate, payer calculation amount | USD 5,000,000 | |
| Fixed rate | 0.17% | |
| Fixed rate day-count fraction | Actual/360 | |
| Fixed rate payer payment dates | March 20, 2005, and thereafter the 20th of each March, June, September, and December | |
| **Floating payments** | | |
| Floating rate payer calculation amount | USD 5,000,000 | |
| Credit event(s) | The following credit event(s) shall apply to this transaction:<br>Bankruptcy<br>Downgrade<br>Failure to pay | |
| Default requirement | USD 10,000,000 as of occurrence of credit event | |
| **Settlement terms** | | |
| Settlement method | Physical settlement | |
| Deliverable obligation category | Bond or loan | |
| Deliverable obligation characteristics | Not subordinated<br>Not contingent<br>Maximum maturity 30 years | |

where *Actual* is the number of days in the quarter. The sum of the present values of these payments through time is the cost of the credit event risk insurance. In other words, the cost of the default risk put option is being paid on an installment plan, with the present value of the quarterly annuity payments being set equal to the cost of the put. There is an important distinction, however. The premium payments are suspended if a credit event occurs during the life of the swap.

Party B, the protection seller, has no obligation unless a credit event occurs. The events specified in Table 19.3 are bankruptcy, rating downgrade, and failure to pay. If a credit event occurs, the contract is settled with physical delivery.[10]

[10] British Bankers' Association (2004, p. 25) reports that 86% of credit derivative contracts have physical settlement.

The protection buyer A delivers the Northrop bond (or one of a number of eligible bonds) at par to the protection seller B and receives USD 10,000,000. As the table shows, eligible deliverable bonds have similar characteristics. The terms of the agreement say that the deliverable bond cannot be a subordinated issue, have embedded options, or have a term to maturity greater than 30 years.

The trade confirmation shown in Table 19.3 does not provide any indication about the motivation for the trade. All we know is that Party A is buying protection (i.e., going short the credit) and Party B is selling protection (i.e., going long the credit). Each side in the transaction could be hedging or speculating. Party A may have initiated the trade to eliminate the credit risk of a Northrop bond held in inventory. Naturally, A could have simply sold the Northrop bond, however, corporate bond markets are fairly illiquid and trading costs are high. Buying protection using a CDS is usually cheaper. In addition, the CDS absorbs the credit risk, but not the encumbrance of legal ownership, of the reference security. On the other side of the trade, rather than buy the bond directly incurring significant trading costs, Party B may have wanted a long position in the Northrop bond.

Quantifying the cost of credit event insurance is difficult, since the number of credit events is large. In the situation where credit event risk is default risk, we can use the Merton (1974) model discussed in Chapter 12 can be used as a starting point. In the Merton framework, we assumed that the firm had a single issue of debt outstanding—zero-coupon bonds maturing at time $T$. We also assumed that the firm's value is log-normally distributed at the end of the bond's life. Under such assumptions, the firm's stock can be modeled as a call option on the value of the firm's assets with an exercise price equal to face value of the bonds and a time to expiration equal to their term to maturity. The stock can be valued using the BSM formula,

$$S = VN(d_1) - Fe^{-rT}N(d_2) \tag{19.1}$$

where

$$d_1 = \frac{\ln(V/Fe^{-rT}) + 0.5\sigma_V^2 T}{\sigma_V\sqrt{T}}$$

$d_2 = d_1 - \sigma_V\sqrt{T}$, $F$ is the face value of the firm's bonds, $V$ is the overall value of the firm, $\sigma_V$ is the volatility rate of the firm, and $r$ is the rate of return on a risk-free bond. With the value of the stock known, the value of the risky bonds is, therefore, $B = V - S$.

In Chapter 12, we also showed that the value of a zero-coupon corporate bond equals the difference between (1) the value of a risk-free zero-coupon bond with face value $F$ and (2) the value of a put that allows the managers of the firm to put the firm's assets to the bondholders if firm value falls below the bonds' face value at maturity, that is,

$$B = Fe^{-rT} - [Fe^{-rT}N(-d_2) - VN(-d_1)] \tag{19.2}$$

To understand the economic intuition underlying why the value of the put equals the default risk premium, note that the expression in squared brackets in (19.2) may be rewritten as

$$e^{-rT}\left[F - Ve^{rT}\frac{N(-d_1)}{N(-d_2)}\right]N(-d_2) \qquad (19.3)$$

In (19.3), the term,

$$Ve^{rT}\frac{N(-d_1)}{N(-d_2)}$$

is the expected firm value at time $T$ conditional on the value of the firm being less than the face value of the bonds, that is, $E(\tilde{V}_T | V_T < F)$. From a corporate bond perspective, this is called the bond's *expected recovery value*—what bondholders expect to receive in the event of default. The *expected loss* of the bond at time $T$ conditional upon default is $F - E(\tilde{V}_T | V_T < F)$, which may be calculated using the term in squared brackets of (19.3). The full expression (19.3) is, therefore, the *present value of the expected loss* on the bond conditional on the value of the firm being less than the bond's face value at time $T$ times the *probability of default*, $\Pr(V_T < F) = N(-d_2)$.

**ILLUSTRATION 19.1** Compute cost of buying default protection.

*Assume that the firm has a current value of 120, and its annual volatility rate is 30%. The firm has two securities outstanding—zero-coupon bonds and common stock. The bonds mature in five years and have a face value of 100. The stock pays no dividends, and the risk-free rate of interest is 5%. Compute the risk-neutral probability of default, the bond's credit spread, and the cost of buying default protection on a quarterly basis.*

In the interest of completeness, we begin by computing the value of the firm's common stock, that is,

OV_CORP_STOCK_FIRM (120, 100, 5, 0.05, 0.30, 1) = 51.98

The value of the firm's bonds is therefore

$$B = 120.00 - 51.98 = 68.02$$

The value of risk-free bonds is

$$B_{\text{risk-free}} = 10e^{-0.05(5)} = 77.88$$

Consequently, the present value of the expected loss conditional on default times the risk-neutral probability of default is 77.88 – 68.02 = 9.86. This is the total cost of buying insurance, which we can amortize in quarterly installments. The promised yield to maturity on the bonds is

$$y = \frac{\ln(100/68.02)}{5} = 7.707\%$$

consequently, the bond's credit spread is 2.707%.

To verify the computation of the insurance premium, we will use equation (19.3). The risk-neutral probability of default can computed using the OPTVAL function,

OV_CORP_PROB_DEFAULT(*firm, face, t, alpha, vf*)

where *firm* is the value of the firm, *face* is the face value of the firm's zero-coupon bonds, *t* is the term to maturity of the bond's in years, *alpha* is the expected rate of appreciation in the value of the firm, and *vf* is the volatility rate of the firm. In a risk-neutral world, the expected rate of appreciation in the value of the firm is set equal to the risk-free interest rate, *r*. Its value is .3786. The expected recovery value conditional upon default is

$$120e^{0.05(5)}\left(\frac{0.1636}{0.3786}\right) = 66.56$$

and may be computed using

OV_CORP_RECOVERY_VALUE (120, 100, 5, 0.05, 0.30) = 66.56

where all of the function arguments are as defined above. The expected loss conditional upon default is 100.00 – 66.56 = 33.44. Alternatively, we can use the function

OV_CORP_EXPECTED_LOSS (120, 100, 5, 0.05, 0.30) = 33.44

The present value of the expected loss conditional upon default times the probability default is

$$e^{-0.05(5)}(33.44)(0./3786) = 9.86.$$[11]

To determine the quarterly payment, we set this amount equal to the present value of an annuity of payments, that is,

$$9.86 = \sum_{t=1}^{20} PAYTe^{-0.05(0.25t)}$$

The quarterly payment is $PAYT = 0.561$.

In the model used to value the cost of protection, we made the implicit assumption that default, if it were to occur, would happen on the bond's maturity date. In reality, default may occur during the life of the bond when the firm's assets deteriorate in value to, say, level $H$. When it does, default occurs and the bondholders receive $H$. While this complicates matters, we provided the solution to this problem in Chapter 8. Instead of the valuing the firm's stock as a standard call option, we value the stock as a knockout or barrier option. Specifically, the firm's stock is a down-and-out call. When the value of the assets sinks down of barrier $H$, the stock's life ends worthless. The value of such a call is given by equation (8.44) in Chapter 8.

**ILLUSTRATION 19.2** Compute cost of buying credit protection with early default.

Assume that the firm has a current value of 120, and its annual volatility rate is 30%. The firm has two securities outstanding—zero-coupon bonds and common stock. The bonds mature in five years and have a face value of 100. The stock pays no dividends, and the risk-

[11] To check this computation, compute the value of the put option on the right-hand side of (19.3) using OV_OPTION_VALUE(120, 10, 5, 0.05, 0.0, 0.30, "p", "e") = 9.86.

free rate of interest is 5%. Compute the bond's credit spread and the total cost of buying default protection assuming the bonds default if the value of the assets drops below 60 during the bond's life or if the value of the firm's assets is below the face value of the bonds at maturity. Explain why the results differ from those in Illustration 19.1.

The value of a down-and-out call option can be computed using the OPTVAL function

OV_NS_BARRIER_OPTION(*s, x, h, t, rebate, r, i, v, TypeFlag*)

where *s* is the asset price, *x* is the exercise price, *h* is the barrier level, *t* is the time to expiration, *r* is the risk-free rate of interest, *i* is the income rate, and *v* is the volatility rate. The *TypeFlag* consists of three contiguous lower case letters. The first is a (c)all/(p)ut indicator, the second is a (d)own/(u) indicator, and the third is a (i)n/(o)ut indicator. For a down-and-out call, *TypeFlag* is "cdo." Given the parameters of this illsutration, the value of a down-and-out call is

OV_NS_BARRIER_OPTION(120, 100, 60, 5, 0, .05, .00, .30, "cdo") = 50.972

and the value of a down-and-in call is

OV_NS_BARRIER_OPTION(120, 100, 60, 5, 0, 0.05, 0.00, 0.30, "cdi") = 1.007

Note that the sum of the values of the down-and-out call and the down-and-in call (with no rebate) equals the value of a standard European-style call option, 51.980.

To find the value of the firm's bonds, we subtract the value of the down-and-out call from the value of the firm, that is,

$$B = 120 - 50.972 = 69.028$$

The bond's promised yield to maturity is 7.413%, and its credit spread is 2.413%. The bond's value increases (yield decreases) from Illustration 19.1 because we have, in essence, imposed the constraint that the bond's value will neven fall below 60. While extremely unlikely, the bond's value in Illustration 19.1 can fall as low as 0.

In some instances, credit default swaps specify that the protection seller pays a pre-specified amount of cash, *CASH*, rather than the difference between the reference price and price in the event of default in the event of default. Again, assuming that the firm has a single issue of debt outstanding—zero-coupon bonds maturing at time *T*, we can value the credit default option as a cash-or-nothing put, that is,

$$p_{con} = CASHe^{-rT}N(-d_2) \tag{19.4}$$

where

$$d_2 = \frac{\ln(V/Fe^{-rT}) - 0.5\sigma_V^2 T}{\sigma_V\sqrt{T}}$$

**ILLUSTRATION 19.3** Value fixed payment credit option.

*Value a credit option that pays 50 if default occurs. Assume that the firm's value is 120 and its volatility rate is 30%. Assume the firm's debt is a five-year, discount bond issue with a principal amount of 100, and the risk-free rate of interest is 5%.*

The value of the fixed payment, put credit option is

$$p_{con} = 50e^{-0.05(5)}N(-d_2) = 14.744$$

where

$$-d_2 = \frac{\ln(120/100e^{-0.05(5)}) - 0.5(0.5^2)5}{0.50\sqrt{5}} = -0.3091$$

and $N(-d_2) = 0.3786$.

## CREDIT-LINKED NOTES

A *credit-linked note* (CLN) is simply a note (or a bond or a loan) with an embedded credit feature. They come in a wide variety of structures. One of the simplest is illustrated in Figure 19.9. In the figure, the CLN issuer, B, buys a corporate or sovereign bond from the issuer, A. The issuer gets paid in cash and is required to make periodic interest payments of, say, 6%. B does not want to incur the credit deterioration and default risk of the bond, so he creates a credit-linked note that he sells to the CLN buyer, C. B receives the cash and promises to pay an 8% coupon if the bond experiences no rating downgrade and a 4% coupon if the bond is downgraded but the bond issuer does not default. In the event the bond defaults, B receives the recovery rate from A and passes it along to C. Presumably, the CLN buyer enters the trade because he believes the probability of a ratings downgrade (or default) is low and wants to earn the incremental coupon interest of 2%.

Credit-linked notes can also be created synthetically using risk-free bonds and a credit default swap. To see an example of a *synthetic credit-linked note* is structured, consider Figure 19.10. In this figure, a bank, A, owns a corporate or a sovereign bond (i.e., the reference asset) and wants to hedge its credit risk. It does so by buying a credit default swap from B. B is a trust whose sole purpose is to issue a note linked to the credit of the reference asset (i.e., a CLN). C wants a synthetic exposure to the reference asset, and, therefore, buys the CLN, paying B in cash. B, in turn, takes the cash, invests it in a risk-free asset. B's role is only as an intermediary. B's profit equals the default premium, $x$%, plus the risk-free return, $y$%, less the coupon interest paid to the CLN holder, $z$%.

The success of the credit-linked note markets, like many other derivatives markets, is driven by three key factors. The first is trading costs. The cash markets for corporate and sovereign bonds are relatively illiquid and trading costs are

**FIGURE 19.9** Credit-linked note.

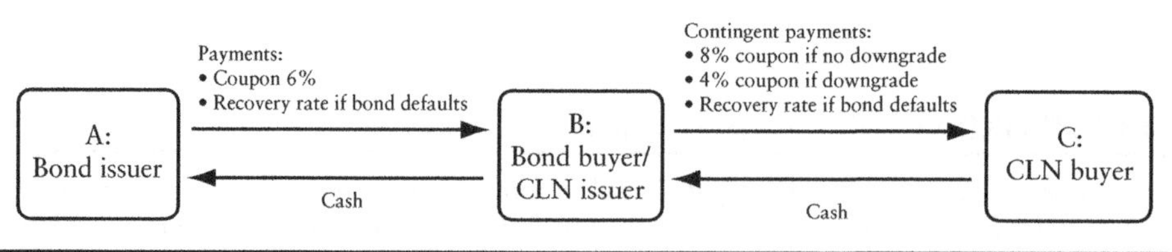

**FIGURE 19.10** Synthetic credit-linked note.

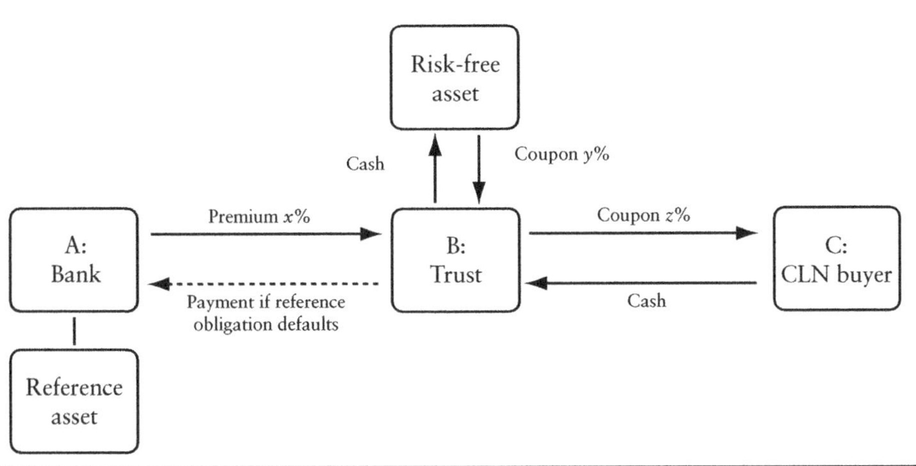


high. Synthetic CLNs can mimic the cash flows of such bonds exactly, but the cost of trading CLNs is lower. Second, CLNs circumvent trading restrictions. Many firms and institutions, for example, are not authorized to engage in derivatives trading or off-balance sheet transactions, and, therefore, are not able to replicate credit exposures synthetically. For these firms, CLNs, being a cash instrument, remain part of the investment opportunity set. Third, CLNs may increase the investment opportunity set for many investors since they can be created on bonds that are publicly traded but in limited supply or not publicly traded at all.

## SYNTHETIC COLLATERALIZED DEBT OBLIGATIONS

In principle, a *collateralized debt obligation* (CDO) has the same structure as a CLN.[12] An intermediary directly or synthetically buys bonds of various issuers and then repackages them as credit-linked instruments that it sells to investors. The key differences between the two products are twofold. First, in place of a single corporate or sovereign bond, a CDO holds a diversified portfolio of bonds. Second, in place of a single credit-linked note, a CDO is usually tranched,[13] providing investors with specific return/risk profiles.

Like CLNs, CDOs involve an intermediary. With CDOs, the types of intermediaries vary. Sometimes it is investment advisory firms. They earn fees based on the amount of assets they manage. By creating a CDO, they can increase their income by increasing its assets under management. Such a CDO is usually called an *arbitrage CDO* because, presumably, there is a spread between the yield it earns on assets and the yield it pays on its debt securities. At other times,

[12] A comprehensive review of CDOs is contained in Lucas, Goodman, and Fabozzi (2006).

[13] *Tranche* is the French word for slice. In CDO markets, the terms *tranche* and *class* are synonymous.

CDOs are created by banks as a way to remove assets from their balance sheets. These are called *balance sheet CDOs*.

Also like CLNs, CDOs come in two basic forms—cash and synthetic. In a *cash CDO*, the intermediary purchases the assets directly, as shown in Figure 19.11. The number of assets purchased varies, but can range up to 100 or more. Some CDOs hold only a single type of bond (e.g., U.S. investment-grade corporate bonds, high-yield corporate bonds, emerging market bonds, and so on). Others include more than one type. The collateral manager is usually required to maintain an average portfolio rating of B or higher.

On the right-hand side of Figure 19.11 are the buyers of the CDO. They are divided into a number of different tranches, with each tranche having a specific return/risk profile. Suppose a CDO issues four classes of securities: (1) senior debt (75% of principal), (2) mezzanine debt (10%), (3) subordinate debt (10%), and (4) equity (5%). Each class protects the ones senior to it from losses on the underlying portfolio. In the event of default losses, the equity holders absorb the first 5% of default losses since they own 5% of the principal of the portfolio. The subordinate debt-holders have 10% of the principal and, hence, absorb the next 10% of default losses. The mezzanine debt have 10% and absorb the next 10% of default losses. Finally, the senior debt has the remaining 75% of principal and absorbs the residual default losses. The sponsor of the CDO usually sets the size of the senior class so that it can attain a triple-A rating. Likewise, the sponsor of a CDO generally designs the other classes so that they achieve successively lower ratings. The equity tranche is sometimes called "toxic waste" because it has significant default risk. A default loss of 4% of the principal of the portfolio, for example, translates into an 80% loss to the equity holders.

**FIGURE 19.11** Cash collateralized debt obligation.

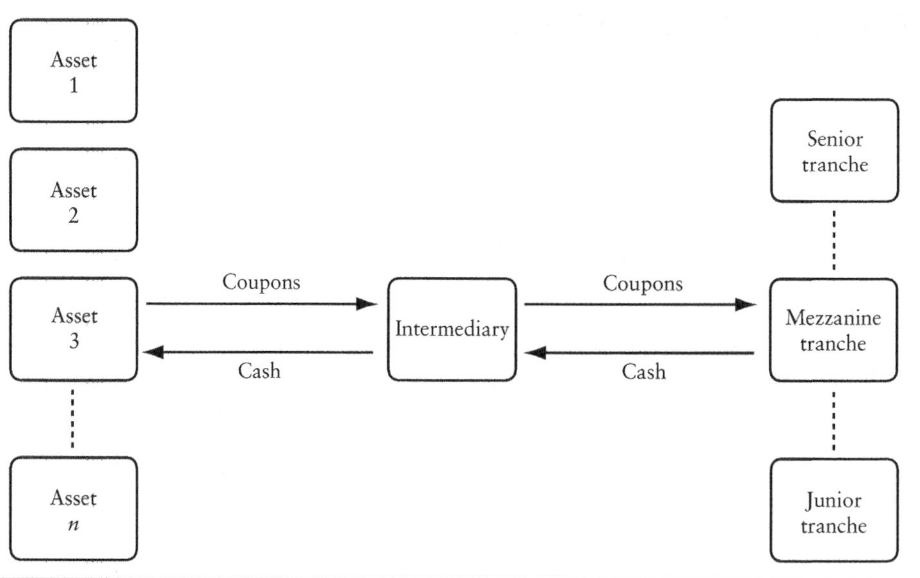

**FIGURE 19.12** Synthetic collateralized debt obligation.

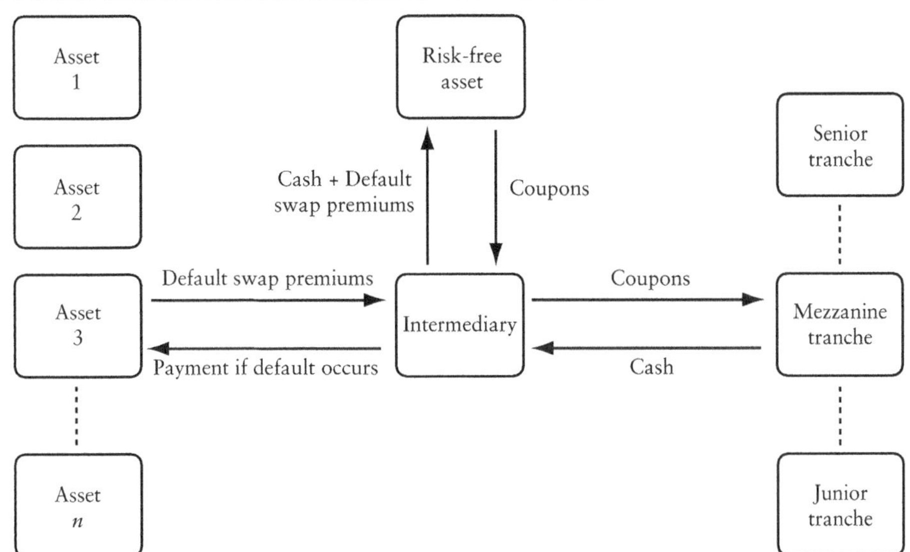


With a *synthetic CDO*, the proceeds from the sale of the CDOs are used to buy risk-free rather than risky bonds. The $n$ different credit risk exposures are created by selling $n$ different credit default swaps. The default risk premiums collected from credit protection buyers together with the cash generated from the sale of the CDOs are placed in risk-free bonds, as shown in Figure 19.12. The coupon payments generated from the risk-free bonds are then used to make the coupon payments to the various tranches of CDO holders. If default occurs, the shortfall is paid from the collateral. The reduction in the amount of collateral is then passed on to the appropriate tranche.

## CREDIT SPREAD FORWARD

A *credit default forward* is a forward contract whose value at expiration depends on a credit spread, that is, the difference between the yield to maturity of a corporate bond and the yield to maturity of a U.S. Treasury bond with a similar coupon interest rate and maturity date.[14] As credit risk rises, the credit spread grows wide, and vice versa. For such contracts, it is important to isolate credit risk from the other factors influencing the bond price. On face appearance, the difference between the yield of a corporate bond and the yield of a comparable U.S. Treasury seems reasonable since subtracting the Treasury yield negates the effect of

[14] Occasionally, the credit spread is erroneously called the *credit risk premium*. This is somewhat misleading in the sense that the credit risk premium is more frequently thought of as the difference between the expected rates of return of a corporate and a Treasury with identical coupons and maturity dates. The credit spread equals the difference between the promised yields to maturity.

interest rate risk. But, this assumes that neither the corporate nor Treasury bonds has any other factor that influences price such a callability, convertibility, extendibility, and so on. If they do, the effects of the option-like features must be modeled. With sovereign bonds, we must control not only for the effects any embedded options but also for the effects of exchange rate risk since the sovereign bond's payments are in a different currency.

## RISK MANAGEMENT LESSON: STATE OF WISCONSIN INVESTMENT BOARD

On March 17, 1995, the State of Wisconsin Investment Board (SWIB) announced that it had incurred a $95 million loss from derivatives trading.[15] The losses arose from a dozen or so swaps based on foreign/domestic interest rate differentials. Specifically, SWIB was betting on the direction of sovereign risk premium movements. While such speculation may seem an odd activity for a money-market fund, we will see precisely how SWIB did it using their Mexican par bond swap contracts as an illustration.

By way of introduction, SWIB is a Wisconsin state agency responsible for investing the assets of the Wisconsin Retirement System, the State Investment Fund (SIF), and five smaller trust funds established by the state. The derivatives losses reported in March 1995 were incurred in the SIF. The $6.7 billion SIF contained operating cash for the state, part of its pension fund, and money from some 1,000 Wisconsin municipalities, county governments, and school districts.[16] For funds managing operating cash, preservation of principal and market liquidity are paramount. SWIB explicitly recognized this fact in its 1994 Annual Report:[17]

> Safety of principal and liquidity in the State Investment Fund are achieved by adherence to rigorous quality standards, careful attention to maturity schedules, and emphasis on high market-ability. Enhanced return is sought through intensive portfolio management, which considers probable changes in the general structure of interest rates.

With the market for risk-free securities being highly competitive, even an extremely successful fund manager would not perform much better than generic money market rates. In the years leading up to the losses, however, SWIB's performance was substantially better than expected. In the 12 years preceding the loss, "state officials say that the fund earned almost one percentage point more than traditional money-market funds."[18] Like in the case of Orange County, AWA Ltd., Barings Bank, and ABN Amro, this should have been a red flag to supervisors. Business activities such as cash management (SWIB and Orange County), minimum-risk foreign currency hedging (AWA Ltd.), stock index futures arbitrage (Barings Bank), and option market making (ABN Amro) are

[15] For details regarding the SWIB controversy, see Chance (1998).
[16] *Wall Street Journal* (March 24, 1995).
[17] SWIB 1994 annual report (p. 21).
[18] *Wall Street Journal* (March 24, 1995).

supposed to be relatively risk-free. If abnormally high returns are earned, chances are that the trading involved risk-taking.

In January 1994, SWIB began entering a series of derivatives trades based on foreign/domestic bond yield differentials. Presumably, these bets were designed to enhance expected return. Some of the contracts were linked to "Brady bonds." These bonds were named after former U.S. Treasury Secretary Nicholas Brady, who in 1989 created a plan to help several countries restructure their external debt into bonds with U.S. Treasury bonds as collateral. In February 1990, Mexico became the first country to issue Brady bonds.

SWIB's first Brady bond swap was linked to the 6.25% coupon Mexican par bond maturing in 2023. The swap was entered on January 27, 1994, and was called a "Stripped Mexican Par Spread." The key terms are summarized in Table 19.4. The swap had a notional amount of $10 million and expired on January 31, 1995. Peculiarly, under the terms of the first swap, SWIB both paid and received six-month LIBOR on a semiannual basis. Naturally, these payments netted to zero and, consequently, they did not contribute to the agreement's economic value. Perhaps, the reason why these periodic payments were included was to give the agreement the appearance of a swap. The only payment in the agreement with any economic significance, however, occurs at expiration when SWIB receives

$$\$10{,}000{,}000 \times \left( \frac{2.95\% - MEXSPD}{2.95\%} \right) \tag{19.5}$$

With only a single payment involved in the structure, the contract is simply a forward contract, not a swap.

Regardless of the misnomer, the terminal payment (19.1) depends on the quantity, 2.95% – *MEXSPD*. If the quantity is positive, SWIB receives the payment, and, if the quantity is negative, SWIB pays. The term, *MEXSPD*, is defined as the difference between (1) the internal rate of return (IRR) of the 6.25% Stripped Collateralized Fixed Rate USD Par Bonds due 2023; and (2) the yield to maturity of the UST 6.25% due 2/15/2003. Here is where the credit risk comes into play. The Brady bonds are USD-denominated, with the principal repayment at the end of the bond's life being guaranteed by the U.S. government.[19] Consequently, the value of a Brady bond can be thought of as being the sum of two components: the present value of a coupon stream discounted at the credit risk-adjusted Mexican yield (U.S. risk-free rate plus a credit risk premium) and the present value of the principal amount discounted at the zero-coupon, U.S. risk-free yield to maturity. Since the second component is nothing but a U.S. strip bond, the terms of the agreement reduce the Mexican par bond price by the market price of a U.S. Treasury strip bond with the same maturity to determine the price of the so-called "Stripped Collateralized Fixed Rate USD Par Bond." Setting the present value of the coupon stream equal to the difference between the Mexican bond price and the UST strip bond price and solving for yield provides the IRR (i.e., the credit risk-adjusted yield on the Mexican par bond). If we fur-

[19] Eighteen months of nearby coupon interest payments were also guaranteed, however, we ignore this consideration in our discussion.

**TABLE 19.4** Selected terms of the stripped Mexican par spread entered by the State of Wisconsin Investment Board on January 24, 1994.

| | |
|---|---|
| Calculation amount | USD 10,000,000.00 |
| Trade date | January 24, 1994 |
| Effective date | January 31, 1994 |
| Termination date | January 31, 1995 |
| **First floating rate payer pays** | |
| First floating rate payer | Bankers Trust Company ("BTCO") |
| Payment dates | Commencing on July 31, 1994 and semiannually thereafter |
| Floating rate option | USD-LIBOR-BAA |
| Designated maturity | 6 months |
| Rounding factor | One-thousandth of 1% |
| Floating rate day convention | Actual/360 |
| Reset dates | The first day of the relevant calculation period |
| **Second floating rate payer** | |
| Second floating rate payer | State of Wisconsin Investment Board State Investment Fund |
| Payment dates | Commencing on July 31, 1994 and semiannually thereafter |
| Floating rate option | USD-LIBOR-BAA |
| Designated maturity | 6 months |
| Rounding factor | One-thousandth of 1% |
| Floating rate day convention | Actual/360 |
| Reset dates | The first day of the relevant calculation period |
| Final exchange amounts | On January 31, 1995, the final exchange amount will be paid in accordance with the following formula: $\text{USD } 10{,}000{,}000.00 \times (2.95\% - \text{MEXSPD})/2.95\%$ If MEXSPD > 2.95%, then SWIB will pay BTCO. If MEXSPD < 2.95%, then BTCO will pay SWIB. Where: "MEXSPD" is the difference, expressed as a percentage, between the Internal Rate of Return of the Stripped Collateralized 6.25% Fixed Rate USD Par Bonds due 2023 issued by the United Mexican States, (the "Mexican Par Bond") and the yield to maturity of the U.S. Treasury Bond 6.25% due February 15, 2003. |

ther subtract the yield to maturity of the UST 6.25% due February 15, 2003, we isolate the risk-premium of Mexican coupon stream over the next 30 years.[20]

For SWIB to enter this swap, they must have held the directional view that the credit risk of Mexico would decline relative to the U.S.[21] But, while we have

[20] The UST 6.25% due February 15, 2003 is presumably chosen to have the same duration as the Mexican par bond coupon stream ending March 31, 2023.

discussed how the agreement isolates the credit risk premium expressed as a percent, we have not discussed the scale of the bet that SWIB was putting into place. Table 19.4 says the notional amount of the swap is \$10 million—a small amount relative to the \$6.7 billion in the fund. But this is no plain-vanilla swap. The expression in parenthesis is a ratio, not an interest rate. It should come as no surprise, therefore, that such swaps are called *ratio swaps*. Note the effect of the ratio. The only economic purpose of the interest rate in the denominator of the ratio is to increase the notional amount of the swap, that is, we can rearrange SWIB's cash receipt (19.5) to read

$$\$338{,}983{,}051 \times (2.95\% - MEXSPD) \tag{19.6}$$

The expression in parenthesis is now an interest rate, as is standard in interest rate swap agreements,[22] but the notional amount of this swap is more than 33 times higher than what is stated in the agreement! If the *MEXSPD* were to move to a level about 300 basis points above 2.95%, the notional amount stated in the original term sheet, \$10 million, would be completely wiped out. It should come as no surprise, therefore, that ratio swaps are also called *leveraged swaps*. For a money-market fund, the potential of losing more than 100% of principal is unusual, to say the least.

The contract's leverage, together with adverse market movements (i.e., being on the wrong side of a big bet), laid the groundwork for disaster. During the course of the year, the *MEXSPD* rose slowly as is shown in the figure below. SWIB entered the agreement when the *MEXSPD* was near its lowest level during 1994. Subsequently during the year, the *MEXSPD* rose to an average level of about 4%. Then, on December 20, 1994, the Economic Growth and Stability Pact (PECE)—a joint government, business and labor body in Mexico—decided to devalue the Mexican peso by 15% to promote economic stability. The credit risk premium of the Mexican par bonds spiked upward, and continued to rise further over the next three months. To stem the tide, SWIB restructured its agreement in May 1994 and then again in February 1995, however, both new structures maintained the directional view that Mexico's credit risk premium would fall. SWIB finally attempted to cut its losses. On March 16, 1995, they entered an off-market, 10-year, fixed-for-floating swap whose value was \$35 million in Bankers Trust's favor. Essentially, this transformed the \$35 million loss into an annuity of monthly payments over a 10-year period. Coincidently, on March 16, 1995, the *MEXSPD* reached its highest level in Figure 19.13—17.15%.

## CREDIT SPREAD OPTIONS

A *credit spread option* is a contract whose value at expiration depends on a the difference between the yield to maturity of a corporate bond and the yield to

[21] Alternatively, if SWIB had a long exposure to the credit risk of Mexico, the swap may have provided a hedge. The composition of the SIF portfolio on June 30, 1994, however, suggests that no such exposure existed. See Chance (1998, p. 6).

[22] Indeed, the payoff is like the inverse floater discussed in Chapter 18.

**FIGURE 19.13** Daily levels of MEXSPD during the period June 23, 1993 through September 22, 1993.

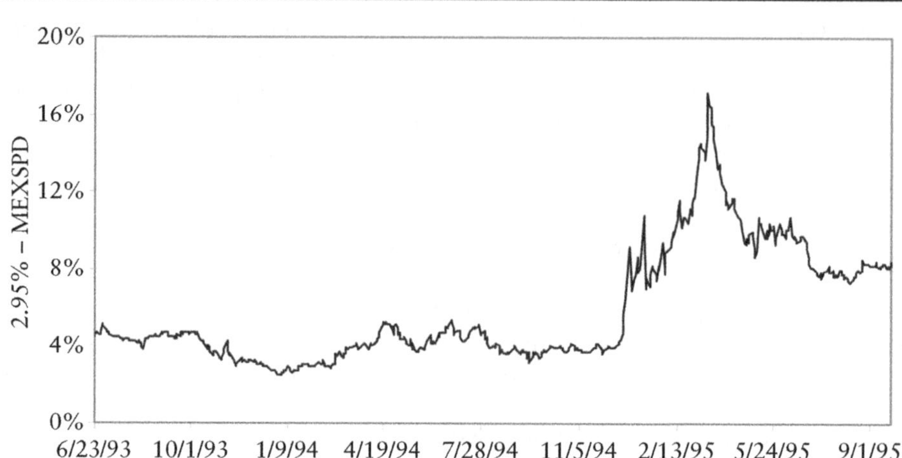


maturity of a U.S. Treasury bond with a similar coupon interest rate and maturity date. A *credit spread call option*, for example, has a payoff of

$$D \max(X - S_T, 0) \quad (19.7)$$

where $S_T$ is the level of the credit spread at the option's expiration, $X$ is the exercise price, and $D$ is a risk factor used to translate the spread into price. $D$ can be closely related to the underlying reference bond's duration. Because the payoff structure (19.7) is expressed in terms of yield, the contingencies are those of a put rather than a call. The call's value increases with an increase in the price of the underlying asset, or, equivalently, a decrease in the yield spread.

Assuming that the credit spread conditional on no default is log-normally distributed at expiration, credit spread options can be valued using the Black (1976) version of the Black-Scholes/Merton (1973) option valuation formulas. Once the Black formula value is computed, we multiply by the probability of no default during the life of the option to arrive at the final option value.

**ILLUSTRATION 19.4** Value credit spread option.

*Compute the value of a three-month European-style credit spread put option with an exercise price of 12%, a risk factor of 5, and a notional amount of \$10 million. Assume the current credit spread is 10%, and its volatility rate is 40%. Assume also that the probability of the firm defaulting during the life of the option is 0.1. The three-month risk-free interest rate is 5%.*

Using the Black (1976) call option valuation formula, the value of a put is

$$p = e^{-0.05(0.25)}[0.11N(d_1) - 0.12N(d_2)] = 0.004948$$

where

$$d_1 = \frac{\ln(0.11/0.12) + 0.5(0.40^2)0.25}{0.40\sqrt{0.25}}$$

and $d_2 = d_1 - 0.40\sqrt{0.25}$. This value can be verified using the OPTVAL function

OV_FOPTION_VALUE(0.11, 0.12, 0.25, 0.05, 0.40, "c", "e") = 0.004948

The put option value assumes a risk factor of 1 and a $1 notional amount. The next step is to scale the value to the terms of the contract. With a risk factor of 5 and a $10 million notional amount, the put option value is

$$0.004948 \times 5 \times 10{,}000{,}000 = 247{,}408$$

Finally, the computed value thus far assumes the firm will not default during the put option's life. If it does, the put will expire worthless. Adjusting for the probability of default/no-default, the put option value is 247,408 × 0.9 = 222,667.

## SUMMARY

Credit derivatives are currently the fastest growing area within the derivatives industry. A *credit derivative* is an agreement that transfers the credit risk of an asset from one party (the *protection buyer*) to another (the *protection seller*). While historically credit risk products focused exclusively on default risk, the payoffs of the products introduced beginning in the early 1990s may be triggered by a variety of credit events including bankruptcy, failure to pay a coupon or to repay the full amount of the bond's principal, an invocation of a cross-default clause such as a more junior bond issue within the firm defaulting, a corporate restructuring that leaves bondholders worse off, and credit deterioration in the form of a downgrade in bond rating. The purpose of this chapter is to provide an overview of the different types of credit derivatives that are now traded in the OTC market and how they are used. We focus on credit default swaps, which constitute the single largest credit derivative contract. In a credit default swap, the protection seller agrees, for an upfront fee or a continuing premium, to compensate the protection buyer upon a defined credit event. Since the buyer retains ownership of the underlying asset, a credit default swap isolates the credit risk inherent in the asset (e.g., the default risk of a corporate bond) from market risk (e.g., the interest rate risk of a corporate bond). We show how credit default swaps are used, in turn, in structuring two other popular types of credit risk products—credit-linked notes (CLNs) and synthetic collateralized debt obligations (CDOs). We also focus on forward and option contracts on credit spreads. Credit spread contracts are contracts whose payoff is proportionally related to the spread between the yield to maturity on a corporate bond and the yield to maturity of a risk-free bond (e.g., U.S. Treasury bond) with same coupon rate and maturity date. The credit spread is a continuous variable that is sensitive to all credit events including bankruptcy, failure to pay, an invocation of a cross-default clause, a corporate restructuring that leaves bondholders worse off, and changes in bond rating.

## REFERENCES AND SUGGESTED READINGS

Acharya, V., and Jennifer Carpenter. 2002. Corporate bond valuation and hedging with stochastic interest rates and endogenous bankruptcy. *Review of Financial Studies* 15: 1355–1383.

Black, Fischer. 1976. The pricing of commodity contracts. *Journal of Financial Economics* 3 (March): 167–179.

Black, Fischer, and John Cox. 1976. Valuing corporate securities: Some effects of bond indenture provisions. *Journal of Finance* 31: 351–367.

Black, Fischer, and Myron Scholes. 1973. The pricing of options and corporate liabilities. *Journal of Political Economy* 81: 637–659.

Bohn, Jeffrey R. 2000. A survey of contingent-claims approaches to risky debt valuation. *Journal of Risk Finance* (Spring): 53–70.

Bohn, Jeffrey R. 2000. An empirical assessment of a simple contingent-claims model for the valuation of risky debt. *Journal of Risk Finance* 1 (Summer): 55–77.

Bohn, Jeffrey R. 1999. Characterizing credit spreads. Working paper, Haas School of Business, University of California, Berkeley.

Campbell, John Y., and Glen B. Taksler. 2003. Equity volatility and corporate bond yields. *Journal of Finance* 58: 2321–2349.

Cooper, Ian A., and Sergei A. Davydenko. 2003. Using yield spreads to estimate expected returns on debt and equity. Working paper. London Business School.

Cornell, Bradford, and Kevin Green. 1991. The investment performance of low-grade bond funds. *Journal of Finance* 46: 29–48.

Crosbie, P., and J. Bohn. 2002. Modeling default risk. Working paper. KMV.

Duffee, Gregory R. 1999. Estimating the price of default risk. *Review of Financial Studies* 12: 197–226.

Duffie, Darryl, and Ken Singleton. 1999. Modeling the term structures of defaultable bonds. *Review of Financial Studies* 12: 687–720.

Geske, Robert. 1979. The valuation of compound options. *Journal of Financial Economics* 7: 63–81.

Huang, Jing-zhi, and Ming Huang. 2003. How much of the corporate-treasury yield spread is due to credit risk? Working paper. Stanford University.

International Swaps and Derivatives Association. 2003. *2003 ISDA Credit Derivatives Definitions*. New York: International Swaps and Derivatives Association.

Jarrow, Robert A., and Stuart Turnbull. 1995. Pricing derivatives on securities subject to credit risk. *Journal of Finance* 50: 53–85.

Leland, Hayne E. 2004. Predictions of default probabilities in structural models of debt. Working paper. Haas School of Business, University of California, Berkeley.

Longstaff, Francis A., and Eduardo S. Schwartz. 1995. Valuing risky debt: A new approach. *Journal of Finance* 50: 789–820.

Lucas, Douglas, J., Laurie S. Goodman, and Frank J. Fabozzi. 2006. *Collateralized Debt Obligations: Strcuture and Analysis*, 2nd ed. Hoboken, NJ: John Wiley & Sons.

Meissner, Gunter. 2005. *Credit Derivative: Application, Pricing, and Risk Management*. Malden, MA: Blackwell.

Merton, Robert C. 1974. On the pricing of corporate debt: The risk structure of interest rates. *Journal of Finance* 29: 449–470.

Tavakoli, Janet M. 1998. *Credit Derivatives: A Guide to Instruments and Applications*. New York: John Wiley & Sons.

Tudela, Merxe, and Garry Young. 2003. A Merton model approach to assessing the default risk of UK public companies. Working paper. Bank of England.

Uhrig-Homburg, Maliese. 2002. Valuation of defaultable claims: A survey. *Schmalenbach Business Review* 54: 24–57.

Vassalou, Maria, and Yuhang Xing. 2004. Default risk in equity returns. *Journal of Finance* 59 (April): 831–868.

# 20

# Valuing Interest Rate Products Numerically

Valuing interest rate derivatives written on short-term bonds is trickier than valuing derivatives on other types of assets for two reasons. First, for an asset such as a stock, a currency or a commodity, price can roam freely through time without constraint. For a fixed income security, however, price is often forced to take a particular level when the security matures. A T-bill, for example, has a value of 100 when it matures, and a T-note has a terminal payment equal to its final coupon interest payment plus the par value. Second, in the fixed income markets, there is often a wide range of securities available on the *same* underlying source of uncertainty. The U.S. Treasury, for example, has T-bills, T-notes and T-bonds with a wide range of maturities. In modeling interest rate dynamics, care must be taken to ensure that all of these securities are simultaneously valued at levels consistent with observed market prices.

The purpose of this chapter is modest—to develop a binomial procedure for valuing interest rate derivative contracts where the short-term interest rate ("short rate") is the single underlying source of interest rate uncertainty. To begin, we discuss a number of constant-parameter short rate processes to lay a foundation for interest rate behavior. While these models are often useful in developing economic intuition regarding interest rate behavior, they produce zero-coupon bond values that are different from the observed market prices, seemingly giving rise to arbitrage opportunities. Consequently, we next turn to no-arbitrage pricing models. These models adjust the parameters of the interest rate process in a manner that produces bond (and interest rate derivatives contract) values equal to observed prices. With the mechanics of no-arbitrage pricing in hand, we then turn to valuing zero-coupon and coupon-bearing bonds, callable bonds, putable bonds, and bond options. Be forewarned, however. While the valuation framework provided in this chapter is intuitive and commonly-applied in practice, it only begins to scratch the surface of the literature focused on no-arbitrage interest rate models. This literature is deep in multifactor theoretical models of interest rate movements and numerical procedures for calibrating the interest rate models and valuing interest rate derivatives.

## CONSTANT-PARAMETER MODELS

In the Black-Scholes (1973)/Merton (1973) model developed in Chapter 5, the price of an asset was assumed to follow the geometric Brownian motion (i.e., equation (5.4)), that is,

$$dS = \alpha S dt + \sigma S dz \tag{20.1}$$

This assumption implies that, over the next infinitesimally small interval of time $dt$, the change in asset price, $dS$, equals an expected price increment (i.e., the product of the instantaneous expected rate of change in asset price, $\alpha$, times the current asset price, $S$, times the length of the interval) plus a random increment proportional to the instantaneous standard deviation of the rate of change in asset price, $\sigma$, times the asset price. Note that, in the assumed process (20.1), the parameters $\alpha$ and $\sigma$ are constants (i.e., do not vary through time or with the level of asset price). In the first part of this section, we develop economic intuition regarding plausible interest rate processes by examining four constant-parameter interest rate processes. In the second part, we show why constant-parameter, short rate models are seldom used in practice.

### Constant-Parameter, Short Rate Processes

The simplest constant-parameter, short rate process that we consider is the arithmetic Brownian motion assumption,

$$dr = a dt + \sigma dz \tag{20.2}$$

where $dr$ is the instantaneous change in the short rate, $a$ is its instantaneous mean, and $\sigma$ is its instantaneous standard deviation. The assumption (20.2) says that the short-rate change over the next increment in time, $\Delta t$, is normally distributed with mean $r + a\Delta t$ and standard deviation $\sigma\sqrt{\Delta t}$.[1] If $a > 0$, the short rate is expected to climb through time, and, if $a < 0$, it is expected to fall. The size of the random change in the rate increases proportionally with $\sigma\sqrt{\Delta t}$.

In terms of describing interest rate dynamics, the process (20.2) has a number of weaknesses. First, the process does nothing to guard against the possibility of the short rate becoming negative. In particular, if $a < 0$, the short rate must eventually become negative. Similarly, the short rate can become negative in the stochastic component of the short-rate movement (i.e., the second term on the right-hand side of (20.2)) has a large negative value. Naturally, in a rationally functioning marketplace, negative interest rates will not arise. In such an environment, individuals would prefer to put cash in their mattresses than hold Treasury bills.

A second weakness of (20.2) is that, if $a > 0$, the short rate is expected to rise without limit. While this assumption may be plausible for asset prices,

[1] For clarity of exposition, think of the short rate $r$ as being the continuously compounded interest rate on a one-year U.S. T-bill and the time increment $\Delta t$ as being equal to one year.

casual empirical observation suggests that interest rates tend to revert toward some long-run mean level through time.[2] This stands to reason from an economic standpoint. When interest rates are high, the demand for borrowed funds subsides, causing interest rates to fall. Conversely, when interest rates are low, the demand for borrowed funds rises, causing interest rates to rise. A third weakness of (20.2) is that the volatility rate is the same, independent of whether interest rates are high or low. From an empirical standpoint, the volatility of interest rates tends to rise with as the level of interest rates rises and falls as the level of interest rates falls.

The next constant-parameter, short-rate process that we consider is the geometric Brownian motion assumption,

$$dr = ardt + \sigma rdz \tag{20.3}$$

introduced by Rendleman and Bartter (1980). In (20.3), $a$ is the instantaneous expected rate of change in the short rate, and $\sigma$ is its instantaneous standard deviation. Note that this specification is identical to the BSM assumption (20.1), that is, Rendleman and Bartter assume that the short rate behaves as if it were an asset price. The process (20.3) circumvents two of the weaknesses associated with (20.2). First, with (20.3), interest rates cannot become negative. One reason is that the expected short rate at the end of the next increment in time is $re^{a\Delta t}$. Even if $a < 0$, the expected short rate remains positive. Another is that the stochastic component of interest rate movements (i.e., the second term on the right-hand side of (20.3)) approaches zero as interest rates fall. Second, the process (20.3) captures the empirical phenomenon that the volatility of interest rates changes ($\sigma r$ in this case) increases with the level of interest rates. The one weakness that (20.3) does not circumvent, however, is that if $a > 0$ the short rate is expected to rise without limit. The process fails to account for the empirical fact (and economic prediction) that interest rates are mean-reverting.

Next is the short-rate process derived by Vasicek (1977),

$$dr = a(b - r)dt + \sigma dz \tag{20.4}$$

where the parameters $a$, $b$ and $\sigma$ are constants. Like (20.2) and (20.3), the change in the short rate has an expected and a random component. Unlike the first terms on the right-hand sides of (20.2) and (20.3) where the short rate is expected to drift upward or downward, however, the first term on the right-hand side of the Vasicek model (20.4) captures mean reversion in the short rate. The long-run mean level of the short rate is $b$, so, if the current short rate $r$ is less than $b$, the short rate is pulled upward, and, if the current short rate is above $b$, it is pulled downward (assuming, of course, that $a$ is positive). The parameter $a$ is called the rate of pull or, simply, pull rate. If the pull rate is 0.5 and the current short rate $r$ is 1% below the long-run mean $b$, we expect that the short rate will increase by 0.5% over the next increment in time. If $a = 0$, the short rate follows arithmetic Brownian motion with a zero mean (i.e., a random walk). Where $a = 1$, the short rate is expected to immediately return to its long-

[2] Recall that we first discussed mean reversion in Chapter 9.

term mean. The last term on the right-hand side accounts for random movements in the short rate. Like (20.2), the random changes in the short rate in (20.4) are a normally distributed and independent of the level of the short rate. This means, like (20.2), the short rate in (20.4) has the prospect of becoming negative and does not account for the fact that the volatility of interest rates changes tends to increase with the level of interest rates and vice versa.

The fourth and final constant-parameter, short rate process that we consider was derived by Cox, Ingersoll, and Ross (1977). The CIR model is specified as

$$dr = a(b - r)dt + \sigma\sqrt{r}dz \tag{20.5}$$

The first term on the right-hand side (20.5) is the mean reversion component introduced by Vasicek. Unlike the Vasicek model, however, the instantaneous standard deviation by the factor $\sqrt{r}$. This overcomes the remaining two deficiencies of the Vasicek model. Specifically, with the random component of the interest rate change defined as $\sigma\sqrt{r}$, (1) the volatility of interest rate movements is directly related to the level of interest rates; and (2) negative interest rates are not possible (i.e., where the short rate falls to zero, the second term on the right-hand side approaches zero, and the short rate is guaranteed to move upward).

### Applying Constant-Parameter Models

All of the constant-parameter models described above can be implemented for valuing bonds and interest rate derivatives. None of them will produce values that are completely consistent with prices observed in the marketplace, however. The reason is that the parameters of the model are constant through time. To see this, consider applying the Vasicek model to value zero-coupon bonds. We begin by approximating (20.4) using the binomial distribution,

$$r_{t+\Delta t} - r_t = \begin{cases} a(b - r_t)dt + \sigma\sqrt{r}dz & \text{with probability} = 1/2 \\ a(b - r_t)dt - \sigma\sqrt{r}dz & \text{with probability} = 1/2 \end{cases} \tag{20.6}$$

Note that, by defining the short-rate movements as (20.6), the vertical distance between the two nodes emanating from $r_t$ equals $2\sigma\sqrt{\Delta t}$.

One disadvantage of using the binomial method to approximate short-rate movements within the Vasicek model is that the binomial lattice does not recombine. To see this, recall the lattice notation from Chapter 9. Specifically, let $r_{i,j}$ be the short rate at time $i$ and vertical node $j$, where $j = 1$ is the lowest node at time $i$. Figure 20.1 contains a two-period, short-rate lattice. Note that at time 2, there are four nodes rather than three since, in general, $r_{2,3} \neq r_{2,2}$. The only instance in which the nodes will recombine (i.e., $r_{2,3} = r_{2,2}$) is where $a = 0$, in which case the short rate follows a simple random walk. The fact that the binomial lattice does not recombine does not mean that the binomial method cannot be used in this context. It only means that the computational exercise is more tedious. With a recombining lattice, the number of possible interest rate nodes is $n + 1$. With a nonrecombining lattice, the number of nodes is $2^n$. Where

**FIGURE 20.1** Two-period lattice for Vasicek model.

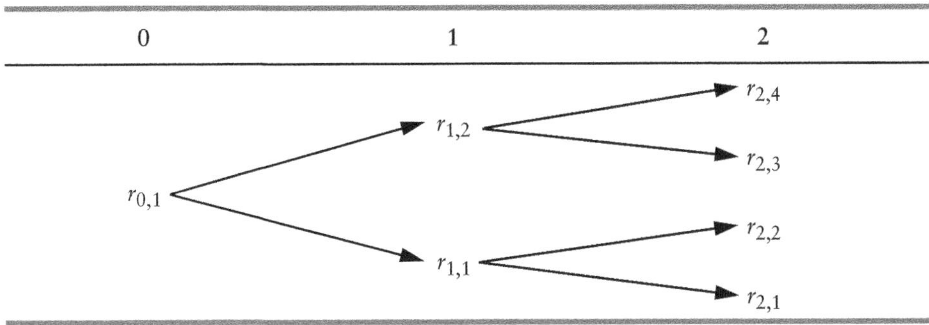


where the nodes at time 1 are

$$r_{1,2} = r_{0,1} + a(b - r_{0,1})\Delta t + \sigma\sqrt{\Delta t}$$

and

$$r_{1,1} = r_{0,1} + a(b - r_{0,1})\Delta t - \sigma\sqrt{\Delta t}$$

and the nodes at time 2 are

$$r_{2,4} = r_{1,2} + a(b - r_{1,2})\Delta t + \sigma\sqrt{\Delta t}$$
$$r_{2,3} = r_{1,2} + a(b - r_{1,2})\Delta t - \sigma\sqrt{\Delta t}$$
$$r_{2,2} = r_{1,1} + a(b - r_{1,1})\Delta t + \sigma\sqrt{\Delta t}$$
$$r_{2,1} = r_{1,1} + a(b - r_{1,1})\Delta t - \sigma\sqrt{\Delta t}$$

Note that, in general, $r_{2,3} \neq r_{2,2}$.

---

the number of time steps is 10 (i.e., $n$ = 10), the number of nodes is 101 for a recombining lattice and 1,024 for a nonrecombining lattice.

Now, let us consider valuing zero-coupon or discount bonds using (20.6). Assume that the zero-coupon yield curve is given by

$$r_i = 0.10 - 0.05e^{0.18(T_i - 1)}$$

where $r_i$ is the continuously compounded, zero-coupon yield rate, and $T_i$ is its time to maturity measured in years. Also assume that we have obtained a history of one-year short rates and have estimated the parameters of the Vasicek model to be $a = 0.5$, $b = 0.06$, and $\sigma = 0.01$, where $b$ and $\sigma$ are annualized rates.[3] Now, let us compute the one-year short rates using Vasicek's mean-reverting process, and then value one-year, two-year, and three-year discount bonds.

[3] Recall that in Chapter 9 we showed how to estimate the parameters of a mean-reverting process using regression analysis.

**FIGURE 20.2** Two-period lattice for Vasicek model assuming the current short rate is 5%, the pull rate is 0.5, the long-run average short rate is 6%, and the volatility rate is 1%. ($r = 0.05$, $a = 0.5$, $b = 0.06$, $\sigma = 0.01$).

| 0 | 1 | 2 |
|---|---|---|
| | | 7.250% |
| | 6.500% | |
| | | 5.250% |
| 5.000% | | |
| | | 6.250% |
| | 4.500% | |
| | | 4.250% |

Figure 20.2 shows the evolution of the short rate under the assumed parameter values. With the current one-year short rate at 5%, the possible one-year short rates in one year are

$$r_{1,2} = 0.05 + 0.5(0.06 - 0.05)1 + 0.01\sqrt{1} = 0.065$$

and

$$r_{1,1} = 0.05 + 0.5(0.06 - 0.05)1 - 0.01\sqrt{1} = 0.045$$

The expected one-year short rates in two years are

$$r_{2,4} = 0.065 + 0.5(0.06 - 0.065)1 + 0.01\sqrt{1} = 0.0725$$

$$r_{2,3} = 0.065 + 0.5(0.06 - 0.065)1 - 0.01\sqrt{1} = 0.0525$$

$$r_{2,2} = 0.045 + 0.5(0.06 - 0.045)1 + 0.01\sqrt{1} = 0.0625$$

and

$$r_{2,1} = 0.045 + 0.5(0.06 - 0.045)1 - 0.01\sqrt{1} = 0.0425$$

Note that the lattice in Figure 20.2 shows the mechanics of short-rate mean reversion at work. Each year, the one-year short-rate jumps up or down by 1% due to the volatility component (i.e., $\pm 0.01\sqrt{1}$ ). Viewed in isolation, this means than standing at $r_{1,2} = 6.5\%$, the one-year short rate will jump to 7.5% or 5.5% with equal probability. But, because the one-year spot rate is above the long-run mean level of 6%, the subsequent one-year spot rates are pulled toward the long-run mean by an amount equal to $0.5(0.06 - 0.065)1 = 0.0025$ or 0.25%. Thus, the nodes $r_{2,4}$ and $r_{2,3}$ are 7.25% and 5.25%, respectively.

Based on the evolution of one-year spot rates displayed in Figure 20.2, we can now compute the values of one-year, two-year, and three-year discount bonds. A one-year discount bond pays 1 in one-year. The one-year short rate is known to be 5%. The value of a one-year discount bond is therefore

$$DBV_1 = e^{-0.05(1)} = 0.95123$$

A two-year, zero-coupon bond pays 1 in year 2. According to the interest rate lattice in Figure 20.2, the evolution of the short rate is (1) 5% over the first year and 6.5% over the second or (2) 5% over the first year and 4.5% over the second, with equal probability. The value of a two-year discount bond is therefore

$$DBV_2 = 0.5e^{-0.05(1)}e^{-0.065(1)} + 0.5e^{-0.05(1)}e^{-0.045(1)} = 0.90037$$

Finally, a three-year discount bond pays 1 in three years. Again, the interest rate lattice in Figure 20.2 describes the possible paths for the short-rate evolution. Four paths are possible, each with equal probability: (1) 5%, 6.5%, and 7.25%, (2) 5%, 6.5%, and 5.25%, (3) 5%, 4.5%, and 6.25%, and (4) 5%, 4.5%, and 4.25%. The value of a three-year discount bond is

$$\begin{aligned} DBV_3 &= 0.25[e^{-0.05(1)}e^{-0.065(1)}e^{-0.0725(1)}] + 0.25[e^{-0.05(1)}e^{-0.065(1)}e^{-0.0525(1)}] \\ &\quad + 0.25[e^{-0.05(1)}e^{-0.045(1)}e^{-0.0625(1)}] + 0.25[e^{-0.05(1)}e^{-0.045(1)}e^{-0.0425(1)}] \\ &= 0.85015 \end{aligned}$$

Now, with the Vasicek model discount bond values in hand, recall that at the outset we assumed the zero-coupon yield curve was given by the relation $R_t = 0.10 - 0.05e^{0.18(t-1)}$. Such a yield curve implies that the zero-coupon bond prices at the outset are

| Years to Maturity | Spot Rate | Discount Bond Price |
|---|---|---|
| 1 | 5.000% | 95.123 |
| 2 | 5.824% | 89.005 |
| 3 | 6.512% | 82.255 |

The one-year discount bond price matches its theoretical value because in applying the Vasicek model we assumed that the one-year short rate was 5%. The two-year and three-year discount bond prices do not match their theoretical values (0.89005 versus 0.90037 and 0.82255 versus 0.85015, respectively), however. The reasons for these apparent arbitrage opportunities are twofold. First, we used historical estimates of the parameters $a$, $b$, and $\sigma$, and, while assuming past parameters are reasonable predictions for the future, they may not be. Second, the Vasicek model assumes that the parameters $a$, $b$, and $\sigma$ are constant through time. Such an assumption will give rise to apparent arbitrage opportunities because the interest rate dynamics modeled by (20.6) are not rich enough to describe the current term structure of zero-coupon interest rates.

**FIGURE 20.3** Discount bonds values based on Vasicek model assuming the current short rate is 5%, the pull rate is 0.5, the long-run average short rate is 6%, and the volatility rate is 1%. ($r$ = 0.05, $a$ = 0.5, $b$ = 0.06, $\sigma$ = 0.01).

One-year discount bond value lattice:

| 0 | 1 |
|---|---|
| | 1 |
| 0.95123 | |
| | 1 |

Two-year discount bond value lattice:

| 0 | 1 | 2 |
|---|---|---|
| | 0.93707 | 1 |
| 0.90037 | | |
| | 0.95600 | 1 |

Three-year discount bond value lattice:

| 0 | 1 | 2 | 3 |
|---|---|---|---|
| | | 0.93007 | 1 |
| | 0.880334 | | |
| | | 0.94885 | 1 |
| 0.85015 | | | |
| | | 0.93941 | 1 |
| | 0.90715 | | |
| | | 0.95839 | 1 |

One possible remedy to this problem is to *calibrate* the short-rate parameters using market prices.[4] More specifically, if we equate the model values of the discount bonds to their observed prices, we can infer the parameters, $a$, $b$, and $\sigma$. In the current illustration, we have two mismatched prices, so we can infer only two of the three model parameters. Suppose that we are willing to accept the fact that $\sigma = 0.01$. We can now solve for the parameters $a$ and $b$ by insisting that the two-year and three-year discount bond values equal their market prices. The parameter values of $a = 0.2440$ and $b = 0.1177$ will make the discount bond values equal their market prices,[5] as shown in Figure 20.4. The apparent arbitrage opportunities have disappeared, however, one is left with the uncomfortable situation that parameter values may not be reasonable from an economic standpoint. Such is the tradeoff created by applying no-arbitrage pricing models.

[4] We used the *calibration* process in earlier chapters when we computed implied standard deviations from option prices.

[5] Solving for the parameters $a$ and $b$ can be accomplished using the Microsoft Excel function, SOLVER.

**FIGURE 20.4** Discount bonds values based on Vasicek model assuming the current short rate is 5%, the pull rate is 0.2440, the long-run average short rate is 11.77%, and the volatility rate is 1%. ($r = 0.05$, $a = 0.2440$, $b = 0.1177$, $\sigma = 0.01$).

One-year discount bond value lattice:

| 0 | 1 |
|---|---|
| | 1 |
| 0.95123 | |
| | 1 |

Two-year discount bond value lattice:

| 0 | 1 | 2 |
|---|---|---|
| | 0.92633 | 1 |
| 0.89005 | | |
| | 0.94504 | 1 |

Three-year discount bond value lattice:

| 0 | 1 | 2 | 3 |
|---|---|---|---|
| | | 0.90794 | 1 |
| | 0.84954 | | |
| | | 0.92628 | 1 |
| 0.82255 | | | |
| | | 0.92177 | 1 |
| | 0.87991 | | |
| | | 0.94039 | 1 |

To emphasize the issue about the plausibility of the parameter estimates, we can extend the illustration to include four discount bond prices. With three mismatched prices, we can infer all three parameters of the Vasicek model. The no-arbitrage parameter values will be $a = 0.2494$, $b = 0.1161$, and $\sigma = -0.00009$. Although all discount bond values now match observed market prices, we are in the unpalatable position of explaining why the estimate of the standard deviation parameter is negative. Clearly, we have reached the limits of this constant-parameter model. Beyond four discount bond prices, it is impossible for the Vasicek model to be used within a no-arbitrage framework. Arbitrage opportunities will appear. The assumed stochastic process is simple not rich enough to capture interest rate movements.

## NO-ARBITRAGE MODELS OF INTEREST RATES

As we have just shown, the chief disadvantage of constant-parameter models is that they cannot, in general, fit today's term structure of zero-coupon rates. In order to ensure that the short-rate dynamics are consistent with prices observed in the marketplace, we allow the parameters of the stochastic process to change through time. This section focuses on the application on *no-arbitrage pricing models.*[6] First, we assume that the changes in the short rate are normally distributed, and then, to prevent the possibility of negative interest rates, we assume the short rate is log-normally distributed (i.e., the logarithm of the short rate is normally distributed).

## Normal Distribution

Suppose we consider the Vasicek model (20.4) with time-varying parameters, that is,

$$dr = a(t)[b(t) - r]dt + \sigma(t)dz \tag{20.7}$$

Note that the pull rate $a(t)$, the long-run mean $b(t)$, and the volatility of the short-rate $\sigma(t)$ are functions of time. The process (20.7) can again be approximated by a binomial process, that is,

$$r_{t+\Delta t} - r_t = \begin{cases} a(t)[b(t) - r]\Delta t + \sigma(t)\sqrt{\Delta t} & \text{with probability} = 1/2 \\ a(t)[b(t) - r]\Delta t - \sigma(t)\sqrt{\Delta t} & \text{with probability} = 1/2 \end{cases} \tag{20.8}$$

As before, we can see that the vertical distance between the two nodes emanating from $r_{i,j}$ in binomial lattice notation is $2\sigma(t)\sqrt{\Delta t}$, that is,

$$r_{i+1,j+1} - r_{i+1,j} = 2\sigma(i)\sqrt{\Delta t} \tag{20.9}$$

Note that the volatility parameter is the local volatility of the one-period short rate in one-period. Thus, if $\Delta t$ is one year, $\sigma(0)$ is volatility of the one-year rate in one year, $\sigma(1)$ is volatility of the one-year rate in two years, $\sigma(2)$ is volatility of the one-year rate in three years, and so on.[7]

To make the binomial lattice procedure more tractable, we impose the restriction that the binomial lattice recombines (i.e., we set $r_{2,3} = r_{2,2}$ in Figure 20.1). This means

$$r_{2,3} = r_{1,2} + a(1)[b(1) - r_{1,2}]\Delta t - \sigma(1)\sqrt{\Delta t} \tag{20.10}$$

and

$$r_{2,2} = r_{1,1} + a(1)[b(1) - r_{1,1}]\Delta t + \sigma(1)\sqrt{\Delta t} \tag{20.11}$$

---

[6] The pioneering work on valuing interest rate derivatives using no-arbitrage pricing models is Ho and Lee (1986).

[7] In this section, we assume that the sequence of volatility estimates is known. In practice, they can be estimated from the prices of caps and floors.

Equating (20.10) and (20.11), rearranging, and simplifying, we get

$$r_{1,2} - r_{1,1} - a(1)(r_{1,2} - r_{1,1})\Delta t = 2\sigma(1)\sqrt{\Delta t} \tag{20.12}$$

Substituting (20.9) into (20.12), we get

$$2\sigma(0)\sqrt{\Delta t} - a(1)[2\sigma(0)\sqrt{\Delta t}]\Delta t = 2\sigma(1)\sqrt{\Delta t}$$

or

$$1 - a(1)\Delta t = \sigma(1)/\sigma(0) \tag{20.13}$$

Note that because we imposed the restriction that the binomial lattice recombines, the mean reversion parameter $a(1)$ is determined by the ratio of the ratio of the local volatility rates at adjacent time steps and need not be estimated separately.

We now turn to the computation of the binomial lattice in a no-arbitrage pricing framework. The key relation in computing the lattice efficiently is that we know the distance between adjacent vertical nodes at each time step (20.9). Begin by considering the possible levels of interest rates at the end of one period. As Figure 20.5 shows, there are two possibilities—$r_{1,1}$ and $r_{1,2} = r_{1,1} + 2\sigma(0)\sqrt{\Delta t}$ with equal probability. Since the volatility parameter and the time increment are known, identifying the numerical values of each of the two nodes is merely a matter of finding $r_{1,1}$. Suppose that the zero-coupon yield curve is described by the relation

$$r_i = 0.10 - 0.05e^{-0.18(T_i - 1)}$$

where $t$ is measured in years and that the volatility rate is $\sigma(t) = 0.01$ for all $t$. Based on the zero-coupon yields, we compute the prices of one-year and two-

**FIGURE 20.5** One-period binomial lattice for no-arbitrage pricing model assuming the short rate is normally distributed.

| 0 | 1 |
|---|---|
| | $r_{1,2} = r_{1,1} + 2\sigma(0)\sqrt{\Delta t}$ |
| $r_{0,1}$ | |
| | $r_{1,1}$ |

where the nodes at time 1 are

$$r_{1,1} = r_{0,1} + a(0)[b(0) - r_{0,1}]\Delta t - \sigma(0)\sqrt{\Delta t} \text{ and}$$
$$r_{1,2} = r_{0,1} + a(0)[b(0) - r_{0,1}]\Delta t - \sigma(0)\sqrt{\Delta t}$$
$$= r_{1,1} + 2\sigma(0)\sqrt{\Delta t}$$

year discount bonds. The one-year discount bond has a price of $DBP_1 = e^{-R(1)1} = e^{-0.05(1)} = 0.95123$ and the two-year discount bond has a price of $DBP_2 = e^{-R(2)2} = e^{-0.05824(2)} = 0.89005$, as summarized in this table:

| Years to Maturity | Spot Rate | Discount Bond Price | Forward Discount Bond Price |
|---|---|---|---|
| 1 | 5.000% | 0.95123 | |
| 2 | 5.824% | 0.89005 | 0.93569 |

Based on the prices the one-year and two-year discount factors, we can compute the forward price of a one-year discount bond in one year as $FBP_{1,1} = DBP_2/DBP_1 = 0.93569$. In the absence of costless arbitrage opportunities, it must be the case that the forward discount bond price from the zero-coupon yield curve must equal the expected discount value in the interest rate lattice. The value of $r_{1,1}$ can therefore be determined by solving

$$\begin{aligned} 0.93569 &= 0.5e^{-r_{1,1}\Delta t} + 0.5e^{(-r_{1,1}+2\sigma(0)\sqrt{\Delta t})\Delta t} \\ &= 0.5e^{-r_{1,1}} + 0.5e^{-r_{1,1}+0.02} \end{aligned}$$

The value can be determined iteratively using SOLVER. The value of $r_{1,1}$ is 5.6523%, and the value of $r_{1,2}$ is 7.6523%, as is shown in Figure 20.6.

We fill out the remaining lattice short-rate binomial lattice by using the same computational procedure recursively. Consider Figure 20.7, which shows the interest rate lattice over two periods. At the end of two periods, we have a

**FIGURE 20.6** One-period binomial lattice for no-arbitrage pricing model assuming the short rate is normally distributed, the zero-coupon yield curve is $R(t) = 0.10 - 0.05e^{-0.18(t-1)}$ where $t$ is measured in years, and the volatility rate is $\sigma(t) = 0.01$ for all $t$.

| 0 | 1 |
|---|---|
| | 7.6523% |
| 5.0000% | |
| | 5.6523% |

**FIGURE 20.7** Two-period binomial lattice for no-arbitrage pricing model assuming the short rate is normally distributed.

| 0 | 1 | 2 |
|---|---|---|
| | | $r_{2,3} = r_{2,1} + 4\sigma(1)\sqrt{\Delta t}$ |
| | $r_{1,2} = r_{1,1} + 2\sigma(0)\sqrt{\Delta t}$ | |
| $r_{0,1}$ | | $r_{2,2} = r_{2,1} + 2\sigma(1)\sqrt{\Delta t}$ |
| | $r_{1,1}$ | |
| | | $r_{2,1}$ |

single unknown, $r_{2,1}$, because we know the distance between adjacent vertical nodes. To solve for its value, we must first compute the forward price of a one-year discount bond in two years, $FDB_{2,1}$. The zero-coupon yield curve tells us its value is 0.92415.

| Years to Maturity | Spot Rate | Discount Bond Price | Forward Discount Bond Price |
|---|---|---|---|
| 1 | 5.000% | 0.95123 | |
| 2 | 5.824% | 0.89005 | 0.93569 |
| 3 | 6.512% | 0.82255 | 0.92415 |
| 4 | 7.086% | 0.75318 | 0.91567 |

In the absence of costless arbitrage opportunities, the forward discount bond price from the zero-coupon yield curve must equal the expected discount price within the interest rate lattice. The value of $r_{2,1}$ can be determined by solving

$$0.92415 = 0.25e^{-r_{2,1}} + 0.5e^{-(r_{2,1}+0.02)} + 0.25e^{-(r_{2,1}+0.04)}$$

The solution to this equation is $r_{2,1} = 0.058976$. The rates at the middle and upper nodes are therefore 0.078976 and 0.098976, respectively. For year 4, the lowest minimum rate is identified by solving for

$$0.91567 = 0.125e^{-r_{3,1}} + 0.375e^{-(r_{3,1}+0.02)} + 0.375e^{-(r_{3,1}+0.04)} + 0.375e^{-(r_{3,1}+0.06)}$$

The solution to this equation is $r_{3,1} = 0.058252$. The complete interest rate lattice over four periods is shown in Figure 20.8.

Note that, in the above computations, we need to identify the probabilities of arriving at binomial lattice node $(i,j)$, where $i$ is the number of the time step, and $j$ is the number of the vertical node (with $j = 1$ being the lowest). The general formula for computing this probability is

$$p_{i,j} = \left(\frac{1}{2}\right)^i \frac{i!}{(j-1)!(i-j+1)!} \tag{20.14}$$

**FIGURE 20.8** Three-period binomial lattice for no-arbitrage pricing model assuming the short rate is normally distributed, the zero-coupon yield curve is $R(t) = 0.10 - 0.05e^{-0.18(t-1)}$ where $t$ is measured in years, and the volatility rate is $\sigma(t) = 0.01$ for all $t$.

| 0 | 1 | 2 | 3 |
|---|---|---|---|
| | | | 11.8252% |
| | | 9.8976% | |
| | 7.6523% | | 9.8252% |
| 5.0000% | | 7.8976% | |
| | 5.6523% | | 7.8252% |
| | | 5.8976% | |
| | | | 5.8252% |

The probabilities of the nodes in the second time step are therefore

$$p_{2,1} = \left(\frac{1}{2}\right)^2 \frac{2!}{(1-1)!(2-1+1)!} = 0.25$$

$$p_{2,2} = \left(\frac{1}{2}\right)^2 \frac{2!}{(2-1)!(2-2+1)!} = 0.5$$

and

$$p_{2,3} = \left(\frac{1}{2}\right)^2 \frac{2!}{(3-1)!(2-3+1)!} = 0.25$$

The no-arbitrage pricing framework described above is interesting in a number of respects. First, the drift in the short rate is dictated by the zero-coupon yield curve. Note that at the end of period one, both possible short rates exceed the short rate a period earlier. This simply reflects the fact that the yield curve is strongly upward sloping. Second, the entire short-rate lattice can be summarized using two vectors. In the first, we record the lowest interest rate node for each time step, $r_i$,1, $i = 1, \ldots, n$. In the second, we record the local volatility rate, $\sigma(i)$, $i = 0, \ldots, n-1$. Third, in computing the interest rate lattice, we required no specific knowledge of the pull rate $a(t)$ or the long-run mean reversion level $b(t)$. The long-run mean reversion is subsumed in matching of the forward discount bond price from the zero-coupon yield to the expected discount bond price procedure. The pull rate $a(t)$ is subsumed by the ratio of the local volatility rates in adjacent periods (see equation (20.14)).

**ILLUSTRATION 20.1** Develop binomial lattice assuming short rate is normally distributed.

*Assume the zero-coupon yield curve is*

$$r_i = 0.12 - 0.06e^{-0.20(T_i - 1)}$$

*and the local volatility function is* $\sigma(i) = 0.015 - 0.00025\ln(1 + T_i)$. *Develop a four-period short-rate lattice where the short rate is a six-month rate.*

The first step in developing the interest rate lattice is to gather the problem information. Based on the zero-coupon yields, we can compute discount bond prices and forward discount bond prices. The problem information used as inputs in developing the interest rate lattice is as follows:

| Years to Maturity | Spot Rate | Discount Bond Price | Forward Discount Bond Rate | Local Volatility Rate |
|---|---|---|---|---|
| 0.5 | 5.369% | 0.97351 | | 1.099% |
| 1 | 6.000% | 0.94176 | 0.96739 | 1.027% |
| 1.5 | 6.571% | 0.90614 | 0.96217 | 0.971% |
| 2 | 7.088% | 0.86784 | 0.95773 | 0.925% |
| 2.5 | 7.555% | 0.82789 | 0.95397 | |

The next step is to identify the lowest interest rate node at each of the four time steps. At time 0, the lowest interest rate node is the spot rate 5.369%. At time 1, the lowest interest rate is determined by solving

$$0.96739 = 0.5e^{-r_{1,1}(0.5)} + 0.5e^{(-r_{1,1} + 2(0.01099)\sqrt{0.5})0.5}$$

The value of $r_{1,1}$ is 5.8557%. The vertical distance between adjacent nodes at the end of period one is $2(0.01099)\sqrt{0.5} = 0.015537$, so $r_{1,2}$ is 7.4094%.

The OPTVAL Library contains a function that determines the minimum short rate at each time step. The function has the syntax

OV_TS_LATTICE_RMIN(*fbp*,*v*,*tinc*,*nstep*,*nl*)

where *fbp* is the forward discount bond price, *v* is the local volatility rate, *tinc* is the length of each time step in years, *nstep* is the number of the current time step, and *nl* is an indicator variable instructing the function to assume the short rate is normally distributed ("N" or "n") or log-normally distributed ("L" or "l"). To perform the above computation, use

OV_TS_LATTICE_RMIN(0.96739,0.01099,.5,1,"n") = 0.058557

The minimum short rate at each time step is:

| Time Step | Years to Maturity | Spot Rate | Discount Bond Price | Forward Discount Bond Price | Local Volatility Rate | Minimum Short Rate |
|---|---|---|---|---|---|---|
| 0 | 0.5 | 5.369% | 0.97351 | | 1.099% | 5.3690% |
| 1 | 1 | 6.000% | 0.94176 | 0.96739 | 1.027% | 5.8557% |
| 2 | 1.5 | 6.571% | 0.90614 | 0.96217 | 0.971% | 6.2636% |
| 3 | 2 | 7.088% | 0.86784 | 0.95773 | 0.925% | 6.5814% |
| 4 | 2.5 | 7.555% | 0.82789 | 0.95397 | | 6.8120% |

The entire short-rate lattice over the two-year period is:

| 0 | 0.5 | 1 | 1.5 | 2 |
|---|---|---|---|---|
| | | | | 12.0465% |
| | | | 10.7007% | |
| | | 9.1676% | | 10.7379% |
| | 7.4094% | | 9.3276% | |
| 5.3690% | | 7.7156% | | 9.4293% |
| | 5.8557% | | 7.9545% | |
| | | 6.2636% | | 8.1206% |
| | | | 6.5814% | |
| | | | | 6.8120% |

## Log-Normal Distribution

The main problem with assuming interest rate changes are normally distributed is that there is some change that interest rates will become negative. A simple remedy to this problem is to assume that interest rates are log-normally distributed or put another way that the logarithm of the interest rate ln$r$ is normally distributed. The modifications to the no-arbitrage pricing procedure are straightforward. The binomial process is

$$\ln r_{t+\Delta t} - \ln r_t = \begin{cases} a(t)[b(t) - \ln r]\Delta t + \sigma(t)\sqrt{\Delta t} & \text{with probability} = 1/2 \\ a(t)[b(t) - \ln r]\Delta t - \sigma(t)\sqrt{\Delta t} & \text{with probability} = 1/2 \end{cases} \tag{20.15}$$

and the distance between adjacent vertical nodes in the binomial lattice is

$$\ln r_{i+1,j+1} - \ln r_{i+1,j} = 2\sigma(i)\sqrt{\Delta t} \tag{20.16}$$

Since we would prefer to have the lattice contain interest rates rather than the logarithm of interest rates, the log of interest rate spacing in (20.17) can be re-written in interest rate form

$$\frac{r_{i+1,j+1}}{r_{i+1,j}} = e^{2\sigma(i)\sqrt{\Delta t}} \tag{20.17}$$

To illustrate the application of this binomial procedure, reconsider the rates zero-coupon yield curve of the running illustration. Furthermore, assume that the volatility rate is 20%.[8] The interest rates in year 2 are determined by solving

$$0.93569 = 0.5e^{-r_{2,1}(1)} + 0.5e^{-[r_{2,1} \times 2\sigma(1)]}$$

The solution for the minimum interest rate is 5.3421%. The volatility rate is 0.20, so the constant proportion between adjacent rates is 1.4918. The interest rate at the upper node at year 2 is therefore 0.053421 × 1.49182 = 0.079695. The full interest rate lattice under the log-normal assumption is provided in Figure 20.9.

**FIGURE 20.9** Two-period binomial lattice for no-arbitrage pricing model assuming the short rate is log-normally distributed.

| 0 | 1 | 2 |
|---|---|---|
| | | $r_{2,3} = r_{2,1}e^{4\sigma(1)\sqrt{\Delta t}}$ |
| | $r_{1,2} = r_{1,1}e^{2\sigma(0)\sqrt{\Delta t}}$ | |
| $r_{0,1}$ | | $r_{2,2} = r_{2,1}e^{2\sigma(1)\sqrt{\Delta t}}$ |
| | $r_{1,1}$ | |
| | | $r_{2,1}$ |

[8] Note that the volatility rate of the change in the logarithm of the interest rate is dramatically higher than the volatility rate of the change in interest rate.

## BOND VALUATION

With the mechanics of generating an interest rate lattice in hand, we now turn to bond valuation. We start with the valuation of zero-coupon bonds, and then generalize the framework to handle coupon-bearing bonds. We then show how the framework can be modified to handle bonds with embedded options such as callable bonds and putable bonds.

### Zero-Coupon Bonds

To value options on bonds in a framework with short-term interest risk as the underlying source of uncertainty requires that we first create a bond price lattice. In order to do so, we extend the interest rate lattice to the end of the bond's life (which may be well beyond the option's life). To illustrate, consider a 4-year discount bond. In year 4, the bond matures with a payment of principal. Assume the principal is 100. In year 3, the short-term interest in the uppermost node is 0.152051. The value of the bond at that interest rate is $100e^{-0.152051(1)} = 85.894$. At the second uppermost node, the bond's value is $100e^{-0.101923(1)} = 90.310$, and so on.

To compute the bond's value in year 2, we must include the probabilities of upward and downward interest rate movements. The value of the bond at the uppermost node in year 2 is computed as

$$e^{-0.113447(1)}\left[\frac{1}{2}\times 85.894+\frac{1}{2}\times 90.310\right] = 78.653$$

The value of the bond at the second uppermost node is

$$e^{-0.076046(1)}\left[\frac{1}{2}\times 90.310+\frac{1}{2}\times 93.396\right] = 84.127$$

The price lattice of the four-year discount bond is shown in Figure 20.10.

**FIGURE 20.10** Three-period binomial lattice for no-arbitrage pricing model assuming the short rate is log-normally distributed, the zero-coupon yield curve is $R(t) = 0.10 - 0.05e^{-0.18(t-1)}$ where $t$ is measured in years, and the volatility rate is $\sigma(t) = 0.20$ for all $t$.

| 0 | 1 | 2 | 3 |
|---|---|---|---|
| | | | 15.2051% |
| | | 11.3447% | |
| | 7.9695% | | 10.1923% |
| 5.0000% | | 7.6046% | |
| | 5.3421% | | 6.8321% |
| | | 5.0975% | |
| | | | 4.5797% |

**FIGURE 20.11** Valuation of a four-year zero-coupon bond using a no-arbitrage pricing model that assumes the short rate is log-normally distributed, the zero-coupon yield curve is $R(t) = 0.10 - 0.05e^{-0.18(t-1)}$ where $t$ is measured in years, and the volatility rate is $\sigma(t) = 0.20$ for all $t$.

| 0 | 1 | 2 | 3 | 4 |
|---|---|---|---|---|
| | | | | 100 |
| | | | 85.894 | |
| | | 78.653 | | 100 |
| | 75.617 | | 90.310 | |
| 75.392 | | 85.127 | | 100 |
| | 82.897 | | 93.396 | |
| | | 89.765 | | 100 |
| | | | 95.524 | |
| | | | | 100 |

## Coupon-Bearing Bonds

The interest rate lattice can be used to value all sorts of bonds. To illustrate its generality, assume that we want to value a four-year coupon-bearing bond with annual coupon payments equal to 6. Again we start at the end of the bond's life. In year 4, the bond matures with a coupon payment of 6 and a repayment of principal of 100. In year 3, the short-term interest in the uppermost node is 0.152051. The value of the bond at that interest rate is $106e^{-0.152051(1)} = 97.048$. At the second uppermost node, the bond's value is $106e^{-0.101923(1)} = 101.729$, and so on.

As we proceed backward in time, we must add in the coupon payments. The value of the bond at the uppermost node in year 2 is

$$e^{-0.113447(1)}\left[\frac{1}{2} \times 97.048 + \frac{1}{2} \times 101.729\right] + 6 = 94.729$$

and at the second uppermost node is

$$e^{-0.076046(1)}\left[\frac{1}{2} \times 101.729 + \frac{1}{2} \times 105.000\right] + 6 = 101.795$$

The price lattice of the four-year coupon-bearing bond is provided in Figure 20.12.

## Callable Bonds

A callable bond is a coupon-bearing bond that allows its issuer to retire the bond before its stated maturity. In general, the call dates of the bond are coupon-payment dates, and the amount that bondholders will be paid is the par value of the bond plus the current coupon.

**FIGURE 20.12** Valuation of a four-year 6% coupon-bearing bond using a no-arbitrage pricing model that assumes the short rate is log-normally distributed, the zero-coupon yield curve is $R(t) = 0.10 - 0.05e^{-0.18(t-1)}$ where $t$ is measured in years, and the volatility rate is $\sigma(t) = 0.20$ for all $t$.

| 0 | 1 | 2 | 3 | 4 |
|---|---|---|---|---|
| | | | | 106 |
| | | | 97.048 | |
| | | 94.729 | | 106 |
| | 96.735 | | 101.729 | |
| 95.899 | | 101.795 | | 106 |
| | 104.897 | | 105.000 | |
| | | 106.853 | | 106 |
| | | | 107.255 | |
| | | | | 106 |

Consider the 6% coupon-bearing bond valued in Figure 20.12. To value the bond, we began at the end of the bond's life and worked backwards, taking the present value of the expected future value of the bond one node at a time. In looking at the values reported at time step 3, note that at the bottom node, the value of the bond is 107.255. If this bond was callable, the issuer would call the bond at this node because calling it would cost 106 while waiting one more period would cost 107.255. Thus in valuing this callable bond, we replace the value at this node with 106, as shown in Figure 20.13, Panel A. Note that the value of the bond at the lowest node at time step 2 has changed from 106.853 in Figure 20.12 to 106.257 in Figure 20.13, Panel A, reflecting the call feature of the bond. But if interest rates evolved in a manner that the firm would find itself at the lowest node at time step 2, it would call the bond since the present value of its expected future value exceeds its immediate redemption value, 106. Again we replace the computed value of the bond, as shown in Figure 20.13, Panel B. Working backward to time 0, we find that the value of the callable bond is 95.707. Comparing this bond value to the noncallable coupon-bearing bond value, we find that from the firm's perspective, the value of the call feature is 0.202.

### Putable Bonds

A putable bond permits the bondholder to sell the bond back to the issuer, usually at the par value of the bond. This put gives the bondholder some protection from loss of principal due to higher interest rates or credit deterioration of the issuer. Putable bonds can be valued straightforwardly using our interest rate lattice procedure. Suppose, for example, that the coupon-bearing bond shown in Figure 20.12 is putable at par by the bondholder. Since the put will be exercised only when the value of the bond falls below par value, we replace only the uppermost node at time step 3, as shown in Figure 20.14, Panel A. Moving back one time step, we see also that the bond will be put back to the issuer at the uppermost node. Therefore as shown in Figure 20.14, Panel B, we replace the

**FIGURE 20.13** Valuation of a four-year 6% coupon-bearing callable bond using a no-arbitrage pricing model that assumes the short rate is log-normally distributed, the zero-coupon yield curve is $R(t) = 0.10 - 0.05e^{-0.18(t-1)}$ where $t$ is measured in years, and the volatility rate is $\sigma(t) = 0.20$ for all $t$.

Panel A:

| 0 | 1 | 2 | 3 | 4 |
|---|---|---|---|---|
| | | | | 106 |
| | | | 97.048 | |
| | | 94.729 | | 106 |
| | 96.735 | | 101.729 | |
| 95.765 | | 101.795 | | 106 |
| | 104.615 | | 105.000 | |
| | | 106.257 | | 106 |
| | | | **106.000** | |
| | | | | 106 |

Panel B:

| 0 | 1 | 2 | 3 | 4 |
|---|---|---|---|---|
| | | | | 106 |
| | | | 97.048 | |
| | | 94.729 | | 106 |
| | 96.735 | | 101.729 | |
| 95.707 | | 101.795 | | 106 |
| | 104.493 | | 105.000 | |
| | | **106.000** | | 106 |
| | | | **106.000** | |
| | | | | 106 |

uppermost node with a value of 100. Finally, at the end of time step 1, the bondholder will exercise his option at the uppermost node, so, again, we replace the computed value of the bond with the exercise proceeds of 100. The value of the putable bond is 97.452. The value of the nonputable coupon-bearing bond is 95.899. The value of the embedded put is therefore 1.447.

## BOND OPTION VALUATION

The interest rate lattice procedure can also be used to value bond options. Assume, for example, that we want to value a two-year European-style put option with an exercise price of 100. Also assume that the option expires just after the coupon is paid in year 2. In year 2, therefore, the put's value will be depend on the ex-coupon bond price, which is the price reported in year 2 less 6. Given that the

**FIGURE 20.14** Valuation of a four-year 6% coupon-bearing puttable bond using a no-arbitrage pricing model that assumes the short rate is log-normally distributed, the zero-coupon yield curve is $R(t) = 0.10 - 0.05e^{-0.18(t-1)}$ where $t$ is measured in years, and the volatility rate is $\sigma(t) = 0.20$ for all $t$.

Panel A:

| 0 | 1 | 2 | 3 | 4 |
|---|---|---|---|---|
| | | | | 106 |
| | | | 100.000 | |
| | | 96.047 | | 106 |
| | 97.343 | | 101.729 | |
| 96.189 | | 101.795 | | 106 |
| | 104.897 | | 105.000 | |
| | | 106.853 | | 106 |
| | | | 107.255 | |
| | | | | 106 |

Panel B:

| 0 | 1 | 2 | 3 | 4 |
|---|---|---|---|---|
| | | | | 106 |
| | | | 100.000 | |
| | | 100.000 | | 106 |
| | 99.169 | | 101.729 | |
| 95.707 | | 101.795 | | 106 |
| | 104.897 | | 105.000 | |
| | | 106.853 | | 106 |
| | | | 107.255 | |
| | | | | 106 |

Panel C:

| 0 | 1 | 2 | 3 | 4 |
|---|---|---|---|---|
| | | | | 106 |
| | | | 100.000 | |
| | | 100.000 | | 106 |
| | 100.000 | | 101.729 | |
| 97.452 | | 101.795 | | 106 |
| | 104.897 | | 105.000 | |
| | | 106.853 | | 106 |
| | | | 107.255 | |
| | | | | 106 |

put is expiring, its values are given by the lower boundary condition max(0,$X$ – $B$), where $X$ is the exercise price of the option and $B$ is the bond price.

| Time | 0 | 1 | 2 |
|---|---|---|---|
| | | max(0,100 – 88.734) = | 11.266 |
| | | | 88.734 |
| | | max(0,100 – 94.798) = | 4.202 |
| | | | 95.798 |
| | | max(0,100 – 100.855) = | 0.000 |
| | | | 100.855 |

The value of the option in year 1 is the present value of the expected future value. At the uppermost node, the computation is

$$e^{-0.0797(1)}\left[\frac{1}{2}\times 11.266+\frac{1}{2}\times 4.202\right] = 7.142$$

At the lowermost node, the computation is

$$e^{-0.0534(1)}\left[\frac{1}{2}\times 4.202+\frac{1}{2}\times 0.000\right] = 1.991$$

The value of the put today is 4.567, as is shown in this figure:

| Time | 0 | 1 | 2 |
|---|---|---|---|
| | | | 11.266 |
| | | | 88.734 |
| | | 7.142 | |
| | 4.567 | | 4.202 |
| | | | 95.798 |
| | | 1.991 | |
| | | | 0.000 |
| | | | 100.855 |

## SUMMARY

The purpose of this chapter is modest—to develop a binomial procedure for valuing interest rate derivative contracts where the short-term interest rate ("short rate") is the single underlying source of interest rate uncertainty. To begin, we discuss a number of constant-parameter, short-rate processes to lay a foundation for interest rate behavior. While these models are often useful in developing economic intuition regarding interest rate behavior, they produce zero-coupon bond values that are different from the observed market prices, seemingly giving rise to arbitrage opportunities. Consequently, we next turn to no-arbitrage pricing models. These models adjust the parameters of the interest rate process in a manner that produces bond (and interest rate derivatives contract) values equal to observed prices. With the mechanics of no-arbitrage pricing in hand, we then turn to valuing zero-coupon and coupon-bearing bonds, callable bonds, putable bonds, and bond options. Be forewarned, however. While the valuation framework provided in this chapter is intuitive and commonly applied in practice, it only begins to scratch the surface of the literature focused on no-arbitrage interest rate models. This literature is deep in multifactor theoretical models of interest rate movements and numerical procedures for calibrating the interest rate models and valuing interest rate derivatives.

## REFERENCES AND SUGGESTED READINGS


Amin, Kausik, and Andrew Morton. 1994. Implied volatility functions in arbitrage-free term structure models. *Journal of Financial Economics* 35: 141–180.

Black, Fischer. 1995. Interest rates as options. *Journal of Finance* 50 (5): 1371–1376.

Black, Fischer, and Piotr Karasinski. 1991. Bond and option pricing when short rates are lognormal. *Financial Analysis Journal* (July–August): 52–59.

Cox, John C., John E. Ingersoll, and Stephen A. Ross. 1985. A theory of the term structure of interest rates. *Econometrica* 53: 385–407.

Heath, David, Robert Jarrow, and Andrew Morton. 1992. Bond pricing and the term structure of interest rates. *Econometrica* 60 (January): 77–105.

Ho, Thomas S. Y., and S. B. Lee. 1986. Term structure movements and pricing interest rate contingent claims. *Journal of Finance* 41: 1011–1029.

Hull, John, and Alan White. 1994. Numerical procedures for implementing term structure models I: Single-factor models. *Journal of Derivatives* 2 (Fall): 7–16.

Hull, John, and Alan White. 1994. Numerical procedures for implementing term structure models II: Two-factor models. *Journal of Derivatives* 2 (Winter): 37–48.

James, Jessica, and Nick Webber. 2000. *Interest Rate Modeling*. Chichester, U.K.: John Wiley & Sons.

Jamshidian, Farshid. 1989. An exact bond option pricing formula. *Journal of Finance* 44 (March): 205–209.

Jarrow, Robert A. 1995. *Modeling Fixed Income Securities and Interest Rate Options*. New York: McGraw-Hill.

Longstaff, Francis A., and Eduardo S. Schwartz. 1992. Interest rate volatility and the term structure: A two factor general equilibrium model. *Journal of Finance* 47 (September): 1259–1282.

Rendleman Jr., Richard J., and Brit J. Bartter. 1980. The pricing of options on debt securities. *Journal of Financial and Quantitative Analysis* 15: 11–24.

Schaefer, S., and Eduardo S. Schwartz. 1987. Time-dependent variance and the pricing of options. *Journal of Finance* 42 (December): 1113–1128.

Tuckman, Bruce. 2002. *Fixed Income Securities*, 2nd ed. Hoboken, NJ: John Wiley & Sons.

Vasicek, Oldrick A. 1977. An equilibrium characterization of the term structure of interest rates. *Journal of Financial Economics* 5: 177–188.

# PART Nine

# Commodity Derivatives

# 21
# Commodity Products

Commodities are physical assets. Examples include precious metals, base metals, energy stores (e.g., crude oil and natural gas), refined products (e.g., heating oil and gasoline), and food (e.g., wheat, and livestock). Commodity derivatives have been traded in over-the-counter markets for centuries. The first modern-day commodity futures exchange began operation in 1865, when the Chicago Board of Trade launched trading of standardized futures contracts calling for the delivery of grain. Other futures exchanges were formed shortly thereafter—the New York Cotton Exchange in 1870 to trade cotton futures, the Chicago Produce Exchange (a forerunner to today's Chicago Mercantile Exchange) in 1874 to trade butter, eggs, and poultry, the London Corn Trade Association in 1878 to trade corn futures in England, and the Winnipeg Commodity Exchange in 1904 to trade oat futures contracts in Canada. With the passage of time, nonagricultural commodities were introduced—precious metal (silver) futures were launched by the Commodity Exchange in the United States in 1933, wool futures by the Sydney Futures Exchange in Australia in 1960, and livestock by the Chicago Mercantile Exchange in 1961. Crude oil and oil products were introduced next—heating oil by the New York Mercantile Exchange in October 1978, crude oil in March 1983, and unleaded gasoline in December 1984. Liquefied propane appeared in August 1987, and electricity in March 1996.

This chapter focuses on derivatives contracts written on commodities. Given their long history, it may seem odd that we have deferred the discussion of commodities derivatives to the end of the book. The reason is that, while their history is long, their trading volume pales by comparison to financial derivatives. During 2003, exchange-traded commodity futures accounted for only 17% of total trading (see Figure 21.1), and exchange-traded commodity options for only 1% of total (see Figure 21.2). Their presence in OTC markets is even less. At the end of December 2003, commodity derivatives accounted for only 1% of the total notional amount outstanding (see Figure 21.3).

This chapter is organized differently than the other product chapters in that the sections of this chapter are arranged by underlying commodity. The reason is that the price relations of commodity derivatives are influenced by idiosyncrasies in the underlying commodity market. Understanding commodity derivatives price behavior therefore involves understanding the factors that influence com-

**FIGURE 21.1** Millions of futures contracts traded on exchanges worldwide during 2003 categorized by type of underlying asset. Total trading volume was 2,848 million contracts.

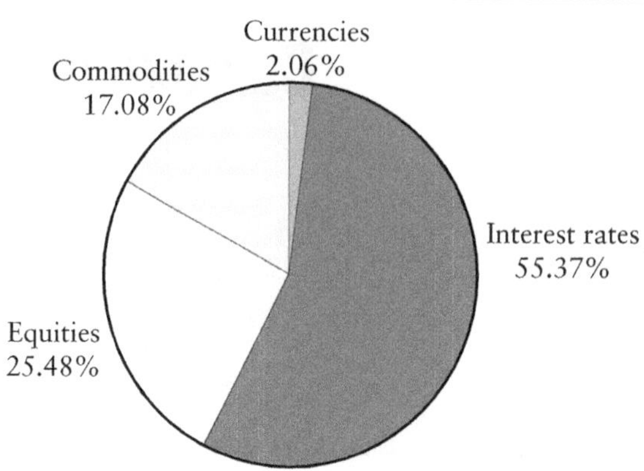


*Source:* Data compiled from Bank for International Settlements (www.bis.org), *BIS Quarterly Review*, June 2004.

**FIGURE 21.2** Millions of options contracts traded on exchanges worldwide during 2003 categorized by type of underlying asset. Total trading volume was 5,210 million contracts.

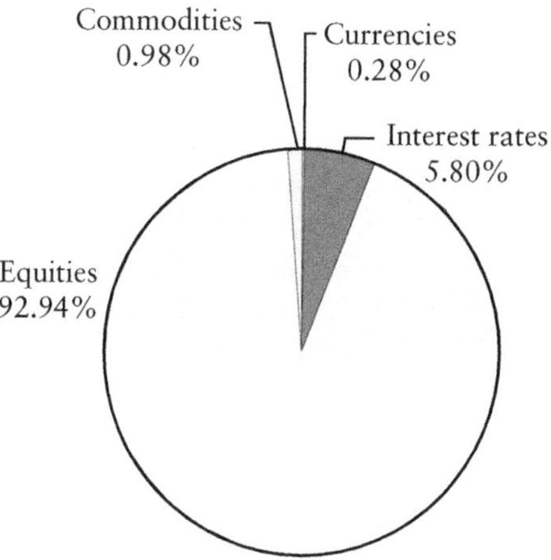


*Source:* Data compiled from Bank for International Settlements (www.bis.org), *BIS Quarterly Review*, June 2004.

modity price behavior. Thus we begin each section with a description of the underlying commodity market, and then provide descriptions of derivatives contract specifications and discussions of common risk management applications.

The sections of the chapter proceed as follows. In the first section, we discuss the fundamental differences between pricing commodity derivatives and pricing financial derivatives. Commodity derivatives require that we consider the storage costs such as warehouse rent and insurance as well as the convenience of having an inventory of the commodity on hand. Neither of these factors played an important role in the pricing of stock, stock index, currency, and interest rate

**FIGURE 21.3** Percentage of total notional amount of derivatives outstanding worldwide on December 2003 by underlying asset category. Total notional amount of derivatives is USD 197.2 trillion.

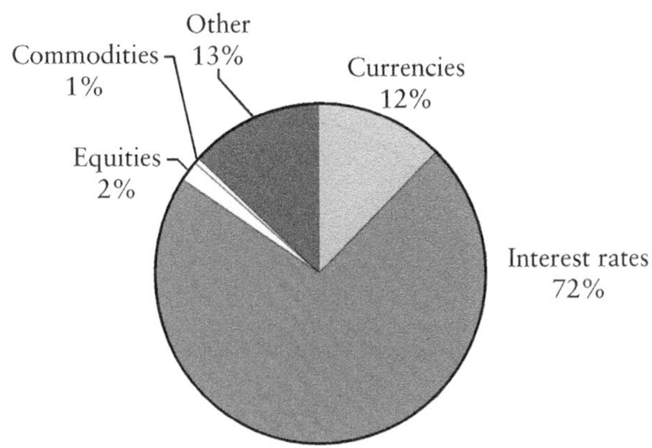


*Source:* Data compiled from Bank for International Settlements (www.bis.org), *BIS Quarterly Review*, June 2004.

derivatives products. The remaining sections are organized by commodity. Figure 21.4 shows commodity futures and futures options trading volume during 2003 by the three major commodity categories—energy, agricultural, and metals. We illustrate the idiosyncrasies of each commodity using an example—petroleum, soybeans, and gold, respectively. Figure 21.5 shows the notional amounts of OTC commodity derivatives outstanding at the end of December 2003. While the breakdown among commodity categories is not as refined, the relative importance of precious metal derivative contracts in the OTC market is apparent.

## NET COST-OF-CARRY RELATION

Chapter 4 contained the development of the no-arbitrage price relations for forwards, futures, and swaps. In the chapters that followed, we used the price relations in a variety of risk management strategies, however, the focus was almost exclusively on financial assets such as stocks and stock portfolios, currencies, and bonds. This section focuses on commodity price risk management, so we begin with a review of the net cost of carry pricing principles.

The *net cost of carry* refers to the difference between the costs and the benefits of holding an asset. A breakfast cereal producer who needs 5,000 bushels of wheat for processing in two months can lock in the price of the wheat today by buying it and carrying it for two months. If he does so, he incurs the opportunity cost of funds. In addition, he will pay *storage costs* such as warehouse rent and insurance. At the same time, by storing wheat, he may accrue *convenience yield*, that is, he may avoid some costs of possible running out of inventory before two months are up and having to pay extra for emergency deliveries or shutting down the production plant. Thus the net cost of carry for a commodity equals interest cost plus storage costs less convenience yield, that is,

**FIGURE 21.4** Proportion of total commodity futures and futures options trading volume in U.S. during 2003 by commodity category. Total futures (futures options) trading volume in 2003 was 200,551,739 (45,377,075) contracts.
Panel A. Futures

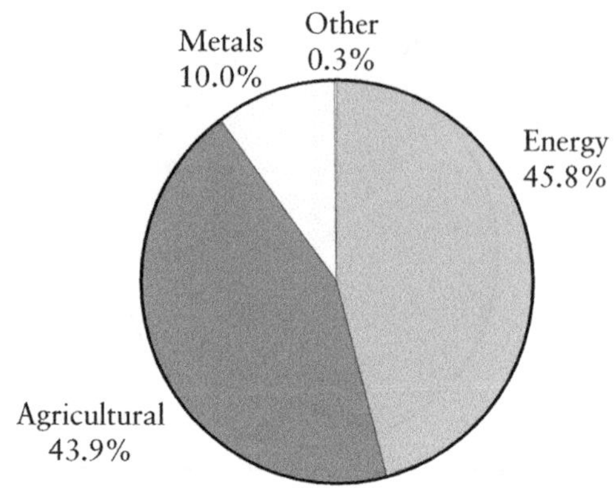


Panel B. Futures options

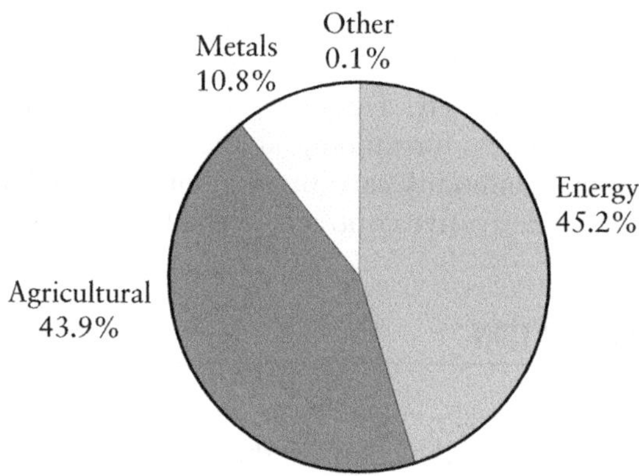


*Source:* Data compiled from Futures Industry Institute, 2005.

$$\text{Net carry costs} = \text{Cost of funds} + \text{Storage cost} - \text{Convenience yield} \tag{21.1}$$

For expositional convenience, we will initially model all costs as constant continuous rates. The value of a cash-and-carry position at time $T$ is $Se^{(r+s-y)T}$, where $r$ is the risk-free interest rate, $s$ is the storage cost rate, and $y$ is the convenience yield rate.

To develop the forward pricing relation for a commodity, we need to consider how commodities are used and the types of traders in the marketplace. Consider a commodity like crude oil. An oil refiner draws convenience yield from holding an inventory of crude to avoid the costs associated with shutting

**FIGURE 21.5** Proportion of total notional amount of commodity derivatives outstanding in OTC markets as of December 31, 2003. Total forwards and swaps (options) notional amount was USD 574B (USD 831B).
Panel A. Forwards and swaps

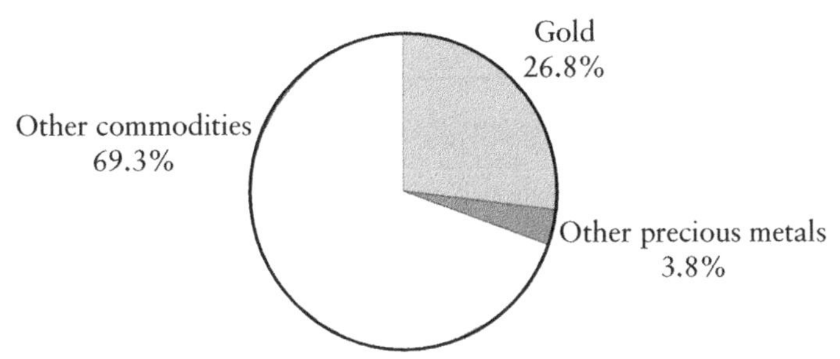


Panel B. Options

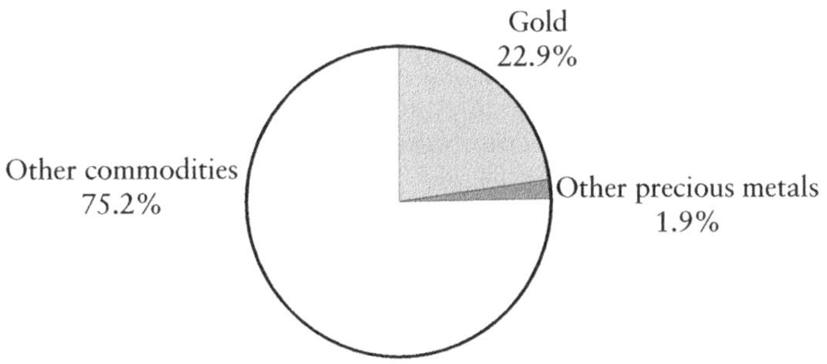


*Source:* Data compiled from Bank for International Settlements (www.bis.org), *BIS Quarterly Review*, June 2004.

down the refinery while more crude oil is pumped in.[1] Thus the refiner's net cost of carry is $r + s - y$. But many market participants do not accrue convenience yield from holding an inventory of crude. Like the refiner, they would incur storage costs, however, since they do not accrue convenience yield, their net carry cost is $r + s$. With these distinctions in mind, we now develop the commodity forward pricing relation.

Recall that, in Chapter 4, we developed the net cost of carry relation,

$$f = Se^{(r-i)T} \tag{21.2}$$

by showing that, if either $f > Se^{(r-i)T}$ or $f < Se^{(r-i)T}$, someone could earn an arbitrage profit. We will use the same approach here to show that the net cost of carry relation for a commodity is

$$Se^{(r+s-y)T} \leq f \leq Se^{(r+s)T} \tag{21.3}$$

[1] Another such cost is lost customer goodwill when deliveries are missed.

**TABLE 21.1** Costless arbitrage trades where $f > Se^{(r+s)T}$.

| Trades | Initial Investment | Value on Day $T$ |
|---|---|---|
| Buy $e^{sT}$ units of commodity | $-Se^{sT}$ | $\tilde{S}_T$ |
| Sell risk-free bonds | $Se^{sT}$ | $-Se^{(r+s)T}$ |
| Sell forward contract | | $-(\tilde{S}_T - f)$ |
| Net portfolio value | 0 | $f - Se^{(r+s)T}$ |

**TABLE 21.2** Arbitrage trades where $f < Se^{(r+s-y)T}$.

| Trades | Initial Investment | Value on Day $T$ |
|---|---|---|
| Sell $e^{(s-y)T}$ units of commodity from inventory | $-Se^{(s-y)T}$ | $\tilde{S}_T$ |
| Buy risk-free bonds | $Se^{(s-y)T}$ | $-Se^{(r+s-y)T}$ |
| Buy forward contract | | $\tilde{S}_T - f$ |
| Net portfolio value | 0 | $f - Se^{(r+s-y)T}$ |

Consider the case where $f > Se^{(r+s)T}$, that is, the forward price is too high relative to the commodity price. To earn an arbitrage profit, we can borrow money at the risk-free rate, buy the commodity, and sell the forward contract to earn $f - Se^{(r+s)T} > 0$. The transactions are shown in Table 21.1. The trading strategy involves no investment and a terminal value that is certain to be positive. We would continue to engage in the strategy until $f \leq Se^{(r+s)T}$.

Now suppose that $f < Se^{(r+s)T}$. The forward price appears to be too low relative to the commodity price, so it appears that we can earn a costless arbitrage profit by selling the commodity, buying risk-free bonds, and buying the forward contract. But therein lies the problem. Unlike financial assets, commodities are frequently in short supply and are unavailable to borrow and sell short. The only person able to execute such an arbitrage is someone, like a refiner, who holds an inventory of the commodity. When the forward price falls below $f < Se^{(r+s-y)T}$, the refiner will find it profitable to sell some of his existing inventory and buy a forward contract, as shown in Table 21.2. The prepaid forward price of the commodity, $fe^{-rT} < Se^{(s-y)T}$ is less than the cost of storing the commodity even after the convenience yield is subtracted.[2]

## Commodity Swap Contracts

An increasingly popular risk management strategy is a commodity swap. Commodity swaps have been around since the mid-1970s, and are an effective means of locking in input and output prices. In a typical fixed-for-floating commodity

[2] One is tempted to reconsider the first inequality in which we engaged in the arbitrage and ask why the refiner, who gathers convenience yield from holding does not step in and buy more of the asset and sell the forward contract. The answer is that the refiner likely holds all the inventory he wants. Additional holdings will only serve to increase storage costs. Without gathering increment convenience yield, the refiner has the same cost structure as we do in executing the arbitrage strategy.

swap, one party agrees to pay a fixed price per unit of the underlying commodity each period throughout the life of the agreement. The length of the contract is negotiable, as is the length of each period during the contract's life (e.g., one month). The contract will also specify the amount to be delivered each period, although the quantity need not be uniform through time. The nature of the settlement each period is also negotiable. Some contracts specify delivery at a particular location. Others are cash-settled with a net payment equal to the difference between the prevailing spot price on the settlement date and the fixed price of the contract times the promised delivery quantity.

## ENERGY: PETROLEUM

Within the energy category, derivative contracts on petroleum are the most active. All exchange-traded contracts in the United States are traded on the New York Mercantile Exchange (NYMEX division). Table 21.3 shows the most active futures and futures options. The petroleum contracts (i.e., crude oil, heating oil, and gasoline) constitute about 74 (56)% of total futures (futures options) trading volume during 2003. Natural gas contracts account for 21.7 (42.6)%. The "other" category includes more than 70 different underlyings including other commodities (e.g., electricity), spreads (e.g., the crack spread), and swaps. While many of these contracts are innovative and potentially useful, none have gathered much interest from a market standpoint. The primary focus of this section is on petroleum and petroleum products.

### Production and Consumption

Petroleum[3] is the generic term applied to oil and oil products. Crude oil is petroleum in its natural state—the dark liquid extracted from the ground—and is the world's largest cash commodity. This is hardly surprising considering our day-

**TABLE 21.3** Summary of New York Mercantile Exchange (NYMEX division) energy futures and futures options trading volume during 2003.

| | Futures | | Futures Options | |
|---|---|---|---|---|
| Commodity | Volume | Percent | Volume | Percent |
| Crude Oil | 45,436,931 | 49.45% | 10,237,121 | 49.90% |
| No. 2 Heating Oil, NY | 11,581,670 | 12.60% | 668,859 | 3.26% |
| Unleaded Reg. Gas., NY | 11,172,050 | 12.16% | 616,245 | 3.00% |
| Natural Gas | 19,037,118 | 20.72% | 8,742,277 | 42.61% |
| Other | 4,654,332 | 5.07% | 250,305 | 1.22% |
| Total | 91,882,101 | 100.00% | 20,514,807 | 100.00% |

*Source:* Data drawn from *Futures Industry Institute*, 2005.

[3] The term *petroleum* is derived from the Latin words *petra*, meaning rock, and *oleum*, meaning oil.

to-day reliance on refined products such as heating oil, gasoline, and jet fuel, not to mention a limitless number of petrochemical-derived products ranging from ball-point pens to toothbrushes and deodorant to lipstick.

Generally speaking, the crude oil refining takes place in the areas where the consumption of petroleum products is highest. One reason for this is that it is cheaper to move crude oil than petroleum product. Another is that it is easier to respond to weather-induced spikes in demand and gauge seasonal shifts. To illustrate this phenomenon, consider Figure 21.6, which shows (1) the production of crude oil by world region and (2) the corresponding refining capacity in

**FIGURE 21.6** World production of crude oil and refining capacity by region for the calendar year 2002.
Panel A. Production

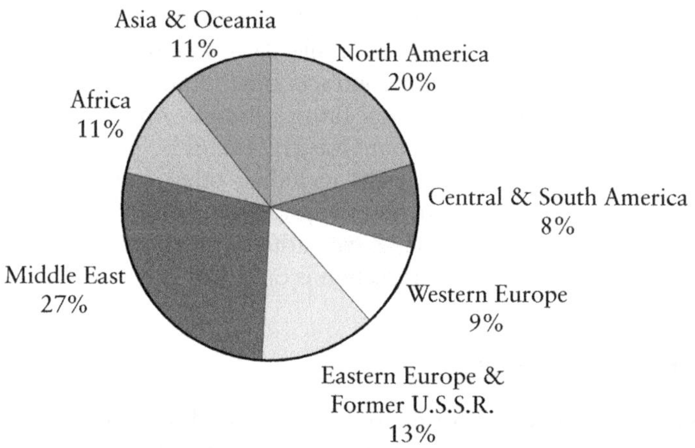


Panel B. Refining capacity

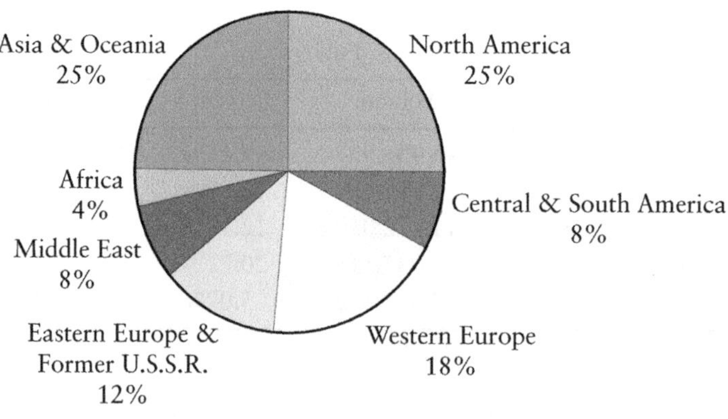


*Source:* Underlying data drawn from Energy Information Administration, *International Energy Annual* 2002.

2002. While the Middle East and Africa produced 38% of the world's oil in 2002, their combined refining capacity was 12%. At the same time, while Asia, North America, and Western Europe account for 40% of production, they have 68% of the world's refining capacity.

The cost of the crude constitutes about 85% of total refining costs. The core refining process is *fractional distillation.* Crude oil is heated until it boils and vaporizes. The vapors are captured in a distillation column, and, as they rise in the column, they cool and condense. Different products condense at different temperatures. The lighter products—liquid petroleum gases, naphtha, and gasoline—are recovered at the lowest temperatures (highest levels within the column). The middle distillates—jet fuel, kerosene, home heating oil, and diesel fuel—are next. Finally, at the lowest levels (highest temperatures), the heaviest products—residuum or residual fuel oil—are recovered. The heavier molecules have fewer uses so they are often further transformed into lighter-end gasoline products by a *catalytic cracking process.* On average, 42 gallons of crude produces 21 gallons of gasoline, 3 gallons of jet fuel, 9 gallons of heating oil and diesel fuel, 4 gallons of lubricants, and 3 gallons of heavier residues.

### Derivatives Markets

The trading of petroleum futures and futures options in the United States is conducted exclusively on the New York Mercantile Exchange (NYMEX). The heating oil futures contract market was launched in December 1978, followed by crude oil in March 1983 and unleaded gasoline futures in December 1984. Relative to many other commodities, petroleum derivatives were late to enter the marketplace. The reason is simple. In the 1960s and 1970s, crude oil prices were tightly controlled by OPEC together with large globally integrated oil companies. With little or no commodity price variability, there is no need for producers and end-users to hedge. By the early 1980s, competition from non-OPEC oil-producing countries began to undermine OPEC's influence on oil markets, and energy prices began to move more freely in response to market conditions. Such an environment creates a new opportunity for risk management tools.

Table 21.4 summarizes the key features of the petroleum futures contracts traded on NYMEX. The crude oil contract calls for the delivery of 1,000 barrels of crude in Cushing, Oklahoma. Several grades of domestic and internationally traded foreign crudes are eligible for delivery. The contracts are traded in an open outcry format on the exchange floor during the day, and electronically at other times. The last day of trading is the third business day prior to the 25th calendar day of the month preceding the delivery month.

The heating oil (also called "no. 2 fuel oil") and gasoline futures contracts call for the delivery of 42,000 gallons in New York Harbor. Note that size of the heating oil and gasoline contracts is the same as the crude oil contract (i.e., 42,000 gallons equals 1,000 barrels). This was done deliberately to facilitate trading of crack spreads. A *crack spread* refers to the simultaneous purchase (sale) of the crude oil futures and sale (purchase) of a heating oil or unleaded gasoline futures. The last day of trading for the heating oil and gasoline contracts is the last business day of the month preceding the delivery month.

**TABLE 21.4** Selected terms of major petroleum futures contracts traded on the New York Mercantile Exchange.

| | Crude Oil (CL) | Heating Oil (HO) | Unleaded Gasoline (HU) |
|---|---|---|---|
| Contract unit | 1,000 barrels (42,000 gallons) | 42,000 gallons (1,000 barrels) | 42,000 gallons (1,000 barrels) |
| Tick size | $.01 per barrel | $.0001 per gallon | $.0001 per gallon |
| Tick value | $10 per contract | $4.20 per contract | $4.20 per contract |
| Trading hours | Open outcry trading is conducted from 10 AM until 2:30 PM. | Open outcry trading is conducted from 10:05 AM until 2:30 PM. | Open outcry trading is conducted from 10:05 AM until 2:30 PM. |
| | After hours trading is conducted via the NYMEX ACCESS internet-based trading platform beginning at 3:15 PM on Mondays through Thursdays and concluding at 9:30 AM the following day. On Sundays, the session begins at 7 PM. | | |
| Contract months | 30 consecutive months plus long-dated futures initially listed at 36, 48, 60, 72, and 84 months prior to delivery. | 18 consecutive months. | 12 consecutive months |
| Last day of trading | Third business day prior to 25th calendar day of month preceding delivery month. | Last business day of month preceding delivery month. | Last business day of month preceding delivery month. |
| Final settlement | Physical | Physical | Physical |

Table 21.5 shows futures settlement prices of the petroleum futures on January 25, 2005. For crude oil futures, contract maturities extend out seven years, although trading volume is quite light in the most distant months. For heating oil futures, the maximum contract tenure is 18 months, and, for gasoline futures, 12 months. The table shows that all three contract markets are in backwardation. This is a common characteristic of energy futures prices. Backwardation implies that there are significant convenience yields on energy products for immediate or near-term delivery. The prices also reflect the seasonal nature of the demand for heating oil and gasoline. With heating oil, for example, demand is highest in the cold winter months. Consequently, we see that the heating oil futures prices reported in Table 21.5 are higher for the contract months November through February than they are for other months during the year. Conversely, gasoline futures prices are highest during the summer months when people travel more.[4]

The NYMEX launched trading of unleaded gasoline futures options in December 1984. The options are American-style, and each contract is written on one underlying futures contract. Exercising a call on the unleaded gasoline futures, for example, means that a long position in one unleaded gasoline futures will appear in your trading account at the end of the day, and you will be marked-to-market at the difference between the futures price and the option's exercise price. The last day of trading of the unleaded gasoline futures contract is the last business day of the month preceding the delivery month of the underlying futures. Options on crude oil and heating oil futures were launched in November 1986 and June 1987, respectively. The terms of the contract are very similar to the unleaded gasoline futures. For details, see www.nymex.com.

### Derivatives Valuation

The valuation of petroleum derivatives follows the principles outlined in the first section of this chapter. Storage costs play a significant role in pricing and convenience yield for refined products varies by time of year as demand rises and falls. In valuing petroleum derivatives and in measuring their risk, the forward curve, as illustrated by the relation between futures prices and their time of expiration in Table 21.5, plays a critical role.

**ILLUSTRATION 21.1** Compute fixed price of commodity swap.

*Based on the heating oil futures prices reported in Table 21.5, compute the fixed price on a heating oil swap that allows you to buy 50,000 gallons of heating oil per week for 26 weeks. Assume that today's date is January 25, 2005 and that the zero-coupon yield curve for risk-free bonds is given by*

$$r_i = 0.0178 + 0.01\ln(1 + T_i)$$

*The first delivery date is February 7, 2005.*

To solve this problem, we assume that the forward curve is given by the structure of futures prices in Table 21.5. The last day of trading of heating oil futures contract is the last day of the month preceding the contract month. Thus, the February 2005 contract expires on January 31, 2005. The points along the forward curve are therefore:

[4] Approximately 75% of gasoline is consumed by individuals.

| Heading Oil Forward Curve | | |
|---|---|---|
| Contract Month | Settlement Price | Time to Expiration |
| Feb-05 | 1.4248 | 0.0192 |
| Mar-05 | 1.4088 | 0.0959 |
| Apr-05 | 1.3608 | 0.1808 |
| May-05 | 1.3153 | 0.2658 |
| Jun-05 | 1.2883 | 0.3507 |
| Jul-05 | 1.2823 | 0.4356 |
| Aug-05 | 1.2833 | 0.5205 |
| Sep-05 | 1.2898 | 0.6055 |
| Oct-05 | 1.2983 | 0.6904 |
| Nov-05 | 1.3068 | 0.7753 |
| Dec-05 | 1.3153 | 0.8603 |
| Jan-06 | 1.3203 | 0.9452 |
| Feb-06 | 1.3133 | 1.0301 |
| Mar-06 | 1.2868 | 1.1151 |
| Apr-06 | 1.2478 | 1.2000 |
| May-06 | 1.2198 | 1.2849 |
| Jun-06 | 1.2013 | 1.3699 |
| Jul-06 | 1.1978 | 1.4548 |

The next step is to set up a table that contains the delivery dates, and the corresponding interest rates and forward prices. The forward prices corresponding to each delivery date can be computed by interpolating between adjacent forward prices. Recall the OPTVAL function

OV_IR_TS_INTERPOLATE(*sterm, term, rate*)

where *sterm* is the time to delivery, *term* is the vector of times to delivery for the forward contracts, and *rate* is the vector of forward prices, performs this operation. With the interest rates and forward prices computed, you compute the discount factor and prepaid forward price for each delivery, and then sum. The results are shown as follows:

| Delivery No. | Delivery Date | Time to Delivery | Interest Rate | Forward Price | Discount Factor | Prepaid Forward | PV of Fixed 1.3321 |
|---|---|---|---|---|---|---|---|
| 1 | 2/7/05 | 0.0356 | 1.815% | 1.4214 | 0.9994 | 1.4205 | 1.3312 |
| 2 | 2/14/05 | 0.0548 | 1.833% | 1.4174 | 0.9990 | 1.4159 | 1.3307 |
| 3 | 2/21/05 | 0.0740 | 1.851% | 1.4134 | 0.9986 | 1.4114 | 1.3302 |
| 4 | 2/28/05 | 0.0932 | 1.869% | 1.4094 | 0.9983 | 1.4069 | 1.3298 |
| 5 | 3/7/05 | 0.1123 | 1.886% | 1.3995 | 0.9979 | 1.3965 | 1.3293 |
| 6 | 3/14/05 | 0.1315 | 1.904% | 1.3887 | 0.9975 | 1.3852 | 1.3287 |
| 7 | 3/21/05 | 0.1507 | 1.920% | 1.3778 | 0.9971 | 1.3739 | 1.3282 |
| 8 | 3/28/05 | 0.1699 | 1.937% | 1.3670 | 0.9967 | 1.3625 | 1.3277 |
| 9 | 4/4/05 | 0.1890 | 1.953% | 1.3564 | 0.9963 | 1.3514 | 1.3272 |

| Delivery No. | Delivery Date | Time to Delivery | Interest Rate | Forward Price | Discount Factor | Prepaid Forward | PV of Fixed 1.3321 |
|---|---|---|---|---|---|---|---|
| 10 | 4/11/05 | 0.2082 | 1.969% | 1.3461 | 0.9959 | 1.3406 | 1.3266 |
| 11 | 4/18/05 | 0.2274 | 1.985% | 1.3358 | 0.9955 | 1.3298 | 1.3261 |
| 12 | 4/25/05 | 0.2466 | 2.000% | 1.3256 | 0.9951 | 1.3191 | 1.3255 |
| 13 | 5/2/05 | 0.2658 | 2.016% | 1.3153 | 0.9947 | 1.3083 | 1.3250 |
| 14 | 5/9/05 | 0.2849 | 2.031% | 1.3092 | 0.9942 | 1.3016 | 1.3244 |
| 15 | 5/16/05 | 0.3041 | 2.046% | 1.3031 | 0.9938 | 1.2950 | 1.3238 |
| 16 | 5/23/05 | 0.3233 | 2.060% | 1.2970 | 0.9934 | 1.2884 | 1.3232 |
| 17 | 5/30/05 | 0.3425 | 2.075% | 1.2909 | 0.9929 | 1.2818 | 1.3226 |
| 18 | 6/6/05 | 0.3616 | 2.089% | 1.2875 | 0.9925 | 1.2778 | 1.3220 |
| 19 | 6/13/05 | 0.3808 | 2.103% | 1.2862 | 0.9920 | 1.2759 | 1.3214 |
| 20 | 6/20/05 | 0.4000 | 2.116% | 1.2848 | 0.9916 | 1.2740 | 1.3208 |
| 21 | 6/27/05 | 0.4192 | 2.130% | 1.2835 | 0.9911 | 1.2721 | 1.3202 |
| 22 | 7/4/05 | 0.4384 | 2.144% | 1.2823 | 0.9906 | 1.2703 | 1.3196 |
| 23 | 7/11/05 | 0.4575 | 2.157% | 1.2826 | 0.9902 | 1.2700 | 1.3190 |
| 24 | 7/18/05 | 0.4767 | 2.170% | 1.2828 | 0.9897 | 1.2696 | 1.3184 |
| 25 | 7/25/05 | 0.4959 | 2.183% | 1.2830 | 0.9892 | 1.2692 | 1.3177 |
| 26 | 8/1/05 | 0.5151 | 2.195% | 1.2832 | 0.9888 | 1.2688 | 1.3171 |
| | | | | Totals | 25.8519 | 34.4366 | 34.4366 |

From Chapter 4, you know that the fixed price on a commodity swap with uniform quantities can be computed by dividing the sum of the prepaid forward prices by the sum of the discount factors, that is,

$$\bar{f} = \frac{34.4366}{25.8519} = 1.3321$$

Another alternative is to set up an additional column in the table that contains the present value of the fixed price and let SOLVER find the price that equates the sum of the present values of the fixed payments to the sum of the prepaid forwards, that is, 34.4366. Finally, OPTVAL contains a function that computes the fixed price on a commodity swap with uniform deliveries each period, that is,

$$\text{OV\_SWAP\_COMMODITY}(t, f, r, vr) = 1.3321$$

where $t$ is the vector of times to delivery, $f$ is the vector of forward prices and $r$ is the vector of risk-free rates corresponding to the delivery times, and $vr$ is an indicator variable that signals the function to determine the swap's value "v" or fixed price "r". The function

$$\text{OV\_SWAP\_COMMODITY\_QUANTITY}(t, f, r, quan, vr)$$

computes the fixed price of a commodity swap where the quantity delivered each period, *quan*, is time-varying.

**TABLE 21.5** Summary of trading activity for NYMEX petroleum complex on Tuesday, January 25, 2005.

| | Crude Oil | | | Heating Oil | | | Unleaded Gasoline | | |
|---|---|---|---|---|---|---|---|---|---|
| | 1,000 Barrels (dollars per barrel) | | | 42,000 Gallons (cents per gallon) | | | 42,000 Gallons (cents per gallon) | | |
| Contract Month | Settlement Price | Total Volume | Open Interest | Settlement Price | Total Volume | Open Interest | Settlement Price | Total Volume | Open Interest |
| Feb-05 | | | | 1.4248 | 23,063 | 26,626 | 1.3445 | 23,094 | 21,704 |
| Mar-05 | 49.64 | 72,155 | 223,551 | 1.4088 | 17,538 | 62,051 | 1.3594 | 22,781 | 56,794 |
| Apr-05 | 49.80 | 39,777 | 68,599 | 1.3608 | 6,288 | 20,270 | 1.4259 | 5,923 | 25,975 |
| May-05 | 49.70 | 21,533 | 30,622 | 1.3153 | 1,684 | 9,249 | 1.4299 | 4,531 | 25,936 |
| Jun-05 | 49.42 | 9,650 | 40,248 | 1.2883 | 963 | 12,267 | 1.4229 | 1,079 | 10,802 |
| Jul-05 | 49.03 | 4,911 | 22,749 | 1.2823 | 250 | 7,923 | 1.4064 | 94 | 5,224 |
| Aug-05 | 48.63 | 633 | 12,674 | 1.2833 | 0 | 3,091 | 1.3799 | 713 | 6,369 |
| Sep-05 | 48.23 | 1,422 | 15,549 | 1.2898 | 5 | 5,895 | 1.3469 | 1,054 | 7,050 |
| Oct-05 | 47.83 | 525 | 11,892 | 1.2983 | 0 | 808 | 1.3054 | 972 | 3,248 |
| Nov-05 | 47.49 | 650 | 15,531 | 1.3068 | 7 | 1,491 | 1.2819 | 115 | 323 |
| Dec-05 | 47.18 | 5,154 | 57,870 | 1.3153 | 405 | 8,253 | 1.2684 | 1 | 1,697 |
| Jan-06 | 46.82 | 122 | 10,804 | 1.3203 | 0 | 1,619 | 1.2629 | 873 | 29 |
| Feb-06 | 46.46 | 54 | 5,242 | 1.3133 | 0 | 737 | | | |
| Mar-06 | 46.13 | 156 | 9,226 | 1.2868 | 80 | 2,355 | | | |
| Apr-06 | 45.84 | 225 | 4,769 | 1.2478 | 0 | 439 | | | |
| May-06 | 45.56 | 0 | 2,690 | 1.2198 | 0 | 410 | | | |
| Jun-06 | 45.28 | 1,487 | 25,683 | 1.2013 | 0 | 567 | | | |
| Jul-06 | 45.04 | 0 | 2,639 | 1.1978 | 0 | 362 | | | |
| Aug-06 | 44.81 | 0 | 1,921 | | | | | | |
| Sep-06 | 44.58 | 145 | 3,823 | | | | | | |
| Oct-06 | 44.36 | 2 | 1,400 | | | | | | |
| Nov-06 | 44.14 | 150 | 1,428 | | | | | | |
| Dec-06 | 43.92 | 2,253 | 39,328 | | | | | | |
| Jan-07 | 43.74 | 0 | 1,711 | | | | | | |
| Feb-07 | 43.57 | 100 | 1,167 | | | | | | |
| Mar-07 | 43.41 | 0 | 743 | | | | | | |
| Apr-07 | 43.25 | 0 | 450 | | | | | | |
| May-07 | 43.10 | 0 | 90 | | | | | | |
| Jun-07 | 42.95 | 50 | 11,537 | | | | | | |
| Dec-07 | 42.14 | 415 | 21,073 | | | | | | |
| Dec-08 | 41.14 | 761 | 23,734 | | | | | | |
| Dec-09 | 40.49 | 106 | 16,842 | | | | | | |
| Dec-10 | 40.06 | 394 | 18,721 | | | | | | |
| Dec-11 | 39.96 | 186 | 2,495 | | | | | | |

*Source:* Information drawn from www.nymex.com.

**Spread Contracts** One unusual feature of the petroleum complex traded on NYMEX is that they list futures and futures options on spreads. Earlier we described the crack spread as being the difference between the price of heating oil (or gasoline) and crude oil. This spread is a petroleum refiner's *gross margin*. Because both the prices of crude oil and the finished products (e.g., heating oil and gasoline) vary with supply and demand in each market, refiners are at risk when, say, the price of crude rises and the product prices remain flat or fall.

To facilitate the risk management needs of refiners, the NYMEX permits trading of the crack spread directly, that is, both legs of the trade are combined into a single futures transaction. They also list crack spread options. Upon exercise, the option holder receives two offsetting futures positions. The exercise of a call option on the heating oil/crude oil crack spread, for example, results in a long heating oil futures/short crude oil futures position.

**ILLUSTRATION 21.2** Compute value of spread option.

*Based on the heating oil and crude oil futures prices reported in Table 21.5, compute the value of an American-style put option on the September 2005 crack spread between the heating oil and crude oil futures. Assume that the option's exercise price is 6, that today's date is January 25, 2005 and that the zero-coupon yield curve for risk-free bonds is given by*

$$r_i = 0.0178 + 0.01\ln(1 + T_i)$$

*Assume also that the volatility rate of the September 2005 heating oil futures is 43.90%, that the volatility rate of the September 2005 crude oil futures is 35.27%, and that the correlation between the heating oil and crude oil returns is 0.85.*

According to its contract specifications, the NYMEX crack spread option expires on the day before the underlying crude oil futures contract.[5] The last day of trading for the crude oil futures contract, in turn, is three business days before the 25th calendar day of the month preceding the delivery month. The crack spread option therefore expires on August 19, 2005 and has 206 days to expiration.

Also according to the contract specifications, the option is expressed in dollars per barrel. Thus the September 2005 heating oil futures price, 1.2898, which is expressed in dollars per gallon, must be multiplied by 42 gallons per barrel. Thus the September 2005 heating oil futures price is 54.17, and the current level of the crack spread is 54.17 – 48.23 = 5.94, that is, the put is slightly in the money.

No valuation equation exists for the NYMEX crack spread options. The reasons are twofold. First, if the heating oil and crude oil futures prices are each lognormally distributed, the difference between the prices (i.e., the crack spread) is not log-normally distributed and the BSM model cannot be applied. Second, the NYMEX options are American-style. You can, however, use numerical methods like the binomial method. A discussion of the procedure is described in Chapter 9. For current purposes, however, you can simply use the OPTVAL function developed for this valuation problem, that is,

OV_APPROX_SPRD_FOPT_BIN(*f1, f2, x, t, r, v1, v2, rho, n, cp, ae*)

where *f1* and *f2* are the heating oil and crude oil futures prices, respectively, *x* is the exercise price of the crack spread option, *t* is its time to expiration, *v1* and *v2* are the volatil-

[5] The most reliable way of finding the product specifications of exchange-traded derivatives is to go directly to the exchange's website. The crack spread specifications were taken from www.nymex.com.

ity rates of heating oil and crude oil, *rho* is the correlation between the rates of return of heating oil and crude oil, *n* is the number of time steps to be used in the binomial valuation, *cp* is a (c)all/(p)ut indicator variable, and *ae* is an (A)merican/(E)uropean-style option type indicator. Using the problem information, we find

OV_APPROX_SPRD_FOPT_BIN(54.17,48.23,6,0.5644,0.0223,0.4390,0.3527,0.85, 100,"p","a") = 3.8558

An option premium of 3.8558 protects its holder in the event that the crack spread falls below 6 between now and August 19, 2005.

### Risk Management Strategies

The strategies used to manage petroleum price risk depend on the nature of the problem. In the petroleum derivatives markets, refiners or producers are big players. They face uncertainty in their input (i.e., crude oil) cost as well as their output (i.e., heating oil and gasoline) sales price. Another important set of players are end-users who hedges to lock-in the price at which he can purchase a commodity. Airlines, for example, frequently hedge to lock in the price of the jet fuel. Rather than demonstrate the mechanics of a particular strategy once again, let us consider what particular firms report that they do.

Firms are required to report the nature of their derivatives use in their financial statements.[6] The passage below is drawn from Southwest Airlines 2003 Annual Report:

> . . . the Company has hedges in place for over 80 percent of its anticipated fuel consumption in 2004 with a combination of derivative instruments that effectively cap prices at about $24 per barrel, including approximately 82 percent of its anticipated requirements for the first quarter 2004. . . . The majority of the Company's near term hedge positions are in the form of option contracts, which protect the Company in the event of rising fuel prices and allow the Company to benefit in the event of declining prices.

Apparently, Southwest's favored strategy is buying call options on jet fuel. In order to cap the purchase price at $24 per barrel, they must have purchased call options with an exercise price of about $24. In the event that the price of jet fuel exceeds $24, Southwest will buy at the market price and exercise their call whose value equals the market price less $24.

American Airlines 2003 Annual Report reveals a similar hedging strategy but not nearly as aggressive:

> As of December 31, 2003, the Company had hedged, with option contracts, approximately 12 percent of its estimated 2004 fuel requirements, or approximately 21 percent of its estimated first quarter 2004 fuel requirements, 16 percent of its second quarter 2004 estimated fuel

[6] The U.S. accounting rules for derivative instruments and hedging activities are contained in FASB Statement No. 133.

> requirements and six percent of its estimated fuel requirements through the remainder of the year. . . . the Company's credit rating has limited its ability to enter certain types of fuel hedge contracts. A further deterioration of its credit rating or liquidity position may negatively affect the Company's ability to hedge fuel in the future.

In reading the first sentence of the passage, one may wonder why American Airlines hedges so little, at least compared with Southwest Airlines. Can the two airlines have completely different views about what the cost and variation of jet fuel prices will be over the next year? Reading a little further into the paragraph provides a different explanation, however. Apparently American Airlines's counterparties are growing increasingly concerned about American's worsening financial condition and are limiting the degree to which they are willing to enter new contracts—risk management of yet a different type!

A couple of other notes regarding the practice of hedging jet fuel costs are worthwhile. First, average-rate derivatives contracts can be very effective and cost-efficient. Consider the airline's risk management problem—it needs a steady flow of jet fuel day by day throughout the year, where the market price it pays each day is uncertain. One hedging alternative is to buy a portfolio of 365 call options with a fixed exercise price (i.e., a cap on the price of fuel throughout the year), with one expiring each day. Assuming the options are cash-settled, the airline receives a cash payment every day that the market price of jet fuel exceeds the exercise price of the call and nothing on the other days. A second hedging alternative is to buy 12 average-rate call options with the same exercise price, with one expiring each month. At the end of the month, the average price of jet fuel over the days during the month is computed. If the average price is above the exercise price of the call, the airline receives the difference in price times the stated quantity over the entire month. The cost of the second alternative is considerably less than the first.

Second, cross-hedging is usually less effective but can be more cost effective. As a practical matter, the market for jet fuel forwards and swaps is not as liquid as it is for heating oil and gasoline. Consequently, airlines are often willing to cross hedge using heating oil contracts to save on trading costs. Why use heating oil rather than gasoline? To answer this question, recall that heating oil and jet fuel are middle distillates in the refining process. Gasoline, on the other hand, is a light distillate. Hence, heating oil and jet fuel are closer substitutes than are gasoline and jet fuel, which means that we expect the heating oil contract to provide a more effective hedge. To test this proposition, we downloaded the weekly prices of jet fuel New York Harbor, crude oil Cushing Oklahoma, heating oil New York Harbor, and unleaded gasoline New Work Harbor from January 1995 though January 2005, compute returns, and estimate cross-correlations. The higher the correlation, the more effective the prospective hedge. Table 21.6 reports the results. As expected, the correlation between the jet fuel and heating oil is 0.844, much higher than the correlation with gasoline, 0.595, or with crude oil, 0.627.

**TABLE 21.6** Correlation between weekly returns of jet fuel, crude oil, heating oil, and gasoline during the period January 1995 through January 2005.

| | Jet fuel | Crude oil | Heating oil | Gasoline |
|---|---|---|---|---|
| Jet fuel | 1 | | | |
| Crude oil | 0.627 | 1 | | |
| Heating oil | 0.844 | 0.575 | 1 | |
| Gasoline | 0.595 | 0.687 | 0.547 | 1 |

## RISK MANAGEMENT LESSONS: MG REFINING & MARKETING

In December 1991, MG Refining and Marketing (MGR&M), a U.S. subsidiary of the Germany conglomerate, Metallgesllschaft AG (MG), embarked on a program in which they committed to deliver petroleum products at fixed prices over a period up to 10 years. To hedge these "long-term, fixed-supply contracts," they purchased short-dated futures contracts and short-term OTC swap agreements[7] with total underlying volume equal to the total commitments, a so-called "one-to-one stacked hedge." When the futures approached maturity, they were "rolled" into new positions by selling the nearby maturing contracts and buying the second nearby, reducing the size of the position by the amount of product delivered that month.

In the early days, this combined marketing/hedging program was very successful. Among the reasons was that the margin between the fixed price and the average spot price was about $.08 per gallon on average. To further capitalize on these seemingly profitable margins, MGR&M expanded the program, taking on larger and ever larger positions. By December 1993, the company had sold forward approximately 160 million barrels (6.72 billion gallons) of petroleum product. Customers included retail gasoline suppliers, large manufacturing firms, and governmental entities. While many end-users were small, customers also included the likes of Chrysler and Browning-Ferris Industries.

Along with the program expansion in 1993 was an unusual and steady decline in petroleum product prices. As Figure 21.7 shows, petroleum product prices were hovering at about the $0.58 per gallon at the beginning of the year, but then they fell to levels well below $0.50. Indeed a sharp drop in late 1993 took the price of heating oil (unleaded gasoline) to $0.4172 ($0.3537).[8] In and of itself, the decline in price should not have been of concern. MGR&M was, after all, hedged. But since MGR&M was long futures and the futures positions were market-to-market each day, MGR&M was facing a severe cash flow drain.[9] On the other side of the hedge, of course, was the increasing value of MGR&M's fixed-supply contracts, however, these gains were not marked-to-market (realized). The firm needed cash to weather the storm. They turned to MG, but MG refused to supply the additional funding. Indeed they replaced

[7] Under the terms of these swap agreements, MGR&M received floating and paid fixed, making them the economic equivalent of a strip of forward contracts.
[8] Both prices reached their lowest levels of the year on December 13, 1993.

**FIGURE 21.7** Daily prices of heating oil and unleaded gasoline over the period February 1, 1993 through January 31, 1994.

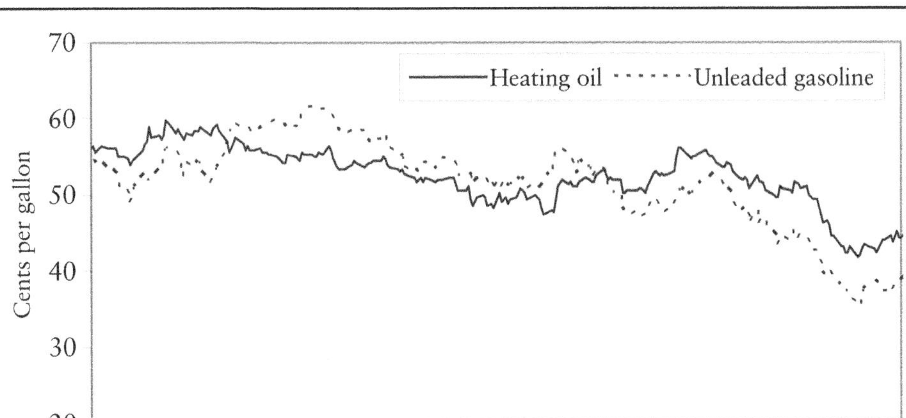


management at MGR&M, closed the futures positions at loss, and *rescinded* the fixed supply contracts. After all was said and done, MGR&M reportedly lost over USD 1.4 billion.

The MGR&M controversy was hotly debated in academic, industry, and regulatory circles. Most of the points of view and specific details regarding corporate actions are contained in a volume of essays edited by Culp and Miller (1999). Our purpose here is to review some basic risk management principles in the context of corporate practice.

This first principle focuses on what it means to hedge. In Chapter 5, we discussed risk-minimizing hedges. These are hedges constructed to reduce price risk to its lowest level independent of any other consideration. But risk minimizing hedges are not always optimal. For one thing, we discussed, in Chapter 3, the tradeoff between expected return and risk and how different individuals/entities will make different decisions depending on their degrees of risk aversion. For another, a subset of market participants may have a comparative advantage in understanding prices (and, therefore, expected returns) in a particular market by having intimate knowledge of supply and demand factors.[10] The management of MGR&M, for example, believed strongly that oil markets should normally be in backwardation and any change to a contango structure would be fleeting. Consequently, they tailored their risk management strategy accordingly, by buying more futures contracts than a risk-minimizing hedge would demand.

The one-to-one stacked hedge employed by MGR&M was not intended to be a risk-minimizing hedge. The ideal risk-minimizing strategy is to buy a strip

[9] For ease of exposition, we talk about the futures contracts as being the only hedge used by MGR&M. As noted earlier, however, OTC swap contracts were also used. While these positions were not marked-to-market daily, provisions are often made for losing counterparties to provide additional collateral when market prices move against them.

[10] See Stulz (1996).

of heating oil and unleaded gasoline futures contracts matching the quantities and delivery dates of the long-term fixed-supply contracts. While on its face, this appears to be a one-to-one hedge ratio, recall that the futures hedges need to be "tailed" by an appropriate discount factor so that the optimal risk-minimizing hedge ratio is below one.[11] In MGR&M's case, a strip hedge was not feasible because, even today, heating oil contracts do not extend beyond eighteen months and unleaded gasoline contracts extend out only one year.[12] In addition, the trading volume in distant contracts is quite modest (see Table 21.5). A second alternative is to cross-hedge using the crude oil futures contracts whose maturities extend out five years or more. But, this would expose MGR&M to considerable basis risk, and, like the petroleum product futures, the distant maturities of the crude futures are not particularly active.

To set a risk-minimizing hedge using only nearby futures contracts requires the use of the regression technique that we described in Chapter 5. Suppose that MGR&M had decided that they wanted to hedge their fixed-supply contract position using only the nearby futures contracts. This practice is not uncommon because the nearby contracts typically offer greater liquidity and lower trading costs. An appropriate way to set the hedge ratio would be to run a regression of the changes in the value of the fixed-supply contracts on the changes in the nearby futures price. If the prices of all futures contract maturities shifted by an equal amount each day, the estimated hedge ratio would be near one. In practice, however, the coefficient estimate will likely be considerably less since the day-to-day price movement in distant contracts is more muted than nearby contracts. With declining correlation between the nearby and distant futures decreasing as maturity increases, fewer and fewer contracts are needed to hedge more distant flows from a risk-minimization standpoint.

In using the one-to-one stacked hedge, MGR&M was clearly banking on a relatively stable pattern of backwardation in the petroleum product markets. If such a pattern persisted through time, the rolling of the futures position from the nearby to second nearby contract would produce an extraordinary gain each month since the price of the nearby contract is above the second nearby in a market with backwardation. In other words, MGR&M was posturing its hedge in such a way that they were willing to accept more risk for the prospect of greater expected return. It should also be noted that if the market moved to contango, the rolling of the futures position from the nearby to the second nearby contract would produce an unrecoverable loss.

Was the bet on market backwardation sensible? Who is to say? Different people hold different views. Figure 21.8 shows the pattern of backwardation in the heating oil market from December 1984 through December 1993. The vertical axis is in dollars per gallon. The value plotted is the difference between the average daily nearby futures contract price and the average daily second nearby futures contract price during each month. Positives values indicate that the market was in backwar-

[11] The mechanics of tailing the futures hedge ratio were discussed in Chapter 4.

[12] If strips of heating oil and unleaded gasoline contracts were available at the time, it is unlikely that MGR&M's sales program would have been so successful since end-users could create "synthetic" fixed supply contracts on their own.

**FIGURE 21.8** Average difference between the price of the nearby and second nearby heating oil futures prices on a monthly basis from December 1984 through December 1993. (Positive value implies backwardation and negative value implies contango.)

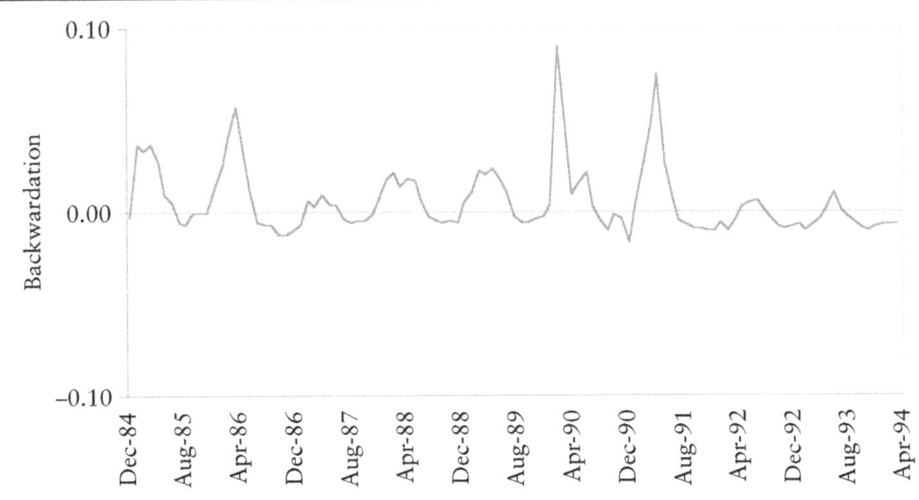


dation; negative values contango. Across the entire horizon, the average difference was about ½ cent. The variation from month to month, however, was considerable.

By comparing Figure 21.7 to Figure 21.8, we can better assess the primary driver behind MGR&M losses. The petroleum product price declines shown in Figure 21.7 are on order of 20 cents per gallon and more. Typical levels of contango, conditional on the market being in contango were well below a penny. Thus, the cumulative effect of the daily marking-to-market of the futures position appears to swamp the size of the average rollover cost. Consequently, the funding crisis appears to have been caused by declining oil prices and the attendant margin calls of the futures market.

Finally, was the situation predictable? Bollen and Whaley (1998) attempt to make this assessment using simulation analysis based on (1) the behavior of the NYMEX heating oil and unleaded gasoline futures contract prices during the period December 1985 through November 1991, the period just before MGR&M began its sales program; and (2) the structure of the fixed supply contracts in MGR&M's book as of December 1993. Their simulation results indicate that, given the structure and size of the positions, the probability of MGR&M needing funding in excess of USD 500 million at some time during the contract lives was in excess of 36%. Understanding and planning for expected funding needs beforehand is critical to being able to maintain a viable hedging strategy.

## AGRICULTURAL: SOYBEANS

Within the agricultural category, derivative contracts on soybeans are the most active. Table 21.7 contains a summary of U.S. futures and futures options trading by underlying agricultural commodity for the year 2003. The agricultural

**TABLE 21.7** Summary of agricultural futures and futures options trading volume in the United States during 2003.

| Product Subcategory | Commodity | Exchange | Futures Volume | Futures Percent | Futures Options Volume | Futures Options Percent |
|---|---|---|---|---|---|---|
| Oilseed | Soybeans | CBT | 17,545,714 | 19.95% | 4,885,399 | 24.53% |
| | Soybean Meal | CBT | 8,158,445 | 9.28% | 546,267 | 2.74% |
| | Soybean Oil | CBT | 7,417,340 | 8.43% | 665,532 | 3.34% |
| | Mini Soybeans | CBT | 250,447 | 0.28% | | 0.00% |
| | Soybeans MIDAM | | 97,163 | 0.11% | | 0.00% |
| | Total oilseed | | 33,469,109 | 38.06% | 6,097,198 | 30.62% |
| Grain | Corn | CBT | 19,118,715 | 21.74% | 4,515,240 | 22.67% |
| | Wheat | CBT | 6,967,416 | 7.92% | 1,788,500 | 8.98% |
| | Wheat | KCBT | 2,632,033 | 2.99% | 465,381 | 2.34% |
| | Spring Wheat | MGE | 1,066,489 | 1.21% | 39,764 | 0.20% |
| | Oats | CBT | 318,898 | 0.36% | 36,163 | 0.18% |
| | Rice | CBT | 265,234 | 0.30% | 34,978 | 0.18% |
| | Mini Corn | CBT | 53,404 | 0.06% | | 0.00% |
| | Corn | MIDAM | 39,555 | 0.04% | | 0.00% |
| | Mini Wheat | CBT | 22,288 | 0.03% | | 0.00% |
| | Hard Red Winter Wheat Index | MGE | 16,535 | 0.02% | 5,773 | 0.03% |
| | Wheat | MIDAM | 5,580 | 0.01% | | 0.00% |
| | National Corn Index | MGE | 3,996 | 0.00% | 1,174 | 0.01% |
| | Total grain | | 30,510,143 | 34.69% | 6,886,973 | 34.58% |
| Foodstuff | Sugar #11 | NYBOT | 7,140,724 | 8.12% | 1,690,190 | 8.49% |
| | Coffee "C" | NYBOT | 3,211,031 | 3.65% | 1,328,081 | 6.67% |
| | Cocoa | NYBOT | 2,128,206 | 2.42% | 497,188 | |
| | Orange Juice, Frozen Concentrate | NYBOT | 652,715 | 0.74% | 195,541 | 0.98% |
| | Class III Milk | CME | 191,351 | 0.22% | 79,901 | 0.40% |
| | Sugar #14 | NYBOT | 133,811 | 0.15% | | 0.00% |
| | Butter | CME | 8,544 | 0.01% | 800 | 0.00% |
| | Mini Coffee | NYBOT | 332 | 0.00% | | 0.00% |
| | Nonfat Dry Milk | CME | 230 | 0.00% | | 0.00% |
| | Class IV Milk | CME | 137 | 0.00% | 41 | 0.00% |
| | Total foodstuff | | 13,467,081 | 15.31% | 3,791,742 | 19.04% |
| Livestock | Live Cattle | CME | 4,436,089 | 5.04% | 664,291 | 3.34% |
| | Lean Hogs | CME | 2,164,155 | 2.46% | 129,227 | 0.65% |
| | Feeder Cattle | CME | 704,852 | 0.80% | 179,347 | 0.90% |
| | Pork Bellies, Frozen | CME | 161,329 | 0.18% | 7,991 | 0.04% |
| | Total livestock | | 7,466,425 | 8.49% | 980,856 | 4.93% |
| | Fiber Cotton #2 | NYBOT | 3,035,992 | 3.45% | 2,157,441 | 10.83% |
| | Total fiber | | 3,035,992 | 3.45% | 2,157,441 | 10.83% |
| Total agricultural commodities | | | 87,948,750 | 100.00% | 19,914,210 | 100.00% |

*Source:* Information drawn from *Futures Industry Institute*, 2005.

commodities are further subcategorized in order to identify precisely where the greatest trading interest resides. As the table shows, the greatest trading interest is in soybeans and soybean products—soybean meal and soybean oil, with 38 (31)% of total agricultural futures (futures options) trading volume during 2003. Like NYMEX and its dominance in the petroleum contract market, the Chicago Board of Trade (CBT) dominates the exchange-traded soybean contract market,[13] as well as other markets such as wheat and corn. The second largest interest is in the grain contracts, which account for 35 (35)% of the agricultural futures (futures options) trading volume.

### Production and Consumption

Soybeans are a relatively new crop in the United States, but not by world standards. They have been grown in China for more than 5,000 and are used to produce a wide variety of soy foods. Gradually soybean production spread across much of the Pacific Basin. Until the early 1930s, however, little soybean production took place outside the Orient. At that time, the Western world began to recognize the value of the soybean as a source of high-protein meal and edible oil. Large-scale production of soybeans in the United States began in the mid-1930s as a result of a trade embargo by China that cut off soybean supply and acreage restrictions placed on cotton, corn, and wheat to curb oversupply.[14]

More than 150 varieties of soybeans grown in the United States. The dominant class in the commercial market (and the class underlying the CBT's futures and futures option contracts) is Yellow soybean. Planting usually takes place in late May or early June, and harvest usually runs from early September through October. The soybean is a bushlike plant that grows to heights ranging from 12 inches to six feet. One of the notable features of the plant is that it has an extensive root system that makes it resistant to drought. After flowering, the plant develops several pods containing beans. Combine machinery is used to harvest and thresh the soybeans. Threshing refers to the process of separating the beans from the pods. After threshing, the beans are dried until they reach a suitable moisture level for storage or processing.

The processing of soybeans into soybean oil and meal is called *crushing*. The first step in the crushing process involves cracking them to remove the hull and then rolling them into full-flat flakes. The rolling process facilitates the second step, solvent extraction of the oil. After the oil has been extracted, the solvent is removed by evaporation and saved for reuse. The flakes are dried, creating defatted soy flakes. Most of the defatted soy flakes are further processed into soybean meal, although they can also be ground to produce other products such as soy flour. As a rule of thumb, one bushel of soybeans (about 60 pounds) yields 11 pounds of oil, 44 pounds of 48% protein meal, and five

---

[13] The Mid American Exchange was an affiliate of the CBOT when it was decommissioned in 2001. At that time, the CBT converted the most viable MidAm financial contracts into mini-sized contracts traded exclusively on the CBT's electronic system. The soybean contract listed in Table 21.7 as being traded on the MidAm is one such contract.

[14] Soybeans seedings were a natural alternative since, like cotton, corn and wheat, soybeans grow best on fertile, sandy loam.

pounds of waste.[15] The main demand for soybean meal is from the livestock industry. Nearly 90% of the soybean meal produced is used to satisfy the basic protein and amino acid requirements of cattle, hogs, and poultry. The major demand for soybean oil is from the food industry, where it is used to produce a variety of products including shortening, margarines, salad oils, and cooking oils. Soybean oil accounts for about 20% of the total world edible oil consumption.

The *gross processing margin* (GPM) of soybeans has seasonal variation. It is usually highest in the fall because of the increased supply from the soybean harvest and the increased demand for soybean meal in anticipation of colder weather, lack of grazing, and heavier livestock feeding requirements. Processing margins tend to decline later in the crop year. As demand for livestock feed declines, soybean meal prices fall, and, as the crop year progresses, soybean prices are higher as a result of lower supplies and the accumulation of carry costs.

### Derivatives Markets

The trading of soybean futures and futures options in the United States is conducted exclusively on the Chicago Board of Trade. The soybean oil futures contract market was launched in October 1936, very shortly after the beginning of the large-scale production of soybeans in the United States noted earlier. The soybean oil futures was launched in July 1950, and the soybean meal futures in August 1951. Table 21.8 summarizes the key features of the soybean futures contract complex. The soybean contract calls for the delivery of 5,000 bushels of soybeans. The deliverable grade is No. 2 yellow, however, No. 1 yellow can be delivered at a premium of six cents per bushel over the contract price, and No. 3 yellow can be delivered at a six cent per bushel discount.[16] The contracts are traded in an open outcry format on the exchange floor during the day, and electronically at other times. The last day of trading is the business day prior to the 15th calendar day of the contract month.

The soybean meal futures contract calls for the delivery of 100 tons (2,000 lbs) of soybean meal with minimum protein of 48%, and the soybean oil contract calls for the delivery of 60,000 pounds of oil. Trading the *crush spread* (called the *Board Crush*) means simultaneously selling (buying) the soybean oil and meal futures contracts and buying (selling) the soybean futures contract. While the Board Crush can be traded in a 1:1:1 ratio (i.e., one soybean futures, one soybean meal futures, and one soybean oil futures), a more precise ratio is 10:11:9. To see this, recall that 60 pounds of soybeans produces 44 pounds of meal and 11 pounds of oil. Thus, 10 soybean futures contracts calls for the delivery of

$$10 \times 5{,}000 \times 60 = 3{,}000{,}000 \text{ pounds of soybeans}$$

[15] Of the five pounds of waste, four pounds are the soybean hulls and one pound is foreign matter (dirt, stones, seeds, etc.).

[16] The short futures right to deliver the cheapest of the deliverable grades is called the *quality option*.

**TABLE 21.8** Selected terms of soybean futures contracts traded on the Chicago Board of Trade (CBT).

| | Soybeans (S) | Soybean Meal (SM) | Soybean Oil (BO) |
|---|---|---|---|
| Contract unit | 5,000 bushels | 100 tons (2,000 lbs/ton) | 60,000 lbs |
| Tick size | 1/4 cent per bushel | 10 cents per ton | 1/100 cent per lb |
| Tick value | $12.50 contract | $10 per contract | $6 per contract |
| Trading hours | Open outcry trading is conducted from 9:30 AM until 1:15 PM, Monday through Friday. Electronic trading is conducted from 7:31 PM until 6:00 AM (CT), Sunday through Friday. | | |
| Contract months | September, November, January, March, May, July, August. | October, December, January, March, May, July, August, September. | October, December, January, March, May, July, August, September. |
| Last day of trading | The business day prior to the 15th calendar day of the contract month. | | |
| Last delivery day | Second business day following the last trading day of the calendar month. | | |
| Final settlement | Physical | Physical | Physical |
| Deliverable grade | No. 2 yellow at par, No. 1 yellow at 6 cents per bushel over contract price, and No. 3 yellow at 6 cents per bushel under contract price. | One grade of soybean meal only with minimum protein of 48%. | Crude soybean oil meeting exchange-approved grades and standards. |

Three million pounds of soybeans yields

$$\frac{44}{60} \times 3{,}000{,}000 = 2{,}200{,}000 \text{ pounds}$$

of soybean meal, and

$$\frac{11}{60} \times 3{,}000{,}000 = 550{,}000 \text{ pounds}$$

of soybean oil. Eleven soybean meal futures calls for the delivery is 2.2 million pounds of meal, and nine soybean oil futures calls for the delivery of 540,000 pounds of oil.

Table 21.9 shows futures settlement prices of the CBT's soybean complex on Thursday, January 25, 2005. The nearby months have the greatest contract volume and open interest. The cost of soybeans appears monotonically increasing from March 2005 through the September 2005 contracts. This arises from the carry costs on existing soybean inventories (from the fall 2004 harvest) as well as that the fact supplies are being depleted. The November 2005 also appears

**TABLE 21.9** Summary of trading activity for CBT's soybean complex on Thursday, January 27, 2005.

| | Soybeans 5,000 bushels (cents per bushel) | | | Soybean Meal 100 tons (dollars per ton) | | | Soybean Oil 60,000 lbs (cents per pound) | | |
|---|---|---|---|---|---|---|---|---|---|
| Contract Month | Settlement Price | Total Volume | Open Interest | Settlement Price | Total Volume | Open Interest | Settlement Price | Total Volume | Open Interest |
| Mar-05 | 515¼ | 35,370 | 132,784 | 19.43 | 10,465 | 76,893 | 154.90 | 13,505 | 54,714 |
| May-05 | 514 | 10,234 | 61,992 | 19.58 | 4,119 | 27,570 | 154.50 | 5,948 | 30,678 |
| Jul-05 | 518½ | 4,366 | 34,537 | 19.74 | 3,501 | 30,414 | 156.90 | 3,556 | 36,202 |
| Aug-05 | 521¾ | 179 | 3,493 | 19.75 | 306 | 5,969 | 158.10 | 331 | 11,261 |
| Sep-05 | 522¼ | 23 | 1,274 | 19.76 | 167 | 5,266 | 159.50 | 214 | 7,995 |
| Oct-05 | | | | 19.80 | 253 | 4,778 | 160.10 | 361 | 7,308 |
| Nov-05 | 531¼ | 1,370 | 19,565 | | | | | | |
| Dec-05 | | | | 19.80 | 863 | 11,963 | 163.00 | 439 | 8,916 |
| Jan-06 | 537½ | 42 | 204 | 19.93 | 65 | 579 | 163.50 | 11 | 360 |
| Mar-06 | 540 | 8 | 109 | 20.02 | 4 | 560 | 166.10 | 102 | 428 |
| May-06 | 538 | 0 | 64 | 20.03 | 0 | 444 | 167.50 | 0 | 99 |
| Jul-06 | | | | 20.05 | 0 | 250 | 170.00 | 0 | 22 |
| Aug-06 | | | | 20.05 | 0 | 92 | | | |
| Sep-06 | | | | 20.10 | 0 | 120 | | | |
| Oct-06 | | | | 20.10 | 0 | 88 | | | |
| Nov-06 | 548 | 1 | 3 | | | | | | |

*Source:* Data drawn from www.cbot.com.

somewhat active. This is the first contract of the next crop year (the fall 2005 harvest). The December 2005 soybean meal and soybean oil contracts correspond to product prices based on the fall 2005 harvest.

The figures in the table also allow us to compute the crush spread per bushel. Consider the March 2005 contract, for example. The cost of soybeans is \$5.1525 per bushel. The price of soybean meal is \$154.90 per ton, which means \$0.07745 per pound. With 44 pounds produced per bushel, the price of meal is \$3.40780 per bushel. Finally, the price of soybean oil is 19.43 cents per pound. With 11 pounds produced per bushel, the price of oil is \$2.1373. The price of the crush spread is therefore \$0.3926 per bushel. In other words, the gross processing margin of soybeans appears to be on order of 39 cents per bushel.

The CBT also lists options contracts on soybeans, soybean meal, and soybean oil. The soybean option contracts were launched in October 1984, and the meal and oil contracts were launched in February 1987. All of the option contracts are American-style, and each contract is written on one underlying futures contract. The last day of trading of all of the contracts is the same—the last Friday preceding the first notice day of the underlying futures contract by at least five business days. For more details regarding the contract specifications, see www.cbt.com.

### Derivatives Valuation

The valuation of petroleum derivatives follows the principles outlined in the first section of this chapter. In the soybean market, storage costs play a significant role in pricing. Consider the prices of the Jul/05 and Aug/05 soybean futures reported in Table 21.9, for example. If we insert them into the cost of carry relation, we get

$$521.75 = 518.50e^{b(1/12)}$$

The implied net cost of carry rate is $b = 7.50\%$. Considering that short-term interest rates are no more than half that rate, we can infer that storage costs are at least 1.625 cents per bushel per month. The forward curves for soybean meal and soybean oil are also upward sloping and in excess of what would be expected given the level of interest rates. Table 21.9 shows little or no evidence that convenience yield plays a significant role in soybean futures pricing.

### Risk Management Strategies

The primary users of soybean contracts are soybean processors. Like other product producers, soybean processors are subject to both input and output risks. A price increase in soybeans increases costs, while declines in soybean oil and meal prices reduce revenue. Futures contracts on all three commodities allow a processor either to hedge each of these price risks separately or to use the crush spread to hedge against an unfavorable change in the gross processing margin. A crush spread involves simultaneously buying futures contracts on soybeans and selling soybean meal and soybean oil futures and is usually done at the 10:11:9 ratio discussed earlier. The soybean position is carried into the delivery month when the soybeans need to be purchased. The short soybean meal and oil futures positions are carried into the months in which the products are sold.

Speculators are also present in the marketplace. Some market participants follow the crush spread quite closely. Figure 21.9 shows the daily levels of the crush spread based on the nearby soybean futures contracts during the period January 2, 2002 through March 22, 2005.[17] When the crush spread becomes less than the actual processing margin, it may be advantageous to put on a *reverse crush spread*—sell the soybean futures and simultaneously buy meal and oil futures. The spread is likely to revert back to a higher level shortly thereafter. The reason is that, if soybean processors are losing money, they will cut back or even stop production. This reduces the supply of soybean product in the marketplace and drives product prices higher. At the same time, with production shut down, processors will demand fewer soybeans, resulting in lower soybean prices. When markets revert back to normal, the reverse spread position can be closed at a profit.

## METALS: GOLD

Within the metals category, derivatives contracts on gold have the largest presence. Table 21.10 shows breakdown of exchange-traded futures and futures options by type of metal. Market interest in precious metals is strongest, with gold being the

**FIGURE 21.9** Daily closing levels of the soybean futures crush spread during the period January 2, 2002 through March 22, 2005. Crush spread is computed on the basis of the nearby settlement prices of the soybean, soybean meal, and soybean oil futures prices.

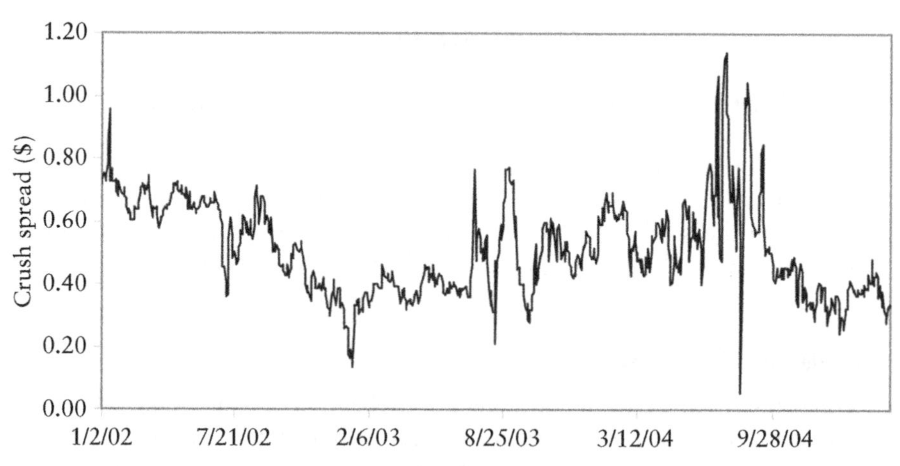


[17] The spike downward in the crush spread on August 12, 2004 resulted from a market reaction to a USDA announcement that the fall 2004 harvest would fall below the average analysts forecast. On that day, the August 2004 futures closed up 50.5 cents a bushel from the previous day's close. The crush margin closed at 5.5 cents.

**TABLE 21.10** Summary of metal futures and futures options trading volume in the U.S. during 2003.

| Metal Subcategory | Commodity | Exchange | Futures | | Futures Options | |
|---|---|---|---|---|---|---|
| | | | Volume | Percent | Volume | Percent |
| Precious | Gold | COMEX | 12,235,689 | 60.91% | 4,310,318 | 87.59% |
| | Silver | COMEX | 4,111,190 | 20.47% | 560,018 | 11.38% |
| | Platinum | NYMEX | 268,305 | 1.34% | 633 | 0.01% |
| | Mini–New York Gold | CBT | 145,173 | 0.72% | | |
| | Palladium | NYMEX | 95,613 | 0.48% | | |
| | Mini–New York Silver | CBT | 34,804 | 0.17% | | |
| | Total precious metal | | 16,890,774 | 84.09% | 4,870,969 | 98.98% |
| Nonprecious | High Grade Copper | COMEX | 3,089,270 | 15.38% | 47,326 | 22.67% |
| | Aluminum | COMEX | 107,490 | 0.54% | 2,679 | 8.98% |
| | Total nonprecious metal | | 3,196,760 | 15.91% | 50,005 | 31.65% |
| Total metal commodities | | | 20,087,534 | 100.00% | 4,920,974 | 100.00% |

*Source:* Information drawn from Futures Industry Institute, 2005.

dominant contract. But even base metals like copper have active markets. Note that, where the NYMEX division of the New York Mercantile Exchange dominates the exchange-traded energy contract markets and the Chicago Board of Trade dominates the exchange-traded agricultural contract markets, the COMEX division of the New York Mercantile Exchange dominates the exchange-traded metals market. In the OTC market, the dominance of gold can be seen both at the precious metals category level specifically and the commodities category level more generally. Figure 21.5, for example, shows that the notional amount of gold forward and swap contracts accounted for 26.8 (22.9)% of the notional value of all commodity forwards and swaps (options) outstanding at the end of 2003. The figure also allows us to infer that 87.6 (92.3)% of the notional amount of the precious metals forwards and swaps (options) were written on gold. With such a large presence in the metals market, therefore, gold is the focus of discussion in our metals category.

### Production

Gold has been mined for thousands of years. The World Gold Council[18] reports that the Egyptians may have produced as much as a metric ton or tonne annually as early as 2000 BCE.[19] Production grew to about five to ten tonnes during the Roman empire, with the ore coming from Spain, Portugal and Africa. Production fell back to about a tonne during the Dark and Middle Ages, with the ore coming largely from the mountains of central Europe. From the middle of the 15th century, the Gold Coast of West Africa (now known as Ghana) became an important source of gold, providing perhaps five to eight tonnes per year. In the early 16th century, the Spanish conquests of Mexico and Peru opened up a further source of gold. By the close of the 17th century, 10 to 12 tonnes a year were provided by the Gold Coast and South America together. Gold was first discovered in Brazil in the mid-16th century but the significant output did not emerge until the early 18th century, considerable supplies began to come from Russia as well, and annual world production was up to 25 tonnes. By 1847, the year before the Californian gold rush, Russian output accounted for 30 to 35 tonnes of the world total of about 75 tonnes. The gold rushes, and later the South African discoveries, radically altered the picture but Russian production continued to rise, reaching around 60 tonnes in 1914.

Today the countries producing gold are many and diverse. South Africa remains the world's largest gold producer, accounting for 15% of the 2,593 tonnes mined in 2003. The United States was second at 12 pecent, and Australia followed with 11%. China had 8%, Russia and Peru were tied at 7%, and Canada followed with 6% of total production. The shares of these and other gold producing countries are shown in Figure 21.10.

---

[18] The World Gold Council is a nonprofit association of the world's leading gold producers dedicated to promote the use of gold. It is headquartered in Geneva, Switzerland and is represented by a network of offices in major centers of gold demand around the world. Its website, www.gold.org, contains a wealth of information regarding the history and use of gold as well as supply and demand statistics. Much of the material in this section is drawn from the myriad of pages and links contained at its website.

[19] One metric ton equals 2,240 pounds.

**FIGURE 21.10** World gold production during 2003 by country. Total world production was 2,593 metric tons.

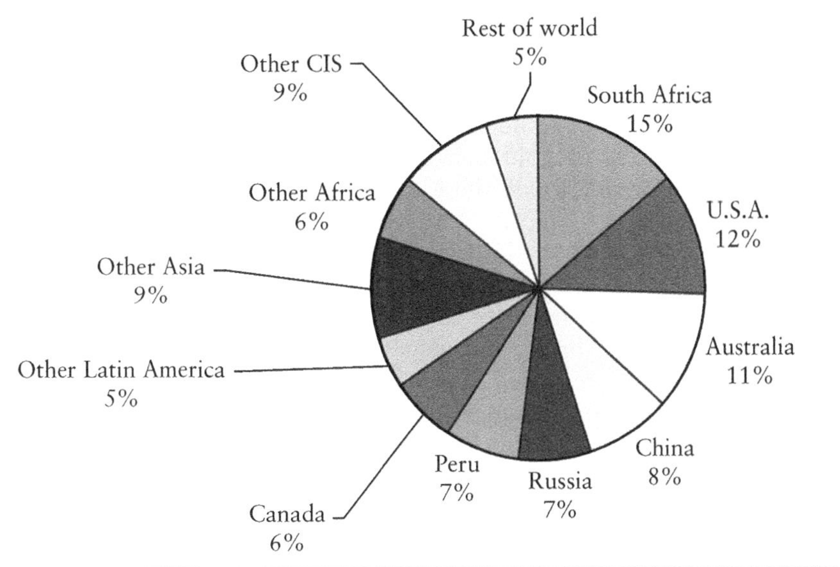


*Source:* Underlying data drawn from *World Gold Council*, www.gold.org, 2004.

**FIGURE 21.11** Demand for gold by use during 2003. Total demand was 3,223 metric tons.

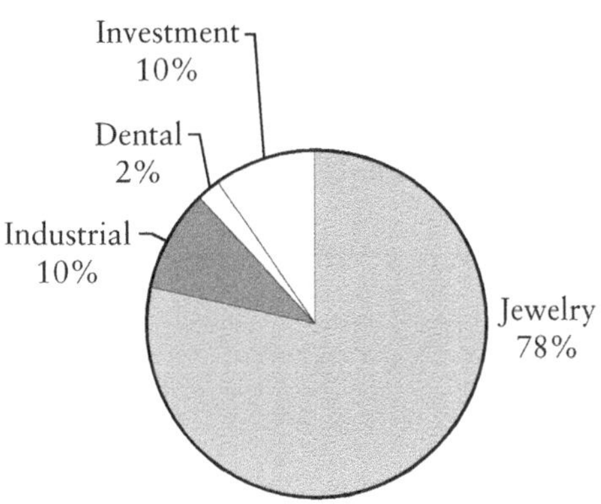


*Source:* Underlying data drawn from *World Gold Council*, www.gold.org, 2004.

## Consumption

The locations of the demand for gold differ significantly from supply. Before focusing on the location of demand, however, it is useful to understand gold's main uses. Figure 21.11 gives a breakdown. Not surprisingly, perhaps, 78% of the 3,223 tonnes of total gold consumption in 2003 was in the manufacture of jewelry. About 10% of gold is used in industrial applications. Gold is an excellent conductor of electricity, is extremely resistant to corrosion, and is one of the most chemically stable of the elements, making it ideally suited for applications in electronic devices such as computers, televisions, DVD players, video cameras, and mobile phone, even with its prohibitive cost. Another 10% is investment in gold bars and coins. The price of gold tends to have a counter-cyclical relation to the level of the stock market, as shown in Figure 21.12. When the stock market falls, investors tend to reduce stock holdings for the "safe haven" of gold, and vice versa. Finally, about 2% of gold consumption is for dental applications.

With nearly 80% of gold consumption being in the form of jewelry, it should not be surprising to see the location of the demand being influenced by cultural considerations. Figure 21.13 shows consumption by country/region. The largest country with the largest consumption of gold is India, accounting for 23% of total world consumption in 2002. Perhaps no other country has gold as deeply woven into the fabric of society. It is commonly involved in weddings, not only adorning the bride, but also constituting a significant value to her dowry. Gold jewelry is regarded as a woman's personal property, and is a means of safeguarding her against financial misfortune and of passing on family wealth along maternal lines. The U.S. demand is next largest at 16%. In the United States, the demand is less culturally tied. The demand is largely as a result of individual wealth and gold's perceived value. It is also used as a hedge against stock market decline. The demands by countries in the Middle East, the South East, Europe, and Greater China follow in size of demand.

### Derivatives Markets

Like in the case of petroleum derivatives, gold derivatives are a relatively recent development. Gold derivatives markets arose in the United States in the 1970s, in the aftermath of two important events. The first was the suspension of the

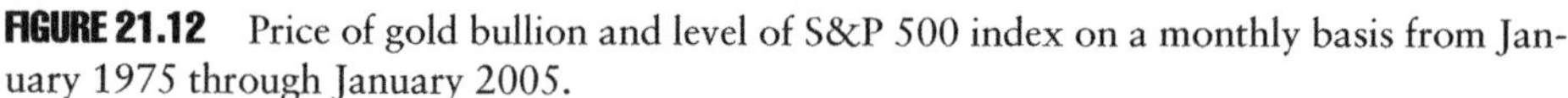

**FIGURE 21.12** Price of gold bullion and level of S&P 500 index on a monthly basis from January 1975 through January 2005.

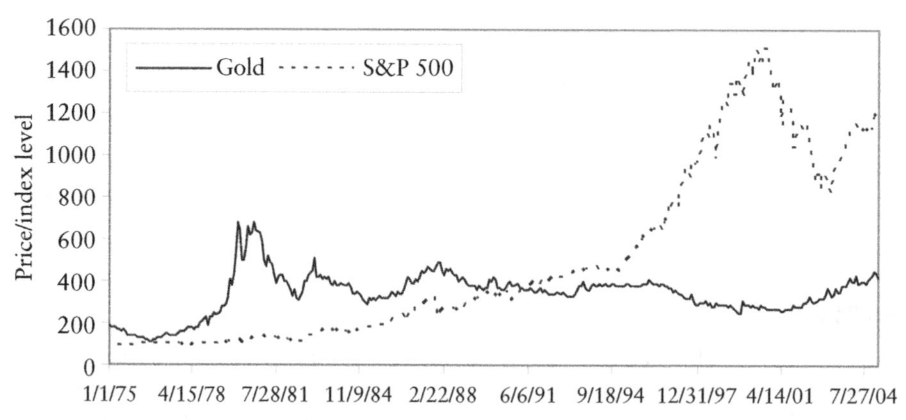


*Source:* Datastream.

**FIGURE 21.13** World gold consumption during 2002 by country.

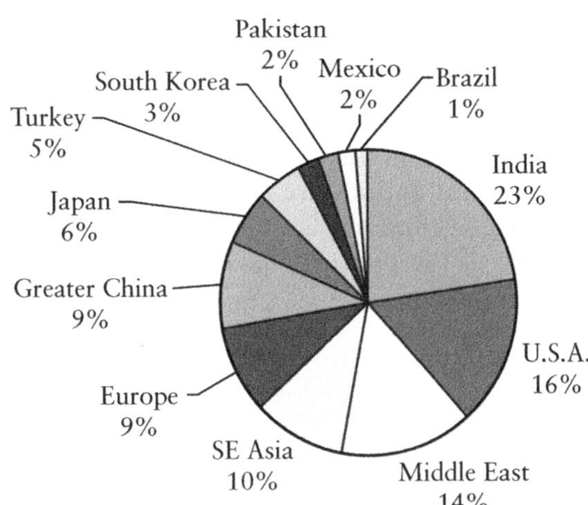


*Source:* Data drawn from *World Gold Council*, www.gold.org, 2004.

Bretton Woods Agreement in 1971. The agreement, originally signed in 1944, fixed all the world's paper currencies to the U.S. dollar, which, in turn, was tied to gold. In 1971, President Nixon effectively cancelled the Bretton Woods agreement by ending its convertibility into gold. The second was lifting of the U.S. ban on private ownership of gold bullion on December 31, 1974. Exchange-traded futures were launched by the Commodity Exchange in New York on the very same day. Futures options followed on October 4, 1982.[20]

The COMEX division of the New York Mercantile Exchange remains the world's largest market for exchange-traded gold contracts. The COMEX futures contract is written on 100 Troy ounces of gold. The contract calls for delivery, and the gold delivered must bear a serial number and identifying stamp of a refiner approved and listed by the exchange. Trading terminates at the close of business on the third to last business day of the maturing delivery month. The first delivery day is the first day of the delivery month; the last delivery day is the last business day of the delivery month.

The COMEX futures option contract is American-style and is written on one COMEX gold futures contract. Option expiration occurs on the fourth business day prior to the underlying futures delivery month. The option may be exercised on any day prior to expiration until one hour after the market close.

[20] In the United States, options on domestic agricultural commodities had been banned by the Commodity Exchange Act of 1936, and it was not until the 1980s that the Commodity Futures Trading Commission took steps to rescind this ban. Specifically, under a pilot program instituted in December 1981, the CFTC approved options for a limited number of futures contracts on commodities *other than* agricultural commodities. It was under this pilot program that the COMEX launched gold futures options. Agricultural futures options were introduced in a second pilot program in March 1984. For further details, see Stoll and Whaley (1985, p. 215).

The OTC market offers a much broader array of gold derivatives products. Forwards and swaps, together with call and put options, are the staple products. But, like with OTC contracts written on other underlying assets, the specific terms of the generic derivatives have limitless flexibility in setting maturity dates, contract size, style of option exercise, and option exercise price. Among the nonstandard forward-style products are spot deferred contracts, participating forwards, advanced premium forwards, and short-term averaging forwards, and, among the nonstandard options are caps and collars, barrier options, and convertible forwards. These contracts are beyond the level of detail appropriate for this, however, many of the products have unique, albeit idiosyncratic, risk management properties.[21]

### Net Cost of Carry Relation

The net cost of carry relation for gold is usually written

$$f = Se^{(r-l)T} \tag{21.4}$$

where $r$ is the zero-coupon rate on a risk-free bond maturing at time $T$, and $l$ is the gold lease rate at the same maturity. Note that this relation more closely resembles the carry relation for a stock index or a currency than a commodity. Neither a storage cost rate nor a convenience yield rate appears in (21.4), as it did in the generic commodity forward pricing relation earlier in the chapter. Storage costs of gold are excluded because gold trades in certificate form. Gold certificates are a means of holding gold without taking physical delivery. They are issued by individual banks, particularly in countries like Germany and Switzerland, and confirm an individual's ownership. The bank, however, holds the metal. In this way, the individual does not incur storage cost or personal security issues, and yet has the ability to unwind his position in a liquid market. Finally, convenience yield does not appear because central banks are the largest holder of gold inventories and accrue no intrinsic benefit from holding the gold.[22]

What does appear in (21.4) and has not appeared before is the gold lease rate. As it turns out, over the past two decades, an active gold loan market has evolved. In a typical gold loan, a mining company borrows gold bullion from a commercial bank to, say, develop a new mine or expand an existing operation. The commercial bank, in turn, borrows the bullion from a central bank. The mining company sells the gold in the spot market, raising the needed cash. In place of paying an interest rate on a cash loan, the borrower pays a *lease rate* on the gold. For each ounce of gold borrowed, the borrower returns $e^{lT}$ when the loan matures. Often the mining company will simultaneously buy a forward contract at the time the loan is drawn. The net position of the combined gold loan/forward position is shown in Table 21.11. Note that the gold loan is equivalent to borrowing cash. The amount borrowed is $Se^{-lT}$, and the amount repaid

[21] Cross (2000) provides desciptions of a large number of the gold derivatives contracts traded in the OTC market.

[22] That is not to say that no one accrues convenience yield from holding gold. Anyone producing a good using gold as a raw material may accrue such a benefit.

**TABLE 21.11** Mechanics of gold loan by mining company.

| Trades | Initial Investment | Value on Day $T$ |
|---|---|---|
| Borrow $e^{-lT}$ ounces of gold | $Se^{-lT}$ | $-\tilde{S}_T$ |
| Buy forward | | $\tilde{S}_T - f$ |
| Net position | $Se^{-lT}$ | $-f$ |

**FIGURE 21.14** Three-month GOFO, LIBOR, and gold lease rates at the beginning of each month during the period January 1998 through January 2005.

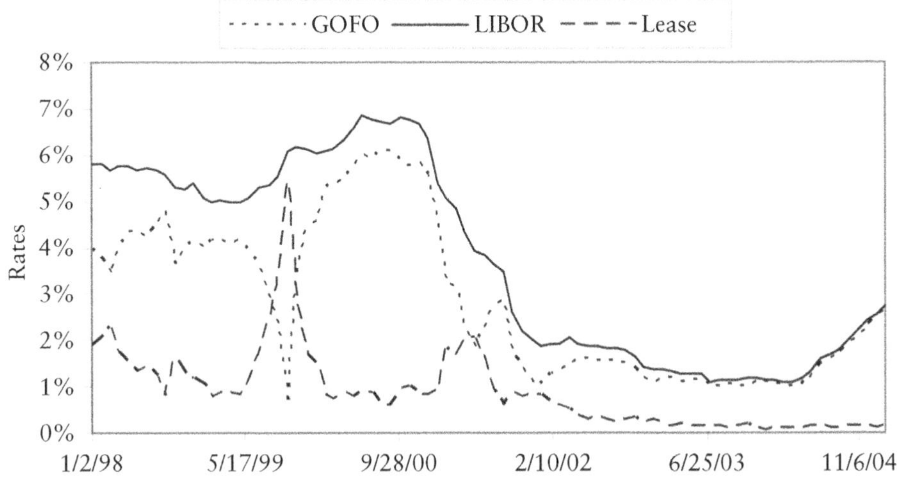


*Source:* Rates drawn from *London Bullion Market Association*, www.lbma.org.

is $f$ at time $T$. Since repayment amount is fixed, the gold loan at rate $l$ is tantamount to a USD loan at rate $r$, that is, $Se^{-lT} = fe^{-rT}$.

In the relation (21.4), the difference between the risk-free interest rate and the gold lease rate is called the *GOFO* or *gold forward rate*, $g$. In general, the GOFO rate is positive because the gold market is in contango (i.e., $f > S$). Unlike base metals, a backwardation (i.e., $f < S$) in the gold market is rare. The reason is simple. Gold is not in short supply. Market participants such as central banks continue to believe that gold remains an important element of global monetary reserves and therefore hold large inventories in reserve.[23] If the forward price of gold happens to slip below the spot price at any point in time, they will simply sell a portion of their inventory in the spot market and enter a forward contract to buy it back again a short time later, and earn an arbitrage profit. Since such trades are easy and relatively cheap to execute, the spot and forward prices would quickly return to the familiar contango structure.

Figure 21.14 shows monthly GOFO, LIBOR, and gold lease rates during the period January 1998 through January 2005. The data were downloaded from

[23] As of September 2002, central banks around the world held about 33,000 tons in reserve.

the London Bullion Market Association website, www.lbma.com. The figure shows that the GOFO rate was positive during the entire period, with an unusual spike downward in the fall of 1999. To understand the reason for this spike, first consider Figure 21.14, which shows the price of gold bullion over a slightly longer interval. What the figure shows is that the price of gold had been falling at a fairly steady rate since mid-1996. The European central banks, with significant inventories of gold, became concerned. On Sunday, September 26, 1999 in Washington, D.C., 15 European central banks agreed to limit sales of gold to 400 tonnes per year over five years as well as limit lending gold to the market to the extent that they had already done so (i.e., no new gold would be placed on deposit). The so-called "Washington Agreement" struck fear into the gold community. From the close of trading on Friday, September 24 to the close of trading in October 5, the gold price shot up by more than USD60. See Figure 21.12. At the same time, the gold lease rate naturally spiked upward. And, with a spike in the lease rate and virtually no change in the LIBOR rate, the *GOFO* rate spiked downward.

### Risk Management Strategies

Important players in the use of gold derivatives contracts are gold refiners. The process of extracting gold ore from a mine and refining it into gold bullion is slow. Indeed, it may take years for the gold in a particular mine to be depleted. Given that the mine's output and output rate over the next few years is all but certain, the only significant risk that a refiner faces is price risk. If the refiner chooses not to hedge, he sells his gold as it is produced at the prevailing spot price. This leaves his future revenue per ounce of gold uncertain, while his cost per ounce of gold is fairly stable. Entering into certain types of derivatives trades can help the refiner manager this gold price risk.

Among the plain-vanilla gold derivatives used by a refiner are forward contracts, call options, and put options. In the gold market, a variety of forward contracts are traded. The simplest is the standard fixed price forward that is commonplace in commodities markets. The refiner agrees to sell a fixed amount of gold at fixed price on a fixed date. Indeed, the refiner may have a strip of these contracts extending out a number of years. Another risk management alternative is to buy out-of-the-money put options to insure the minimum price at which future production will be sold. While this is an effective strategy, it is expensive in the sense that the put premiums must be paid at the outset. To subsidize this cost, the refiner often simultaneously sells out-of-the-money call options in the same quantities and with the same maturity dates. The call premium is used, at least in part, to cover the purchase of the puts. Zero-cost collars are easily designed by tailoring the exercise prices of the options.

**ILLUSTRATION 21.3** Determine cap exercise price on collar agreement in competitive OTC gold and gold derivatives market.

*Suppose that you are a gold refiner and want to hedge the price at which you will sell your monthly production over the next 12 months. Currently, the zero-coupon yield curve for risk-free bonds is*

$$r_i = 0.04 + 0.01\ln(1 + T_i)$$

*the term structure of GOFO rates is*

$$g_i = 0.03 + 0.009\ln(1 + T_i)$$

*and the term structure of the gold volatility rate is*

$$\sigma_i = 0.15 + 0.05\ln(1 + T_i)$$

*If the current gold price USD 400 per ounce and you want to sell all 12 deliveries at a minimum price of USD 390 per ounce, what is the maximum price that you should expect to receive? Assume the amount of production is uniform from month to month and all deliveries are at month-end.*

The first step is to transform the above three term structures into option valuation parameters for each maturity option. You use the zero-coupon and GOFO yield curves to deduce the term structure of forward prices. Recall

$$f_i = Se^{g_i T_i}$$

Thus based upon the problem information, the term-specific option valuation parameters are as summarized here:

| Month | Years to Expiration | Risk-Free Rate | GOFO Rate | Forward Price | Volatility Rate |
|---|---|---|---|---|---|
| 0 | 0.000000 | 4.00% | 3.00% | 400.00 | 15.00% |
| 1 | 0.083333 | 4.08% | 3.07% | 401.03 | 14.60% |
| 2 | 0.166667 | 4.15% | 3.14% | 402.10 | 14.23% |
| 3 | 0.250000 | 4.22% | 3.20% | 403.21 | 13.88% |
| 4 | 0.333333 | 4.29% | 3.26% | 404.37 | 13.56% |
| 5 | 0.416667 | 4.35% | 3.31% | 405.56 | 13.26% |
| 6 | 0.500000 | 4.41% | 3.36% | 406.79 | 12.97% |
| 7 | 0.583333 | 4.46% | 3.41% | 408.04 | 12.70% |
| 8 | 0.666667 | 4.51% | 3.46% | 409.33 | 12.45% |
| 9 | 0.750000 | 4.56% | 3.50% | 410.65 | 12.20% |
| 10 | 0.833333 | 4.61% | 3.55% | 411.99 | 11.97% |
| 11 | 0.916667 | 4.65% | 3.59% | 413.37 | 11.75% |
| 12 | 1.000000 | 4.69% | 3.62% | 414.76 | 11.53% |

The next step is to compute the value of the floor on the sales price of gold. This value is computed as the sum of 12 European-style put option values, one corresponding to each monthly delivery. Since you have the forward prices of gold, you can value the options directly from the forward curve using the OPTVAL function

OV_FOPTION_VALUE(*f*, *x*, *t*, *r*, *v*, *cp*, *ae*)

where *f* is the forward price, *x* is the exercise price, *t* is the time to expiration, *r* is the risk-free rate of interest, *v* is the volatility rate, *cp*, is a (c)all/(p)ut indicator, and *ae* is an indicator variable for whether the option is (A)merican- or (E)uropean-style . For the first option in the series, the value of the put is

OV_FOPTION_VALUE(401.03, 390, 0.08333, 0.0408, 0.1460, "p", "e") = 2.5319

Repeating the valuation procedure for the remaining 11 put options, you find that the sum of the put option values is 82.5243. The individual put option values are shown in the table below.

The final step is to compute the value of the cap on the sales price of gold. Since you do not have the exercise price of the calls, you must set up your Excel worksheet in a fashion that relies on a particular cell as containing the exercise price. You then use *SOLVER* to identify the call exercise price that makes the sum of the call premiums also equal to 82.5243. That exercise price is 428.72, as shown:

| | | | | | | Exercise Prices | |
|---|---|---|---|---|---|---|---|
| | | | | | | 390.00 | 428.72 |
| Month | Years to Expiration | Risk-Free Rate | GOFO Rate | Forward Price | Volatility Rate | Put Value | Call Value |
| 0 | 0.000000 | 4.00% | 3.00% | 400.00 | 15.00% | | |
| 1 | 0.083333 | 4.08% | 3.07% | 401.03 | 14.60% | 2.5319 | 0.4199 |
| 2 | 0.166667 | 4.15% | 3.14% | 402.10 | 14.23% | 4.3380 | 1.6318 |
| 3 | 0.250000 | 4.22% | 3.20% | 403.21 | 13.88% | 5.5566 | 2.9551 |
| 4 | 0.333333 | 4.29% | 3.26% | 404.37 | 13.56% | 6.4268 | 4.2370 |
| 5 | 0.416667 | 4.35% | 3.31% | 405.56 | 13.26% | 7.0611 | 5.4529 |
| 6 | 0.500000 | 4.41% | 3.36% | 406.79 | 12.97% | 7.5235 | 6.6049 |
| 7 | 0.583333 | 4.46% | 3.41% | 408.04 | 12.70% | 7.8545 | 7.7009 |
| 8 | 0.666667 | 4.51% | 3.46% | 409.33 | 12.45% | 8.0822 | 8.7492 |
| 9 | 0.750000 | 4.56% | 3.50% | 410.65 | 12.20% | 8.2266 | 9.7574 |
| 10 | 0.833333 | 4.61% | 3.55% | 411.99 | 11.97% | 8.3031 | 10.7323 |
| 11 | 0.916667 | 4.65% | 3.59% | 413.37 | 11.75% | 8.3233 | 11.6794 |
| 12 | 1.000000 | 4.69% | 3.62% | 414.76 | 11.53% | 8.2967 | 12.6036 |
| | | | | Sum of premiums | | 82.5243 | 82.5243 |

## OTHER: WINE

OTC markets for wine futures have existed in the United States for decades, beginning with French wines in the 1970s and including Californian wines in the late 1980s. Customers execute contracts with wine merchants for the delivery of fixed number of bottles of vintage wine from a particular château (e.g., the 2003 Château Margaux). In essence, the customer buys the wine after it is made, but before it is bottled. Cask samples of wines are made available for tasting to wine journalists and the large wholesale buyers in the spring following the vintage. The wine is generally bottled and shipped about two years later.

The term *wine futures* is a misnomer. The contracts are actually prepaid forward contracts. Upon agreeing to terms with a wine merchant, the customer is required to pay the merchant in full, as much as two years before delivery. Do not expect significant cost savings. The buyer's contract with the wine merchant is only one mark-up in a chain. The wine merchant, in turn, has a futures contract with the distributor, who in turn has a futures contract with an importer, who has a futures contract with a broker. Only the broker deals directly with the château.

From château to consumer, the total markup in price may be several hundred percent, just as if the customer had purchased the wine off the store shelf.

In a typical year, the wines are released in a sequence of tranches, with each tranche being priced at a different level depending on how the previous one sold. In good vintages, the initial release prices are usually the lowest at which the wines will ever be sold. But what is and what is not a good vintage is not known until the wine has matured. The 1997 Bordeaux, for example, had an initial release price that was too high, and its price declined in the following years. The 2000 Bordeaux, on the other hand, had an initial release price that was too low. Even those buying in the second and third tranches saw prices appreciate quickly. Thus buying wine futures is speculation in most cases (no pun intended), except, of course, if the contract is used as a means of acquiring a highly allocated, small-production wine that may never see a store shelf. For a wine producer, selling wine futures may be an effective short hedge in which he receives cash upfront for a delivery that will not be made for two years.

## SUMMARY

This chapter focuses on derivatives contracts written on commodities. It is organized differently than the other product chapters in that the sections of the chapter are arranged by underlying commodity. The reason is that the price relations of commodity derivatives are influenced by idiosyncrasies in the underlying commodity market. Understanding commodity derivatives price behavior, therefore, involves understanding the factors that influence commodity price behavior. At the outset, we discuss the fundamental differences between pricing commodity derivatives and pricing financial derivatives. Commodity derivatives require that we consider the storage costs such as warehouse rent and insurance as well as the convenience of having an inventory of the commodity on hand. Neither of these factors played an important role in the pricing of stock, stock index, currency, and interest rate derivatives products. We then turn to derivative contracts written on the three major commodity categories—energy, agricultural, and metals. We illustrate the idiosyncrasies of each commodity using an example—petroleum, soybeans, and gold, respectively.

## REFERENCES AND SUGGESTED READINGS

Bollen, Nicolas P. B., and Robert E. Whaley. 1998. Simulating supply. *Risk* 11: 143–147.

Chicago Board of Trade. 1994. *Commodities Trading Manual.* Chicago: Chicago Board of Trade.

Cross, Jessica. 1994. *New Frontiers in Gold: The Derivatives Revolution*, 1st ed. London: Cromwell Press.

Culp, Christopher L., and Merton H. Miller. 1999. *Corporate Hedging in Theory and Practice: Lessons From Metallgesellschaft.* London: Risk Books.

Neuberger, Anthony. 2001. *Gold Derivatives: The Market Impact.* London: World Gold Council.

Stoll, Hans R., and Robert E. Whaley. 1985. The new options markets. in *Futures Markets: Their Economic Role.* Edited by Anne Peck. Washington, DC: American Enterprise Institute.

Stulz, Rene M. 1996. Rethinking risk management. *Journal of Applied Corporate Finance* 9 (Fall): 8–24.

Tufano, Peter. 1996. Who manages risk? An empirical examination of risk management strategies in the gold mining industry. *Journal of Finance* 51: 1097–1137.

# PART Ten

# Lessons Learned

# 22
# Key Lessons

The sheer length of this book may give the impression that derivatives are a long and complicated subject. If it were a murder mystery, we might expect hundreds of characters and a complex story line. The irony is that the characters are few—two main characters, a forward and an option, and two supporting characters, a risk-free bond and the underlying asset. And the story line is simple: Two perfect substitutes must have the same price and, therefore, price dynamics. Consequently, the price risk of one instrument can be managed using the other.

This book is about risk management using derivative contracts, that is, how derivatives can be used to effectively manage the different types of risks faced by individuals, corporations, governments, and governmental agencies in their day-to-day operations. For corporate producers such as oil refiners, managing price risk of input costs (i.e., crude oil) as well as output prices (i.e., heating oil and unleaded gasoline) are relevant. For end-users such as airlines, managing its exposure to jet fuel prices is important. Depending upon user, some risks may be acceptable, while others may not. A gold company, for example, may have a thorough understanding of the world's supply and demand for gold production and, consequently, may be better able to predict gold price movements in the short- and long-run. On the other hand, it may have little or no awareness of probable movements in exchange rates. For this company to accept the gold price risk exposure and, at the same time, to hedge foreign currency risk exposure of sales commitments in a different currency is perfectly sensible.

The key lessons of this book are few:

1. **Derivatives markets exist because of high trading costs and/or trading restrictions/regulations in the underlying asset market.** A firm with floating rate debt can convert it into fixed rate debt using an interest rate swap at only a small fraction of the cost of floating a fixed rate bond issue. A wheat farmer can sell his unharvested crop in the spring even though the underlying grain does not yet exist by selling wheat futures. A hedge fund can shed the interest rate risk of a junk bond portfolio by selling interest rate futures. The ability to transfer risk in a cost-effective manner is derivatives markets' *raison d'etre*.

2. **The expected return/risk relation for derivative contracts, like risky assets, is governed by the capital asset pricing model.** In financial economics, the capital asset pricing model (CAPM) provides the structural relation between expected return and risk. This relation is central to the understanding risk management using derivative contracts. The motives for trading derivatives contracts are twofold. Hedging refers to reducing risk, and speculation refers to placing a directional bet. What is critical, however, is that risk management is synonymous with expected return/risk management. As the CAPM shows, in equilibrium, we cannot move one without moving the other.
3. **The absence of costless arbitrage opportunities (i.e., the law of one price) ensures that derivative contract price is inextricably linked to the prices of the underlying asset and risk-free bonds.** A cereal producer, for example, may require wheat for production in two months and wants to lock in its cost today. He has two possible strategies. First, he can buy the wheat in the spot market and carry it for two months. Second, he can buy a two-month forward contract. Since both of these strategies provide an inventory of wheat in two months at a price known today, the cost of the two alternatives must be the same. Otherwise, costless arbitrage profits are possible.
4. **The no-arbitrage price relation between a derivative contract and its underlying asset ensures that derivative contracts are effective risk-management tools.** If we know the structure of the price relation between the derivative and its underlying asset, we can precisely measure the change in the price of the derivative with respect to a change in the price of the asset (i.e., the derivative contract's price risk with respect to unexpected movements in the asset price). If we can measure risk accurately, we can use derivative contracts to manage asset price risk effectively.
5. **The key insight into derivative contract valuation is that a risk-free hedge can be formed between a derivatives contract and its underlying asset.** If a risk-free hedge between a derivative contract and its underlying asset can be formed, derivative contract valuation does not depend on individual risk preferences and, hence, need not depend on estimating expected risk-adjusted returns.[1] Consequently, we can approach derivative contract valuation as if all individuals are risk-neutral. In a risk-neutral world, all assets are expected to have a rate of return equal to their risk-free rate of interest, and the need to estimate risk-adjusted rates of return is eliminated.
6. **Only two basic types of derivatives exist—a forward and an option.** Even though a seemingly endless number of derivative product structures trade in the marketplace, all of them are nothing more than portfolios of basic forward and option contracts. In some instances, the construction of the portfolio is obvious. A protected equity note, for example, is a portfolio of risk-free bonds and an index call. In other instances, the construction is less obvious. An index put option can be replicated dynamically using a stock index futures contract and risk-free bonds.
7. **Valuing and measuring the risk of complex derivatives is made possible by valuation by replication.** Since the cash flow contingencies of complex derivatives

[1] If a risk-free hedge can be formed between two risky securities, the securities are *redundant*, and each can be priced in relation to the other as if investors are risk-neutral.

can be replicated using a portfolio of basic forward and option positions, the law of one price dictates that the value (risk) of such a contract equals the sum of the values (risks) of the constituent forward and option positions. An important corollary to this rule is that, if all of the contingencies of a particular contract cannot be modeled, its value and risk cannot be computed accurately and the contract should not be avoided.

8. **Derivatives valuation and risk measurement principles are not asset-specific.** The valuation equations/methods and risk management strategies for foreign currency derivatives are no different than those used for stock derivatives, stock index derivatives, interest rate derivatives, and commodity derivatives. The only distinction between the different underlying assets is the net cost of carry parameter. The net cost of carry is the cost of holding an asset through time. One carry cost common to all assets is the opportunity cost of funds. To come up with the purchase price, we must either borrow money or liquidate existing interest-bearing assets. The remaining costs/benefits are asset specific. For a commodity such as wheat, storage costs (e.g., rent and insurance) are incurred. At the same time, certain benefits may accrue. By storing wheat, we may avoid some costs of possible running out of our regular inventory before two months are up and having to pay extra for emergency deliveries, that is, we may accrue convenience yield. For a financial asset or security such as a stock or a bond, income (yield) may accrue in the form of quarterly cash dividends or semi-annual coupon payments. Thus, the net cost of carry of an asset equals interest cost plus (less) any other costs (benefits) that accrue while holding the asset.
9. **Accurate parameter estimation is critical in applying derivative contract valuation models.** Statistics and regression analysis play important roles in the application of derivative contract valuation models. In valuing long-term employee stock options, for example, it is necessary to estimate the expected future volatility rate over the remaining life of the option. One approach is doing so is to estimate the parameter using a long time-series of historical return data. Choosing the length of the series, the frequency of the data, and the formula for computing the historical volatility rate are among the statistical decisions that must be made in arriving at the parameter estimate. The degree of comfort that we should feel with this estimate can be measured by computing its confidence interval. Testing the robustness of the estimate across estimation methods can also provide valuable insights regarding the stationarity of the parameter through time.
10. **So-called "derivative disasters" reported in the financial press did not arise from a failing in the performance of a derivative contract or the market in which it traded.** In recounting "derivatives disasters" in various chapters of the book, the main conclusion is that they were largely "management disasters," brought about by a lack of meaningful internal controls and/or supervision. From the money market management activities of Orange County and the State of Wisconsin Investment Board to the stock index arbitrage activities conducted by Barings Bank in Singapore, and from the currency hedging activities by AWA Ltd in Australia to the foreign currency option market making operations of ABN Amro in New York, one common theme emerges—huge bets can produce huge losses. With proper internal control and supervision, the bets would never have been taken.

# Appendices

# APPENDIX A
# Elementary Statistics

The purpose of this appendix is to provide a quick and informative review of elementary statistics. Statistics is used in almost every facet of every life form aviation to weather prediction. In the field of finance, one of its primary uses is to characterize the rate of return distributions of risky securities or portfolios of securities, although the principles apply to prices changes, earnings, or cash flows of almost any sort. To clarify the use of the statistical concepts used in this appendix, numerous illustrations are provided. To make the concepts in the illustrations as usable as possible, we demonstrate how the computations the computations can be performed using Microsoft Excel add-ins.

## OBJECTIVES

After reviewing this Appendix, you should be able to:

1. Understand the difference between a population and a sample.
2. Understand the statistical properties of a probability distribution.
3. Understand the properties of expectation operators.
4. Estimate properties of population from a sample of observations drawn from the distribution.
5. Understand the properties of important continuous distributions including the normal distribution, the chi-square distribution, the *t*-distribution, and the *F*-distribution.
6. Test the hypothesis that a given data series approximates the normal distribution.
7. Test the hypothesis that the mean of a population is zero.
8. Test the hypothesis that the means of two samples are equal when the samples have equal and unequal variances.
9. Test the hypothesis that the means in a paired sample are equal.
10. Understand the distinction between Type I and Type II errors in statistical inference.
11. Understand *p*-values and the power of tests.
12. Test the hypothesis that the variance of two samples are equal.

13. Test the hypothesis that a time series is autocorrelated.
14. Understand the relevance of the Central Limit Theorem in statistical inference.

## POPULATION VERSUS SAMPLE

The need for statistics stems from a lack of complete information about a particular process. Statisticians refer to the total collection of observations or measurements from the process as the (finite- *or* infinite-sized) *population.* Data taken from the population via a particular study or experiment make up a (finite-sized) *sample.*

In practice, Greek letters are commonly used to denote quantities that characterize the population (such as $\mu$ or $\sigma$). These values are referred to as parameters and are generally considered to be fixed and unknown. Parameter estimates, denoted here by Greek letters with hats (such as $\hat{\mu}$ or $\hat{\sigma}$), are statistics calculated from the sample that are used as a best guess for the true parameter. Because we may never know the values of the true population parameters, we associate a value known a *standard error,* denoted $s_{\hat{\mu}}$, with each estimate. Thus in using statistical methods, we can obtain estimates for the relevant parameters and also quantify their uncertainty.

### Summary of the Statistical Method

1. Identify the problem of interest.
2. Draw a random sample from the population.
3. Perform statistical tests on the sampled data.
4. Make inferences about the relevant population.

## RANDOM VARIABLES

A *random variable* is a variable that takes on different values, each with a probability less than or equal to 1. The process that generates a random variable is called a *probability distribution.* It can be thought of as a list of all possible values of the variable and the probability that each will occur. A coin toss, for example, can be interpreted as a random variable generated from a *binomial probability distribution.*

A *discrete random variable* may take on only a specific number of real values. Consider the outcomes from rolling a pair of dice. The possible outcomes range from 2 to 12. If the dice are fair, each side of each die has an equal probability (i.e., a one in six chance) of appearing. If we enumerate all possible outcomes, a total of 2 can appear with only one combination—(1,1), a total of 3 can appear with two combinations—(1,2) and (2,1), a total of four can appear with three combinations—(1,3), (2,2), and (3,1), and so on. Figure A.1, Panel A shows the *frequency distribution* of possible outcomes. A value of 7 appears most frequently at $f_7 = 6$. The total number of possible outcomes is

$$\sum_{i=2}^{12} f_i = 36$$

If we rescale the frequencies so they add up to one, that is,

$$\sum_{i=2}^{12} \frac{f_i}{36} = \sum_{i=2}^{12} p_i = 1$$

we obtain the *discrete probability density function* (or discrete pdf) shown in Figure A.1, Panel B.

**FIGURE A.1** Frequency and probability distributions of outcomes from rolling a pair of fair dice.
Panel A. Frequency distribution

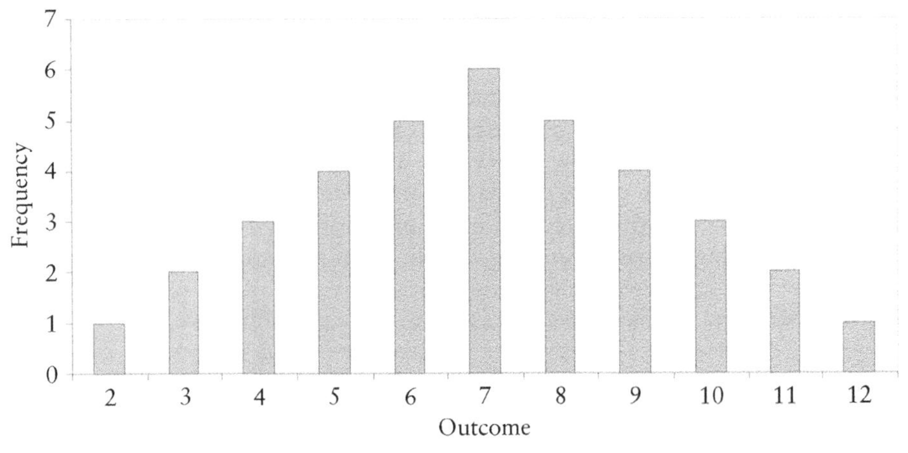


Panel B. Probability distribution

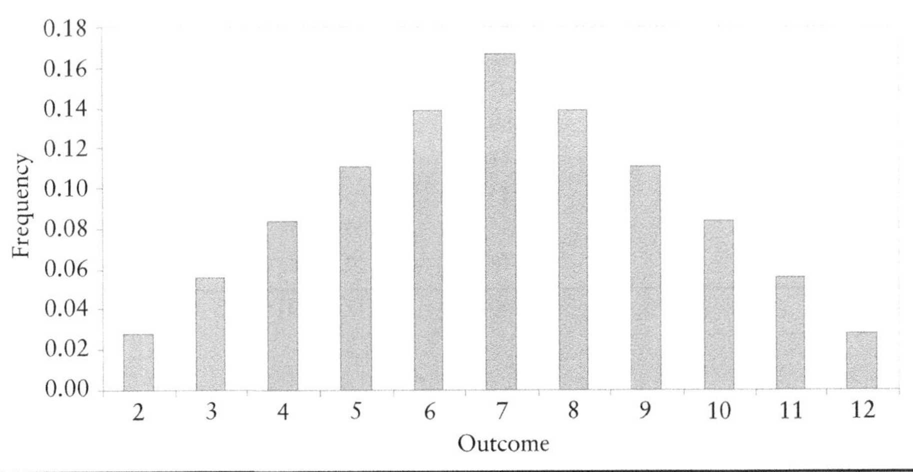

## Mean

A probability distribution is often characterized by its mean and variance.[1] The definitions of mean and variance, in turn, are defined in terms of the *expectations operator E*. Assume that $X_1, X_2, X_3, \ldots, X_N$ represent the $N$ possible outcomes associated with the random variable $X$ (i.e., the *population*). The *mean* or *expected value* of X, denoted $\mu_X$, is defined as

$$\mu_X = E(X) = \sum_{i=1}^{N} p_i X_i \qquad \text{(A.1)}$$

where $p_i$ is the probability that $X_i$ occurs, and the sum of the probabilities equals 1, that is,

$$\sum_{i=1}^{N} p_i = 1$$

Note that the mean is simply a weighted average of the possible outcomes, where the probabilities serve as outcome weights. Table A.1 shows the individual terms of the summation (A.1) for the above dice rolling illustration. The mean is 7. Note that $\mu_X$ is the mean of the population and is distinct from the *sample mean*, which is the average of the outcomes in a sample of size $n$ (where $n < N$) drawn from the underlying distribution. The sample mean is denoted $\hat{\mu}_X$.

**TABLE A.1** Mean and variance of outcomes from rolling a pair of fair dice.

| Outcome, $X_i$ | Frequency, $f_i$ | Probability, $p_i$ | Expected Value, $p_i X_i$ | Variance, $p_i[X_i - E(X)]^2$ |
|---|---|---|---|---|
| 2 | 1 | 0.0278 | 0.0556 | 0.6944 |
| 3 | 2 | 0.0556 | 0.1667 | 0.8889 |
| 4 | 3 | 0.0833 | 0.3333 | 0.7500 |
| 5 | 4 | 0.1111 | 0.5556 | 0.4444 |
| 6 | 5 | 0.1389 | 0.8333 | 0.1389 |
| 7 | 6 | 0.1667 | 1.1667 | 0.0000 |
| 8 | 5 | 0.1389 | 1.1111 | 0.1389 |
| 9 | 4 | 0.1111 | 1.0000 | 0.4444 |
| 10 | 3 | 0.0833 | 0.8333 | 0.7500 |
| 11 | 2 | 0.0556 | 0.6111 | 0.8889 |
| 12 | 1 | 0.0278 | 0.3333 | 0.6944 |
| Total | 36 | 1.0000 | 7.0000 | 5.8333 |

[1] Indeed, under the capital asset pricing model discussed in Chapter 3, risky securities/portfolios are evaluated solely on the basis of these two parameters.

### Variance and Standard Deviation

The *variance* of a random variable measures the dispersion of the distribution around the mean. The variance, denoted $\sigma_X^2$, is defined as

$$Var(X) = \sigma_X^2 = E[X - E(X)]^2 = \sum_{i=1}^{N} p_i[X_i - E(X)]^2 \tag{A.2}$$

Like the mean, the variance is a weighted average of the squares of the deviations of the outcomes on $X$ from its expected value, with the probabilities serving as weights. Table A.1 also shows the individual terms of the summation (A-2) for the dice rolling illustration. The variance is 5.8333. The (positive) square root of the variance is called the *standard deviation.* The standard deviation (or variance) of a rate of return distribution is a commonly used measure of the total risk of a security.

### Covariance and Correlation

In many applications in this book, we are interested in the *joint distribution* of $X$ with a second random variable $Y$. With a joint distribution, the outcomes are in terms of both $X$ and $Y$, and the probabilities are joint probabilities of the $X$-$Y$ pair occurring. The *covariance* of $X$ and $Y$, denoted $\sigma_{XY}$, is defined as

$$\begin{aligned} Cov(X, Y) &= \sigma_{XY} = E[(X - E(X))(Y - E(Y))] \\ &= \sum_{i=1}^{N} \sum_{j=1}^{N} p_{ij}(X_i - E(X))(Y_j - E(Y)) \end{aligned} \tag{A.3}$$

where $p_{ij}$ represents the joint probability of $X$ and $Y$ occurring. The *covariance* is a measure of the linear association between $X$ and $Y$. Covariance is positive when both variables are above and below their means at the same time and is negative when $X$ is above its mean when $Y$ is below its mean. Figure A.2 shows the association between two variables $X$ and $Y$ when the covariance is positive and negative.

Note that the covariance depends on the units in which $X$ and $Y$ are measured. To make the covariance *scale-free,* the association between $X$ and $Y$ is often expressed in terms of the *correlation coefficient,*

$$\rho_{XY} = \frac{\sigma_{XY}}{\sigma_X \sigma_Y} \tag{A.4}$$

The correlation coefficient always lies between –1 and +1.

**FIGURE A.2** Positive and negative covariance between two random variables.
Panel A. Positive covariance

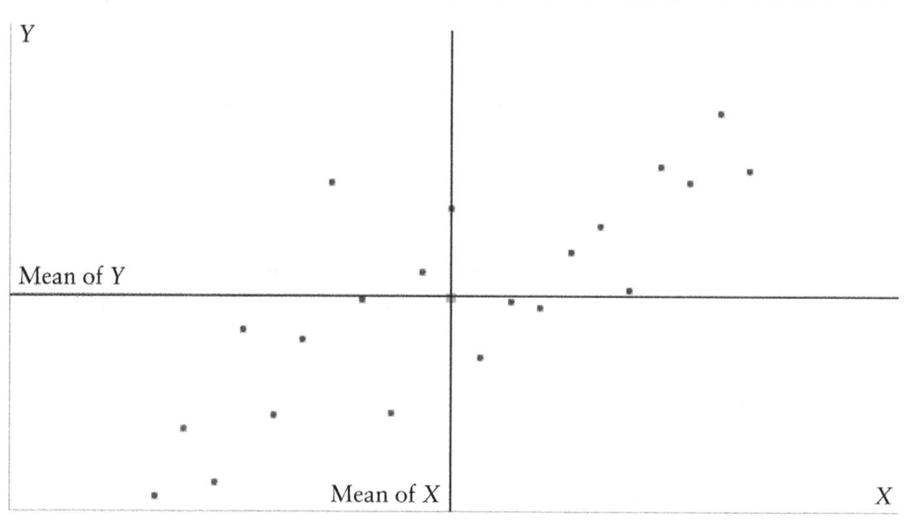


Panel B. Negative covariance

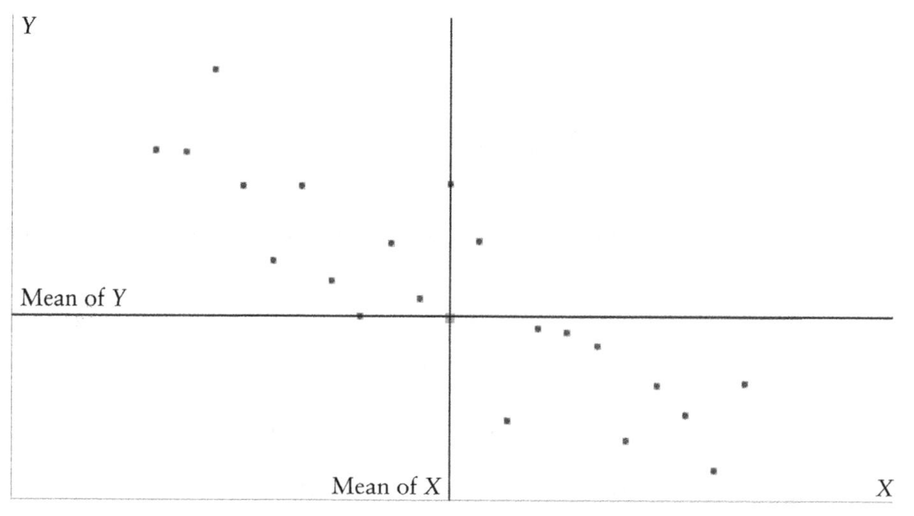


### Semivariance and Semi-Standard Deviation

The *semivariance* of a random variable measures the dispersion of the distribution around a constant $B_X$ for only part of the probability distribution. The *lower semivariance*, for example, is

$$\text{Lower semivariance} = E[\min(X - B_X, 0)^2] = \sum_{i=1}^{N} p_i[\min(X_i - B_X, 0)^2] \quad (A.5)$$

The (positive) square root of the semi-variance is called the *semistandard deviation* or, sometimes, the *semideviation*. Lower semistandard deviation of return, where is set equal to the risk-free rate of interest, is a less commonly-used, but more intuitively appealing, risk measure.

### Semicovariance and Semicorrelation

Like semivariance is to variance, semicovariance is to covariance. The *lower semicovariance* of $X$ and $Y$ is defined as

$$\begin{aligned}\text{Semicovariance} &= E[\min(X - B_X, 0)\min(Y - B_Y, 0)] \\ &= \sum_{i=1}^{N}\sum_{j=1}^{N} p_{ij}\min(X_i - B_X, 0)\min(Y_j - B_Y, 0)\end{aligned} \quad (A.6)$$

where $p_{ij}$ represents the joint probability of $X$ and $Y$ occurring and $B_X$ and $B_Y$ are the boundaries for variables $X$ and $Y$. The lower *semicorrelation coefficient* is

$$\text{Lower semicorrelation} = \frac{\text{Lower semicovariance}}{\text{Lower semideviation}_X \text{Lower semideviation}_Y} \quad (A.7)$$

and always lies between –1 and +1.

### Skewness

The *skewness* of a random variable measures the degree of asymmetry of the distribution around the mean. The skewness, denoted $\gamma_1$, is third standardized moment of the distribution and is defined as

$$\text{Skew}(X) = \gamma_1 = \frac{E[X - E(X)]^3}{\sigma^3} = \frac{1}{\sigma^3}\sum_{i=1}^{N} p_i[X_i - E(X)]^3 \quad (A.8)$$

where $\sigma$ is the standard deviation of the distribution. Generally speaking, a distribution is positively skewed (right-skewed) if the higher tail is longer and negatively skewed (left-skewed) if the lower tail is longer.

### Kurtosis

The *kurtosis* of a random variable measures the degree of the "peakedness" of the distribution around the mean. The kurtosis, denoted $\gamma_2$, is fourth standardized moment of the distribution and is defined as

$$Kurt(X) = \gamma_2 = \frac{E[X - E(X)]^4}{\sigma^4} = \frac{1}{\sigma^4} \sum_{i=1}^{N} p_i [X_i - E(X)]^4 \qquad \text{(A.9)}$$

where $\sigma$ is the standard deviation. In most statistical software, excess kurtosis rather than kurtosis is reported. *Excess kurtosis* is defined as $\gamma_2 - 3$. For a normal distribution, excess kurtosis equals 0. Positive excess kurtosis implies that the distribution of $X$ is more peaked in the center than the normal and has fatter tails. Such a distribution is said to be "leptokurtic." Negative excess kurtosis implies that the distribution of $X$ is flatter in the middle and has smaller tails. Such a distribution is said to be "platykurtic." Finally, when excess kurtosis equals zero (like the normal), the distribution is said to be "mesokurtic."

## PROPERTIES OF EXPECTATION OPERATORS

Many finance applications, particularly those associated with portfolio selection, involve using expectations of the parameters of future security rate of return distributions. Since a security portfolio is nothing more than a weighted sum of its constituent securities, we are interested in understanding how random security returns aggregate into portfolios. Table A.2 presents some key properties of expectations operators. In the table, $X$ and $Y$ are assumed to be random variables, and $a$ and $b$ are assumed to be known constants. In the remainder of this section, we use these results in examining the properties of the formulas we use to estimate the parameters of probability distributions.

## ESTIMATION

Means, variances, and covariances are measured with certainty only if we have the population (i.e., all possible outcomes) at our disposal. More typically, however, we have a *sample* from the population and want to make inferences about the population. In this section, assume we have a sample of $n$ data points from

**TABLE A.2** Key properties of expectations operators. $X$ and $Y$ are random variables, and $a$ and $b$ are known constants.

| | |
|---|---|
| $E(aX + b) = aE(X) + b$ | (P-1) |
| $E[(aX)^2] = a^2E(X^2)$ | (P-2) |
| $Var(aX + b) = a^2Var(X)$ | (P-3) |
| $E(X + Y) = E(X) + E(Y)$ | (P-4) |
| $Var(X + Y) = Var(X) + Var(Y) + 2\ Cov(X,Y)$ | (P-5) |
| **Also, if $X$ and $Y$ are independent,** | |
| $E(XY) = E(X)E(Y)$ | (P-6) |
| $Cov(X,Y) = 0$ | (P-7) |

the population. Our objective is to estimate characteristics of the population, and then attempt to draw conclusions about the population parameters. An *estimator* is the formula used to estimate a population parameter; an *estimate* is the value obtained from an estimator for a particular sample.

### Estimator of Mean

An estimator is said to be *unbiased* if the expected value of the estimator is equal to the population parameter. The estimator of the sample mean is

$$\hat{\mu}_X = \frac{1}{n}\sum_{i=1}^{n} X_i \qquad \text{(A.10)}$$

This estimator is unbiased since its expected value equals the population mean, that is,

$$\begin{aligned} E(\hat{\mu}_X) &= E\left(\frac{1}{n}\sum_{i=1}^{n} X_i\right) = \frac{1}{n}E\left(\sum_{i=1}^{n} X_i\right) \\ &= \frac{1}{n}\sum_{i=1}^{n} E(X_i) = \frac{1}{n}\sum_{i=1}^{n} \mu_X = \frac{1}{n}n\mu_X = \mu_X \end{aligned}$$

### Estimator of Variance

The unbiased estimator of the variance of a random variable is

$$\hat{\sigma}_X^2 = \frac{1}{n-1}\sum_{i=1}^{n} (X_i - \hat{\mu}_X)^2 \qquad \text{(A.11)}$$

The reason $n - 1$ (rather than $n$) appears in the denominator is that, in order to compute the sample variance, the sample mean must first be computed. This places a constraint on the $n$ data points in the sample. That is, the $n$ observations must sum to $n$ times the computed mean, $\hat{\mu}_X$. This leaves $n - 1$ unconstrained observations with which to estimate the sample variance.

### Estimator of Covariance and Correlation

The unbiased estimator for sample covariance is

$$\hat{\sigma}_{XY} = \frac{1}{n-1}\sum_{i=1}^{n} (X_i - \hat{\mu}_X)(Y_i - \hat{\mu}_Y) \qquad \text{(A.12)}$$

The adjustment to the denominator is made because, in calculating the sum of the products of the deviations in $X$ and $Y$, there are $n$ observations on the joint outcomes of $X$ and $Y$ and thus $n$ independent pieces of information. One piece of information is used to calculate the means of $X$ and $Y$, however. The sum of all $n$ observations is constrained to be equal to $n$ times the means of $X$ and $Y$, respectively. As a result, there are degrees of freedom.

Finally, the *sample correlation coefficient* between the two variables is

$$\hat{\rho}_{XY} = \frac{\sum_{i=1}^{n}(X_i - \hat{\mu}_X)(Y_i - \hat{\mu}_Y)}{\sqrt{\sum_{i=1}^{n}(X_i - \hat{\mu}_X)^2 \sum_{i=1}^{n}(Y_i - \hat{\mu}_Y)^2}} = \frac{\hat{\sigma}_{XY}}{\hat{\sigma}_X\hat{\sigma}_Y} \tag{A.13}$$

## Estimator of Lower Semivariance

An estimator of sample semivariance is

$$\text{Lower semivariance} = \frac{1}{n}\sum_{i=1}^{n}\min(X_i - B_X, 0)^2 \tag{A.14}$$

The (positive) square root of the estimate of the semivariance provides our estimate of the semistandard deviation. In applying (A.12) to return distributions, the most common choices for $B_X$ are the risk-free rate of interest and zero. The choice of the risk-free rate is intuitive in the sense that it says we are only concerned about holding a risky asset to the extent that its return might be below what can be earned by placing the investment funds in a risk-free asset.

## Estimators of Semicovariance and Semicorrelation

An estimator of sample semicovariance is

$$\text{Lower semicovariance} = \frac{1}{n}\sum_{i=1}^{n}\sum_{j=1}^{n}\min(X_i - B_X, 0)\min(Y_j - B_Y, 0) \tag{A.15}$$

where $B_X$ and $B_Y$ are the upper boundaries of variables $X$ and $Y$. The estimator of the lower semicorrelation coefficient is

$$\text{Lower semicorrelation} = \frac{\text{Lower semicovariance}}{\text{Lower semideviation}_X \text{Lower semideviation}_Y} \tag{A.16}$$

and always lies between –1 and +1.

### Estimator of Skewness

An estimator of sample skewness is

$$\hat{\gamma}_1 = \frac{n}{(n-1)(n-2)}\sum_{i=1}^{n}\left(\frac{X_i - \hat{\mu}_X}{\hat{\sigma}_X}\right)^3 \tag{A.17}$$

where $\hat{\sigma}_X$ is the estimated standard deviation of the distribution.[2] Positive skewness implies that the distribution has a long tail to the right, and negative skewness implies that it has a long tail to the left. Many financial models incorporate the behavioral assumption that investors gain satisfaction from positive skewness in the rate of return distribution, holding other factors constant.

### Estimator of Kurtosis

An estimator of sample excess kurtosis is

$$\hat{\gamma}_2 = \left\{\frac{n(n+1)}{(n-1)(n-2)(n-3)}\sum_{i=1}^{n}\left(\frac{X_i - \hat{\mu}_X}{\hat{\sigma}_X}\right)^4\right\} - \frac{3(n-1)^2}{(n-2)(n-3)} \tag{A.18}$$

Excess kurtosis characterizes the peakedness or flatness of a distribution relative to the normal distribution. Positive kurtosis indicates a relatively peaked distribution, and negative kurtosis indicates a relatively flat distribution.

**ILLUSTRATION A.1** Estimate mean, variance, standard deviation, skewness, and excess kurtosis of monthly stock returns for IBM.

*The worksheet **A1** in the Excel file, **A Illustrations.xls**, contains 60 months of returns for IBM and a value-weighted stock market index over the period January 2000 through December 2004. Estimate the mean, variance, standard deviation, skewness, and kurtosis of IBM's return series. Use the standard Excel statistical functions to perform your computations. Comment on the levels of skewness and kurtosis.*

To begin, examine the contents of the data file illustrated on the following page. The first column contains the date of the month-end. The next two columns contain the rates of return of IBM's stock and a value-weighted stock market index. Note that rows 7 through 60 have been compressed some that the file contents can be displayed on one page. You can adjust the height to see the contents of the cells if necessary.

[2] While it is beyond the scope of this appendix, the $1/(n-1)$ allows for the fact that a degree of freedom has been used in estimating the mean, and $n/(n-2)$ is a small sample bias adjustment.

| | A | B | C |
|---|---|---|---|
| 1 | **Monthly holding period returns (2000-2004)** | | |
| 2 | | Returns | |
| 3 | Month | IBM | VW index |
| 4 | 20000131 | 0.04056 | -0.03980 |
| 5 | 20000229 | -0.08356 | 0.03180 |
| 6 | 20000331 | 0.14842 | 0.05350 |
| 61 | 20041029 | 0.04677 | 0.01780 |
| 62 | 20041130 | 0.05203 | 0.04830 |
| 63 | 20041231 | 0.04605 | 0.03520 |

Rather than perform the computations of each estimator, we will rely on Microsoft Excel add-ins. Some are part of the Excel add-in function library provided by Microsoft. Others are part of the OPTVAL add-in function library that is part of the CD that accompanies this book. The same approach is used to apply the functions from either library.

The first step in applying an add-in function is to click on the "Insert" menu and select "Function" as shown:

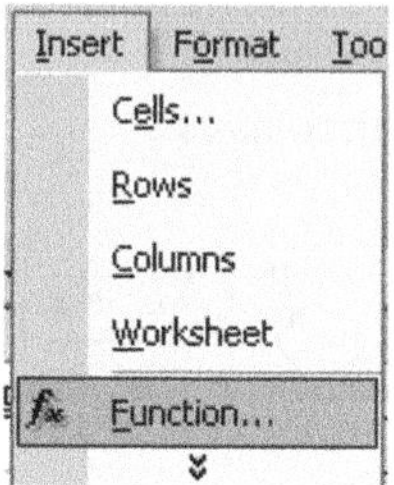


Clicking on "Function" will cause a menu to appear. The menu contains the different sub-libraries of add-ins that are available. "All" contains the entire set of add-in functions. It is so lengthy, it is cumbersome to use. In the Insert Function dialog box as shown, "All" are the functions separated into categories according to their general purpose. For this illustration, we need functions from the "Statistical" category.

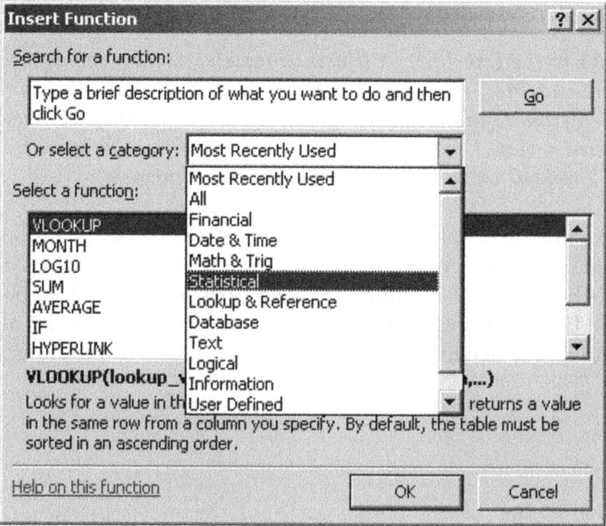


Clicking on "Statistical" will provide a list of statistical functions. The "Average" function is used to compute the estimate of the mean using (A-10). When we click on the function name, the following form appears. To insert the IBM return series in computing the mean, simply place the cursor in the Function Arguments dialog box to the right of Number1 and highlight the cells B4 through B63 as shown, and then click "OK":

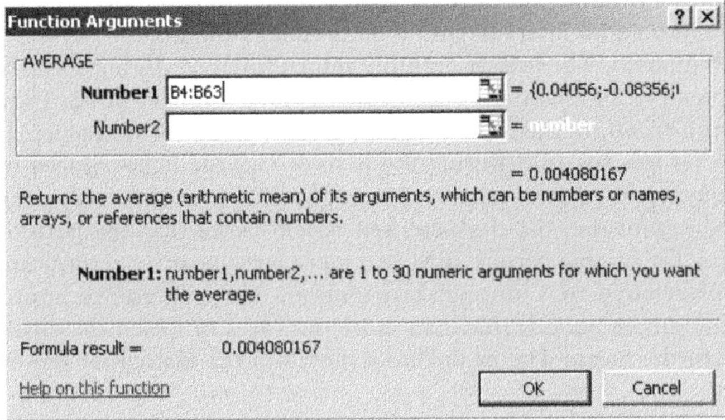


The illustration that follows summarizes the results. Note that the contents of cell B67 is the mean monthly return of IBM, 0.00408. Cell C67 contains the mean return of the market index and involves the function call "=AVERAGE(C4:C63)".

For your convenience, the Excel function names of all of the remaining estimators are provided in column D. An inspection of the worksheet shows that cells B67 through B71 have the following function calls:

=AVERAGE(B4:B63)
=VAR(B4:B63)
=STDEV(B4:B63)
=SKEW(B4:B63)
=KURT(B4:B63)

The estimated skewness of IBM's observed monthly returns is 0.96509. Positive skewness implies that the return distribution is asymmetric and has a long tail on the right. The estimated kurtosis is 2.44513. Positive excess kurtosis implies that the return distribution is more peaked than the normal and has fatter tails.

B67 =AVERAGE(B4:B63)

| | A | B | C | D |
|---|---|---|---|---|
| 1 | **Monthly holding period returns (2000-2004)** | | | |
| 2 | | Returns | | |
| 3 | Month | IBM | VW index | |
| 4 | 20000131 | 0.04056 | -0.03980 | |
| 5 | 20000229 | -0.08356 | 0.03180 | |
| 6 | 20000331 | 0.14842 | 0.05350 | |
| 61 | 20041029 | 0.04677 | 0.01780 | |
| 62 | 20041130 | 0.05203 | 0.04830 | |
| 63 | 20041231 | 0.04605 | 0.03520 | |
| 64 | | | | |
| 65 | | | | Excel |
| 66 | | Parameter estimates | | function |
| 67 | Mean | 0.00408 | 0.00018 | AVERAGE |
| 68 | Variance | 0.01077 | 0.00242 | VAR |
| 69 | Standard deviation | 0.10378 | 0.04924 | STDEV |
| 70 | Skewness | 0.96509 | -0.31475 | SKEW |
| 71 | Kurtosis | 2.44513 | -0.58410 | KURT |

To understand the meaning of the skewness and kurtosis parameter values in relation to the shape of the return distribution, it is useful to plot a *histogram*. A histogram typically divides the distance between the minimum and maximum values of the sample of observations into equal intervals and then tabulates the number of observations that fall within each interval. The lowest monthly return for IBM during the sample period is –22.6% in September 2002 and the highest is 35.4% in October 2002. The total number of monthly returns is 60. In the following figure, we display the frequency distribution of actual monthly returns for IBM during the period (i.e., the light-colored bars). We also shown the frequency of returns that is expected if IBM's returns were normally distributed during the period (i.e. the dark-colored bars).[3] Note that the patterns are just as expected. During the sample period, IBM had more large positive returns and fewer large negative returns relative to a normal distribution. This represents positive skewness. Also, during the sample period, IBM had more instances in which the observed monthly was very close to the mean. The peakedness shown in the histogram represents positive excess kurtosis.

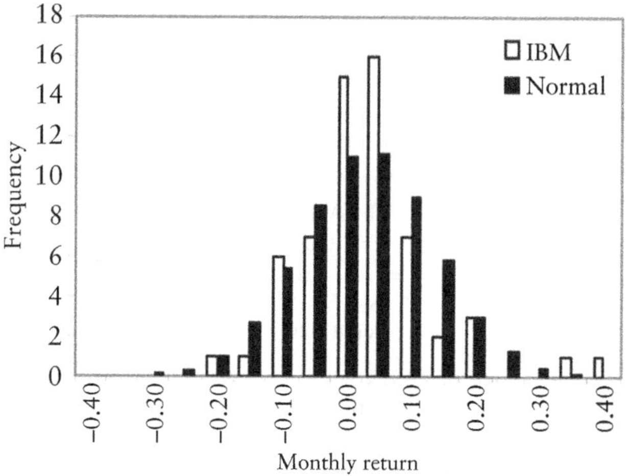


**ILLUSTRATION A.2** Estimate covariance and correlation between IBM and stock market index returns.

*Using the monthly returns reported in the* ***A2*** *worksheet of the Excel file,* ***A Illustrations.xls****, estimate the covariance and correlation between the IBM and market return series. Use the standard Excel statistical functions to perform your computations.*

As noted earlier in this appendix, covariance and correlation measure the association between two random variables. To get a sense of the relation between two variables, it is useful to plot the series against one another. The figure below shows us that, when the market return is positive, IBM's return is positive, and, when the market return is negative, IBM's return is negative. In other words, the returns of two series are positively correlated (have positive covariance).

[3] The mean and the standard deviation of the normal distribution are set equal to the mean and the standard deviation estimated for the sample, 0.00408 and 0.10378, respectively.

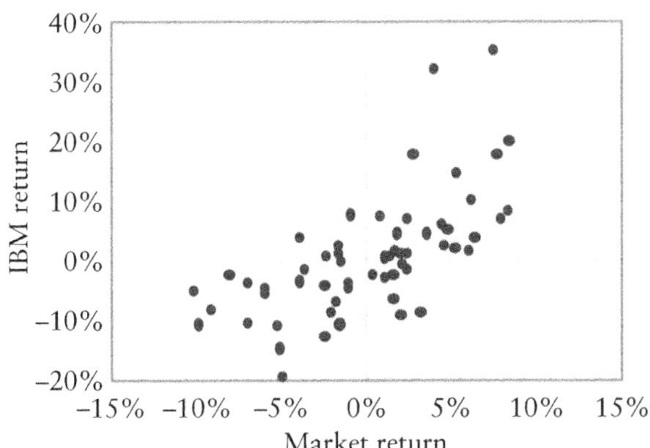


The Excel functions for computing the covariance (A-12) and correlation (A-13) are COVAR and CORREL, respectively. Using the information in the worksheet *A2*, the estimates of covariance and correlation are:

B67 fx =COVAR(B4:B63,C4:C63)

| | A | B | C |
|---|---|---|---|
| 1 | **Monthly holding period returns (2000-2004)** | | |
| 2 | | Returns | |
| 3 | Month | IBM | VW index |
| 4 | 20000131 | 0.04056 | -0.03980 |
| 5 | 20000229 | -0.08356 | 0.03180 |
| 6 | 20000331 | 0.14842 | 0.05350 |
| 61 | 20041029 | 0.04677 | 0.01780 |
| 62 | 20041130 | 0.05203 | 0.04830 |
| 63 | 20041231 | 0.04605 | 0.03520 |
| 64 | | | |
| 65 | | Parameter | Excel |
| 66 | | estimate | function |
| 67 | Covariance | 0.00344 | COVAR |
| 68 | Correlation | 0.68415 | CORREL |

The estimated correlation is 0.68415, which implies that the returns are strongly positively correlated.

**ILLUSTRATION A.3** Estimate semivariance and semistandard deviation of return distributions. Also estimate semicovariance and semicorrelation.

*Using the information provided in the worksheet A3 in the Excel file,* ***A Illustrations.xls****, estimate semivariance and semistandard deviation of the return series for IBM and the market. Also, estimate semicovariance and semicorrelation between IBM and stock market index returns. Compare the correlation and semicorrelation estimates and comment on the difference.*

The "Statistical" library in Excel contains the most commonly-used statistical functions in applications from all disciplines. This book focuses exclusively on finance applications, and certain useful statistical functions are not included in the Excel statistical library. Consequently, these functions are included in the OPTVAL function library.

To use the OPTVAL functions, we click on the "User Defined" option in the Insert Function menu as shown:

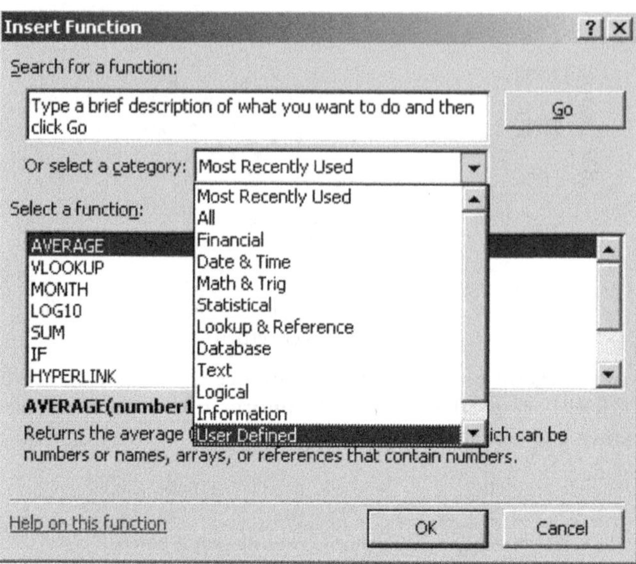


What will appear is the list of user-defined functions. They are clustered together in the menu by virtue of the fact that they begin with the prefix "OV_". The next term in the function name describes the category. The statistical functions in the OPTVAL library begin with "OV_STAT_" as shown:

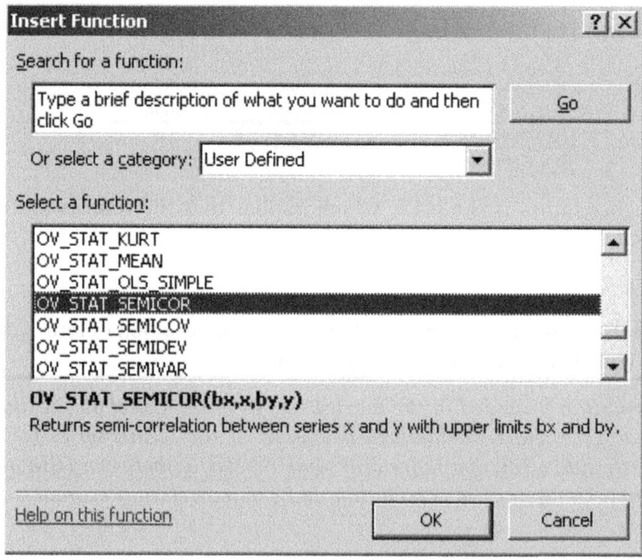


The remaining part of the name corresponds to the nature of the computation. The worksheet below illustrates the use of the lower semi-correlation function. The syntax of the function is

$$\text{OV\_STAT\_SEMICOR}(bx, x, by, y)$$

where $bx$ is the upper bound on the observations of $x$, $x$ is a vector containing the observations of $x$, $by$ is the upper bound on the observations of $y$, and $y$ is the vector of $y$ observations.

A summary of the computations is contained in the illustration that follows. Interestingly, the lower semicorrelation estimate, 0.73313, is greater than the correlation, 0.68415. The fact that both correlations are positive indicates that IBM and the market tend to move together, however, the fact that the lower semicorrelation is higher means that the relation is strongest when prices fall. This is type of behavior is not uncommon in financial markets. A declining market sometimes causes investors to leave a particular asset class in favor of a safer one (e.g., sells stocks and buy Treasury bills).

B69 =OV_STAT_SEMICOV(0,B4:B63,0,C4:C63)

| | A | B | C | D |
|---|---|---|---|---|
| 1 | **Monthly holding period returns (2000-2004)** | | | |
| 2 | | Returns | | |
| 3 | Month | IBM | VW index | |
| 4 | 20000131 | 0.04056 | -0.03980 | |
| 5 | 20000229 | -0.08356 | 0.03180 | |
| 6 | 20000331 | 0.14842 | 0.05350 | |
| 61 | 20041029 | 0.04677 | 0.01780 | |
| 62 | 20041130 | 0.05203 | 0.04830 | |
| 63 | 20041231 | 0.04605 | 0.03520 | |
| 64 | | | | |
| 65 | | | | OPTVAL |
| 66 | | Parameter estimates | | function |
| 67 | Semi-variance | 0.00383 | 0.00131 | OV_STAT_SEMIVAR |
| 68 | Semi-deviation | 0.06190 | 0.03620 | OV_STAT_SEMIDEV |
| 69 | Semi-covariance | 0.00164 | | OV_STAT_SEMICOV |
| 70 | Semi-correlation | 0.73313 | | OV_STAT_SEMICOR |

## PROBABILITY DISTRIBUTIONS

In the remainder of this appendix, we work with four specific *continuous* density functions—the normal, chi-squared, $t$, and $F$ distributions.[4] Unlike a discrete density function, a continuous random variable can take on any value from the real number line from $-\infty$ to $+\infty$. We use the normal distribution to develop measures of risk. We use the remaining three distributions to help develop a framework for understanding the role of measurement error in security valuation and risk measurement.

### Normal Distribution

The *normal distribution* is important for a number of reasons. First, it is symmetric and bell-shaped, and closely approximates many empirical distributions such as security returns and cash flows. Second, it is fully described by its mean

[4] In Chapter 7, we also use the log-normal distribution in describing the distribution of future security prices.

and variance, so we need not worry about other properties such as skewness and kurtosis. Third, if two (or more) random variables are normally distributed with identical means and variances, any weighted sum of these variables will be normally distributed.

The *normal distribution* is a continuous bell-shaped probability distribution whose density function is given by

$$p(X_i) = \frac{1}{\sqrt{2\pi\sigma_X^2}} e^{\left[-\frac{1}{2\sigma_X^2}(X_i - \mu_X)^2\right]} \tag{A.19}$$

where $\mu_X$ and $\sigma_X$ are the mean and standard deviation of $X$. In the special case where $\mu_X = 0$ and $\sigma_X = 1$, the resulting random variable (usually denoted $z$) has a *standard normal density function*,

$$n(z) = \frac{1}{\sqrt{2\pi}} e^{-z^2/2} \tag{A.20}$$

Figure A.3, Panel A plots $n(z)$ as a function of $z$. Note that all normal distributions can be be transformed into the standard (or unit) normal distribution using the relation, $z_i = (X_i - \mu_X)/\sigma_X$.

To compute the probability that a random drawing from a standard normal distribution will fall below a level $a$, we integrate (A.20) over the range from $-\infty$ to $a$, that is,

$$\begin{aligned} \Pr(\tilde{z} < a) &= \int_{-\infty}^{a} \frac{1}{\sqrt{2\pi}} e^{-z^2/2} dz \\ &= N(a) \end{aligned} \tag{A.21}$$

The usual way in which values of $N(a)$ have been available in matrices like Tables C.1A and 1B in Appendix C of this book. Appendix C contains all of the statistical tables that we will need in hypothesis testing and building confidence intervals. In Table C.1A, for example, $N(-2.00) = 0.0228$. This means that the chance that a random drawing from a standard normal distribution will have a value more than two standard deviation below the mean is 2.28%. Since the standard normal distribution is symmetric and centered on 0, this also means that the chance that a random drawing from a standard normal distribution will have a value more than two standard deviation above the mean is 2.28%. To check this, we can turn to Table C.1B, where we find that $N(2.00) = 0.9772$, that is, the chance that a random drawing from a standard normal distribution will have a value less than two standard deviations above the mean is 97.72%. The complement of this value is, of course, 2.28%. The chance that a random drawing from a standard normal distribution will have a value in the range plus or minus two standard deviations from the mean is 97.72 – 2.28 = 95.44%.

**FIGURE A.3** Standard normal distribution function and cumulative standard normal density function.
Panel A. Standard normal

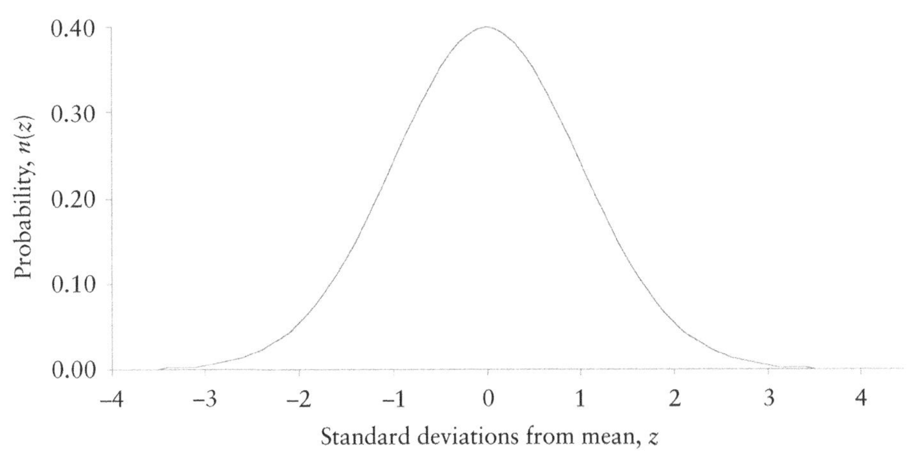


Panel B. Cumulative standard normal

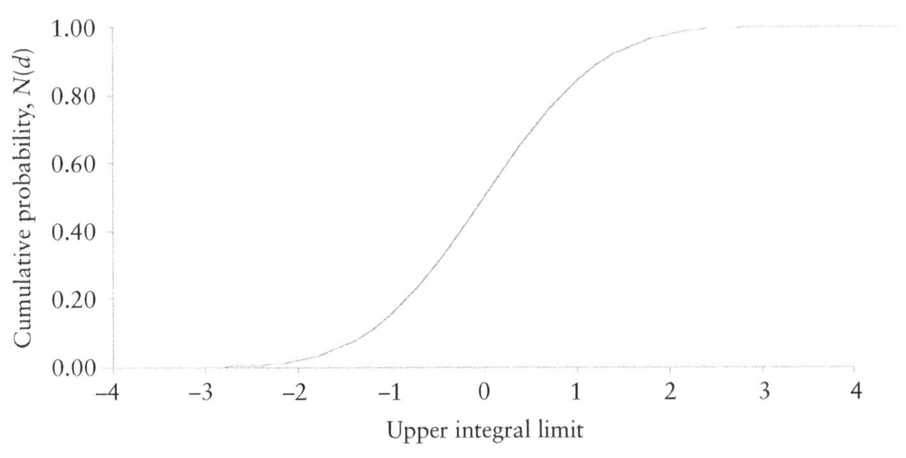


In recent years, commonly used statistical software packages have begun to include functions for evaluating the integral (A.21). Microsoft Excel, for example, has an add-in function called NORMSDIST that computes the cumulative standard normal probability, $N(a)$. The following illustration shows how the function is called as well as sample values. Note that the values correspond to the values reported in Tables C.1A and 1B. Figure C.1, Panel B shows the cumulative probability $N(a)$ as a function of $a$.

| B4 | | fx =NORMSDIST(A4) |
|---|---|---|
| | A | B | C |
| 1 | a | Probability | |
| 2 | -0.55 | 0.2912 | |
| 3 | 0.00 | 0.5000 | |
| 4 | 1.65 | 0.9505 | |

Closely related to the NORMSDIST function is the NORMSINV function, which computes the inverse of the cumulative standard normal density function. Suppose we are interested in determining the level of *a* that makes the cumulative probability equal to 5%, that is,

$$\int_{-\infty}^{a^*} \frac{1}{\sqrt{2\pi}} e^{-z^2/2} dz = 0.05$$

Using $a = 0.05$ in the inverse function shows that NORMSINV(0.05) = –1.645. This imples that the chance of a random drawing from a standard normal distribution producing a value at or below –1.645 standard deviations below the mean is 5%. Alternatively, it implies that we are 95% confident that a random drawing from a standard normal distribution will produce a value exceeding –1.645. This illustration shows sample functions calls and values:

| B4 | | fx =NORMSINV(A4) |
|---|---|---|
| | A | B | C |
| 1 | Probability | a | |
| 2 | 0.2912 | -0.55 | |
| 3 | 0.5000 | 0.00 | |
| 4 | 0.9505 | 1.65 | |

**ILLUSTRATION A.4** Compute maximum possible loss over next month with 95% confidence.

*Assume you hold $10 million of IBM's stock as of December 31, 2004. Based on the returns that appear in the worksheet* ***A4*** *in the Excel file,* ***A Illustrations.xls,*** *compute the expected maximum (or "worst loss") that we can expect to occur over the next month with 95% confidence. How does the result change if you assume IBM's returns are normally distributed?*

As a risk manager, you will be often placed in situations in which you will need to quantify the level of risk you face. There are a variety of ways to go about this task, and we will discuss several in the chapters of the text. The one discussed here is called *Value-at-Risk* or simply *VAR*. What VAR attempts to measure is the maximum dollar loss we can expect to incur over the given period of time at a particular confidence level.

**Empirical Distribution**

One way we can go about estimating this quantity is to use the realized *empirical distribution*, that is, the distribution of returns as they appeared in the recent past. The intuition is that, unless there is reason to believe otherwise, the next observed return should be drawn from the same distribution.

The worksheet *A4* contains the most recent 60 months of IBM stock returns. Each return in the series is assumed to have an equal chance of occurring again. Suppose we order the returns from lowest to highest. With 60 return observations, the number of intervals between observations is 59. Hence, the probability of falling into a particular interval is 1/59 or 1.695%. The first few observations in the ordered return series together with their receptive probabilities are:

**Monthly holding period returns (2000–2004)**

| Month | IBM return | Cumulative probability |
|---|---|---|
| 20020930 | –0.22645 | 0 |
| 20020430 | –0.19462 | 0.01695 |
| 20000929 | –0.14773 | 0.03390 |
| 20001031 | –0.12444 | 0.05085 |
| 20021231 | –0.10838 | 0.06780 |
| 20020131 | –0.10805 | 0.08475 |

Since no return below –22.645% appeared in the 60-month history, the probability that a drawing from this distribution will have a value below –22.645% is 0.[5] The probability that a drawing from this distribution will have a value below –12.444% is 0.05085. The cumulative probability function for this empirical distribution is:

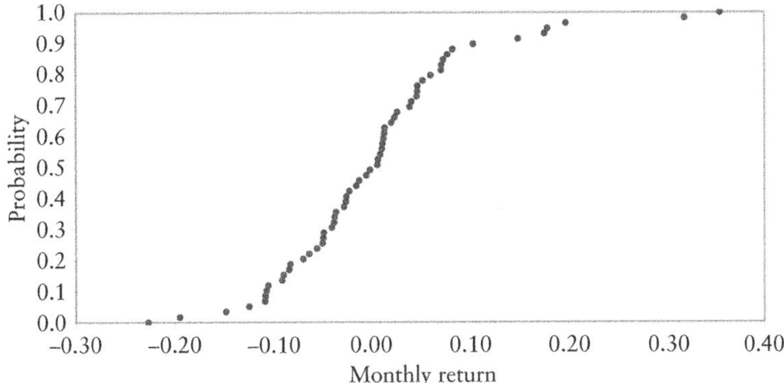


The question is, however, what is the critical return below which there is a 5% chance of occurrence. Looking at the above table, the critical return lies somewhere in the range between –14.773% and –12.444%. To find exactly where, we interpolate using the cumulative probabilities as weights, that is,

$$-14.773\left(\frac{0.05085-0.05000}{0.05085-0.03390}\right)-12.444\left(\frac{0.05000-0.03390}{0.05085-0.03390}\right) = -12.560\%$$

In other words, based on the empirical distribution of IBM's returns, the chance of experiencing a return of –12.560% or less over the next month is 5%. Alternatively, we are

[5] The fact that no return below –22.645% has been observed does not mean that no returns will ever fall below that level. This is a weakness of using the empirical distribution approach to estimating VAR.

95% confident that the worst loss we will experience over the next month is –12.560% of the portfolio value or $1,256,045.

As it turns out, another Excel statistical function can compute this critical return directly. The syntax of the function is

PERCENTILE(*array*,*k*)

where *array* is the vector of monthly returns and *k* is the probability level. In using this function, there is no need to arrange the monthly return series in ascending order. In the event that the critical return falls between observed returns (as it does in this illustration), the function performs the interpolation automatically. To verify this result, consider the following:

B65 =PERCENTILE($B$3:$B$62,$B$64)

| | A | B | C | D |
|---|---|---|---|---|
| 1 | | IBM | | |
| 2 | Month | return | | |
| 3 | 20000131 | 0.04056 | | |
| 4 | 20000229 | -0.08356 | | |
| 5 | 20000331 | 0.14842 | | |
| 60 | 20041029 | 0.04677 | | |
| 61 | 20041130 | 0.05203 | | |
| 62 | 20041231 | 0.04605 | | |
| 63 | | | | |
| 64 | Percentile | 0.05000 | | |
| 65 | Critical return *R** | -12.560% | | |
| 66 | Portfolio value | 10,000,000 | | |
| 67 | Value-at-risk | -1,256,045.00 | | |

**Normal distribution**

A second approach to estimating value-at-risk is to assume that security returns have a parametric distribution. The most common assumption in this regard is that returns are normal distributed. Consequently, the only parameters we need to characterize the distribution are the mean and the standard deviation. To find these values, we rely the historical returns, and then work with the mechanics of the normal distribution to do the rest.

The mean and standard deviation of IBM returns over the sample period were 0.00408 and 0.10378, respectively. From the discussion of the standard normal distribution earlier, we know that we can use the NORMSINV function to find the critical value of $a^*$ such that $n(a^*) = 0.05$, as shown in the following figure. From an earlier illustration, we know that the critical value of $a^*$ is –1.645. Thus, the critical return (i.e., the worst loss over the next month with 95% confidence) is

$$R^* = 0.00408 - 1.65(0.10378) = -0.16662$$

and the VAR under the assumption of normally distributed returns is $1,666,200. This number exceeds the VAR under the empirical distribution because the empirical distribution is positively skewed. The normal distribution assigns a greater chance of large negative returns.

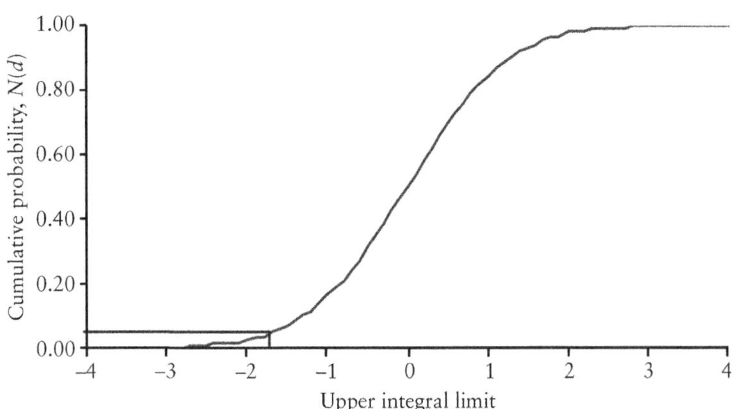


It is also worth nothing that we need not compute the critical return $R^*$ by hand, as we did above. Excel has add-in functions, NORMDIST and NORMINV, that allow the user to prespecify the mean and standard deviation of the normal distribution directly. Thus where NORMSINV returns the critical value of $a^*$ where the mean and standard deviation are 0 and 1, respectively, NORMINV returns the critical value of $R^*$ where the mean and standard deviation are $\hat{\mu}_R$ and $\hat{\sigma}_R$, respectively. Applying the problem parameters, we get:

B7 =NORMINV($B$6,$B$2,$B$3)

| | A | B | C |
|---|---|---|---|
| 1 | Portfolio value | 10,000,000 | |
| 2 | Expected return | 0.408% | |
| 3 | Standard deviation | 10.378% | |
| 4 | | | |
| 5 | Confidence level | 95.00% | |
| 6 | Probability of lower tail | 5.00% | |
| 7 | Critical return *R** | -16.662% | |
| 8 | Value-at-risk | -1,666,229.09 | |

Finally, it is worth noting that VAR is generally defined as the dollar loss relative to the mean. In some instances, however, users prefer to define VAR as the *absolute* dollar loss relative to 0, with no reference to expected value. We can easily accommodate this convention by setting the mean equal to 0 in the above spreadsheet. The absolute dollar VAR is about $1.7 million.

B7 =NORMINV($B$6,$B$2,$B$3)

| | A | B | C |
|---|---|---|---|
| 1 | Portfolio value | 10,000,000 | |
| 2 | Expected return | 0.000% | |
| 3 | Standard deviation | 10.378% | |
| 4 | | | |
| 5 | Confidence level | 95.00% | |
| 6 | Probability of lower tail | 5.00% | |
| 7 | Critical return *R** | -17.070% | |
| 8 | Value-at-risk | -1,707,029.09 | |

## Chi-Square Distribution

The *chi-square distribution* plays a key role in many statistical tests. One important application is in the context of answering the question: "Are two sets of data drawn from the same distribution function?" In Illustration A.4, for example, can we test whether the sample of IBM stock returns are drawn from a normal distribution? Below we define the chi-square distribution and its probabilities, and then apply it in tests for distributional differences.

Formally defined, a variable that is the sum of the squares of $n$ independent drawings from a standard normal distribution, that is,

$$\chi_n^2 = X_1^2 + X_2^2 + \cdots + X_n^2 \tag{A.22}$$

is said to have a the chi-square distribution with $n$ degrees of freedom. The shape of the distribution changes with the number of degrees of freedom, as is shown in Figure A.4. With few degrees of freedom, the distribution is highly positively skewed. As the number of degrees of freedom grows large, the distribution becomes more and more symmetric.

Table A.4 reports the probability that the sum of squared of $n$ random standard normal variables will be greater than the critical value $\chi_n^2$. To interpret the table, consider the case where the number of degrees of freedom is 10 and the probability level $\alpha$ is 0.05. The critical $\chi^2$ value is 18.31. This means that the chance of observing a sample $\chi_{10}^2$ value exceeding 18.31 is less than 5%, or, alternatively, we are 95% confident that the sample $\chi_{10}^2$ will be less than 18.31. Figure A.5 illustrates. The darkened tail to the right contains 5% of the area under the $\chi^2$ distribution. The lower bound of this tail is the critical value 18.31. It is also worth noting that Excel has a statistical function that computes the critical value of $\chi_n^2$. Its syntax is

**FIGURE A.4** Chi-square ($\chi^2$) distribution with various degrees of freedom.

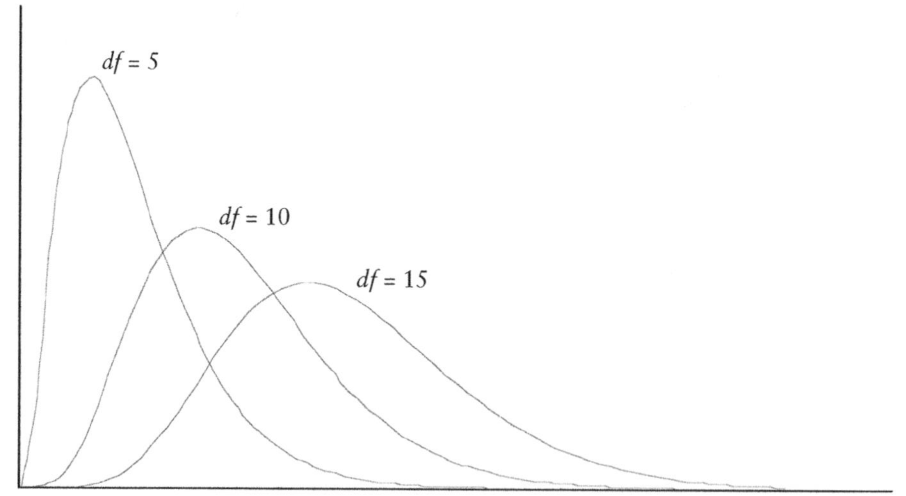

**FIGURE A.5** Critical chi-square value at 5% probability level and 10 degrees of freedom.

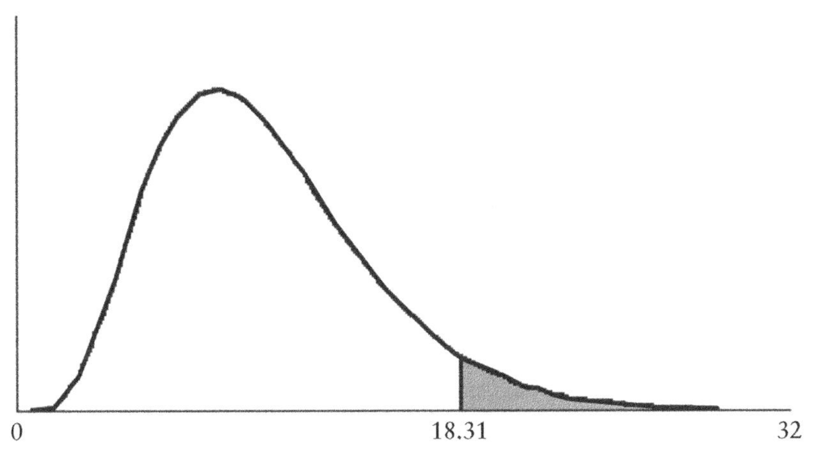


CHINV(*Probability, Deg_freedom*)

where *Probability* is the chosen significance level, and *Deg_freedom* is the number of degrees of freedom. CHINV(0.05,10) = 18.31.

**Tests for Normality** One particularly important application of the chi-square distribution is in tests of normality. One simple way of distinguishing between the distributions of two samples is to compute the statistic,

$$\chi^2 = \sum_{i=1}^{n} \frac{(F_i - f_i)^2}{f_i} \tag{A.23}$$

where $n$ is the number of bins, $F_i$ is the number of events observed in the $i$th bin, and $f_i$ is the expected number under some known distribution such as the normal.[6] In this particular case, the terms in (A.23) are not individually normal, however, if either the number of bins is large or the number of events in each bin is large, the chi-square probability function is a good approximation to the distribution of (A.23). To test the null hypothesis that the sampling distribution is normal, we compute the test statistic (A.23) and compare the value against the critical values reported in Table C.2 in Appendix C.

This is the first of many hypothesis tests that we will perform in this appendix. It is important to note that, *before* any testing is done, we must preset the desired level of significance of our test. The choice of the level of significance, denoted by $\alpha$, represents the probability of rejecting the null hypothesis when the null hypothesis is, in fact, true. It is our choice, however, conventional levels in statistical analyses are 5% or 1%.

[6] As a practical matter, any term in (A.19) where $n_i = 0$ is ignored.

**ILLUSTRATION A.5** Test for normality of stock market returns.

*The worksheet A5 in the Excel file,* ***A Illustrations.xls****, contains 60 months of returns for a value-weighted stock market index over the period January 2000 through December 2004. Test the null hypothesis that these returns were drawn from a normal distribution.*

The first step in performing such a test using binned data is to create the binned data. In creating binned data, it is useful to begin with an understanding of the distributions summary statistics. For the 60-monthly market index returns:

| | Parameter Estimate | Excel Function |
|---|---|---|
| Mean | 0.00018 | AVERAGE |
| Standard deviation | 0.04924 | STDEV |
| Minimum | –0.10250 | MIN |
| Maximum | 0.08390 | MAX |

The range of monthly returns is from –10.250% to 8.390%.

The choice of bins is arbitrary. Based upon the range of observations, we will define the bins to be in 2.5% increments and the range to be from –12.5% to 12.5%. With the bins defined, we then count the number of observations in each bin, that is, identify the $F_i$'s, $i = 1, \ldots, 11$ for use in (A.23).

Next we need to identify the number of observations expected in each bin assuming the monthly returns are normally distributed. The first bin includes all monthly return observations below –12.5%. Under a normal distribution with mean 0.018% and standard deviation 4.924%, the probability of drawing a return below –12.5% is 0.0055. With 60 total return observations, the expected number to fall in this first category is $f_1$ = 0.330. Note that this value need not be integer. The second bin includes all monthly return observations between –12.5% and –10.0%. Under a normal distribution with mean .018% and standard deviation 4.924%, the probability of drawing a return between –12.5% and –10.0% is 0.0154. With 60 total return observations, the expected number to fall in this second category is $f_2$ = 0.926. The remaining cells in the column are computed in the same manner. The frequencies of observed versus expected numbers of observations in each bin is as follows:

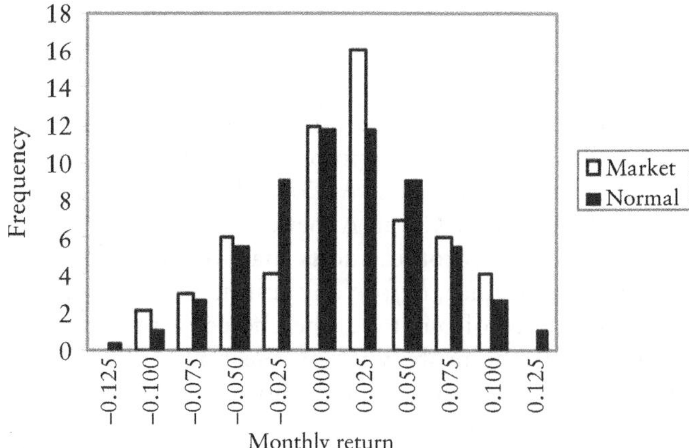


Finally, we compute the individual terms in (A.23) and sum. The computed chi-square value is 8.385. Comparing this value to the critical values reported for 11 degrees of freedom in Table C.2, we find that it lies somewhere between the 10 and 90 percentile values. In other words, we cannot reject the hypothesis that the value-weighted market returns were drawn from a normal distribution. Excel also has a function for computing the chi-square probability. Its syntax is

CHIDIST(*x*, *deg_freedom*)

where $x$ is the computed chi-square value and *deg_freedom* is the number of degrees of freedom. In the current illustration, CHIDIST(8.385,11) = 0.6784.

Before proceeding further, it is important to digress and discuss the concept of a $p$-value, which we have just applied in Illustration A.5 (i.e., the CHIDIST function computes the $p$-value for a $\chi^2$ distribution). As we have noted, the standard procedure for reporting the statistical significance of results of hypothesis testing is to compare the test statistic to the critical value determined at the 5% or 1% significance level. In recent years, however, it has become more common to report $p$-values (probability values). A $p$-value describes the exact significance level associated with a particular test statistic. Thus, a $p$-value of 0.6784 indicates that a coefficient is statistically significant at the 0.6784 level. In the context of a chi-square test with 11 degrees of freedom, this means that 67.84% of the $\chi^2$ distribution lies above 8.385. For purposes of hypothesis testing, we compare the $p$-value with our demanded level of significance, say, $\alpha = 0.05$. Since $0.6784 > 0.05$, we cannot reject the null hypothesis that the market return distribution is normal. Rejection requires that the $p$-value is less than $\alpha$.

The test statistic (A.23) is useful in demonstrating the intuition underlying why a chi-square test is useful in distinguishing whether there are meaningful differences between the underlying distributions of two samples of data. In the practice, however, we frequently have data that are drawn from continuous distributions. Arbitrarily grouping data into bins involves loss of information. In addition, the selection of bins is arbitrary. For this reason, a considerable amount of energy has been devoted to develop alternative statistics for testing whether a particular sample is drawn from a normal distribution. One well-known test for normality is the Jarque-Bera (1980, 1987) statistic:

$$JB = \frac{n}{6}[\hat{\gamma}_1^2 + \hat{\gamma}_2^2/4] \tag{A.24}$$

where $n$ is the number of sample observations and $\hat{\gamma}_1$ and $\hat{\gamma}_2$ are the sample skewness (A.17) and excess kurtosis (A.18), respectively. The $JB$ statistic follows a chi-square distribution with 2 degrees of freedom. If the $JB$ statistic is greater than the critical value of the chi-square, we reject the null hypothesis of normality.

**ILLUSTRATION A.6** Jarque-Bera test for normality of stock market returns.

*The worksheet A6 of the Excel file,* ***A Illustrations.xls****, contains 60 months of returns for a value-weighted stock market index over the period January 2000 through December 2004. Test the null hypothesis that the returns were drawn from a normal distribution using the Jarque-Bera test statisitic.*

To compute the Jarque-Bera test statistic, we need estimates of the skewness and excess kurtosis of the return distribution. Using the appropriate Excel functions for computing (A.17) and (A.18), we find $\hat{\gamma}_1 = -0.31475$ and $\hat{\gamma}_2 = -0.58410$. Thus, the JB statistic is

$$JB = \frac{60}{6}(-0.31475^2 + (-0.58410)^2/4) = 1.8436$$

At 2 degrees of freedom, the sample $\chi^2$ lies in the range between the 10 and 90 percentiles, which means we cannot reject the null hypothesis that the market returns are normally distributed. This conclusion can be confirmed using the Excel function, CHIDIST(1.8436,2) = 0.3978.

### *t*-Distribution

The *Student t-distribution*[7] or, simply, *t-distribution* also plays a key role in statistical analyses. We know from the discussion thus far in this appendix that, in general, we are interested in knowing the parameters of a population but we can neither (a) observe the parameters directly nor (b) observe all of the elements in the distribution. Consequently, we rely upon a sample of observations and statistical analysis to infer the population parameters. The sample mean (A-10), for example, is our "best guess" of the population mean, however, it is a guess. The *t-distribution* helps us quantify the accuracy with which the sample mean estimates the population (or "true") mean.

The random variable,

$$t = \frac{z}{\sqrt{Z/N}} \tag{A.25}$$

is said to have a $t$-distribution with $N$ degrees of freedom if (a) $z$ is normally distributed with mean 0 and variance 1, (b) $Z$ is distributed as chi-square with $N$ degrees of freedom, and (c) $X$ and $Z$ are independent. Like the standard normal distribution, the $t$-distribution is symmetric. Unlike the normal distribution, the $t$-distribution has fat tails when the number of degrees of freedom is small. Figure A.6 illustrates. Although both are centered at 0, the $t$-distribution has greater variance.

Table C.3 in Appendix C contains percentiles of the $t$-distribution. The panel heading, *Probability*, is probability that a positive $t$ value will exceed each number in the table in absolute value and is therefore appropriate in one-tailed test. See Figure A.7, Panel A. For a one-tailed test with 10 degrees of freedom and a significance level of $\alpha = 0.05$, the critical $t$-value $t_\alpha$ is 1.812, that is, the probability that the $t$-value exceeds 1.812 in absolute value is 5%. For a two-tailed test with 10 degrees of freedom and a significance level of $\alpha = 0.05$, the critical $t$-value $t_{\alpha/2} = 2.228$, that is, the probability that the $t$-value is below −2.228 *or* above 2.228 is 5%—2.5% in each tail. See Figure A.7, Panel B.

[7] The $t$-distribution was derived by William Sealey Gosset in 1908 while he was working at he Guinness brewery in Dublin. He was not allowed to publish under his own name, so the paper was written under the pseudonym "Student." See Student (1908) and http://en.wikipedia.org/wiki/Student%27s_t-distribution.

**FIGURE A.6** Student $t$-distribution versus normal distribution.

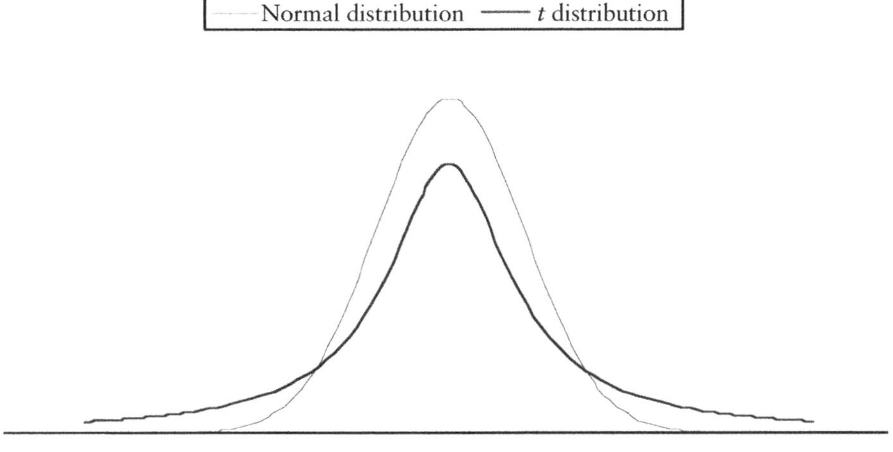


**FIGURE A.7** Critical values $t$-distribution at 10 degrees of freedom for one-tailed and two-tailed tests at the 5% level.
Panel A. One-tailed test.

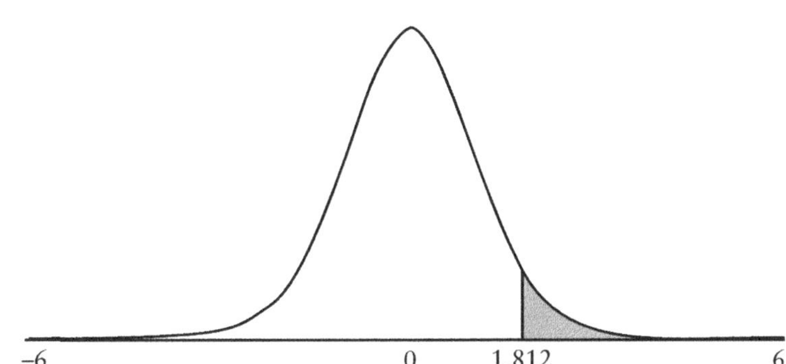

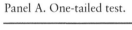

Panel B. Two-tailed test.

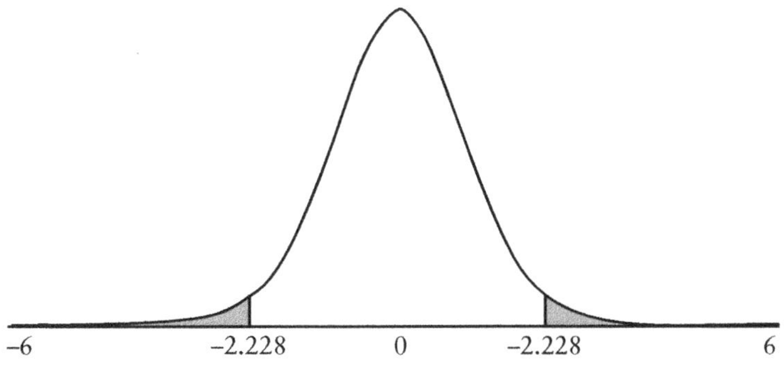

To understand how (A.21) helps us, note that the variance of the sample mean is

$$\begin{aligned} Var(\hat{\mu}_X) &= Var\left(\frac{1}{n}\sum_{i=1}^{n} X_i\right) = \frac{1}{n^2}\sum_{i=1}^{n} Var(X_i) \\ &= \frac{1}{n^2} n\sigma_X^2 = \frac{1}{n}\sigma_X \end{aligned} \tag{A.26}$$

where $n$ is the sample size. The standard deviation of the sample mean is therefore

$$\sigma_{\hat{\mu}_X} = \sigma_X/\sqrt{n} \tag{A.27}$$

Recall that any linear combination of normal distributions is a normal distribution. If $X$ is normally distributed with mean $\mu_X$ and standard deviation $\sigma_X$, then

$$\frac{\hat{\mu}_X - \mu_X}{\sigma_{\hat{\mu}_X}} = \frac{\hat{\mu}_X - \mu_X}{\sigma_X/\sqrt{n}} \tag{A.28}$$

is normally distributed with mean 0 and standard deviation 1. We use (A.28) in the numerator of (A.25).

Focusing now on the denominator of (A.25), we know that $(n-1)\hat{\sigma}_X^2/\sigma_X^2$ follows a chi-square distribution with $n - 1$ degrees of freedom. Combining results in (A.25) and simplifying, we find that

$$t = \frac{\dfrac{\hat{\mu}_X - \mu_X}{\sigma_X/\sqrt{n}}}{\sqrt{\dfrac{(n-1)\hat{\sigma}_X^2}{\sigma_X^2}/(n-1)}} = \frac{\hat{\mu}_X - \mu_X}{\hat{\sigma}_X/\sqrt{n}} = \frac{\hat{\mu}_X - \mu_X}{s_{\hat{\mu}_X}} \tag{A.29}$$

has a $t$-distribution with $n$ degrees of freedom. Consequently, we can test whether the mean of a random variable is equal to any particular number using the rightmost term in (A.29), even when the variance of the random variable is unknown. The denominator in the expression, $s_{\hat{\mu}_X}$, is called the *standard error of the estimate.* Note that the standard error becomes small as the sample size grows large. The intuition for this result is that, the more information you gather in estimating the mean, the more reliable your estimate will be.

**Test for Zero Mean** Perhaps the most common use of the $t$-statistic is in testing the null hypothesis that the mean of the population is different from zero. Such a test is a special case of (A.29), that is,

$$t = \frac{\hat{\mu}_X}{s_{\hat{\mu}_X}} \tag{A.30}$$

The $(1 - \alpha)\%$ *confidence interval* for the mean of the population is

$$\mu_X \leq \hat{\mu}_X + t_{\alpha,\, df} s_{\hat{\mu}_X} \tag{A.31}$$

where $t_{\alpha,df}$ is the critical $t$-value corresponding to $df$ degrees of freedom and a desired level of probability $\alpha$ (or desired level of confidence, $1 - \alpha$).

**ILLUSTRATION A.7** Test hypothesis mean is equal to 0.

*The worksheet A7 of the Excel file,* ***A Illustrations.xls,*** *contains 60 months of returns for IBM during the period January 2000 through December 2004. Test the null hypothesis that these mean monthly return equals 0 at the 5% probability level. Also, compute the 95% confidence interval for the mean monthly return for IBM.*

The first test is to compute the mean and standard deviation of the sample of 60 return observations: $\hat{\mu}_X = 0.00408$ and $\hat{\sigma}_X = 0.10378$. Next we compute the standard error of $\hat{\mu}_X$:

$$s_{\hat{\mu}_X} = \hat{\sigma}_X / \sqrt{n} = 0.10378/\sqrt{60} = 0.01340$$

Finally, compute the $t$-statistic: $t = 0.00408/0.01340 = 0.305$. The OPTVAL library contains a function for computing a $t$-test of the mean from a pre-specified constant. Its syntax is

OV_STAT_TCNST(*x, cnst, out*)

where $x$ is the vector of sample observations, *cnst* is the prespecified constant, and *out* is an indicator variable instructing the output to be aligned horizontally ("h" or "H") or vertically ("v" or "V"). The output of the function (the $t$-ratio and the number of degrees of freedom) is written to two adjacent cells, and both must be highlighted when entering the input information. Then press Shift, Ctrl, and Enter simultaneously.

With 59 degrees of freedom and a 5% probability level, the critical $t$-value is about 2.00. (The critical $t$-value reported in Table C.3 is 2.000 at 60 degrees of freedom. No value is reported for 59 degrees of freedom). Since the absolute value of 0.305 is less than 2.00, we do not reject the hypothesis that the mean monthly return for IBM is 0. Note that Excel has an add-in function that allows a more accurate value of the critical value. The syntax of the function is

TINV(*probability, deg_freedom*)

where *probability* is the desired level of probability in a two-tailed test and *deg_freedom* is the number of degrees of freedom. TINV(0.05, 59) = 2.001, which is very close to our approximate value obtained from Table C.3. Finally, we can use the computed $t$-ratio directly in the Excel add-in,

TDIST(*x, deg_freedom, tails*)

where $x$ is the $t$-ratio, *deg_freedom* is the number of degrees of freedom, and *tails* is 1 or 2, depending upon whether you want to perform a one- or two-tailed test. TDIST(0.30453,

59, 2) = 0.762, which means there is a 76.2% probability that the true difference between the population mean and 0 lies outside the range –0.30453 and 0.30453.

B76 =TDIST(B73,B74,2)

| | A | B | C |
|---|---|---|---|
| 1 | | IBM | |
| 2 | Month | return | |
| 3 | 20000131 | 0.04056 | |
| 4 | 20000229 | -0.08356 | |
| 5 | 20000331 | 0.14842 | |
| 60 | 20041029 | 0.04677 | |
| 61 | 20041130 | 0.05203 | |
| 62 | 20041231 | 0.04605 | |
| 63 | | | |
| 64 | | Parameter | |
| 65 | | estimate | |
| 66 | No. of observations | 60 | |
| 67 | Mean | 0.00408 | |
| 68 | Standard deviation | 0.10378 | |
| 69 | Standard error | 0.01340 | |
| 70 | | | |
| 71 | *Hypothesis test* | | |
| 72 | *t*-ratio (by hand) | 0.30453 | |
| 73 | *t*-ratio (OPTVAL) | 0.30453 | |
| 74 | df | 59 | |
| 75 | Inverse of *t* | 2.001 | |
| 76 | 2-tailed probability | 0.762 | |

The 95% confidence interval for the mean of IBM's monthly returns is closely related to the test of the null hypothesis that the mean return equals zero. Substituting the problem parameters into (A.27), we find that

$$\mu_X \leq 0.00408 \pm 2.001(0.01340) = (-0.02273, 0.03089)$$

In other words, based on the 60 months of sample information, we are 95% confident that the "true" mean monthly return of IBM is somewhere between –2.273% and 3.089%—not a high degree of precision indeed. Since 0% is contained within the confidence interval, the null hypothesis that the mean return is 0% cannot be rejected at the 5% level of probability. Similarly, the null hypothesis that the mean monthly return of IBM is 3% cannot be rejected since, it too, falls within the 95% confidence interval.

**Test for Equivalence of Means** Tests of the equivalence of two means come in two forms. The distinction is driven by the decision about whether it is reasonable to assume the two distributions have the same variance. If two distributions are thought to have the same variance, the appropriate test statistic is

$$t = \frac{\hat{\mu}_X - \hat{\mu}_Y}{\hat{\sigma}_D} \tag{A.32}$$

where

$$\hat{\sigma}_D = \sqrt{\frac{\hat{\sigma}_X^2(n_X - 1) + \hat{\sigma}_Y^2(n_Y - 1)}{n_X + n_Y - 2}\left(\frac{1}{n_X} + \frac{1}{n_Y}\right)} \tag{A.33}$$

We evaluate the significance of this $t$-value for the Student's distribution with $n_X + n_Y - 2$ degrees of freedom. Note that, if $Y$ is a constant 0, the expression for the standard error becomes

$$\hat{\sigma}_D = \sqrt{\frac{\hat{\sigma}_X^2(n_X - 1)}{n_X - 1}\left(\frac{1}{n_X}\right)} = \hat{\sigma}_X/\sqrt{n_X} = s_{\hat{\mu}_X}$$

which is identical to the standard error in (A.30).

Often there is no reason to believe that the variances of $a$ and $b$ are equal. In this instance, the $t$-test for the difference in means must be modified. The relevant $t$-statistic for unequal variance is

$$t = \frac{\hat{\mu}_X - \hat{\mu}_Y}{\sqrt{\hat{\sigma}_X/n_X + \hat{\sigma}_Y/n_Y}} \tag{A.34}$$

where this statistic is *approximately* as Student's $t$ with a number of degrees of freedom equal to

$$df = \frac{(\hat{\sigma}_X^2/n_X + \hat{\sigma}_Y^2/n_Y)^2}{\frac{(\hat{\sigma}_Y^2/n_Y)^2}{n_X - 1} + \frac{(\hat{\sigma}_X^2/n_X)^2}{n_X - 1}} \tag{A.35}$$

Note that expression for determining the number of degrees of freedom (A.35) is, in general, not an integer—there is no reason it has to be.

**ILLUSTRATION A.8** Test hypothesis difference in means is 0.

*The worksheet A8 of the Excel file,* ***A Illustrations.xls,*** *contains 60 months of returns for IBM during the period January 2000 through December 2004. Test the null hypothesis that the mean during the first 30 months is no different than the mean return in the second 60 months. First, assume the variances of the two samples are equal, and then assume the variances are different.*

After computing the mean and variance of each sample, we can perform the computations by hand using equations (A.32) through (A.35). But both computations can also be performed using the OPTVAL function

OV_STAT_TMEANS($x$, $y$, *ind*, *out*)

where $x$ and $y$ are the vectors of sample observations for the two samples, *ind* is an indicator variable instructing the function to assume equal variances ("y" or "Y") or unequal variances ("n" or "N"), and *out* is an indicator variable instructing the function to return the output horizontally ("h" or "H") or vertically ("v" or "V"). Again, the output is the $t$-ratio and the number of degrees of freedom and so two adjacent cells must be highlighted when the function is called. The results are shown below.

The results indicate that there is little reason to believe that (1) the mean return for IBM is different in the two sample periods; and (2) different variances have an important effect on the testing procedure. Under the assumption that the variances are the same across samples, the $t$-ratio for testing the null hypothesis that the means are the same is –0.804. Since the critical value of the $t$-distribution corresponding to a two-tailed test and 58 degrees of freedom is $t_{0.05/2,58} = 2.002$. Since the absolute value of the $t$-ratio is less than 2.002, we cannot reject the hypothesis that the means are the same. Alternatively, since the $p$-value, 0.425, is greater than the demanded level of significance, 0.05, the null cannot be rejected.

D43 fx {=OV_STAT_TMEANS(B4:B33,D4:D33,"N","V")}

| | A | B | C | D |
|---|---|---|---|---|
| 1 | Sample 1 (30 observations) | | Sample 2 (30 observations) | |
| 2 | | IBM | | IBM |
| 3 | Month | return | Month | return |
| 4 | 20000131 | 0.04056 | 20020731 | -0.02222 |
| 5 | 20000229 | -0.08356 | 20020830 | 0.07287 |
| 6 | 20000331 | 0.14842 | 20020930 | -0.22645 |
| 31 | 20020430 | -0.19462 | 20041029 | 0.04677 |
| 32 | 20020531 | -0.03773 | 20041130 | 0.05203 |
| 33 | 20020628 | -0.10503 | 20041231 | 0.04605 |
| 34 | | | | |
| 35 | | Parameter | | Parameter |
| 36 | | estimate | | estimate |
| 37 | No. of obs. | 30 | | 30 |
| 38 | Mean | -0.00673 | | 0.01489 |
| 39 | Standard deviation | 0.11646 | | 0.09006 |
| 40 | | | | |
| 41 | *Hypothesis test* | *Same variances* | | *Different variances* |
| 42 | $t$-ratio (by hand) | -0.804 | | -0.260 |
| 43 | $t$-ratio (OPTVAL) | -0.804 | | -0.260 |
| 44 | df | 58.000 | | 54.548 |
| 45 | tinv | 2.002 | | 2.005 |
| 46 | 2-tailed probability | 0.425 | | 0.796 |

**Test for Equivalence of Means in a Paired Sample** Paired comparisons in finance-related problems are not infrequent. Suppose, for example, two stocks have done particularly well during a specified period of time, but that, during the same period, the stock market did particularly well. Is the performance of the two stocks different in a meaningful way?

To answer this question, we can, again, rely on a $t$-test. The $t$-ratio is

$$t = \frac{\hat{\mu}_X - \hat{\mu}_Y}{\hat{\sigma}_D} \tag{A.36}$$

and is evaluated with degrees of freedom. The definition of the denominator is

$$\hat{\sigma}_D = \left( \frac{\hat{\sigma}_X^2 + \hat{\sigma}_Y^2 - 2\hat{\sigma}_{XY}}{n-1} \right)^{0.5} \tag{A.37}$$

that is, the standard error of the difference in returns of X and Y. A little reflection will tell you why this is appropriate. Since both $a$ and $b$ may co-vary with some factor, we need to abstract from that factor. Thus, we reduce the variance in the numerator of (A.37) by the amount of the covariation in determining whether the difference is indeed significant.

**ILLUSTRATION A.9** Test hypothesis difference between means in paired sample.

*The worksheet A9 of the Excel file,* ***A Illustrations.xls,*** *contains 60 months of returns for IBM and GM during the sample period January 2000 through December 2004. Test the null hypothesis that the mean of IBM's returns is different from the mean of GM's returns.*

Summary statistics for the return series are shown in the table below. Since individual stock returns tend to covary with the market, they tend to covary with each other. To check if this is the case, we can compute the correlation between the return series. The estimated correlation coefficient is 0.294, which indicates that, when testing for a difference between the mean returns of the two stocks, it is appropriate to use a test statistic that accounts for the contemporaneous relation between the series.

With the information provided in the summary table, we can compute the $t$-ratio using (A.36) and (A.37). The $t$-ratio is 0.300. Using a two-tailed test with 59 degrees of freedom and $\alpha = 0.05$, we cannot reject the hypothesis that the mean returns of IBM and GM are the same. The OPTVAL library contains a function for computing the $t$-ratio directly without us having to perform the intermediate computations. Its syntax is

OV_STAT_TPMEANS($x$, $y$, *out*)

where $x$ and $y$ are the vectors containing the pairs of observations vectors, and *out* is an indicator variable instructing the function to return the output horizontally ("h" or "H") or vertically ("v" or "V"). The output of the function is the $t$-ratio and the number of degrees of freedom.

| | **Parameter Estimates** | |
|---|---|---|
| No. of obs. | 60 | 60 |
| Mean | 0.00408 | –0.00078 |
| Standard deviation | 0.10378 | 0.10721 |
| Variance | 0.01077 | 0.01149 |
| Covariance | 0.00321 | |

| **Correlation Matrix** | **IBM** | **GM** |
|---|---|---|
| IBM | 1 | |
| GM | 0.294 | 1 |

| **Hypothesis Test** | |
|---|---|
| $t$-ratio | 0.300 |
| df | 59 |
| tinv | 2.001 |
| 2-tailed probability | 0.765 |

### Type I and Type II Errors and the Power of a Test

With the rules for conducting hypothesis tests and building confidence intervals in hand, we are in a position to discuss two more subtle statistical issues. The first is Type I and Type II errors. Recall that, in the illustrations of this appendix, we preset the desired level of significance of the test *before* the test was performed. The choice of the level of significance $\alpha$ (usually 5% or 1%) represents the probability of rejecting the null hypothesis when the null hypothesis is, in fact, true. This type of mistake is called *Type I error. Type II error*, on the other hand, refers to the probability that the null hypothesis is not refuted when it should be.

To more clearly distinguish between the two types of errors, consider changing the level of significance in a test from 5% to 1%. Obviously, the probability of incorrectly rejecting the null hypothesis (Type I error) falls from 5% to 1%. At the same time, the probability of a Type II error increases. The lower the value of $\alpha$, the wider the range of outcomes within the confidence interval, and the greater our inability to distinguish between values contained within the interval. If the true population parameter is 3 and the confidence interval is (–5,+5), a significance test will not reject the null hypothesis that the parameter is 0, even though we know that it is not. Thus, in selecting the level of significance, we face a trade off. As we lower the probability of Type I error, we increase the probability of Type II error. The choice between the two types of errors depends on the particular problem. In finance applications, we usually choose a low level of significance and, hence, a low probability of Type I error.

Closely related to Type I and Type II errors is the concept of the power of a test. Suppose that we fail to reject the hypothesis that the population parameter is 0. Consider the possible reasons for this "failure." One obvious reason is that the null hypothesis is true. Another possibility is that the null hypothesis is false, but the particular data set used for the test happens to be consistent with the null. The statistical concept that helps us evaluate the importance of the second explanation is the *power of a test. Power* is the probability of rejecting the null hypothesis when it is in fact false and is, therefore, equal to one minus the probability of a Type II error (i.e., one minus the probability that one will accept the null hypothesis as true when it is in fact false). Note that power depends not only on the size of the effect that has been measured, but also on the number of observations in the sample. Holding other factors constant, the larger the effect and the larger the sample size, the more powerful the test. When a statistical analysis with relatively low power fails to show a significant $p$-value, we should not be hasty in concluding that there is no effect. We must allow for the fact that the study may be inconclusive because the data set is not rich enough sufficient to allow us to distinguish between the null and alternative hypotheses.

### *F* Distribution

Formally defined, $(X/n_1)/(Y/n_2)$ is distributed according to an *F distribution* with $n_1$ and $n_2$ degrees of freedom if $X$ and $Y$ are independent and distributed as chi square with $n_1$ and $n_2$ degrees of freedom, respectively. The $F$-distribution is skewed to the right, as shown in Figure A.8. The exact shape will depend on the numbers of degrees of freedom in the numerator and the denominator. The fig-

**FIGURE A.8** *F*-distribution with (5,10) and (10,20) degrees of freedom.

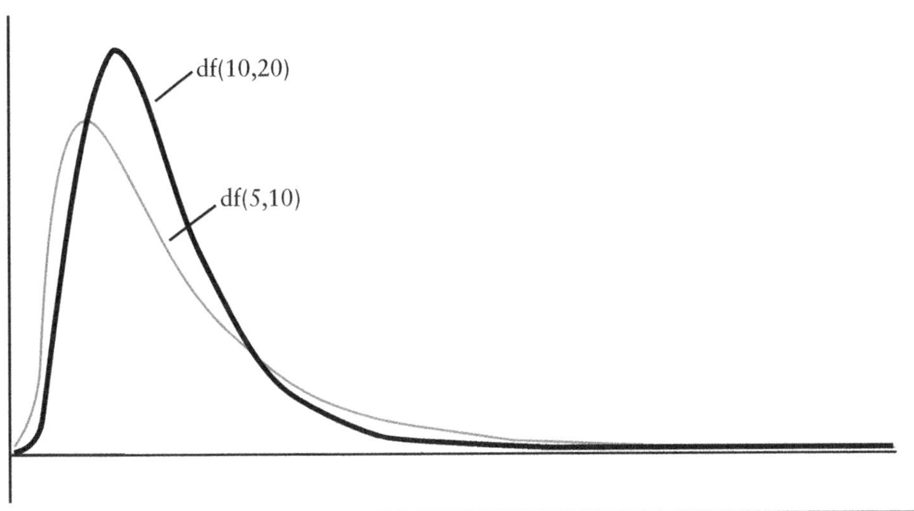


ure displays an *F*-distribution with 5 and 10 degrees of freedom and another with 10 and 20 degrees of freedom. The latter distribution is less skewed.

**Test for Equivalence of Variances** The *F*-distribution is commonly used in tests of the equality of two variances. The *F*-statistic is always tabulated with the larger estimate of variance in the numerator and the smaller estimate in the denominator. Thus assuming

$$\hat{\sigma}_X^2 > \hat{\sigma}_Y^2$$

the *F*-statistic is

$$F = \frac{\hat{\sigma}_X^2}{\hat{\sigma}_Y^2} \tag{A.38}$$

with $n_X - 1$ and $n_Y - 1$ degrees of freedom. The resulting ratio is always greater than 1, and provides information about the upper tail of the *F*-distribution. The greater the difference between the two variances, the greater the *F*-statistic. Thus, a large value of *F* implies that it is unlikely that the two error variances are equal. Tables C.4A and C.4B summarize critical *F*-values under 5% and 1% probability levels. Note that the tables are arranged with the columns representing different numbers of degrees of freedom in the numerator and the rows representing different numbers of degrees of freedom in the denominator. To illustrate applying the tables, assume the number of degrees of freedom in the numerator and the denominator is 10 and that we preset the level of significance to $\alpha = 0.05$. The critical $F$-value in Table C.4A is 2.98, which means that if the $F$-statistic from the test exceeds 2.98, we reject the null hypothesis that the two variances are equal at the 0.05 probability level. If the $F$-statistic exceeds 4.85, we also reject the null hypothesis that the two variances are equal at the 0.01 probability level (see Table C.4B).

**ILLUSTRATION A.10** Test for difference in variances of stock return series.

*The worksheet **A10** of the Excel file, **A Illustrations.xls**, contains 60 months of returns for IBM and the market portfolio during the sample period January 2000 through December 2004. Test the null hypothesis that the variance of IBM's returns is different from the variance of the returns of the market at the .05 probability level.*

Summary statistics for the return series are shown in the table below. The variance of IBM returns is considerably larger than the variance of the market returns, so we place IBM in the numerator. The $F$-statistic is

$$F = \frac{0.01077/(60-1)}{0.00242/(60-1)} = 4.4432$$

With $\alpha = 0.05$ and 59 degrees of freedom in both the numerator and the denominator, the critical value $F_{0.05,59,59}$ is 1.5400. The closest value in Table C.4A is $F_{0.05,60,60} = 1.53$. The exact value was obtained using the Excel function

FINV(*probability,deg_freedom1,deg_freedom2*)

where *probability* is the preset significance level, and *deg_freedom1* and *deg_freedom2* are the number of degrees of freedom in the numerator and denominator, respectively. FINV(0.05,59,59) = 1.5400. Finally, Excel also has a function for computing the $p$-value of an $F$-statistic directly. Its syntax is

FDIST (*x,deg_freedom1,deg_freedom2*)

where $x$ is the sample $F$-statistic. As it turns out, FDIST(4.4432,59,59) = 0.0000. The null hypothesis that the variances of the two series are equal is soundly rejected.

| Month | IBM Return | Market Return |
|---|---|---|
| 20000131 | 0.04056 | –0.03977 |
| 20000229 | –0.08356 | 0.03178 |
| 20000331 | 0.14842 | 0.05353 |
| 20041029 | 0.04677 | 0.01780 |
| 20041130 | 0.05203 | 0.04826 |
| 20041231 | 0.04605 | 0.03518 |

| | Parameter Estimates | |
|---|---|---|
| No. of obs. | 60 | 60 |
| Mean | 0.00408 | 0.00018 |
| Standard deviation | 0.10378 | 0.04924 |
| Variance | 0.01077 | 0.00242 |

| Hypothesis Test | | |
|---|---|---|
| F-statistic (by hand) | 4.4432 | |
| df(num,den) | 59 | 59 |
| finv | 1.5400 | |
| Probability | 0.0000 | |

## Test for Autocorrelation

In the study of finance, another key property of the returns (besides normality) is *independence*—past returns carry no information regarding current and future returns. The usual way of testing for whether returns are independently distributed is by calculating the *sample autocorrelation function*

$$\hat{\rho}_k = \frac{\sum_{t=1}^{T-k} (X_t - \overline{X})(X_{t+k} - \overline{X})}{\sum_{t=1}^{T-k} (X_t - \overline{X})^2} \tag{A.39}$$

where $T$ is the number of observations in the time series. If the returns are independent, the lag $k$ autocorrelation should be zero. To test whether a particular value of the autocorrelation function $\rho_k$ is equal to zero, we use a Bartlett test. Under the null hypothesis that the time series is *white noise,* the sample autocorrelation coefficients are approximately normally distributed with mean zero and standard deviation $1/\sqrt{T}$. For the S&P 500 monthly returns in our sample, the autocorrelation function is:

| Lag | 1 | 2 | 3 | 4 | 5 |
|---|---|---|---|---|---|
| Autocorrelation | -0.0785 | -0.0409 | 0.0314 | -0.0570 | -0.0180 |
| Standard deviation | 0.0783 | 0.0783 | 0.0783 | 0.0783 | 0.0783 |

It is computed using the OPTVAL function

OV_STAT_AUTOCORREL(*k*, *x*, *out*)

where $k$ is the maximum number of lags, $x$ is the time series, and *out* is an indicator variable set equal to 0 if the output array is to be returned horizontally and 1 if the array is to be returned vertically. With 163 monthly returns in the time series, the standard error is $1/\sqrt{163} = 0.07833$. In other words, the absolute magnitude of an autocorrelation coefficient would have to be greater than $0.07833 \times 2 = 0.15665$ in order to sure that the autocorrelation coefficient is not zero with 95% confidence. The sample autocorrelation function indicates that none of the true coefficients are different from zero. Box and Pierce developed a $Q$ statistic for testing the *joint* hypothesis that *all* the autocorrelation coefficients are zero, that is,

$$Q = T \sum_{k=1}^{K} \hat{\rho}_k^2 \tag{A.40}$$

where $Q$ is (approximately) distributed as chi-square with $K$ degrees of freedom. The OPTVAL function

OV_STAT_BOX_PIERCE (*k*, *x*, *out*)

computes the chi-squared statistics for different values of $k$. The results for the S&P 500 monthly returns are

| Lag | 1 | 2 | 3 | 4 | 5 |
|---|---|---|---|---|---|
| Autocorrelation | –0.0785 | –0.0409 | 0.0314 | –0.0570 | –0.0180 |
| Standard deviation | 0.0783 | 0.0783 | 0.0783 | 0.0783 | 0.0783 |
| Box-Pierce Q statistic | 1.0051 | 1.2778 | 1.4386 | 1.9675 | 2.0205 |
| Critical chi-square level | 2.7055 | 4.6052 | 6.2514 | 7.7794 | 9.2364 |

The levels of the $Q$-statistic are well below their critical levels at the 90% confidence level, so we cannot reject the hypothesis that all the *true* autocorrelation coefficients are equal to zero.

## Central Limit Theorem

Earlier we stated that the parameters of the distribution are certain if the entire population is known (i.e., $n = N$). Intuitively, therefore, this must mean that, as the sample size grows large, the estimate of the mean should converge on the population mean. This intuition, which holds for probability distributions with finite means, can be summed up formally as:

> **The central limit theorem.** If the random variable $X$ has mean $\mu_X$ and variance $\sigma_X^2$, then the sampling distribution of $\hat{\mu}_X$ becomes approximately normal with mean $\mu_X$ and variance $\sigma_X^2/n$ as $n$ increases.

In other words, for sufficiently large sample sizes, we can rely on the normality assumption, which greatly simplifies statistical tests. The central limit theorem will prove useful in assessing the performance of option trading strategies in Chapter 10.

## REFERENCES AND SUGGESTED READINGS

Abramowitz, Milton, and Irene A. Stegum. 1972. *Handbook of Mathematical Functions*, 10th ed. Washington, DC: National Bureau of Standards.

Bartlett, M. S. 1946. On the theoretical specification of sampling properties of autocorrelated time series. *Journal of the Royal Statistical Society, Series B8* 27.

Intriligator, Michael D. 1978. *Econometric Techniques, and Applications*. Englewood Cliffs, NJ: Prenctice-Hall.

Jarque, C. M., and A. K. Bera. 1987. A test of normality of observations and regression residuals, *International Statistical Review* 11: 351–360.

Jarque, C. M., and A. K. Bera. 1980. Efficient tests of normality, homoscedasticity and serial dependence of regression residuals. *Economic Letters* 6, 255–259.

Joanes, D. N., and C. A. Gill. 1998. Comparing measures of sample skewness and kurtosis. *Journal of the Royal Statistical Society (Series D): The Statistician* 47: 183–189 .

Jorion, Philippe. 1997. *Value at Risk*. Homewood, IL: Irwin.

Kennedy, Peter. 1992. *A Guide to Econometrics*, 3rd ed. Cambridge, MA: MIT Press.

Kmenta, Jan. 1971. *Elements of Econometrics*. New York: Macmillan.

Pindyck, Robert S., and Daniel L. Rubinfeld. 1998. *Econometric Models and Economic Forecasts*, 4th ed. Boston: Irwin/McGraw-Hill.

Press, W. H., S. A. Teukolsky, W. T. Vetterling, and B. P. Flannery. 1992. *Numerical Recipes in FORTRAN: The Art of Scientific Computing*, 2nd ed. Cambridge: Cambridge University Press.

Student (W. S. Gosset). 1908. The probable error of a mean. *Biometrika* 6 (1): 1–25.

APPENDIX B

# Regression Analysis[1]

The purpose of this appendix is to provide a quick and informative review of ordinary least squares (OLS) regression. OLS regression is used in almost every field imaginable, from anthropology to zoology. In the field of finance, the most common application of OLS regression is estimating betas for individual stocks. In the finance subfield of derivatives risk management, OLS regression is frequently used in identifying risk-minimizing hedge ratios. In this appendix, we review OLS regression by discussing topics such as regression estimation, testing, and prediction using both simple and multiple regression models. To avoid unnecessary repetition, the content of Appendix A, "Elementary Statistics," is assumed to be background knowledge.

## OBJECTIVES

After reviewing this appendix, you should be able to:

1. State and understand the four OLS regression assumptions.
2. Estimate a simple OLS regression model from summary statistics.
3. Interpret OLS regression and ANOVA results from a statistical software package.
4. Perform hypothesis tests and construct confidence intervals for individual regression coefficients.
5. Perform hypothesis tests on an entire model.
6. Calculate and interpret the $R$-squared and adjusted $R$-squared for a model.
7. Choose from among a collection of models based on explanatory power and parsimony.
8. Recognize when model assumptions are violated and understand the consequences.

[1] I am grateful to Jon Stroud for providing assistance in developing this appendix. Nick Bollen, Emma Rasiel, and Tom Smith also provided valuable comments and suggestions.

## SIMPLE LINEAR REGRESSION

The goal of regression is to learn about a relation between variables. Pay attention to the adjectives used when describing the word regression. They provide important information regarding the structure of the model being investigated. In this section, we focus on simple linear regression. The term *simple* refers to the fact that we have only *two* variables, $X$ and $Y$, and the term *linear* refers to the fact that the relation between the variables will be represented by a *line*. In contrast to simple linear regression, *multiple* regression involves more than two variables, and *nonlinear* regression involves a relation between $X$ and $Y$ that is not a straight line.

In simple linear regression, $X$ appears on the right-hand side of the equation and is called the *independent variable*. Other names for it include *explanatory variable* and *predictor variable*. On the left-hand side is $Y$, the *dependent variable* or *response variable*. In regression, $X$ is assumed to be nonrandom (taking on values that are fixed by the investigator). $Y$ depends linearly on $X$ but also has a random component, $\varepsilon$. Thus the relation between $X$ and $Y$ in a simple linear regression is written

$$Y_i = \beta_0 + \beta_1 X_i + \varepsilon_i \tag{B.1}$$

where $\beta_0$ represents the intercept of the regression line, $\beta_1$ represents the slope, and $i$ represents the $i$th pair of observations of the variables $X$ and $Y$. We have assumed only that the relation between $X$ and $Y$ is linear and that the values of $X$ are nonrandom or fixed.

The remaining regression assumptions pertain to the error term, $\varepsilon_i$. First, the expected value of $\varepsilon_i$ is 0 and the variance of $\varepsilon_i$ is constant across observations, that is, $E(\varepsilon_i) = 0$ and $Var(\varepsilon_i) = \sigma^2$. Note that, if $X$ is nonrandom, the error term will have constant variance if and only if the response variable $Y$ has constant variance. The constant variance assumption is commonly referred to as *homoscedasticity* and is the basis for *ordinary* least squares regression estimation. "Ordinary" applies because every observation of $Y_i$ has equal variance and is therefore given equal weight in the estimation of the model. In contrast, if the response variable $Y_i$ and the error term $\varepsilon_i$ have nonconstant variance (i.e., are *heteroscedastic*), a *weighted* least squares approach is appropriate. This allows observations with smaller variances to be given more weight than those with larger variances.

The second assumption governing the residual error term is that the errors are independent of one another, that is, $\text{Cov}(\varepsilon_i,\varepsilon_j) = 0$ for $i \neq j$. Violation of this assumption induces *autocorrelation* or *serial correlation,* a problem frequently encountered in time-series data. Finally, the residual errors are assumed to be normally distributed. Because the $X$'s are nonrandom, this assumption implies that the response variable $Y$ is also normally distributed.

The OLS regression assumptions are summarized in the following statement:

$$Y_i = \beta_0 + \beta_1 X_i + \varepsilon_i \quad \varepsilon_i \overset{\text{iid}}{\sim} N(0, \sigma^2) \tag{B.2}$$

The relation between $X$ and $Y$ is linear and the values of $X$ are fixed. The expression, $\varepsilon_i \overset{iid}{\sim} N(0, \sigma^2)$, means that the errors are independent and identically distributed (*iid*), where $N(0,\sigma^2)$ signifies the distribution is normal with mean 0 and variance $\sigma^2$.

---

### OLS Regression Assumptions

1. The relation between $X$ and $Y$ is linear.
2. The error term $\varepsilon$ is independent, identically (normally) distributed with mean 0 and constant variance $\sigma^2$.

---

Before moving on to model estimation, it is important to clarify one commonly misinterpreted point about linear regression. "Linear" refers to the fact that the regression equation is linear in the parameters, and not necessarily in the variables. Consider, for example, a nonlinear model such as

$$Y_i = e^{\beta_0 + \beta_1 X_i + \varepsilon_i}$$

On face appearance, linear regression seems inappropriate. Such a model, however, is *inherently linear* in the sense that it may be re-specified as the linear model,

$$\ln Y_i = \beta_0 + \beta_1 X_i + \varepsilon_i$$

Nonlinear models that can be re-specified into a linear form using only a transformation of the $X$ or $Y$ variables are still considered to be linear.

### Ordinary Least Squares (OLS) Estimation

Under the condition that our data satisfy the three assumptions of OLS regression, we can proceed by estimating the model in the following way. First, we denote the estimated regression line by

$$\hat{Y} = \hat{\beta}_0 + \hat{\beta}_1 X$$

where $\hat{\beta}_0$ represents our best guess for the true intercept $\beta_0$, $\hat{\beta}_1$ is our best guess for the population slope $\beta_1$, and $\hat{Y}$ is the predicted value of $Y$ that falls along the regression line. In order to calculate this line, all we need to do is choose values of $\hat{\beta}_0$ and $\hat{\beta}_1$. This is done here using a method known as *ordinary least square* (OLS) estimation. As noted earlier, "ordinary" arises because every observation is assumed to have equal variance and is therefore given equal weight in the estimation of the model.[2] "Least squares" is used because we will choose the line that minimizes the squared distances between the observed and

[2] The application of regression techniques sometimes requires weighting observations unequally. For an explanation of *weighted least squares* regression, see Pindyck and Rubinfeld (1998).

the predicted response variables. Defining the sample residual $e_i$ as $Y_i - \hat{Y}_i$, the OLS requirement is explained in the next section.

### OLS Requirement

The sum of the squared residuals,

$$\sum_{i=1}^{n} e_i^2$$

is minimized.

Among other things, minimizing the sum of squares errors implies that the sum of the regression errors (and the average error, for that matter) will be equal to zero. This means that the regression can be re-expressed in deviations from the mean form. That is, if the mean in the regression model (B.2) is 0, the mean value of $Y$ is

$$\overline{Y} = \beta_0 + \beta_1\overline{X} \tag{B.3}$$

where $\overline{X}$ is the mean of $X$. Taking the difference between the expressions,

$$\begin{aligned} Y_i - \overline{Y} &= \beta_0 + \beta_1 X_i + e_i - \beta_0 - \beta_1\overline{X} \\ &= \beta_1(X_i - \overline{X}) + e_i \end{aligned}$$

Expressing the deviations from the mean as $y_i = Y_i - \overline{Y}$ and $x_i = X_i - \overline{X}$, the regression equation becomes

$$y_i = \beta_1 x_i + e_i \tag{B.4}$$

Next, the least squares *estimators* of $\beta_0$ and $\beta_1$ are identified. To do so, write the sum of squared errors,

$$\sum_{i=1}^{n} e_i^2$$

as

$$\begin{aligned} \sum_{i=1}^{n} e_i^2 &= \sum_{i=1}^{n} (y_i - \beta_1 x_i)^2 \\ &= \sum_{i=1}^{n} (y_i^2 + \beta_1^2 x_i^2 - 2\beta_1 x_i y_i) \end{aligned} \tag{B.5}$$

Differentiating (B.5) with respect to $\beta_1$,

$$\frac{d\sum_{i=1}^{n} e_i^2}{d\beta_1} = \sum_{i=1}^{n}(2\beta_1 x_i^2 - 2x_i y_i) \tag{B.6}$$

Setting (B.6) equal to 0, simplifying, and rearranging provides the least squares estimator of the slope coefficient, that is,

$$\hat{\beta}_1 = \frac{\sum_{i=1}^{n} x_i y_i}{\sum_{i=1}^{n} x_i^2} \tag{B.7}$$

Because the mean residual error is zero, the estimator for the intercept follows from (B.3), that is,

$$\hat{\beta}_0 = \overline{Y} - \hat{\beta}_1 \overline{X} \tag{B.8}$$

**ILLUSTRATION B.1** Estimate beta for common stock.

*A common application of simple linear regression in finance is estimating a stock's beta coefficient or relative systematic risk.*[3] *A stock's beta is the slope coefficient in a regression of a stock's return on the return of the market portfolio. Suppose you are interested in the relation between General Electric's (ticker symbol: GE) stock return and the return of the S&P 500 portfolio. To learn more about the relation, you collect annual return data for both series over the period January 1985 through December 2004. The data are contained in the worksheet* ***B-1*** *in the Excel file* ***B Illustrations.xls****. Find the OLS regression line and interpret the coefficients* $\hat{\beta}_0$ *and* $\hat{\beta}_1$ *where the dependent variable is GE's annual return and the independent variable X is the S&P 500 return.*

The first step in applying the regression coefficient estimators (B.7) and (B.8) is to compute the means of $X$ and $Y$. Next, compute the deviations from the mean for the $X$ and $Y$ variables. Denote them as $x$ and $y$. Finally, compute the products of the deviations, that is, $xx$, $yy$, and $xy$. The results are:

[3] The theoretical importance of beta is motivated by the capital asset pricing model discussed in Chapter 3.

| Year Ending | Annual Returns GE Y | S&P 500 X | Deviations from Mean y | x | Products xy | yy | xx |
|---|---|---|---|---|---|---|---|
| 12/31/1985 | 0.33066 | 0.2633 | 0.1268 | 0.1470 | 0.0186 | 0.0161 | 0.0216 |
| 12/31/1986 | 0.21803 | 0.1462 | 0.0141 | 0.0298 | 0.0004 | 0.0002 | 0.0009 |
| 12/31/1987 | 0.05246 | 0.0203 | –0.1514 | –0.0961 | 0.0146 | 0.0229 | 0.0092 |
| 12/30/1988 | 0.04895 | 0.1240 | –0.1549 | 0.0076 | –0.0012 | 0.0240 | 0.0001 |
| 12/29/1989 | 0.48758 | 0.2725 | 0.2837 | 0.1561 | 0.0443 | 0.0805 | 0.0244 |
| 12/31/1990 | –0.08170 | –0.0656 | –0.2856 | –0.1820 | 0.0520 | 0.0816 | 0.0331 |
| 12/31/1991 | 0.37194 | 0.2631 | 0.1680 | 0.1467 | 0.0247 | 0.0282 | 0.0215 |
| 12/31/1992 | 0.15068 | 0.0446 | –0.0532 | –0.0717 | 0.0038 | 0.0028 | 0.0051 |
| 12/31/1993 | 0.26017 | 0.0705 | 0.0563 | –0.0458 | –0.0026 | 0.0032 | 0.0021 |
| 12/30/1994 | 0.00252 | –0.0154 | –0.2014 | –0.1318 | 0.0265 | 0.0406 | 0.0174 |
| 12/29/1995 | 0.45125 | 0.3411 | 0.2474 | 0.2247 | 0.0556 | 0.0612 | 0.0505 |
| 12/31/1996 | 0.40347 | 0.2026 | 0.1996 | 0.0862 | 0.0172 | 0.0398 | 0.0074 |
| 12/31/1997 | 0.50937 | 0.3101 | 0.3055 | 0.1937 | 0.0592 | 0.0933 | 0.0375 |
| 12/31/1998 | 0.40974 | 0.2667 | 0.2058 | 0.1503 | 0.0309 | 0.0424 | 0.0226 |
| 12/31/1999 | 0.53542 | 0.1953 | 0.3315 | 0.0789 | 0.0261 | 0.1099 | 0.0062 |
| 12/29/2000 | –0.06041 | –0.1014 | –0.2643 | –0.2178 | 0.0576 | 0.0699 | 0.0474 |
| 12/31/2001 | –0.15021 | –0.1304 | –0.3541 | –0.2468 | 0.0874 | 0.1254 | 0.0609 |
| 12/31/2002 | –0.37653 | –0.2336 | –0.5804 | –0.3500 | 0.2032 | 0.3369 | 0.1225 |
| 12/31/2003 | 0.30742 | 0.2638 | 0.1035 | 0.1474 | 0.0153 | 0.0107 | 0.0217 |
| 12/31/2004 | 0.20708 | 0.0899 | 0.0032 | –0.0265 | –0.0001 | 0.0000 | 0.0007 |
| Mean | 0.20390 | 0.1164 | | | | | |
| Total | | | 0.0000 | 0.0000 | 0.7335 | 1.1895 | 0.5130 |

Based on these results, the estimate of the slope is

$$\hat{\beta}_1 = \frac{\sum_{i=1}^{n} x_i y_i}{\sum_{i=1}^{n} x_i^2} = \frac{0.7335}{0.5130} = 1.4298$$

and the estimate of the intercept is

$$\hat{\beta}_0 = \bar{Y} - \hat{\beta}_1 \bar{X} = 0.2039 - 1.4298(0.1164) = 0.0375$$

Combining results, the estimated OLS regression line is

$$\hat{Y}_i = 0.0375 + 1.4298 X_i$$

The actual returns of GE conditional on the returns of the S&P 500 and the returns predicted by the regression line are summarized in the figure below. The line segment represents the "best" (i.e., least squares) fit of a line drawn through the pairs of actual returns. Note that the line segment is drawn only through the range of observed values of the S&P 500 return. The reason is that regression is only valid over the range of the data, that is, S&P 500 returns in the range between the sample's minimum and maximum returns (−0.2336,0.3411). The slope coefficient $\hat{\beta}_1$ can be interpreted as follows: for an increase of 1% in S&P 500 return, the return on GE will change by about 1.4298%. Stocks like GE with $\beta_1 < 1$ are called *aggressive stocks* because they do better than the market when the market goes up, and worse than the market when the market goes down. Stocks with are called *defensive stocks* for the opposite reasons.

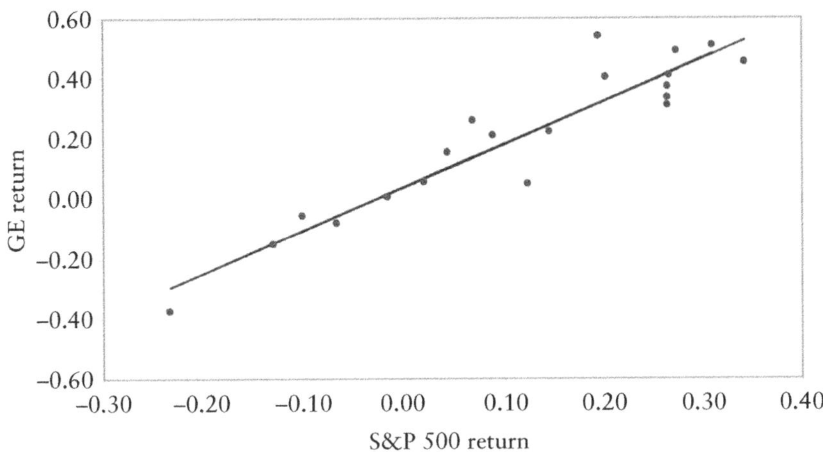


### Hypothesis Tests for Individual Regression Parameters

After a model has been fitted, we may wish to test whether the independent variable has a significant effect on the response variable. This can be done by testing the hypothesis that the parameter $\beta_1$ equals zero. If the slope of the regression line is zero, this implies that there is no linear relation between $X$ and $Y$; in this case, the "true" regression line is $E(Y|X) = \beta_0$, and we are just as well off using the sample mean, $\bar{Y}$, to predict future $Y$'s. A population slope not equal to zero implies that the variables are somehow linearly correlated. A regression line with slope greater than zero means that $X$ has a positive effect on $Y$, and one with a downward slope implies a negative relation between the two variables. We can test for any of these relations using the data collected in our sample.

Suppose we are interested in learning about a relation between two variables. The variables are believed to be linearly related, but it is not known whether the relation is negative or positive. A two-tailed hypothesis test can be used to check whether the population slope is equal to or unequal to zero. (If we had an idea that the slope was either positive or negative, then we would use a one-tailed test). But before any testing is done, we must preset a desired level of the test, denoted by $\alpha$. In our case, $\alpha$ represents the probability of incorrectly concluding that the two variables are related in some linear manner ($\beta_1 \neq 0$), when in fact they are not ($\beta_1 = 0$). A researcher can formalize these possibilities by specifying two different hypotheses: a null hypothesis, denoted $H_0$, and an alternative hypothesis, denoted $H_1$. The alternative hypothesis usually represents what the researcher is trying to prove, for example, that the variables are related; and the null hypothesis usually refers to the status quo, or the accepted state of the world. So, in our example, we would choose the null hypothesis to be $H_0 : \beta_1 = 0$ and the alternative as $H_1 : \beta_1 \neq 0$. Thus once we have stated our null and alternative hypotheses, specified the level of the test, and collected the data, we can formally test our beliefs.

Based on our sample, the best guess for the "true" slope of the regression line is $\hat{\beta}_1$. There is, however, error associated this estimate. This inaccuracy can be quantified by the standard error of the estimate, $s_{\hat{\beta}_1}$, which is defined as

$$s_{\hat{\beta}_1} = \frac{s}{\sqrt{\sum_{i=1}^{n} x_i^2}} \tag{B.9}$$

where

$$s = \sqrt{\frac{\sum_{i=1}^{n} e_i^2}{n-2}} \tag{B.10}$$

is an estimate for $\sigma$, the standard deviation of the error. Using this measure of uncertainty, we can standardize our parameter estimate to get the test statistic,

$$t = \hat{\beta}_1 / s_{\hat{\beta}_1}$$

which follows a $t$-distribution with $n - 2$ degrees of freedom. If the absolute value of $\hat{\beta}_1$ is much larger than its standard error, then $t$ will also grow large in absolute value, indicating that $\beta_1$ is different than zero. A large positive value of the test statistic is evidence of a positive relation, whereas a large negative value of the test statistic is a strong indication of a negative relation. Because the test statistic has a $t$-distribution, we can set cutoffs, or critical values, for rejecting the null hypothesis for any specified level of significance. The table that follows gives the rejection rules for three types of hypothesis tests of the regression line slope. Given a probability $\alpha$ that a $t$-distributed random variable (with $n - 2$ degrees of freedom) is greater than some *critical value* $t_\alpha$, the following rules apply:

**Common Hypothesis Tests for the Slope of a Regression Line**

| Null Hypothesis | Alternative Hypothesis | Rejection Rule |
|---|---|---|
| $H_0$: $\beta_1 = 0$ | $H_1$: $\beta_1 \neq 0$ | Reject $H_0$ if $\|t\| > t_{\alpha/2}$ |
| $H_0$: $\beta_1 = 0$ | $H_1$: $\beta_1 > 0$ | Reject $H_0$ if $t > t_\alpha$ |
| $H_0$: $\beta_1 = 0$ | $H_1$: $\beta_1 < 0$ | Reject $H_0$ if $t < -t_\alpha$ |

Recall the critical $t$-values for different levels of $\alpha$ were tabulated in Table A.5 of Appendix A. Note that the first row of the table represents a "two-tailed" hypothesis test. Since the alternative hypothesis, $\beta_1 \neq 0$, does not specify whether $\beta_1$ is greater than or less than 0, we compare the absolute value of the $t$-statistic with the critical $t$-value corresponding to a probability $\alpha/2$, that is, $\alpha/2$ in each tail of the two tails of the distribution.

We can use a similar procedure to perform hypothesis tests on the intercept. We specify the null and alternative hypotheses involving $\beta_0$, select the level of significance, and calculate $\hat{\beta}_0$ according to the formula given above, and its standard error using

$$s_{\hat{\beta}_0} = s\sqrt{\frac{1}{n} + \frac{\overline{X}^2}{\sum_{i=1}^{n} x_i^2}} \tag{B.11}$$

Then

$$t = (\hat{\beta}_0 - c)/s_{\hat{\beta}_0}$$

is the test statistic for the null hypothesis $H_0 : \beta_0 = c$ that the intercept is equal to some value $c$. (This is more general than the decision rules for the slope. For the slope, an investigator usually wants to ascertain whether it is equal to something other than zero. To avoid confusion, the tests of $\beta_1$ assume that $c$ is always equal to zero.) It should also be noted that, in a simple regression setting, hypothesis tests for the slope are far more common than for the intercept.

**Common Hypothesis Tests for the Intercept of a Regression Line**

| Null Hypothesis | Alternative Hypothesis | Rejection Rule |
|---|---|---|
| $H_0$: $\beta_0 = c$ | $H_1$: $\beta_0 \neq c$ | Reject $H_0$ if $\lvert t \rvert > t_{\alpha/2}$ |
| $H_0$: $\beta_0 = c$ | $H_1$: $\beta_0 > c$ | Reject $H_0$ if $t > t_\alpha$ |
| $H_0$: $\beta_0 = c$ | $H_1$: $\beta_0 < c$ | Reject $H_0$ if $t < -t_\alpha$ |

**ILLUSTRATION B.2** Test hypothesis that slope and intercept are zero.

*Using the return data from Illustration B.1, perform a hypothesis test of $H_0 : \beta_1 = 0$ versus $H_1 : \beta_1 \neq 0$ at the $\alpha = 0.05$ level of significance. Also test the hypothesis $H_0 : \beta_0 = 0$ versus $H_1 : \beta_0 > 0$ at the $\alpha = 0.05$ level of significance.*

The first step is to calculate the squared errors in the regression. Using the estimated intercept and the slope coefficients, the errors and squared errors are as follows:

| Year Ending | Annual Returns GE Y | S&P 500 X | Predicted Y | $e$ | $e^2$ |
|---|---|---|---|---|---|
| 12/31/1985 | 0.3307 | 0.2633 | 0.4140 | −0.0833 | 0.0069 |
| 12/31/1986 | 0.2180 | 0.1462 | 0.2465 | −0.0285 | 0.0008 |
| 12/31/1987 | 0.0525 | 0.0203 | 0.0665 | −0.0140 | 0.0002 |
| 12/30/1988 | 0.0490 | 0.1240 | 0.2148 | −0.1659 | 0.0275 |
| 12/29/1989 | 0.4876 | 0.2725 | 0.4271 | 0.0604 | 0.0037 |
| 12/31/1990 | −0.0817 | −0.0656 | −0.0563 | −0.0254 | 0.0006 |
| 12/31/1991 | 0.3719 | 0.2631 | 0.4137 | −0.0417 | 0.0017 |
| 12/31/1992 | 0.1507 | 0.0446 | 0.1013 | 0.0494 | 0.0024 |
| 12/31/1993 | 0.2602 | 0.0705 | 0.1384 | 0.1218 | 0.0148 |
| 12/30/1994 | 0.0025 | −0.0154 | 0.0155 | −0.0129 | 0.0002 |
| 12/29/1995 | 0.4512 | 0.3411 | 0.5252 | −0.0740 | 0.0055 |
| 12/31/1996 | 0.4035 | 0.2026 | 0.3272 | 0.0763 | 0.0058 |
| 12/31/1997 | 0.5094 | 0.3101 | 0.4809 | 0.0285 | 0.0008 |
| 12/31/1998 | 0.4097 | 0.2667 | 0.4188 | −0.0091 | 0.0001 |
| 12/31/1999 | 0.5354 | 0.1953 | 0.3167 | 0.2187 | 0.0479 |
| 12/29/2000 | −0.0604 | −0.1014 | −0.1075 | 0.0471 | 0.0022 |
| 12/31/2001 | −0.1502 | −0.1304 | −0.1490 | −0.0012 | 0.0000 |
| 12/31/2002 | −0.3765 | −0.2336 | −0.2966 | −0.0799 | 0.0064 |
| 12/31/2003 | 0.3074 | 0.2638 | 0.4147 | −0.1073 | 0.0115 |
| 12/31/2004 | 0.2071 | 0.0899 | 0.1661 | 0.0410 | 0.0017 |
| Mean | 0.2039 | 0.1164 | 0.2039 | 0.0000 | |
| Total | | | | | 0.1408 |

Note that the sum of the errors is zero, as expected. The sum of the squared errors is 0.1408.

Next we apply (B.10) to obtain the standard error of the estimate,

$$s = \sqrt{\frac{\sum_{i=1}^{n} e_i^2}{n-2}} = \sqrt{\frac{0.1408}{20-2}} = 0.0884$$

The standard error of the slope coefficient from (B.9) is

$$s_{\hat{\beta}_1} = \frac{s}{\sqrt{\sum_{i=1}^{n} x_i^2}} = \frac{0.0884}{\sqrt{0.5130}} = 0.1235$$

Under the null hypothesis that the slope is zero, the test statistic, $t$, is

$$t = \frac{\hat{\beta}_1}{s_{\hat{\beta}_1}} = \frac{1.4298}{0.1235} = 11.5799$$

Since we are performing a two-tailed test at the 5% probability level, we look up the critical $t$-value at a probability level of $\alpha/2$ or 2.5% and 18 degrees of freedom. From Table C.3 in Appendix C, we see that the critical value is $t_{\alpha/2} = 2.101$. Since our sample $t$-statistic, 11.5799, exceeds the critical value, we can reject the null hypothesis that $\beta_1 = 0$.

The procedure for testing the null hypothesis that $\beta_0 = 0$ follows a similar procedure. The standard error of the intercept from (B.11) is

$$s_{\hat{\beta}_0} = s\sqrt{\frac{1}{n} + \frac{\overline{X}^2}{\sum_{i=1}^{n} x_i^2}} = 0.0884\sqrt{\frac{1}{20} + \frac{0.1164^2}{0.5130}} = 0.0244$$

The $t$-statistic is therefore

$$t = \frac{\hat{\beta}_0}{s_{\hat{\beta}_0}} = \frac{0.0375}{0.0244} = 1.5335$$

Since we are testing the null against the alternative hypothesis that $\beta_0 > 0$, a one-tailed test is appropriate. From Table C.3, the critical $t$-value for a one-tailed test at the 5% significance level is $t_\alpha = 1.734$. Since the sample $t$-statistic, 1.5335, is not greater than 1.734, we cannot reject the null hypothesis that the intercept is zero.

## Confidence Intervals

The idea of constructing confidence intervals is very much related to that of hypothesis testing. Again we are usually interested in finding out whether the independent variable in the regression has a significant effect on the dependent variable. But this time, instead of using a test statistic and critical value, we construct intervals and attempt to "pin down" the true value of a parameter and base our inferences on that. The tools used in constructing confidence intervals are identical to those used in hypothesis testing as previously shown.

To calculate a confidence interval for the slope of the regression line, we need only three things: the point estimate for the parameter, the standard error of the estimate, and the confidence coefficient that is taken from a $t$-distribution with $n - 2$ degrees of freedom. The interval itself is just the estimate of the parameter plus or minus some margin, which is related to the standard error of the estimate and the selected level of confidence.

**Confidence Intervals for the Intercept and Slope of a Regression Line**

| Parameter | Interval Size | Confidence Interval |
|---|---|---|
| Intercept | $(1 - \alpha)\%$ | $\hat{\beta}_0 \pm t_{\alpha/2} s_{\hat{\beta}_0}$ |
| Slope | $(1 - \alpha)\%$ | $\hat{\beta}_1 \pm t_{\alpha/2} s_{\hat{\beta}_1}$ |

The confidence coefficient, $\alpha$, identical to the critical value used in hypothesis testing, is based on a $t$-distribution with $n - 2$ degrees of freedom and is chosen by the modeler to give a specified level of confidence. Clearly, a larger interval will yield a higher level of confidence and vice versa. The most common confidence widths are 90%, 95%, and 99%.

After the formulas above are used to construct confidence intervals for a population parameter, one can check to see if a certain value of interest falls in the interval. If we are testing that the independent variable has an effect on Y, for example, we should construct a confidence interval for the slope. If zero is contained in the interval, then the data does not give sufficient evidence that $X$ has an effect on Y. Conversely, if the interval does not contain zero, then there is evidence that the two variables are related at the $\alpha$ level of confidence. The conclusions obtained from building confidence intervals will give the exact same results as using hypothesis tests.

**ILLUSTRATION B.3** Compute confidence interval for slope.

*Using the return data from Illustration B.1, compute a 95% confidence interval for $\beta_1$. Does the interval contain zero?*

A 95% confidence interval for $\beta_1$ is given by $\hat{\beta}_1 \pm t_{\alpha/2}s(\hat{\beta}_1)$. The $t$-statistic again comes from a $t$-distribution with 18 degrees of freedom. The critical t-value is 2.101. The estimate and the standard error of $\beta_1$ are as calculated above. Therefore a 95% interval is

$$1.4298 \pm 2.101(0.1235) = (1.1704, 1.6892)$$

Note that the 95% confidence interval for $\beta_1$ ranges from 1.1704 to 1.6892 and does not include 0. We should not be surprised by this result since we had already concluded that $\beta_1$ is not equal to zero by virtue of a $t$-test. By the same logic, we also know that $\beta_1$ is not equal to 1 at the 5% probability level.

## Prediction

Another reason for using ordinary least squares regression is to predict future observations. Forecasting sales as a function of marketing expenses is an example. Prediction can be summarized in one paragraph in the following way. Once a linear model has been fitted using previous data, our best guess of $Y$ (call it $\hat{Y}_p$) for a specified value of $X$ (call it $X_p$) is

$$\hat{Y}_p = \hat{\beta}_0 - \hat{\beta}_1 X_p$$

We can also quantify our uncertainty about the estimate with a prediction interval. A $(1 - \alpha)$% confidence interval for a new observation $Y_p$ is $\hat{Y}_p \pm t_{\alpha/2}s_p$ where the standard error of the prediction is

$$s_p = s\sqrt{1 + \frac{1}{n} + \frac{(X_p - \overline{X})^2}{\sum_{i=1}^{n} x_i^2}} \tag{B.12}$$

A warning about prediction, however. The estimates and intervals for new values of $Y$ are only valid if $X_p$ falls within the range of the $X$ values used in the regression. Extrapolation must be treated with extreme caution.

**ILLUSTRATION B.4** Develop stock return prediction based on market return.

*Using the return data from Illustration B.1, compute the predicted annualized rate of return for GE assuming the return on the S&P 500 is 30%. Compute the return assuming the S&P 500 return is 40%. Which predicted is more reliable, and why? Show that your intuition is consistent with the confidence interval of each of the predictions.*

For a 30% S&P 500 return, GE's predicted return is

$$\hat{Y}_p = 0.0375 + 1.4298(0.30) = 46.64\%$$

For a 40% S&P 500 return, GE's predicted return is

$$\hat{Y}_p = 0.0375 + 1.4298(0.40) = 60.94\%$$

The predicted return for the 30% S&P 500 return is more believable. This is because the 40% S&P 500 return falls well outside the range of our data. The minimum and maximum S&P 500 returns in the sample are –23.36% and 34.11%, respectively.

The 95% confidence interval for each of our predictions confirms our intuition. For the 30% S&P 500 return, the standard error of the prediction is

$$s_p = s\sqrt{1 + \frac{1}{n} + \frac{(X_p - \bar{X})^2}{\sum_{i=1}^{n} x_i^2}} = 0.0884\sqrt{1 + \frac{1}{20} + \frac{(0.30 - 0.1164)^2}{0.5130}} = 0.0934$$

and the 95% confidence interval is

$$0.4664 \pm 2.101(0.0934) = (0.2703, 0.6626)$$

For the 40% S&P 500 return, the confidence interval is

$$0.6094 \pm 2.101(0.0971) = (0.4054, 0.8134)$$

Note that we are more confident in our prediction of GE stock return (i.e., the range of the confidence interval is 39.23%) when the S&P 500 return is 30% than we are when the S&P 500 return is 40% and the range is 40.80%.

## Goodness of Fit

Another important aspect of regression analysis is model testing. This can be used when trying to assess a model's predictive power or when choosing between two or more models. A common way to measure goodness of fit is by decomposing the sum of squares of the data into the amount explained by the model and the amount left unexplained. The higher the amount explained by the model, the better the model. The decomposition is done as follows. For a single variable $Y$ with $n$ observations, the *total sum of squares* is given by

$$SST = \sum_{i=1}^{n} y_i^2$$

Once we have fitted a model, we obtain the fitted values, $\hat{Y}_i = \hat{\beta}_0 + \hat{\beta}_1 X_i$, for each observation of $X$. The squared distances between these predictions and the overall mean $\bar{Y}$ give the *regression* or *explained sum of squares,*

$$SSR = \sum_{i=1}^{n} \left(\hat{Y}_i - \bar{Y}\right)^2 = \sum_{i=1}^{n} \hat{y}_i^2$$

which is the amount of the $SST$ explained by the model. Finally, the part left unexplained by the model, called the *error* or *residual sum of squares* is just

$$SSE = \sum_{i=1}^{n} \left(\hat{Y}_i - \bar{Y}\right)^2 = \sum_{i=1}^{n} \hat{y}_i^2$$

By Pythagorus' Theorem, the regression and error sum of squares must add up to the total sum of squares. This type of decomposition is closely related to ANOVA, or *analysis of variance*, and is frequently used to determine how well an estimated model fits the data.

To illustrate, consider now a model that perfectly predicts all the data points, i.e., $\hat{Y}_i = Y_i$ for all $i$. In this case, the regression sum of squares equals the total sum of squares and the error sum of squares equals zero—a perfect fit. On the other hand, a model with an estimated slope $\hat{\beta}_1 = 0$ will have no predictive power at all (because $\hat{Y}_i = \hat{\beta}_0$ for all $i$), and therefore the total sum of squares will equal the error sum of squares, leaving the variation explained by the model as zero.

**R-Squared** A commonly used indicator of regression goodness of fit is the $R^2$ statistic. It is also referred to as the *coefficient of determination* and represents the proportion of the total variation that is explained by the model. In the case of simple linear regression, $R^2$ is the square of the correlation between $X$ and $Y$. The $R^2$ is simply the ratio of the regression sum of squares ($SSR$) to the total sum of squares ($SST$):

$$R^2 = \frac{SSR}{SST} = \frac{\sum_{i=1}^{n} \hat{y}_i^2}{\sum_{i=1}^{n} \hat{y}_i^2}$$

Since the range of $SSR$ is 0 to $SST$, the range of $R^2$ is from 0 to 1. A perfect model fit will yield an $R^2$ of 1, and a model with no explanatory power whatsoever gives $R^2 = 0$. In general, a model with a high $R^2$ is preferred to one with a low one.

**ILLUSTRATION B.5** Compute sums of squares and $R$-square.

*Using the return data from Illustration B.1, compute the total sum of squares (SST), the regression sum of squares (SSR), and the error sum of squares (SSE) for our estimated return prediction model. Also, compute the regression* R-*squared.*

| $Y_i$ | $X_i$ | $y_i$ | $y_i^2$ | $\hat{Y}_i$ | $e_i$ | $e_i^2$ | $\hat{y}_i$ | $\hat{y}_i^2$ |
|---|---|---|---|---|---|---|---|---|
| 0.3307 | 0.2633 | 0.1268 | 0.0161 | 0.4140 | −0.0833 | 0.0069 | 0.2101 | 0.0441 |
| 0.2180 | 0.1462 | 0.0141 | 0.0002 | 0.2465 | −0.0285 | 0.0008 | 0.0426 | 0.0018 |
| 0.0525 | 0.0203 | −0.1514 | 0.0229 | 0.0665 | −0.0140 | 0.0002 | −0.1374 | 0.0189 |
| 0.0490 | 0.1240 | −0.1549 | 0.0240 | 0.2148 | −0.1659 | 0.0275 | 0.0109 | 0.0001 |
| 0.4876 | 0.2725 | 0.2837 | 0.0805 | 0.4271 | 0.0604 | 0.0037 | 0.2233 | 0.0498 |
| −0.0817 | −0.0656 | −0.2856 | 0.0816 | −0.0563 | −0.0254 | 0.0006 | −0.2602 | 0.0677 |
| 0.3719 | 0.2631 | 0.1680 | 0.0282 | 0.4137 | −0.0417 | 0.0017 | 0.2098 | 0.0440 |
| 0.1507 | 0.0446 | −0.0532 | 0.0028 | 0.1013 | 0.0494 | 0.0024 | −0.1026 | 0.0105 |
| 0.2602 | 0.0705 | 0.0563 | 0.0032 | 0.1384 | 0.1218 | 0.0148 | −0.0655 | 0.0043 |
| 0.0025 | −0.0154 | −0.2014 | 0.0406 | 0.0155 | −0.0129 | 0.0002 | −0.1884 | 0.0355 |
| 0.4512 | 0.3411 | 0.2474 | 0.0612 | 0.5252 | −0.0740 | 0.0055 | 0.3213 | 0.1032 |
| 0.4035 | 0.2026 | 0.1996 | 0.0398 | 0.3272 | 0.0763 | 0.0058 | 0.1233 | 0.0152 |
| 0.5094 | 0.3101 | 0.3055 | 0.0933 | 0.4809 | 0.0285 | 0.0008 | 0.2770 | 0.0767 |
| 0.4097 | 0.2667 | 0.2058 | 0.0424 | 0.4188 | −0.0091 | 0.0001 | 0.2149 | 0.0462 |
| 0.5354 | 0.1953 | 0.3315 | 0.1099 | 0.3167 | 0.2187 | 0.0479 | 0.1128 | 0.0127 |
| −0.0604 | −0.1014 | −0.2643 | 0.0699 | −0.1075 | 0.0471 | 0.0022 | −0.3114 | 0.0970 |
| −0.1502 | −0.1304 | −0.3541 | 0.1254 | −0.1490 | −0.0012 | 0.0000 | −0.3529 | 0.1245 |
| −0.3765 | −0.2336 | −0.5804 | 0.3369 | −0.2966 | −0.0799 | 0.0064 | −0.5005 | 0.2505 |
| 0.3074 | 0.2638 | 0.1035 | 0.0107 | 0.4147 | −0.1073 | 0.0115 | 0.2108 | 0.0444 |
| 0.2071 | 0.0899 | 0.0032 | 0.0000 | 0.1661 | 0.0410 | 0.0017 | −0.0378 | 0.0014 |
| Total | | 0.0000 | 1.1895 | | 0.0000 | 0.1408 | 0.0000 | 1.0487 |

The table above shows the raw computations of the sums of squared errors. The sum of the squared deviations of $Y_i$ about its mean ($SST$) is 1.1895, the sum of squared errors ($SSE$) is 0.1408, and the regression sum of squares ($SSR$) is 1.0487. The regression $R^2$ is therefore

$$R^2 = \frac{SSR}{SST} = \frac{1.0487}{1.1895} = 0.8817 \text{ or } 88.17\%.$$

## Applying a Regression Program

The purpose of reviewing simple linear regression in such detail is to remove the mystery of regression analysis. A summary of all of the simple linear regression estimation formulas is contained in Table B.1. In practice, all of these formulas are preprogrammed in a number of different regression software packages. Microsoft Excel 2003, for example, has linear regression as one of its data analysis functions. Below we illustrate the application of the regression analysis function.

**TABLE B.1** Summary of simple linear regression estimation formulas.

| | | | |
|---|---|---|---|
| Estimator for slope: | $\hat{\beta}_1 = \frac{\sum_{i=1}^{n} x_i y_i}{\sum_{i=1}^{n} x_i^2}$ | Standard error: | $s(\hat{\beta}_1) = \frac{s}{\sqrt{\sum_{i=1}^{n} x_i^2}}$ |
| Estimator for intercept: | $\hat{\beta}_0 = \overline{Y} - \hat{\beta}_1 \overline{X}$ | Standard error: | $s(\hat{\beta}_0) = s\sqrt{\frac{1}{n} + \frac{\overline{X}^2}{\sum_{i=1}^{n} x_i^2}}$ |
| Prediction: | $\hat{Y}_p = \hat{\beta}_0 - \hat{\beta}_1 X_p$ | Standard error: | $s_p = s\sqrt{1 + \frac{1}{n} + \frac{(X_p - \overline{X})^2}{\sum_{i=1}^{n} x_i^2}}$ |
| Standard error of the estimate: | $s = \sqrt{\frac{\sum_{i=1}^{n} e_i^2}{n-2}}$ | | |
| *R*-squared: | $R^2 = \frac{\text{Explained variation}}{\text{Total variation}} = \frac{\sum_{i=1}^{n} \hat{y}_i^2}{\sum_{i=1}^{n} y_i^2}$ | | |

**ILLUSTRATION B.6** Estimate simple linear regression using Excel regression routine.

*Estimate the ordinary least squares regression of GE's stock returns on the returns of the S&P 500 using the Microsoft Excel regression function. The return data are included in worksheet **B6** of the Excel file, **B Illustrations.xls**.*

The first step is to click Data Analysis in the Tools menu.



| | A | B | C |
|---|---|---|---|
| 1 | | Annual returns | |
| 2 | Year | GE | S&P 500 |
| 3 | ending | Y | X |
| 4 | 19851231 | 0.3307 | 0.2633 |
| 5 | 19861231 | 0.2180 | 0.1462 |
| 6 | 19871231 | 0.0525 | 0.0203 |

From the Data Analysis dialog box, AnalysisTools list, click Regression.

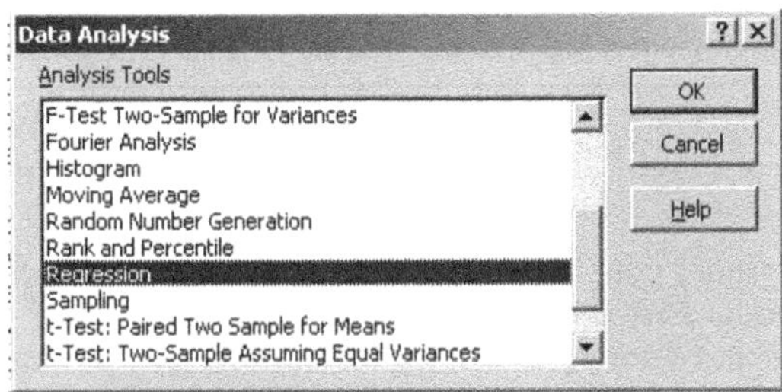


When the Regression dialog box appears, enter the vector of $Y$ observations in the Input Y Range, and the vector $X$ observations in the Input X Range. Click the Output Range option button under the Output options, and then enter the location of the cell which will be the upper left-hand corner of the output panel of results. Click OK.

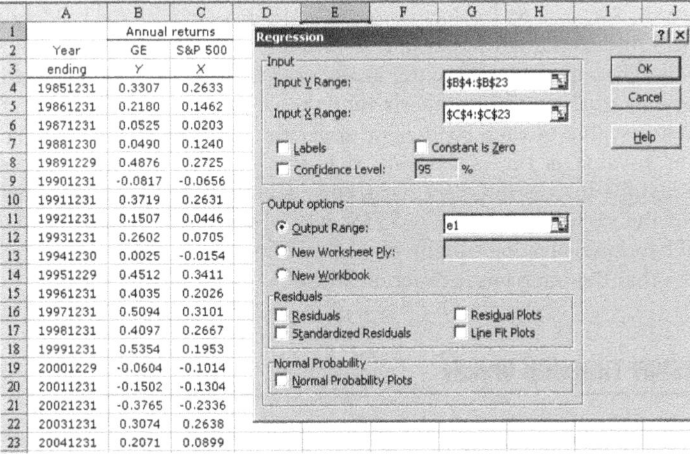


| | A | B | C |
|---|---|---|---|
| 1 | | Annual returns | |
| 2 | Year | GE | S&P 500 |
| 3 | ending | Y | X |
| 4 | 19851231 | 0.3307 | 0.2633 |
| 5 | 19861231 | 0.2180 | 0.1462 |
| 6 | 19871231 | 0.0525 | 0.0203 |
| 7 | 19881230 | 0.0490 | 0.1240 |
| 8 | 19891229 | 0.4876 | 0.2725 |
| 9 | 19901231 | -0.0817 | -0.0656 |
| 10 | 19911231 | 0.3719 | 0.2631 |
| 11 | 19921231 | 0.1507 | 0.0446 |
| 12 | 19931231 | 0.2602 | 0.0705 |
| 13 | 19941230 | 0.0025 | -0.0154 |
| 14 | 19951229 | 0.4512 | 0.3411 |
| 15 | 19961231 | 0.4035 | 0.2026 |
| 16 | 19971231 | 0.5094 | 0.3101 |
| 17 | 19981231 | 0.4097 | 0.2667 |
| 18 | 19991231 | 0.5354 | 0.1953 |
| 19 | 20001229 | -0.0604 | -0.1014 |
| 20 | 20011231 | -0.1502 | -0.1304 |
| 21 | 20021231 | -0.3765 | -0.2336 |
| 22 | 20031231 | 0.3074 | 0.2638 |
| 23 | 20041231 | 0.2071 | 0.0899 |

The following results will appear.

| Summary Output | |
|---|---|
| **Regression Statistics** | |
| Multiple $R$ | 0.9390 |
| $R$-Square | 0.8817 |
| Adjusted $R$-Square | 0.8751 |
| Standard Error | 0.0884 |
| Observations | 20 |

ANOVA

| | *df* | *SS* | *MS* | *F* | Significance *F* |
|---|---|---|---|---|---|
| Regression | 1 | 1.0487 | 1.0487 | 134.10 | 0.0000 |
| Residual | 18 | 0.1408 | 0.0078 | | |
| Total | 19 | 1.1895 | | | |

| | Coefficients | Std. Error | *t* Stat | P-value | Lower 95% | Upper 95% |
|---|---|---|---|---|---|---|
| Intercept | 0.0375 | 0.0244 | 1.5335 | 0.1425 | –0.0139 | 0.0888 |
| X Variable 1 | 1.4298 | 0.1235 | 11.5799 | 0.0000 | 1.1704 | 1.6892 |

In the first table of results, note that our computations are consistent with the reported values $R^2$ and the standard error of the regression. The "multiple $R$" is simply the square root of $R^2$. Finally, we have not yet discussed the adjusted $R^2$. We will do so in the multiple regression analysis section that follows. It is an important statistic for deciding between competing model specifications.

The second table is labeled ANOVA, short for analysis of variance. Like the adjusted $R^2$, the ANOVA results are most typically used in a multiple regression context. At this juncture, it is sufficient to recognize only that ANOVA results are based on the sums of squares computations that we discussed earlier. Note that, in our computations in earlier illustrations, we identified the *SSR*, *SSE*, and *SST* values reported in the column with the heading *SS*.

The third table contains the parameter estimates, standard errors, and 95% confidence intervals. The reported values are, again, consistent with our computations. The $t$-ratios correspond to the null hypothesis that the coefficient is 0. The Excel regression also reports the $p$-value of each coefficient under the null hypothesis that the coefficient equals 0. The $p$-value is the probability that the sample $t$-statistic was observed by chance. The $p$-value for the intercept term, for example, is 0.1425. This means that the probability of the sample $t$-statistic, 1.5335, was observed by chance is 14.25%. Since conventional hypothesis testing usually involves 5% or 1% cutoff levels, we cannot reject the hypothesis that the intercept is different from 0.

## OLS REGRESSION THROUGH ORIGIN

On occasion, it is necessary to consider a simple regression whose intercept term, for economic reasons, equals zero, that is,

$$Y_i = \beta_1 X_i + \varepsilon_i \tag{B.13}$$

As before, the error term $\varepsilon_i$ is assumed to be independent, identically (normally) distributed with mean zero and constant variance. The least squares estimator of $\beta_1$ is

$$\hat{\beta}_1 = \frac{\sum_{i=1}^{n} X_i Y_i}{\sum_{i=1}^{n} X_i^2} \tag{B.14}$$

which is similar to (B.7) except the levels of $X_i$ and $Y_i$ are used rather than their deviations from their respective means. The standard error of the estimate, $s(\hat{\beta}_1)$, is defined as

$$s(\hat{\beta}_1) = \frac{s}{\sqrt{\sum_{i=1}^{n} X_i^2}} \tag{B.15}$$

where

$$s = \sqrt{\frac{\sum_{i=1}^{n} e_i^2}{n-1}} \tag{B.16}$$

The standard error of the prediction is

$$s_p = s\sqrt{1 + \frac{X_p^2}{\sum_{i=1}^{n} X_i^2}} \tag{B.17}$$

**ILLUSTRATION B.7** Estimate simple linear regression through the origin using Excel regression routine.

*Estimate the ordinary least squares regression through the origin of GE's stock returns on the returns of the S&P 500 using the Microsoft Excel regression function. The return data are included in worksheet* ***B7*** *of the Excel file,* ***B Illustrations.xls****.*

The steps in applying the Excel regression function are the same as in Illustration B.6, except that when the regression dialog box appears, Constant is Zero option.

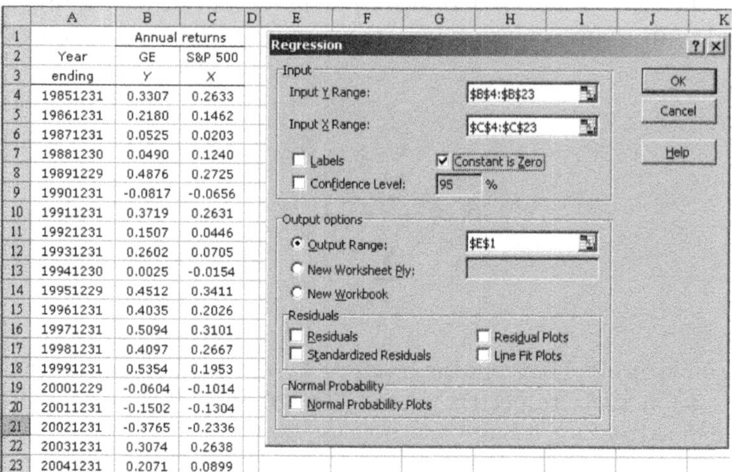

| | Annual returns | |
|---|---|---|
| Year | GE | S&P 500 |
| ending | Y | X |
| 19851231 | 0.3307 | 0.2633 |
| 19861231 | 0.2180 | 0.1462 |
| 19871231 | 0.0525 | 0.0203 |
| 19881230 | 0.0490 | 0.1240 |
| 19891229 | 0.4876 | 0.2725 |
| 19901231 | -0.0817 | -0.0656 |
| 19911231 | 0.3719 | 0.2631 |
| 19921231 | 0.1507 | 0.0446 |
| 19931231 | 0.2602 | 0.0705 |
| 19941230 | 0.0025 | -0.0154 |
| 19951229 | 0.4512 | 0.3411 |
| 19961231 | 0.4035 | 0.2026 |
| 19971231 | 0.5094 | 0.3101 |
| 19981231 | 0.4097 | 0.2667 |
| 19991231 | 0.5354 | 0.1953 |
| 20001229 | -0.0604 | -0.1014 |
| 20011231 | -0.1502 | -0.1304 |
| 20021231 | -0.3765 | -0.2336 |
| 20031231 | 0.3074 | 0.2638 |
| 20041231 | 0.2071 | 0.0899 |



The regressions results are as follows:

| Summary Output | |
|---|---|
| **Regression Statistics** | |
| Multiple *R* | 0.9307 |
| *R* Square | 0.8662 |
| Adjusted *R* Square | 0.8136 |
| Standard Error | 0.0915 |
| Observations | 20 |

ANOVA

| | df | SS | MS | F | Significance *F* |
|---|---|---|---|---|---|
| Regression | 1 | 1.0304 | 1.0304 | 122.9939 | 0.0000 |
| Residual | 19 | 0.1592 | 0.0084 | | |
| Total | 20 | 1.1895 | | | |

| | Coefficients | Std. Error | t Stat | P-value | Lower 95% | Upper 95% |
|---|---|---|---|---|---|---|
| Intercept | 0 | #N/A | #N/A | #N/A | #N/A | #N/A |
| X Variable 1 | 1.5411 | 0.1034 | 14.9079 | 0.0000 | 1.3248 | 1.7575 |

As the results show, the intercept term no longer appears. The estimated slope coefficient, 1.5411, is slightly greater than the slope estimated in Illustration B-6, 1.4298, since we have forced the regression line through 0, as shown in the following figure:

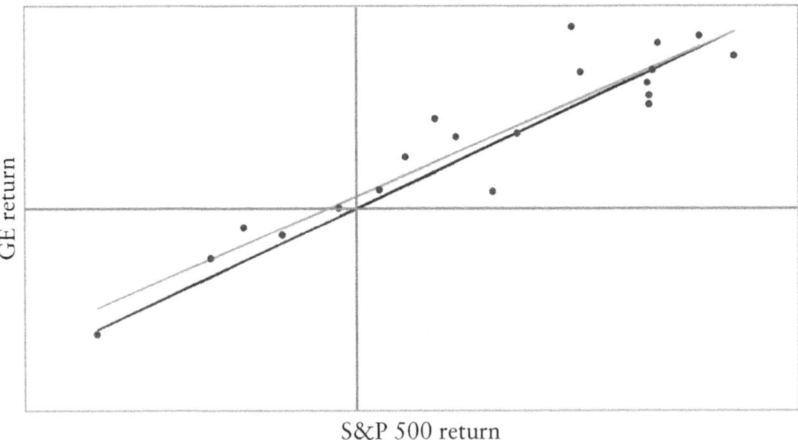


**TABLE B.2** Summary of simple linear regression through the origin estimation formulas.

| | | | |
|---|---|---|---|
| Estimator for slope: | $\hat{\beta}_1 = \dfrac{\sum_{i=1}^{n} X_i Y_i}{\sum_{i=1}^{n} X_i^2}$ | Standard error: | $s(\hat{\beta}_1) = \dfrac{s}{\sqrt{\sum_{i=1}^{n} X_i^2}}$ |
| Prediction: | $\hat{Y}_p = \hat{\beta}_1 X_p$ | Standard error: | $s_p = s\sqrt{1 + \dfrac{X_p^2}{\sum_{i=1}^{n} X_i^2}}$ |
| Standard error of the estimate: | $s = \sqrt{\dfrac{\sum_{i=1}^{n} e_i^2}{n-1}}$ | | |

## MULTIPLE LINEAR REGRESSION

Analogous to simple linear regression models, we can fit a model using two or more explanatory variables of the form

$$Y_i = \beta_0 + \beta_1 X_{1i} + \cdots + \beta_k X_{ki} + \varepsilon_i \tag{B.18}$$

where $k$ denotes the number of independent variables in the model, $Y$ is the dependent variable, $X_1, \cdots, X_k$ are the independent variables, and $\beta_0, \beta_1, \cdots, \beta_k$ are the $k + 1$ regression coefficients. This is referred to as a *multiple linear regression model* because the equation is linear in the parameters. Note that $X_2, \cdots, X_k$ could all be functions of $X_1$ such as $X_1^2$ or $\ln X_1$ and this would still be considered a linear model. The idea of multiple regression is that one independent variable may not be enough to predict *Y* effectively, so additional variables are added to give more explanatory power to the model.

### Model Assumptions

The assumptions for multiple linear regression are essentially the same as the five we used in simple regression model. First, the relation between *X* and *Y* is assumed to be linear except that now there are multiple *X*s, as shown in (B.18). Second, the values of the *X*s are nonrandom. In addition, we require that there is no exact linear relation among any of the independent variables. Finally, the error term $\varepsilon$ is assumed to be independent and identically (normally) distributed with mean 0 and constant variance $\sigma^2$.

### Estimation

Multiple linear regression models are fitted using ordinary least squares in a similar manner to their simple regression analogues. Again, the requirement is that the sum of squared errors (*SSE*) is minimized. Estimation of the parameters in the case $k > 1$ involves using linear algebra and matrix inversion, so the calculations are nearly impossible to perform by hand. Luckily, most statistical software packages have built-in estimation routines so these models can be fitted quite easily.

### Hypothesis Tests for Individual Parameters

Once we have fit a multiple regression model, we may wish to find out whether a particular independent variable has a significant effect on *Y*. We can do this by testing the hypothesis that the corresponding parameter value is equal to zero. The procedure for these tests is almost identical to the case of simple regression models, except that, in a more general sense, the test statistic,

$$t = \hat{\beta}_i / s_{\hat{\beta}_i}$$

has a *t*-distribution with $n - k - 1$ degrees of freedom. Most regression software packages automatically provide the parameter estimates, standard errors, *t*-ratios, and *p*-values when a linear regression is performed.

**ILLUSTRATION B.8** Test difference between two means using dummy variable.

*The worksheet **B8** of the Excel file, **B Illustrations.xls**, contains 60 months of returns for IBM during the period January 2000 through December 2004. In Illustration A.8 of Appendix A, we used this data to test the null hypothesis that the mean during the first 30 months is no different than the mean return in the second 60 months. Assuming the variances of the two samples are equal, usea dummy variable regression to perform the same statistical test.*

The test the difference between means using regression analysis, we must create a dummy (or binary) variable to use as an independent variable. The construction of a dummy variable is simple—it is set equal to either 0 or 1 depending on a particular criterion. In the current illustration, we set the dummy equal to 0 during the first 30 months and 1 during the second. We then regress the 60 months of IBM stock returns on the 60 dummy variable observations and find following results:

| Summary Output | |
|---|---|
| **Regression Statistics** | |
| Multiple *R* | 0.10499 |
| *R*-Square | 0.01102 |
| Adjusted *R*-Square | –0.00603 |
| Standard Error | 0.10410 |
| Observations | 60 |

ANOVA

| | *df* | *SS* | *MS* | F | Significance *F* |
|---|---|---|---|---|---|
| Regression | 1 | 0.00701 | 0.00701 | 0.64647 | 0.42466 |
| Residual | 58 | 0.62849 | 0.01084 | | |
| Total | 59 | 0.63549 | | | |

| | Coefficients | Std. Error | *t* Stat | *P*-value | Lower 95% | Upper 95% |
|---|---|---|---|---|---|---|
| Intercept | –0.00673 | 0.01901 | –0.35385 | 0.72473 | –0.04477 | 0.03132 |
| X Variable 1 | 0.02161 | 0.02688 | 0.80403 | 0.42466 | –0.03219 | 0.07541 |

To interpret these results, recognize that the dummy equals 0 in the first half of the sample. This means that the average value of the dummy variable in the first half of the sample must also equal 0, and that the average monthly return equals the intercept term, –0.00673, that is,

$$\begin{aligned}\bar{Y} &= \hat{\beta}_0 + \hat{\beta}_1 \bar{X}\\ &= -0.00673 + 0.02161(0)\\ &= -0.00673\end{aligned}$$

During the second half of the sample, the average value of the dummy variable is 1. Consequently, the average monthly return during the second half is

$$\begin{aligned}\bar{Y} &= \hat{\beta}_0 + \hat{\beta}_1 \bar{X}\\ &= -0.00673 + 0.02161(1)\\ &= 0.01488\end{aligned}$$

Note that these values conform exactly to the results shown in Illustration A.8.

To test if there is a significant difference in the means of the two samples, we simply use the estimated slope coefficient and its standard error. To see this, recognize that the intercept applies to the returns over the entire 60-month sample and that the slope applies to only the second half of the sample. This means that the slope can be interpreted as the incremental mean return in the second half of the sample. Hence, the reported $t$-ratio for the slope tests the null hypothesis that there is a difference in the means of the two sub-periods. At $t = 0.804$, the $p$-value is 0.425 so we do not reject the null. Note that these values are, again, identical to those we computed in Illustration A.8.

**ILLUSTRATION B.9** Test stationarity of return relation using dummy variable slope-shifter.

*In the regression of GE's returns on the returns of the S&P 500, it is implicitly assumed that the intercept and slope coefficients are constant through time. Often in such time series, there is reason to believe that the relation has changed in some way during the sample period, and you want to test whether it has. Test the null hypothesis that the coefficient $\beta_1$ is the same during the first half of the sample than the second half of the sample. The return data are included in worksheet,* ***B9****, of the Excel file,* ***B Illustrations.xls****.*

The worksheet contains the returns of GE and the S&P 500. It also contains an additional variable called a *dummy variable slope-shifter.* Note that this variable is 0 during the first half of the sample period, and is equal to the market return during the second half. When we run the regression of GE's returns on the two independent variables, the "beta" of GE during the first half of the sample is $\beta_1$ and the beta during the second half of the sample is $\beta_1 + \beta_2$. Thus, to test the hypotheses that the slope coefficient has changed, we perform a $t$-test on the slope coefficient $\beta_2$. If the coefficient is not different from 0 in the statistical sense, the null hypothesis that the relative systematic risk of GE has not changed from the first half of the period to the second cannot be rejected.

To perform the regression in Microsoft Excel, we follow the same steps as before(see the Regression dialog box illustrated below). The only distinction is that the in the Input X Range, we highlight both columns C and D, which contain the two independent variables in our regression. If we click OK, the multiple regression will be performed. Before turning to the results, however, the fact that the independent variables must be in adjacent columns is a limitation of the regression function in Excel. In multiple regression problems, it is often the case that the researcher has many more variables than is necessary. Having the flexibility to use, say, the second, fourth, and ninth columns of data as independent variables without editing the file would be useful. Excel demands that you rearrange the data so that the independent variables are in adjacent columns. For this reason, Excel is not frequently used in academic research or other large-scale applications. For our purposes, however, it is more than adequate.

| | A | B | C | D |
|---|---|---|---|---|
| 1 | | Annual returns | | Slope |
| 2 | Year | GE | S&P 500 | dummy |
| 3 | ending | Y | X1 | X2 |
| 4 | 19851231 | 0.3307 | 0.2633 | 0 |
| 5 | 19861231 | 0.2180 | 0.1462 | 0 |
| 6 | 19871231 | 0.0525 | 0.0203 | 0 |
| 7 | 19881230 | 0.0490 | 0.1240 | 0 |
| 8 | 19891229 | 0.4876 | 0.2725 | 0 |
| 9 | 19901231 | -0.0817 | -0.0656 | 0 |
| 10 | 19911231 | 0.3719 | 0.2631 | 0 |
| 11 | 19921231 | 0.1507 | 0.0446 | 0 |
| 12 | 19931231 | 0.2602 | 0.0705 | 0 |
| 13 | 19941230 | 0.0025 | -0.0154 | 0 |
| 14 | 19951229 | 0.4512 | 0.3411 | 0.3411 |
| 15 | 19961231 | 0.4035 | 0.2026 | 0.2026 |
| 16 | 19971231 | 0.5094 | 0.3101 | 0.3101 |
| 17 | 19981231 | 0.4097 | 0.2667 | 0.2667 |
| 18 | 19991231 | 0.5354 | 0.1953 | 0.1953 |
| 19 | 20001229 | -0.0604 | -0.1014 | -0.1014 |
| 20 | 20011231 | -0.1502 | -0.1304 | -0.1304 |
| 21 | 20021231 | -0.3765 | -0.2336 | -0.2336 |
| 22 | 20031231 | 0.3074 | 0.2638 | 0.2638 |
| 23 | 20041231 | 0.2071 | 0.0899 | 0.0899 |

Regression
Input
Input Y Range: $B$4:$B$23
Input X Range: $C$4:$D$23
Labels
Constant is Zero
Confidence Level: 95 %
Output options
Output Range: $F$1
New Worksheet Ply:
New Workbook
Residuals
Residuals
Residual Plots
Standardized Residuals
Line Fit Plots
Normal Probability
Normal Probability Plots
OK
Cancel
Help

The regression results are reported below. Turning immediately to the slope coefficient for $X_2$, we see that the coefficient estimate is 0.1745, the $t$-ratio is 0.7935, and the $p$-value is 0.4384. Using a 5% significance level ($\alpha = 0.05$), the null hypothesis that $\beta_2 = 0$ cannot be rejected. In other words, there is no reason to believe the relation between GE's returns and the returns of the S&P 500 has changed through time, at least with respect to the two halves of the sample.

| Summary Output | |
|---|---|
| **Regression Statistics** | |
| Multiple $R$ | 0.9412 |
| $R$ Square | 0.8859 |
| Adjusted $R$ Square | 0.8725 |
| Standard Error | 0.0894 |
| Observations | 20 |

ANOVA

| | *df* | *SS* | *MS* | *F* | Significance *F* |
|---|---|---|---|---|---|
| Regression | 2 | 1.0538 | 0.5269 | 65.9832 | 0.0000 |
| Residual | 17 | 0.1357 | 0.0080 | | |
| Total | 19 | 1.1895 | | | |

| | Coefficients | Std. Error | *t* Stat | *P*-value | Lower 95% | Upper 95% |
|---|---|---|---|---|---|---|
| Intercept | 0.0421 | 0.0254 | 1.6594 | 0.1154 | –0.0114 | 0.0957 |
| X Variable 1 | 1.2998 | 0.2060 | 6.3102 | 0.0000 | 0.8652 | 1.7344 |
| X Variable 2 | 0.1745 | 0.2199 | 0.7935 | 0.4384 | –0.2895 | 0.6386 |

### Confidence Intervals

In a similar vein to hypothesis testing, we can also learn about the effects of individual explanatory variables by constructing confidence intervals. For each of the $k + 1$ parameters in the model, we can obtain interval estimates using the regression output from software packages in the following manner:

$$\text{A } (1 - \alpha)\% \text{ confidence interval for } \beta_i \text{ is: } \hat{\beta}_i \pm t_{\alpha/2} s_{\hat{\beta}_i}$$

To see whether the $i$th explanatory variable has an effect on $Y$, we check for the presence of zero in the confidence interval for $\beta_i$.

### Hypothesis Tests for Significant Overall Regression

In addition to testing whether individual explanatory variables have an effect on $Y$, we may also want to check whether the model as a whole has significant predictive power. We can do this using an $F$-test, where the null hypothesis under question is that all coefficients are equal to zero: $H_0$: $\beta_1 = \beta_2 = \cdots = \beta_k = 0$. This is compared with the alternative hypothesis that at least one of the coefficients is nonzero. The test statistic here is denoted by $F$, which can be regarded as a *signal-to-noise* ratio. The signal refers to the portion of the variation explained by the model, and the noise relates to the part left unexplained. The $F$-test can also be understood by examining the following generic analysis of variance (ANOVA) table resulting from a linear regression procedure:

ANOVA Table

| Source | Sum of Squares | Degrees of Freedom | Mean-Squared Error | F-ratio |
|---|---|---|---|---|
| Regression | $SSR$ | $k$ | $SSR/k$ | $\dfrac{SSR/k}{SSE/(n-k-1)}$ |
| Error | $SSE$ | $n-k-1$ | $SSE/(n-k-1)$ | |
| Total | $SST$ | $n-1$ | $SST/(n-1)$ | |

An analysis of variance table like the one above is standard output from most software packages when a regression procedure is performed. The first column shows how the total variation of $Y$ is decomposed: *Regression*, the part explained by the model; *Error*, the part unexplained by the model; and, *Total*, both parts put together. In the *Sum of Squares* column, $SSR$, $SSE$, and $SST$ stand for regression, error, and total sum of squares, respectively. The *Degrees of Freedom* (*df*) are divided up as follows: total degrees of freedom are the number of observations minus one (which is lost because the overall mean, $\bar{Y}$, is estimated); degrees of freedom for the regression are equal to the number of explanatory variables in the model; and the difference between the two gives the degrees pf freedom of the error. The error *df* is also the degrees of freedom on which $t$-test for individual parameter significance is based. The *Mean-Squared Error* column gives essentially the average sum of squares for each source. Note that the mean-squared total is the unbiased estimate for the variance of $Y$. The $F$-statistic in column five can be thought of as the signal-to-noise ratio: the regression mean squared, $SSR/k$, being the signal, and the error mean squared, $SSE/(n-k-1)$, as the noise. If the $F$-statistic gets very high, this means that the regression is explaining a large proportion of the variance, and, if it gets quite low, this indicates that a great deal is left unexplained by the model. Therefore we reject the null hypothesis of a useless model if $F$ is large enough. And for any given level of significance, we can find the critical value of $F$ using an $F$-distribution with $k$ and $n-k-1$ degrees of freedom. Critical values of the $F$-distribution are reported in Table C.4 of Appendix C.

### Prediction

For any combination of independent variables lying in the range of the observed $X$'s, we can obtain point estimates and predictions intervals by using a formula similar to the one given for the simple regression case. The only difference is that in the standard error, which depends on the distance from the prediction point, $X_p$ and the mean, $\bar{X}$, we need to incorporate the fact that this should be measured in $k$-dimensional space. However, most statistical software packages provide this output, so again no matrix algebra is necessary.

### Model Selection and Goodness of Fit

**$R$-Squared and Adjusted $R$-Squared** Just as for a simple regression, goodness-of-fit analysis for multiple regression is commonly based on the sum of squares decomposition. The coefficient of determination, $R^2$, is widely used because of its ease of interpretation. $R^2$ can be quite misleading, however, because it increases monotonically with $k$. In other words, as each additional independent variable is added to the model, the coefficient of determination must either increase or remain the same. This becomes a problem when extraneous variables are included in the model solely to boost the value of $R^2$, ignoring scientific or statistical indications that they do not belong. Parsimony, or economy of explanation, is of great value to an investigator because it greatly eases the burden of understanding and interpreting the model. Therefore, we commonly use a related statistic, the adjusted-$R^2$, to take into account the size of the model when assessing goodness of fit in a multiple regression.

The adjusted-$R^2$, denoted by $\bar{R}^2$, is given by the formula,

$$\bar{R}^2 = 1 - \frac{Var(e)}{Var(Y)} = 1 - \frac{SSE/(n-k-1)}{SST/(n-1)} = 1 - (1 - R^2)\left(\frac{n-1}{n-k-1}\right) \tag{B.19}$$

where $k$ is the number of independent variables in the model. We can see that the adjusted-$R^2$ is always less than or equal to $R^2$. (It only equals $R^2$ when the model has only an intercept.) It is also possible for $\bar{R}^2$ to be negative. The advantage of the adjusted-$R^2$ is that it penalizes the model for including variables that do not provide information about $Y$. Note that, for two models with the same $R^2$ but different $k$, the $\bar{R}^2$ will be larger for the smaller model. This is intended to ensure that the issue of parsimony is addressed in the model selection process.

**ILLUSTRATION B.10** Test purchasing power parity.

*Purchasing power parity (PPP) is a simple arbitrage relation that says the price of a commodity or security in one country equals the price of the same commodity or security in another after adjusting for the rate of exchange in the currency. Suppose we are considering the price of a stock index in euros, $S_{EURO}$, and the price of the same index in USD, $S_{USD}$. The PPP relation is*

$$S_{EUR,t} = S_{USD,t} \times S_{EURO/USD,t} \tag{a}$$

*where $S_{EURO/USD}$ is the price in Euros for one USD. Since the equation is nonlinear, we cannot test it directly using OLS regression. PPP is, however, intrinsically linear. Taking the natural logarithm of both sides, we get*

$$\ln(S_{EUR,t}) = \ln(S_{USD,t}) + \ln(S_{EUR/USD,t}) \qquad (b)$$

*To avoid issues of nonstationarity (see Chapter 5), the logged PPP relation is usually tested in differenced form. Since the differenced in logged prices is a continuous return, for example,*

$$R_{EUR,t} \equiv \ln(S_{EUR,t}/S_{EUR,t-1}) \equiv \ln(S_{EUR,t}) - \ln(S_{EUR,t-1}) \qquad (c)$$

*we can test PPP by running the OLS regression,*

$$R_{EUR,t} = \beta_0 + \beta_1 R_{USD,t} + \beta_2 R_{EUR/USD,t} + \varepsilon_t \qquad (d)$$

*The worksheet* ***B10*** *in the Excel file* ***B Illustrations.xls*** *contains the monthly returns of the DAX 30, the S&P 500, and the EUR/USD exchange rate over the period January 2000 through January 2006. The DAX 30 is a diversified portfolio of German stocks, and the S&P 500 is a diversified portfolio of U.S. stocks. Use the returns on these portfolios to proxy for the returns on equities in each country. Test the PPP relation.*

The regression results are as follows:

**Summary Output**

| Regression Statistics | |
|---|---|
| Multiple $R$ | 0.7855 |
| $R$-Square | 0.6170 |
| Adjusted $R$-Square | 0.6059 |
| Standard Error | 0.0452 |
| Observations | 72 |

ANOVA

| | *df* | *SS* | *MS* | *F* | Significance *F* |
|---|---|---|---|---|---|
| Regression | 2 | 0.22752 | 0.11376 | 55.57159 | 0.00000 |
| Residual | 69 | 0.14125 | 0.00205 | | |
| Total | 71 | 0.36879 | | | |

| | Coefficients | Std. Error | *t* Stat | *P*-value | Lower 95% | Upper 95% |
|---|---|---|---|---|---|---|
| Intercept | −0.00087 | 0.00535 | −0.16196 | 0.87181 | −0.01154 | 0.00981 |
| X Variable 1 | 1.29608 | 0.12626 | 10.26480 | 0.00000 | 1.04419 | 1.54797 |
| X Variable 2 | 0.53488 | 0.18234 | 2.93332 | 0.00455 | 0.17111 | 0.89864 |

These results are interesting in a number of respects. First, note that the adjusted $R$-square is 60.59%. This means that the S&P 500 and exchange rate returns explain 60.59% of the variance in the DAX 30 returns. Second, note that both slope coefficients are significantly different from 0 at the 5% level. Indeed, both coefficients are significant at the .5%. This means both regressors have a significant effect on the dependent variable. Third, we are reject the joint hypothesis that $\beta_1 = 0$ *and* $\beta_2 = 0$. The $F$-statistic is

55.57, and its $p$-value is less than 0.000005. Fourth, the intercept term is not significantly different from 0. This is not unexpected. Comparing the regression equation (d) with the logged PPP relation (b), it should be obvious that expected values of the coefficients are: $\beta_0 = 0$, and $\beta_1 = \beta_2 = 1$.

This last observation is somewhat discomforting. Although we have shown that the slope coefficients are different from 0, a test of PPP requires that we test the null hypothesis that the coefficients $\beta_1$ and $\beta_2$ are equal to 1. Performing $t$-tests on these hypothesis also rejects these hypotheses, so, technically, the PPP relation is rejected.

The most likely reason that we reject PPP is that the DAX 30 and S&P 500 stock indexes are not perfect substitutes. The DAX 30 consists of only 30 high market capitalization stocks and is not particularly well-diversified. The S&P 500, on the other hand, is well-diversified and accounts for more than 70% of the total market value of all stocks traded in the U.S. What the regression results do show, however, is that the rate of return on the DAX does systematically covary with U.S. stock return (its beta is 1.66) and with change in the EUR/USD exchange rate.

## Specification Errors

Implicit in the specification of the multiple regression model (B.13) are the assumptions that we know the identity of all of the $k$ relevant explanatory variables, and that their relation with the dependent variable is linear. But, since regression is by its nature exploratory, we need to be concerned about the "correctness" of our specification. What impact does failing to include a relevant explanatory variable have on estimation? Along the same line, what is the effect of including an explanatory variable that does not belong in the regression model? Finally, what is the effect of estimating a linear relation when the actual relation is nonlinear? We address each of these issues in turn.

**Omitting Relevant Explanatory Variables** Failing to include a relevant explanatory variable can have serious implications. To see this, assume that the "true" model is

$$y_i = \beta_1 x_{1i} + \beta_2 x_{2i} + \varepsilon_i \tag{B.20}$$

where the variables are expressed as deviations from their means. Now suppose that, instead of estimating (B.20), we estimate

$$y_i = \beta_1^* x_{1i} + \varepsilon_i^* \tag{B.21}$$

What are the implications?

We know from our discussion of simple linear regression that the estimated slope in (B.21) is

$$\hat{\beta}_1 = \frac{\sum_{i=1}^{n} x_i y_i}{\sum_{i=1}^{n} x_i^2} \tag{B.22}$$

Substituting (B.20) for $y_i$, we obtain

$$\hat{\beta}_1^* = \frac{\beta_1 \sum_{i=1}^{n} x_{1i}^2 + \beta_2 \sum_{i=1}^{n} x_{1i}x_{2i} + \sum_{i=1}^{n} x_{1i}\varepsilon_i}{\sum_{i=1}^{n} x_{1i}^2}$$

$$= \beta_1 + \frac{\beta_2 \sum_{i=1}^{n} x_{1i}x_{2i}}{\sum_{i=1}^{n} x_{1i}^2} + \frac{\sum_{i=1}^{n} x_{1i}\varepsilon_i}{\sum_{i=1}^{n} x_{1i}^2} \tag{B.23}$$

Since $X_1$ is fixed and the expected value of the error is 0, the expected value of the estimated slope is

$$E\left(\hat{\beta}_1^*\right) = \beta_1 + \beta_2 \frac{\sum_{i=1}^{n} x_{1i}x_{2i}}{\sum_{i=1}^{n} x_{1i}^2} \tag{B.24}$$

This means that, in general, the estimated slope parameter in (B.21) will be biased. The direction of the bias depends on the product of $\beta_2$ and the covariance between the independent variables. If $\beta_2$ and the covariance are both positive, the estimated slope will be upward biased. The intuition for this is that the estimated slope picks up not only the co-variation of $y_i$ with $x_{1i}$ but also some of the co-variation of $y_i$ with $x_{2i}$. Only in the event that the correlation between the independent variables is zero will the estimated slope be unbiased.

The standard error of the estimate will also be biased. In the case of estimating (B.21) when (B.20) is the correct model, the standard error of $\hat{\beta}_1^*$ will be less than the standard error of $\hat{\beta}_1$. We thereby run the risk of rejecting the null hypothesis that the slope parameter is 0 when in reality it is.

**ILLUSTRATION B.11** Examine effect of omitted variable in regression specification.

*In Illustration B.10, we estimated a multiple regression model with the return on the DAX 30 as the dependent variable and the returns of the S&P 500 and the EUR/USD exchange rate as the independent variables. Estimate the simple linear regression of DAX 30 returns on S&P 500 returns, and comment on the difference in results.*

The regression results are as follows:

| Summary Output | |
|---|---|
| **Regression Statistics** | |
| Multiple $R$ | 0.7545 |
| $R$ Square | 0.5692 |
| Adjusted $R$ Square | 0.5631 |
| Standard Error | 0.0476 |
| Observations | 72 |

ANOVA

| | df | SS | MS | F | Significance $F$ |
|---|---|---|---|---|---|
| Regression | 1 | 0.20990 | 0.20990 | 92.49113 | 0.00000 |
| Residual | 70 | 0.15886 | 0.00227 | | |
| Total | 71 | 0.36876 | | | |

| | Coefficients | Std. Error | $t$ Stat | $P$-value | Lower 95% | Upper 95% |
|---|---|---|---|---|---|---|
| Intercept | −0.00195 | 0.00562 | −0.34756 | 0.72921 | −0.01317 | 0.00926 |
| X Variable 1 | 1.27685 | 0.13277 | 9.61723 | 0.00000 | 1.01205 | 1.54164 |

Comparing these results with those of Illustration B.10 shows at least two interesting facts. First, the adjusted $R$-square value falls from 60.59% to 56.31%. As noted earlier, the adjusted $R$-square value is often used as a criterion for choosing among competing models with the same dependent variable. Based on the results, the model in Illustration B.10 is preferred. Second, the estimated slope coefficient is now 1.27685 versus 1.29608 in Illustration B.10. This is the omitted variable bias just discussed. Equation (B.24) shows the nature of the bias. Since we know $\beta_2$ is positive, the bias in (B.24) depends on the sign of the covariance term in the numerator of the last term on the right hand side. Since the estimated coefficient falls in value from 1.29608 to 1.27685 (i.e., the bias is negative), we can deduce that the correlation between the returns of the S&P 500 and the EUR/USD exchange rate is negative. Indeed, if we compute the correlation matrix for the three return series, we find that:

| | DAX30 | S&P 500 | EUR/USD |
|---|---|---|---|
| DAX30 | 1 | | |
| S&P 500 | 0.7545 | 1 | |
| EUR/USD | 0.1791 | −0.0519 | 1 |

The correlation between the returns of the S&P 500 and the EUR/USD is negative, as expected. Its level is only −0.0519, thus the degree of bias is modest. The higher the correlation, the greater the bias. The only circumstance in which no bias occurs is if the correlation is 0—a highly unlikely event.

**Including Irrelevant Explanatory Variables** The effects of including an irrelevant variable are much less serious. The estimated parameters of the relevant explanatory variables remain unbiased. The only cost, so to speak, is that the standard errors of the estimates will be larger than they should be, making it more difficult to reject the null hypothesis of a zero slope parameter. Thus, if you reject the null in the presence of irrelevant variables, you can be quite confident of your decision.

**Nonlinearities** A separate discussion of the effects of nonlinearity is unwarranted. Fitting a linear regression to a nonlinear relation is a special case of the omitted variables discussed above. We can expect bias in the estimated coefficients, and the standard errors to be smaller than appropriate.

### Multicollinearity

Multicollinearity arises when two or more variables are highly correlated with each other. While it is possible to obtain least squares estimates of the regression coefficients, the interpretation of the coefficients is difficult. Recall that the interpretation of a regression coefficient is the change in $Y$ with respect to a change in $X_1$, *holding other factors constant*. The presence of multicollinearity means that other factors are not being held constant. If $X_1$ and $X_2$ are highly correlated, a change in $X_1$ implies a change in $X_2$, and vice versa.

A rule of thumb states that multicollinearity is likely to be a problem if a simple correlation between the two variables is larger than the correlation of either or both variables with the dependent variable. Such a rule may be reasonable when there are only two independent variables in the regression. With more than two independent variables, however, simple correlations will not detect a more complicated linear relation among variables. Perhaps the simplest way to detect if multicollinearity is a problem is to examine the standard errors of the coefficients. If several coefficients have high standard errors, and dropping one or more variables from the equation lowers the standard errors of the remaining variables, multicollinearity will usually be the source of the problem.

### Violations of Disturbance Assumption

OLS regression assumes that the relation between dependent and independent variables is linear and that the error term $\varepsilon$ is independent and identically (normally) distributed with mean 0 and constant variance $\sigma^2$. These assumptions can be violated in four ways: (1) the relation is nonlinear, (2) the error variance may not be constant, (3) the residual errors may be correlated, and (4) the errors may not be normally distributed. Below we discuss how to detect such violations, explain the consequences of each violation, and suggest remedies to fix or, at least mitigate, the effects of the violation.

**Nonlinearity** Plotting the relation between the $Y$ and $X$ variables is a useful first step in regression analysis. Among other things, it allows us to uncover potential nonlinearities in the data. To illustrate, consider the $(X,Y)$ points plotted in the figure that follows. The solid line in the figure is the "best fit" obtained from the simple regression of $Y$ on $X$, that is,

$$Y_i = \beta_0 + \beta_1 X_i + \varepsilon_i$$

Obviously, the relation between $Y$ and $X$ is not linear. Where the level of $X$ is near 0, the level of $Y$ tends to be below its predicted level. For levels of $X$ between 0 and 150, the levels of $Y$ are above predicted, and, for levels of $X$ above 200, the levels are below predicted. If the model was "correct," the $(X,Y)$ points should be symmetrically distributed around the fitted line. Nonlinearity is usually revealed through a "bowed" pattern of residuals such as seen below (i.e., the model makes systematic errors whenever it is making unusually large or small predictions).

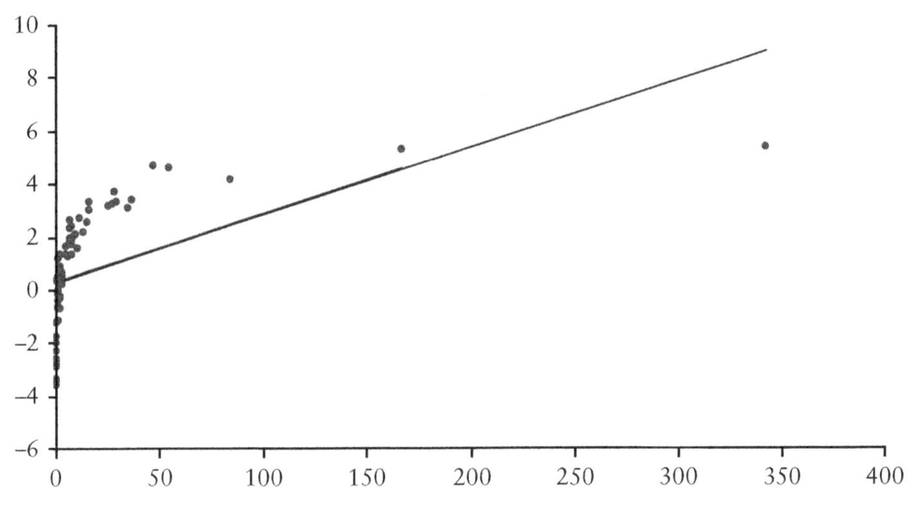


To remedy the problem, we may want to consider applying a *nonlinear transformation* to the dependent and/or independent variables. In the figure above, note that all of the values of $X$ are positive and that the pattern of points looks like a log transformation. We may therefore want to consider applying a log transformation to the $X$ variable. Another possibility to consider is adding another regressor which is a nonlinear function of one of the other variables. Since we have regressed $Y$ on $X$, we may want to regress $Y$ on both $X$ and $X^2$. Note that, unlike the log transformation, this transformation can be applied even when $X$ and/or $Y$ have negative values.

As it turns out, the relation in the above figure is intrinsically linear. The figure below shows () points as well as the regression line,

$$Y_i = \beta_0 + \beta_1 \ln X_i + \varepsilon_i$$

fitted through the pairs of coordinates. Note that the residuals are now symmetrically distributed around the fitted line. This gives us comfort that we have uncovered the "correct" specification.[4]

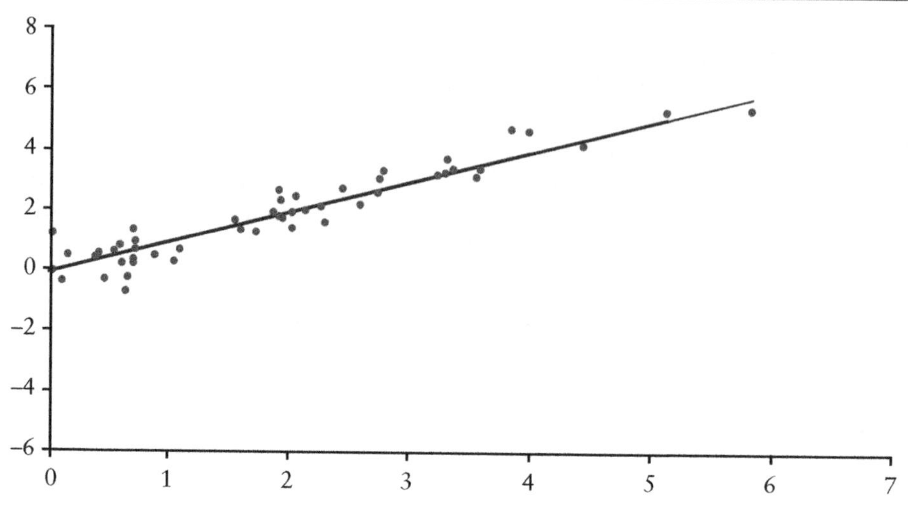


**Heteroscedasticity** Detecting a violation of the constant variance (or homoscedastic) error assumption is also facilitated by a plot of the residuals around the fitted values of $Y$. If the residuals have a constant variance at different levels of prediction, the error term is homoscedastic. If the residuals appear fan-shaped, as shown in the figure on the next page, heteroscedasticity may be a problem. A popular test for the presence of heteroscedasticity is the Goldfeld-Quandt (1965) test. The steps are as follows:

1. Order the data by the $X_i$ observations.
2. Omit the $c$ central observations.[5]
3. Fit separate regressions to the first $(n - c)/2$ and the last $(n - c)/2$ observations. Naturally, $(n - c)/2$ must exceed the number of parameters to be estimated.
4. Compute the ratio $R = SSE_2/SSE_1$, where $SSE_1$ and $SSE_2$ are the sum of squared errors from the first and second regressions, respectively.[6] Under the assumption of homoscedasticity, $R$ has an $F$ distribution with $(n - c)/2$ and $(n - c)/2$ degrees of freedom in the numerator and the denominator, respectively. If $R$ exceeds the critical value reported in Table C.4 of Appendix C, we reject the null hypothesis that the error variance is the same in both subsamples.

[4] In financial economics, model specification is usually driven by theoretical considerations.

[5] The power of the test depends on the choice of $c$. The greater the value of $c$, the lower the power of the test. On the other hand, the lower the value of $c$, the greater the power, however, the more likely the residual variances will move closer together.

[6] As discussed in Appendix A, we place the largest $SSE$ in the numerator. That is, the notation implicitly assumes $SSE_2 > SSE_1$.

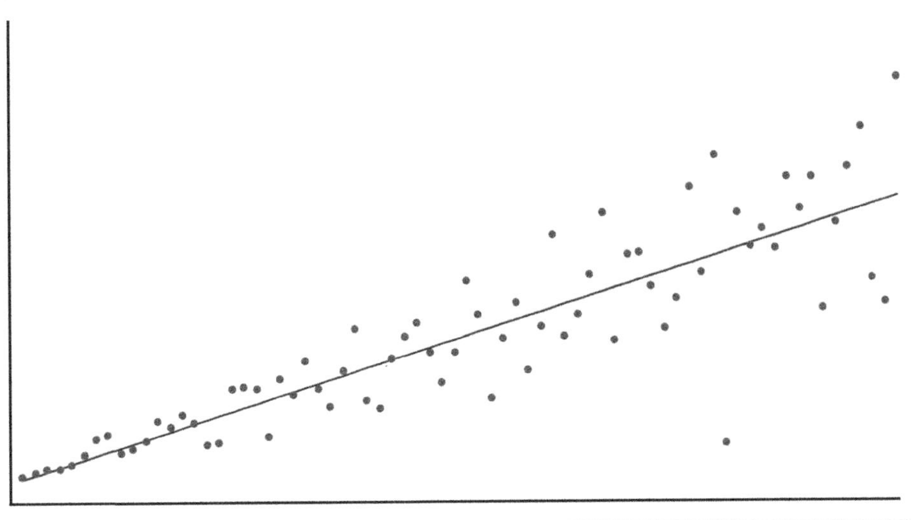

With a heteroscedastic error term, ordinary least squares estimation places greater weight on observations with large error variances than on those with small error variances. This implicit weighting occurs because the sum of the squared residuals associated with the large variance error terms is likely to be substantially greater than the sum of the squared residuals associated with small error variances. This means that, while the parameter estimates remain unbiased, the standard errors of the parameter estimates will be biased.

Correcting for heteroscedasticity is possible using *weighted least squares* estimation. To illustrate, suppose that the error variances in the regression,

$$Y_i = \beta_0 + \beta_1 X_{1i} + \cdots + \beta_k X_{ki} + \varepsilon_i \tag{B.25}$$

vary directly with one of the explanatory variables, say, $X_{i,1}$, that is,

$$Var(\varepsilon_i) = CX_{1i}^2$$

where C is a nonzero constant. To correct for heteroscedasticity, we multiply the terms of the regression by the inverse of $X_{1i}$, and run the regression,

$$\frac{Y_i}{X_{1i}} = \beta_0 \frac{1}{X_{1i}} + \beta_1 + \cdots + \beta_k \frac{X_{ki}}{X_{1i}} + \frac{\varepsilon_i}{X_{1i}} \tag{B.26}$$

The error term in the transformed regression model,

$$\varepsilon_i^* = \frac{\varepsilon_i}{X_{1i}}$$

now has constant variance, that is,

$$Var(\varepsilon_i^*) = Var\left(\frac{\varepsilon_i}{X_{1i}}\right) = \frac{1}{X_{1i}}Var(\varepsilon_i) = C \qquad \text{(B.27)}$$

Uncovering the form of the heteroscedasticity is sometimes difficult since the error variance may be a nonlinear function of one of the independent variables, or it may be a function of some other variables, $Z$, not included in the regression model. Standard econometric textbooks offer guidance on appropriate correction procedures.[7] After the structure of the error variance is determined, however, variable transformations in a weighted least squares framework rectifies the problem.

**Serial Correlation** Violations of the error independence assumption are most often found in time series data.[8] A common method for their detection is the Durbin-Watson (1951) test. The $DW$-statistic looks at the sum of squared differences between subsequent residuals to see if they are, on average, too close together or too far apart. The $DW$-statistic tests the null hypothesis of no autocorrelation among the dependent variable against the alternative of autocorrelated data. The test statistic is

$$DW = \frac{\sum_{i=2}^{n}(e_i - e_{i-1})^2}{\sum_{i=1}^{n}e_i^2} \qquad \text{(B.28)}$$

where $e_i$ is the $i$th time-ordered residual from the model. Note that the numerator will be small when subsequent errors are similar (positively correlated) and will be large when they tend to be far apart (negatively correlated). The level of the $DW$-statistic is approximately $2(1 - \rho)$, where $\rho$ is the first-order autocorrelation of the residuals. Thus, a $DW$-statistic close to 2 indicates the residuals are uncorrelated.

In using the Durbin-Watson test of the null hypothesis that there is no serial correlation in the residuals, we must use a table of critical values such as those reported in Table C.5 of Appendix C for the five percent significance level. The rules for applying these values are as follows. If we are checking for positive autocorrelation, the null hypothesis is rejected if $DW < d_l$ and is accepted if $DW > d_u$. Between $d_l$ and $d_u$ the results are inconclusive. For a simple linear regression ($k = 2$) using 60 observations ($n = 60$), the critical values are $d_l = 1.51$ and $d_u = 1.65$. Thus, if $DW < 1.51$, we reject the null hypothesis of no serial correla-

[7] See, for example, Pindyck and Rubinfeld (1998, pp. 148–159).

[8] Any serial correlation in the errors of a cross-sectional regression can be eliminated by shuffling the order of the data.

tion in favor of the alternative hypothesis that there exists positive autocorrelation, and, if $DW > 1.65$, we accept the null. If $1.51 < DW < 1.65$, we cannot say one way or the other. If we are checking for negative autocorrelation, we view matters from an endpoint of 4 rather than an endpoint of 0. That is, the null hypothesis is rejected if $DW > 4 - d_l$ and is accepted if $DW < 4 - d_u$. Between $4 - d_u$ and $4 - d_l$ the results are inconclusive. For a simple linear regression ($k = 2$) using 60 observations ($n = 60$), the critical values are 2.35 and 2.49. If $DW > 2.49$, we reject the null hypothesis of no serial correlation in favor of the alternative hypothesis that there exists negative autocorrelation, and, if $DW < 2.35$, we accept the null. The results are inconclusive where $2.35 < DW < 2.49$.

The presence of serial correlation does not bias the parameter estimates. It does, however, affect the standard errors of the estimates. In the presence of positive serial correlation, the standard errors will be smaller than they should be, potentially causing us to reject the null when we should not. To understand possible correction procedures, consider the nature of the problem. Under the assumption the error term is serially correlated, the regression model is

$$Y_t = \beta_0 + \beta_1 X_{1t} + \cdots + \beta_k X_{kt} + \varepsilon_t \tag{B.29}$$

where

$$\varepsilon_t = \rho\varepsilon_t + \upsilon_t \tag{B.30}$$

$\rho$ is the first-order serial-correlation, and $\upsilon_t$ is normally distributed with zero mean and constant variance and is independent of other errors through time. Since equation (B.29) holds for all time periods, we can write

$$Y_{t-1} = \beta_0 + \beta_1 X_{1t-1} + \cdots + \beta_k X_{kt-1} + \varepsilon_{t-1} \tag{B.31}$$

Multiplying (B.31) by $\rho$ and subtracting it from (B.29), we get

$$Y_t^* = \beta_0(1-\rho) + \beta_1 X_{1t}^* + \cdots + \beta_k X_{kt}^* + v_t \tag{B.32}$$

where the asterisks denote *generalized differences*. The variable $X_{1t}^*$, for example, is defined as $X_{1t}^* = X_{1t} - \rho X_{1t-1}$. Since the error term in (B.32) is independent through time, the standard errors of the regression model (B.32) will be unbiased.

To implement the correction procedure, we need to estimate $\rho$. One simple procedure, called the Hildreth-Lu (1960) procedure, is to set $\rho$ to a grid of different values between 0 and 1 (e.g., 0, 0.1, 0.2, ..., 1) and estimate (B.32) for each assumed value. Based upon the regression results, we choose the value of $\rho'$ that produces the lowest sum of squared errors, and then set up a new, more refined grid that searches in the neighborhood of $\rho'$ to find a new value that minimizes the sum of squared errors. The procedure is repeated until the desired degree of accuracy is attained. Another approach, called the Cochrane-Orcutt (1949), is to estimate $\rho$ from the residuals of (B.29), that is,

$$e_t = \rho e_{t-1} + v_t \tag{B.33}$$

and then use the estimated serial correlation in the estimation of the generalized difference model (B.32). Using the estimated parameters from (B.32), we generate a new set of residuals from the original regression equation (B.29), re-estimate (B.33) to obtain a new estimate of $\rho$, and then reestimate (B.32). The procedure is repeated iteratively until the new estimates of $\rho$ differ from the old ones by, say, 0.005 or less, or after 10 to 20 iterations.

**Nonnormality** A violation of the normality assumption is particularly serious. The reason is simple. Since parameter estimation is based on the minimization of the sum of *squared errors*, a few extreme observations can exert a disproportionate influence on the parameter estimates and their standard errors. One way to test for normally distributed errors is to use a *normal probability plot* of the residuals. A normal probability plot is a plot of the fractiles of error distribution versus the fractiles of a normal distribution having the same mean and variance. If the distribution is normal, the points on this plot should fall close to the diagonal line. A "bow-shaped" pattern of deviations from the diagonal indicates that the residuals have excessive skewness (i.e., they are not symmetrically distributed, with too many large errors in the same direction). An "S-shaped" pattern of deviations indicates that the residuals have excessive kurtosis (i.e., there are either two many or two few large errors in both directions).

Violations of normality often arise either because (1) the distributions of the dependent and/or independent variables are nonnormal, and/or (2) the linearity assumption is violated. In such cases, a nonlinear transformation of variables might cure both problems. In some cases, the problem with the residual distribution is mainly due to one or two very large errors called *outliers*. Outliers should be scrutinized closely. If they are merely errors or if they can be explained as unique events not likely to be repeated, you may have cause to remove them.

## REFERENCES AND SUGGESTED READINGS

Cochrane, D., and G. H. Orcutt. 1949. Application of least-squares regressions to relationships containing autocorrelated error terms. *Journal of teh American Statistical Association* 44: 32–61.

Durbin, J., and G. S. Watson. 1951. Testing for serial correlation in least squares regression. *Biometrika* 38: 159–177.

Goldfeld, S. M., and R. E. Quandt. 1965. Some tests for homoscedasticity. *Journal of the American Statistical Society* 60: 539–547.

Hildreth, G., and J. Y. Lu. 1960. Demand relations with autocorrelated disturbances. *Michigan State University Agricultural Experiment Station Technical Bulletin* 276.

Intriligator, Michael D. 1978. *Econometric Techniques, and Applications*. Englewood Cliffs, NJ: Prenctice-Hall.

Jarque, C. M., and A. K. Bera. 1987. A test of normality of observations and regression residuals. *International Statistical Review* 11: 351–360.

Jarque, C. M., and A. K. Bera. 1980. Efficient tests of normality, homoscedasticity and serial dependence of regression residuals. *Economic Letters* 6: 255–259.

Kennedy, Peter. 1992. *A Guide to Econometrics*, 3rd ed. Cambridge, MA: MIT Press.

Kmenta, Jan. 1971. *Elements of Econometrics*. New York: Macmillan Publishing Co.

Pindyck, Robert S., and Daniel L. Rubinfeld. 1998. *Econometric Models and Economic Forecasts*, 4th ed. Boston: Irwin/McGraw-Hill.

# APPENDIX C
# Statistical Tables

The appendix includes statistical tables that are commonly used in testing hypotheses and building confidence intervals. In order of appearance, the tables are:

TABLE C.1A: Area under standard normal distribution from minus infinity to $a$ for values of $a < 0$.

TABLE C.1B: Area under standard normal distribution from minus infinity to $a$ for values of $a > 0$.

TABLE C.2: Critical values of the chi-square ($\chi^2$) distribution for given levels of probability that the $\chi^2$ will exceed table entry.

TABLE C.3: Critical values of the $t$-distribution for given levels of probability that the $t$-value will exceed table entry.

TABLE C.4A: Critical values of the $F$-distribution for 5% probability level ($\alpha = .05$) that the $F$-statistic will exceed table entry.

TABLE C.4B: Critical values of the $F$-distribution for 1% probability level ($\alpha = .01$) that the $F$-statistic will exceed table entry.

TABLE C.5: 5% significance points of $d_l$ and $d_u$ for Durbin-Watson test statistic.

**TABLE C.1A** Area under standard normal distribution from minus infinity to $a$ for values of $a < 0$.

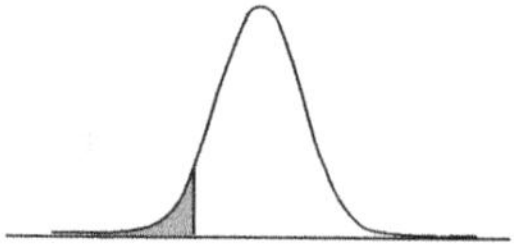

| $a$ | 0.00 | 0.01 | 0.02 | 0.03 | 0.04 | 0.05 | 0.06 | 0.07 | 0.08 | 0.09 |
|---|---|---|---|---|---|---|---|---|---|---|
| –3.0 | 0.0013 | 0.0014 | 0.0014 | 0.0015 | 0.0015 | 0.0016 | 0.0016 | 0.0017 | 0.0018 | 0.0018 |
| –2.9 | 0.0019 | 0.0019 | 0.0020 | 0.0021 | 0.0021 | 0.0022 | 0.0023 | 0.0023 | 0.0024 | 0.0025 |
| –2.8 | 0.0026 | 0.0026 | 0.0027 | 0.0028 | 0.0029 | 0.0030 | 0.0031 | 0.0032 | 0.0033 | 0.0034 |
| –2.7 | 0.0035 | 0.0036 | 0.0037 | 0.0038 | 0.0039 | 0.0040 | 0.0041 | 0.0043 | 0.0044 | 0.0045 |
| –2.6 | 0.0047 | 0.0048 | 0.0049 | 0.0051 | 0.0052 | 0.0054 | 0.0055 | 0.0057 | 0.0059 | 0.0060 |
| –2.5 | 0.0062 | 0.0064 | 0.0066 | 0.0068 | 0.0069 | 0.0071 | 0.0073 | 0.0075 | 0.0078 | 0.0080 |
| –2.4 | 0.0082 | 0.0084 | 0.0087 | 0.0089 | 0.0091 | 0.0094 | 0.0096 | 0.0099 | 0.0102 | 0.0104 |
| –2.3 | 0.0107 | 0.0110 | 0.0113 | 0.0116 | 0.0119 | 0.0122 | 0.0125 | 0.0129 | 0.0132 | 0.0136 |
| –2.2 | 0.0139 | 0.0143 | 0.0146 | 0.0150 | 0.0154 | 0.0158 | 0.0162 | 0.0166 | 0.0170 | 0.0174 |
| –2.1 | 0.0179 | 0.0183 | 0.0188 | 0.0192 | 0.0197 | 0.0202 | 0.0207 | 0.0212 | 0.0217 | 0.0222 |
| –2.0 | 0.0228 | 0.0233 | 0.0239 | 0.0244 | 0.0250 | 0.0256 | 0.0262 | 0.0268 | 0.0274 | 0.0281 |
| –1.9 | 0.0287 | 0.0294 | 0.0301 | 0.0307 | 0.0314 | 0.0322 | 0.0329 | 0.0336 | 0.0344 | 0.0351 |
| –1.8 | 0.0359 | 0.0367 | 0.0375 | 0.0384 | 0.0392 | 0.0401 | 0.0409 | 0.0418 | 0.0427 | 0.0436 |
| –1.7 | 0.0446 | 0.0455 | 0.0465 | 0.0475 | 0.0485 | 0.0495 | 0.0505 | 0.0516 | 0.0526 | 0.0537 |
| –1.6 | 0.0548 | 0.0559 | 0.0571 | 0.0582 | 0.0594 | 0.0606 | 0.0618 | 0.0630 | 0.0643 | 0.0655 |
| –1.5 | 0.0668 | 0.0681 | 0.0694 | 0.0708 | 0.0721 | 0.0735 | 0.0749 | 0.0764 | 0.0778 | 0.0793 |
| –1.4 | 0.0808 | 0.0823 | 0.0838 | 0.0853 | 0.0869 | 0.0885 | 0.0901 | 0.0918 | 0.0934 | 0.0951 |
| –1.3 | 0.0968 | 0.0985 | 0.1003 | 0.1020 | 0.1038 | 0.1056 | 0.1075 | 0.1093 | 0.1112 | 0.1131 |
| –1.2 | 0.1151 | 0.1170 | 0.1190 | 0.1210 | 0.1230 | 0.1251 | 0.1271 | 0.1292 | 0.1314 | 0.1335 |
| –1.1 | 0.1357 | 0.1379 | 0.1401 | 0.1423 | 0.1446 | 0.1469 | 0.1492 | 0.1515 | 0.1539 | 0.1562 |
| –1.0 | 0.1587 | 0.1611 | 0.1635 | 0.1660 | 0.1685 | 0.1711 | 0.1736 | 0.1762 | 0.1788 | 0.1814 |
| –0.9 | 0.1841 | 0.1867 | 0.1894 | 0.1922 | 0.1949 | 0.1977 | 0.2005 | 0.2033 | 0.2061 | 0.2090 |
| –0.8 | 0.2119 | 0.2148 | 0.2177 | 0.2206 | 0.2236 | 0.2266 | 0.2296 | 0.2327 | 0.2358 | 0.2389 |
| –0.7 | 0.2420 | 0.2451 | 0.2483 | 0.2514 | 0.2546 | 0.2578 | 0.2611 | 0.2643 | 0.2676 | 0.2709 |
| –0.6 | 0.2743 | 0.2776 | 0.2810 | 0.2843 | 0.2877 | 0.2912 | 0.2946 | 0.2981 | 0.3015 | 0.3050 |
| –0.5 | 0.3085 | 0.3121 | 0.3156 | 0.3192 | 0.3228 | 0.3264 | 0.3300 | 0.3336 | 0.3372 | 0.3409 |
| –0.4 | 0.3446 | 0.3483 | 0.3520 | 0.3557 | 0.3594 | 0.3632 | 0.3669 | 0.3707 | 0.3745 | 0.3783 |
| –0.3 | 0.3821 | 0.3859 | 0.3897 | 0.3936 | 0.3974 | 0.4013 | 0.4052 | 0.4090 | 0.4129 | 0.4168 |
| –0.2 | 0.4207 | 0.4247 | 0.4286 | 0.4325 | 0.4364 | 0.4404 | 0.4443 | 0.4483 | 0.4522 | 0.4562 |
| –0.1 | 0.4602 | 0.4641 | 0.4681 | 0.4721 | 0.4761 | 0.4801 | 0.4840 | 0.4880 | 0.4920 | 0.4960 |

**TABLE C.1B** Area under standard normal distribution from minus infinity to *a* for values of *a* > 0.

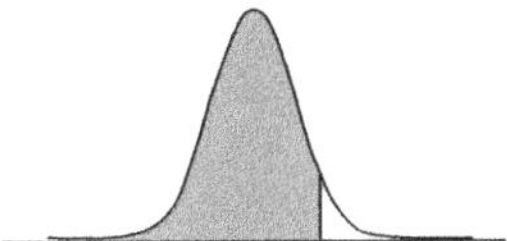

| *a* | 0.00 | 0.01 | 0.02 | 0.03 | 0.04 | 0.05 | 0.06 | 0.07 | 0.08 | 0.09 |
|---|---|---|---|---|---|---|---|---|---|---|
| 0.0 | 0.5000 | 0.5040 | 0.5080 | 0.5120 | 0.5160 | 0.5199 | 0.5239 | 0.5279 | 0.5319 | 0.5359 |
| 0.1 | 0.5398 | 0.5438 | 0.5478 | 0.5517 | 0.5557 | 0.5596 | 0.5636 | 0.5675 | 0.5714 | 0.5753 |
| 0.2 | 0.5793 | 0.5832 | 0.5871 | 0.5910 | 0.5948 | 0.5987 | 0.6026 | 0.6064 | 0.6103 | 0.6141 |
| 0.3 | 0.6179 | 0.6217 | 0.6255 | 0.6293 | 0.6331 | 0.6368 | 0.6406 | 0.6443 | 0.6480 | 0.6517 |
| 0.4 | 0.6554 | 0.6591 | 0.6628 | 0.6664 | 0.6700 | 0.6736 | 0.6772 | 0.6808 | 0.6844 | 0.6879 |
| 0.5 | 0.6915 | 0.6950 | 0.6985 | 0.7019 | 0.7054 | 0.7088 | 0.7123 | 0.7157 | 0.7190 | 0.7224 |
| 0.6 | 0.7257 | 0.7291 | 0.7324 | 0.7357 | 0.7389 | 0.7422 | 0.7454 | 0.7486 | 0.7517 | 0.7549 |
| 0.7 | 0.7580 | 0.7611 | 0.7642 | 0.7673 | 0.7704 | 0.7734 | 0.7764 | 0.7794 | 0.7823 | 0.7852 |
| 0.8 | 0.7881 | 0.7910 | 0.7939 | 0.7967 | 0.7995 | 0.8023 | 0.8051 | 0.8078 | 0.8106 | 0.8133 |
| 0.9 | 0.8159 | 0.8186 | 0.8212 | 0.8238 | 0.8264 | 0.8289 | 0.8315 | 0.8340 | 0.8365 | 0.8389 |
| 1.0 | 0.8413 | 0.8438 | 0.8461 | 0.8485 | 0.8508 | 0.8531 | 0.8554 | 0.8577 | 0.8599 | 0.8621 |
| 1.1 | 0.8643 | 0.8665 | 0.8686 | 0.8708 | 0.8729 | 0.8749 | 0.8770 | 0.8790 | 0.8810 | 0.8830 |
| 1.2 | 0.8849 | 0.8869 | 0.8888 | 0.8907 | 0.8925 | 0.8944 | 0.8962 | 0.8980 | 0.8997 | 0.9015 |
| 1.3 | 0.9032 | 0.9049 | 0.9066 | 0.9082 | 0.9099 | 0.9115 | 0.9131 | 0.9147 | 0.9162 | 0.9177 |
| 1.4 | 0.9192 | 0.9207 | 0.9222 | 0.9236 | 0.9251 | 0.9265 | 0.9279 | 0.9292 | 0.9306 | 0.9319 |
| 1.5 | 0.9332 | 0.9345 | 0.9357 | 0.9370 | 0.9382 | 0.9394 | 0.9406 | 0.9418 | 0.9429 | 0.9441 |
| 1.6 | 0.9452 | 0.9463 | 0.9474 | 0.9484 | 0.9495 | 0.9505 | 0.9515 | 0.9525 | 0.9535 | 0.9545 |
| 1.7 | 0.9554 | 0.9564 | 0.9573 | 0.9582 | 0.9591 | 0.9599 | 0.9608 | 0.9616 | 0.9625 | 0.9633 |
| 1.8 | 0.9641 | 0.9649 | 0.9656 | 0.9664 | 0.9671 | 0.9678 | 0.9686 | 0.9693 | 0.9699 | 0.9706 |
| 1.9 | 0.9713 | 0.9719 | 0.9726 | 0.9732 | 0.9738 | 0.9744 | 0.9750 | 0.9756 | 0.9761 | 0.9767 |
| 2.0 | 0.9772 | 0.9778 | 0.9783 | 0.9788 | 0.9793 | 0.9798 | 0.9803 | 0.9808 | 0.9812 | 0.9817 |
| 2.1 | 0.9821 | 0.9826 | 0.9830 | 0.9834 | 0.9838 | 0.9842 | 0.9846 | 0.9850 | 0.9854 | 0.9857 |
| 2.2 | 0.9861 | 0.9864 | 0.9868 | 0.9871 | 0.9875 | 0.9878 | 0.9881 | 0.9884 | 0.9887 | 0.9890 |
| 2.3 | 0.9893 | 0.9896 | 0.9898 | 0.9901 | 0.9904 | 0.9906 | 0.9909 | 0.9911 | 0.9913 | 0.9916 |
| 2.4 | 0.9918 | 0.9920 | 0.9922 | 0.9925 | 0.9927 | 0.9929 | 0.9931 | 0.9932 | 0.9934 | 0.9936 |
| 2.5 | 0.9938 | 0.9940 | 0.9941 | 0.9943 | 0.9945 | 0.9946 | 0.9948 | 0.9949 | 0.9951 | 0.9952 |
| 2.6 | 0.9953 | 0.9955 | 0.9956 | 0.9957 | 0.9959 | 0.9960 | 0.9961 | 0.9962 | 0.9963 | 0.9964 |
| 2.7 | 0.9965 | 0.9966 | 0.9967 | 0.9968 | 0.9969 | 0.9970 | 0.9971 | 0.9972 | 0.9973 | 0.9974 |
| 2.8 | 0.9974 | 0.9975 | 0.9976 | 0.9977 | 0.9977 | 0.9978 | 0.9979 | 0.9979 | 0.9980 | 0.9981 |
| 2.9 | 0.9981 | 0.9982 | 0.9982 | 0.9983 | 0.9984 | 0.9984 | 0.9985 | 0.9985 | 0.9986 | 0.9986 |
| 3.0 | 0.9987 | 0.9987 | 0.9987 | 0.9988 | 0.9988 | 0.9989 | 0.9989 | 0.9989 | 0.9990 | 0.9990 |

**TABLE C.2** Critical values of the chi-square ($\chi^2$) distribution for given levels of probability that the $\chi^2$ will exceed table entry. Using a significance level of $\alpha = 0.05$, the critical chi-square value assuming 10 degrees of freedom $\chi^2_{10}$ is 18.31, that is, the probability that a drawing from a chi-square distribution with 10 degrees of freedom will exceed 18.31 is 5%.

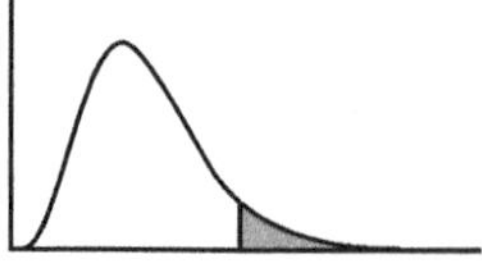

| Degrees of Freedom | Probability of a Value at Least as Large as the Table Entry | | | | | | | | | |
|---|---|---|---|---|---|---|---|---|---|---|
| | 0.995 | 0.990 | 0.975 | 0.950 | 0.900 | 0.100 | 0.050 | 0.025 | 0.010 | 0.005 |
| 1 | 0.0000 | 0.0002 | 0.0010 | 0.0039 | 0.0158 | 2.71 | 3.84 | 5.02 | 6.63 | 7.88 |
| 2 | 0.0100 | 0.0201 | 0.0506 | 0.1026 | 0.2107 | 4.61 | 5.99 | 7.38 | 9.21 | 10.60 |
| 3 | 0.0717 | 0.1150 | 0.2160 | 0.3520 | 0.5840 | 6.25 | 7.81 | 9.35 | 11.34 | 12.84 |
| 4 | 0.2070 | 0.2970 | 0.4840 | 0.7110 | 1.0600 | 7.78 | 9.49 | 11.14 | 13.28 | 14.86 |
| 5 | 0.4120 | 0.5540 | 0.8310 | 1.1500 | 1.6100 | 9.24 | 11.07 | 12.83 | 15.09 | 16.75 |
| 6 | 0.6760 | 0.8720 | 1.2400 | 1.6400 | 2.2000 | 10.64 | 12.59 | 14.45 | 16.81 | 18.55 |
| 7 | 0.9890 | 1.2400 | 1.6900 | 2.1700 | 2.8300 | 12.02 | 14.07 | 16.01 | 18.48 | 20.28 |
| 8 | 1.3400 | 1.6500 | 2.1800 | 2.7300 | 3.4900 | 13.36 | 15.51 | 17.53 | 20.09 | 21.95 |
| 9 | 1.7300 | 2.0900 | 2.7000 | 3.3300 | 4.1700 | 14.68 | 16.92 | 19.02 | 21.67 | 23.59 |
| 10 | 2.1600 | 2.5600 | 3.2500 | 3.9400 | 4.8700 | 15.99 | 18.31 | 20.48 | 23.21 | 25.19 |
| 11 | 2.6000 | 3.0500 | 3.8200 | 4.5700 | 5.5800 | 17.28 | 19.68 | 21.92 | 24.72 | 26.76 |
| 12 | 3.0700 | 3.5700 | 4.4000 | 5.2300 | 6.3000 | 18.55 | 21.03 | 23.34 | 26.22 | 28.30 |
| 13 | 3.5700 | 4.1100 | 5.0100 | 5.8900 | 7.0400 | 19.81 | 22.36 | 24.74 | 27.69 | 29.82 |
| 14 | 4.0700 | 4.6600 | 5.6300 | 6.5700 | 7.7900 | 21.06 | 23.68 | 26.12 | 29.14 | 31.32 |
| 15 | 4.6000 | 5.2300 | 6.2600 | 7.2600 | 8.5500 | 22.31 | 25.00 | 27.49 | 30.58 | 32.80 |
| 16 | 5.1400 | 5.8100 | 6.9100 | 7.9600 | 9.3100 | 23.54 | 26.30 | 28.85 | 32.00 | 34.27 |
| 18 | 6.2600 | 7.0100 | 8.2300 | 9.3900 | 10.8600 | 25.99 | 28.87 | 31.53 | 34.81 | 37.16 |
| 20 | 7.4300 | 8.2600 | 9.5900 | 10.8500 | 12.4400 | 28.41 | 31.41 | 34.17 | 37.57 | 40.00 |
| 24 | 9.8900 | 10.8600 | 12.4000 | 13.8500 | 15.6600 | 33.20 | 36.42 | 39.36 | 42.98 | 45.56 |
| 30 | 13.7900 | 14.9500 | 16.7900 | 18.4900 | 20.6000 | 40.26 | 43.77 | 46.98 | 50.89 | 53.67 |
| 40 | 20.7100 | 22.1600 | 24.4300 | 26.5100 | 29.0500 | 51.81 | 55.76 | 59.34 | 63.69 | 66.77 |
| 60 | 35.5300 | 37.4800 | 40.4800 | 43.1900 | 46.4600 | 74.40 | 79.08 | 83.30 | 88.38 | 91.95 |
| 120 | 83.8500 | 86.9200 | 91.5700 | 95.7000 | 100.6200 | 140.23 | 146.57 | 152.21 | 158.95 | 163.65 |

**TABLE C.3** Critical values of the *t*-distribution for given levels of probability that the *t*-value will exceed table entry. For a one-tailed test with 10 degrees of freedom and a significance level of $\alpha = 0.05$, the critical *t*-value $t_\alpha$ is 1.812, that is, the probability that the *t*-value exceeds 1.812 in absolute value is 5%. For a two-tailed test with 10 degrees of freedom and a significance level of $\alpha = 0.05$, the critical *t*-value $t_{\alpha/2}$ 2.228, that is, the probability that the *t*-value is below −2.228 *or* above 2.228 is 5%—2.5% in each tail.

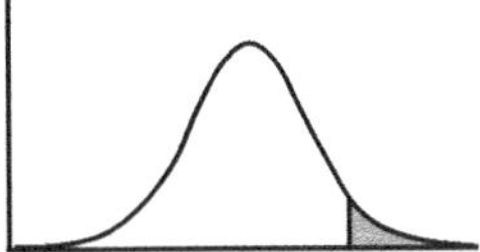

| Degrees of Freedom | Probability of a Value at Least as Large as the Table Entry | | | | | | |
|---|---|---|---|---|---|---|---|
| | 0.400 | 0.200 | 0.100 | 0.050 | 0.025 | 0.010 | 0.005 |
| 1 | 0.325 | 1.376 | 3.078 | 6.314 | 12.706 | 31.821 | 63.656 |
| 2 | 0.289 | 1.061 | 1.886 | 2.920 | 4.303 | 6.965 | 9.925 |
| 3 | 0.277 | 0.978 | 1.638 | 2.353 | 3.182 | 4.541 | 5.841 |
| 4 | 0.271 | 0.941 | 1.533 | 2.132 | 2.776 | 3.747 | 4.604 |
| 5 | 0.267 | 0.920 | 1.476 | 2.015 | 2.571 | 3.365 | 4.032 |
| 6 | 0.265 | 0.906 | 1.440 | 1.943 | 2.447 | 3.143 | 3.707 |
| 7 | 0.263 | 0.896 | 1.415 | 1.895 | 2.365 | 2.998 | 3.499 |
| 8 | 0.262 | 0.889 | 1.397 | 1.860 | 2.306 | 2.896 | 3.355 |
| 9 | 0.261 | 0.883 | 1.383 | 1.833 | 2.262 | 2.821 | 3.250 |
| 10 | 0.260 | 0.879 | 1.372 | 1.812 | 2.228 | 2.764 | 3.169 |
| 11 | 0.260 | 0.876 | 1.363 | 1.796 | 2.201 | 2.718 | 3.106 |
| 12 | 0.259 | 0.873 | 1.356 | 1.782 | 2.179 | 2.681 | 3.055 |
| 13 | 0.259 | 0.870 | 1.350 | 1.771 | 2.160 | 2.650 | 3.012 |
| 14 | 0.258 | 0.868 | 1.345 | 1.761 | 2.145 | 2.624 | 2.977 |
| 15 | 0.258 | 0.866 | 1.341 | 1.753 | 2.131 | 2.602 | 2.947 |
| 16 | 0.258 | 0.865 | 1.337 | 1.746 | 2.120 | 2.583 | 2.921 |
| 17 | 0.257 | 0.863 | 1.333 | 1.740 | 2.110 | 2.567 | 2.898 |
| 18 | 0.257 | 0.862 | 1.330 | 1.734 | 2.101 | 2.552 | 2.878 |
| 19 | 0.257 | 0.861 | 1.328 | 1.729 | 2.093 | 2.539 | 2.861 |
| 20 | 0.257 | 0.860 | 1.325 | 1.725 | 2.086 | 2.528 | 2.845 |
| 21 | 0.257 | 0.859 | 1.323 | 1.721 | 2.080 | 2.518 | 2.831 |
| 22 | 0.256 | 0.858 | 1.321 | 1.717 | 2.074 | 2.508 | 2.819 |
| 23 | 0.256 | 0.858 | 1.319 | 1.714 | 2.069 | 2.500 | 2.807 |
| 24 | 0.256 | 0.857 | 1.318 | 1.711 | 2.064 | 2.492 | 2.797 |
| 25 | 0.256 | 0.856 | 1.316 | 1.708 | 2.060 | 2.485 | 2.787 |
| 26 | 0.256 | 0.856 | 1.315 | 1.706 | 2.056 | 2.479 | 2.779 |
| 27 | 0.256 | 0.855 | 1.314 | 1.703 | 2.052 | 2.473 | 2.771 |
| 28 | 0.256 | 0.855 | 1.313 | 1.701 | 2.048 | 2.467 | 2.763 |
| 29 | 0.256 | 0.854 | 1.311 | 1.699 | 2.045 | 2.462 | 2.756 |
| 30 | 0.256 | 0.854 | 1.310 | 1.697 | 2.042 | 2.457 | 2.750 |
| 40 | 0.255 | 0.851 | 1.303 | 1.684 | 2.021 | 2.423 | 2.704 |
| 60 | 0.254 | 0.848 | 1.296 | 1.671 | 2.000 | 2.390 | 2.660 |
| 120 | 0.254 | 0.845 | 1.289 | 1.658 | 1.980 | 2.358 | 2.617 |
| ∞ | 0.253 | 0.842 | 1.282 | 1.645 | 1.960 | 2.327 | 7.500 |

**TABLE C.4A** Critical values of the *F*-distribution for 5% probability level () that the *F*-statistic will exceed table entry. The critical *F*-value assuming 10 degrees of freedom in the numerator and 10 degrees of freedom in the denominator is 2.98, that is, the probability that a drawing from a *F*-distribution with 10 degrees of freedom in the numerator and 10 degrees of freedom will exceed 2.98 is 5%.

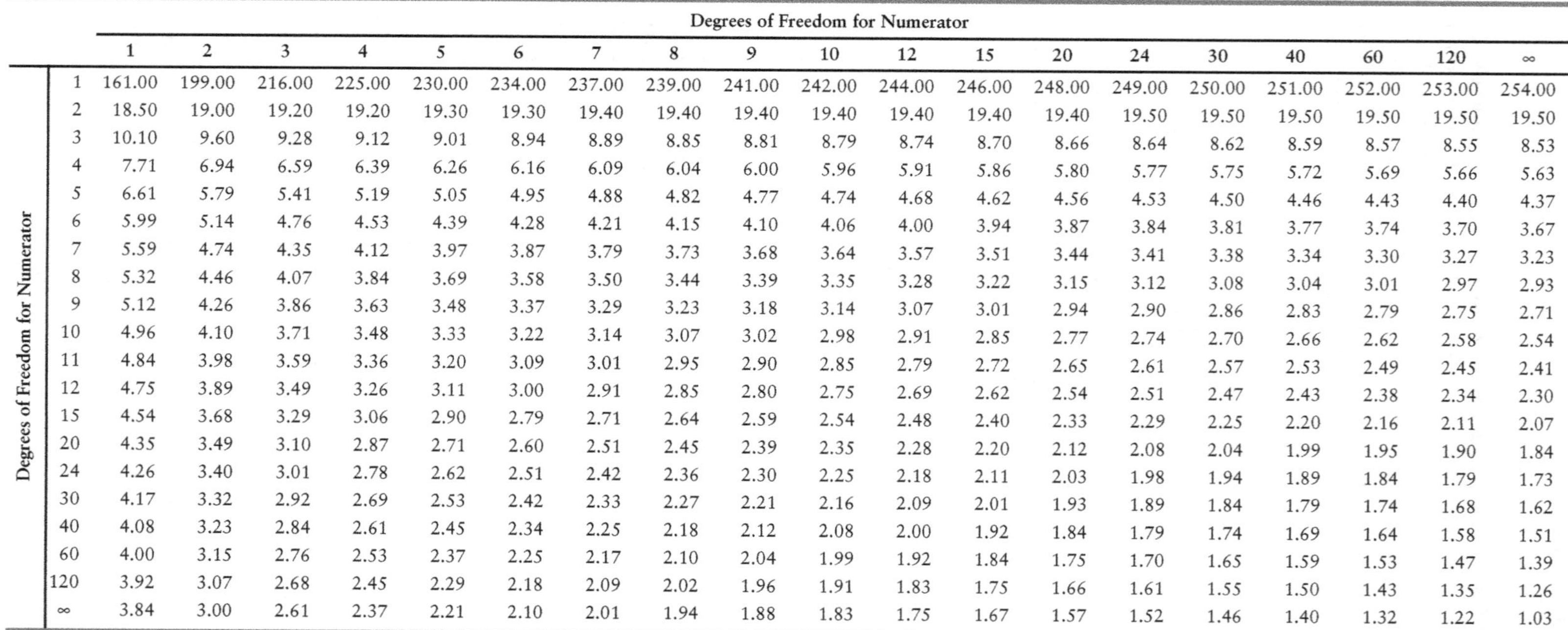

| Degrees of Freedom for Numerator | Degrees of Freedom for Numerator | | | | | | | | | | | | | | | | | | |
|---|---|---|---|---|---|---|---|---|---|---|---|---|---|---|---|---|---|---|---|
| | 1 | 2 | 3 | 4 | 5 | 6 | 7 | 8 | 9 | 10 | 12 | 15 | 20 | 24 | 30 | 40 | 60 | 120 | ∞ |
| 1 | 161.00 | 199.00 | 216.00 | 225.00 | 230.00 | 234.00 | 237.00 | 239.00 | 241.00 | 242.00 | 244.00 | 246.00 | 248.00 | 249.00 | 250.00 | 251.00 | 252.00 | 253.00 | 254.00 |
| 2 | 18.50 | 19.00 | 19.20 | 19.20 | 19.30 | 19.30 | 19.40 | 19.40 | 19.40 | 19.40 | 19.40 | 19.40 | 19.40 | 19.50 | 19.50 | 19.50 | 19.50 | 19.50 | 19.50 |
| 3 | 10.10 | 9.60 | 9.28 | 9.12 | 9.01 | 8.94 | 8.89 | 8.85 | 8.81 | 8.79 | 8.74 | 8.70 | 8.66 | 8.64 | 8.62 | 8.59 | 8.57 | 8.55 | 8.53 |
| 4 | 7.71 | 6.94 | 6.59 | 6.39 | 6.26 | 6.16 | 6.09 | 6.04 | 6.00 | 5.96 | 5.91 | 5.86 | 5.80 | 5.77 | 5.75 | 5.72 | 5.69 | 5.66 | 5.63 |
| 5 | 6.61 | 5.79 | 5.41 | 5.19 | 5.05 | 4.95 | 4.88 | 4.82 | 4.77 | 4.74 | 4.68 | 4.62 | 4.56 | 4.53 | 4.50 | 4.46 | 4.43 | 4.40 | 4.37 |
| 6 | 5.99 | 5.14 | 4.76 | 4.53 | 4.39 | 4.28 | 4.21 | 4.15 | 4.10 | 4.06 | 4.00 | 3.94 | 3.87 | 3.84 | 3.81 | 3.77 | 3.74 | 3.70 | 3.67 |
| 7 | 5.59 | 4.74 | 4.35 | 4.12 | 3.97 | 3.87 | 3.79 | 3.73 | 3.68 | 3.64 | 3.57 | 3.51 | 3.44 | 3.41 | 3.38 | 3.34 | 3.30 | 3.27 | 3.23 |
| 8 | 5.32 | 4.46 | 4.07 | 3.84 | 3.69 | 3.58 | 3.50 | 3.44 | 3.39 | 3.35 | 3.28 | 3.22 | 3.15 | 3.12 | 3.08 | 3.04 | 3.01 | 2.97 | 2.93 |
| 9 | 5.12 | 4.26 | 3.86 | 3.63 | 3.48 | 3.37 | 3.29 | 3.23 | 3.18 | 3.14 | 3.07 | 3.01 | 2.94 | 2.90 | 2.86 | 2.83 | 2.79 | 2.75 | 2.71 |
| 10 | 4.96 | 4.10 | 3.71 | 3.48 | 3.33 | 3.22 | 3.14 | 3.07 | 3.02 | 2.98 | 2.91 | 2.85 | 2.77 | 2.74 | 2.70 | 2.66 | 2.62 | 2.58 | 2.54 |
| 11 | 4.84 | 3.98 | 3.59 | 3.36 | 3.20 | 3.09 | 3.01 | 2.95 | 2.90 | 2.85 | 2.79 | 2.72 | 2.65 | 2.61 | 2.57 | 2.53 | 2.49 | 2.45 | 2.41 |
| 12 | 4.75 | 3.89 | 3.49 | 3.26 | 3.11 | 3.00 | 2.91 | 2.85 | 2.80 | 2.75 | 2.69 | 2.62 | 2.54 | 2.51 | 2.47 | 2.43 | 2.38 | 2.34 | 2.30 |
| 15 | 4.54 | 3.68 | 3.29 | 3.06 | 2.90 | 2.79 | 2.71 | 2.64 | 2.59 | 2.54 | 2.48 | 2.40 | 2.33 | 2.29 | 2.25 | 2.20 | 2.16 | 2.11 | 2.07 |
| 20 | 4.35 | 3.49 | 3.10 | 2.87 | 2.71 | 2.60 | 2.51 | 2.45 | 2.39 | 2.35 | 2.28 | 2.20 | 2.12 | 2.08 | 2.04 | 1.99 | 1.95 | 1.90 | 1.84 |
| 24 | 4.26 | 3.40 | 3.01 | 2.78 | 2.62 | 2.51 | 2.42 | 2.36 | 2.30 | 2.25 | 2.18 | 2.11 | 2.03 | 1.98 | 1.94 | 1.89 | 1.84 | 1.79 | 1.73 |
| 30 | 4.17 | 3.32 | 2.92 | 2.69 | 2.53 | 2.42 | 2.33 | 2.27 | 2.21 | 2.16 | 2.09 | 2.01 | 1.93 | 1.89 | 1.84 | 1.79 | 1.74 | 1.68 | 1.62 |
| 40 | 4.08 | 3.23 | 2.84 | 2.61 | 2.45 | 2.34 | 2.25 | 2.18 | 2.12 | 2.08 | 2.00 | 1.92 | 1.84 | 1.79 | 1.74 | 1.69 | 1.64 | 1.58 | 1.51 |
| 60 | 4.00 | 3.15 | 2.76 | 2.53 | 2.37 | 2.25 | 2.17 | 2.10 | 2.04 | 1.99 | 1.92 | 1.84 | 1.75 | 1.70 | 1.65 | 1.59 | 1.53 | 1.47 | 1.39 |
| 120 | 3.92 | 3.07 | 2.68 | 2.45 | 2.29 | 2.18 | 2.09 | 2.02 | 1.96 | 1.91 | 1.83 | 1.75 | 1.66 | 1.61 | 1.55 | 1.50 | 1.43 | 1.35 | 1.26 |
| ∞ | 3.84 | 3.00 | 2.61 | 2.37 | 2.21 | 2.10 | 2.01 | 1.94 | 1.88 | 1.83 | 1.75 | 1.67 | 1.57 | 1.52 | 1.46 | 1.40 | 1.32 | 1.22 | 1.03 |

**TABLE C.4B** Critical values of the $F$-distribution for 1% probability level ($\alpha = 0.01$) **that the $F$-statistic will exceed table entry.** The critical $F$-value assuming 10 degrees of freedom in the numerator and 10 degrees of freedom in the denominator $F_{0.05,\,10,10}$ is 4.85, that is, the probability that a drawing from a $F$-distribution with 10 degrees of freedom in the numerator and 10 degrees of freedom will exceed 4.85 is 1%.

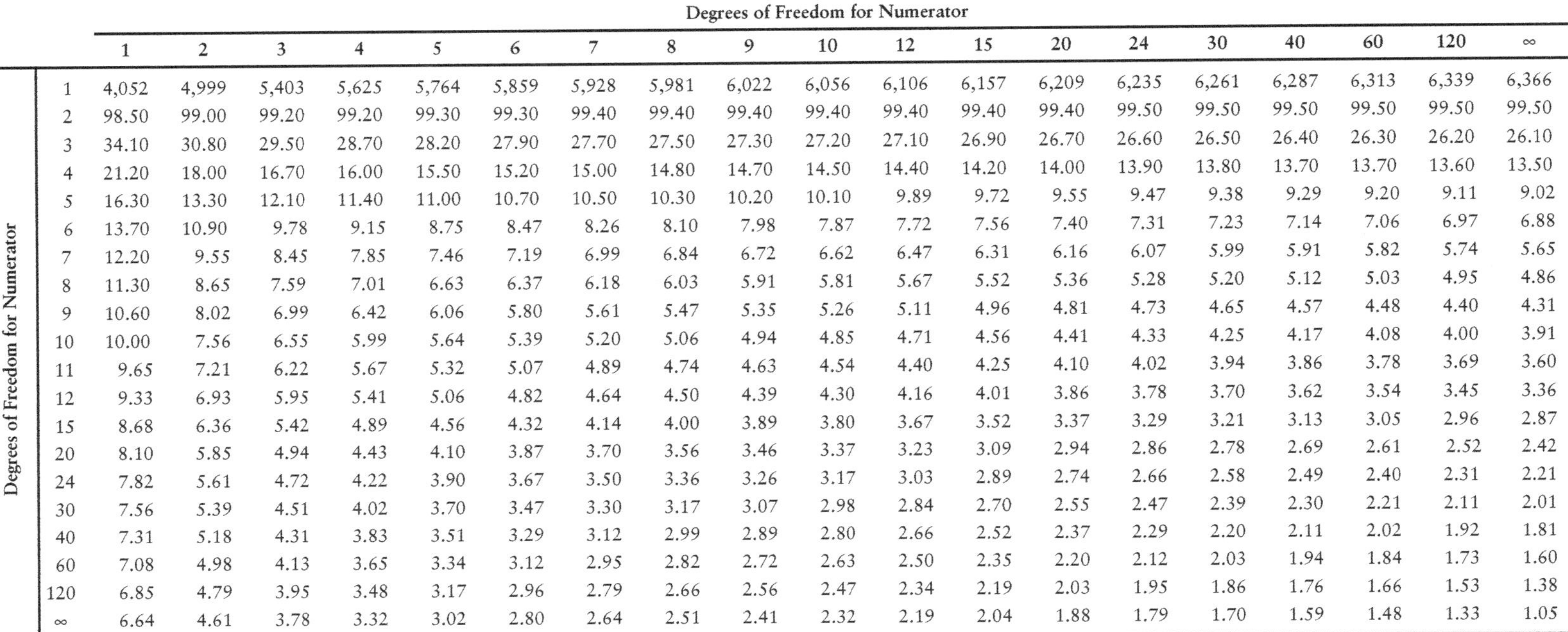

| Degrees of Freedom for Numerator | Degrees of Freedom for Numerator | | | | | | | | | | | | | | | | | | |
|---|---|---|---|---|---|---|---|---|---|---|---|---|---|---|---|---|---|---|---|
| | 1 | 2 | 3 | 4 | 5 | 6 | 7 | 8 | 9 | 10 | 12 | 15 | 20 | 24 | 30 | 40 | 60 | 120 | ∞ |
| 1 | 4,052 | 4,999 | 5,403 | 5,625 | 5,764 | 5,859 | 5,928 | 5,981 | 6,022 | 6,056 | 6,106 | 6,157 | 6,209 | 6,235 | 6,261 | 6,287 | 6,313 | 6,339 | 6,366 |
| 2 | 98.50 | 99.00 | 99.20 | 99.20 | 99.30 | 99.30 | 99.40 | 99.40 | 99.40 | 99.40 | 99.40 | 99.40 | 99.40 | 99.50 | 99.50 | 99.50 | 99.50 | 99.50 | 99.50 |
| 3 | 34.10 | 30.80 | 29.50 | 28.70 | 28.20 | 27.90 | 27.70 | 27.50 | 27.30 | 27.20 | 27.10 | 26.90 | 26.70 | 26.60 | 26.50 | 26.40 | 26.30 | 26.20 | 26.10 |
| 4 | 21.20 | 18.00 | 16.70 | 16.00 | 15.50 | 15.20 | 15.00 | 14.80 | 14.70 | 14.50 | 14.40 | 14.20 | 14.00 | 13.90 | 13.80 | 13.70 | 13.70 | 13.60 | 13.50 |
| 5 | 16.30 | 13.30 | 12.10 | 11.40 | 11.00 | 10.70 | 10.50 | 10.30 | 10.20 | 10.10 | 9.89 | 9.72 | 9.55 | 9.47 | 9.38 | 9.29 | 9.20 | 9.11 | 9.02 |
| 6 | 13.70 | 10.90 | 9.78 | 9.15 | 8.75 | 8.47 | 8.26 | 8.10 | 7.98 | 7.87 | 7.72 | 7.56 | 7.40 | 7.31 | 7.23 | 7.14 | 7.06 | 6.97 | 6.88 |
| 7 | 12.20 | 9.55 | 8.45 | 7.85 | 7.46 | 7.19 | 6.99 | 6.84 | 6.72 | 6.62 | 6.47 | 6.31 | 6.16 | 6.07 | 5.99 | 5.91 | 5.82 | 5.74 | 5.65 |
| 8 | 11.30 | 8.65 | 7.59 | 7.01 | 6.63 | 6.37 | 6.18 | 6.03 | 5.91 | 5.81 | 5.67 | 5.52 | 5.36 | 5.28 | 5.20 | 5.12 | 5.03 | 4.95 | 4.86 |
| 9 | 10.60 | 8.02 | 6.99 | 6.42 | 6.06 | 5.80 | 5.61 | 5.47 | 5.35 | 5.26 | 5.11 | 4.96 | 4.81 | 4.73 | 4.65 | 4.57 | 4.48 | 4.40 | 4.31 |
| 10 | 10.00 | 7.56 | 6.55 | 5.99 | 5.64 | 5.39 | 5.20 | 5.06 | 4.94 | 4.85 | 4.71 | 4.56 | 4.41 | 4.33 | 4.25 | 4.17 | 4.08 | 4.00 | 3.91 |
| 11 | 9.65 | 7.21 | 6.22 | 5.67 | 5.32 | 5.07 | 4.89 | 4.74 | 4.63 | 4.54 | 4.40 | 4.25 | 4.10 | 4.02 | 3.94 | 3.86 | 3.78 | 3.69 | 3.60 |
| 12 | 9.33 | 6.93 | 5.95 | 5.41 | 5.06 | 4.82 | 4.64 | 4.50 | 4.39 | 4.30 | 4.16 | 4.01 | 3.86 | 3.78 | 3.70 | 3.62 | 3.54 | 3.45 | 3.36 |
| 15 | 8.68 | 6.36 | 5.42 | 4.89 | 4.56 | 4.32 | 4.14 | 4.00 | 3.89 | 3.80 | 3.67 | 3.52 | 3.37 | 3.29 | 3.21 | 3.13 | 3.05 | 2.96 | 2.87 |
| 20 | 8.10 | 5.85 | 4.94 | 4.43 | 4.10 | 3.87 | 3.70 | 3.56 | 3.46 | 3.37 | 3.23 | 3.09 | 2.94 | 2.86 | 2.78 | 2.69 | 2.61 | 2.52 | 2.42 |
| 24 | 7.82 | 5.61 | 4.72 | 4.22 | 3.90 | 3.67 | 3.50 | 3.36 | 3.26 | 3.17 | 3.03 | 2.89 | 2.74 | 2.66 | 2.58 | 2.49 | 2.40 | 2.31 | 2.21 |
| 30 | 7.56 | 5.39 | 4.51 | 4.02 | 3.70 | 3.47 | 3.30 | 3.17 | 3.07 | 2.98 | 2.84 | 2.70 | 2.55 | 2.47 | 2.39 | 2.30 | 2.21 | 2.11 | 2.01 |
| 40 | 7.31 | 5.18 | 4.31 | 3.83 | 3.51 | 3.29 | 3.12 | 2.99 | 2.89 | 2.80 | 2.66 | 2.52 | 2.37 | 2.29 | 2.20 | 2.11 | 2.02 | 1.92 | 1.81 |
| 60 | 7.08 | 4.98 | 4.13 | 3.65 | 3.34 | 3.12 | 2.95 | 2.82 | 2.72 | 2.63 | 2.50 | 2.35 | 2.20 | 2.12 | 2.03 | 1.94 | 1.84 | 1.73 | 1.60 |
| 120 | 6.85 | 4.79 | 3.95 | 3.48 | 3.17 | 2.96 | 2.79 | 2.66 | 2.56 | 2.47 | 2.34 | 2.19 | 2.03 | 1.95 | 1.86 | 1.76 | 1.66 | 1.53 | 1.38 |
| ∞ | 6.64 | 4.61 | 3.78 | 3.32 | 3.02 | 2.80 | 2.64 | 2.51 | 2.41 | 2.32 | 2.19 | 2.04 | 1.88 | 1.79 | 1.70 | 1.59 | 1.48 | 1.33 | 1.05 |

**TABLE C.5** 5% significance points of $d_l$ and $d_u$ for Durbin-Watson test statistic.

| | $k = 1$ | | $k = 2$ | | $k = 3$ | | $k = 4$ | | $k = 5$ | |
|---|---|---|---|---|---|---|---|---|---|---|
| $n$ | $d_l$ | $d_u$ | $d_l$ | $d_u$ | $d_l$ | $d_u$ | $d_l$ | $d_u$ | $d_l$ | $d_u$ |
| 15 | 1.08 | 1.36 | 0.95 | 1.54 | 0.82 | 1.75 | 0.69 | 1.97 | 0.56 | 2.21 |
| 16 | 1.10 | 1.37 | 0.98 | 1.54 | 0.86 | 1.73 | 0.74 | 1.93 | 0.62 | 2.15 |
| 17 | 1.13 | 1.38 | 1.02 | 1.54 | 0.90 | 1.71 | 0.78 | 1.90 | 0.67 | 2.10 |
| 18 | 1.16 | 1.39 | 1.05 | 1.53 | 0.93 | 1.69 | 0.82 | 1.87 | 0.71 | 2.06 |
| 19 | 1.18 | 1.40 | 1.08 | 1.53 | 0.97 | 1.68 | 0.86 | 1.85 | 0.75 | 2.02 |
| 20 | 1.20 | 1.41 | 1.10 | 1.54 | 1.00 | 1.68 | 0.90 | 1.83 | 0.79 | 1.99 |
| 21 | 1.22 | 1.42 | 1.13 | 1.54 | 1.03 | 1.67 | 0.93 | 1.81 | 0.83 | 1.96 |
| 22 | 1.24 | 1.43 | 1.15 | 1.54 | 1.05 | 1.66 | 0.96 | 1.80 | 0.86 | 1.94 |
| 23 | 1.26 | 1.44 | 1.17 | 1.54 | 1.08 | 1.66 | 0.99 | 1.79 | 0.90 | 1.92 |
| 24 | 1.27 | 1.45 | 1.19 | 1.55 | 1.10 | 1.66 | 1.01 | 1.78 | 0.93 | 1.90 |
| 25 | 1.29 | 1.45 | 1.21 | 1.55 | 1.12 | 1.66 | 1.04 | 1.77 | 0.95 | 1.89 |
| 26 | 1.30 | 1.46 | 1.22 | 1.55 | 1.14 | 1.65 | 1.06 | 1.76 | 0.98 | 1.88 |
| 27 | 1.32 | 1.47 | 1.24 | 1.56 | 1.16 | 1.65 | 1.08 | 1.76 | 1.01 | 1.86 |
| 28 | 1.33 | 1.48 | 1.26 | 1.56 | 1.18 | 1.65 | 1.10 | 1.75 | 1.03 | 1.85 |
| 29 | 1.34 | 1.48 | 1.27 | 1.56 | 1.20 | 1.65 | 1.12 | 1.74 | 1.05 | 1.84 |
| 30 | 1.35 | 1.49 | 1.28 | 1.57 | 1.21 | 1.65 | 1.14 | 1.74 | 1.07 | 1.83 |
| 31 | 1.36 | 1.50 | 1.30 | 1.57 | 1.23 | 1.65 | 1.16 | 1.74 | 1.09 | 1.83 |
| 32 | 1.37 | 1.50 | 1.31 | 1.57 | 1.24 | 1.65 | 1.18 | 1.73 | 1.11 | 1.82 |
| 33 | 1.38 | 1.51 | 1.32 | 1.58 | 1.26 | 1.65 | 1.19 | 1.73 | 1.13 | 1.81 |
| 34 | 1.39 | 1.51 | 1.33 | 1.58 | 1.27 | 1.65 | 1.21 | 1.73 | 1.15 | 1.81 |
| 35 | 1.40 | 1.52 | 1.34 | 1.53 | 1.28 | 1.65 | 1.22 | 1.73 | 1.16 | 1.80 |
| 36 | 1.41 | 1.52 | 1.35 | 1.59 | 1.29 | 1.65 | 1.24 | 1.73 | 1.18 | 1.80 |
| 37 | 1.42 | 1.53 | 1.36 | 1.59 | 1.31 | 1.66 | 1.25 | 1.72 | 1.19 | 1.80 |
| 38 | 1.43 | 1.54 | 1.37 | 1.59 | 1.32 | 1.66 | 1.26 | 1.72 | 1.21 | 1.79 |
| 39 | 1.43 | 1.54 | 1.38 | 1.60 | 1.33 | 1.66 | 1.27 | 1.72 | 1.22 | 1.79 |
| 40 | 1.44 | 1.54 | 1.39 | 1.60 | 1.34 | 1.66 | 1.29 | 1.72 | 1.23 | 1.79 |
| 45 | 1.48 | 1.57 | 1.43 | 1.62 | 1.38 | 1.67 | 1.34 | 1.72 | 1.29 | 1.78 |
| 50 | 1.50 | 1.59 | 1.46 | 1.63 | 1.42 | 1.67 | 1.38 | 1.72 | 1.34 | 1.77 |
| 55 | 1.53 | 1.60 | 1.49 | 1.64 | 1.45 | 1.68 | 1.41 | 1.72 | 1.38 | 1.77 |
| 60 | 1.55 | 1.62 | 1.51 | 1.65 | 1.48 | 1.69 | 1.44 | 1.73 | 1.41 | 1.77 |
| 65 | 1.57 | 1.63 | 1.54 | 1.66 | 1.50 | 1.70 | 1.47 | 1.73 | 1.44 | 1.77 |
| 70 | 1.58 | 1.64 | 1.55 | 1.67 | 1.52 | 1.70 | 1.49 | 1.74 | 1.46 | 1.77 |
| 75 | 1.60 | 1.65 | 1.57 | 1.68 | 1.54 | 1.71 | 1.51 | 1.74 | 1.49 | 1.77 |
| 80 | 1.61 | 1.66 | 1.59 | 1.69 | 1.56 | 1.72 | 1.53 | 1.74 | 1.51 | 1.77 |
| 85 | 1.62 | 1.67 | 1.60 | 1.70 | 1.57 | 1.72 | 1.55 | 1.75 | 1.52 | 1.77 |
| 90 | 1.63 | 1.68 | 1.61 | 1.70 | 1.59 | 1.73 | 1.57 | 1.75 | 1.54 | 1.78 |
| 95 | 0.10 | 1.69 | 1.62 | 1.71 | 1.60 | 1.73 | 1.58 | 1.75 | 1.56 | 1.78 |
| 100 | 1.65 | 11.69 | 1.63 | 1.72 | 1.61 | 1.74 | 1.59 | 1.76 | 1.57 | 1.78 |

*Note:* $n$ is the number of observations, and $k$ is the number of explanatory variables including the intercept.
*Source:* J. Durbin and G.S. Watson, "Testing for Serial Correlation in Least Squares Regression," *Biometrika* 38 (1951), 159–177.

# D

# Glossary of Derivatives-Related Terms[1]

**accrued interest** The amount of coupon interest income accumulated on a coupon-bearing bond since the last coupon payment date.

**all-or-none (AON) order** An order that must be filled in its entirety or not at all.

**American option** See *American-style option.*

**American-style option** An option that can be exercised at any time up to and including the expiration day.

**amortizing swap** A swap whose notional principal decreases through time.

**anticipatory hedge** A hedge placed in anticipation of making a transaction in spot market on future date (e.g., a breakfast cereal producer may want to lock in the price of the grain that he needs three months from now).

**arbitrage** The simultaneous purchase or sale of perfect substitutes at different prices.

**arbitrager** Someone who engages in arbitrage.

**arbitrageur** Same as arbitrager.

**Asian option** An option whose payoff is determined by the average price of asset during specified period.

**ask price** The price at which a market maker stands ready to sell.

**asset allocation** The investment decision regarding how to allocate funds across different asset categories (e.g., stocks, bonds, commodities, real estate).

**asset-or-nothing option** An option whose payoff is the underlying asset contingent on the underlying asset price being greater than or less than the critical price.

**assignment** The procedure by which option seller is notified of buyer's intention to exercise.

**at-the-money** An option whose exercise price is approximately equal to current underlying asset price.

**automatic exercise** The automatic exercise of an in-the-money option at expiration made by clearinghouse.

**average option** See *Asian option.*

**backwardation** A futures market in which the futures prices decline monotonically from the nearby to the distant contract months.

**balance sheet risk** The risk from balance sheet entries' denominations in different currencies.

**bank discounts** See *discounts.*
**barrier option** An option whose payoff depends upon payoff to an ordinary option and whether a prespecified barrier has been touched or crossed (e.g., down-and-in, down-and-out, up-and-in, and up-and-out options).
**basis** The difference between spot price and futures price.
**basis mispricing** The difference between the actual and theoretical basis.
**basis point** One-hundredth of a percentage point (i.e., 0.01%).
**basis rate swap** An exchange of floating-rate cash flows from two securities.
**basis risk** The uncertainty in the comovements of the spot and future prices. Equals the sum of the grade and time basis.
**basis risk, grade** The uncertainty about futures prices of roughly comparable goods.
**basis risk, time** The uncertainty about the difference between the futures price and the underlying asset's price.
**bear market** A market in which prices are falling.
**bear spread** An option spread that increases in value as the underlying asset price falls.
**Bermuda option** An option that can be exercised at a fixed number of points during the option's life (i.e., Bermuda is between Europe and America).
**beta** A measure of the risk of a security or portfolio relative to the market as a whole.
**bid price** The price at which a market maker is willing to buy immediately.
**binary option** An option whose payoff is one dollar if the option expires in the money and zero otherwise.
**binomial model** An option pricing model in which the underlying asset moves discretely through the option's life. At each point in time, the underlying asset price moves up or down.
**Black model** A model for valuing European-style forward or futures options. Assumes that the underlying forward or futures price is lognormally distributed at the option's expiration.
**Black-Scholes model** A model for valuing European-style options on nondividend-paying stocks. Assumes that the underlying stock price is lognormally distributed at the option's expiration.
**block trade** The purchase or sale of at least 10,000 shares of stock in one trade.
**bond equivalent yield** A yield calculation based on a 365-day rather than a 360-day year to allow comparison between the T-bill and other Treasury securities.
**bond option** An option to buy or sell a bond.
**borrowing portfolio** A portfolio with a positive weight on the risky asset(s) and a negative weight on the risk-free asset.
**box** A spread involving buying a call and selling a put at one exercise price, and selling a call and buying a put at another. All four options have the same underlying asset and expiration date.
**brand new issue** The first time shares in a privately owned firm are sold to the public.
**breakeven asset price** The asset price at which a derivatives position has a zero profit.

**broker** A person who executes a transaction on behalf of a customer. The fee charged by the broker is usually called a commission and is usually quoted on a per contract basis.

**Brownian motion** A stochastic process whose increments are normally distributed with zero mean and variance proportional to time.

**bull spread** A spread that increases in value as the underlying asset price rises.

**butterfly spread** An option position consisting of one long call at a particular exercise price, another otherwise identical long call at a different exercise price, and two otherwise identical short calls at an exercise price between the other two.

**buy/write** Buying the asset and selling a call option written on the asset simultaneously.

**buyer (fixed-for-floating swaps)** The party that pays the fixed rate stream in a fixed-for-floating rate swap.

**buying collateral** Accepting the collateral for a loan in a repo contract.

**calculation amount** The notional amount upon which the interest payment cash flow is computed.

**calendar spread** An option position that consists of buying an option with a given expiration date and the sale of an otherwise identical option with a different expiration date.

**calibration** Empirical adjustment of model parameters to match observed market prices.

**call option** An option that provides the buyer with the right to purchase the underlying asset at a fixed price (i.e., the exercise price) within a specified period of time (i.e., the time remaining to expiration).

**callable bond** A bond whose issuer has the right to redeem the bond prior to its maturity date.

**callable swap** An interest rate swap in which one party has the right to cancel the swap at a certain time without any additional costs.

**cap** A contract between a borrower and lender whereby the borrower is assured that he will not have to pay more than some maximum interest rate on borrowed funds. This type of contract is analogous to a series of European interest rate call options.

**capital asset pricing model (CAPM)** A model that specifies the expected return on an asset as a function of the risk-free rate, the expected return on the market, and the asset's beta or systematic risk. The CAPM was originally developed by Sharpe (1964) and Lintner (1965).

**capital market line** The linear relation between expected return and risk for efficient portfolios.

**caplet** An interest rate cap contract for a specific instance of time.

**cash and carry** A trading strategy in which an asset is purchased with borrowed funds and a futures contract is sold. The position is held to the futures contract expiration.

**cash equivalent** The risk-free dollar amount that offers the same level of satisfaction as holding a risky position.

**cash market** See *spot market*.

**cash settlement** A settlement procedure whereby derivative contracts are settled in cash and without physical delivery.

**cash settlement** The difference between spot and forward price paid in cash at expiration. See *delivery settlement.*

**cash-or-nothing option** An option whose payoff is a fixed amount of cash contingent on the underlying asset price being greater than or less than the exercise price.

**catalytic cracking** The splitting of longer hydrocarbon chains into shorter, lighter gasoline using chemical catalytes.

**centralized market** A market that brings together buyers and sellers with the help of an intermediary, thereby lowering search costs.

**chart analysis** The use of graphs and charts to analyze historical prices and trading behavior in an attempt to predict future price movements.

**cheapest-to-deliver** The T-bond or T-note that, if delivered on the CBT's T-bond or T-note futures contract, has the smallest difference between the invoice price and the cost of the bond.

**chooser option** An option that provides its holder with the right to pick either a call option or a put option.

**circuit breaker** A trading halt in the stock market or stock index futures market precipitated by a large price change in the index or futures are large.

**clearinghouse** A firm that guarantees the performance of both parties to a derivative contract, collects margins, and maintains recorders of the parties to all transactions.

**cliquet option** See *ratchet option.*

**collar** A contract between a borrower and lender whereby the borrower is assured that he will not have to pay more than some maximum interest rate on borrowed funds and the lender is assured that he will not have to receive less than some minimum interest rate on lent funds. This type of contract is analogous to a series of European interest rate call and put options.

**commission** A fee paid to the broker for executing a trade. The commission is usually quoted on a per contract basis.

**commission broker** A trader who executes transactions for customers. The fee for his service is the commission rate.

**commodity** A physical asset such as wheat, gold or crude oil.

**commodity derivative** A derivative written on a commodity or physical asset.

**commodity fund** A professionally managed fund that trades commodity futures and option contracts.

**commodity futures** A futures contract written on a physical commodity (e.g., wheat, gold, crude oil).

**Commodity Futures Trading Commission (CFTC)** The federal agency that regulates futures and futures option trading in the United States.

**commodity option** An option contract written on a physical commodity. Since few such options exist, the term is most frequently used to describe an option on a commodity futures.

**commodity swap** A swap in which the cash flows on at least one leg are based on a commodity price.

**commodity trading advisor** An individual who specializes in offering advice regarding the trading of futures or futures options.

**compound option** An option on an option.

**compounding** The accumulation of value over time as earlier rate payments also earn the same rate of return as the initial investment.
**constant yield swap** An interest rate swap with two floating rate legs.
**contango** A futures market in which the futures prices rise monotonically from the nearby to the distant contract months.
**contingency order** An order that becomes effective only when a certain market condition is met.
**contingent-pay option** An option in which the premium is paid at expiration and only if the option being in the money.
**continuous compounding** A model under which interest accrues continuously, that is, the compounding periods grow arbitrarily small.
**continuous trading** A market in which trading takes place continuously in time.
**continuously compounded mean return** The logarithm of the expected return over a time period
**continuously compounded return, mean of** The expectation of the logarithm of the returns over a time period. Identical to the continuously compounded mean return if returns are not variable across time.
**contractual obligation** One whose terms cannot be altered.
**convenience value** The value of having a commodity in inventory for its use in production.
**convergence** The reduction in the futures basis as the spot and futures prices to come together as a futures contract approaches expiration.
**conversion** An arbitrage that consists of: (1) selling a call and (2) buying a synthetic call.
**conversion factor** An adjustment factor applied to the settlement price of the CBT's T-bond contract that converts the price of an eligible T-bond into the price of an 6% nominally required for delivery. Also applies to the CBT's T-note futures contract.
**convertible bond** A corporate bond that provides its holder with the right to convert the bond into shares of the firm at a fixed rate.
**convexity** A measure of a bond's price sensitivity to changes in the bond's yield.
**corner** A market situation in which a trader or group of traders attempt to acquire the available supply of an asset.
**cost of carry** The cost of holding an asset. This includes interest cost plus (less) any costs (benefits) from holding the asset (e.g., warehouse rent and insurance for physical assets and dividend income and coupon payments for financial assets).
**costless arbitrage** A self-financing arbitrage strategy.
**counterparty** The opposite party in a derivative contract.
**counterparty risk** The risk that a counterparty will default.
**coupon** The periodic (usually semiannual) interest payment on a coupon-bearing bond.
**coupon bond** Same as *coupon-bearing bond.*
**coupon rate** The stated interest rate on a coupon-bearing bond.
**coupon swap** See *fixed-for-floating rate swap.*
**coupon-bearing bond** A bond that has periodic coupon payments as well as repayment of principal at maturity.
**covariance** A statistical measure of the association between two random variables.

**covered call** Trading strategy that consists (1) buying the underlying asset, and (2) selling a call option. Also called *buy-write.*

**covered write** Same as *covered call.*

**crack spread** A spread that consists of: (1) buying (selling) crude oil futures and (2) selling (buying) heating oil or gasoline futures.

**credit derivative** An agreement concerning the transfer of credit risk between a buyer and seller of this protection.

**credit event** Any event related to a credit risk realization.

**credit risk** The risk of a loss arising from default or credit downgrade of a counterparty.

**credit-linked note** A composite security structured to behave like a particular reference security.

**cross-hedging** Any hedge where the asset being hedged is not the specific asset underlying the futures contract.

**cross-rate option** A foreign currency option where the numeraire is not dollars, but a foreign currency.

**cross-rate relation** Same as *triangular arbitrage.*

**crush spread** A spread that consists of: (1) buying (selling) soybean futures and (2) selling (buying) soybean oil or soymeal futures.

**crushing** Processing soybeans into soybean oil and soy meal.

**cubic spline interpolation** An interpolation method with a piecewise-defined interpolant of polynomials of the third degree.

**cum-dividend** A stock trading before a cash dividend is paid.

**currency option** An option to buy currency.

**currency swap** A swap in which the interest payments on at least one leg are tied to a foreign currency.

**daily price limit** An exchange-imposed rule governing the maximum absolute daily price movement on a futures contract.

**daily settlement** Same as *marking-to-market.*

**day order** An order that is canceled if it is not filled by the end of the trading day.

**day trader** A trader who closes out all positions by the close of the trading day.

**dealer** A person or firm who makes a market in a particular asset or derivative contract.

**deep market** A market in which large trades can be executed with little impact on price.

**default-free** An asset with no risk of default (e.g., U.S. Treasury securities).

**deferred swap** Same as a *forward swap.*

**delivery** Closing a derivative contract position by delivering the asset specified in the contract (e.g., a trader who is short wheat futures at the futures expiration must deliver the wheat to the trader who is long the futures contract).

**delivery date** The date on which the underlying asset is exchanged for cash payment.

**delivery month** The calendar month during which delivery on a futures contract must be made.

**delivery settlement** The conclusion of a forward contract through the exchange of physical underlying commodity at set price on expiration.

**delta** The change in the option's model value induced by a change in the underlying asset price.

**delta-neutral** A portfolio whose value is insensitive to movements in the asset price.

**derivative** Same as *derivative contract.*

**derivative contract** A financial contract that specifies the terms of a future transaction (or set of transactions) in some underlying asset. The term, "derivative," arises because the value of this contract is "derived" from the underlying asset price.

**Designated Order Turnaround (DOT)** The NYSE's system for expediting stock transactions.

**diagonal spread** An option spread in which the options on the same underlying asset differ by both time to expiration and exercise price.

**digital option** See *binary option.*

**dilution factor** The proportion of the firm owned by warrant holders if they exercise their warrants.

**discount** The method of quoting U.S. Treasury bill prices.

**discount bond** A zero-coupon bond.

**discount factor** The present value of one dollar to be received at a future date.

**dividend** A cash payment made to common stock holder.

**dividend capture** A strategy of buying the stock before a dividend issue and selling immediately after, capturing part of the dividend payment.

**dividend declaration date** The date of a dividend announcement.

**dividend payment date** The date on which a declared dividend is paid.

**dividend protection** A feature on an over-the-counter stock option whereby the exercise price is reduced by the amount of the dividend on an ex-dividend day.

**dividend yield** The cash dividends paid on a stock or stock index expressed as a percentage of the stock price or index level.

**doubling** A gambling strategy to double the amount bet each time a loss occurs.

**down-and-in option** An option that becomes a standard option only if the price of the underlying asset falls below the barrier. Otherwise, it expires worthless.

**down-and-out option** A standard option that becomes worthless if the price of the underlying asset falls below the barrier. Otherwise, it expires normally.

**downtick** A price decrease equal to one tick.

**dual trading** The practice of a floor trader on a futures exchange trading for a customer as well as on his or her own account.

**duration** The weighted average of the maturities of the bond's cash flows, where the weights are the fractions of the bond's price that the cash flows in each time period represent. Equals the percent change in bond price for an infinitely small change in yield.

**DV01** Equals the change in bond price if the yield changes by one basis point.

**dynamic hedge** A hedge strategy maintained by dynamically rebalancing portfolio weights.

**dynamic portfolio insurance** Portfolio insurance by synthetically creating a put

**early exercise** Exercising an American option prior to the expiration date.

**early exercise premium** The economic value of the right to exercise an American-style option early. Equals the difference between the value of an American-style option and an otherwise comparable European-style option.

**effective date** The first day of the term of a contract made between two parties.

**effective interest rate** The annualized rate of interest on an investment that has multiple compounding periods per year.
**efficient portfolio** A portfolio that has the lowest risk for a given level of expected return.
**employee stock option** A call option on the firm's stock awarded to an employee.
**employee stock purchase plan** An award given to employees that provides the right to buy the firm's stock at a discount.
**end-of-month option** The right to deliver any day during the last remaining business days of the month after the futures contract has ceased trading.
**equity basis swap** An exchange of cash flows from two different equity indices.
**equity option** An option on an individual stock or a stock index.
**equity swap** A swap in which one leg involves a series of cash flows that are linked to equity.
**errors-in-the-variables problem** The effect of measurement errors in the independent variables on the t-statistics of an OLS regression.
**eta** The percentage change in the option's model value induced by a percentage change in the underlying asset price.
**Eurodollar** See *Eurodollar time deposit.*
**Eurodollar contracts** Derivative contracts written on Eurodollar time deposits.
**Eurodollar futures contract** Futures contract written on a Eurodollar time deposit.
**Eurodollar time deposit** U.S. dollar deposit in a European bank.
**European Currency Unit (ECU)** A composite measure of a U.S. dollar exchange rate based on a weighted-average of European currency rates.
**European option** See *European-style option.*
**European-style option** An option that can be exercised only at expiration.
**exchange option** The right to exchange one asset for another.
**exchange rate** The rate at which a unit of one currency is exchanged for another.
**ex-dividend date** The date on which a stock trades without its current dividend embedded in price.
**exercise** Refers to the option holder executing his right. A call option holder, for example, "exercises" by notifying his broker and paying the exercise price in cash. In return, he receives the underlying asset.
**exercise price** The price at which the underlying asset is bought or sold if the option is exercised.
**exotic option** An option whose terms are nonstandard.
**expectations theory** A term structure theory under which forward rates are the market's expectation of future spot rates.
**expected recovery value** The amount a bondholder expects to receive in the event of default.
**expected utility of terminal wealth** The "best guess" of an agent's utility of wealth after the realization of payoffs.
**expected value** The "best guess" of the future value of an asset.
**expiration** The time and date on which the derivative contract expires.
**expiration date** The date on which the derivative contract expires.
**ex-split date** The date on which the stock split takes effect.
**extendible bond** A bond whose holder has an option to extend its term-to-maturity.
**face value** The principal amount of a bond repaid at the bond's maturity.

**fair bet** A gamble that has an expected outcome of zero.

**fair value** Same as theoretical value or model value.

**feasibility** Whether an outcome of an objective function is possible under the given constraints.

**fill-or-kill (FOK) order** An order that must be filled immediately and in its entirety. Failing this, the order is canceled.

**financial asset** See *security.*

**financial futures** A futures contract written on a financial asset (e.g., stocks, bonds, foreign currencies).

**fixed-against-floating swap** See *fixed-for-floating rate swap.*

**fixed-for-floating rate swap** An exchange of a fixed rate cash flow and a floating rate between two parties.

**fixed income securities** A security with prespecified interest payments (e.g., a coupon-bearing bond).

**flat volatility** A forward volatility curve that is invariant with respect to maturity.

**floating rate note** A bond that pays interest based on a floating interest rate.

**floating rate option** An option on a floating rate cash flow such as LIBOR.

**floating rate, day-count fraction** The fraction of a year equal to a bond's designated maturity.

**floor** A contract between a borrower and lender whereby the lender is assured that he will not have to receive less than some minimum interest rate on lent funds. This type of contract is analogous to a series of European interest rate put options.

**floor broker** A trader who executes orders on behalf of customers on the floor of an exchange.

**floor trader** A member of an exchange who trades on the floor of the exchange.

**floorlet** An interest rate floor contract for a specific instance in time.

**foreign currency derivatives** Derivative contracts written on foreign currency spot exchange rates (e.g., forwards, futures, options, swaps).

**forward commitment** See *forward contract.*

**forward contract** A financial contract that requires its buyer to purchase an underlying asset at a fixed price on a fixed future date. No cash flows is paid until the delivery date.

**forward curve** The relation between forward prices and maturity.

**forward discount factor** A discount factor for a cash flow at a future date.

**forward exchange rate** The value one unit of a currency in terms of another (e.g., the U.S. dollar cost of one British pound (the "USD/GBP" exchange rate) might be 1.60 USD, while the British pound cost of a U.S. dollar (the "GBP/USD" exchange rate) is 0.625 GBP).

**forward market** A market in which forward contracts are traded.

**forward option** An option on a forward contract.

**forward premium** A positive difference between the forward price and the current spot price.

**forward price** The delivery price written in a forward contract.

**forward rate of interest** An interest rate on a loan that begins at a future date.

**forward swap** A forward contract to enter into a swap.

**forward transaction** An exchange agreement to take place in the future. See *forward contract.*

**forward volatility** The volatility of forward interest rates.
**forward volatility curve** The relation between forward volatilities and maturity.
**forward start option** An option contract that begins at a future date.
**forward start swap** An interest rate swap that begins at a future date.
**fractional distillation** The process of splitting crude oil into various hydrocarbons such as gasoline by the boiling point properties of each compound.
**frictionless markets** Markets that operate without trading impediments such as transaction costs or position limits.
**front-running** Trading ahead of someone who has private information or an order size that is likely to move the current market price.
**full carry** The term used to describe the relation between the futures price and the spot price when the futures prices equals exactly the spot price plus the costs of carry.
**fundamental analysis** Predicting price movements based on the fundamental factors influencing an asset's value.
**Futures commission merchant** A firm in the business of executing futures and/or futures options transactions for customers.
**futures contract** An agreement between two parties, a buyer and a seller, to exchange an asset or currency at a later date at price fixed today. Distinguished from a forward contract by virtue of the futures exchange's daily settlement procedure (i.e., marking to market).
**futures option** An option to buy or sell a futures contract.
**futures price** The delivery price written in a futures contract.
**futures-style settlement** A settlement procedure used by an exchange in which buying a contract requires no immediate cash outlay. Cash settlement is made daily based on the change in the contract price.
**gamma** The change in the option's delta induced by a change in the asset price.
**gamma-neutral** A portfolio whose delta is insensitive to movements in the asset price.
**gap option** An option under which the payoff amount and the payoff occurrence are determined by two separate constants.
**Garman-Kohlhagen model** A model for valuing European-style foreign currency options.
**GLOBEX** The CME's automated trading system in which bids and offers are entered into a computer and executed electronically.
**going long** To buy.
**going short** To sell.
**gold forward rate (GOFO)** The difference between the risk-free interest rate and the lease rate on gold.
**good-till-cancelled (GTC) order** An order that remains in effect until cancelled. Usually used with stop orders or limit orders.
**grade** A measure of a commodity's quality.
**Greeks** The sensitivities of option values to changes in its input parameters.
**gross (processing) margin** The difference between the revenue from and costs of producing.
**guarantee** A contract in which the seller accepts the responsibility of the buyer's payment obligation in case of default.
**guts** A strangle where both the call and the put are in-the-money.

**haircut** Lending a fraction of the collateral's value in a repo to protect the lender.
**hedge** A trade that reduces the risk of the individual or firm's current position.
**hedge position** Selling (buying) the futures while holding a long (short) position in the underlying.
**hedger** A trader who attempts to reduce his risk.
**hedging** Reduce risk.
**historical volatility** Volatility estimated using historical return data.
**holding period** The time period over which a portfolio is held.
**horizontal option spread** Buying and selling call or put options with the same exercise price but different expiration dates.
**horizontal spread** Same as *calendar spread.*
**hybrid** A derivatives contract that has characteristics of multiple basic derivatives.
**immediate-or-cancel (IOC) order** An order that must be filled immediately or it will be canceled. IOC orders need not be filled in their entirety.
**immunization** A bond portfolio hedging strategy designed to immunize the bond portfolio value from changes in the level of interest rates.
**implicit volatility** See *implied volatility.*
**implied financing cost** The difference between the minimum share price and the cash advance amount in a variable prepaid forward contract.
**implied forward discount factor** A discount factor implied by two spot discount factors at different maturities.
**implied forward rate** A forward rate of interest implied by two spot rates of different maturities (e.g., the forward rate on a one-year loan in one year is implied by the prevailing spot rates on a one-year and a two-year loan).
**implied repo rate** The cost of financing a cash-and-carry position implied by the relation between a T-bond and a *t*-bond futures contract.
**implied standard deviation (ISD)** See *implied volatility.*
**implied volatility** The standard deviation of asset return obtained by setting the market price of an option equal to the value given by a particular option pricing model.
**index amortized swap** An interest rate swap whose notional amount is amortized over the life of the swap.
**index arbitrage** The arbitrage between a stock index futures and the portfolio of stocks that underlie the futures.
**index option** An option whose underlying asset is an index.
**index participations** Securities that behave as if they were units in a particular stock index portfolio.
**initial margin** The minimum amount of money that a customer must deposit with his or her futures broker to establish a futures or options position. Margin is required to guarantee that a customer honor his or her contract obligations and may be deposited in the form of interest-bearing securities.
**institutional customer** A customer that is a firm or a fund rather than an individual investor. See also *retail customer.*
**interbank** Business transactions conducted between banks.
**interest rate cap** An OTC contract that protects a borrower from floating rates above a certain level.
**interest rate collar** Buying an interest rate cap and selling an interest rate floor.

**interest rate derivative** A derivative security whose value depends on the level of or the difference between interest rates.
**interest rate floor** An OTC contract that protects a lender from floating rates below a certain level.
**interest rate futures** A futures contract on an interest rate instrument.
**interest rate option** An option contract on an interest rate instrument.
**interest rate parity** An arbitrage relation that holds between foreign currency spot prices and interest rates.
**interest rate parity** An arbitrage relation equating the forward premium or discount on an exchange rate to the difference between the short-term interest rates in the two countries.
**interest rate swap** A swap in which interest payments are exchanged.
**intermarket spread** A spread with derivatives on different, but related, underlying assets.
**internal rate of return** The interest rate that equates the present value of the future cash flows with the market price (e.g., the yield to maturity on a coupon-bearing bond).
**in-the-money** A call (put) option whose exercise price is less (greater) than the underlying asset price.
**intracommodity spread** A spread between two futures contracts written on the same commodity but with different delivery months.
**intrinsic value** The amount by which an option is in-the-money or zero, whichever is greater.
**invoice price** The actual price that a T-bond futures buyer pays to the seller at delivery.
**Johnson-Shad Agreement** The 1982 agreement between CFTC chairman Phillip McBryde Johnson and SEC chairman John Shad providing trading in stock futures.
**kappa** See *vega*.
**lambda** See *vega*.
**last trade price** The price of the last transaction of the day.
**lattice** A tree that models the movement of asset prices or interest rates through time in discrete jumps.
**law of one price** The economic principle that two identical assets must have the same price.
**lease rate** The interest paid on a physical asset borrowed.
**leg** One side of an arbitrage or spread position.
**lending portfolio** A portfolio with positive weight on the risk-free asset as well as the risky asset(s).
**leverage** Borrowing to finance the purchase of an asset.
**leveraged swap** A swap whose fluctuations can exceed the notional amount.
**limit down** Maximum allowable daily price decrease for an exchange-traded contract.
**limit move** Maximum allowable daily price movement for an exchange-traded contract.
**limit order** An order to be filled at a specified price or better.
**limit up** Maximum allowable daily price increase for an exchange-traded contract.

**linear interpolation** A weighted average of two endpoints as an estimation of some point in the line segment between them.
**liquid market** A market in which trades can be executed quickly.
**liquidity** See liquid market.
**liquidity preference theory** A term structure theory in which long-term rates exceed short-term rates because lender preference for short-term loans.
**local** Another name for a market maker on a futures or futures option exchange.
**locked market** A market in which trading has been suspended because prices have reached their limit.
**lognormal distribution** A probability-distribution for a random variable $x$ such that the natural logarithm of $x$ has a normal distribution.
**London Interbank Offer Rate (LIBOR)** The interest rate on a Eurodollar time deposit.
**long** A position created by buying.
**long hedge** A hedge involving a short position in the spot market and a long position in the futures.
**long-term equity anticipation securities (LEAPS)** Options on stocks and stock indexes with times to expiration of more than one year.
**lookback call option** An option whose payoff at expiration is the asset price less the minimum price that the asset has had over the life of the option.
**lookback put option** An option whose payoff at expiration is the maximum price that the asset has had over the life of the option less than asset price.
**lower bound** An arbitrage relation governing the lowest possible price of an option.
**macrohedge** A hedge of the firm's combined risk exposure of all of its assets and liabilities.
**maintenance margin** The minimum amount of money that must be kept in a margin account on any day other than the day of a transaction.
**margin** Funds deposited in a margin account to ensure contract performance.
**margin call** A demand for additional margin funds.
**margining system** The requirement of a good-faith collateral deposit upon entering a futures position for both parties.
**market efficiency** A market in which the price of an asset reflects its true economic value.
**market frictions** Conditions in the market that restrict trading (e.g., trading costs, price limits, up-tick rules).
**market integrity** The safe, fair, and efficient operation of markets to encourage investor participation.
**market maker** Someone who stands ready to immediately buy (at the bid price) or sell (at the ask price).
**market order** An order to be filled immediately at the current market price.
**market portfolio** The portfolio consisting of all risky assets in the market.
**market price of risk** The premium investors demand to bear risk.
**market segmentation theory** A term structure theory based on the supply and demand in long-term and short-term interest rate markets.
**market timing** A trading strategy based on predicting the directional moves in the underlying asset price.
**market transparency** See *transparency*.

**market-if-touched (MIT) order** An order that becomes a market order if price touches or crosses a pre-specified level.

**market-indexed security** A derivative contract that pays a minimum return plus a given percentage of any change in the market above a certain level.

**market-on-close (MOC) order** An order to be filled close as possible to the close of trading.

**Markowitz efficiency frontier** The set of risk-minimizing portfolios for a range of return levels.

**mark-to-market** See *daily settlement.*

**maturity date** See *expiration date.*

**microhedge** A hedge of an individual asset's (rather the firm's overall) risk exposure.

**minimum selling price** The lowest price the agent would be willing to accept for his position.

**minimum variance hedge** See *optimal hedge.*

**money market** The market for short-term securities.

**money market hedge** A hedge by switching currencies.

**money spread** A spread that consists of: (1) buying one option and (2) selling an otherwise identical option with a different exercise price.

**Monte Carlo simulation** A probabilistic simulation of the possible changes in the price of an asset over a period of time.

**multiple listing** A security or derivative contract that is traded on more than one exchange.

**naked** A long or short position with no offsetting hedge.

**naked call** See *uncovered call.*

**naked option position** An option position with no offsetting hedge.

**natural hedge** An endogenous negative correlation that reduces revenue risk such as the relationship between price and quantity.

**nearby contract** The futures contract with the shortest time to expiration.

**net cost of carry** The difference between the benefits and costs associated with holding an asset through time.

**net cost of carry relation** The comparison between buying the asset in the futures market and holding it by buying at the spot.

**net present value** The present value of an investment's cash flows less the initial cost of the investment.

**netting** Aggregating all payments between two counterparties.

**no-arbitrage pricing models** Models based on the premise that securities with identical payoffs should have identical values.

**nonlinear programming problem** The mathematical process of maximizing (minimizing) an objective function bounded by a system of equalities and inequalities.

**nonstandard option** An exotic option.

**normal distribution** The standard bell-shaped probability distribution.

**notional principal** The principal amount a loan or a bond.

**obligation to pay fixed** The reference for terms "buyer" and "seller" in fixed-for-floating swaps. See buyer, seller (fixed-for-floating rate swap).

**offset** See *offsetting order.*

**offsetting order** A liquidating trade that has exactly the opposite terms of an outstanding position.
**omega** Same as *vega*.
**one-cancels-the-other (OCO) order** Two orders submitted simultaneously. If either is filled, the other is canceled.
**open interest** The number of derivative contracts that have been established and not yet been offset or exercised.
**open outcry** Trading in a pit in which bids and offers are indicated by shouting.
**optimal hedge** The number of derivative contracts that should be bought or sold in order to minimize the risk of changes in the value of the overall portfolio.
**option** A contract that provides the right to buy or sell an asset at a specified price (i.e., the exercise price) over a specified period (i.e., the time remaining to expiration).
**option class** All of the options of a particular type (call or put) on a given stock, index, currency, or futures commodity.
**option contract** See *option*.
**option on futures** See *futures option*.
**option premium** The price of an option.
**option series** One of the options within an option class. Uniquely identified by (1) the option type (call or put), (2) the exercise price, and (3) the expiration day.
**option type** An option is designated as either a call or a put.
**option writer** Someone who sells an option.
**options clearing corporation (OCC)** The firm that operates as the clearinghouse for U.S. option exchanges.
**order book official (OBO)** An exchange official responsible for opening rotation and maintaining the limit order book.
**ordinary least squares** An optimization technique to find the best fit line through a set of points.
**OTC derivatives** Derivatives traded in the over-the-counter market, that is, negotiated between private parties.
**out trade** A trade made on an exchange that cannot processed due to conflicting terms reported by the two parties involved in the trade.
**out-of-the-money** A call (put) option whose exercise price is greater (less) than the underlying asset price.
**outright position** A position involving only the future contract, but not the underlying or related securities.
**overnight repo** A repurchase agreement with a maturity of one night. See also *repo*.
**overpriced** A condition in which the market price of a security or derivative exceeds its model value.
**over-the-counter (OTC) market** A market for securities or derivatives not conducted on an organized exchange.
**overwrite** Sale of call option against an existing asset position.
**par bond yield** The coupon interest rate that makes the bond price equal its face value. The yield-to-maturity equals the coupon rate if the bond is selling at par.
**par bond yield curve** The relation between par bond yields and their terms to maturity.
**par grade** The standard grade of the commodity underlying the futures contract.

**par swap rate** The fixed rate on a plain vanilla interest rate swap that sets the value of the swap to zero.
**par value** See *face value.*
**partial expectation** An expectation taken conditionally.
**participation percentage** The percentage of asset return earned by the holder of participation derivative.
**passive hedge** A hedge that consists of buying/selling derivatives and holding them to expiration.
**passive portfolio insurance** Portfolio insurance by buying an index put option.
**path dependent option** An option whose value depends upon the path that the underlying asset prices takes over over the life of the option.
**paylater option** See *contingent option.*
**payoff** The amount of money received from a transaction at the end of the holding period.
**perfect substitute** An asset that is the equivalent of (and can thus be substituted for) another.
**physical asset** See *commodity.*
**pit** An octagonally or hexagonally shaped, multi-tiered station on a trading floor where a specific group of contracts trade.
**plain vanilla interest rate swap** An interest rate swap where one side receives fixed-rate payments and pays floating rate, and the other side receives the floating rate and pays the fixed rate.
**portfolio** A set of securities.
**portfolio insurance** Index option trading strategy designed to provide a minimum or floor value of a portfolio at a future date.
**portfolio theory** The study of how individuals choose to allocate their wealth among risky assets.
**position** The composition of a trader's portfolio.
**position limit** An exchange rule limiting the maximum number of contracts an individual can hold.
**position trader** A trader who typically holds a position for longer than a day.
**preferred habitat theory** See *market segmentation theory.*
**futures premium** The difference between the futures and spot index prices assuming open markets.
**option premium** The price of an option.
**price limit** An exchange rule limiting the maximum price increase or decrease on a particular contract during one trading day.
**price risk** The risk of not knowing the level of price at some future date.
**primary market** The market for assets when they are originally issued and not previously traded among the public. In contrast to secondary market.
**profit diagram** A figure showing the profit of a derivative position at expiration.
**program trading** The simultaneous purchase or sale of a portfolio of securities (usually stocks). Usually requires the use of computers and high-speed communications lines.
**protected equity note** A discount bond-like contract providing a guaranteed rate of return on the principal plus a fraction of upside return on an underlying such as a stock index. Also known as a principal-protected note, capital guarantee note, safe return certificate, equity-linked note, or index-linked note.

**protective put** An investment strategy involving buying a put to limit possible declines in the price of the underlying asset.

**pure discount bond** See *discount bond.*

**put option** An option that provides the buyer with the right to sell the underlying asset at a fixed price (i.e., the exercise price) within a specified period of time (i.e., the time remaining to expiration).

**putable swap** An interest rate swap where one side has an opportunity to cancel the swap.

**put-call parity** An arbitrage relation linking the prices of a call, a put with the same exercise price, and the underlying asset.

**quadratic approximation** A numerical method for approximating the value of American-style options. See Barone-Adesi and Whaley (1987).

**quality option** An option that provides the right to deliver any one of a number of eligible assets.

**quantity risk** The risk of not knowing the quantity of an asset at some future date.

**quoted bid-ask spread** The difference between the market maker's ask and bid price quotes.

**ratchet option** A sequence of forward-start options.

**rate capped swap** An interest rate swap in which the floating rate is capped.

**ratio spread** A spread in which the number of contracts is chosen in such a way that the overall position is delta-neutral.

**ratio swap** A swap contract where the effective interest rate is determined by a ratio of two other rates.

**ratio vertical spread** A ratio spread in which more contracts are sold than are purchased, with all contracts having the same underlying and expiration date.

**real asset** A tangible asset such as real estate or a natural resource.

**replicating portfolio** A portfolio of assets which replicates the cash flows of a derivative contract.

**repo** See *repurchase agreement.*

**repurchase agreement (repo)** An agreement between two parties under which one party agrees to sell and then later buy a security on an agreed-upon date and at an agreed-upon price. The difference between the original sale price and the subsequent repurchase price is in effect the interest on a loan, which, when expressed as an interest rate, is commonly known as the repo rate.

**reset date** The date on which the floating rate on an interest rate swap is reset.

**retail automatic execution system (RAES)** A computerized system used by the CBOE to expedite the filling of public orders.

**retail customer** A customer that is an individual rather than a firm or a fund. See also institutional customer.

**retractable bond** A bond whose holder can choose to redeem prior maturity.

**reversal** See reverse conversion.

**reverse conversion** An arbitrage that consists of (1) buying a call and (2) selling a synthetic call.

**reverse crush spread** The opposite of a crush spread, selling soybean futures and buying soy product futures.

**reverse repo (reverse)** See *reverse repurchase agreement.*

**reverse repurchase agreement** The counterparty's position in a repo transaction, lending the asset in question.

**reversing in** See *buying collateral.*
**reversing out** See *selling collateral.*
**rho (carry)** The change in the option's delta induced by a change in the cost-of-carry rate.
**rho (carry)-neutral** A portfolio whose delta is insensitive to movements in the cost-of-carry rate.
**rho (interest)** The change in the option's delta induced by a change in the interest rate.
**rho (interest)-neutral** A portfolio whose delta is insensitive to movements in the interest rate.
**rights** See *warrants.*
**risk aversion** The characteristic that, holding other factors constant, individuals want to avoid risk.
**risk preferences** An investor's attitude toward risk.
**risk premium** The additional return risk-averse investors expect for assuming risk.
**risk tolerance** The maximum amount of risk measurable in standard deviations that an investor is willing to take.
**risk-free rate** A default-free interest rate.
**riskless rate** A default-free interest rate.
**risk-minimizer** An investor who minimizes portfolio risk.
**risk-neutral investor** An investor who is indifferent toward risk.
**risk-neutral valuation** Computing the value of an asset or derivative contract under the assumption that investors are risk-neutral.
**Roll model** An American-style call option model with one known dividend paid on the underlying stock.
**sale-repurchase agreement** See *repurchase agreement.*
**scalper** An exchange trader who attempts to profit by buying at the bid and selling at the offer.
**scratch trade** A zero-profit trade designed to adjust a dealer's inventory.
**seasoned new issue** An additional issue of already publicly traded securities.
**seat** A term used to refer to a membership on an exchange.
**secondary market** The market for assets that were issued previously.
**Securities Exchange Commission (SEC)** The federal agency responsible for regulating securities markets and listed option markets in the United States.
**security** A certificate of ownership of an investment.
**security market line** The linear relation between expected return and market risk for individual securities and derivatives. One of the results of the capital asset pricing model.
**self-financing trading strategy** A trading strategy that has no cash inflows or outflows prior to its liquidation.
**seller (fixed-for-floating swaps)** The party that pays the floating interest rate stream in a fixed-for-floating rate swap.
**selling collateral** The buyer's selling of securities to provide collateral for the loan in a repo.
**series** See *option series.*
**settlement price** The end-of-day price established by the exchange clearinghouse used in marking-to-market futures contract positions.

**shareholder record date** The date at which an individual must have held the stock in order to receive an announced dividend.
**short** A position created by selling.
**short hedge** A hedge involving a long position in the spot market and a short position in the futures.
**short sale** A trading strategy in which an investor borrows a security from a broker and sells the security. At a later date, the investor buys back the security and returns it to the broker.
**short squeeze** A speculative strategy that manipulates prices by making it difficult for agents with a short futures position to unwind through the purchase of large amounts of both the underlying commodity and related futures contracts. Recall that a short futures position may be exited by either delivering the underlying, or going long an offsetting number of futures. Once demand for these securities drives prices up, the party attempting the short squeeze can realize gains by selling.
**short volatility** A portfolio with a negative vega that will decrease in value if volatility increases.
**simple interest rate** An interest rate which does not include compounding.
**simple return** The income from holding a security divided by its initial cost.
**specialist** A market maker given exclusive rights by an exchange to make a market in a specified asset.
**speculation** A trading position established to profit from a directional move in the price of an asset.
**speculative bubble** A rapid increase in price due to a rush of buyers unrelated to fundamental qualities of a security but hoping to profit from the price trend.
**speculative gain** A profit made on a strategy that relies on a directional price move.
**speculator** A trader who hopes to profit from a directional move in the price of an asset.
**spot exchange rate** The current rate of exchange of one unit of a currency for another.
**spot market** The market for an asset that involves the immediate sale and delivery of the asset.
**spot price** The price on an asset for immediate delivery.
**spot rate** An interest rate on a loan that begins immediately.
**spread** A trading strategy that consists of buying one contract and selling another similar contract.
**spreader** A trader who engages in spread transactions.
**stack hedge** A hedge in which short-term futures contracts are used to hedge long-term commitments.
**Standard and Poor's 500 Index (S&P 500)** A market-value weighted stock price index consisting of 500 NYSE, AMEX, and NASDAQ-traded stocks.
**standard deviation** A measure of the dispersion of a random variable around its mean. It is equal to the square root of the variance.
**standard option** An ordinary call or put option.
**static hedge** See *passive hedge*.
**stock dividend** A dividend paid with additional shares of the stock.
**stock index** An index created from the prices of a specific portfolio of stocks.

**stock index futures** A futures contract written on a stock index.
**stock index option** An option contract on a stock index.
**stock option** An option contract on a common stock.
**stock price collar** Avoiding some of the downside risk of stock ownership by financing out-of-the-money put purchases with out-of-the-money call sales, while enjoying other benefits of ownership like voting rights and dividend payments.
**stock split** A situation where a company reduces its share price and increases its number of shares outstanding by issuing additional shares on a pro rata basis to each existing shareholder. The product of the old share price and the old number of shares outstanding equals the product of the new share price and the new number of shares outstanding.
**stock valuation formula** A formula for determining a present value of the future cash flows from a stock.
**stock-style settlement** A settlement procedure used by an exchange in which buying a contract requires immediate and full payment of the asset price.
**stop-limit order** Same as *stop-loss order.*
**stop-loss order** An order to buy or sell if the price touches or crosses at pre-specified level.
**storage** The act of holding a commodity or asset for a period of time.
**storage costs** The costs to storing a commodity. These include warehouse rent, insurance, and spoilage.
**straddle** An option position consisting of a long (short) call and a long (short) put with the same exercise price and time to expiration. Sometimes called a volatility spread.
**strangle** An option position consisting of a long (short) call and a long (short) put with the same time to expiration but with the call's exercise price exceeding that of the put.
**strap** A trading strategy that consists of: (1) buying (selling) two calls and (2) buying (selling) one put, where all options are written on the same underlying asset and have the same exercise price and expiration date.
**strike price** See *exercise price.*
**strike spread** See *money spread.*
**striking price** See *exercise price.*
**strip** A trading strategy that consists of: (1) buying (selling) one call and (2) buying (selling) two puts, where all options are written on the same underlying asset and have the same exercise price and expiration date.
**strip hedge** A hedge in which a series of futures contracts of successively longer expirations are bought or sold.
**stripped bond** A bond which was originally coupon-bearing but whose coupons and principal repayment have been separated and are selling as individual discount bonds.
**swap contract** A derivative contract that involves exchanging cash flow streams.
**swap dealer** A firm that makes a market in swaps.
**swap rate** The loss rate for exchanging units of currencies at a future date.
**swaption** An option on a swap.
**switching option** See *quality option.*

**synthetic asset** A long (short) call together with a short (long) put where both options have the same underlying, exercise price, and expiration date.

**synthetic derivative** A portfolio of traded securities that replicates the cash flows of a derivative contract.

**synthetic long call** Generated by buying the underlying asset and buying the put with the same exercise price. The cost of the position is financed at the short-term interest rate.

**synthetic long put** Generated by selling the underlying asset and buying a call put. The net proceeds from establishing the position are invested at the short-term interest rate.

**synthetic short call** Generated by selling the underlying asset and selling a put. The proceeds from the sale are invested at the short-term interest rate.

**synthetic short put** Generated by buying the underlying asset and selling a call. The net cost of establishing the position is financed at the short-term interest rate.

**tailing the hedge** Adjusting the hedging ratio to account for the interest paid or received from the daily settlement of the futures position.

**target duration** The desired level of interest rate risk (i.e., duration) of a bond portfolio.

**T-bill** See *Treasury bill.*

**T-bill futures** See *Treasury bill futures.*

**T-bond** See *Treasury bond.*

**T-bond futures** See *Treasury bond futures.*

**technical analysis** Prediction of future price movements based on an analysis of past prices and trading volumes.

**term repo** A repurchase agreement with a maturity of more than one day.

**term structure of forward exchange rates** Relation between exchange rates and time to maturity

**term structure of interest rates** Relation between zero-coupon interest rates and time to maturity.

**term structure of spot rates** See term structure of interest rates

**termination date** The day on which a contract between two parties expires.

**theoretical value** An option value generated by a theoretical model.

**theta** The change in the option's model value induced by a change in time to expiration.

**theta-neutral** A portfolio whose value is insensitive to movements in time.

**tick** The minimum permissible price fluctuation.

**tick size** See *tick.*

**time premium** See *time value.*

**time spread** See *calendar spread.*

**time value** The difference between the option's price and its value if it were exercised for certain on the expiration date.

**time value decay** The erosion of an option's time value through time.

**timing option** The right to deliver a T-bond on any day during the CBT's T-bond futures delivery month.

**T-note** See *Treasury bond.*

**T-notes futures** See *Treasury note futures.*

**total rate of return swap** A swap contract that encompasses both cash flows and value changes of an asset.
**trade date** The day on which a contract is made between two parties.
**trading halt** A temporary suspension of trading when the price of a futures or an asset has moved by a predetermined amount.
**transaction costs** The costs of trading. Usually consists of two components: a broker's commission and a market maker's bid/ask spread.
**transparency** The observability of the pricing information for a contract.
**Treasury bill** A short-term discount bond issued by the U.S. government.
**Treasury bill futures** A futures contract written on Treasury bills.
**Treasury bond** A coupon-bearing bond issued by the U.S. government. Have terms to maturity exceeding 10 years.
**Treasury bond futures** A futures contract written on Treasury bonds.
**Treasury note** A coupon-bearing bond issued by the U.S. government. Have terms to maturity between two and 10 years.
**Treasury note futures** A futures contract written on Treasury notes.
**Treasury strips** A zero-coupon bond created by "stripping" the interest and principal payments from Treasury notes and bonds.
**triangular arbitrage** The arbitrage relation linking the exchange rates of three currencies.
**trinomial model** Similar to the binomial model, the underlying asset moves discretely through the option's life. At each point in time, the underlying asset price moves to one of three levels.
**unbiased expectations theory** See *expectations theory.*
**uncovered option** Writing a call or a put without an offsetting position in the underlying asset.
**underlying** The instrument underlying the derivative contract.
**underpriced** A condition in which the market price of a security or derivative is below its model value.
**underwrite** To buy a securities issue from a company and resell it to private investors at a profit.
**unsystematic risk** The risk of a security that is not explained by market movements.
**unwinding** To exit a current position in the market through an offsetting transaction.
**up-and-in option** For up-and-in options, an upper level (barrier) is specified for the asset price on which the option is written. For a up-and-in call (put) option the contract becomes a standard call (put) option if the price of the underlying asset goes above the barrier. If the price of the underlying asset never goes above the barrier during the life of the contract, the contract expires worthless.
**up-and-out option** An option that expires automatically when the asset price on which the option is written hits a predefined barrier.
**uptick** A price increase equal to one tick.
**uptick rule** A rule in the stock market which prohibits short sales except when the last trade had a price increase.
**utility of wealth function** A measure of the satisfaction an agent derives from a level of wealth.

**valuation-by-replication** The method of finding a portfolio of known value with identical payoffs in all states. By the principle of no-arbitrage, the replicated asset should have the same value.

**variable prepaid forward contract** A contract for the future sale of a contingent number of shares for a prepaid sum.

**variance** A measure of the dispersion of a random variable around its mean.

**variation margin** The gains or losses on open futures position when it is market-to-market.

**vega** The change in the option's model value induced by a change in volatility.

**vega-neutral** A portfolio whose value is insensitive to movements in volatility.

**vertical bear spread** A spread that consists of: (1) buying a call (put) and (2) selling a call (put) with a lower exercise price. The options have the same expiration date.

**vertical bull spread** A spread that consists of: (1) buying a call (put) and (2) selling a call (put) with a higher exercise price. The options have the same expiration date.

**vertical spread** See *money spread.*

**vesting period** A time period during which received employee stock options cannot be exercised.

**volatility** The standard deviation of return on an annualized basis.

**volatility spread** See *straddle.*

**volume** Number of contracts traded in a particular interval of time.

**vulnerable derivative** A derivative contract with default risk.

**warrant** A contract issued by a firm that allows the holder to buy its underlying stock at a predetermined price within a specified amount of time.

**wealth constraint** The property that the proportions of an investor's allocations to various assets must sum to one.

**wild card option** An option that arises in a derivative contract when the settlement price of the contract is established before the market is closed. For example, wildcard options are embedded in the CBT's T-bond futures and the CBOE's S&P 100 options.

**write an option** Sell an option.

**yield** See *yield-to-maturity.*

**yield curve** The relation between the yield-to-maturity and term-to-maturity for bonds with a comparable degree of default risk (usually U.S. government securities).

**yield risk** A producer's uncertainty about the amount of commodity that will be produced in the future.

**yield-to-maturity** The discount rate that equates the present value of the bond's cash flow stream to its market price.

**zero-coupon bond** A bond that makes no interest or coupon payments. Also called a pure discount bond.

**zero-coupon yield curve** See *term structure of interest rates.*

**zero-sum game** A game in which payoffs to all players sum to zero (i.e., one person's win comes with another's loss).

# About the CD-ROM

## INTRODUCTION

This appendix provides you with information on the contents of the CD that accompanies this book. For the latest and greatest information, please refer to the ReadMe file located at the root of the CD.

## SYSTEM REQUIREMENTS

- A computer with an Intel Pentium processor running at 233 MHz or faster (Intel Pentium III recommended)
- 128 megabytes (MB) of RAM or greater
- Microsoft Windows 2000 with Service Pack 3 (SP3), Windows XP, or later
- Microsoft Excel 2003
- A CD-ROM drive

*NOTE:* Older versions of Microsoft Excel may also work, but are not guaranteed. Many popular spreadsheet programs are capable of reading Microsoft Excel files. However, users should be aware that a slight amount of formatting might be lost when using a program other than Microsoft Word.

## USING THE CD WITH WINDOWS

To install the items from the CD to your hard drive, follow these steps:

1. Insert the CD into your computer's CD-ROM drive.
2. The CD-ROM interface will appear. The interface provides a simple point-and-click way to explore the contents of the CD.

---

*Publisher's note:* Wiley publishes in a variety of print and electronic formats and by print-on-demand. If this book refers to media such as a CD or DVD that is not included in the version you purchased, you may download this material at http://booksupport.wiley.com. For more information about Wiley products, visit www.wiley.com.

If the opening screen of the CD-ROM does not appear automatically, follow these steps to access the CD:

1. Click the Start button on the left end of the taskbar and then choose Run from the menu that pops up.
2. In the dialog box that appears, type ***d*:\setup.exe**. (If your CD-ROM drive is not drive d, fill in the appropriate letter in place of *d*.) This brings up the CD Interface described in the preceding set of steps.

## WHAT'S ON THE CD

The CD contains two subdirectories: Content and OPTVAL.

### Content

The Content subdirectory contains end-of-chapter questions and problems as well as Microsoft Excel files that contain data for use on end-of-chapter problems. The contents of each of the Excel files are described in the end-of-chapter problem.

### OPTVAL™

The accompanying book, as well as the end-of-chapter problems on this CD ROM, makes extensive use of OPTVAL™. OPTVAL is a library of Microsoft Excel Visual Basic Add-Ins designed to perform a wide range of valuation, risk measurement, and statistical computations. The logic in doing so is simple. By facilitating the computation of value/risk, the OPTVAL functions allow the reader to focus on the economic understanding of solving the valuation and risk management problems rather than the computational mechanics of valuation and risk measurement.

More specifically, accurate and reliable valuation/risk measurement has two important computational steps. The first is performing all of the computations that go into generating a model value conditional on knowing the values of the model's parameters. In some instances such as valuing a simple forward or futures contract, the numbers of intermediate computations are hundreds, perhaps, thousands. In other instances such as valuing an option on a dividend-paying stock, they are many. The second is estimating model parameters. All valuation models are function analytical or numerical functions of a set of parameters. Reliably estimating many of these parameters such as expected future return volatility involves collecting histories of price data and then applying statistical techniques. OPTVAL also contains a host of statistical functions to supplement what is already available in Microsoft Excel.

The add-in functions contained in OPTVAL are introduced and applied in each chapter's illustrations. In the early chapters of the book, the illustrations show all of the intermediate computations involved in addressing the valuation/ risk measurement problem at hand as well as the OPTVAL function that allows the reader to find the solution without seeing the intermediate computations. This two-step procedure is designed to allow the reader to develop confidence that OPTVAL functions are not merely a "black box" but rather a set of computational routines that the reader can verify, if he or she chooses to do so. As the chapters progress, less emphasis is placed on showing intermediate steps and more emphasis is placed on addressing important, everyday valuation/risk management problems.

### Installing Add-Ins on Your Computer

Before you can use an add-in, you must first install it on your computer and then load it into Excel. Add-ins (*.xla files) are installed by default in one of the following places:

- The Library folder or one of its subfolders in the Microsoft Office/Office folder.
- The Documents and Settings/<user name>/Application Data/Microsoft/AddIns folder.

The administrator for your company's network can designate other locations for add-in programs. See your administrator for more information.

### Loading Add-Ins into Excel

After installing an add-in, you must load it into Excel. Loading an add-in makes the feature available in Excel and adds any associated commands to the appropriate menus. To load the OPTVAL Function Library in Excel, go to the *Tools* menu and select *Add-Ins*. Select the OPTVAL Function Library and click *OK*.

### Unloading Add-Ins from Excel

To conserve memory and improve performance, unload add-ins you don't use often. Unloading an add-in removes its features and commands from Excel, but the add-in program remains on your computer so you can easily reload it. When you unload an add-in program, it remains in memory until you restart Excel.

## CUSTOMER CARE

If you have trouble with the CD-ROM, please call the Wiley Product Technical Support phone number at (800) 762-2974. Outside the United States, call 1(317) 572-3994. You can also contact Wiley Product Technical Support at **http://support.wiley.com**. John Wiley & Sons will provide technical support only for installation and other general quality control items. For technical support on the applications themselves, consult the program's vendor or author.

To place additional orders or to request information about other Wiley products, please call (877) 762-2974.

# Index

Printed and bound by CPI Group (UK) Ltd, Croydon, CR0 4YY

23/04/2025

14660936-0001